February 24–27, 2014
Haifa, Israel

I0028878

Association for Computing Machinery

Advancing Computing as a Science & Profession

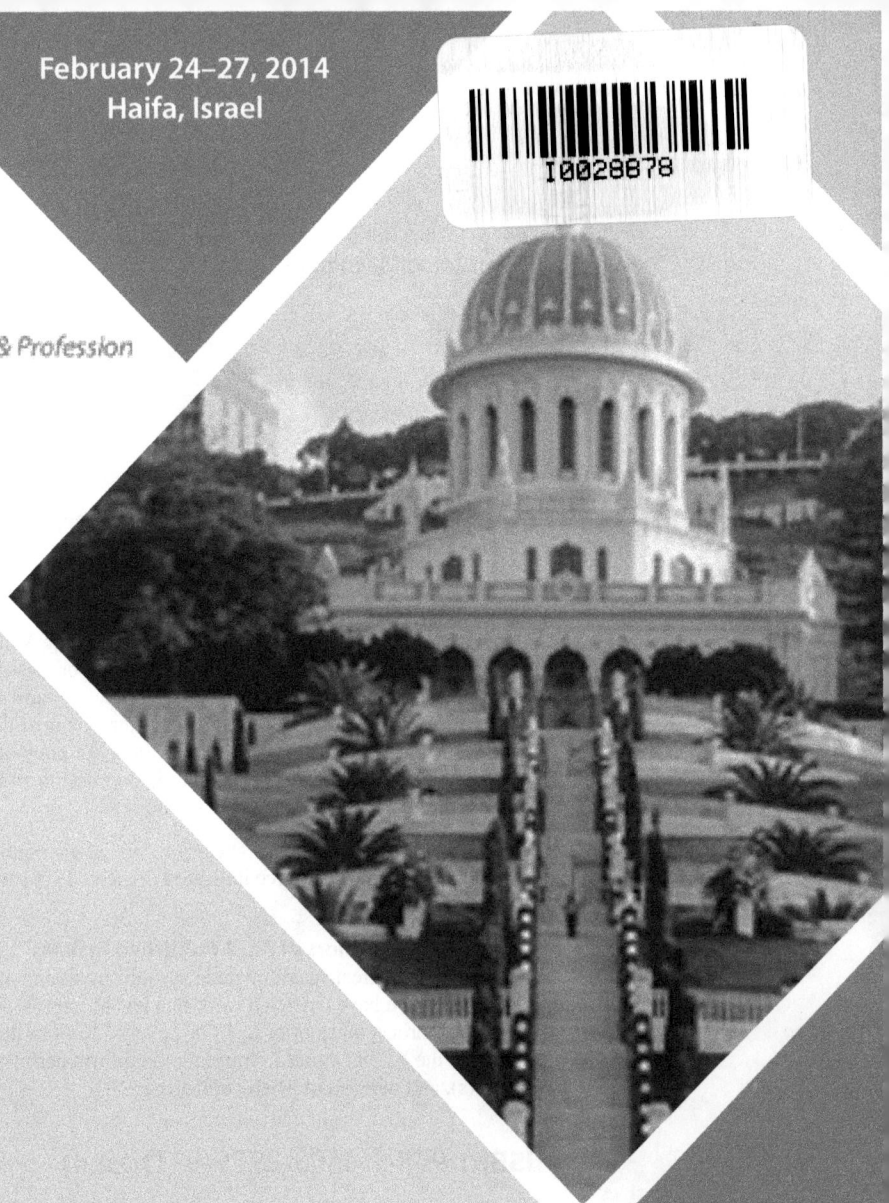

IUI'14

Proceedings of the 19th International Conference on
Intelligent User Interfaces

Sponsored by:

ACM SIGAI and ACM SIGCHI

Supported by:

IBM, RedWhale Software, Microsoft Research, HAIFA Municipality, CRI, University of Haifa, Tel Aviv University and AAAI

**Association for
Computing Machinery**

Advancing Computing as a Science & Profession

The Association for Computing Machinery
2 Penn Plaza, Suite 701
New York, New York 10121-0701

Notice to Past Authors of ACM-Published Articles
ACM intends to create a complete electronic archive of all articles and/or other material previously published by ACM. If you have written a work that has been previously published by ACM in any journal or conference proceedings prior to 1978, or any SIG Newsletter at any time, and you do NOT want this work to appear in the ACM Digital Library, please inform permissions@acm.org, stating the title of the work, the author(s), and where and when published.

ISBN: 978-1-4503-2729-9 (Digital)

ISBN: 978-1-4503-3113-5 (Print)

Additional copies may be ordered prepaid from:

ACM Order Department
PO Box 30777
New York, NY 10087-0777, USA

Phone: 1-800-342-6626 (USA and Canada)
+1-212-626-0500 (Global)
Fax: +1-212-944-1318
E-mail: acmhelp@acm.org
Hours of Operation: 8:30 am – 4:30 pm ET

Printed in the USA

Welcome

It is our great pleasure to welcome you to the *2014 International Conference on Intelligent User Interfaces (IUI'14)*. It is the nineteenth IUI conference, continuing its tradition of being the principal international forum for reporting outstanding research at the intersection of Human-Computer Interaction (HCI) and Artificial Intelligence (AI). The work that appears at IUI bridges these two fields and also delves into related fields, such as psychology, cognitive science, computer graphics, the arts, and many others. Members of the IUI community are interested in improving the symbiosis between humans and computers, and in making systems adapt to humans rather then the other way round.

The call for papers attracted 191 submissions from Asia, America, Europe, Africa, and Australia. The program committee accepted 46 papers, covering a diverse set of topics, reflected in the session titles "From Touch through Air to Brain", "Learning and Skills", "Intelligent Visual Interaction", "Users and Motion", "Leveraging Social Competencies", "Adaptive User Interfaces" and a special session with papers that honor the memory of John Riedl, who left us too early. A great attraction of the conference is provided by the scientific keynotes: Professor Wolfgang Wahlster opens the conference program with a keynote on "Multiadaptive Interfaces to Cyber-Physical Environments", Professor Noam Tractinsky's second day keynote is on "Visual Aesthetics of Interactive Technologies" and the last day keynote, by Professor Mark Billinghurst is on "Using AR to Create Empathic Experiences". In addition we are pleased to offer an invited talk by a relevant industry speaker, Yanki Margalit: "Startup nation and the Makers revolution. Intelligent user interfaces and the future of the Israeli hi-tech". We also have 11 posters and an excellent demonstration program consisting of 27 demos. In addition, the conference provides four very interesting workshops and a student consortium.

The conference could be organized only with the help of a large number of individuals who volunteered a lot of their own time and enthusiasm. Their names can be found in the following pages. The local organization has worked very hard and a big thank you goes to all people who helped overcome all sorts of problems. We must also thank our senior program committee for coordinating the review process and all the members of the program committee for providing high quality reviews. And, most important, we must thank the authors for providing the content of this conference, and also those whose papers could not be included in the 24% selected for the program. Finally, we must thank our sponsors, ACM, SIGCHI and SIGART, AAAI, our generous corporate supporters, IBM, our Platinum sponsor, and the rest of our corporate sponsors, Microsoft Research and RedWhale Software, and our academic and municipal sponsors, the Municipality of Haifa and Haifa Tourist Board, Tel Aviv University, the University of Haifa and the Caesarea Rothschild Institute for Interdisciplinary Applications of Computer Science.

We hope you will find the program interesting and thought-provoking. We also hope the conference will provide you with a valuable opportunity to share ideas with other researchers and practitioners from around the world, leading to further advancements in the field of IUI.

Tsvi Kuflik
IUI'14
General Co-Chair
The University of Haifa, Israel

Oliviero Stock
IUI'14
General Co-Chair
FBK, Trento, Italy

Joyce Chai
IUI'14 Program Co-Chair
Michigan State University, USA

Antonio Krüger
IUI'14 Program Co-Chair
DFKI, Saarbrücken, Germany

Table of Contents

Session 7: Leveraging Social Competencies

Session Chair: Cecile Paris *(CSIRO)*

Session 8: Adaptive User Interfaces

Session Chair: Michelle Zhou *(IBM Research)*

Session 9: Posters

IUI 2014 Conference Organization

General Chairs: Tsvi Kuflik (The University of Haifa, Israel)
Oliviero Stock (FBK-IRST, Italy)

Program Chairs: Joyce Chai (Michigan State University)
Antonio Krüger (Saarland University and DFKI GmbH, Germany)

Workshop Chairs: Ido Guy (IBM Research Haifa, Israel)
Tracy Hammond (Texas A&M University, USA)

Demo/Industry Chairs: Doron Friedman (IDC, Israel)
Massimo Zancanaro (FBK-IRST, Italy)
Claudia Goldman (General Motors Advanced Technical Center, Israel)

Students Consortium Chairs: Shlomo Berkovsky (NICTA, Australia)
Helmut Prendinger (National Institute of Informatics, Japan)

Local Arrangements Chairs: Joel Lanir (The University of Haifa, Israel)
Eran Toch (Tel Aviv University, Israel)

Publicity Chair: Nava Tintarev (University of Aberdeen, UK)

Treasurer Chair: Melinda Gervasio (SRI International, USA)

Sponsorship Chair: Doug Riecken (Columbia University, USA)

Social Media Chair: Angel Puerta (RedWhale Software, USA)

Senior Program Committee: Saleema Amershi *(Microsoft Research at Richmond, USA)*
Liliana Ardissono (University of Torino, Italy)
Sumit Basu (Microsoft Research, USA)
Shlomo Berkovsky (NICTA, Australia)
Mark Billinghurst (HIT Lab, New Zealand)
Marco Blumendorf (TU-Berlin, Germany)
Dan Bohus (Microsoft Research, USA)
Andrea Bunt (University of Manitoba, Canada)
Gaelle Calvary (Grenoble Institute of Technology, France)
Fang Chen (NICTA, Australia)
Keith Cheverst (Lancaster University, UK)
Cristina Conati (University of British Columbia, Canada)
Jill Freyne (CSIRO, Australia)
Wai-Tat Fu (University of Illinois at Urbana-Champaign, USA)
Paul Groth (VU University Amsterdam, Netherlands)
Tracy Hammond (Texas A&M University, USA)
Michael Johnston (AT&T Labs Research, USA)
Joaquim Jorge (Technical University of Lisbon, Portugal)
Per Ola Kristensson (University of St Andrews, UK)
Bob Kummerfeld (University of Sydney, Australia)
Henry Lieberman (Massachusetts Institute of Technology, USA)
Kris Luyten (Hasselt University, Belgium)
Jalal Mahmud (IBM Research, USA)
Joachim Meyer (Tel Aviv University, Israel)
Yukiko Nakano Seikei University
Petteri Nurmi (Helsinki Institute for Information Technology, Finland)
Nuria Oliver (Telefonica R&D, Spain)
Shimei Pan (IBM Research, USA)
Cecile Paris (CSIRO, Australia)
Fabio Paterno (CNR-ISTI, Italy)
Beryl Plimmer (University of Auckland, New Zealand)
Helmut Prendinger (National Institute of Informatics, Japan)
Frank Shipman (Texas A&M University, USA)
Daniel Sonntag (DFKI, Germany)
Robert St. Amant (North Carolina State University, USA)
Chen Yu (Indiana University, USA)
Massimo Zancanaro (FBK - Fondazione Bruno Kessler, Italy)
Michelle Zhou (IBM Almaden Research Center, USA)
Ingrid Zukerman (Monash University, Australia)

IUI 2014 Technical Program Committee

Safurah Abdul Jalil *(University of Auckland, New Zealand)*

Aaron Adler *(BBN Technologies, USA)*

Christine Alvarado *(Harvey Mudd College, USA)*

Lisa Anthony *(University of Florida, USA)*

Lora Aroyo *(VU University Amsterdam, Netherlands)*

Tyler Baldwin *(Michigan State University, USA)*

Joerg Baus *(DFKI, Germany)*

Rachel Blagojevic *(University of Auckland, New Zealand)*

Matthias Böhmer *(DFKI, Germany)*

Francesca Bonin *(Trinity College Dublin, Ireland)*

Francois Bouchet *(Université Pierre et Marie Curie, France)*

Jim Burton *(University of Brighton, UK)*

Maya Cakmak *(University of Washington, USA)*

Juan Pablo Carrascal *(Universitat Pompeu Fabra, Spain)*

Marc Cavazza *(Teeside University, UK)*

Federica Cena *(University of Torino, Italy)*

Pablo Cesar *(CWI (Centrum voor Wiskunde en Informatica), Netherlands)*

Li Chen *(Hong Kong Baptist University (HKBU), China)*

Karen Church *(Telefonica Research, Spain)*

Karin Coninx *(Hasselt University, Belgium)*

Céline Coutrix *(Université Joseph Fourier, France)*

Florian Daiber *(DFKI, Germany)*

Victor de Boer *(VU University Amsterdam, Netherlands)*

Nadja De Carolis *(University of Bari, Italy)*

Alexander De Luca *(Munich University, Germany)*

Rodrigo de Oliveira *(Telefonica Research, Spain)*

Aidan Delaney *(University of Brighton, UK)*

Michael Feld *(DFKI, Germany)*

Rebecca Fiebrink *(Princeton University, USA)*

Christopher Fry *(MIT, USA)*

Sven Gehring *(DFKI, Germany)*

cristina gena *(University of Torino, Italy)*

Giuseppe Ghiani *(ISTI-CNR, Italy)*

Andreas Girgensohn *(FX Palo Alto Laboratory, USA)*

David Gotz *(IBM Research, USA)*

Ricardo Gutierrez-Osuna *(Texas A&M University, USA)*

Michiel Hildebrand *(VU University Amsterdam, Netherlands)*

Jochen Huber *(MIT, USA)*

Arne Jonsson *(Linköping University, Sweden)*

Alexandros Karatzoglou *(Telefonica Research, Spain)*

Frederic Kerber *(DFKI, Germany)*

Franziska Klügl *(Örebro University, Sweden)*

W. Bradley Knox *(MIT, USA)*

Kazunori Komatani *(Graduate School of Engineering, Japan)*

Stefan Kopp *(University of Bielefeld, Germany)*

Tsvi Kuflik *(University of Haifa, Israel)*

Timothy Lebo *(Rensselaer Polytechnic Institute, USA)*

Grzegorz Lehmann *(DAI-Lab, Germany)*

Luis A. Leiva *(Universitat Politècnica de València, Spain)*

Henry A. Lieberman *(MIT, USA)*

Markus Löchtefeld *(DFKI, Germany)*

Pasquale Lops *(University of Bari, Italy)*

Jie Lu *(IBM Research, USA)*

Maurizio Marchese *(University of Trento, Italy)*

Roberto Martinez Maldonado *(University of Sydney, Australia)*

Kasia Muldner *(CIDSE, USA)*

Michael Nebeling *(ETH Zürich, Switzerland)*

John O'Donovan *(University of California, USA)*

Tihomir Orehovacki *(University of Zagreb, Hungary)*

Jason Orlosky *(Osaka University, Japan)*

Denise Paradowski *(DFKI, Germany)*

Brandon Paulson *(Texas A&M University, USA)*

Steve Pettifier *(The University of Manchester, UK)*

Martin Pielot *(OFFIS, Germany)*

Luiz Pizzato *(The University of Sydney, Australia)*

Till Plumbaum *(DAI-Lab, Germany)*

Frederic Raber *(DFKI, Germany)*

Martin Raubal *(ETH Zürich, Switzerland)*

Norbert Reithinger *(DFKI, Germany)*

Mark Riedl *(Georgia Institute of Technology, USA)*

Jose San Pedro *(The Pennsylvania State University, USA)*

Michael Schellenbach *(Max Planck Institute for Human Development, Germany)*

IUI 2014 Sponsors & Supporters

Sponsors:

Platinum Supporter:

Other Supporters:

Multiadaptive Interfaces to Cyber-Physical Environments

Wolfgang Wahlster
German Research Center for Artificial Intelligence (DFKI)
Campus D3 2
D-66123 Saarbrücken, Germany
wahlster@dfki.de

ABSTRACT

Networked cyber-physical systems are the basis for intelligent environments in a variety of settings such as smart factories, smart transportation systems, smart shops, and smart buildings. However, one of the remaining grand challenges for the Internet of Things is to transform the way how humans interact with and control such cyber-physical environments (CPE). A major goal of our research is the creation of a multiadaptive dialogue management system that is adaptive in multiple ways: adaptive to various CPE, adaptive to diverse modality combinations, adaptive to a variety of interaction metaphors, and adaptive to diverse task domains and user models. We support multiparty communication and deal simultaneously with many independent and mobile users or groups of users with a joint intention in the same smart environment, instead of a single user in the traditional HCI paradigm. In human-environment interfaces for CPE, the physical interaction of the users with artifacts in the environment must be taken into account as a key situational factor for dialogue understanding. Since complex CPE such as smart urban environments are systems of systems of systems, multiscale interface technologies for near field and distant interaction with different scope and granularity are needed. Since each CPE includes a large variety of sensors and actuators, the dialogue management system has to select dynamically the best sensors for input analysis and the best actuators for rendering output information at each time cycle, instead of a fixed set of input and output devices in traditional UI design.

We will illustrate our approach to multiadaptive interaction with cyber-physical production systems in dirty, oily, and noisy smart factory environments and demonstrate our innovative user interfaces combining glasses, leap motion technology and mobile eye-trackers. We argue that active semantic product memories will play a key role in the upcoming fourth industrial revolution based on cyber-physical production systems. Low-cost and compact digital storage, sensors and radio modules make it possible to embed a digital memory into a product for recording all relevant events throughout the entire lifecycle of the artifact.

By capturing and interpreting ambient conditions and user actions, such computationally enhanced products have a data shadow and are able to perceive and control their environment, to analyze their observations and to communicate with other smart objects and human users about their lifelog data. In contrast to the classical centralized production planning and manufacturing execution systems, this leads to decentralized production logic, where the emerging product with its object memory is not only a central information container, but also an observer, a negotiator, and an agent in the production process. A semantic service architecture based on a production ontology and ubiquitous microweb servers realizes intelligent matchmaking processes between emerging products, production tools and factory workers. We illustrate this revolutionary production architecture with examples from DFKI's fully operational Smart Factory.

In addition, we present our recent results for advanced driver assistance of smart cars in cyber-physical transportation environments. Since for interfaces to smart factories and smart connected vehicles safety is a major concern, we show how dynamic models of cognitive load can lead to advanced attention management that increases workplace and driving safety.

Author Keywords

Multimodal Interfaces; Multiadaptive Dialogue Management; Cyber-Physical Environment; Human-Environment Communication.

ACM Classification Keywords

H.5.2 User Interfaces (D.2.2, H.1.2, I.3.6)

BIO

Wolfgang Wahlster is the Director of DFKI and a Professor of Computer Science at Saarland University. He has published more than 200 technical papers and 10 books on user modeling, multimodal user interfaces and instrumented environments. He is a Fellow of AAAI, ECCAI, and GI. In 2001, he received the German Future Prize from the President of Germany for his work on intelligent user interfaces. He is a member of the Royal Swedish Academy of Sciences and the German National Academy. In 2013, he received the IJCAI Donald Walker Distinguished Service Award for his substantial contributions, as well as his extensive service to the field of AI throughout his career.

REFERENCE

Wahlster, W.: The Semantic Product Memory: An Interactive Black Box for Smart Objects. In: Wahlster, W. (ed): SemProM: Foundations of Semantic Product Memories for the Internet of Things. Heidelberg, New York, Tokyo: Springer 2013, p. 3-21.

Visual Aesthetics of Interactive Technologies

Noam Tractinsky
Information Systems Engineering
Ben-Gurion University of the Negev
noamt@bgu.ac.il

ABSTRACT

One of the defining characteristics of interactive technologies in the new millennium is the emergence of aesthetic considerations as a major factor in the development of systems and products. Following almost two decades of empirical research in this area we have now a better grasp of this trend and its potential effects on users and societal processes. This talk will open with a brief overview of my early encounters with this phenomenon and of early studies of visual aesthetics of interactive systems, emphasizing the findings regarding its influence on people's perceptions of usability. I will offer explanations about the importance of the role that aesthetics plays in interactive systems from at least three major perspectives: the design of systems and artifacts, psychological processes and biases, and practical and business consideration. Finally, I will discuss the limitation of our current knowledge and challenges for future research and practice.

Author Keywords

Visual aesthetics; interactive technologies; design; psychology; practice

ACM Classification Keywords

H.5.2 User Interfaces

BIO

Noam Tractinsky is an Associate Professor at the department of Information Systems Engineering at Ben-Gurion University of the Negev. He is interested in the study of phenomena associated with the interaction of people and computers. He has studied the effects of the visual aesthetics of interactive technology, including some of the earliest studies in this area. His current research interests also include the effects of using cell-phones while driving, theoretical and measurement aspects of usability and user experience, and the design and use of computerized interventions in reminiscence therapy for Alzheimer's patients.

IUI'14, February 24–27, 2014, Haifa, Israel.
ACM 978-1-4503-2184-6/14/02.
http://dx.doi.org/10.1145/2557500.2568056

Using Augmented Reality to Create Empathic Experiences

Mark Billinghurst
The HIT Lab NZ
University of Canterbury, ILAM Road
Christchurch 8041, New Zealand
mark.billinghurst@hitlabnz.org

ABSTRACT

Intelligent user interfaces have traditionally been used to create systems that respond intelligently to user input. However there is a recent trend towards Empathic Interfaces that are designed to go beyond understanding user input and to recognize emotional state and user feelings. In this presentation we explore how Augmented Reality (AR) can be used to convey that emotional state and so allow users to capture and share emotional experiences. In this way AR not only overlays virtual imagery on the real world, but also can create deeper understanding of user's experience at particular locations and points in time. The recent emergence of truly wearable systems, such as Google Glass, provide a platform for Empathic Communication using AR. Examples will be shown from research conducted at the HIT Lab NZ and other research organizations, and key areas for future research described.

Author Keywords

Augmented Reality; Empathic Computing; Collaboration.

ACM Classification Keywords

H.5.1. [Multimedia Information Systems]: Artificial, augmented, and virtual realities; H.5.3. [Group and Organization Interfaces]: Collaborative computing.

BIOGRAPHY

Professor Mark Billinghurst is Director of the Human Interface Technology Laboratory New Zealand (HIT Lab NZ) at the University of Canterbury where he leads research developing innovative computer interfaces that explore how virtual and real worlds can be merged. With a PhD from the University of Washington, he has previously worked at ATR Research Labs in Japan, the MIT Media Laboratory, Nokia and Google. He has published over 250 technical papers and won a number of awards including the 2013 IEEE VR Award for Technical Achievement in research and commercialization of Augmented Reality technology, and the 2012 ISMAR 10 Year Lasting Impact Award. In 2013 he was elected as a Fellow of the Royal Society of New Zealand.

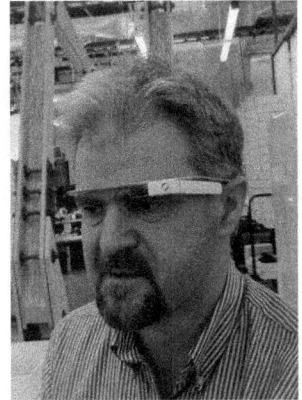

IUI'14, February 24–27, 2014, Haifa, Israel.
ACM 978-1-4503-2184-6/14/02.
http://dx.doi.org/10.1145/2557500.2568057

Who Have Got Answers? Growing the Pool of Answerers in a Smart Enterprise Social QA System

Lin Luo[1] Fei Wang[2] Michelle X. Zhou[2] Ying Xin Pan[1] Hang Chen[1]
[1]IBM Research – China, [2]IBM Research – Almaden
{luolin, panyingx, chenhch}@cn.ibm.com, {wangfe, mzhou}@us.ibm.com

ABSTRACT

On top of an enterprise social platform, we are building a smart social QA system that automatically routes questions to suitable employees who are willing, able, and ready to provide answers. Due to a lack of social QA history (training data) to start with, in this paper, we present an optimization-based approach that recommends both active (seed) and inactive (prospect) answerers for a given question. Our approach includes three parts. First, it uses a predictive model to find top-ranked seed answerers by their fitness, including their ability and willingness, to answer a question. Second, it uses distance metric learning to discover prospects most similar to the seeds identified in the first step. Third, it uses a constraint-based approach to balance the selection of both seeds and prospects identified in the first two steps. As a result, not only does our solution route questions to top-matched active users, but it also engages inactive users to grow the pool of answerers. Our real-world experiments that routed 114 questions to 684 people identified from 400,000+ employees included 641 prospects (93.7%) and achieved about 70% answering rate with 83% of answers received a lot/full confidence.

Author Keywords
Social QA; answerer recommendation; question routing.

ACM Classification Keywords
H.5.m. Information interfaces and presentation (e.g., HCI): Miscellaneous.

INTRODUCTION
Social Question-Answering (QA) sites, such as Quora, have become very popular, as they leverage the power of the crowd to provide an effective channel for people to seek information and share knowledge [4]. Due to a large number of questions posted, one active research topic on Social QA is how to route the questions to the right answerers so that askers can obtain satisfying answers timely [2, 4].

There is much work on recommending suitable answerers for a given question based on people's past question-answering behavior [2, 6, 11, 20]. Most work however requires large amounts of training data—extensive user question-answering activities—to match questions with suitable answerers. For example, Dror et al. train their model based on the activities of 169,000+ users over 1.25 million questions on Yahoo! Answers [2]. However, not every Social QA site generates user activities at this scale. For example, the Social QA site launched within our company has about 5000 registered users, among which 3000 have *no* answering activities at all and only about 1% (48) are very active by providing nearly 50% of the answers for over 31% of the questions (one question may receive multiple answers). Due to limited user activities at such sites, existing approaches may fail to find suitable answerers for a given question or tend to overburden a small number of active users.

To address the challenges described above and foster user participation at an enterprise Social QA site, we are building a Smart Social QA system that recommends both active and inactive users for a given question. Here we use the term *seeds* to refer to the most active users who have had extensive question-answering activities. We use the term *prospects* to refer to those in a company who could become potential answerers but have only limited or no past Social QA activities. In our current implementation, a user is qualified as a seed if she has answered at least 10 questions in the past. Any employee who is on our company's social platform, IBM Connect, is considered a prospect.

We develop an optimization-based approach to recommend both seeds and prospects in three steps. First, we build a statistical model to predict a person's fitness for a given question based on her ability (expertise), willingness, and readiness to answer the question. Similar to existing work [2, 20], we assess one's ability and readiness for answering a question based on her past social QA activities. Moreover, we evaluate the person's willingness to help others in general, as previous work shows that such willingness impacts a person's likelihood to respond to a request [12]. To model a person's willingness, we compute a variety of features, including one's *promptness* to respond to any request on social media and personality traits such as *friendliness*.

Second, we use distance metric learning to identify a set of prospects who are most *similar* to the seeds identified in the first step. Their similarity is computed by comparing a wide variety of their traits, including their demographics, organizational roles, and personality. This step promotes pros-

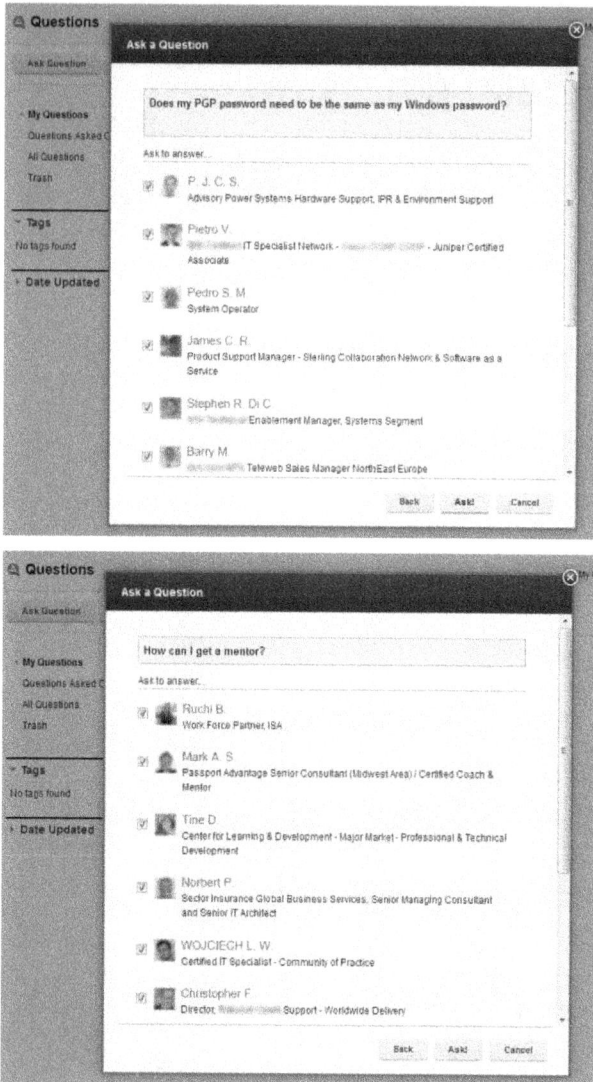

Figure 1. Recommending answerers to a user. Top (a): a question that requires certain domain knowledge. Bottom (b): a more general question that solicits others' opinions.

pects as potential answerers, who may rank low in the first step due to their limited QA activities but share certain similar traits of the seeds identified in the first step.

Third, based on the results of steps 1 and 2, we develop a constraint-based approach to select the top-N ranked answerers, including both seeds and prospects such that their combined fitness to answer the question and the diversity of their QA activeness are maximized. Choosing answerers with varied levels of activeness diversifies the routing targets. As a result, we can grow the pool of answerers gradually by involving more prospects. In turn, these "light users" can contribute more to the communities and help maintain the overall healthiness of a Social QA system [16, 19].

Currently, our Smart Social QA system is built on top of an existing enterprise social platform, IBM Connect, used by over 400,000 employees at IBM. On such a platform, em-

ployees can form communities and publish blogs. Based on their past Social QA activities, we have identified 48 seeds who have provided over 50% of answers for over 31% questions. And the rest of users (400,000+) are considered prospects. Using our system, a user posts a question and automatically receives a set of recommended potential answerers. Due to the nuanced social dynamics in an enterprise (e.g., an asker may not wish to route his questions to certain people) and the imperfections in our routing algorithm, we allow users to explicitly select/deselect among the system-recommended answerers to route a question to.

Figure 1 shows the user interface of our system where an asker views the recommended answerers for his submitted question. Currently, top-6 matched answerers are recommended, which often include both seeds (2 on the top in Figure 1a) and prospects (4 on the bottom).

To the best of our knowledge, our work is the first on recommending inactive users in an enterprise Social QA setting. It thus offers three unique contributions.

1) We use a rich set of features, including one's personality traits that have never been used before, to accurately measure a person's overall fitness for answering a question. As shown later, our approach outperforms the method that uses only expertise modeling.

2) We use distance metric learning to automatically discover prospect answerers *similar to* seeds, even if they have very limited or no past Social QA activities.

3) Our optimization-based answerer recommendation not only ensures the overall fitness of the potential answerers for a question, but also helps grow the answerer pool by involving inactive users while protecting a small number of active users from social fatigue.

We have conducted an extensive set of experiments, including a live study involving 684 recommended answerers from over 400,000 employees to respond to 114 questions posed by our colleagues. The study results demonstrate the effectiveness of our work. In the rest of the paper, we first provide a brief discussion of the related work before giving an overview our system. We then present our optimization-based approach to answerer recommendation and describe our experiments and their results.

RELATED WORK

Our work is directly related to numerous research efforts in Social QA, in particular, the efforts on recommending proper answerers for a given question. These efforts fall into two broad categories. The first category of work focuses on using one's Social QA activities (e.g., answers to questions) to infer a person's ability (expertise) to answer a particular question [6, 11, 20]. Since a person may still ignore a routed question even if he is capable of answering it, the second category of work uses additional factors, such as time of routing and asker-answerer social ties [2, 10, 25], to estimate the person's likelihood to answer a question. However, most approaches rely on people's existing QA behavior to recommend potential answerers.

In contrast, our work uses one's Social QA activities *and* non-QA characteristics, including personality traits, to model the person's fitness to answer a question. As a result, our approach can recommend inactive users who have no or very limited Social QA activities as potential answerers. In addition, our focus is on facilitating social QA activities in an enterprise, which presents unique challenges (e.g., limited employee participation) and also opportunities (e.g., additional organizational or employee information) that existing social QA systems have never addressed.

Related to our work on identifying prospect answerers based on their similarity to seed answerers, there are several research efforts on modeling early experts in the context of Social QA [16, 21, 25]. Compared to these works, we model the potentials of prospect answerers from a wider variety of aspects, including their expertise, willingness, and readiness (availability) to help others. Moreover, existing works still rely on one's past Social QA activities, e.g., quantity and frequency of contributions, to infer their early potential. In contrast, we assess one's potential even if the person has no past Social QA activities.

To overcome the data sparsity problem when existing Social QA activities are limited, researchers have come up with various solutions. For example, Richardson et al. augment user profiles by using the users' email archives [20], while Horowitz et al. enrich users' profiles with their social data, including information extracted from the users' blogs and their social networks [8]. Similar to these works, we also leverage additional data sources, e.g., a user's posts and votes in an online forum, to enrich the user's profile. However, we extend existing work by modeling deeper user traits, such as one's willingness to help, to infer the overall fitness of potential answerers.

More recently, there are works on deriving one's personality traits from social media [5, 12]. While we leverage these findings to infer one's personality traits, our focus is on the use of these traits to recommend suitable answerers in an enterprise Social QA system.

SYSTEM OVERVIEW

Figure 2 shows the overview of our Smart Social QA system and its key components. Our system is built on top of the IBM Connect social platform deployed in our company. The platform supports various social applications, including micro-blogging, blogging, and discussion forum. Since this platform did not have a dedicated Social QA application, a standalone Social QA service, called Answers@T, was created for employees to submit questions and receive answers. To model a potential answerer, we have used the data from IBM Connect and Answers@T. Since *all* 400,000+ employees registered on IBM Connect are potential answerers, we compute each person's ability, willingness, and readi-

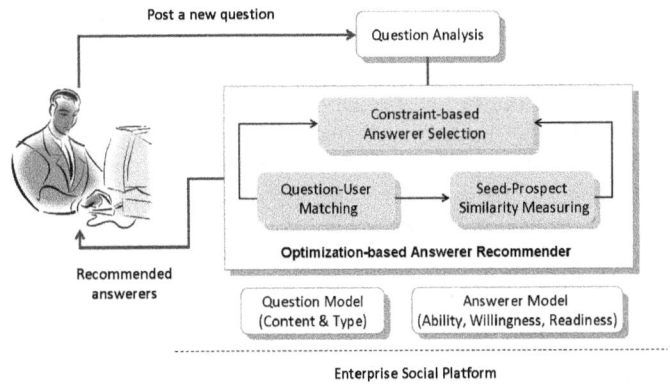

Figure 2. System overview.

ness based on his social QA activities and/or general social activities (e.g., micro-blogging and forum posts).

Using IBM Connect, a user can pose a question in his social activity stream (i.e., micro-blogging stream). Upon receiving the question, our system extracts a set of features to characterize the question (e.g., a term vector capturing the content of the question). Based on the computed features of a user and the question, it uses the *question-user matching* module to compute the fitness of the user for this question[1]. By their fitness, the system keeps the top-M ranked users in the candidate pool that is empty initially. If there are *seeds* among the top-M candidates, our system uses the *seed-prospect similarity measuring* to find the *prospects* similar to each qualified seed. Our system adds the top-N most similar prospects into the candidate pool. Finally, our system uses a *constraint-based selection* to recommend the top-K people from the candidate pool by maximizing the combined fitness and the diversity of the chosen candidates. The asker can then decide whether to route her question to all or a sub-set of the top-K recommended answerers.

OUR APPROACH

We develop an optimization-based approach to answerer recommendation. Before presenting our approach, we describe the data we collected to build our models, and the features used to model a question and a potential answerer.

Data Collection

We model answerers based on two data sets. One is collected from the IBM Connect social platform that did not support Social QA service, and the other is from a standalone internal Social QA system, Answers@T.

From IBM Connect, we collected 420,722 posts and 635,942 comments/ replies created by over 400,000+ registered users. From Answers@T, we collected 2,892 questions and 4,207 answers generated by 1,732 askers and 1,091 answerers among 4,872 registered users.

---

[1] Since we have 400,000+ potential answerers, we use clustering to group people together and filter out unfit groups before computing the fitness of individuals in the remaining groups to reduce computational cost.

Question Modeling

We characterize a question by two aspects: *content* and *type*. We extract a term vector to describe the content of a question. To construct a term vector, we remove stop words and apply Part-Of-Speech (POS) tagging to retain only nouns, adverb, and adjectives. We then characterize a question by its type. We hypothesize that the type of question would affect the answerer selection criteria. Two people coded all the questions collected from Answers@T (inter-coder reliability with Cohen's Kappa = 0.92), and categorized the questions into three types based on the amount of knowledge or skills required to answer them.

The first type of question (Type I) is on a specific topic, which requires in-depth knowledge about the topic to answer a Type I question. A sample question in this category is: "*My web server just crashed and got error code CXV0003. What should I do?*". The second type (Type II) is more general but still requires certain domain knowledge that many employees possess. A sample Type I question is "*How could I connect to a printer near my office?*". The third type (Type III) includes general questions that often solicit one's opinions and most employees should be able to answer them. A typical question in this category is "*Where can I find a mentor?*".

Currently, an asker can explicitly indicate the type of her question during submission. By default, the question type is Type I. In the future, our system will infer a question's type based on all previously submitted questions.

As seen later, the content vector is used to assess a person's ability to answer a question, and the question type is used to weigh the person's various traits, since different types of questions require different answerers (e.g., one's ability weighs more for Type I questions).

Answerer Modeling

We model a person's ability, willingness, and readiness to answer a question. Table 1 lists the features used.

Ability. One's *ability* measures whether the person has sufficient expertise or knowledge to answer an intended question. Similar to many existing approaches [2, 8, 20], ours approximates a user's ability in part based on her generated content, including her asked questions, provided answers, and posted comments. From each type of content, we extract a term vector to measure the ability.

Besides user-generated content, we also used three features from an employee's profile, including organization, geography, and friend network, to approximate one's ability. Our rationale is that within an enterprise it is more likely that people may share similar skills or expertise, if they belong to the same organization (e.g., the sales group), geographical region, or social network (e.g., belonging to the same text analytics online community).

		QA-related	Non-QA related
Ability	Content	*Previous questions and answers (title, details, tags, etc.)*	*forum posts, replies, comments, profiles*
	Other	*geography, organization, and social network*	
Willingness	Activeness	*# of answers*	*# of posts* *# of replies* *# of microblogs* *# of comments* *# of friends* *# of votes*
	Personality	*103 LIWC + Big 5 personality features*	
Readiness		*activity recency, work state, current load (e.g., # questions routed).*	

Table 1. Features used for modeling answerers.

Willingness. Even if a person is able to answer a question, the person may be unwilling to answer the question [12]. It is thus important to gauge a person's willingness to respond to a routed question. Built on the previous work [12, 17], we estimate one's willingness from two aspects: social activeness and personality traits.

Social activeness measures the level of social activities a person has generated, including the number of answers and posts provided, which have been identified as significant predictors for one's response to requests [17]. In addition, one's *personality traits*, including one's friendliness, indicate a person's likelihood to respond [12]. Based on the previous work [12, 18, 23], we computed 103 personality traits for each user using at least 3000 words from their generated content. The 103 attributes cover 68 Linguistic Inquiry of Word Count (LIWC) attributes and 35 Big5 personality attributes [12].

Readiness. Even if a person is willing and able to answer a question, she may not be ready to answer it at the time of the request or within a given time window. To route a question to a right person at the right time, we also model a person's readiness to answer a question. We use several types of information, including the person's work state (e.g., out of office) and current load (e.g., the number of questions already routed to the person).

Optimization-based Answerer Recommendation

We develop an optimization-based approach to answerer recommendation, which consists of three parts. First, it uses a statistical model to predict the fitness of a person for answering a given question. By their fitness, it selects the top-M ranked candidates, including both seeds and prospects. Second, it uses distance metric learning to identify top-N suitable prospects who are most similar to the seeds identified in the first step. Third, it uses a constraint-based approach to select a mix of top-K seeds and prospects such that their combined fitness for answering the question and overall diversity of their activeness are maximized.

Algorithm 1 Question routing algorithm

Require: $f : q \times u \rightarrow R$ question-user matching func.
$d_M : u \times u \rightarrow R$ user-user distance func.

Require: A question q with known type t,
M ← 50, N ← 100, K ← 6

1: Rank all users according to $f(q,u)$, find all seed answerers s_j among top M users.
2: **if** s_j is not empty in 2 **then**
3:   For each $s_j \leftarrow 1$ to J, find top N prospects who are closest to s_j according to d_M^t.
4:   Pool all those prospects and top N users, sort them according to sum of the first two terms of optimization function in Eqn (2), find K users which maximize the energy function.
5: **else**
6:   Sort top M users according to f, find K users which maximize the energy function.
7: **end if**

Figure 3. Summary of our question routing algorithm.

Figure 3 summarizes our question routing algorithm and its key steps.

Predicting Answerer Fitness for a Question

To predict a person's fitness for answering a question, we have trained statistical models based on the question-answering data collected from Answers@T.

Data Set. Because of the sparse data (i.e., most of users did not have any question-answering activities), we used only the questions that the seeds answered as the positive samples for training. There were 48 seeds, each of whom answered at least 10 questions. Finding negative samples was tricky, since there might be many reasons why a question was not answered by a seed and it is difficult to associate an unanswered question with a particular seed. We thus searched for the time (t) when a seed answered a question, and then identified L (now L=5) unanswered questions posted around the same time ($t \pm \partial$) as the negative samples for this seed. Our heuristic is that the seed would have also seen these questions but chose not to answer them. Since there were many more negative examples than positive ones, we used under-sampling to obtain an equal number (N=2050) of positive and negative samples.

Feature Selection. For each question and seed, we computed a set of features as described above. To improve the performance of our models, we analyzed the significance of each feature by computing its. χ^2 value to determine its discriminative power [23]. We eliminated the features that did not contribute significantly to the result. We identified 67 significant features, including 47 personality features, such as *friendliness, cooperation, agreeableness,* and *altruism.*

Statistical Models. We randomly split the data set into training (90%) and testing (10%) sets. We trained several statistical models, including SVM, Random Forest, Linear Regression, and Logistic Regression, to predict one's fit-

ness to answer a given question. From our experimental results, logistic regression performed the best. We thus use this model in our current implementation.

Generalized Model for Prospects. When we tried to apply the model trained for the seeds to predict a prospect's fitness for answering a question, we found that these models over-fit. This is because our model was trained on seeds' activities (48 seeds and 4100 examples) and most of the 400,000+ prospects did not generate sufficient training data. To address this problem, we performed point bi-serial correlation analysis and used the correlation coefficients of the significant features as the weights to build a more generalized prediction model to predict the fitness of a prospect.

However, when applying the generalized model to predict a seed's fitness, the model may not be as accurate as the original model trained on the seeds' social QA activities. We thus use a two-step process to predict a seed's fitness. We first use the original model built for seeds to predict a seed's fitness. We then apply the generalized model to the identified seeds determined by the original model. As a result, we leverage the first model to obtain more accurate fitness ranks for seeds, while using the second model to "normalize" the fitness scores of both seeds and prospects.

By their predicted fitness, our system keeps the top-M ranked candidates in a candidate pool that is empty initially.

Identifying Prospects by Similarity Measuring

Using our fitness prediction model described above, most prospects are often ranked low by their fitness score due to their limited or missing QA activities. To "promote" suitable prospects as potential answerers, we develop a similarity model that discovers a set of prospects who are *most similar to* the qualified seeds found by our fitness model.

Data Set. To compute prospect-seed similarity, we used the QA data collected from Answers@T as our training set. If a question was answered by more than one person, we considered each pair of answerers as similar answerers and labeled this pair as a positive example. To form the negative training set, for each pair of users labeled as "positive" sample, we randomly picked 6 pairs of users (one of them being in the "positive" pair) who had never answered the same questions before. For each type of question, our training set initially contained around 4000 positive examples and 24,000 negative examples. We then used oversampling to obtain an equal number (N=24,000) of positive and negative examples [26].

Model Training of Metric Learning. Although there are many ways to measure the similarity between a seed and a prospect, e.g., by demographics and behavior, our goal is to define a similarity metric that helps identify prospects who would *behave similarly* as a seed does in a Social QA context. To do so, we adopt the "distance metric learning" [22], which automatically learns a pair-wise metric function:

11

$$d_M(u,u') = \sqrt{(u-u')M(u-u')}, \qquad (1)$$

where u and u' are feature vectors of a pair of users, M is positive semi-definite (PSD) matrix M, also known as Mahalanobis matrix [24].

Unlike other similarity measures, e.g. Cosine similarity, Mahalanobis distance allows the relative importance of various features to be *automatically* learned from the training samples. In other words, the distance metric learning keeps instances of the same class close while pushing instances of different classes far away. As a result, this model promotes prospects who have limited social QA activities but are very similar to certain seeds, since it takes into account a number of user features (e.g., personality and organization) in its pair-wise, feature-based constraints.

We use information-theoretic metric learning (ITML) [1] to learn the function for the following reasons. First, ITML can handle a wide variety of constraints and can also optionally incorporate a prior on the distance function. Second, it is fast and scalable as our data is of very large quantity. Third, the online version of the algorithm can handle streaming data well. This is important since our live Social QA system must handle constant updates of a QA history.

As mentioned earlier, different types of questions may require different types of answerers. We thus train the prospect-seed similarity model by each type of question. The ITML training took less than 2 secs on a typical PC to learn the Mahalanobis distance matrix for each question type.

Constraint-based Answerer Selection
Based on the results of steps 1 and 2, we select the top-K ranked users such that their combined fitness to answer the question and the diversity of their QA activeness are maximized. As mentioned earlier, choosing users with varied levels of activeness ensures that a question is routed to both seeds and prospects. The overall answerer selection process can be modeled as an optimization problem. Formally, given a question q, we find a set of prospects p_i and seeds s_j such that the following holds:

$$U^* = \underset{p_i, s_j}{argmax} \sum_{i=1}^{K} f(s_i, q)$$
$$+ \sum_{j=1}^{L} \left(f(p_j, q) + \alpha \cdot \sum_{i=1}^{K} f(s_i, q) * (1 - d_M(s_i, p_j)) \right)$$
$$+ \beta H(\{a_{s_1}, \cdots, a_{s_K}, a_{p_1}, \cdots, a_{p_j}\}), \qquad (2)$$

where $U^* = \{p_i^*, s_j^*\}$ is the set of potential answerers that optimizes the energy function. The first term of the function measures the fitness of all seed candidates for question q; the second term computes the fitness of all prospect candidates and their similarity to those highly ranked seeds by their fitness score. The similarity measure between a prospect and a seed, $1 - d_M(s_j, p_i)$, is used to boost the prospect's chance to be selected. Specifically, we let a prospect "borrow" the fitness score of a seed as a gain if the prospect is similar enough to the seed. If the fitness score of a prospect is too low, the "contribution" of this term will also be low. In such cases, the seeds, rather than the most similar prospects, would most probably be selected. The third term represents the divergence constraint by candidates' activeness. We use an information theoretic measure, Shannon entropy of the activeness a_{p_i} over all candidates as our diversity constraint. In other words, the more diverse level of activities that the selected candidates have, the more uniformly distributed the random variable is, and the higher the Shannon entropy is. α and β are the weight parameters that control the contributions of each term. They are estimated empirically based on the training data.

Our constraint-based model is designed to handle many different cases in a systematic manner. For example, there are cases where no qualified seed answerers are discovered in Step 1 (e.g., all seed answerers are ranked very low by their fitness score). This may very well happen for new questions that require knowledge previously not present in the social QA history. In these cases, the similarity measuring in the second term will be skipped, since the higher ranked users are already prospects, and our system can directly select those prospects according to the diversity constraint. On the other hand, no prospects may be found similar enough to any selected seeds according to the second term, in which cases only the seeds will be selected by the 1st and 3rd terms.

Note that the third term, our diversity constraint, is still very useful even when balancing the selection among just a set of seeds/prospects alone. Our goal is to find a set of people with varied levels of activity to make sure that we do not overburden the more active ones while fostering the participation of less active ones.

EXPERIMENTS
We have conducted both cross-validation experiments and empirical studies to validate our approach.

Cross Validation
Since our collected Social QA data set did not contain ground truth for measuring the accuracy of recommending a prospect who has very limited or no past Social QA activities, we used the data set to evaluate the recommendation accuracy for only seeds. We have conducted 10-fold cross-validation experiments using all the 2050 answers (for 901 questions) provided by the seeds.

Accuracy Metric
While the traditional precision and recall measure assesses the quality of *all* retrieved items, we want to measure the quality of partial results (seeds only). For each question, we thus computed *coverage rate*, which measures the overlap

between our top-K recommended seeds and the seeds who actually answered the question (ground truth).

Results

Table 2 shows our experimental results. We compared our approach with a baseline that used only seeds' expertise/ability (tag-based) to make recommendations as most other systems do. As shown, our approach outperformed the baseline significantly. This implies that additional features beyond one's expertise, such as their willingness and readiness to answer questions, help better predict one's overall fitness for being an answerer of a question.

Empirical Study

To demonstrate the value of our work in the real world, we also designed and conducted an empirical study. We first collected 150 questions from about 50 colleagues. Among the 150 questions received, there were 52, 52, and 46 questions in Type I (requiring subject matter expertise), Type II (requiring general domain knowledge), and Type III (general questions that any employee can answer), respectively.

We manually went through all the submitted questions and filtered out those that were too vague (e.g., we had trouble parsing them) or too easy (e.g., answers can be found easily on Google). After the filtering, we submitted the remainder of 114 questions (42 Type I, 38 Type II, and 34 Type III) to our system[2]. For each question, our system recommended the top-6 potential answerers. To avoid overburdening the answerers, in this experiment our system recommended each potential answerer *once* to answer only one question. As a result, our system identified a total of 684 potential answerers, with 43 seeds (6.3%) and 641 prospects (93.7%), for the 114 submitted questions. We then contacted and asked each of them to conduct a survey.

Survey Method

We designed a survey to assess the quality of our recommendation by soliciting the responses from the recommended answerers. Our survey included three parts. The first part asked a potential answerer to tell us whether she would be able to answer the routed question, when she would be able to answer the question, her actual answer to the question, and her self-assessed confidence in her answer. The second part solicited input from those who would not be able to answer the question or could not answer the question at the time of request. We asked the person to choose or state main reasons why she could not answer the routed question and the preferred time window she might be able to answer the question. The third part inquired about the desired features of a Social Q&A system for potential answerers, including whether they would like to receive question routing notifications in the future, what additional information they would wish to know (e.g., time constraint and asker information), when and which channel they prefer

	Top-3	Top-5	Top-10
Our approach	44.9%	56.3%	73.9%
Baseline	27.8%	36.8%	60.1%

Table 2. 10-fold cross validation for coverage rate.

to receive routing notifications, and whether and how often they would want to receive periodical reminders.

We invited all 684 recommended answerers via email to conduct the survey. Based on the survey results, we randomly chose 50 submitted questions that received answers, and sent the 90 collected answers of these questions to the original 27 askers. We asked the askers to rate the quality of the answers on a 5-likert scale, 1 being "Totally Unacceptable", and 5 being the "Excellent answer".

Results and Findings

From the 684 recommended answerers, we received 303 completed surveys submitted by 22 recommended seeds and 281 prospects. These responses generated 201 answers to 112 questions by 22 recommended seeds and 187 prospects. Among the 112 questions answered, there were 42 Type I, 36 Type II, and 34 Type III questions. From 201 answers received, Type I, II, and III questions received 82, 56, and 63 answers, respectively. On average, each question received 1.8 answers. Table 3 shows the evaluation of 90 answers from 27 askers. There are 63.3% (57/90) answers received the satisfactory rating 4 or above, and 73.3% (66/90) answers received the rating 3 or above.

Based on the survey results, 75% of them indicated that they were able to answer the routed question, 9% were not sure, and only 16% could not answer the question. When asked how confident they had in their answers, over 80% reported a lot/full confidence. Our analysis also showed that the answerer confidence and askers' satisfaction rating are significantly correlated with coefficient 0.369 ($p < .001$).

For those (16%) who indicated that they could not answer the routed question, we also asked them whether they knew others who might know the answer. 19 out of 70 stated so, 14 provided email addresses of those people, and 11 were willing to forward the question to them.

Overall 88.3% of participants also expressed that they

	Asker Satisfaction Rating (1-5)				
	1 Totally unacceptable	2 Barely acceptable	3 Neutral	4 Good	5 Excellent
Seed	1	0	1	2	4
Prospect	9	14	8	31	20
Total	10	14	9	33	24

Table 3. Asker satisfaction rating for 90 answers.

---

[2] Although our system is already online and we could let the askers to submit their questions themselves, we were still going through company approvals (e.g., privacy training) before its company-wide deployment.

would like to receive question routing notifications in the future as long as the routing frequency is reasonable.

Seeds vs. Prospects. Since our goal is to involve inactive users in Social QA, we examined and compared the responses from the recommended seeds and prospects (Table 4). We used two metrics to assess their responses. First, we computed *response rate*, the percentage of recommended answerers who took our survey. Second, we calculated *answering rate*, the percentage of people who provided answers to the routed question in the survey. Table 4 shows the comparisons of these two rates for the recommended seeds and prospects. The seeds had a higher response rate (51.1% vs. 43.8%), while the prospects had a slightly higher answering rate (66.5% vs. 63.6%). In addition, the answerer self-rated confidence in their answers (rated a lot and full confidence) and the askers' rating about the quality of the received answers (rated 4 and 5) were also similar.

It is interesting to notice that the recommended prospects showed a slightly higher level of willingness to answer the question (69.4% vs. 63.6%), which is consistent with their higher answering rate. On the other hand, the recommended seeds produced a higher asker satisfaction (75% vs. 62.2%), which may not be surprising since the seeds have had much more experience in answering questions. Overall, the results imply that our recommended prospects are *able* and *willing* to answer routed questions, and most of their produced answers were also acceptable (62.2% asker satisfaction).

Our study also provided us with valuable ground truth about our prospects' social QA behavior, which was not available before. We can then use the data in the future to fine-tune our model, e.g., learning different feature weights for seeds and prospects in our fitness prediction model.

Effects of Question Type. We were also curious about how other factors might have impacted the results. We found that the *question type* had a significant impact on several aspects. By ANOVA test, question type had a significant impact on the number of answers received (F=4.428, df=2, p<.05). The post-hoc tests indicated that Type I (M = 3.12) received significantly more answers than Type II & III (median = 2.47, p<.05 and M = 2.44, p<.05). The non-parametric Kruskal-Wallis test showed that question type also had a significant effect on answer response time (p<.001). Post-hoc tests indicated Type 1 (median = 17 hours) and Type III (median = 1.7 hours) had significant differences (p<.001) and Type I questions needed more time. From these results, it seems that Type I questions would require more time to receive answers but have a high chance to get an answer. On the opposite, it is more difficult for Type III questions to receive an answer. But if someone is willing to answer it, s/he would answer it quickly.

We have two hypotheses regarding to Type III questions. One is that not everyone is willing to give out an opinion but if someone decides to do so, she would do it promptly. The other is that some users may find Type III questions too general (or as someone commented "a silly question"), while Type I questions are more challenging, as they require more technical skills or knowledge. The latter might be true in an IT company like ours, it is unclear to us whether such phenomenon holds in other enterprises.

Nevertheless, these results will be useful for a Social QA system to predict the probability and estimate the time taken to receive an answer for a given type of question. Such function would also provide askers with much more information about the Social QA system itself and let them know in advance what to expect (i.e., the likelihood for a question to get an answer and how long it would take).

Answerer Preferences. In the survey, we also asked the participants their preferences of receiving question routing notifications. In terms of *when* they would prefer to receive question notifications, 44% had no preferences, 34.3 preferred either start (Monday) or end of week (Friday), and 21.7% preferred to receive notifications in the morning. In addition, 85.8% preferred to receive notifications via email and 35.8% also wished to receive notifications posted on the existing social platform. 38.6% also preferred to receive a weekly reminder. We also asked what additional information would be helpful to the answerers. The top-4 rated items were: time constraint (72.1%), question source (68.9%), asker information (64.2%), and question status (55.9%). For the asker information, the top-2 rated items were: job information (85.3%) and social relationship (44.80%). Such information is invaluable, as it can be used to tune our system and improve its answerer response rate.

Compared with Answers@T. As mentioned earlier, Answers@T is a stand-alone Social QA service deployed in our company. Since Answers@T completely relies on volunteers to find and answer the submitted questions instead of actively identifying potential answerers as our system does, we compared the performance of Answers@T and that of ours based on our empirical study. Notably, each question on Answers@T received 1.45 answers on average, while ours received 1.8 answers. In addition, the acceptance rate (askers rated the answers acceptable) for Answers@T is 53.1%, while ours is around 63.3%. These results indicate that our routing is useful and improves pure self-selected Social QA service.

	Seed	Prospect
Response Rate	51.1% (22/43)	43.8%(281/641)
Answering Rate	63.6% (14/22)	66.5% (187/281)
Confidence	85.7% (12/14)	84.0% (157/ 187)
Willingness	63.6% (14/22)	69.4%(195/281)
Asker Satisfaction	75% (6/8)	62.2% (51/82)

Table 4. Responses of seeds and prospects.

DISCUSSION

Here we discuss several observations made in our field study and in our real-world deployment. We also note the current limitations in our approach, which bear design implications of developing a smart Social QA system.

Handling Cold Start: The Worst Case Scenario

Our system is specifically designed to address "cold start" problem where the majority of users have very limited or no past Social QA activities. However, we still expect that the users have exhibited certain *other* social behavior, e.g., blogging and forum posts, which can be used to gauge their willingness, ability, and readiness to answer a question. In our current implementation, we leveraged the non-Social QA activities occurred in our enterprise social platform to model our prospects. However, in the process of deploying our system for one of our customers, we found that we had no data to draw upon, since there was no existing social platform used in that company.

We have thought of several alternatives to handle this "worst case scenario". One is to use other internal data sources, e.g., emails and employee records. The other is to use external data sources, such as public social media sites like Twitter. Both have their own unique challenges. The first one may require the access to confidential or private information, while the latter often requires entity resolution that links an employee's identity with his external social media IDs. It thus would be interesting to investigate what other features or data sources can be easily obtained and are also helpful for predicting one's Social QA behavior.

Extensibility

Since our goal is to deploy our system to any company who wants to support Social QA, we have examined the extensibility of our approach from several aspects. First, our models are domain independent, although we have trained ours using the data from our company. However, certain customization will still be required when adopting our system to a different environment in several areas.

First, our answerer fitness prediction model relies on both the question and answerer features. We currently used simple natural language processing (NLP) to extract these features. Depending on the line of business, certain terms may be more important than others. For example, common legal jargons may be considered stop words in a law firm but rather important in other contexts. In addition, each company may have its own set of jargons that may need to be captured (e.g., "cloud computing" together instead of being treated as two separate words). In short, our model may need to be re-trained (e.g., a new set of stop words) in a new context.

Second, although our prospect-seed similarity model is general, it may need to be extended to suit a specific business setting. For example, our current model does not consider the similarity of people's roles (e.g., customer advocate) or positions held in a company (e.g., development manager). Such information could be useful for identifying prospects especially if they have limited social activities.

Third, depending on a business context, we may need to extend our constraint-based answerer selection by incorporating new constraints. For example, Type III questions are generally soliciting someone's subjective opinion in public. Such opinions expressed in public even still within an enterprise may bear serious consequences (e.g., opinions expressed in a financial institute or law firm). In such cases, we may want to add new selection constraints, e.g., routing these questions to only designated answerers.

Fourth, our current goal is to help foster Social QA activities within an enterprise. Nonetheless, our approach is quite general and can be easily adopted in other social platforms, e.g., Facebook and Twitter. Since an enterprise social platform does provide information that may not be available on a public social platform (e.g., organizational information), we would need to replace the features computed based on such information with different features.

Answerer Engagement

Our current work has focused on how to recommend suitable answerers for a question. Once a set of potential answerers is identified, currently our system generates an email message based on a template and sends the question to the recommended answerers. Based on our survey results, we can tune our system to better suit the preferences of an answerer, e.g., providing the additional required information and timing the message. Depending on a user's personality traits including his motivation, the notification message can be further customized. For example, the message to an extrovert person may stress the social reward to be received, while the message to an altruistic person may stress the benefits of the answer to his colleagues.

Personalized Question Asking

In our current system, we assume all askers are the same and want the same. This may not be true in the real world. For example, certain askers may desire fast but partial answers to their questions, while others may prefer to wait for a perfect answer. Moreover, askers may wish to get an answer from someone who is similar or dissimilar to themselves. A future research topic would be to model the askers and truly understand their needs and wishes in a Social QA setting. Using the asker model, the answerer recommendation can then incorporate the preferences/constraints of each asker and tailor the recommendation results to the asker.

CONCLUSION

In this paper, we have presented a Smart Social QA system in an enterprise setting. Due to the limited awareness and participation in an enterprise Social QA site, we develop an optimization-based approach to answerer recommendation. Our approach includes three parts. First, it uses a statistical model to predict the fitness of a potential answerer, including his ability (expertise), willingness, and readiness to answer the question. Based on the predicted fitness, it selects the top-N

ranked candidates. If the top-N candidates contain *seeds* (most active answerers), our system then uses distance metric learning to automatically discover top-M *prospects* (less active answerers) that are most similar to each identified seed. Combining the top-N and top-M candidates from the previous two steps, it uses a constraint-based approach to select the final top-K potential answerers such that their combined fitness for the question and diversity of activity level are maximized. These top-N people are then recommended to the asker to route her question to.

As a result, not only can our solution find top-matched answerers for a given question, but it can also involve less active users including inactive ones in Social QA to help grow the pool of answerers. Our extensive algorithmic and live experiments have demonstrated the value of our work, which can select a mix of seeds and prospects from over 400,000 employees, and achieve about 70% answering rate and asker satisfaction rate.

ACKNOWLEDGEMENT

We thank Min Li, Shi Wan Zhao, Chang Yan Chi, Jeffrey Nichols, Jalal Mahmud, Thomas Schaeck, and Aditya Pal for their inspiring suggestions on this work. We also thank our study participants for providing help on the surveys.

REFERENCES

1. Davis, J., Kulis, B., Jain, P., Sra, S. and Dhillon, I., "Information-theoretic metric learning," in Proceedings of International Conference on Machine Learning (ICML), 2007.

2. Dror, G., Koren, Y., Maarek, Y., and Szpektor, I., I want to answer, who has a question? Yahoo! Answers recommender system. *KDD'11*, 1109-1117.

3. Ehrlich, K., Lin, C., and Griffiths-Fisher, V., Searching for experts in the enterprise: combining text and social network analysis. *Group'07*, 117-126.

4. Gazan, R. Social Q&A. *J. of the Amer. Soc. for Info. Sci. & Tech.*, Advances in Information Science, 2011.

5. Golbeck, J. Robles, C., Edmondson, M., Turner, K. 2011. Predicting Personality from Twitter. In *Proc. IEEE SocialCom.*

6. Guo, J., Xu, S., Bao, S., and Yu, Y., Tapping on the potential of Q&A community by recommending answer providers. *CIKM '08*, 921-930.

7. Guy, I., Zwerdling, N., Ronen, I., Carmel, D., and Uiel, E., Social media recommendation based on people and tags, *SIGIR'10*, 194-201.

8. Horowitz, E., and Kamvar, S. D., The anatomy of a large-scale social search engine. *WWW'10*, 431-440.

9. Krishna, V. and Rani, T. On the Classification of Imbalanced Datasets. International Journal of Computer Science and Technology, Vol, 2: 145-148, 2011.

10. Liu, Q., and Agichtein, E., Modeling answerer behavior in collaborative question answering systems. *ECIR'01*, 67-79.

11. Liu, X., Croft, W. B., and Koll, M., Finding experts in community-based question-answering services, *CIKM'05*, 315-316.

12. Mahmud, J., Zhou, M.X., Maggido, N., and Nichols, J. Recommending Targeted Strangers from Whom to Solicit Information on Social Media. *Proc. IUI 2013*, 37-48.

13. Mamykina, L., Manoim, B., Mittal, M., Hripcsak, G., and Hartmann, B. Design lessons from the fastest Q&A site in the West. *CHI '11*, 2857-2866.

14. Morris, M. R., Teevan, J., and Panovich, K., What do people ask their social networks, and why? A survey study of status message Q&A behavior, *CHI'10*, 1739-1748.

15. Muller, M. Lurking as personal trait or situational disposition? Lurking and contributing in enterprise social media, *CSCW'12*, 253-256

16. Pal, A., Farzan, R., Konstan, J. A., and Kraut, R. E., Early detection of potential experts in question answering communities, *UMAP'11*, 231-242.

17. Pan, Y., Luo, L. Chi, C., and Liao, Q. To answer or not: what What non-QA social activities can tell? CSCW 2013.

18. Pennebaker, J.W., Francis, M.E., and Booth, R.J. Linguistic Inquiry and Word Count. *Erlbaum Publishers*, 2001.

19. Qu, M., Qiu, G., He, X., Zhang, C., Wu, H., Bu, J., and Chen, C. Probabilistic question recommendation for question answering communities. *WWW '09*, 1229-1230.

20. Richardson, M., and White, R. W., Supporting synchronous social Q&A throughout the question lifecycle, *WWW'11*, 755-764.

21. Sung J., Lee, J. and Lee, U. Booming Up the Long Tails: Discovering Potentially Contributive Users in Community-Based Question Answering Services. *Proc. ICWSM 2013.*

22. Xing, E., Ng, A., Jordan, M., and Russel, S. Distance metric learning, with application to clustering with side-information. Proc. *NIPS' 2002*, 505-512.

23. Yang, Y., and Pedersen, O.J. A Comparative Study on Feature Selection in Text Categorization. In *Proc. ICML*, 1997.

24. Yarkoni, Tal. Personality in 100,000 words: A largescale analysis of personality and word usage among bloggers. Journal of Research in Personality 2000.

25. Zhang, J., Ackerman, M. S., Adamic, L., and Nam, K. K., QuME: a mechanism to support expertise finding in online help-seeking communities, *Proc. UIST'07*, 111-114.

26. Zhou, Z. M., Lan, M., Niu, Z. Y., and Yu, Y., Exploiting user profile information for answer ranking in cQA, *WWW2012 Companion.*

Improving Business Rating Predictions Using Graph Based Features

Amit Tiroshi[*†], **Shlomo Berkovsky**[*‡], **Mohamed Ali Kaafar**[*],
David Vallet[*], **Terence Chen**[*], **Tsvi Kuflik**[†]

[*]NICTA, Australia   [†]University of Haifa, Israel   [‡]CSIRO, Australia

[*]firstname.lastname@nicta.com.au   [†]atiroshi,tsvikak@is.haifa.ac.il

ABSTRACT

Many types of recommender systems rely on a rich ensemble of user, item, and context features when generating recommendations for users. The features can be either manually engineered or automatically extracted from the available data, such that feature engineering becomes an important part of the recommendation process. In this work, we propose to leverage graph based representation of the data in order to generate and automatically populate features. We represent the standard user-item rating matrix and some domain metadata, as graph vertices and edges. Then, we apply a suite of graph theory and network analysis metrics to the graph based data representation, in order to populate features that augment the original user-item ratings data. The augmented data is fed into a classifier that predicts unknown user ratings, which are used for the generation of recommendations. We evaluate the proposed methodology using the recently released Yelp business ratings dataset. Our results indicate that the automatically populated graph features facilitate more accurate and robust predictions, with respect to both the variability and sparsity of ratings.

ACM Classification Keywords

H.3.3 Information Storage and Retrieval: Information Filtering

Author Keywords

Recommender Systems, Graph-Based Recommendations, Feature Extraction.

INTRODUCTION

Many widely-used recommendation approaches, e.g., collaborative filtering and matrix factorization, rely – in their base form – on statistical correlations in the available user ratings for items. However, prior research has

IUI'14, February 24–27, 2014, Haifa, Israel.
Copyright © 2014 ACM 978-1-4503-2184-6/14/02...$15.00.
http://dx.doi.org/10.1145/2557500.2557526

shown that the accuracy of recommendations can be improved through augmenting the ratings with a variety of user and item features [5, 2]. Examples of systems that exploit data features in the recommendation process include content-based [22], knowledge-based [26], conversational [9], and context-aware recommenders [1], to name a few. Augmenting the data and incorporating additional features allow the recommender to address a range of issues, such as contextual dependencies, explanations and persuasion, bootstrapping and cold-start, diversity, and others.

Generating features (often referred to as *feature engineering*), populating their values, and incorporating them in the recommendation process is, however, not a straightforward process. Firstly, features that shed a new light on the data and encompass a new knowledge, should to be conceived. It is not clear a priori what features are more promising than others, and have the potential to lead to the new knowledge. Secondly, the new features need to be populated for as large as possible portions of the data. This may be a tedious task that is either done by human experts, e.g., through crowdsourcing or focus groups, or requires a substantial domain knowledge, e.g., ontologies or domain-specific databases like IMDB. Thirdly, the contribution of the new features to the recommender should be evaluated, in order to assess to what extent each of the features improves the system's performance and in which conditions.

Previous research into automatic feature generation focused primarily on combining multiple sets of features together [18, 13]. A more recent work proposed to extract new features from the available Social Network user profiles, and leverage these features in the recommendation process [25]. In here, we extend and thoroughly evaluate the ideas presented in [25], and consider a scenario, where new features are extracted and populated through looking at the data from a cardinally different perspective. Specifically, we represent a fairly standard collaborative filtering dataset of user ratings for items (containing also limited metadata: item location and category) using a graph-based structure. The users, items, and metadata entities are considered as the graph vertices, whereas the available user-item ratings and item categorization are the graph edges. Then, we apply a suite of widely-used graph theory and network analysis metrics

[10], to automatically generate and populate additional features for the users and items. Finally, we feed both the original rating data and the newly populated graph features into a Random Forest regression model [7], in order to predict unknown user ratings and inform the recommendations.

We evaluate our approach using a publicly available dataset of user reviews for businesses, recently released by Yelp for the ACM Recommender Systems Conference 2013 challenge.[1] The dataset contains thousands of user reviews for businesses, which are accompanied by numeric ratings. We focus primarily on the ratings and model the dataset using two representations: as a bipartite (user and business vertices) and a tripartite[2] (user, business, and metadata vertices) non-directional graph. We extract and populate a set of user and business related features and use these features to predict unknown user ratings for businesses. Our results show that augmenting the rating data with the graph features improves the accuracy of the generated recommendations. We also investigate which features, combinations of features, and graph representation contribute most to the accuracy of the recommender, and how this contribution is affected by various parameters of the input data, such as the variability and the sparsity of ratings.

In summary, the main contributions of our work are three-fold. Firstly, we present and demonstrate an approach for augmenting the collaborative user-item rating data with automatically populated graph-based features. Secondly, we provide a strong empirical evidence in favor of incorporating these features into the prediction and recommendation process. Thirdly, we evaluate the accuracy of the rating predictions for various degrees of variability and sparsity in the data.

METHODOLOGY

In this section we present our method for predicting business ratings. This consists of two components. Firstly, we represent the data using a graph model and use this model to augment and populate features used by the prediction mechanism. Secondly, we apply the Random Forest regression method to predict user ratings for businesses. In the following sub-sections we present these components.

Graph Model and Feature Extraction

The original Yelp dataset (will be elaborately presented and characterized in the next section) inherently contains a limited number of features, e.g., average user/business rating and business category, which can be leveraged to predict unknown ratings. In order to enrich the set of features used by the predictor, we represent

---

[1]http://recsys.acm.org/recsys13/recsys-2013-challenge/

[2]Our use of the "tripartite graph" notation is slightly inconsistent with the canonic definition, such that the "bipartite graph with metadata nodes" notation would be more appropriate. However, for the sake of brevity we stick to the bipartite and tripartite terminology.

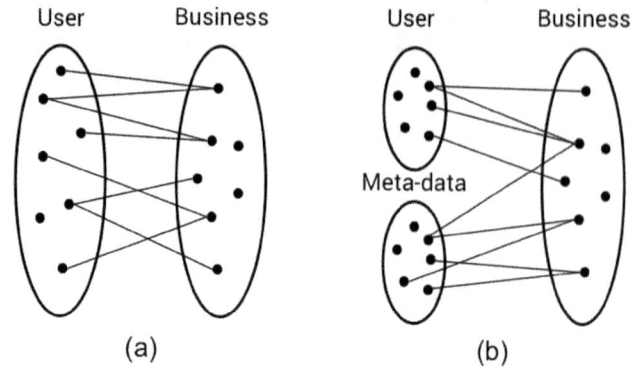

Figure 1. Two graph models: (a) bipartite graph (b) tripartite graph

the data using a graph model. Two models were implemented and evaluated: a *bipartite* model with vertices U and B representing users and businesses, and a *tripartite* model with vertices U, B, and M representing users, businesses, and metadata items, respectively. The models are illustrated in Figure 1.

More formally, the bipartite graph is defined as G = {U, B, E}, where U = $\{u_i \mid i$ is a user} and B = $\{b_j \mid j$ is a business} are the vertex sets in the two partitions of G. Vertices u_i and b_j are connected by edge e_{ij} if j was reviewed by i, i.e., E = $\{e_{ij} \mid i$ reviewed $j\}$. Similarly, the tripartite graph is defined by G = {U, B, M, E}. In this case, the vertex sets represent users U = $\{u_i \mid i$ is a user}, businesses B = $\{b_j \mid j$ is a business}, and metadata items M = $\{M_c \cup M_l\}$, where $M_c = \{c_m \mid m$ is the category(ies) of $j\}$, e.g., shopping, food, automotive, and $M_l = \{l_n \mid n$ is the location of $j\}$. As for the edges E of the graph, e_{ij} edges represent, in similar to the bipartite graph, user reviews for businesses, but e_{jc} represent business categories and e_{jn} represent business locations. All the edges in both types of graph are not labeled.

Every review in the dataset provided by user i for business j contributes to multiple features. We aggregate the features into three groups (see Figure 2).

- *Basic* features include only the unique identifiers of i and j.

- *Extended* features include: number of reviews by i, average rating of i, number of reviews for j, number of categories $|\{m\}|$ with which j is associated, average number of businesses in $\{m\}$, average rating of businesses in $\{m\}$, and location n of j.

- *Graph* features include: degree centrality [6], average neighbor degree [4], PageRank score [20], clustering coefficient [15], and node redundancy [15]. These five features are populated for both user nodes u_i and business nodes b_j, whereas an additional shortest path feature is computed for the pairs of nodes (u_i, b_j). Note that the graph features are populated separately for the bipartite and tripartite graph representations.

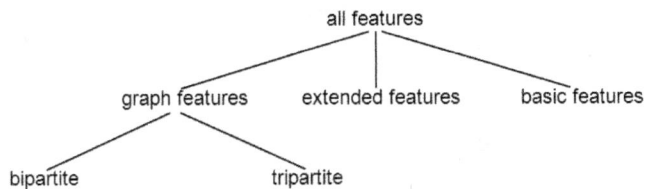

Figure 2. Feature classes

Degree centrality (or, simply, node degree) quantifies the importance of a node through the number of other nodes, to which it is connected. Hence, in the bipartite graph, degree centrality of a user node u_i is the activity of i, i.e., the number of businesses that i reviewed, and for a business node b_j it is the popularity of j, i.e., the number of users who reviewed it. In the tripartite graph, the number of categories $|\{m\}|$ of j plus 1 (business location) are added to degree centrality of b_j.

As the name suggests, *average neighbor degree* measures the average degree of nodes, to which a node is connected. In the bipartite graph, this metric communicates for u_i – the average popularity of businesses that i reviewed, and for b_j – the average activity of users who reviewed j. Note that in the tripartite graph, the average neighbor degree of b_j also incorporates the popularity of categories $\{m\}$ of j and the number of businesses sharing the same location n as j.

PageRank is a widely-used recursive metric that quantifies the importance of nodes in a graph. For a user node u_i, the PageRank score is computed through PageRank of the businesses $\{b_j\}$ which i reviewed, and, likewise, for a business node b_j – through PageRank of the users $\{u_i\}$ who reviewed j, of the categories with which j is associated, and of the location of j. In the tripartite graph, the PageRank scores of the business category nodes $\{c_m\}$ and of the location node l_n also affect PageRank of a business node b_j.

Clustering coefficient measures the density of a node's immediate subgraph as the ratio between the observed and possible number of cliques. Since cliques are impossible in the bipartite graph, clustering coefficient measures the density of "squares" in the graph, i.e., the portion of pairs of businesses j_x and j_y that are both reviewed by a pair of users i_a and i_b, and, respectively, the portion of pairs of users i_a and i_b that reviewed a pair of businesses j_x and j_y. Since no edges between u_i and $\{c_m\}$ (or, u_i and l_n) exist in the tripartite graph, clustering coefficient is meaningful only for the b_j nodes, where it is reduced to the bipartite variant.

Similarly, *node redundancy* shows what fraction of a node's pairs of neighbors are linked to the same other node. In the bipartite graph, node redundancy communicates for u_{i_a} - the portion of pairs of businesses that i_a reviewed that were both reviewed by another user i_b, and for b_{j_x} - the portion of pairs of users who reviewed j_x and also both reviewed another business j_y. In the tripartite graph, redundancy of business nodes also incorporates pairs of categories of j, with which some other businesses are associated as well.

Note that the graph based features are extracted and generated offline, i.e. not as part of the recommendation process, and, as such, the added computational overhead does not affect online recommendations.

Predicting Business Ratings

We apply the Random Forest regression model for the generation of the predictions of user ratings for businesses [7]. Random Forest is a popular ensemble classification algorithm that combines a set of binary decision trees. At the training stage, each tree is constructed using a portion of the training data and a subset of data features. Given a fixed set of features F that model the training data, $\log |F|$ features and about 2/3 of the training data are randomly selected by the algorithm to construct each tree. Within the forest trees, each node uses for the decision making only one feature $f \in F$, which is the top performing feature out of the selected subset of features.

At the classification stage, the test data items are run through all the trees in the trained forest. The class of a test item is determined by the majority voting of the terminal nodes reached when traversing the trees. In case of a regression model, which is applied for predictions of continuous values rather than discrete class labels, the predicted score is computed as a linear combination of the scores of the terminal nodes.

It should be noted that the ensemble of trees in Random Forest and the selection of the best performing feature in each node inherently eliminate the need for feature selection. Since every node uses for decision making a single top performing feature, the accurate predictive features get naturally selected in many nodes. Hence, these features have a strong impact on the classifier, such that the ensemble of multiple trees virtually substitutes the feature selection process. We refer the readers to [7] for an elaborate presentation of the Random Forest algorithm.

DATASET

The dataset used in this work is a public dataset released by Yelp for the ACM Recommender Systems Conference 2013 challenge. For our analysis, we filtered out users with less than 5 reviews (representing 21% of users), which results in 9,464 users providing 171,003 reviews and the corresponding ratings for 11,197 businesses.

Table 1 summarizes the basic statistics of users and businesses in the dataset. The average number of reviews per user stands at 18.07 (median=9) and the average number of reviews per business is 15.27 (median=5). Despite the high number of categories in the dataset, the average number of categories with which a business is associated is only 2.68. Every business is also associated with a single location.

	mean	std	min	25%	50%	75%	max
#reviews per user	18.07	29.60	5	6	9	17	588
#reviews per business	15.27	32.43	1	3	5	13	528
#categories per business	2.68	1.14	0	2	2	3	10

Table 1. Basic data statistics

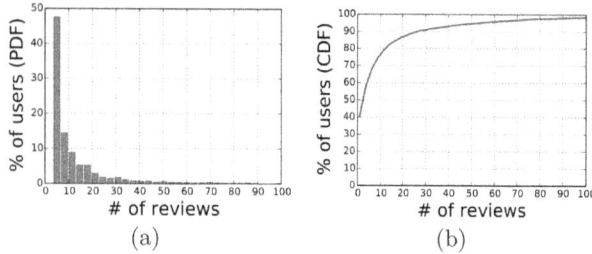

(a)   (b)

Figure 3. PDF and CDF of number of reviews per user

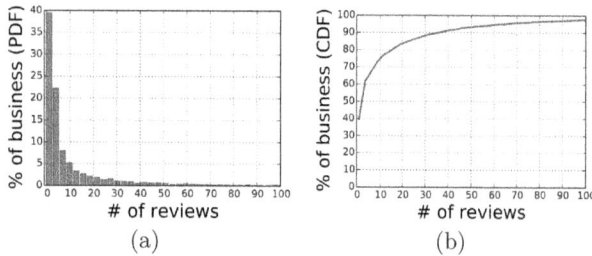

(a)   (b)

Figure 4. PDF and CDF of number of reviews per business

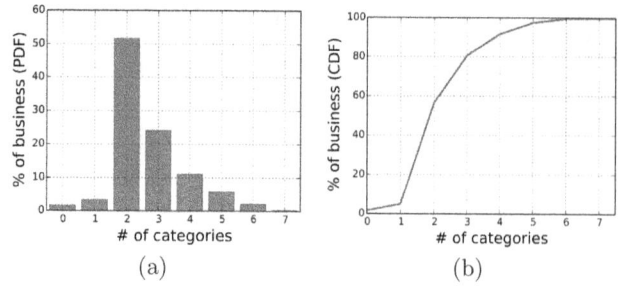

(a)   (b)

Figure 5. PDF and CDF of number of categories per business

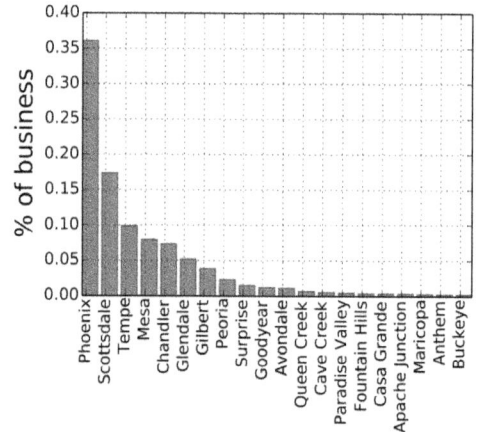

Figure 6. Location distribution of businesses across top-20 cities (overall, there are 62 cities)

Figure 3 illustrates the distribution of the number of reviews (and ratings) per user. The Cumulative Distribution Function (CDF) plot reveals a long tail distribution of the user degree with more than 75% of the users providing less than 10 reviews. Likewise, we observe in Figure 4 the distribution of the number of reviews per business. Only 24% of businesses attract more than 10 reviews, while only a few businesses (less than 2%) have a relatively higher number of reviews (more than 100). Hence, the cold-start problem manifests to some extent even in the filtered dataset.

Now, we characterize the distribution of business categories and locations in the dataset, which are considered as metadata information. Figure 5 illustrates the Probability Distribution Function (PDF) and CDF of the number of categories per business. We observe that the majority of businesses in the dataset are associated with less than three categories: more than half of the businesses have two categories and almost 25% have three. We also observe in Figure 6 that 97.6% of the businesses are located in the top-20 cities, with Phoenix alone being associated with 36% of businesses.

In order to evaluate whether the business category has any impact on the number of reviews and on the average rating, we show in Table 2 the top-25 categories and the corresponding average rating. The "Restaurants" category is by far the most popular with 4,467 businesses, where we observe on average 26.52 reviews per business with average rating of 3.45. Several other categories (marked in bold) obtain a higher average rating,

but have a substantially lower number of reviews per business. We computed the Spearman's Correlation coefficient between the average number of reviews per business and the average rating within the categories that are associated with 50 businesses or more. The computation shows a moderate correlation of 0.38, which suggests that the number of reviews per business influences the average rating assigned by the reviewers.

We then further study the impact of the number and the variability of reviews on the rating values. We examine in Figure 7(a) the distribution of the average rating as a function of the number of reviews that each business receives. We observe that although there is a trend slightly increasing from 1 to 4 with the increase of the median number of reviews, the distribution of the number of reviews is too skewed to argue for a clear impact. However, we observe in Figure 7(b), which shows the standard deviation of the average ratings, that both very high and low ratings generally imply a low deviation of ratings. This suggests that users mainly provide consistent ratings when reviewing businesses on the extreme sides of the scale, i.e., either very good or very bad businesses.

We also depict in Figure 8 the distributions of the average rating for users and for businesses, and the overall distribution of ratings in the dataset. More than 55% of the average user ratings range between 3 and 4. Combining this observation with the previously discussed distri-

order	category	# business	avg reviews/business	avg rating
1	Restaurants	4467	26.52	3.45
2	Shopping	1646	7.15	3.75
3	Food	1606	16.53	3.77
4	Beauty & Spas	721	4.54	**3.97**
5	Nightlife	637	36.67	3.5
6	Mexican	623	23.25	3.47
7	Automotive	529	3.83	3.67
8	Bars	515	40.58	3.46
9	Active Life	504	8.73	**3.99**
10	American (Traditional)	476	27.52	3.32
11	Fashion	474	7.23	3.74
12	Pizza	453	23.96	3.44
13	Health & Medical	428	2.86	**3.99**
14	Event Planning & Services	419	9.34	3.66
15	Fast Food	384	7.26	3.1
16	Sandwiches	380	23.12	3.6
17	Home Services	369	3.01	3.66
18	Hotels & Travel	345	10.45	3.44
19	American (New)	339	52.79	3.58
20	Grocery	332	13.61	3.6
21	Coffee & Tea	322	20.09	3.77
22	Arts & Entertainment	298	22.06	3.87
23	Local Services	296	3.89	3.88
24	Chinese	287	19.16	3.36
25	Burgers	259	26.71	3.34

Table 2. Average number of reviews and average rating for top-25 business categories.

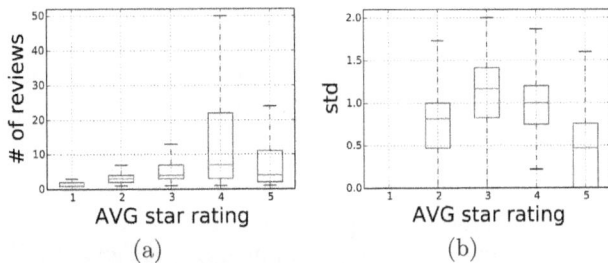

(a)　　　　(b)

Figure 7. Distribution of the number of review and of standard deviation of ratings

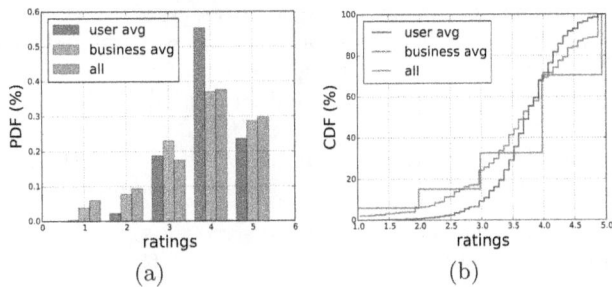

(a)　　　　(b)

Figure 8. PDF and CDF of user average ratings, business rating and all ratings

bution of ratings (almost 20% of user ratings are 3 and more than 35% are 4), we conclude that about half of the users consistently provide ratings between 3 and 4. This indicates that the average user rating could be an important indicator for rating predictions.

The observed average business rating distribution follows closely the overall rating distribution, with only a few businesses receiving a low rating. In fact, more than 80% of the average business scores are greater than 3. While in this case we do not observe a consistent behavior of users across rating different businesses, we posit that the average business rating could also be a valuable indicator to consider when predicting ratings.

RESULTS

In this section, we evaluate the accuracy of the recommendations and analyze the impact of graph features on the accuracy of the recommender. We use in the evaluation the Yelp dataset characterized in the previous section (recall that users who provided less than 5 ratings were excluded from the evaluation).

We perform a 5-fold cross validation and, therefore, split the ratings into 80% training and 20% test sets. For each fold, we train the predictive model using both the original features encapsulated in the review data and the new graph features. The basic and extended features are populated directly from the reviews. The graph features are populated from the bipartite and tripartite graph representations of the data and they are used to augment the basic and extended features.

We use an offline evaluation to optimize the parameters of the Random Forest regressor and set the number of trees to 100, and the number of features to select from at each node to 1. We measure the predictive accuracy of various combination of features (will be detailed in the next sub-section) using the RMSE metric and apply a paired t-test to validate statistical significance [24].

Graph Features Effectiveness

In this section, we study the contribution of the graph based features to the overall accuracy of the recommendations. We analyze how different types of features affect rating predictions and how they complement each other. Table 3 compares the RMSE values obtained by the recommender when different groups of features are used to train the Random Forest model. We show in the table four feature groups (basic, extended, bipartite, and tripartite), as well as some of their combinations.

First and foremost, we would like to highlight the closeness of the RMSE scores obtained by various combinations: the difference between the best and the worst performing combination is less than 10%. This is explained primarily by the low variance of user ratings, which was discussed in the previous section. Since most ratings given by a user are similar, they are highly predictable using simple methods like user/business average that perform reasonably accurately. This phenomenon is not peculiar to the Yelp dataset and got widely recognized in the Netflix Prize challenge [14]. As such, the complex mechanism of Random Forest has only a confined space for improvement.

Directly comparing the standalone performance of the two groups of graph features, bipartite vs. tripartite, we observe that the bipartite features produce more accurate predictions than the tripartite ones. When both bipartite and tripartite features are combined into graph features, there is a further slight improvement in performance over each of the two groups individually. Although the improvement is modest, it is statistically significant, p<0.001. This suggests that the bipartite fea-

features combination	features	RMSE
all_features	basic ∪ extended ∪ graph	1.076667
allexcept_tripartite	basic ∪ extended ∪ bipartite	1.077535
allexcept_basic	extended ∪ graph	1.082222
extended_and_bipartite	extended ∪ bipartite	1.085074
allexcept_bipartite	basic ∪ extended ∪ tripartite	1.089689
extended_and_tripartite	extended ∪ tripartite	1.107377
allexcept_extended	basic ∪ graph	1.109540
graph	bipartite ∪ tripartite	1.114891
allexcept_graph	basic ∪ extended	1.117572
bipartite		1.118867
tripartite		1.132601
basic		1.180921
extended		1.185396

Table 3. RMSE per selected feature combinations

tures may benefit, albeit minimally, from the availability of the tripartite features.

We now analyze how graph features contribute to the overall accuracy of the predictions. As expected, the best performance is achieved when all the groups of features are combined. By observing the accuracy differences when various groups of features are combined, there is a number of findings that support our hypothesis that graph features overall contribute to the accuracy of the recommendations. Firstly, when analyzing the performance of each group of features, we conclude that the two graph features (bipartite and tripartite) perform noticeably better than the other two groups features (basic and extended). The combination of graph features outperforms slightly, although statistically significantly, the combination of the basic and extended features.

When analyzing the impact of each feature group as a whole, we exclude a group from the overall set of features and measure the difference in performance with respect to the all_features run. We refer to these variants as allexcept_*group*, where *group* is the combination of features that is excluded from the computation. We observe that when graph features are excluded, the predictions are less accurate than when the basic and/or extended features are excluded. This indicates that graph features do provide additional information, which is not covered by the basic and extended features, and this information improves the accuracy of the generated recommendations.

There is also further evidence that the combination of bipartite and tripartite features is beneficial: we observe that the exclusion of tripartite features has a minor impact on the accuracy (allexcept_tripartite), whereas the exclusion of bipartite features (allexcept_bipartite) has a stronger impact. However, it should be noted that when both the groups of graph features are excluded (allexcept_graph), the impact on the accuracy is much stronger, which suggests that their combination benefits the system more than each one of them individually.

In order to evaluate the significance of the results, we perform a paired t-test using the RMSE values obtained for the various group combinations. The vast major-

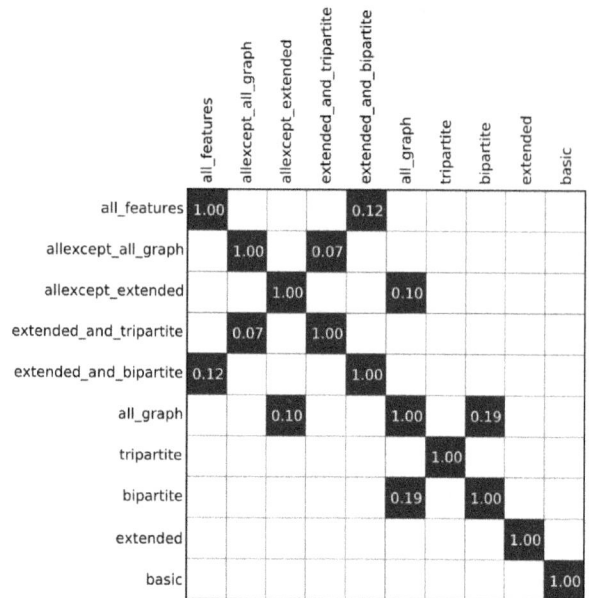

Figure 9. Significance of various combinations (white cells - significant, dark cells - not significant with p-value)

ity of differences are significant, p<0.001, whereas those that are not significant are highlighted in Figure 9. Two conclusions can be drawn from the failed tests: (1) the performance of bipartite features is not different from the performance of graph features, which indicates the prevalence of the bipartite features over the tripartite ones, when these two groups are considered individually; and (2) the combination of extended and bipartite features produces results that are not different from a combination of all the groups of features, which indicates that extended and bipartite features are the most important groups of features for the recommender.

Delving one level deeper, we analyze the contribution of individual features to the accuracy of the predictions. For this, we analyze the importance scores of the individual features, as computed by the Random Forest model. Table 4 summarizes the importance scores of the top features. We observe that two most important features are, as expected, user and business average ratings. We would like to highlight that these two features account together to more than 43% of the overall feature importance. The third and fourth features are related, respectively, to the tripartite and bipartite graph representations. This is an important finding, which suggests that features from both representations are within the short list of features considered by Random Forest. The fifth feature, business review count, is related to business popularity, which is also important in the context of rating predictions. Note that the PageRank score in the bipartite and tripartite graphs are ranked fourth and sixth, respectively, which means that the topography of the graphs provides a valuable information.

feature	import.	feature group
business_avg_rating	0.2228	extended
user_average_stars	0.2085	extended
business_tripartite_avg_ne_deg	0.0467	tripartite
business_bipartite_pagerank	0.0457	bipartite
business_review_count	0.0410	extended
business_tripartite_pagerank	0.0394	tripartite
business_bipartite_clustering_coeff.	0.0337	bipartite
business_main_category_degree	0.0334	extended
business_main_category_avg_stars	0.0313	extended
business_main_category	0.0311	extended
business_avg_degree_of_categories	0.0296	extended
business_bipartite_degree_centrality	0.0283	bipartite
business_avg_stars_of_categories	0.0264	extended
business_tripartite_degree_centrality	0.0255	tripartite
business_bipartite_avg_ne_deg	0.0203	bipartite
business_bipartite_node_redundancy	0.0152	bipartite
user_bipartite_avg_ne_deg	0.0147	bipartite
user_bipartite_node_redundancy	0.0129	bipartite

Table 4. Relative importance of individual features for all_features combination

While feature importance scores in Table 4 show that the average user and business ratings are pivotal for accurate predictions, we posit that these may not perform well when predicting ratings for businesses with high variability of ratings. We will investigate this question in the following subsection.

Robustness to Variability

In this experiment we assess the robustness of various groups of features when predicting ratings for businesses with a high variability of ratings. For this, we split the businesses to equally sized buckets based on the standard deviation (STD) of the business ratings, and compute the RMSE scores for each feature combination and each bucket of businesses. The results of this experiment are summarized in Figure 10, where only a small selection of most interesting for our analysis feature combinations is shown. The left columns refers to buckets with low STD of ratings and right columns to buckets with high STD.

The experiment shows that the behavior of the graph features differs from the behavior of the basic and extended features extracted from the original rating data. While graph features achieve a low accuracy in the low STD buckets, i.e., they struggle to generate accurate predictions for businesses with stable ratings, they perform remarkably well in the high STD buckets, where dominant features like average user/business rating included in the extended features group, struggle to generate accurate predictions. The all_features combination manages to effectively balance between the benefits of the extended and graph features and across the board achieves the highest overall accuracy. The difference in performance in the high STD buckets between all_features and allexcept_graph features clearly shows that the graph features complement data-driven features by allowing for more accurate predictions to be generated for businesses with highly variable ratings.

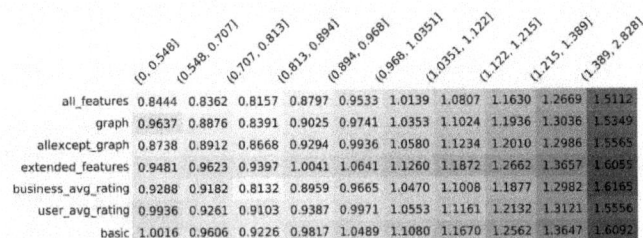

	(0, 0.548]	(0.548, 0.707]	(0.707, 0.813]	(0.813, 0.894]	(0.894, 0.968]	(0.968, 1.035]	(1.035, 1.122]	(1.122, 1.215]	(1.215, 1.389]	(1.389, 2.828]
all_features	0.8444	0.8362	0.8157	0.8797	0.9533	1.0139	1.0807	1.1630	1.2669	1.5112
graph	0.9637	0.8876	0.8391	0.9025	0.9741	1.0353	1.1024	1.1936	1.3036	1.5349
allexcept_graph	0.8738	0.8912	0.8668	0.9294	0.9936	1.0580	1.1234	1.2010	1.2986	1.5565
extended_features	0.9481	0.9623	0.9397	1.0041	1.0641	1.1260	1.1872	1.2662	1.3657	1.6055
business_avg_rating	0.9288	0.9182	0.8132	0.8959	0.9665	1.0470	1.1008	1.1877	1.2982	1.6185
user_avg_rating	0.9936	0.9261	0.9103	0.9387	0.9971	1.0553	1.1161	1.2132	1.3121	1.5556
basic	1.0016	0.9606	0.9226	0.9817	1.0489	1.1080	1.1670	1.2562	1.3647	1.6092

Figure 10. RMSE of the buckets (by STD) for selected combinations

In summary, graph features seem more robust when predicting ratings for businesses with variable ratings. However, how is their performance affected by the rating data sparsity? In the next section we will investigate the performance of the graph features at various levels of data sparsity, specifically, when a little rating data is available about a user/business.

Robustness to Sparsity

In this experiment we evaluate the performance of the recommender when predicting ratings for users/businesses with a low number of training ratings. We follow a methodology similar to the one used in the previous sub-section and split users/businesses into equally sized buckets. But this time, the split is done according to the number of ratings available. Figure 11 summarizes the RMSE scores obtained for each feature combination and each bucket of users, while Figure 12 focuses on businesses. The left columns refers to buckets with high sparsity of ratings and right columns to buckets with low sparsity.

Generally, the performance of the recommender improves as more ratings are available for a user/business, and this trend is consistent across all the evaluated combinations of features. Again, we can clearly see the contribution of the graph features. Comparing the performance of the all_features and the allexcept_graph combinations, we observe that the graph features complement other data-driven features and improve the performance of the recommender. Adding graph features yields a noticeable improvement in the business split, while also in the user split the effect is positive. Although other features such as the business and user average ratings perform well overall, they perform poorly when there is little training data. Focusing on the important predictive features, we notice that graph features outperform across the board individual features like user and business averages, which can be observed both for the user and business split.

Finally, we carry out an experiment that focuses on the business cold-start use case.[3] To this end, we split the businesses into 2 groups: those having more training ratings than test ratings and vice versa. We measure the accuracy of the ratings predictions using all the features

---

[3]The user cold-start evaluation is impossible, as we filtered from our dataset users with fewer than 5 ratings.

	(4, 5]	(5, 8]	(8, 11]	(11, 17]	(17, 25]	(25, 39]	(39, 58]	(58, 83]	(83, 140]	(140, 471]
all_features	1.2020	1.1693	1.1345	1.1181	1.0813	1.0599	1.0219	1.0177	0.9962	0.9130
graph	1.2447	1.2107	1.1694	1.1600	1.1158	1.0981	1.0555	1.0530	1.0305	0.9561
allexcept_graph	1.2545	1.2243	1.1807	1.1632	1.1230	1.0976	1.0650	1.0540	1.0349	0.9547
extended_features	1.3026	1.2812	1.2498	1.2287	1.1867	1.1700	1.1411	1.1253	1.1091	1.0111
business_avg_rating	1.2695	1.2206	1.1893	1.1765	1.1441	1.1209	1.0837	1.0839	1.0630	0.9914
user_avg_rating	1.2755	1.2462	1.1862	1.1789	1.1355	1.1156	1.0738	1.0807	1.0485	0.9839
basic	1.3000	1.2671	1.2276	1.2220	1.1810	1.1724	1.1212	1.1299	1.1081	1.0330

Figure 11. RMSE of the buckets (by number of user ratings) for selected combinations

	(0, 3]	(3, 9]	(9, 17]	(17, 27]	(27, 38]	(38, 53]	(53, 74]	(74, 103]	(103, 169]	(169, 440]
all_features	1.2894	1.1258	1.0727	1.0711	1.0700	1.0473	1.0238	1.0350	1.0125	0.9697
graph	1.3334	1.1983	1.1352	1.1164	1.1097	1.0801	1.0499	1.0551	1.0261	0.9867
allexcept_graph	1.3861	1.1513	1.0980	1.1078	1.1060	1.0802	1.0658	1.0813	1.0577	1.0109
extended_features	1.4514	1.1965	1.1536	1.1718	1.1746	1.1576	1.1388	1.1511	1.1330	1.0647
business_avg_rating	1.5984	1.1805	1.1050	1.0939	1.0931	1.0667	1.0419	1.0531	1.0206	0.9745
user_avg_rating	1.3434	1.2155	1.1604	1.1379	1.1392	1.1049	1.0797	1.0818	1.0587	1.0119
basic	1.3976	1.2656	1.2007	1.1703	1.1686	1.1469	1.1233	1.1304	1.0901	1.0617

Figure 12. RMSE of the buckets (by number of business ratings) for selected combinations

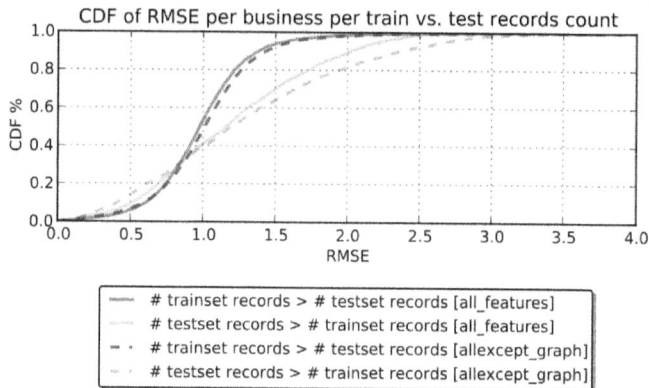

Figure 13. CDF of RMSE for business predictions. Businesses split based on the number of ratings in training and test set

(all_features) and all the features except for the graph features (allexcept_graph). The results of this experiment are shown in Figure 13.

We observe that in the setting, where there are more training than test ratings, i.e., enough training data for informed predictions, the accuracy of the predictions in the all_features and allexcept_graph cases is comparable. However, when there are more test ratings than training ratings, i.e., in the business cold-start setting, the exclusion of graph features degrades the accuracy of the predictions, as shown by the lower CDF curve starting from approximately RMSE=1.

Hence, we conclude that in addition to strengthening the robustness to rating variability, graph features also strengthen the robustness to data sparsity and unavailability of sufficient training data. This is an important finding, which indicates that graph features have the potential to alleviate the cold-start problem of recommender systems.

RELATED WORK
Applying machine learning and data mining techniques to user modeling and recommender systems applications has been the subject of many early studies [23, 28, 21, 27]. The two major challenges for applying machine learning techniques to those tasks, small datasets and lack of labeled data, are less of an issue nowadays [3]. Large and labeled datasets are being publicly released quite often, e.g., the Netflix Prize dataset, Movielens, Yelp dataset that was used in this work, and many other datasets.

Larger and richer datasets bring with them the possibility of using more complex machine learning techniques

that take into consideration a large set of features. The Netflix Prize winning team, for example, modeled the temporal dynamics, confidence levels, and implicit feedback features using the supplied dataset, and applied matrix factorization [14]. An ensemble method was then used to combine those features into a single model. The effectiveness of having more data and more features facilitates machine learning techniques achieving accurate results, which was discussed in [11]. Since extracting features from the data is considered a challenge [3], studies looked into ways of automatically engineering and populating features.

Previous work has investigated automatic feature generation by combining existing features using arithmetic functions such as min, max, average, and others [18]. In that work, a specific language for defining features was presented, where a feature was described by a set of inputs, their types, construction blocks, and the produced output. A framework for generating a feature space using the feature language as input was evaluated. The evaluation showed that the framework outperformed legacy feature generation algorithms in terms of accuracy. The main difference between the presented framework and its predecessors was that the framework was generic and applicable to multiple tasks and machine learning approaches. A review of other key feature generation methods was also provided, including task-oriented feature generation approaches and other construction methods (for instance, using boolean combinations [13]).

Only a few previous works incorporated graph features into machine learning and data mining applications [16, 17]. In [16], the recommendation problem was defined as a link prediction problem, and a similarity score between users and items nodes was computed using random walks. Items were then ranked based on their similarity scores, and top scoring items were recommended to users. Compared to other non-graph based similarity ranking methods, this approach was shown to outperform others using the True Positives vs. False Negatives metric. A similar random walk metric was used in [17], complemented by additional graph metrics based on the graph structure. These metrics were used for the purpose of link prediction and property values prediction in semantic descriptive graphs (RDF) using an SVM-based machine learning technique. Experimental results showed that the graph structure features in use were competitive to other graph structure features. It was also noted that the new defined features were not dataset-specific but could be applied to any RDF graph, while previously known structure based features were dataset-specific.

Our work also defines dataset agnostic graph-based features. However, the studied features are generic and not dependent on a known graph schema, such as RDF. In addition, we extend the set of generated features beyond random walks and tree structures, with a variety of metrics based on local neighborhood and global popularity. Finally, our evaluation focuses on the effect of the generated features on rating prediction and recommendation. Since the recommendation domain is tightly connected to graphs (e.g., social recommendations, people recommenders, nearest neighbors notion of collaborative filtering, and so forth), it is natural to evaluate the contribution of the graph based features to the accuracy of ratings predictions, and, in turn, of the generated recommendations.

Regarding the dataset used in this work, Yelp's service and other published or proprietary datasets have been explored in several works. Although these works are not directly related to predicting ratings or recommending, they may shed more light on the service and the released datasets. In [12] the motivations for using Yelp was discussed. Key usage patterns that emerged from an online user study were: to retrieve information regarding businesses and to serve as a form of entertainment (by engaging in a collaborative reviewing of businesses). Another work explored a different aspect of Yelp, by studying its mechanism for filtering out fake reviews [19]. According to the evaluation results, which were subsequently confirmed by Yelp, approximately a quarter of the submitted reviews were filtered due to suspicion of being fake. Another study examined the effect that a site like Groupon had on business reviews in Yelp [8]. Their results showed that, contrary to the common belief, users of Groupon provided more balanced and detailed reviews than other Yelp users.

CONCLUSIONS

In this work, we examined how additional features can be extracted from a graph-based representation of a user-to-item rating dataset. Using the state-of-the-art machine learning methods and widely-used graph theory metrics, we designed, implemented, and evaluated a model that was applied to predict user ratings. We validated our approach using a publicly available dataset of user reviews for businesses.

The evaluation showed that when augmenting basic data-driven features with graph features (considering both bipartite or tripartite graph representation models) improved the accuracy of the generated predictions. We verified that the studied graph features were robust to data variability and sparsity. This could be credited to the augmentation of the graph structure, be it a user vertex, a business vertex, or an edge, that captured an intrinsic valuable information that might not be uncovered otherwise due to data sparsity.

We observed that bipartite graph features were superior to the tripartite ones and led to a higher accuracy of the rating predictions, which suggested that the use of a more complex graph representation might also introduce noise. Combining the two representations, however, yield a higher accuracy, such that the best overall results were achieved when combining the graph features with other data-driven features.

Although, as observed in this paper, the ratings in the Yelp dataset in use did not exhibit variance high enough to expect a substantial improvement in accuracy, it was interesting to note that graph features did improve the accuracy of predictions for businesses with a high variability of ratings.

The graph features used in this work were deliberately kept simple, although more complex features can potentially yield more accurate predictions. Despite this, the obtained results demonstrate the effectiveness of the graph representation of the ratings data and the benefits of augmenting the original data-driven features with the graph features. The graph representation of the data is generic enough to allow the applicability of the proposed technique to other datasets, which argues in favor of the generalization of the graph features and their necessity to improve the recommendation accuracy. Nevertheless, more sophisticated graph features extraction may result in a better representativeness of the data, and, in turn, in a better predictive accuracy. Analyzing how different types of data are influenced by the graph features is left as future work.

Another modification that remains beyond the scope of this work pertains to graph representation incorporating user-to-user and business-to-business relationships. Although neither the bipartite nor the tripartite graph allow edges within the user/business subgraphs, these edges naturally exist, e.g., user friendship and business similarity. A new method for modeling these edges should be developed and their contribution should be evaluated.

Also, in our work we did not label any of the graph edges. However, additional data pertaining to the graph edges is available, e.g., numeric scores of the reviews, strength of ties between users, or domain metadata relationships. If incorporated into the prediction mechanism, both the within-partition edges and their type may affect the graph features and potentially improve the accuracy of the predictions.

REFERENCES

1. G. Adomavicius and A. Tuzhilin. Context-aware recommender systems. In *Recommender systems handbook*, pages 217–253. Springer, 2011.

2. X. Amatriain, A. Jaimes, N. Oliver, and J. M. Pujol. Data mining methods for recommender systems. In *Recommender Systems Handbook*, pages 39–71. 2011.

3. M. Anderson, D. Antenucci, V. Bittorf, M. Burgess, M. J. Cafarella, A. Kumar, F. Niu, Y. Park, C. Ré, and C. Zhang. Brainwash: A data system for feature engineering. In *CIDR*, 2013.

4. A. Barrat, M. Barthelemy, R. Pastor-Satorras, and A. Vespignani. The Architecture of Complex Weighted Networks. *PNAS*, 2004.

5. S. Berkovsky, T. Kuflik, and F. Ricci. Cross-technique mediation of user models. In *AH*, pages 21–30, 2006.

6. S. P. Borgatti and D. S. Halgin. Analyzing Affiliation Networks. *The Sage handbook of social network analysis*, 2011.

7. L. Breiman. Random forests. *Machine learning*, 45(1):5–32, 2001.

8. J. W. Byers, M. Mitzenmacher, and G. Zervas. The groupon effect on yelp ratings: A root cause analysis. In *Proceedings of the 13th ACM Conference on Electronic Commerce*, pages 248–265. ACM, 2012.

9. L. Chen and P. Pu. Critiquing-based recommenders: survey and emerging trends. *User Model. User-Adapt. Interact.*, 22(1-2):125–150, 2012.

10. A. Hagberg, P. Swart, and D. S Chult. Exploring network structure, dynamics, and function using networkx. Technical report, LANL, 2008.

11. A. Halevy, P. Norvig, and F. Pereira. The unreasonable effectiveness of data. *Intelligent Systems, IEEE*, 24(2):8–12, 2009.

12. A. Hicks, S. Comp, J. Horovitz, M. Hovarter, M. Miki, and J. L. Bevan. Why people use yelp. com: An exploration of uses and gratifications. *Computers in Human Behavior*, 2012.

13. Y.-J. Hu and D. Kibler. Generation of attributes for learning algorithms. In *AAAI/IAAI, Vol. 1*, pages 806–811, 1996.

14. Y. Koren, R. Bell, and C. Volinsky. Matrix factorization techniques for recommender systems. *Computer*, 42(8):30–37, 2009.

15. M. Latapy, C. Magnien, and N. D. Vecchio. Basic notions for the analysis of large two-mode networks. *Social Networks*, 2008.

16. X. Li and H. Chen. Recommendation as link prediction: a graph kernel-based machine learning approach. In *Proceedings of the 9th ACM/IEEE-CS joint conference on Digital libraries*, pages 213–216. ACM, 2009.

17. U. Lösch, S. Bloehdorn, and A. Rettinger. Graph kernels for rdf data. In *The Semantic Web: Research and Applications*, pages 134–148. Springer, 2012.

18. S. Markovitch and D. Rosenstein. Feature generation using general constructor functions. *Machine Learning*, 49(1):59–98, 2002.

19. A. Mukherjee, V. Venkataraman, B. Liu, and N. Glance. What yelp fake review filter might be doing. In *Seventh International AAAI Conference on Weblogs and Social Media*, 2013.

20. L. Page, S. Brin, R. Motwani, and T. Winograd. The pagerank citation ranking: Bringing order to the web. Technical Report 1999-66, Stanford InfoLab, 1999.

21. M. Pazzani and D. Billsus. Learning and revising user profiles: The identification of interesting web sites. *Machine learning*, 27(3):313–331, 1997.

22. M. J. Pazzani and D. Billsus. Content-based recommendation systems. In *The adaptive web*, pages 325–341. Springer, 2007.

23. W. Pohl. Labour-machine learning for user modeling. In *HCI (2)*, pages 27–30. Citeseer, 1997.

24. G. Shani and A. Gunawardana. Evaluating recommendation systems. In *Recommender Systems Handbook*, pages 257–297. Springer, 2011.

25. A. Tiroshi, S. Berkovsky, M. A. Kaafar, T. Chen, and T. Kuflik. Cross social networks interests predictions based on graph features. In *RecSys*, 2013.

26. S. Trewin. Knowledge-based recommender systems. *Encyclopedia of library and information science*, 69(Supplement 32):69, 2000.

27. G. I. Webb, M. J. Pazzani, and D. Billsus. Machine learning for user modeling. *User modeling and user-adapted interaction*, 11(1-2):19–29, 2001.

28. I. Zukerman and D. W. Albrecht. Predictive statistical models for user modeling. *User Modeling and User-Adapted Interaction*, 11(1-2):5–18, 2001.

Improving Government Services with Social Media Feedback

Stephen Wan and Cécile Paris
The CSIRO Computational Informatics Division
Sydney, Australia
firstname.lastname@csiro.au

ABSTRACT

Social media is an invaluable source of feedback not just about consumer products and services but also about the effectiveness of government services. Our aim is to help analysts identify how government services can be improved based on citizen-contributed feedback found in publically available social media. We present ongoing research for a social media monitoring interactive prototype with federated search and text analysis functionality. The prototype, developed to fit the workflow of social media monitors in the government sector, collects, analyses, and provides overviews of social media content. It facilitates relevance judgements on specific social media posts to decide whether or not to engage online. Our user log analysis validates the original design requirements and indicates ongoing utility to our federated search approach.

Author Keywords

Social Media Monitoring, Federated Search, Natural Language Processing, eGovernment

ACM Classification Keywords

H.5.m. Information Interfaces and Presentation (e.g. HCI)

INTRODUCTION

Social media is fast becoming an important means for community engagement and public communication. It empowers the ordinary web user to become not just a consumer but also a producer of information, potentially encouraging further contributions from other users. For example, microblogs (e.g., Twitter[1]), blogs and discussion forums are often used to share advice, opinion, and commentary. As a result, social media is an invaluable source of feedback not just about consumer products and services but also about the effectiveness of government services.

In the government sector, it has been recognised that social media tools can facilitate the delivery of government services [6]. We are working with various government departments to

---

[1] www.twitter.com

IUI'14, February 24–27, 2014, Haifa, Israel.
ACM 978-1-4503-2184-6/14/02.
http://dx.doi.org/10.1145/2557500.2557513

find feedback in publically available social media that suggests how existing services can be improved, and to identify opportunities to improve information dissemination about the services to which the public are entitled. Research-wise, we aim to support social media monitoring activities through the design and development of tools that couple text analysis technology with flexible, easy-to-use interfaces. Ultimately our hope is that the tools can be deployed seamlessly within existing social media monitoring workflows.

Our user study of social media monitoring for government services [8] defines some of the core tasks involved. In short, the monitoring activity requires sifting through social media search results (for example, a comment, microblog or blog), judging it for relevance, identifying the underlying issues, and potentially acting upon the content to engage with an online community. These issues may reveal how existing services are performing, highlighting potential areas of improvement for both the services themselves and the departments' communications about them. Through social media monitoring, media and communication teams aim to identify both the reach of their own communication, and the forums/media to target so that information dissemination about service entitlements reaches the appropriate audiences. Finally, they also look for opportunities to engage directly with online communities to make sure that information about government services being shared by citizens is correct.

The study also found that dealing with multiple applications, each corresponding to a separate social media platform, is time-consuming and can introduce problems in consistent engagement with online communities. Ideally, within a single application, social media monitors would perform the core tasks above and gain insights as to how content from one social media platform interacts with another. As an example of how such associations arise, consider the case of a government press release which triggers subsequent news articles. These articles can in turn evoke discussions and comments on news sites, opinion blogs and social networking sites, to name but a few. Each of these items may require the attention of a social media monitor, but judging how to respond to these posts may be made more difficult if these are presented in isolation, as is currently done in most search engine results.

We introduce a social media monitoring prototype, Vizie, that presents 1) a single federated search interface for different social media platforms that allows users to understand why information is collected and where the content came from, and 2) a unified analysis of the aggregated data to support data exploration. The analyses, using methods from Natural Language Processing (NLP), serve to help media monitors find commonly discussed issues across different types of social media and assist in identifying opportunities for engagement with online communities.

In this paper, we present Vizie and describe the technical and real world challenges involved in producing a tool that is used by 17 government departments. We analyse the aggregate user log statistics to examine the effect of introducing a federated search interface on query reformulations. Our analysis reveals the following:

1. Our prototype design, a novel combination of interactive interfaces, NLP and information retrieval capabilities, has demonstrated utility, as indicated by stable usage patterns spanning over 18 months.

2. The usage patterns validate the design of the prototype in facilitating overview and engagement activities.

3. Stable usage is associated with well-defined monitoring goals, as reflected by maintenance and refinement of queries queries.

RELATED WORK

To our knowledge, federated search approaches to social media monitoring, where a uniform query interface and a corresponding analysis is presented to the user, have not been explored in-depth within the research community. Whilst there are a number of tools available online to perform social media monitoring (for example, GoogleAlerts[2] and Socialmention[3]), these generally focus on a retrieval task that does not necessarily include data exploration. For example, although SocialMention retrieves content from various social media platforms, it does not easily allow content from one platform to be compared to another, nor is there an analysis to guide the user on salient issues and topics within the search results. Existing tools for general search and analysis, including SocialMention, are generally limited to showing trending words. This kind of analysis is typically presented as a ranked list. Our interface provides the user with a sense of the volume associated with major clusters of data, and how this changes across time.

There are a variety of tools dedicated to a specific social media platforms. Tools like TwitterMap[4] can present twitter content with geotag data on maps to highlight what is being discussed in a particular region. Software such as Tweetdeck[5] can be used to monitor microblog conversations on a topic. Analytics about the rise and fall of particular terms can be presented as graphs using tools like Hootsuite[6], which offers a microblog and social network dashboard for Facebook[7] and Twitter. Whilst Hootsuite and Tweetdeck are popular, this forces social media monitors interested in a diverse range of

social media platforms to use a number of tools and websites in an *ad hoc* manner to obtain an overall impression of the data, resulting in multiple views of collected social media.

Within the academic community, there are a number of systems and tools that help identify what in Twitter might be of importance. For example, TweetStand classifies Tweets into news or junk [15], while the system by Sriram *et al.* [16] classifies Tweets into five generic categories: news, events, opinions, deals, and private messages. These works differ from ours in that they are not geared towards facilitating specific social media tasks, and they handle only Twitter content. In contrast, our work considers many social media channels, and the data analysis is intended to help the user with specific monitoring tasks.

Some related research work is aimed at providing an overview of content by applying Bayesian topic modelling approaches to social media content, for example, on Twitter [10], on discussion forums [13], and on bookmarking sites [11]. However, these have not yet been deployed widely for general use in an end-user application.

There are some notable systems that present contentful overview analyses of online text. The Newssift tool[8], by the Financial times, performed topic analysis on news articles matching a query. Unfortunately, this site was closed down in February 2010. Berstein *et al.* [3] describe a social media tool that highlights related discussions across Twitter. By treating Tweets as queries, a set of related documents can be retrieved from search engines to overcome data sparseness issues. Although the work of [3] shares a similarity in application and in the use of topic-based clustering, our research differs in examining multiple social media types.

Within the context of government-based social media monitoring, there is work that exploits social media for emergency situation management, in particular to identify Tweets that might be useful to detect an emergency or help support a response to an emergency (for example, see [14, 18, 1, 20]). In our work, we are not looking specifically at emergency crisis, and, again, we are interested in monitoring a wide range of social media channels.

Finally, the TweetGathering prototype [21], which focuses solely on Twitter data, is designed to help journalists gather news, using an interactive interface and techniques from NLP. The prototype was shown to journalists for evaluation, but, to our knowledge, it was not used in their jobs. In contrast, our prototype monitors all social media information, not just news. Furthermore, our evaluation is based on user log data.

GOVERNMENT SERVICES AND SOCIAL MEDIA

Although government social media monitors often use a number of the tools described above, their monitoring task involves more than simple brand monitoring or identifying the relevant buzzwords to engage with an intended audience. Often there is a desire to improve existing government services, by identifying service feedback discussed in online discussions and potentially engage with the community.

---

[2]www.google.com/alerts. At the time of initial design, Google Alerts search results were available as an RSS feed that could be used for data analysis. As of July 2013, this is no longer the case.
[3]www.socialmention.com
[4]www.twittermap.com
[5]www.tweetdeck.com
[6]www.hootsuit.com
[7]www.facebook.com

[8]www.newssift.com

Collecting social media content is not straightforward, however. Queries pertaining to government services may be ambiguous in meaning, resulting in the collection of non-relevant content. For example, the department in charge of social services cannot simply use a query such as "social welfare". This would retrieve content from all across the world. Using the official name of the benefit may help narrow the focus to a country, if the name is unique. However, official names for services are also subject to misspellings and colloquial references. For example, "bereavement benefit" may simply be referred to as "payment" for the "death" of a close relative.

This ambiguity is exacerbated by the problem that the collected social media is heterogeneous in nature, given that each social media platform is marketed towards a niche in online communication. Consequently, a search query designed to retrieve specific content on one platform may perform poorly on another. For example, the query "school kids bonus", the name of a benefit to help Australian families with the cost of schooling, retrieves Facebook statuses requesting information about the social benefit, whereas retrieved Twitter statuses includes political commentary.

Finding online discussions with useful feedback is a daunting task given the volume of social media content. In addition, the user requirements identified in [8] suggests that it is problematic for social media monitors to juggle together the existing tools. Ideally, users would have access to a single content overview, regardless of media type (blogs, microblogs, news, forums, etc) to help them identify what issues are being currently discussed online. From that overview, they should be able to drill in to access relevant content.

Furthermore, social media monitors need to identify when to engage with online communities. For example, someone may post a question about a government service on a site like Yahoo!Answers[9]. Ideally, other online community members would help to answer each other's questions. Occasionally, however, incorrect answers may be posted. These require the social media monitor to engage with the relevant community to address the problem, an engagement which may then be retrieved in future web searches. This is particularly relevant in a government scenario, as policy changes may affect the eligibility rules of various services for citizens, rendering some information outdated [8]. With the advent of microblogs and ubiquitous computing devices, relevant content grows rapidly, making social media monitoring increasingly difficult. Without any dedicated social media tools for analysis and aggregation of data, dealing with this burgeoning data is difficult.

Our prototype is designed to address these problems. However, the design of tools to support such tasks is not immediately straightforward. The real world constraints are challenging and range from 1) designing an affordable but scalable architecture to handle hundreds of users spread across a number of government departments; 2) compliance with the terms of service of social media platforms; and 3) choosing

analysis methods that are appropriate for the data collected, in terms of scalability of volume and time to process.

The first constraint influences how we design the system to ensure that the load placed by one department does not negatively impact the user experience of another. It also has a bearing on how data is stored to keep each department's collected data separate. The second constraint affects how much data we collect from a specific platform. Finally, the third constraint forces us to use text analysis methods that are domain independent given that the services and activities of the participating departments span many areas of public life. In addition, the system must be able to analyse large quantities of textual data on limited computing resources.

AN OVERVIEW OF VIZIE'S KEY FEATURES

The prototype Vizie, designed to be used by a social media monitoring team, provides a single point-of-entry to both data collection and data analysis interfaces. These are realised as a novel combination of interactive and collaborative interfaces which rely on NLP and information retrieval techniques, including language identification[10], clustering algorithms (based on keywords or Latent Dirichlet Allocation (LDA) [4]), discussion summarisation [19], keyword and keyphrase detection (based on [7]), and extractive summarisation [9].

The various pages of the User Interface (UI) are implemented as a combination of several web components including navigation menus, graphs, search interfaces, etc. Each page also has options for the user to interact with in order to examine the data. Viewing these pages and interacting with the prototype are user events which are logged for further study. We return to this analysis below. We now describe how this functionality is exposed in the prototype's interfaces, particularly with respect to the requirements outlined above.

A Social Media Federated-Search Interface

To make the problem of collecting data of different social media types easier, we created a single federated search interface where the same query is issued to multiple social media platforms. In this way, we retrieve only publically available content. We use the Application Programming Interfaces (APIs) of the various platforms like Twitter, Facebook, YouTube, LinkedIn, and Instagram. For image and video data, our prototype only processes the textual content found in descriptions and comments. In addition, we utilise the API of the SocialMention social media search engine to collect data. This is particularly helpful in collecting data in the recent past if there are technical difficulties, either within our system or with a specific API. Finally, data can be collected by specifying RSS or ATOM feeds. These feeds are checked hourly for new content.

In addition to these data collection methods, the prototype collects data across from different social media platforms by downloading all linked content. The prototype reconstructs discussion threads based on the "in-reply-to" associations found in the metadata returned by each platform for retrieved

---

[9]http://answers.yahoo.com

[10]https://code.google.com/p/language-detection

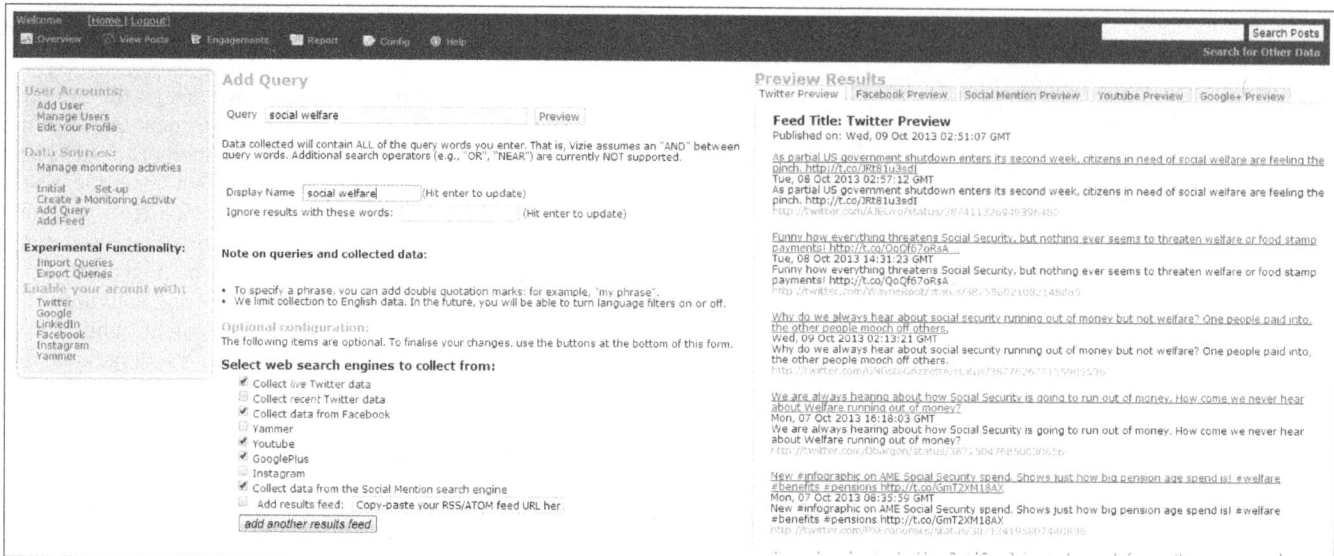

Figure 1. The query registration interface. The form allows the specification of complex queries which are then issued to a number of social media platforms. Previews for collected results are presented on the right to allow the user to refine the query through the use of exclusion terms and additional contextual query terms.

posts. For example, if a Tweet mentioning the query term is part of a discussion, the system will attempt to download the conversational context for that post.

Similarly, if a data has a shortened URL, the link is resolved and the linked web content is captured since it provides the context for some online commentary. Given the transient nature of the web, the system stores snapshots of the webpage, if possible, to archive the content, a legal requirement for many government departments. The data archived by the prototype is not available for public dissemination, and the user takes responsibility for the use of any data collected by the prototype, which is available to them only.

As system designers, one problem we find is that users do not always spend a great deal of time in manually refining queries. Often, our users are extremely time-poor. Some users, such as those involved in government policy, are not in fact part of a media and communications group, and they perform their social media monitoring activities as an extra task in addition to their normal daily activity. For example, the user may *a priori* have a query in mind, such as the official name of a service. In a naive user interface, this might then be entered into the system without verifying that the query is appropriate (e.g., as in our previous "bereavement" example). In some cases, the query term may simply not be one that is adopted by the online public. The user must then wait for a period of time 1) for new content to be created by the online public, and 2) for the system to collect data. The user can then be frustrated if, after this period, no relevant data is collected.

To alleviate this problem, our prototype provides previews of data to indicate what content is likely to be collected. In Figure 1, we present our interface for registering a query within the prototype. To the right, a series of panels presents previews for each of the platforms. The previews give the user an idea of what information from each platform will be col-

lected. If this does not match their expectations, they can then reformulate the queries as appropriate. This is necessary as a query issued to one platform (like Twitter) may not suit another (for example, Facebook) and may result in very different content being collected. The system is designed so that the user is forced to vet the preview results before data collection and analysis. This is important as the more non-relevant data that is collected, the harder it is for subsequent automated data analyses to provide useful results.

The problem of finding a query that will work in federated search is further complicated by the fact that each platform's API has a different query language. For example, the search-based streaming API for Twitter does not support phrasal queries. In addition, boolean operators such as AND and OR are not available in a uniform manner across each platform, making it difficult for users to issue complex queries with multiple terms.

As shown in Figure 1, the prototype's interface uses a form to collect the parameters of the complex query. The top text field can be used to provide one or more words, any of which may be scoped within phrasal markers (double quotation marks). In the interface, we indicate that a conjunction is used for each query term or phrase. At this stage, we do not allow disjunction, which can, in any case, be achieved by registering variations within the prototype as a separate query. We adopt this position because a preview interface would otherwise be overly complicated; the user would not know which part of the disjunction is contributing to the results. Finally, the form also provides fields for the NOT operator which can be used to exclude content to refine the query. To the right, the previews of data to be collected from each social media platform are presented.

The previews and the data collected are passed through a series of filters designed to enforce the query constraints captured through the form in Figure 1. These filters are necessary to uniformly impose query constraints on the data returned by the various APIs, given that each API provides a different query language. In addition, we presently use an existing language filter to restrict data collection to English content[11].

Overviews for Exploring Collected Data

Once the data is collected, the prototype presents a single overview of the aggregate data, based on analyses providing the major data clusters. This can be used to sift and explore the data, either to find feedback or opportunities for engagement, or else to further refine queries by understanding what data is eventually collected. The overview is available in both a textual and visual interactive interfaces.

The analysis includes a categorisation of each social media post to specify its media type. For example, YouTube and Vimeo content would be labelled as video. The microblog category includes predominantly Twitter data but also contains some Identica posts. Given that Facebook is the only social network that we currently support, it is given its own label. The other categories currently in use include blogs, pictures, comments, government, press releases, social network profiles, questions, bookmarks, and forums. We also use a miscellaneous category for content that cannot be identified.

The overviews are created by grouping posts according to keywords, where a salient keyword is chosen for each post. To select a single keyword to represent a post, candidate keywords are first generated using various cues such as word length, capitalisation, and membership within an indicative phrase. Phrases are provided by a rule-based keyphrase identifier that delimits the post into phrases based on stopwords. To select the single keyword to assign the post to a group, the system first checks if any of the keywords has a match in a list of specific terms that are of interest to the user. If not, the system chooses the one that is most popular (as measured by frequency) within a one week window. In this way, groupings can capture the streaming nature of social media data.

This data grouping approach, a surrogate for a clustering algorithm, was chosen as it is 1) fast and 2) easily deployed on the low powered virtual machines that we dedicate per department. More in-depth but computationally expensive analyses, for example a clustering provided by LDA [4], are available on-demand.

The overviews are then presented for a series of days, typically the preceding week. Figure 2 shows the interactive textual version of this overview, which can be displayed on devices without Java or Flash, including government computers and handheld smart devices. The overview is in a mode designed to maximise screen to show the top eight to ten groupings of data, indicated with a keyword, and to show the proportions between groupings for a single day and *within* a specific social media type.

In this figure, data about countryside fires was collected using the queries such as "#ausheatwave", "#bushfire", "#heatwave", "#nswfires", "#safires", "#sydneyheatwave", "#tas-

---
[11]https://code.google.com/p/language-detection

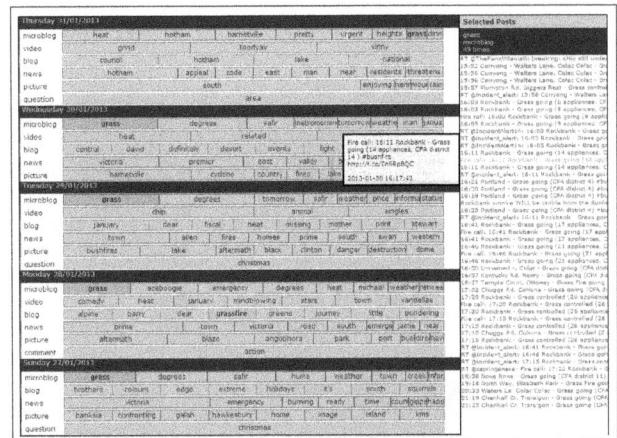

Figure 2. A textual overview of retrieved social media content. The overview is designed to make full use of the screen to highlight the cluster labels. The large panel to the right shows the cluster currently selected. The small pop-up window presents a preview of an individual post. The user can drill down to a specific post from that panel.

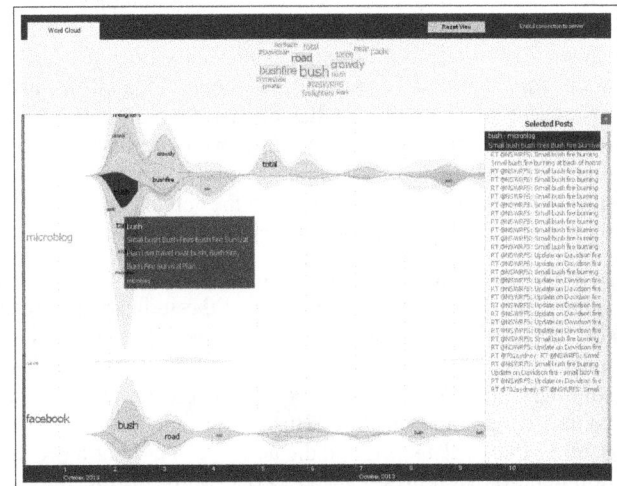

Figure 3. A visual overview of social media about rural fire services.

fires", "#vicfires", and "@NSWRFS". A different colour is assigned to each mediatype — for example, green for blogs and blue for microblogs. In this figure, the users has selected one of the keywords "grass". The interface highlights all mentions of that string throughout the week to allow the user to gauge its prominence across the week. To the right of the overview, a listing shows the posts included in one of the groupings for the keyword "grass", each represented by a snippet of text. Hovering over the post will show more of the text and clicking on it will take the user to the archived content for that post.

The visual overview, presented in Figure 3, allows the cluster sizes to be compared across days. It is inspired by the Stacked Graphs visualisation [5] but differs from it in terms of the smoothing methods used to produce curves, and in our use of the multiple stacked graphs to show different channels of data.

Although the prototype generates both versions of the overview from the same data, the visual overview is able to

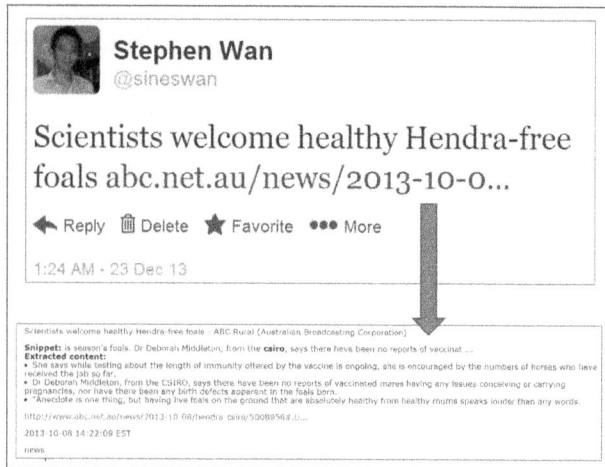

Figure 4. A summary of the news article that is linked to from the shortened URL is presented to the user as context to the Twitter discussion.

show some of the smaller clusters, as our interactive visualisation affords a zoom-in-zoom-out interaction. Figure 3 shows the visualisation zoomed to a level to show discussions about rural fires on Twitter and Facebook. This allows users to inspect some of the smaller clusters, which can be useful when the social media monitor is trying to find problems and issues as they are beginning to trend. As in the textual overview, the user can drill down to the actual post content if they deem it relevant and worth reading further.

In both the textual and visual overviews, multi-document summaries are presented that include the indicative phrases for each keyword. The pop-up in Figure 3 presents a summary for the cluster under the mouse pointer. In this case, the summary provides more context for the cluster label "bush" containing key phrases like "Bush fire" and "Bush Fire Prevention Plan". This might indicate to the user that a prevention plan for rural fires is the key concept for the cluster.

Supporting Online Engagements and Reporting

The user requirements [8] discussed above indicated that engagement with the online community was important. To support this activity, the prototype assists with relevance judgements for each post, in which the user must decide if the content is such that an engagement is required (for example, to provide a correction to user-contributed information). The interface also supports record keeping to archive the engagements that have been made, since the archival of correspondence is usually required by government departments.

To support relevance judgements, where possible, we provide the context that triggers online discussions. For example, shortened URLs might indicate the web content that led to a Twitter discussion. In Figure 4, we present a Tweet in the top half of the figure with such a link embedded within it. To help the social media monitor decide how to react to the post, we provide as much context to the Tweet as possible, including a summary of the news article that is linked to, as this might be quite lengthy to read. For our summarisation of the news article, we employ a generic sentence extraction summariser which utilises centroid-based methods (for example, [9]).

Although not shown in this figure, if the post is part of a discussion, the prototype presents the number of discussion turns and, if possible, the extracted date of posting. These help the user to appraise the discussions potential viewership and thus impact. Using thread summarisation methods, the system also shows sentences related to the key issues, as selected by vector space methods that rely on contentful word repetition across various discussion turns (for example, [19]). We are currently researching question-answer summarisation methods for discussion summaries as in [12].

The prototype also facilitates other tasks such as report generation and search within the collected data. To make it easier to manage the collected data, we provide a simple filing system to the user. The data collected is automatically tagged with a series of user categories that organise the queries used with the social media platforms. These categories, which we call Monitoring Activities, typically specify the different foci of a data collection exercise. For example, a monitoring activity for "rural fires" might be created in addition to one entitled "fire prevention public education", each housing different queries for the social media platforms. These groupings help divide the data collected from the queries into different subsets, which can be analysed and reported on separately. These subsets of data can also be exported for the user to analyse with other tools.

USER LOG ANALYSIS

We originally developed our prototype to support one specific government department and worked with the communication team in that department to design the tool, ensuring it would fit their work environment. However, since 2012, we released the prototype to 17 government departments and have about 200 registered users.

Our users are all busy professionals with heavy workloads. As a result, we cannot perform a formal task-based evaluation of our tool, for example, to see whether it helps them cover a larger space of social media posts they would cover otherwise, or to do this faster. Instead, we consider the fact that some have continuously used the tool in their daily activities for about 18 months now as evidence of the utility and effectiveness of the tool. We present here a user log analysis which looks at the amount of data that was collected and the average number of times a user logs in the tool. We then examine general patterns in the actions performed by users, looking at the types of functionality users employ on average.

General Usage Patterns

Our user logs for the prototype span a total of 18 months and include the usage data of about 200 registered users spread across around 17 government departments. Each department is given an instance of the prototype that is independent from the others, allowing us to examine usage per department. During this period, we collected 45 million posts. Of these, over half were from Twitter.

The departments started using the prototype at different times, with the majority starting in June 2012. The rapid growth around March 2013 in the number of posts collected

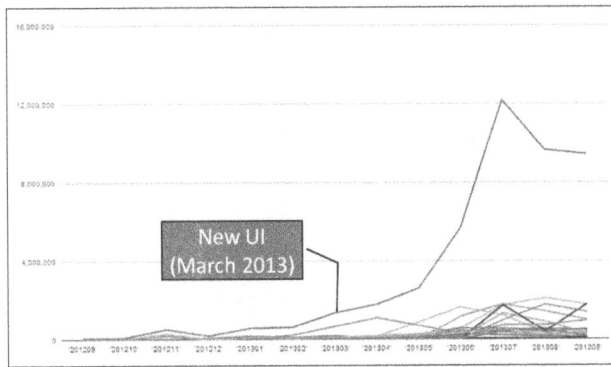

Figure 5. Number of posts collected each month in a 18 month window.

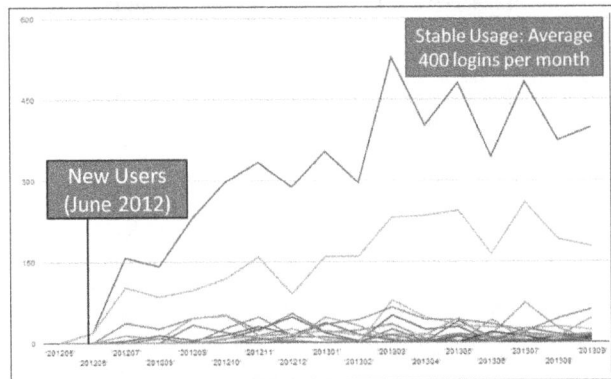

Figure 6. Number of logins over 18 months.

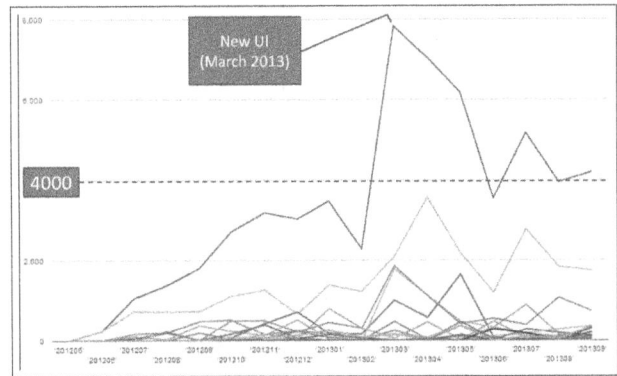

Figure 7. Number of prototype UI components viewed.

shown in Figure 5 is attributed to the introduction of the federated search interface. The top blue curve in Figures 5 to 7 represents the aggregate over the departments. The other lines represent a specific department.

Prior to March 2013, users had to enter each site to monitor separately. The new interface essentially automates the collection from multiple platforms. Since users typically would not exhaustively provide URLs for data collection, this resulted in more posts being collected. It also has an impact on query refinement, as we shall see. To handle this growth in data collection, we also redesigned our infrastructure to deal with the collection, storage and analysis of this growth of data.

The main indicator of stable usage by a department is the number of logins to the system, as shown in Figure 6. Most of the government departments started using the prototype in mid-2012, explaining the rapid growth then. The aggregate logins reach a plateau of about 400 logins a month, indicating that in general we have a stable user base. This is despite some login patterns indicating that a handful of departments have tried the prototype once but decided not to use it. The stable usage suggested by the graph indicates that the users find value in the prototype to the extent that they logged back in regularly throughout the 18 months to use its functionality.

Similarly, the number of prototype UI components (recall these are combined to form pages in the web application) viewed by users reaches a stable level of around 4000 components per month, as shown in Figure 7. On average, each user

session with the prototype involves viewing 10 components, which corresponds to viewing a number of pages. We interpret this to indicate that the user is doing more than logging in; rather they are examining the data collected.

The system's federated search interface, which allows users to preview data from different platforms, was released gradually (with one API added after another) from March to May. We note that shortly after the time that the federated search interface was introduced there is an initial drop in components viewed around June 2013. However, this stabilises around August 2013.

We interpret this graph as showing how the users adapt to the new behaviour of the system, which, by automating the issuing of queries to the various platforms via the federated search interface, dramatically increases the number of posts collected. This interface can save the user time in collecting content, but it can also increase the number of non-relevant posts collected. Shortly before usage stabilisation, we observed that users returned to the configuration pages of the prototype to refine their queries, as presented in Figure 8. The stable usage suggests that users were able to deal with the complex task of query formulation, using the preview facility in the federated interface to vet the data collected from each platform.

Indeed, qualitative feedback from the departments using our prototype are encouraging. Yatu Widders, Communications Advisor at the National Mental Health Commission (NMHC) has said "With the Commission having a mandate and commitment to speaking to the broader Australian community on issues of mental health and suicide prevention, Vizie has provided unique insights into what topics are being discussed and are of interest to a diverse range of groups, beyond just the health and Government sectors."[12]

Similarly, Amanda Dennett, Senior Social Media Adviser, Department of Human Services (DHS), said "VIZIE has really helped increase our exposure and credibility in the social media space. With student forums for example, it's gone from students thinking 'why are you here', to them now waiting to receive the official response because they know we are online. It has certainly helped us address misinformation out

---

[12]Public remarks in a letter, 2013.

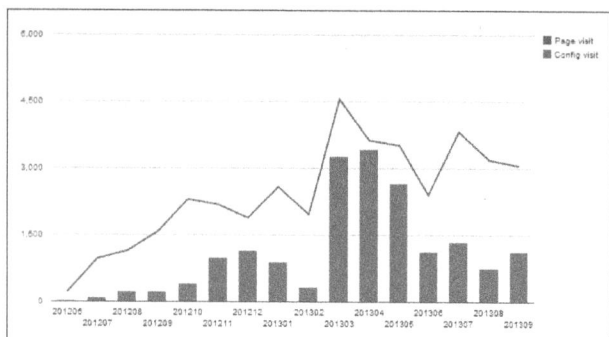

Figure 8. The period from March to May 2013 was associated with query adjustments following the gradual deployment of the federated search interface. The blue line indicates non-config prototype usage (as measured by interface page views) and the red bars indicates the number of config pages viewed.

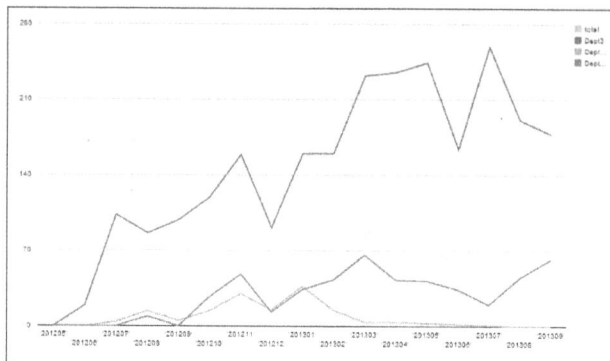

Figure 10. Login patterns for three user groups. The usage for the NMHC (yellow) is event-driven and peaks in late 2012 but then drops away in 2013. For the DHS (red) and SLNSW (green) the usage is on-going.

there and proactively provide the information that people are looking for."[13]

Interaction Patterns within the Prototype

We can investigate the primary types of interactions further using a server log inspection tool [17] that shows usage patterns for a website. In Figure 9, we present a visualisation from this tool showing the top 100 ways that users interact with the prototype. These interaction patterns are aggregations of individual user sessions.

After users log in, they are presented with a *home* screen containing a dashboard showing a summary of content for the last 24 hours. The main use of the system after viewing this *home* screen is to make relevance judgements on social media posts (see the *listPost* box) and also to record engagements with the online community (see the *listEngagement* box) which validates part of the original intended use of the prototype for managing online engagement.

Users also drill down to individual posts, search across the collected data (including using the advanced search interface within the prototype), and use the overview visualisation. Interestingly, we observe alternations between *config* and *home* screens, in which the user configures the system with queries for federated search, and then returns to the home page within the prototype. The repeated visits to the config page suggests that query refinement for federated search to multiple social media platforms is not a trivial task.

Three Case Studies of Query Maintenance

The user groups of each of the departments now covers a diverse set of interests, ranging from media and communications units to data archivists, to name but a few. This represents a range of monitoring information needs relating to the government services associated with the department, and we find that users have appropriated the prototype for their purposes. Some of the services are citizen focused, for example, the applications for and delivery of social benefits. Others are public services like documentation or knowledge management with other government and professional bodies as the key stakeholders.

---

[13]Excerpt taken from a CSIRO and DHS brochure, 2013.

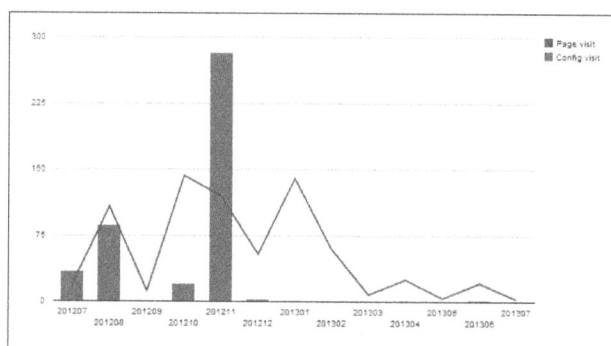

Figure 11. An example of query configuration and monitoring for events.

We can divide our user groups into categories depending on the type of social media monitoring being performed. Monitoring tasks can be event-driven or on-going. Figure 10 compares the login patterns of three organisations: the National Mental Health Commission (NMHC) is an example of event-driven monitoring whilst the other two examples, the Department of Human Services (DHS) and the State Library of New South Wales (SLNSW), perform on-going social media monitoring.

The NMHC is a government body set up to assess and document the state of mental health services in Australia. They used Vizie to monitor the social media feedback to an annual report from journalists, health professionals and the public alike. In particular, Vizie provided insights about what vocabulary the community used to discuss health issues, since professional vocabulary is not always adopted by the public. Figure 11 shows the interaction between configuration of Vizie and usage, with two main configuration events in August and November 2012 in preparation for the release of the report in late November, followed by a monitoring period into early 2013.

As an example of an on-going monitoring task, SLNSW has a mandate to collect and preserve documents that reflect lives of citizens, for use by researchers now and in the future. SLNSW staff are currently trialling Vizie to collect social media content that is significant to major events in a specific region. This complements existing web archival projects

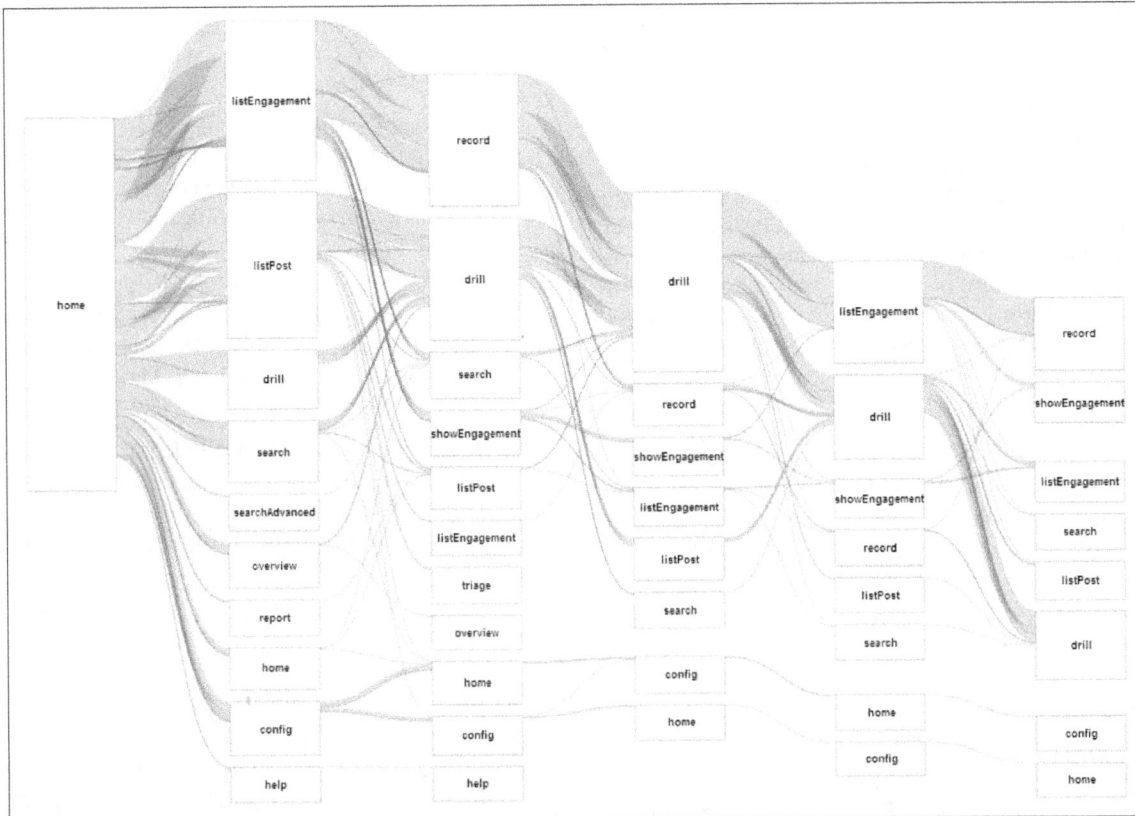

Figure 9. Interaction patterns within the prototype. Most of the components of the UI are self-explanatory. The remaining items are defined as follows: *home* **is the user's landing page within the web application;** *listEngagement* **shows a list of archived engagements;** *listPost* **displays the most recent posts in reverse chronological order; and** *drill* **is the action of viewing the actual content of a post.**

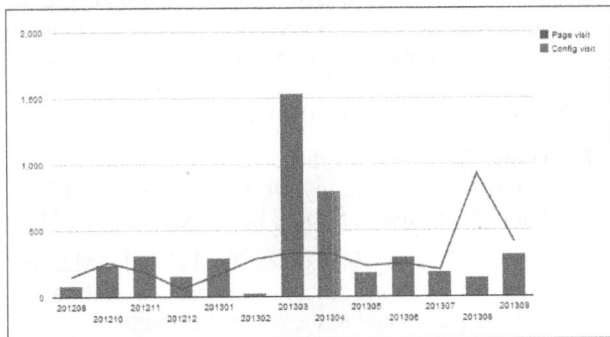

Figure 12. An example of query configuration and monitoring to archive social media descriptions of life unfolds with respect to major event in a region.

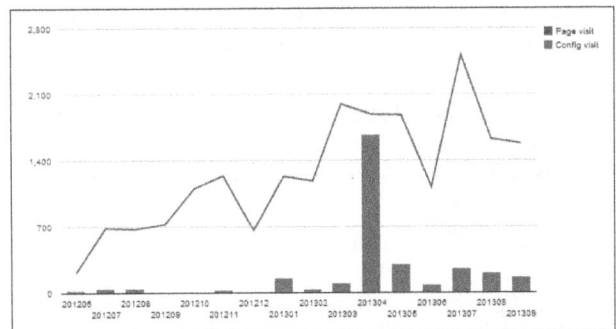

Figure 13. An example of query configuration and monitoring to capture social media feedback about a stable set of government services.

which were started before the advent of social media. In addition to the query adjustments following the introduction of the federated search interface, Figure 12 shows how this user group redefines its queries regularly for this task reflecting the rapidly adaptation to major events as they unfold. The SLNSW framework for defining queries to capture this data for prosperity's sake is introduced in [2].

The DHS has a social media monitoring group with one central coordinator and a team of media monitors. The team has an interest in providing accurate information about social welfare services. As such, they regularly examine online

discussions to answer questions and to ensure that the information provided by other members of the public is accurate. Figure 13 shows how refinement takes place for a stable set of queries about a government service, with one major refinement taking place in April 2013 as a result of the new interface change.

CONCLUSION

In this paper, we described a social media monitoring prototype, Vizie, for improving government services based on published user requirements. The prototype uses single federated search interface for users to submit queries to different social media platforms, and provides an overview of the aggregated results. From an analysis of users logs from nearly 200 registered users across 17 government departments, we are able to show utility. The analysis and qualitative feedback suggests that Vizie is able to support data exploration and to facilitate relevance judgments of online discussions that might lead to engagement with an online community. We investigated the interaction between complex query formulation and federated search for social media platforms. The analysis revealed encouraging changes in behaviour suggesting that the federated search interface is useful in managing how queries are issued to different platforms. Finally, we presented case studies illustrating query maintenance strategies for three social media monitoring scenarios.

REFERENCES

1. Abel, F., Hauff, C., Houben, G.-J., Stronkman, R., and Tao, K. Semantics + filtering + search = twitcident. exploring information in social web streams. In *Proc. of the 23rd ACM Conference on Hypertext and social media*, ACM (New York, NY, USA, 2012), 285–294.

2. Barwick, K., Joseph, M., Paris, C., and Wan, S. Hunters and collectors: seeking social media content for cultural heritage collections. In *VALA 2014: Streaming With Possibilities* (2014).

3. Bernstein, M. S., Suh, B., Hong, L., Chen, J., Kairam, S., and Chi, E. H. Eddi: interactive topic-based browsing of social status streams. In *Proc. of the 23nd annual ACM symposium on User Interface Software and Technology*, ACM (New York, NY, USA, 2010), 303–312.

4. Blei, D. M., Ng, A. Y., and Jordan, M. I. Latent dirichlet allocation. *J. Mach. Learn. Res. 3* (March 2003), 993–1022.

5. Byron, L., and Wattenberg, M. Stacked Graphs – Geometry & Aesthetics. *IEEE Transactions on Visualization and Computer Graphics 14*, 6 (2008), 1245–1252.

6. Government 2.0 Taskforce. Engage: Getting on with government 2.0. World Wide Web: http://gov2.net.au/files/2009/12/Draft-Government-2-0-Report-release.pdf, December 22 2009. Last viewed 29th January 2010.

7. Kupiec, J., Pedersen, J., and Chen, F. A trainable document summarizer. In *Proc. of the 18th Annual International ACM SIGIR*, Text Summarization (1995), 68–73.

8. Paris, C., and Wan, S. Listening to the community: social media monitoring tasks for improving government services. In *Proc. of the 2011 CHI Extended Abstracts*, ACM (New York, NY, USA, 2011), 2095–2100.

9. Radev, D., Otterbacher, J., and H. Qi, D. T. MEAD ReDUCs: Michigan at DUC 2003. In *Document Understanding Conference 2003: Workshop on Text Summarization* (Edmonton, Canada, May 2003).

10. Ramage, D., Dumais, S., and Liebling, D. Characterizing microblogs with topic models. In *ICWSM* (2010).

11. Ramage, D., Hall, D., Nallapati, R., and Manning, C. D. Labeled LDA: A supervised topic model for credit attribution in multi-labeled corpora. In *Proc. of the 2009 Conference on EMNLP* (Singapore, August 2009), 248–256.

12. Rambow, O., Shrestha, L., Chen, J., and Laurdisen, C. Summarizing email threads. In *HLT-NAACL 2004: Short Papers*, D. M. Susan Dumais and S. Roukos, Eds. (Boston, Massachusetts, USA, May 2 - May 7 2004), 105–108.

13. Rossi, R., and Neville, J. Modeling the evolution of discussion topics and communication to improve relational classification. In *SOMA 2010: Workshop on Social Media Analytics* (Washington, DC, July 2010).

14. Sakaki, T., Okazaki, M., and Matsuo, Y. Earthquake shakes twitter users: real-time event detection by social sensors. In *Proc. of the 19th International Conference on World Wide Web*, WWW '10, ACM (New York, NY, USA, 2010), 851–860.

15. Sankaranarayanan, J., Samet, H., Teitler, B. E., Lieberman, M. D., and Sperling, J. Twitterstand: news in tweets. In *Proc. of the 17th ACM SIGSPATIAL International Conference on Advances in Geographic Information Systems*, GIS '09, ACM (New York, NY, USA, 2009), 42–51.

16. Sriram, B., Fuhry, D., Demir, E., Ferhatosmanoglu, H., and Demirbas, M. Short text classification in twitter to improve information filtering. In *Proc. of the 33rd Annual International ACM SIGIR*, SIGIR '10, ACM (New York, NY, USA, 2010), 841–842.

17. Thomas, P. Explaining difficulty navigating a website using page view data. In *ADCS*, A. Trotman, S. J. Cunningham, and L. Sitbon, Eds., ACM (2012), 31–38.

18. Verma, S., Vieweg, S., Corvey, W., Palen, L., Martin, J., Palmer, M., Schram, A., and Anderson, K. Natural language processing to the rescue? extracting "situational awareness" tweets during mass emergency. In *ICWSM* (2011).

19. Wan, S., and McKeown, K. Generating overview summaries of ongoing email thread discussions. In *COLING '04* (Morristown, NJ, USA, 2004), 549.

20. Yin, J., Lampert, A., Cameron, M., Robinson, B., and Power, R. Using social media to enhance emergency situation awareness. *IEEE Intelligent Systems 27*, 6 (2012), 52–59.

21. Zubiaga, A., Ji, H., and Knight, K. Curating and contextualizing twitter stories to assist with social newsgathering. In *Proc. of the 2013 IUI*, IUI '13, ACM (New York, NY, USA, 2013), 213–224.

Toward Crowdsourcing Micro-Level Behavior Annotations: The Challenges of Interface, Training, and Generalization

Sunghyun Park, Philippa Shoemark, and Louis-Philippe Morency

Institute for Creative Technologies

University of Southern California

12015 Waterfront Dr., Los Angeles, CA 90094

{park, morency}@ict.usc.edu, pjshoemark@gmail.com

ABSTRACT

Research that involves human behavior analysis usually requires laborious and costly efforts for obtaining micro-level behavior annotations on a large video corpus. With the emerging paradigm of crowdsourcing however, these efforts can be considerably reduced. We first present OCTAB (Online Crowdsourcing Tool for Annotations of Behaviors), a web-based annotation tool that allows precise and convenient behavior annotations in videos, directly portable to popular crowdsourcing platforms. As part of OCTAB, we introduce a training module with specialized visualizations. The training module's design was inspired by an observational study of local experienced coders, and it enables an iterative procedure for effectively training crowd workers online. Finally, we present an extensive set of experiments that evaluates the feasibility of our crowdsourcing approach for obtaining micro-level behavior annotations in videos, showing the reliability improvement in annotation accuracy when properly training online crowd workers. We also show the generalization of our training approach to a new independent video corpus.

Author Keywords

Crowdsourcing; micro-level annotations; behavior annotations; inter-rater reliability; training crowd workers

ACM Classification Keywords

H.5.2. Information interfaces and presentation: User Interfaces.

General Terms

Design; Experimentation; Human Factors; Measurement.

INTRODUCTION

Annotating multimedia content is becoming an important part of many recent research problems, including multimedia event recognition [21], video retrieval and classification [13], and human behavior analysis [19]. Supervised learning approaches applied to these research problems usually require a large number of annotated video sequences. While some of these algorithms are applied at

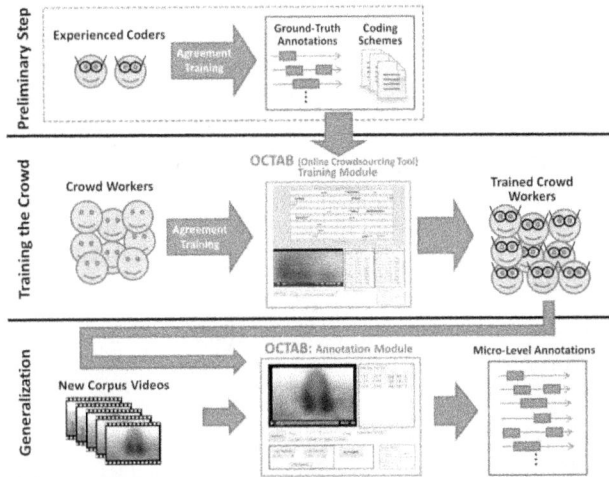

Figure 1. Overview of our approach for crowdsourcing micro-level behavior annotations in videos, with a focus on our web interface called OCTAB, which (1) includes a module specifically designed to train crowd workers online and (2) generalizes to new independent video corpora.

the video or scene level (referred to as macro-level annotations), many of these problems need micro-level annotations, where the precise start and end times of an event or behavior need to be identified. These annotation efforts, which are usually carried out with experienced local coders, are very costly both in terms of budget and time.

In recent years, there has been an explosive growth in the research and use of crowdsourcing paradigm, fueled by convenient online crowdsourcing environments like Amazon Mechanical Turk. In the research community, crowdsourcing is already being actively used for many types of tasks, including image labeling [18] and linguistic annotations [17]. When crowdsourcing micro-level human behavior annotations in videos, three main challenges emerge: interface, training crowd workers online, and generalization. Firstly, there is a need of a web interface that allows crowd workers to accurately and efficiently annotate micro-level behavioral events while keeping the interface simple and intuitive. Secondly, there should be an effective web interface and procedure for training crowd workers online that can simulate the environment experienced local coders use when discussing and reaching

OCTAB Interface: Annotation Module

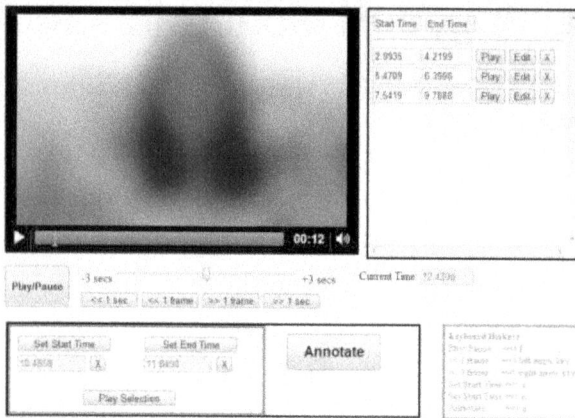

Figure 2. The first component of OCTAB (Online Crowdsourcing Tool for Annotations of Behaviors) is a web annotation module that allows crowd workers to make precise micro-level annotations of human behaviors or events in videos.

agreement. Lastly, the training of online workers should generalize across datasets if we want this approach to be widely applicable.

In this paper, we present OCTAB (Online Crowdsourcing Tool for Annotations of Behaviors), a web-based annotation tool that allows precise and convenient behavior annotations in videos, directly portable to popular crowdsourcing platforms such as Amazon Mechanical Turk (see Figure 1). In addition, we introduce a training module with specialized visualizations and an iterative procedure for effectively training crowd workers online, inspired by an observational study of experienced local coders reaching agreement. Finally, we present an extensive set of experiments that evaluates the feasibility of. our crowdsourcing approach for obtaining micro-level behavior annotations in videos, showing the reliability improvement in annotation accuracy when properly training online crowd workers. We also show the generalization of our training approach to a new independent corpus.

RELATED WORK

Crowdsourcing has gained much attention lately, and a survey paper by Yuen et al. [31] and another by Quinn and Bederson [22] present a general overview of the topics on crowdsourcing and human computation, and many interesting applications [2, 9, 32] are appearing that take advantage of the new paradigm. Regarding Amazon Mechanical Turk, Mason and Suri [15] provided detailed explanations on using the platform for conducting behavioral research, and Ross et al. [25] showed changing demographics of the people using the platform.

Quality control is a critical issue with crowdsourcing. Downs et al. [5] and Rashtchian et al. [23] showed the benefit of a screening/qualification process, Le et al. [12]

showed an approach of adding a training period in designing a study, and Sheng et al. [26] explored repeated labeling of data for more reliability. By comparing annotations (none of them on videos) obtained with crowdsourcing and those with expert annotators, several [6, 7, 14, 18, 23, 27] have reported across different domains that they could obtain good quality annotations through crowdsourcing. In our work, we incorporate most of these quality control measures and further show novel experimental results of comparing micro-level annotations in videos obtained by crowdsourcing with those done by experienced local annotators.

As for crowdsourcing video-related tasks, Wu et al. [30] worked on obtaining video summarizations, Biel and Gatica-Perez [3] on macro-labeling impressions of vloggers in videos, and Riek et al. [24] on macro-labeling social contexts in video scenes. However, none of them were concerned with micro-level annotations. Probably most relevant pieces of work in terms of our web interface were done by Vondrick et al. [29] and Spiro et al. [28], whose interfaces allowed micro-level motion tracking and were also used with Amazon Mechanical Turk. However, their interfaces only put an emphasis on motion tracking, while our interface is concerned with identifying and segmenting behavioral events in videos. Although there are quite a number of software for making complicated annotations on videos [4], such full-fledged tools are not suitable to be used for crowdsourcing due to a relatively steep learning curve and the difficulty of incorporating them into web-based crowdsourcing platforms.

Krippendorff's alpha has been previously used to measure inter-rater reliability of video annotations both at a macro-level [24] (label on the whole video clip) and micro-level [8] . In this paper, we follow the approach taken in [8] at a micro-level, but we further explore the stability and reliability of the alpha at different temporal resolutions. The approach taken in [20] is also used for disagreement analysis to supplement the alpha because the alpha cannot show the types of disagreement between coders, which can be critical information for effectively training crowd workers.

To our knowledge, we are the first to introduce an effective interface with specialized visualizations to train crowd workers online, by extensively showing the feasibility of training crowd workers to obtain micro-level behavior annotations in videos and demonstrating generalizability of training across different video corpora.

ONLINE CROWDSOURCING TOOL FOR ANNOTATIONS OF BEHAVIORS (OCTAB)

We developed OCTAB[1] (Online Crowdsourcing Tool for Annotations of Behaviors), a web-based annotation tool for

---

[1] OCTAB will be made freely available for research at http://multicomp.ict.usc.edu/

OCTAB Interface: Training Module

(1) Overall Bar-Graph Visualization Component

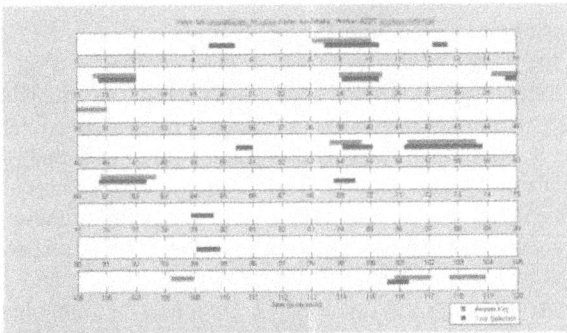

(2) Side-By-Side Review Component

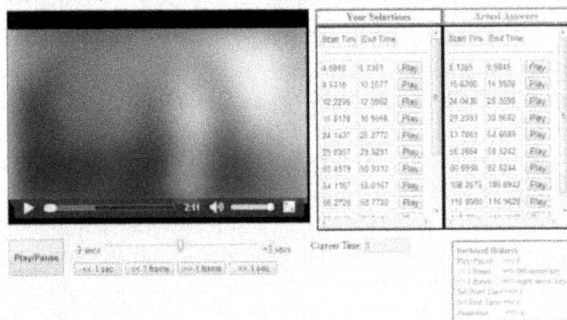

Figure 3. The second module of OCTAB to effectively train crowd workers online by giving them a quick overall visualization of disagreement (top) and the ability to review both ground-truth and their attempted annotations side-by-side (bottom).

making convenient and precise micro-level annotations in videos. It consists of two main modules. The first module is a HTML-based web interface that allows an annotator to conveniently navigate in a video to annotate micro-level human behaviors or events (see Figure 2). The second module was designed for training crowd workers online, inspired by observing how experienced local coders train themselves to reach agreement (see Figure 3).

Annotation Module (Micro-Level Behavior Annotations)

OCTAB is intended for annotating a single behavior on a single video at a time, and it is based on HTML5 and JavaScript, providing all the basic functionalities of a web video player (HTML5 supports three video types of MP4, WebM, and Ogg). We considered the following three main aspects in our design of the annotation module of OCTAB.

Precision

For accurate micro-level annotations on videos, annotators need to have frame-level precision in identifying the start and end time points of an event. To address this requirement, the interface provides the annotator with 4 buttons for moving 1 second backward/forward and 1 frame backward/forward from the current time in the video, as well as a slider bar that offers frame-level navigation in the

range from -3 to +3 seconds. Once the annotator identifies a behavior or event to annotate, he/she can use the navigation control buttons to pinpoint and select the behavior or event's start and end times. Then, he/she can play the selection to verify and press a button to save the selection as a valid annotation. Although intended for annotating a single behavior on a single video at a time, it should be noted that this interface also allows annotations of multiple behavior tiers or intensities with a simple addition of radio buttons, and it can be even configured to support any arbitrary annotation tasks with additional radio buttons, sliders, text boxes, etc.

Integrability

Popular annotation software applications like ELAN or ANVIL [4] allow annotators to make sophisticated annotations on video and audio files, but they are not suitable for the purpose of crowdsourcing. They have a relatively steep learning curve to use and cannot be used with online crowdsourcing platforms like Amazon Mechanical Turk. OCTAB was written directly in HTML so that it can be easily used to create a template task page when using online crowdsourcing platforms.

Usability

Annotating videos often involves moving around in a video to check, re-evaluate and edit previously made annotations. A special section in the annotation module displays a list of all saved annotations, and the annotator can always go back and work on previously made annotations by replaying, editing or deleting any annotations. For convenience and speed in making annotations, most controls in the interface have hotkeys associated with them, and the interface's functionalities are kept to the minimal level with an intuitive layout to minimize confusion.

Training Module (Training Crowd Workers Online)

The challenge of training crowd workers for annotation tasks arises mainly due to the lack of physical interaction that local coders enjoy when training themselves in person according to a coding scheme. In order to have an effective design of this training module, we first observed how experienced local coders work together to reach agreement. Then, we created needed visualizations and a training procedure to translate the findings to effectively train crowd workers online.

Observational Study of Experienced Local Coders' Training

As a preliminary step, we performed an observational study of two experienced local coders reaching agreement on behavior annotations for 5 short YouTube videos of people giving movie reviews. The coders annotated a total of 4 behaviors, the same ones used in our experiments: gaze away, pause filler, frown, and headshake (see Experiment section).

We observed that experienced local coders sit together to devise a coding scheme, which is a precise description of an annotation task. Then, they individually try annotating according to the coding scheme on a training video. After computing their agreement, they again sit head-to-head to review their annotations together, replay all of their annotations multiple times side by side, engage in discussions, and make appropriate modifications to the coding scheme as needed. This process is iterated with more training videos one after another until the agreement consistently reaches a satisfactory level determined by researchers.

From the observational study, we noted that our online training module should concentrate on two key functionalities in order to simulate how local coders train themselves. Firstly, crowd workers should have an overall visualization that enables them to quickly compare their annotations with each other (or with ground-truth annotations). Secondly, crowd workers should also be able to efficiently review (play the video and see all instances of) both ground-truth and their attempted annotations side-by-side.

Design of Online Training Modules

The first necessary functionality noted during the observational study is reflected in our training module with an overall bar-graph visualization on a time line that not only informs crowd workers with an overall picture of their mistakes in identification of a behavior but also in its segmentation (see Overall Bar-Graph Visualization Component from Figure 3). The second functionality is reflected with a modified version of the behavior annotation module in which crowd workers can review both ground-truth annotations and their attempted annotations side-by-side by repeatedly playing any of those annotation instances in the video (see Side-by-Side Review Component from Figure 3). This training module is generated automatically with scripts.

PROCEDURE FOR CROWDSOURCING MICRO-LEVEL BEHAVIOR ANNOTATIONS IN VIDEOS

Given our interactive web interface for training crowd workers and annotating micro-level behaviors in videos, we propose 4 main steps to successfully train new crowd workers: Obtaining coding schemes and ground-truth annotations, recruiting and screening workers, training workers online, and obtaining repeated annotations if necessary.

Obtaining Coding Schemes / Ground-Truth Annotations

If no trained online workers are available, the first step is to work with experienced local coders to create a coding scheme and annotating a small set of training videos. As will be shown, this step of creating a coding scheme with annotated training examples is only necessary if the behavior to annotate is new. During this step, the local coders train themselves on the training videos until their agreement reach a satisfactory level (see Experiments section for more details about agreement measures during their training sessions). The resulting annotations from these training videos will be used as ground-truth annotations for training crowd workers. If trained online

workers are available for the desired behavior or if a coding scheme and annotated training set already exist, this step can be skipped.

Recruiting / Screening Crowd Workers

In recruiting crowd workers, it is suggested to first try recruiting from a forum such as www.mturk.com, where many serious crowd workers reside. It is also beneficial to use a relatively unambiguous annotation task that still requires close attention to detail at the frame level to check if a crowd worker is able to annotate with frame-level precision. For example, gaze away behavior is a relatively easy behavior to identify with unambiguous start and end times, but it requires one to pay attention at the frame level. Measuring agreement performance on this type of tasks can be a good threshold point for screening crowd workers.

Training Crowd Workers Online

For training crowd workers, we propose an iterative procedure where workers first annotate a video with OCTAB annotation module and then receive feedback with the training module. This gives them a chance to learn and improve with each training video using the overall bar-graph visualization and side-by-side review components. Once crowd workers consistently perform at the agreement level on par with the agreement between local coders, they are tagged as properly trained. For our study, we used Time-Slice Krippendorff's alpha (described in the Experiment section) to measure agreement, and we set the satisfactory alpha level at 0.80 for relatively clear behaviors and 0.70 for harder ones.

Unique vs. Repeated Annotations

When annotators are trained to strongly agree with each other, future annotations can be obtained with one annotator per video. With properly trained crowd workers, it could be the case that having only one worker annotate per video is sufficient to obtain quality annotations. However, for relatively harder behaviors to annotate, it may be necessary to make repeated annotations with multiple workers per video and take a majority vote approach. In fact, it could be possible to take this approach with even untrained crowd workers and obtain annotations with satisfactory quality. We show the effect of training and having repeated annotations with an extensive set of experiments in this paper.

EXPERIMENTS

We designed our experiments to evaluate the performance and user experience of our OCTAB interface for online crowd annotations. We particularly put a focus on the effect of training crowd workers and also tested the generalization of our training procedure by having workers trained on one dataset and have them tested on another independent dataset.

Evaluation Methods

We used Time-Slice Krippendorff's alpha [8] as our main evaluation metric for measuring inter-rater reliability of micro-level annotations in videos. Krippendorff's alpha is

Event Agreement Metric

From the reference point of Coder A　　　　*From the reference point of Coder B*

Coder A
Coder B
2 agreed instances

Coder A
Coder B
4 agreed instances

$$\text{Event Agreement} = \frac{Total\ Number\ of\ Agreed\ Events}{Total\ Number\ of\ Identified\ Events} = \frac{2+4}{2+5} = 85.7\%$$

Segmentation Agreement Metric

Coder A
Coder B

$$\text{Segmentation Agreement} = \frac{Total\ \#\ of\ Agreed\ Slices\ Within\ Agreed\ Events}{Total\ \#\ of\ Slices\ Within\ Agreed\ Events} = \frac{3}{9} = 33.3\%$$

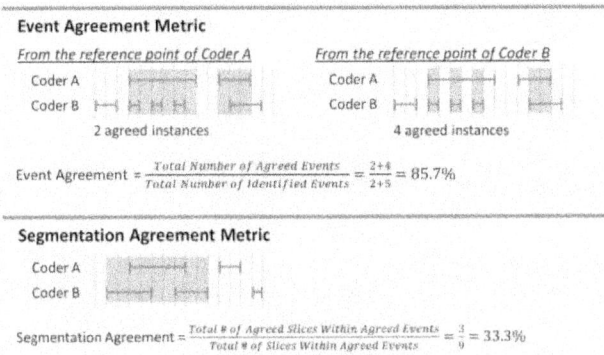

Figure 4. Definition of the event and segmentation agreement metrics with examples.

particularly suited for crowdsourcing because it can handle multiple annotators at the same time and also account for missing data. We further used two supplementary metrics to analyze the types of disagreement between coders, which can be very helpful in determining whether coder disagreement stems from inaccurate identification of behaviors or from imprecise segmentation [20].

Time-Slice Krippendorff's Alpha
Our first measure, Krippendorff's alpha [10], is a generalized chance-corrected agreement coefficient that can be calculated between two or more annotators. The general formula for the alpha is the following:

$$\alpha = 1 - \frac{D_o}{D_e} \qquad (1)$$

where D_o, or observed disagreement, is the amount of pairwise disagreement observed between the annotators, and D_e, or expected disagreement, is the level of disagreement expected by chance as calculated from the data. The coefficient alpha itself is a measure of agreement ranging from -1 to 1, where 1 is perfect agreement (zero observed disagreement), 0 is chance-level agreement, and values lower than 0 indicate systematic disagreement.

The alpha works by looking separately at the agreement on individual annotation instances. For micro-level annotations, we treat each time slice (e.g., 1 frame per slice) as a separate annotation instance, with a binary annotation indicating presence or absence of a specific behavior (such as a frown). While it is the case that adjacent frames tend to have similar annotations, our experiments show that the alpha is not very sensitive to the sampling rate of the time slice. The agreement is calculated separately for each annotated behavior.

Applying the alpha to individual time slices means that the measure can only assess whether the annotators agree that at a certain time point a behavior takes place, not whether they agree about the segmentation or the individuation of behaviors (whether a certain time span contains one or two instances of a frown); this drawback has been pointed out by Krippendorff [11]. To supplement the alpha, we use two

additional measures which are intended to capture agreement on the individuation of annotated behaviors.

Disagreement Type Analysis
As mentioned in the previous section, Time-Slice Krippendorff's alpha does not differentiate between disagreement caused by misalignment of the annotations or that caused by direct event disagreement. To better understand these annotation differences, we use two new metrics (see Figure 4), which can be valuable information when deciding whether crowd workers' training should concentrate on better behavior identification, segmentation, or both.

- *Event Agreement Metric.* An agreed event is defined as when there is an overlap of identified events in two annotations. In other words, agreed events are those that both annotators jointly identified. Depending on which annotation is taken as the reference point however, the number of agreed events could be different (see Figure 4). For this reason, we compute the percentage of agreed behavior events between the two annotations by dividing the total number of agreed events from both reference points by the total number of identified events from both reference points.

- *Segmentation Agreement Metric.* Another informative measure in gauging the agreement between two annotators is to see how precisely they segmented the boundary of the same annotation event. To compute the segmentation precision, we look at the time windows of agreed behavior events from both reference points combined and compute agreement within the time windows only (see Figure 4). The percentage is computed by dividing the number of agreed time slices by the number of total time slices within the time window of agreed events.

Datasets
From YouTube, which is a video-sharing website where users can upload and share videos, about 360 videos of people giving movie reviews were collected. Each video was annotated by two coders to determine the sentiment of the reviews (negative, neutral, and positive). From those videos, 20 videos were selected for this study that were both gender-balanced and sentiment-balanced (to have various expressions). Additionally, 5 more videos were randomly selected and used for training purposes. Each video showed a frontal, upper-body shot of a different person talking. Since all of the videos appeared to have been recorded using a webcam, it should be noted that the overall quality of the videos was not ideal but still fair enough to discern various facial expressions and eye gaze. For the 20 videos that were used in the actual experiments, the frame rate was at 30 frames per second and the video length ranged from 60 to 180 seconds, averaging at 138 seconds. The 5 training videos had the same frame rate, averaging at 106 seconds in length.

To show the generalization of our training procedure, a second dataset was created with 10 clipped videos from the Semaine corpus [16], which is a well-known video corpus in the research communities focusing on emotion, affective computing, and human behavior analysis. The purpose of this second dataset was to investigate if the effect of training crowd workers on one dataset can be transferred to another dataset for annotating human behaviors. These videos also showed a frontal, upper-body shot of a person speaking, and the frame rate was also at 30 frames per second, averaging at 150 seconds in length.

Annotated Behaviors

From behaviors that were relatively common and frequent in all the videos, we selected 4 different types of behaviors to annotate based on their variety (one for eyes, one for facial expressions, one for head movements, and one for verbal cues) and difficulty. These behaviors are all very frequently annotated behaviors for research involving human behavior analysis. The descriptions of the behaviors in our coding schemes were adapted from the MUMIN multimodal coding scheme [1].

- Gaze away: eye gaze is directed away from the camera.

- Pause filler: the person says "um..." or "uh..."

- Frown: the eyebrows contract and move toward the nose.

- Headshake: a repeated rotation of the head from one side to the other.

Experimental Design

We used Amazon Mechanical Turk (AMT) for our experiments, which is arguably the most well-known and widely used platform for crowdsourcing. The main idea behind AMT is to distribute small tasks at which humans are proficient and computers are still incompetent to a crowd of workers worldwide. Using AMT's web interface, the "requesters" can design and publish tasks online, which are called HITs for Human Intelligence Tasks. In designing HITs, the requesters can set various options to restrict access to specific kinds of workers, set the number of unique workers to work on them, and set the amount of monetary reward. Moreover, a HIT template can be created, and one can define variables whose values will vary from HIT to HIT, which becomes very useful in creating a batch of similar HITs but with different videos. We created a HIT template with OCTAB annotation interface integrated and batch created all of our HITs with the videos in our YouTube and Semaine datasets. A total of 19 workers participated in our experiments, who worked for an effective hourly wage between $4 and $6 for compensation. The reader is referred to [15] for more detail on using AMT.

Experienced Local Coders

Two experienced local coders were recruited for this study, and the agreement between them after training was considered as the gold standard in our experiments. They devised coding schemes for the 4 behaviors to annotate, and

they trained themselves to reach agreement on the 5 YouTube videos set aside for training purposes only. They trained on one video at a time until agreement (measured with Time-Slice Krippendorff's alpha) reached a threshold of 0.80 (or very close) for all behaviors with the exception of headshake behavior because the local coders could not manage to reach 0.80 for some training videos even after 3 trials. However, the average alpha level for headshake behavior across the 5 training videos still reached 0.80. We performed a more detailed analysis of the types of errors in our experiments (see Results section) to better understand this challenge with headshake behavior (see Figure 7, bottom part).

After training, each of the local coders used the same environment as crowd workers to annotate all the videos from the YouTube and Semaine datasets across all the behaviors. Since agreement between the local coders was high, the final annotations from one of the local coders during training were used as ground-truth annotations to train crowd workers online.

Untrained Crowd Workers

To compare our approach with a scenario where crowd workers are untrained, we selected a total of 12 workers to participate as untrained crowd workers. As mentioned earlier, they were screened using an annotation test for gaze away behavior. This brief screening process was only to make sure that they could pay attention to frame-level detail, and no training sessions were given. They were provided with the coding schemes drafted by the two local coders, and they made a combined effort to annotate all the videos from only the YouTube dataset across all the behaviors.

Trained Crowd Workers

A total of 7 workers, who were not involved as untrained crowd workers, participated as trained crowd workers. They were trained with the same 5 YouTube videos that local coders used for training. After each training video, workers received e-mail feedback with our OCTAB training module, generated automatically with scripts. Workers were considered trained when they reached the same alpha thresholds used for experienced local coders. The training process involved only at most 1 trial per training video for gaze away and pause filler behaviors. For frown behavior, each worker took mostly 1 trial per video to reach the alpha threshold on average across all training videos, and it took about 2 to 3 trials per training video for headshake behavior. The trained workers were provided with the coding schemes drafted by the two local coders and annotated all the videos across all the behaviors from the YouTube dataset first. Then, they similarly annotated the Semaine dataset to investigate if the effect of training crowd workers for annotating human behaviors on one dataset can be transferred to annotating a different and independent dataset. The crowd workers were not informed that these videos were from a different dataset.

- OCTAB: Annotation Module

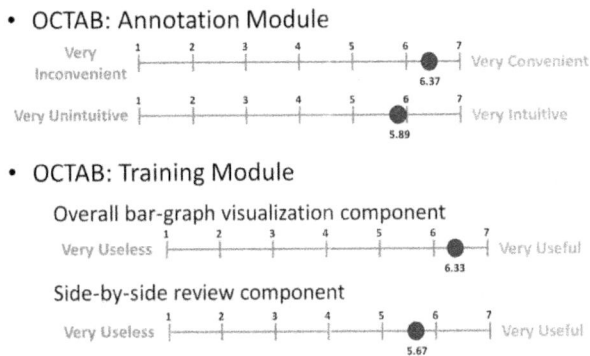

- OCTAB: Training Module

Overall bar-graph visualization component

Side-by-side review component

Figure 5. The user experience ratings of our OCTAB interface.

Repeated Annotations

For both of the above-mentioned conditions with untrained and trained crowd workers, 3 repeated annotations were obtained to investigate the benefit of taking a majority vote approach.

Annotation Strategies

For each dataset, we compared the agreement performance of three annotation approaches: *experts*, *crowdsourced unique*, and *crowdsourced majority*.

Experts. We had two local experienced coders who each produced a complete set of annotations for each dataset. The agreement between the two local coders was considered as the gold standard in our experiments. We refer to these sets as *experts* in the next section.

Crowdsourced Unique. From crowd workers, we obtained 3 repeated annotation sets from different workers per behavior per video. By randomly permuting the order in the 3 annotation sets, we created 3 complete sets of crowdsourced annotations for each dataset, which we refer to as *crowdsourced unique*.

Crowdsourced Majority. The 3 complete sets of crowdsourced annotations can be combined to make another complete set using majority voting, where a time slice (or frame) is judged annotated if at least 2 out of 3 workers agreed. We refer to this set as *crowdsourced majority* for each dataset.

We compared agreement in three different combinations: (1) within *experts* so that we have a baseline, (2) *experts* vs. *crowdsourced unique* to see if having one worker annotate per video is sufficient, and (3) *experts* vs. *crowdsourced majority* to see the benefit of having repeated annotations and performing a majority vote. The agreement comparison was performed for the YouTube dataset with untrained crowd workers, the YouTube dataset with trained crowd workers, and the Semaine dataset with trained crowd workers.

RESULTS AND DISCUSSIONS

This section highlights five main research problems studied during our experiments: the user experience ratings of

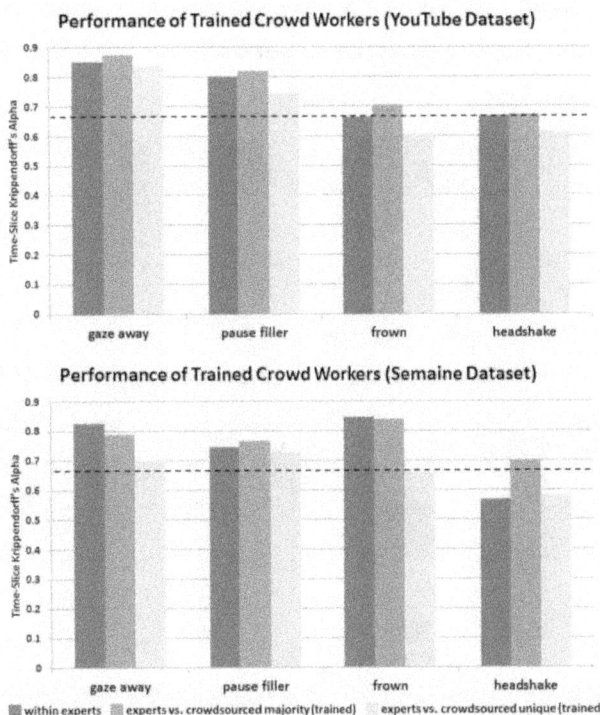

Figure 6. The performance of the trained crowd workers on the YouTube dataset (top) and the Semaine dataset (bottom). The dotted lines indicate the agreement alpha threshold point at 0.667.

OCTAB annotation and training modules, the performance of trained crowd workers, the performance of untrained crowd workers, the analysis of the types of disagreement, and the sensitivity analysis of Time-Slice Krippendorff's alpha measure to test its stability and reliability.

It should be noted that researchers in social sciences usually consider macro-level annotation data with a Krippendorff's alpha value equal to or above 0.80 as reliable and in high agreement, and they consider data with an alpha value equal to or above 0.667 but lower than 0.80 as reliable only to draw tentative conclusions [10]. These threshold points, however, are somewhat arbitrary, and it is controversial whether the same standards are fair to hold for judging the reliability and quality of micro-level (frame-level) behavior annotations. Keeping this in mind, we nevertheless use the 0.667 threshold as the standard of quality in the remainder of this section.

User Experience Ratings of OCTAB

The 19 crowd workers who participated in the experiments completed a survey to evaluate OCTAB annotation and training modules and the behavior annotation tasks (see Figure 5). On a 7-point Likert scale to rate OCTAB annotation module's convenience (from very inconvenient at 1 to very convenient at 7) and intuitiveness (from very unintuitive at 1 to very intuitive at 7), the mean score was 6.37 (n = 19, sd = 0.74) for convenience and 5.89 (n = 19, sd = 0.91) for intuitiveness. For OCTAB's training module,

Performance of Untrained Crowd Workers (YouTube Dataset)

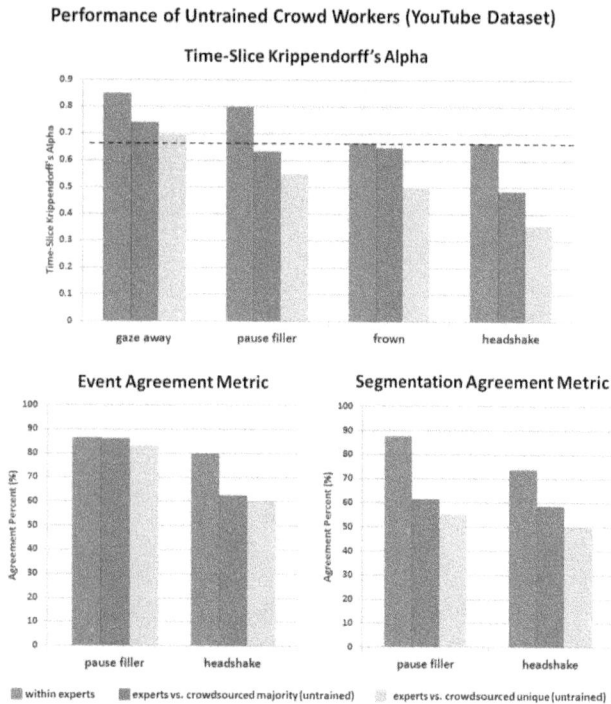

Figure 7. The performance of untrained crowd workers on the YouTube dataset. The dotted line indicates the agreement alpha threshold at 0.667.

the mean score on usefulness (from very useless at 1 and very useful at 7) was 6.33 (n = 6 sd = 0.47) for the bar graph visualization and 5.67 (n = 6, sd = 1.97) for the side-by-side review component. These evaluation results show high usability of our OCTAB interface.

The crowd workers also evaluated the difficulty of each behavior to annotate (from very difficult at 1 to very easy at 7), and the mean score was 6.42 (n = 19, sd = 0.82) for gaze away behavior, 5.71 (n = 14, sd = 1.33) for pause filler behavior, 3.94 (n = 16, sd = 2.05) for frown behavior, and 3.64 (n = 14, sd = 1.59) for headshake behavior. Not surprisingly, the reported difficulty level correlated with the general agreement performance of each behavior.

Performance of Trained Crowd Workers
For the YouTube dataset, on which the crowd workers were trained to perform the annotation tasks, the performance of *crowdsourced majority* was striking. For all behaviors, the average agreement between individual experienced local coders and *crowdsourced majority* was higher than between the two local coders themselves (see Figure 6). The average alpha between *experts* and *crowdsourced majority* reached above the 0.667 threshold for all behaviors, specifically 0.87 for gaze away behavior, 0.82 for pause filler behavior, 0.70 for frown behavior, and 0.67 for headshake behavior. These results show that crowdsourcing can be a very effective tool for researchers in obtaining high-quality behavior annotations, provided that proper training sessions were given and 3 repeated annotations were obtained to take a majority vote approach. For relatively unambiguous

Trained vs. Untrained Crowd Workers (YouTube Dataset)

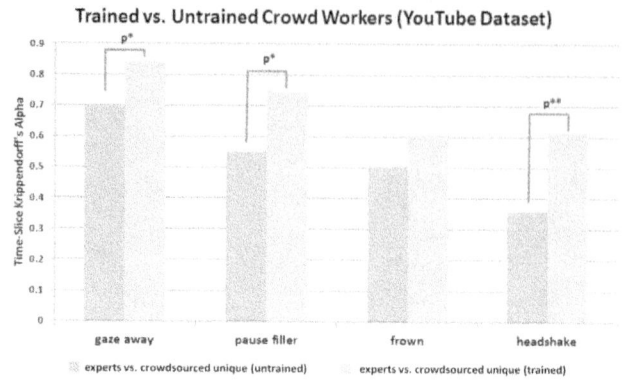

Figure 8. The performance comparison between the untrained and trained crowd workers on the YouTube dataset (t-tests showed statistically significant difference at p* < 0.01 and p** < 0.001).

behaviors, such as gaze away and pause filler behaviors, the result indicates that repeated annotations are actually unnecessary and having one worker annotate per video is sufficient to obtain high-quality annotations.

When the crowd workers, who were trained on the YouTube dataset, performed the same annotation tasks on different videos in the Semaine dataset, we could observe the effect of training actually transferrable. The agreement between *experts* and *crowdsourced majority* was almost equal to or higher than between *experts* themselves except for gaze away behavior. This exception is most likely due to the speakers in the Semaine videos not talking directly toward the camera as was the case in YouTube dataset. The speakers in the Semaine dataset talk to an interlocutor (invisible in videos) and this difference probably introduced much confusion in deciding what makes a gaze away behavior in the changed setting because the coding scheme was the same for both datasets. Nevertheless, the average alpha between *experts* and *crowdsourced majority* was still high at 0.79 for gaze away, 0.77 for pause filler, 0.84 for frown, and 0.70 for headshake. We can also observe a similar trend that having only one worker annotate per video is sufficient to obtain high-quality annotations for gaze away and pause filler behaviors.

Performance of Untrained Crowd Workers
The performance of the untrained crowd workers on the YouTube dataset shows that both *crowdsourced unique* and *crowdsourced majority* reached the agreement alpha threshold of 0.667 for gaze away behavior (see Figure 7). The agreement between *experts* and *crowdsourced majority* reached very close to the 0.667 threshold for pause filler and frown behaviors, and it should be noted that it is not uncommon for an alpha value of 0.60 to have well over 85% of agreement at the frame-level without chance correction, which is by no means a low agreement.

The result also shows the benefit of disagreement analysis with event and segmentation agreement metrics. For instance, the disagreement analysis reveals that the source

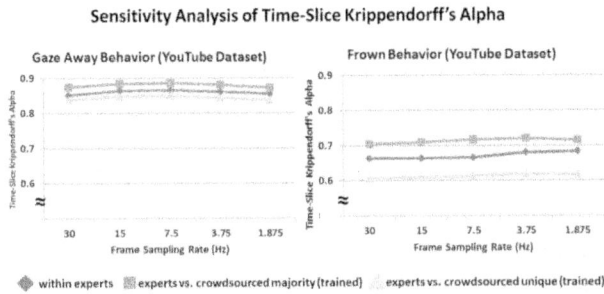

Figure 9. Sensitivity analysis of Time-Slice Krippendorff's alpha across different frame sampling rate.

of the low alpha value for crowd workers in annotating pause filler behavior was not in behavior identification but in segmentation. In other words, the untrained crowd workers were just as proficient as the experienced local coders in identifying instances of pause filler behavior. However, for headshake behavior, the disagreement analysis shows that the untrained crowd workers had problems of both identifying and segmenting behaviors correctly compared to the experienced local coders. This analysis is aligned with our previous observation that experienced local coders also had trouble agreeing with an alpha threshold at 0.80.

Trained vs. Untrained Crowd Workers

We emphasize the effect of training in Figure 8, which shows the average agreement alpha values between *experts* and trained *crowdsourced unique* and also between *experts* and untrained *crowdsourced unique*. By training crowd workers, their agreement performance on the YouTube dataset improved with a statistical significance at $p < 0.01$ for gaze away and pause filler behaviors and at $p < 0.001$ for headshake behavior (statistical significance computed with t-tests).

Time-Slice Krippendorff's Alpha

For all behaviors, Time-Slice Krippendorff's alpha was shown to be a stable measure that stayed consistent across different sizes of time slices, and we show the results for gaze away and frown behaviors on the YouTube dataset in Figure 9. For this experiment, annotation sets created at lower frame rate were up-sampled using a majority vote technique, where each time slice was considered annotated if at least 50% of the slice was annotated.

CONCLUSIONS

This paper presents a novel web interface and training procedure for crowdsourcing micro-level behavior annotations in videos and shows that such annotations can achieve a quality comparable to those done by experienced local coders. Specifically, we presented an effective web tool called OCTAB for crowdsourcing micro-level behavior annotations online, which consists of a convenient and precise annotation module and a training module that give crowd workers the ability to quickly get trained by seeing first an overall view of their errors and then performing side-by-side review of their annotations against ground-

truth annotations. Our results from an extensive set of experiments showed the feasibility of our crowdsourcing approach for obtaining micro-level behavior annotations in videos, showing the reliability improvement in annotation accuracy when properly training online crowd workers. We also investigated the generalization of our training approach to a new video corpus, showing that our training procedure is transferrable across different independent video corpora.

ACKNOWLEDGMENTS

This material is based upon work supported by the National Science Foundation under Grant No. IIS-1118018 and the U.S. Army Research, Development, and Engineering Command (RDECOM). The content does not necessarily reflect the position or the policy of the Government, and no official endorsement should be inferred.

We thank the USC Annenberg Graduate Fellowship Program for supporting the first author's graduate studies.

REFERENCES

1. Allwood, J., Cerrato, L., Dybkjaer, L., Jokinen, K., Navarretta, C., and Paggio, P. The MUMIN multimodal coding scheme. *Proc. Workshop on Multimodal Corpora and Annotation 2004.*

2. Bernstein, M., Brandt, J., Miller, R., and Karger, D. Crowds in two seconds: Enabling realtime crowd-powered interfaces. *Proc. UIST 2011*, 33-42.

3. Biel, J. I. and Gatica-Perez, D. The good, the bad, and the angry: Analyzing crowdsourced impressions of vloggers. *Proc. ICWSM 2012*, 407-410.

4. Dasiopoulou, S., Giannakidou, E., Litos, G., Malasioti, P., and Kompatsiaris, Y. A survey of semantic image and video annotation tools. *Knowledge-Driven Multimedia Information Extraction and Ontology Evolution, Lecture Notes in Computer Science 6050* (2011), 196-239.

5. Downs, J. S., Holbrook, M. B., Sheng, S., and Cranor, L. F. Are your participants gaming the system?: screening mechanical turk workers. *Proc. CHI 2010*, 2399-2402.

6. Gao, Q. and Vogel, S. Consensus versus expertise: A case study of word alignment with Mechanical Turk. *Proc. CSLDAMT 2010*, 30-34.

7. Hsueh, P. Y., Melville, P., and Sindhwani, V. Data quality from crowdsourcing: A study of annotation selection criteria. *Proc. ALLNP 2009*, 27-35.

8. Kang, S., Gratch, J., Sidner, C., Artstein, R., Huang, L., Morency, L. Towards building a virtual counselor: Modeling nonverbal behavior during intimate self-disclosure. *Proc. AAMAS 2012*, 63-70.

9. Kim, J., Nguyen, P., Weir, S., Guo, P., Miller, R., and Gajos, K. Crowdsourcing step-by-step information

extraction to enhance existing how-to videos. *Proc. CHI 2014*.

10. Krippendorff, K. *Content Analysis: An Introduction to Its Methodology*. Sage, Beverly Hills, CA, 2004.

11. Krippendorff, K. On the reliability of unitizing contiguous data. *Sociological Methodology 25* (1995), 47-76.

12. Le, J., Edmonds, A., Hester, V., and Biewald, L. Ensuring quality in crowdsourced search relevance evaluation: The effects of training question distribution. *Proc. SIGIR CSE 2010*, 21-26.

13. Lew, M. S., Sebe, N., Djeraba, C., and Jain, R. Content-based multimedia information retrieval: State of the art and challenges. *ACM T. Multim. Comput. 2*, 1 (2006), 1-19.

14. Marge, M., Banerjee, S., and Rudnicky, A. I. Using the Amazon Mechanical Turk for transcription of spoken language. *Proc. ICASSP 2010*, 5270-5273.

15. Mason, W. and Suri, S. Conducting behavioral research on Amazon's Mechanical Turk. *Behavior Research Methods 44*, 1 (2012), 1-23.

16. McKeown, G., Valstar, M.F., Cowie, R., and Pantic, M. The SEMAINE corpus of emotionally coloured character interactions. *Proc. ICME 2010*, 1079-1084.

17. Novotney, S. and Callison-Burch, C. Cheap, fast and good enough: Automatic speech recognition with non-expert transcription. *Proc. HLT 2010*, 207-215.

18. Nowak, S. and Ruger, S. How reliable are annotations via crowdsourcing: A study about inter-annotator agreement for multi-label image annotation. *Proc. MIR 2010*, 557-566.

19. Pantic, M., Pentland, A., Nijholt, A., and Huang, T. Human computing and machine understanding of human behavior: A survey. *Proc. ICMI 2006*, 239-248.

20. Park, S., Mohammadi, G., Artstein, R., and Morency, L.-P. Crowdsourcing micro-level multimedia annotations: The challenge of evaluation and interface. *Proc. CrowdMM 2012*, 29-34.

21. Poppe, R. A survey on vision-based human action recognition. *Image Vision Comput. 28*, 6 (2010), 976-990.

22. Quinn, A. J. and Bederson, B. B. Human computation: A survey and taxonomy of a growing field. *Proc. CHI 2011*, 1403-1412.

23. Rashtchian, C., Young, P., Hodosh, M., and Hockenmaier, J. Collecting image annotations using Amazon's Mechanical Turk. *Proc. CSLDAMT 2010*, 139-147.

24. Riek, L., O'Connor, M., and Robinson, P. Guess what? A game for affective annotation of video using crowd sourcing. *Proc. ACII 2011*, 277-285.

25. Ross, J., Irani, L., Silberman, M., Zaldivar, A., and Tomlinson, B. Who are the crowdworkers?: Shifting demographics in Mechanical Turk. *Proc. Ext. Abstracts CHI 2010*, 2863-2872.

26. Sheng, V. S., Provost, F., and Ipeirotis, P. G. Get another label? Improving data quality and data mining using multiple, noisy labelers. *Proc. KDD 2008*, 614-622.

27. Snow, R., O'Connor, B., Jurafsky, D. and Ng, A. Y. Cheap and fast but is it good?: Evaluating non-expert annotations for natural language tasks. *Proc. EMNLP 2008*, 254-263.

28. Spiro, I., Taylor, G., Williams, G., and Bregler, C. Hands by hand: Crowd-sourced motion tracking for gesture annotation. *Proc. CVPRW 2010*, 17-24.

29. Vondrick, C., Ramanan, D., and Patterson, D. Efficiently scaling up video annotation with crowdsourced marketplaces. *Computer Vision - ECCV 2010 6314*, 610-623.

30. Wu, S. Y., Thawonmas, R., and Chen, K. T. Video summarization via crowdsourcing. *Proc. Ext. Abstracts CHI 2011*, 1531-1536.

31. Yuen, M. C., King, I., and Leung, K. S. A survey of crowdsourcing systems. *Proc. SocialComp 2011*, 766-773.

32. Zhang, H., Law, E., Miller, R., Gajos, K., Parkes, D., and Horvitz, E. Human computation tasks with global constraints. *Proc. CHI 2012*, 217-226.

Left and Right Hand Distinction for Multi-Touch Tabletop Interactions

Zhensong Zhang[1] Fengjun Zhang[1,2*] Hui Chen[1,2]
[1]Beijing Key Lab of Human-Computer Interaction
Institute of Software
Chinese Academy of Sciences
zzs@iel.iscas.ac.cn
{fengjun, chenhui}@iscas.ac.cn

Jiasheng Liu[3] Hongan Wang[1,2] Guozhong Dai[1,2]
[2]State Key Laboratory of Computer Science
Institute of Software
Chinese Academy of Sciences
{wha, dgz}@iel.iscas.ac.cn
[3]Information Center, Guodian Finance Co., Ltd.
liujiasheng@cgdc.com.cn

ABSTRACT

In multi-touch interactive systems, it is of great significance to distinguish which hand of the user is touching the surface in real time. Left-right hand distinction is essential for recognizing the multi-finger gestures and further fully exploring the potential of bimanual interaction. However, left-right hand distinction is beyond the capability of most existing multi-touch systems. In this paper, we present a new method for left and right hand distinction based on the human anatomy, work area, finger orientation and finger position. Considering the ergonomics principles of gesture designing, the body-forearm triangle model was proposed. Furthermore, a heuristic algorithm was introduced to group multi-touch contact points and then made left-right hand distinction. A dataset of 2880 images has been set up to evaluate the proposed left-right hand distinction method. The experimental results demonstrate that our method can guarantee the high recognition accuracy and real time performance in freely bimanual multi-touch interactions.

Author Keywords

Left-right hand distinction; multi-touch interaction; bimanual interaction.

ACM Classification Keywords

H.5.2. Information interfaces and presentation: User Interfaces-*Ergonomics, Interaction styles, User-centered design.*

General Terms

Human Factors; Design.

INTRODUCTION

Over the past years, computer-vision based multi-touch surfaces are becoming prevalent in our daily life [2, 7, 8, 11,

Note: *Corresponding author. Tel.: +86-10-62661574

21]. Multi-touch interactions extend traditional desktop interactions through allowing direct-touch with bare fingers. Therefore, designing natural interactions with multi-touch interactive surfaces has attracted increasing attention in recent years.

The advantage of interactive surfaces provides new opportunities for freely bimanual interactions. Moscovich and Hughes [18] demonstrated that usually one-handed input and two-handed input are not exchangeable since they have different meanings. Especially, their studies indicated that unimanual multi-touch manipulation is suitable for moving, rotating, and stretching an object, while two hands perform better than one at tasks which require separate control of two points. According to Guiard [13], asymmetric but bimanual interactions are among humans' most skilled manual activities. In fact, we are quite familiar with using both our hands in very different manners in our daily lives, such as playing violin and using scissors.

However, most existing multi-touch tabletop systems relied only on contact locations and the movement of fingertips; they provided little information about which hand was touching the display, hence limited the naturalness of the interactions. The limited scopes of information without left-right hand distinction constrain the interaction vocabulary and narrow the potential natural input bandwidth of bimanual interactions.

Since quite few hardware devices or software frameworks provide handedness information, the objective of our work is to group multi-touch contacts into a user's left or right hand to fully explore the potential of bimanual interactions. The observations show that finger orientation [8, 15, 25, 26, 30] may be a potential input dimension for detecting finger handedness and extending the design space for natural interactions on interactive surfaces. Besides, ergonomics, especially work area [3, 12, 23], should be taken into account when designing touch gestures [19, 29]. Surprisingly, although there have some researches on bimanual interactions [2, 8, 11, 25], very few exploit the work area for interactions.

In this paper, a new left and right hand distinction method is proposed based on both the finger orientation observation and natural ergonomics work area design principles. It is a simple but effective method of multi-touch tabletop interactions that can detect multiple touches, group the touch points, and further map the touch points to their associated joined hand without resorting to additional hardware. Left and right hand distinction can assign different work to different hands, enable asymmetric bimanual interaction [13], enrich semantic information, enhance user-friendliness of multi-touch screens and enrich the gesture vocabulary. The main contributions of our work are summarized as follows:

• A body-forearm triangle interaction model was proposed based on the human anatomy, normal comfort work area and ergonomics principles of gesture designing;

• A heuristic algorithm clustering multiple finger touches into groups, and distinguishing between left hand and right hand even when not all of the fingers from a given hand are placed on the surface;

• A dataset of multi-touch gestures with 2880 images was set up. The recognition accuracy and time performance of our method were tested on the dataset. The results demonstrated that one-handed or two-handed multi-touch gestures composed by arbitrary fingers can be identified in real time by the proposed method.

RELATED WORK

Computer vision-based interactive tabletop techniques are most popular because of their scalability, low cost and ease of setup. However, in most vision-based techniques [21], such as Laser Light Plane Illumination (LLP), frustrated total internal reflection (FTIR) [14] and diffused illumination (DI), touch areas are recognized as blobs of light, therefore, touch discrimination is essential in multi-touch interactions.

Current available solutions to touch discrimination rely mostly on hardware. One of the earliest commercially available tabletop systems that supported discriminating touches was DiamondTouch [9], which used a technique where a circuit was capacitively closed when a user touched the surface, by which it associated touch regions to a specific user. This technology supports user identifications and bimanual interactions. Dohse et al. [10] distinguished and identified users by using skin color segmentation with a peripheral overhead camera. Ackad et al. [1] used the Kinect sensor and mobile phones to continuously track and identify different users, however, it didn't make hand discrimination of users. Some other hardware-based methods also require that the users wear the necessary devices, for example, both Meyer and Schmidt's IdWristbands [17] and Roth et al.'s IR ring [22] emitted a coded signal as identifiers. Marquardt et al. [16] employed the gloves equipped with fiducials that enabled recognition of markers together with their orientations, hence finger

orientations were derived. Hand and user detection were also achieved in this way. However, these methods rely on external devices, which impede the compactness of the setup and also introduce additionally heavily processing to the pipeline [10].

Software-based systems with the existing hardware of a common vision-based tabletop are also proposed. Considering the positional information for the fingertips, distance based distinction methods are most widely used. Ewerling et al. [11] developed an approach for finger identification and hand distinction on optical multi-touch devices, their approach relied on the Maximally Stable Extremal Regions algorithm for detecting user's fingertips. Nevertheless, their method is more computationally intensive than common blob detection methods. Bojan et al. [5] proposed a biometric method which was based only on the touch coordinates for user identification on multi-touch displays. Au and Tai [2] presented a simple finger registration method, which could distinguish which hand and fingers were touching the interactive surface directly from the positions of the contact points. While this method only works when all the five fingers are touching the surface in a natural pose, and it cannot tackle two hand distinctions.

Several other systems employed finger orientations to extend natural interactions. Malik et al. [15] firstly explored finger orientations in their Visual Touchpad system, the entire hand of the user was tracked by two overhead cameras, hence the finger orientations were derived. Considering the dynamics of the finger landing process, Wang et al. [26] proposed an algorithm for detecting finger orientations from contact information in real time. Zhang et al. [30] used the orientations of the touching fingers for discriminating user touches on vision-based tabletop systems. Dang et al. [8] developed heuristics based on constraints applied to the touch position with finger orientations and mapped fingers to their associated joined hands. Walther-Franks et al. [25] proposed a decision tree to classify fingertip configurations on optical interactive surfaces. Their system provides fingertip registration with less than five fingers present. However, their detection rate is only 80%, which is still too low for tabletop interaction.

Besides using the positions of the contact regions and finger orientations, researchers have also developed methods that extract additional context information for new interactions. Boring et al. [6] and Benko et al. [4] explored the use of contact size to enable rich interactions. ShapeTouch presented by Cao et al. [7] directly utilized contact shape to manipulate objects. Wilson et al. [28] leveraged the contact contours to expand the interaction vocabulary, with which they could manipulate digital objects. Wang and Ren [27] empirically investigated and evaluated several finger properties using a FTIR-based multi-touch surface, they concluded that the shape of the finger contact area, the size of the contact area and the orientation of the contact finger are useful for designing natural multi-touch gestures.

Rather than rely on additional hardware or consider finger properties individually, in this work, we utilize the three aspects together for left and right hand discrimination: 1) both finger orientations and touch positions; 2) the anatomy of human hands and fingers; and 3) natural comfort work areas [3, 12, 23] when interacting with multi-touch tabletop.

LEFT AND RIGHT HAND DISTINCTION ALGORITHM

In this section, we will introduce left and right hand distinction algorithm in detail. First, we will present the basic assumptions used in the algorithm. Second, we will describe a method that detects the orientation of finger contact based on the shape of the contact area. Third, several constraints in grouping finger contacts will be explained. Finally, based on the two groups, we can then perform left and right hand distinction.

Basic Assumptions

Based on existing ergonomics researches [3, 12, 13, 20, 23, 24] and observations of interactions on multi-touch tabletop, three assumptions of our left and right hand distinction method are proposed.

The three assumptions are derived from the movement of kinematic chain of upper limb [13], including angular movement of the wrist, natural work area considering movement of elbow and shoulder. The ergonomics normal range of the angular movements of the wrist [24] is given in assumption 1. Then the normal area [3, 12, 23], which can be reached easily in natural interactions, is given in assumption 2. After that, body-forearm triangle model is proposed based on the observations in assumption 3.

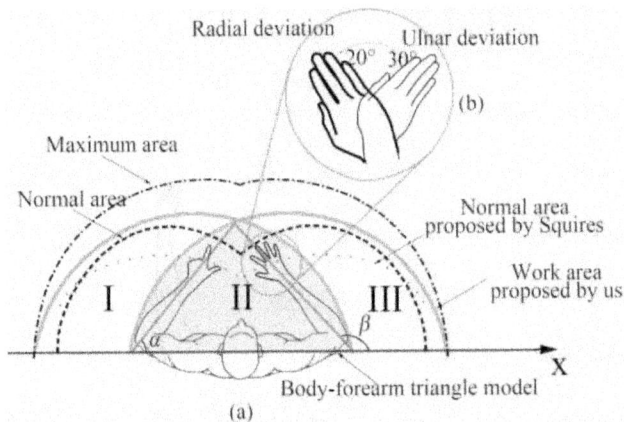

Figure 1. Basic assumptions: (a) working areas; and (b) the angular range of wrist movements.

Assumption 1 **(Ergonomics forearm movements assumption)**: The user naturally places his/her hand(s) on the surface, with his/her wrist(s), elbow(s) and shoulder(s) relaxed, the angular range of wrist movements [24] is shown in Figure 1(b), the orientation of forearm is estimated by the average orientation of finger contacts.

This assumption is in accordance with ergonomics [20]. Nielsen et al. [20] pointed out that the human based gesture approach should be ergonomic, i.e. not physically stressing when used often. They furthermore concluded six main principles in ergonomics, among which are avoiding outer positions, relaxing muscles and avoiding internal and external forces on joints that may stop body fluids. According to these principles, when designing touch interactions, the human hand cannot be utilized beyond the limits of its inner structure despite its dexterity.

Assumption 2 **(Work area assumption)**: According to Barnes and Squires's theory, we divide the work area into three parts (in Figure 1(a)) : I) the left work area, only left hand can reach this area; II) the public work area, both hands can reach this work area; and III) the right work area, only right hand can reach this area. Obviously, these parts depend on the length of the user's hand as well as his/her position, therefore the users are asked to identify their work areas before interaction with the multi-touch tabletop when he/she moves or uses our system for the first time.

Figure 1(a) shows the maximal and normal areas proposed by Barnes [3] and Squires [23], and work area proposed by us. Farley [12] and Barnes [3] proposed maximum and normal areas in horizontal work surface area. Maximum area is defined as the area that could be reached by extending the arm from the shoulder, shown in dash-and-dot line. Normal area is defined as the area which can be conveniently reached with a sweep of the forearm while the upper arm hangs in a natural position at the side, shown in dashed line. Squires [23] also took into account the dynamic interaction of the movement of the forearm as the elbow also is moving, and the normal area proposed by Squires is shown in dotted line. In practice, the user will not fully extend his/her arm(s) or fix his/her elbow(s) when interacting with tabletop, therefore we define work area as the area which both include normal area and can be easily reached, shown in orange solid line.

Assumption 3 **(Body-forearm triangle assumption)**: According to our observation, we suppose that the body and the forearms form a triangle, termed as body-forearm triangle, in the public area during natural interactions, shown as the blue triangle in Figure 1(a)).

In Figure 1(a), α and β are the orientations of the left forearm and the right forearm, respectively. When a user interacts with the tabletop using two hands, it is always true that $\beta > \alpha$. Hence if we can calculate the orientations of two forearms, we can easily tell left hand from right hand by comparing their orientations, the hand that has the smaller orientation is left hand, and the other one is right hand. When a user interacts with the tabletop using only one hand, there are three cases: 1) if the touch contacts occur in the left work area, then these touch contacts belong to left hand; 2) if the touch contacts occur in the right work area, then these touch contacts belong to right hand; and 3) if the touch contacts occur in the public area, the orientation of the hand is estimated as θ, if $\theta > 90°$, then these contacts belong to right hand, otherwise, they belong to left hand.

Finger Orientation Detection

Despite various multi-touch hardware systems, computer-vision based multi-touch technologies are considered in this paper, such as LLP-based multi-touch table (Laser Light Plane). Depending on the particular LLP-setup, only the finger contacts are visible. The captured image in Figure 2(a) stems from a LLP-based table. Since our left-right hand distinction algorithm depends highly on the orientation of finger contact, it's very important to calculate right orientations for all contacts.

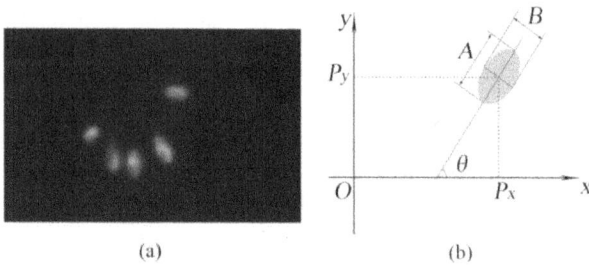

Figure 2. Finger orientation: (a) image captured by a camera from the LLP-based table; (b) finger contact region fitted to an ellipse.

The position and orientation of a detected finger contact area is defined in Figure 2(b). The major axis A, minor axis B and slant angle θ ($0° \leq \theta \leq 180°$) describe the shape of the ellipse; and (P_x, P_y) is the center coordinate of the finger contact. The finger contact blob appears as an elliptic shape which can be perfectly fitted to an ellipse using least-square fitting, as in Figure 2(a). Equation (1) describes the fitted ellipse, where a and b are one-half of the ellipse's major axis A and minor axis B respectively [26].

$$\left(\frac{(x-P_x)\cos\theta+(y-P_y)\sin\theta}{a}\right)^2 + \left(\frac{(y-P_y)\cos\theta-(x-P_x)\sin\theta}{b}\right)^2 = 1 \quad (1)$$

As explained in [26, 27], only oblique touches are considered in our algorithm. Hence we need to determine whether the finger is currently in an oblique touch state to generate reliable finger orientation, similar to [26], area and aspect ratio are used to identify an oblique touch. The identification criteria is shown in Equation (2), where t_a and t_b are empirical thresholds of touch area, and t_s is empirical threshold of aspect ratio.

$$\begin{cases} t_b > area > t_a \\ aspect\ ratio = \dfrac{A}{B} > t_s \end{cases} \quad (2)$$

An oblique touch should meet both criteria in Equation (2), otherwise the touch contact will be discarded. Based on pilot experiments and ergonomics [26], t_a is set to be 100 mm^2, t_b is set to be 500 mm^2, and t_s is set to be 120% in our

prototype system. For an area smaller than t_a, we consider the contact to be vertical or accidental touch; for an area bigger than t_b, we consider that user's fingers are placed too close together; in this case, the finger contacts are merged to one contact area resulting in unreliable detection.

In this step, positions and orientations of all touch contacts as well as their distance between each other are calculated.

Finger Contacts Grouping

Due to the fact that thumb always has the largest spanning angle and its orientation is of large difference with other four fingers, it's hard to tell whether a contact belongs to left hand or right hand solely from its orientation. As a result, when more than one contacts are detected, we have to cluster the finger contacts first, all the contacts from one hand should be clustered in the same group. Both finger orientation and the distance between two contacts are used for clustering the contacts from the same hand into one group.

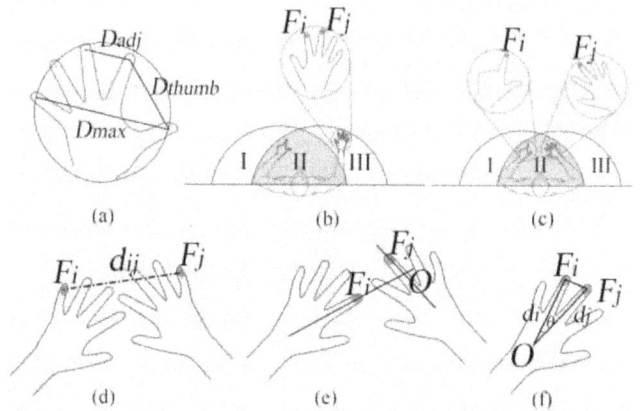

Figure 3. Finger grouping constraints: (a) some thresholds; and (b-f) constraints of touch contacts.

To better describe our algorithm, as depicted in Figure 3, we denote D_{adj} as the maximal distance of adjacent fingers (except thumb) from same hand, D_{thumb} as the farthest distance a thumb can have to the other fingers from same hand, D_{max} as the maximal distance of any two fingers from same hand, O as the intersection point of finger contact F_i to F_j, d_{ij} as the distance from contact F_i to contact F_j, d_i as the length of OF_i, d_j as the length of OF_j. Based on prior trials, D_{adj} is empirically set to be 40 mm, D_{thumb} is empirically set to be 80 mm, D_{max} is empirically set to be 100 mm in our system. Nevertheless, these thresholds are user specific, in fact, these thresholds may be unreasonable for a child. One potential solution is to register hand before interactions as in [2, 11]. In registration, the user is asked to open his/her palm and his/her fingers fully stretched apart as shown in Figure 3(a), then places his/her hand on the interactive surface, D_{adj}, D_{thumb} and D_{max} can be easily derived when five fingertips are detected. Different from [2, 11], the user only has to register his/her hand once before his/her first interaction in our system. All contacts during interactions are clustered into two groups according to the following four constraints:

***Constraint* 1 (Consistent area constraint):** For contacts F_i and F_j, based on Barnes and Squires's theory, if both contacts are in the left part of the user's work area as explained in ***Assumption* 3**, these two contacts belong to the same group, furthermore, they belong to left hand. This is also true when both contacts are in the right part of the user's work area, shown in Figure 3(b).

***Constraint* 2 (Maximum distance constraint):** If $d_{ij} > D_{max}$, the two touch contacts are certainly from different hands. When two hands are far away from each other, this step can effectively cluster contacts belonging to the same hand into one group, as shown in Figure 3(c). When two hands are close enough, fingers can be partly divided into two groups. Such as in Figure 3(d), finger F_i and finger F_j are from different hands.

***Constraint* 3 (Minimum distance constraint):** The distance (d_i and d_j) from the intersection point O to finger contacts (F_i and F_j) should all be larger than a minimum finger length threshold λ. That is if one is smaller than the threshold λ, i.e. $d_i < \lambda$ or $d_j < \lambda$, then finger contact F_i and finger contact F_j come from two different hands. Generally, the threshold λ is set to be the minimum of the average length of thumbs and that of pinkies. In our system, λ is empirically set to be 50 mm. Figure 3(e) sketches this case.

***Constraint* 4 (Angle constraint):** If $d_{ij} < D_{adj}$, the interior angle θ between the orientations of the two fingers is taken into consideration. The basic idea behind this constraint is to estimate a proper angle range of two fingers in the same hand. According to the law of cosines, Equation (3) can be derived (in Figure 3(f)),

$$\theta = \arccos\left(\frac{d_i^2 + d_j^2 - d_{ij}^2}{2 \times d_i \times d_j}\right) \qquad (3)$$

where $d_i \in [a_0, a_1]$ and $d_j \in [b_0, b_1]$.

If the range of d_i and d_j are known, given a specific d_{ij}, the range of θ can be estimated according to Equation (3). The range of d_i and d_j are estimated using Equation (4), then the proper angle ranges of two fingers from the same hand (θ_0 and θ_1) are estimated by Equation (5).

We can easily figure out the range of d_i and d_j are the same, i.e. $a_0 = b_0$ and $a_1 = b_1$. As explained in ***Constraint* 3**, $d_i \geq \lambda$ and $d_j \geq \lambda$, hence $a_0 = b_0 = \lambda$. In a vision-based tabletop system, if two fingers are too close when interaction, then these two finger contacts may merge into one big contact area, which violate the area criterion in Equation (2), thus finger orientation cannot be detected. In our observation, in order to correctly detect finger orientation, the centers of adjacent fingertips should be at least 20 mm apart, d_i and d_j are supposed to reach the upper length boundary in this

situation. To estimate the value of a_1 and b_1, we let both d_i and d_j be x in Equation (3), thus:

$$x = \frac{d_{ij}}{\sqrt{2 \times (1 - \cos(\theta))}} \qquad (4)$$

Our prior experiments show that θ is at least 5° when d_{ij} approximates 20 mm. Hence we set d_{ij} to be 20 mm and θ to be 5° in Equation (4) to estimate the upper bound of d_i and d_j (i.e. a_1 and b_1) to be 230 mm.

In our prototype system, a_0 and b_0 are empirically set to be 50mm, a_1 and b_1 are empirically set to be 230 mm. Furthermore, the range of θ has

$$\theta_0 = \arccos(\tfrac{a_1^2 + b_1^2 - d_{ij}^2}{2a_1 b_1}) \leq \theta \leq \arccos(\tfrac{a_0^2 + b_0^2 - d_{ij}^2}{2a_0 b_0}) = \theta_1 \qquad (5)$$

It won't be hard for us to derive that F_i and F_j are from different hands if $\theta < \theta_0$ or $\theta > \theta_1$.

Based on these constraints and heuristics, the touch contacts are divided into two groups.

Left and Right Hand Distinction

Wobbrock and Colleagues [29] outlined 27 different gesture commands performing on a tabletop interactive surface. Murugappan et al. [19] further studied these hand poses, and concluded that 1) the majority of gestures are performed with one, two, three or five finger touch points; 2) almost all the one-finger interactions are performed using the fore-finger; 3) for two-finger interactions, the fingers used are thumb-fore fingers and fore-middle fingers; 4) for three-finger interactions, the finger combinations used are thumb-fore-middle and fore-middle-ring; and 5) for four-finger interactions, the finger combinations are thumb-fore-middle-ring and fore-middle-ring-and-little. Based on the above observations, and taking bimanual and asymmetric interactions into account, we propose 80 gestures including $(1 + 2 + 2 + 2 + 1) \times 2 = 16$ one-handed gestures and $(1 + 2 + 2 + 2 + 1)^2 = 64$ two-handed gestures to be detected in our system.

The clustered groups are then used to distinguish left hand contacts from right hand contacts. Since there are only two groups of touch contacts, if one group of them is recognized, the remaining group is determined. The left and right hand distinction steps are as follows:

***Step* 1**: Figure out the centroid of the either group of touch contacts. According to our body-forearm triangle model, if the centroid locates in the left work area, then this group of touch contacts belongs to left hand; if the centroid locates in the right work area, then this group of touch contacts belongs to right hand; if both centroids locate in the public work area, then go to ***Step* 2**.

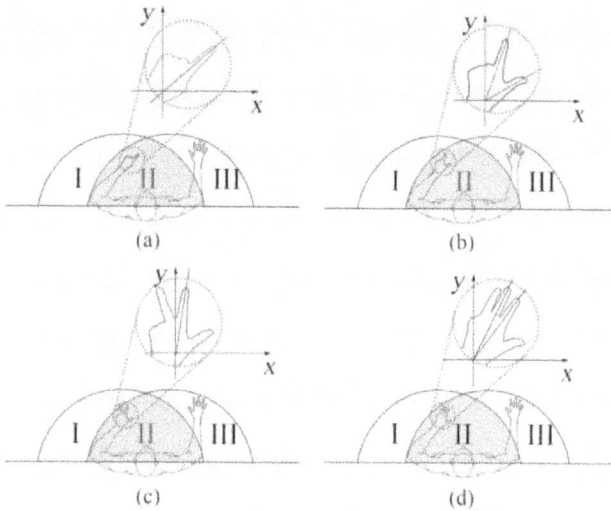

Figure 4. Hand orientation estimation.

Step 2: Compute the orientation of the group while the centroid of the group of touch contacts locates in the public work area. When there is only one contact in the group (Figure 4(a)), the orientation of the group equals to that of the contact; when there are two contacts in the group (Figure 4(b)), the orientation of the group equals to the mean orientation angle of contacts; when there are more than 2 contacts in the group (Figure 4(c-d)), the group orientation is the mean orientation angle of the contacts without the maximum and minimum orientations.

Step 3: Make left and right hand distinction based on the **body-forearm triangle assumption**. If there is only one group, the orientation of the group is estimated as θ, if $\theta > 90°$, then these contacts belong to right hand, otherwise, they belong to left hand. If there are two groups of contacts, α and β are the orientations of group one and group two, respectively. If $\beta > \alpha$, then the contacts of group one belong to the left hand, while the contacts of group two belong to the right hand, and vice versa.

A concrete example of our left and right hand distinction algorithm is shown in Figure 5. Figure 5(a) is a raw image captured by Flycap, the image is firstly preprocessed by background removal and image binarization (Figure 5(b)). Secondly, finger orientations are calculated by detecting contacts blobs and fitting the blobs into ellipses, as shown in Figure 5(c). Thirdly, the contacts points are classified into two groups in Figure 5(d), where the finger grouping result is represented by the colored digits, yellow digits belong to one group, while purple digits belong to another group. Finally, we perform left and right hand distinction (Figure 5(e)), the left and right hand distinction result is indicated by the colored ellipses, red ellipses indicate that this group of contacts belongs to left hand, while green ellipses indicate that this group of contacts belongs to right hand.

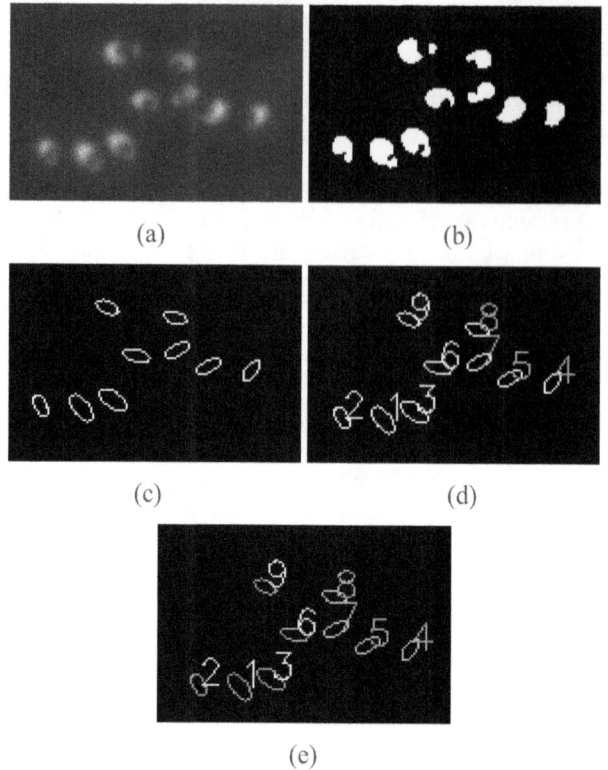

Figure 5. A concrete example of our left and right hand distinction algorithm.

EXPERIMENTS

Experimental evaluations were conducted to assess the performance of our proposed left and right hand distinction algorithm.

Apparatus

We conducted the experiment on LLP (Laser Light Plane Illumination, LLP) based multi-touch interactive tabletop, shown in Figure 6. The tabletop device rear-projects images with a resolution of 1024×768 pixels onto a surface with size 140 cm × 104 cm. The tabletop was connected to a personal compter with 2.4 GHz processor and 2GB RAM, the operating system is 32-bit Windows XP Professional 2002 Service Pack 3.

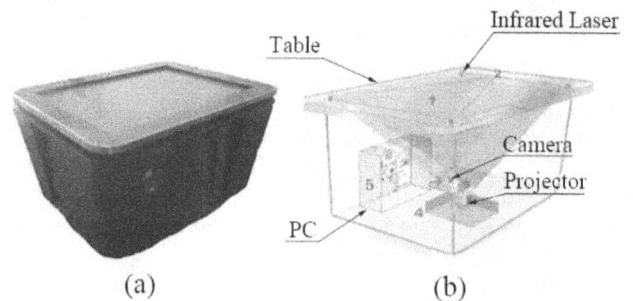

Figure 6. LLP-based multi-touch table: (a) appearance; (b) internal components.

Participants

12 graduate students (6 males and 6 females, aged between 23 and 29) with a mean age of 25.2 (std. dev. = 3.1) were involved in this study. 2 participants were left-handed (1 male and 1 female). All of the participants had experience in using multi-touch user interfaces. None of them had used the system we developed in this work prior to the experiments.

Task & Design

At the beginning of experiments, all of the participants were given a brief demonstration of how the task could be done using various finger gestures. The participants stood in front of the tabletop and were asked to adopt a position that felt natural and comfortable for them. Since detecting finger orientations was a component of our left-right hand distinction system, we didn't provide any visual feedback; hence the participants had to rely on their subjective perception of the finger orientation completely.

The participants were asked to perform the proposed 80 gestures and were reminded to touch the screen in a natural and comfortable way. When they posed a gesture, the user input image was recorded via software named Flycap. At the same time, the actual gestures were recorded by a camera to verify our left-right hand distinction result. The participants had to lift their fingers before performing the next gesture. Participants performed each gesture with three repetitions, and in one of which they were reminded to put their fingers closer.

Thus a dataset consisting of multi-touch gestures was set up, and the total images consisted of: 12 participants × 80 gestures × 3 repetitions = 2880 images in total.

Criteria

The hand discrimination accuracy and time performance are assessed with the following criteria:

1) **Grouping Accuracy (GA):** GA = (the number of correctly grouped fingers) / (the number of all contacts);

2) The **Precision** in left-right hand **Distinction** after **Grouping** contact points (PDG): PDG = (the number of contacts that are successfully mapped to their joined hands) / (the number of correctly grouped fingers);

3) The **Overall Handedness Identification Accuracy** (OHIA): OHIA = GA × PDG = (the number of contacts that are successfully mapped to their joined hands) / (the number of all contacts);

4) **Execution Time (ET).**

Results

Several experimental cases are shown in Figure 7, for every subfigure, the original image is shown in the left, while the results of finger contacts grouping and left-right hand distinction are shown in the right. The finger grouping result is represented by the colored digits, white represents no group information, yellow represents one group, while purple represents the other group; the left and right hand distinction result is represented by the colored ellipses, red ellipse represents that this contact belongs to left hand, while green ellipse represents that this contact belongs to right hand. Even when there is only one finger touching the tabletop, as shown in Figure 7(a)(b), our algorithm can effectively provide the handedness information. Figure 7(c) shows the case that two touch contacts from the same hands, while Figure 7(d) shows the case that two touch contacts come from the different hand. Similarly, Figure 7(e-o) indicates some possible combinations of input gestures from three to ten fingers. Besides, our method support both unimanual gestures, such as in Figure 7(a-c)(e)(i), and bimanual gestures, such as in Figure 7(d)(f)(g-h)(j-o). The results show that one-handed or two-handed multi-touch gestures composed by arbitrary fingers can be identified by our proposed method.

We collected 12 × 80 × 3 = 2880 images in the experiment, seven of which were discarded because of the mis-operation by the users. In experiment, we manually annotated 2873 images with 15501 touch contacts, during which 14759 contacts were grouped correctly by our algorithm, the precision in clustering contacts was 95.2%; Based on correctly grouping, 14165 contacts were correctly mapped to their associate joined hand, the accuracy rate was 96.0%; The average recognition rate of our proposed method was about 91.4% which improved dramatically comparing to that of decision tree-based method [25], whose detection rate was 80%. Figure 8 shows the precision in correct clustering contacts (GA), the precision in left-right hand distinction after correctly grouping contact points (PDG) and the precision in mapping contact points to the associate joined hands (OHIA) from 1 finger to 10 fingers. Our result reveal accuracy rate as high as 97.2% when there is only 1 contact, comparing to Literature [19], we can not only map single contact to its associate joined hand, but also have a higher success rate, which supports our body-forearm triangle interaction model; as expected, when it comes to 2 contacts, we achieve a lowest precision of 90 % in correctly clustering fingers (GA), and a lowest precision of 86.4% in mapping contact points to the associate joined hands (OHIA); along with the increase of the number of contacts, the precision in correctly clustering the contacts and mapping contacts to their associate joined hands increase. When it comes to 10 contacts, we observe 98.9% recognition rate for grouping fingers (GA) and 98.3% for left-right hand distinction (OHIA).

Figure 9 shows the execution times with respect to the simultaneous number of contacts. The reported execution times include all steps of our proposed method as well as image preprocessing. We started measuring just after loading the images into memory and stopped when all processing steps had been executed. In order to minimize the influence of external factors, the record images were processed three times and we took the average times as performance measures. It took 11.55 ms on average (std. dev. = 2.30 ms) with a maximum of 16ms to detect handedness, which met the requirement of real-time interaction on tabletop.

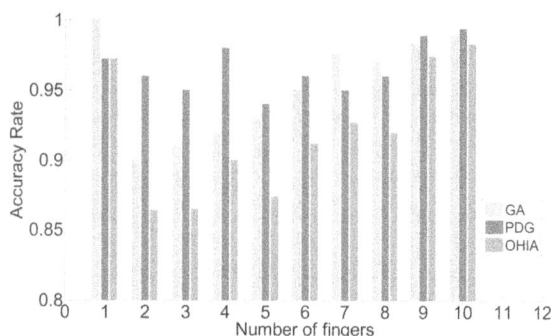

Figure 8. The precision in clustering contacts and mapping contacts to their associate joined hands.

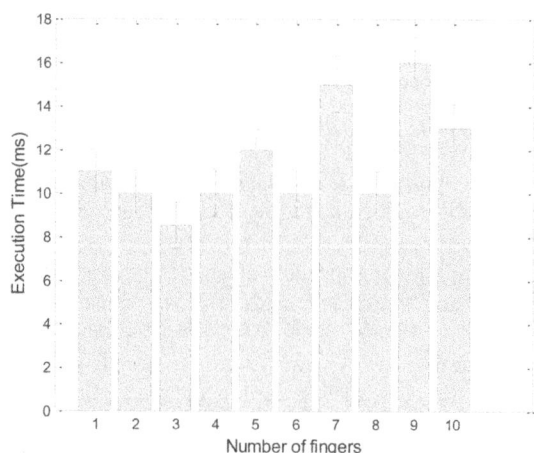

Figure 9. Execution times with respect to the simultaneous number of contacts involved in the processing.

Discussion
When the number of contacts is less than five, there is relative less information for us to use to group fingers, therefore most of our errors stemmed from false finger orientation. There is no overlapping and adhesion when there is only one contact, resulting in correct finger orientation at high recognition rate. In the case of 2 contacts, contacts grouping usually failed in the presence of overlapping and adhesion when user performs fore-middle finger gestures. The case that mistaking one hand's fore-finger as the thumb of the other hand didn't happen. One possible reason might be that this posture is not natural or comfortable for the users. We also observed that the accuracy increases as the number of finger contacts increases. When there are many contacts, the accuracy of handedness detection (OHIA) may be affected by adhesion, when contacts points are too close, our algorithm may fail. The major reason is that it will cause wrong finger orientation detection. In order to generate reliable finger

orientation, we adopt Equation (2) to avoid the situation when two contacts points are too close. In our experiment, this situation happened very few, about less than 10 times in our collected dataset with 2880 images. One potential solution to this problem is to consider continuous frames. Because the contacts points may be too close in current frame, but they may be far enough to be distinguished in next frame.

Our proposed method has several limitations, it only deals with one user, and it may be desirable to consider collaborative use with the multi-touch systems and moving scenarios. Our method only deals with one image in our current study; it may also be interesting to consider multiple frames in our future work. What's more, our algorithm relies heavily on the detection of finger, especially finger orientation, hence a false detection for finger orientation may result in a false left-right hand distinction. Future studies are needed to explore reliable finger orientation detection.

CONCLUSION
In this research work, we designed and implemented a simple but robust software-based method for finger handedness distinction on optical interactive surfaces. We take both the contacts and the complete arm-hand-chain into consideration. Using data gathered from 12 users on an LLP multi-touch display, our system reported an accuracy of 91.4% in detecting finger handedness. Our prototype system demonstrates that it is possible to provide finger handedness distinction capabilities on every multi-touch display, and we also believe that detecting handedness of fingers will enrich designs of multi-touch interactions.

ACKNOWLEDGEMENT
The work described in this paper was supported by several grants, including the National Fundamental Research Grant of Science and Technology under 973 Project 2013CB329305, and the National Natural Science Foundation of China under Grant (NSFC 61173059, 61135003, 61203276, and 61232013).

REFERENCES
1. Ackad, C., Clayphan, A., Maldonado, R.M. and Kay, J. Seamless and continuous user identification for interactive tabletops using personal device handshaking and body tracking. *Ext. Abstracts CHI 2012*, ACM Press (2012), 1775-1780.

2. Au, O.K. and Tai, C. Multitouch finger registration and its applications. In *Proc. OzCHI 2010*, ACM Press (2010), 41-48.

3. Barnes, R.M. and Barnes, R.M. Motion and time study. Wiley (1958).

4. Benko, H., Wilson, A.D., and Baudisch, P. Precise selection techniques for multi-touch screens. In *Proc. CHI 2006*, ACM Press (2006), 1263-1272.

5. Blažica, B., Vladušič, D., and Mladenić, D. MTi: A method for user identification for multitouch displays. *International Journal of Human-Computer Studies 71*, 6 (2013), 691-702.

6. Boring, S., Ledo, D., Chen, X., Marquardt, N., Tang, A., and Greenberg, S. The fat thumb: using the thumb's contact size for single-handed mobile interaction. In *Proc. MobileHCI 2012*, ACM Press (2012), 39-48.

7. Cao, X., Wilson, A.D., Balakrishnan, R., Hinckley, K., and Hudson, S.E. ShapeTouch: Leveraging contact shape on interactive surfaces. In *Proc. TABLETOP 2008*, IEEE (2008), 129-136.

8. Dang, C.T., Straub, M., and André, E. Hand distinction for multi-touch tabletop interaction. In *Proc. ITS 2009*, ACM Press (2009), 101-108.

9. Dietz, P. and Leigh, D. DiamondTouch: a multi-user touch technology. In *Proc. UIST 2001*, ACM Press (2001), 219-226.

10. Dohse, K.C., Dohse, T., Still, J.D., and Parkhurst, D.J. Enhancing multi-user interaction with multi-touch tabletop displays using hand tracking. In *Proc. ACHI 2008*, IEEE (2008), 297-302.

11. Ewerling, P., Kulik, A., and Froehlich, B. Finger and hand detection for multi-touch interfaces based on maximally stable extremal regions. In *Proc. ITS 2012*, ACM Press (2012), 173-182.

12. Farley, R.R. Some principles of methods and motion study as used in development work. *General Motors Engineering Journal 2*, 6 (1955), 20-25.

13. Guiard, Y. Asymmetric division of labor in human skilled bimanual action: The kinematic chain as a model. *Journal of motor behavior*, 19 (1987), 486-517.

14. Han, J.Y. Low-cost multi-touch sensing through frustrated total internal reflection. In *Proc. UIST 2005*, ACM Press (2005), 115-118.

15. Malik, S. and Laszlo, J. Visual touchpad: a two-handed gestural input device. In *Proc. ICMI 2004*, ACM Press (2004), 289-296.

16. Marquardt, N., Kiemer, J., and Greenberg, S. What caused that touch?: expressive interaction with a surface through fiduciary-tagged gloves. In *Proc. ITS 2010*, ACM Press (2010), 139-142.

17. Meyer, T. and Schmidt, D. IdWristbands: IR-based user identification on multi-touch surfaces. In *Proc. ITS 2010*, ACM Press (2010), 277-278.

18. Moscovich, T. and Hughes, J.F. Indirect mappings of multi-touch input using one and two hands. In *Proc. CHI 2008*, ACM Press (2008), 1275-1284.

19. Murugappan, S., Elmqvist, N., and Ramani, K. Extended multitouch: recovering touch posture and differentiating users using a depth camera. In *Proc. UIST 2012*, ACM Press (2012), 487-496.

20. Nielsen, M., Störring, M., Moeslund, T.B., and Granum, E. A procedure for developing intuitive and ergonomic gesture interfaces for HCI. *Gesture-Based Communication in Human-Computer Interaction*, Springer Berlin Heidelberg (2004), 409-420.

21. Multi-Touch Technologies. Community Release. http://nuicode.com/attachments/download/115/Multi-Touch_Technologies_v1.01.pdf.

22. Roth, V., Schmidt, P., and Güldenring, B. The IR ring: authenticating users' touches on a multi-touch display. In *Proc. UIST 2010*, ACM Press (2010), 259-262.

23. Squires, P. The shape of the normal work area. *USN Submarine Medical Research Laboratory Report 15*, 4 (1956).

24. Tsandilas, T., Dubois, E., and Raynal, M. *Modeless Pointing with Low-Precision Wrist Movements*. In *Proc. INTERACT 2013*, IEEE (2013), 494-511.

25. Walther-Franks, B., Herrlich, M., Aust, M., and Malaka, R. Left and right hand distinction for multi-touch displays. *Smart Graphics 2011*, Springer Berlin Heidelberg (2011), 155-158.

26. Wang, F., Cao, X., Ren, X., and Irani, P. Detecting and leveraging finger orientation for interaction with direct-touch surfaces. In *Proc. UIST 2009*, ACM Press (2009), 23-32.

27. Wang, F. and Ren, X. Empirical evaluation for finger input properties in multi-touch interaction. In *Proc. CHI 2009*, ACM Press (2009), 1063-1072.

28. Wilson, A.D., Izadi, S., Hilliges, O., Garcia-Mendoza, A., and Kirk, D. Bringing physics to the surface. In *Proc. UIST 2008*, ACM Press (2008), 67-76.

29. Wobbrock, J.O., Morris, M. R., and Wilson, A.D. User-defined gestures for surface computing. In *Proc. CHI 2009*, ACM Press (2009), 1083-1092.

30. Zhang, H., Yang, X.D., Ens, B., Liang, H.N., Boulanger, P., and Irani, P. See me, see you: a lightweight method for discriminating user touches on tabletop displays. In *Proc. CHI 2012*, ACM Press (2012), 2327-2336.

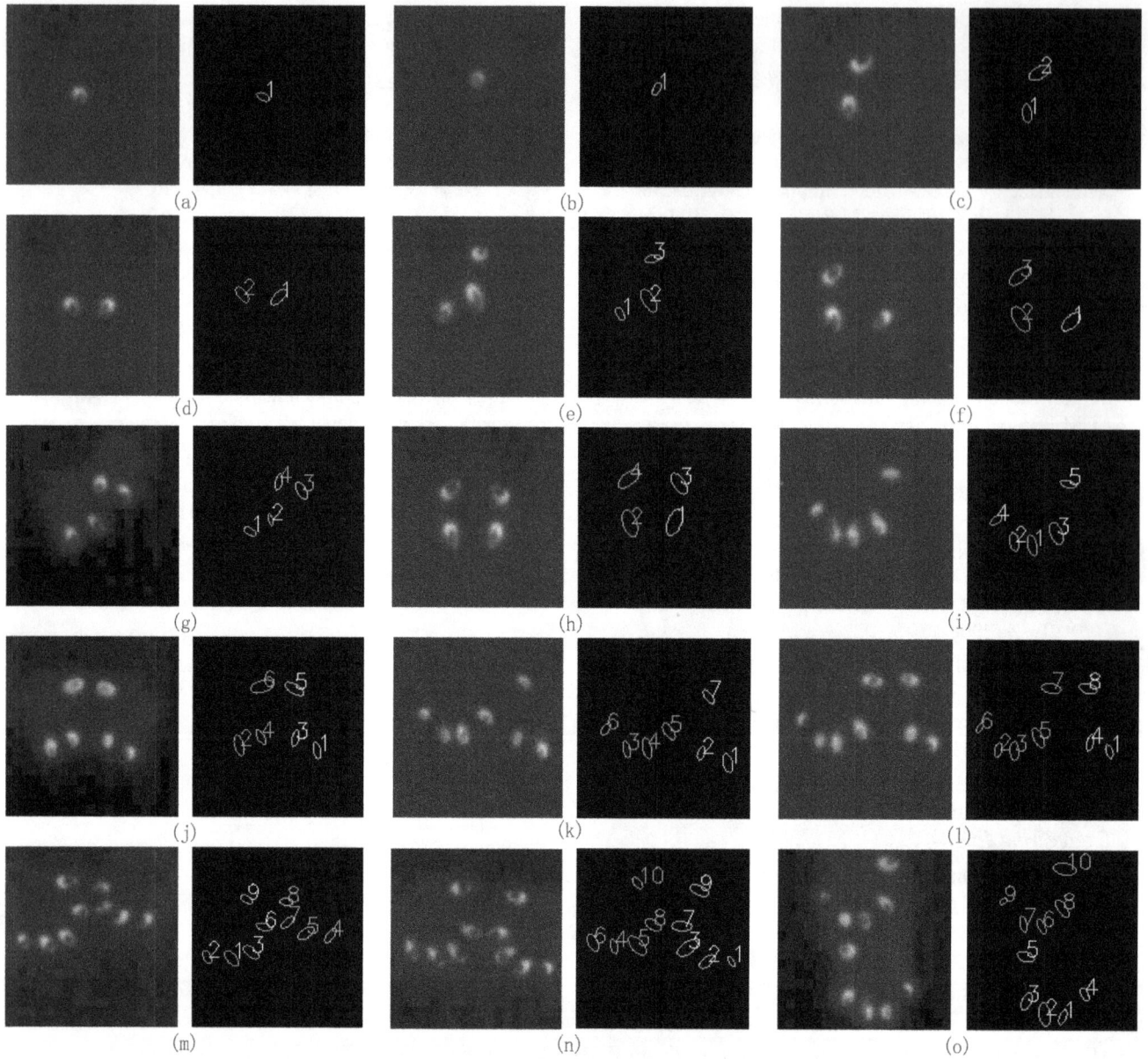

Figure 7. Experiments of finger grouping and left-right hand distinction.

Improving Accuracy in Back-of-Device Multitouch Typing: A Clustering-based Approach to Keyboard Updating

Daniel Buschek[1,2], Oliver Schoenleben[1], Antti Oulasvirta[3,4]

[1]Helsinki Institute for Information Technology HIIT, Aalto University; [2]University of Munich (LMU)
[3]Max Planck Institute for Informatics; [4]Saarland University

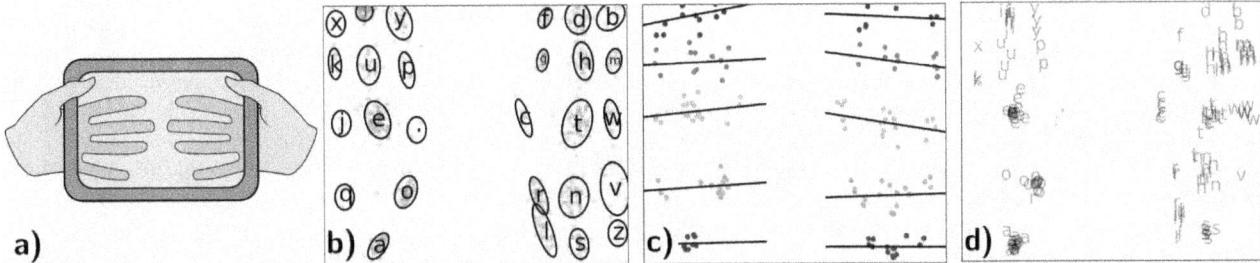

Figure 1. We present a method for ten-finger typing on the back of a tablet with a capacitive multitouch sensor (a). b) Gaussian Bayes learns keys from labelled touches and c) hand modelling assigns *new* unlabelled touches to fingers, represented as lines. Both models are combined in a clustering method to predict characters for touches (d) and adapt keys when hand postures change during typing. We further improve predictions with language models.

ABSTRACT

Recent work has shown that a multitouch sensor attached to the back of a handheld device can allow rapid typing engaging all ten fingers. However, high error rates remain a problem, because the user can not see or feel key-targets on the back. We propose a machine learning approach that can significantly improve accuracy. The method considers hand anatomy and movement ranges of fingers. The key insight is a combination of keyboard and hand models in a hierarchical clustering method. This enables dynamic re-estimation of key-locations while typing to account for changes in hand postures and movement ranges of fingers. We also show that accuracy can be further improved with language models. Results from a user study show improvements of over 40% compared to the previously deployed "naïve" approach. We examine entropy as a touch precision metric with respect to typing experience. We also find that the QWERTY layout is not ideal. Finally, we conclude with ideas for further improvements.

Author Keywords

Machine Learning; Classification; Clustering; Touch; Typing; Back-of-Device

ACM Classification Keywords

H.5.2 Information Interfaces and Presentation: Input devices and strategies (e.g. mouse, touchscreen)

INTRODUCTION

Low text entry rates are a recognised problem for mobile devices. Recent research has explored back-of-device interaction with multitouch sensors [3, 30, 34, 35]. Potential benefits of this concept for mobile text entry are: 1) faster typing rates engaging all ten fingers, 2) releasing display space for applications on the front. However, realising these benefits remains a challenge. Related work used physical keys on the back [18, 29]. Folding the layout in two rotated halves [29] retains the finger-to-key assignments, known from three-row keyboards like QWERTY or the Dvorak Standard Keyboard (DSK). Unfortunately, the demonstrated mean typing speeds were low (15 wpm), and the addition of physical keys breaks the familiar form factor of the device. The *Sandwich Keyboard* [28] deployed a multitouch sensor that followed this concept without extra buttons to keep the familiar form factor. A user study with training showed promising typing speeds (QWERTY: 26 wpm, DSK: 46 wpm). Users reached about 70% of their speeds for physical keyboards. However, error rates were higher than with other methods: about 12% after 7 hours of training. To make this approach a valuable alternative to existing text entry methods, further work is needed to decrease the proportion of errors.

This paper provides an extended modelling framework for typing with a capacitive multitouch sensor on the back (see Figure 1). Our approach can reduce errors by over 40%. We analyse sources of errors and propose ways to locate and remedy them. In contrast to previous work, our approach explicitly models the user's hands and adapts keyboards to changing touch behaviour during typing without collecting new labelled training data. Varying hand locations and angles relative to the device, as well as finger tremor and movement variance lead to different touch locations for the same key. These factors may change dynamically between typing sessions and while typing. Addressing them is important to make keyboards more robust with respect to mobility and individual differences in behaviour and anatomy.

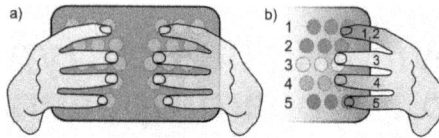

Figure 2. A folded multitouch keyboard [28] on the back (a) with finger-to-key assignments (b). Each key is associated with one character, depending on the layout (e.g. QWERTY). Keys in this figure are not personalised; our approach adapts locations and sizes of keys to the user.

Approach and Related Work

The goal of this work is to improve touch classification accuracy for a folded back-of-device soft keyboard (Figure 2). Our approach utilises machine learning methods to specifically address three kinds of variability: First, we model touch location distributions around targets, the keys (Figure 1b). Second, we account for ongoing changes in hand postures and finger placement behaviour with keyboard updates, facilitated by a hand model (Figure 1c). Third, we train models on user-specific data to respect variance between users. The resulting system predicts characters for the touches (Figure 1d).

We assume a one-to-one mapping of keys to characters. Combined with the folded version of a known layout like QWERTY, this is argued to enable transfer of users' existing motor programs from physical keyboards [28]. This also defines the prediction task: each touch (at x, y) must be mapped to a character. Our approach models keyboard, hands and language.

Keyboard model: Our keyboard model personalises key-locations and sizes based on the user's touch distributions. Matching keys with the user's personal touch behaviour can be expected to improve classification. Related work on personalised key-targets for soft keyboards mostly uses a Gaussian Bayes classifier [1, 15, 25, 36]. It models keys with (bivariate) Gaussian distributions, as justified by evidence for front screen interaction [13, 32]. For typing on a tabletop, distance-based classification had been proposed based on a study with expert typists [11], before the same authors switched to decision trees [10]. For our approach, we evaluated these and other methods on the back using data from novice and expert typists. We considered different touch features and classifiers. Gaussian Bayes was confirmed as a preferable classifier with touch locations on the back as well. Only Support Vector Machines (SVMs) had slightly better accuracy, but at the price of high computational costs, because multiple SVMs need to be trained for more than two classes (keys). Without extensions, they also lack probabilistic output. Costly computations are undesirable for mobile devices and probabilistic predictions can be combined with language models. Most importantly, the Bayes model provides explicit key-locations, which can be updated with our hand model and clustering approach.

Hand model: Our hand model estimates finger locations from unlabelled touches and predicts which touch belongs to which finger. It supports keyboard adaptation when hand postures change during typing. This dynamic adaptation improves touch classification. In general, adapting classifiers to varying user behaviour requires new training data, ideally in each session. This may be unacceptable to the user. Related work on soft keyboards for mobile devices has proposed to collect training data from free typing, using the current mo-

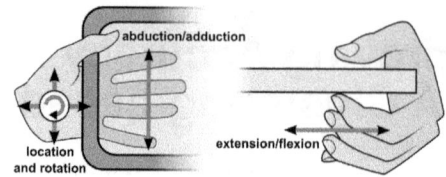

Figure 3. Sources of variance in typing touch locations.

del's predictions to label the touches [2]. However, this implies to trust the same model we want to update, which is inappropriate if we expect dynamically changing behaviour. Another approach trained multiple supervised models in advance, then selected the most specific one in each context to achieve adaptation [36]. Unfortunately, this method assumed discrete hand postures (e.g. one/two thumb), but typing postures on the back are continuous (see Figure 3).

We propose a *keyboard updating* approach, which does not rely on labelled touches. It has two parts. First, we utilise touch-to-finger assignments from the hand model and knowledge about the layout (e.g. QWERTY) to cluster unlabelled new touches. Second, we find the optimal pairing of existing keys and new cluster locations to update the keyboard.

We compare our approach to two simple methods and the *Sandwich Keyboard* algorithm [28]. It predicts the closest key for each touch and compares its prediction to the ground-truth key. If the prediction was correct, the key is moved towards the touch location. Incorrect predictions move it away.

Language model: Language context improves classification for ambiguous touch locations, because not all characters are equally likely to continue previously entered text. We build on existing work on language modelling for soft keyboards to predict characters from both touches and language context [13, 15, 25]. Our approach is two-fold. First, we use n-grams to improve key disambiguation during typing as in related work [13, 15]. Second, we infer words from touch sequences with Hidden Markov Models (HMMs) and use dictionaries [22, 25] to correct them. Auto-correction is a common feature of modern devices (e.g. the Android stock keyboard [14]).

We further examine touch density and entropy of probabilistic keyboard models. We discuss entropy as a metric for touch precision while typing. These methods allow us to gain insight into differences between users and layouts.

KEYBOARD MODEL

To classify touches into keys, a formal representation of touch events is required. We evaluated these **features** (Figure 4a):

- *downX, downY, upX, upY*: Touch locations when meeting and leaving the surface.
- *travelX, travelY, travelAngle*: Distances and angle between touch down and up.
- *distanceToPrev, angleToPrev*: Distance and angle between two following touches.
- *touchDuration, timeDifference*: Time between down and up and time between two following touches.

The list is not exhaustive. Other sensors may provide new features. Our model uses *upX, upY*, based on feature evaluation.

A **touch classifier** can learn to statistically associate touch feature values with keys. It is trained on labelled touches, which means that the ground-truth key for each training touch is known. The trained classifier can then predict keys for future unlabelled touches. We use Gaussian Bayes, which models each key with a (bivariate) normal distribution, see Figure 1b). This model is defined by Bayes' Theorem:

$$p(k|t) = \frac{p(t|k)p(k)}{p(t)}$$

$p(t|k) \sim \mathcal{N}(\mu, \Sigma)$ is the *likelihood* of touch t given key k. $p(k)$ models *prior* believe in k. $p(t)$ is a normalisation factor:

$$p(t) = \sum_{k \in K} p(t|k)p(k), \text{ for the set of all keys } K.$$

The *posterior* $p(k|t)$ gives the probability of keys after observing t. However, only the numerator is needed to find the most probable key k', which is the classification decision:

$$k' = \operatorname*{argmax}_{k \in K} \left(\frac{p(t|k)p(k)}{p(t)} \right) = \operatorname*{argmax}_{k \in K} \left(p(t|k)p(k) \right)$$

To train the model, the likelihood $p(t|k) \sim \mathcal{N}(\mu, \Sigma)$ is derived from all touches with label k: μ is their average location, Σ is their covariance. The prior $p(k)$ is given by the relative frequency of characters in the language or training text.

We propose to consider sparse training data. Keys for uncommon characters may have few training touches. This leads to poor estimates for their likelihood distributions $p(t|k)$. We solve this problem with a fallback to a default distribution. If there are less than *minPoints* training touches for a key k, the covariance matrix of $p(t|k)$ is not estimated from those touches. It is rather set to a default matrix with zero covariance and variance d. Thus, d defines a default key-size.

HAND MODEL AND KEYBOARD UPDATING

We present a simple hand model for back-of-device typing. It uses a set of lines to represent possible fingertip locations for each digit finger. Line orientations and locations are learned from touches. As a result, our model captures location and rotation of the hand relative to the device. We use this context knowledge to facilitate keyboard updates while typing with changing hand postures.

Each hand is represented by five straight lines. Each digit finger is modelled as one line, thumbs are not needed. However, the index finger gets two lines; it serves two rows of keys in the folded layout (Figure 2). The hand model θ is defined as:

$$\theta = [\theta^i], \theta^i = (\theta^i_1, \theta^i_2)^T, 1 \le i \le 5$$

θ^i defines the i-th line with intercept θ^i_1 and slope θ^i_2. Lines ordered vertically (Figure 4b): θ^1, θ^2 define the index finger, θ^3 is the middle finger, θ^4 the ring finger, θ^5 the small finger.

Learning Fingers with k-Lines

To learn the parameters of the presented hand model, we have to fit finger-lines to touch locations. Intuitively, our method takes a first informed guess to place initial lines. They are then refined iteratively. Each iterative step has two parts. First, each touch is assigned to its closest line. Second, slope and

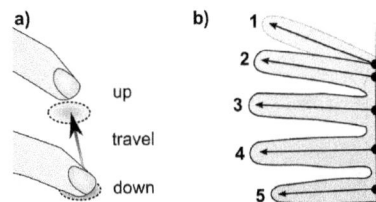

Figure 4. A touch event (a) and the hand model (b) with lines indicating slopes and intercepts along the touch surface edge on the back. The index finger is modelled with two lines to account for the abducted stance used to reach the second row of keys (compare to Figure 2).

intercept of each line are updated to fit the assigned touches. The algorithm terminates, when no more changes occurred.

The algorithm uses an iterative optimisation method similar to k-Means. It is referred to as k-Lines in related work [5]. A detailed description of our procedure is given below:

1. Initialisation: Initial slopes are set to 0 (horizontal fingers). Intercepts are initialised with k-Means using only y-values of the touches. We define k lines $\theta^i = (c_i, 0)^T$. c_i is the i-th cluster-mean of the k-Means clustering. Cluster-means are sorted to match the finger indices described for the hand model. Then, we start an optimisation loop with two steps.

2. Fitting touches to lines: The first step of each iteration assigns each touch $t = (t_x, t_y)^T$ to its closest line:

$$line(t) = \operatorname*{argmin}_{1 \le i \le k} distance(t, \theta^i) = \operatorname*{argmin}_{1 \le i \le k} \frac{|\theta^i_1 + \theta^i_2 t_x - t_y|}{\sqrt{\theta^{i^2}_2 + 1}}$$

3. Fitting lines to touches: The second iterative step fits k lines to the touches, using linear regression with basis functions. We create a design matrix X and target vector y per line:

Let T_i denote the set of all touches t assigned to the i-th line. The $N \times M$ design matrix X_i for the i-th line is defined as:

$$X_i = [x_{nm}], x_{nm} = \Phi_m(t_n), t_n \in T_i$$

Φ_m denotes the m-th of M basis functions. Each of the $N = |T_i|$ rows of X_i contains one touch, each column one feature. For straight finger-lines, we set $\Phi_1(t) = 1$ (bias) and $\Phi_2(t) = t_x$ (linear term). The algorithm is flexible: Other Φ and corresponding distance measures could model different assumptions, for example a quadratic component: $\Phi_3(t) = t^2_x$.

Next, y_i is defined as the vector of the y-values of all touches $t = (t_x, t_y)^T \in T_i$. Finally, X_i and y_i are used with least-squares:

$$\theta^i = (X_i^T X_i + \lambda I)^{-1} X_i^T y_i$$

With Φ_1, Φ_2 as described above, $\theta^i \in \mathbb{R}^{2 \times 1}$ represents a straight line with intercept θ^i_1 and slope θ^i_2. λ penalises large θ and restricts the model to avoid steep slopes (indicate crossing fingers) and intercepts beyond the device borders.

4. Termination: Steps 2 and 3 are executed repeatedly, until no further changes to the line assignments occurred since the last iteration. For physical finger assignments, simply merge the two clusters of the index finger lines. This completes the desired output of the algorithm - finger assignments and the final hand model θ. Figure 1c) shows an example result.

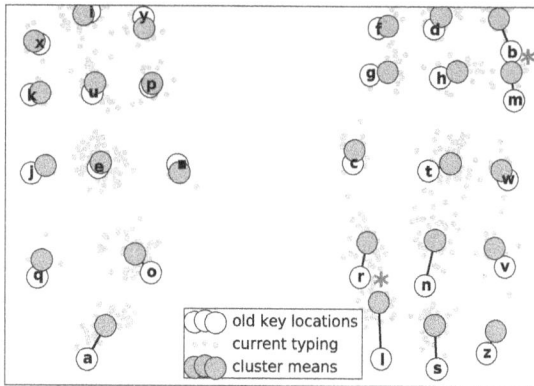

Figure 5. Update example: An existing keyboard (white) is updated by clustering the incoming unlabelled touches (grey). Their cluster means (orange) define new key-locations. They are labelled by pairing them with the old keys, minimising the global sum of distances. Asterisks (*) point out examples for the importance of an optimal pairing per finger: Simply assigning the closest of all old keys would not have worked here.

Keyboard Updating

Touch behaviour can vary between or during typing sessions (see Figure 3). A personalised keyboard model has to adapt its keys to these changes or the mismatch of old key-locations and new touch locations will increase touch classification errors. Collecting new labelled data to retrain the model is not an option, because training phases interrupt the user. New touches from the user's ongoing free typing may inform the model instead, but they lack labels. Hence, it is unknown which touch should update which key.

We solve this problem with a combination of keyboard and hand models in a clustering method. This allows the system to use unlabelled touches to update the keyboard and avoids to bother the user with new training phases. Our approach has two parts. First, clustering finds unlabelled key-locations. Second, existing labelled keys are paired with the new locations. We then move each key to its new location.

Standard clustering methods (e.g. k-Means) can not fully utilise context knowledge about layout and hands. Hence, we propose a custom *hierarchical clustering algorithm*:

1. **Hands:** If hands do not overlap, they are trivially given by the touches' relative locations to the device center.

2. **Fingers:** Our hand model is used to cluster touches of each hand by fingers. Figure 1c) shows an example.

3. **Keys:** Touches of each finger are clustered into keys with k-Means, initialised with key-locations of the existing model.

Our hand model enables the important second step; the method can search for key-clusters *per finger*, not just per hand. The method needs at least one touch per key, because the number of clusters is fixed. This can be ensured by adding key-locations of the existing keyboard to the new touches.

After clustering, each existing key is associated with a new cluster mean. The solution to this set-matching problem is a pairing which minimises the sum of distances, see Figure 5. One may try all possible pairings or use the Hungarian Method [20]. Fingers can be treated separately.

Each key is then moved to its corresponding cluster mean. Updates can be scheduled regularly during typing. We chose the end of sentences in this work. The updated model is then used to classify future touches - until its next update.

LANGUAGE MODEL

In case of ambiguous touch locations, language properties can help to infer user intention. Language models can thus complement models of touch behaviour. We use n-gram models, Hidden Markov Models (HMMs) and dictionaries. We do not model relationships between words here (e.g. word n-grams).

We use character n-gram models as priors like related work [12, 13] to predict $p(k_n|k_1k_2...k_{n-1})$, the probability of key k_n given the last $n-1$ predictions $k_1, k_2, ..., k_{n-1}$. The Bayes model combines this with the touch likelihood $p(t|k_n)$:

$$p(k_n|t) = \frac{p(t|k_n)p(k_n|k_1k_2...k_{n-1})}{p(t)}$$

Training is the same as before. The n-gram model itself is trained on a large text corpus.

We also propose word evaluation, which resembles autocorrection: HMMs extend the Bayes model with state transitions to find the most likely state sequence (word), given the observation sequence (touches). We refer to related work [24] for a detailed description. Following their notation, we set up the HMM $\lambda = (A, B, \pi)$ with known information: Initial probabilities π are character frequencies of the language (unigram model). The transition matrix A is given by a bigram model. Emissions B are the likelihood distributions $p(t|k)$ from the Bayes model. In addition, dictionaries can correct mistyped or misclassified words [22, 25]. They use large training text to suggest candidates, which are ranked by similarity to the input. We further rank equally similar candidates by touch probability, not by training text frequency. The input is then corrected with the best candidate.

DATA COLLECTION

To evaluate the method, we collected three datasets. They are summarised in table 1. Dataset D_1 was provided by [28] from their *Sandwich Keyboard*. We refer to their work for details on apparatus and study design. In summary, two tablets were fixed back-to-back to enable touch interaction from both sides. Experienced ten-finger typists completed a training procedure using the folded versions of their layout over the course of 8 one-hour meetings. Each meeting contained multiple typing sessions. A session is defined as continuous typing without putting the tablet down. Users typed bigrams, word drills and sentences (from [31]) shown on the front screen in a sitting position. Errors were detected with an adaptive recogniser and marked with red lines under the corresponding letter in the prompt. Users reached typing speeds of 26 wpm (QWERTY) and 46 wpm (DSK). We used the 19 typing sessions without keyboard visualisation on the front, no backspacing and only sentences (about 20 per session).

We also obtained 10 typing sessions from an expert user with 70 wpm after 35 hours of training on the *Sandwich Keyboard*. This dataset E was collected as a "stress test'" for keyboard updating. It has two special properties in comparison to the other datasets and is thus only used to evaluate keyboard updating and hand models: First, the user *consciously* varied hand postures to provoke large cross-session changes. Second, sessions consisted of 40 sentences with about 40% *pangrams*. This helps to evaluate that the concepts work for all keys. However, we do not use this data to evaluate language models, since pangrams distort language properties.

Dataset D_2 was collected with a prototype and study design similar to D_1 [28]. It used a touch panel on the back, resulting in a slimmer and lighter device. In contrast to D_1, 5 *novice* users were recruited. They had not learned an official blind ten-finger typing method in the past. In the study, 2 used QWERTY, 3 DSK. We assigned 2 of our 5 users to QWERTY, because DSK was better in previous work [28]. A backspace key was available and users were encouraged to correct *cognitive* errors, like confusing fingers with respect to the layout. We excluded backspaced touches from evaluation. Participants completed 9 one-hour meetings similar to D_1. One of the users had only 7 meetings, due to time constraints on the user's side. We still use this data, since individual performances are never compared between users. Users reached 13.5 wpm on average - much slower than in D_1. We explain this result with the lack of prior ten-finger typing experience. We noticed that users still had to think about the relative locations of the keys during their last sessions, slowing them down. We also measured average speeds with a laptop keyboard (32.8 wpm) and the default Android keyboard on the front (21.5 wpm). As in D_1, we only used data from invisible keyboards (20 sessions, $\sim$ 25 sentences each). Overall, we collected about 40,000 touches from 12 users.

RESULTS

All results were computed on the described datasets. We used the Weka Machine Learning environment [16] for feature evaluation and the comparison of classifiers. Significance is reported at $p \leq 0.05$. We use t-tests and pair conditions per session and also per outlier filtering tolerance or cross-validation fold, where applicable. Note that the different numbers of sessions lead to different degrees of freedoms for the datasets.

Feature Selection

In *single feature evaluation*, classifiers were trained on one feature at a time. This indicates a feature's own explanatory power, see [10]. Results are summarised in Table 2. Location features (*downX, downY, upX, upY*) performed best. Only one other feature, *angleToPrev*, performed considerably better than the baseline across all classifiers and datasets.

Correlation-based feature selection (CFS, [17]) examines data to select feature subsets. It selected touch location features and *angleToPrev* for all sessions. For D_1, *timeDiff* appeared in subsets for 4 of 19 sessions, all other features were selected in only one session each. In D_2, *distanceToPrev* appeared in 2 of 20 sessions, *timeDiff* once, other features never.

Finally, we applied *wrapper feature selection* [19], which greedily adds the best feature to the existing subset, using classifiers; here Naïve Bayes, decision trees, k-Nearest-Neighbours (kNN, $k = 5$) and Support Vector Machines (SVM). All selected subsets had touch location features. For

Dataset	Sessions	Subjects	Typing experience
D_1	19	3 DSK 3 QWERTY	Experts
D_2	20	3 DSK, 2 QWERTY	Novices
E	10	1 DSK	Back-of-device expert

Table 1. Overview of the datasets used in this evaluation.

	Classification accuracy (%)					
Feature	Dataset D_1			Dataset D_2		
	NB	Tree	kNN	NB	Tree	kNN
downY	54.9	52.2	51.4	40.2	37.1	34.5
downX	48.5	45.9	44.5	40.3	38.3	36.6
upY	55.2	52.1	51.3	40.3	37.4	33.9
upX	48.3	46.2	44.5	40.9	38.1	36.9
angleToPrev	23.0	32.0	32.7	21.4	26.3	26.2
travelY	14.0	14.2	14.3	11.6	12.1	12.1
travelX	13.6	15.1	14.4	11.7	12.2	11.9
travelAngle	12.7	16.1	15.7	10.3	12.4	12.4
distanceToPrev	13.9	17.4	17.1	13.2	12.8	12.4
touchDuration	13.9	12.8	12.2	10.8	10.8	10.1
timeDifference	13.2	12.1	11.4	11.8	10.0	10.1
Majority Classifier	12.1			10.8		

Table 2. Classification accuracy with 10-fold-cross-validation using only one feature, averaged over all sessions of each dataset. The majority classifier (baseline) predicts the most common class for each session.

D_1 and Bayes, subsets for 10 of 19 sessions solely comprised of locations. With decision trees, *travelY* (7 sessions) and *distanceToPrev* (6) were the most common non-location features. For D_2 and Bayes, subsets for 14 of 20 sessions contained only locations. With decision trees, *travelY* and *angleToPrev* had 6 sessions each, followed by *distanceToPrev* (5). kNN and SVM almost exclusively selected locations.

Overall, touch locations and *angleToPrev* were favoured by single feature evaluation and CFS. The wrapper approach confirmed touch locations, but not *angleToPrev*. In conclusion, we chose only locations (*upX, upY*) for this work.

Touch Classification

We tested classifiers with 10-fold cross-validation per session. Datasets were preprocessed to facilitate an evaluation of methods, not user-skill: We removed spaces, since this key was operated by the right thumb on the front and hence trivial to recognise. Touches with a *local outlier factor* (LOF, [6]) exceeding an outlier threshold OT were removed. We expect outliers to coincide with cognitive user-errors (e.g. confusing finger-to-key assignments for the layout). We report results in simple error rate. Values in the text are given for $OT = 2.5$, a conservative upper bound for points in a Gaussian cluster [6].

Model comparison: Figure 6a) shows results for D_1: Decision Tree (10.6% average error rate) and Random Forest (10.0%) were outperformed by kNN (9.3%) and Naïve Bayes (9.1%). SVMs ranked first (linear 8.6%, radial basis functions - RBF: 8.4%). D_2 confirmed this ranking, see Figure 6b). All results improved with stricter outlier threshold. For $OT = 1.1$, more than a third of the touches were outliers. This is clearly unlikely to reflect the true number of (cognitive) user-errors, but indicates expectations for more precise typing. Figure 6 shows that the classifiers' ranking was mostly independent of outlier removal. This could not have been observed with fixed outlier thresholds found in evaluations of touch behaviour in related work on soft keyboards [1, 11, 36].

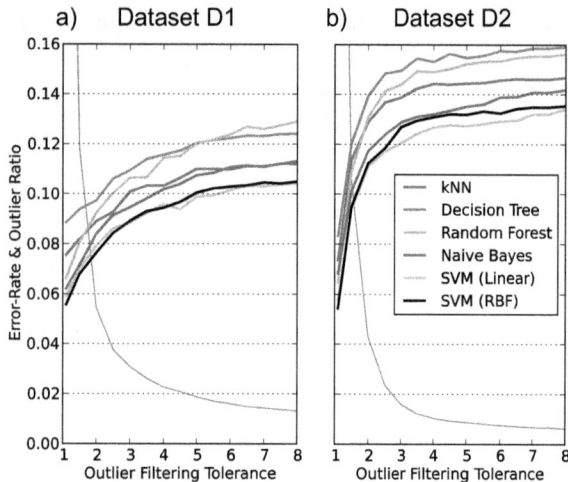

Figure 6. Average error rates of different classifiers as a function of outlier filtering tolerance (LOF-score, [6]), computed with 10-fold cross-validation per session. Falling grey lines indicate the ratios of outliers.

Comparison to related work: We evaluated key predictions from the *Sandwich Keyboard* algorithm (SWK) as *recorded* by the authors of related work [28]. We observed 10.7% (D_1) and 20.6% (D_2). These results were *optimistic*, since they had used ground-truth labels for adaptation during the study. We then slightly adjusted the SWK algorithm to be able to use a training set and perform predictions without ground-truth labels. This modification allowed for cross-validation and a direct comparison with Naïve Bayes. It significantly outperformed SWK (D_1: $t(284) = -6.16$, D_2: $t(299) = -11.72$). Their average error rates at $OT = 2.5$ were 9.1% vs 9.8% (D_1) and 12.4% vs 14.4% (D_2). Note that our SWK performed better than the recorded results, since we estimated initial keys with training sets, not just with single touches by the user.

Sparse data: We modified the Bayes model to account for sparse data. If a key had less than *minPoints* training touches, its distribution used a default variance of 400. We considered two values (5, 15) for *minPoints*. All values are subject to further optimisation. *minPoints* = 5 significantly improved error rates (D_1: $t(284) = -8.04$, D_2: $t(299) = -9.75$). *minPoints* = 15 only achieved this for D_1 (D_1: $t(284) = -9.15$, D_2: $t(299) = 2.81$). There was no significant difference between the SVM and the improved Bayes model for D_1 ($t(284) = 0.08$). The SVM was significantly better for $D2$ ($t(299) = -4.56$). This indicates that Bayes suffered from sparse training data in comparison to the SVM. Our simple extension partly remedied this problem. A practical conclusion is that enough training data per key should be collected to make this unnecessary.

Covariance: We compared Bayes with and without covariance between x and y. Covariance significantly improved error rates with *minPoints* = 15 (D_1: $t(284) = -4.53$, D_2: $t(299) = -6.66$). Their average error rates at $OT = 2.5$ were 8.4% vs 8.6% on D_1 and 12.1% vs 12.5% on D_2. Covariance was worse than no covariance with *minPoints* = 5, but this was only significant for D_1 (D_1: $t(284) = 2.67$, D_2: $t(299) = 0.93$). The observation that covariance only improved classifiers with *minPoints* = 15 demonstrates that estimating the additional parameters for covariance requires more touches per key.

Classifier	Error Rate MSD (%)	
	Dataset D_1	Dataset D_2
Bigram model ($n = 2$)	10.06	9.51
Trigram model ($n = 3$)	9.87	9.48
4-gram model	10.08	10.07
5-gram model	10.05	10.13
Baseline: Naïve Bayes	11.50	11.14

Table 3. Performances of Naïve Bayes with *n*-gram language models.

Classifier	Error Rate MSD (%)	
	Dataset D_1	Dataset D_2
HMM	9.19	8.79
HMM & Dictionary	6.87	6.09
Naïve Bayes & Dictionary	7.70	6.86
Naïve Bayes, trigram & Dictionary	6.99	6.58
Baseline: Naïve Bayes	11.50	11.14

Table 4. Performances for word by word touch classification.

In summary, we identified Gaussian (Naïve) Bayes and Support Vector Machines as the most promising classifiers. Covariance between x and y can be considered if enough training touches per key are available (here > 15). Improvements for sparse training data can be achieved with a default key-size. For D_1, no significant difference was found between improved Bayes and SVM. We favour Bayes; it is computationally cheap in both training and prediction, provides probabilities and inherent handling of more than two classes. In contrast to SVMs, Bayes also offers explicit representations of key-locations, which can be updated with our clustering approach. In general, models performed better for the experienced typists (D_1) than the novices (D_2). This confirms that typing skill is transferred from a traditional keyboard to the *Sandwich Keyboard* [28].

Language Models

Language enhanced *character prediction* was evaluated with 10-fold cross-validation. Folds consisted of whole phrases. Outliers ($OT = 2.5$) were removed from training phrases, but not from test phrases, because removing single characters would have damaged the text for language model evaluation. Spaces remained in the data for the same reason. Results are given in *error-rate$_{MSD}$*, the Damerau-Levenshtein (minimal string) distance [9, 21] of predicted and expected text. *n*-gram models were built with NLTK [4]. All models were trained on the "big.txt" file from Peter Norvig [22]. It contains >1M words from public domain sources.

Table 3 shows that all models improved the baselines. Trigram models performed best with significant improvements to the baselines (D_1: $t(189) = -6.22$, D_2: $t(199) = -8.27$).

We implemented HMMs and dictionaries for *word prediction* in Python. Dictionaries followed Peter Norvig's concept [22]. Table 4 shows that all approaches outperformed the baseline. *HMM & Dictionary* performed best with significant improvements to the baselines (D_1: $t(189) = -11.14$, D_2: $t(199) = -15.15$). It also outperformed *Trigrams & Dictionary*, but only significantly for D_2 (D_1: $t(189) = -0.42$, D_2: $t(199) = -2.38$). Without dictionaries, HMMs outperformed trigrams (see Table 3) significantly (D_1: $t(189) = -3.41$, D_2: $t(199) = -4.44$).

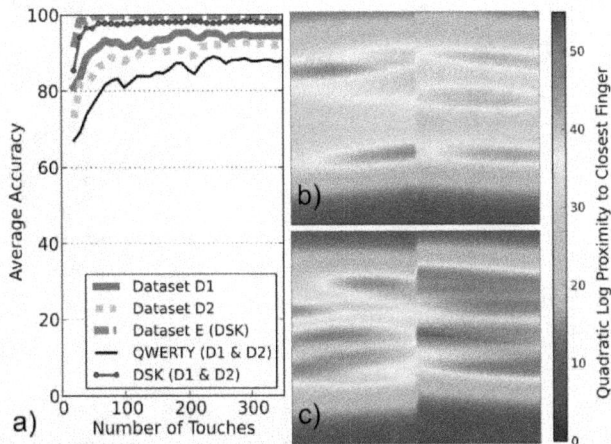

Figure 7. Left: a) Accuracy of touch-to-finger assignments with k-Lines, as a function of the observed number of touches. Right: (log) average proximity of pixels to the nearest finger-line, split by layout. Red is close. These plots indicate that finger locations found with this hand model were spread further apart and varied around more distinct areas of the touch surface for b) DSK than c) QWERTY.

| Classifier | Error Rate (%) | | | | | |
| | same session | | cross-session | | cross-user | |
	D_1	D_2	D_1	D_2	D_1	D_2
Naïve Bayes	9.14	12.40	33.96	25.49	65.40	51.80
Decision Tree	10.61	14.83	33.18	27.86	60.40	52.70
kNN ($k = 5$)	9.27	13.67	30.90	26.27	54.24	48.79
SVM	8.43	11.87	30.85	26.40	59.21	51.15

Table 5. Cross-user (same layout) and cross-session applications.

| Method | Error Rate MSD (%) | | |
	D_1	D_2	E
Baseline: No Updates (Naïve Bayes)	28.92	20.94	39.37
Baseline: *Sandwich Keyboard* algorithm	24.54	19.05	28.90
Distribution Updates	28.03	19.75	38.23
Fast Location Updates	26.82	17.77	31.01
Clustering Updates	20.12	16.68	16.82

Table 6. Performance of (updated) Naïve Bayes across sessions, averaged over all possible cross-session combinations for all users.

In conclusion, n-gram models, HMMs and dictionaries significantly improved the Bayes classifier. Higher order n-gram models may perform better with more training text (see [8, 27]). In contrast to our model comparison (Figure 6), this evaluation included spaces and outliers to keep language properties unchanged. As a result, the ranking of the datasets reversed; we now observed lower error rates for D_2 than for D_1. This indicates that outliers had a larger impact on data without backspacing (D_1). Since users in $D2$ were encouraged to backspace cognitive errors, this also shows that outlier filtering with LOF [6] can indeed remove such user-errors.

User- and Session-Specificity
We trained classifiers on touches of one session (i.e. typing without putting the tablet down) and applied them to touches of another one. Spaces and outliers ($OT = 2.5$) were removed. The observed high error rates (Table 5) show that typing behaviour was *user-specific*, supporting personalised keyboards. It was also *session-specific*. In practice, the cross-session case is the default, since it is impractical for users to retrain their keyboard before each typing session. We conclude that updating keyboard models across sessions is vital in this context.

Finding Fingers
We evaluated touch-to-finger assignments from our hand model. Expected text and layout defined the ground-truth. For example, "f" is the left index finger for QWERTY. Outliers were removed from the data ($OT = 2.5$).

Figure 7a) shows that accuracy improved with more touches. For D_1, up to 95.3% average accuracy was observed after 200 touches. For D_2, 92.6% was reached at 290 touches. With 20 touches, the algorithm achieved 81.1% (D_1) and 73.0% (D_2). With 30 touches, results for D_2 already reached 82.0%. For the expert user (E), it achieved 91.5% with 20 touches and consistently more than 99% after 50 touches. We observed significantly higher accuracy for DSK than QWERTY users

($t(33) = 19.60$). This could be seen as a limitation of the algorithm, but also as one of the layout: Finger modelling revealed that DSK facilitates more precise movements and therefore clearer finger separation in this context. Figures 7b) and c) summarise fingers by layout. Derived finger locations showed showed more cluttered fingers for QWERTY, and more distinctive regions for DSK.

Keyboard Model Updating
We evaluated our clustering approach in comparison to the *Sandwich Keyboard* algorithm and two naïve methods: The first one, *Distribution Updates*, adds each touch to the distribution of its predicted key. The second one, *Fast Location Updates*, adjusts the predicted key's location, based on the average of its existing mean and new touches. Hence, it weights each touch of the current session as much as all touches of the training session, leading to faster adaptation. We consider these methods naïve, because they use new data *touch by touch*. In contrast, clustering uses all new touches in each update. Figure 8a) shows intermediate results, Table 6 final results over the full sessions. Figure 8b) visualises key-movements.

Clustering Updates significantly improved error rates for both baselines: *No Updates* (D_1: $t(47) = -4.95$, D_2: $t(59) = -16.68$, E: $t(89) = -16.76$) and the *Sandwich Keyboard* algorithm (D_1: $t(47) = -2.55$, D_2: $t(59) = -4.54$, E: $t(89) = -8.51$). After 150 touches, a typical short message, clustering had already decreased error rates of Naïve Bayes by 4.93% on D_1, 2.19% on D_2 and 10.53% on E.

In contrast, overall improvements with *Distribution Updates* were small (Table 6). *Fast Location Updates* performed better, but was outperformed by *Clustering Updates* (on all datasets) and the *Sandwich Keyboard* algorithm (on D_1 and E).

The expert user tried different hand postures as a "stress test" for updating. Hence, cross-session variance is the highest for E. Clustering handled it well, in contrast to the other approaches (see Table 6). Experienced typists (D_1) showed higher session-specificity than novices (D_2). Novices placed fingers more slowly and consciously, because they were still learning movements and memorising the keys. Thus, their typing behaviour appeared more stable across sessions. This indica-

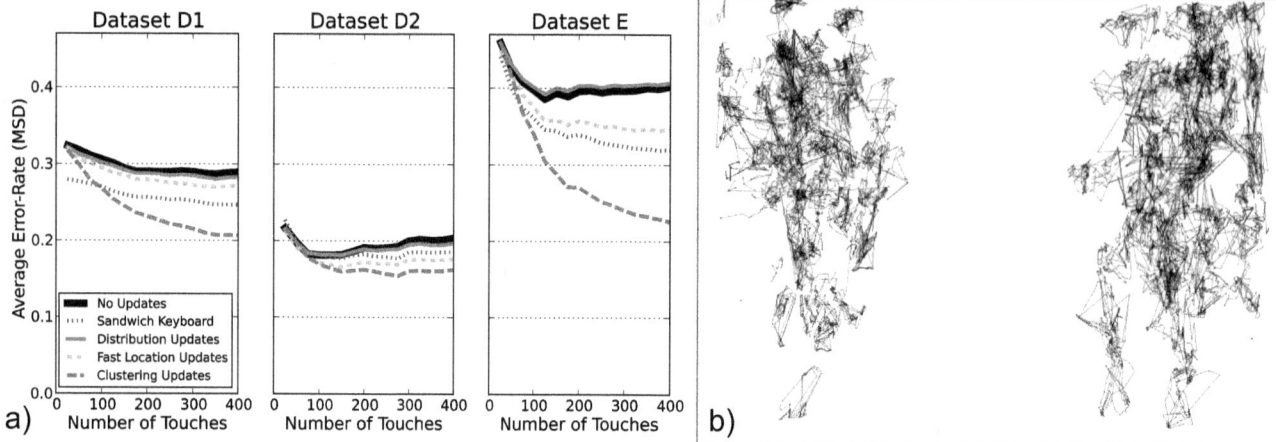

Figure 8. Left (a): Error rates after x touches, averaged over all cross-session combinations. Plots are limited to the first 400 touches to ensure that they always represent *all* sessions. Table 6 shows results over the full lengths. For D_1, the *Sandwich Keyboard* algorithm started noticeably better than the other methods after only $x = 25$ touches: It was used to detect and mark errors in this study. Hence, users initially adapted to this model. Clustering updates still outperformed it after about 100 touches. Right (b): All key-movement paths from clustering updates on dataset D_2, revealing that back-of-device typing is highly dynamic. The long and overlapping traces show that touch behaviour greatly varies during typing and between users.

tes that dealing with cross-session variance may become even more important with increasing experience, at least in this unrestricted setting with no visual or tactile posture cues.

Regarding computational demands, an update with about 500 touches took less than 300 ms with our unoptimised Python script on a modern laptop. We expect faster processing with optimised and precompiled code. Clustering with our concept can also be performed in its own thread. Keys can then be updated almost instantaneously once the results are available.

Discussion

In our user study, Gaussian Bayes was identified as a preferred *keyboard model* on the back. Touch locations were the only useful features here, but the model is flexible and could be used with other features, too. It currently handles sparse training data with a simple fallback threshold (*minPoints*). A more complete Bayesian approach could employ conjugate priors instead [15]. Future model comparisons could also rigorously optimise hyperparameters. New sensors or raw touch data present further interesting opportunities [26].

We observed accurate touch-to-finger assignments with our *hand model*, especially for DSK users ($> 95\%$). The current model neglects more complex hand properties like finger joints, but can be learned solely from touch data. We used it to adapt key-locations to changing hand postures during typing. Updating the full key-distributions (i.e. shape, size) is left to further investigation.

Language models greatly improved classification accuracy, despite their limitations. We did not consider relationships between words and used only character n-grams. We expect further improvements with extended language modelling techniques and more training text.

All methods were evaluated offline on collected user data. Our dataset contained only 12 users, but we observed an interesting range of typing experience and up to 9 hours of training per participant. Next, we plan to test our approach online to explore how users and adaptive keyboards interact.

ANALYSING PERSONALISED KEYBOARD MODELS

The described Bayes model was used to predict keys for touches. We present two simple methods to further analyse the information captured in such a probabilistic model and facilitate a keyboard-wide analysis of typing touch behaviour.

Keyboard Touch Likelihood

Intuitively, touches are more likely to belong to the typing process if they appear in regions where many typing touches have been observed so far. We refer to this touch density as *keyboard touch likelihood*, because it is high if the touch is close to *any* key. Hence, this models a keyboard's *surface*. Figure 9 shows examples.

For a touch location $t \in \mathbb{R}^{2 \times 1}$, and distributions $p(t|k)$ for the set of keys K, the *keyboard touch likelihood* L_t is defined as:

$$L_t = \frac{1}{|K|} \sum_{k \in K} p(t|k)$$

Formally, this describes a Gaussian Mixture Model. Keyboards could filter touches with low L, since they are unlikely to be aimed at keys. Unintended touches on the back may occur from carrying the device between typing sessions.

Keyboard Entropy

Observing entropy of probabilistic keyboard models can reveal areas of ambiguous touch behaviour. Entropy is high for ambiguous touches and low for clear key-presses. Hence, high entropy is found where keys "overlap" and indicates *edges* of soft keyboards. Figure 10 shows examples.

Formally, for touch $t \in \mathbb{R}^{2 \times 1}$ and model $p(k|t)$, entropy S_t is:

$$S_t = - \sum_{k \in K} p(k|t) \ln p(k|t), \text{ for the set of all keys } K.$$

We can also compute an average, for example over all pixels, which reflects overall ambiguity: Precise and consistent typing touch behaviour produces smaller values, sloppy typing

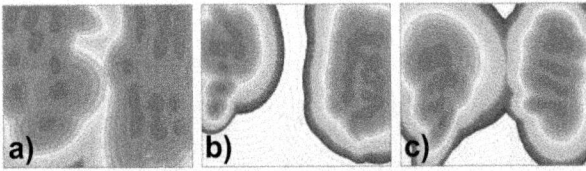

Figure 9. Keyboard touch log-likelihood from different sessions of: a) a novice user, whose hands drifted upwards over the course of the session; b) a more experienced typist; c) the expert user. Red indicates high touch density, white marks regions below the chosen colour scale.

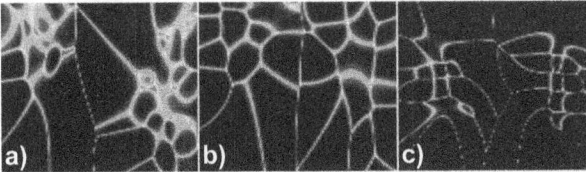

Figure 10. Posterior entropy of Gaussian Bayes keyboard models of: a) a novice user's first try (average entropy 0.18), b) the same user after more training (0.11), and c) the expert user (0.05). Red indicates high entropy and marks regions of "overlapping" keys - the keyboard's edges.

larger ones. Hence, this yields a metric for typing touch precision. In comparison to error rates, cognitively confusing two keys does not matter here, as long as the key-press itself is accurate. We propose to examine entropy to complement existing measures, like error rate and speed.

Observations on Touch Distributions

Modelling typing touch density was presented to examine soft keyboard surfaces. We studied individual sessions (see Figure 9), and observed great variations between users, which can not only be attributed to different hand sizes. Experienced typists showed a tendency to place keys closer together than novices. We propose a simple filter-application: Touches in regions of low density could be ignored, since they are unlikely to be intended typing behaviour. Back-of-device interaction seems prone to generate non-typing touches, for example when carrying the device or putting it down.

We further proposed posterior entropy to examine soft keyboard edges and to define a metric for typing precision. We evaluated average entropies for all sessions: The expert *Sandwich Keyboard* user (E) had a mean of 0.06. The experienced ten-finger typists from D_1 scored second with mean 0.09, followed by the novice typists from D_2 with mean 0.16. One-way ANOVA showed a significant effect of typing experience ($F_{2,46} = 24.46$, $p < 0.001$). These results show that posterior entropy can reflect touch precision, related to typing experience. Figure 10 visualises examples.

CONCLUSIONS

We presented a multi-model approach with keyboard, hand and language models to improve error rates for back-of-device typing. Our evaluation revealed insights into the contributions of the individual modelling assumptions. Considering touch variance per key improved the previous distance-based approach. *n*-grams provided useful character context, but dictionaries achieved even larger improvements. Word prediction was slightly better if touch sequences were first processed by a HMM. Hence, language strongly supports inference for this back-of-device soft keyboard, and a close combination of touch and language modelling is desirable.

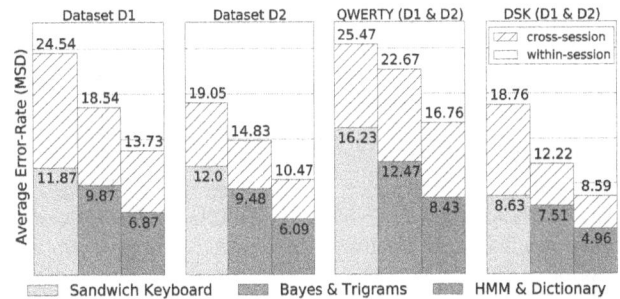

Figure 11. Best practice approaches across sessions and within (cross-validation). Our methods used clustering updates for the cross-session cases. The baseline is given by the *Sandwich Keyboard* algorithm. Splitting the data by layout reveals a superiority of DSK users.

Finally, our hierarchical clustering method updated keyboards while typing. The clustering approach reconsidered all previous touches in each update. It handled unlabelled free typing data without trusting the possibly outdated current keyboard model when deriving the new key-locations. This significantly outperformed previous adaptation methods, which only considered new information touch by touch, and had to trust the current model to label these new touches first. Hence, we conclude that clustering methods can significantly improve accuracy for dynamic typing with touch, compared to only addressing it as a static classification problem.

Best Practice Approaches

Putting the pieces together, we arrive at the following best practices: Bayes with trigram models *per touch*, HMMs and dictionary for *word predictions*, clustering for keyboard updating *across sessions*. Figure 11 shows the results.

Including word correction, we reduced errors by > 40% compared to previous work [28]. Using the DSK layout, this constitutes the best and recommended case (4.96% within sessions, 8.59% across). In comparison, previous work [28] reported 9.8% for DSK users (within their final sessions), using ground-truth labels of the touches to update the keyboard.

Outliers were not removed from the test sets here to keep the text unchanged for language model evaluation. Thus, user-errors likely remained in the data and these results could be considered pessimistic from a modelling point of view.

Future Work

We expect that the lessons learned here can be useful on a broader scale. In particular, we found that normal distributions can also model touches aiming at occluded key-targets on the back, complementing previous work for the front [32]. Our hand model and updating method could prove interesting for other soft keyboards, for example on tabletops. Touch density and entropy discussed here can reveal areas of activity and potential mistakes for interfaces in which targets (e.g. buttons) can be described with touch distributions.

We conclude with ideas for further improvements: Touch classification and finger modelling results suggested a superiority of DSK. Better layouts could be derived with optimisation methods [23]. Touch offset models [7, 33] might help to account for targeting errors. Besides machine learning, refined user training and tactile (back-of-device) markers could improve speed and precision. Visualisations on the front screen can help the user, too, but would cover screen space. A static keyboard should be compared to the personalised version to investigate more restricted typing behaviour as well.

ACKNOWLEDGEMENTS

This work was supported by the Academy of Finland, the EIT ICT Labs, and the Cluster of Excellence for Multimodal Computing and Interaction at Saarland University.

REFERENCES

1. Azenkot, S., and Zhai, S. Touch behavior with different postures on soft smartphone keyboards. In *Proceedings of the 14th international conference on Human-computer interaction with mobile devices and services* (2012), 251–260.

2. Baldwin, T., and Chai, J. Towards online adaptation and personalization of key-target resizing for mobile devices. In *Proceedings of the 2012 ACM international conference on Intelligent User Interfaces* (2012), 11–20.

3. Baudisch, P., and Chu, G. Back-of-device interaction allows creating very small touch devices. In *Proceedings of the SIGCHI Conference on Human Factors in Computing Systems* (2009), 1923–1932.

4. Bird, S., Klein, E., and Loper, E. *Natural Language Processing with Python.* O'Reilly Media Inc., 2009.

5. Bobrowski, L. K-Lines Clustering with Convex and Piecewise Linear (CPL) Functions. *Mathematical Modelling 7*, 1 (2012), 108–111.

6. Breunig, M. M., Kriegel, H.-P., Ng, R. T., and Sander, J. LOF: identifying density-based local outliers. *Proceedings of the 2000 ACM SIGMOD international conference on Management of data* (2000), 93–104.

7. Buschek, D., Rogers, S., and Murray-Smith, R. User-Specific Touch Models in a Cross-Device Context. In *Proceedings of the 15th international conference on Human-computer interaction with mobile devices and services* (2013), 382–391.

8. Chen, S. F., and Goodman, J. An empirical study of smoothing techniques for language modeling. *Proceedings of the 34th annual meeting on Association for Computational Linguistics* (1996), 310–318.

9. Damerau, F. J. A technique for computer detection and correction of spelling errors. *Communications of the ACM 7*, 3 (1964), 171–176.

10. Findlater, L., and Wobbrock, J. O. Personalized input: improving ten-finger touchscreen typing through automatic adaptation. In *Proceedings of the SIGCHI Conference on Human Factors in Computing Systems* (2012), 815–824.

11. Findlater, L., Wobbrock, J. O., and Wigdor, D. Typing on flat glass. In *Proceedings of the SIGCHI Conference on Human Factors in Computing Systems* (2011), 2453–2462.

12. Goel, M., Jansen, A., and Mandel, T. ContextType: Using Hand Posture Information to Improve Mobile Touch Screen Text Entry. In *Proceedings of the SIGCHI Conference on Human Factors in Computing Systems* (2013), 2795–2798.

13. Goodman, J. T., Venolia, G., Steury, K., and Parker, C. Language modeling for soft keyboards. In *Proceedings of the 7th international conference on Intelligent user interfaces*, ACM Press (New York, New York, USA, Jan. 2002), 194–195.

14. Google. Google keyboard. https://play.google.com/store/apps/details?id=com.google.android.inputmethod.latin (date accessed 08.10.2013).

15. Gunawardana, A., Paek, T., and Meek, C. Usability guided key-target resizing for soft keyboards. In *Proceedings of the 15th international conference on Intelligent user interfaces* (Feb. 2010), 111–118.

16. Hall, M., National, H., Frank, E., Holmes, G., Pfahringer, B., Reutemann, P., and Witten, I. H. The WEKA Data Mining Software: An Update. *SIGKDD Explorations 11*, 1 (2009), 10–18.

17. Hall, M. A. *Correlation-based feature selection for machine learning.* PhD thesis, University of Waikato, 1999.

18. Kim, H., Row, Y., and Lee, G. Back Keyboard: A Physical Keyboard on Backside of Mobile Phone using QWERTY. In *CHI '12 Extended Abstracts on Human Factors in Computing Systems* (2012), 1583–1588.

19. Kohavi, Ron and John, G. H. Wrappers for feature subset selection. *Artificial Intelligence 97*, 1 (1997), 273–324.

20. Kuhn, H. W. The Hungarian method for the assignment problem. *Naval Research Logistics Quarterly 2*, 1-2 (1955), 83–97.

21. Levenshtein, V. I. Binary codes capable of correcting deletions, insertions and reversals. *Soviet physics doklady 10*, 8 (1966), 845–848.

22. Norvig, P. How to write a spelling corrector. http://norvig.com/spell-correct.html (date accessed 16.09.2013).

23. Oulasvirta, A., Reichel, A., Li, W., Zhang, Y., Bachynskyi, M., Vertanen, K., and Kristensson, P. O. Improving two-thumb text entry on touchscreen devices. In *Proceedings of the SIGCHI Conference on Human Factors in Computing Systems* (2013), 2765–2774.

24. Rabiner, L. R. A Tutorial on Hidden Markov Models and Selected Applications in Speech Recognition. *Proceedings of the IEEE 77*, 2 (1989), 257–286.

25. Rashid, D. R., and Smith, N. A. Relative keyboard input system. In *Proceedings of the 13th international conference on Intelligent user interfaces* (Jan. 2008), 397–400.

26. Rogers, S., Williamson, J., Stewart, C., and Murray-Smith, R. AnglePose: Robust, Precise Capacitive Touch Tracking via 3D Orientation Estimation. In *Proceedings of the SIGCHI Conference on Human Factors in Computing Systems* (2011), 2575–2584.

27. Rosenfeld, R. Two decades of statistical language modeling: Where do we go from here? *Proceedings of the IEEE 88*, 8 (2000), 1270–1278.

28. Schoenleben, O., and Oulasvirta, A. SandwichKeyboard: Fast Ten-Finger Typing on a Mobile Device with Adaptive Touch Sensing on the Back Side. In *Proceedings of the 15th international conference on Human-computer interaction with mobile devices and services* (2013), 175–178.

29. Scott, J., Izadi, S., Rezai, L. S., Ruszkowski, D., Bi, X., and Balakrishnan, R. RearType: Text Entry Using Keys on the Back of a Device. In *Proceedings of the 12th international conference on Human computer interaction with mobile devices and services* (2010), 171–180.

30. Shen, E.-l., Tsai, S.-s., Chu, H.-h., Hsu, J. Y.-j., and Chen, C.-w. Double-side multi-touch input for mobile devices. In *CHI '09 Extended Abstracts on Human Factors in Computing Systems* (2009), 4339–4344.

31. Vertanen, K., and Kristensson, P. O. A versatile dataset for text entry evaluations based on genuine mobile emails. *Proceedings of the 13th International Conference on Human Computer Interaction with Mobile Devices and Services* (2011), 295–298.

32. Wang, F., and Ren, X. Empirical evaluation for finger input properties in multi-touch interaction. In *Proceedings of the SIGCHI Conference on Human Factors in Computing Systems* (2009), 1063–1072.

33. Weir, D., Rogers, S., Murray-Smith, R., and Löchtefeld, M. A user-specific machine learning approach for improving touch accuracy on mobile devices. In *Proceedings of the 25th annual ACM symposium on User interface software and technology* (2012), 465–476.

34. Wobbrock, J. O., Myers, B. A., and Aung, H. H. The performance of hand postures in front- and back-of-device interaction for mobile computing. *International Journal of Human-Computer Studies 66*, 12 (2008), 857–875.

35. Wolf, K., Müller-Tomfelde, C., Cheng, K., and Wechsung, I. Does proprioception guide back-of-device pointing as well as vision? In *CHI '12 Extended Abstracts on Human Factors in Computing Systems* (2012), 1739–1744.

36. Yin, Y., Ouyang, T. Y., Partridge, K., and Zhai, S. Making touchscreen keyboards adaptive to keys, hand postures, and individuals: a hierarchical spatial backoff model approach. In *Proceedings of the SIGCHI Conference on Human Factors in Computing Systems* (2013), 2775–2784.

User Identification Using Raw Sensor Data From Typing on Interactive Displays

Philipp Mock
University of Tübingen
Sand 13, 72076 Tübingen,
Germany
philipp.mock@uni-
tuebingen.de

Jörg Edelmann
Knowledge Media Research
Center
Schleichstraße 6, 72076
Tübingen, Germany
j.edelmann@iwm-kmrc.de

**Andreas Schilling, Wolfgang
Rosenstiel**
University of Tübingen
schilling@uni-tuebingen.de,
rosenstiel@informatik.uni-
tuebingen.de

ABSTRACT
Personalized soft-keyboards which adapt to a user's individual typing behavior can reduce typing errors on interactive displays. In multi-user scenarios a personalized model has to be loaded for each participant. In this paper we describe a user identification technique that is based on raw sensor data from an optical touch screen. For classification of users we use a multi-class support vector machine that is trained with grayscale images from the optical sensor. Our implementation can identify a specific user from a set of 12 users with an average accuracy of 97.51% after one keystroke. It can be used to automatically select individual typing models during free-text entry. The resulting authentication process is completely implicit. We furthermore describe how the approach can be extended to automatic loading of personal information and settings.

Author Keywords
User identification; interactive displays; machine learning

ACM Classification Keywords
H.5.2 Information Interfaces and Presentation: User Interfaces - Input devices and strategies.

INTRODUCTION
With multi-touch screens having entered the mass consumer market several years ago, there has also been a rise of multi-touch devices with larger screen diagonals. As these devices are well suited for multi-user scenarios, they have encouraged the development of a rich set of collaborative applications. Among these, several make intensive use of text input [1, 14]. Since typing on a software keyboard is difficult due to the lack of haptic feedback, dedicated hardware keyboards are still frequently used. Current research tries to compensate for this drawback by exploiting the additional sensory information, which an interactive screen provides. Thereby, it could be shown that typing speed and accuracy could be improved

by training individual keyboard models [6, 7]. For collaborative applications the use of individual models imposes the problem of having to determine which user is currently typing in which screen area. A one-time training session which is necessary to generate the data for an individual model can be justified, as it improves typing performance significantly. However, the need to authenticate oneself at the beginning of each session or, in case of multiple users sharing a keyboard, even repeatedly in between, places a burden on the practicability of using individual adaption in collaborative scenarios. The same holds true for personal devices, which are regularly used by more than one person, for example, tablets. Ideally, a user should be able to start typing right away, without worrying about which keyboard model is currently active.

Following this, instead of an explicit authentication procedure, this paper presents a method of implicitly identifying a user while he or she is typing on the soft-keyboard. This is accomplished by analyzing the complete sensory information that is captured on each keystroke. We found that the way users hit the different keys of a virtual keyboard is highly individual. In this paper, we describe the design and implementation of a user identification technique based on raw sensor data from an optical touch screen device. We provide an in depth analysis of typing data from 12 users. This data was used to train two different types of user classifiers. We discuss the results of the resulting classifiers and describe how the presented techniques should be applied in practice. Finally, we analyze the implications of this work for security applications.

RELATED WORK
The extraction of biometrics from keystroke dynamics for authentication or password hardening has been thoroughly researched on traditional hardware keyboards. Typically features like inter-keystroke flight times, key press hold times and sometimes rhythm are combined with statistical methods [17], support vector machines [23] or neural networks [18]. A good overview of the field of research can be found in Banerjee et al. [2]. An extension of the approach with pressure data obtained from a touch pad has been presented by Saevanee et al. [20]. Their results indicate that pressure data can contain more discriminative information than keystroke dynamics.

As to user identification on multi-touch devices, there have been diverse approaches in hard- and software: Diamond-Touch is a system for user identification of up to four users working on a front-projected tabletop system [5]. It is based on capacitive coupling between a transmitter array under the screen's surface and a receiver that is located in each user's chair. In contrast, Fiberio identifies a user by using a special fiber optic screen material that can sense a user's fingerprints [15]. A sensing approach which evaluates impedance profiles of a person to distinguish between users is presented by Harrison et al. [12]. Schmidt et al. use hand-contours on an optical multi-touch screen to extract biometrics [21]. The system uses a SVM trained with characteristic features to identify known users. In contrast to the above, it does not rely on additional hardware. In [19], Sae-Bae et al. analyze a gesture-based approach for user authentication that achieves 90% accuracy for single gestures. De Luca et al. use dynamic time warping to investigate the potential of exploiting individual touch patterns for shape based authentication systems on smart phones [4]. An approach for continuous authentication on smart phones, is presented by Frank et al. [9]. The proposed classifiers are trained with navigational touch strokes and achieve between 0% and 4% equal error rates.

A solution for textual input on a touch screen, which omits the problem of identifying typists directly on the screen, is presented by Hartmann et al. [13]. The authors' idea is to augment an interactive display with traditional keyboard and mice. The input devices are placed upon the screen and function as a proxy for user identity. The collaboration system Pictionaire [14] also uses this technique.

INDIVIDUAL TYPING PATTERNS

Due to the lack of haptic feedback on virtual keyboards, key press distributions can vary heavily in between users. This is particularly true for touch typists, which tend to not look at the key layout during typing. Findlater et al. [8] could observe this behavior among 20 expert typists, who entered text with an on-screen keyboard. Furthermore, they also found that the key press distributions were spatially consistent within an individual. Accordingly, they presented a classification technique that uses features extracted from key presses on a touch screen to dynamically adapt to individual typing patterns of a user [7]. Edelmann et al. [6] use the complete sensory information of an optical touch device to train individual SVM based classifiers to improve typing accuracies both for touch and non-touch typists. They also found that key press distributions vary in between users. Moreover, a classifier trained only from touch images showed significant differences in performance when trained with a typist's own data instead of data from other users. This is a strong indicator that raw sensor information from an optical touch screen in fact contains valuable information for distinguishing users.

Data Acquisition Procedure

We use a data acquisition approach as described by Edelmann et al. [6] to generate a dataset of individual typing behavior from multiple users: A simulated classifier was used in combination with an on-screen keyboard with standard QWERTY

layout. To generate labeled data, each participant was presented text that consisted of standard phrases from MacKenzie and Soukoreff [16] and pangram sentences at a 4:1 ratio. The classifier reported imprecise input as correct, as long as the location of a key press was not too far from the designated position (3.6% of the total amount of keypresses were rejected). That way, users were expected to type as if they were confronted with an ideal classifier, thus following their natural typing habits.

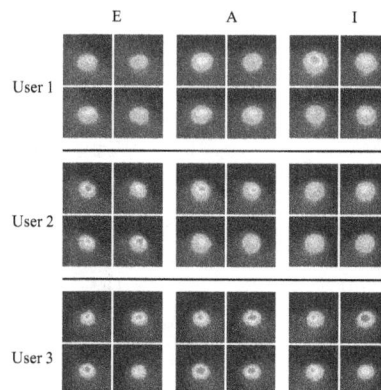

Figure 1. Raw sensor data for three different keys from three different users in comparison.

The data acquisition procedure was carried out on an FTIR [11] touch sensor using a camera with 640x480 at 60fps. For each occurring keystroke, a 42x42 pixel grayscale image centered around the touch position was saved. Apart from that, the position and a timestamp for the beginning and ending of each touch event were recorded. 12 participants (age 16 to 35, 2 female) had 5 minutes to get familiar with the system. Afterwards, three sessions of 10 minutes each with 5-10 minute breaks in between were conducted. At an average typing speed of 40 words per minute, an average total of around 3500 keystrokes were collected per user.

Data Analysis

To validate the assumption that fingerprints on an optical touch screen contain information that can be exploited for user identification, as a first step, the collected data was analyzed for separability. Prior research has shown that sensor data from one user can be used to improve key classification [6]. In order to determine whether user classification from this data is also feasible, we compute a separability criterion for both cases.

The data was grouped into samples corresponding to one user and one key on the virtual keyboard. Then, the separability criterion was computed for one user across all keys and additionally for one key across all users. The classes were the keys in the first and the users in the latter case. The used criterion is derived from the scatter matrices, reflecting the within- and between-class scatter. For class C_k, the scatter matrix can be calculated as:

$$S_k = \sum_{x \in C_k} (x - \mu_k)(x - \mu_k)^T$$

where μ_k is the mean of class C_k. The within-class scatter matrix S_W is calculated as the summation of S_k across all classes. The between-class matrix is calculated as:

$$S_B = \sum_{k=1}^{K} (\mu_k - \mu)(\mu_k - \mu)^T$$

where μ is the total mean. The criterion J_d using the eigenvalues of $S_W^{-1} S_B$ that was used as an estimation for class separability is: $J_d = tr[S_W^{-1} S_B]$. The results confirmed the suitability of the touch image data for user identification, as the class separability J_d for the different keys per user as classes (290.71) was lower than for the different users per key (306.49). In other words, users should be better distinguishable than keys. Since touch sensor images have already been successfully used for key classification, we expect the data to perform equally as good for user classification.

We also considered using key press hold and inter-key flight times, but discarded it within the early stages of our evaluation. Monrose's and Rubin's research results [17] argue in favor of using structured text instead of free-text entry when using keystroke dynamics for user authentication. According to their results, recognition based on text input in an unconstrained condition is expected to vary greatly. Our analysis is in accord with that. Consequently, we chose to focus on the value of touch sensor data completely.

USER IDENTIFICATION

When using individual keyboard models for multiple users on a single device, an author has to authenticate him- or herself to the system before the model which has been adapted to his or her personal typing behavior can be used. We propose an alternative approach to explicitly selecting a username from a list of known users or entering one's name into a textfield. Our idea is to reuse the data sets, which have been used to train the individual models, and train a classifier that is able to distinguish between users. Following this idea, the selection of individual models works as follows: After approaching the system, a user simply starts typing, without telling the system his or her identity. Initially, no model is selected and a general key classifier is used (e.g., key boundaries). After a few strokes, the user classifier determines which user is currently typing and seamlessly switches to the corresponding individual keyboard. From then on, the user can use his or her optimized model and subsequent keystrokes can be recorded to refine the model at a later time. By selecting keyboard models this way, after the initial training phase, the on-screen keyboard can be used just like a non-personalized version. When multiple virtual keyboards are used in a collaborative scenario, a different model can be selected for each user.

Prior research shows that distributions of position and image based data differ substantially for different keys [6]. Accordingly, the user identification technique which is presented in this work is composed of multiple classifiers: One for each visible key. This allows to correctly model the differences between users key-wise. However, it also makes a prior key classification step necessary, as we have to detect the correct

key in order to chose the correct user classifier. The complete process is illustrated in Figure 2.

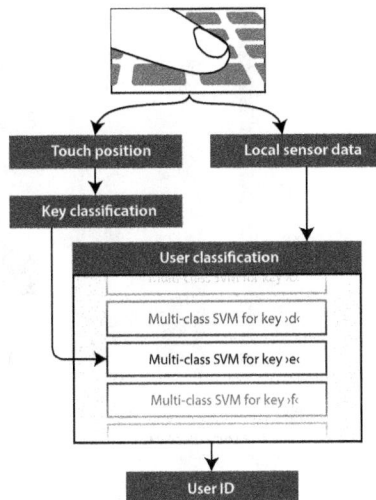

Figure 2. The complete user classification process: In a first step, the pressed key label is determined and the corresponding user classifier is chosen. In a second step, a user ID is determined for the current keystroke.

Key Classification

Due to the lack of haptic feedback, imprecise typing is to be expected. This is taken into account by the way our data set was obtained. Since the simulated classifier gave correct feedback for most imprecise keystrokes, the data set contains some sloppy typing, as well as hand drift. Consequently, naive key boundary checks or nearest neighbor approaches yield relatively poor results. A majority voting from the individual classifiers is also ineligible, because most classifiers are likely to come to a wrong solution. We found that a classifier based on average bivariate Gaussian distributions for keystroke positions improved overall accuracy. However, the best results could be achieved by multiplying the probabilities of the Gaussian distributions with those of a language model and choosing the best overall decision. For this purpose, we used a 5-gram language model using Kneser-Ney smoothing as described by Goodman [10]. It was trained with 2.4 million words from random Wikipedia articles.

Multi-Class SVM Classification

The 42x42 pixels per touch image result in a large feature space. Support Vector Machines (SVM) are large margin classifiers that can handle large amounts of features. Consequently, we use a multi-class SVM approach with the known users as classes for our analysis. A dedicated SVM was trained for each key on the virtual keyboard. The recorded typing data was split into two equal parts for training and testing the classifiers. The implementation was done in Matlab using the libSVM [3] toolbox.

Gaussian kernel functions tended to overfit the training data as we use a feature set that is relatively large in comparison to the amount of samples. According to this, we use a linear SVM whose parameters were optimized by cross validation.

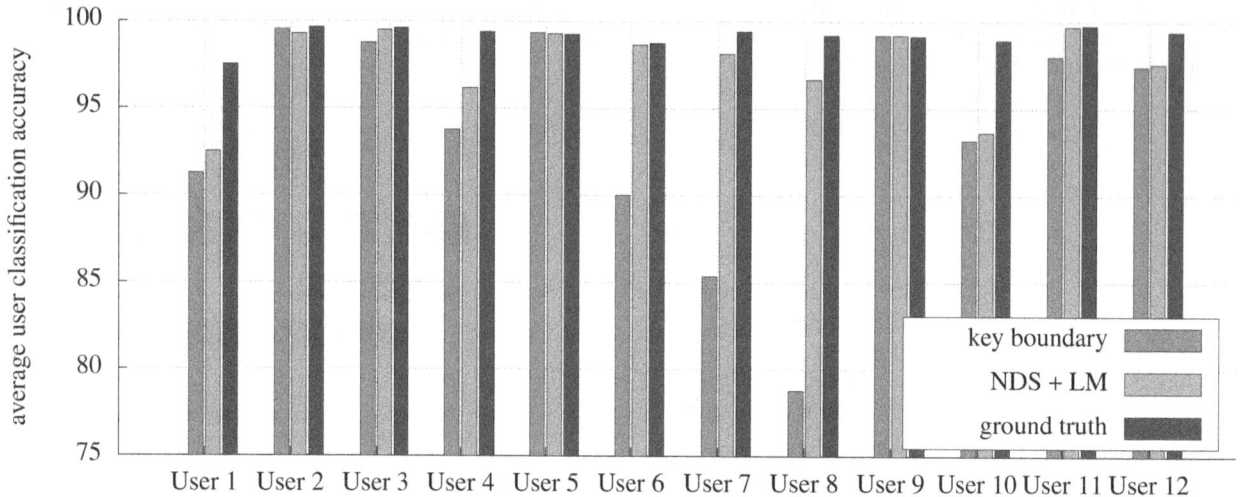

Figure 3. Accuracies of the multi-class SVMs for user identification across all participants from a single keystroke. It is particularly noticeable, that all results are well above 90% using NDS + LM for prior key classification. Please note that the y-axis starts at 75 percent.

The evaluation was performed with three different key labeling techniques to select the proper classifier: a naive boundary check (*key boundary*), a combination of aggregated bivariate Gaussian distributions and a language model (*NDS + LM*), and the correct labels that were available from the data acquisition process (*ground truth*). In practice, ground truth data will not be available for free-text entry. Still, using it is a worthwhile evaluation to investigate the maximum potential of the presented user identification technique.

DETECTION OF UNKNOWN USERS

Using multi-class SVM classification, unknown users will always be classified as one user for which training data is available. This is undesirable for two reasons: First, a new user might not be aware that the on-screen keyboard features personalization. If he or she just starts using the system without training it beforehand, a classifier will be loaded that resembles his or her typing behavior most closely. However, this does not mean that it will produce good results. Second, a collaborative system or a personal system with multiple users might also provide personal preferences or user specific information, like a typing history or an address book. This information should not be accessible for unknown users. In consequence, new users have to be identified, if we also want to support automatic selection of data apart from a personalized keyboard model.

The confidence values that libSVM provides for a decision of the multi-class SVM cannot be used, because they only give information about the relative similarity of new touch input to the classified class as compared to other classes. In other words, input from a new user might get high confidence values from one class despite strongly differing from the training data, as long as it differs even more from the other classes. By contrast, a one-class SVM [22] can be used for novelty detection. That is, it can be used to identify typing data from an author that was previously unknown to the system. Such a classifier is trained with data from a single class. It deter-

mines the hyperplane that separates this data from the origin with maximum margin. A ν parameter is used to control the tradeoff between maximizing the distance to the origin and the amount of data inside the region separated by the hyperplane. It directly influences the false acceptance rate (FAR) and false rejection rate (FRR) of the classifier. As for the kernel, a third degree radial basis function was chosen. A separate one-class SVM is trained for each key and each user. It can be used in the same way as the multi-class classifiers described in the preceding section.

RESULTS

In the following, the performance of the individual classifiers will be presented. This includes average and personal classification accuracies for the identification of known users, as well as for the detection of unregistered users after a single keystroke. In addition, the probabilities for making a correct decision after a longer sequence of letters will be examined.

Classification Results

User Identification using multi-class SVMs per key yielded very good overall results. The average accuracy of the per-key classifiers with data from all 12 participants is 99.16% for theoretical *ground truth* labeling. The *NDS + LM* key classification approach results in 97.52% average accuracy and naive *key boundary* still gives 93.71%. We did not observe any structural differences between the performance of individual keys across all users (best and worst performing keys are only 2.08% apart). Accordingly, differences between keys were not investigated further. It has to be noted that not all key misclassifications lead to a wrong decision of the user classifiers (average error of *key boundary* is 23%). The individual classification accuracies across all 12 users are shown in Figure 3. The influence of the key classifier on the overall performance largely depends on how imprecise a user's input is in the first place. What stands out is the high accuracy throughout all users.

In order to evaluate the performance of unknown user rejection, two statistics have been computed for the one-class SVM approach: false rejection rate (FRR) and false acceptance rate (FAR). FRR is the percentage of input that was typed by the correct user for any given one-class SVM, but still detected as an outlier and thus rejected. FAR is the percentage of input that an unknown user entered that was still being accepted by one of the classifiers. The performance of the presented approach is illustrated in a receiver operator characteristic (ROC) curve (see Figure 4). The equal error rate (EER), at which accept and reject errors are equal, is 12.3 on average. However, this value varies a lot when looking at specific user combinations. For a great number of combinations between classifier and unknown user, the EER is nearly 0. On the other hand, there are combinations which are harder to discriminate from correct input. The "worst case" combination of user and classifier is also shown in Figure 4. EER is 38.7 for that case.

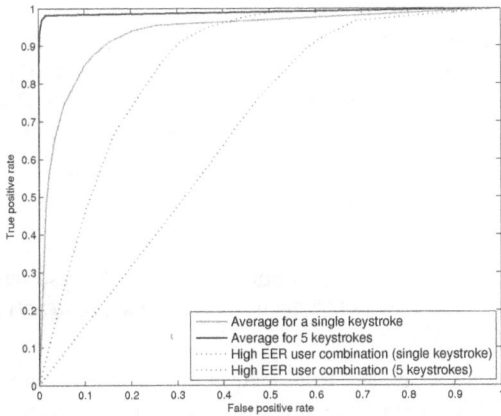

Figure 4. ROC curve for the one-class SVM classifiers. Green and blue curves are the average results. The dotted lines in red and magenta represent the pair of classifier and unknown user with the highest equal error rate.

Results for longer sequences

The results of the preceding section are decisions after a single keystroke. However, a system does not need to decide upon which user is currently typing as early as that. In fact, there is some variation in the personal typing habits of each user, so the decision should only be made, when sufficient data has been collected to ensure a correct classification.

For longer sequences, the correct user will be identified, if for n letters at least $\lfloor n/2 \rfloor + 1$ letters are correctly assigned to a user. This can be formulated as a Bernoulli process. The probability $P(Z \geq k)$ of making at least k correct guesses with probability p from n decisions is:

$$P(Z \geq k) = 1 - \sum_{i=0}^{k} \binom{n}{k} p^i (1-p)^{n-i}$$

where Z is the random variable that assigns the results of the Bernoulli process its score. Table 1 shows the average probabilities of a multi-class SVM majority voting for sequences of 5, 10, 15 and 20 letters. This can be applied to the one-class SVMs in the same way (see Figure 4 for results with n = 5).

Key Classifier	n = 5	n = 10	n = 15	n = 20
Key boundary	96.52	99.98	99.99	100
NDS + LM	99.41	99.99	100	100
Ground truth	99.93	100	100	100

Table 1. Average accuracies of a majority voting of the multi-class SVM classifiers for letter sequences with length n (in %).

DISCUSSION AND LIMITATIONS

The results of our evaluation show that the sensory information that an optical touch screen provides can successfully be used to distinguish between typists. The presented multi-class SVM approach produced excellent results for a data set of unrestricted typing from 12 users. The evaluation of the multi-class SVMs showed high accuracies even for a single keystroke, when combined with the *NDS + LM* key classifier (97.52% correct decisions). After more than 10 strokes, a user can be identified assuredly from among the 12 participants.

The one-class SVM approach that was used for detection of unregistered users showed good overall results, as well. With an average ratio of 99.12% true positives compared to less than 0.0001% false matches after 10 keystrokes, it can be used in a two-step method for automatic loading of a personalized keyboard models in a multi-user scenario: For the first 9 keystrokes no personal model is loaded and a standard key classifier is used (in our case *NDS + LM*). After 10 keystrokes, the one-class SVMs decide whether the current user has already trained a personal keyboard model. If so, the correct user is determined by the multi-class SVMs. The system can now proceed with the personalized model and other selected user preferences.

Due to high FAR of the one-class SVM classification for a few user combinations we do not recommend to use it as a security mechanism alone. Consequently, sensitive information that should not be presented to other users should not be loaded automatically as described above. However, we do not expect the proposed technique to perform any worse when used for structured text. On the contrary, typing behavior should be even more individual for text that is typed very often, like passwords or one's own name. This is why we see huge potential in using raw sensor information for password hardening. Of course, this has to be validated with a different set of typing data. Here, common attacks like "shoulder surfing" have to be considered, as touch screens are often used in public areas. For security applications, we suggest to use raw sensor data in combination with keystroke dynamics.

So far, the presented user identification technique was only tested on an optical device. As mentioned above, it would be interesting to use the presented approach on a tablet computer. We assume that similar results are possible on a capacitive screen, but this is yet to be tested.

CONCLUSION AND FUTURE WORK

In this paper we presented a user identification technique for optical touch screens that can be used to automatically select individual keyboard models or user preferences. It uses raw data from the optical sensor to train SVM classifiers for each visible key on the keyboard. These classifiers can recognize the current user from all known users with high accuracy after a few keystrokes. In addition, we investigated how unknown users can be recognized using one-class SVMs trained with the same data. Moreover, we described how these two approaches can be combined and discussed the implications of our results for security applications.

As to future work, we want to implement a testing environment for long-term studies in order to further investigate the potential of raw sensor data for typing applications on interactive displays. We plan to conduct studies both with optical and capacitive touch sensors to validate the transferability of the approach to different devices, in particular tablet computers. With regard to security applications, we also want to acquire an extensive data set for entry of fixed-text, such as passphrases or a user's name. These studies will be carried out with implementations of the classifiers presented in this work in combination with comparable approaches based on features like hold and flight times. We thereby want to investigate how touch sensor data can complement keystroke dynamics for password hardening. A special focus will be on the effectiveness of shoulder surfing attacks. That is, how easily different characteristics of typing behavior can be imitated by observers.

ACKNOWLEDGEMENTS

This project is funded in part by the "Wettbewerbsfonds 2011" of the Leibniz Association.

REFERENCES

1. Amershi, S., and Morris, M. R. Cosearch: a system for co-located collaborative web search. In *Proc. CHI 2008*, ACM (2008), 1647–1656.

2. Banerjee, S. P., and Woodard, D. L. Biometric authentication and identification using keystroke dynamics: A survey. *Journal of Pattern Recognition Research 7* (2012), 116–139.

3. Chang, C.-C., and Lin, C.-J. Libsvm: a library for support vector machines. *ACM TIST 2*, 3 (2011), 27.

4. De Luca, A., Hang, A., Brudy, F., Lindner, C., and Hussmann, H. Touch me once and i know it's you!: Implicit authentication based on touch screen patterns. In *Proc. CHI 2012*, ACM (2012), 987–996.

5. Dietz, P., and Leigh, D. Diamondtouch: a multi-user touch technology. In *Proc. UIST 2001*, ACM (2001), 219–226.

6. Edelmann, J., Mock, P., Schilling, A., Gerjets, P., Rosenstiel, W., and Strasser, W. Towards the keyboard of oz: learning individual soft-keyboard models from raw optical sensor data. In *Proc. ITS 2012*, ACM (2012), 163–172.

7. Findlater, L., and Wobbrock, J. Personalized input: improving ten-finger touchscreen typing through automatic adaptation. In *Proc. CHI 2012*, ACM (2012), 815–824.

8. Findlater, L., Wobbrock, J. O., and Wigdor, D. Typing on flat glass: examining ten-finger expert typing patterns on touch surfaces. In *Proc. CHI 2011*, ACM (2011), 2453–2462.

9. Frank, M., Biedert, R., Ma, E., Martinovic, I., and Song, D. Touchalytics: On the applicability of touchscreen input as a behavioral biometric for continuous authentication. *Information Forensics and Security 8*, 1 (2013), 136–148.

10. Goodman, J. T. A bit of progress in language modeling. *Computer Speech & Language 15*, 4 (2001), 403–434.

11. Han, J. Y. Low-cost multi-touch sensing through frustrated total internal reflection. In *Proc. UIST 2005*, ACM (2005), 115–118.

12. Harrison, C., Sato, M., and Poupyrev, I. Capacitive fingerprinting: Exploring user differentiation by sensing electrical properties of the human body. In *Proc. UIST 2012*, ACM (2012), 537–544.

13. Hartmann, B., Morris, M. R., Benko, H., and Wilson, A. D. Augmenting interactive tables with mice & keyboards. In *Proc. UIST 2009*, ACM (2009), 149–152.

14. Hartmann, B., Morris, M. R., Benko, H., and Wilson, A. D. Pictionaire: supporting collaborative design work by integrating physical and digital artifacts. In *Proc. CSCW 2010*, ACM (2010), 421–424.

15. Holz, C., and Baudisch, P. Fiberio: a touchscreen that senses fingerprints. In *Proc. UIST 2013*, ACM (2013), 41–50.

16. MacKenzie, I. S., and Soukoreff, R. W. Phrase sets for evaluating text entry techniques. In *Ext. abstracts CHI 2003*, ACM (2003), 754–755.

17. Monrose, F., and Rubin, A. D. Keystroke dynamics as a biometric for authentication. *Future Generation Computer Systems 16*, 4 (2000), 351–359.

18. Obaidat, M. S., and Sadoun, B. Verification of computer users using keystroke dynamics. *Systems, Man, and Cybernetics, Part B: Cybernetics, IEEE Transactions on 27*, 2 (1997), 261–269.

19. Sae-Bae, N., Ahmed, K., Isbister, K., and Memon, N. Biometric-rich gestures: A novel approach to authentication on multi-touch devices. In *Proc. CHI 2012*, ACM (2012), 977–986.

20. Saevanee, H., and Bhattarakosol, P. Authenticating user using keystroke dynamics and finger pressure. In *Proc. CCNC 2009*, IEEE (2009), 1–2.

21. Schmidt, D., Chong, M. K., and Gellersen, H. Handsdown: hand-contour-based user identification for interactive surfaces. In *Proc. NordiCHI 2010*, ACM (2010), 432–441.

22. Schölkopf, B., Platt, J. C., Shawe-Taylor, J., Smola, A. J., and Williamson, R. C. Estimating the support of a high-dimensional distribution. *Neural computation 13*, 7 (2001), 1443–1471.

23. Yu, E., and Cho, S. Keystroke dynamics identity verification - its problems and practical solutions. *Computers & Security 23*, 5 (2004), 428–440.

Teaching Motion Gestures via Recognizer Feedback

Ankit Kamal
University of Waterloo
Waterloo, ON, Canada
a6kamal@uwaterloo.ca

Yang Li
Google Research
Mountain View, CA, USA
yangli@acm.org

Edward Lank
University of Waterloo
Waterloo, ON, Canada
lank@cs.uwaterloo.ca

ABSTRACT

When using motion gestures, 3D movements of a mobile phone, as an input modality, one significant challenge is how to teach end users the movement parameters necessary to successfully issue a command. Is a simple video or image depicting movement of a smartphone sufficient? Or do we need three-dimensional depictions of movement on external screens to train users? In this paper, we explore mechanisms to teach end users motion gestures, examining two factors. The first factor is how to represent motion gestures: as icons that describe movement, video that depicts movement using the smartphone screen, or a Kinect-based teaching mechanism that captures and depicts the gesture on an external display in three-dimensional space. The second factor we explore is recognizer feedback, i.e. a simple representation of the proximity of a motion gesture to the desired motion gesture based on a distance metric extracted from the recognizer. We show that, by combining video with recognizer feedback, participants master motion gestures equally quickly as end users that learn using a Kinect. These results demonstrate the viability of training end users to perform motion gestures using only the smartphone display.

Author Keywords

Motion Gestures; sensors; smartphone; Android; Recognizer feedback.

ACM Classification Keywords

H.5.2. User Interfaces – Interaction Styles.

General Terms

Human Factors; Design; Experimentation.

INTRODUCTION

Hand motion—pointing, gesturing, grasping, shaking, tapping—is a rich channel of communication. We point and gesture while we talk; we grasp tools to extend our capabilities; we grasp, rotate, and shake items to explore them. Inspired by these everyday movements to extend

conversation, researchers [13, 14, 16, 17, 18] have begun to explore motion gestures, i.e. deliberate movements to issue commands to a device, as an input modality. Motion gestures have been applied to, for example, large-screen displays, desktop computers, and smartphones.

In this paper, we are particularly interested in motion gestures as an input modality for modern smartphones. The reasons for this are twofold. First, modern smartphones contain an evolving set of sensors for recognizing movement of the phone, including accelerometers, gyroscopes and cameras, so the technology already exists to support motion gesture input. Second, using a motion gesture provides many attendant benefits, including an expanded input space and the ability to issue commands eyes-free without using the touch screen by leveraging proprioception [14].

One of the most significant barriers to widespread adoption of motion gesture input involves teaching end-users to perform motion gestures. Motion gestures are not self-revealing; end-users need to be taught the set of motion gestures supported by a smartphone device. As well, for each of these gestures, end-users need to understand exactly how to perform the gestures to ensure maximum recognition accuracy. Constraints on movement include the shape of the movement of the motion gesture (its three-dimensional path in space) and the kinematics of the motion gesture (the tolerances for fast or slow motion gestures).

The process of instructing and correcting the actions of a learner is typically called scaffolding. Scaffolding involves both a depiction of the desired activity and assessment to correct inaccuracies. Many questions arise when considering how to depict motion gestures. Can we simply show icons of motion gestures that depict movement (see Ruiz et al. [17]). Do we instead need to show a brief video of movement on the smartphone display? Or do we require an external display to see movement in larger scale? Alongside techniques for depicting the form of a motion gesture, recognizing a motion gesture involves contrasting the gesture performed with some desired template, i.e. providing some form of feedback that guides a user more quickly to the correct action. We wish to also understand how feedback can be used to help a user converge to the ideal motion gesture more quickly.

In this paper, we contrast three techniques for teaching motion gestures: icons, smartphone videos, or Kinect plus videos on external displays. For each of these techniques, we also study the effect that simple recognizer feedback – more specifically a visualization of the distance between a desired template and the actual input movement of the user – on the ability of end-users to accurately perform motion gestures.

We show that Kinect-based instruction, where the movement is displayed as a 3D wireframe and participant movement is captured and replicated for direct contrast teaches motion gestures very quickly for a group of participants. As well, for Kinect-based feedback, the presence of a visualization of recognizer distance had limited effect on accuracy, primarily because the Kinect's contrasting of input motion from template was sufficient. However, we also show that, while video on a smartphone screen is worse than Kinect, video on a smartphone screen plus a simple visualization of recognizer feedback causes the smartphone video condition to converge to the performance of Kinect-based instruction.

The significance of these results lies in the training of end-users on motion gestures as input to smartphones. Before embarking on this research, we were unsure whether it was possible to train end users effectively on motion gestures without someone present to demonstrate the motion gestures, or without external hardware (e.g. a Kinect) to allow users to master the kinematics of the motion gesture commands. Given our results, it now seems plausible to construct a teaching aid for motion gestures that uses only the smartphone display.

The remainder of this paper is organized as follows. We first highlight related work in motion gestures and on techniques for teaching gestures. Next we detail a series of pilot studies and a final study evaluating techniques for teaching motion gestures. Finally, we discuss our results and their implications more fully.

RELATED WORK

Free-space hand gesture interaction (as in the movie *Minority Report*) has been perceived of as a novel, futuristic input technique, despite known problems with fatigue, i.e. gorilla arm. Bolt designed a "put-that-there" system in 1980 that combined pointing with voice commands [3]. Vogel and Balakrishnan [18] explored the design space for freehand gestural interaction for large vertical displays.

Motion gestures are a known, albeit underutilized, technique for controlling smartphones. Hinckley et al. [7] proposed using tilt on mobile devices to allow a user to change screen orientation—a feature now commonly found on many smartphones. In addition to navigation, tilt sensors have also been used for text input [8] and accessing data on virtual shelves around a user [11]. Commercially, the use of a shake motion gesture to shuffle music is one common example of controlling a smartphone or personal music player (e.g. iPod) via a motion gesture. As well, some modern smartphones allow the user to place the smartphone face-down on a desk to mute the ringtone for an incoming

phone call. Finally, the Google App for iPhone turns on voice search if the iPhone is brought to your ear.

Previous research on motion gestures

Ruiz et al. [17] created a taxonomy describing the attributes of smartphone motion gestures and their natural mappings onto smartphone commands. They showed that a consensus exists among users on parameters of movement and on mappings of motion gestures onto commands. They also enumerated a user-defined motion-gesture set for smartphone input.

Alongside work on motion gesture input, Ruiz and Li [16] explored how best to discriminate between deliberate motion gestures and everyday movement of a smartphone. They proposed "DoubleFlip", a motion gesture designed as an input delimiter for smartphone motion gestures. The DoubleFlip delimiter is performed by quickly rotating the wrist such that the phone's display is facing away from the user and back to the original position with the display of the phone facing the user. They showed that DoubleFlip is easy to invoke and unlikely to be accidentally invoked by users.

Negulescu et al. [14] analyzed the relative cognitive cost of taps, surface gestures, and motion gestures for distracted input on smartphone devices. They show that there is no significant difference in reaction time for motion gestures, taps, or surface gestures on smartphones, and that the use of motion gestures results in participants in a study spending significantly less time looking at the smartphone during walking than taps, even with eyes-free optimized input interfaces.

Negulescu et al. [13] also explored techniques for limiting false positives and false negatives for motion gesture input. They devised a "bi-level threshold" recognizer which helped lower the rate of recognition failures by accepting either a tightly thresholded gesture or two consecutive gestures recognized by a looser-threshold model.

Previous research on teaching surface gestures

Our research in this paper focuses specifically on teaching motion gestures to smartphone users. Significant past work exists in teaching users gestural input languages. Kurtenbach's [10] Marking menus, an extension of pie menus [5], combine feed-forward and feedback to provide a fluent transition between novice and expert use. Marking menus take advantage of novice user's hesitation when they are unsure of a gesture or command. Users flick the pen or mouse in a particular direction in order to indicate a command. After a "press and wait" gesture, a circular feed-forward display appears around the mouse cursor, showing each available command. Highlighting the current selected item during input provides feedback on how a user's input is being interpreted. This approach offers a good compromise between learning and efficient use. Novices often pause to take advantage of the feed-forward display. As they become experts, they move more quickly and no longer needing the feed-forward menu, significantly increase overall performance.

In the same vein as marking menus, Bau et al. [2] designed a dynamic guide called "Octopocus" that combines on-screen feed-forward and feedback to help users learn, execute and remember surface gesture sets. Octopocus continuously updates the state of the recognition algorithm by gradually modifying the thickness of possible gesture paths, based on its 'consumable error rate'. They show that users can better learn, execute and remember gesture sets if one reveals, during input, what is normally an opaque process, the current state of recognition, and represents gestures in a graphical form that shows the optimal path for the remaining alternatives.

One challenge with gesture-based systems is that end-users need to be made aware of the gestures that can be performed to invoke commands. Alongside this awareness, as users are learning the mechanics of gestures, they must also have the opportunity to practice and receive feedback on the gestures they attempt. To satisfy these goals, Bragdon et al. [4] designed a unique training system, GestureBar, which can be incorporated into gesture-based systems for pen-tablet computers. GestureBar is, conceptually, a simple scratch pad which allows the user to select a gesture and then attempt the gesture within a region of the display. Feedback depicting the deviation between desired input and the user's input is displayed so the user can modify and correct any errors in the pen strokes that they draw on the screen. In their research, Bragdon et al. describe the design iterations, the final GestureBar system, and its effectiveness as a training tool based on subjective user feedback.

One of our goals is to adapt aspects of the training systems described above to motion gestures on Smartphones. However, how we communicate motion gestures to end users is somewhat ambiguous. With Marking menus, Octopus, and GestureBar, because users were drawing on a two-dimensional surface, the system could render the two-dimensional shape. Users could start out with an animation of the movement, then over time simply see the final, complete gesture. However, a smartphone cannot move itself through space. Communicating the relative displacement obviously requires some form of a movie that displays motion relative to the end-user. To the best of our knowledge, no previous research has been done to train people to perform motion gestures.

GESTURE RECOGNIZER DESIGN

Ruiz et al. [17] note that, when end-users design motion gestures, the gestures they select tend to be simple (non-compound), single-axis movements with low kinematic impulse. As a result, we base our study around four single-axis gestures – *right flick, left flick, flick up towards face* and *flick down away from face*.

Our four gestures were chosen from the user defined set in Ruiz et al. [17], and we would argue that they represent the simplest set of useful motion gestures for smartphone control. Nominally, the gestures correspond to next,

previous, zoom-in and zoom-out gestures respectively. Essentially, we chose the gestures we did because these are the types of gestures – single axis, low kinematic impulse – users specify when we elicit gestures from them [17].

Our recognizer was developed in Java using the Android SDK [1] for use on Nexus S phones with an ARM Cortex A8 1GHz processor and a three-axis accelerometer. Sensor input, i.e. filtered acceleration data, is matched to gesture templates using Dynamic Time Warping (DTW) [12]. DTW is a dynamic programming algorithm that measures the similarity of two time series with temporal dynamics [12] when given a function for calculating the distance between the two time samples. The result is a warp distance that can be used to determine how similar a set is to the reference set. A warp distance of 0 (zero) indicates absolute identical sets. The bigger the distance, the more different the sets are. Our implementation of our gesture recognizer uses a weighted Euclidean distance function for calculating the distance between the quantized time series of acceleration data to the a template. As a full discussion of DTW is beyond the scope of this paper, we refer the reader to Wobbrock et al. [19] for more information. The sampling rate of acceleration data was 32 Hz.

One challenge with the gestures we select is that, because they are single-axis and because they have low kinematic impulse, the gestures are virtually indistinguishable from everyday movement of a smartphone. The typical way designers of recognizers address a collision between noise and signal is via a tight criterion function to discriminate true positives from false positives [13]. The challenge with a tight criterion function is the propensity to cause false negatives. In other words, seeking to avoid accidental activation of a motion gesture, we require greater precision in the performance of a motion gesture. This, in turn, makes it more essential to teach end users the careful kinematics needed to successfully invoke a motion gesture; otherwise, they repeatedly fail to invoke their desired motion gesture.

To simulate this tight criterion function, the DTW templates for each gesture type were created by an expert user, specifically one of the authors of this paper. The expert performed the correct gesture 20 times. Each gesture was compared to the 19 other gestures using DTW. Then, the average warp distance for the respective gesture was calculated, and the gesture with lowest average warp distance from all other gestures was selected as the gesture template for that particular gesture. This is a common approach found in related work (Kar et al. [9]). In a second step, the selected gesture template was compared to the remaining 19 gestures. The 19 warp distances were then used to calculate the mean, median, minimum, maximum and standard deviation of distances. These values were used to calculate the threshold of the DTW Distance metric within which an input gesture is considered as valid. The result of the use of a single expert user is that, to successfully invoke a motion gesture on a smartphone, the

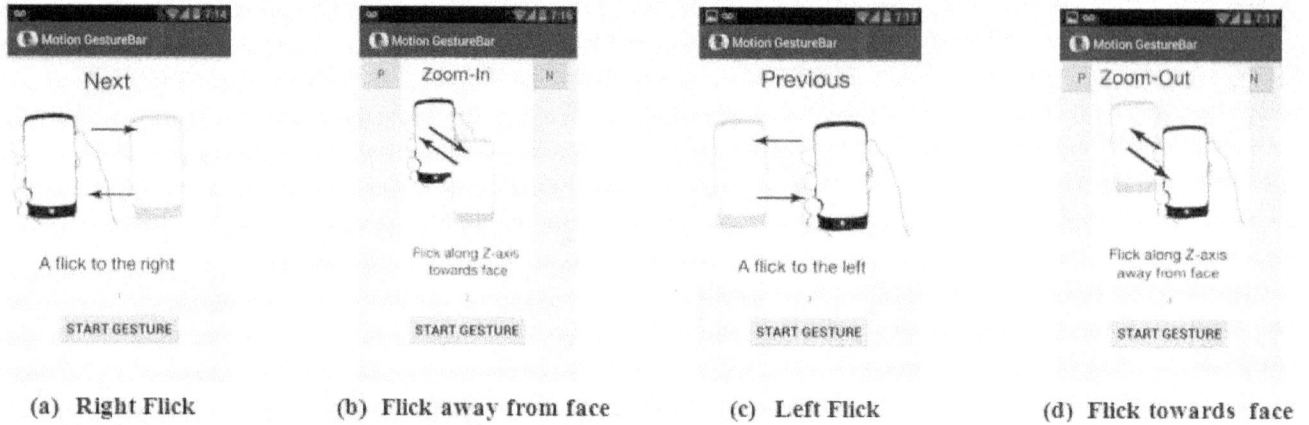

(a) **Right Flick**   (b) **Flick away from face**   (c) **Left Flick**   (d) **Flick towards face**

Figure 1: Iconic representation of the motion gestures

end-user must perform the gesture in nearly the same manner as the expert from whom the template was elicited.

In the following sections, we describe our experiments where we explore various types of mechanisms to teach end users motion gestures, examining two factors. The first factor we explore is how to represent motion gestures: as icons that describe movement, video that depicts movement using the smartphone screen, or as video on an external screen. The second factor we explore is feedback, i.e. a simple representation of the proximity of a motion gesture to the desired motion gesture based either on a distance metric extracted from the recognizer or based upon movement tracked by Kinect.

PRELIMINARY STUDY: DEPICTING MOTION GESTURES

We performed a preliminary study to compare the performance of two basic representations of motion gestures as teaching methods: icons describing the movement (see Ruiz et al. [17]) and short videos depicting the movement on the smartphone screen. Feedback mechanisms were not explored in this study. The reason for conducting this study was to check if very basic representations of the motion gesture, e.g. icons or simple videos, are sufficient to teach motion gestures.

Participants

We recruited 12 participants (8 male, 4 female, ages 20 -35) from the general student body of our institution. We advertised the study widely to get a sample of participants with diverse backgrounds and levels of experience using computers. All participants owned a smartphone. and knew what motion gestures were, but not with respect to movement of the smartphone device. All were familiar with motion gestures pertaining to the Nintendo Wii or Kinect based games, but none were familiar with smartphone-based motion gestures (beyond shake-to-shuffle).

Experimental Design

We used a between-subjects design with the two conditions - teaching via icons and via videos. The reason for choosing a between-subjects design is that if a user masters a gesture using one technique, the evaluation of the other technique becomes invalid. Six participants were asked to perform motion gestures based on the iconic representation of the motion gesture shown and the other six were asked to perform gestures based on the video shown on the phone. The iconic representations that were displayed on the Android device are shown in Figure 1. These iconic representations of the motion gestures were taken from the user-defined set created in the work done by Ruiz et al. [17]. The videos of gestures were captured from gestures performed by an expert user, and they depict the gesture used for the correct template in our recognizer from an eyes-view. i.e. as if one was looking at the smartphone while performing the gesture, Figure 2.

Figure 2: A screen-grab of the video on the phone describing the correct motion gesture

Procedure

Each participant was asked to perform four blocks (corresponding to the four gesture types) of thirty gestures each, i.e., 4 x 30 = 120 gestures. The order of the blocks of gestures to be performed was presented randomly. We did not give any hint to our participants regarding the correct gesture. When our DTW recognizer recognized a correct gesture, a beep sound was generated, indicating the completion of the correct gesture. Participants could refer to the icons or watch the videos as many times as they wanted. A total of 4 x 30 x 12 = 1440 gestures were performed.

Metrics

We extracted two metrics from our participants:

No. of correct gestures: The number of correct gestures out of the total of 120 performed by each user. This is a measure of performance of the user.

Average converging gesture count: This value is the average number of gestures it took for the participant to converge (or learn) to the correct gesture. Convergence is essentially, the point after which the gesture is performed consistently correctly. In our data, it works out to reaching 80 - 100% success rate, and represents the speed of learning a specific gesture.

Results

Figure 3 shows the number of correct gestures (out of 120) performed by all 12 participants for the two conditions – videos and icons. A Student's t–test showed significant differences for the number of correct gestures performed. Participants performed significantly better ($p < .001$) in terms of number of correct gestures performed with videos (M = 98.5, S.D = 1.87) versus icons (M = 83, S.D = 3.74). Figure 4 shows the average number of gestures (out of 30) over the four kinds of gestures at which the participants converged to the correct gesture. A Student's t–test showed significant differences for the average converging gesture count. Participants performed significantly better ($p < .001$) in terms of average number of gestures to converge to the correct gesture with videos (M = 5.5, S.D = 0.55) than with icons (M = 9.5, S.D = 1.04). The primary reasons for not performing a correct gesture were differences in speed and direction (acceleration of the device along a particular axis to be precise). If the DTW distance (which was based on acceleration along a particular axis) was within a specified threshold, then the gesture was considered correct.

Our initial results indicate that, by only showing icons, participants take a significant amount of time to converge to the correct gesture (10 gestures on an average) and perform poorly. Videos perform significantly better (6 gestures on an average) than icons as a teaching method, but scope for improvement exists. In the next section, we describe a set of designs that support feedback on the accuracy of performing motion gestures. We also evaluate our mechanisms for teaching gestures and assessing gesture accuracy.

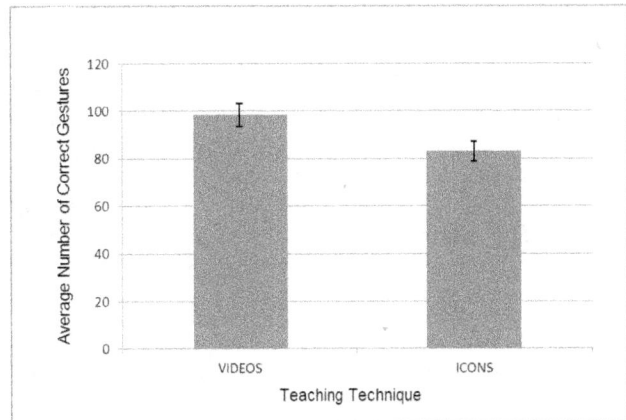

Figure 3: Average number of correct gestures (out of 120) performed by participants. 95% CI shown

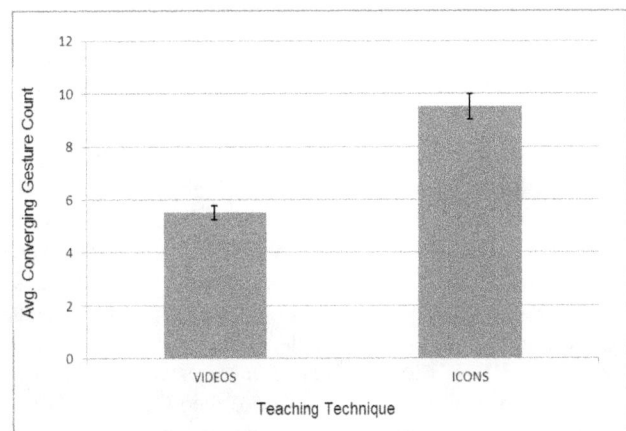

Figure 4: Average gesture count (out of 30) over the four types of gestures at which participants converged to the correct gesture. 95% CI shown

EVALUATION OF TECHNIQUES TO TEACH MOTION GESTURES

Our second user study explores additional representations of motion gestures, specifically examining the presentation of motion gestures on an external screen. We also explore additional feedback mechanisms for depicting motion gestures. These include using the Kinect to provide feedback, and also providing feedback from our recognizer using a distance metric extracted from the DTW algorithm.

Recognizer feedback design

In their work on bi-level thresholding, Negulescu et al. [13] note that, when users repeated fail to perform a motion gesture, they begin to vary the parameters of movement, attempting, essentially, to re-acquire the correct movement parameters needed to perform the motion gesture. We use the term *annealing* to describe this process of exploration.

Feedback that allows end users to assess the accuracy of a gesture exists on a continuum, from simple to more complex forms. The simplest form of feedback is some indication of correct versus incorrect from a recognizer.

earlier study, we advertised the study widely to get a sample of participants with diverse backgrounds and levels of experience using computers. All participants owned a smartphone and knew what motion gestures were, but not with respect to movement of the smartphone device. Some of the participants were familiar with some hand gestures above the screen that can be performed on the Samsung Galaxy S4 Android device. All participants were remunerated with a $10 Tim Horton's gift card after the completion of the experiment.

Experimental Design

We again used a between-subjects design for this study. The rationale for choosing a between-subjects design is that, if a user masters a gesture using one technique, the evaluation of the other technique becomes invalid. In this experiment, we evaluate the following 5 motion gesture teaching techniques – icons with DTW feedback, videos, videos with DTW feedback, Kinect, and Kinect with DTW feedback. We did not evaluate icons as a teaching mechanism in this study due to their poor performance in our preliminary study.

PROCEDURE

As in the preliminary study, the gestures that the participants were asked to do were *right flick, left flick, flick towards the face* and *flick away from face*. Participants were required to perform the gesture presented to them 30 times. Thus, each participant was asked to do four blocks (corresponding to the four gesture types) of thirty gestures, i.e., 4 x 30 = 120 gestures. Each gesture block was presented to them randomly. We described the presentation and feedback mechanisms for the desired gesture, but did not provide any guidance on when or how to use feedback during the experiment. The goal of the participants was to perform as many correct gestures as possible. Given 50 participants in our study, for each of the 5 teaching/feedback mechanisms, we had 10 participants. Thus a total of 4 x 30 x 50 = 6000 gestures were performed, 1200 per feedback mechanism. In the case of the Kinect with DTW feedback, the DTW feedback, was displayed on the smartphone after each gesture. After performing all the gestures, each participant was asked to complete an exit questionnaire, followed by a semi-structured interview. The questionnaire examined the subjective preferences of our participants, and the interview was intended to obtain their opinion on motion gestures in general as an input modality for smartphones.

Metrics

As in our previous study, we capture the following measures:

No. of correct gestures: The number of correct gestures out of the total of 120 performed by each user. This is a measure of performance of the user.

Average converging gesture count: This value is the average number of gestures it took for the participant to converge (or learn) to the correct gesture. Convergence is

essentially, the point after which the gesture is performed consistently correctly. In our data, it works out to reaching 80 - 100% success rate, and measures how quickly users can learn motion gestures.

Results

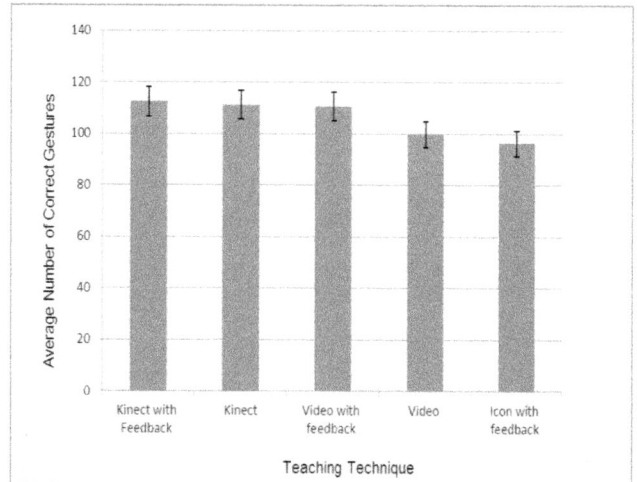

Figure 7: Average number of correct gestures (out of 120) performed by participants. 95% CI shown

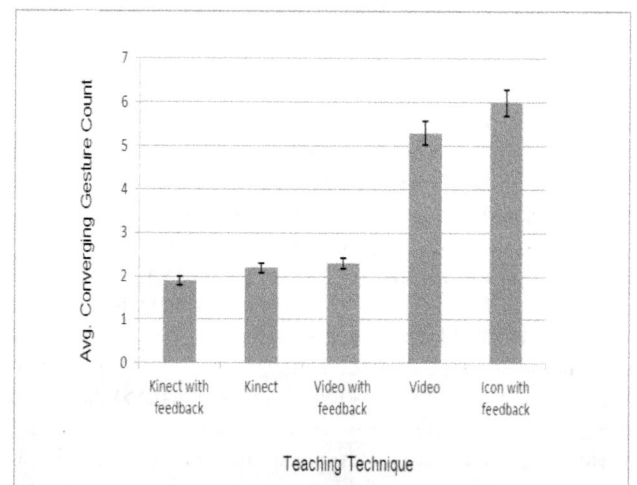

Figure 8: Average gesture count (out of 30) over the four types of gestures at which participants converged to the correct gesture. 95% CI shown

Figure 7 shows the number of correct gestures (out of 120) performed by all 50 participants for the 5 teaching mechanisms - icons with the DTW feedback, videos, videos with DTW feedback, Kinect, and Kinect with DTW feedback. A one-way analysis of variance shows that teaching technique had a significant effect on number of correct gestures performed ($F_{4,45} = 43.9$, $p < 0.001$). Post-hoc analysis using Bonferroni correction showed earlier study, we advertised the study widely to get a sample of participants with diverse backgrounds and levels of experience using computers. All participants owned a smartphone and knew what motion gestures were, but not with respect to movement of the smartphone device. Some of the participants were familiar with some hand gestures above the screen that can be performed on the Samsung Galaxy S4 Android device. All participants were remunerated with a $10 Tim Horton's gift card after the completion of the experiment.

Experimental Design

We again used a between-subjects design for this study. The rationale for choosing a between-subjects design is that, if a user masters a gesture using one technique, the evaluation of the other technique becomes invalid. In this experiment, we evaluate the following 5 motion gesture teaching techniques – icons with DTW feedback, videos, videos with DTW feedback, Kinect, and Kinect with DTW feedback. We did not evaluate icons as a teaching mechanism in this study due to their poor performance in our preliminary study.

PROCEDURE

As in the preliminary study, the gestures that the participants were asked to do were *right flick, left flick, flick towards the face* and *flick away from face*. Participants were required to perform the gesture presented to them 30 times. Thus, each participant was asked to do four blocks (corresponding to the four gesture types) of thirty gestures, i.e., 4 x 30 = 120 gestures. Each gesture block was presented to them randomly. We described the presentation and feedback mechanisms for the desired gesture, but did not provide any guidance on when or how to use feedback during the experiment. The goal of the participants was to perform as many correct gestures as possible. Given 50 participants in our study, for each of the 5 teaching/feedback mechanisms, we had 10 participants. Thus a total of 4 x 30 x 50 = 6000 gestures were performed, 1200 per feedback mechanism. In the case of the Kinect with DTW feedback, the DTW feedback, was displayed on the smartphone after each gesture. After performing all the gestures, each participant was asked to complete an exit questionnaire, followed by a semi-structured interview. The questionnaire examined the subjective preferences of our participants, and the interview was intended to obtain their opinion on motion gestures in general as an input modality for smartphones.

Metrics

As in our previous study, we capture the following measures:

No. of correct gestures: The number of correct gestures out of the total of 120 performed by each user. This is a measure of performance of the user.

Average converging gesture count: This value is the average number of gestures it took for the participant to converge (or learn) to the correct gesture. Convergence is

essentially, the point after which the gesture is performed consistently correctly. In our data, it works out to reaching 80 - 100% success rate, and measures how quickly users can learn motion gestures.

Results

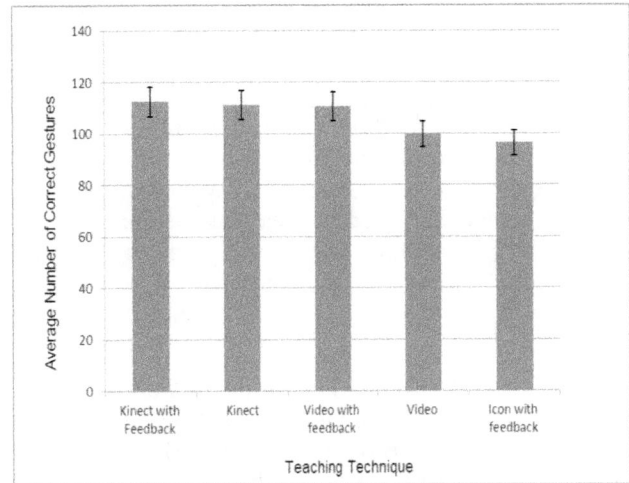

Figure 7: Average number of correct gestures (out of 120) performed by participants. 95% CI shown

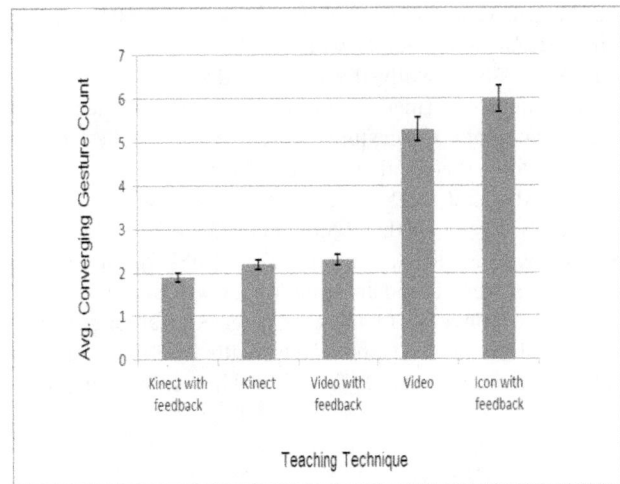

Figure 8: Average gesture count (out of 30) over the four types of gestures at which participants converged to the correct gesture. 95% CI shown

Figure 7 shows the number of correct gestures (out of 120) performed by all 50 participants for the 5 teaching mechanisms - icons with the DTW feedback, videos, videos with DTW feedback, Kinect, and Kinect with DTW feedback. A one-way analysis of variance shows that teaching technique had a significant effect on number of correct gestures performed ($F_{4,45} = 43.9$, $p < 0.001$). Post-hoc analysis using Bonferroni correction showed significant differences between Kinect with feedback and videos (p < 0.001), Kinect with feedback and icons with feedback (p < 0.001), Kinect and videos (p < 0.001), Kinect and icons with feedback(p < 0.001), videos with feedback and icons with feedback(p < 0.001) and finally between videos with feedback and videos(p < 0.001). Participants performed significantly better in terms of number of correct gestures with video with feedback (M = 110.7, S.D. = 3.5), Kinect (M = 111.3, S.D. = 3.4) and Kinect with feedback (M=112.5, S.D. = 2.9) than with videos (M = 99.8, S.D. = 3.5) or icons with feedback (M = 96.3, S.D. = 4.2). No significant differences were found in terms of number of correct gestures among Kinect with DTW feedback, Kinect, and videos with DTW feedback teaching mechanisms (p = 1.00 for all). This shows that, by combining video with DTW feedback, participants perform almost equally well as end users that learn using a Kinect or Kinect with DTW feedback.

Figure 8 shows the average number of gestures (out of 30) over the four kinds of gestures at which the participants converged to the correct gesture. A one-way analysis of variance shows that the teaching technique had a significant effect on the average converging gesture count ($F_{4,45}$ = 37.9, p < 0.001). Post-hoc analysis using Bonferroni correction showed significant differences between Kinect with feedback and videos (p < 0.001), Kinect with feedback and icons with feedback (p < 0.001), Kinect and videos (p < 0.001), Kinect and icons with feedback (p < 0.001), videos with feedback and icons with feedback (p < 0.001) and between videos with feedback videos (p < 0.001). Participants performed significantly better in terms of average number of gestures to converge to the correct gesture with video with feedback (M = 2.3, S.D. = 1.15), Kinect (M = 2.2, S.D. = 1.03) and Kinect with feedback (M=1.9, S.D. = 0.73) than with videos (M = 5.3, S.D. = 1.2) or icons with feedback (M = 6, S.D. = 1.05). No significant differences were found in terms of the average number of gestures to converge to the correct gesture among Kinect with feedback, Kinect and videos with feedback teaching mechanisms (p = 1.00 for all). This shows that, by combining video with DTW feedback, participants perform equally quickly (i.e., just after 2 incorrect gestures) as end users that learn using a Kinect or Kinect with DTW feedback.

These results demonstrate the viability of training end users to perform motion gestures using only the smartphone display. In particular, given some graphical representation of distance from correct gesture and a video depicting kinematics of movement, participants performed as well and learned as quickly as participants trained using full graphical feedback via the Kinect.

Subjective preferences of exit questionnaire
We further examined the subjective preferences of our participants via an exit questionnaire. Participants were to circle choices on a Likert Scale from -3 to 3. The following questions were asked in the questionnaire:

1. How did you like the motion gesture teaching technique in this experiment? Here, a rating of -3 corresponded to very poor and 3 to very good.

2. Would you like to have motion gestures for device commands along with surface gestures? Here, a rating of -3 corresponded to least preferred and 3 to most preferred.

Figure 9 shows the results of the first question. i.e., How much did the participant like the teaching technique. A one-way analysis of variance shows that teaching technique had a significant effect on the average rating of how much the users liked it ($F_{4,45}$ = 6.142, p < 0.001).

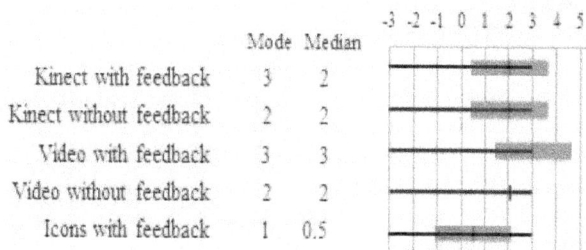

Figure 9: Median Likert rating from -3 to 3 for how much participants liked the teaching technique. The bars show 95% CI for median

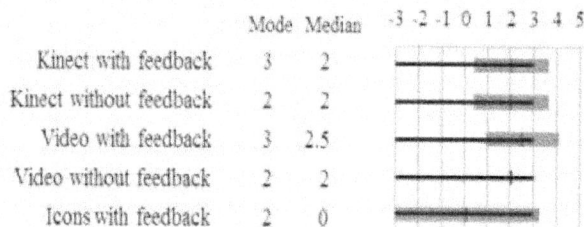

Figure 10: Median Likert rating from -3 to 3 for participant's opinion of motion gestures as an input modality along with surface gestures. The bars show 95% CI for median

Post-hoc analysis using Bonferroni correction showed significant differences between Kinect with feedback and icons with feedback (p < 0.05), Kinect and icons with feedback (p < 0.05), videos with feedback and icons with feedback (p < 0.05) and finally, videos and icons with feedback (p < 0.05). Participants gave significantly better ratings for video (M = 2.1, S.D. = 0.87), video with feedback (M = 2.4, S.D. = 1.15), Kinect (M = 1.7, S.D. = 0.96) and Kinect with feedback (M=1.9, S.D. = 1.28) than icons with feedback (M = 0.1, S.D. = 1.37). Video with feedback got the highest average ratings. One of the reasons for this could be that videos along with the recognizer feedback are much more suitable to display on the smartphone and no external display is needed.

Figure 10 shows the results of the second question. i.e., if participants would like to have motion gestures as an input modality along with touch (surface) gestures. A one-way analysis of variance again shows that teaching technique had a significant effect on the average rating of whether participants would like to have motion gestures as an input modality along with surface gestures ($F_{4,45}$ = 5.045, p < 0.05). Post-hoc analysis using Bonferroni correction showed significant differences between Kinect with feedback and icons with feedback (p < 0.05), videos with feedback and icons with feedback (p < 0.05) and finally, between videos and icons with feedback (p < 0.05). Participants gave significantly better ratings in the case of video (M = 1.5, S.D. = 1.5), video with feedback (M = 2.4, S.D. = 0.69) and Kinect with feedback (M= 2, S.D. = 1.05) than icons with feedback (M = 0.3, S.D. = 1.7)

Again, video with feedback got the highest average ratings, higher than both the Kinect-based teaching mechanisms. One of the reasons for this could be that videos along with the recognizer feedback are much more believable as a prospective teaching method on the smartphone than those that require any external display like the Kinect based-mechanisms.

User's opinions on motion gestures
We also conducted an exit semi-structured interview after each participant completed the experiment. Transcripts of the recorded interviews were used to identify common themes that emerged from our study.

Subtle gestures
16 out of 50 participants commented about the kind of motion involved in the motion gesture. A common theme that emerged was that the gesture should involve as little movement as possible.

Well, I mean motion gestures are ok and all, but I would rather use my wrist than using my arm.[P28].

The four kinds of gestures in this study did involve some lateral and vertical arm movement. Participants felt that too much arm movement in any gesture would be strenuous and might also invade an adjoining person's private space.

If I'm in a packed place or say on the bus, my arm might accidentally bump into the person next to me while doing the gesture. [P12].

Social Acceptability
36 out of 50 participants indicated their fondness for motion gestures and mentioned that, just like any new technology, motion gestures would eventually be accepted and used in public.

I don't mind these in public. I think they're pretty cool. [P21]

I think motion gestures could go mainstream really soon. It's kind of a cool new technology after all. Eventually everyone would be using them. [P40]

However a few of the participants indicated that motion gestures may become "awkward" in public places.

I would feel weird doing them in public. If all of us start doing motion gestures, it'll feel like a crazy world.[P3]

Fatigue
12 out of 50 participants mentioned that with prolonged use, motion gestures may cause some damage to the arm, especially for older people.

With prolonged use, my arms could pain and the older folks, say my grandfather, wouldn't want to do these at all. [P11]

Individual privacy
9 out of 50 participants indicated that, if motion gestures are standardized, then observers may be more aware of their actions, i.e. that the observability of motion gestures may result in a loss of privacy.

If all motion gestures are the same, your motion might indicate what you're doing. Other people might see me doing actions on the phone which I, you know, don't want to show them. [P12]

False positives/negatives
The last theme that came up from the quotes of many participants (33 out of 50) was the problem of false positives and negatives. Participants mentioned the problem of distinguishing everyday motion from motion gestures and minimizing false positives. They also said that the recognizer should be very responsive and should have a minimal false negative rate.

What if I'm like, running with the phone in my pocket or maybe stretching? Then if I accidentally start calling someone, that would be a big problem. [P35]

As we note earlier, significant past work addresses the question of balancing false positives and false negatives [13, 16].

Gamification of Recognizer Feedback
31 out of 50 participants indicated that one of the reasons they liked the DTW feedback in our study was that it challenged them to get the arrow point to the correct (green) area of the bar and as high as possible on each attempt.

I felt like, you know, I can totally do this. I just didn't want to let that arrow to drop down. It was fun. [P17]

DISCUSSION AND LIMITATIONS
Our experiments demonstrate that, as a teaching mechanism, showing a video of a desired gesture on the phone along with some feedback of how close a gesture is to optimal can effectively aid learning of motion gestures. This clearly demonstrates the viability of training end users to perform motion gestures using only the smartphone display.

We acknowledge that the four gestures in our evaluation were simple gestures, requiring only lateral or vertical motion of the phone. For complicated gestures, e.g. gestures using twists or curves, only providing feedback about how close a person is to the desired gesture may not be sufficient.

CONCLUSION

This paper addresses the challenge of teaching people to do motion gestures. Specifically, we examine two factors. The first factor is how to represent motion gestures: as icons that describe movement, video that depicts movement using the smartphone screen, or a Kinect-based teaching mechanism that captures and depicts the gesture on an external display in three-dimensional space. The second factor we examine is recognizer feedback, i.e. a simple representation of the proximity of a motion gesture to the desired motion gesture based on a distance metric extracted from the recognizer. We show that, by combining video with recognizer feedback, participants master motion gestures almost equally quickly as end users that learn using a Kinect and perform equally well.

ACKNOWLEDGEMENTS

We thank the participants in our studies. Funding for this research was provided by the Natural Science and Engineering Research Council of Canada (NSERC), the Networks of Centres of Excellence Program (NCE-GRAND), the Ontario Ministry of Innovation, and the Google Faculty Fellowship Program.

REFERENCES

1. *Android Open Source Project*. Google Inc.

2. Bau, O., and Mackay,W., "OctoPocus: A Dynamic Guide for Learning Gesture-Based Command Sets.", *Proc. of UIST'08*, 37-46.

3. Bolt, R. "Put-that-there: Voice and gesture at the graphics interface." *Proc. Computer Graphics*, 14:3, 1980, 262- 270

4. Bragdon, A., Zeleznik, R., Williamson, B., Miller, T., and Laviola, J. J., "Gesturebar: improving the approachability of gesture-based interfaces." *Proc. CHI 2009*, 2269–2278.

5. Callahan, J., Hopkins, D., Weiser, M. & Shneiderman, B.,"An empirical comparison of pie vs. linear menus", *Proc. CHI'88*, 95-100.

6. Bucolo, S., Billinghurst, M. and Sickinger, D., "User experiences with mobile phone camera game interfaces," *Proc, MUM 2005*, 87-94.

7. Hinckley, K., Pierce, J., Sinclair, M., and Horvitz, E. "Sensing techniques for mobile interaction." *Proc. UIST 2000*, 91–100.

8. Jones, E., Alexander, J., Andreou, A., Irani, P., and Subramanian, S. "GesText: Accelerometer-based Gestural Text-Entry Systems." *Proc. CHI 2010*, 2173-2182.

9. Kar, B., Dutta, P. K., Basu, T. K., Vielhauer, C., Dittmann, J., "DTW based verification scheme of biometric signatures", *Proc. ICIT 2006*, 381-386.

10. Kurtenbach, G. (1993) "The Design and Evaluation of Marking Menus", *Ph. D. Thesis*, Dept. of Computer Science, University of Toronto.

11. Li, F., Dearman, D., Truong, K.N. "Virtual Shelves: Interactions with Orientation Aware Devices." *Proc. UIST 2009*, 125-128.

12. Myers, C. and Rabiner, L., "A comparative study of several dynamic time-warping algorithms for connected word recognition", *The Bell System Tech Journal 60*, 7 (1981), 1389- 1409.

13. Negulescu, M., Ruiz, J., and Lank, E., "A Recognition Safety Net: Bi-Level Thresholding for Mobile Motion Gestures", *Proc. MobileHCI 2012, 147-150.*

14. Negulescu, M., Ruiz, J., Li., Y. and Lank, E., "Tap, Swipe, Move: Attentional Demands for Distracted Smartphone Input", *Proc. AVI 2012, 173-180.*

15. *nuiCapture Analyze*, Cadavid Concepts Inc.

16. Ruiz, J. and Li, Y., "DoubleFlip: a motion gesture delimiter for mobile interaction", *Proc. CHI 2011*, 2717–2720.

17. Ruiz, J., Li, Y. and Lank, E., "User-Defined Motion Gestures for Mobile Interaction", *Proc. CHI 2011*,197 - 206.

18. Vogel, D., and Balakrishnan, R. "Distant freehand pointing and clicking on very large high resolution displays." *Proc., UIST 2005,* 33-42.

19. Wobbrock, J.O., Wilson, A.D., and Li, Y., "Gestures without libraries, toolkits or training: a $1 recognizer for user interface prototypes", *Proc. of UIST '07*, ACM (2007), 159–168.

A Brain-Computer Interface for High-Level Remote Control of an Autonomous, Reinforcement-Learning-Based Robotic System for Reaching and Grasping

Thomas Lampe[*‡]
tlampe@informatik.uni-freiburg.de

Lukas D. J. Fiederer[†‡]
lukas.fiederer@uniklinik-freiburg.de

Martin Voelker[†]
martin.voelker@uniklinik-freiburg.de

Alexander Knorr[†]
alexander.knorr@uniklinik-freiburg.de

Martin Riedmiller[*]
riedmiller@informatik.uni-freiburg.de

Tonio Ball[†]
tonio.ball@uniklinik-freiburg.de

ABSTRACT

We present an Internet-based brain-computer interface (BCI) for controlling an intelligent robotic device with autonomous reinforcement-learning. BCI control was achieved through dry-electrode electroencephalography (EEG) obtained during imaginary movements. Rather than using low-level direct motor control, we employed a high-level control scheme of the robot, acquired via reinforcement learning, to keep the users cognitive load low while allowing control a reaching-grasping task with multiple degrees of freedom. High-level commands were obtained by classification of EEG responses using an artificial neural network approach utilizing time-frequency features and conveyed through an intuitive user interface. The novel combination of a rapidly operational dry electrode setup, autonomous control and Internet connectivity made it possible to conveniently interface subjects in an EEG laboratory with remote robotic devices in a closed-loop setup with online visual feedback of the robots actions to the subject. The same approach is also suitable to provide home-bound patients with the possibility to control state-of-the-art robotic devices currently confined to a research environment. Thereby, our BCI approach could help severely paralyzed patients by facilitating patient-centered research of new means of communication, mobility and independence.

Author Keywords

Semi-autonomous systems; Robots; Camera-based UIs; Machine Learning and Data Mining

ACM Classification Keywords

H.5.2. Information Interfaces and Presentation (e.g. HCI): User Interfaces

[*]Albert-Ludwigs-University Freiburg, Machine Learning Lab, Georges-Köhler-Allee 79, 79110 Freiburg, Germany
[†]Albert-Ludwigs-University Freiburg, iEEG and Brain Imaging Group, Engelbergerstr. 21, 79108 Freiburg, Germany
[‡]These authors contributed equally.

General Terms

Human Factors; Experimentation

INTRODUCTION

The use of brain-computer interfaces (BCIs) for robot control has become an integral field of research in recent years, intimately blending neuroscience and robotics. One central application that has received much attention is the control of prosthetic actuators by disabled individuals. Systems have developed far enough to enable tetraplegic patients to interact with the world [4, 7] by translating neuronal activity measured in the motor cortex into control signals steering external effectors such as a robotic device.

While the relevance and clinical promise of such work can hardly be emphasized enough, one drawback of BCIs relying on low-level motor control such as during reaching-grasping tasks is the limited accuracy that can be achieved with current BCI techniques, even after extensive training. To ameliorate the problem of limited accuracy, cognitive BCI approaches combined with autonomous intelligent systems have been proposed [12].

In this framework, a user should ideally only have to control the system on a higher level, the intuitive vision being that one would only need to think of *what* to do, not how to do it. The actuator would then perform the detailed action by itself to achieve the specified goal. Such a high-level approach would reduce the cognitive load required of the user. As a result, semi-autonomous systems would be intuitive to use and might be adapted to more quickly.

Here, we developed and tested an intuitive user interface that can be controlled via electroencephalography (EEG) signals to perform a reaching-grasping task carried out by an autonomous, reinforcement-learning-based robotic system. Motor-imagery-related EEG changes classified in single trials were used to select the target object to be grasped. An autonomous robotic arm then performed the desired action without the need for low-level control by the user.

While previous BCI research has to a large extent focused on improving recording and decoding techniques and has made tremendous progress in these fields, relatively little work so far has been devoted to the development and refinement of dedicated user interfaces for experimental and emerging clinical BCI applications [1]. Here, we present a user interface that is based on automatic image segmentation to identify graspable objects within the range of the robotic arm. In the video stream presented to the subjects, graspable objects are overlaid with a selection box that can be moved among the set of identified objects based on BCI commands issued by the user.

On the control side, we made use of reinforcement learning (RL) [18] to acquire most of the needed grasping skills only through trial-and-error. While not strictly necessary for the principal idea of an intelligent prosthesis, such an approach is desirable, as it allows the adaption of the system to changes in the environment or in the robot itself. Furthermore, this approach does not require engineering of the control skills. Thus, rather than merely shifting the learning required from the user to an expert programmer or engineer, we leave it entirely to the machine.

On the EEG side, our emphasis was on testing a comfortable and quickly usable setup, rather than optimizing decoding accuracy. Particularly, by using dry EEG electrodes, which are attached fast and easily and do not need electrode gel or scalp scraping, we avoided exposing subjects and patients to an uncomfortable situation. While the present dry electrode-based EEG setup is not meant to replace such approaches aimed at high accuracy, it proved to be useful for extensive testing and optimization of the user interface.

The novelty of our approach lies in the combination of camera-based visual servoing control with reinforcement learning in a brain-computer interface. Additionally, we used dry electrodes for EEG control based on multi-class decoding, instead of wet electrodes as typically used in similar previous EEG-based BCIs. To the best of our knowledge, no dry electrodes have been used before for a system that is as quick to set up while allowing detection of four motor imagery classes, and no such system has incorporated reinforcement learning, which adds extra potential for user adaptability. Other remote BCI systems were also mostly aimed at mobile navigation (ex. [5]). Some works have used an arm for manipulation, but either involved an SSVEP interface rather than one based on motor imagery [3] or employed direct kinematic motor control for fewer degrees of freedom (DOFs) [6].

The feasibility of robot control was demonstrated in three subjects. In addition, a larger study with screen cursor instead of robot control was performed in order to further quantify the reliability of the dry-electrode-based EEG control.

SYSTEM ARCHITECTURE

The general setup we propose assumes that a user is attached to EEG hardware. A semi-autonomous robotic device is to be controlled remotely while situated at another location.

As an example of such a setup, we considered the case of the Jaco robotic arm (Kinova, Montreal, Canada), capable of grasping colored balls in its working area. Instead of the arm being controlled directly, the user merely needed to choose the specific object to be manipulated through high-level EEG commands. Once an object had been chosen, it was autonomously picked up through the behaviors elaborated on in

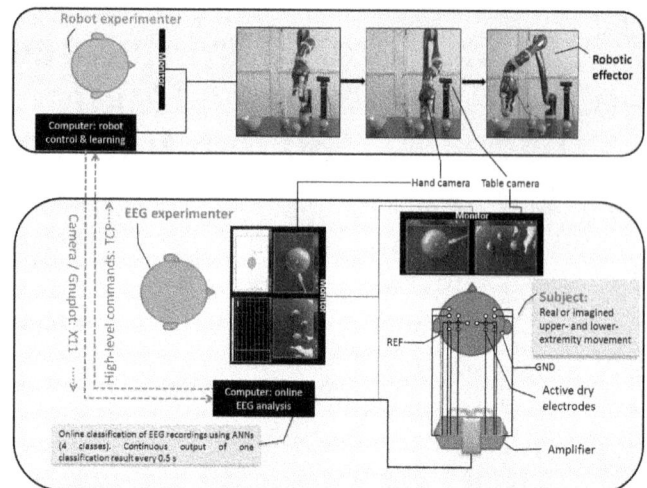

Figure 1. Schematic representation of experimental setup. Subjects and robot are located several kilometers apart and connected through the Internet by TCP/IP and X-forwarding. EEG Subjects see the online video stream of hand and table cameras of the robot arm. The EEG experimenter sees both video streams, the sent data and the ongoing EEG recordings. The robot experimenter sees both video streams, the received data and the flow of robotic control. GND: ground; REF: reference; ANN: artificial neural network.

the next section. An overview of the architecture is illustrated in Figure 1.

Users were presented with two webcam views, one showing a hand view and the other a scene view (c.f. Figure 2c & b, respectively). Objects recognized in either camera were framed with selection boxes. Three types of BCI events which conceptually corresponded to *left*, *right* and *confirmation* were then used to select the desired target from these objects. Left and right signals were forwarded directly to the vision module, which selected the object next to the currently tracked one in the given direction. In this way, a user could cycle through available targets. Confirmation events were processed by the control system itself, and cause it to toggle through a series of process stages.

Initially, the arm was in a waiting position, with the user selecting the object to grasp in the table camera's view. A first confirmation triggered the actuator's approach towards a position located close to the target. The view then switched to the hand-mounted camera to allow the user to choose again between multiple close objects or to amend incorrect choices in the first attempt before performing the actual grasp. Once ready, a second confirmation started the short-range controller that grasps the object and picks it up. Then, the user would issue two more confirmation events, launching hand-coded feed-forward behaviors that moved the arm over a drop point and opened the gripper, respectively, before the cycle restarted.

Communication between decoder and robot controller was realized via a custom TCP/IP interface. Here, the commands sent to the controller were strings of either $[0\ 0]$ for no action, $[0\ 1]$ for right, $[0\ -1]$ for left, or $[1\ 0]$ for confirmation. These specific commands were ultimately arbitrary and easily exchanged or extended. The numeric coding was used

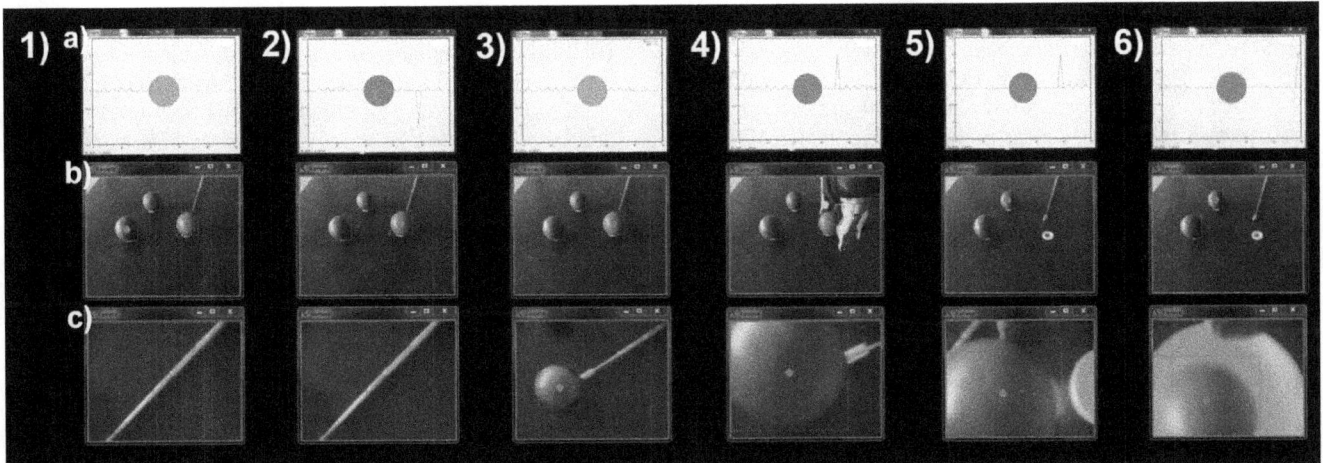

Figure 2. Windows of the control interface. Subjects see (b) & (c), both experimenters see all three windows. (a) Overview of recognized events and lock status during the last 5 seconds: Blue spikes indicate recent confirmation events, red spikes pointing downwards or upwards imply movement of the selection box to the next or preceding ball in the sequence, respectively. Small red spikes and the red circle indicate the lock state. (b) Desk cameras view. The target object to be grasped is indicated by a metal pointer. (c) View from camera inside the robotic hand. 1) Start, the user is supposed to pick up the ball on the bottom right as indicated by the pointer. 2) Decoding of right hand movement, cursor in the desk camera (b) jumps to the right. 3) Decoding of toe movement, i.e., a conformation event; the robotic arm moves toward the target ball, control switches to the hand camera (c). 4) Confirmation event causes the robotic arm to pick up the ball. 5) Another conformation event lets the robotic hand to move over a bowl, and a last conformation in 6) causes the robotic hand drop the ball.

here simply for ease of processing on the robotic side, which needed to transform any command into such a sequence for its internal representation. In principle, any high-level command string could have been be used, such as look_left. After each command, the locking signal [0.1 0.1] was sent to prevent sending commands multiple times. Sent commands were displayed online to the user for greater feedback (Figure 2). This graph, as well as the live camera streams, were accessed on the users side via X11-forwarding.

ROBOT CONTROL

The physical system was centered around a Kinova Jaco robotic arm, a therapeutic model commonly used by individuals capable of using their hands but lacking arm strength, and designed for installation on a wheelchair.

The autonomous control of this robotic system followed an identical approach to that described in previous work [8]. Two separate modules were responsible for the actual grasping behavior of the arm. The first, dubbed the *long-range* controller, realized a coarse mapping to bring the actuator close to a target object using the camera mounted on the table. It was therefore activated after the initial target selection by the user. In the second stage, a more precise *short-range* controller took over using a visual servoing approach to perform the fine movements needed for a secure grasp.

To train the autonomous agent, techniques of both supervised and reinforcement learning were used. The network that constituted the long-range controller was trained in a supervised fashion, i.e. by recording sets of input and desired output. Specifically, it realized a mapping from object locations in the stationary camera to kinematic positions of the actuator in the horizontal plane. In contrast, the short-range controller was trained using reinforcement learning. Thus the system learned an ideal grasp policy by interacting with the environ-

ment and learning from success and error. The arm started at a random position over the working area, with the likewise randomly placed object being visible in the hand camera. Episodes alternated between greedy exploitation of the current policy and ϵ-greedy exploration with $\epsilon = 0.2$. After each episode, the policy was updated using Neural Fitted Q-Iteration [16], a batch algorithm that achieves comparatively quick and efficient learning with few observations.

BRAIN-COMPUTER INTERFACE

The brain-computer interface developed to control the robotic arm is based on movement-related changes in EEG power [15]. We examined both real and imagined movements. Real movements usually elicit more easily detectable brain responses than imagined ones and are thus useful especially in early stages of BCI projects. Imagined movements as a rule produce less pronounced brain activity but might be closer to the signals available in paralyzed patients. Finger tapping (alternatively touching the thumb with all 4 fingers) and toe clenching were used to elicit EEG responses. The four decoded classes were left hand finger tapping, right hand finger tapping, both toe clenching and the relaxed state where no motor imagery was performed. The commands relayed to the robot controller were related to movement in the following manner: finger tapping navigates the object selection box in the direction of the corresponding hand; toe clenching was used as the confirmation signal for object selection and action trigger. No action was elicited when the relaxed state was decoded.

Signal acquisition

EEG was acquired at 512 Hz using two g.USBamp amplifiers in combination with 16 g.SAHARA dry active electrodes (both GUGER TECHNOLOGIES, Graz, Austria). Electrode locations according to the 10-10 system [14] were C1, C3, C5, Fc3, Fc5, F5, C2, C4, C6, Fc4, Fc6, Cp4,

Cp6 and F6 with the reference (REF) on the left mastoid and the ground (GND) electrode on the right mastoid. Additionally, electrooculography (EOG) was recorded with four Ag/AgCl ring electrodes, two for horizontal and two for vertical eye movements, as well as myoelectrography (EMG) with two Ag/AgCl ring electrodes per arm and two for one leg. BCI2000 was used [17] to interface amplifier and signal processing in MATLAB (MathWorks, Natick, MA).

Stimulus presentation

Prior to the measurement, the subject was instructed to sit as motionlessly as possible and to minimize blinking rate while fixating a fixation point on the screen. During offline trials the subjects were shown arrows pointing left, right or down (in lieu of a confirm icon) for 5 seconds; the interval between the stimuli randomly alternated from 5 s to 10 s. When only the fixation mark was shown on the screen, the subject had to relax; this defined the rest-state. If either left or right arrows were shown, the subject had to tap or imagine tapping fingers of the corresponding hand. When the down arrow was shown, the subject had to move or imagine moving all his toes in a grabbing way. For each subject, 220 trials per conditions were recorded for both real and imagined movements, resulting in 880 offline trials.

During online trials subjects had to move a cursor from the center of the screen to one of four targets located on the four edges of the screen. The cursor moved to the decoded target in one single step. Left and right hand (imagined) finger tapping was used to move left and right, respectively. Downwards movement was achieved with (imagined) toe movements and upwards movement by relaxing. Again, upward and downward cursor movements were used due to the lack of a visualization for relaxation and confirmation events, respectively. The timing of online trials was as follows. 1 s rest, followed by 6.5 s feedback accumulation after which decoding was performed for minimally 2 s with a timeout of 5 s. If the correct target was hit it was highlighted for 1 s. Timed out trials were not evaluated. For subjects S1-3, 54 trials per condition were recorded for both real and imagined movements, resulting in 216 online trials. Online trials of subjects 4-5 were aborted after fewer trials once it became apparent that no control was possible.

EEG Preprocessing

First the common average was subtracted from all EEG channels. The signal was then filtered using 6th order high-pass and notch Butterworth filters with a cut-off frequency of 1 Hz and 48–52 Hz, respectively. Using the *MultiTaper method* [19], time-resolved spectral magnitude was calculated with a sliding 1-s window and time-steps of 500 ms. Pre-whitening was applied to prevent frequency shifts. The data was then normalized to have 0 mean and a standard deviation of 1.

Channels for decoding were selected based on the average amplitudes of movement-related responses, i.e., without referring to class differences in order to avoid circularity. To do so the the preprocessed offline trials were cut 3 s before the start and 5 s after the end of the stimulus. Baseline removal was achieved by dividing each trial by the mean of the

first 500 ms of all trials. Following, median trials for each condition and channel were calculated. Cp3 and Cp4 showed the strongest alpha band depression during imagined or real hand movement over all subjects. This observation was underpinned by p-values calculated for 8-30 Hz with the sign test, which were smallest in these channels.

Offline Classification

To classify rest, left finger, right finger and toe (imagined) movements, the Neural Network Toolbox of MATLAB was used to create an artificial neural network (ANN) with 198 inputs, 20 hidden neurons and 4 outputs. The *patternnet-function*, which creates a feed-forward neural network, was used. The neural network was then trained on the 198 previously selected features. Bayesian regulation backpropagation was used as training method. It uses the *Levenberg-Marquardt optimization*, which is known to generate networks that generalize well [10]. The network accuracy was tested using 10-fold cross-validation; p-values for the classification accuracies were calculated against chance level (25%) using the binomial cumulative distribution function in MATLAB. The four outputs of the network range from -1 to 1 and the one with the highest score was chosen as decoded class.

Online Classification

In experiments with online control the classification method was identical to its offline counterpart. The ANNs were trained on the whole offline data first and then retrained on 10 trials per condition using the online paradigm before further online testing. In contrast to offline, the same output class had to be decoded four times consecutively as well as having an output score above 0.3 before being accepted. p-values for the classification accuracies were also calculated against chance level (25%).

RESULTS

Five healthy subjects (S1-5) with no previous experience with BCI participated in this study, which was approved by the Ethics Committee of the University Medical Center Freiburg and conducted after the subjects gave their written informed consent.

The subjects were two females and three males, all right-handed; their age ranged from 23 to 30 years.

Mean offline decoding accuracy was significantly above chance level (chance $25\%, p \ll 10^{-16}$) for all 5 subjects in both real and imagined movements. For real movements, mean offline accuracy ranged from 36.9% to 71.8%. For imagined movements, mean online accuracy ranged from 37.0% to 53.2%. Mean online decoding accuracy was significantly above chance (chance $25\%, p < 10^{-14}$) for Subjects 1-3. Their accuracy ranged from 60.6-74.4% and from 50.2-60.4% for real and imagined movements, respectively. Detailed results per subject are shown in Table 1. Median spectra and single trial spectra of electrode Cp3 for right hand finger tapping and toe clenching of S1 are shown in Figure 3. Even on single trial level, both movements show distinct patterns. Subjects 4 and 5 did not produce accuracies above chance level (chance $25\%, p > 0.1$) during the online sessions.

Subj.	Sex	Age	Offline						Online					
			# trials		Mean accuracy		p-value		# trials		Mean accuracy		p-value	
			real	imag.	real	imag.	real	imag.	real	imag.	real	imag.	real	imag.
S1	M	23	880	880	71.8%	47.4%	$< 10^{-16}$	$< 10^{-16}$	202	204	61.4%	58.8%	$< 10^{-16}$	$< 10^{-16}$
S2	M	26	880	720	63.6%	48.2%	$< 10^{-16}$	$< 10^{-16}$	213	207	60.6%	60.4%	$< 10^{-16}$	$< 10^{-16}$
S3	F	23	880	880	61.3%	53.2%	$< 10^{-16}$	$< 10^{-16}$	211	203	74.4%	50.2%	$< 10^{-16}$	$< 10^{-14}$
S4	F	24	880	880	36.9%	37%	$< 10^{-16}$	$< 10^{-16}$	22	57	22.7%	28.1%	0.59	0.31
S5	M	30	880	880	44.3%	43.1%	$< 10^{-16}$	$< 10^{-16}$	57	76	26.3%	30.3%	0.42	0.15

Table 1. Accuracies and trial numbers per subject. All subjects were right-handed. In the offline setting, the number of trials denotes the trials used for training and validating the classifier, in the online setting the number of test trials.

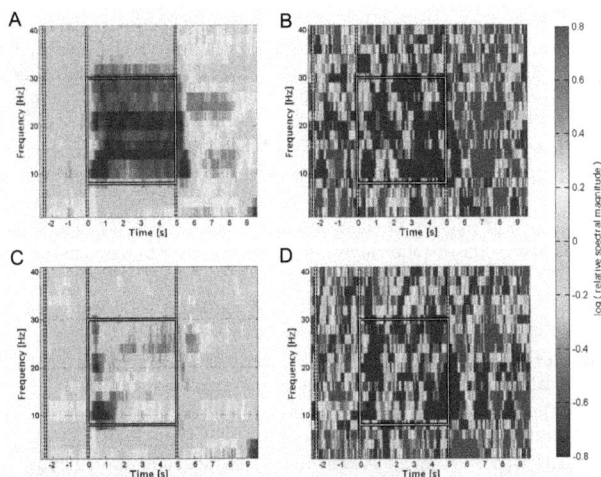

Figure 3. Time-frequency EEG responses for hand and toe movement of S1. All plots show channel Cp3. A: Median of 220 trials, right hand movement. B: Single trial, right hand movement. C: Median of 220 trials, toe movement. D: Single trial, toe movement. The vertical lines indicate the end of the baseline (-2.5 s), stimulus onset (0 s) and offset (5 s); the rectangle defines the area which was used to train the ANN (8-30 Hz, 0-5 s).

Subjects 1-3 were subsequently invited to try controlling the Jaco robotic arm based on the same successful online control as described above. Due to the relatively long duration of the entire process (setup, BCI training and robot calibration) subjects tended to become fatigued. As a result, only a limited number of trials with online robot control could be performed for each subject. While this precluded the calculation of accuracy measures, all subjects achieved robot control with a similar success rate as in the previous online cursor control. Despite the limited reliability in the detection of single events, subjects were usually able to successfully grasp the target object due to the ability to simply either amend incorrect commands. In addition, the fact that the selection list wrapped around at the ends enabled them to simply move the opposite direction if one was not recognized properly. Naturally, this also means that there was often no objectively correct action as the users could pursue two paths to the same goal.

DISCUSSION

In the present study, we have developed and tested an intuitive interface that allows users to convey high-level control signals via a BCI to an intelligent robotic device. Objects detected in a camera image were marked so that they could be selected by the user using motor imagery as commands, and the actual grasp was performed by the autonomous robot controller trained via reinforcement learning. This augmented reality approach proved to be intuitive; all subjects in our study quickly learned to navigate the interface.

Signal detection was robust enough to allow users to grasp intended objects, although dry electrodes were used for greater ease of setup of the system. Movement-related EEG recordings showed the classical suppression in the alpha and beta frequency ranges in a very pronounced manner (Figure 3). We achieved good online and offline decoding in the majority of subjects based on single-trial classification of movement-related spectral power changes in these frequencies, both during real and imagined upper- and lower-extremity movements. While the accuracy achieved in the present study was not perfect, the main goal of providing subjects with a substantial sense of control was reached.

The results presented here are the first to employ this type of dry electrodes for four-class classification. Comparable electrodes have become commercially available only recently, precluding a direct comparison with other systems using devices that provide markedly different signal quality. State-of-the-art four class decoding using wet electrodes can achieve higher accuracies between 60-90 %, depending on whether decoding is offline, online, continuous or not, as well as the number of electrodes used [2, 23]. However, the ease-of-use can make up for the reduced accuracy if the focus of a system lies on comfort and rapid deployability like in our case.

Beyond the basic application demonstrated here, this approach can be extended in various respects. On the robotic side, different grasp types may be inferred for one object and presented in a symbolic form, replacing the simple selection box in the current study. Furthermore, other robotic systems like mobile and/or humanoid robots could be integrated in the setup to share tasks. Preliminary work in our labs has recently been successful at using a mobile humanoid robot for a fetch-and-carry task.

On the EEG side, our focus thus far has been on establishing a comfortable and quickly usable setup, rather than optimizing the decoding accuracy. Although having achieved good online and offline decoding in the majority of subjects, decoding performance can likely be further increased using a range of established EEG interfacing techniques, such as sophisticated channel and feature selection, spatial filtering, and adaptive decoding [13, 9, 20]. A further performance boost can be expected from moving to intracranial (invasive) control signals, such as the electrocorticogram (ECoG) recoded from the brain surface, intracortical local field potentials, or single-neuron activity [22, 11]. Although invasive measurements are usually associated with low-level paradigms, their robustness and high accuracy make them very interesting signal sources for high-level BCIs. Whether high-level control would still provide an advantage with them remains to be investigated in future work. It is also worth noting that the remote nature of the system would be even more justified, since there are restrictions on using robotic equipment in the vicinity of implanted patients.

A noteworthy feature of the BCI system used in our study is that it combined three (potentially) adaptive entities: the users brain, the decoder, and the autonomous agent. Firstly, to train the autonomous agent, techniques of both supervised and reinforcement learning were used (see Methods), and could be employed to adapt behaviors if conditions of the system or requirements change, such as in case of damage to the hardware. Secondly, although the employed decoder was not continually adapting, it was updated based on new data from each online session before starting the next session, thus effectively adapting on the time scale corresponding to the duration of individual experimental sessions. And finally, although learning and adaptivity on the users side was not assessed in the present study, there is a large and growing body of evidence that learning on the neuronal level occurs during BCI control and is essential for its success [21]. An interaction between these three adaptive systems leads to potentially interesting co-adaptivity scenarios that go beyond the dual co-adaptivity problems previously addressed in the BCI context.

In summary, here we have presented a novel BCI setup that is centered on an intuitive user interface based on an augmented reality approach. This interface links signals derived from dry-electrode EEG recordings to control an intelligent robotic device for reaching and grasping. While not meant to replace approaches aimed at high accuracy, such as systems based on intracranial signals, the setup proved to be very useful for extensive testing and optimization of the user interface. This platform is well suited for the development of clinical BCI systems in which interface properties have to be tailored to patient's needs and their individual environment.

ACKNOWLEDGMENT

This work was partly supported by the BrainLinks-BrainTools Cluster of Excellence funded by the German Research Foundation (DFG, grant number EXC 1086) and by the German Federal Ministry of Education and Research grant 16SV5834 NASS to the University of Freiburg. We also thank the anonymous reviewers for their useful suggestions which helped improve the final paper.

REFERENCES

1. Allison, B. Z., Leeb, R., Brunner, C., Müller-Putz, G. R., Bauernfeind, G., Kelly, J. W., and Neuper, C. Toward smarter BCIs: extending BCIs through hybridization and intelligent control. *Journal of Neural Engineering 9* (2012), 1.

2. Brunner, C., Naeem, M., Leeb, R., Graimann, B., and Pfurtscheller, G. Spatial filtering and selection of optimized components in four class motor imagery EEG data using independent components analysis. *Pattern Recognition Letters 28*, 8 (2007), 957–964.

3. Bryan, M., Green, J., Chung, M., Chang, L. Y., Scherer, R., Smith, J. R., and Rao, R. P. N. An adaptive brain-computer interface for humanoid robot control. In *Humanoids* (2011), 199–204.

4. Collinger, J. L., Wodlinger, B., Downey, J. E., Wang, W., Tyler-Kabara, E. C., Weber, D. J., McMorland, A. J. C., Velliste, M., Boninger, M. L., and Schwartz, A. B. High-performance neuroprosthetic control by an individual with tetraplegia. *The Lancet 381*, 9866 (2013), 557–564.

5. Escolano, C., Antelis, J., and Minguez, J. Human brain-teleoperated robot between remote places. In *Robotics and Automation, 2009. ICRA '09. IEEE International Conference on* (2009), 4430–4437.

6. Ferreira, A., Bastos-Filho, T., Sarcinelli-Filho, M., Cheein, F., Postigo, J., and Carelli, R. Teleoperation of an industrial manipulator through a tcp/ip channel using eeg signals. In *Industrial Electronics, 2006 IEEE International Symposium on*, vol. 4 (2006), 3066–3071.

7. Hochberg, L. R., Bacher, D., Jarosiewicz, B., Masse, N. Y., Simeral, J. D., Vogel, J., Haddadin, S., Cash, J. L. S. S., van der Smagt, P., and Donoghue, J. P. Reach and grasp by people with tetraplegia using a neurally controlled robotic arm. *Nature 485*, 7398 (2012), 372–375.

8. Lampe, T., and Riedmiller, M. Acquiring visual servoing reaching and grasping skills using neural reinforcement learning. *IEEE International Joint Conference on Neural Networks (IJCNN)* (2013).

9. Lotte, F., Congedo, M., Lcuyer, A., Lamarche, F., and Arnaldi, B. A review of classification algorithms for EEG-based brain-computer interfaces. *Journal of Neural Engineering 4*, 2 (2007), R1–R13.

10. MacKay, D. J. C. A practical bayesian framework for backpropagation networks. *Neural Computation 4*, 3 (1992), 448–472.

11. Moran, D. Evolution of brain-computer interface: action potentials, local field potentials and electrocorticograms. *Current Opinions in Neurobiology 20*, 6 (2010), 741–745.

12. Musallam, S., Corneil, B. D., Greger, B., Scherberger, H., and Andersen, R. A. Cognitive control signals for neural prosthetics. *Science 305* (2004), 258–262.

13. Neuper, C., Müller-Putz, G. R., Scherer, R., and Pfurtscheller, G. Motor imagery and EEG-based control of spelling devices and neuroprostheses. *Progress in Brain Research 159* (2006), 393–409.

14. Oostenveld, R., and Praamstra, P. The five percent electrode system for high-resolution EEG and ERP measurements. *Clinical Neurophysiology 112*, 4 (2001), 713–719.

15. Pfurtscheller, G., and F.H. Lopes da Silva. Event-related EEG/MEG synchronization and desynchronization: basic principles. *Clinical Neurophysiology 110*, 11 (1999), 1842–1857.

16. Riedmiller, M. Neural fitted Q iteration – first experiences with a data efficient neural reinforcement learning method. In *European Conference on Machine Learning*, Springer (2005), 317–328.

17. Schalk, G., Mcfarl, D. J., Hinterberger, T., Birbaumer, N., and Wolpaw, J. R. BCI2000: A general-purpose brain-computer interface (BCI) system. *IEEE Transactions on Biomedical Engineering 51* (2004), 2004.

18. Sutton, R. S., and Barto, A. G. *Reinforcement Learning: An Introduction (Adaptive Computation and Machine Learning)*. A Bradford Book, 1998.

19. Thomson, D. Spectrum estimation and harmonic analysis. *Proceedings of the IEEE 70*, 9 (1982), 1055–1096.

20. Vidaurre, C., Kawanabe, M., von Bünau, P., Blankertz, B., and Müller, K. R. Toward unsupervised adaptation of LDA for brain-computer interfaces. *IEEE Transactions on Biomedical Engineering 58*, 3 (2011), 587–597.

21. Vidaurre, C., Sannelli, C., Müller, K. R., and Blankertz, B. Machine-learning-based coadaptive calibration for brain-computer interfaces. *Neural Computation 16* (2010).

22. Waldert, S., Pistohl, T., Braun, C., Ball, T., Aertsen, A., and Mehring, C. A review on directional information in neural signals for brain-machine interfaces. *Journal of Physiology – Paris 103*, 3–5 (2009), 244–254.

23. Wang, D., Miao, D., and Blohm, G. Multi-class motor imagery EEG decoding for brain-computer interfaces. *Frontiers in Neuroprosthetics 6* (2012), 151.

Mimetic Interaction Spaces :
Controlling Distant Displays in Pervasive Environments

Hanae Rateau
Universite Lille 1, Villeneuve
d'Ascq, France
Cite Scientifique, 59655
Villeneuve d'Ascq
hanae.rateau@inria.fr

Laurent Grisoni
Universite Lille 1, Villeneuve
d'Ascq, France
Cite Scientifique, 59655
Villeneuve d'Ascq
laurent.grisoni@lifl.fr

Bruno De Araujo
INRIA Lille
40, avenue Halley - Bat A -
Park Plaza 59650 Villeneuve
d'Ascq
bdearaujo@gmail.com

ABSTRACT

Pervasive computing is a vision that has been an inspiring long-term target for many years now. Interaction techniques that allow one user to efficiently control many screens, or that allow several users to collaborate on one distant screen, are still hot topics, and are often considered as two different questions. Standard approaches require a strong coupling between the physical location of input device, and users. We propose to consider these two questions through the same basic concept, that uncouples physical location and user input, using a mid-air approach. We present the concept of mimetic interaction spaces (MIS), a dynamic user-definition of an imaginary input space thanks to an iconic gesture, that can be used to define mid-air interaction techniques. We describe a participative design user-study, that shows this technique has interesting acceptability and elicit some definition and deletion gestures. We finally describe a design space for MIS-based interaction, and show how such concept may be used for multi-screen control, as well as screen sharing in pervasive environments.

Author Keywords

gestural interaction ; mid-air gestures; contactless interaction

ACM Classification Keywords

H.5.2 User Interfaces: Ergonomics, Evaluation / methodology, Interaction styles, User-centered design

General Terms

Human Factors; Design; Measurement.

INTRODUCTION

Grasping the mouse, or touching the pad, is currently, by far, the most common way to start interacting with an application. Such paradigms imply both proximity between user and interactive system. For interaction situations in which distance between user and screen can not be avoided(e.g distant screen),

and instrumented interaction may be difficult to deploy (public displays), or limiting (family in front of connected TV, work meetings, etc ...), mid-air gestural interaction appears to have great potential for such contexts.

Pervasive environments are contexts in which fluid interaction has a key role to play for M. Wieser's vision to be reached. We need always-available, (ideally) low-instrumented, interaction techniques, that would permit users interacting with several displays; we also need techniques that allow collaboration in the same room for a given task on the same display. Mid-air interaction still has several drawbacks that are not overcome yet; moreover it is still poorly understood, quite apart from elementary tasks [13]. A common (wrong) approach is to think about mid-air gestures as "touch at a distance", as stated in [14].

We generalize, in this article, the idea of predefined plane for mid-air interaction with distant display, and present the concept of *MIS gestures*. Instead of interacting in a pre-defined static space, we allow the user to create and delete his own interaction space at any time and place thanks to a simple gesture that mimics the interaction space.

This article first presents a user study that provides some elements of knowledge about how users, in a participative design approach, would potentially use such systems. In our results, we show that users validate the idea of a planar MIS, and that most users that run the experiment instinctively state that plane position is user-defined and dynamic (can be both created and deleted). We also show that users easily integrate mental representation of interaction MIS, since user-defined deletion gestures take plane location into account.

Finally, we provide guidelines for MIS gestures in mid-air interaction techniques. We also describe the design space associated to the presented concept, and describe the proof of concept of MIS interaction that illustrates 2 key scenarios.

RELATED WORK

Although the proposed concept is novel, we can find in literature other works that relate, on some aspects, to MIS.

Mid-air Interaction. Several virtual interaction volume techniques have been proposed in the past years. All in different contexts of use and with different properties.

Hilliges et al.[7] propose a static extension of the 2D display that allows the user to perform 3D gestures above the screen. There is a direct mapping between the hand above the surface and the output (shadows displayed). As long as the system can detect the user's hands, the user can manipulate objects of the 3D scene. In that case, the interaction volume is static, always active and of a predefined size (here the screen size).

In [6], Gustafson et al. propose a system with no visual feedback. Screen is replaced by short term memory. The user defines dynamically the space in which he wants to interact with a non-dominant hand posture as a reference point. Interactions start with a posture and stop when the user releases the pose. Three studies show that the more time spent, the more degraded memory. But using the non dominant hand as a reference point improves performance. In our concept of MIS, the short term memory is maintained by the visual feedback and the reference point is not compulsory anymore as showed in [2].

The work in [10] presents a virtual touch panel named Air-Touch Panel. The user has to form an L-shape with his left hand to define a virtual panel and then can interact with an AirTouch panel-based intelligent TV: changing channels and volume. In this work, the panel has a pre-defined size the user cannot control but he can define the position and the orientation of the panel. Our work is a generalization of the AirTouch Panel concept.

MIS interaction. To our knowledge, there is no existing studies on how users may create or delete interaction subspaces. However, some work on multitouch interaction can give some hints.

In [15] several participants conceived imaginary areas around the screen with particular properties, as clipboard or a trash can. Similarly, some of them also imagine invisible widgets and reused them. The mental representation of invisible interfaces is not unnatural or too much exotic to users. In this same study, participants mostly preferred one-hand gestures as in [11] for the efficiency/simplicity and energy saving.

In [10] the authors also conducted two studies. The first is related to what kind of click gesture will be more appropriate. Results showed that, considering the average miss-clicks, the tapping gesture is the worst, the left hand click is the more tiring and a specific gesture, which is stretching the thumb away from the index, has the highest satisfaction rate. Interestingly, in [4], the air tap is the preferred gesture to click in mid-air. The second study investigates the more appropriate size of panel to avoid miss click and satisfy user's comfort. The 24" panel was the more appropriate size. Concerning the size, in [9], Kattinakere et al. study and model a steering law for 3D gestures in above-the-surface layers, resting the hand on the surface. Results suggest that a layer should be at least 2 cm thick and that steering along more than 35 cm generates more errors.

Methodology for Eliciting gestures. We chose to carry out a gesture elicitation study, as in several prior work, in order to see how potential users could use the MISs, and what they could expect.

The methodology proposed by Nielsen et al. in [12] consists in identifying "the functions that will be evoked" by the gestures, which are in our work a creation, click and deletion functions, then, finding "the most appropriate gesture for each of those functions" by an analysis phase of the gestures performed by the users. In [15], Wobbrock et al. conducted a similar study in the context of gesture-based surface computing. They identified 27 common commands and the participants had to choose a gesture for each of these. In [11], which is the follow up of [15], the authors concluded "that participatory design methodologies [...] should be applied to gesture design".

Gesture classification. Cadoz [3] suggested a classification regarding the function of the gestures which are complementary and dependent : semiotics (modification), ergotic (perception) and epistemic (communication). But these are not appropriate for our domain. Karam and Schraefel proposed a classification adapted to HCI based on gesture styles : deictic, manipulative, semaphoric(with a cultural meaning like thumb up for OK), gesticulation(conversational gesture), sign language, multiple(combined) gestures styles. Aigner et al. presented in [1] a modified taxonomy of Karam and schraefel [8] adapted to gesture elicitation study in mid-air without speech command or sign language.

MIMETIC INTERACTION SPACES: CONCEPT DESCRIPTION

We present here the concept of Mimetic Interaction Spaces (MIS) and *MIS gestures*. A MIS is a delimited sub-space of the user's space, used to perform interaction gestures. It can be of arbitrary dimension i.e. a 1D curve, a 2D shape or a finite volume depending on the application. The chosen sub-space is simple enough so that it is possible to evaluate whether or not user's hand is within this sub-space and if gestures shall be taken into account for interaction or not. The *MIS gestures* are defined as the set of user's gestures which can be performed within such space, to interact with it, as well as to create or delete it. It may relate (but not necessarily) to a physical object, or an imaginary representation of it. By gesturing on or in the MIS, the user can interact with a distant screen, e.g control a mouse cursor on an invisible touchpad (planar MIS). We think this concept is interesting because it is more specific than the standard understanding of mid-air interaction, while obviously leaving quite an interesting design space to distant display control (shape type, dimension, space localization regarding user and display, multiple spaces, etc... see further description in this article).

Formal Definition of MIS, and MIS-based interaction technique

From the concept of MISs, we first define formally a MIS as a virtual object with four characteristic components detailed as follows: *geometric definition (GD), input reference frame (IRF), action reference frame (ARF), interaction attributes (IA)*. Each of these components are described below. We define a *MIS-based interaction technique* as a particular set of these four components.

Geometric definition (GD)

We defined here the elementary geometric aspects of a MIS: shape, orientation, scale, position. They are expressed relative to the input frame of reference of the MIS they describe.

Input Reference Frame (IRF)

This is the coordinate frame that links MIS to the physical world in which the user evolves. In the general case, a MIS can be anchored to an *entity* of the real world, possible entities being user's body or a part of it (e.g hand, head,...), or any identified object or the world (fixed position). If this entity moves, then the MIS moves as well. A MIS may have multiple IRFs. Then, a main IRF must be declared for the primary properties. Plus, it can be changed during interaction, using specific command gesture associated to the MIS.

Action Reference Frame (ARF)

This is the coordinate frame that links MIS to the display with which user is willing to interact. A MIS can have multiple ARFs. A default ARF is defined, that may be changed during interaction.

Interaction Attributes (IA)

The interaction attributes gather all properties that may be necessary to define the interaction technique based on the MIS defined by a set (GD, IRF, ARF). They may relate to human factors, data acquisition specificity, or any additional element that needs to be taken into account to define interaction technique. Such attributes may vary, both from numbers, types and values, depending on the interaction techniques we target.

USER STUDY

Our user study was designed to collect gesture data that could be used to define *MISs* and question the users on what they could expect of MIS interaction. In order to perform such study without suggesting any solution, we decided to simulate distant screens using a large curved screen (5.96 meters by 2.43 meters).Using such environment, we are able to project images of displays at different locations and of different sizes. By doing so, we expected to represent daily scenarios in an abstract way such as using a computer screen or a television at home or in collaborative working sessions.... The remaining of the section describes our experimental protocol and how it relates to our concept of *MIS* interaction. With their agreement, all participant sessions have been videotaped using a Kinect camera in front of the user and a video camera on the side recording a different point of view and sound.

Protocol

Participants had to define 90 areas corresponding to projected virtual screens of two different sizes : 32 inches and 55 inches. Each virtual screen were displayed 3 times at 15 different positions on the large screen. They could take a break every 10 trials to avoid fatigue.

For each trial, participants had to define, by a gesture or a posture, an area they thought was the most relevant and comfortable to control the shown virtual screen. Then they had to touch it as if they were interacting with the virtual screen. They were told the virtual screen could be either a computer

screen or a television. The only constraint was that they were not allowed to walk but they could turn around. After the repetitive trials, they were asked to tell which gesture they preferred during the experiment. Then they had to imagine a gesture they would perform to delete an area they have previously defined.

Participants

18 participants volunteered for the study (4 female). 8 participants worked in HCI. They were between the ages of 22 and 43 (mean: 27.6). Two participants were left-handed and one was ambidextrous. All participants used a PC and 39 % of them used tactile devices almost everyday (mostly smartphones).However, only 28 % of the participants played video games regularly. Even if they were not gamers, all of them had already tried and knew 3D gestures using the Wiimote, the Kinect, the Eyetoy or the PS Move.

Gesture Classification

To classify the different gestures performed by the participants, we used the gesture taxonomy proposed by the Aigner et al. [1] and depicted in Figure 1. This taxonomy proposes four different classes of gestures: pointing, semaphoric, pantomimic and iconic.

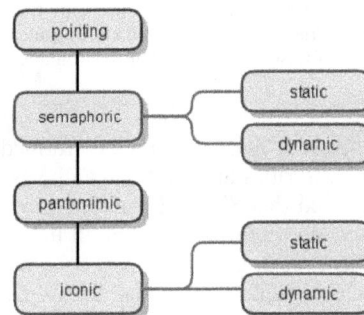

Figure 1. Classification used to analyse the gestures made in the user study.

While *pointing* gestures are mostly used to name an object or a direction, *semaphoric* gestures are gestures that are meaningful. There are *static* semaphoric gestures like the thumb-up posture that means "OK", and *dynamic* semaphoric gesture like waving the index finger sideways to mean "no". Note that these meanings are strongly dependent of the cultural background and experience of the user. *Pantomimic* gestures refer to gestures used to mimic an action like grabbing an imaginary object and rotating it. Finally *iconic* gestures represent informative gestures. They inform about the properties of an object like specifying a size or a shape. There are static iconic gestures and dynamic gestures. Unlike semaphoric gestures, no common knowledge of the user's past experience is needed to understand these kind of gestures.

Results

This section presents the results and observations of our study. We decouple our analysis into three parts related to the *MIS interaction* basic steps which are: the gestures to create it, how users can interact with it and finally how participants propose to delete it.

Interaction space creation gesture

We analyzed the video of each participant and described each gesture performed along the 90 trials of the experiment using the gesture taxonomy presented by Figure 1 and complemented with the information about which hands were used, hand postures and the relationship between the location of the gesture and the user field of view or any significant body part. We choose to discard any isolated gesture performed or slightly different variants from the same gesture.

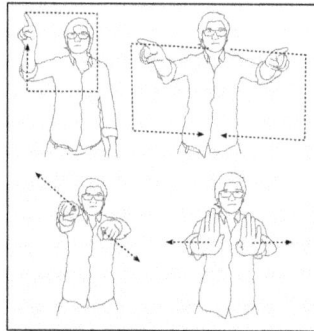

Figure 2. Frequent creation gestures proposed by the user: defining a rectangular area using one or both hands (top) and using an opening gesture in its field of view with diagonal or horizontal symmetric gesture (bottom).

Looking to the set of the 33 gestures performed by all users, 71 % of them describes an area that can be assimilated to a plane. We noticed that 89 % of users performed iconic dynamic gestures, representing 60 % of all the gestures. They mostly represent rectangular shapes (66 %) or opening gesture (28 %) along a line or diagonal delimiting the size of a frame as depicted by Figure 2. Circular motions such as circles and waving in front or around the user were less common (9 %).

Regarding hand usage, we noticed that 33 % of them exclusively defined gestures using one hand, 33 % using both hands and 33 % mixing both approaches while performing the several trials. While all unimanual gestures were mainly done using the dominant hand, most of bimanual gestures described symmetrical movements or poses. Only three users presented gestures following the asymmetric bimanual Guiard model [5]. While performing the gestures, we noticed that most of participants used a reduced set of hand poses shown in Figure 3. Index finger pointing to the screen, and mimic of a pencil were prominent among participants (77 %) compared to both L shape (27 %) and open flat hand postures (33 %).

About display position influence, we noticed that most of the participant aligned their field of view prior to start the gesture by rotating both the head and body. However, 39 % of the users depicted gestures in a fixed position regarding their body. The preferred approach (61 % of users) was to create vertical planes aligned with the field of view or the projected screen by drawing rectangles or defining static frames. In the case of horizontal or oblique planes independently of the

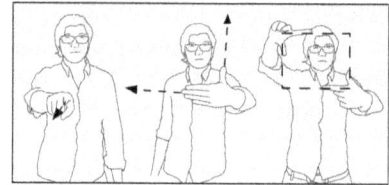

Figure 3.   The 3 main hand postures. From left to right: pointing to a given direction, flat hand posture defining a spatial reference, two L hand postures delimiting an area.

screen position or field of view user was never looking at his hands while performing the gesture.

Interacting on a MIS

For each trial, we asked the participants to touch or interact on the previously defined interaction area. They mainly simulated drawing or small push actions close to the area defined as shows Figure 4. Users touched the imaginary space using their dominant hand, except one with both hands. We noticed three different major hand poses: pointing using the index finger, pointing using a flat hand and pushing using an open hand with a percentage of 56, 22 and 17 respectively. People using an open or a flat posture tend to push, grab or swipe close to the MIS definition. While participants using their index finger tried to mimic drawing short scribbles or push small imaginary buttons. These behaviors showed a strong materialization of the MIS as a physical tool.

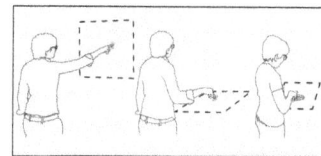

Figure 4. Common touch gestures proposed by the subjects: pointing on a vertical or horizontal imaginary area and touching the non dominant hand as a reference.

Deleting a MIS

At the end of experiment, we asked participants to propose a delete gesture considering that their interaction zone creation was persistent. Looking to the 23 gestures collected, we noticed a strong usage of pantomimic gestures since most of users materialized the interaction MIS. 23 % of the proposals do not fit in this classification such as leaving the interactive area, waiting for it to disappear, drawing a cross or using the inverse of creation movement. For users that used non dominant hand as a support to interact, the area shall disappear just by removing the hand. Figure 5 illustrates the main proposed gestures.

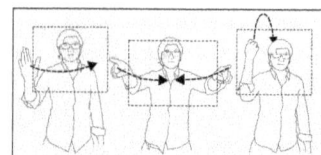

Figure 5.   Participants delete gesture proposals: pushing the area with one hand, closing the MIS using both hand or throwing it away to a given location.

Observations

From the current user study, we can highlight the following observations and remarks to implement MIS based applications and better take advantage of the design space offered by such concept.

Make MIS planar, and dynamic : most of users spontaneously create planar MISs, and take for granted that they can specify them in arbitrary position, without any experience.

User tends to turn in the direction of the screen : in that case, MIS tends to be vertical, and directly relates to the field of view of user. In case where users do not orientate themselves in the direction of the screen, MIS is created horizontally, for indirect interaction.

Gesture for creating and deleting MISs can be parameterized gestures: for most users, these gestures specify both a *command* (e.g create subspace) and some *parameters* of the command (e.g some geometric features such as MIS location for creation), in the same gesture.

User has proper mental perception of MISs he/she creates Since all users provided delete gestures that start in a location devoted to the MIS that was previously created. The MIS became real.

DESIGN SPACE

From previous experiment observations and the MIS formal definition, we explore the design space according the four components defining a MIS. The mentioned variations can be combined to provide a large and flexible set of mis-based interaction techniques.

On Geometric Definition One specific shape could represent one specific range of possible actions. A plane may refer to a 2D control of a cursor, whereas a sphere, for example, may suggest a rotation control of virtual objects. As well, a particular orientation may refer to a particular action. Different dimensions could allow more or less accuracy.

On Input Reference Frame Attaching a MIS to the world as a reference frame of input links it to the world. Even if the user moves, the MIS will not. If the MIS is associated and linked to the user, the latter can move around the environment keeping the MIS next to him at the same position regarding his position. The MIS could also be attached to a physical object. The MIS will remain attached to the object and then can be shared in a collaboration context.

On Action Reference Frame As explained in the section , Action Reference Frame links MIS to the display it controls. It can be associated to a static display or the ARF can also be associated to moving display. In this latter configuration, whatever the position of the display, the MIS still controls it. The ARF may be re-affected in a multiple displays configuration.

On Interaction Attributes In this section, only very few "properties" of the MIS are addressed. These attributes may enable bimanual gestures, tuning of the sensitivity of the MIS, relative or absolute mapping, 3D or 2D input . . .

MIS PROOF OF CONCEPT

Following the observations resulting from our user study, we devised an application as a proof of concept to let one or more users interact with one or more distant displays.

Several key scenarios were possible to implement regarding both the number of users and the number of screens. The one user interacting with one screen scenario, the one user with multiple screens scenario and the multiple users with one screen scenario.

The application consisted of providing to two users the capacity to control and share the mouse cursor between several displays allowing to interact with any content displayed by the screens. We chose to implement a planar MISs solution defined by rectangular gestures since such gestures were the most common among our user study. The application was implemented as a daemon sending mouse inputs directly to the operating system (Microsoft Windows 7).

To track the user's gestures, we chose to rely on a wireless magnetic based tracking system i.e. Liberty LATUS system from Polhemus complemented with a button to emulate the mouse click as depicted in Figure 6. Such solution was preferred to non intrusive tracking solutions such as the Microsoft Kinect depth sensor, in order to obtain reliable positions and orientations of the user's hand. However, our MIS concept could be used in a more pervasive environment using several cameras to track users in a non-intrusive way. All input data were streamed to our software daemon using a TUIO client approach.

Figure 6. The user is only equipped with (a) a tracker and (b) a wired button.

The details of the implementation are discussed in the following chronologically from creation gesture to deletion gesture.

Application

The detection of a MIS creation gesture is made through 3 steps analyzing the user's hand motion. **First**, both the beginning and the end of a gesture are triggered based on threshold values over the hand acceleration. All the positions and orientations retrieved in between these two events are recorded tracking user gestures. **The second step** is the computation of the plane thanks to a least square method. We then define the origin, the normal and construct the reference frame of the plane from the average of the orientation vectors of the user's hand during the gesture to get the "up direction" (i.e y-axis) and the "right direction" (i.e x-axis) as depicted by Figure 7. The dimensions are computed by projecting the gesture points on the newly defined plane and computing the aligned bounding box on its reference frame. **Finally** to detect rectangular shape creation gesture, we use the 1$ recognizer on the 2D path corresponding to the projection of the 3D hand positions on the pre-computed plane. A pop-up on the screen informs the user the MIS is created.

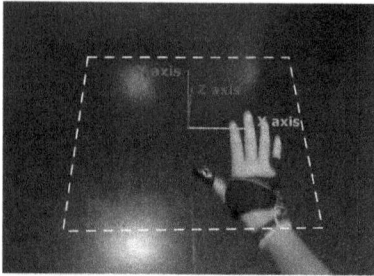

Figure 7. The frame of reference of a MIS

Once the MIS is created, each 3D position received is then treated regarding the MIS. When the hand is near enough from the MIS, we allow the user to control the mouse cursor with his hand. The mapping between the hand position in the MIS and the mouse cursor position on the screen is absolute.

Currently this proof of concept was defined to track two users max and interact with two screens. When the MIS is created by a user, it is automatically attached to the closer screen regarding the user's position. The directional swipe gesture allows to change such default binding.

To delete such space, we choose to detect horizontal swipe gestures starting within the MIS and finishing out of it with a given velocity and along the x-axis of the plane.

CONCLUSION

We presented elements of knowledge about mid-air interaction with distant displays. We introduced the concept of *MIS gestures*, that we think is a flexible approach to mid-air interaction within pervasive environments, as the associated design space is quite large. We showed that MIS gestures are, to the highest acceptability, planar and dynamic. The application developed allows to see few interesting possibilities among all of possible MIS-based interaction techniques.

As future work, a final complete set of questions related to MIS is the practical application of such concept to collaborative, co-located interaction contexts, e.g. such as command centers. Studies of uses of MIS within such contexts would be interesting in order to understand how to take the best from the presented concept, adapted to collaborative environments.

Also, an in-depth study of the possible applications of MIS may highlight, within all mid-air possible interaction contexts, some specific subsets, that opens new research directions. Interaction techniques, visual feedback, reachable interaction precision taking into account distance of view, are interesting questions in this context.

REFERENCES

1. Aigner, R., Wigdor, D., Benko, H., Haller, M., Lindbauer, D., Ion, A., Zhao, S., and Koh, J. T. K. V. Understanding mid-air hand gestures: A study of human preferences in usage of gesture types for hci. Tech. Rep. MSR-TR-2012-11, Redmond, WA, USA, Nov 2012.

2. Balakrishnan, R., and Hinckley, K. The role of kinesthetic reference frames in two-handed input performance. In *Proceedings of UIST '99*, ACM (New York, NY, USA, 1999), 171–178.

3. Cadoz, C. Le geste canal de communication homme/machine: la communication instrumentale. *TSI. Technique et science informatiques 13*, 1 (1994), 31–61.

4. Camp, F., Schick, A., and Stiefelhagen, R. How to click in mid-air. In *Proc. of HCII 2013* (July 2013), 78–86.

5. Guiard, Y. Asymmetric division of labor in human skilled bimanual action: The kinematic chain as a model, 1987.

6. Gustafson, S., Bierwirth, D., and Baudisch, P. Imaginary interfaces: spatial interaction with empty hands and without visual feedback. In *Proceedings of UIST '10*, ACM (NY, USA, 2010), 3–12.

7. Hilliges, O., Izadi, S., Wilson, A. D., Hodges, S., Garcia-Mendoza, A., and Butz, A. Interactions in the air: adding further depth to interactive tabletops. In *Proc. of UIST '09*, ACM (NY, USA, 2009), 139–148.

8. Karam, M., and m. c. schraefel. A taxonomy of gestures in human computer interactions. Technical report, University of Southampton, 2005.

9. Kattinakere, R. S., Grossman, T., and Subramanian, S. Modeling steering within above-the-surface interaction layers. In *Proceedings of CHI '07*, ACM (New York, NY, USA, 2007), 317–326.

10. Lin, S.-Y., Shie, C.-K., Chen, S.-C., and Hung, Y.-P. Airtouch panel: A re-anchorable virtual touch panel. In *Proceedings of ACM Multimedia 2013 (ACM MM)*, ACM (october 2013), 625–628.

11. Morris, M., Wobbrock, J., and Wilson, A. Understanding users' preferences for surface gestures. In *Proceedings of GI '10* (Toronto, Canada, 2010), 261–268.

12. Nielsen, M., Moeslund, T., Störring, M., and Granum, E. A procedure for developing intuitive and ergonomic gesture interfaces for hci. In *Proc. of the 5th Internation Gesture Workshop*, GW 2003 (2003).

13. Ren, G., and O'Neill, E. 3d selection with freehand gesture. *Computers & Graphics 37*, 3 (2013), 101 – 120.

14. Wigdor, D., and Wixon, D. *Brave NUI World: Designing Natural User Interfaces for Touch and Gesture*, 1st ed. Morgan Kaufmann Publishers Inc., San Francisco, CA, USA, 2011.

15. Wobbrock, J., Morris, M., and Wilson, A. User-defined gestures for surface computing. In *Proc. of CHI '09*, ACM (NY, USA, 2009), 1083–1092.

Recognition of Understanding Level and Language Skill using Measurements of Reading Behavior

Pascual Martínez-Gómez
The University of Tokyo
National Institute of Informatics
pascual@nii.ac.jp

Akiko Aizawa
The University of Tokyo
National Institute of Informatics
aizawa@nii.ac.jp

ABSTRACT
The reading act is an intimate and elusive process that is important to understand. Psycholinguists have long studied the effects of task, personal or document characteristics on reading behavior. An essential factor in the success of those studies lies in the capability of analyzing eye-movements. These studies aim to recognize causal effects on patterns of eye-movements, by contriving variations in task, personal or document characteristics. In this work, we follow the opposite direction. We present a formal framework to recognize reader's level of understanding and language skill given measurements of reading behavior via eye-gaze data. We show significant error reductions to recognize these attributes and provide a detailed study of the most discriminative features.

Author Keywords
Reading behavior; eye-tracking; cognitive and user profiling

ACM Classification Keywords
H.1.2 Information Systems: User/Machine Systems

INTRODUCTION
Reading is a fundamental activity that is not well understood, since it involves complex and unobservable cognitive processes. The mechanism behind those cognitive processes is determined by personal attributes of the reader such as the native language or background knowledge, and influences reading behavior. The analysis of eye-movements to measure reading behavior has been extensively studied in the psycholinguistic literature [48] and has been shown to reflect online cognitive processing [30, 39] when reading text. Current eye-trackers allow to record areas of attention unobtrusively, which may reveal personal interests on the content in that text area or individual difficulties to integrate information.

Document characteristics such as lexical difficulty [39], syntactic complexity [17] or semantic ambiguity [49] also proved

to influence reading behavior and their effects were successfully observed analyzing eye-movements. The common strategy was to carefully contrive words or sentences that manifest the linguistic variation under study and to observe the effect on fixation times or regression events of readers. Analyzing eye-movements is, however, a challenging task due to variable and systematic errors introduced by eye-trackers [25] and the difficulty to align fixation events to words in a text. For this reason, most studies investigating the influence of linguistic features on reading behavior were limited to isolated words or sentences. The Dundee corpus [31] was one of the earliest attempts to enable quantitative analysis of eye-movements in natural reading tasks, where subjects read documents splitted into screens containing five lines of text.

The objectives of these analyses typically follow two directions. The first category consists in integrating measurements of eye-movements across subjects to obtain a *general* model of reading behavior. Examples of this category are the estimation of cognitive cost models [51], recognition of machine translation and text quality [18, 5]. Contrarily, works in the second category aim to model *individual* differences in reading behavior among subjects to discriminate them according to certain personal attributes. Using eye-movements to build individual models contributed to create personalized applications without the need of explicit user feedback, such as recommendation and summarization systems [54, 55], document filtering [12] and query expansion [13].

Our work is motivated by the latter objective, where we aim to recognize task or personal attributes such as language skill or reader's level of understanding given measurements of eye-movement and characteristics of the document. Thus, we can state our hypothesis as:

Hypothesis: A combination of eye-movement features and document characteristics are predictive of language skill and level of understanding.

The contribution of this work is to propose a formal and general framework to build recognizers (predictors) of personal and task attributes given measurements of reading behavior via eye-movements and document characteristics. We also provide a detailed study of the most discriminative features to recognize target attributes and characterize readers according to their patterns of reading behavior.

In the next section, we review similar efforts to recognize personal and task attributes in behavioral disciplines. In Methodology section, we describe the rationale behind our features of eye-movement and linguistic characteristics of documents. Then, we introduce our framework to combine these features. In Experiments section, we assess the recognition performance of our systems, study feature importance and characterize readers according to their reading behaviors. We dedicate Discussion section to discuss the limitations and degree of success achieved by our feature set in this recognition task and the implications of our findings. Finally, a summary of our conclusions can be found in the last section.

RELATED WORK

In human behavioral sciences, researchers strive to understand what influences human behavior. Systematic analyses are typically performed via controlled environmental conditions or via naturalistic observations. Recent advances in sensor technology allow to measure changes in body temperature, galvanic skin fluctuations or superficial brain electrical activity, which are signals that help to describe and quantify human behavior. From a computational perspective, there have been recent investigations in integrating these measurements to analyze their relationships to external stimuli. In [35], researchers attempted to recognize an intimate human quality such as "affect" using a combination of facial images with prosodic and spectral features from the voice. In [3], they also tried to recognize emotions using other behavior measurements such as brainwaves or mouse movements.

In sociolinguistics, much has been investigated about observable effects of author's characteristics in written productions [34, 4]. The electronic availability of large collections of text in blogs on internet has also inspired practitioners of computational linguistics to investigate effects of author's attributes in their written productions [50, 1, 11]. They showed that age and gender are reflected as variations in language style and content, and they had different degrees of success in recognizing those author's attributes. These works were followed by others that used more sophisticated features such as patterns in sequences of Part of Speech (POS) tags [43], or that aimed to recognize other personal attributes such as regional origin or political orientations from Twitter [47]. To recognize age, gender and native language, other forms of modern informal communications were successfully used such as conversation transcripts and e-mail [22] or transcribed telephone conversations [8]. As has been shown, spontaneous or personal expressions can potentially reflect personal characteristics that would otherwise be difficult to recognize. In [40], researchers attempted to recognize reading performance, which is a slightly different target attribute in nature since it depends both on the person and the task. They examined atypical pauses in transcriptions of temporally aligned prosodic speech to recognize reading skill. While individual differences may reflect reading performance, reading hesitations of a sufficiently large population would reveal actual difficulties associated to the text being read.

Our work shares the objectives described above, in that we aim to recognize a personal attribute such as English language skill, and a task attribute such as level of understanding. We described how human behavior expressions such as written text or transcribed speech has been used to recognize personal

and task attributes. In this work we use measurements on eye-movements when reading, which are a more subtle and unconscious modality of human behavior expression.

There are several factors that influence eye-movements and that have been traditionally investigated. The first factor relates to the characteristics of the stimuli, such as linguistic features of the text or objects in an image. The second factor involves task characteristics such as objective (e.g. memorize, understand, etc.) or time constraints. Refer to [48] for a careful review. Personal attributes have also proved to influence eye-movements. In [28], subjects from different ages were exposed to emotional stimuli and the researchers analyzed the patterns of eye-movements to discover attentional preference. Differences in patterns of eye-movements have also been reported in the context of autism studies [7].

Eye-movements were also used as implicit feedback in usability studies and information foraging [23, 16]. There is a growing interest in the community of information retrieval to understand what personal and task characteristics influence user behavior as reflected by eye-movements [44, 36, 2]. The common approach is to consider eye-movements as a dependent variable of personal or task characteristics and test for significance in eye-movement variability between different personal or task conditions. This approach follows a causal reasoning since eye-movements are the result of an interaction between the subject and the stimuli. In our work, however, our independent variables are measurements on eye-movements, and we aim to recognize unobservable personal and task latent attributes given these measurements. Although we do not attempt to model the causal relationship between personal and task attributes to eye-movements, we will be able to provide an idea of what are the features of reading behavior that best characterize different personal or task attributes from a computational perspective.

Although regularities in eye-movements across subjects have been reported in eye-tracking research [24], we aim to infer individualities from the observation of reading behavior. To our knowledge, there are only two works that attempted to recognize personal or task attributes from measurements of eye-movements in natural reading tasks. In [38], every reading session was represented using a fixed-size feature vector where each component contained the fixation time on a certain linguistic feature. They found that a projection of these fixed-size feature vectors onto two or three principal components led to a separation of subjects according to their document understanding. Although the idea was promising, they did not provide a formal evaluation nor a hypothesis test to complement their results, due to the small number of subjects (9) in their experimentation. The work in [33] proposed to compute the distribution of fixation time on every word with the intention to infer language ability. However, no evaluation was carried out to measure the success of the approach.

In our work, we aim to recognize document understanding and language ability, as we think those attributes might be important for user profiling given measurements of eye-movements in a naturalistic reading environment. To that end, we use a wide array of gaze and linguistic features. The work in [29] provides an extensive summary of the most relevant gaze features traditionally used in the eye-tracking literature. We borrow features that are suitable for reading tasks and develop some other specific features for this occasion. We provide a formal evaluation of the recognition capabilities to infer personal and task latent attributes given measurements of eye-movements from 39 subjects. Then, we study the most relevant features of reading behavior that contribute to the recognition task and characterize readers with different levels of understanding using their patterns of reading behavior.

METHODOLOGY

We proceed to describe the latent personal and task attributes that we aim to recognize, and motivate the features that were used as our predictors. Then, we describe our recognition systems and the method to select the most relevant features.

Personal and task latent attributes

We work under the assumption that personal and task attributes are reflected in reading behavior. We define personal and task *latent* attributes as those attributes of the user or the task that cannot be directly observed by our system. In this work, our personal attributes are a subjective and objective measurement of English language skill:

English: Self-reported language ability in English measured in three levels: beginner, intermediate or advanced.

ToE: English language ability as measured by a normalized score in either the Test of English for International Communication (TOEIC) or Test of English as a Foreign Language (TOEFL), scaled to mean = 0 and standard deviation = 1.

The task attribute that we aim to recognize relates to "understanding", which depends on the reader and the text:

Understanding: A quantification of document understanding using an exhaustive questionnaire after reading every document, scaled to mean = 0 and standard deviation = 1.

Binarized understanding: Reading sessions where subjects' understandings are below the first quartile or above the third quartile are labeled as "low" or "high" level of understanding.

Feature extraction

We divide our features into two groups. The first group contains features that are computed solely from gaze data, such as sequence of fixations, saccades or changes in pupil diameters. The second group consists of features that combine gaze data and linguistic information, such as the proportion of fixation time on prepositions or long words.

Gaze features

Our gaze features are related to fixations, saccades and pupil dilations. Fixations are short periods of time (between 200 and 300 milliseconds), where eyes gaze to a still location and are typically associated to lexical decoding. Saccades are rapid eye-movements used to change the fixation location. Although lexical processes may also occur during saccadic eye-movements [27], saccade length may also be an effective signal to recognize skilled readers in syntactic integration. Pupil dilation has proved to reflect cognitive effort in certain

tasks [45]. However, pupil response may have some delays and obey to conditions other than textual content, such as luminosity or contrast in different screen locations, but they are included in this study due to their potential discrimination power. We collected several statistics of this features.

Number of fixations: Skilled readers have an increased ability of identifying words in the parafoveal region of the gaze point. Thus, the number of fixations per 100 words may reflect reading skill or education level.

Reading time: Total reading time per 100 words is a rough measure of information processing speed. A long reading time may reflect difficulties in understanding or a careful interpretation of the content which may lead to greater comprehension. Although this feature might be an ambiguous predictor of how well a subject understands a document, it may reflect how familiar the subject is to the topic of the text.

Average fixation time and **standard deviation of fixation time**: Cognitive effort in early stages of reading such as lexical decoding might be reflected by larger fixation times. Since fixation time has a large variability during a reading session, we compute the average and the standard deviation to obtain some information about the distribution.

Maximum fixation time: Some mental processes might be blocking and prevent the reader to proceed until they are resolved. We extract the maximum fixation time from every session to account for these potentially blocking situations.

Fixation mean velocity and **fixation mean acceleration**: Confident readers may produce longer saccades to advance faster along the text. We compute the mean of the first and second derivatives of fixation locations with respect to x and y coordinates, obtaining the fixation mean velocity and acceleration in x and y coordinates (four features).

Saccade median length: There are different types of saccadic eye-movements. Forward saccades are the most common type in sequential reading; regressions are backward saccades to previously read content; and return sweeps are used to proceed to the beginning of the next line. The length of saccades may give a sense of reader skill in navigating across the text, but the average of saccade length is dominated by few long return sweeps. Thus, we compute the median saccade length to exclude return sweeps from this feature.

Number of regressions: There are multiple possible causes of regressions in natural reading, such as resolving coreferences or semantic contradictions. The number of regressions per 100 words may reflect hesitations in integrating new information or other reading difficulties.

Pupil max-min diff: To quantify cognitive effort, we measure the difference between the maximum and minimum diameter of the pupil during the reading of a document [45].

Pupil standard deviation: Variations in pupil response to visual stimuli may reveal genuine intention of understanding. Thus, we compute the standard deviation of pupil dilations.

Pupil mean velocity and **pupil mean acceleration**: The velocity and acceleration of changes in the pupil diameter may

Linguistic feature	Short description	Type	Binary
All uppercase	Tokens with all letters capitalized	Lexical	Yes
Contains uppercase	Tokens with at least one letter capitalized	Lexical	Yes
Numbers	Token with at least one digit (e.g. protein name)	Lexical	Yes
Word length	Number of syllables	Lexical	No
Perplexity	Lexical surprise as given by an N-gram language model	Lexical/Syntactic	No
Prepositions	Whether the token is a preposition	Syntactic	Yes
Verbs	Whether the token is a verb	Syntactic	Yes
Nouns	Whether the token is a noun	Syntactic	Yes
Terminal nodes	Ratio of terminal nodes to non-terminal nodes in HPSG parse tree	Syntactic	No
Dependency distance	Maximum syntactic dependency distance spanning current token	Syntactic	No
Dependency density	Number of dependencies spanning current token	Syntactic	No
FoM	Figure of merit in building HPSG parse tree for sentence of current token	Syntactic	No
Sentence length	Number of words in sentence of current token	Syntactic	No
Passive	Verbs or verb phrases in passive form	Syntactic	Yes
Named entity	Names of person, location or organization	Semantic	Yes
Height hypernym	Quantification of concreteness of term	Semantic	No
General	Tokens appearing in list of general and common words	Semantic	Yes
Academic	Tokens appearing in list of academic words	Semantic	Yes
Out of Vocabulary	Tokens not appearing in any list of words	Semantic	Yes
Coreference distance	Maximum coreference distance spanning current token	Discourse	No
Lexical chains	Number of active lexical chains at current token	Discourse	No
Discourse connectors	Whether the token is (part of) a discourse connector	Discourse	Yes
Line feed	Token at the beginning or the end of a line (not sentence)	Physical	Yes

Table 1: Linguistic features used to compute fixation time distribution. Linguistic features were mainly of lexical, syntactic, semantic and discourse nature. About half of the features were binary, while the rest were normalized in the interval $[0, 1]$.

also reflect the intensity of cognitive effort. We compute these two features as the first and second derivative of the pupil diameter from the sequence of fixations.

Linguistic features

The assumption behind this type of features is that the proportion of fixation duration on certain linguistic features is different among different types of readers. For example, fixating 200 milliseconds on a verb might be the typical reading behavior of a native reader, but fixating 200 milliseconds on a preposition may reveal language difficulties. There are multiple gaze features that could be measured on different text locations, such as fixation time, number of regressions or pupil dilation. However, gaze features related to regressions or pupil dilations on text locations are difficult to interpret. In the case of regressions, they may occur several words or sentences after their actual cause, when the reader does not expect to recover from processing errors anymore. In the case of pupil dilations, they might be caused by changes in brightness in different physical locations. For this reason, our only gaze feature on text locations will be the duration of fixations.

We characterize text locations by the linguistic features they contain. Some linguistic features are binary, such as whether a word is a "verb" or a "preposition". Other features are quantified using real numbers that ultimately can be normalized to be in the range $[0, 1]$, such as "sentence length". Intuitively, linguistic features that span more than one word or that are very frequent are more likely to accumulate longer fixation times. To account for frequent features and to preserve simplicity, all linguistic features are defined at word level, such

that every word in the span of a certain feature is quantified as the whole span[1]. Let t_j be the total amount of fixation time on word w_j, and let $f_{i,j}$ be the quantification of linguistic feature i at word w_j[2]. Then, we can estimate the normalized fixation time on linguistic feature i, T_i as:

$$T_i = \frac{\sum_j t_j \cdot f_{i,j}}{(\sum_j t_j) \cdot (\sum_j f_{i,j})} \quad (1)$$

T_i will account for the proportion of the total amount of fixation time that every linguistic feature i attracts from the reader, and they will be used as predictive signals to recognize personal and task latent attributes. The list of linguistic features can be found in Table 1. A graphical example of proportions of fixation times on linguistic feature "lexical chains" can be found in Figure 1.

Latent attribute recognition

We can formulate the problem of recognizing personal and task latent attributes as a pattern recognition problem where, given measurements of reading behavior, our objective is to predict the value of the target attributes. Some latent attributes such as "ToE" scores or the quantification of "understanding" are real numbers, and we will perform the recognition in the form of a regression. Other latent attributes such as

---

[1] In the case of the feature "sentence length", every word has its feature value equal to the length of its sentence.
[2] For feature "is noun", $f_{\text{noun},j} = 1$ if w_j is a noun.

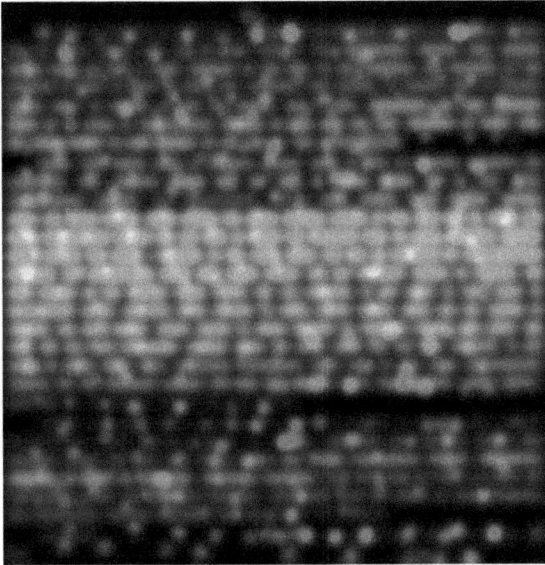

Figure 1: Fixation times (red) on a quantification of active lexical chains (green) of a single reader. Larger fixation times are displayed as intense red points. Density of active lexical chains at every token (rectangular shapes) is proportional to intensity of green color. Fixation and text overlaps in yellow.

self-reported English skill (three levels) or "binarized understanding" take values within a limited set of classes. In this case, the recognition will take the form of a classification.

Formally, let $x_1, \ldots, x_p$ be the feature measurements of reading behavior described above, and let $y_1, \ldots, y_q$ be the values of personal and task latent attributes of a subject reading a certain document. The objective is to construct mechanisms f_i that are capable to predict attributes y_i:

$$\hat{y}_i = f_i(x_1, \ldots, x_p) \qquad (2)$$

We measure the degree of success in recognizing latent attribute y_i by quantifying errors of its prediction mechanism:

$$\text{error}_i = \text{difference}(y_i, \hat{y}_i) \qquad (3)$$

where the difference between the predicted attribute value $\hat{y}_i$ and the actual attribute value y_i is the arithmetic difference between their numerical values in a regression task, or a $0-1$ error if their classes differ in a classification task.

We use two models to build recognition mechanisms of latent attributes, namely Support Vector Machines (SVM) [14, 19] and Random Forests [10]. Both models are capable of performing classification and regression, but they are based in substantially different ideas.

Support Vector Machines build a hyper-tube for regression or a separating hyper-plane for classification and apply non-linear transformations to input feature values. Parameters for regression and classification are estimated with the objective of reducing the error on the training set. When estimating the regression or classification parameters, a certain degree C of mispredicted training observations might be allowed, which controls overfitting and increases performance on unseen data. Another aspect of Support Vector Machines that has to be decided is the non-linear transformation function of the input feature values. The parameter C an the non-linear transformation function are usually application-dependent.

Random Forests are built by growing a multitude of classification or regression decision trees with a controlled variance. Variability in the trees is introduced by two techniques that complement each other. The first one consists in growing each tree with a different random subsample of the training set. The second technique consists in using a different number of m randomly selected features to split decision nodes at each tree. Predictions of Random Forests are computed as the mode or average in classification or regression, respectively. The error rate in random forests depends on the correlation between trees and the predictive strength of individual trees. Both factors are controlled by m, which can be estimated well from a disjoint set of training samples at each tree.

In the recognition of latent attributes such as level of understanding or language skill, some features may contain information that is useful to recognize the latent attribute, but other features may not be discriminative and simply add noise to the model. In order to estimate the usefulness or importance of each feature j to recognize each attribute y_i, we used the permutation test technique of Random Forests. For every tree, we randomly exclude about $1/3$ of the training data into a separate subset called out-of-bag samples, and we grow the tree with the remaining $2/3$ of the data. For every tree, we compute classification or regression for the out-of-bag samples. Then, we randomly permute the value of feature j for these samples, and compute the new decision at every tree. Importance of feature j can be computed as the difference between the number of correct votes for the original out-of-bag sample and the number of correct votes for the out-of-bag sample with perturbed feature j, normalized by the number of trees. The feature set in our decision functions f_i will consist of features with positive importance.

EXPERIMENTS

Data

Document characteristics
There were 2 documents on 3 topics (6 in total), about economics, nutrition and astronomy written in English. Documents contained 22.5 sentences and 469 words on average. The text of each document was displayed entirely on a single 23" screen with a resolution of 1920×1080 px. The font family of the text was Courier New with a font size of 16px and line height of 30px. The upper left corner of the text was located at pixels $(500, 24)$ and the bottom right corner at $(1400, 980)$, displayed at a distance of 70 cm from the reader.

We computed proportions of fixation times on linguistic features from Table 1. Lexical and Part of Speech (POS) features were averaged at word level to obtain a single estimation for every document. As an example, feature "Numbers" denotes the percentage of tokens that contain digits. Named entities, percentage of prepositions, nouns and verbs were extracted using the NLTK toolkit [6]. Word lengths (in syllables) were computed using the CMU pronunciation dictionary [52], and word perplexity was computed using Google 5-grams [9] with deleted interpolation. To estimate syntactic difficulty [26], we computed maximum dependency densities and average distance between dependents, using a dependency parser [32]. To estimate phrase-based syntactic difficulty, we computed terminal node to non-terminal node ratio, figure of merit of parsing surprise and average number of passive clauses using an HPSG parser [42]. We obtained the height of hypernyms, as a measure of term concreteness, by computing the average distance between lemmas to the most abstract term in WordNet [20]. Features "General", "Academic" and "Out of Vocabulary" denote the average number of words in the General Word Service List [53], in the Academic Word List [15], or in none of them. Linguistic features related to discourse were the average distance between mentions and their referents, maximum number of active lexical chains [21] (both computed using a coreference resolver [46]), and the percentage of tokens that are discourse connectors from a hand-crafted list of 279 connectors.

Documents had different text lengths and linguistic characteristics. For that purpose, we normalized our measurements, first by document and then across all reading sessions. Thus, all feature values of pure gaze and fixation proportions on linguistic features were centered and scaled, to have mean $= 0$ and standard deviation $= 0$.

Eye-tracking sessions

We collected fixation times on every word using the eye-tracker Tobii TX300, and used a text-gaze aligner [37] to correct systematic errors introduced by the eye-tracker. No chinrest was used, to favor naturalistic reading behavior. There were 40 subjects participating in our study, but one of them was discarded due to unrecoverable calibration errors. From a manual inspection of eye-data quality, we found that 20% of sessions displayed an excellent tracking signal and perfect text-gaze alignment. About 70% of sessions had good eye-data quality but displayed text-gaze misalignments in some parts of the screen. The remaining sessions displayed poor tracking signal and strong text-gaze misalignments. Although eye-tracking errors and text-gaze misalignments may influence negatively on the recognition accuracy, we decided to include all data in our experiments since errors are a common factor in naturalistic applications of eye-tracking.

The two documents of each topic were randomly flipped for each reader, and the three topics were also randomly permuted. A questionnaire was presented in the web browser after reading each document, and subjects answered 8 single and multiple choice questions related to the document. The average duration of a reading and question-answering session was 1 hour, and subjects were compensated with the equivalent to 20 US dollars in cash. We collected data from 234 eye-tracking sessions (39 subjects $\times$ 6 documents), which was later splitted into training and test sets following a leaving-one-out cross-validation to evaluate our recognition systems.

There were 12 female and 27 male subjects, with ages ranging from 22 to 65 years (avg. 30 years, std. 8.4). Most subjects were non-native English speakers linked to academia, with varying language skills and background knowledge. All readers self-reported on their own English language skill. Thus, our data set for this personal attribute consisted in 234 observations. We had 22 readers reporting on their TOEFL or TOEIC scores, and thus we had 132 reading sessions annotated with a normalized score of English language skill. For the recognition of quantified understanding score, all readers were tested with questionnaires after reading each text. Thus, all 234 reading sessions were used as data points for this attribute. The binarized version of understanding ("understanding bin") consisted in the first and fourth quartile of quantified understanding scores, corresponding to 127 reading sessions from 38 different readers.

To inform our baseline, we used the prior on the training data for the target attribute. That is, for classification, we obtain the most common class in the training data and use it to predict the class of the test sample. For regression, the baseline computes the average value of the target attribute on the training data (e.g. average understanding score), and uses it to assign such score to the test sample. SVMs used an RBF kernel and the parameter C was estimated from the training data. Random Forests were estimated using 500 trees.

Results

Figure 2 compares system performance to our baseline in a leaving-one-out cross-validation. That is, at every iteration, the reading session of one subject is selected as a test sample and all remaining reading sessions are used as a training set. To avoid overfitting and other biases, all other reading sessions of the test subject are removed from the training data.

Random Forests recognized English language skill (ToE) with a statistically significant (p-value $= 0.015$) lower error than baseline. However, neither SVMs nor Random Forests found patterns in reading behavior that are discriminative of self-reported English skill. To our surprise, the correlation between self-reported English skill and the normalized ToE score is -0.39, which shows considerable differences in our subject's perceptions of their own English language ability. In the regression task of recognizing the normalized text understanding score, our algorithms did not capture any meaningful pattern that helps to predict this task attribute. In the binary classification task of recognizing text understanding level, the systems obtained significant (p-values $< 10^{-6}$) error reductions when discriminating between readers with high and low levels of understanding. We also computed the t-test significance of error reductions in this task, when comparing to a baseline with 50% of error, and obtained p-values below $4 \cdot 10^{-4}$ for both SVM and Random Forest methods. This suggests that recognizing a binarized understanding level is a substantially easier task than its regression counterpart.

Variable importance

Table 2 displays the top 10 most discriminative features for attributes that we succeeded to recognize. In general, pure gaze features proved to be more discriminative than fixation time

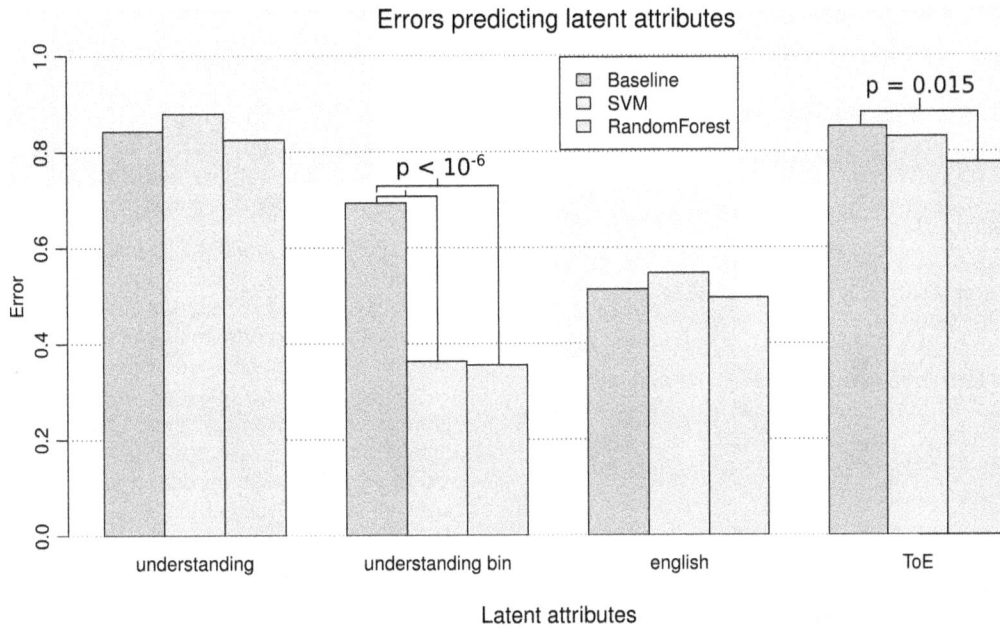

Figure 2: Average error in recognizing latent attributes using Baseline, SVMs and Random Forests. Statistically significant error reductions are labeled with their p-values computed using Wilcoxon paired t-test. Our systems had a considerable success when recognizing the binary classification of understanding level (understanding bin), and mild but significant error reduction in recognizing English language skill as measured by a test of English (ToE).

No.	ToE	understanding bin
1	reading time	fixation average
2	saccade median length	saccade median length
3	fixation mean acceleration x	fixation mean acceleration x
4	fixation std	discourse connectors
5	fixation mean velocity y	fixation std
6	fixation average	fixation mean velocity x
7	num regressions	num fixations
8	pupil mean velocity	reading time
9	fixation mean acceleration y	pupil mean acceleration
10	num fixations	num regressions

Table 2: Top 10 most discriminative features to recognize English language skill (ToE) and level of understanding (understanding bin), sorted in descending order of discriminative power. Pure gaze features are in general more discriminative than proportions of fixation time on linguistic features.

on quantifications of linguistic features. In the task of recognizing English language skill (ToE), reading time proved to be a very discriminant feature in our laboratory conditions, since subjects were probably well motivated to complete the reading task. However, these conditions may not hold when users can be driven by different reading objectives. Other very discriminative features were "saccade median length" and "fixation mean acceleration x", which are two similar features that measure the distance between two or three consecutive fixations. The fourth and sixth most discriminative features in recognizing ToE were "fixation std" and "fixation average", which relate to the duration of fixations and their variability during the reading session. These features have been reported to correlate with speed in lexical processing in the literature on psycholinguistics [48].

In the binary classification task of recognizing the level of understanding, the most discriminative features were "fixation average", "saccade median length" and "fixation mean acceleration x", which relate to fixation durations and the distance between consecutive fixations. A discriminative feature of different nature was the proportion of fixation time on "discourse connectors", whose importance in text comprehension was already suggested in [41]. The ninth most discriminative feature is related to pupil dilations, which was found to correlate with cognitive effort in memory tasks [45].

Characterization of readers

Studies on variable importance help us to discover what discriminative features play an important role in the recognition of reader's latent attributes. However, such studies fail at giving us information on the actual relationship between each feature and the latent attribute of interest. For brevity and simplicity, we computed the Wilcoxon t-test of differences in feature values between readers with a low and high level of understanding. Results can be observed in Table 3.

Readers that displayed lower level of understanding were characterized by having significantly larger average fixation durations and larger variance on this duration, which might be related to slower word recognition or lexical processing time. Readers with lower level of understanding were also characterized by smaller saccade median length and fixation mean acceleration on the x-coordinates, which may be related to difficulties in syntactic integration and also reflect limited lexical processing in the parafovea. They also fixated longer discourse connectors and had longer overall reading times than subjects with higher level of understanding. Although

No.	Feature	low vs. high	p-value
1	fixation average	>	$2 \cdot 10^{-4}$
2	saccade median length	<	$3 \cdot 10^{-6}$
3	fixation mean acceleration x	<	$3 \cdot 10^{-4}$
4	discourse connectors	>	$6 \cdot 10^{-4}$
5	fixation std	>	$2 \cdot 10^{-5}$
6	fixation mean velocity x	<	$2 \cdot 10^{-4}$
7	num fixations	>	0.06
8	reading time	>	$4 \cdot 10^{-3}$
9	pupil mean acceleration	>	0.17
10	num regressions	<	0.44

Table 3: Characterization of readers with a low and high level of understanding. Column "low vs. high" indicates whether each feature has a larger value (>) for readers with a low level of understanding or vice versa (<). P-values are computed using the Wilcoxon t-test.

the variable importance method ranked "pupil mean acceleration" and "num regressions" as important features, there were no statistically significant value differences of those features for different levels of understanding. This may suggest that these features might be effective to discriminate readers only when they are combined with other features.

DISCUSSION AND FUTURE WORK

As presented in Figure 2, there was a small but significant reduction in recognition error of English skill as measured by a normalized test of English (ToE), but no error reductions were achieved when recognizing self-reported English skill (english). Surprisingly, there was no positive correlation between self-reported English skill and English skill as measured by tests. Under the assumption that tests of English (as given by TOEFL and TOEIC) are consistent across subjects, a possible explanation for a lack of positive correlation is that our readers were not consistent in their self-assessment of language ability. For that reason, our machine learning methods may have had difficulties in finding characterizing patterns to discriminate different levels of self-reported English skill.

We did not achieve error reductions in the regression task of recognizing reader's understanding score, but we achieved significant error reductions when discriminating readers with low and high level of understanding. While personal attributes might be available in personalized reading environments, the level of understanding remains latent, and gaining capabilities to recognize it has advantages in adaptive applications and information recommenders.

In Table 2 we showed that pure gaze features are more discriminative than proportions of fixation times on linguistic features. The reason could be that small calibration drifts have a strong negative effect on the correct alignment between fixation locations to actual fixated words. Most pure gaze features are not strongly affected by small to moderate calibration drifts, making them more robust features for these recognition tasks. However, personal differences in processing text with certain characteristics have been studied in the literature, and they might be potentially informative features if accurate eye-tracking data is available.

In Table 3 we displayed the differences in feature values between readers with low and high level of understanding. Some features did not show strong statistical significance in their values between the two reader populations. However, the optimal predictive mechanism may consist of a non-linear function of those features, and Random Forest were capable of discovering those non-linear relationships.

Our experiments could be extended by including a larger number of subjects, possibly to recognize a wider set of attributes. Quality of eye-tracking data and text-gaze alignment are affected by experimental conditions such as the use of a chin-rest to prevent head movements, or displaying less lines per screen to reduce text-gaze misalignments. We favored naturalistic reading conditions to preserve validity in general applications, but recent advances in eye-tracking error correction would benefit similar applications. Other extensions could consist in investigating gaze patterns on non-textual regions or combining other modalities such as face micromovements or body pose to recognize latent personal attributes.

We found evidence that eye-movements contain patterns that are useful to recognize reader's level of understanding and language skill, but their direct application to information recommendation and adaptive systems may still be challenging. Our work could be extended by making actual use of the positive gaze patterns, to recommend easier-to-read documents for users with low language skill, or activate reading assistance when users display gaze patterns of low understanding. Recognizing understanding on a certain topic would also help us to discover topic familiarity, useful to build refined user models of the World. We believe in the importance of gaining capabilities to recognize personal and task attributes given observations of reading behavior, and we hope this work can initiate us in that research direction.

CONCLUSIONS

We presented a framework to recognize English language skill and level of understanding given measurements of reading behavior. We achieved a small but significant error reduction in recognizing English language skill as measured by TOEFL or TOEIC, but failed at recognizing self-reported English skill, probably due to inconsistencies between self-assessment of English ability by our readers.

We did not achieve error reductions in the recognition of the exact quantification of reader's understanding with respect to our baseline based on priors. However, we obtained significant recognition performance in the task of discriminating between readers with low and high level of understanding, which is unprecedented given measurements of reading behavior. We believe our findings have potential applications in adaptive and recommendation systems.

We analyzed the most discriminative features of reading behavior in recognizing our target latent attributes. We found that pure gaze features are more discriminative than proportions of fixation times on different linguistic features, and we showed a characterization of the readers in our study that showed low and high levels of understanding.

REFERENCES

1. Argamon, S., Koppel, M., Pennebaker, J., and Schler, J. Mining the blogosphere: age, gender, and the varieties of self-expression. *First Monday 12*, 9 (2007).

2. Aula, A., Majaranta, P., and Räihä, K.-J. Eye-tracking reveals the personal styles for search result evaluation. In *Human-Computer Interaction-INTERACT 2005*. Springer, 2005, 1058–1061.

3. Azcarraga, J., and Suarez, M. T. Predicting academic emotions based on brainwaves, mouse behaviour and personality profile. In *PRICAI 2012: Trends in Artificial Intelligence*. Springer, 2012, 728–733.

4. Biber, D., and Finegan, E. *Sociolinguistic perspectives on register*. Oxford University Press Oxford, 1994.

5. Biedert, R., Dengel, A., Elshamy, M., and Buscher, G. Towards robust gaze-based objective quality measures for text. In *Proceedings of the Symposium on Eye Tracking Research and Applications*, Association for Computational Linguistics (2012), 201–204.

6. Bird, Steven, E. L., and Klein, E. *Natural Language Processing with Python*. O'Reilly Media Inc, 2009.

7. Boraston, Z., and Blakemore, S.-J. The application of eye-tracking technology in the study of autism. *The Journal of Physiology 581*, 3 (2007), 893–898.

8. Boulis, C., and Ostendorf, M. A quantitative analysis of lexical differences between genders in telephone conversations. In *Proceedings of the 43rd Annual Meeting on Association for Computational Linguistics*, ACL '05, Association for Computational Linguistics (Stroudsburg, PA, USA, 2005), 435–442.

9. Brants, T., and Franz, A. Web 1T 5-gram version 1, 2006.

10. Breiman, L. Random forests. *Machine learning 45*, 1 (2001), 5–32.

11. Burger, J. D., and Henderson, J. C. An exploration of observable features related to blogger age. In *Computational Approaches to Analyzing Weblogs: Papers from the 2006 AAAI Spring Symposium* (2006), 15–20.

12. Buscher, G., and Dengel, A. Gaze-based filtering of relevant document segments. In *International World Wide Web Conference (WWW)* (2009).

13. Buscher, G., Dengel, A., and van Elst, L. Query expansion using gaze-based feedback on the subdocument level. In *ACM Special Interest Group on Information Retrieval (SIGIR)* (2008).

14. Cortes, C., and Vapnik, V. Support-vector networks. *Machine learning 20*, 3 (1995), 273–297.

15. Coxhead, A. *An academic word list*, vol. 18. School of Linguistics and Applied Language Studies, Victoria University of Wellington, 1998.

16. Cutrell, E., and Guan, Z. What are you looking for?: an eye-tracking study of information usage in web search. In *Proceedings of the SIGCHI conference on Human factors in computing systems*, ACM (2007), 407–416.

17. Demberg, V., and Keller, F. Data from eye-tracking corpora as evidence for theories of syntactic processing complexity. *Cognition 109*, 2 (2008), 193 – 210.

18. Doherty, S., O'Brien, S., and Carl, M. Eye tracking as an MT evaluation technique. *Machine Translation 24* (2010), 1–13. 10.1007/s10590-010-9070-9.

19. Drucker, H., Burges, C. J., Kaufman, L., Smola, A., and Vapnik, V. Support vector regression machines. *Advances in neural information processing systems* (1997), 155–161.

20. Fellbaum, C. WordNet. *Theory and Applications of Ontology: Computer Applications* (2010), 231–243.

21. Feng, L., Jansche, M., Huenerfauth, M., and Elhadad, N. A comparison of features for automatic readability assessment. In *Proceedings of the 23rd International Conference on Computational Linguistics: Posters*, Association for Computational Linguistics (2010), 276–284.

22. Garera, N., and Yarowsky, D. Modeling latent biographic attributes in conversational genres. In *Proceedings of the Joint Conference of the 47th Annual Meeting of the ACL and the 4th International Joint Conference on Natural Language Processing of the AFNLP: Volume 2 - Volume 2*, ACL '09, Association for Computational Linguistics (Stroudsburg, PA, USA, 2009), 710–718.

23. Granka, L. A., Joachims, T., and Gay, G. Eye-tracking analysis of user behavior in WWW search. In *Proceedings of the 27th annual international ACM SIGIR conference on Research and development in information retrieval*, SIGIR '04, ACM (New York, NY, USA, 2004), 478–479.

24. Hayhoe, M. M., Ballard, D. H., Triesch, J., Shinoda, H., Aivar, P., and Sullivan, B. Vision in natural and virtual environments. In *Proceedings of the 2002 symposium on Eye tracking research & applications*, ETRA '02, ACM (New York, NY, USA, 2002), 7–13.

25. Hornof, A., and Halverson, T. Cleaning up systematic error in eye-tracking data by using required fixation locations. *Behavior Research Methods 34* (2002), 592–604. 10.3758/BF03195487.

26. Hudson, R. Measuring syntactic difficulty. *Manuscript, University College, London* (1995).

27. Irwin, D. E. Lexical processing during saccadic eye movements. *Cognitive Psychology 36*, 1 (1998), 1–27.

28. Isaacowitz, D. M., Wadlinger, H. A., Goren, D., and Wilson, H. R. Selective preference in visual fixation away from negative images in old age? an eye-tracking study. *Psychology and aging 21*, 1 (2006), 40.

29. Jacob, R. J., and Karn, K. S. Eye tracking in human-computer interaction and usability research: Ready to deliver the promises. *Mind 2*, 3 (2003), 4.

30. Just, M. A., and Carpenter, P. A. Eye fixations and cognitive processes. *Cognitive Psychology 8*, 4 (1976), 441–480.

31. Kennedy, A., and Pynte, J. Parafoveal-on-foveal effects in normal reading. *Vision Research 45* (2005), 153–168.

32. Klein, D., and Manning, C. D. Accurate unlexicalized parsing. In *Proceedings of the 41st Annual Meeting on Association for Computational Linguistics*, Association for Computational Linguistics (2003), 423–430.

33. Kunze, K., Kawaichi, H., Yoshimura, K., and Kise, K. Towards inferring language expertise using eye tracking. In *CHI'13 Extended Abstracts on Human Factors in Computing Systems*, ACM (2013), 217–222.

34. Labov, W. *Sociolinguistic patterns*, vol. 4. Philadelphia: University of Pennsylvania Press, 1972.

35. Lee, N. N., Cu, J., and Suarez, M. T. A real-time, multimodal, and dimensional affect recognition system. In *PRICAI 2012: Trends in Artificial Intelligence*, P. Anthony, M. Ishizuka, and D. Lukose, Eds., vol. 7458 of *Lecture Notes in Computer Science*. Springer Berlin Heidelberg, 2012, 241–249.

36. Lorigo, L., Pan, B., Hembrooke, H., Joachims, T., Granka, L., and Gay, G. The influence of task and gender on search and evaluation behavior using Google. *Information Processing & Management 42*, 4 (2006), 1123–1131.

37. Martínez-Gómez, P., Chen, C., Hara, T., Kano, Y., and Aizawa, A. Image registration for text-gaze alignment. In *Proceedings of the 2012 ACM international conference on Intelligent User Interfaces*, IUI '12, ACM (New York, NY, USA, 2012), 257–260.

38. Martínez-Gómez, P., Hara, T., and Aizawa, A. Recognizing personal characteristics of readers using eye-movements and text features. In *Proceedings of COLING* (Mumbai, India, December 2012), 1747–1762.

39. McDonald, S. A., and Shillcock, R. C. Eye movements reveal the on-line computation of lexical probabilities during reading. *Psychological Science 14*, 6 (2003), 648–652.

40. Medero, J., and Ostendorf, M. Atypical prosodic structure as an indicator of reading level and text difficulty. In *Proceedings of NAACL-HLT* (2013), 715–720.

41. Millis, K. K., and Just, M. A. The influence of connectives on sentence comprehension. *Journal of Memory and Language 33*, 1 (1994), 128–147.

42. Miyao, Y., and Tsujii, J. Feature forest models for probabilistic HPSG parsing. *Computational Linguistics 34* (March 2008), 35–80.

43. Mukherjee, A., and Liu, B. Improving gender classification of blog authors. In *Proceedings of the 2010 Conference on Empirical Methods in Natural Language Processing*, EMNLP '10, Association for Computational Linguistics (Stroudsburg, PA, USA, 2010), 207–217.

44. Pan, B., Hembrooke, H. A., Gay, G. K., Granka, L. A., Feusner, M. K., and Newman, J. K. The determinants of web page viewing behavior: an eye-tracking study. In *Proceedings of the 2004 symposium on Eye tracking research & applications*, ACM (2004), 147–154.

45. Piquado, T., Isaacowitz, D., and Wingfield, A. Pupillometry as a measure of cognitive effort in younger and older adults. *Psychophysiology 47*, 3 (2010), 560–569.

46. Raghunathan, K., Lee, H., Rangarajan, S., Chambers, N., Surdeanu, M., Jurafsky, D., and Manning, C. A multi-pass sieve for coreference resolution. In *Proceedings of the 2010 Conference on Empirical Methods in Natural Language Processing*, Association for Computational Linguistics (2010), 492–501.

47. Rao, D., Yarowsky, D., Shreevats, A., and Gupta, M. Classifying latent user attributes in twitter. In *Proceedings of the 2nd international workshop on Search and mining user-generated contents*, SMUC '10, ACM (New York, NY, USA, 2010), 37–44.

48. Rayner, K. Eye movements in reading and information processing: 20 years of research. *Psychological Bulletin 124* (Nov. 1998), 372–422.

49. Rayner, K., Carlson, M., and Frazier, L. The interaction of syntax and semantics during sentence processing: eye movements in the analysis of semantically biased sentences. *Journal of Verbal Learning and Verbal Behavior 22*, 3 (1983), 358 – 374.

50. Schler, J., Koppel, M., Argamon, S., and Pennebaker, J. Effects of age and gender on blogging. In *Proceedings of 2006 AAAI Spring Symposium on Computational Approaches for Analyzing Weblogs* (2006), 199–205.

51. Tomanek, K., Hahn, U., Lohmann, S., and Ziegler, J. A cognitive cost model of annotations based on eye-tracking data. In *Proceedings of the 48th Annual Meeting of the Association for Computational Linguistics*, ACL '10, Association for Computational Linguistics (Stroudsburg, PA, USA, 2010), 1158–1167.

52. Weide, R. The CMU pronunciation dictionary, release 0.6, 1998.

53. West, M., and Jeffery, G. B. *A general service list of English words: with semantic frequencies and a supplementary word-list for the writing of popular science and technology*. Longmans, Green London, 1953.

54. Xu, S., Jiang, H., and Lau, F. C. Personalized online document, image and video recommendation via commodity eye-tracking. In *ACM Recommender Systems (RecSys)* (2008).

55. Xu, S., Jiang, H., and Lau, F. C. User-oriented document summarization through vision-based eye-tracking. In *International Conference on Intelligent User Interfaces (IUI)* (2009).

Towards Facilitating User Skill Acquisition - Identifying Untrained Visualization Users through Eye Tracking

Dereck Toker, Ben Steichen, Matthew Gingerich, Cristina Conati, Giuseppe Carenini

Department of Computer Science,
University of British Columbia, Vancouver, Canada
{dtoker, steichen, majugi, conati, carenini}@cs.ubc.ca

ABSTRACT

A key challenge for information visualization designers lies in developing systems that best support users in terms of their individual abilities, needs, and preferences. However, most visualizations require users to first gather a certain set of skills before they can efficiently process the displayed information. This paper presents a first step towards designing visualizations that provide personalized support in order to ease the so-called 'learning curve' during a user's skill acquisition phase. We present prediction models, trained on users' gaze data, that can identify if users are still in the skill acquisition phase or if they have gained the necessary abilities. The paper first reveals that users exhibit the learning curve even during the usage of simple information visualizations, and then shows that we can generate reasonably accurate predictions about a user's skill acquisition using solely their eye gaze behavior.

Author Keywords

Skill Acquisition; Information Visualization; Eye-tracking; Machine Learning; Adaptation.

ACM Classification Keywords

H.5.m.

General Terms

Human Factors; Measurement.

INTRODUCTION

Individual user abilities, needs, and preferences have been shown to play an important role in the effectiveness of many human-computer interaction and information visualization systems. User differences can include medium- to long-term characteristics such as interests, personality, or cognitive abilities, as well as more short-term states such as cognitive load or affect. The benefits of dynamically adapting to these differences have already been demonstrated in a variety of human-computer interaction tasks and applications, such as menu based interfaces, web search, desktop assistance, or human learning [13]. One important characteristic that has received

less attention (in terms of adaptation) is a user's experience or competence with a system, especially in the information visualization area. In particular, most visualizations typically require users to first acquire a certain set of skills, gained through practice, before they can efficiently process the displayed information

The long-term goal of the research presented in this paper is to devise visualizations that can ease the so-called 'learning curve' through adaptive support during a user's skill acquisition phase. Such support may include preventing untrained users from accessing advanced features, providing tooltips, offering tutorials, etc. As with any user-adaptive system design, the key challenges of this endeavor lie in (i) measuring the effect that a target user's characteristics (in our case *skills in using a given visualization*) have on user performance, (ii) detecting these characteristics in real-time, and (iii) providing adaptive help to best support the user's current needs and abilities.

In this paper, we focus on challenges (i) and (ii), namely on verifying the effect and supporting the detection of a user's skill acquisition with information visualizations. With respect to skill acquisition detection, we investigate the value of user eye gaze information as a data source, because visual scanning and processing are fundamental components of working with any information visualization system (and the only components for non-interactive visualizations). Our research questions are as follows:

1) To what extent can a user's skill level be predicted in real-time, using solely eye gaze data?

2) Which eye gaze features are most predictive?

3) To what extent is knowledge about the user's current visualization required for these predictions?

In order to answer these research questions, we leveraged data obtained from a study that involved users performing low-level visualization tasks with simple bar graphs. The paper shows that, despite our best efforts to control for any learning/ordering effects, participants indeed exhibited a learning curve even with these simple visualizations. The paper then shows that we can generate reasonably accurate predictions about a user's skill acquisition using classifiers that are trained solely based on eye gaze data. In particular, we show that from the outset (i.e., after only seeing a small part of a user's gaze data) our classifiers outperform a simple baseline, and that accuracies can reach up to 64%. To investigate the generalizability of our approach, we provide comparative results for classifiers that use *Visualization-Specific* features versus *Generic* feature sets, and we show that some the most predictive features are in fact visualization-independent.

RELATED WORK

Effects of Individual Differences on User Performance with Visualizations

Recent visualization research has shown that user characteristics can significantly influence user performance. There is substantial evidence that cognitive measures such as *perceptual speed*, *visual working memory* and *verbal working memory* influence user effectiveness and satisfaction when working with a visualization [25][27]. The personality trait known as *locus of control* (internal vs. external) has been shown to impact visualization performance (e.g., [29]). Several researchers have looked at the impact of *domain expertise* on performance with visualizations (i.e., a user's expertise in the task domain, as opposed to expertise with the visualization itself). For example, Dillon [9] discusses how domain expertise (e.g., experience reading academic journals in cognitive science) has been repeatedly shown to play a significant role in predicting performance with various visual navigation tools, and that this should be taken into account when designing visualization systems. Similarly, domain expertise consisting of measuring prior technical training (e.g., in statistics, psychology, etc.) has been shown to play a significant role in visualization performance, e.g., [16][19].

System Expertise in Adaptive Systems & Skill Acquisition

Outside information visualization, there has also been work on modeling and adapting to a user's *system expertise*, i.e. to the user's level of familiarity with the interactive system being used. For example, Bunt et al. [5] devised and evaluated MICA, a mixed-initiative GUI-customization tool that provided suggestions on how to personalize the menus of a word processor, by considering, among other factors, the user's expertise with the word processor. Expertise levels were defined based on how much time a user took to perform menu selections with the interface. However, the ability to track a user's system expertise in real time was not implemented. An evaluation of MICA, in which expertise was assessed via a pre-questionnaire, showed better performance with and higher preference for MICA compared to a version that provided the customization functionality without personalized suggestions. Linton & Shaefer [17] generated a model of expert usage of a word processor based on the frequency, sequence, and number of distinct menu commands displayed by the users of the application. This model was then used to generate recommendations on which functionalities to use for users who diverged from the expert model. In this paper, we

contribute to this line of work by looking at system expertise with a visualization, and at whether we can track how it evolves during usage, a problem that to our knowledge has yet to be addressed in research of user-adaptive interaction.

In perceptual psychology, numerous theoretical models exist on this topic of expertise, or *skill acquisition* (see [1] for an overview). While it is not within the scope of this paper to argue for the correctness or fit of any of these theories, we focus on the fact that a typical method used in psychology for tracking how user performance improves with practice is by using a *learning curve* [23]. Learning curves are also frequently used in HCI to compare and evaluate the effectiveness of various systems, including information visualization systems (e.g., [28][22][20]). In this paper, we leverage the concept of learning curve as a way to identify two broad stages of a user's skill acquisition, which we then use to evaluate the detection of a user's skill using eye-gaze data.

Eye-tracking in User Modeling for Adaptive Systems

Several studies have examined the value of using eye tracking data as an input source for real-time modeling of relevant user characteristics. For example, Qu & Johnson [21] showed that user gaze behaviors can help predict users' motivation during interaction with an intelligent tutoring system. Kardan et al. [14] and Bondareva et al. [4] showed that eye tracking data can be used to predict student learning with two different educational environments, and that this prediction can be performed early enough to possibly provide adaptive interventions that can foster learning. D'Mello et al. [8] evaluated an intelligent tutoring system that both detected and reacted to students' lack of attention based on gaze patterns. They found that this gaze-reactive tutor had a positive impact on student learning. Bednarik et al. [3] used eye tracking features in order to predict users' problem-solving strategies (e.g., evaluation, intention, planning, etc.), as well as user performance while solving a visual puzzle. They examined the effect of window-size on feature extraction, and found that, in general, increased window sizes led to an improvement in classification. Conati & Merten [7] combined gaze data with information on user's actions to predict user meta-cognitive behavior (e.g., self-explanation) within an exploratory learning environment. Steichen et al. [24] showed very positive results in using gaze data to recognize in real time a user's tasks and cognitive traits (e.g., perceptual speed, verbal working memory) while interacting with two simple visualizations (bar and radar graphs). Similar to the work in [24], the data we use in this paper comes from a study involving users who perform low-level visualization tasks using simple bar graph visualizations. Here, however, we use gaze data to predict a *user's skill acquisition phase* in working with the visualization.

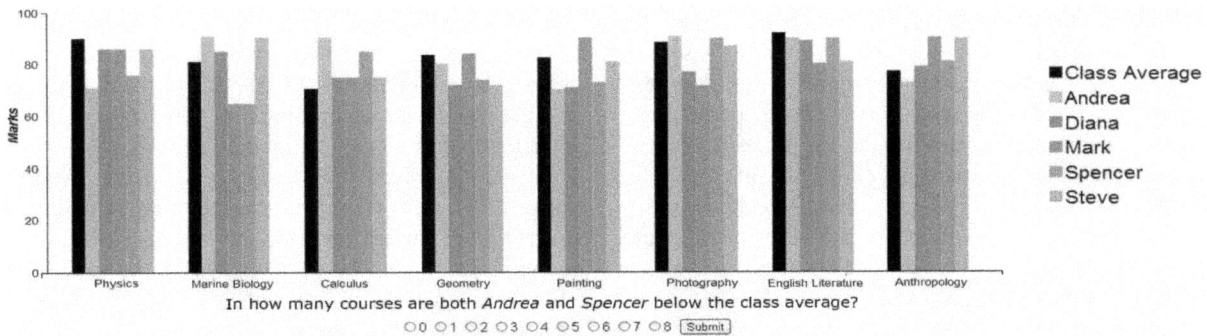

Figure 1. Example bar graph visualization as used in the experimental task

USER STUDY

In this section, we provide an overview of the study we conducted to gather empirical data (including eye tracking data) about bar graph processing. The primary purpose of this study was to investigate the relative effectiveness of several 'visual prompts' designed to help visualization processing, as well as the relative effect of different user traits and task complexity [6]. Here, we leverage the data from this study to investigate user skill acquisition with simple visualizations. In the next few sections, we provide a summary of the main components of the study sufficient for the purposes of this paper.

Experimental Visualizations and Tasks

In the study, participants were given bar graph visualizations, along with textual questions for them to answer, relating to the displayed data (see Figure 1). We selected bar graphs as the information visualization for this study because (i) they are a very common and basic visualization, and (ii) there is already research that shows that several types of individual differences can play a role in the effectiveness of bar graphs [25], suggesting that user-adaptive techniques could be of benefit. As mentioned above, some of the visualizations (fully randomized) contained one of four highlighting interventions (see Figure 2) designed to guide the user's focus to a specific subset of data within the bar graph that is relevant to answer the associated question. The experimental software was fully automated and ran in a web-browser, with the visualizations and interventions being programmed using the D3 visualization framework [7]. The experiment was conducted on an Intel Core i7, 3.4GHz, with 4GB of RAM, connected to a Tobii T120 eye-tracker as the main display.

The study tasks involved comparing individuals against a group average (data points in the bar graph) on a set of dimensions (data series in the bar graph). For variety, the task questions were drawn from four different domains. All tasks involved the same number of data points (six, including the average) and series (eight). Two types of tasks were chosen from a set of primitive data analysis tasks that Amar et al. [2] identifies as "largely capturing people's activities while employing information visualization". The first task type was Retrieve Value (a relatively simple task),

which consisted of retrieving a specific individual in the target domain and comparing it against the group average; (e.g., "Is Michael's grade in *Chemistry* above the class average for that course?"). The second task type was Compute Derived Value (a more complex task type), which required users to first perform a set of comparisons, and then compute an aggregate of the comparison outcomes; (e.g., "In how many cities is the movie *Vampire Attack* above the average revenue and the movie *How to Date Your Friends* below it?").

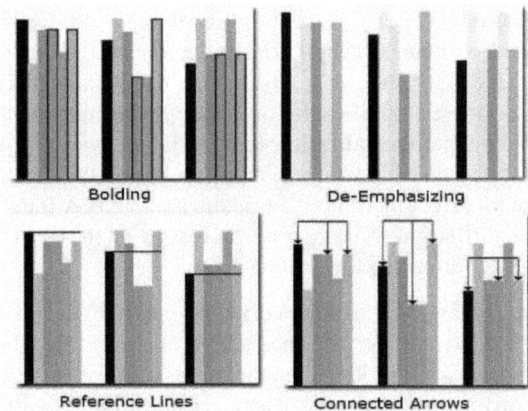

Figure 2. Example visualizations with added prompts

Study procedure

The study had 62 subjects, ranging in age from 18 to 42. Participants were mostly recruited via dedicated systems at our university, resulting in a variety of students from diverse backgrounds (e.g., Psychology, Forestry, Computer Science, Finance, Fine Art, German, Commerce). We also recruited 7 non-student participants such as a non-profit community connector, a 3D artist, and an air combat systems officer. The experiment was a within-subjects study, fitting in a single session lasting at most 90 minutes, with each participant completing a total of 80 trials covering combinations of task type and visual prompts.

Participants began by completing a number of pre-study questionnaires and cognitive tests (not used in this paper). Next, participants underwent a training phase to expose them to bar graphs, the study tasks, and the visual prompts. The training phase first involved familiarizing users with all of the features of our visualization layout (e.g., x-axis, y-axis, legend mapping, labels, bars etc.), followed by a series of practice tasks that exposed users to the various task types as well as the layout of the interventions. Participants then underwent a calibration phase for the eye-tracker, before starting the study trials. Participants performed 40 of the 80 study trials, followed by a 5-minute break. After the break, the eye-tracker was re-calibrated and the participant performed the remaining 40 trials. The 80 trials were fully randomized in terms of experimental conditions (i.e., task complexity, interventions). Lastly, participants took a post-questionnaire designed to gauge their evaluations of each intervention's usefulness, as well as their relative preferences (not used in this paper).

EVIDENCE OF SKILL ACQUISITION: MAIN EFFECT OF TRIAL ORDER

A prior analysis of the study data (based on an ANOVA repeated measures) revealed interesting effects of interventions, task type, and user characteristics on performance (see [6]). However, despite our best efforts to control for any learning/ordering effects, (e.g., by training each user with the visualization system at the beginning of the study as well as by fully randomizing the experimental conditions), a General Linear Model repeated measures revealed a main effect of trial order on task completion time, ($F_{79,1142}$= 6.85, $p < .001$). This result indicates that users improved significantly over time, independently from the other experimental factors (e.g., task type, visual prompt type). Note that for task accuracy (measured for each trial as either correct/incorrect), a Friedman's ANOVA indicated no main effect of trial order on accuracy, ($\chi^2(62)$= 115.83, $p = .262$), likely due to a ceiling effect.

Figure 3 shows the learning curve for our study data, which plots the average performance across all users over the 80 study tasks, in order of completion (i.e., average user performance on the ith trial, where i ranges from 1 to 80).

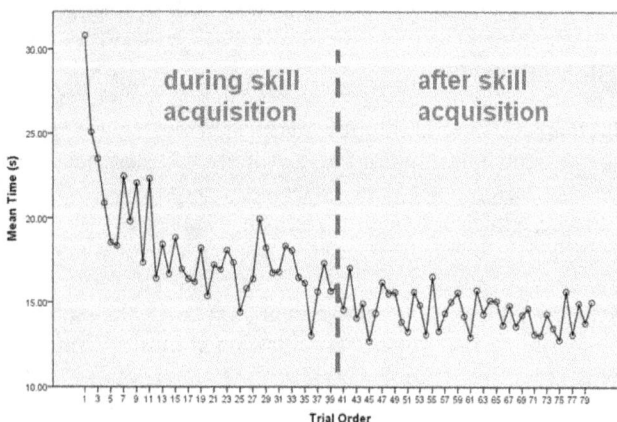

Figure 3. Learning curve showing performance improvement. The blue line separates trials into two general stages of skill acquisition, which we call *during* and *after*

The curve clearly indicates an improvement in performance, as characterized by a descending slope for roughly the first half of the trials (left of the dotted blue line in figure 5). In the second half of trials (right of the dotted blue line), however, performance appears to stabilize (as indicated by a reduced variance across trials). These results suggest that users were acquiring relevant skills during the initial part of the experiment, and that the skills are related to the processing of the visualizations, because the learning effects in Figure 3 are independent of both the type of task performed and the intervention received (recall that the actual task and intervention type seen for the ith trial varied across users, because of randomization). The presence of this learning effect therefore suggests that it may be useful to track and facilitate a user's skill acquisition phase when working with a visualization. In the next section, we present the classifiers we built to detect a user's skill acquisition phase using a user's eye gaze data.

CLASSIFIERS FOR SKILL ACQUISITION DURING VISUALIZATION PROCESSING.

Classification Labels

Because participants were given a break at the halfway point in the study (after 40 trials), and much of the skill acquisition effects in Figure 3 appeared to happen during this first part of the study, we opted to use this break as the boundary to generate labels for classification of skill acquisition. The 40 trials before the break are hence labeled *during* (skill acquisition), and the 40 trials after the break are labeled *after* (skill acquisition). This choice is further supported by the fact that the difference in completion time between the two phases (i.e., *during* vs. *after*) is statistically significant (using an ANOVA, $p < .001$). The average completion time for tasks *during* skill acquisition was 18.2s (SD=10.7), whereas the average performance *after* skill acquisition was 14.4s (SD=8.2). Conceptually, trials labeled as *during* represent instances where (in general) a user is still practicing/undergoing skill acquisition with the visualization system, whereas trials *after* represent instances where a user has become practiced/competent. The benefit of labeling the trials in this manner, as opposed to defining skill acquisition in terms of some fixed value(s) of time, is that the labels are thus relative, meaning that this definition can be expanded to other visualization (and non-visualization) systems. Specifically, we envision labeling additional task interaction data sets taken from other visualization systems, where the concept of *during* skill acquisition and *after* skill acquisition can be transferred relative to the sets of tasks being performed for that given interface.

Eye tracking measures & features

An eye-tracker captures gaze information through fixations (i.e., maintaining gaze at one point on the screen) and saccades (i.e., a quick movement of gaze from one fixation point to another), which can be processed and analyzed to derive attention patterns. Following the approach in [14] and [24], we generated a large set of eye-tracking features by calculating statistics upon basic eye-tracking measures (see Table 1 & Table 2).

Table 1. Basic Gaze Measures

Basic gaze measures	Description
Fixation Count	Count of number of fixations
Fixation Duration	Time duration of an individual fixation
Saccade Length	Distance between the two fixations delimiting the saccade (d in Figure 4)
Relative Saccade Angles	The angle between the two consecutive saccades (e.g., angle y in Figure 4)
Absolute Saccade Angles	The angle between a saccade and the horizontal (e.g., angle x in Figure 4)

Of these basic measures, *Fixation Count* and *Fixation Duration* are widely used in eye tracking studies. In addition, we included *Saccade Length* (e.g., distance d in Figure 4); *Relative Saccades Angle* (e.g., angle y in Figure 4); and *Absolute Saccade Angle* (e.g., angle x in Figure 4); as suggested in [10], because these measures are potentially useful for summarizing trends in user attention patterns within a specific interaction window, e.g., if the user's gaze follows a planned sequence (as opposed to being scattered).

The raw gaze data from the Tobii eye tracker was processed using our open-source data analysis toolkit, which is freely available for download and extension by the research community[1]. The toolkit computes features such as sum, average, and standard deviation over the eye tracking measures with respect to (i) the overall screen, to get a sense of the complete interaction with the task (*Overall Features* from now on) and (ii) specific areas of interest (AOI), identifying sub-parts of the interface that may be relevant for understanding a user's attention processes (*AOI-level Features* from now on). The total range of features computed by EMDAT is shown in Table 2.

Table 2. Features calculated based on basic gaze measures

Overall Features
Total Number of Fixations, Fixation rate
Sum, Mean, Std. deviation of Fixation Durations
Sum, Mean, Std. deviation of Saccade Length
Sum, Mean, Std. deviation of Relative Saccade Angles
Sum, Mean, Std. deviation of Absolute Saccade Angles

AOI-level Features (for each AOI)
Total number of fixations in AOI
Sum & Mean of fixation durations in AOI
Time to first fixation in AOI
Time to last fixation in AOI
Longest fixation in AOI
Number of Transitions From this AOI to every other AOI ($n*(n-1)$ separate measures, where n is the number of AOIs)

[1] http://www.cs.ubc.ca/~skardan/EMDAT/

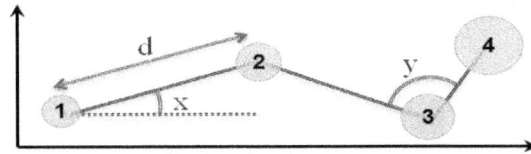

Figure 4. Saccade based eye measures

AOI definitions

Visualization-specific AOIs can be useful for gaining detailed insights on how certain visualization components are being processed by users (e.g., Toker et al. *[26]* found that users spend more time looking at the legend AOI during difficult tasks). Additionally, [4] and *[24]* have shown that by including visualization-specific AOIs, higher classification accuracy can be achieved in terms of predicting properties such as learning gain, cognitive abilities, visualization type, and task type. In our study, the *Visualization-Specific* set contained the following 6 AOIs:

- *High Area*: covers the upper half of the data elements of the visualization which corresponds to a rectangle over the top half of the vertical bars.
- *Low Area*: covers the lower half of the data elements.
- *Labels*: covers the data labels.
- *Question Text*: covers the text describing the task to be performed.
- *Legend*: covers the legend, which shows the mapping between the data series and the color of the visualization elements.
- *Answer Input*: covers the task response radio buttons and submit button.

Since one of the aims of this paper is to investigate how accurately we can predict user task acquisition independent of the visualization (research question 3), we also explore the possibility of making predictions using *Generic AOI* sets, which are not defined in terms of any particular visualization or interface. Specifically, we analyze if any of them may be suitable/adequate alternatives to the *Visualization-Specific* AOIs. In total we devised *5 Generic AOI* sets (referred to as *2x2, 3x3, 4x4, 5x5,* and *X grid*), with each of them consisting of grid-like AOIs and differing only in terms of granularity/layout (see Figure 5).

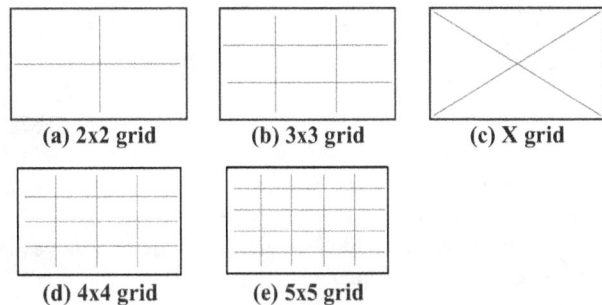

(a) 2x2 grid	(b) 3x3 grid	(c) X grid
(d) 4x4 grid	(e) 5x5 grid	

Figure 5. Generic AOI grids

Data sets and evaluation process

Similar to the analysis performed in [24], the goal of our classification experiments is to predict the correct labels (in our case *during* vs. *after*) for individual user trials based on eye tracking features. In order to explore the potential of classifying users while they are engaged in a task (to be able to then provide dynamic help), we generated a number of datasets that simulated partial observation of a user's eye gaze data. In the next section, we will first look at datasets generated based on *percentage* of the overall interaction during a trial (e.g., 10%, 20%, etc.), and then at datasets generated based on *absolute time* intervals (e.g., 1sec, 2sec, etc.).

Additionally, in order to study the importance of having knowledge regarding which specific visualization (e.g., bar graph) a user is currently engaged with, we compare the classification performance between each of the various AOI sets defined in the previous section, i.e., the *Visualization-Specific* set, the 5 *Generic* sets, as well as a classifier with no AOIs ('*None*'). As a baseline, we use a simple classifier that always selects the most likely class.

For each of our classification experiments, we used the WEKA data mining toolkit [11] for model learning and evaluation. In particular, we used a Logistic Regression classifier, both for its simplicity, and because it has previously been found to be the best performing classifier for experiments involving eye gaze data [4][24]. For all our experiments, classification accuracy is computed using 10-fold cross validation.

CLASSIFICATION RESULTS

Percentage-based Time Intervals

To evaluate how feasible it is to classify a user's skill acquisition phase from gaze data, we first generated datasets consisting of incremental percentages (time intervals) of interaction data, following an approach proposed in [4][14][24]. This approach is a good proof of concept to determine classification accuracy given different amount of interaction data, without having to worry about variances in users' completion times, e.g., it allows us to verify whether the first 10%, 20% etc., of a user's interaction are particularly good for the given classification task.

The results of these analyses are shown for each AOI set in Figure 6. The trends in the figure show that the *Visualization-Specific* classifier generally performs best, indicating that, not surprisingly, knowing which visualization the user is working with improves skill acquisition detection. A one-way ANOVA with AOI-type as the independent variable (8 levels), and the *average over time accuracy* as the dependent measure shows that there is indeed a statistically significant effect of AOI-type on classification accuracy ($F_{7,783}= 162.7$, $p < .001$). Bonferroni-adjusted pairwise comparisons further qualify these effects as follows:

- All classifiers are significantly better than the baseline classifier ($p < .001$);
- The *Visualization-Specific* classifier (M=62.7, SD=1.0) performs significantly better than all the *Generic AOI* classifiers (M=60.59, SD=0.7) and the *None* classifier (M=59.8, SD=0.6) ($p < .001$);
- The *3x3 AOI* classifier (M=61.1, SD=1.2) performs significantly better than *None* (M=59.8, SD=0.6) ($p < .001$);
- There are no other significant differences among the *None* and *Generic AOI* classifiers.

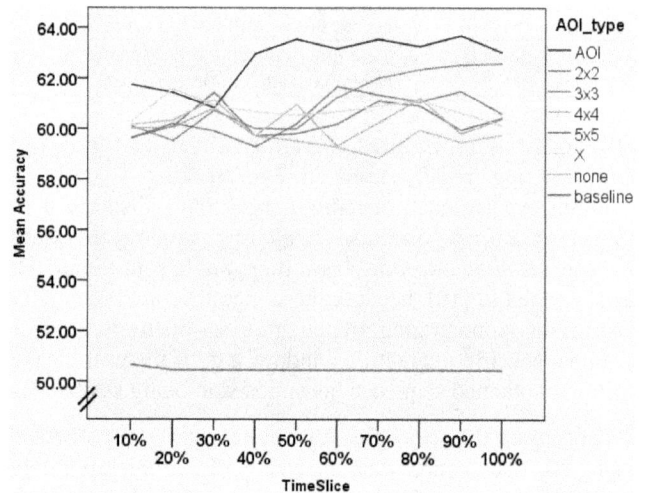

Figure 6. Classification accuracy of user skill acquisition state using percentage-based eye tracking features

Although our results indicate that visualization-specific gaze features can significantly improve the classification of skill acquisition, it should be noted that the 'specific' AOIs in our visualizations could easily be transferred to different visualizations, since they mainly consist of common visualization components (e.g., labels, legend). However, if the goal is to design visualization-independent classifiers (i.e., not just common visualizations), our results indicate that classifiers based on generic AOIs also perform reasonably well, considering that this is based purely on generic eye gaze features (which could potentially be combined with other sources such as interaction or mouse-tracking data). The results also suggest that the AOI granularity needs to strike a compromise between specificity and sensitivity. In particular, results indicate that using the 3x3 grid is the best generic AOI alternative given that it is the only set that performed significantly better than using no AOI information. This points to a possible tradeoff between having too few AOIs (i.e., not enough precision to track meaningful gaze movements across AOIs) versus too many AOIs (i.e., granularity being too fine-grained and gaze movements becoming too noisy across small AOIs).

Absolute Time Intervals

While the approach described in the previous section (i.e., investigating classification accuracy based on percentage of available data) can give valuable insights into trends and patterns of classification accuracy, it requires a task to be fully completed in order to determine what constitutes 100% of the interaction. In practice, a real-time classifier needs to make predictions without knowledge of when the target task will be completed. For this reason, we also generated partial observation datasets based on absolute lengths of interaction times, i.e., the first 1000ms, 2000s, 3000ms, etc. of each trial. These datasets can therefore be seen as more realistic in terms of evaluating classification accuracies *while* a user is interacting with (i.e., looking at) the visualization. One particular challenge in using this approach is that users do not necessarily complete tasks in the same time. Thus, as we train classifiers with increasing absolute time intervals, there is the question of how to deal with participants that have already finished a task prior to the current time interval, specifically whether they should be included in the training sets for time intervals longer than their completion time or not. Based on comparative tests (which we will not present in the paper), we found that we can obtain better results by retaining the full data set across all classification time slices, even if some users in the training set have finished before a specific time cut-off. One simple explanation for this result could be that the reduction of the training set may leave the classification algorithm with too few examples to learn from, particularly for longer trials.

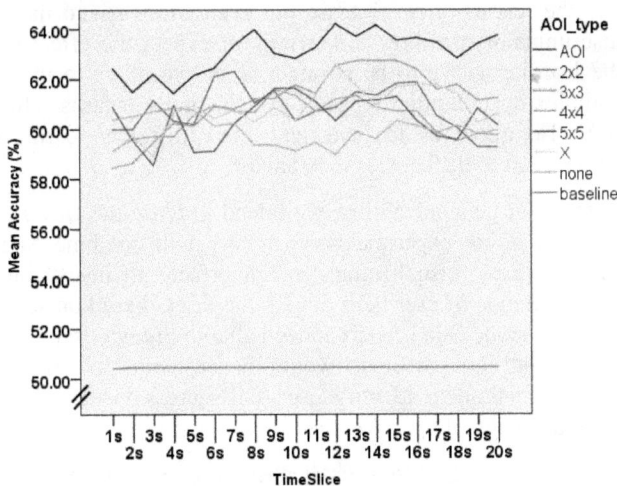

Figure 7. Classification accuracy using absolute time to generate eye tracking features

Similar to the percentage-based experiments, we computed the classification accuracy over incremental time slices (in this case 20 absolute-time intervals, from 1000ms to 20000ms) for each of the seven AOI sets. The resulting overtime trends are shown in Figure 7. In general, we see that the *Visualization-Specific* classifier generates the best accuracy right from the beginning, and that all classifiers comfortably outperform the baseline classifier, reaching accuracies of up to 64%. Also, some classifiers already reach over 60% accuracy after only seeing a few seconds of eye tracking data, hence providing very encouraging results

for our long-term goal of developing user-adaptive systems during a user's system usage. Similarly, while the *Visualization-Specific* classifier performs best overall, it is worth noting that all classifiers perform in the region of 60% across all time intervals (including the classifier with no AOI information), which could potentially be combined with other sources such as interaction or mouse-tracking data to achieve even higher accuracies (and hence drive a user-adaptive system).

We also compared the average over time performance between both the *percentage-based* and the *absolute-time-based* segmentation approaches. We ran a 2 (percent/absolute) by 8 (AOI-Type) ANOVA with classification accuracy as the dependent measure. Results indicated no significant differences between the percentage and absolute time classifiers ($F_{1,44}= 1.04$, $p = .314$). The main effect of AOI-Type, however, is again significant ($F_{7,2357}= 408.8$, $p < .001$), and Bonferroni adjusted pairwise comparisons yield identical results as reported in the previous subsection, i.e. showing that *Visualization-specific* classifiers perform best, and that the 3x3 is the best performing *Generic* AOI set. The lack of a statistically significant difference between percentage and absolute time slices is also interesting, because it indicates that the percentage-based approach (often used in prior research) is not gaining an unrealistic/unfair advantage from the fact that it potentially encodes the task length in the eye gaze features (e.g. longer trials having a higher number of fixations in the first 10%, hence being indicative of a *during* trial).

Feature Selection

In addition to examining the different accuracies of classifiers, we are also interested in studying which features are most predictive for skill acquisition classification (research question 2). In particular, we want to qualify the differences in behavior *during* and *after* skill acquisition. We therefore ran feature selections for each time slice using the correlation-based feature selection (CFS) method described in [12], which picks the top attributes (on average 10 for our data sets) based on the individual predictive ability of each feature along with the degree of redundancy between them. We then generated frequency tables across all time slices to analyze which features were chosen most often. We repeated this process for both percentage-based and absolute-time classifier sets. Across each of the classifiers, there were five eye-gaze features that consistently appeared across time slices, and which were particularly influential during the early stages. In particular, high values for *standard deviation of relative path angles*, *sum of absolute path angles*, as well as *sum of relative path angles* were found to be indicative of users *during* skill acquisition. This supports prior hypotheses that state that 'relative angles within a scan path indicate the directness of scanning, and therefore the complexity or uncertainty of the task and page layout' [10], since untrained users would typically be more uncertain about how to read the visualization and hence perceive the task to be more complex (a result that was also found in [4]). Similarly, we found that high values of *sum of path distances* and *mean of absolute path angles* were found to be predictive of trials *after* skill acquisition. This may indicate that trained users have more confident gazes, since their individual paths are longer and hence more 'assertive'. During longer time slices (especially after 15000 ms), *Visualization-Specific* AOIs became increasingly important for classification, for example with *during* trials spending significantly more time in the *question text*.

Overall, these results explain why even the classifier with no AOI information (i.e. '*none*') performed comparably well for early time slices (since the five features above were all AOI independent), whereas the *Visualization-Specific* classifier became increasingly accurate during the later stages of trials.

DISCUSSION & FUTURE WORK

This paper has presented our initial steps towards facilitating adaptive help to ease a user's learning curve.

First of all, we have verified that even with simple visualizations, it is possible to identify a significant difference in performance based on the amount of practice a user has had with the system, regardless of other experimental conditions. We have tracked this performance difference using a learning curve, which allowed us to split user trials into two general stages of skill acquisition (*during* and *after* skill acquisition).

Second, this paper has explored the feasibility of building an online classifier that aims to make predictions *while* a user is using a visualization for a short task. We have shown that from the outset, our gaze-based classifiers outperform a simple baseline, and that even after observing only a few seconds of gaze data, we can make predictions with up to 60% accuracy. While these accuracies may not be high enough yet for driving a user-adaptive system, it is worth noting again that in this paper we have solely used gaze data, and that the combination of this data with complementary input features such as interaction data, mouse-tracking data, or other user characteristics is likely to improve prediction accuracies (as shown in [15]).

Third, in order to investigate the generalizability of detecting user skill acquisition across different types of visualizations and other interfaces, we have provided initial results on the relative performance of a *Visualization-Specific* AOI set (less generalizable) compared to *Generic* AOIs (applicable to any user interface). Results of this analysis have shown that, while visualization-specific AOI sets are the most predictive overall (as to be expected), reasonably accurate predictions can be achieved without detailed knowledge of the visualization/interface. In particular, we showed that the generic 3x3 AOI grid performed best overall (compared to more/less fine-grained

grids), indicating that there is a trade-off in terms of having too few AOIs versus too many AOIs.

While these are already encouraging results, there are many alternative methods that we plan to apply in future work in order to build realistic user-adaptive systems. For example, while our time-slices are currently of a 'cumulative' nature, we can investigate 'sliding window' classifiers to see if there are particular segments (e.g., in the middle of a user's system usage) that are more discriminative. Similarly, in this paper we have only attempted to predict a user's skill level based on individual trials (with trials consisting of very short periods of 'interaction'), which is arguably a very difficult task for data-driven classification. An alternative that we envision is to classify based on longer periods of user gaze data, for example through combining a number of trials to form longer interaction periods. Another alternative could be to track gaze behavior over such longer periods, and then classify users based on particular *changes* in behaviors.

Similarly, while the simple two-way split has given us some initial insights into the feasibility of user classification, as well as the behavioral differences that accompany a user's skill level, there are a number of potential enhancements to explore. For example, since the learning curve follows a typical power law [18] (see Figure 3), we may investigate alternative splits (e.g., labeling the first 20 trials as *during* and the rest as *after*) to tease out even stronger and more discriminatory features. Likewise, we expect the effect of the learning curve to be stronger when we move to more complex or unfamiliar types of visualizations or tasks. This will also allow us to investigate how different learning curves map to differences in behavior.

In terms of generalizability, we intend to reuse the *Generic* AOIs in future experiments, where we will combine data from different visualizations and interfaces to investigate general trends of user behavior. If classifiers based on such heterogeneous data sets are indeed able to predict user skill acquisition, our methods would hence point towards a general method to identify user skill across visualization systems in general.

Lastly, future research challenges also lie in devising adaptive mechanisms that can actually aid users during the skill acquisition phase. Such challenges include, for example, choosing the type of adaptation to use (e.g., tooltips vs. reducing interface functionalities), as well as analyzing the relative benefits and drawbacks of such adaptations (e.g., adaptation effectiveness vs. intrusiveness).

REFERENCES

1. Adams, J.A. Historical review and appraisal of research on the learning, retention, and transfer of human motor skills. *Psychological Bulletin 101*, 1 (1987), 41–74.

2. Amar, R., Eagan, J., and Stasko, J. Low-Level Components of Analytic Activity in Information Visualization. *Proceedings of the Proceedings of the 2005 IEEE Symposium on Information Visualization*, IEEE Computer Society (2005), 15–.

3. Bednarik, R., Eivazi, S., and Vrzakova, H. A Computational Approach for Prediction of Problem-Solving Behavior Using Support Vector Machines and Eye-Tracking Data. In Y.I. Nakano, C. Conati and T. Bader, eds., *Eye Gaze in Intelligent User Interfaces*. Springer London, London, 2013, 111–134.

4. Bondareva, D., Conati, C., Feyzi-Behnagh, R., Harley, J.M., Azevedo, R., and Bouchet, F. Inferring Learning from Gaze Data during Interaction with an Environment to Support Self-Regulated Learning. In H.C. Lane, K. Yacef, J. Mostow and P. Pavlik, eds., *Artificial Intelligence in Education*. Springer Berlin Heidelberg, 2013, 229–238.

5. Bunt, A., Conati, C., and McGrenere, J. Supporting interface customization using a mixed-initiative approach. ACM Press (2007), 92.

6. Carenini, G., Conati, C., Hoque, E., Steichen, B., Toker, D., and Enns, J.T. Highlighting Interventions and User Differences: Informing Adaptive Information Visualization Support. (2013), (accepted).

7. Conati, C. and Merten, C. Eye-tracking for user modeling in exploratory learning environments: An empirical evaluation. *Knowledge-Based Systems 20*, 6 (2007), 557–574.

8. D'Mello, S., Olney, A., Williams, C., and Hays, P. Gaze tutor: A gaze-reactive intelligent tutoring system. *International Journal of Human-Computer Studies 70*, 5 (2012), 377–398.

9. Dillon, A. Spatial-semantics: How users derive shape from information space. *Journal of the American Society for Information Science 51*, 6 (2000), 521–528.

10. Goldberg, J.H. and Helfman, J.I. Comparing information graphics: a critical look at eye tracking. *Proceedings of the 3rd BELIV'10 Workshop: BEyond time and errors: novel evaLuation methods for Information Visualization*, ACM (2010), 71–78.

11. Hall, M., Frank, E., Holmes, G., Pfahringer, B., Reutemann, P., and Witten, I.H. The WEKA data mining software: an update. *SIGKDD Explor. Newsl. 11*, 1 (2009), 10–18.

12. Hall, M. Correlation-based Feature Selection for Machine Learning. 1999. http://www.cs.waikato.ac.nz/~mhall/thesis.pdf.

13. Jameson, A. The human-computer interaction handbook. In J.A. Jacko and A. Sears, eds., L. Erlbaum Associates Inc., Hillsdale, NJ, USA, 2003, 305–330.

14. Kardan, S. and Conati, C. Exploring gaze data for determining user learning with an interactive simulation. *In: Proc. of UMAP, 20th Int. Conf. on User Modeling, Adaptation, and Personalization*, (2012), 126–138.

15. Kardan, S. and Conati, C. Comparing and Combining Eye Gaze and Interface Actions for Determining User Learning with an Interactive Simulation. *In: Proc. of UMAP, 21st Int. Conf. on User Modeling, Adaptation and Personalization*, (2013).

16. Lewandowsky, S. and Spence, I. Discriminating Strata in Scatterplots. *Journal of the American Statistical Association 84*, 407 (1989), 682–688.

17. Linton, F. and Schaefer, H.-P. Recommender Systems for Learning: Building User and Expert Models through Long-Term Observation of Application Use. *User Modeling and User-Adapted Interaction 10*, 2-3 (2000), 181–208.

18. Logan, G.D. Shapes of reaction-time distributions and shapes of learning curves: A test of the instance theory of automaticity. *Journal of Experimental Psychology: Learning, Memory, and Cognition 18*, 5 (1992), 883–914.

19. McDonald, S. and Stevenson, R.J. Navigation in hyperspace: An evaluation of the effects of navigational tools and subject matter expertise on browsing and information retrieval in hypertext. *Interacting with Computers 10*, 2 (1998), 129–142.

20. Pascual-Cid, V., Vigentini, L., and Quixal, M. Visualising Virtual Learning Environments: Case Studies of the Website Exploration Tool. IEEE (2010), 149–155.

21. Qu, L. and Johnson, W.L. Detecting the Learner's Motivational States in An Interactive Learning Environment. *Proceedings of the 2005 conference on Artificial Intelligence in Education: Supporting Learning through Intelligent and Socially Informed Technology*, IOS Press (2005), 547–554.

22. Saraiya, P., North, C., and Duca, K. An Insight-Based Methodology for Evaluating Bioinformatics Visualizations. *IEEE Transactions on Visualization and Computer Graphics 11*, 4 (2005), 443–456.

23. Speelman, C. and Kirsner, K. *Beyond the Learning Curve*. Oxford University Press, 2005.

24. Steichen, B., Carenini, G., and Conati, C. User-adaptive information visualization: using eye gaze data to infer visualization tasks and user cognitive abilities. *Proceedings of the 2013 international conference on Intelligent user interfaces*, ACM (2013), 317–328.

25. Toker, D., Conati, C., Carenini, G., and Haraty, M. Towards adaptive information visualization: on the influence of user characteristics. *Proceedings of the 20th international conference on User Modeling, Adaptation, and Personalization*, Springer-Verlag (2012), 274–285.

26. Toker, D., Conati, C., Steichen, B., and Carenini, G. Individual user characteristics and information visualization: connecting the dots through eye tracking. *Proceedings of the SIGCHI Conference on Human Factors in Computing Systems*, ACM (2013), 295–304.

27. Velez, M.C., Silver, D., and Tremaine, M. Understanding visualization through spatial ability differences. *IEEE Visualization, 2005. VIS 05*, (2005), 511–518.

28. Zhu, Y. Measuring effective data visualization. In *Advances in Visual Computing*. Springer, 2007, 652–661.

29. Ziemkiewicz, C., Crouser, R.J., Yauilla, A.R., Su, S.L., Ribarsky, W., and Chang, R. How locus of control influences compatibility with visualization style. *2011 IEEE Conference on Visual Analytics Science and Technology (VAST)*, (2011), 81–90.

Active Learning of Intuitive Control Knobs for Synthesizers Using Gaussian Processes

Cheng-Zhi Anna Huang
Harvard University
czhuang@fas.harvard.edu

David Duvenaud
University of Cambridge
dkd23@cam.ac.uk

Kenneth C. Arnold
Harvard University
kcarnold@seas.harvard.edu

Brenton Partridge
Harvard University
bapartridge@seas.harvard.edu

Josiah W. Oberholtzer
Harvard University
josiah.oberholtzer@gmail.com

Krzysztof Z. Gajos
Harvard University
kgajos@seas.harvard.edu

ABSTRACT

Typical synthesizers only provide controls to the low-level parameters of sound-synthesis, such as wave-shapes or filter envelopes. In contrast, composers often want to adjust and express higher-level qualities, such as how 'scary' or 'steady' sounds are perceived to be.

We develop a system which allows users to directly control abstract, high-level qualities of sounds. To do this, our system learns functions that map from synthesizer control settings to perceived levels of high-level qualities. Given these functions, our system can generate high-level knobs that directly adjust sounds to have more or less of those qualities. We model the functions mapping from control-parameters to the degree of each high-level quality using Gaussian processes, a nonparametric Bayesian model. These models can adjust to the complexity of the function being learned, account for nonlinear interaction between control-parameters, and allow us to characterize the uncertainty about the functions being learned.

By tracking uncertainty about the functions being learned, we can use active learning to quickly calibrate the tool, by querying the user about the sounds the system expects to most improve its performance. We show through simulations that this model-based active learning approach learns high-level knobs on certain classes of target concepts faster than several baselines, and give examples of the resulting automatically-constructed knobs which adjust levels of non-linear, high-level concepts.

Author Keywords

Intuitive Control Knobs; Synthesizers; Sound Synthesis; Sound Design; Intelligent Interactive Systems; User Interfaces; Active Learning; Preference Learning; Gaussian Processes.

ACM Classification Keywords

H.5.5. [Sound and Music Computing]: Methodologies and Techniques; Signal Analysis, Synthesis, and Processing

INTRODUCTION

Composers and sound designers use synthesizers to create sounds with spectral and temporal dynamics beyond what is possible through acoustic instruments or recorded sounds. These users generally seek not just to create a certain sound, but rather a collection of related sounds, by transforming a set of sounds in semantically meaningful directions. The ability to intuitively adjust only the relevant qualities of a set of sounds is paramount to the artist's workflow. However, synthesizers are particularly difficult for artists to interact with, since their many parameters must often be adjusted in complex ways in order to change just a single semantically-meaningful aspect of a sound. This often forces a shift in the user's attention from expressing their high-level goals to the low-level trial-and-error tweaking of control parameters.

Several strategies have been developed to address this problem: First, providing the user with pre-set sounds having various qualities, such as "bright acoustic piano" or "dark acoustic piano". Second, interpolating between existing sounds, by averaging the low-level control settings which generate those sounds. Third, expert-engineered high-level knobs for directly controlling relatively intuitive aspects of sounds, such as Waves' OneKnobs, mostly used in the context of production to "brighten" or "phatten" tracks and mixes, and which under the hood controls sound-treatment modules such as equalizers, compressors, and resonators.

However, synthesizers can support more complex concepts, such as those that are multi-modal. For example there are different kinds of "scary" sounds, such as low rumbling, cold chilly wind-like sounds. And we might want different ways to adjust the "scariness" of a sound depending on what kind it is. For example, if a sound is directional, we might make it more "scary" by making it more aggressive. If a sound is more of an ambient pulsating sound, we can make it warble in more irregular ways or more high pitched, or perhaps add some eerie metallic "clicks" to its foreground.

In this paper, we explicitly model high-level sound qualities in order to allow users to automatically adjust arbitrary sounds to have desired levels of those qualities. We define a high-level concept as a function that maps from a high-dimensional control space to the perceived level of that quality. With such mappings, we can generate a high-level knob which directly adjusts sounds to have more or less of a given quality. These knobs are generated for each sound by constructing a path through control space which increases (or decreases) the level of the learned function. Such paths allow composers to move towards and away from sounds along perceptually meaningful dimensions. To learn such functions for a high-level concept, we learn from user ratings of sounds generated by the synthesizer.

In order to learn from a small number of user interactions, we take an active learning approach to assisting a user in finding points in the control-parameter space to demonstrate a high-level concept. The user first informs the system which sorts of sounds she wants to be able to modify and to which ranges. At any point in teaching the system a high-level concept, the user can ask the system where it wants to learn about the high-level concept the most. The system queries the user on the sound that it believes can most improve its ability to adjust the high-level quality for the given set of sounds. The user can listen to the sound and respond by rating how much they think the sound has the high-level quality. We have prototyped a user interface to allow users to express this rating by allowing them to organize sounds on a continuous one-dimensional space to indicate how much they think the sounds carry a particular high-level quality.

Our formulation can be applied to other domains where a user wants to build a layer of richer, personalized controls on top of the parameters provided by the original system.

RELATED WORK

We describe related work in computer-assisted sound design and music composition that uses the metaphor of knobs (one-dimensional, continuous controls), and also other kinds of interfaces and interactions that assist users in working with synthesizers. Our active-learning approach is informed by work in active learning in general, and active data selection, and Bayesian optimization.

High-level knobs

There have been a number of works on learning high-level "knobs" for audio editing tools such as equalizers and reverberators. [21,24,25] treat a knob as a fixed linear mapping between a low-level control and a high-level quality. They adopt a weighting-function procedure widely used in psychoacoustics to tune hearing aids, which operates by correlating gain in each frequency bin to a user's perceptual ratings.

Instead of mapping directly between parameters of a specific reverberator and user ratings, [22] derived nonlinear mappings from low-level controls to reverberation measures such as "echoness", which can be generalized onto different reverberators with similar parameterizations. Their system then learns linear mappings from reverberation measures to perceptual qualities such as "boomy". As sound modification on synthesizers is more complex and their parameterizations

vary drastically across different synthesizers, it is more difficult to engineer a set of high-level functions *a priori*. Instead, we use the expressiveness of nonparametric methods to model the covariance structure between controls and to adjust to the complexity of functions being learned.

As user ratings for different high-level qualities may be correlated, [22] uses transfer learning to incorporate concepts taught by prior users. In this setting, each user rates only a subset of example sounds to train a user-concept, and the system fills in the rest of the ratings by weighting ratings of other user-concepts by their distances to the current user-concept. To choose the subset of sounds to query a user, the work uses active learning by selecting sounds that most differentiate between previously learned user-concepts. [3] crowd-sources many more user-concepts to study which equalizer descriptors are widely-agreed-upon and which are true audio synonyms. Our method takes an active-learning approach to help a user more quickly teach a concept from scratch, with the objective of maximizing test-time performance, defined as the ability to construct high-level knobs that can adjust desired qualities in sounds with high certainty.

In additional to the "knobs" metaphor for interaction, [17] uses a 2D self-organizing map to place concepts with similar ratings close to each other, so that users can directly explore the semantic space instead of control space. [8] allows users to interact with different supervised learning algorithms to define mappings from arbitrary controllers to synthesis parameters. [7] describes a play-along mode where the user first composes a sequence of synthesis parameters and then gestures along as it is being played back. The parameter-gesture pairs become training data for learning a mapping that supports the reversed interaction. Instead of relying on user data, [14] applies data mining to existing presets to provide autocompletion. For example, as a user adjusts the controls, other statistically related controls adjusts itself accordingly.

A complementary interaction is when the user is not searching for a desired sound, but already has an audio recording of a target sound at hand, and wants the machine to automatically generate a synthesizer setting that approximates that sound. With such a setting, the sound is no longer canned, but can be manipulated in real-time using the synthesizer controllers. This is often achieved by minimizing the difference between the timbral trajectories of the synthesized and the target sound. As synthesizer controls are high dimensional and highly nonlinear, optimization techniques such as genetic algorithms or particle swarm optimization are often used to search through different synthesis structures and to perform parameter estimation, as in [10, 11, 16, 28]. These techniques also allow users to control a synthesizer by directly specifying values for acoustic features [12].

The "knobs" metaphor is also used in computer-assisted composition for helping users adjust high-level qualities of symbolic representations of music. For example, [18] exposes the log weighting between transition matrices in hidden Markov models trained on major ("happy") and minor ("sad") songs, as an intuitive knob for adjusting how "happy" an accompaniment sounds. [20] adjusts melodies to be more or less 'tonal', 'serial', or 'brown' by moving closer or further away from that concept's decision boundary.

Active learning

A number of systems have explored using active learning for assisting users in defining personalized concepts [1,9,21]. For example, [9] supports users in interactively defining concepts for re-ranking web images search results, and presents users the option of classifying images that are closest to the decision boundary between positive and negative classes, using a nearest-neighbor approach. They also use a heuristic to actively select images that explore new weightings in their distance metrics on low-level features used in computer vision.

More generally, one of the goals of active data selection is to select data that reduces the uncertainty the most on some parameters of interest, given past observations. For example, we can aim to maximize the expected information gain on model parameters by selecting data where the the posterior predictive variance is the highest [15]. Alternatively, the goal could be to minimize generalization error by choosing data that minimizes the overall variance of the predictor [4]. Both of these criteria have been employed in active Gaussian process GP regression, by leveraging the variance on the posterior predictive marginal distribution of GPs [26]. [13] adapts this approach into a classification setting of visual object category recognition, defines a covariance function that reflects local features for object and image representations, and then actively selects data closest to the decision boundary.

However, for settings where we are not given a set of examples a priori to select from, we need to first propose a set of queries from a continuous space, which is the case for our work. Furthermore, the objective may be more specific than reducing uncertainty on parameters. More generally, active learning is the setting where a model and an associated goodness (or loss) is first defined and then the goal is to query a next point that is predicted to result in a future model that produces the highest goodness (or equivalently lowest loss).

In our work, we define a new utility function for our domain by formalizing what the user would desire during test time. Our utility function captures how confident a model is in producing the desired knob paths for adjusting a given set of starting sounds. As in [19] and [2], our system learns in an iterative manner, and at each iteration we query the user with the point that maximizes the tool's expected utility. While [2] uses Bayesian optimization to search globally to help users in procedural animation to find the best parameter setting, our goal is to focus learning in regions that are expected to later allow us to best fulfill user requests. As in [27], we compute the expected utility of a point by sampling its values from the current distribution, and evaluate the model's expected confidence in adjusting sounds, conditioned on fantasized ratings.

OVERVIEW OF METHOD

We treat a high-level concept as a function that maps from synthesizer control parameter space $\mathbf{x} \in \mathbb{R}^D$ to perceived $y \in \mathbb{R}$ levels of that quality. If we knew this function $f(\mathbf{x})$, we could automatically adjust that concept on a preset $\mathbf{x}_s$ to

a desired level y_d of that quality by moving $\mathbf{x}_s$ to a nearby location that has the desired quality level. A knob would move $\mathbf{x}$ along a continuous path through control-parameter space corresponding to increasing and decreasing levels of $f(\mathbf{x})$.

Since we do not know $f(\mathbf{x})$, we start with a probabilistic model of $f(\mathbf{x})$ and refine it with user feedback. Because the domain of f will be high-dimensional, learning the function over its whole domain would require an impractical amount of user feedback. Instead, we focus our learning in high-level knob space by asking for user feedback only in the parts of the control parameter space that is relevant to improving the paths for the high-level knobs.

To guide the acquisition of user feedback, we first specify how we expect the system will be used (which sorts of sounds will be modified, and the expected range of modifications). We can then estimate how well the tool can be expected to fulfill the user's request, given the different queries made to the user during training time. We can then ask the user for the feedback which is most expected to improve the test-time performance of the system. In short, we will use active learning to select the queries made to the user in order to determine f in places which will be expected to improve the utility of the tool the most.

Determining good user queries requires two steps: first, proposing a set of possible user queries, then ranking those queries by how much they are expected to improve the utility of the tool. For the former, we develop a heuristic which proposes points nearby points visited during path optimizations. Second, to estimate a candidate's expected impact of the utility of the system, we sample from the current posterior marginal distribution of f and, for each sample, evaluate the utility of the system as if we had actually made that observation. The candidate point that maximizes for expected utility of the system is chosen for user feedback.

MODELING HIGH-LEVEL KNOBS

We model the function f mapping from control parameters to high-level concepts probabilistically with Gaussian process (GP) priors [23]. In contrast to previous approaches which learned linear mappings [21], the non-parametric nature of GPs allows us to learn a function whose complexity can grow to match that of the function being learned. We use a zero-mean prior and the standard squared-exponential kernel:

$$f \sim GP(0, k)$$
$$k(\mathbf{x}, \mathbf{x}') = \sigma_y^2 \exp(-\frac{(\mathbf{x} - \mathbf{x}')^2}{2\ell^2}) + \sigma_n^2 \delta_{ii'}$$

The kernel is parameterized by lengthscales ℓ, which specify the typical distances along which each dimension of f varies, and by the amplitude and noise variances σ_y^2 and σ_n^2, respectively. We denote these parameters collectively as θ.

GP regression is an appropriate tool for this problem for two reasons: First, it provides everywhere a closed-form estimate of the remaining uncertainty about the function being learned, which is necessary for estimating the expected performance of the model. Second, the marginal likelihood gives us a principled way to choose the parameters of the kernel.

Integrating over hyperparameters

Typically, the parameters of the kernel are estimated by maximum likelihood. However, when there are very few datapoints, these point estimates are known to drastically over-estimate lengthscales, leading to an under-estimate of uncertainty about the function itself. As we need a useful estimate of uncertainty even conditioned on only a few data points, we must also characterize our uncertainty about the lengthscales of the GP. Therefore we take a fully-Bayesian approach by approximately integrating over hyperparameters using a Sobol sequence.

Our approximate integration over kernel parameters means that our predictive marginal posterior of f at a given point $\mathbf{x}^\star$ is a weighted sum of GP posteriors:

$$P(y^*|\mathbf{x}^*, \mathbf{X}, \mathbf{y}) = \int P(y^*|\mathbf{x}^*, \mathbf{X}, \mathbf{y}, \theta) P(\theta|\mathbf{X}, \mathbf{y}) d\theta$$

$$P(\theta|\mathbf{X}, \mathbf{y}) = \frac{P(\mathbf{y}|\mathbf{X}, \theta) P(\theta)}{\int P(\mathbf{y}|\mathbf{X}, \theta') P(\theta') d\theta'}$$

The mean and variance of the posterior marginal at $\mathbf{x}^*$ is given below. $\mu_i(\mathbf{x}^*)$ and $\sigma_i^2(\mathbf{x}^*)$ are the posterior mean and variance of the GP with a single set of hyperparameters θ_i.

$$\mu_i(\mathbf{x}^*) = \mathbf{k}_{\theta_i}(\mathbf{X}, \mathbf{x})^T \mathbf{K}_{\theta_i}^{-1}(\mathbf{X}, \mathbf{X}) \mathbf{y}$$

$$\sigma_i^2(\mathbf{x}^*) = \mathbf{k}_{\theta_i}(\mathbf{x}, \mathbf{x}) - \mathbf{k}_{\theta_i}(\mathbf{X}, \mathbf{x})^T \mathbf{K}_{\theta_i}^{-1} \mathbf{k}_{\theta_i}(\mathbf{X}, \mathbf{x})$$

$$\mu(\mathbf{x}^*) = \sum_{i=1}^{M} P(\theta_i|\mathbf{X}, \mathbf{y}) \mu_i(\mathbf{x}^*)$$

$$\sigma^2(\mathbf{x}^*) = \sum_{i=1}^{M} P(\theta_i|\mathbf{X}, \mathbf{y}) \left([\mu_i(\mathbf{x}^*) - \mu(\mathbf{x}^*)]^2 + \sigma_i^2(\mathbf{x}^*) \right)$$

To sample a y^* given x^*, we first sample which set of hyperparameters to use, and then sample from the predictive marginal posterior given just that set of hyperparameters.

Knob paths

Once we have an estimate of the function defining a high-level quality, we can generate a knob which varies that quality for a preset sound by finding a path from the preset through control-parameter space corresponding to increasing and decreasing levels of the learned function. We generate such paths by first locally optimizing for each of a set of equally-spaced desired quality levels $\mathbf{y}_d$ spanning from the lowest user rating to the highest, then linearly interpolate between these points. In our experiments, we used 8 equally spaced levels. The objective of this optimization is to minimize the squared difference between the posterior predictive mean and a desired knob level y_d when starting from a control-parameter setting $\mathbf{x}_s$. We denote the control-parameter setting returned by the optimizer as $\mathbf{x}_{sd}$.

$$\mathbf{x}_{sd} = \arg \min_{\mathbf{x}^*} (y_d - \mu(y^*|\mathbf{x}^*, \mathbf{X}, \mathbf{y}))^2 \qquad (1)$$

In future work, we plan to take uncertainty into account while optimizing for desired knob levels, and explicitly optimizing for desirable properties for knobs such as smoothness.

ACTIVE LEARNING

Our system learns in an iterative manner: At each iteration, we choose a point at which to query the user, based on the current model of f. We then update the model of f, and re-query the user. To determine which point to query the user at, we first propose a set of *candidate points*, whose expected impact on the utility of the system we will estimate. After estimating these utilities, we then query the user at the best candidate point.

Evaluating the expected utility of a point

Given a set of *candidate points*, we need to decide which one can most help us improve the utility of our model. Formally, we define *utility* $\mathcal{U}$ as the total mass within ϵ-wide bins centered at the desired knob levels $\mathbf{y}_d$ for all presets $\mathbf{X}_s$.

$$\mathcal{U}(\mathbf{X}, \mathbf{y}) = \sum_{s=1}^{S} \sum_{d=1}^{L} [P(y_{sd} > (y_d + \epsilon)|\mathbf{x}_{sd}, \mathbf{X}, \mathbf{y})$$
$$- P(y_{sd} > (y_d - \epsilon)|\mathbf{x}_{sd}, \mathbf{X}, \mathbf{y})] \qquad (2)$$

This expression can be intuitively thought of as the probability that we will be able to give the user a sound with the desired high-level quality by moving along the learned paths.

Reoptimizing hyperparameters under fantasies

To evaluate the expected impact of a candidate $\mathbf{x}_c$ on our system, we sample the current posterior predictive marginal distribution $P(y_c|\mathbf{x}_c, \mathbf{X}, \mathbf{y})$ for what the possible perceived y_c could be. In order to more accurately evaluate expected utilities, we retrain our model for each sample by re-optimizing the hyperparameters on the GP prior as if we had seen this additional observation, resulting in a fantasized posterior predictive marginal distribution of $P(y^*|\mathbf{x}^*, \mathbf{x}_c, y_c, \mathbf{X}, \mathbf{y})$ on which the desired knob levels are optimized. Intuitively, the hyperparameter re-optimization is helpful because it accounts for the fact that new queries can potentially change our estimates of the lengthscales, which can drastically change our model's predictions. This is essential early on when we have not yet seen much data, and are very uncertain about the lengthscales.

$$\mathbf{E}(\mathcal{U}|\mathbf{x}_c, \mathbf{X}, \mathbf{y}) = \int \mathcal{U}(\mathbf{x}_c, y_c, \mathbf{X}, \mathbf{y}) P(y_c|\mathbf{x}_c, \mathbf{X}, \mathbf{y}) \mathrm{d}y_c \qquad (3)$$

Proposing candidate points

Intuitively, we want to learn more about points that can potentially improve the knob paths. We use a heuristic for generating candidate points which are likely to be useful: We sample points nearby those visited by the truncated-Newton optimizer while determining the knob paths.

Because we expect f to vary slowly in directions which have long lengthscales, we heuristically add gaussian noise to candidates $\mathbf{X}_c$ with variances proportional to the length scales of that dimension. Hence, to determine the noise for a particular candidate x_c, we first sample a set of length scales according to their marginal likelihood. Then, for each dimension d, we sample from a gaussian with variance proportional to the lengthscale l^d of that dimension. We reject any points that fall outside the domain of the synthesizer.

$$\epsilon_c^d \sim \mathcal{N}(0, \frac{l^d}{2})$$
$$\mathbf{x}_c^d \leftarrow \mathbf{x}_c^d + \epsilon_c^d$$

To further increase the potential information gain, we also heuristically include as candidate points the peaks on the posterior variance of f that are reachable through the truncated optimizer from the given set of presets $\mathbf{X}_s$.

The active-learning algorithm and its variations

Algorithm 1 outlines our procedure for how to decide where the query the user next for feedback. Both `for` loops can be parallelized. Figure 1 shows a synthetic 1D visualization of some the steps involved.

Algorithm 1 Choosing the next point $\mathbf{x_r}$ for user to rate

---

Input: $\mathcal{D} = \{\mathbf{X}, \mathbf{y}\}$, $\mathbf{X}_s$, $\mathbf{y}_d$, n_c: num of candidates, n_m: num of monte carlo samples
Train full-bayes GP with $\mathcal{D}$
Optimize (1) for $\mathbf{X}_{sd}^{path}$ on GP given $\mathbf{y}_d$ and $\mathbf{X}_s$
Randomly choose n_c candidates $\mathbf{X}_c$ from points
   visited during the previous optimization step
for $i = 1$ **to** n_c **do**
  for $j = 1$ **to** n_m **do**
    Sample $y_{c_{ij}} \sim \mathcal{GP}(y|\mathbf{X}_{c_i}, \mathcal{D})$
    Fantasize $\hat{GP}_{c_i}$ by training it with $y_{c_{ij}}, \mathbf{X}_{c_i}, \mathcal{D}$
    Optimize (1) for $\mathbf{X}_{sd_{ij}}^{path}$ on $\hat{GP}_{c_i}$ given $\mathbf{y}_d$ and $\mathbf{X}_s$
    Compute $\mathcal{U}_{ij}$ by (2)
  end for
  $\mathbf{E}(\mathcal{U}_i) = \frac{1}{n_m} \sum_{j=1}^{n_m} \mathcal{U}_{ij}$
end for
minIndex $= \arg\min \mathbf{E}(\mathcal{U}_i)$
$\mathbf{x}_r = \mathbf{X}_{c_{minIndex}}$

We later refer to our full-fledged path-informed model-based active-learning procedure as "active learning (re-opt)". We also experimented with a number of simplifications, both as baselines to compare against, and also because they can have shorter run times and so can be more naturally integrated into interactive systems. "Active learning" takes out the step of reoptimizing hyperparameters after each fantasized outcome. "Path entropy" skips the fantasizing step all together, and chooses the point that has the highest variance from the set of proposed candidate points, while "Path random" simply chooses a point at random from the proposed points.

USER INTERFACE AND INTERACTION

In order to support users in defining their own high-level concepts, we have prototyped a user interface that allows users to demonstrate high-level concepts with examples. The user can communicate how much a sound carries a high-level concept by placing it accordingly into a box, as shown in Figure 2, where the horizontal axis indicates an increasing level of a high-level concept from left to right. This allows users to rate sounds in reference to each other, to correct previous ratings, and also to re-adjust their overall scales.

If the user has some prior knowledge of which control parameters might give rise to a high-level concept, she can help the machine reduce the dimensionality of the problem by selecting a subset of parameters, as illustrated by labels 1 and 2 in Figure 2. The user can also make such decisions later on in the process as she gains more experience with the synthesizer.

As the user has accumulated a number of points in the box, the user can ask the machine to learn the concept and apply it to a starting sound in order to check how well the machine is understanding the concept. This can be performed at the interface by first hitting the "play" button, at which point the system trains the model and then optimizes for a path through the sound to increasing and decreasing levels of the learned concept. The system has been set to optimize for three discrete levels on the learned function. Both these four points and the original sound are added to the box and placed horizontally at where the model believes it should be. These points are the "darker" row of dots labeled as 7 in Figure 2, where the second dot from the left is the original sound. The user then has the option of correcting these points by moving them left or right, and the moved points become a new data point for training the high-level concept. The user can now move the slider above the box to adjust her sound according to the learned concept, and see how it controls the synth control parameters.

Assisting the user with active learning

The user can specify how she expects to use the system by first choosing a set of presets she wishes to modify. This can be indicated in the interface by suppressing those presets, labeled as 3 in Figure 2. Then at each iteration, the user can ask for different kinds of assistance by clicking on the corresponding helper buttons. For example, the "next filler random" button labeled as 5 calls for the "path random" variation of our active-learning algorithm to propose the next point to evaluate. A new control parameter setting is then added as a dot to the box, placed at a horizontal position where the model currently believes how much of the high-level concept it carries. The user can help refine the model by correcting these points.

EXPERIMENTS AND EVALUATIONS

We ran a preliminary pilot study with two composers to collect high-level concepts. We evaluate our method in two parts: how well our model captures these high-level concepts, and how quickly our active-learning approach is able to learn these high-level knobs compared to other baselines. For each concept, we show a few examples of knob paths.

Pilot study with two composers

The task was for users to build a knob for a high-level quality such as "scariness" that she wishes to more directly control during sound synthesis. First, the user was prompted to choose a set of preset sounds on which she would test the high-level knob. The user was then asked to identify a set of examples on the synthesizer that carries varying degrees of that high-level quality. Users interacted with our interface shown in Figure 2, with the option of asking for suggested examples from the lightweight variation "path random" of

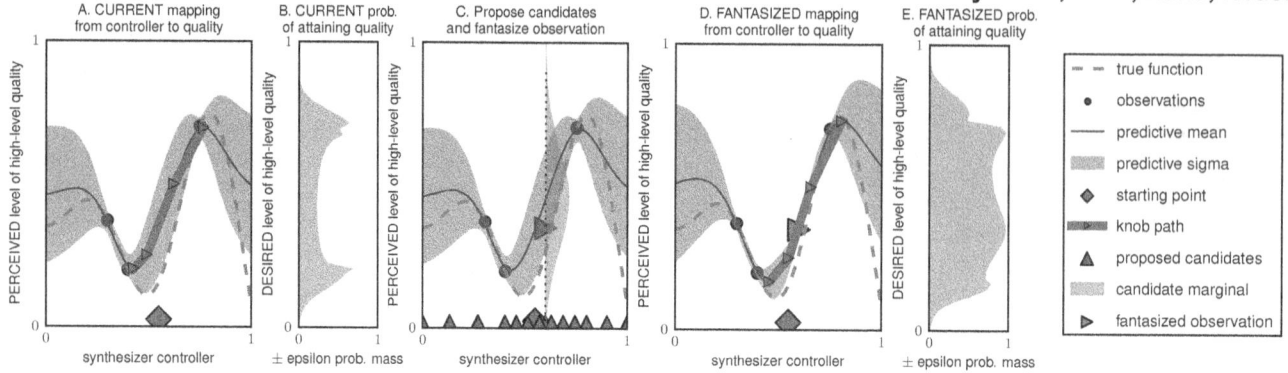

Figure 1. Synthetic 1D example of an 1-sample evaluation of the expected utility of a proposed candidate, where the model's utility increased from (B) to (E). Plots A, C, D refer to mappings from control-parameter (x-axis) to a high-level quality (y-axis). Plots B, E refer to the model's confidence in attaining desired levels of a high-level quality (y-axis) measured by the $\pm \epsilon$ probability mass (x-axis) from the mean of the predictive marginal for the corresponding control-parameter on the knob path (green line in preceding plot). (A) Current mapping from synth controller to high-level quality, given three ratings of perceived levels of high-level quality. The green diamond is a sound in the synth control space that is to be adjusted. (C) Proposed candidates shown as magenta triangles on x-axis. The Gaussian predictive marginal of one of the candidates is shown and the red-triangle shows a sample from that distribution. (D) The mapping after fitting the model with the addition fantasized observation (red-triangle).

our active-learning. The interface allows users to specify the amount of a perceived quality in a sound by moving the dot that represents it on a one-dimensional axis. The synthesizer used for the user studies is a representative software synth named FreeAlpha, from Linplug.

Modeling high-level concepts

From these two pilot studies, we collected three examples of nonlinear concepts on synthesizers, "pulsation", "guitar-like" and "scary". The first and third are multimodal, while the second is unimodal. They range from concrete to abstract. The "pulsation" concept was obtained by querying a single user uniformly on a 8x8 grid in the control-parameter space of 2 synth controls. As we wanted to use this concept for our later simulations, we did not want to bias the input distribution with any of the methods that were being compared in the simulations. For the "guitar-like" and "scary", the user was free to interact with our interface and ask for suggested queries from the "path-random" variation of our active-learning method.

We first illustrate these concepts and then show cross-validation results on how our model performs when trying to predict how users would rate a sound.

Example concept 1: "pulsation"
We want to learn about how two control parameters, the rate of low frequency modulation FM and amplitude modulation AM, interact to produce different degrees of perceived "pulsation". Turning either of these controls up increases pulsation up to a point where modulation becomes so fast that we can not perceive distinctive vibratos anymore, but instead we hear a timbral color change. Moreover, they interact in how they give rise to perceived "pulsation". When FM is low, it dominates our perception, and turning up AM does not give any effect. However when FM is so high that we cannot hear the pulsation anymore, for example the diamond in the lower right corner of Figure 7, turning AM up in the lower ranges allows us to add more "pulsation" to our colored sound. We can observe this effect on the response surface of the mean of

the GP conditioned on a grid of 8x8 user ratings on these two control dimensions, shown in Figure 7.

Example concept 2: "guitar-like"
Figure 3, left, shows the learned model of the "guitar-like" quality, over 2 of the the 4 control dimensions. The GP characterizes this quality as peaking when the attack time on the amplitude envelope is short, the "cut-off" on the bandpass filter is low, the frequency of a low-frequency oscillator (LFO) is medium, and the detune on the chorus is high. Colloquially, a guitar-like has a "sharp attack", with some warble in the release, and is coloured with some "detuned harmony". In the space of these four control-parameters, this function is unimodal, which means all paths will be maximized at the same point, as shown in figure 3, left.

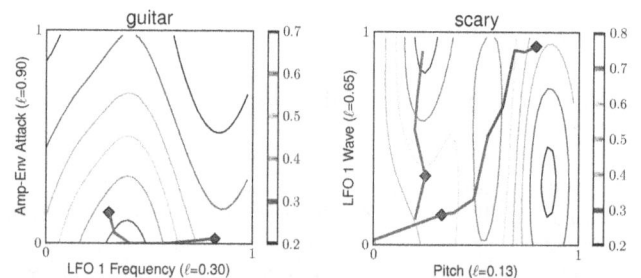

Figure 3. Visualizations of high-level concepts. Contours represent the full-Bayes GP posterior mean of the degree of the high-level quality as a function of synthesizer controls. Red, blue and green lines represent paths through control-space which vary the high-level quality, starting from sounds denoted by black diamonds. Left: 2D slice of posterior mean of "guitar-like" function, and knob paths. Right: 2D slice of posterior of "scary" function.

Example concept 3: "scary"
We model this quality as a function of four different control-parameters: the depth of a filter envelope, the waveshape and the frequency of the LFO, and the main pitch of the synth. In figure 3, right, we show a slice of the mean of a GP conditioned on user ratings. In this slice, both the LFO frequency and the depth of the filter envelope are fixed at 0.7 which

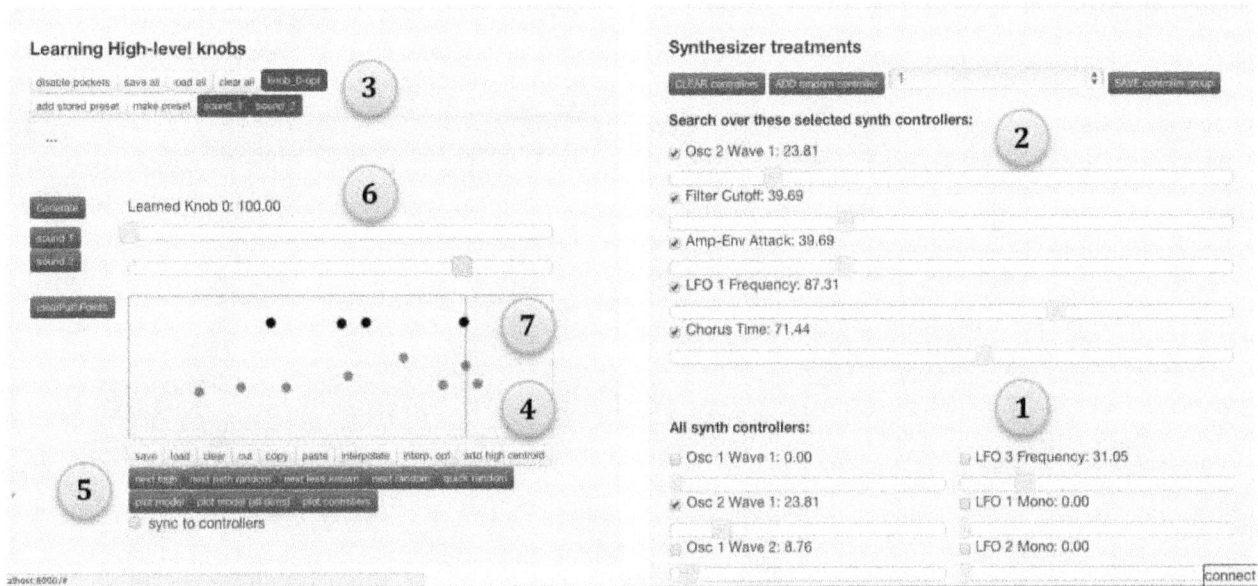

Figure 2. User interface for learning and applying high-level knobs to sounds. (1) Sliders for adjusting the low-level control-parameters on the synthesizer directly. There are a total of 64, many are cropped in this screenshot for space. Users can choose a subset of low-level controls to optimize over by checking the checkboxes, and these controls will pop up in region (2). (3) Preset buttons for users to choose as starting sounds. Users can also instantiate new sounds as buttons. (4) Box for users to give ratings to sounds. The horizontal axis of the box reflects how much a sound carries a high-level concept, increasing from left to right. Each training example is represented as a dot and corresponds to a particular synthesizer control-parameter setting. Users can click on buttons in region (5) to ask the tool to suggest sounds to add as training examples. (6) Sliders for adjusting high-level qualities in sounds directly once the model is trained. They are like macro knobs that control the low-level synthesizer parameters in region (2). Each slider corresponds to a knob path that is specific to a starting preset in region (3). (7) The row of darker dots correspond to optimized points on the high-level knob path.

corresponds to a steady pulsating rumbling base sound. As the LFO parameter increases, the waveshape becomes more complex, for example going from sine waves, to sawtooth, and finally to a much noisier wave, introducing hisses into the foreground making the sound more scary. As the main pitch of the synth increases, the volume of the "scary" sound body also increases. However, if the pitch is increased too much, the sound becomes much thinner and loses its force. In between the two modes, the foreground hissing and the background rumbling merge, and the sound becomes slightly less scary.

Predicting user ratings

We compare predictive performance of our GP-based model to other models on held-out user ratings. The results are shown in Table 1, where we see that for multimodal qualities "pulsating" and "scary", our model predicts user ratings better than support vector regression (SVR) with a radial basis kernel, decision tree regression (DTR), and linear regression. Although the predictive performance of the GP is not uniformly better than other regression techniques, the probabilistic nature of the GP enables active learning, and the smooth function estimates it provides enable us to compute continuous adjustment paths. Future work will revisit the covariance function used in our model, in order to allow it to capture more structure.

Evaluating active learning

To evaluate our path-informed model-based active-learning algorithm, we run simulations on two functions to compare

quality \model	GP	SVR	DTR	LINEAR
pulsating (n=64, d=2)	**0.036**	0.051	0.051	0.073
guitar-like (n=31, d=4)	0.042	0.029	**0.026**	0.040
scary (n=64, d=4)	**0.065**	0.068	0.116	0.071

Table 1. Comparing the 10-fold cross-validation mean-squared error of different models on user ratings of different high-level qualities. n is the number of ratings, and d is the number of control parameters being varied. Each quality's ratings were gathered from a single user. Users rate sounds by placing sounds on a one-dimensional interface.

their performances to several baselines. We used IPython's parallel framework to evaluate the expected utility of each candidate in parallel, corresponding to the outer for loop in Algorithm 1. We first started with a simple synthetic function, and then ran another set of simulations on a function learned from user ratings. We show that our method in the former case is able to learn target concepts faster according to the metric we define below in Eqn. (4) by focusing on regions most relevant to the knob paths. For the latter function, even though our method did not learn faster than some baselines according to our current metric, it performed qualitatively better by being able to identify multiple modes, and to route different starting points to their nearby peaks. In future work, we need to define an error metric that captures the multimodal nature of synthesizer concepts. We also wish to devise a metric that depends on relative perceptions. For example, a user may be less concerned about a knob giving a sound that is exactly 0.5 "scary", if there even exists such a notion, but instead she might be more concerned if moving a knob in one part of its range changes the sound a lot more than some other parts.

As a start, we define *error* as the sum of absolute differences between the desired levels $\mathbf{y}_d$ and the actual levels of the points returned when optimizing for the desired levels, summing over the knob paths for all starting points $\mathbf{X}_s$. $\mathbf{X}_i$ and $\mathbf{y}_i$ denotes the accumulated points the models have evaluated up to iteration i plus all the starting points $\mathbf{X}_s$. f here is the function that simulates the human rating. In the first experiment, this function is a synthetic function, while in the second experiment, this function is the mean of a GP conditioned on the 8x8 grid of user-ratings of the "pulsation" concept.

$$err(\mathbf{X_i}, \mathbf{y_i}, \mathbf{X_s}, \mathbf{y_d}) = \sum_{s=1}^{S} \sum_{d=1}^{L} |\mathbf{f}(\mathbf{x_{sd}}) - \mu(\mathbf{y_{sd}}|\mathbf{x_{sd}}, \mathbf{X_i}, \mathbf{y_i})|$$

(4)

We compare our method to several baselines, including proposing points according to the latin hypercubes, and an "entropy" baseline that proposes as the next point the mode on the variance of the posterior predictive marginal of the GP, by running local optimizers from the initial presets. We also compare between several variations of our path-informed active-learning method. "Active learning (re-opt)" re-optimizes the hyperparameters after each fantasized outcome, while "active learning" does not. The "path random" variation skips the fantasizing step, and choose at random a point from the set of proposed candidate points, which were originally randomly sampled from points nearby those visited by the truncated-Newton optimizer while determining the knobs paths. The "path entropy" variation also skips the fantasizing step, and chooses the point that has the highest variance among the proposed candidate points.

In both of the experiments, the number of candidates proposed was 15 and the number of Monte Carlo samples taken for each candidate was 30. The simulations were initialized with simulated ratings of 2 to 3 preset control-parameter settings, which corresponds to the sounds to be adjusted by the knob paths. The experiments were terminated when the performance started to plateau Figure 4 or when the model began to pick up the multimodality of the rating function Figure 4. For all our active-learning variations, the means and standard errors are averaged across five runs.

Experiment 1: Synthetic function
The synthetic function simulates a concept where most of the space does not give rise to its quality. The function was originally two-dimensional. In order to experiment with how the algorithm would perform in higher dimensions, we artificially added two more dummy dimensions, whose values do not affect the function. Figure 4 shows the performance of our method and other baselines as the models iteratively adds more data observations.

Figure 4 shows that our active-learning methods are able to learn high-level knobs faster under our error metric Eqn. (4). Furthermore, the downward curves of the active-learning methods show that they are able to iteratively improve and refine the model, while for other techniques the lines rise and

fall with much higher error. Figure 5 shows the different response surfaces at the ninth iteration. We can see that our active learning approach was able to focus the evaluations in the region that is most relevant to the knob paths.

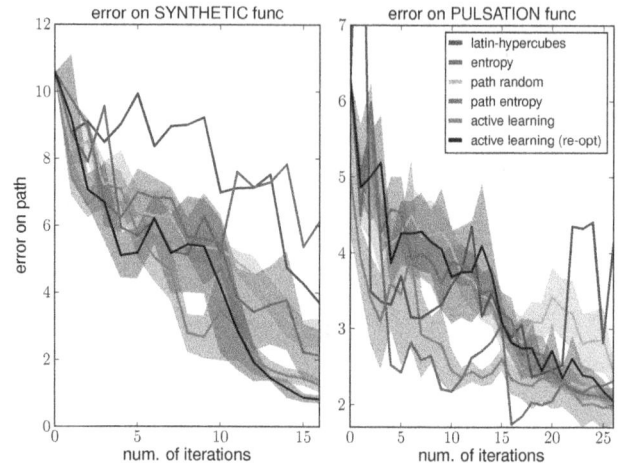

Figure 4. *Error* for active-learning variations and baselines on predicting knob paths on synthetic function (left), and "pulsation" function (right). Solid lines represent the mean, and shaded colors show the standard error over 5 runs.

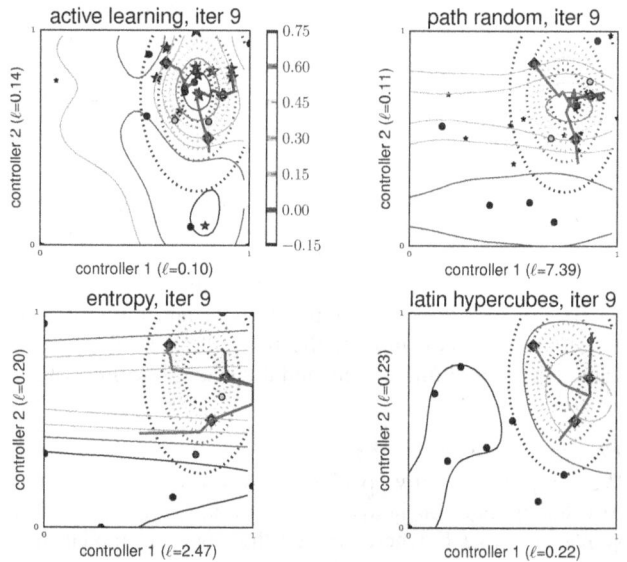

Figure 5. In the synthetic experiment, the full-Bayes GP posterior mean for different methods after 9 more observations beyond initialization. ℓs on the X and Y axes give the lengthscales of the corresponding low-level controllers under MLE. Dotted contour lines represent the target function. Dots indicate observations, and stars correspond to proposed candidates, which only applies to the active-learning methods.

The objective of our active-learning approach is to reduce the uncertainty on the knob paths, as opposed to learning the function everywhere. Figure 6 shows how well our "active-learning (re-opt)" method and the "entropy" baseline predicts the true function over the entire space. We evaluate the two corresponding GPs at 1000 locations given by the Sobol sequence, and plot these predicted values against those of the true function. This true function has a lot of low regions around zero, corresponding to the whitespace in Figure 5 without dotted contours. Only about a quarter of the space is occupied by a Gaussian bump. This shape is typical of mappings on synthesizers where most of the sounds in a space have none of a certain quality, and only a small part of the space gives rise to that quality. However, a model would have a low mean-squared error if it simply predicted low values everywhere. This is undesirable for constructing knobs, because the knob would be very flat and would not be able to make much adjustments to sounds. We see that in this case, our active-learning method is still able to predict well over a wider range of levels. Hence, if a user is able to find a sound that begins to have some of her desired qualities, then our tool will be able to give her knobs that can help her increase or decrease that degree, and this adjustment is often challenging for users to perform manually because low-level controls interact.

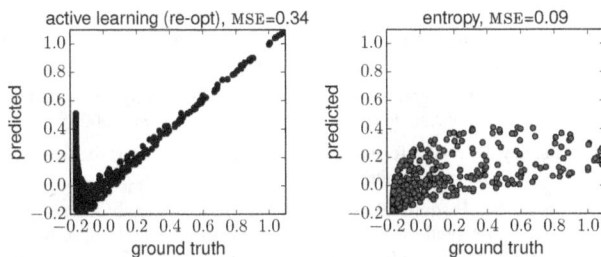

Figure 6. In the synthetic experiment, a comparison of how active learning and the "entropy" baseline predict the target function over the entire space. MSE corresponds to the mean-squared error.

Experiment 2: "Pulsation" function
The function learned from perceptual data is based on user ratings of sounds in terms of their "pulsation" - a high-level concept where amplitude and frequency modulation interact to give a non-trivial response surface. The user was queried at an 8x8 grid on two synth control parameters, and the mean of a GP conditioned on these ratings was used during comparison of learning procedures. We also artificially added two more dummy dimensions to this function, whose values do not affect the function.

Figure 4 shows the performance of our method and other baselines as the models iteratively adds more observations. According to our current error metric, the "entropy" baseline reaches the lowest error the quickest, at iteration 16. However, it was not able to discover that the concept is actually multimodal, as shown in Figure 7. In contrast, the best iteration from our active learning (with hyperparameter re-optimization) was able to learn that there was more than one mode in the concept, and routed the starting points to their nearest peak, as shown in Figure 7. Figure 7 shows the functions learned by the different techniques when we terminated the experiments at iteration 27.

DISCUSSION
We now discuss a few observations and lessons learned from our experiments. Currently, we assume users are able to identify a small subset of relevant low-level controls, and our

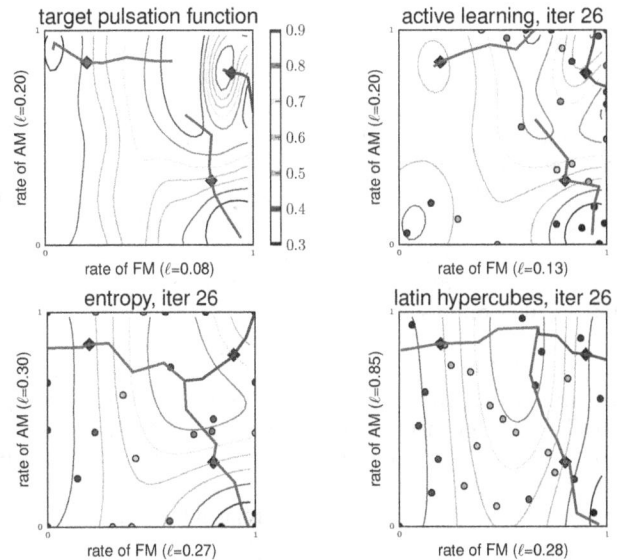

Figure 7. In the "pulsation" experiment, the full-Bayes GP posterior means for different methods after 26 more observations beyond initialization. Note the upper-left subplot shows the target function.

method focuses on learning the nonlinear interaction between these controls. To scale to higher-dimensional settings, we will have to encode domain knowledge into the covariance structure of our priors. For example on equalizers, adjusting gains for neighboring frequency bins vary perceptually in similar ways, we can parameterize the distance metric in our kernel by the Malahanobis distance to explicitly model covariance between dimensions. Alternatively, if we know the kinds of interaction between controls vary in different parts of the control space, we can call for a non-stationary kernel. See [6] for insights on how to choose the structural form of the kernel.

Moreover, our method for constructing knob paths is still naive, as it only optimizes separately for different knob values and there is no guarantee that the resultant path is coherent. For example, a path could jump around in the control space due to the many-to-one mapping from control space to musical concept. In the future, we plan to regularize our paths and optimize for a path as a whole so that we can control its perceived smoothness.

Furthermore, our user studies are still preliminary. More human-in-the-loop experiments are needed to better understand how users use our procedure to help them build personal control knobs. Casual observations show that users construct preferences on-the-fly, and they alternate between phases of exploration and refinement, analogous to phases of divergent and convergent thinking [5]. For example, one composer requested sounds from our lightweight "path random" active-learning procedure to refine his "guitar-like" knob, after a dozen of sounds he felt the need to explore whether different kinds of "guitar-like" qualities existed. So he switched to using our entropy-based procedure to try to touch the boundaries of the space, and was pleased that it gave him sounds that he had never heard before. Second, the listening mode of the user often evolves. Initially, users tend to react intuitively to sounds, but later on, they begin to listen more analytically, and explicitly reason and weigh sonic attributes when rating sounds. For example, a sound may have a "sharp attack" like a guitar but may "warble" too quickly to be one, and a composer may still rate it above average because it possess at least one of the main characters of a guitar sound. Third, as user preferences may change and in light of new possibilities, the re-rating of existing sounds becomes necessary, and one composer requested for a feature to "shave off" similar sounds, so that the new ratings and new sounds can have more influence.

CONCLUSION

Composers seek to explore sounds along intuitive and personal sonic dimensions, but synthesizers can often only be controlled through low-level controls that interact in complex ways. Inspired by this mismatch, we proposed a novel formulation of high-level knobs that treats a knob as a dynamic mapping that allows us to adjust different sounds along different paths in the control space. In this paper, we presented two building blocks towards realizing such knobs. We adopted the expressiveness of a fully-Bayesian nonparametric model, Gaussian processes, to model the rich perceptual world of synthesizers, where there are many ways to achieve a certain musical quality.

Second, to assist users in finding the set of examples to demonstrate a high-level concept, we derived a model-based active learning algorithm that queries the user in order to improve knob paths, and we showed in simulation that it is more effective for learning high-level knobs. Our procedure is modular, allowing us in the future to swap in different knob path formulations. As there are often multiple ways of achieving a certain desired effect, as shown by the multi-modality of our example concepts, we are considering a variation that we call "branching" knobs, which would provide the user with multiple paths for adjusting a sound, some with endpoints at modes further away or higher than others. This allows composers to explore a wider palette of related sounds, and to trade off between achieving a desired adjustment and preserving different aspects of the original sound. Last by not least, our formulation is general, and can be applied to any other domain for users to construct and calibrate a layer of richer, personalized controls on top of the parameters provided by the original system.

REFERENCES

1. Amershi, S., Fogarty, J., Kapoor, A., and Tan, D. Effective End-User Interaction with Machine Learning. *AAAI* (2011).

2. Brochu, E., Brochu, T., and de Freitas, N. A bayesian interactive optimization approach to procedural animation design. In *Proceedings of the ACM SIGGRAPH* (2010).

3. Cartwright, M., and Pardo, B. Social-eq: Crowdsourcing an equalization descriptor map. In *Proceedings of the International Society for Music Information Retreival Conference* (2013).

4. Cohn, D. Neural network exploration using optimal experiment design. *Neural Networks 9*, 6 (1996).

5. Cropley, A. In praise of convergent thinking. *Creativity Research Journal 18*, 3 (2006).

6. Duvenaud, D., Lloyd, J. R., Grosse, R., Tenenbaum, J. B., and Ghahramani, Z. Structure discovery in nonparametric regression through compositional kernel search. In *Proceedings of International Conference on Machine Learning* (2013).

7. Fiebrink, R., Cook, P. R., and Trueman, D. Play-along mapping of musical controllers. In *Proceedings of the International Computer Music Conference* (2009).

8. Fiebrink, R., Trueman, D., and Cook, P. R. A meta-instrument for interactive, on-the-fly machine learning. In *Proceedings of the New Interfaces for Musical Expression* (2009).

9. Fogarty, J., Tan, D., Kapoor, A., and Winder, S. Cueflik: Interactive concept learning in image search. In *Proceedings of the SIGCHI Conference on Human Factors in Computing Systems* (2008).

10. Garcia, R. A. Automatic design of sound synthesis techniques by means of genetic programming. In *Audio Engineering Society Convention 113* (2002).

11. Heise, S., Hlatky, M., and Loviscach, J. Automatic cloning of recorded sounds by software synthesizers. In *Audio Engineering Society Convention 127* (2009).

12. Hoffman, M., and Cook, P. R. Feature-based synthesis: mapping acoustic and perceptual features onto synthesis parameters. In *Proceedings of the International Computer Music Conference* (2006).

13. Kapoor, A., Grauman, K., Urtasun, R., and Darrell, T. Active learning with gaussian processes for object categorization. In *Proceedings of the IEEE International Conference on Computer Vision* (2007).

14. Loviscach, J. Programming a music synthesizer through data mining. In *Proceedings of New Interfaces for Musical Expression* (2008).

15. MacKay, D. J. C. Information-based objective functions for active data selection. *Neural Computation 4* (1992).

16. Macret, M., Pasquier, P., and Smyth, T. Automatic calibration of modified fm synthesis to harmonic sounds using genetic algorithms. In *Proceedings of the 9th Sound and Music Computing Conference* (2012).

17. Mecklenburg, S., and Loviscach, J. subjeqt: Controlling an equalizer through subjective terms. In *CHI Extended Abstracts on Human Factors in Computing Systems* (2006).

18. Morris, D., Simon, I., and Basu, S. Exposing parameters of a trained dynamic model for interactive music creation. In *Proceedings of the National Conference on Artificial intelligence*, AAAI (2008).

19. Osborne, M. A., Garnett, R., and Roberts, S. J. Active data selection for sensor networks with faults and changepoints. *International Conference on Advanced Information Networking and Applications* (2010).

20. Pachet, F. Description-based design of melodies. *Computer Music Journal 33*, 4 (2009).

21. Pardo, B., Little, D., and Gergle, D. Building a personalized audio equalizer interface with transfer learning and active learning. In *Proceedings of the ACM workshop on Music information retrieval with user-centered and multimodal strategies* (2012).

22. Rafii, Z., and Pardo, B. Learning to control a reverberator using subjective perceptual descriptors. In *Proceedings of the International Society for Music Information Retrieval Conference* (2009).

23. Rasmussen, C. E., and Williams, C. K. I. *Gaussian processes for machine learning*. MIT Press, 2006.

24. Sabin, A. T., and Pardo, B. A method for rapid personalization of audio equalization parameters. In *Proceedings of the ACM International Conference on Multimedia* (2009).

25. Sabin, A. T., Rafii, Z., and Pardo, B. Weighting-function-based rapid mapping of descriptors to audio processing parameters. *Journal of the Audio Engineering Society 59*, 6 (2011).

26. Seo, S., Wallat, M., and Graepel, T. Gaussian process regression: Active data selection and test point rejection. *International Joint Conference on Neural Networks IJCNN* (2000).

27. Snoek, J., Larochelle, H., and Adams, R. P. Practical bayesian optimization of machine learning algorithms. In *Neural Information Processing Systems* (2012).

28. Yee-King, M. J. An autonomous timbre matching improviser. In *Proceedings of the International Computer Music Conference* (2011).

Visualizing Expert Solutions in Exploratory Learning Environments

Or Seri and Ya'akov (Kobi) Gal

Department of Brain and Cognitive Sciences,
Department of Information Systems Engineering,
Ben-Gurion University, Beer Sheva, Israel
or.seri@gmail.com, kobig@bgu.ac.il

ABSTRACT

Exploratory Learning Environments (ELE) are open-ended and flexible software, supporting interaction styles that include exogenous actions and trial-and-error. This paper shows that using AI techniques to visualize worked examples in ELEs improves students' generalization of mathematical concepts across problems, as measured by their performance. Students were exposed to a worked example of a problem solution using an ELE for statistics education. One group in the study was presented with a hierarchical plan of relevant activities that emphasized the sub-goals and the structure relating to the solution. This visualization used an AI algorithm to match a log of activities in the ELEs to ideal solutions. We measured students' performance when using the ELE to solve new problems that required generalization of concepts introduced in the example solution. The results showed that students who were shown the plan visualization significantly outperformed other students who were presented with a step-by-step list of actions in the software used to generate the same solution to the example problem. Analysis of students' explanations of the problem solution shows that the students in the former condition also demonstrated deeper understanding of the solution process. These results demonstrate the benefit to students when using AI technology to visualize worked examples in ELEs and suggests future applications of this approach to actively support students' learning and teachers' understanding of students' activities.

Author Keywords

Plan recognition; exploratory learning environments; visualizations of students' interactions; worked examples.

IUI'14, February 24–27, 2014, Haifa, Israel.
Copyright © 2014 ACM 978-1-4503-2184-6/14/02$15.00.
http://dx.doi.org/10.1145/2557500.2557520

ACM Classification Keywords

H.5.m. Information interfaces and presentation (e.g., HCI): D.2.2: Design tools and techniques

INTRODUCTION

Modern educational software is open-ended and flexible, allowing students to build scientific models and examine properties of the models [1,10]. Such Exploratory Learning Environments (ELE) provide a rich educational experience for students, and are generally used in classes too large for teachers to monitor all students and provide assistance when needed [18]. Thus, there is a need to develop techniques that recognize and visualize students' activities in a way that supports students in their work and contributes to their learning by using the software.

Past work has demonstrated that showing expert solutions to students enhances their ability to generalize solution concepts to new problems [2,5,6]. Although such "worked examples" approaches have been shown to be an important instructional tool [22], they have not been applied to open-ended educational software. This paper shows that using existing AI techniques to visualize worked examples in ELEs can contribute significantly to students' problem solving. We based our empirical study on an ELE for statistics education that allows students to solve problems by building stochastic models of the world, running the models and analyzing the results.

The study involved first-year undergraduate students enrolled in a statistics and probability course for engineering majors at Ben Gurion University of the Negev. Students were presented with a solution to an example problem in probability theory. Some students were presented with a visualization that deconstructed the solution into a hierarchy of labeled components called a plan. We used a recent plan recognition algorithm from the literature to generate the plan automatically [16]. These components made explicit the relationship between sets of actions in the solution, and emphasized mathematical concepts used in the solution (e.g., computing the sum of a random variable). Another group of students were presented with an ordered list of the actions comprising the solution to the problem. Such a list represents the sole option currently available for extracting log activities from the software post-hoc.

Both groups of students were subsequently asked to use the ELE to solve new problems that were gradually more difficult than the example problem and required to generalize mathematical concepts. Students' performance for the new problems were analyzed using several measures, including the length of interaction time with the ELE, the number of actions performed on the ELE, and the ratio of redundant actions which did not play a part in the solution and represent mistakes and exploratory activities. We used plan recognition in two ways. First, to generate the visualization of the example problem that was shown to students. Second, to analyze students' performance on the test problems.

The results showed that students who were presented with the plan visualization outperformed those students who were presented with the list of activities for all of these measures. The effect of the plan visualization was most pronounced for those students whose academic level of achievement in the course was above average. Further analysis shows that the students shown the plan visualization were more likely to explain solutions to the example problem using sub-goals, which has been suggested to facilitate the generalization of mathematical concepts to solve new problems. This is the first work to demonstrate the benefit of combining AI techniques with intelligent user interfaces for supporting students' use of ELEs.

RELATED WORKS

Our study relates to two different areas of prior work: learning by worked examples and visualizing students' interactions with educational software. We relate each of these areas to our study in turn.

Worked examples are an instructional technique that provides students with an expert's solution to a task or a problem using a step-by-step demonstration [2,9]. This approach commonly involves displaying problem instances as well as expert solutions to the problems that demonstrate concepts and principles that commonly recur in other problem solving instances. Worked examples have been shown to provide effective instructional strategies for teaching complex problem-solving skills [23] and are widely accepted as an effective learning technique [2]. For example, it was shown that using worked examples in a college-level math class was found to be more effective for students than solving practice problems [22]. In particular, students who were presented with expert solutions to problems were more likely to successfully transfer acquired techniques to new problems, and to generalize mathematical concepts relating to the solution. In contrast, students using practice problems made more mistakes and adopted fewer sophisticated strategies when solving new problems [11, 21].

Catrambone and Holyoke [7] found that using cues in worked examples to indicate steps in the expert solution that go together ("sub-goals") positively affected students' generalization abilities to solve new problems. Specifically, students were presented with sub-goals that labeled solution concepts (like "computing the average") in solutions to statistics problems. These students were more likely to adopt and use these concepts when solving advanced problems than students who were not shown the labels in the expert solution. In addition, students who were presented with sub-goals were more likely to refer to them when providing a self-explanation of how they solved problems. Our work is first to extend the worked-examples approach to ELEs.

The visualization method described in this paper relates to prior approaches for analyzing and assessing students' interactions with educational software. Some approaches work on-line, visualizing predefined features of students' interactions to teachers. Examples include the student tracking tool [19] and the FORMID-Observer [16]. Other systems work post-hoc, and generate reports to teachers based on students' complete interaction histories. Relevant examples include the ASSISTment system [14] and Student Inspector [20]. These visualization methods do not provide a hierarchy of activities, and are dependent on diagnosis of the students' activities by the software. The plan-based visualization method described in this paper provides a deeper, structured analysis of students' problem-solving behavior, it is independent of the ELEs and has been used to visualize students' interactions in ELEs for statistics and chemistry [15,24].

Lastly, we mention a work showing that organizing knowledge in a hierarchical fashion facilitates cognitive tasks such as recall and knowledge modification [13]. This work did not use learned examples or educational software in the experiment design.

The TinkerPlots Domain

TinkerPlots is an ELE used internationally to teach students in grades 4 through 8 about statistics and probability [17]. It provides students with a toolkit to actively model stochastic events, and to create and investigate a large variety of statistical models. It is an extremely flexible application, allowing for data to be modeled, generated, and analyzed in many ways using an open-ended interface for designing stochastic models, running the models, and displaying and analyzing the results.

The all-purpose sampling object in TinkerPlots is called a Sampler. A Sampler is an object into which the user can place random devices, including spinners and mixers, in order to create a stochastic model of the world. We demonstrate TinkerPlots using the following example problem, called EXAM, used to introduce the software to students.

Figure 1: Solving the EXAM problem using TinkerPlots

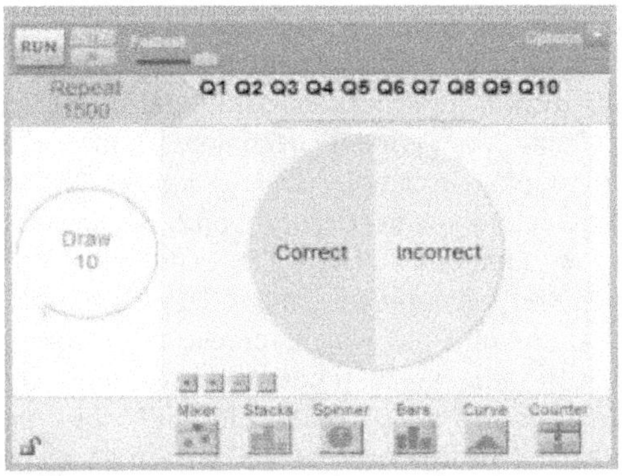

Figure 1(a) Sampler with Spinner Device

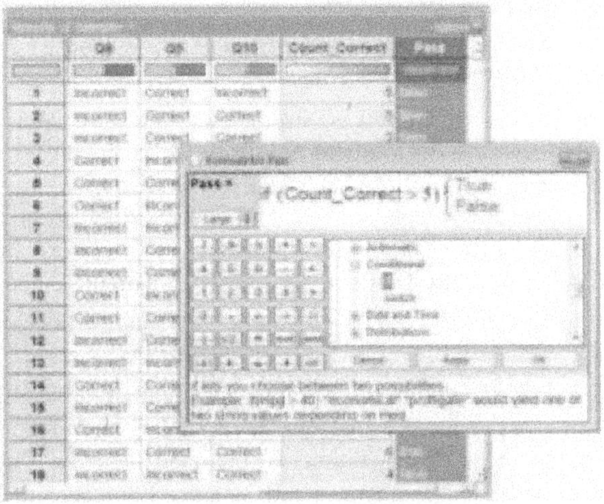

Figure 1(b) Results table and function window

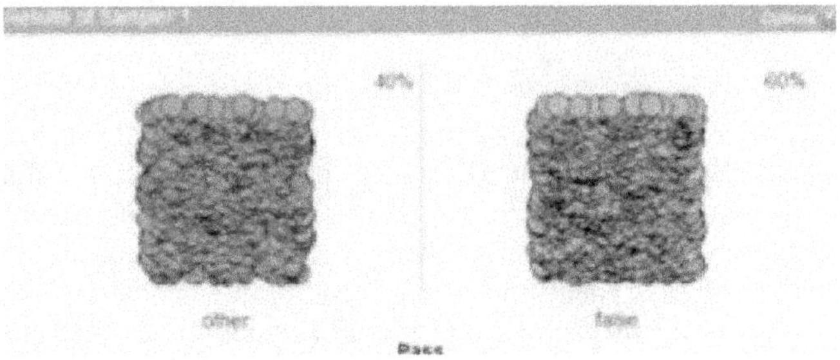

Figure 1(c) Plot and plot toolbar

"John is taking a multiple-choice exam. There are two possible answers for each question (only one of the answers is correct), and 10 questions in the exam. To pass the exam John needs to answer at least 60% of the questions correctly. John did not study for the exam and uses a coin-toss to answer each question. Build a TinkerPlots model of John's answers in the exam, and use the model to compute the probability that John will pass the exam."

Figure 1 shows one approach to solving this problem using TinkerPlots. The sampler mechanism is shown in Figure 1(a). It contains a device with two elements (Correct and Incorrect) for describing the choice for each question in the

exam. The parameter "Draw" (number of draws) in the sampler is set to 10 to represent 10 questions. The parameter "Repeat" (number of repetitions) in the sampler is set to 1,500 so that the number of samples will produce a representative sample. When a sampler is run, it generates data that is sampled according to the distribution defined by the parameters of its model. In our example, running the sampler (by clicking the "Run" button on the top-left corner of the sampler) will generate a results table which includes 1,500 instances of 10 questions each.

Figure 1(b) shows the second stage for solving the problem. To facilitate the analysis of the generated data, two new functions are created (called *attributes* in TinkerPlots) and added to the results table. The first attribute, called "Count Correct", counts the number of correctly answered questions in each instance. The second attribute, called "Pass", equals true when the test was passed (i.e., the value of "Count Correct" was greater than 5).

The last stage of the solution is shown in Figure 1(c). To compute the probability of passing the test, a Plot object is created and the values of the "Pass" attribute are projected onto the plot. This creates a histogram of the "Pass" attribute and shows the percentages of the different values, which is the solution to the problem.

The flexibility of the TinkerPlots systems affords multiple ways of solving the EXAM problem. For example, a single attribute for counting the number of successful answers in the exam is also possible. In addition, TinkerPlots supports exploratory actions and mistakes, which are not a salient part of an ideal solution to the problem. These actions are referred to as *redundant actions* in this paper.

Plan Recognition

Monitoring students' learning in ELEs is essential for the quality of education and contributes to effectiveness of teaching and learning. A key component for this activity is the activity log: a chronological record of all the student's interactions with a system. Analyzing the logs in ELEs allows to understand the student's work.

A common method to extract the student's activity from logs is *Plan Recognition*, an approach to infer a hierarchy that best describes an agent's activities given observations of its actions and a predefined grammar. In the TinkerPlots ELE, this grammar is problem-specific and represents a set of ideal activities for solving the problem. Plan recognition in ELEs is a computationally hard problem, arising from the complex nature of students' interactions with TinkerPlots which includes exploration, exogenous actions and mistakes. We used a novel plan recognition algorithm in the study that was tailored to recognize students' activities for ELEs [15]. The algorithm provides a single encompassing plan that best describes the student's activity with TinkerPlots. We use this inferred plan for two purposes: for generating the plan that visualizes the expert solution to the problem, and for analyzing students' activities with the software.

EMPIRICAL METHODOLOGY

Our hypothesis was that showing a hierarchical presentation of sample problems in TinkerPlots will improve students' performance on new problems when compared to a default presentation method that consisted of an ordered list of their activities. Specifically, we expected students who were shown the hierarchical presentation to be able to solve new problems more quickly, with fewer mistakes and with committing less redundant actions when compared to students who were shown the list.

Visualization Methods

We will use the following example problem, called COIN, to describe the visualizations we used in the study:

"A fair coin with a side of '0' and a side of '1' is tossed 3 times. What is the average expected sum of the tosses?"

The first visualization method showed the ideal interactions as a hierarchy of activities called a *Plan*. The most fundamental components in a plan are called *basic actions*. These are atomic actions, which cannot be decomposed further. A few examples of basic actions in TinkerPlots are: adding a sampler, changing the name of a device, adding elements to a spinner, or running a sampler. The logs of users' interactions comprise a list of basic actions. While such a list provides a complete account of a student's interaction with the software, it fails to provide a high-level description that can be useful for a teacher. This log is the sole option for showing solutions to problems in TinkerPlots without additional analysis. For example, one sequence of basic actions may constitute the activity of "creating a sampler for solving the COIN problem;" another sequence may constitute the activity of "plotting the results of the run on a graph;" while other action sequences may actually be exploratory actions and mistakes.

To be able to describe these higher-level activities, we introduce the notion of *complex actions*, which represent sub-goals in the students' solution process. Complex actions describe abstract activities that can be decomposed into sub-actions, which can themselves be basic actions or other complex actions. Examples of complex actions in TinkerPlots are: adding a spinner with six equally weighted events to a sampler, or displaying and formatting sampler data on a plot.

The Plan is an inferred hierarchical representation of the actions performed in TinkerPlots in order to solve the presented problem. Figure 2 shows part of a plan visualization of a worked example of a solution to the COIN problem as a tree of basic actions (leaf nodes) and complex actions (parent nodes).[1] The root of the plan

(*Correct_Solution*) decomposes into three constituent complex actions for creating the coin model (*Create_Coin_Model*), running the model (*Generate_Results*) and computing the average sum of tosses (*Compute_Average_Sum*). In turn, the complex action Create_Coin_Model decomposes into the basic action of adding a sampler (*add_sampler*), the complex action of creating a coin (*Create_Coin*), the basic action of setting the number of times the experiment should be repeated (*set_repetitions*) and the complex action Create_Tosses_of_Coin which represents the basic action of setting the number of times the coin should be tossed (*set_draws_in_sampler*). The "leaves" of the tree correspond to the student's action sequences recorded by TinkerPlots. Actions appear in left-to-right order in a way that is consistent with the temporal order of students' activities. For expository convenience, only part of the plan is shown in the Figure (for example, the *Compute_Sum* complex action is not presented).

The plan visualization was introduced to the students using an interactive tool, allowing to "drill down" to reveal the constituents actions of each node in the tree. Clicking on any node also displays additional information about the action parameters relating to the action in the Information Panel at the bottom of the screen. To illustrate, Figure 2 shows the element index and the temporal position in the log of the *Change_Element_in_Device* action.

The *List* visualization presented students with a bulleted list of the basic actions performed to solve the example problem. This visualization is obtained from a linear sequence of temporally ordered actions. It represents the default support that is currently available to students using the software. A partial list of these actions is shown in Figure 3.

Participants

The study involved 61 first-year undergraduate students enrolled in a statistics and probability course for engineering majors at Ben Gurion University of the Negev. The study was carried out during the middle of the semester after the students had acquired basic knowledge of probability theory and undergone a midterm. All students were given a home exercise to familiarize with TinkerPlots.[2] The students were divided into two groups based on their academic achievements in the midterm quiz. Group1 (30 students) refers to those students whose grade was above average, while Group2 (31 students) refers to those students whose grade was below average. We randomly assigned half of the students in each group to the Plan or List conditions. In total, 32 students were presented with a Plan solution, and 29 were presented with a list solution.

---

[1] This is a snapshot of the application showing the expert solution to the students in the study.

[2] The homework problems were not related in any way to the problems in this study.

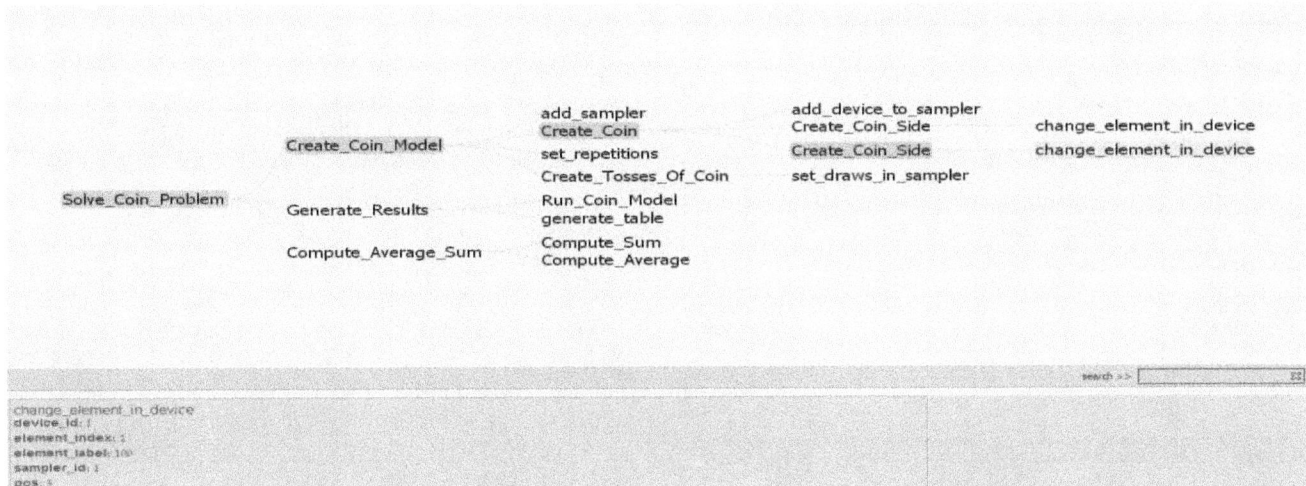

Figure 2: Plan visualization of the expert solution for the COIN problem

There was no significant difference in the standard deviations of the grade between the two groups.

Procedure

The study was conducted in a designated lab in which each student was situated in front of a computer. In the first part of the study, all students were provided with the COIN problem description in writing, and the expert solution to the problem was subsequently presented to them using the List or Plan visualization, depending on their assigned condition. In addition, all students were shown an (identical) snapshot of the TinkerPlots desktop following the solution procedure. The students were asked several comprehension questions about the solution, such as whether (and why) the interaction shown to them constitutes a correct solution to the COIN problem; to indicate the role in the solution of one of the actions in interaction; to explain the solution to "a friend" using free text. There were two purposes for these questions: First, to confirm that the students comprehended the solution. Second, to compare between students' self-explanations of the solution to the COIN problem in the two experimental conditions. Students were allocated up to 20 minutes to complete this part of the study.

In the second part of the study, students were asked to solve two new problems in sequence using TinkerPlots. Students were allocated up to 30 minutes to complete this part of the study. The problems were taken from the curriculum of an introductory course in probability. We wanted the problems to be non-trivial, but still possible to solve by the majority of students in the allocated 30 minutes. We chose problems whose solutions exhibited similar concepts (reasoning about combinations and events in sample space). The first problem, called WHEEL was purposely chosen to be similar to the COIN problem in that its solution required computing the expectation of a random variable, albeit in a different context.

Each time Mary spins the wheel-of-fortune, she will earn between 1 and 8 points, depending on the result of the spin

(each result is equiprobable). Mary spins the wheel four times and her score sums the results. (1) What is the average (expected) score for Mary? (2) What is the probability that Mary's score will be exactly 8 points higher than this average?

The second problem, called DICE, was harder: it did not mention explicitly the notion of expectation, and it required to reason about the disjunction of complex events that relate to the sample space.

John and Mary compete in a dice-tossing game. They take turns tossing a die, and sum the result of each toss. The winner is the first to accumulate more than 10 points. Compute the probability that (1) John will win after two rounds of the game. (2) Either John or Mary will win after two rounds of the game.

Students were asked to answer a survey about how their respective visualization assisted them in solving the TinkerPlots problems. We collected the TinkerPlots log from each student's interactions as well a snapshot of their desktop recording during the activity. We did not randomize the order of questions to control for the problem difficulty on performance.

RESULTS

We hypothesized that students assigned to the plan condition would exhibit better performance than students assigned to the list condition when using TinkerPlots to solve the DICE problem (which was more difficult and required generalization). In contrast, we did not expect to see an effect for the WHEEL problem (which was structurally similar to the practice problem). Consequently we expected the WHEEL problem to be successfully solved by all the students regardless of their assigned condition.

We measured student performance using the following metrics: the length of interaction (in minutes); the total number of actions in an interaction; the ratio of *redundant actions* in an interaction, which represent mistakes and

```
Add device 1 to sampler1
Change the label of element 0 in device 1 in sampler 1 to "0"
Change the label of element 1 in device 1 in sampler 1 to "1"
Set the repetitions in sampler 1 to "1500"
Set the draws in sampler 1 to "3"
Run sampler 1 and generate columns Draw1,Draw2 and Draw3
Add an attribute named "Sum" to table 2
Edit the formula of attribute "Sum" in table 2 to  Draw1+Draw2+Draw3
Add plot 3
Drag the attribute "Sum" to plot 3
Divide the values in plot 3
Average on plot 3 of attribute "Sum"
```

Figure 3: List visualization of the expert solution to the COIN problem

exogenous actions that do not play a part in the student's solution.

We provide a description of students' performance for the DICE problem. All of the results we report below were statistically significant in the $p<0.05$ range using a non-parameterized two-tailed Mann-Whitney test.

We found that the plan visualization significantly improved students' performance across all measures. These results are summarized in Table 4. Specifically, the average interaction length of the students in the Plan condition (AVG=9.01 min, SD=3.92) was significantly shorter than the average interaction length for students in the List condition (AVG=12.47 min, SD=6.6). The total number of actions in a student's interaction (AVG=39.65, SD=11.79) was significantly lower than the total number of actions in the List condition (AVG=57.069, SD=32.628). The ratio of redundant actions of the Plan condition (28%) was significantly lower than the ratio of redundant actions for students in the List condition (46%).

When breaking down these results according to the students' academic level, we found the effects also held for students whose midterm grade was above average (Group1). Specifically, the average interaction length of Group1 students in the Plan condition (AVG=7.76 min, SD=3.54) was significantly shorter than the interaction length for Group1 students in the List condition (AVG=12.56 min, SD=5.01). The total number of actions in a student's interaction of students in the Plan condition (AVG=36.25, SD=9.497) was significantly lower than the total number of actions in the List condition (AVG=62.429, SD=34.669). The ratio of redundant actions for Group1 students in the Plan condition (22%) was significantly lower than for Group1 students in the List condition (48%).

The Plan visualization also affected students with a midterm grade below average (Group2), but this effect was less pronounced. Specifically, the average interaction length of Group2 students in the Plan condition (AVG=10.25 min, SD=3.98) was shorter than the average interaction length for Group2 students in the List condition (AVG=12.38 min,

SD=7.39). Although the number of total actions in the Plan condition (AVG=47, SD=12.01) was slightly higher than in the List condition (AVG=43.66, SD=18.11), the ratio of redundant actions in the Plan condition (33%) was lower than the ratio of redundant actions in the List condition (43%).

As hypothesized, we did not observe a significant effect of the plan visualization on students' performance for the WHEEL problem. Specifically, there was no significant difference between the average interaction length of students in the Plan condition (AVG=9.96 min, SD=5.17) and the List condition (AVG=10.29 min, SD=3.67); no significant difference between the total number of actions in the Plan condition (AVG=46.34, SD=13.99) and the List condition (AVG=44.83, SD=15.71); and no significant difference between the ratio of redundant actions for students in the Plan condition (71%) and students in the List condition (70%).

We end this section with a description of common errors and redundant actions. Most students were able to solve both of the problems correctly. The most common error by far was computing the average of a random variable (e.g., average value of dice tosses) rather than the average of the sum of the random variables (e.g., average value of the sum of dice tosses). We did not find an effect of the visualization type on the types of errors performed by students. Specifically, there were four students in the Plan condition and seven students in the List condition were not able to solve the COIN problem correctly. Eight students in the Plan condition and seven students in the List condition did not solve the DICE problem correctly. We also did not find a significant difference in students' academic level for this measure. The most common redundant actions in both conditions were the creation of unnecessary objects (e.g., a plot or sampler object that was not subsequently used in the solution) and unnecessary repetitions of actions (e.g., running a sampler or displaying the percentage of averages in the plot several times.)

DISCUSSION

As shown by the results, the students in the Plan condition were able to achieve better performance for all measures in the more difficult problem (DICE) as compared to students in the List condition. This improvement was consistent and uniform as can be attested by the standard deviations for all measures, which were lower for the Plan condition than for the List condition. This confirms our hypothesis that using hierarchical representations to visualize worked examples assists students in their problem solving when interacting with ELEs. This also suggests that the open-ended and flexible nature of the ELE settings requires more elaborate visualizations of expert solutions that highlight organizing knowledge at different level of detail.

The visualization effect was most pronounced for the DICE problem, which required more complex reasoning and generalization of the concepts than the WHEEL and COIN

	Time (min)	Number of Actions	Redundancy
Plan	**9.01**	**39.65**	**28%**
List	12.47	57.06	46%

Table 4: Performance measures on DICE problem for students in Plan and List conditions

problems. This indicates that visualizing the hierarchical aspect of the example facilitates students' ability to generalize mathematical and structural concepts across new problems (in our case, the use of expectation to reason about events in the sample space). This is in line with findings that labeled solution may result in transfer of mathematical knowledge [3,4] and suggest that worked examples may be used as an effective instructional tool when interacting with open-ended and flexible educational software.

We can attribute the lack of a significant effect of the plan visualization for the WHEEL problem to the fact that it was the first one that students solved during the study; as such it exhibited more exploratory activities and mistakes, which lowered students' performance regardless of their academic level.

Interestingly, the effect of the visualization was more pronounced for students of stronger academic background (Group1). This finding aligns with a past study [6] showing that learners with a stronger math background were more able to self-explain their solution, which is believed to be a contributing factor to students' ability to generalize from worked examples.[3] However, given that the overall effect was also demonstrable for weaker students (Group2), we contend that more practice problems may help to generate a more pronounced effect of the plan visualization for this group. We plan to study this hypothesis in future work.

We now turn to analyzing students' explanations of solutions. Past studies have suggested that generating self-explanations facilitates students' learning and generalizations from worked examples [8,5]. There were striking differences in the way students explained the solution to the COIN problem based on their respective visualization condition. Overall, 75% of the students in the Plan condition used and referred to sub-goals when describing the solution to the COIN problem, as compared to 66% of the List students.

In our study, sub-goals represent higher-level activities such as generating and running a sampler, projecting the results to a plot, and computing the average sum of a random variable. These activities recur in all three of the problems in the study, and recognizing and internalizing these concepts may have contributed to the success of the plan

---

[3] They were also more likely to refer to sub-goals when explaining the solution.

visualization. The students in the List condition were far less likely to use such concepts when describing the problem.

We illustrate the use of sub-goal referral by quoting from one of the student's explanations in the Plan visualization condition, which provided a two-step separation of the solution: *"...The results of the 3 tosses were summed... a graph was created to show this sum, and then the Average button was clicked to find out the average sum."* In total, only 18% of the students in the Plan condition made incorrect references to sub-goals in their explanations (for example, referring to the average of the tosses instead of the average of the sum of the tosses), while 35% in the List condition made such incorrect references.

Interestingly, the effects of the plan visualization on sub-goal referrals were significant for weaker students (Group2) but not for stronger students (Group1). Specifically, in Group2, 71% of students in the Plan condition referred to sub-goals when explaining their solution, as opposed to 53% of the students in the List condition. In Group1, 80% of the students in the Plan condition and 79% of the students in the List condition referred to sub-goals. Also, the academically stronger students were more likely to refer to sub-goals than the weaker students regardless of the visualization condition. This relates to findings in the literature that correlate the use of sub-goals in students' self-explanations to their academic level [6].

CONCLUSION AND FUTURE WORK

This paper studied how visualizing expert solutions of example problems to students affects their performance when solving new problems using open-ended and flexible educational software. The flexible nature of such software provides students with a rich educational environment but poses significant challenges to teachers and researchers who wish to understand how students are using the software. One group in the study was presented with a hierarchical plan of relevant activities that emphasized the sub-goals and the structure relating to the solution. The hierarchy was generated using a plan recognition algorithm from the literature. The other group was presented with an ordered list of actions comprising the solution. The results show that those students who were presented with the hierarchical visualization were able to solve new problems more quickly and with higher solution quality than the students presented with the ordered list when solving new problems in terms of interaction length and efficiency. They were also more likely to refer to important structural elements of the solution when explaining it. The results demonstrate the benefit of combining AI techniques with intelligent user interfaces to better support teachers and students using ELEs.

In future work, we will study the effects of visualizing students with their own solutions on their problem solving and explore new types of visualizations that emphasize temporal information relating to their solutions.

REFERENCES

1. Amershi, S., & Conati, C. (2006). *Automatic recognition of learner groups in exploratory learning environments. Intelligent Tutoring Systems*, 463-472.

2. Atkinson, R. K., Derry, S. J., Renkl, A., & Wortham, D. (2000). Learning from Examples: Instructional Principles from the Worked Examples Research. *Review of Educational Research* , 70 (2), 181-214.

3. Catrambone, R. (1994). Improving examples to improve transfer to novel problems. *Memory & Cognition*, 22, 606-615.

4. Catrambone, R. (1995). Aiding subgoal learning: Effects on transfer. *Journal of Educational Psychology*, 87, 5-17.

5. Catrambone, R. (1996). Generalizing solution procedures learned from examples. *Journal of Experimental Psychology: Learning, Memory, and Cognition*, 22, 1020-1031.

6. Catrambone, R. (1998). The Subgoal Learning Model: Creating Better Examples So That Students Can Solve Novel Problems. *Journal of Experimental Psychology*, 127 (4), 355-376.

7. Catrambone, R., & Holyoak, K. J. (1990). Learning and subgoals and methods for solving probability problems. *Memory & Cognition*, 18, 593-603.

8. Chi, M. T., de Leeuw, N., Chiu, M. H., & Vancher, L. (1994). Eliciting self-explanations improves understanding. *Cognitive Science*, 18, 439-477.

9. Clark, R.C., Nguyen, F., & Sweller, J. (2011). Efficiency in learning: evidence-based guidelines to manage cognitive load. San Francisco: Pfeiffer.

10. Cocea, M., Gutierrez-Santos, S., & Magoulas, G. D. (2008). The challenge of intelligent support in exploratory learning environments: A study of the scenarios. *Proceedings of the 1st International Workshop in Intelligent Support for Exploratory Environments on European Conference on Technology Enhanced Learning.*

11. Cooper, G., & Sweller, J. (1987). Effects of schema acquisition and rule automation on mathematical problem-solving transfer. *Journal of Educational Psychology*, 79 (4), 347–362.

12. Dufresne, R. J., Gerace, W. J., Hardiman, P. T., & Mestre, J. P. (1992). Constraining novices to perform expertlike problem analyses: Effects on schema acquisition. *The Journal of the Learning Sciences*, 2, 307-331.

13. Eylon, B., & Reif, F. (1984). Effects of knowledge organization on task performance. *Cognition and Instruction*, 1, 5-44.

14. Feng, M., & Heffernan, N. T. (2007). Towards live informing and automatic analyzing of student learning: Reporting in assistment system. *Journal of Interactive Learning Research*, 18(2), 207-230.

15. Gal Y., Reddy, S., Shieber, S., Rubin, A., & Grosz, B. (2012). Plan Recognition in Exploratory Domains. Artificial Intelligence Journal (AIJ), 176(1), 2270-2290.

16. Gueraud V., Adam, J.M., Lejeune, A., Dubois, M., & Mandran, N (2009). Teachers need support too: Formid-observer, a exible environment for supervising simulation-based learning situations. In *Proceedings of the 2nd International Workshop on Intelligent Support for Exploratory Environments* (part of AIED 2009), 19-28.

17. Konold, C., & Miller, C. (2004). TinkerPlots Dynamic Data Exploration 1.0. Key Curriculum Press.

18. Pawar, U.S., Pal, J., & Toyama, K. (2007). Multiple Mice for Computers in Education in Developing Countries. *Conference on Information and Communication Technologies and Development*, 64-71.

19. Pearce-Lazard, D., Poulovassilis, A., & Geraniou, E. (2010). The design of teacher assistance tools in an exploratory learning environment for mathematics generalisation. *Sustaining TEL: From Innovation to Learning and Practice*, 260-275.

20. Scheuer, O., & Zinn, C. (2007). How did the e-learning session go? the student inspector. *Proceeding of the 2007 conference on Artificial Intelligence in Education*, 487-494, Amsterdam, The Netherlands, IOS Press.

21. Sweller, J., & Cooper, G. (1985). The use of worked examples as a substitute for problem solving in learning algebra. *Cognition and Instruction* , 2 (1), 59-89.

22. Sweller, J., Van Merriënboer, J., & Paas, F. (1998). Cognitive architecture and instructional design. *Educational Psychology Review*, 10, 251-296.

23. Van Merriënboer, J. (1997). Training Complex Cognitive Skills: a Four-Component Instructional Design Model for Technical Training. *Educational Technology Publications*.

24. Amir, O. & Gal, Y. (2011). Plan recognition in virtual laboratories. *Proceedings of the 22nd International Joint Conference on Artificial Intelligence* (IJCAI), Barcelona, Spain, 2392-2397.

Expediting Expertise: Supporting Informal Social Learning in the Enterprise

Jennifer Lai, Jie Lu, Shimei Pan, Danny Soroker, Mercan Topkara, Justin Weisz,
Jeff Boston, Jason Crawford

IBM Thomas J. Watson Research Center

1101 Kitchawan Road, Yorktown Heights, NY 10598

{jlai, jielu, shimei, soroker, mtopkara, jweisz, daddyb, ccjason}@us.ibm.com

ABSTRACT

In this paper, we present Expediting Expertise, a system designed to provide structured support to the otherwise informal process of social learning in the enterprise. It employs a data-driven approach where online content is automatically analyzed and categorized into relevant topics, topic-specific user expertise is calculated by comparing the models of individual users against those of the experts, and personalized recommendation of learning activities is created accordingly to facilitate expertise development. The system's UI is designed to provide users with ongoing feedback of current expertise, progress, and comparison with others. Learning recommendation is visualized with an interactive treemap which presents estimated return on investment and distance to current expertise for each recommended learning activity. Evaluation of the system showed very positive results.

Author Keywords

Expertise, learning, personalized, social, informal, assessment, recommendation.

ACM Classification Keywords

H.5.m [Information Interfaces and Presentation]: Miscellaneous.

General Terms

Algorithms; Design; Experimentation.

INTRODUCTION

Expertise development is critical to knowledge workers who continually improve their knowledge and skills to stay current with changing technologies. It is typical for knowledge workers to learn on the job through informal learning as much as (and sometimes more than) from formal learning [31]. Informal learning through knowledge sharing and interaction with social software (e.g. online communities, wikis and file sharing) has emerged as an important form of learning to help knowledge workers increase their expertise [4, 18, 22]. Informal social learning has the advantage of providing a more personalized, open, dynamic, and knowledge-pull model of learning, as opposed to the one-size-fits-all, centralized, static, top-down and knowledge-push model of formal curriculum-based learning [11]. However, the effectiveness of informal learning in an online social environment is often hindered by two problems. First, because voluntary contribution accounts for a large amount of content in social software, the available content often lacks organization and quality control [23]. Without guidance, it is challenging for users to identify suitable learning materials. Second, no feedback is given to learners regarding their current expertise level and distance to their target level of expertise. As a result, learners may question their progress and stop before reaching their goal.

To address these problems, we have built the Expediting Expertise (EE) system that aims to provide structured support to informal social learning in the enterprise. The approach taken by the system is data-driven and grounded in Social Learning theory, which suggests that people learn in a social context by modeling and observing others (in our case, experts) [6, 8, 16]. With this approach, online content is automatically analyzed and categorized into relevant topics to provide users with an overview of the main subjects contained in the target domain. Individuals' expertise scores in these topics are computed by comparing activity and word vector based models built from users' online activities with the same models for experts to help users identify expertise gaps and give them ongoing feedback during expertise development. Learning recommendation is created by taking into consideration content relevancy along with social factors (e.g., popularity, ratings, and related expert activities), and further personalized based on individual user models.

The benefits of this data-driven and social-oriented approach are multifold. First, it requires little effort for domain customization, making the system easily applicable to a wide range of subjects and skills. Second, it allows the natural evolution of domain knowledge (e.g. emerging topics, expanding expertise) to be automatically captured and seamlessly handled, which provides adaptability and flexibility. Third, it creates a concrete social measure of

IUI '14, February 24–27, 2014, Haifa, Israel.
Copyright 2014 ACM 978-1-4503-2184-6/14/02...$15.00.
http://dx.doi.org/10.1145/2557500.2557539

expertise by modeling and quantifying social participation and contribution. This not only encourages learners to actively contribute to the growth of their expertise, but also motivates experts to engage more in knowledge sharing and increase their digital eminence.

Our ultimate goal is to create an adaptive, engaging, and rewarding social learning environment that provides personalized learning feedback and guidance with an intuitive interface. For the work reported in this paper, we focus on the following aspects: dynamically modeling users' social learning activities; computing and presenting expertise scores to provide continuous feedback; and creating a personalized learning roadmap that is easy to follow and interact with.

Our work has three main contributions:

1. We developed a system built on top of existing enterprise social software to provide structured support to informal social learning. It is the first of this kind known to us.

2. We proposed a data-driven approach to automatically collect and organize learning materials and objectively assess users' expertise to provide instant and continuous feedback. It enables a learning solution that is more adaptive, personalized, and less costly to build and maintain than traditional e-learning systems.

3. We designed a web UI that employs interactive and intuitive graphical visualizations to present expertise assessment and learning recommendation to facilitate effective system-user interaction.

RELATED WORK

Traditional E-Learning Systems

Learning management system (LMS) is the traditional approach to e-learning. Learning in LMS is organized as courses (a.k.a. curriculum). Traditional LMS is mainly used for formal learning and is considered incompetent for supporting e-learning in the new era when learning is viewed as a self-governed, problem-based and collaborative social process [12].

Intelligent tutoring system (ITS) [17, 25, 26] is developed to support learning of a particular subject or skill. ITS dynamically builds a student model as the learning process advances and compares it against a pre-determined domain model, which serves as a source of expert knowledge and a standard for evaluating the student's performance. Based on the comparison result, the system provides timely customized instruction or feedback to the learner. ITS is expensive to develop and implement in general [2, 24, 25, 28]. It is particularly difficult and time-consuming to develop the domain model (i.e., the concepts, rules, and problem-solving strategies of the domain to be learned), which requires structured and well-defined domain knowledge [24, 25]. Only recently Educational Data Mining emerged as a research field that explores the application of data mining and machine learning techniques

for domain modeling [14]. Similar to ITS, our system dynamically builds a user model for each learner and compares it against a domain model to provide personalized feedback and recommendation. The data-driven approach adopted by our system makes it much easier and less costly to create and dynamically update the domain model.

Social Learning

Web 2.0 and collaboration technologies (e.g., social networking, wiki, blog, forum) have gained increasing popularity in social learning and brought profound impact to education [19, 29]. Existing collaboration and social software tools primarily focus on basic content sharing features such as file sharing, rating, commenting, tagging and searching, which are not tailored specifically to support learning. The work presented in [32] pointed out the needs for new social learning technologies to help learners find the right content, connect with the right people, and to motivate participation. Vassileva et al. described different approaches to motivate users to participate in social computing applications [33], and explored recommendation techniques for e-learning focused discussion forums [1]. Despotakis et al. conducted automatic semantic analysis to capture viewpoints and enable visual exploration of the conceptual spaces of user-generated content [13]. In comparison, the focus of our work is on supporting informal social learning with automatic and dynamic expertise assessment and progress checking, and creation and visualization of personalized learning roadmaps.

Expert Finding

Expert finding systems have been developed to answer questions like "who are the experts on topic X?" Two main approaches are employed to automatically identify experts [5, 27, 30]. The first approach models one's expertise based on all the materials s/he is associated with, and then uses information retrieval methods to rank individual expertise models by their relevancy to the topic. The second approach first locates materials highly relevant to the topic, and then builds and ranks expertise models only for those who are associated with these materials. Despite the differences, both approaches have demonstrated the effectiveness of using content (text and metadata) associated with a person to assess this person's expertise on different topics. In comparison, our system is capable of identifying experts for topics derived from available content based on user expertise models created from activities associated with this content. However, the main purpose of this functionality is to facilitate social interactions in learning, not to find experts for specific Q&A.

Recommender Systems

The field of recommender systems is very rich and over years, many algorithms (e.g., collaborative filtering [9, 20], content [3, 21] and social based [10] recommendation) have been developed to support applications ranging from movie, music and book recommendation to news filtering. In this work, we primarily use content and social based strategies in learning recommendation. Unlike typical recommender systems that suggest a list of ranked items, our system characterizes the utility of each recommended learning item along two dimensions: return on investment and distance to the user's current expertise. It then employs an interactive treemap visualization to present both dimensions simultaneously.

MODEL REPRESENTATIONS

Topic Model

Topics provide a form of guidance to help users navigate through the learning space. The system employs a three-step process to create a model representation that associates individual documents with topics. In the first step, the system uses unsupervised statistical text analytics to infer topic distribution from the collection of documents in the target domain. This automatic topic analysis step reduces the manual effort needed to organize content. Topics created at this step are referred to as *system topics*. In the second step, domain leaders map system topics to a set of *labeled topics*. Each labeled topic corresponds to one or more system topics. This human validation step ensures the quality of the topic model and produces easier to understand topic labels and descriptions. In the third step, the system creates a topic-specific word vector for every <document, labeled topic> pair. This representation serves as the basis for creating topic-specific user and domain models. Since both expertise assessment and learning recommendation are conducted at the labeled topic level, labeled topics are simply referred to as *topics* in the later sections of this paper unless otherwise noted.

Specifically, in the first step, Latent Dirichlet Allocation (LDA) [7] is conducted over the collection of documents to infer topic assignment for every word token in each document. Based on the topic assignment, two types of information are derived: topic-specific word distribution Φ and document-specific topic distribution Θ.

In the second step, domain leaders inspect top-ranked words and documents associated with each of the system topics (derived from Φ and Θ respectively), and label them to produce a set of labeled topics. Multiple system topics may be given the same label, essentially merging them to a single topic. Incoherent system topics may be removed.

In the third step, a word vector representation $V_{d,t}$ is created for every document d on every labeled topic t. The ith dimension of $V_{d,t}$ corresponds to a unique word w_i in the vocabulary of the document collection. Let k_j denote the jth word token in document d, $T_s(k_j)$ denote the system topic assigned to k_j in the first step, $T(T_s(k_j))$ denote the labeled topic associated with $T_s(k_j)$ in the second step, then:

$$V_{d,t}(i) = \sum_j (I(w_i = k_j) \times I(T(T_s(k_j)) = t)) \qquad (1)$$

where $I(x = y)$ denotes the indicator function that returns 1 when x is equal to y and 0 otherwise. In other words, $V_{d,t}(i)$

is the count of all the words in d that are equal to w_i and have a topic assignment equal to t. The overall topic strength $S_{d,t}$ of document d for labeled topic t is the L1-norm (sum) of $V_{d,t}$:

$$S_{d,t} = \left\| V_{d,t} \right\|_1 \qquad (2)$$

The system uses the above formula instead of Θ to compute the topic strength in order to give equal weight to each topic-related word, regardless of the length of the document that contains the word.

User Model

User modeling infers users' expertise based on the content associated with their knowledge sharing (e.g. author, comment) and acquisition (e.g. read, download) activities in the enterprise social environment. Even though models built this way may not fully capture all aspects of individuals' expertise, previous success of expert finding systems [5, 27, 30] show that they provide more reliable and granular representations of expertise than the expertise profiles created based on manual/self assessment, and we believe that they are sufficient for the purpose of providing users feedback and guidance in social learning.

Individual user models are built at the topic level to represent topic-specific user expertise. The model of user u for topic t has two parts. The first part captures the strength of various user activities in relation to the topic. It is represented with a multi-dimensional activity vector $A_{u,t}$ where the mth dimension corresponds to an activity type a_m (e.g. create-wiki, read-blog), and its value measures to what degree the user's activities of type a_m is about topic t:

$$A_{u,t}(m) = L(\sum_{d \in D(u,a_m)} S_{d,t}) \times \omega(a_m) \qquad (3)$$

$$L(x) = \frac{1}{1 + a \times e^{-b \times x}} \qquad (4)$$

where $D(u, a_m)$ denotes the set of documents associated with user u through activity type a_m, $S_{d,t}$ is the topic strength of document d for topic t (see the previous section), L is a logistic function to control the scale of the value, and $\omega(a_m)$ is the weight of activity type a_m. Activity type weight reflects the different levels of expertise required/implied by different types of activities. Its value is the product of empirically determined action type weight and content type weight. For instance, the action type of "create" has a higher weight (e.g. 1.0) than "read" (e.g. 0.4), and the content type of "wiki" has a higher weight (e.g. 0.8) than "forum" (e.g. 0.6).

The second part of the topic-specific user model captures the user's familiarity with the terminologies of the topic. It is represented with a word vector $W_{u,t}$ where the ith dimension corresponds to a unique word w_i:

$$W_{u,t}(i) = \sum_m (\omega(a_m) \times \sum_{d \in D(u,a_m)} V_{d,t}(i)) \qquad (5)$$

In other words, $W_{u,t}$ is the weighted sum of the topic-specific word vectors for all the documents associated with the user.

Topic-Specific Domain Model

A topic-specific domain model is an amalgam of experts' activities and knowledge related to a specific topic in the target domain. It is created by aggregating individual topic-specific user models of those who are identified as experts for the topic. Specifically, for each topic t, the activity and word vectors $A_{u,t}$ and $W_{u,t}$ of the experts for this topic are averaged to create the vector representations $A_{e,t}$ and $W_{e,t}$, which are stored in the topic-specific domain model for t.

The identification of experts for a topic is a combination of automatic and manual effort. First, the system ranks all users based on the L1-norm values of their activity vectors for the topic and outputs a list of top-ranked users as candidate experts. Second, domain leaders select one or more candidates from the list and designate them as experts. This procedure ensures that the experts (whom all others are compared against) are both well established and have a prominent digital presence in the domain.

EXPERTISE ASSESSMENT

The goal of expertise assessment is to create a quantified measure of expertise to help users keep track of their current status, progress, and distance to target expertise when they engage in social learning activities to improve their expertise. We chose to use a relative measure of expertise as it is easier to interpret and understand in the social context. Specifically, expertise assessment of a user for a topic takes the form of an expertise score with its value ranging from 0% to 100% to indicate the user's relative expertise level when compared against the aggregate expertise of the experts for the topic (a.k.a. topic-specific domain model). Below we describe the method to calculate expertise scores and the research work around the presentation of expertise scores at the user interface.

Creation

The system evaluates a user's expertise for a topic from three aspects. The first aspect assesses the user's overall activity level for the topic in relative to the aggregate expert activity level:

$$S_1 = \min\{1, \frac{\|A_{u,t}\|_1}{\|A_{e,t}\|_1}\} \qquad (6)$$

where $A_{u,t}$ denotes the activity vector from the user's model for topic t, $A_{e,t}$ denotes the aggregate expert activity vector from the topic-specific domain model, and $\|\bullet\|_1$ denotes the L1-norm (sum) of the vector.

The second aspect compares the user and the experts at a finer granularity by measuring how closely the user's activities resemble the aggregate expert activities. It is calculated as:

$$S_2 = 1 - \sqrt{\frac{\sum_m (\max\{0, A_{e,t}(m) - A_{u,t}(m)\})^2}{\sum_m A_{e,t}(m)^2}} \qquad (7)$$

The third aspect estimates the user's familiarity with the topic by calculating the similarity between the user's topic-specific word vector $W_{u,t}$ and the aggregate expert's topic-specific word vector $W_{e,t}$:

$$S_3 = 1 - \sqrt{\frac{\sum_i (\max\{0, W_{e,t}(i) - W_{u,t}(i)\})^2}{\sum_i W_{e,t}(i)^2}} \qquad (8)$$

The final expertise score S of a user u for a topic t is the average of S_1, S_2, and S_3.

New user activities and/or expert activities cause expertise scores to change. Scores can not only increase, but also decrease. For example, when there are new expert activities but no new activities from a user, the user gets into the situation of "if you are not getting better, you are getting worse."

Presentation

The user interface design for displaying expertise scores aims to find a graphical presentation that maximizes the users' trust in the system's expertise assessment and their perceived utility of the system. We explored the effects of different graphical presentations of expertise scores on trust and perceived system utility with a controlled experiment (N=60). Our results indicated that the users' trust in the system's assessment of their expertise increased when the scores were presented in an exact percentage format (e.g. 35%) instead of a range format (e.g. 30-40%). We also tested the effects of providing social comparison, and observed that the users found more utility in the system when they were provided with an average score next to their scores. Whether the average score was above or below their scores did not have a significant effect on their response. These results on increased perception in the utility of the system align with the literature on social comparison [8].

Based on the results of this experiment, our design decision was to present the expertise score of a user for a topic in an exact percentage format, together with the average score calculated based on the expertise scores of all users with non-zero scores for the topic.

To further apply ideas from social learning, the design of the user interface includes a list of experts for each topic. Names and expertise scores of these experts are displayed under their pictures (hyperlinked to their profiles in an enterprise social network), informing users of who the experts are and how far his/her expertise score for a topic is from those of the experts. This design decision was based on several social learning concepts such as being able to find models (experts), as well as providing a way to easily reach out to experts to ask questions.

Figure 1 illustrates how we implemented the "My Interests" page at the user interface based on these design decisions. The page displays four types of information: 1) the topics

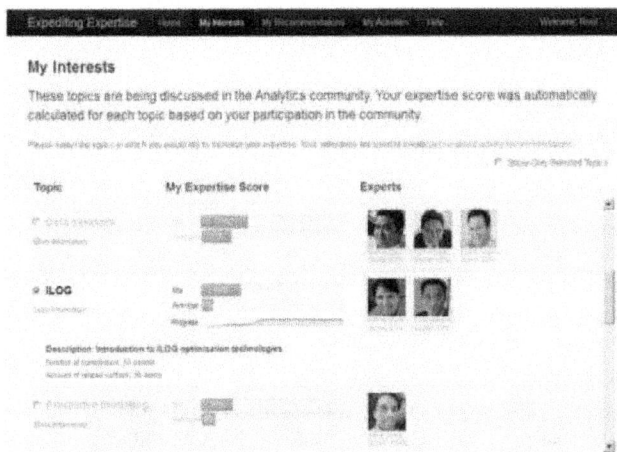

Figure 1. EE user interface – "My Interests"

available for learning, 2) the user selection of the topics s/he is interested in learning (which can be changed at any time during learning), 3) topic-specific expertise scores, and 4) the experts for each topic. All the information is organized into sections, where each section corresponds to one topic, listed in alphabetical order based on topic labels.

Clicking on "More Information" below the label of a topic expands the section for this topic to display a description of the topic, the number of documents related to the topic, and the number of content contributors for the topic.

The charts in the central portion of each topic section show the user's expertise score for the topic, along with the average expertise score as a comparison. The interface provides a sparkline of the progress of the user, which gives the user an idea about the changes to her/his expertise score over time. More detail on the exact value and time of those score changes can be obtained by hovering over different points on the progress chart. As the user progresses through learning, the scores are dynamically updated.

The "My Activities" page (not shown here due to space limitation) lists all of the user's activities recorded by the system. This helps the user track his/her progress and gives an idea of what are included in the user model used to compute his/her expertise scores. The user can choose to have the list categorized by action type (e.g. read, author), or content type (e.g. wiki, blog, forum, file).

LEARNING RECOMMENDATION

The goal of learning recommendation is to create personalized learning roadmaps that can provide users guidance on what to learn and help them get the most learning benefits out of the time and effort spent. The recommendation is on a topic basis and takes the form of learning activities. Each recommended learning activity is associated with two different dimensions of information: *ROI* (**r**eturn **o**n **i**nvestment) to provide an estimate of "the bang for the buck" provided by this activity, and *DUCE*

(**d**istance to the **u**ser's **c**urrent **e**xpertise) to give some idea about how familiar the user is with this activity. Both *ROI* and *DUCE* values can change over time as a result of the user's evolving expertise and the related social learning activities of other users. Below we describe the algorithm for creating the recommended learning activities, and the design for presenting them at the user interface.

Creation

To create personalized learning recommendation for a topic, the system first generates two candidate activity lists, one for reading activities and the other for creation activities. While reading activities aim to help users acquire knowledge, the purpose of creation activities is mainly to encourage users to demonstrate and share expertise for others to benefit from social learning. The system ranks the activities from both lists together based on their *ROI* values and recommends the top-ranked activities (up to a value or rank threshold). Below we describe separately the creation of each list and the calculation of the *ROI* and *DUCE* values for each recommended activity.

Reading Activity Recommendation
The *ROI* value of a reading activity for a topic is a combination of the following factors related to the recommended document to read:

- Relevance R: the topic strength $S_{d,t}$ of the document
- Importance I: the weighted count of expert activities associated with the document, with each count weighted by the action type (e.g., read, create)
- Popularity P: the count of user activities associated with the document by all users
- Average rating A: the product of the average relevance rating and the average helpfulness rating of the document
- Type T: the weight (empirically determined) of the content type (e.g. wiki, blog)
- Size S: the length (word count) of the document

The value of each factor is scaled to be between 0 and 1 using Formula 4, where the normalizing parameters a and b are set to different values for different factors.

The *ROI* value is calculated as:

$$ROI = \frac{R \times I \times P \times A \times T}{S} \qquad (9)$$

To measure the familiarity of a user u with a recommended document d, we compute *DUCE* (distance to the user's current expertise) as the distance between the user's topic-specific word vector $W_{u,t}$ and the topic-specific word vector $V_{d,t}$ of the recommended document:

$$DUCE = \sqrt{\frac{\sum_i (\max\{0, V_{d,t}(i) - W_{u,t}(i)\})^2}{\sum_i V_{d,t}(i)^2}} \qquad (10)$$

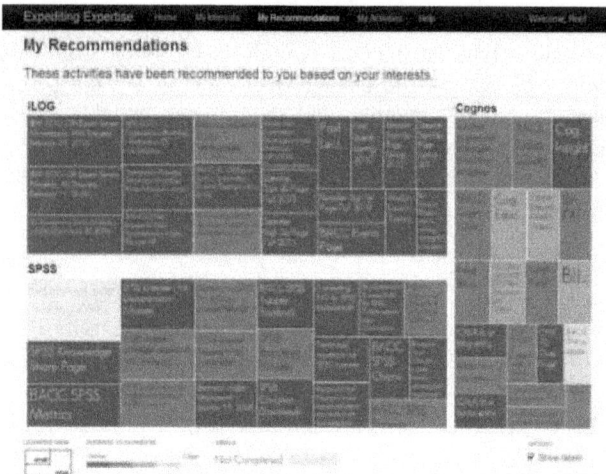

Figure 2. EE user interface – "My Recommendations"

Creation Activity Recommendation

The system recommends four types of creation activity: create a blog entry, create a wiki page, create a new forum post, and create a reply to an existing forum post. For the first three types of creation activity, because there is no content associated with them, the *ROI* value is calculated as the product of the user's expertise score for the topic and the popularity of the data source (i.e. total number of user activities) where the content is to be created. The idea is to encourage (via a high *ROI* value) users with high expertise scores to share their knowledge by creating content in the data source of high popularity and potentially high impact. The *DUCE* value is the inverse of the normalized count of the same type of activities by the user on the topic, assuming that the user is more familiar with a creation activity if s/he has conducted similar activities for the topic previously.

The last type of creation activity (i.e. create a reply to an existing forum post) is recommended to users with expertise scores above a threshold for the topic. Content from the existing forum post is used to calculate the *ROI* and *DUCE* values using the methods described in the previous section.

Presentation

The user interface design for presenting learning recommendation has two main goals. First, it aims to provide an easy-to-follow visual guidance to help the users to prioritize the learning activities for improving expertise. Second, the presentation aims to give the users an overview of their expertise strengths and gaps across topics, so they can easily assess current status and track progress as the presentation gets updated over time.

With the above goals in mind, we chose to present learning recommendation in the form of an interactive treemap for two reasons. First, compared with traditional list views, a treemap provides a more compact and visually appealing

display which gives the users more information at a glance. Second, it enables simultaneous presentation of multiple data dimensions with size, color, and grouping, which can be utilized in a straightforward manner to display the *ROI*, *DUCE*, and topic information.

Figure 2 illustrates how we implemented the "My Recommendations" page at the user interface. The recommendation treemap groups learning activities by topic and renders only activities for the user-selected topics. Each recommended learning activity is depicted as a box in the treemap, labeled with document title if it is a reading activity or activity type such as "create a wiki" if it is a creation activity. The *ROI* and *DUCE* values of the activity are mapped to the size and color dimensions of the corresponding box respectively. Bigger boxes correspond to greater *ROI* values, and darker boxes correspond to greater *DUCE* values (different *DUCE* values are binned with each bin mapped to a different shade of the same color, which is blue in our case). Completed activities are marked gray to differentiate them from those that had not yet been completed. As a result, when a user completes more activities and the distance between the recommended activities and the user's expertise becomes smaller due to increased user expertise, the color distribution of the treemap gets lighter, which resembles a cleaner plate. This makes it easy for the user to quickly assess his/her progress. Our design choice for the color distribution also enables the system to avoid any restrictions for color-blind users.

Clicking on a recommendation box opens up an overlay modal window which provides an overview of the recommended learning activity. It displays a snippet from the content (for reading activity), content type (e.g., wiki, blog, forum), degree of estimated learning gain (return on investment), popularity, and an estimation of the time (in minutes) needed to complete the activity if it is a reading activity (calculated based on the word count of the associated document). The overview is intended to let the user know more about the recommended activity to help him/her decide whether to follow the recommendation to complete it.

For a reading activity, there is a "Read Now" button which when clicked on opens a new browser tab to display the content to read. For a creation activity, the window shows a "Create Now" button instead, which takes the user to the online data source where s/he can create new content. The user can spend as much time as s/he wants/needs to complete the activity in the new browser tab.

After the user is finished with the activity, s/he can simply close the new tab and return to the "My Recommendations" page, where the same overlay window is updated to enable user ratings of the activity in terms of its relevancy to the topic and helpfulness to the user's learning. The ratings will be incorporated into the calculation when the system creates new recommendations for this user and others. Another update to the overlay window is its buttons. For a reading

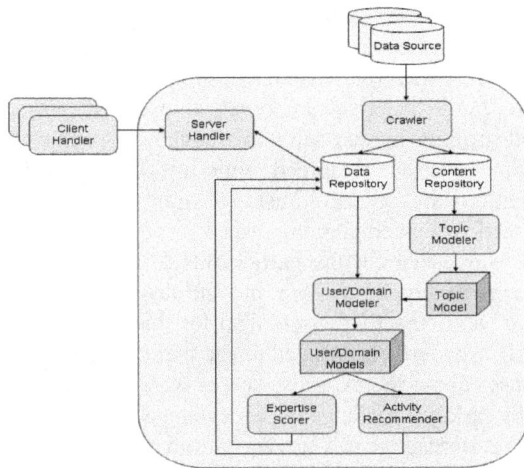

Figure 3. EE system architecture and flow

activity, the user is required to explicitly mark the activity as completed by clicking on the "Mark as Read and Close" button (which replaces the "Read Now" button) to close the overlay window. The treemap is automatically updated to color the corresponding box gray, indicating that the activity has been completed. For a creation activity, the user is not required to mark it as completed as creation activities are automatically detected and tracked by the system. The user can simply click on the "Close" button to close the overlay window. The color of the corresponding box will only be updated after the system recalculates the *DUCE* value of the recommended creation activity based on the updated user model which includes the new creation activity. It turns lighter over time as the user creates more content, but never gray (which signals "completed") in order to encourage the users to keep contributing to content.

SYSTEM ARCHITECTURE AND FLOW

Figure 3 illustrates the architecture and flow of the system integrating all the components described above to support informal social learning. First we describe the back-end process. It starts with the *crawler* gathering data it has not seen before from available data sources in the target domain and extracting documents (e.g. wikis, blogs, forum posts, files) as well as time-stamped user activities associated with each document. Document metadata and activities are stored in the *data repository*, while document text is stored in the *content repository*. The *topic modeler* retrieves data from the content repository and conducts text analytics to create the *topic model* if there isn't one already, or to fold new documents into the existing topic model otherwise. The *user/domain modeler* accesses the data repository and the topic model to build topic-specific *user models*. Individual topic-specific models of the users who are identified as experts for a topic are aggregated to create the topic-specific *domain model* of the topic. The *expertise scorer* computes topic-specific expertise scores for each user. The *activity recommender* creates a list of recommended learning activities for each <user, topic>.

Each learning activity has the attributes of activity type, link to the content (for reading) or to the data source (for creation), and the *ROI* and *DUCE* values. Both expertise scores and recommended learning activities are recorded in the data repository. Periodically (e.g. overnight) the back-end process is re-executed to gather new content/activities, and update models, expertise scores, and recommendations.

On the front-end, each of the three main pages has its own *client hander* to provide the UI functionality for the page. Each client handler communicates with the centralized *server handler* using a set of REST APIs and JSON-formatted data to retrieve the data to be displayed and report user interaction to the back-end for processing.

USER STUDY

Methodology

We conducted a controlled laboratory study to collect data on the user experience with the Expediting Expertise (EE) system. The user study was designed to evaluate to which degree the system meets the original design goals, and to gather feedback on how the system could be improved.

We crawled data (documents and activities) from two internally public communities dedicated to data analytics products and services in an enterprise social platform. We chose these communities based on the high level of activities. The data set contains 2,533 documents (including wiki pages, blog posts, forum entries, and files), and 10,755 activities (including create, update, comment, and download) from 4,748 community members. We set the number of system topics (a configurable parameter) to 30 for the automatic topic modeling step. A domain expert mapped these system topics to 13 labeled topics by merging related topics together during the human validation step.

Due to the geographically dispersed nature of the community members, it turned out to be difficult to run a laboratory study with the actual members. Therefore, we chose data from three community members with various degrees of activities ("active", "moderate", "inactive") and mapped them to three hypothetical users of the EE system. The topics of interest for learning were pre-selected prior to the evaluation to keep the setup same for all participants.

There were a total of three exercise sessions (one per each hypothetical user) in the study. For each exercise, the study participants were asked to log in to the system as one of the hypothetical users and perform three tasks. Each task required the participants to explore one page of the system (i.e., "My Activities", "My Interests", and "My Recommendations") and answer 9 questions using the information available on that page (e.g., number of documents authored, topic with the highest expertise score, recommended learning activity with the highest *ROI/DUCE* value and its content type, popularity, or estimated completion time). A full list of these questions is omitted here due to space limitation. The error rate of the answers to these questions provides objective measures of the participants' understanding of EE's main features. Each task also included 3 questions asking for subjective evaluation of the expertise scores and recommendation for the associated hypothetical user on a 5-point Likert scale (e.g. "the recommendation map gives the user an idea of his/her overall expertise strengths and gaps for the selected topics"). The order of the exercises (hypothetical users) was randomly selected for each participant.

For the main study, we recruited 10 participants from a large international corporation, 7 of who were male and 3 were female. Before performing the exercises, each user was given a tutorial on EE, during which s/he was instructed to log in to the system using a test account and visit all of the main pages. The users had time to freely explore all the features at the UI. For each exercise in the study, the participants read the descriptions of the tasks and the questions they needed to answer in print form. After the participants completed all three exercises, we asked them to fill out an exit survey of 10 questions that aimed to collect feedback on the overall system. The questions were structured to ask about degrees of agreement with a number of statements regarding the expertise scores, the recommendation map and the overall system, measured using a 5-point Likert scale (from "strongly disagree" to "strongly agree").

Results

In this section we report on objective and subjective data collected from the lab study.

The training time varied from 5 minutes to 18 minutes across the users, with an average of 11 minutes. In spite of this very brief training time, all participants were able to complete their exercises with few difficulties. The total exercise completion time varied from 6 minutes to 27 minutes, with an average of 14 minutes. There was no significant variance among the completion time of different exercises by a single participant. Almost all participants answered all task questions correctly. Only one participant made a mistake on answering one question in his last exercise, where he was asked to identify the recommended learning activity that provided the most learning gain (return on investment) for a topic. This same participant had correctly answered the same question for other topics in his two earlier exercises. Overall, the short exercise completion time and the low error rate indicate that the users could easily understand and interact with the system.

9 out of 10 participants indicated that they understood that the expertise scores were a relative measure calculated based on a comparison of the user's activities against activities of others in the communities. All participants agreed/strongly agreed that the expertise scores would be helpful in keeping track of the user's current status, progress, and target in expertise building. However, their opinions varied regarding whether 'the expertise scores are

an accurate representation of the hypothetical user's expertise as reflected in his/her activities listed on the "My Activities" page' (our actual question text). For both the "active" and "inactive" hypothetical users, 8 participants agreed/strongly agreed with this statement, while only 2 participants strongly agreed with this statement for the "moderate" hypothetical user, 7 remained neutral, 1 disagreed. The average rating was 3.90 out of 5. We believe that it was easier for the participants to judge the relation between the expertise score and the activity level for the "active" and "inactive" users than for the "moderate" user. Overall, we were encouraged to see that the majority of the responses about the expertise scores were positive, and felt that by asking participants to evaluate the hypothetical users' expertise scores given the available data, these responses were relatively objective and free of any bias that may be introduced (if we asked them to evaluate their own expertise scores) due to people's desire to be seen in the best possible light (e.g. social desirability bias, selective self-presentation effect).

All participants agreed that it would be useful to have the recommendation map personalized based on the user's background, and the meanings of the color and size of the boxes in the recommendation map were easy to understand. 9 out of 10 participants agreed that it was helpful to have *ROI* and *DUCE* information for each recommended learning activity, and it was easy to prioritize learning activities (i.e. determining which to focus on first) based on such information. All except one user (who remained neutral) agreed that they would prefer the recommendation map to the list style display of recommended learning activities. One user commented: *"List is dull."* Another user said *"I like the map view but lists are sometimes useful too. Both views should be available."* 9 out of 10 participants agreed that the recommended learning activities were relevant to the topics. Only one user found it difficult to judge relevancy mentioning that he was not familiar with the domain chosen for the study. We saw a slight drop in the participants' agreement with the statement of "the recommendation map would give the user an idea of his/her overall expertise strengths and gaps for the topics" when the hypothetical user's activity level was lower. While all agreed or strongly agreed with this statement in the "active" user's case, that number was 8 for the "moderate" user, and 7 for the "inactive" user.

For the overall assessment of the system, all participants agreed that they found the user interface intuitive and easy to use, and that they would use the tool for their own expertise building if available, and recommend it to others.

For all the study results, we performed one-sample t-tests comparing means to the midpoint of the Likert scales (3) and found them all statistically significant ($p < .005$).

DISCUSSION

Content

Because the primary goal of the Expediting Expertise system is to support informal social learning, we have largely focused on content organically created in social environments (i.e., content created by and shared with peers and colleagues). We use topic modeling to automatically group content into topics and assess content quality based on a number of factors such as relevancy to topic, popularity, and user ratings. This effort helps structuralizing content and making it more suitable for learning, but it is only the start. One of our user study participants pointed out that even though the recommendation map provided an intuitive roadmap for learning about a topic, the lack of information about how different pieces of content about this topic are related to each other could still make learners feel at loss, especially if they are new to the topic and want to start with the basics. This suggests a need for granular structures on content within topic boundaries. However, it is a challenge to obtain such structures automatically without extensive domain knowledge.

One way to address this issue is that, instead of focusing purely on informal learning, we could explore technologies to associate organically created content with curated content (including formal training materials) wherever available to synergistically blend formal and informal learning. Because information such as dependency and difficulty is more easily available for curated content, utilizing content and metadata created for formal learning could help to better access the quality and suitableness of particular informal learning content, which would result in more effective learning. An additional benefit of blending formal and informal learning is that it allows users to easily access different types of learning materials that are complementary to each other in one setting without having to go to different places.

One should note that although there has been work on integrating social learning into existing learning management systems, organically created content is still largely viewed as supplementary to formal learning content. As a result, it is not systematically analyzed and its use is limited. We would argue that organically created content should be put on an equal footing with formal learning content in terms of the attention it should receive, so users can benefit more from knowledge and experience of others, especially for fast growing areas where formal learning content is scarce.

Assessment

One common feedback from our users was that the usefulness of expertise scores and personalization of learning recommendation mostly depend on how accurate a user model is in representing one's expertise. Since the system infers a user's expertise based on what s/he does, it is important to build user models based on comprehensive sources of user activity information. A feature that allows users to provide information about their activities and associate content (e.g. a publication authored) through user interface would enable the system to build more accurate user models by incorporating information from sources that are otherwise unknown or ignored.

A concern frequently raised about expertise assessment was whether it could have a negative impact on employee performance evaluation. Users tended to be more critical of the accuracy of expertise scores and less willing to make their scores visible to others when they perceived that the scores would be associated with the evaluation of their job performance. Therefore, it is important to emphasize the learning support purpose of expertise assessment for the system to be successfully adopted.

Recommendation

Several users called for a more granular personalization of learning recommendation than what *ROI* (size) and *DUCE* (color) values could provide in the recommendation map. They commented that a more useful recommendation would require an understanding of the user's goal and preferences in learning. Their feedback suggests that learning recommendation should be created based not only on what the user knows and doesn't know, but also on what s/he needs/wants to know. To deal with the cold start or data sparsity problems, the recommendation could be based on activities and preferences from people who are "similar" to the target user (e.g. people in the same job role or from the user's personal social network) by adapting collaborative filtering techniques.

Other features suggested for learning recommendation include providing a more dynamic and adaptive Amazon style recommendation based on the specific learning activity the user is currently focusing on, and enabling users to bookmark/pin a particular recommendation for easy access at a later time.

CONCLUSION

In this paper, we present Expediting Expertise, a system that facilitates continuous expertise building in the enterprise by providing a social environment to support personalized informal learning. It employs a data-driven approach to automatically organize learning materials, concretely measure users' current expertise levels in their topics of interest and create personalized recommendations of learning activities. This approach requires minimal domain customization and automatically captures the evolution of domain knowledge. The system's web UI presents expertise assessment and learning recommendation using graphical visualizations to facilitate effective system-user interaction. Results from our user study demonstrate the usefulness of our main design features and the effectiveness of the overall system.

REFERENCES

1. Abel, F., Bittencourt, I., Costa, E., Henze, N., Krause, D. and Vassileva J. (2010). Recommendations in online discussion forums for e-learning systems. *IEEE Transactions on Learning Technologies*, 3(2):165–176.

2. Anderson, J.R., Corbett, A.T., Koedinger, K.R. and Pelletier, R. (1995). Cognitive tutors: Lessons learned. *The Journal of the Learning Sciences*, 4:167–207.

3. Antonopoulus, N., Salter, J. (2006). Cinema screen recommender agent: Combining collaborative and content-based filtering. *IEEE Intelligent Systems*, 35–41.

4. Ballantyne, N.J. and Quinn, K. (2006). Informal learning and the social web. *http://informallearning.pbworks.com/w/page/19914104/FrontPage*.

5. Balog, K., Azzopardi, L. and de Rijke M. (2006). Formal models for expert finding in enterprise corpora. In *SIGIR '06*.

6. Bandura, A. (1977). Self-efficacy: Toward a unifying theory of behavioral change. *Psychological Review*, 84(2):191–215.

7. Blei, D., Ng, A. and Jordan, M (2003). Latent dirichlet allocation. *Journal of Machine Learning Research*, 3:993–1022.

8. Buunk, B.P., Collins, R.L., Taylor, S.E., Van Yperen N.W. and Dakof, G.A. (1990). The affective consequences of social comparison: Either direction has its ups and downs. *Journal of Personality and Social Psychology*, 59(6):1238–1249.

9. Candillier, L., Meyer, F., Boullé, M. (2007). Comparing state-of-the-art collaborative filtering systems. *Lecture Notes in Computer Sciece*, 4571: 548–562.

10. Carmagnola, F., Vernero, F., Grillo, P. (2009). SoNARS: A social networks-based algorithm for social recommender systems. In *Proceedings of the 17th International Conference on User Modeling, Adaptation, and Personalization*, 223–234.

11. Chatti, M.A. and Jarke, M. (2007). The future of e-learning: A shift to knowledge networking and social software. *International Journal of Knowledge and Learning*, 3(4/5):404–420.

12. Dalsgarrd, C. (2006). Social software: e-learning beyond learning management systems. *European Journal of Open, Distance, and E-Learning*.

13. Despotakis, D., Dimitrova, V., Lau, L., Thakker, D., Ascolese, A. And Pannese, L. (2013). ViewS in user generated content for enriching learning environments: A semantic sensing approach. *International Journal of Artificial Intelligence in Education*, (7926):121–130.

14. Educational Data Mining. *http://www.educationaldatamining.org*.

15. Enterprise Strategy Group. (2012). Research report: Social enterprise adoption trends. *http://www.esg-global.com/research-reports/social-enterprise-adoption-trends/*.

16. Festinger, L. (1954). A theory of social comparison processes. *Human Relations*, 7(2):117–140.

17. Freedman, R. (2000). What is an intelligent tutoring system? *Intelligence*, 11(3):15–16.

18. Gary, B. (2004). Informal learning in an online community of practice. *Journal of Distance Education*, 19(1):20–35.

19. Greenhow, C., Robelia, B., Hughes, J. (2009). Learning, teaching, and scholarship in a digital age web 2.0 and classroom research: What path should we take now? *Educ Res* 38(4):246–259.

20. Herlocker, J., Konstan, J., Borchers, A., Riedl, J. (1999). An algorithmic framework for performing collaborative filtering. In *SIGIR '99*, 230–237.

21. Lang, K. (1995). NewsWeeder: learning to filter netnews. In *Proceedings of the 12th International Conference on Machine Learning*, 331–339.

22. Mason, R. and Rennie, F. (2007). Using Web 2.0 for learning in the community. *The Internet and higher education*, 10(3):196–203.

23. Minocha, S. (2009). Role of social software tools in education: A literature review. *Education and Training*, 51(5/6):353–369.

24. Murray, T. (1999). Authoring intelligent tutoring systems: An analysis of the state of the art. *International Journal of Artificial Intelligence in Education (IJAIED)*, 10:98–129.

25. Nkambou, R., Mizoguchi, R. and Bourdeau, J. (2010). Advances in intelligent tutoring systems. Heidelberg: Springer.

26. Nwana, H.S. (1990). Intelligent tutoring systems: An overview. *Artificial Intelligence Review*, 4:251–277.

27. Petkova, D. and Croft W.B. (2006). Hierarchical language models for expert finding in enterprise corpora. In *ICTAI '06*.

28. Polson, M.C. and Richardson, J.J. (1988). Foundations of Intelligent Tutoring Systems. Lawrence Erlbaum.

29. Ravenscroft, A. (2009). Social software, web 2.0 and learning: status and implications of an evolving paradigm. *Journal of Computer Assisted Learning*, 25(1):1–5.

30. Seid, D.Y. and Kobsa, A. (2003). Expert finding systems for organizations: Problem and domain analysis and the DEMOIR approach. *Journal of Organizational Computing and Electronic Commerce*, 13(1):1–24.

31. Shank, P. (2012). Smart companies support informal learning. The eLearning Guild.

32. Vassileva, J. (2008). Toward social learning environments. *IEEE Transactions on Learning Technologies*, 1(4):199–214.

33. Vassileva, J. (2012). Motivating participation in social computing applications: a user modeling perspective. *User Modeling and User-Adapted Interaction*, 22(1–2):177–201.

SpiderEyes: Designing Attention- and Proximity-Aware Collaborative Interfaces for Wall-Sized Displays

Jakub Dostal, Uta Hinrichs, Per Ola Kristensson and Aaron Quigley
University of St Andrews
St Andrews, Fife, United Kingdom
{jd67, uh3, pok, aquigley}@st-andrews.ac.uk

Figure 1. An illustration of our attention- and proximity-aware collaborative visualisation interface in-use. The first image shows three people using the system in parallel. The second image shows two users forming a group. The third image shows an exploration by a single user.

ABSTRACT

With the proliferation of large multi-faceted datasets, a critical question is how to design collaborative environments, in which this data can be analysed in an efficient and insightful manner. Exploiting people's movements and distance to the data display and to collaborators, proxemic interactions can potentially support such scenarios in a fluid and seamless way, supporting both tightly coupled collaboration as well as parallel explorations. In this paper we introduce the concept of collaborative proxemics: enabling groups of people to collaboratively use attention- and proximity-aware applications. To help designers create such applications we have developed SpiderEyes: a system and toolkit for designing attention- and proximity-aware collaborative interfaces for wall-sized displays. SpiderEyes is based on low-cost technology and allows accurate markerless attention-aware tracking of multiple people interacting in front of a display in real-time. We discuss how this toolkit can be applied to design attention- and proximity-aware collaborative scenarios around large wall-sized displays, and how the information visualisation pipeline can be extended to incorporate proxemic interactions.

Author Keywords

Collaborative proxemics; attention-aware user interfaces

ACM Classification Keywords

H.5.3. Information Interfaces and Presentation: Group and Organization Interfaces – Collaborative computing

INTRODUCTION

With the advent of affordable, accurate, and efficient depth sensors and computer vision systems, proximity-aware interfaces that can track a user's position relative to a display become feasible (e.g. [3, 11]). In the same vein, proxemic toolkits and techniques leveraging the proxemic relations between people and objects (digital and physical) have emerged in the literature (e.g. [6, 7, 17]). However, using proxemics to support collaborative scenarios around large vertical displays is still an unexplored area. Further, it is non-trivial to implement attention- and proximity-aware interfaces for collaboration.

In this paper we introduce the concept of collaborative proxemics: enabling groups of people to collaboratively use attention- and proximity-aware applications. We present a toolkit that enables markerless attention-aware tracking of multiple users by combining data from a Kinect depth sensor and an off-the-shelf RGB camera. Our toolkit tracks up to four people in real time. People's body positions and eye-pair locations are estimated with an error less than 10 cm and within a range between 0.5–5 meters from the display. Our toolkit allows developers to easily create both native and web-based applications leveraging multi-user proxemic interactions. As part of the the toolkit, we also present a web-based tool for implementing proximity- and attention-aware visualisation applications. We describe how these tools can be used to create novel visualisation applications.

We then present an analysis of how our toolkit can be used to support collaborative scenarios. We introduce visualisation-based scenarios and explore how proxemic interactions can be leveraged to support parallel and collaborative exploration of large multi-faceted datasets on a wall-sized display. We describe how proxemic interactions can be used to navigate and combine different visualisation layers with varying levels of detail and context in co-located collaborative scenarios.

RELATED WORK

Previous work has discussed different dimensions that proxemics introduce to the interaction between people and interactive objects. This work has included both absolute and relative *positions* of people and objects, which implies *distance*, *orientation*, *movement*, and *identity* [3]. In this paper, we focus on how the relative position to the display and to other people in front of the display, as well as knowledge about people's orientation to the display, can be used to support collaborative scenarios (see Figure 2).

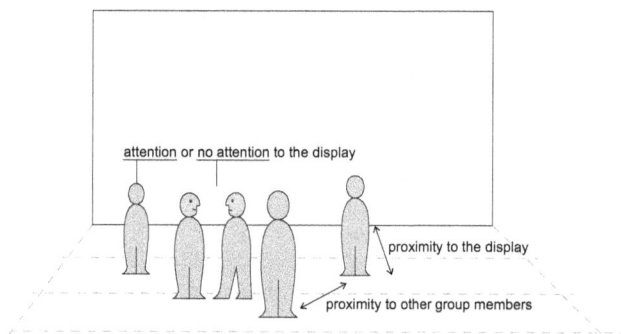

Figure 2. Using proxemics to support collaborative scenarios.

A direct parameter that can be used to drive proxemic interactions with a wall-sized display is the distance of people to the display. Previous work on proxemic interactions has described a variety of techniques and example scenarios of how the absolute and relative position of people to a stationary display can drive interactions [2, 3, 12, 14, 16, 18, 22].

Prior systems have adjusted the size or magnification factor of information as people move closer to or away from the display [5, 12, 14, 15, 19]. The distance to the display has also been used as a parameter to adjust the amount of information displayed, or to help users navigate visual information [2, 3, 22]. Finally, the type of information on the display can be adjusted based on people's distance to the display, an approach that some previous research has explored [14, 18, 22].

In the context of multi-user interactive whiteboards, the technique "Field of View" developed by Seifried et al. [20] takes people's distance to the display into account to determine the horizontal impact area of undo/redo actions: being closer to the display results in a smaller field of view and, therefore, a narrower impact area.

In our work, we expand our understanding of proxemic interactions by demonstrating how the distance to the display can be used to support *collaborative* information analysis. We call this *collaborative proxemics*.

THE SPIDEREYES TOOLKIT

We contribute a novel, attention- and proximity-aware multi-user tracking toolkit. The features of the toolkit include:

Multi-User Tracking: The toolkit tracks up to four users in real-time.

Separates Foreground and Background Activity: The toolkit uses computer vision to track users' eyes and uses this information to separate users actively engaging with the system from users in the background attending to other activities or just passing by.

Markerless Tracking: The system does not use any markers to track users and does not require any calibration for users to be tracked.

Easy Setup: The toolkit only relies on a single depth camera (e.g. a Kinect) and a high-resolution RGB camera, making it easy to set up and deploy in a variety of environments.

Programming Language Independent: The tracking system communicates its results in a programming language independent format, which allows designers to use a programming language of their choice.

Distributed Deployment: The tracking system can be deployed on a different computer than the application that uses it. This allows developers more flexibility and independence from specific deployment environments.

Visualisation Design Tool: The toolkit contains a web-based tool for designing visualisation sets. It allows designers to make their existing visualisations attention- and proximity-aware.

The toolkit is realised via two components. The first component is a multi-user tracking system. Developers can use this component to obtain real-time information about multiple users' positions and attention-aware statuses in relation to a large wall-sized display. The second component is a design tool that enables toolkit users to design attention-aware visualisation applications.

Toolkit Component 1: Tracking System

It is difficult to develop attention- and proximity-aware markerless multi-user tracking systems. To enable designers to easily create new attention- and proximity-aware interfaces we have therefore created a flexible toolkit that provides easy-to-use programming abstractions. While the bulk of our system is written in C++, our toolkit runs either a TCP/IP or a WebSockets server, which enables both native applications and browser-based applications to use the data. The scenarios we have described in this paper have all been implemented using this toolkit.

Currently, the tracking system is configured by defining several simple parameters about the environment in a text file.

```
{
"timestamp": 0003030300,
"users": [
  {"userid": 1,
   "position": {"x": 1234, "y": 1750, "z": 1063},
   "orientation": {"x": 0, "y": 0, "z": -1},
   "confidence": 1},
  {"userid": 1,
   "position": {"x": -570, "y": 1640, "z": 1534},
   "orientation": {"x": 0, "y": 0, "z": 0},
   "confidence": 0}
]
}
```

Figure 3. Example JSON object sent by the tracking system. The time-stamp is in milliseconds since the system has been initialised; position is in millimeters; orientation is reported as a unit vector. Both position and orientation are in sensor coordinates. Confidence is in the interval 0-1 (values reported by the system: 1 = full detection: eye-pair and individual eyes are detected; 0.8 = partial detection: only the eye-pair is detected; 0 = no detection).

Designers can choose from several tracking algorithms (Computer Vision (CV) only, multi-user Kinect-CV fusion, or single-user Kinect-CV fusion) as well as configuring the data output (TCP/IP server, WebSockets server, or local logging). Once the system is running, the server sends the tracking results to all connected clients as a valid JSON object. See Figure 3 for an example of a data point.

Toolkit Component 2: Visualisation Design Tool

The visualisation design tool is web-based and written in JavaScript. The use of the design tool requires setting the values of several parameters and the implementation of a single function. The following parameters can be set (Figure 4 provides an example implementation for the *Vis-Active Display* with *Constant Zoom*):

Viewport Sizing (*entity_size_type*): *fraction* This parameter gives each active user an equal fraction of the display space. *angle* will dynamically resize the viewports so that they occupy equal visual angles for all active users.

Layer Magnification (*layer_zoom_type*):   This parameter defines which of the magnification methods described in the scenarios section should be used for the visualisation layers. Possible values are: *physical, constant, amplified*. For *constant*, an additional parameter that defines the desired visual angle must be set (*layer_angle*). For *amplified*, the amplification ratio (*zoom_amplification*) and neutral point (*amplified_midpoint_distance*) need to be set.

Default Visualisations (*generateVisualisationSet(uid)*): This function allows the designer to define the visualisations and their distance boundaries, for each user. Each detail layer is defined by the *url* to its content (which can be an image or a URL to a webpage) and the *start* and *end* distance boundaries for its visibility.

Grouping Distance (*group_distance*): This parameter defines the maximum distance between a pair of users for them to be considered a group by the system.

Our visualisation design tool automatically manages the creation of the application itself. In addition, it also provides the

```
var entity_size_type = "angle";
var layer_zoom_type = "constant";
var layer_angle = 20.0; //in degrees
var amplified_midpoint_distance = 1500; //mm
var zoom_amplification = 0.5; //1.0 = neutral
var group_distance = 400; //mm

function generateVisualisationSet(uid) {
  var words = new detailLayer("w.svg", 0, 5000);
  var heat = new detailLayer("h.svg", 0, 5000);
  var clusters = new detailLayer("c.svg", 0,
      5000);
  var default_visLayer = new visualisationLayer();
  switch(uid) {
  case 1: {
    default_visLayer.addLayer(words);
    break; }
  case 2: {
    default_visLayer.addLayer(heat);
    break; }
  case 3: {
    default_visLayer.addLayer(clusters);
    break; }
  case 4: {
    default_visLayer.addLayer(heat);
    break; }
  }
  var result = new visualisationSet();
  result.addLayer(default_visLayer);
  return result;
}
```

Figure 4. Code listing for the JavaScript API used for implementing the scenarios. In this code sample, the *generateVisualisationSet()* function implements the passive scenario with constant zoom and a different visualisation for each user.

following functions. The tool automatically distinguishes active users and people passing by in the background and foreground based on whether their visual attention is on the display or not and only displays visualisations for active users.

TRACKING ALGORITHMS

In this section we describe our system algorithms that underpins our toolkit. We use depth sensing (in our case a Kinect) *in combination* with computer vision algorithms to detect the users' eyes in regular RGB camera streams. The tracking system consists of four separate parts: user identification, head position tracking, attention detection, distance estimation and distance estimate correction. Some of parts of the tracking system are based on preliminary earlier work by Dostal el al. [8], which describes an approach to fusing data from a depth camera and an RGB camera for distance estimation.

In our implementation, we use the OpenCV and OpenNI frameworks coupled with our custom code. OpenCV offers implementations of standard computer vision algorithms as well as access to camera hardware. OpenNI allows us to work with the Kinect depth sensor and its data.

User Identification

To track multiple users, it is essential to have a robust user identification system. We use the Kinect's depth-based blob segmentation accessible from OpenNI as it has proved more reliable and less resource intensive compared to a computer

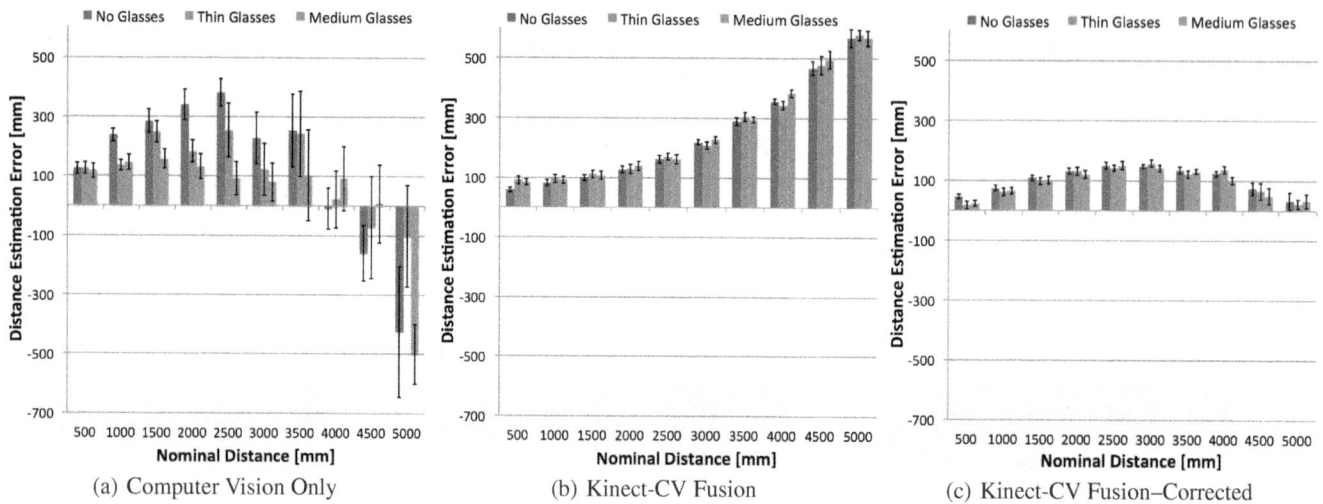

(a) Computer Vision Only   (b) Kinect-CV Fusion   (c) Kinect-CV Fusion–Corrected

Figure 5. Mean distance estimation error using computer vision-only, using computer vision-guided fusion with a Kinect depth sensor, and using computer vision-guided fusion with a Kinect depth sensor and applying a pre-computed linear regression correction model. Error bars show standard error. The three conditions in the experiment were participants wearing no glasses, glasses with a thin rim, and glasses with a rim of medium thickness.

vision approach. Due to the use of depth data, this approach is relatively robust to body occlusion and fast movement. However, this approach may lead to misidentification of users when they leave the field of view and later rejoin at a different distance. We have tested user identification with up to four users.

Head Position Tracking

After a user has been identified, we establish the position of the head within the depth/RGB images. This is a necessary step that allows our system to perform multi-user tracking in real time. This is because it enables us to significantly reduce the search area within the images. The tracking is accomplished with a cascade of three head position predictors. The primary predictor uses past data from our computer vision-based attention detector (described in the next section). If the position of the user's eye-pair is known, we use it as the centre of the search area. If the eye-pair data is not available, the secondary predictor is based on the skeleton data from the depth camera. We use the head joint as the centre of the search area. If the skeleton data is not available, then the tertiary predictor attempts to predict where the head is from the depth blob used to identify the user.

Attention Detection

Once the search area for the likely position of the user's head has been established, we translate the rectangular search area into the coordinate space of the RGB camera and perform a search for the user's eyes. We use the OpenCV implementation of the Viola-Jones feature tracking algorithm [21] to identify the users' eyes. Our algorithm is an extension of previous work [6, 8, 9], which uses eye-pair and single-eye classifiers and a custom tracking algorithm to provide coarse-grained gaze- and user-tracking.

In the first stage of the search a classifier attempts to locate the user's eye-pair. If successful, the second stage classifiers attempt to confirm the result by locating the left and right eye

separately in the left and right halves of the eye-pair area. The confidence of the attention detector depends on which of the search stages were successful. The system will report either a full detection (both first and second stage detections were successful), a partial detection (only the eye-pair was detected), or no detection. The detector will also report detailed information about the detected eyes. This is used for distance estimation. It can also be used for head position tracking in the future.

Distance Estimation

Distance estimation is performed by a cascade of estimators that use available sensor data. All of the estimators estimate the distance from points within the depth data, the only difference is the method of choosing the sampling points. The primary estimator uses the points between the eyes translated into the coordinate space of the depth camera, if the eye-pair data from the attention detector is available. The secondary estimator uses points between the head and neck joint of the skeleton data if it is available. The tertiary estimator uses the mean distance of the top 25% of the user's blob if only the depth-segmented user blob is available.

Distance Estimation Correction Model

In the evaluation of our system (described later in this section), we found that the Kinect depth camera systematically over-estimates actual distances exponentially as a function of nominal distance (see Figure 5(b)). We therefore use a pre-computed correction model that adjusts the overestimation error using a linear regression model. The linear regression correction model is[1]: $y = 0.9005x$. Using experimental data we found that this correction model explains 99% of the variance of the overestimation error ($R^2 = 0.99$). The final result is that when users are between 0.5 and 5 metres away from the

---

[1]The model for figure 5(c) also includes an offset of 48.411 mm to account for the distance between user's feet and their eyes.

display, our system can reliably estimate their distance from the display with an error of less than 10 cm (see Figure 5(c)).

Tracking Latency

Using a 2.8GHz Quad-Core Intel Core i5 processor we can track four users with a latency of approximately 30–40 ms at 20–30 fps, which results in a system that is both scalable and fast. To speed up the tracking of multiple users to this level we have parallelised the tracking procedure. As we mentioned before, we use the OpenCV implementation of the Viola-Jones feature tracker and OpenNI to access the Kinect data. Unfortunately, OpenCV and OpenNI are difficult to multithread due to critical data structures being exposed in shared memory without appropriate locking mechanisms.

We work around this by using a series of locks around OpenCV and OpenNI's core data structures and by spinning off a separate worker thread for each user we are tracking. This enables multiple users to be tracked at approximately the same speed as a single user if there are enough available cores on the machine performing the tracking.

Advantages

It is possible to perform fast tracking of multiple users using just the Kinect data or by estimating a distance directly from a blob obtained from the depth data in the usermap (although this is non-trivial and body occlusion is a serious problem). However, our Computer Vision-Kinect fusion procedure provides three distinct advantages to designers of attention- and proximity-aware interfaces.

First, we can obtain a more specific and accurate distance estimation compared to what is possible using just the Kinect skeleton interface. The range obtainable using our system is between 50 cm and 5 metres compared to the Kinect skeleton's range between 80 cm and 4 metres. For our system, 5 metres is the maximum range we tested; the actual maximum range is likely even greater. The limitation is the availability of user blobs from the OpenNI user tracker (which starts to degrade at around 4.5 m) rather than the distance estimation procedure. The spatial resolution of the Kinect depth data at 8 metres is still < 20 cm [1]. The other limitation is the image resolution of the RGB camera. The maximum distance at which an eye-pair can be detected depends on the amount of pixels occupied by the eye-pair of the tracked person in the image. For a person with 60 mm pupil distance, using a 5 megapixel (2592×1944 pixels) image taken with a camera with a 62° horizontal field of view, the maximum theoretical distance at which the person can be detected is approximately 684 cm.

Second, our system is attention-aware, which means the system can tell whether a user is looking at the screen or not. This information is not possible to obtain from the Kinect skeleton data as it only provides a single point for the head joint. Our approach makes it possible to design a wide range of attention-aware interfaces. For example, it is possible to enable the interface to visualise display changes when the user is reengaging with the display (e.g. [8]).

Third, as the system is attention-aware it can distinguish between people actively viewing the system and people that are casually passing by or are standing in the background, engaged in other activities. This makes the system more practical in open office and large laboratory environments. In general, we believe systems that are able to separate "attentive signals" from background signals are crucial for real-world adoption of markerless proximity-aware interfaces.

Evaluation

To evaluate the potential of fusing computer vision and depth sensing we conducted an experiment. We recruited eight participants (three females and five males; their ages ranged from 21 to 39) from our university campus. The experiment followed a within-subjects design with two factors: Glasses (participants wearing no glasses, participants wearing glasses with a thin frame, and participants wearing glasses with a thick frame) and Sensor (Computer Vision Only, Kinect-CV Fusion, and Kinect-CV Fusion Corrected). The Computer Vision Only condition used the distance of the participant's pupils that was available from the attention detector to estimate distance using a 5 megapixel (2592×1944 pixels) image taken with a Logitech C910 RGB camera. The Kinect-CV Fusion condition used the fusion algorithm we have previously described, without the pre-computed correction model. The Kinect-CV Fusion Corrected condition used the correction model.

We positioned the RGB camera on top of the Kinect sensor. We also marked the floor at 50 cm intervals at a range from 50 cm to 5 metres. Each participant was asked to stand with their feet aligned to each of the distance markers, while the study administrator manually read the distance value from each of the sensors. We repeated the process for each participant three times. Each time the participant either wore glasses with thin or thick frames, or no glasses at all.

Figures 5(a), 5(b) and 5(c) show the distance estimation error for Computer Vision Only, Kinect-CV Fusion, and Kinect-CV Fusion Corrected respectively. In each case, the perfect performance would be represented by a constant error of approximately 5 cm (due to the difference in the position between the tips of the feet of the participants and their eyes). As is evident in the figure, the final system that uses the linear regression correction model resulted in an estimation error less than 10 cm for a range between 0.5 and 5 metres. The evaluation also showed that the system can accurately detect the user even if the user wears glasses.

USING THE TOOLKIT

We now illustrate example scenarios of how proxemic interactions can be leveraged for individual and collaborative activities around large wall-sized displays. Previously, Jakobsen et al. [14, 15] introduced proxemic interactions with information visualisations but concentrated on single-user scenarios. While we believe that proxemic interactions can potentially be applied to a number of different collaborative scenarios, we focus on a collaborative setting where a small group of information workers explore a multi-faceted dataset

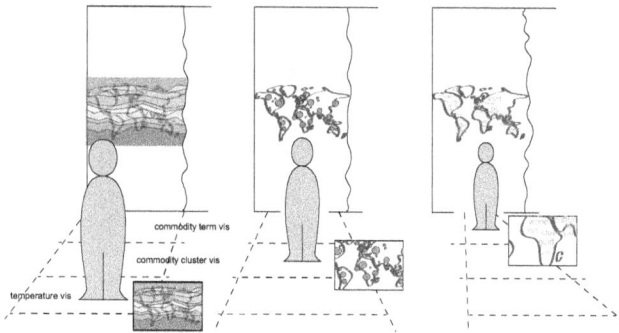

Figure 6. *Vis-Active* **Display: proximity to the display determines the type of visualisation.**

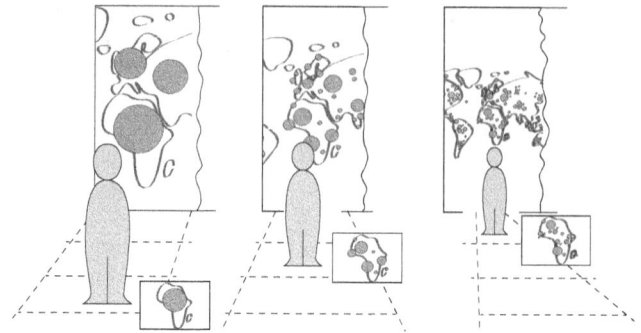

Figure 7. *Detail-Active* **Display with** *Constant Zoom*: **proximity to the display determines the level of data granularity.**

from different perspectives, using a variety of visual representations.

General Considerations
We considered mapping the distance between people and the display to three different parameters: visualisation type, detail level and zoom level.

Mapping Proxemics to Visualisation Type (Vis-Active)
Depending on the distance to the display the visualisation type can be adjusted. For example, people far away from the display can see the temperature layer. However, as they get closer to the display, the temperature layer can be replaced by a commodity cluster visualisation. Directly in front of the display people can see a commodity word cloud (see Figure 6).

Mapping Proxemics to Detail Level (Detail-Active)
Similarly to the adjustment of visualisation depending on the distance to the display, the amount of detail shown within the same visualisation can be adjusted. See Figure 7 for an example.

Mapping Proxemics to Zoom Level
Depending on the distance to the display the zoom-level of the visualisation can be adjusted. We distinguish three different variations:

Physical Zoom. The visualisation layer does not actively react to people's movements in front of the display but retains a constant width and height at all times. However, people's proximity to the display naturally increases or decreases the (perceived) size of information represented in the visualisation layer (see Figure 8).

Constant Zoom. The viewing angle of the visualisation layer is kept constant no matter how close people are to the display. That is, the size of the visualisation layer (width and height) is actively changed as people move back and forth in front of the display in such a way that the perceived size of the represented information remains constant at all times (see Figure 7 and Figure 9).

Amplified Zoom. The visualisation layer is scaled up or down depending on people's proximity to the display. As people move closer, the visualisation layer enlarges, providing

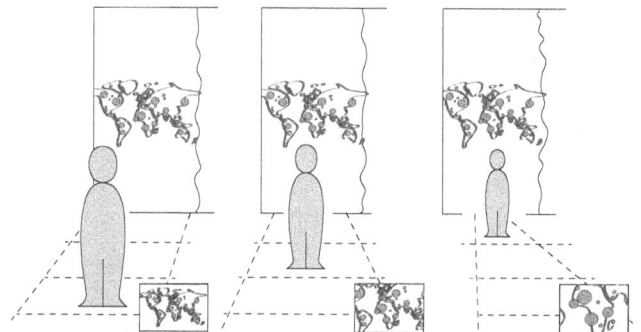

Figure 8. *Physical Zoom*: **The visualisation layer remains the same size.**

a magnified view on the information represented (see Figure 10).

These three different proxemic-based parameter mappings can be combined in different ways, resulting in nine different scenarios: *Vis-Active* with *Physical, Constant* or *Amplified Zoom, Detail-Active* with *Physical, Constant* or *Amplified Zoom* and complex *Vis-and-Detail-Active* scenarios with *Physical, Constant* or *Amplified Zoom*. We describe four of the nine scenarios in detail to point out the potential advantages and disadvantages of the parameter combinations.

Scenario 1: Vis-Active with Physical Zoom
On the *Vis-Active* Display (see Figure 6), the visualisation layer changes based on an individual's distance to the display while the size of the visualisation remains constant. The mapping between proximity and visualisation type can be continuous with the visual layers blending into each other as people move towards and away from the display.

In a multi-user scenario (see Figure 11) the visualisations change as group members move toward and away from the display. One of the possible advantages of this setup is that it supports independent explorations by users: each user can easily shift between visualisation views, and the continuous blending of visualisations even allows each user to explore correlations within the different data sets and perspectives. A possible disadvantage is that in collaborative situations, users cannot easily blend different types of visualisations while standing next to each other because they would need to be at different vertical distances from the display. According to

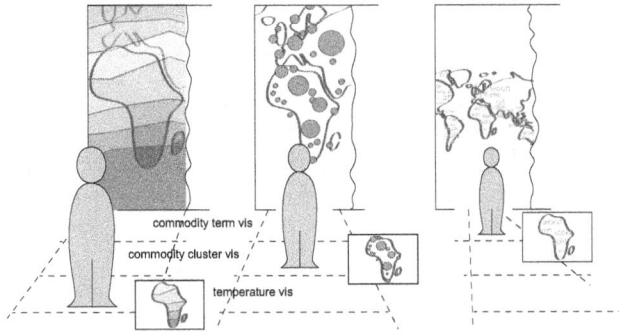

Figure 9. *Vis-Active* Display with *Constant Zoom*: the proximity to the display determines the type of visualisation while people's viewing angle remains stable.

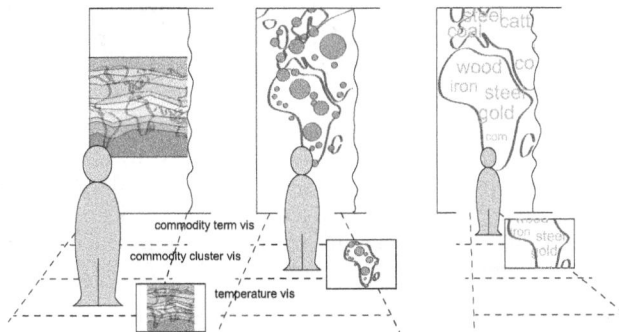

Figure 11. *Vis-Active* Display with *Physical Zoom*: multi-user scenario.

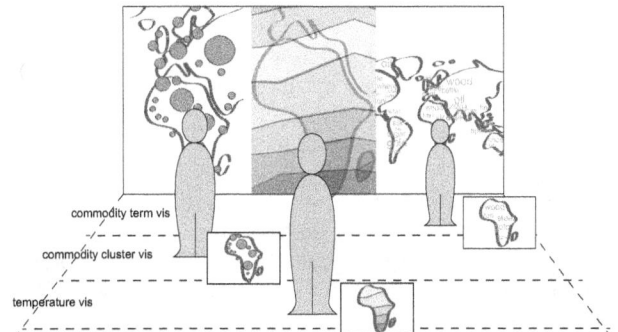

Figure 10. *Vis-Active* Display with *Amplified Zoom*: the proximity to the display determines (1) the type of visualization and (2) the amount of context/magnification level of information.

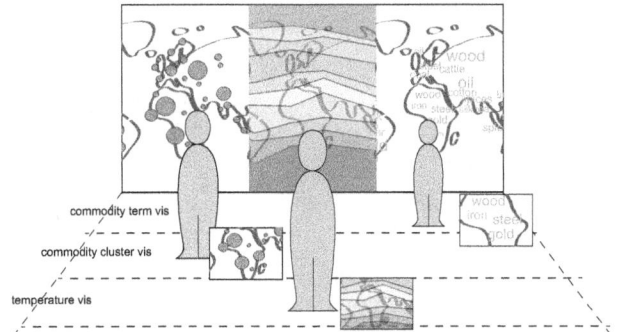

Figure 12. *Vis-Active* Display with *Constant Zoom*: multi-user scenario.

findings by Hawkey et al. [13], forcing group members to position themselves at different vertical positions in front of the display may hamper communication and coordination, which are important factors in more closely coupled collaborative work phases.

Scenario 2: Vis-Active with Constant Zoom

In Scenario 2 we adjust the type of visualisation layer as people move back and forth in front of the display while adjusting its size to keep people's viewing angle constant.

As shown in Figure 9, more context information can be added to the display as a person moves closer—because the viewing angle remains constant as a person moves toward the display, the (physical) size of information in focus does not change. This can facilitate direct interaction with information when close to the display because information is visible in a constrained space; people do not have to reach far or crouch to manipulate particular data of interest, something that has been reported as problematic on large wall-sized displays that show map representations [13].

In a multi-user setting of the *Vis-Active* with *Constant Zoom* scenario (see Figure 12), users standing at different distances from the display will see different types of visualisation layers. At the same time, their viewing angle remains stable as they move towards or away from the display. Similarly to Scenario 1, in a collaborative scenario, individual users can

work on different data perspectives and explore different visualisations at the same time, while each group member can observe the visualisations that their collaborators are working on in their periphery. This may inspire further explorations of their own visualisation. However, the constant viewing angle has the limitation that comparisons of size between data items in the different visualisations are difficult if group members stand in different zones since the viewing angle remains constant with changing distances to the display. However, as group members start to collaborate in a more closely coupled way on two different visualisations, for instance to actively compare trends within different data, it is likely that they will choose to stand in horizontal proximity, according to previous studies [13].

Scenario 3: Vis-Active with Amplified Zoom

Figure 10 shows a version of the *Vis-Active* scenario that is effectively the inverse of Scenario 2: more context information is shown from afar, while content becomes magnified as the person moves closer to the display. Note that in both variations, the type of visualisation is also changed according to the distance to the display, as described in Scenario 2. Also, while the magnification behaviour is inverted, the advantages and disadvantages when used by multiple users are likely to be similar as with *Constant Zoom* in Scenario 2.

Scenario 4: Detail-Active Display

In Scenario 4, the *Detail-Active* Display (see Figure 7), the level of data detail within the same visualisation is changed

Figure 13. *Detail-Active* Display with *Constant Zoom*: multi-user scenario.

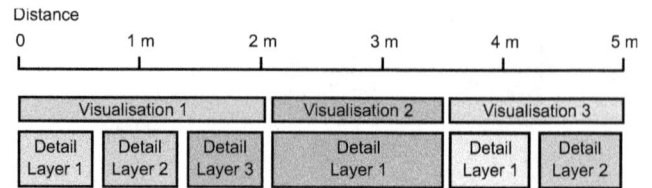

Figure 14. An illustration of a complex visualisation set consisting of three visualisations with each visualisation using a different amount of detail layers.

CASE STUDY

Using the D3 JavaScript library we modified a well known information visualisation to realise a proximity-aware visualisation using the SpiderEyes toolkit. The purpose was to evaluate the difficulty of interfacing our toolkit with an established information visualisation framework. For this, we selected the "Wealth and Health of Nations" example[2], which visualises a complex, high-dimensional dataset (country, per-capita income, life expectancy, population size, and time). In our example, we mapped the lateral movement along the horizontal axis to the temporal dimension of the dataset. Stepping from one side to another in front of the wall-sized display changed the displayed data to a specific year. This case study visualisation can be seen in Figure 15, Figure 16, and in the supplemental video of this paper.

Many alternative designs are also possible. Here we list a few examples. The forward and backward physical movements can be mapped to a scale/zoom mechanism, such as *Constant Zoom*. While *Constant Zoom* is used, the lateral movements along the horizontal axis may also be mapped to a translation function, moving the position of the visualisation on the display so that it is always centred in front of the user.

as people move toward and away from the display. We assume that showing more detail of the data can be helpful when people are close to the display for perceptual and interaction reasons. Standing close to the display makes it possible to *perceive* more subtle nuances and distinguishable features within the data that may not even be visible from further away, even if they would be represented. Furthermore, people may want to engage in more elaborate active explorations (e.g. via direct-touch), in which case it makes sense to show more data and, therefore, provide a more fine-grained visualisation of the dataset. We only depict one variation of the *Detail-Active* Display, which uses *Constant Zoom* and directly corresponds to the concept shown in Figure 13. Further variations using *Physical Zoom* and *Amplified Zoom* are also possible and are analogous to Scenarios 2 and 3, respectively.

In the multi-user *Detail-Active* Display with *Constant Zoom* scenario, group members could, again, focus on different (previously chosen) visualisations, which will remain the same as they move back and forth in front of the display (see Figure 13). The level of detail for each individual group member and the viewport on the visualisation change as a group member's distance to the display is altered. In a collaborative scenario, providing different levels of detail along with different types of visualisations can be beneficial: similar to the other scenarios we described, group members can work in parallel to explore different perspectives of the data. In more closely-coupled collaborative phases which may be about discussing particular patterns or discoveries, it can be beneficial to have different levels of detail on the data available and blend visualisations as we described in Scenario 1.

Uniting the Design of the Scenarios

The *Vis-Active* and *Detail-Active* scenarios can be seen as two special cases of a single hierarchical structure. Each detail layer is essentially the same visualisation with a different amount of detail visible. Therefore, each visualisation layer in the *Vis-Active* scenario can be defined as a visualisation layer containing only a single detail layer. This means that we can unite the scenarios by defining the visualisation set as a set of one or more visualisation layers, each of which contains one or more detail layers. Figure 14 is an example design of a complex *Vis-Detail-Active* visualisation set.

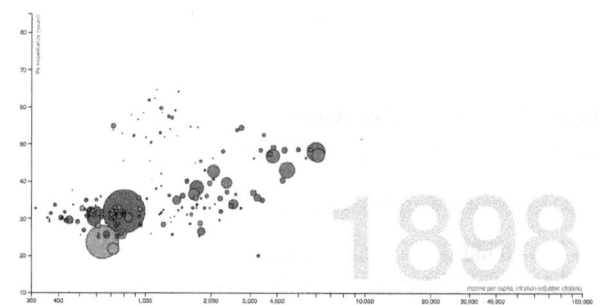

Figure 15. The example D3 visualisation used as a case study.

EXTENDING THE INFOVIS PIPELINE

Numerous authors have built on, and extended, the original Information Visualisation Pipeline as a means the decompose and better conceptualise the tasks and sub-tasks involved in representing data in a graphical form [4]. Each model emphasises different aspects of the problem, analysis, scale of data, domain, or indeed the current understanding of data use. Fry [10] extended the pipeline to emphasise seven stages, or elements of design, to be considered when moving from data to display.

---

[2]`http://bost.ocks.org/mike/nations/`

Figure 16. The example D3 visualisation explored by a user.

We have conducted an initial evaluation of this pipeline with respect to the influence of proxemics, proximity-aware interactions, and related forms of physical interaction with displayed information. The results of this preliminary exploration are shown in Figure 17. The Fry [10] information visualisation pipeline consists of seven stages. The acquisition stage is concerned with the collection or input of data from a source. In the parsing stage, data is converted into a desired internal format. The filtering stage removes data that will not be relevant for a particular visualisation. The mining stage generates higher level abstractions or compound measures from the filtered data. The representation stage is concerned with the design decisions around the section of the appropriate visual structures for presentation of data. The refinement stage optimises the visual form of the data using a set of design practices or contextual information to maximise impact of the visualisation. Finally, the interaction stage deals with any interaction mechanisms or techniques related to the visual form of the visualisation itself [10].

Our analysis of this pipeline suggests that, with the exception of the parsing stage, all other stages can be directly or indirectly affected when physical interaction systems, such as proxemic-based interactions, are introduced. Figure 17 provides a summary of the relationships between such interactions in this pipeline. Here the interaction stage is directly affected in a wide variety of ways. Direct manipulation of the viewpoint for the data and associated movement, as well as scaling and zoom, belong to this stage. The scenarios in this paper describe some of the possible proxemic mappings to these parameters. The changes to these parameters also indirectly influence the acquisition stage, as additional data may have to be provided when the change occurs. Working backwards through the pipeline, the refinement stage can be indirectly influenced when changes in position between the users and the display may render parts of the visualisation unintelligible, thereby forcing a change in refinement or representation. The influence of proxemic mappings on the representation stage is best exemplified in the *Vis-Active* scenarios, which show different types of representations as the user moves through the space. The mining stage is influenced directly through the higher number of dimensions that can be displayed compared to other non-proxemic views, as shown in our D3 visualisation example. This allows for navigation

along all the standard axes, as well as time. Additionally, the *Detail-Active* scenarios show an example that directly influences both the filtering and mining stages via the need for clustering and other grouping and filtering mechanisms. The application of these mechanisms may also trigger a further data acquisition when transitioning from a low-detail to a high-detail view, thus indirectly influencing the acquisition stage.

Our points of interconnection between individual and group physical movements with respect to information visualisation are exploratory in nature and requires further study and evaluation. However, we believe the results of this exploration are valuable as a starting point for a more detailed inquiry.

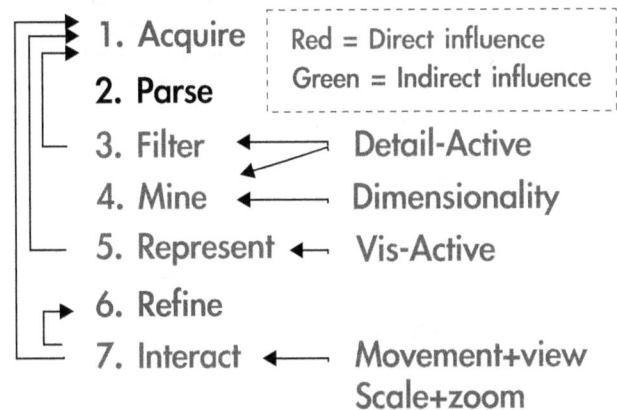

Figure 17. The information visualisation pipeline adapted to proxemic interactions.

LIMITATIONS AND FUTURE WORK

A series of user studies are necessary to fully understand the limitations and capabilities of our system and application scenarios. A particularly fruitful avenue of future research might be to investigate how groups of people negotiate the sharing of the space in collaborative attention- and proximity-aware user interfaces.

A limitation of the current work is that the application scenarios presented in the paper might underutilise the potential of attention-driven interactions. In our currently implemented application scenarios, users' visual attention is only used to filter out passers-by. This is an important function because distinguishing between users engaging with our system and users that are present in the background is a critical practical issue in a deployed system. Nevertheless, one direction of future work is to embed the visual attention detection feature in our toolkit more deeply into the application scenarios.

All application scenarios we have presented in this paper are grounded on existing evidence from the research literature. We believe these application scenarios form a sensible starting point for better understanding the design space of collaborative attention- and proximity-aware user interfaces. A more extensive classification and validated design space exploration can in the future serve as a foundation for collaborative proxemics.

CONCLUSIONS

In this paper we have introduced the concept of collaborative proxemics: enabling groups of people to collaboratively use attention- and proximity-aware applications. To help designers we have developed SpiderEyes: a toolkit that enables people to design proximity- and attention-aware co-located collaborative interfaces. We have presented an analysis of how proxemics can be used to support collaborative scenarios and we have introduced visualisation-based scenarios that explore how proxemic interactions can be used to support parallel and collaborative exploration of large multi-faceted datasets on a wall-sized display.

The SpiderEyes toolkit uses our novel tracking system that provides fast and accurate markerless attention- and proximity-aware tracking of up to four users at 30 frames per second. It also includes a visualisation design tool that allows designers to easily augment their visualisations with attention- and proximity-awareness with minimal programming efforts. We exemplified this by interfacing SpiderEyes with an example from the D3 JavaScript library. Finally, we extended the infovis pipeline so that it supports proxemics.

The SpiderEyes toolkit can be downloaded here: `http:// sachi.cs.st-andrews.ac.uk/software/spidereyes`

ACKNOWLEDGEMENTS

This work was supported by the Scottish Informatics and Computer Science Alliance (SICSA).

REFERENCES

1. Andersen, M., Jensen, T., Lisouski, P., Mortensen, A., Hansen, M., Gregersen, T., and Ahrendt, P. Kinect Depth Sensor Evaluation for Computer Vision Applications. Tech. rep., Department of Engineering, Aarhus University, Denmark, 2012.

2. Ball, R., North, C., and Bowman, D. A. Move to Improve: Promoting Physical Navigation to Increase User Performance with Large Displays. In *Proc. CHI'07*, ACM (2007), 191–200.

3. Ballendat, T., Marquardt, N., and Greenberg, S. Proxemic Interaction: Designing for a Proximity and Orientation-Aware Environment. In *Proc. ITS'10*, ACM (2010), 121–130.

4. Card, S. K., Mackinlay, J. D., and Shneiderman, B., Eds. *Readings in information visualization: using vision to think*. Morgan Kaufmann Publishers Inc., 1999.

5. Clark, A., Dünser, A., Billinghurst, M., Piumsomboon, T., and Altimira, D. Seamless Interaction in Space. In *Proc. OzCHI'11*, ACM (2011), 88–97.

6. Dostal, J., Kristensson, P. O., and Quigley, A. Estimating and using absolute and relative viewing distance in interactive systems. *Pervasive and Mobile Computing* (July 2012).

7. Dostal, J., Kristensson, P. O., and Quigley, A. Multi-view proxemics: distance and position sensitive interaction. In *Proc. PerDis'13*, ACM (2013), 1–6.

8. Dostal, J., Kristensson, P. O., and Quigley, A. Subtle Gaze-Dependent Techniques for Visualising Display Changes in Multi-Display Environments. In *Proc. IUI'13*, ACM (2013), 137–147.

9. Dostal, J., Kristensson, P. O., and Quigley, A. The Potential of Fusing Computer Vision and Depth Sensing for Accurate Distance Estimation. In *CHI'13 Extended Abstracts*, ACM (2013), 1257–1262.

10. Fry, B. *Visualizing Data*, 1st ed. O'Reilly Media, 2007.

11. Greenberg, S., Marquardt, N., Ballendat, T., Diaz-Marino, R., and Wang, M. Proxemic Interactions: The New Ubicomp? *ACM Interactions 18*, 1 (2010), 42–50.

12. Harrison, C., and Dey, A. K. Lean and Zoom: Proximity-Aware User Interface and Content Magnification. In *Proc. CHI'08*, ACM (2008), 8–11.

13. Hawkey, K., Kellar, M., Reilly, D., Whalen, T., and Inkpen, K. M. The Proximity Factor: Impact of Distance on Co-Located Collaboration. In *Proc. Group'05*, ACM (2005), 31–40.

14. Jakobsen, M. R., and Hornbæk, K. Proxemics for Information Visualization on Wall-Sized Displays. In *Proxemics'12: Workshop in Conjunction with NordiCHI'12* (2012).

15. Jakobsen, M. R., Sahlemariam, H. Y., Knudsen, S., and Hornbæk, K. Information Visualization and Proxemics: Design Opportunities and Empirical Findings. *IEEE Transactions on Visualization and Computer Graphics 19* (2013), 2386–95.

16. Ju, W., Lee, B. A., and Klemmer, S. R. Range: Exploring Implicit Interaction through Electronic Whiteboard Design. In *Proc. CSCW'08*, ACM (2008), 17–26.

17. Marquardt, N., Ballendat, T., Boring, S., Greenberg, S., and Hinckley, K. Gradual engagement: facilitating information exchange between digital devices as a function of proximity. In *Proc. ITS'12*, ACM (2012), 31–40.

18. Prante, T., Röcker, C., Streitz, N. A., Stenzel, R., Magerkurth, C., van Alphen, D., and Plewe, D. A. Hello.Wall—Beyond Ambient Displays. In *Adj. Proc. UbiComp'03* (2003), 277–278.

19. Rädle, R., Butscher, S., Huber, S., and Reiterer, H. Navigation Concepts for ZUIs Using Proxemic Interactions. In *Proxemics'12: Workshop in Conjunction with NordiCHI'12* (2012).

20. Seifried, T., Rendl, C., Haller, M., and Scott, S. D. Regional Undo/Redo Techniques for Large Interactive Surfaces. In *Proc. CHI'12*, ACM (2012), 2855–2864.

21. Viola, P., and Jones, M. J. Robust Real-Time Face Detection. *International Journal of Computer Vision 57*, 2 (2004), 137–154.

22. Vogel, D., and Balakrishnan, R. Interactive Public Ambient Displays: Transitioning from Implicit to Explicit, Public to Personal, Interaction with Multiple Users. In *Proc. UIST'07*, ACM (2007), 137–146.

Frequence: Interactive Mining and Visualization of Temporal Frequent Event Sequences

Adam Perer
IBM T.J. Watson Research Center
Yorktown Heights, New York, USA
adam.perer@us.ibm.com

Fei Wang
IBM T.J. Watson Research Center
Yorktown Heights, New York, USA
fwang@us.ibm.com

ABSTRACT

Extracting insights from temporal event sequences is an important challenge. In particular, mining frequent patterns from event sequences is a desired capability for many domains. However, most techniques for mining frequent patterns are ineffective for real-world data that may be low-resolution, concurrent, or feature many types of events, or the algorithms may produce results too complex to interpret. To address these challenges, we propose Frequence, an intelligent user interface that integrates data mining and visualization in an interactive hierarchical information exploration system for finding frequent patterns from longitudinal event sequences. Frequence features a novel frequent sequence mining algorithm to handle multiple levels-of-detail, temporal context, concurrency, and outcome analysis. Frequence also features a visual interface designed to support insights, and support exploration of patterns of the level-of-detail relevant to users. Frequence's effectiveness is demonstrated with two use cases: medical research mining event sequences from clinical records to understand the progression of a disease, and social network research using frequent sequences from Foursquare to understand the mobility of people in an urban environment.

Author Keywords

Visual Analytics, Frequent Sequence Mining, Temporal Visualization

ACM Classification Keywords

H.5.m. Information Interfaces and Presentation (e.g. HCI): Miscellaneous

INTRODUCTION

One of the challenges of the Big Data era is to leverage the voluminous data that is being captured to drive decision making and insights. Common to such data are temporal events, data points with both a timestamp and event type, so understanding patterns of temporal event sequences is an important problem to many. For example, medical researchers wish to leverage the data captured by electronic health records to determine if certain sequences of medical events correlate with positive outcomes. Similarly, city government officials wish

to leverage the temporal data collected from their transportation systems, call centers, and law enforcement agencies to improve their cities' services.

However, despite the availability of temporal data and the common desire to extract knowledge, mining patterns from temporal event sequences is still a fundamental challenge in data mining [7]. Frequent Sequence Mining (FSM) techniques have emerged in the data mining community to find sets of frequently occurring subsequences. However, these algorithms often have constraints that limit its applicability to real-world data:

- **Level of Detail.** Temporal events are often recorded at a specific level-of-detail to record maximum information about an event's type. FSM techniques applied to data with a large dictionary of event types will often suffer from computational complexity. Perhaps even more of a fundamental problem is that patterns extracted from a specific level-of-detail may impair an interpretable overview of patterns for users. In order for mining techniques to be technically feasible and usable, we propose multiple levels-of-detail should be available to users.

- **Temporal Context.** Many FSM techniques ignore the temporal context associated with data, and instead focus on the pure sequentiality of events. However, for certain real-world scenarios, if a certain amount of time elasped between events, the events should not be considered as part of the same sequence, even if events are technically sequential in the event log. We propose mining techniques need to take into consideration the temporal context of users.

- **Concurrency.** Many FSM algorithms suffer from pattern explosion when there are many concurrent events. This is particularly troubling for real-world data, as many systems may record data in low-resolution precision, such as a day, and many events may occur on the same day. For other datasets, even when there is extreme temporal precision to data (e.g. millisecond precision), the exact order of events may be irrelevant, so if they occur within a domain-relevant time window, they should be treated as concurrent. We propose mining techniques need to handle concurrency.

- **Outcome.** Many FSM algorithms are agnostic to the types of patterns mined. However, in real-world data, analysts may not just need a list of patterns but instead how each of the patterns correlate to an outcome measure. We propose mining techniques need to support outcome analysis.

In this paper, we enhance a fast and popular FSM algorithm to handle these real-world needs to serve actionable insights.

But to support each need properly, the parameters should be flexible to derive from user hypotheses or evolve during an iterative data exploration process. In order to support flexible decision making, we present *Frequence*, a intelligent user interface designed to reach actionable insights by integrating visualization with interactive mining algorithms.

We demonstrate Frequence's utility in two real-world use cases: a medical informatics researcher using frequent sequences in electronic medical records to understand the progression of a disease among patients, and a social network researcher using frequent sequences from a location-based social network to understand the relationship between online popularity and offline mobility throughout urban environments.

Concretely, Frequence's contributions include both **a novel algorithm** for Frequent Sequence Mining whose design handles real-world constraints of level-of-detail, temporal context, concurrency, and outcome, and **a novel intelligent user interface** that integrates mining and visualization to support interactive parameterization and exploration to reach insights.

This paper begins with related work, providing an overview of sequence mining and visualization techniques. Next, an overview of the design of Frequence is described, as well as the iterative workflow it supports. Then, Frequence's sequence mining algorithms are described as well as its novel enhancements. Next, Frequence's visual interface is described in terms of its visual encoding and interactive UI to parameterize the analytics. Then, use cases are described to demonstrate Frequence's utility on real-world data. Finally, this paper concludes with a discussion of future work.

RELATED WORK

There has been little work that integrates techniques for mining and visualizing frequent event sequences, so we present prior work on mining and visualization separately.

Mining Frequent Event Sequences

Frequent Sequence Mining (FSM) is a popular technique for finding sets of frequently occurring subsequences from a larger set of temporal event sequences. It is challenging since one may need to examine a combinatorially explosive number of possible frequent subsequences.

FSM has been researched for a long time and many approaches have been proposed. Initially, most of the approaches (e.g., Generalized Sequential Pattern miner (GSP) [1]) are *A priori*-like [1], which utilizes the fact that any super-pattern of a non-frequent pattern cannot be frequent. These approaches start by constructing a frequent pattern set (the appearance frequencies of the patterns included are above a certain percentage threshold) containing only one event, then they grow those patterns pass by pass, with each pass appending one single event to the detected patterns from last pass, until no frequent patterns can be found. This type of approach can be computationally expensive due to the huge candidate sequence set and multiple database scans. Many strategies have been proposed to make FSM more efficient

and practical. For example, *PrefixSpan* (Prefix-projected Sequential PAtterN mining) [8] explores prefix projection in FSM to reduce the efforts of candidate subsequence generation. *SPADE* (Sequential PAttern Discovery using Equivalence classes) [17] utilizes combinatorial properties to decompose the original problem into smaller sub-problems, that can be independently solved in main-memory using efficient lattice search techniques, which greatly reduces the number of database scans. *SPAM* (Sequential Pattern Mining) [3] designs a smart bitmap based representation for those event sequences, so that all event sequences become 0-1 strings, and all operations needed for FSM will become bitwise AND/OR operations. This makes the FSM procedure much more efficient. However, despite these improvements, there are still some difficulties for applying such algorithms directly to real world data, especially when there are concurrent events or temporal constraints. Frequence's FSM algorithm enhances SPAM to support these user needs.

Temporal Event Sequence Visualizations

There has been a great body of work in the visualization community designing techniques for temporal event sequences. A common approach is to place records on a series of horizontal timelines to show multiple records in parallel [2, 9] and support interactive search [6, 13, 16], filtering [13], and clustering [4]. Recently, LifeFlow [15] introduced a way to aggregate multiple event sequences into a tree, and Outflow [14] later designed a way to aggregate events into a graph, as well as integrating statistics.

The visual design of Frequence's visualization is similar to Sankey [10] and alluvial [11] diagrams. However, these diagrams focus on the flow of resources, as Sankey diagrams ignore sequential ordering whereas alluvial diagrams were designed to show how network structures change over time. Outflow also looks visually similar to our approach, however, Outflow aggregates subsequences and outcomes [14]. In Frequence, each subsequence is represented as an individual edge to provide an overview of all sequences and their individual outcomes and support, as we support user tasks to find meaningful individual sequences. Furthermore, only Frequence supports navigation by level-of-detail which is a novel contribution to prior approaches.

SYSTEM DESIGN AND WORKFLOW

Frequence's intelligent user interface is designed to put users at the center of both analytics and visualization. In line with many advanced visual interfaces, Frequence supports the common browsing and searching strategy of the Visual Information Seeking Mantra, which suggests to support *Overview first, Zoom and Filter, then Details-on-Demand* [12]. When users begin their exploration, as illustrated in Figure 6, they are first shown frequent patterns at a coarse level-of-detail to give them an overview. If they discover an pattern of interest, they can select the pattern and then zoom and filter to see the underlying patterns at a finer level-of-detail. Whenever users want more information about a particular pattern, at any level-of-detail, they can select it to get details-on-demand, which include statistics about the pattern's frequency, outcome, and the events composed within.

However, parallel to browsing and searching, Frequence also supports interaction with the analytics to support a refinement strategy, where users can adapt the mining algorithm based upon their data-driven hypotheses to generate more meaningful patterns to explore. By interactively refining parameters of the mining algorithm, such as temporal context, outcome measures, and other temporal constraints, users can be empowered to make sure they are reaching meaningful results.

In the next section, we explain the novel frequent pattern mining algorithms necessary to support this iterative workflow.

MINING FREQUENT PATTERNS

Frequence's frequent pattern mining algorithm is based on the SPAM algorithm [3], with several enhancements. In order to understand the enhancements, we first provide an overview of the SPAM algorithm.

The goal of Frequent Sequence Mining (FSM) is to mine *frequent* subsequences from a set of event sequences. Formally, event sequences and subsequences are defined as follows:

Definition 1. An event sequence $\theta = \langle \theta_1, \theta_2, \cdots, \theta_m \rangle (\theta_i \in \mathcal{D})$ is an ordered list of events, where $\mathcal{D}$ is the event dictionary and θ_i happened no later than θ_{i+1}.

Definition 2. A sequence $\tau = \langle \tau_1, \tau_2, \cdots, \tau_{m_\tau} \rangle$ is said to be a subsequence of another sequence $\theta = \langle \theta_1, \theta_2, \cdots, \theta_{m_\theta} \rangle$, denoted by $\tau \subseteq \theta$ if $\exists i_1, i_2, \cdots, i_m$ such that $1 \leqslant i_1 \leqslant i_2 \leqslant \cdots \leqslant i_m \leqslant m_\theta$ and $\tau_1 = \theta_{i_1}, \tau_2 = \theta_{i_2}, \cdots, \tau_{m_\tau} = \theta_{i_m}$.

Support is the measure that determines whether a subsequence is frequent or not:

Definition 3. Given a set of event sequences $\mathcal{S} = \{\theta_1, \theta_2, \cdots, \theta_n\}$, the support of a sequence τ is the percentage of the sequences in $\mathcal{S}$ which have τ as a subsequence.

With the above definition, we say a subsequence (or temporal pattern) is *frequent* for sequence set $\mathcal{S}$ if its appearance percentage in $\mathcal{S}$ is above a certain pre-specified support value.

As described in our overview of related work, most FSM algorithms adopt a *pattern growing* strategy, which is illustrated in Figure 1. Initially, the algorithms start with an empty frequent pattern set $\mathcal{F} = \{\}$, then each single event in the event dictionary $\mathcal{D}$ is checked, and the events that are frequent are added to $\mathcal{F}$. These patterns are referred to as frequent patterns of *length* 1, as the length of a pattern is defined as the number of events it contains. The pattern can be grown with two types of extensions: an *S-extension* and an *I-extension* [3]:

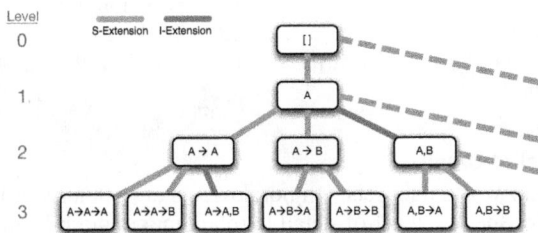

Figure 1. A graphical illustration of the pattern growing procedure.

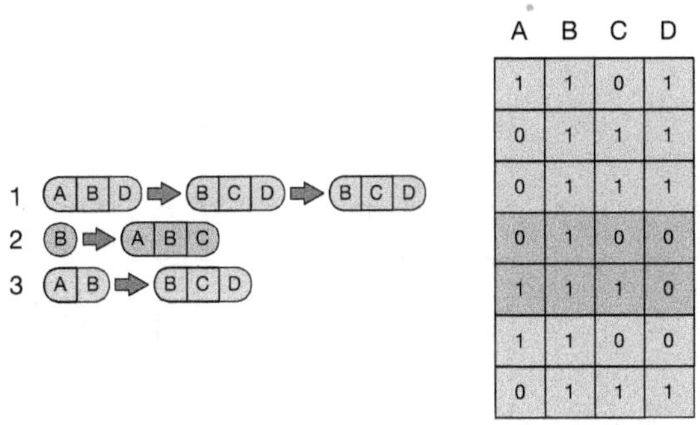

Figure 2. An example of the bitmap representation of the sequences, where there are four different events and three sequences.

Definition 4. An S-extension of a sequence $\tau = \langle \tau_1, \tau_2, \cdots, \tau_{m_\tau} \rangle$ with event θ, denoted by $\tau \rightarrow \theta$, is to append θ at the end of τ so that θ happens after τ_{m_τ}.

Definition 5. An I-extension of a sequence $\tau = \langle \tau_1, \tau_2, \cdots, \tau_{m_\tau} \rangle$ with event θ, denoted by τ, θ, is to append θ at the end of τ so that θ and τ_{m_τ} happen concurrently.

After a pattern growing stage, all candidate patterns of length 2 are obtained and the frequent ones are added to $\mathcal{F}$. Then the algorithm grows each pattern of length 2 via an S-extension and an I-extension to get the frequent patterns of length 3, and the pattern growing procedure repeats until no more frequent patterns are found. If one considers the complete pattern growing process as a tree (see Figure 1), then the procedure can be seen as a *breadth-first search* on that tree, which checks the tree level-by-level. A *depth-first search* strategy has also been proposed [3], which checks the tree branch by branch, and can be a more efficient recursion procedure for long sequences.

SPAM is able to be computationally efficient by using a *bitmap representation* for event sequences [3], which is illustrated in Figure 2. In this representation, a sequence θ is represented as a $|\theta| \times |\mathcal{D}|$ bitmap $\mathcal{B}(\theta)$, where $|\theta|$ is the length of θ and $|\mathcal{D}|$ is the size of $\mathcal{D}$, such that $\mathcal{B}(\theta)(i,j) = 1$ if the j-th event in $\mathcal{D}$ happened at the i-th timestamp of θ, otherwise $\mathcal{B}(\theta)(i,j) = 0$. With this representation, both S-extensions and I-extensions can be performed with a bitwise AND operation. Figure 3 shows how to extend event A with event B for the example in Figure 2. For an S-extension, the first appearance of A in each sequence is detected, so the corresponding bit value is changed to 0 and all the following bits to 1 (denoted as $T(A)$), and then an AND-operation is executed between the bitmap vectors of $T(A)$ and B. For an I-extension, an AND-operation is directly executed between the bitmap vectors of A and B. After the extension, the value of 1 will exist in each sequence if the extended pattern exists in those sequences. Therefore, the appearance frequency of the extended pattern is simply the number of sequences that have a value of 1.

Temporal Context

Although SPAM uses a smart bitmap representation to make the FSM procedure efficient, it does not take into consideration the temporal context of detected patterns. This is problematic for real-world applications, as patterns lasting years

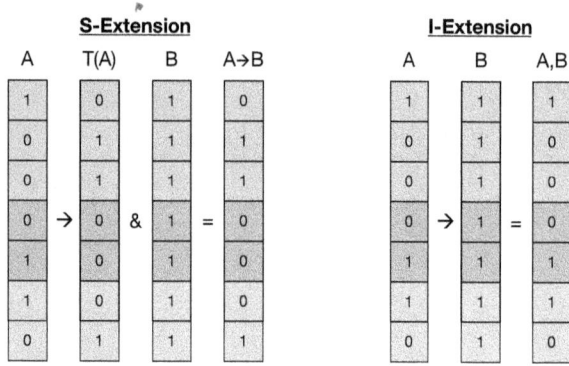

S-Extension

A   T(A)   B   A→B

I-Extension

A   B   A,B

Figure 3. An example of S-extension and I-extension of event A with event B for the example sequences in Figure 2.

and other patterns lasting days may have completely different meanings in different contexts, but SPAM would treat them equivalently.

In order to make SPAM capable of detecting temporal patterns within a temporal context (that is, within the threshold of a user-defined duration), we propose the following enhancement: Suppose that there is an explicit timestamp associated with every event in every sequence, then when a candidate pattern appears in a specific sequence, the pattern must not only appear, but also its duration in the sequence should be below the threshold. Specifically, we define the pattern duration in a sequence as:

Definition 6. Let $\tau = \langle \tau_1, \tau_2, \cdots, \tau_{m_\tau} \rangle$ be a candidate pattern of sequence $\theta = \langle \theta_1, \theta_2, \cdots, \theta_{m_\theta} \rangle$, where each event θ_i is associated with timestamp t_i, and $(i_1, i_2, \cdots, i_m)$ be a set of indices of θ satisfying $1 \leqslant i_1 \leqslant i_2 \leqslant \cdots \leqslant i_m \leqslant m_\theta$ and $\tau_1 = \theta_{i_1}, \tau_2 = \theta_{i_2}, \cdots, \tau_{m_\tau} = \theta_{i_m}$, then the duration of τ in θ is $min_{(i_1, i_2, \cdots, i_m)} (t_{i_m} - t_{i_1})$.

Algorithm 1 summarizes the our enhanced SPAM approach, which we call *Time-Aware SPAM*. Note that in step 3 and step 8 of the **Pattern_Grow** subroutine, when checking the appearance frequencies of τ_S / τ_I, there is a requirement that patterns should both appear in the counted sequence and their duration should be shorter than L.

Concurrency

A bottleneck for Time-Aware SPAM occurs when events happen at the same time, as this greatly increases the search tree size in the pattern growing procedure. This is particularly problematic as concurrent events are often common in real-world applications. For example, the finest resolution of temporal data in many Electronic Health Records systems is a *day*, and during a day, multiple medical events may occur to a patient (e.g. a patient often gets multiple lab tests during a single lab visit). For other datasets, even when there is extreme temporal precision to data (e.g. millisecond precision), the analyst may not be concerned about the exact order of events, as long as they occurred within a domain-relevant time window.

To alleviate this problem, we pre-process event sequences prior to Time-Aware SPAM to contain pattern explosion. As there can be many *Concurrent Event Sets* (CESs) contained in

---

Algorithm 1 Time-Aware SPAM

Require: Sequence set $\mathcal{S} = \{\theta_1, \theta_2, \cdots, \theta_n\}$, Support value α, Pattern duration L

1. Construct bitmap representations for all sequences in $\mathcal{S}$
2. Set the output frequent pattern set $\mathcal{F} = \{\}$
3. Count all the single event frequencies, and add the ones whose frequencies above α to $\mathcal{F}$
4. **For** every event $\theta \in \mathcal{F}$
5.   Do **Pattern_Grow**$(\theta, \mathcal{F}, \mathcal{F}, L)$
6. Output $\mathcal{F}$

Pattern_Grow$(\tau, \mathcal{S}_n, \mathcal{I}_n, L)$
1. $\mathcal{S}_t = \{\}, \mathcal{I}_t = \{\}$
2. **For** every $\theta \in \mathcal{S}_n$
3.   **if** τ_S=S_extension(τ, θ) is frequent w.r.t. L
4. $\mathcal{S}_t = \mathcal{S}_t \cup \theta$, add τ_S to output pattern set
5. **For** every $\theta \in \mathcal{S}_t$
6.   **Pattern_Grow**$(\tau_S, \mathcal{S}_t, \mathcal{S}_t \succeq \theta)$
7. **For** every $\theta \in \mathcal{I}_n$
8.   **if** τ_I=I_extension(τ, θ) is frequent w.r.t. L
9. $\mathcal{I}_t = \mathcal{I}_t \cup \theta$, , add τ_I to output pattern set

10. **For** every $\theta \in \mathcal{I}_t$
11.   **Pattern_Grow**$(\tau_I, \mathcal{S}_t, \mathcal{I}_t \succeq \theta)$

---

event sequences, the first step is to detect the frequent *Event Packages* (EPs) that are frequent subsets of CESs. If we treat each CES in every event sequence as a *transaction*, then the problem of detecting EPs is equivalent to the problem of *frequent item set mining* [1], and each detected EP can be used as a *super event*. Then, a greedy approach is applied based on *Two-Way Sorting* to break down each CES as a combination of regular and super events, such that the number of events contained in each CES is greatly reduced.

To better explain the process of breaking down CESs, we provide the following example: Suppose there exists a CES ABCDE that needs to be broken down using the detected EPs (shown in the center of Figure 4). The algorithm then sorts the packages according to the two-way sorting strategy as shown in Figure 4 – that is, the EPs are first sorted according to their cardinalities. Then, for packages with the same cardinality, they are sorted with respect to their appearance frequency. To breakdown ABCDE, the algorithm first finds the *longest* event packages that are subsets. In this case, ABC and ACE are the longest packages which are subsets of ABCDE. Then, because ABC occurs more frequently than ACE, ABC is selected as a super event contained in ABCDE. Besides ABC, the rest of the events are DE. Then the procedure is applied again to break down ABCDE as ABC,D, E. Using this technique, there are only 3 super events in ABCDE after the break-down procedure. The full details of the algorithm are described in Algorithm 2.

Level of Detail

In real-world data sets, temporal events are often recorded at a very specific level-of-detail to retain maximum information about an event. However, applying many FSM techniques (e.g. [17, 3, 8]) or Time-Aware SPAM to data with a large

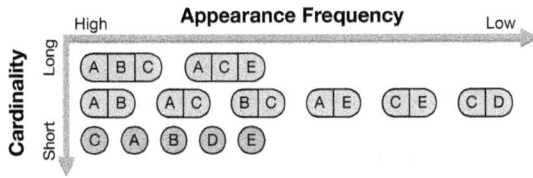

Figure 4. A graphical illustration of how the two-way sorting procedure works. We first sort the mined event packages according to their cardinalities, and then for the packages with the same cardinality, we sort them according to their frequencies.

Algorithm 2 Breaking Down a CES

Require: An CES S to be broken down into frequent Event Packages (EPs).

1: Sort the detected EPs into buckets according to their cardinalities (number of events contained), such that the packages within the same bucket have the same cardinality.
2: Sort the packages within the same bucket with their appearance frequencies in the patient traces.
3: $\mathcal{O} = \emptyset$
4: **for** Every bucket $\mathcal{B}$ **do**
5:   **if** length($\mathcal{B}$) < length(S) **then**
6:     **for** Every EP $\mathcal{E}$ in $\mathcal{B}$ **do**
7:       **if** $\mathcal{E}$ is a subset of S **then**
8:         Add $\mathcal{E}$ to $\mathcal{O}$, Set $S = S \backslash \mathcal{E}$
9:         **if** $S == \emptyset$ **then**
10:           **Return** $\mathcal{O}$
11:         **else**
12:           Return to Step 4
13:         **end if**
14:       **end if**
15:     **end for**
16:   **end if**
17: **end for**

---

dictionary of event types will often suffer from computational complexity. Technical complexity aside, another fundamental problem is patterns extracted from a fine levels-of-detail may impair gaining an interpretable overview from the results. In order for mining to be technically feasible and usable, Frequence is able to mine data on multiple levels-of-detail.

For each level-of-detail available, Frequence runs its mining algorithm on event sequences using the event dictionary available for each level-of-detail. Typically, levels-of-detail are hierarchical and thus the coarse level will likely have a small event dictionary. In this case, special techniques for handling concurrency or collapsing event sets may not be required to remain performant. However, for finer levels-of-detail, large data sets may require such features to be computationally feasible. That said, in practice, if an overview of coarse patterns are shown first, a coarse pattern of interest may be selected to focus on, and then Frequence only needs to mine from the cohort that matched the coarse pattern, which drastically reduces the number of sequences and event types. Frequence's iterative workflow was designed to support this type of exploration.

Outcome

Once a set of frequent patterns has been identified, correlations between the mined patterns and the event sequences' outcome measure can be identified. For example, in a medical informatics scenario, analysts may be curious how certain patterns correlate with discrete outcome variables (e.g., deceased vs. alive) or continuous ones (e.g., blood pressure measurements).

To enable outcome analysis, a *Bag-of-Pattern* (BoP) representation is constructed for each event sequence. Formally, given a set of n frequent patterns, the BoP representation is an n-dimensional vector, where the i-th element of that vector stores the frequency of the i-th pattern within the corresponding event sequence. If there are m event sequences, then we construct an $m \times n$ sequence-pattern matrix $\mathbf{X} = [\mathbf{x}_1, \mathbf{x}_2, \cdots, \mathbf{x}_n]$ whose (j, i)-th element indicates the number of times the i-th pattern appeared in the j-th event sequence. Thus, the i-th column $\mathbf{x}_j$ summarizes the frequency of the i-th pattern in all m sequences. We can also construct an m-dimensional sequence outcome vector $\mathbf{y}$, such that y_j is the outcome of the j-th event sequence. For example, with a binary outcome, $y_i \in \{+1, -1\}$, +1 represents a positive outcome whereas -1 represents a negative outcome. Given this formulation, statistics are then computed to measure the correlation between each $\mathbf{x}_i$ and $\mathbf{y}$ to measure the informativeness of the i-th pattern in terms of predicting a sequence's outcome. Frequence has implemented a variety of statistical measures including Pearson correlation, P-value, information gain, and odds ratio.

FREQUENCE'S VISUAL USER INTERFACE

Frequence is a web-based interface that features a visualization panel in the center of the interface to navigate the visualization, as well as a panel on the left side of the interface to control the interactive analytics.

Interactive Visualization

Frequence mines sequential knowledge temporal from event sequences so analysts can gain insights. However, the quantity of patterns discovered is often too large for users to make sense of them. The goal of Frequence is not only to mine the patterns but also to present the data in a user-centric way so that the patterns mined can be utilized in real-world settings. Information visualization is an effective way of communicating complex data, and thus the key part of the Frequence UI is a flow visualization.

We describe the characteristics of our visualization using Figure 5 as an illustrative example. In this example, the patterns are sequences of places that users have traveled, and each user has an outcome measure of popularity. This type of data will be subsequentially described in more detail as a use-case.

Events in the frequent sequences are represented as nodes, and event nodes that belong to the same sequence are connected by edges. The nodes and edges are positioned using a modified Sankey diagram layout [10]. However, while Sankey layouts aggregate common subsequences into a single edge, such an aggregation in Frequence would make it impossible to reach insights about individual patterns.

Temporal Event Sequence	Outcome	Support
Arts & Entertainment→Food→Travel & Transport	Unpopular	0.25
Arts & Entertainment→Food→Nightlife Spot	Popular	0.50
Shop & Service→Food→Nightlife Spot	Popular	0.50
Food→Outdoors & Recreation	Neutral	0.25

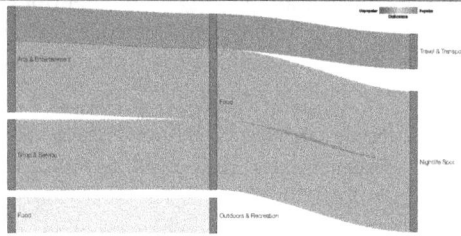

Figure 5. An illustrative example of Frequence's visual encoding for a set of frequent patterns. Patterns are represented by a sequence of nodes (events) connected by edges (event subsequences). Patterns are colored according to their correlation with users' outcomes.

Thus, in Frequence, subsequences are represented as individual edges. For instance, the simple pattern `Food →
Outdoors&Recreation`, is visualized as a `Food` node connected to a `Outdoors&Recreation` node, as shown at the bottom of Figure 5. Patterns that share similar subsequences, such as `Arts&Entertainment → Food → NightlifeSpot` and `Arts&Entertainment → Food → Travel&Transport`, involve two edges from `Arts&Entertainment` to `Food` representing each subsequence. Thus, prominent subsequences also become visually prominent due to the thickness of the combined multiple edges.

Of course, not all event subsequences are equal as some correlate to a positive outcome, whereas others correlate to a negative outcome, as determined by Frequence's outcome analytics. The visualization uses color to encode each pattern's association with an associated outcome. For this scenario, the patterns that occur more often with popular users (those who have a lot of followers on Twitter) are more blue. The patterns that occur more often with unpopular users (those who have few followers) are more red. The neutral patterns that appear common to both popular and unpopular users are gray.

The frequency of each pattern also varies, and the visualization uses the thickness of edges to encode how often each pattern occurs using the pattern's support, as defined in Definition 3. For instance, in the example shown in Figure 5, the pattern `Arts&Entertainment → Food → Travel&Transport` has a support of 0.25, which is why its thickness is half the size of `Arts&Entertainment → Food → NightlifeSpot`, which has a support of 0.5.

Users can interact with the visualization by moving their mouseover an edge, which will display statistics, such as support and outcome, about the pattern the edge represents. If users click a node, all patterns that do not match the selected node have their opacity diminished so users can focus on patterns that match the user's specification. Users can specify a frequent pattern of interest by clicking on multiple nodes until their pattern is fully selected. Once a pattern is selected, users can use this selection to zoom and filter. Frequence supports two ways to zoom and filter. The first way is by *cohort*, which constrains the dataset to the population that has the selected pattern, and shows the most frequent patterns among

that population. The second way is by *pattern*, which uses the whole population, but only mines events that feature the subtypes of the selected pattern. This latter option is useful for navigating hierarchical levels-of-detail.

Interactive Analytics

In addition to exploring patterns using the visualization, users can also adapt and modify the mining algorithm according to their needs by using the control panel located on the left-side of the interface.

By default, the *Statistics* section is selected to show a statistical overview of various aspects of the dataset and patterns. Users can navigate to the *Pattern Definition* section to refine the patterns being mined. Here, users can adjust the support value for patterns, to focus the analytics on either stronger or weaker patterns. By selecting the *Level of Detail* panel, users can change the level-of-detail of the displayed patterns, and choose if filtering is by cohort or by pattern. The *Outcome* panel allows users to select an outcome variable, as well as a threshold on that variable to segment the population. Here, users can also interactively filter the visualization using a range slider to focus on positive or negative patterns. The *Temporal Context* panel allows users to turn on temporal constraints, such as concurrency. This panel also features a slider to specify the time duration for events to be considered concurrent. The *Database* panel allows users choose from where to load their data.

USE CASE: LOCATION SHARING SOCIAL NETWORKS

Some social network researchers are curious about the relationship between people's online social media personas and their offline activities. While mobility data has been difficult to uncover in the past, this is changing due to the proliferation of Location Sharing Services (LSS), where people broadcast the places they visit. One such LSS is Foursquare, a service that allows users to "check-in" at different venues to save and share their locations to friends. According to Foursquare[1], there are over 40 million users and over 4.5 billion check-ins with Foursquare, as of September 2013. A corpus of a subset of Foursquare data was made publicly available[5], which contains over 200,000 users and over 22 million check-ins, and which was imported into Frequence.

In this use case, the researcher was interested in understanding the behavior of users in New York City (NYC), so the analysis described here is limited to check-ins within the boroughs of Manhattan, Queens, and Brooklyn. This was done by filtering all check-ins to fall within a bounding box of latitude and longitude coordinates, surrounding the city. After the geographical filtering, the size of the NYC-constrained database consisted of 17,739 users with 419,023 check-ins in 17,182 unique venues over 11 months. Each unique venue was augmented with Foursquare's hierarchy of 9 top-level categories and 289 sub-level categories, retrieved using Foursquare's Venue Search API[2] to create three levels-of-data on which to mine.

---

[1]http://www.foursquare.com/about

[2]http://developer.foursquare.com/docs/venues/search

The goal of the analysis was to understand if certain patterns of mobility correlate with popularity to procure evidence for their hypothesis that people who are popular in social media go to different places in different sequences than people who were less popular. In order to gain a proxy for social popularity, users' Foursquare accounts are unified with their Twitter accounts, and the number of Twitter followers was used as a metric of popularity. All Foursquare users in the database had an active Twitter account, and used Twitter to broadcast their check-ins. The analyst was only interested in users who were active users of Twitter, so users that had less than 1000 tweets in their lifetime were filtered out[3]. The median number of Twitter followers for a user the dataset was 265, so the analyst used the Outcome panel to consider patterns by users greater than 265 to be popular, and less than 265 to be unpopular. The analyst also used the Temporal Context panel to constrain event sequences within a 6-hour time window so that only events that occured within that same window were considered a part of the same event sequence. Each of these constraints were determined by rapidly testing multiple hypotheses, and the constraints evolved from original hypotheses to different sensible parameters based upon data exploration.

With the parameters tuned from interactive exploration, an overview of patterns at the coarsest level-of-detail is shown at the top of Figure 6. Interestingly, many of the patterns associated with popular social media users (the blue patterns) contain a `Shop&Service` event. The analyst was also interested in the unpopular patterns, and selected one of the red patterns for further inspection. After selecting the red `Professional&OtherPlaces` → `Food` pattern, the researcher used it as a cohort filter to show patterns only from people who have this pattern. Again, the analyst was interested in understanding patterns among less popular users, and to focus on these patterns, the analyst filtered to only the red patterns, shown in the middle of Figure 6. The analyst determines that `Office` → `Hotel` correlates with the least popular social media users, and uses this pattern as a cohort filter to mine only users who have this pattern. The bottom of Figure 6 shows the patterns at the finest level of detail, where the names of the actual venues are now visible to the researcher. No specific offices are frequent enough to appear in the patterns, due to the countless companies spread throughout the city, but certain hotels (e.g. the W Hotel in Times Square) do appear and correlate to unpopular users, whereas most popular patterns are those tied with Shopping (e.g. Macy's, H&M). The researcher remarked the potential applications of these findings to marketing professionals, who wish to understand who frequents their venues, and their ability to communicate to their individual social media audiences.

While the researcher acknowledges these insights only apply to a specific demographic that uses Foursquare and broadcasts their check-ins on Twitter, this case study demonstrates the utility of Frequence for exploring temporal patterns of human mobility and reaching insights.

USE CASE: MEDICAL INFORMATICS

Due to a large number of medical institutions adopting Electronic Health Records (EHRs), the opportunities to analyze and derive insights from medical data has never been greater. In particular, clinicians and clinical researchers are very interested in understanding patterns of medical events that often lead to positive or negative outcomes, so that they can understand or improve their clinical practices.

This use case involves a team of clinicians and clinical researchers interested in determining if there are particular patterns that lead to patients with lung disease developing sepsis, a potentially deadly medical condition. The institution used a set of 2,336 patients diagnosed with lung disease, each with longitudinal events of diagnostic codes (which encode symptoms, causes, and signs of diseases using ICD-9 standards [4]). ICD-9 codes are organized according to a meaningful hierarchy and this hierarchy was utilized by Frequence as multiple levels of detail.

Of the patients with lung disease, 483 developed sepsis within six months of their diagnosis of lung disease, whereas 1,853 managed to not contract the condition. Prior to using Frequence, the clinical researchers had difficulty drawing any conclusions between these two cohorts, as both types of patients tend to share many of the same diagnosis codes. However, the researchers were interested in mining for frequent patterns to see if the order of these diagnoses has any effect on their patients.

At the top of Figure 7, the coarsest patterns for all of the lung disease patients are shown. The clinician was particularly interested in cardiovascular complications, and noticed that the pattern `CardiacDisorders` → `SymptomDisorders` was common yet neutral (that is, this pattern was common to patients who did and did not end up contracting sepsis). After selecting this pattern and filtering by cohort to see the matching patients, the finer level of detail (Level 1) allowed the clinician to see more detailed cardiac conditions, such as cardiac dysrhythmia and heart failure. Other complications, such as acute renal failure (which medical literature suggests is linked to developing sepsis), also appear. However, the clinician is interested in the patterns that led to patients not developing sepsis, and filtered to the positive patterns in the middle of Figure 7. Surprised to see the pattern `HeartFailure` → `LungDiseases`, the clinician filtered to the cohort that matched this pattern and pivoted to Level 2, as shown in the bottom of Figure 7. The clinician immediately noticed that patterns that featured both Atrial Fibrillation and Acute Respiratory Failure are red, which is sensible, as medical literature suggests both are risk factors for sepsis. However, the clinician found it interesting that patterns beginning with Acute Respiratory Failure alone were not predictive of sepsis, but rather what happened next in the sequence was more predictive. From the Acute Respiratory Failure node in the first column of the visualization, the patterns diverge into red and blue, making it clear that what happens immediately after such Acute Respiratory Failure will likely determine if the patient will get sepsis or not.

---

[3]On average, there were 2144 tweets per user in the NYC dataset, before filtering.

[4]http://www.who.int/classifications/icd/

CONCLUSION AND FUTURE WORK

This paper presents Frequence, a novel visual interface designed to mine and visualize frequent event sequences from temporal events. Frequence includes a novel FSM algorithm to handle real-world data requirements to serve actionable insights. Frequence also supports iterative and flexible exploration with a visual interface where users can explore results and refine parameters of the mining algorithm.

We demonstrate Frequence's utility in two real-world use cases: a medical researcher using frequent sequences in Electronic Medical Records to understand the relationship between the progression of a disease and patient outcomes, and a social network researcher using frequent sequences from a Location-based Sharing Service to understand the relationship between online popularity and offline mobility throughout urban environments.

While these use cases show that Frequence can lead to insights, many topics remain for future work. While Frequence supports interactive parameterization of the mining algorithm, choosing the right parameters might be a challenge for some users. A next goal of Frequence is to augment the user interface with visual feedback to act as a preview of how the parameters will affect mining. An additional item for future work reflects the scalability of our frequent sequence mining algorithm. Although our bitmap-based approach is computationally efficient, as data sets get larger and larger, new approaches will be necessary for Frequence to remain scalable. We plan to investigate applying our algorithm to a cloud-based distributed architecture, as the hierarchical aspects of our mining algorithm are well-suited for such an environment. Finally, a more comprehensive user evaluation is critical to understanding the relationship between analytics and visualization in Frequence. We plan to deploy Frequence to domain partners to conduct longitudinal case studies, where we capture how the capabilities of Frequence affect their workflow and help them reach insights.

REFERENCES

1. Agrawal, R., and Srikant, R. Fast algorithms for mining association rules in large databases. In *Proceedings of the 20th International Conference on Very Large Data Bases* (1994), 487–499.

2. Aigner, W., Miksch, S., Thurnher, B., and Biffl, S. Planninglines: novel glyphs for representing temporal uncertainties and their evaluation. In *Information Visualisation, 2005. Proceedings. Ninth International Conference on* (2005), 457–463.

3. Ayres, J., Gehrke, J. E., Yiu, T., and Flannick, J. Sequential pattern mining using bitmaps. 429–435.

4. Burch, M., Beck, F., and Diehl, S. Timeline trees: visualizing sequences of transactions in information hierarchies. In *Proceedings of the working conference on Advanced visual interfaces*, AVI '08, ACM (New York, NY, USA, 2008), 75–82.

5. Cheng, Z., Caverlee, J., Lee, K., and Sui, D. Z. Exploring millions of footprints in location sharing services. *AAAI ICWSM* (2011).

6. Fails, J., Karlson, A., Shahamat, L., and Shneiderman, B. A visual interface for multivariate temporal data: Finding patterns of events across multiple histories. In *Visual Analytics Science And Technology, 2006 IEEE Symposium On* (2006), 167–174.

7. Mitsa, T. *Temporal Data Mining*, 1st ed. Chapman & Hall/CRC, 2010.

8. Pei, J., Han, J., Mortazavi-Asl, B., Wang, J., Pinto, H., Chen, Q., Dayal, U., and Hsu, M. Mining sequential patterns by pattern-growth: The prefixspan approach. *IEEE Transactions on Knowledge and Data Engineering 16*, 11 (2004), 1424–1440.

9. Plaisant, C., Milash, B., Rose, A., Widoff, S., and Shneiderman, B. Lifelines: visualizing personal histories. In *Proceedings of the SIGCHI Conference on Human Factors in Computing Systems*, CHI '96, ACM (New York, NY, USA, 1996), 221–227.

10. Riehmann, P., Hanfler, M., and Froehlich, B. Interactive sankey diagrams. In *IEEE InfoVis* (2005), 233–240.

11. Rosvall, M., and Bergstrom, C. T. Mapping change in large networks. *PLoS ONE 5*, 1 (01 2010), e8694.

12. Shneiderman, B. The eyes have it: a task by data type taxonomy for information visualizations. In *Visual Languages, 1996. Proceedings., IEEE Symposium on* (1996), 336–343.

13. Wang, T. D., Plaisant, C., Quinn, A. J., Stanchak, R., Murphy, S., and Shneiderman, B. Aligning temporal data by sentinel events: discovering patterns in electronic health records. In *Proceedings of the SIGCHI Conference on Human Factors in Computing Systems*, CHI '08, ACM (New York, NY, USA, 2008), 457–466.

14. Wongsuphasawat, K., and Gotz, D. Exploring flow, factors, and outcomes of temporal event sequences with the outflow visualization. In *IEEE InfoVis* (2012).

15. Wongsuphasawat, K., Guerra Gómez, J. A., Plaisant, C., Wang, T. D., Taieb-Maimon, M., and Shneiderman, B. Lifeflow: visualizing an overview of event sequences. In *Proceedings of the SIGCHI Conference on Human Factors in Computing Systems*, CHI '11, ACM (New York, NY, USA, 2011), 1747–1756.

16. Wongsuphasawat, K., and Shneiderman, B. Finding comparable temporal categorical records: A similarity measure with an interactive visualization. In *Visual Analytics Science and Technology, 2009. VAST 2009. IEEE Symposium on* (2009), 27–34.

17. Zaki, M. J. Spade: An efficient algorithm for mining frequent sequences. *Machine Learning 42*, 1/2 (2001), 31–60.

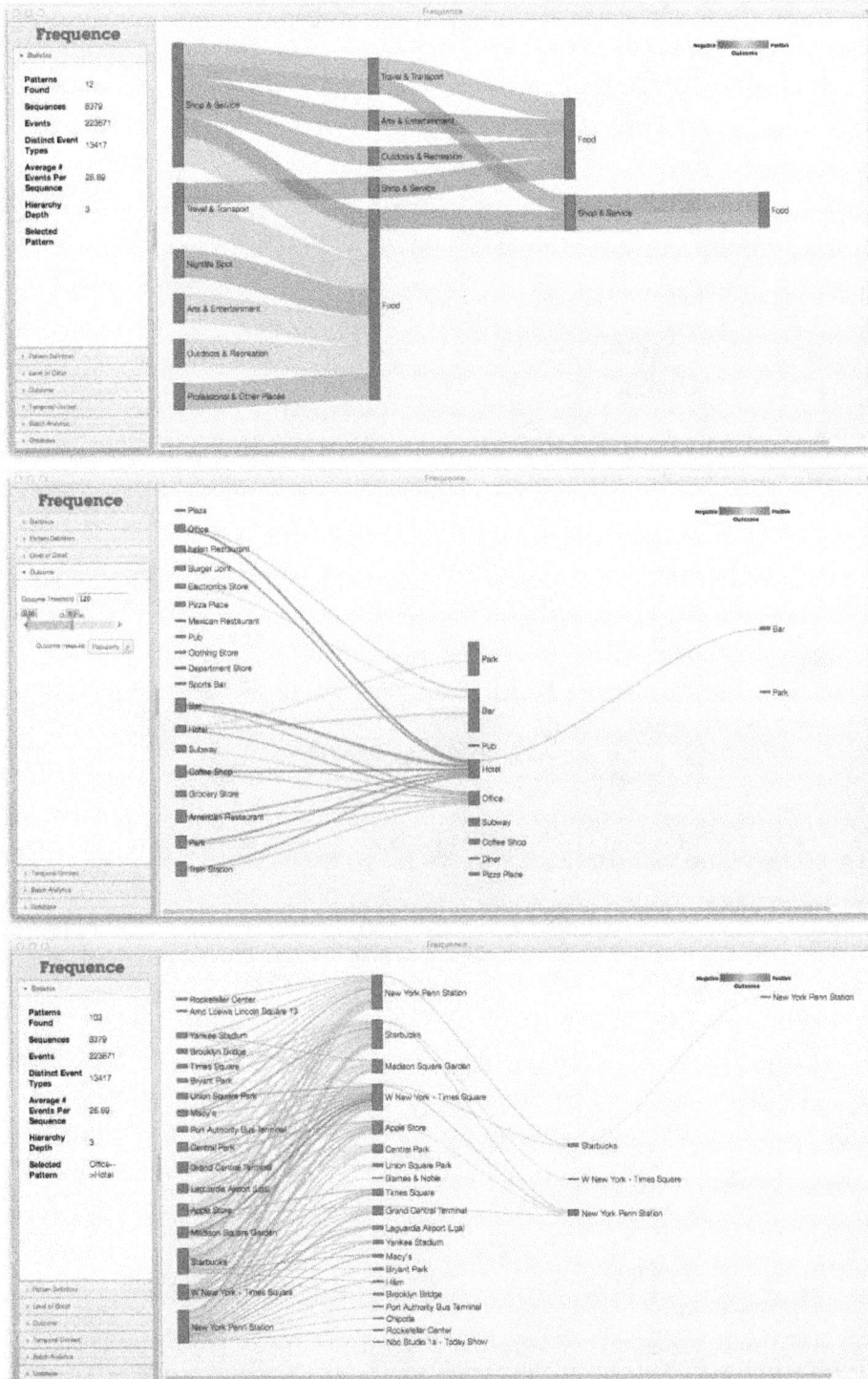

Figure 6. The exploration process of the Foursquare dataset with Frequence. The top figure shows an overview of the coarsest patterns. The middle figure shows a filtered view of unpopular patterns at a finer level-of-detail for the cohort who matched the Professional&OtherPlaces → Food sequence. The bottom figure shows the patterns at the finest level of detail, where the names of the actual venues become visible, after filtering to the cohort who have the Office → Hotel pattern.

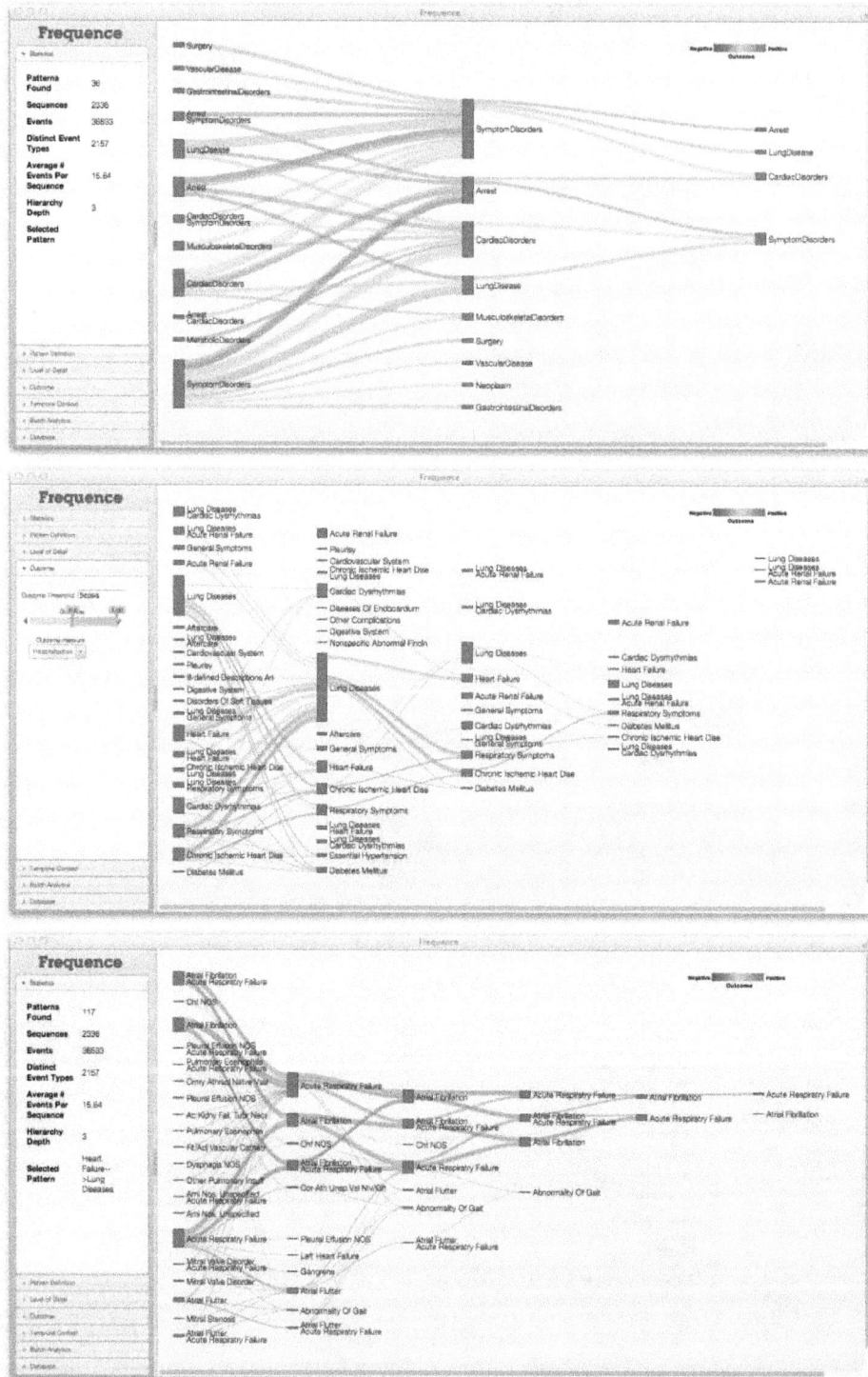

Figure 7. The exploration process of the lung disease patient dataset with Frequence. The top figure shows an overview of the coarsest patterns. The middle figure shows the positive patterns at a finer level-of-detail for the cohort who matched the `CardiacDisorders` → `SymptomDisorders` sequence. The bottom figure shows the patterns at the finest level of detail, after selecting `HeartFailure` → `LungDiseases`.

Time-Offset Interaction with a Holocaust Survivor

Ron Artstein[1] David Traum[1] Oleg Alexander[1] Anton Leuski[1] Andrew Jones[1] Kallirroi Georgila[1]
Paul Debevec[1] William Swartout[1] Heather Maio[2] Stephen Smith[3]

[1]USC Institute for Creative Technologies, 12015 Waterfront Drive, Playa Vista CA 90094-2536, USA
[2]Conscience Display, 1023 Fifth Street, Coronado CA 92118, USA
[3]USC Shoah Foundation, 650 West 35th Street, Suite 114, Los Angeles CA 90089-2571, USA
{artstein|traum|oalexander|leuski|jones|kgeorgila|debevec|swartout}@ict.usc.edu
consciencedisplay@gmail.com   smithsd@dornsife.usc.edu

ABSTRACT

Time-offset interaction is a new technology that allows for two-way communication with a person who is not available for conversation in real time: a large set of statements are prepared in advance, and users access these statements through natural conversation that mimics face-to-face interaction. Conversational reactions to user questions are retrieved through a statistical classifier, using technology that is similar to previous interactive systems with synthetic characters; however, all of the retrieved utterances are genuine statements by a real person. Recordings of answers, listening and idle behaviors, and blending techniques are used to create a persistent visual image of the person throughout the interaction. A proof-of-concept has been implemented using the likeness of Pinchas Gutter, a Holocaust survivor, enabling short conversations about his family, his religious views, and resistance. This proof-of-concept has been shown to dozens of people, from school children to Holocaust scholars, with many commenting on the impact of the experience and potential for this kind of interface.

Author Keywords

Agents and intelligent systems; Computer-mediated communication; E-Learning and education; Multi-modal interfaces; Dialogue systems; Holocaust testimony preservation

ACM Classification Keywords

H.5.2 Information Interfaces and Presentation: User Interfaces – *Natural language*; H.5.1 Information Interfaces and Presentation: Multimedia Information Systems – *Artificial, augmented, and virtual realities*; I.3.3 Computer Graphics: Picture/Image Generation

INTRODUCTION

Recently, a number of computer interfaces (e.g., skype, facetime, hangouts) have been created to allow people in different locations to engage in multi-modal conversational interaction. However all of these require that all conversation participants be available at the same time. If participants are available at different times, current interfaces generally only allow a single message exchange, before waiting for another participant to sign on and reply.

We introduce a new interface for allowing limited interactive conversations with participants who are not currently available for interaction, but who have been able to record relevant material previously. Existing dialogue system technology is used to organize the recorded material such that new partners can engage in conversational interaction with the participant. This "time-offset interaction" allows the intimacy, relevance and interactiveness of conversation for material and participants who were once only accessible via unidirectional communication. This concept has appeared in a number of science fiction and fantasy movies, including *Superman* (1978, and several subsequent versions), in which Superman is able to ask questions and receive instructions from his long dead father; *I, Robot*, in which the Police Detective Del Spooner (played by Will Smith) is able to question a holographic representation of the recently deceased Dr. Alfred Lanning (played by James Cromwell); and *Harry Potter*, in which people in pictures are able to hold conversations with viewers of the picture.

Technology borrowed from Virtual Humans [4] provides many of the basic elements needed to make this idea a reality. We adapt elements from the publicly available Virtual Human Toolkit [5][1] as well as a new video player and video-blending techniques to create a time-offset interaction interface.

One area where time-offset interaction can make a real difference is in introducing new learners to the Holocaust though direct conversational interaction with survivors, who relay their personal experiences as related to specific concerns of the learners. Today this happens frequently, as survivors visit school classrooms, museums, and public lectures. Given the advancing age of the survivors, physical interaction will no

---

[1]http://vhtoolkit.ict.usc.edu

longer be possible in the near future, but time-offset interaction can preserve much of the interaction style and impact of these encounters.

In this paper, we describe a first proof of concept of a time-offset interaction interface. This proof of concept is the first stage in the *New Dimensions in Testimony* project [7], which will allow people to verbally ask questions to a persistent representation of Pinchas Gutter, a Holocaust survivor, and receive his answers to questions on a range of topics. The current proof of concept is limited in scope – appropriate for a demonstration of the concept, delivered by someone who knows approximately what to ask. Future work involves improving both the fidelity of the display, as well as the breadth of available interactions and accessibility for a broad user group.

In the next section, we describe the user experience, including displays for both audience and demonstrator, and a sample dialogue. The following sections describe the system architecture, the recording and video processing used to create a persistent conversational presence, and a small evaluation of the language processing performance. Finally, we sketch the next steps, that will lead to a more generally usable system for a broad range of naive interactors.

USER EXPERIENCE

The proof-of-concept system is designed to be shown to an audience by a trained demonstrator. It is typically run from a laptop computer, projecting the survivor onto an external display while keeping all the controls on the laptop's built-in display, invisible to the audience (we have tested on both Windows and Mac OS, and on a variety of laptops, including the MacBook Air). The external display is typically a projector screen or large television, but can be any computer display depending on availability; for natural interaction it is usually preferable to show the survivor close to life size, and this can be achieved by rotating a large-screen television to portrait orientation, when feasible.

The system is composed of several components running in separate windows (see the system architecture section below), but a demonstrator typically sets it up with only minimal interaction with three components.

1. The Launcher window (a component of the Virtual Human Toolkit [5]) is used to start the demo.

2. The survivor display (an instance of a video player) is positioned on the external display, and maximized to occupy the full display (Figure 1).

3. The audio acquisition client (also a component of the Virtual Human Toolkit) is brought into focus, and the mouse cursor is moved to the push-to-talk region (Figure 2).

After the initial setup, no further interaction is required with the window displays, and the remainder of the demo consists of natural conversation between the demonstrator and the survivor. The demonstrator talks to the survivor through a microphone, using a mouse or similar pointing device for push-to-talk (push while talking, release when done). The

Figure 1. Pinchas Gutter, a holocaust survivor, as he appears on the screen talking to an audience ©University of Southern California

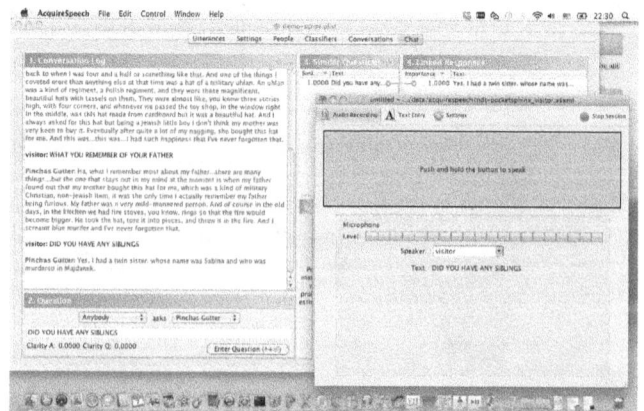

Figure 2. A typical demonstrator screen: the acquisition client is in focus, with NPCEditor in the background ©University of Southern California

2	Opening sequence	2	Survival and coping
3	Childhood	2	Resistance
3	Sister	2	Closing sequence
2	Religion	3	Off-topic

Table 1. Survivor utterances in the proof-of-concept, by topic

microphone is typically a head-mounted close-talking device, though for informal demos the built-in laptop microphone can be used as well. For a large audience, a wireless microphone and mouse can be used, eliminating all physical contact between the demonstrator and the computer, and allowing the demonstrator to assume an ideal position while talking to the survivor and to the audience.

A typical demo will start by greeting the survivor, and proceed with a series of questions depending on the allotted time and the interests of the audience. The present proof-of-concept has 19 statements by the survivor, any of which can be solicited at any time by a question asked by the demonstrator. The statements fall into natural short blocks that form coherent mini-conversations (see Table 1), allowing the demonstrator and survivor to explore a topic in some depth. Three of the survivor's statements are of special status: they are "off-topic" responses which are used when the survivor fails to understand the demonstrator's utterance, in order to deflect the question when the survivor does not have an appropriate answer. An example short demo is provided in the video accompanying the submission, and transcribed in Figure 3. Following the interaction, if the audience is technically inclined, the demonstrator can also drag some of the component windows to the external display to show how the system works.

SYSTEM ARCHITECTURE

Figure 4 shows the system architecture, which makes use of several components from the Virtual Human Toolkit [5], including a module launcher and the VHMsg messaging system, built on top of ActiveMQ.[2] The system consists of automatic speech recognition modules (ASR) – the client and the server; a natural language understanding and response selection module (NLU); and a rendering module (Video Player) that displays the response for the survivor. The individual modules are separate applications that communicate with each other using the ActiveMQ messaging platform. This design allows us to reconfigure the system efficiently and reuse the modules in different projects. The Launcher allows the user to start and stop the individual modules if necessary.

We deliver the system as a single application. When the user double clicks to launch the application, the application starts the ActiveMQ process, starts the Launcher, and the other four components. Termination is done in reverse order: when the user quits the main application, it shuts down individual modules and then terminates the ActiveMQ process. The Video Player module was specifically created for this project; we adapted and customized the other modules from the Virtual Human Toolkit. As the system is intended to be used by people who are not computer experts, the main user interface

---
[2]http://activemq.apache.org

Demonstrator	Hello Pinchas.
Survivor	Hello.
Demonstrator	Can I ask you some questions?
Survivor	You can ask me any questions you would like.
Demonstrator	Growing up, did you have any siblings?
Survivor	Yes, I had a twin sister, whose name was Sabina, and who was murdered in Majdanek.
Demonstrator	Do you remember Sabina?
Survivor	I only remember the plait that she had, she was blonde, blue eyed, just like we all were, my mother were. And when we arrived in Majdanek she was separated from my mother and was put amongst the children. I was together with my father. My father told me to say I was eighteen years old and she must have spotted my mother standing amongst the adult women who were also separated and I saw her too and I saw my sister suddenly running towards my mother. She embraced her. And from that time on, whenever I think of my sister, the only thing that I can see, the only thing that I can visualize, is just that braid, blonde, long, plait and nothing else.
Demonstrator	Pinchas, why do you tell your story?
Survivor	I tell my story for the purpose of improving humanity, if that's possible. Even drop by drop by drop. You know, like a drop of water falls on a stone and it erodes a little bit and smooths it out. So hopefully by me telling my story over and over again, I will achieve, hopefully achieve the purpose of making humanity or the world a better place to live in.
Demonstrator	Thank you, Pinchas, for sharing your story with us.
Survivor	Thank you very much for listening to me.

Figure 3. A short demo (transcription of the accompanying video)

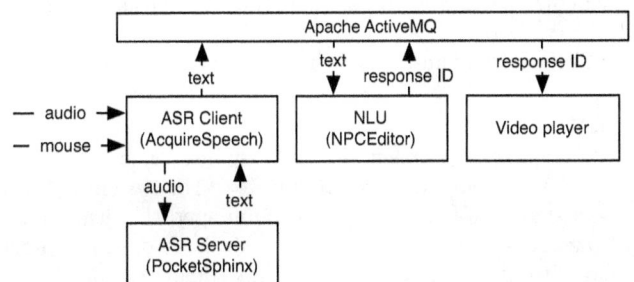

Figure 4. System architecture. We omitted the Launcher and the control events among modules for clarity. ©University of Southern California

challenge was to hide the system complexity from the user by integrating the modules together and making the process of launching and terminating the application as seamless as possible. In the rest of the section we summarize the design of the individual modules.

ASR Client

The speech recognition part of the system consists of two modules: a client and a server. The client, called Acquire-Speech, presents a GUI front end to the user. The ASR currently operates in push-to-talk mode: the user presses a button on the AcquireSpeech window before she starts speaking and releases the button once she is done. AcquireSpeech collects the audio data that arrives from the microphone between the mouse press and release and forwards the data to the server at 0.25 second intervals. In our experiments we observed that users often start speaking before they press the push-to-talk button and release the button before they finish their sentence. This observation led us to modify the AcquireSpeech to extend the recorded audio interval by adding a short segment of recording before the button is pressed and after the button is released. The client listens to the audio constantly and keeps track of the most recent 0.25 seconds of audio in a buffer. When the user presses the button, the application sends the data from the buffer to the server. When the user releases the button, AcquireSpeech keeps recording and sending for another 0.25 seconds. AcquireSpeech is a highly modular and customizable application that allows us to adapt its interface to projects (e.g., [10]) that can use multiple recording sources, recognition engines, and control buttons. The system can be customized to automatically log the audio in files.

ASR Server

Many speech recognition systems are compatible with the VH Toolkit, and could easily be used in this type of application [8]. For the proof of concept, we use CMU PocketSphinx speech recognizer.[3] Using the PocketSphinx libraries we created a server application that accepts a digital audio stream over a TCP connection and sends back the recognition results. The language model (back-off 3-gram) was trained on a set of 81 questions written by the system developers using the CMU Statistical Language Modeling toolkit [2]. Each of the 81 questions corresponded to one of the 19 survivor responses noted in Table 1. For US English speakers we used the Wall Street Journal (WSJ) acoustic models distributed by CMU. For British English speakers we used acoustic models trained with the WSJCAM0 corpus [11]. The CMU pronouncing dictionary v0.7a [12] was used as the main dictionary with the addition of domain-dependent words, such as names.

NLU

For language understanding and response selection we use an NLU system called NPCEditor [6]. The system is based on a statistical language classification approach, using ideas from cross-lingual information retrieval. A designer specifies a list of system responses and links them to some training set utterances. The system uses this data to make an implicit

dictionary. When the system receives a new utterance, it applies the dictionary to construct a representation of the most likely response. It compares that response representation to each response in its database and returns a list of matching responses. NPCEditor also knows when it does not know the answer: when the score of the best matching response is below a specified threshold, the classifier returns an empty list. This approach has been shown to be both robust to the errors in ASR output and very effective for implementing simple conversational agents [6].

In addition to the language classifier, NPCEditor includes a dialogue manager that processes the classification results and picks the actual response that is presented to the user. For example, when the classification list is empty, NPCEditor returns one of the responses specified as "off-topic" – e.g., "The question that you asked me, I am afraid I won't be able to answer." When the list contains several responses, the dialogue manager attempts to pick a response that the user has not heard yet. NPCEditor sends the selected response identifier to the Video Player via the ActiveMQ connection.

Video Player

The final module of the system is a custom Video Player. It has one video clip for each survivor response and a collection of 1–2 second "idle" clips, which serve to create listening and waiting behaviors when one of the longer response clips is not playing. Creation of these clips is described in the next section. The Video Player is based on the libraries from the VLC project[4] and is capable of playing MP4-encoded files. When the system is idle, the player plays a sequence of randomly chosen idle clips. Once it receives a response ID from NPCEditor, it selects, schedules, and plays back the appropriate response video clip.

RECORDING PROCESS AND VIDEO PROCESSING

Capture

We captured a long form interview with the survivor illuminated by the Light Stage 6 device [1]. The Light Stage 6 device is a geodesic dome approximately 26 feet in diameter. There are approximately 660 individually controllable light sources mounted on every vertex of the dome. For this shoot we set all the lights to the same intensity, resulting in an even illumination of the survivor. We shot with a RED Epic camera mounted in portrait orientation. The footage was then edited and converted to a set of individual video clips, one response per clip.

Transitions

To create seamless transitions between clips, we asked the survivor to always start and end a response in the same "neutral pose". We morphed the start and end frames of each video clip to a single neutral pose frame. We also created short "idle" clips, 1–2 seconds each, using the morph transitions as connective tissue. The morph transitions were computed automatically using optical flow. However, we found that sometimes the optical flow failed on frames which were too dissimilar. In addition, even when the morphs worked

---

[3]http://cmusphinx.sourceforge.net

[4]http://www.videolan.org/vlc/index.html

	#Utterances	Word Error Rate (%)	Robustness (%)
US	39	21	95
UK	65	17	89
All	104	19	91

Table 2. Speech recognition and NLU performance

well, the motion appeared too linear and not natural. This convinced us that a more sophisticated transition system was needed.

EVALUATION

Speech recognition

For speech recognition our main evaluation metric was word error rate (WER). The WER is calculated by comparing the speech recognition output with what the speaker actually said (transcription), and can be formulated as follows:

$$\text{WER} = \frac{\text{Substitutions} + \text{Deletions} + \text{Insertions}}{\text{Length of transcription string}}$$

Table 2 shows speech recognition results for two demonstrators of the system, one from US and one from UK, as well as the average WER. The lower the WER the better. This evaluation is based on 104 utterances, consisting of several extended demos from each speaker.

Natural language understanding

We measure the NLU's ASR robustness by passing through the NPCEditor both the speech recognition output and the transcription and counting the number of matches between the two outputs. Intuitively this is a measure of how much ASR errors will impact NLU results. NLU ASR robustness can be formulated as follows:

$$\text{NLU ASR Robustness} = \frac{\text{Number of matches}}{\text{Number of utterances}}$$

The same utterances that were used for calculating the WER were also used for calculating the NLU ASR Robustness. Table 2 shows the Robustness for the two demonstrators as well as the average Robustness; the higher the Robustness the better. Since the NLU ASR Robustness is much higher than ASR accuracy $(1 - \text{WER})$, we can see that the NLU can recover from a high percentage of ASR errors without impacting the overall performance. For a demo system, demonstrators can be trained to say things that the NLU would be able to understand, so ASR NLU robustness is the dominant factor in performance. For less experienced users, domain coverage would also be very important, as users might not know how to formulate questions in a way that could be understood (whether or not the ASR performance is good).

The above results show that the system performs well and allows for successful system-user interactions. In the future we intend to experiment with different language and acoustic models and to perform a rigorous evaluation with more users.

User reactions

Probably the most important evaluation of the proof of concept is its impact on viewers of the system. While we have not undergone a formal study of viewer reactions, the system has been demonstrated to hundreds of people, individually, in small groups, and in larger presentations with dozens of audience members. The reaction has been quite positive, both to the concept of time-offset interactions, the specific interface, the content from the survivor, and possible other uses of this kind of interface.

FUTURE WORK

We intend to extend the proof-of-concept into a full prototype, which will provide a richer experience and allow the survivor to interact with people who are not trained as demonstrators. The extensions will include an enhanced graphic display environment, and additional interactive content.

Graphics improvements

We will design and implement an improved video recording process for the survivor testimony which will allow for holographic video projection, 3D stereo display, and multi-view high definition archiving. The goal of the process is to record the appearance of the survivor giving their testimony in as "future-proof" a manner as possible, with the greatest possible fidelity and repurposeability, that reasonable expense will allow.

The survivor will be comfortably seated, attractively illuminated, and recorded by a semicircular array of 50 high-definition video cameras. These will provide video streams of the testimony from all angles from left profile to frontal to right profile. The views along this arc will be sufficiently closely spaced to allow "optical flow" image processing algorithms to realistically synthesize any possible camera position along the arc; the result will be a dataset which can be used by a state-of-the-art life-sized autostereoscopic holographic display system, or viewed interactively on a PC from a user-directed angle, providing a solid sense of three-dimensional presence.

In addition to the semicircular arc of angles, approximately ten of the cameras will be dedicated to recording additional special views of the survivor. These include cameras which will record close-up video of the survivor's face and hands, and cameras which will record additional viewpoints to enable 3D geometric shape information for each frame of the survivor's testimony. Two of the frontal cameras will be placed in optimal positions to record left-eye/right-eye 3D stereo video.

When the subject is available, we will additionally perform a Light Stage 6 full-body geometry and reflectance scan of them wearing the same clothing in which they are interviewed, as well as Light Stage X [3] facial scans of key facial expressions with submillimeter accuracy. These datasets will document the appearance of the survivor with the best technology available today, and could be used in the future to enhance the resolution of the recorded survivor testimony video.

In order to make the transitions between responses appear as seamless as possible, the application will include a transition system based on cluster analysis of the video frames. The application can run on a 2D monitor or a 3D monitor requiring 3D glasses. The video could also be projected on a 2D screen or a 3D screen (requiring each viewer to wear 3D glasses) at life size.

Finally, additional processing and rendering of the acquired dynamic performance and static reference data will enable, in the not-too-distant-future, for the survivor to be faithfully rendered to match the lighting conditions of any museum or classroom environment, providing the closest possible impression of the survivor being present within the same space and lighting of the participating audience's environment.

Content enhancements

In order to hold coherent conversations with uninitiated people, the survivor will need to record many more statements than are available at present, which would provide answers to the most common questions people want to ask. The full prototype will include additional content on the existing topics of family, religion and resistance, as well as other topics of common interest. But in order to address the common questions (rather than topics), we need to find out what these questions actually are.

Data collection forms a crucial step when transitioning a synthetic character from private demonstration to public interaction, because the language understanding components need to know not only *what* information people want from the character, but also *how* they ask for it in conversation. Preparing a person for interacting with the public will require a similar collection of the actual language people use. To collect the data, we plan to build a mock-up system with only voice recordings of the survivor, to allow expeditious and inexpensive addition of content. To save development time and cost we will use a person to select the survivor's statements in real time rather than trained speech recognition and language understanding ("Wizard of Oz" scenario). The mock-up will be taken to target audiences (e.g., schools, museums), and will be extended iteratively with additional survivor statements until a large set of "frequently asked questions" are identified. Based on these questions we will design the interview for the video recording sessions, so that the recorded statements will be the ones most frequently sought out by the public. Based on experience with museum interactions with synthetic characters [9, 10], we believe that a set of several hundred statements on a small number of select topics can provide sufficient content to allow the survivor to keep sustained interactions with the public well into the future.

ACKNOWLEDGMENTS

Creation of the proof-of-concept was made possible by generous donations from private foundations and individuals. We are extremely grateful to the Pears Foundation, Alan Shay, Lucy Goldman, and the Wolfson Foundation for their support. Special thanks to Pinchas Gutter for sharing his story, and for his tireless efforts to educate the world about the Holocaust.

REFERENCES

1. Chabert, C.-F., Einarsson, P., Jones, A., Lamond, B., Ma, A., Sylwan, S., Hawkins, T., and Debevec, P. Relighting human locomotion with flowed reflectance fields. In *SIGGRAPH 06: ACM SIGGRAPH 2006 Sketches*, ACM (2006), 76.

2. Clarkson, P., and Rosenfeld, R. Statistical language modeling using the CMU-Cambridge toolkit. In *Proc. of Eurospeech* (Rhodes, Greece, 1997).

3. Ghosh, A., Fyffe, G., Tunwattanapong, B., Busch, J., Yu, X., and Debevec, P. Multiview face capture using polarized spherical gradient illumination. In *Proceedings of the 2011 SIGGRAPH Asia Conference*, SA '11, ACM (New York, NY, USA, 2011), 129:1–129:10.

4. Gratch, J., Rickel, J., Andre, E., Cassell, J., Petajan, E., and Badler, N. Creating interactive virtual humans: Some assembly required. *IEEE Intelligent Systems* (2002), 54–63.

5. Hartholt, A., Traum, D., Marsella, S. C., Shapiro, A., Stratou, G., Leuski, A., Morency, L.-P., and Gratch, J. All together now: Introducing the virtual human toolkit. In *International Conference on Intelligent Virtual Humans* (Edinburgh, UK, Aug. 2013).

6. Leuski, A., and Traum, D. Practical language processing for virtual humans. In *Proceedings of the 22nd Annual Conference on Innovative Applications of Artificial Intelligence (IAAI-10)* (2010).

7. Maio, H., Traum, D., and Debevec, P. New dimensions in testimony. *PastForward*, Summer (2012), 22–26.

8. Morbini, F., Audhkhasi, K., Sagae, K., Artstein, R., Can, D., Georgiou, P., Narayanan, S., Leuski, A., and Traum, D. Which ASR should I choose for my dialogue system? In *Proceedings of the SIGDIAL 2013 Conference* (Metz, France, August 2013), 394–403.

9. Robinson, S., Traum, D., Ittycheriah, M., and Henderer, J. What would you ask a conversational agent? Observations of human-agent dialogues in a museum setting. In *Proceedings of the Sixth International Conference on Language Resources and Evaluation (LREC)* (Marrakech, Morocco, 2008).

10. Traum, D., Aggarwal, P., Artstein, R., Foutz, S., Gerten, J., Katsamanis, A., Leuski, A., Noren, D., and Swartout, W. Ada and Grace: Direct interaction with museum visitors. In *Intelligent Virtual Agents: 12th International Conference, IVA 2012, Santa Cruz, CA, USA, September 12–14, 2012 Proceedings*, Y. Nakano, M. Neff, A. Paiva, and M. Walker, Eds., vol. 7502 of *Lecture Notes in Artificial Intelligence*, Springer (Heidelberg, September 2012), 245–251.

11. Vertanen, K. Baseline WSJ acoustic models for HTK and Sphinx: Training recipes and recognition experiments. Tech. rep., Cavendish Laboratory, University of Cambridge, 2006.

12. Weide, R. The CMU pronouncing dictionary, 2008.

Hierarchical Route Maps for Efficient Navigation

Fangzhou Wang [1]
fzw@acm.org

Yang Li [2]
yangli@acm.org

Daisuke Sakamoto [1]
d.sakamoto@acm.org

Takeo Igarashi [1,3]
takeo@acm.org

[1]The University of Tokyo

[2]Google Research

[3]JST ERATO Igarashi Design Interface Project

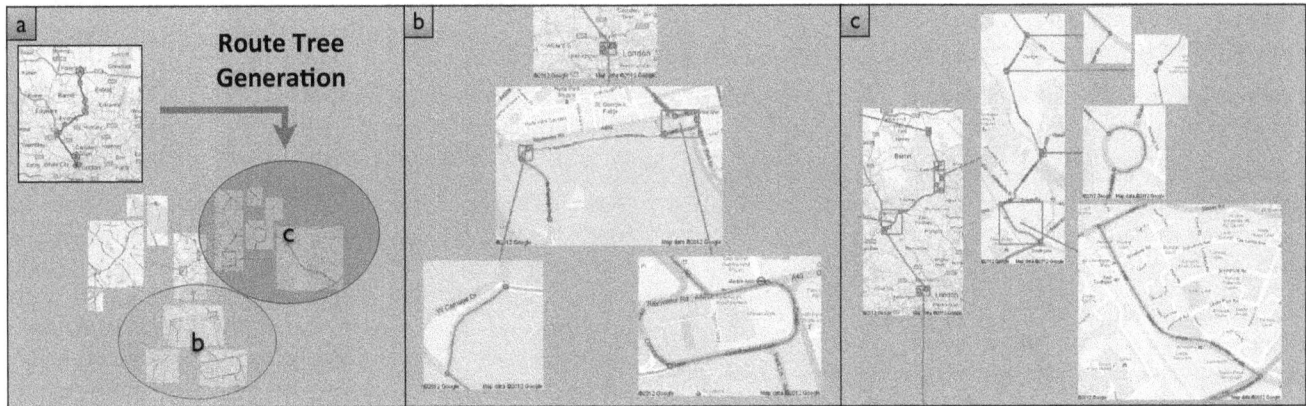

Figure 1: An example of Route Tree. The proposed algorithm automatically extracts meaningful multi scale views of a route and organizes those views into a hierarchical structure to support efficient navigation. (a) shows the original route and a complete overview of the Route Tree generated form the route, (b) and (c) show close-up view of the Route Tree. Note that these are visualization of the internal data structure and the end-users do not see them directly.

ABSTRACT

One of the difficulties with standard route maps is accessing to multi-scale routing information. The user needs to display maps in both a large scale to see details and a small scale to see an overview, but this requires tedious interaction such as zooming in and out. We propose to use a hierarchical structure for a route map, called a "Route Tree", to address this problem, and describe an algorithm to automatically construct such a structure. A Route Tree is a hierarchical grouping of all small route segments to allow quick access to meaningful large and small-scale views. We propose two Route Tree applications, "RouteZoom" for interactive map browsing and "TreePrint" for route information printing, to show the applicability and usability of the structure. We conducted a preliminary user study on RouteZoom, and the results showed that RouteZoom significantly lowers the interaction cost for obtaining information from a map compared to a traditional interactive map.

Author Keywords

Route Map Visualization; View Extraction; Multi-scale Navigation.

ACM Classification Keywords

H5.2 [Information interfaces and presentation]: User Interfaces. - Graphical user interfaces.

INTRODUCTION

A route map presents route information to guide users from one place to another. Various systems have been developed for automatically generating route maps. These systems have been conventionally implemented in car navigation systems with a local map database. The use of web-based route map generation systems, such as Google Maps [9], has become commonplace for various types of users recently as smart phones and tablet PCs become popular. However, several usability problems still remain with these map systems.

One problem with standard map systems is the lack of support for presenting multi-scale information. For example, when users want to see an overview of the entire route, a smaller scale view is preferred. On the other hand, when they want to get detailed information on points of interest (POIs) such as turning points or junctions, they would prefer a larger scale view to see more details. However, standard paper-printed route maps or interactive route map systems in a modern map system [9, 19] require the user to manually change both scale and position in the map to get a desirable view, which can be very tedious. Therefore, it is desirable to provide an easy way to access various meaningful views with different scales and positions in the route.

We propose to pre-compute a hierarchical structure for a route map (called a "Route Tree") to provide quick access to such meaningful views (Figure 1). The important features of our hierarchical structure are as follows:

Feature 1. Each node represents a part of its parent view in a larger scale, while the root node represents a complete view of the whole route.

Feature 2. For every part of the route, there is a node that visualizes the part in the necessary scale.

Feature 3. The number of nodes in the tree is made as small as possible, while keeping an appropriate view size (size of the rendered result on the screen or print) for each node.

We present an algorithm for automatically constructing a Route Tree. It starts with an over-segmented tree and iteratively simplifies it by taking balance between compactness and readability. A Route Tree itself is raw tree data, and it can be used in various applications. In this paper, we implemented an interactive map browsing system called RouteZoom to demonstrate the effectiveness of a RouteTree.

Our method is designed to address the situation where a user needs to actively learn or explore an area or route. It is different from but complements automatic uses of maps systems such as Turn-by-Turn navigation used in car navigation in which a user passively receives step-by-step instructions from the system. The contributions of this work are summarized as follows.

1. A novel hierarchical structure for route maps called a Route Tree.

2. A fast algorithm to construct the Route Tree with a few parameters given by the user to control the results.

3. Two useful route map applications that exploit Route Trees, respectively improved a conventional route map browsing system and a route map printing system.

RELATED WORK

Route map visualization
Agrawala et al. [1] have proposed a system to render a route map that mimics handwriting maps made by humans. This approach focuses on conveying precise information about POIs and an abstract overview of the complete route. To achieve the goal, it distorts the geographic shape and length of the route and takes away detailed context around the route. However, the lack of contextual information outside the route makes it difficult for users to turn back to the precise route when they mistakenly choose a wrong one, or to determine their precise position in the route map from information such as landmarks around them or the shape of the road. Furthermore, the distorted representation makes it

difficult to use the map in combination with advanced services such as aerial photo views.

Several existing web-based map systems [9, 19] are able to print a step-by-step guide showing all POIs and corresponding verbal directions along the route. Karnick et al. [16] proposed a method of putting detailed views of POIs in the route around the complete overview of the route. This can be problematic because the user might want to see the map in some intermediate scales. Furthermore, some of the detailed views are almost the same and therefore redundant because the method shows a detailed view for each POI even in a case where it is possible to show multiple POIs in a single view.

Several previous studies [22, 25] attempted to exploit the user's prior knowledge about the route in order to produce a more simplified, useful route for users. Other studies [5, 11] propose methods that combine videos or images with conventional route maps to enrich the user's knowledge about the route. There are also systems that generate Goal-oriented route maps such as tourist maps [10] or Destination-oriented maps [18] rather than Start-to-Goal route maps.

Hierarchical map structure
There are several studies on hierarchical structures for map visualization. However, most of them discuss how to automatically make a series of multi-scale map images from geographic data while including information in an appropriate level of detail (e.g., [20, 27]). They do not use them for route map visualization. Studies have been made on hierarchical structures and route maps, but most of them focus not on visualization but on human cognition on routes and its application to generating verbal route directions [17, 26]. Our work differs from these studies in that our method generates a series of maps with appropriate detail in different scales for a route map, and uses them for interactive browsing or compact printing.

Map browsing interface
Various methods have been proposed for interactively browsing maps in different scales. Some of them [2, 4] integrated maps of multiple scales into one screen using Focus+Context techniques such as Furnas' fisheye [7]. Others adopt Overview+Detail techniques to arrange pictures of different levels of focus and size [12, 15]. Another approach is to extend conventional panning and zooming interfaces. Igarashi et al. [13] proposed a method to automatically change zoom level depending on the scrolling speed for map navigation. Zhao et al. [28] proposed to implicitly bookmark user's view on the map to accelerate browsing speed. Both of the latter two techniques rely only on general user input and do not leverage semantic information associated with routes. Pindat et al. [23] proposed content-aware adaptive fisheye lens that changes its way of zooming depending on its focus on map. However, the study focuses on interface design and does

not discuss in detail how to pre-compute the necessary semantic information it requires from a map.

Robbins et al. [24] proposed a system called "ZoneZoom", which provides an effective way of navigation on a mobile display. It divides the screen into several areas and allows the user to recursively zoom into them. Though they suggested in their study that their method could be well applied to map navigation, they did not discuss a method to automatically compute zoomable areas. We apply their method as the basis of our user interface for RouteZoom application, but the zoomable areas are automatically computed by our method.

ROUTE TREE CONSTRUCTION

The construction process consists of three steps: 1) Scale Evaluation, 2) Initial Tree Construction, and 3) Optimization (Figure 2). The input route data is taken from a route-search engine (e.g., Google Directions API [8], NavEngine [21]), which includes information such as the road's geographic shape, the type of road, and POIs. First, we extract a set of "route segments" from the input route data, which represent short, straight lines in the route, and use this information to assign scale values to the segments (Scale Evaluation). Second, we construct an initial tree by hierarchically organizing the route segments depending on their scales (Initial Tree Construction). Since this tree is over-segmented, we optimize the nodes to an appropriate number and size of view to get the final tree (Optimization).

Scale Evaluation

The route shape is initially given as a polyline, and we divide the polyline into short, straight segments with nearly equal lengths. Next, we evaluate a scale value for every route segment. A scale value indicates the minimum scale necessary to present enough information about the segment in the map. For example, motorway segments are visible in a small scale, but small street segments need to be in a

POI Road	NoPOI	Turn	Branch	Continue
Motorway	7	11	17	10
Primary	9	13	17	12
Secondary	10	14	17	13
Local	14	18	17	17
...	...	...	...	...

Table 1: Example look-up table for Type(R)

larger scale to be visible, because in smaller scale it is usually not rendered on the map. A scale value is an integer ranging from 0 to around 20 (depending on the map) and determines the approximate translation ratio from latitude/longitude coordinates to pixel coordinates in the map as

$$(x,y) = \left(f(lat,lon), g(lat,lon) \right)$$

$$f(lat,lon) = \frac{2^{Scale+8}}{360} \cdot (lon - A)$$

$$g(lat,lon) = \frac{2^{Scale+8}}{360 \cdot \cos(lat)} \cdot (B - lat)$$

where x and y respectively indicate horizontal and vertical coordinates in the map image, and lat and lon indicate latitude and longitude coordinates. A and B respectively indicate longitude and latitude at the top left of the map image [3].

We use the following function to evaluate the scale:

$$Scale(R) = \max\{Type(R), Dist(R)\}$$

where R indicates a route segment.

Type(R) returns a scale value of the segment defined by the road type and the type of POI it contains. It depends on the input map data. Table 1 shows the definition for Google Maps. A larger scale value is defined for segments that contain POIs, because those segments usually need a higher scale to be visualized. It returns different values depending on the type of POI (e.g., turning point, branch of roads, continue to a different street), because each of them has a different level of importance for the user and a different scale value for visualization. *Dist(R)* is added in order to prevent neighboring POIs from being too close in the rendered view. It measures the distance between R and neighboring POIs, and returns a minimum scale value to make the distance larger than a predefined value (we use 30 pixels in our implementation) on the screen.

Initial Tree Construction

Figure 3 shows an overview of the method in this step. We first prepare a copy of segmented routes for each scale value within the defined range (Figure 3a). We remove all segments whose scale is smaller than the scale level associated with each copy (Figure 3b). We then group adjacent route segments in each scale level, making nodes (Figure 3c). Each node is associated with a scale level.

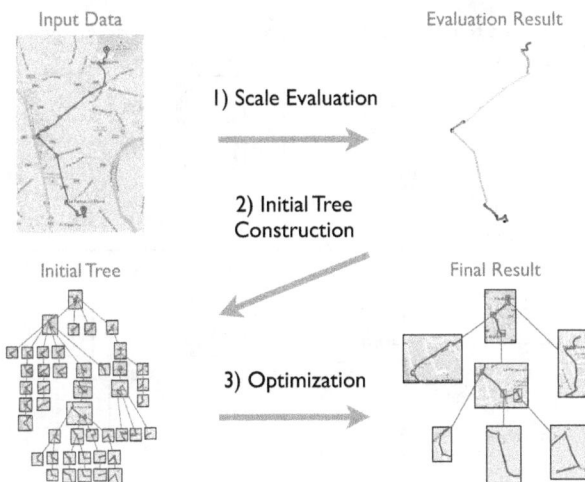

Figure 2: Overview of Route Tree construction process.

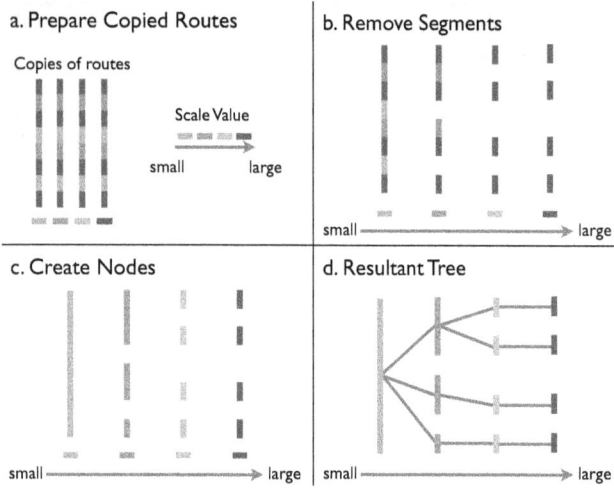

Figure 3: Initial tree construction process.

Finally, an initial Route Tree is created by connecting each node on the basis of the containment relationship among the segments (Figure 3d).

Optimization

The initial tree is over-segmented and each node is too small at this point. We therefore optimize the tree by minimizing a cost function to reduce the number and increase the size of nodes.

Cost Functions

The definition of the cost function is as follows:

$$\cos t(t) = \sum_{n \in t} \begin{cases} 10^{15} & (score(n) \leq 0) \\ 1 / score(n) & (score(n) > 0) \end{cases}$$

$$score(n) = \alpha \cdot nodesize(n) + \beta \cdot childsize(n)$$

where t represents a Route Tree and n represents its node. We set $\alpha=0.5$ and $\beta=0.5$ for weighting parameters α, β in our implementation. The score function $nodesize(n)$ is a restriction against the view size of node n and $childsize(n)$ is one against that of the child nodes of n. Increasing parameter α or decreasing β will better preserve every node size to be similar but randomize the size of area every child nodes indicates in its parent view, and vice vasa. The greater the returned $score(n)$ value is and the smaller the number of nodes n in tree t is, the less is the $cost(t)$ that is returned. The definition and graph plot of $nodesize(n)$ are as follows:

$$nodesize(n) = \begin{cases} \exp(A \cdot (s(n) - p \cdot M_{max})) & (s(n) < M_{min}) \\ B \cdot (s(n) - p \cdot M_{max})^2 + 1.0 & (M_{min} \leq s(n) \leq M_{max}) \\ C \cdot (s(n) - p \cdot M_{max})^2 + 1.0 & (M_{max} < s(n)) \end{cases}$$

$$A = \frac{\log(a)}{M_{min} - p \cdot M_{max}}, B = \frac{a - 1.0}{(M_{min} - p \cdot M_{max})^2}, C = \frac{b - 1.0}{(M_{min} - p \cdot M_{max})^2}$$

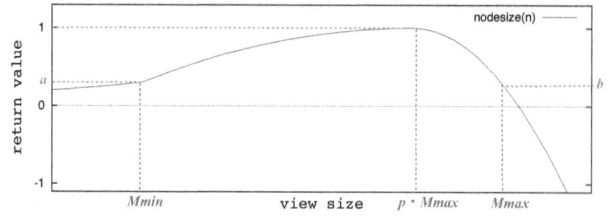

where a, b, and p are values ranging from 0.0 to 1.0, M_{min} and M_{max} are respectively the minimum and maximum limit of the node size, and $s(n)$ represents the size of node n. All these parameters are application-specific i.e. different values are set for different applications. The function sets the ideal node size to $p \cdot M_{max}$ and gives a negative value as a penalty when the size exceeds its defined limit M_{max} too much.

The definition of $childsize(n)$ are as follows:

$$childsize(n) = \exp\left(\frac{(M_{max} / s'(n) - m)^2}{2 \cdot \sigma^2}\right)$$

where $s'(n)$ is the size of node n in its parent view. The function sets the ideal child node size to be $1/m$ of the M_{max} in its parent view, and thus avoids the problem of the area a child node indicates being too large or too small in its parent view.

GA Optimization

We use a genetic algorithm (GA) for the optimization. The basic idea is to repeatedly apply the following four operations to the tree in order to reduce the number and increase the size of nodes.

1. Integrate a node to its child nodes (Figure 4a).

2. Integrate a node to its adjacent node (Figure 4b).

3. Increment the scale value of a node (Figure 4c).

4. Add 10 segments (5 for each side) to a node (Figure 4d).

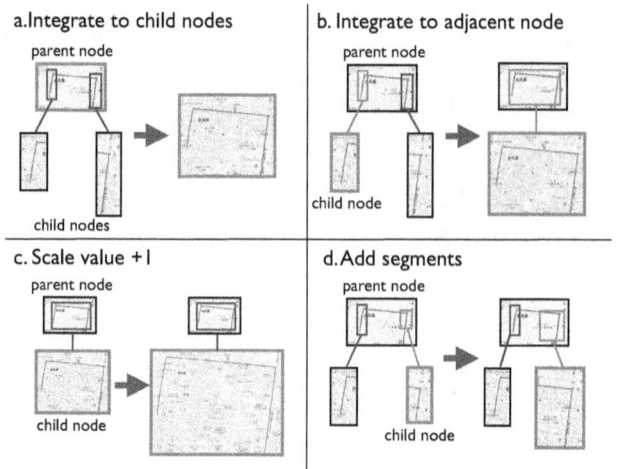

Figure 4: Operations in optimization process.

The algorithm first prepares 500 candidate trees by randomly applying the four operations to the initial tree. It then iteratively reduces the cost of the trees by applying crossover and mutation. The probabilities for crossover and mutation are respectively 0.5 and 0.3. Crossover randomly mixes two selected trees and mutation randomly applies one of the four operations to each node in the selected tree with a probability of 0.1. We use a simple roulette-wheel selection process to make successive generations, and the fitness of each seed is defined as the inverse of the cost evaluated by the Route Tree cost function, After repeating the process 1000 times, the algorithm returns the tree with the lowest score as the final solution.

ROUTE TREE APPLICATIONS

We implemented two Route Tree applications: "RouteZoom" for interactively browsing route maps on a display, and "TreePrint" for printing routing information. We will describe the details of each application respectively in the following two subsections.

RouteZoom

Real-time navigation systems automatically move the map view according to the current position. However, the users may want to browse the map under certain circumstances, e.g., to allow them to 1) memorize directions for parts of the route they are unfamiliar with, and 2) see information for the next few turns to prepare their mind during driving. Therefore, it is still important to improve techniques for browsing route maps for developing better navigation systems.

Figure 5 shows the user interface and functions of RouteZoom. The system has two main functions, the first of which is "smart zoom". With this function, the system automatically suggests areas in the main map that the user may want to zoom in on to see the details. The user has only to select a suggested area to get a detailed view of it. The user can also get an appropriate zoomed-out view by right-clicking on the map or selecting the (-) command at the bottom right corner. Note that this function not only scales the view but also slides it to efficiently show the route, while in a standard map application the user has to adjust the view position manually after changing the scale. The second function is "smart slide". With this function, the user can move forward or backward along the route by selecting a command button on the top or bottom of the parent view. The position and scale are automatically adjusted after the slide.

The construction process is as follows. First, we construct a Route Tree from the route. We set construction parameters M_{max}=800x600px, M_{min}=50x50px, a=0.1, b=0.0, p=0.9, m=5, σ=1.0. Second, we trace the parent-child relationship in the tree to construct the smart-zoom function. Third, we scan the Route Tree from the root to the leaves and connect each POI in the route to nodes that contain it. The smart-slide function gathers nodes connected to the POIs that are

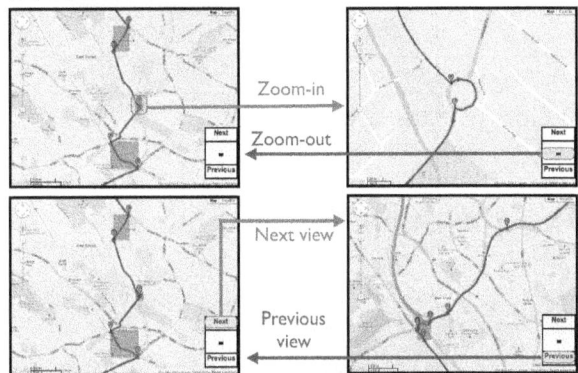

Figure 5: (a) User interface of RouteZoom (b) Smart zoom and smart slide functions in RouteZoom.

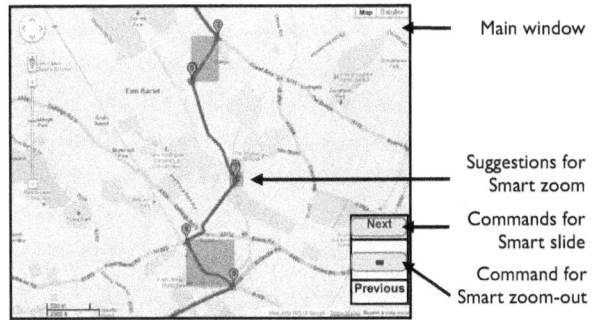

next or previous to the current viewport. From the gathered nodes it then chooses one target node that has the nearest scale value to the current view scale. If the difference between the scale value of a target node and that of the current view is less than 3, it simply slides the view to the target node. In case the difference is greater than or equal to 3 we maintain the current scale and slide the view to the next or previous POI's position.

TreePrint

Although real-time navigation systems are very common these days, there are still strong needs to print out route maps in some situations. We conducted an informal survey to ask 20 daily map users whether they use a printed route map. Surprisingly, 16 of them answered, "Sometimes *I may need to print out a route map*" and two answered, "I *often print out a route map*", while only two answered, "Not *necessary at all*". They listed several cases when they needed to print out maps such as traveling abroad in a rented car without a car-navigation system, making a backup for a cell phone low on battery power or a low-accuracy GPS, or just wanting to save money for their cell-phone Internet connection.

The TreePrint system produces a collection of map images for showing route information in three levels of views. It produces a complete overview of a route, detailed views for each POI, and mid-scale views between them. Figure 6a

(a) TreePrint layout

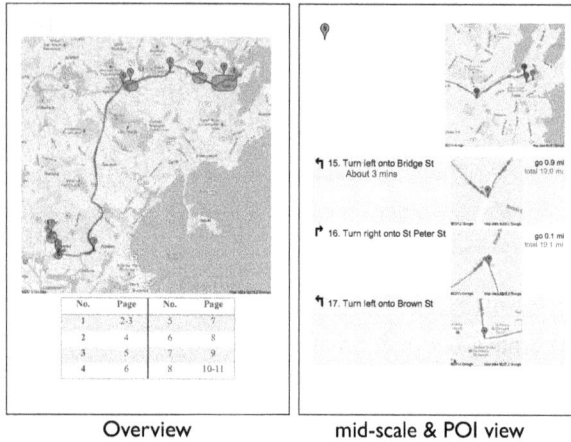

No.	Page	No.	Page
1	2-3	5	7
2	4	6	8
3	5	7	9
4	6	8	10-11

Overview   mid-scale & POI view

(b) Google Maps layout

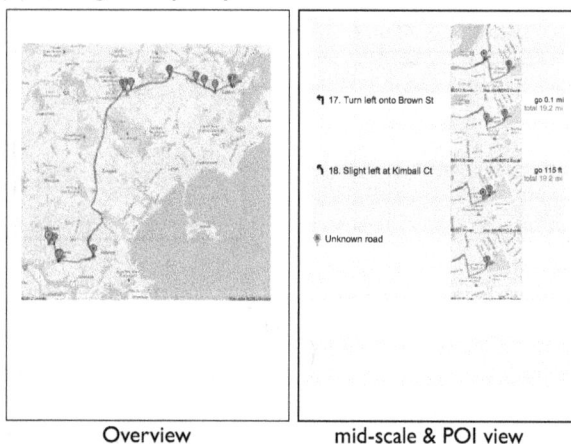

Overview   mid-scale & POI view

Figure 6: Comparison of (a) TreePrint layout (b) Google Maps printing layout. For comparison, POI markers in Google Maps layout overview are manually added. The texts are enlarged from original size for better visual presentation.

shows an example of a layout printed using map images produced by TreePrint. A complete overview of the route is printed on the first page. Mid-scale views are indicated on the view with their index numbers. The user can refer to the table shown at the bottom to jump to pages with more detailed information about the indicated view. Currently our route tree implementation only generates individual map images and the final layout with text description is manually generated. However, it will not be difficult to automatically generate this simple layout given the sufficient text instruction and icon image resources in modern map systems.

The advantage of enabling a Route Tree to print is that it optimizes the map views depending on the information it contains, while the conventional printing method in a modern map system produces map images with fixed scale regardless of the information they contain. The optimization process avoids the producing of multiple similar views or views with excessively small scale. Furthermore, mid-scale

views clarify the spatial relationships between multiple POIs, such as the road shape or the distance between them. This is a clear improvement over conventional systems that have difficulty in visualizing this information when multiple POIs are concentrated in a short part within a long route.

The TreePrint application first produces a Route Tree for the route it prints. The root node of the tree, nodes with depth 1, and nodes with depth 2 respectively represent a complete overview, mid-scale view, and POI-level views. We set construction parameters M_{max} and M_{min} depending on the depth of the node, which is defined by the map size on each view level. We set the same a, b, p, σ values used to construct RouteZoom, while setting larger m value $m=16$ to reduce the depth of the tree. After Route Tree construction, we set the depth of all leaf nodes to be 2 by iteratively removing parent nodes of leaf nodes whose depths are larger than 2, and adding a child node for leaf nodes whose depths are less than 2. We set the scale value as 15 for newly added children with depth 1 and one greater than its parent node' s scale for depth 2.

RESULTS

Figure 7a shows an example of view transitions in RouteZoom and Figure 7b shows an example of printouts generated by TreePrint. These results are generated from identical route from The Community College of Baltimore to Sinai Hospital of Baltimore.

In Figure 7a, views for which a higher scale is needed to see the details are automatically suggested in each of the views. These views are appropriately connected and the user can use the smart-zoom and smart-slide functions to achieve easy and quick browsing of the route map. The red arrows in the figure suggest zooming transitions between the parent and child views while the blue arrows suggest sliding transitions.

In Figure 7b, the mid-scale view on pages 2-7 effectively visualizes the spatial relationship between each of the POIs, and enables each POI view to have a larger scale to give detailed information without losing context information of the route. The clear hierarchical indexing between complete overview, mid-scale view, and detailed POI view extract views necessary to the user.

EVALUATION

We conducted a user study for RouteZoom by comparing them with conventional methods. RouteZoom is basically an extension of a conventional route map browsing technique, and they both use similar types of map images for presenting information. Therefore, there is essentially no difference in the amount of information they can provide. The difference is in the speed at which correct information can be gotten and the interaction cost needed to get it. Thus, our goal in this user study is to confirm the following two hypotheses:

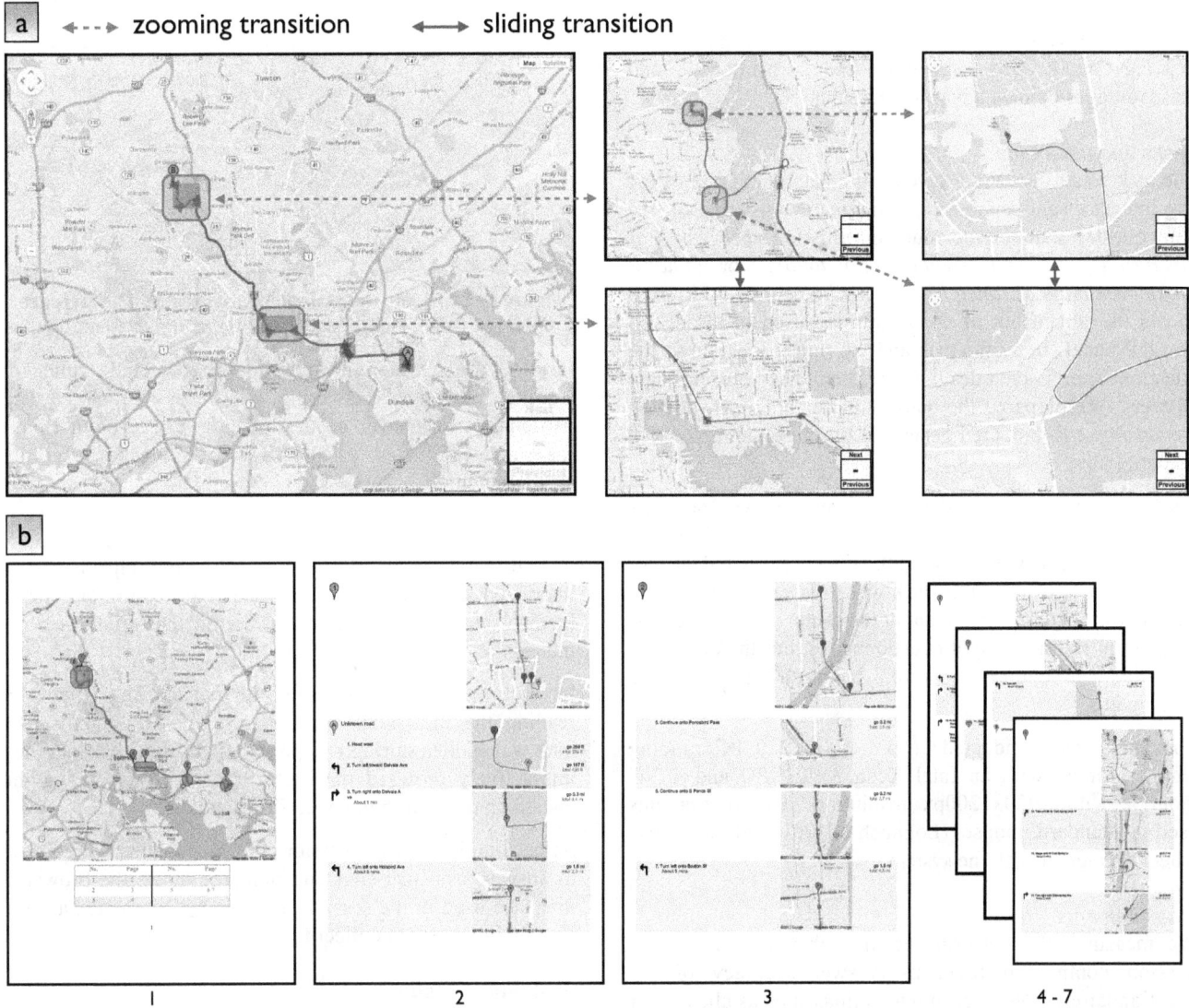

Figure 7: (a) Resultant view transitions on RouteZoom. Note that the user can also zoom-out to parent view by right click or clicking (-) command button on bottom-right of the map. (b) Example printing layout using map images generated by TreePrint.

H_1 The user can gain accurate route information in a shorter time using RouteZoom than using Baseline.

H_2 The user can gain accurate route information with a smaller number of interactions and in a shorter interaction time using RouteZoom than using Baseline interface.

To confirm these two hypotheses, we asked participants to work on a route information-searching task to measure the task completion time to operationalize H_1, and the number of interactions and the interaction time taken to complete the task to operationalize H_2. Note that H_1 concerns the overall time for completing a task while H_2 only concerns the portion of the task in which the user interacts with the route map. We recruited sixteen participants (twelve males, four females) from an IT corporate environment to conduct this study.

Interfaces
Two interfaces were compared in the study:

RouteZoom: The RouteZoom interface allows the participants to fully use the functions of the application that we described in the previous section.

Baseline: The Baseline interface allows the participants to pan the map by mouse dragging and to zoom by double clicking or scrolling the mouse wheel.

Although more advanced browsing interfaces such as multiview or fisheye exist, we chose a simple one-view panning and zooming interface as the Baseline interface. This is because 1) the Baseline interface is the one having the most basic and popular interaction style among conventional map systems [9, 19] and 2) our method of adding semantic view extraction to navigation interface is orthogonal to advanced methods such as multiview or fisheye. They are not mutually exclusive and it is possible to combined with our method. Our study thus complements existing work [6] showing the advantages and disadvantages of such advanced methods.

Tasks and Apparatus

The task was to browse a given route map using one of the two interfaces and answer a questionnaire consisting of five item questions about the route information such as *"For this turn X, which is the right direction to take"*, or *"What is the approximate distance from turn X to turn Y?"* Figure 8 shows the screenshot of the system we used in the study. The left panel shows the map and the right panel shows the questionnaire. Each questionnaire item has four possible answers. We prepared the questionnaires before inspecting the resulting Route Tree generated by the system to avoid potential bias.

Each participant was asked to complete two sessions sequentially, one session using the Baseline interface and the other using RouteZoom. Each session consisted of four trials, for each of which the task was to browse a route map and answer a questionnaire about the route. All participants worked on the same eight questionnaires, but the order and condition assignments were balanced among the participants.

The study was conducted on a Lenovo S20 PC running Ubuntu Linux, with an Intel Xeon 3690 CPU and a 24" monitor with 1920x1200px resolution. The participants used a standard mouse (Logitech G400) with a mouse wheel to interact with the system.

Measurements

We measured the performance of each participant by 1) Session completion time, 2) Answer accuracy of the questionnaire, 3) Number of interactions such as clicking or mouse wheel rolling, and 4) Interaction time for operating the map. Note that while the session completion time addresses the total time taken for completing all tasks in the

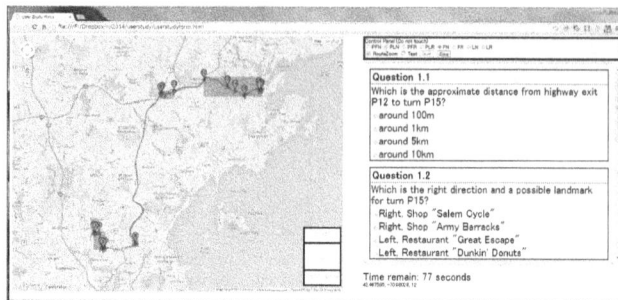

Figure 8: Experimental system for user study. The texts are enlarged from original size for better visual presentation.

session, the interaction time does not include time for reading maps and answering questions. We also asked participants to answer a questionnaire with 7-point Likert scale and conducted an interview for subjective usability measurements.

Procedures

Before starting each session, the participants were instructed to complete two practice trials to familiarize themselves with the system and the browsing interface for the session.

In each trial in the session, the participants began by reading the in-session questionnaire for 30 seconds (the map was hidden during this preparation time) and then they interactively browsed the route map while answering the questionnaire within the next 90 seconds.

After completing each session, the participants were asked to answer a post-session questionnaire about the browsing interface used in the session. Finally, we conducted a post-session interview to collect feedbacks.

Evaluation Results

Figure 9a shows the quantitative results for mean session completion time, answer accuracy, number of interactions, and map interaction time taken. The post-session

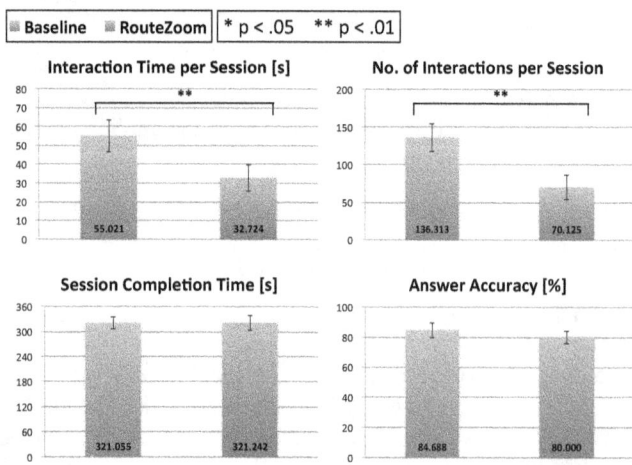

(a) Objective Measurements

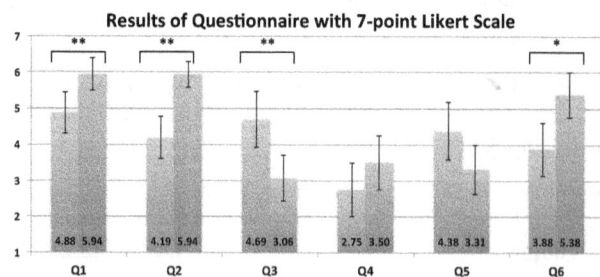

No.	Questions	p
Q1	I can quickly browse route maps with this method.	.008
Q2	It is easy to browse route maps with this method.	.000
Q3	This method requires much operation to browse a route map.	.007
Q4	A lot of training is necessary to use this method.	.171
Q5	I get tired when operating maps with this method.	.129
Q6	I want to use this method in the future.	.010

(b) Subjective Evaluations

Figure 9: Results for RouteZoom user study.

questionnaire results (7-point Likert scale) are shown in Figure 9b along with the questions asked. We respectively used a paired t-test and a Wilcoxon signed-rank test to analyze the quantitative and qualitative results.

Objective Measurements
There were no significant differences in the session completion time for a session (p=.979), meaning that H_1 was not supported. On the other hand, there were significant differences in both map interaction time taken (p=.000) and number of interactions (p=.000), while there were no significant differences in the answer accuracy (p=.141). This demonstrates hypothesis H_2 was supported.

Table 2 shows detail of interaction time taken and number of interactions per session for each interface. The results shows that more zoom interactions are replaced by automatic zooming ((z_a-z_b)/z_a=0.70 in time and 0.68 in number) than pan interactions by automatic panning ((p_a-p_b)/p_a=0.50 and 0.57). On the other hand, the replaced interaction cost is reduced more efficiently by automatic panning (p_b'/(p_a-p_b)=0.20 in time and 0.12 in number) than automatic zooming (z_b'/(z_a-z_b)=0.42 and 0.31).

One possible reason H_1 was not supported is that the users' behavior was mostly affected by the given time constraint (90 sec per question set) and not by the technique. The users apparently used the extra time due to the reduced interaction time to work on problems longer. This did not contribute to improved answer accuracy because most of the mistakes were the result of fundamental misunderstandings about the route information.

Although H_1 was not supported in our study, the reduced number of interactions and interaction time by RouteZoom would have considerable impact on navigation safety, because less interaction cost will greatly help to prevent the user from being distracted from their driving or walking. It may also have a positive impact on the session completion time in terms of practical conditions, because many car navigation systems adopt more adverse input conditions than those in our user study (high performance wheel mouse and large display).

Subjective Evaluations
The post-session questionnaire results showed that on the whole the participants preferred RouteZoom to the Baseline

Method	Baseline (a)		RouteZoom (b)	
	Time (s)	No.	Time (s)	No.
Zoom (z)	28.33	90.44	8.42	29.38
Pan (p)	26.69	45.88	13.22	19.75
Auto zoom (z')	-	-	8.33	18.88
Auto pan (p')	-	-	2.76	3.06

Table 2: Comparison of interaction costs between two interfaces. Note that smart slide function in RouteZoom not only automatically pans the view but may also zoom it.

interface (Figure 9b). In particular, they felt RouteZoom was a *"quicker"* way to browse the route maps than the Baseline method. This is probably because the users had to constantly move their hands and fingers to change the view with the Baseline method and thus felt the time taken for the interaction was the bottleneck. RouteZoom removed this bottleneck and was positively received by the users.

The results also show that the users felt it was easier to browse route maps with fewer operations when using RouteZoom. This corresponds to the reduced interaction-cost shown in the quantitative results. With respect to the learning effort needed for using these two methods, the results for Q4 show that although the participants were already familiar with the conventional method, for them there was no significant difference between the two methods. This indicates that RouteZoom is easy to learn. The participants also indicated they would like to use RouteZoom in the future.

In addition to answering the structured post-session questionnaire, participants were asked to give comments and suggestions about RouteZoom in the post-study interview. We received many positive comments, such as that RouteZoom was *"quick and easy"* and that it provided *"good positioning to appropriate views."* They also pointed out usability issues that we can improve on, such as *"Sometimes suggestions in the map were too small to read easily."* It is worth mentioning that while several participants highly preferred the smart slide function, several others never used it during the study and commented that they did not want to shift their focus from the map to the command button at the bottom left corner. We can easily address this issue by providing a keyboard shortcut for triggering the function.

DESIGN IMPLICATIONS
A Route Tree is a general representation with various possible applications, which is not limited to two applications we proposed in this paper. For example, advanced browsing techniques such as multiview control and fisheye zooming can be applied to a Route Tree. We can enable users to select suggested areas on the parent view to instantly change not only the position but also the zoom level of the detailed view. By enabling the Route Tree to support the fisheye technique, we can allow the system users to automatically change the zoom level depending on the position of the fisheye lens on the map.

A Route Tree also enables the user to control the route map by giving voice commands such as *"Zoom in to area 1"*, *"Zoom out"*, or *"(Slide to) next"*. This would be much faster and less distracting for the users than existing voice-enhanced browsing methods (e.g., [14]), because most of them require the user to constantly focus on the display.

A Route Tree could also improve the automatic view transition function provided by real-time step-by-step navigation system. It would reduce the number of view transitions by optimizing the number of views to a minimum while preserving necessary information for the users. This would provide a less stressful navigation experience to the user.

CONCLUSION

We proposed a hierarchical structure for route maps called a "Route Tree." It helps users to move back and forth across multiple views with different scale levels and positions in a map. We also proposed an algorithm to automatically construct a Route Tree and two Route Tree applications. These are "RouteZoom", an interactive map application where the user interactively browses a hierarchical map, and "TreePrint", which uses the hierarchical structure to generate 3 kinds of map images suitable for printing out. We conducted a user study with RouteZoom. The results showed that the application effectively reduces users' map interaction costs and is well perceived by the user in terms of its quickness and easiness to use.

REFERENCES

1. Agrawala, M. and Stolte, C. Rendering effective route maps. In *Proc. SIGGRAPH 2001*, ACM Press (2001), 241-249.

2. Appert, C., Chapuis, O., and Pietriga, E. High-precision magnification lenses. In *Proc. CHI 2010*, ACM Press (2010), 273–282.

3. Bing Maps Tile System. http://msdn.microsoft.com/en-us/library/bb259689.aspx.

4. Carpendale, M. S. T., Ligh, J. and Pattison, E. Achieving higher magnification in context. In *Proc. UIST 2004*, ACM Press (2004), 71–80.

5. Chen, B., Neubert, B., Ofek, E., Deussen, O., and Cohen, M.F. Integrated videos and maps for driving directions. In *Proc. UIST 2009*, ACM Press (2009), 223-232.

6. Cockburn, A., Karison, A., and Bederson, B.B. A review of overview+detail, zooming, and focus+context interfaces. ACM Computing Surveys 41, 1 (2008), 2:1-2:31.

7. Furnas, G.W. Generalized fisheye views. *ACM SIGCHI Bulletin 17*, 4 (1986), 16-23.

8. Google Directions API. *https://developers.google.com/maps/documentation/directions/*.

9. Google Maps. http://maps.google.com/.

10. Grabler, F., Agrawala, M., Sumner, R.W., and Pauly, M. Automatic generation of tourist maps. *ACM TOG 27*, 3 (2008), 100:1–100:11.

11. Hirtle, S.C. and Srinivas, S. Enriching spatial knowledge through a multiattribute locational system. In *Proc. ICSC 2010*, Springer-Verlag (2010), 279-288.

12. Hornbæk, K. Bederson, B. B. and Plaisant, C. Navigation patterns and usability of zoomable user interfaces with and without an overview. *ACM TOCHI 9*, 4 (2002), 362–389.

13. Igarashi, T. and Hinckley, K. Speed-dependent automatic zooming for browsing large documents. In *Proc. UIST 2000*, ACM Press (2000), 139-148.

14. Igarashi.T. and Hughes, J.F. "Voice as Sound: Using Non-verbal Voice Input for Interactive Control" In *Proc. UIST 2001*, ACM Press (2001), 155-156.

15. Javed, W., Ghani, S., and Elmqvist, N. PolyZoom: Multiscale and Multifocus Exploration in 2D Visual Spaces. In *Proc. CHI 2012*, ACM Press (2012), 287-296.

16. Karnick, P., Cline, D., Jeschke, S., Razdan, A., and Wonka, P. Route visualization using detail lenses. *IEEE TVCG 16*, 2 (2009), 235-247.

17. Klippel, A., Hansen, S., Richter, K., and Winter, S. Urban granularities—a data structure for cognitively ergonomic route directions. *GeoInformatica 13*, 2 (2008), 223-247.

18. Kopf, J., Agrawala, M., Bargeron, D. Salesin, D., and Cohen, M. Automatic generation of destination maps. *ACM TOG 29*, 6 (2010), 158:1–158:12.

19. MapQuest. http://www.mapquest.com/.

20. Martinez, A. Automated insetting: An expert component embedded in the census bureau's map production system. In *Proc. AutoCarto 9*, CaGIS (1989), 181-190.

21. NavEngine. http://developers.cloudmade.com/projects/show/navengine.

22. Patel, K., Chen, M.Y., Smith, I., and Landay, J.A. Personalizing routes. In *Proc. UIST 2006*, ACM Press (2006), 187-190.

23. Pindat, C., Pietriga, E., Chapuis, O., and Puech, C. JellyLens: content-aware adaptive lenses. In *Proc. UIST 2012*, ACM Press (2012), 261-270.

24. Robbins, D.C., Cutrell, E., Sarin, R., and Horvitz, E. ZoneZoom. In *Proc. AVI 2004*, ACM Press (2004), 231-234.

25. Schmid, F. Knowledge-based wayfinding maps for small display cartography. *JLBS 2*, 1 (2008), 57-83.

26. Tenbrink, T. and Winter, S. Variable Granularity in Route Directions. *Spatial Cognition & Computation 9*, 1 (2009), 64-93.

27. Timpf, S. Hierarchical Structures in Map Series, Ph.D Thesis. Technical University of Vienna, Institute for Geoinformation, 1998.

28. Zhao, J., Wigdor, D., and Balakrishnan, R. TrailMap: facilitating information seeking in a multi-scale digital map via implicit bookmarking. In *Proc. CHI 2013*, ACM Press (2013), 3009-3018.

STAR-CITY:
Semantic Traffic Analytics and Reasoning for CITY *

Freddy Lécué, Simone Tallevi-Diotallevi, Jer Hayes, Robert Tucker,
Veli Bicer, Marco Luca Sbodio, Pierpaolo Tommasi
IBM Research, Smarter Cities Technology Centre
Dublin, Ireland
firstname.lastname@ie.ibm.com

ABSTRACT

This paper presents STAR-CITY, a system supporting semantic traffic analytics and reasoning for city. STAR-CITY, which integrates (human and machine-based) sensor data using variety of formats, velocities and volumes, has been designed to provide insight on historical and real-time traffic conditions, all supporting efficient urban planning. Our system demonstrates how the severity of road traffic congestion can be smoothly analyzed, diagnosed, explored and predicted using semantic web technologies. We present how semantic diagnosis and predictive reasoning, both using and interpreting semantics of data to deliver useful, accurate and consistent inferences, have been exploited and adapted systematized in an intelligent user interface. Our prototype of semantics-aware traffic analytics and reasoning, experimented in Dublin City Ireland, works and scales efficiently with historical together with real live and heterogeneous stream data.

Author Keywords

Intelligent user interfaces; semantic web; semantic reasoning; automated system; transportation

ACM Classification Keywords

H.5.2. [Information Interfaces and Presentation]: User Interfaces; I.2.4. [Knowledge Representation Formalisms and Methods].

INTRODUCTION

As the number of vehicles on the road steadily increases and the expansion of roadways remains static, congestion in cities and urban areas became one of the major transportation issues in most industrial countries [20]. Urban traffic costs 5.5 billion hours of travel delay and 2.9 billion gallons of wasted fuel in the USA only, all at the price of $121 billion per year.

*The research leading to these results has received funding from the European Union's Seventh Framework Programme (FP7/2007-2013) under grant agreement ID 318201 (SIMPLI-CITY).

Even worse, the costs of extra time and wasted fuel has quintupled over the past 30 years. It also used to stress and frustrate motorists, encouraging road rage and reducing health of motorists [12]. All of them, among others, are examples of negative effects of congestion in cities.

Two ways can be considered to reduce congestion [4]; one is to improve the infrastructure e.g., by increasing the road capacity, but this requires enormous expenditure. Another solution is to determine where, when, and why congestion will be occurring, which will support transportation departments to proactively manage the traffic before congestion is reached e.g., changing traffic light strategy, re-routing.

STAR-CITY[1,2] (**S**emantic **T**raffic **A**nalytics and **R**easoning for **CITY**), as a system which integrates heterogeneous data in terms of format variety (structured and unstructured data), velocity (static and stream data) and volume (large amount of historical data), has been mainly designed to provide such insights on historical and real-time traffic conditions. Most of the existing modern traffic systems such as US TrafficView[3] [17], Italian 5T[4] mainly focus on monitoring traffic status in cities using dedicated sensors (e.g., loop indiction detectors), all exposing numerical data. Others, more citizen-centric such as the traffic layer of Google Maps provide real-time traffic conditions and estimation but do not deliver insight to interpret historical and real-time traffic conditions. Basic in-depth but semantics-less state-of-the-art analytics are employed, limiting also large scale real-time data integration. Therefore, context-aware computing together with reusability of the underlying data is quite limited.

STAR-CITY tackles these limitations by interpreting the semantics of contextual information and then deriving innovative and easy-to-explore insights. In particular STAR-CITY, designed as a web-based application, extends state-of-the-art traffic systems by seamlessly and smoothly integrating and augmenting the following in an intelligent user interface:

(i) in-depth *analysis* of historical and real-time road traffic conditions, which supports any spatio-temporal comparison of road traffic conditions,

[1] Video (.avi, .mov, m4v format) available: http://goo.gl/TuwNyL
[2] Live system: http://dublinked.ie/sandbox/star-city/
[3] https://trafficview.org/
[4] http://www.5t.torino.it/5t/

(ii) *diagnosis* [9], which aims at connecting road traffic congestion to its causes through explanations,

(iii) *contextual exploration* [6], deriving spatio-temporal similarities of traffic congestion and its diagnosis,

(iv) more accurate traffic *forecasting* using recent theoretical research work in contextual predictive reasoning [13].

The system is used on a daily and real-time basis to understand how traffic condition is evolving over time / space, but also why. From a city planning perspective, the diagnosis part is used for understanding which events causes what types of congestion. Thus they can better plan events in the city.

The novelty of STAR-CITY lies in the ability of the system to ingest highly heterogeneous real-time data (c.f., Table 1) and perform various types of inferences i.e., analysis, diagnosis, exploration and prediction. These inferences are all elaborated through a combination of various types of reasoning i.e., (i) semantic based i.e., distributed ontology classification-based subsumption [16], (ii) rules-based i.e., pattern association [13], (iii) machine learning-based i.e., entities search [6] and (iv) sensor stream-based i.e., correlation [13].

STAR-CITY completely relies on the W3C semantic Web stack e.g., OWL 2 (Web Ontology Language) and RDF (Resource Description Framework) for representing semantics of information and delivering inference outcomes. Currently applied in the context of Dublin City, STAR-CITY can scale to any other city, which exposes data sensors of any kind.

This paper is organized as follows: The next section presents the Dublin city context. Then we sketch in-use scenarios for STAR-CITY, and describe its main technologies. The next section reports some experimental results regarding scalability and accuracy. Finally we briefly comment on related work, draw some conclusions and talks about future directions.

CONTEXT: TRANSPORTATION IN DUBLIN CITY

Table 1 reports all data sources processed by STAR-CITY in the Dublin scenario with respect to their velocity i.e., static, quasi stream, stream. They report various types of information coming from static or dynamic sensors, exposed as open, public data and described along heterogeneous formats.

The *journey times* data stream is used for (i) monitoring road traffic flow (i.e., free, moderate, heavy, stopped) between static sensors, and (ii) deriving congestion and its severity (i.e., spatial and temporal representation of traffic queues [5]) across 47 routes and its 732 points in Dublin city (updated every minute), all in real-time. Analyzing, diagnosing exploring and predicting the characteristics of this stream consists in interpreting, contextualizing and correlating its content with these six exogenous data sources: (1) *road weather condition* which captures specific features of roads conditions in Dublin city e.g., road temperature along 11 static stations, (2) *weather information* e.g., general condition, temperature, precipitation along 19 static stations, (3) *Dublin bus stream* which senses location, speed, delay of 1000 buses every 20 seconds, (4) *social media feeds* which relate traffic-related information e.g., accident, delays, last minute road closure from reputable sources, with an average of 132 tweets per day, (5) *road works and maintenance* which plan roads disruptions,

their type, duration and (potential) impact on traffic, with an average of 59 road works per day, all updated on a weekly basis, (6) *social events* which characterize events of various type e.g., music, sport, politics, family, with an average of 187 events per day, all updated on a daily basis. In the following we will denote by "*city events*" all types of events in a city i.e., social events, road works and incidents.

Figure 1 spatially represents the static traffic-related sensors of Table 1: journey times, road condition, weather stations. The ESRI SHAPE file of Dublin city, describing spatial-related elements, is used for identifying nearby roads and their spatial-based segment representation.

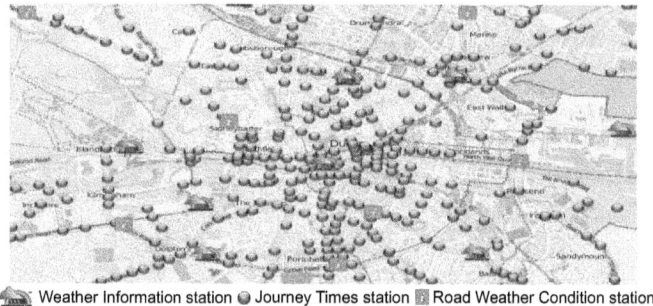

🚗 Weather Information station ◉ Journey Times station ▣ Road Weather Condition station

Figure 1: Static Traffic-related Sensors in Dublin (color print)

STAR-CITY SCENARIO, CHALLENGES AND APPROACH

The STAR-CITY system is illustrated through a list of scenarios, where each highlights actions that any city manager is required to perform on a daily basis. Existing systems fails in supporting these scenarios because of the not-so-easy tasks of data integration and underlying contextual semantic reasoning. The use of semantic web technologies is transparent to end-users. However such technologies are strongly required to (i) encode semantic information through real-time transformation, (ii) compile and deliver contextual analysis, diagnosis, exploration and prediction form such heterogenous data sets. All user interactions (UI) are achieved through simple UI paradigms e.g., spatial and temporal selection for initialization (respectively ①, ② and ③ in Figure 2), where similar time intervals over several days can be selected e.g., from 10 : 00 to 17 : 00 in ②. All results, delivered by analysis, diagnosis, exploration and prediction, are dynamically exported as parallel, spider, pie, graph-based and time-series charts.

For each scenario, we sketch its (i) description, (ii) motivation, (iii) challenge, together with (iv) the STAR-CITY approach, its (v) scalability and (vi) limitation.

Spatio-Temporal Analysis of Traffic Status

• *Description & Motivation*: City traffic managers are interested in both historical and real-time information of traffic status (discretized as free, low, moderate, heavy, stopped flow) in order to visually extract the pulse of the city traffic together with its context at any time and space.

• *Challenge*: In a context of real-time information, stream journey times data needs to be processed in real-time while fast aggregation (average, max, min) is required for historical

Type	Sens-ing	Data Source	Description	Format	Temporal Frequency (s)	Size per day (GBytes)	Data Provider (all open data)
Stream Data	Static	Journey times across Dublin City (47 routes)	Dublin Traffic Department's TRIPS system[a]	CSV	60	0.1	Dublin City Council via dublinked.ie[b]
		Road Weather Condition (11 stations)		CSV	600	0.1	NRA[c]
		Real-time Weather Information (19 stations)		CSV	[5, 600] (depending on stations)	[0.050, 1.5] (depending on stations)	Wunderground[d]
	Dynamic	Dublin Bus Stream	Vehicle activity (GPS location, line number, delay, stop flag)	SIRI: XML-based[e]	20	4-6	Dublin City Council via dublinked.ie[f]
		Social-Media Related Feeds	Reputable sources of road traffic conditions in Dublin City	Tweets	600	0.001 (approx. 150 tweets per day)	LiveDrive[g] Aaroadwatch[h] GardaTraffic[i]
Quasi Stream	Dynamic	Road Works and Maintenance		PDF	Updated once a week	0.001	Dublin City Council[j]
		Events in Dublin City	Planned events with small attendance	XML	Updated once a day	0.001	Eventbrite[k]
			Planned events with large attendance			0.05	Eventful[l]
Static	Static	Dublin City Map (listing of type, junctions, GPS coordinate)		ESRI SHAPE	No	0.1	Open StreetMap[m]

[a] Travel-time Reporting Integrated Performance System - http://www.advantechdesign.com.au/trips

[b] http://dublinked.ie/datastore/datasets/dataset-215.php

[c] NRA - National Roads Authority - http://www.nratraffic.ie/weather

[d] http://www.wunderground.com/weather/api/

[e] Service Interface for Real Time Information - http://siri.org.uk

[f] http://dublinked.com/datastore/datasets/dataset-289.php

[g] https://twitter.com/LiveDrive

[h] https://twitter.com/aaroadwatch

[i] https://twitter.com/GardaTraffic

[j] http://www.dublincity.ie/RoadsandTraffic/ScheduledDisruptions/Documents/TrafficNews.pdf

[k] https://www.eventbrite.com/api

[l] http://api.eventful.com

[m] http://download.geofabrik.de/europe/ireland-and-northern-ireland.html

Table 1: (Raw) Data Sources for Dublin City Traffic Prediction Scenario

analysis of traffic status. In both contexts rules-based mechanisms are required to capture and infer traffic status.

• *Approach*: It consists in discretizing numerical values of travel time (described through road, link, sensors) in traffic status with rules-based mechanisms. Intuitively, rules are encoded using SWRL (Semantic Web Rule language[5]) rules (associated ontologies and rules available[6]). Contrary to state-of-the-art approaches, the traffic condition is not only established based on historical information but also based on contextual information. Our system could, for example, trigger the rule (1) *"the traffic flow of road r_1 is heavy if its travel time is much longer than usual and if r_1 is adjacent to a road r_2 where an accident occurs and the humidity is optimum"*. This rule connects the *journey times*, *social media* and *weather information* data streams together with historical information.

$HeavyTrafficFlow(s) \leftarrow$
    $Road(r_1) \wedge Road(r_2) \wedge isAdjacentTo(r_1, r_2) \wedge$
    $TravelTime(r_1, t_1) \wedge TravelTimeMax(r_1, m_1) \wedge$
    $lessThan(m_1, t_1) \wedge$
    $hasWeatherPhenomenon(r_1, w) \wedge OptimunHuminidity(w) \wedge$
    $hasTravelStatus(r_1, s) \wedge hasTrafficPhenomenon(r_2, a) \wedge$
    $RoadTrafficAccident(a)$ (1)

[5] http://www.w3.org/Submission/SWRL/
[6] http://goo.gl/5TbTT2

The component ⑤ in Figure 2 embeds the results in a parallel chart, where the status (green, yellow, orange, red and black coloring) of each road segment together with its distance, minimal, maximal and average travel time are reported. Some weather information ④ can be also displayed to understand the context of the analysis. The table, reported as ⑥, gives a detailed view, where a selection of a row highlights the corresponding elements in both the parallel chart and the map. The pie chart ⑦ establishes the proportion of road traffic status in the boundary box ③.

• *Scalability*: On the server side the approach is scalable up to twenty weeks (i.e., through appropriate selection of ① and ② in Figure 2) of aggregated journey travel time.

• *Limitation*: The search and aggregation over tens of months become more challenging because of the large number of journey travel time data and SWRL-based reasoning to be processed. This can be partially resolved by pre-aggregating journey travel time e.g., every 30 minutes instead of 1 minute.

Spatio-Temporal Diagnosis of Traffic Status

• *Description*: How to identify the nature and cause of traffic congestion in real-time? How to capture diagnosis results on a spatial and (historical) temporal basis? The diagnosis component, selected from tabs ⑧, addresses these challenges.

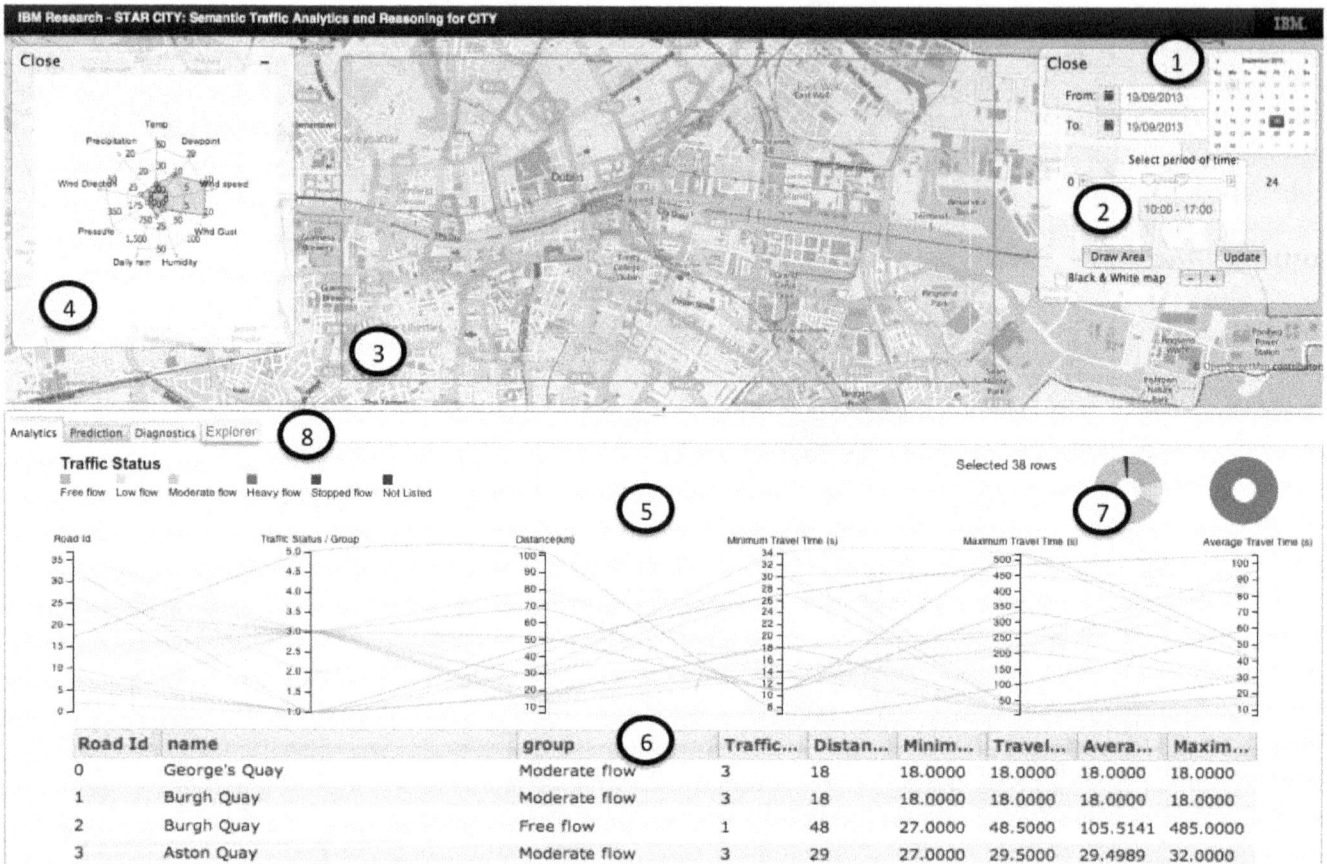

Figure 2: Interface of STAR-CITY. ①, ②: Temporal (Date and Time) context (subject to user selection), ③: Spatial (Map Area) context (subject to user selection), ④: Weather context for the spatio-temporal analysis, ⑤: Travel time status vs. historical min., max., average travel time (segments are select-able), ⑥: Detailed version of travel time information (records are select-able with automated update on the parallel chart and map),⑦: Spatio-temporal proportion of travel time status. ⑧: Tab-based selection of analytics and reasoning: prediction, diagnosis, exploration. (color print).

- *Motivation*: These are general questions which cannot be answered by existing state-of-the-art traffic systems, but of really importance for city managers to better understand and plan her/his cities at any time.

- *Challenge*: Such question remains open because (i) relevant data sets (e.g., road works, social events, incidents), (ii) their correlation (e.g., road works and social events connected to the same city area) and (iii) historical traffic conditions (e.g., road works and congestion in Canal street on July 24th, 2013) are not fully open, integrated and jointly exploited.

- *Approach* (Figure 3): STAR-CITY exploits the semantics of streams exposed by sensors and its underlying data.

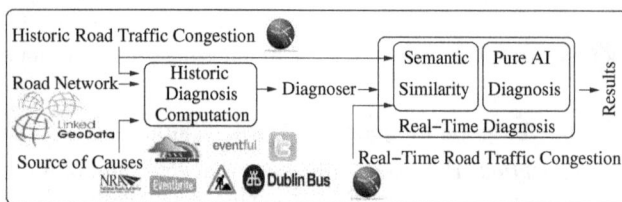

Figure 3: Diagnosis Approach Overview.

It compiles off-line all historic diagnosis information into a deterministic finite state machine, following the structure of Dublin road network (using linkgeodata.org). The network is used (i) to properly connect roads and (ii) for exploiting congestion propagation. The state machine is augmented with respect to all semantic-augmented city events and weather conditions where a subset of them are connected to past congestion and the probability with which they have caused it. The real-time diagnosis of traffic condition is performed by analyzing the historical versions of the state machines to retrieve similar contexts i.e., congestion, potential explanation (i.e., city events), weather information. The similarity is estimated by comparing semantic descriptions of the context.

STAR-CITY extends [9] by supporting both scalable real-time and historical aggregation of traffic congestion anomalies and its diagnosis results (Figures 4-6). Figure 4 illustrates the number of traffic congestion (red-highlighted number) which has been retrieved given the time window. In addition to a spatial representation of traffic conditions and their diagnosis (red and blue icons for respectively congestion and diagnosis in Figure 5), STAR-CITY exposes a spider chart (⑫ and ⑭) together with pie charts (⑬ and ⑮) to compile and compare the impact of city events on the traffic conditions in Figure 6. ②2 (respectively ③3) represents all types (respectively subtypes) of city events occurring in the selected area of the city while ④4 (respectively ⑤5) captures all types (respectively subtypes) of city events which negatively impact (i.e., diagnose) the traffic conditions. E.g., most of congestion is due to social events ④4 i.e., 72% and more particularly music events ⑤5 although 34% of city events are road works in the spatio-temporal context of Figure 6. All results in Figures 4, 5, 6 can be interpreted by city managers to understand how traffic condition is impacted by any type of city event.

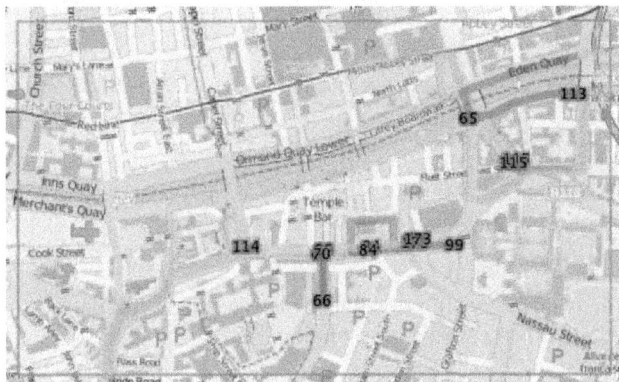

Figure 4: Traffic Congestion Anomaly. The red-highlighted numbers refer to the number of traffic congestion in the spatio-temporal context of Figure 2 (color print).

• *Scalability*: Diagnosis reasoning strongly relies on classification of semantic stream data in Table 1. Classification, or the computation of subsumption hierarchies for classes and properties of the semantic representations, is required to quickly determine semantic matching (or similarity) of contexts (e.g., city events, weather context) in real-time. The scalability of diagnosis is ensured through a distributed classification [16] of individual contexts. All rules, which are required for classification, are distributed across various nodes based on their types. Fast processing and search is also ensures through spatial and temporal indexes of all anomalies (i.e., traffic congestion), city events and contexts. DB2 Temporal and Spatial extensions[7] are combined for this challenge.

• *Limitation*: The current implementation is limited to OWL EL[8] as semantic encoding of city events for the computation of semantic similarity. The OWL 2 EL profile is designed as a subset of OWL 2 that is suitable in our context since ontology classification can be decided in polynomial time, hence scalable. The on-the-fly integration of new data sources (e.g., city events and context), exposed as raw data, with our semantic representation of data in Table 1 is not straightforward. In addition it requires not only a careful semantic integration at spatio-temporal level but also an appropriate alignment of vocabularies. The latter will ensure a seamless integration, which is required by the matching-based diagnosis reasoning component. Finally, a large number of historical data is required to reach good results: 458 days of data in our context.

[7]http://www-03.ibm.com/software/products/us/en/db2spaext/
[8]http://www.w3.org/TR/owl2-profiles/

Spatio-Temporal Exploration of Contextual Information

• *Description*: STAR-CITY enables the city managers to explore contextual information related to some city events and traffic conditions. The exploration is achieved on a temporal dimension where similar traffic conditions and their diagnosis can be easily retrieved based on historical semantic data.

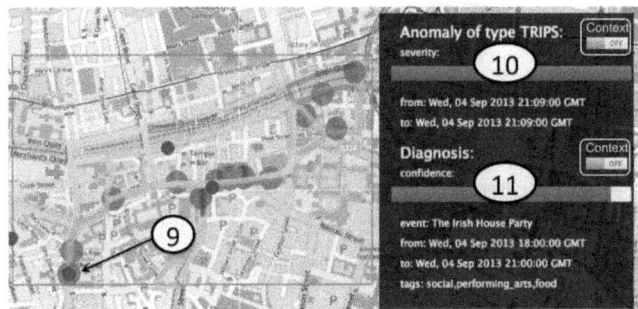

Figure 5: Diagnosis Interpretation. An example of traffic congestion (red points) where one i.e., ⑨9 is diagnosed by 4 (blue points) explanations. ⑩10: Detailed descriptions (severity, date, time) of congestion, ⑪11: Detailed description (city event name, date, time, type) of diagnosis (color print).

• *Motivation*: It gives an in-depth understanding of similar city events and their impact on a temporal basis. Contrary to the pure diagnosis component (Figures 4, 5, 6), the STAR-CITY explorer gives the city managers the ability to easily retrieve not only past but also similar snapshots and contexts of traffic conditions, its congestion, city events and diagnosis.

• *Challenge*: Retrieving the relevant contextual information over heterogeneous and vast city data is a challenging task since classical search techniques are limited in terms of (i) identifying the information needs of the city managers, (ii) handling the contextual information to find similar settings which occurred in the past, and (iii) utilizing heterogeneous and semantic data to retrieve accurate information.

• *Approach*: We address these issues by using semantic search technologies [6]. It extends them significantly to handle both the context (i.e., type of congestion severity, type of diagnosis) and spatio-temporal dimensions. As a first step, the city manager selects the context is interested in. To this end, the toggle switch of either the anomaly or diagnosis needs to be on. For example, the diagnosis in Figure 7 is selected as the context of the exploration c.f., ⑯16. By default the context is empty and can be filled by any anomaly and diagnosis. Once the context is captured and the explorer tab is selected, the system formulates a contextual semantic query is formulated to identify the actual information needed by the city manager. The context sets up the constraints of the query. Then, it retrieves the relevant information (e.g., diagnosis, traffic conditions) that occurred in a similar context by using its underlying semantic search engine and displays the search results on the map. E.g., only diagnosis of type "social", "performing_arts", and "food", similar to ⑰17, causing a past congestion in the area is retrieved in ⑱18 of Figure 7.

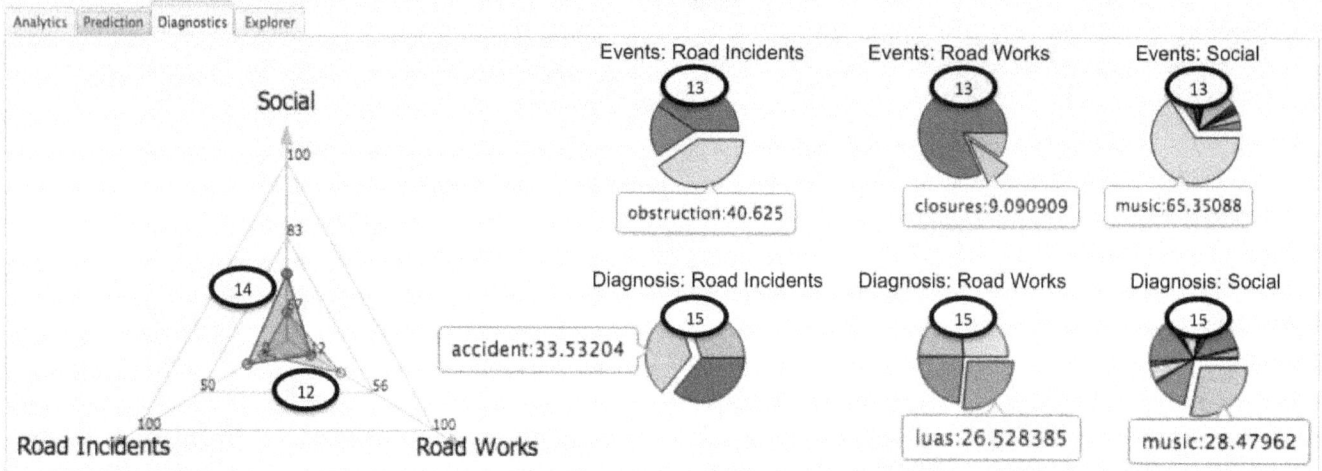

Figure 6: STAR-CITY Diagnosis: Impact of City Events on Traffic Conditions. ②: Proportion of city events which occurs in the spatio-temporal context, ③: Clustering and proportion of city events by subtypes, ④: Proportion of diagnosis (i.e, types of city events which cause a traffic congestion), ⑤ Clustering and proportion of diagnosis by subtypes (color print).

The STAR-CITY explorer provides insight about similar city events (or past congestion) in in the city (or of close proximity) with similar (i) time of the day, and (ii) weather context.

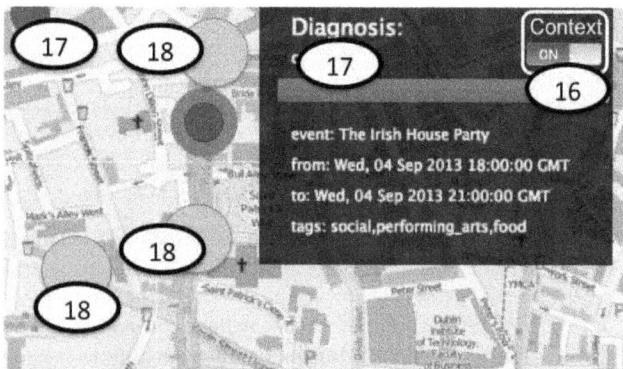

Figure 7: STAR-CITY Explorer. ⑥: Context capture on diagnosis, ⑦: Diagnosis as context, ⑧: Similar diagnosis of historical traffic congestion in the selected area (color print).

• *Scalability*: Similarly to diagnosis, the scalability of the explorer is ensured by the OWL 2 EL descriptions.

• *Limitation*: The temporal similarity is strictly based on time intervals. In other words the exploration is achieved on all city events and anomalies that meet this time interval. Some refinements of our approach are required to capture more generic and flexible temporal aspects such as anomalies and diagnosis during *rush hours*, *bank holidays*, *week-end*.

Traffic Status Prediction

• *Description*: Prediction, or the problem of estimating future observations given some historical information, is an important inference task required by city traffic managers.

• *Motivation*: It determines the future states of roads segments, which will support transportation departments and

their managers to proactively manage the traffic before congestion is reached e.g., changing traffic light strategy.

• *Challenge*: All existing approaches e.g., [21] have been mainly designed for very fast processing and mining of (syntactic and numerical) raw data from sensors. However they rarely utilize exogenous sources of information for adjusting estimated prediction. Inclement weather condition, a concert event, a car accident, peak hours are examples of external factors that strongly impact traffic flow and congestion [8]. They also all fail in using and interpreting underlying semantics of data, making prediction not as accurate and consistent as it could be, specially when data streams are characterized by texts (hence semantics), or sudden changes over time.

• *Approach*: STAR-CITY shows that the integration of numerous sensors, which expose heterogenous, exogenous and raw data streams such as weather information, road works, social events or incidents is a way forward to improve accuracy and consistency of traffic congestion prediction. For the sake of clarity Algorithm 1, illustrated with Figure 8, sketches the approach of predicting travel time data stream $\mathcal{O}_m^n$ at point of time $j \in [m, n]$ using weather information data stream $\mathcal{P}_m^n$ only, all using semantic representations. The approach mainly consists of: (i) auto-correlation of data on a time basis (lines 5, 6 - ⓐ in Figure 8) for retrieving all similar past weather conditions, (ii) association rules mining (lines 7-10 - ⓕ in Figure 8) for inferring correlation and rules between past weather condition and travel time e.g., rule (1) which explicits how weather condition may impact traffic status on road r_1, (iii) validation of prediction results in $\mathcal{O}_m^n(j)$ by analyzing its semantic consistency i.e., checking that no conflict of knowledge is occurring (e.g., free flow prediction while all connected roads are all congested). All prediction rules are extracted through association mining of semantic descriptions (across streams). Then they are filtered based on their occurrence (i.e., support) and confidence in line 9. The rule (1), extended with temporal dimension, is one example of such semantic rules[9]. The rule encoding is not new, but their inference at semantic level is. In the context of social media, all tweets are semantically described (if possible) through incidents, accident, obstruction, closures by analyzing their content. Their semantics is then associated with knowledge from other sources e.g., weather condition, traffic condition, types of events to infer weighted recurring rules.

Algorithm 1: Context-aware Travel Time Prediction (sketch)

1 **Input**: (i) Travel time data stream $\mathcal{O}_m^n$ (from time m to n) to be predicted, (ii) Weather data stream $\mathcal{P}_m^n$ used as context, (iii) Point of prediction time $j \in [m,n]$, (iv) Min. threshold of prediction rule support m_s, confidence m_c.

2 **Result**: $\mathcal{P}_m^n(j)$: Travel time predicted at point of time j.

3 **begin**

4     $\mathcal{R} \leftarrow \emptyset$; % Initialization of prediction rules set.

5   % Auto-correlation of contextual weather information.

6     $\tilde{\mathcal{P}}_m^n \leftarrow$ retrieve all similar contexts of $\mathcal{P}_m^n(j)$ in $[m,n]$;

7   % Stream association rules between $\tilde{\mathcal{P}}_m^n$ and $\mathcal{O}_m^n$.

8   **foreach** rule $\rho \in \tilde{\mathcal{P}}_m^n(k) \times \mathcal{O}_m^n(k), \forall k \in [m,n]$ **do**

9   **if** $support(\rho) > m_s \wedge confidence(\rho) > m_c$ **then**

10           $\mathcal{R} \leftarrow \mathcal{R} \cup \{\rho\}$;

11   % Semantic evaluation of rule $\rho \in \mathcal{R}$ at point of time j.

12   **foreach** $\rho \in \mathcal{R}$ of the form $\mathcal{G} \twoheadrightarrow h$ **do**

13   **if** h in semantically consistent with $\mathcal{O}_m^n(j)$ **then**

14   Apply rule ρ at point of time j of $\mathcal{O}_m^n$;

15   **return** $\mathcal{O}_m^n(j)$;

Figure 9 illustrates how predictions are handled in STAR-CITY. The future status of road segments (of the selected boundary box) and their proportion are reported up to five hours ahead. Different visualizations are offered i.e., area, bar, line, scatter to provide better comparison experiences.

• *Scalability*: Similarly to diagnosis and exploration, the scalability of prediction is coupled with the polynomial-time characteristics of subsumption-based reasoning in OWL 2 EL. Subsumption and classification are achieved to derive the consistency of prediction in line 13 of Algorithm 1. Scalability is not issue in our context, but could be with high through-put sensors (which can be the case in highly modern cities, or with private city traffic companies).

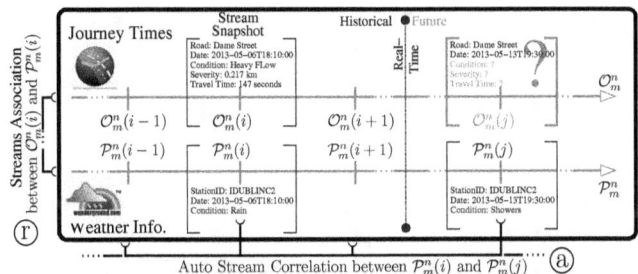

Figure 8: Context-Aware Travel Time Prediction. Capture of (i) records along one weather station and (ii) travel condition between two sensors on Dame Street at time i and j.

---

[9]Some example of semantic rules are publicly reported: http://goo.gl/5TbTT2

• *Limitation*: In the real world, sensors exhibit noise i.e., they do not observe the world perfectly. The causes range from malfunctioning, mis-calibration, to network issues and attrition breakdown. Noisy data needs to be detected early to avoid unnecessary semantic enrichment, which could lead to more important problems at prediction time. Indeed travel time associated to noisy context would lead to noisy model for prediction, reaching to completely inaccurate prediction. We partially addressed this problem by integrating some *custom filter operators* to check validity of data. The integration of new data, as context, needs a careful analysis of historical data in order to identify the most appropriate filters, avoiding as much noise as possible. Other drawbacks of the algorithms are: (i) impact of the context (i.e., stream data) , (ii) impact of the configuration of Algorithm 1 e.g., min. threshold, support, confidence, which all impact precision.

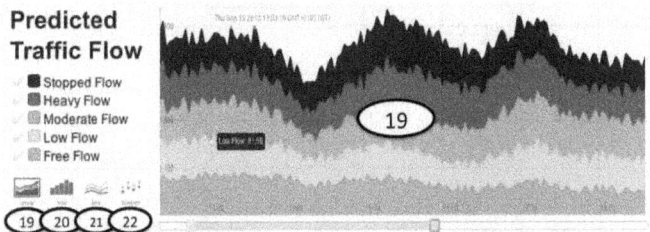

Figure 9: Prediction of Traffic Status. (19): area-, (20): bar-, (21): line-, (22): scatter-based visualization (color print).

STAR-CITY TECHNOLOGIES

This section sketches the main technologies behind STAR-CITY with a focus on the innovative reasoning parts, and details of the web-based application.

Semantic Representation

The model we consider to represent static background knowledge and semantics of data stream is provided by an ontology, encoded in OWL 2 EL. The selection of the W3C standard OWL 2 EL profile has been guided by (i) the expressivity which was required to model semantics of data in Table 1, (ii) the scalability of the underlying basic reasoning mechanisms we needed (c.f., scalability challenges of diagnosis, exploration and prediction). Semantic technologies were used to compare and evaluate different context e.g., events (and their properties: venue, category, size, types / subtypes), weather information (highly / moderate / low windy, rainy; good / moderate / bad weather condition). More importantly they were required for (automatically) designing, learning, applying rules at reasoning time for analysis, diagnosis and prediction components. At the end, all interfaces of STAR-CITY produces and consumes semantic representation of data. All interactions of STAR-CITY are possible because of the semantic engine, which runs behind the scene. For instance, the spatio-temporal exploration of diagnosis is only possible if the underlying data is described with semantics.

Semantic Enrichment

All raw data streams in Table 1 are served as real-time OWL 2 EL ontology streams (i.e., stream of semantic-encoded data) [13] by using InfoSphere Streams [7]. Different mapping strategies are used depending on the data format. For instance

XSLT for XML, Typifier [15] for tweeter feeds or custom OWL 2 EL mapping for CSV have been used. All the ontology streams have the same static background knowledge to capture time (W3C Time Ontology[10]), space (W3C Geo Ontology[11]) but differ only in some domain-related vocabularies e.g., traffic flow type, weather phenomenon, event type, road work, incident. These ontologies, publicly available[6], have been mainly used for enriching raw data (and its context), facilitating its integration and comparison over time. The main innovation is related to the real-time transformation of stream data using a stream processing engine. STAR-CITY provides a generic mechanism for enriching real-time raw data using a pre-defined mapping descriptor.

Knowledge Extraction
The main challenges were related to (i) variety of update frequency of streams, (ii) heterogenous data format, (iii) difficulty to re-use existing vocabularies for data description, (iv) noisy sensors. We addressed them (i) by achieving real-time access, transformation, aggregation and (semantic) correlation of stream data, (ii) and (iii) by using semantic representation, and (iv) by removing outliers using historical data.

Distributed Semantic Reasoning
The matching-based computation of context similarity, which is crucial in diagnosis and prediction components of STAR-CITY, is ensured by real-time semantic classification of ontology streams. Such classification is achieved by distributing all the standard completion OWL 2 EL rules [2] across various nodes based on their types. Each node is dedicated to at most one type of axioms and runs its appropriate rules.

Semantic Stream Reasoning
Real-time semantic comparison and matching of stream snapshots (i.e., stream at one point of time) are operated through stream reasoning. Such computing is required by predictive reasoning, real-time diagnosis and exploration for elaborating semantic context (city events, weather information) similarity and correlation over time, all in real-time. The stream correlation is established by comparing the number of changes between snapshots. This is unique to STAR-CITY for establishing context-aware diagnosis, exploration and prediction.

Semantic Rule Association and Mining
Predictive reasoning is achieved following state-of-the-art principles i.e., rules association mining. The generation of association rules between streams snapshots is based on a semantic extension of Apriori [1], aiming at supporting subsumption for determining association rules. Contrary to the initial version of Apriori which infers associations between data instances, the association in STAR-CITY is achieved between their descriptions e.g., type of city events, weather, congestion. Rules are encoded in SWRL, and all consequents of each rule are validated though consistency checking (c.f., line 13 in Algorithm 1). This ensures to obtain consistent and accurate prediction results (c.f., Experimental Results).

---

[10]http://www.w3.org/TR/owl-time/
[11]http://www.w3.org/2003/01/geo/

Web-based Application
• *REST Interface*: All functionalities of STAR-CITY are exposed through REST services, providing component-ization, evolve-ability via loose coupling and hypertext.

• *Web User Interface*: STAR-CITY strongly relies on HTML, CSS, Javascript (Dojo toolkit, D3, JQuery libraries) to produce an appealing user interface. Time-series, spider charts together with parallel charts are examples where Dojo and D3 components were combined with HTML and CSS.

• *Deployment*: Our technology stack is based on (i) well-established commercial components e.g., InfoSphere Streams [7] for stream enrichment and processing, WebSphere as the HTTP/Application Server and (ii) state-of-the-art components such as OpenLayers[12] as an open source JavaScript library for displaying dynamic map data, pssh for parallel distribution of reasoning, Jena TDB[13] as RDF store.

EXPERIMENTAL RESULTS
We do not evaluate the UI paradigm of STAR-CITY, which is simple and based on well-established and common-sense design i.e., (i) map-based exploration for spatial search, (ii) classic pie, spider charts for analytics results. We focus on the scalability and accuracy of the results that STAR-CITY delivers. We highlight the diagnosis and predictive reasoning, as the most critical and resource consuming components of STAR-CITY. Experiments were run on a server of 4 Intel(R) Xeon(R) X5650, 2.67GHz cores and 6GB RAM.

Open Data Context
Live stream data (Table 1), transformed in OWL/RDF (Table 2) using a static knowledge[6], are used to experiment STAR-CITY. Diagnosis and prediction are experimented on a basis of 458 days (from July 4th, 2012 to October $4th$, 2013).

Data Stream	Update (seconds)	Raw Update Size (KB)	Semantic Update Size (KB)	Semantic Update #RDF Triples	Semantic Conversion (millseconds)
[a] Journey Times	60	20.2	6, 102	63, 000	0.61
[b] Bus	40	66.8	1, 766	11, 000	0.415
[c] Weather	300	2.2	267	1, 140	0.189
[d] Road Works	weekly	146.6	77.9	820	3.988
[e] Social Events	daily	240.7	297	612	1.018
[f] Road Weather	600	715.7	181	660	0.068
[g] Incident	600	0.2	1.0	7	0.002

Table 2: Stream Datasets Details (average figures).

Diagnosis Experimentation
• *Scalability*: Figure 10 presents the computation time for diagnosing a congested road by varying the context i.e., number of historical $|H|$, real-time $|R|$ city events occurring per day.

The historical modeling of the diagnoser is strongly impacted by the number of historical city events while the real-time diagnosis remains constant. The modeling part compiles all

---

[12]http://openlayers.org/
[13]http://jena.apache.org/documentation/tdb/index.html

diagnosis results and evaluates semantic similarity between H and R (after semantic classification) while on-line diagnosis consists in retrieving diagnosis on a spatio-temporal basis. In our context 589 traffic congestion (out of 732 road segments) i.e., maximum number of congested road segments we captured over 458 days (which occurred on December 21st, 2012) have been diagnosed in less than 6 minutes.

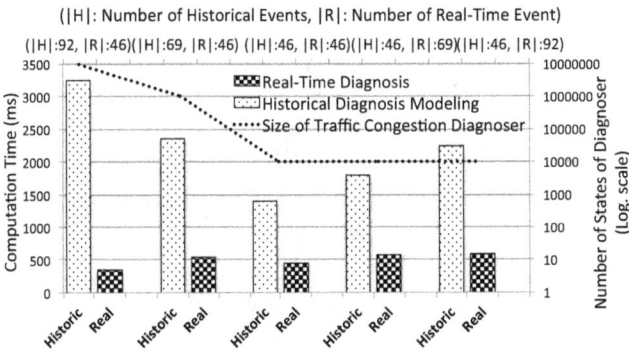

Figure 10: Scalability of Diagnosis (on a basis of 50 runs).

• *Accuracy*: Table 3 depicts the precision and recall of returned diagnosis results by varying the proportion of historical city events $|H|$ in the diagnoser. We report the ratio of up to 10 diagnosis results identified and compared against those estimated by transportation experts (used as ground truth).

Ratio of Historical City Events $|H|$ (%)	10	20	30	40	50	60	70	80	90	100
Precision (%)	24	29	36	43	51	63	70	79	88	94
Recall (%)	11	18	25	35	39	51	59	68	75	89

Table 3: Accuracy of Diagnosis (on a basis of 50 runs).

• *Lessons Learned*: Reducing the number of historical events decreases the computation time, but also decreases accuracy. The more similar historical events the higher the probability to catch accurate diagnosis. The computational performance is mainly impacted by the expressivity of the semantics as it impacts semantic classification and similarity computation.

Prediction Experimentation

The objective is to predict the severity of traffic congestion (i.e., *journey times* stream data) on some Dublin roads in the next 2 hours using contextual information from city events and weather information (Table 2). The evaluation is achieved using different contextual information i.e., [a], [a,b], [a,b,c], [a,b,c,d], [a,b,c,d,e], [a,b,c,d,e,f], [a,b,c,d,e,f,g] in Table 2, to evaluate their impacts on scalability and accuracy.

• *Scalability* : Figure 11 reports the scalability of our approach, noted [X14] and compares its computation time with a state-of-the-art approach [18] in predictive analytics. [18] scales better than our approach in all contextual configurations. Our approach requires some non-negligible computation time for reasoning on top of the semantics-enriched data. The identification of significant rules is strongly impacted by the number of potential rules, which grows exponentially with the number of semantic representations in streams (secondary vertical axis). Once all rules are identified, consistent prediction is delivered from $1.5s$ to $2.7s$.

• *Accuracy*: Figure 12 reports the prediction accuracy of both approaches [18] and [X14]. The accuracy is measured by comparing predictions (severity of congestion) with real-time situations in Dublin City, where results can be easily extracted and compared from the raw and semantic data in respectively [18] and our approach. The more the number of contexts the better the accuracy of prediction for both approaches. However our approach reaches a better accuracy when text-related context [d,e,g] are interpreted. On contrary [18] cannot take any benefit of their semantics. Overall, our approach obtains a better accuracy, mainly because all the rules are pruned based on the consistency of their consequent. By enforcing their consistency, we ensure that rules are selected based on the surrounding context i.e., exogenous data streams.

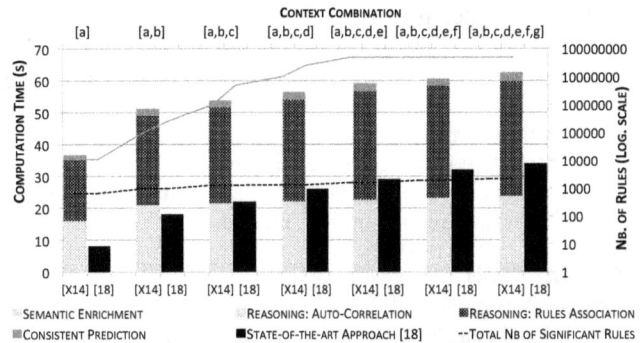

Figure 11: Scalability of Prediction (on a basis of 50 runs).

• *Lessons Learned*: Our experimental results emphasize the advantage of using semantic Web technologies for journey times prediction i.e., accuracy, but also point out the scalability limitation, specially compared to pure statistical approaches. In particular the more contexts (as streams) the more rules which positively (resp. negatively) impacts accuracy (resp. scalability). Since state-of-the-art approaches fail to encode text-based streams in pure value-based time series, they simply fail to interpret their semantics. On contrary, our approach interprets their semantics to enrich the prediction model, ensuring more accurate prediction.

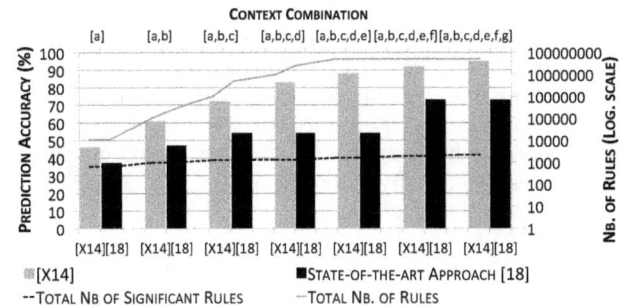

Figure 12: Accuracy of Prediction.

RELATED WORK

There are many traffic control systems, as standalone applications e.g., Italian 5T[4], which supports city traffic managers in her/his day-to-day tasks. They usually provide tools for (i) monitoring roads infrastructure and its traffic, (ii) detecting, visualizing [7] or predicting [21] traffic congestion through stream data and optimization mechanisms using existing data mining [14] or machine learning approaches [3]. However they do not expose toolkits for smoothly analyzing and easily exploring traffic data on various combinations of contexts i.e., spatial, temporal, event-based.

More importantly most of traffic control systems rarely capture insight from the integration of heterogenous open data sources e.g., context-aware diagnosis, prediction. STAR-CITY extends recent works in traffic diagnosis [9] by supporting both scalable (i) real-time and (ii) historical compilation of traffic congestion and its explanations (Figures 4-6). In most of data stream mining applications, prediction is estimated by (i) correlating current and past data (e.g., travel times for traffic application), (ii) identifying patterns using different distance metrics [10], and (iii) selecting rules that are used for predicting future conditions [19]. These approaches are designed for very fast processing and mining of (syntactic and numerical) raw data from sensors. However they rarely utilize exogenous sources of information for adjusting estimated prediction. Recent research works [11] have integrated tweeter feeds to improve travel time prediction, but the integration remains limited and ahdoc.

CONCLUSION

This paper presented STAR-CITY, an innovative system which has been designed as an intelligent user interface for (i) seamlessly aggregating heterogeneous real-time data and more importantly (ii) delivering integrated contextual analysis, diagnosis, exploration and prediction of traffic conditions in Dublin City, while being scalable to any city and contexts that involve sensor data. STAR-CITY delivers insight to interpret historical and real-time traffic conditions, making road traffic easier to be managed and supporting efficient urban planning. Thus STAR-CITY supports city managers in understanding effects of city events on traffic conditions in order to take corrective actions. The experiments have shown scalable, accurate and consistent analysis, diagnosis, exploration and prediction of traffic conditions.

As emphasized in the *Limitation* sections, handling (i) data summarization, (ii) flexible data integration, (iii) advanced temporal similarity, (iv) noisy data stream are future domains of investigation. UI-related future works are (i) types-based exploration (e.g., by impact of congestion), (ii) integration of diagnosis in prediction results, (iii) automated update of diagnosis i.e., when a zone is selected users want diagnosis to show up automatically without activating any buttons.

REFERENCES

1. Agrawal, R., and Srikant, R. Fast algorithms for mining association rules in large databases. In *VLDB* (1994), 487–499.

2. Baader, F., Brandt, S., and Lutz, C. Pushing the el envelope. In *IJCAI* (2005), 364–369.

3. Babu, S., and Widom, J. Continuous queries over data streams. *SIGMOD Record 30*, 3 (2001), 109–120.

4. Bando, M., Hasebe, K., Nakayama, A., Shibata, A., and Sugiyama, Y. Dynamical model of traffic congestion and numerical simulation. *Physical Review E 51* (1995), 1035–1042.

5. Banks, J. H. Freeway speed-flow-concentration relationships: More evidence and interpretations. In *Transportation Research Record* (1992), 53–60.

6. Bicer, V., Tran, T., Abecker, A., and Nedkov, R. Koios: Utilizing semantic search for easy-access and visualization of structured environmental data. In *ISWC (2)* (2011), 1–16.

7. Biem, A., Bouillet, E., Feng, H., Ranganathan, A., Riabov, A., Verscheure, O., Koutsopoulos, H. N., and Moran, C. Ibm infosphere streams for scalable, real-time, intelligent transportation services. In *SIGMOD* (2010), 1093–1104.

8. Cairns, S., Hass-Klau, C., and Goodwin, P. *Traffic impact of highway capacity reductions: Assessment of the evidence*. Landor Publishing, 1998.

9. Daly, E. M., Lécué, F., and Bicer, V. Westland row why so slow?: fusing social media and linked data sources for understanding real-time traffic conditions. In *IUI* (2013), 203–212.

10. Gehrke, J., Korn, F., and Srivastava, D. On computing correlated aggregates over continual data streams. In *SIGMOD Conference* (2001), 13–24.

11. He, J., Shen, W., Divakaruni, P., Wynter, L., and Lawrence, R. Improving traffic prediction with tweet semantics. In *IJCAI* (2013).

12. Lajunen, T., Parker, D., and Summala, H. Does traffic congestion increase driver aggression? *Transportation Research Part F: Traffic Psychology and Behaviour 2*, 4 (1999), 225–236.

13. Lecue, F., and Pan, J. Z. Predicting knowledge in an ontology stream. In *IJCAI* (2013), 2662–2669.

14. Luo, C., Thakkar, H., Wang, H., and Zaniolo, C. A native extension of sql for mining data streams. In *SIGMOD Conference* (2005), 873–875.

15. Ma, Y., Tran, T., and Bicer, V. Typifier: Inferring the type semantics of structured data. In *ICDE* (2013).

16. Mutharaju, R. Very large scale owl reasoning through distributed computation. In *ISWC* (2012), 407–414.

17. Nadeem, T., Dashtinezhad, S., Liao, C., and Iftode, L. Trafficview: traffic data dissemination using car-to-car communication. *ACM SIGMOBILE Mobile Computing and Communications Review 8*, 3 (2004), 6–19.

18. Papadimitriou, S., Sun, J., and Faloutsos, C. Streaming pattern discovery in multiple time-series. In *VLDB* (2005), 697–708.

19. Schrader, C. C., Kornhauser, A. L., and Friese, L. M. Using historical information in forecasting travel times. *Transportation Research Board 51* (2004), 1035–1042.

20. Schrank, D., Eisele, B., and Lomax, T. 2012 urban mobility report. http://goo.gl/Ke2xU, 2012.

21. Wang, H., Fan, W., Yu, P. S., and Han, J. Mining concept-drifting data streams using ensemble classifiers. In *KDD* (2003), 226–235.

Location Sharing Preference: Analysis and Personalized Recommendation

Jierui Xie
Samsung Research Center
San Jose, CA, USA
jierui.xie@samsung.com

Bart Piet Knijnenburg
University of California, Irvine
Irvine, CA, USA
bart.k@uci.edu

Hongxia Jin
Samsung Research Center
San Jose, CA, USA
hongxia.jin@samsung.com

ABSTRACT

Location-based systems are becoming more popular with the explosive growth in popularity of smart phones. However, the user adoption of these systems is hindered by growing user concerns about privacy. To design better location-based systems that attract more user adoption and protect users from information under/overexposure, it is highly desirable to understand users' location sharing and privacy preferences.

This paper makes two main contributions. First, by studying users' location sharing privacy preferences with three groups of people (i.e., Family, Friend and Colleague) in different contexts, including check-in time, companion and emotion, we reveal that location sharing behaviors are highly dynamic, context-aware, audience-aware and personal. In particular, we find that emotion and companion are good contextual predictors of privacy preferences. Moreover, we find that there are strong similarities or correlations among contexts and groups.

Our second contribution is to show, in light of the user study, that despite the dynamic and context-dependent nature of location sharing, it is still possible to predict a user's in-situ sharing preference in various contexts. More specifically, we explore whether it is possible to give users a personalized recommendation of the sharing setting they are most likely to prefer, based on context similarity, group correlation and collective check-in preference. PPRec, the proposed recommendation algorithm that incorporates the above three elements, delivers personalized recommendations that could be helpful to reduce both user's burden and privacy risk. It also provides additional insights into the relative usefulness of different personal and contextual factors in predicting users' sharing behavior.

Author Keywords

Location sharing; privacy; user behavior; recommendation

ACM Classification Keywords

H.5.m. Information Interfaces and Presentation (e.g. HCI): Miscellaneous

INTRODUCTION

[1]Location-sharing services (LSS) enable users to share their location with their friends, which may result in a range of social benefits [21]. However, research suggests that LSS users are plagued by a myriad of privacy concerns, which causes them to significantly limit their amount of location-sharing [3, 16]. While sites such as Facebook allow users fine-grained control over who can see their profiles, it is difficult for average users to specify this kind of detailed policy because specifying user preferences is tedious and very time-consuming work [10, 25]. Studies have consistently shown that users struggle to express and maintain such policies [1, 6, 11, 20, 26], due in part to complex and unusable interfaces [26]. Arguably, we should help users in this decision [15, 7] to alleviate their burden on configuration [14].

A careful simplification of a system's privacy controls [32] can strike a balance between control and complexity. When there are many decisions to make, one can group decisions for which users are expected to have similar preferences. For example, Knijnenburg et al [15] found that information disclosure behavior is multidimensional; certain types of information are almost always disclosed (or withheld) in conjunction. This knowledge could be used to reduce the number of sharing decisions.

When, for a given decision, the user has to choose from many available options, one can suggest a certain subset of options [13]. Arguably, this suggested subset is not the same for every user and every situation (otherwise a smaller number of options would suffice to begin with), but has to be tailored to the user's privacy preferences and the current context. This is thus essentially a recommendation problem: a recommender system collects knowledge about users, uses it to predict their preference of each of the available options, and then presents to each user a short list of options that he/she is most likely to choose. Consequently, recommender systems are said to reduce the choice overload that users may experience when having to choose from a large list of options [5, 17].

Although recommender systems have been around for over two decades and their application to privacy has been proposed [18], very few efforts have been made towards the actual implementation of a privacy recommender. One recent example is the work by [13] on a location-sharing privacy recommender that tried to reduce the number of location-sharing actions (e.g. 'share with nearby friends', 'keep my location private') the user could choose from when checking in. They

---

[1]Bart participated in this research as part of his summer internship at the Samsung research center.

Attribute	Distribution
Age	18 to 24 (21.42%), 25 to 34 (45.23%), 35 to 44 (20.23%), 45 to 54 (5.95%), 55 to 64 (7.14%)
Marital Status	married (40.47%), not married (59.52%)
Gender	male (57.14%), female (42.85%)
Concern Level	Very Concerned (39%), Moderately (41%), Slightly (15%), Not Care (5%)

Table 1. Demographics of Participants.

Audience	Sharing Settings
Family	Not share (1), Spouse (2), Immediate (3), Nearby (4), All (5)
Friend	Not share (1), Close (2), Acquaintances (3), Nearby (4), All (5)
Colleague	Not share (1), Close (2), Manager (3), Nearby (4), All (5)

Table 2. Audience and sharing settings.

elicited the user's evaluation of the activity they are engaging in (an arguably easier task than choosing among sharing options), and used it to predict a subset of sharing actions the user would be most likely to choose from. They were able to make this prediction with high accuracy, but users seemed to dislike the extra step they had to take to evaluate the activity. [13] therefore suggested to create a recommender that would be able to predict the sharing action with alternative information about the user.

The current paper follows this suggestion. In this paper we argue that people have different tendencies to disclose their locations in different contexts, such as location type, time, companion, and how they feel at the moment. We thus explore how this readily available *contextual* information can be used to predict the user's sharing preferences. Using this information allows us to recommend sharing actions like [13], without other extra efforts.

LOCATION SHARING BEHAVIOR STUDY

We conducted online user experiments to test our hypotheses about user location sharing preferences. Our main hypothesis is that sharing behaviors are dynamic, complex and personal; the context-awareness and audience-awareness contribute important parts to the sharing dynamics. In the study, we considered twenty location *semantics* (e.g, restaurant, instead of a specific shop name) covering a diversity of situations in our daily life. Aside from the location itself, user check-in behaviors are also influenced by many other contextual factors such as time [33], *companion* and *emotion*. The companion aspect is inspired by Facebook's 'Who are you with' feature; The impact of this feature has not yet been fully studied. Facebook also recently introduced a way to express emotion in a post, and how expressing a personal emotion at a particular location drives the sharing behavior is also not yet fully understood. In this paper, we explore how sharing behaviors change along these different dimensions.

Data Collection

We recruited a total of 1088 participants using Amazon Mechanical Turk[2], a popular crowdsourcing site. To guarantee the quality of the data, we restricted participants to people in USA with high reputation and having used any form of location sharing services. The demographics are shown in Table 1.

---

[2]https://www.mturk.com/mturk/.

Due to the difficulty of collecting privacy preference data from existing LSS, participants in the experiments were asked to imagine using a location-sharing tool. Participants were presented a **scenario** (context, status update) and were asked to select one sharing **setting** (or option) for each of three **groups** of recipients (i.e., audience). Available settings are listed in Table 2. Each participant was randomly assigned ten scenarios.

Depending on what context is associated with an update, we have five experiments as described in Table 3. In all experiments, users would imagine checking in at several types of locations. We selected twenty **location semantics** that are supported by Google Places[3]: Airport, Art Gallery, Bank, Bar, Bus Station, Casino, Cemetery, Church, Company Building, Convention Center, Hospital, Hotel, Law Firm, Library, Movie Theater, Police Station, Restaurant, Shopping Mall, Spa, Workplace. In experiment 2 we also provided the specific time of the check-in, in experiment 3 we told participants who their companion at the location was, and in experiment 4 we described both time and companion. Finally, in experiment 5 participants were given either a positive or a negative status update (extracted from a Gowalla dataset[4]); in all other experiments the status updates were neutral.

Note that given the nature of the online crowdsourcing platform, the presented scenarios (and therefore the data and analyses) are based on users' imagined and expressed behavior rather than their actual behaviors. Thus, there are limitations compared to real world applications. This paper aims to provide a preliminary study on the connection between user privacy preferences and automatic recommendation, and hopefully motivates future field studies in this direction.

Location Sensitive Sharing Patterns: Impact of Time, Companion and Emotion

Prior to the study, we asked users about their general privacy concern towards using LSS, which is chosen from 'Very Concerned', 'Moderately', 'Slightly', and 'Not Care'. The corresponding distribution is shown in Table 1, which indicates majority of the participants (%80) are at least moderately concerned about their privacy.

---

[3]https://developers.google.com/places.
[4]The Gowalla check-ins dataset was collected from June to October 2010. The dataset consisted of 104,875 users and 4,744,089 total locations visited over all users.

Study	Context	# of participants N	# of selections $|R|$	Example status updates
1	location	84	840	I am at a ART GALLERY at the exhibition of Van Gogh
2	location + time	133	1376	I am at a HOSPITAL on MONDAY MORNING waiting for test reports ...
3	location + companion	244	2440	I am at a BAR with FRIENDS having a beer ...
4	location + time + companion	510	4969	I am at a CHURCH with FAMILY on WEEKEND
5	location+emotion	117	1170	[negative] I am at a MOVIE THEATER. I've seen a lot of bad film and this one is really a piece of crap :(. [positive] I am at a RESTAURANT. Dinner at Acquerello. Mmmm! This is what I was looking forward to! :)

Table 3. Experiments and scenarios.

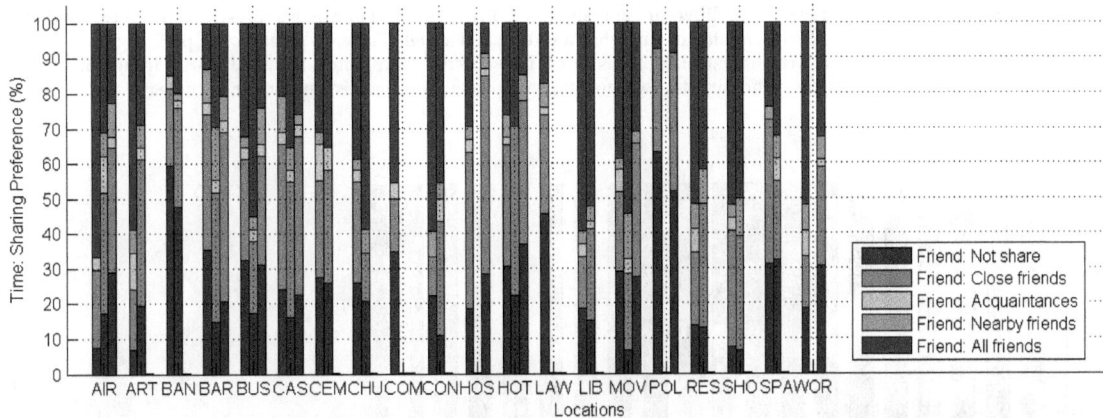

Figure 1. The preferences for sharing with friends at different times (Experiment 2). The x-axis represents the abbreviated location names. The y-axis is the sharing preference in terms of the fraction of time that a setting is selected. For each location, we present the distributions over all settings for three values of time. The first stacked bar is weekday, the second is weekend, and the third is at night. We omit some of these sub-dimensions if they are not applicable to a location, e.g., night is omitted for art gallery.

In this section, we present detailed findings/patterns regarding two aspects, i.e., the variability of location-sharing behavior per audience between different contexts. We focus on the extent and direction of sharing preference shifts regarding each of these contextual factors. Figures 1-3 summarize the **sharing preference** for each sharing settings as the fraction of time a setting was selected. Due to space limitations, we restrict ourselves here to 'friends' as the audience. Different audiences are compared in a later section.

Time dimension: We study three values for time : *weekday*, *weekend* and *night* [5]. Sharing preference is found to be time sensitive in many locations.

In Figure 1, we show the preference for sharing with friends. The frequency of using the 'Not share' setting is lower on weekend compared with weekday, e.g., at a bar, bus station, and movie theater[6]. This is also true for church, which is a place many people visit on the weekend. In contrast, people prefer higher levels of privacy at the airport and art gallery on

the weekend (i.e., they share less). Sharing at night is typically more conservative (i.e., sharing 'All' is less frequent.). Examples include hospital and workplace.

Companion dimension: We explore the impact of companion considering seven values (i.e., *alone, family, kids, spouse, girlfriend, friends, colleagues*). Figure 2 summarizes the sharing behaviors with one's friend group when *alone*, with *family*, *friends* and *colleagues*. (We defer the analyses of other values to the next section.) Sharing behavior depends heavily on who the companion is. When with friends, people are more open to share, e.g., at a casino, church, convention center, hospital, library, movie theater police station, and shopping mall. On the other hand, when people are alone, they seem to be less willing to share their updates to the public. This is true for 17 out of 20 locations.

Emotion dimension: We study scenarios involving a wide range of emotions, e.g., *happiness, sadness, angry, disgusted*, and so on [9]. To aid interpretation, results are cast onto two sub-dimensions: *positive* and *negative*. Figure 3 summarizes the results for sharing with the friend group. The influence of emotion is more predictable than time or companion given a location. People tend to either share nothing or everything when a scenario is associated with emotions. For instance,

---

[5]We remove some times that are not common or do not make sense for some locations.

[6]Unless otherwise specified, conclusions are drawn based on Chi-squared test at a 0.05 level of α.

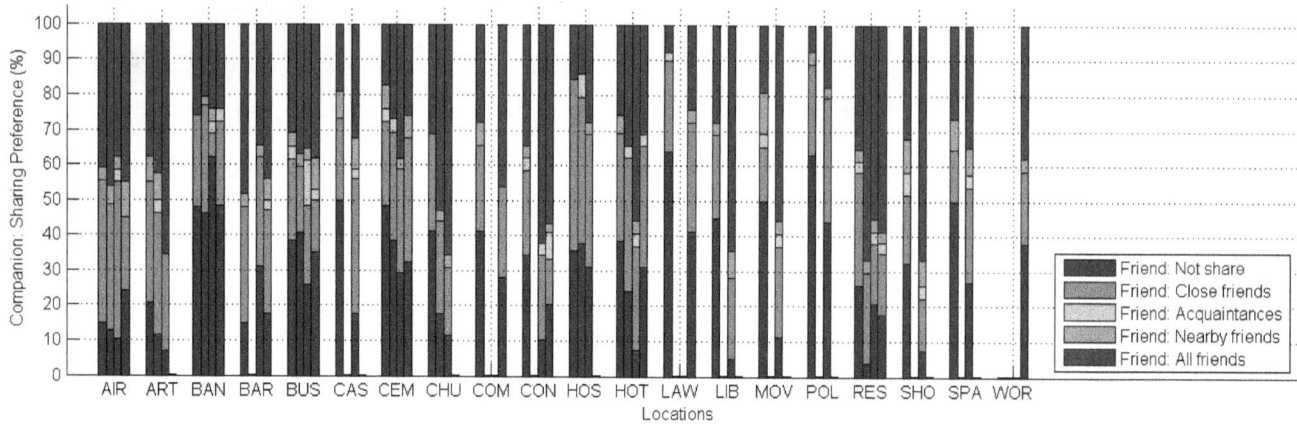

Figure 2. The preferences for sharing with friends with different companions (Experiment 3). The x-axis represents the abbreviated location names. The y-axis is the sharing preference in terms of the fraction of time that a setting is selected. For each location, we present the distributions over all settings for four sub-dimensions in companion. The first stacked bar is alone, the second is with family, the third is with friend, and the fourth is with colleague. We omit some of these sub-dimensions if they are not common in practice, e.g., colleague is omitted for art gallery.

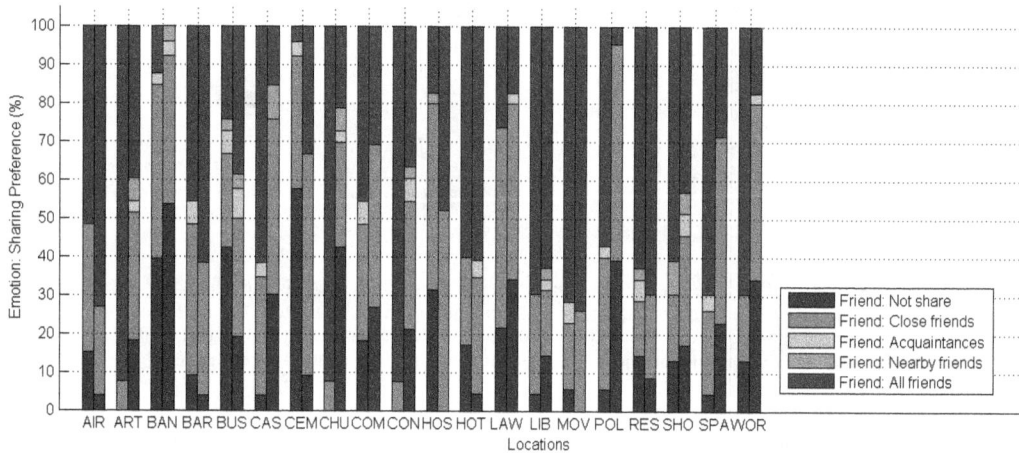

Figure 3. The preference for sharing with friends with different emotions (Experiment 5). The x-axis represents the abbreviated location names. The y-axis is the sharing preference in terms of the fraction of time that a setting is selected. For each location, we present the distributions over all settings for two sub-dimensions in emotion. The first stacked bar is positive, and the second is negative.

when at a library or airport, people tend to select the 'Share with All' setting most of the time no matter whether they are happy or not (no significant difference). In contrast, sharing at a law firm and cemetery are predictably restricted regardless of the emotion. For art gallery, church and convention center, people almost always share with everyone when they are in a positive mood.

Audience-aware Sharing Patterns and Shift in Privacy Behaviors

As expected, sharing is also related to the target audience. In this section, we will provide a quantity for characterizing the direction and the amount of the shift in privacy behaviors with different audiences. Given two different contexts, X and Y, we define the Privacy Behavior Drift (PBD) as the divergence in the skewnesses of two corresponding privacy preference distributions. In statistics, skewness is a measure of the extent to which a probability distribution leans to one side of the

mean. Typically, a negative value indicates the tail on the left side of the probability distribution is longer than the right side.

We first map the privacy settings to numbers (i.e., $\{1, 2, 3, 4, 5\}$), whose values reflect the degree of concern (See Table 2). The smaller the value, the more concerned (e.g., 1 for 'Not share' and 5 for 'Share All') in that a smaller audience is reached. Note that the mapping here is a coarse conversion with limitations. Formally, the PBD is given as

$$PBD(X,Y) = \frac{\frac{1}{n_1}\sum_{i=1}^{n_1}(x_i - \bar{x})^3}{\left(\frac{1}{n_1}\sum_{i=1}^{n_1}(x_i - \bar{x})^2\right)^{1.5}} - \frac{\frac{1}{n_2}\sum_{i=1}^{n_2}(y_i - \bar{y})^3}{\left(\frac{1}{n_2}\sum_{i=1}^{n_2}(y_i - \bar{y})^2\right)^{1}}$$

(1)

Clusters	Locations
1st cluster	Airport, Bus Station, Art Gallery, Movie Theater, Shopping Mall, Restaurant, Library, Hotel, Cemetery, Church
2nd cluster	Bar, Casino, Spa, Hospital
3rd cluster	Police Station, Law Firm, Bank
4th cluster	Company Building, Convention Center, Workplace

Table 4. Similarity in location semantic discovered by clustering.

where n_1 and n_2 are sample sizes in X and Y, $\bar{x}$ and $\bar{y}$ are sample means. The first and second terms on the RHS are the standard skewnesses of X and Y, respectively.

Since we are interested in evaluating how much change occurs when extra contextual information other than location itself is introduced, the preference distribution for which only location is considered is denoted by X, and distributions for which other contextual factors are considered are denoted by Y in Eq.(1). *Positive values indicate a shift toward less disclosure and vice versa.* We measured the significance of the PBD based on KL-divergence between two estimated distributions with respect to statistic $\frac{n_1+n_2}{log_2 e} D(p_x \| p_y) \chi^2_{|\Re_v-1|}$ as proposed by [12] [7]. Figures 4, 5 and 6 show the aggregated PBD, which is averaged over all locations.

The results demonstrate the audience-aware property of the sharing behavior, and confirm our previous observations. In fact, many patterns could be observed from PBDs. Here we just list a few. For example, people are more concerned about sharing with the colleague group in most contexts (positive PBD in Figures 4, 5 and 6). Along the companion dimension (Figure 5): In general, when people are with a particular member from a group (e.g., family), they are more open to other members in the same group (see the negative PBDs in Figure 5); People tend to be less open when they are alone or with someone who is special, e.g., spouse/girlfriend; When people are accompanied by kids, they also become more prudent. Along the emotion dimension (Figure 6): When the feeling is positive, people tend to share much more with family and friends; When the feeling is negative, people share less with the colleague group. Along the time dimension (Figure 4): On weekdays, people tend to be more willing to share a location with family and friends (negative PBD), but are concerned about sharing with colleagues (positive PBD). Late at night, people are generally more careful about their sharing behaviors (especially at a bar or casino), evidenced by positive PBDs in all groups.

Similarity and Correlation in Behaviors and Contexts

To conclude the behavioral study, we discuss three additional regularities in users' behavior.

First, we have observed relatively consistent sharing patterns for location semantics with similar characteristics. For example, among our 20 location semantics, we can infer the higher level semantic (latent characteristic) of these locations

---
[7]The statistic has a χ^2 distribution with $|\Re_v-1|$ degrees of freedom.

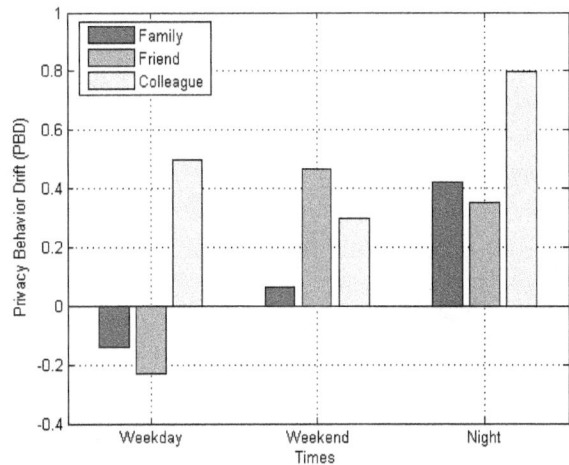

Figure 4. The privacy behavior drift (PBD) along the time dimension for different recipient groups. PBD is averaged over all locations. Positive values indicate less disclosure and, vice versa.

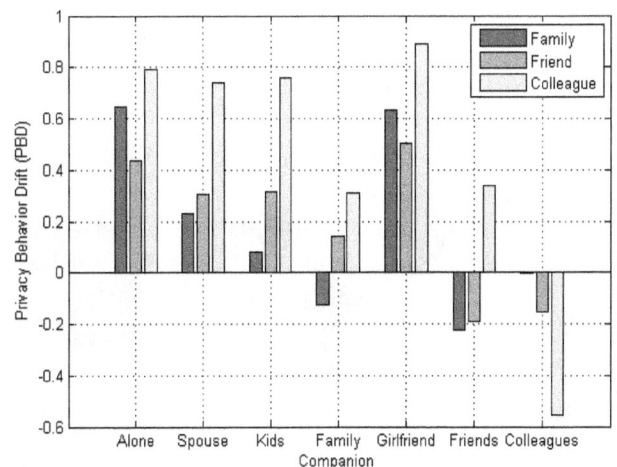

Figure 5. The privacy behavior drift (PBD) along the companion dimension for different recipient groups. PBD is averaged over all locations. Positive values indicate less disclosure and, vice versa.

from users' sharing behaviors. More specifically, Based on clustering results (we used the K-means algorithm with user preference as features), four groups with similar characteristic are discovered, representing work related places, public places and highly private and security related places (see Table 4).

Second, sharing preferences may differ per social group, but the preferences per group may be correlated. To verify and quantify how much knowledge is gained by knowing our participants' preference for other groups, we measure the *information gain* for each of the three group pairs, (family, friend), (family, colleague) and (friend, colleague). Figure 7 verifies the existence of strong correlation and high predictability. Among these three groups, family is closely related to friend, and friend is closely related to colleague. In other words, there is a high chance that one can infer the preference in one group by knowing the sharing preference in another group.

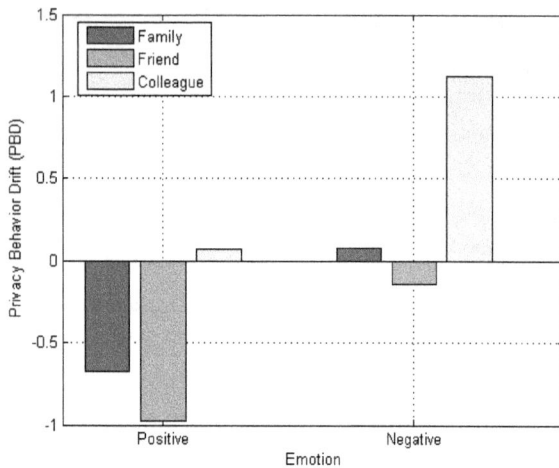

Figure 6. The privacy behavior drift (PBD) along the emotion dimension for different recipient groups. PBD is averaged over all locations. Positive values indicate less disclosure and, vice versa.

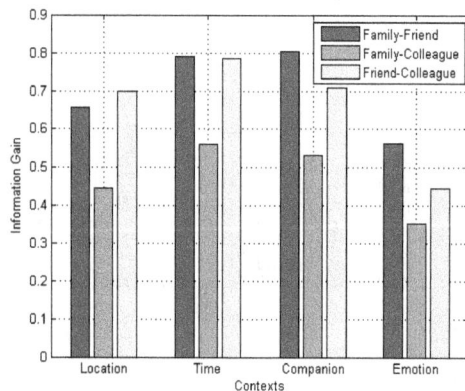

Figure 7. High predictabilities between recipient groups measured by information gain.

Third, although the sharing preferences in a specific context (e.g., at night) might be saliently diverse, in reality, there is typically a group of people who share a similar preference. Therefore, we expect that collective behavior could provide useful insights for predicting individual preferences. This is an approach we turn to in the next section, where we develop a privacy recommender.

PRIVACY SETTING RECOMMENDATION
One useful way to leverage our results regarding the context-dependent nature of information disclosure is to help users by providing them the right privacy configurations. This can be considered as a recommendation or prediction problem. The variability in users' disclosure preferences inevitably imposes great challenges in predicting their sharing behaviors. For example: (1) Users' behaviors depend on a specific combination of locations and other contexts. Given that there are a number of locations and contexts, and each one has multiple values, the scenario space is potentially huge. This makes a static pre-configuration of settings for all location preferences impractical. (2) Users' behaviors seem to depend on various recipients making this a multi-variate prediction problem. (3)

Sharing preferences are typically highly personal, and therefore personalized recommendation is desired.

All these challenges imply that providing accurate recommendation is a non-trivial task. Fortunately, in the behavioral study we have observed strong similarities or correlations among users, contexts, and groups, which enables effective solutions.

PPRec - A Personalized Privacy Recommender
In this section, we introduce PPRec, a personalized recommender that predicts the most likely privacy setting for a user given a specific *scenario*. A scenario is defined as a specific combination of location and any other contexts (i.e., time, companion, emotion or any mixture of them). The prominent challenge here lies in the large number of scenarios and the limited amount of information about user sharing history (we observe at most 9 other sharing instances), which is challenging for any recommendation algorithm. Inspired by the above observations, PPRec combined information from three spaces: users, scenarios (therefore locations and contexts) and recipient groups to take advantage of various correlations. PPRec integrates collaborative filtering and learning, and it is a hybrid of traditional user-based and item-based algorithms. Our goal for developing PPRec is to provide a proof of concept for a privacy recommender, and also to investigate the relative contribution of each contextual factor to the recommendation process.

Notations and Definitions
The set of users in the system is denoted by U, and the set of scenarios by I. We denote the settings matrix by R ($|U| \times |I|$) and write S the set of possible values for a setting. Here, $S = \{$ Not share, Spouse, Immediate, Nearby, All $\}$ in the family group (similar for other groups, see Table 2). The selection made by any user $u \in U$ for a particular scenario $i \in I$ is denoted by r_{ui}.

Problem Definition: We are interested in finding, for a particular user u, the *most* likely privacy setting for a new scenario i. Given some history settings for some scenarios, we define the problem as a multi-class classification problem. Therefore, the ultimate goal is to learn a function $O : U \times I \rightarrow S$ that predicts the privacy setting $\hat{r}_{ui}$ of a user u for a new scenario i.

Our method blends user-based and item-based nearest neighbor techniques. In our method, the similarity between two scenarios is implicitly embedded in the similarity of all users' selections for these scenarios. The individual privacy preferences are predicted by identifying other users/scenarios with similar behaviors/characteristics. Formally, we predict $\hat{r}_{ui}$ using the privacy settings selected for i by k users most similar to u (denoted by $N_i(u)$) and also k scenarios most similar to i that are rated by u (denoted by $N_u(i)$). The similarity between two users u and v is denoted by w_{uv}, and the similarity between two scenarios i and j is denoted by w_{ij}. The prediction is made by having all nearest neighbors (both user-based and item-based) vote on a setting $r \in S$. The classifier is defined as

$$\hat{r}_{ui} = O(u,i) = \arg\max_r f_r(u,i), \qquad (2)$$

where f_r is the sum of the weighted votes from nearest neighbors on a setting r.

$$f_r(u,i) = \sum_{v \in N_i(u)} \delta_1(r_{vi}, r) \cdot g_{uv} + \sum_{j \in N_u(i)} \delta_1(r_{uj}, r) \cdot g_{ij}, \qquad (3)$$

where $\delta_1(a,b)$ is 1 if $a = b$, 0 otherwise. As a result, the value of r with the highest vote is recommended to the user.

In light of our analyses of recipient group correlation, we take into account dependence across groups. More specifically, we define a linear function g_{uv} to integrate correlations between u and v in the target group (e.g., family) and two external groups (e.g., friend and colleague with respect to family) as

$$g_{uv}(\theta_1^u, \theta_2^u; u, v) = w_{uv} + \theta_1^u w_{uv}^1 + \theta_2^u w_{uv}^2, \qquad (4)$$

where w_{uv}^1 and w_{uv}^2 are similarities in other groups, parameters θ_1^u and θ_2^u are the strengths of the cross-group dependence. g_{uv} is called the *interpolation* weights defined for each user u.

Similarly, we define the interpolation weights for two neighboring scenarios i and j as

$$g_{ij}(\theta_1^u, \theta_2^u; i, j) = w_{ij} + \theta_1^u w_{ij}^1 + \theta_2^u w_{ij}^2, \qquad (5)$$

Note that the cross-group dependence variable is designed to be the same for users and scenarios, which balances these two spaces depending on the training data.

Multi-class Learning

Given the above development of our classifier, we need to estimate the *cross-group dependence strength*, $\{\theta_x^u | u \in U, x \in \{1, 2\}\}$ from the data. Given N users, this requires $2N$ parameters. We employ the conventional RMSE as the evaluation measure for the learning. The goal is to minimize the RMSE with regularization. Let the estimated privacy setting be:

$$\hat{r}_{ui} = O(u, i; \theta_1^u, \theta_2^u), \qquad (6)$$

which has an error $e_{ui} = r_{ui} - \hat{r}_{ui} \, \forall (u, i) \in R_{train}$. To avoid overfitting, we regularize this error with regularization factor λ

$$E_{ui} = \frac{1}{2}(e_{ui}^2 + \lambda \left[(\theta_1^u)^2 + (\theta_2^u)^2\right]). \qquad (7)$$

Summing over all errors gives us the Sum of Squared Errors (SSE), and minimizing this function is equivalent to minimizing the $RMSE = \sqrt{SSE/|R_{train}|}$.

$$(\theta_1^{*u}, \theta_2^{*u}) = \arg\min_{(\theta_1^u, \theta_2^u)} RMSE \qquad (8)$$

We adopt the incremental gradient descent method [27] for learning. Suppose we are given an example $(u, i, r_{ui}) \in R_{train}$, we first compute the gradient of E_{ui},

$$\begin{aligned} \frac{\partial E_{ui}}{\partial \theta_x^u} &= e_{ui}e'_{ui} + \lambda\theta_x^u \\ &= [O(u,i; \theta_1^u, \theta_2^u) - r_{ui}]O(u, i; \theta_1^u, \theta_2^u)' \\ &\quad + \lambda\theta_x^u. \end{aligned} \qquad (9)$$

We then update the parameters in the negative direction of the gradient using

$$\theta_x^u = \theta_x^u - \eta\frac{\partial E_{ui}}{\partial \theta_x^u}, \forall x \in \{1, 2\}, \qquad (10)$$

where η is the learning rate. For the pseudo codes of the algorithm, refer to Alg. 1.

Algorithm 1 : PPRec

1: Input: R_{train} training set, η learning rate (0.005), λ regularization factor (0.01)
2: Ouput: $\theta_1^{*u}, \theta_2^{*u}$
3: partition R_{train} into R' and validation set R''
4: initialize θ_1^u, θ_2^u with small random values from (0, 0.01)
5: **repeat**
6:     **for** each (u, i, r_{ui}) **do**
7:         compute E_{ui} according to Eq.(7)
8:         compute the gradient of E_{ui} according to Eq.(9)
9:         update θ_1^u, θ_2^u according to Eq.(10)
10:     **end for**
11:     calculate the RMSE on R''
12:     if the RMSE is better than in any previous epoch
13:         $\theta_1^{*u} = \theta_1^u, \theta_2^{*u} = \theta_2^u$
14: **until** RMSE does not decrease during 5 epochs

Function O for Multi-class Prediction

In Eq.(2) (therefore, in Eq.(6)), f_r is the *cumulative* vote and the weight from a neighbor user v (or item j) is counted only when r_{vi} (or r_{uj}) equals to the class label r under consideration, determined by δ_1 in Eq.(3).

To output the r that has the largest value (f_r) as the desired class label, the following multiple conditions have to be true at the same time.

$$(f_r - f_1) \geq 0, (f_r - f_2) \geq 0, \ldots, (f_r - f_{|S|}) \geq 0$$

For notational simplicity, we define $h_{rk}(\theta_1^u, \theta_2^u) = f_r - f_k$ and $d_{rk}(\theta_1^u, \theta_2^u) = \delta_2(h_{rk})$, where $\delta_2(x) = 0$ if $x < 0$, 1 otherwise. In other words, the following equation needs to be 1 (true).

$$p_r(\theta_1^u, \theta_2^u) = \prod_{k=1}^{|S|} d_{rk}, \qquad (11)$$

where $|S|$ is the number privacy settings.

Without loss of generality, we assume that no more than one f_k achieves the maximum value. If Eq.(11) is evaluated to be true, then we expect to output exactly r given by $q_r(\theta_1^u, \theta_2^u) = rp_r$, 0 otherwise. To search the target r among all possible settings in S, we sum over different $q'_r s$, leading to

$$O(u, i; \theta_1^u, \theta_2^u) = \sum_{r=1}^{|S|} q_r. \qquad (12)$$

As a result, the classifier outputs only one valid class label r.

So far, Eq.(12) is non-differentiable. To make the first derivative in this function possible for our classifier, we approximate δ_1 and δ_2 with continuous functions $\tilde{\delta}_1$ and $\tilde{\delta}_2$ given by

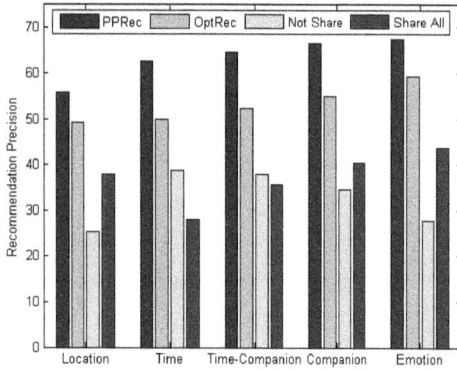

Figure 8. Comparing the recommendation precisions of PPRec, OptRec and configuration with default values (share all or not share).

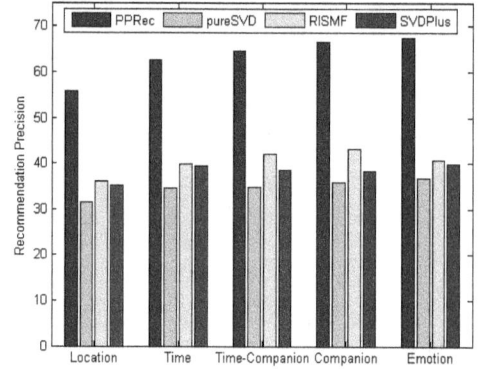

Figure 9. Comparing the recommendation precisions of PPRec and other collaborative filtering recommenders.

$\tilde{\delta}_1(x,r) = 1 - tanh(K_1(x-r))$, $\tilde{\delta}_2 = \frac{1}{1+e^{-K_2 x}}$, where K_1 and K_2 are the amplification constant set to 1000. We also have $\frac{d\tilde{\delta}_2(x)}{dx} = K_2 \tilde{\delta}_2 (1 - \tilde{\delta}_2)$.

Thus, the first derivatives of O with respect to θ_1^u and θ_2^u are given as

$$\frac{\partial O(u,i;\theta_1^u,\theta_2^u)}{\partial \theta_x^u} = \sum_{r=1}^{|S|} 2r \left(\prod_{k=1}^{|S|} d_{rk}(\theta_1^u,\theta_2^u) \right) \quad (13)$$
$$\cdot \left(\sum_{k=1}^{|S|} \frac{\frac{\partial \tilde{\delta}_2(h_{rk}(\theta_1^u,\theta_2^u))}{\partial h_{rk}(\theta_1^u,\theta_2^u)} \cdot \frac{\partial h_{rk}(\theta_1^u,\theta_2^u)}{\partial \theta_x^u}}{d_{rk}(\theta_1^u,\theta_2^u)} \right) .$$

Up to this point, we complete all derivations that are required for learning.

Experiments

We apply PPRec to the location experiment datasets (denoted as R_i). For dataset sizes (e.g., the number of users N, and the number of check-ins $|R|$), refer to Table 3. The average number of locations rated by each user is about 10. We use 10-fold cross validation. To avoid the case of not having training data for a user, we preserve 10% of each user's ratings for testing in each fold.

In the experiment, we fix the learning rate to 0.005, and use cross validation to identify the best setting for k (neighborhood size) and λ, which is found to be $k = 5$ and $\lambda = 0.1$ (regularization factor). We adopt the prediction *accuracy* (or precision)[8] as the performance measure in our study.

The similarity measure (for w_{uv} and w_{ij}) is found to be an important factor for achieving better performance[9]. We used

the Humming similarity which offers the best performance compared to cosine similarity, and Euclidean similarity[10].

First, we compare the performance of PPRec with some baselines. The first baseline, OptRec, predicts individual sharing settings based on the population's average preferences given in Figures 1, 2, and 3. That is, it selects the most popular setting for a scenario. We compare with two naive default configurations as well. One is to always share with 'All', and the other is to always 'Not Share'. These two baselines are used as the default setting in most existing LSS platforms.

As shown in Figure 8, default configurations do not seem to capture in-situ user preference well and their performances are not comparable to PPRec. With significant improvement over these two baselines in different contexts, it suggests that it is possible to use PPRec to improve the quality of default-based privacy management, reducing the risk of being over-exposed[11] (e.g., due to default Share All policy) and under-exposed (e.g., due to default Not Share policy) in existing systems. Moreover, PPRec beats OptRec, which is based on aggregated statistics, by 19.40% on average ($p = 0.002$[12]). It suggests that recommendation of privacy configuration could be improved by introducing personalization as in PPRec.

We also compare our algorithms with other collaborative filtering algorithms to illustrate the advantage of incorporating domain specific knowledge (e.g., the group correlation). The first one is pureSVD [8], which decomposes R into user and item factors. To provide a full matrix, we impute the missing data with the average value for each location. The second algorithm is RISMF[27], which is similar to pureSVD but considers only the available ratings and is trained with regularization. It similar to RSVD [22]. The third algorithm is SVD++ [19], in which extra implicit feedback is incorporated. The

---

[8] A *hit* occurs when the user accepts a presented setting in a recommendation; otherwise a *miss*. The *precision* is defined as fraction of hits over the total number of recommendations. The precision in Figures 8 and 9 is averaged over all locations.

[9] The similarity is based on the subset of locations two users have both 'visited'.

[10] Note that the popular Pearson Correlation (PC) is not suitable in our data, because there are users who share all locations to everyone, and there are users who share no locations to anyone. In either case, the variance is zeros and the PC is not applicable.

[11] As discussed in [28], we made the assumption that people typically do not change the default.

[12] Tests of significance are based on Student's t-test.

values for parameters like the number of factors and the regularization factors are obtained via cross-validation.

Compared to pureSVD, RISMF and SVD++, PPRec achieves significant improvement of 82.69% ($p < 0.001$), 57.21% ($p < 0.001$), and 65.61% ($p < 0.001$), respectively as shown in Figure 9. Also, it is interesting that these algorithms do not perform much better than the baselines.

Beyond Precision

Based on the performance of PPRec (personalized algorithm) and OptRec (non-personalized algorithm), we roughly compare the importance of three contexts (time, companion and emotion) in terms of prediction accuracy. It appears that emotion is most useful for predicting sharing behavior followed by companion and time.

This observation might serve as a simple guideline for feature selection for multiple contexts scenarios in other similar tasks. Moreover, companion and emotion have not been used in LSS until their recent inclusion in Facebook's status updates. However, our results suggest that if location-sharing services want to predict users' sharing preferences (e.g., in order to provide sharing recommendations), they should probably incorporate companion and emotion as input variables in their check-in interface, because these variables allow for a more accurate prediction.

RELATED WORK

Location sharing and privacy have been studied in recent decades. Research has shown that the primary privacy concerns surrounding location sharing include context and use [31, 2]. It also found that a greater degree of rule expressiveness may increase the efficiency of sharing information without violating users' personal privacy preferences [4]. [30] investigates how location characteristics and tracking method influence privacy. The results show that users appear more comfortable sharing their presence at locations visited by a large and diverse set of people. In this paper, we focus on privacy preferences as a variable of location semantic, and different from other work, we estimate the interaction between location and contextual information including emotion and companion.

Recently, grouping mechanisms have been found to offer a balance between privacy control and configuration burden [23]. We share similar vision with [23], and we focus on exploring audience-based sharing preference and privacy. Providing default privacy settings or automated suggestions has gained increasing attentions [24, 29]. Ravichandran et al. [24] studied the problem of predicting a user's privacy preferences based on location and time of day. However, they did not evaluate to what degree this information influences the prediction.

CONCLUSION

We have presented series of user experiments investigating sharing patterns for context-aware location sharing. We focus on understanding how different contextual factors affect users' location sharing preferences. We show that

users' location privacy preferences are highly context sensitive, location semantic specific and audience-aware. We find that users' location sharing preferences are strongly correlated between the three groups of recipients we studied. We designed a prediction algorithm (PPRec) that can be used to help users configure their privacy settings. Arguably such a 'sharing recommendation' would reduce the burden of manually specifying complex fine-grained privacy policies. We conclude that user preferences are predictable and that algorithms like PPRec could help improve the quality of default privacy management, reducing the risk of being over-exposed or under-exposed. In this paper, we focus on predicting the best setting among a set of given options for a given set of audiences. Designing the best audience grouping and the ideal set of sharing options is not our main focus. However, these are non-trivial tasks that have great impact on the user experience [16]. We would like study in depth a better and smarter audience grouping mechanism.

Although the use of hypothetical scenarios, evaluated by Amazon Mechanical Turk workers, does provide important insights in privacy research as demonstrated in this paper, there are limitations in expressed privacy concerns regarding hypothetical scenarios versus actual in-situ user responses. This motivates our future work on conducting a field study with similar contexts and methods described in this paper. Our offline evaluation of PPRec has shown advantage in achieving reasonably good precision, but the explanation of the recommendation and users' satisfaction with PPRec are open issues that are missing in this work. We are currently conducting a study focusing on user satisfaction with sharing recommendations. This study also considers explanations, which we believe are important for understanding how to build trust between users and a good recommender.

Based on our current findings, we hypothesize that location-sharing recommenders have a great potential for satisfying users' privacy concerns in a user-friendly way: they allow users to exercise more powerful (finer-grained) privacy control, but at the same time alleviate some of the decision burden by reducing the number of location-sharing options the user has to choose from.

REFERENCES

1. Alessandro Acquisti, R. G. Imagined communities: Awareness, information sharing, and privacy on the facebook. *Lecture Notes in Computer Science 4258* (2006), 36–58.

2. Barkhuus et al, L. From awareness to repartee: sharing location within social groups. In *SIGCHI* (2008), 497–506.

3. Benisch, M., Kelley, P. G., and Sadeh, N. Capturing location-privacy preferences: Quantifying accuracy and user-burden tradeoffs. *Journal of Personal and Ubiquitous Computing 15*, 7 (2011), 679–694.

4. Benisch, M., Kelley, P. G., Sadeh, N., Sandholm, T., Tsai, J., Cranor, L. F., and Drielsma, P. H. The impact of expressiveness on the effectiveness of privacy

mechanisms for location-sharing. In *SOUPS* (2009), 22:1–22:1.

5. Bollen, D., Knijnenburg, B. P., Willemsen, M. C., and Graus, M. Understanding choice overload in recommender systems. In *ACM RecSys* (2010), 63–70.

6. Church, L., Anderson, J., Bonneau, J., and Stajano, F. Privacy stories: confidence in privacy behaviors through end user programming. In *SOUPS* (2009), 20:1–20:1.

7. Consolvo, S., Smith, I. E., Matthews, T., LaMarca, A., Tabert, J., and Powledge, P. Location disclosure to social relations: why, when, & what people want to share. In *CHI* (2005), 81–90.

8. Cremonesi, P., Koren, Y., and Turrin, R. Performance of recommender algorithms on top-n recommendation tasks. In *ACM Recsys* (2010), 39–46.

9. Ekman, P. *Emotions Revealed: Understanding Faces and Feelings*. Weidenfeld & Nicolson, June 2004.

10. Fang, L., and LeFevre, K. Privacy wizards for social networking sites. In *WWW* (2010), 351–360.

11. Gross, R., and Acquisti, A. Information revelation and privacy in online social networks. In *ACM WPES* (2005), 71–80.

12. Jakulin, A., and Bratko, I. Testing the Significance of Attribute Interactions. In *ICML* (2004), 409–416.

13. Knijnenburg, B. P., and Jin, H. The persuasive effect of privacy recommendations for location sharing services. In *Pre-ICIS Workshop on HCI Research in MIS, http://bit.ly/SigHCI2013* (2013).

14. Knijnenburg, B. P., and Kobsa, A. Making decisions about privacy: Information disclosure in context-aware recommender systems. *ACM Trans. Interact. Intell. Syst. 3*, 3 (2013), 20:1–20:23.

15. Knijnenburg, B. P., Kobsa, A., and Jin, H. Dimensionality of information disclosure behavior. *IJHCS 71*, 12 (2013), 1144–1162.

16. Knijnenburg, B. P., Kobsa, A., and Jin, H. Preference-based Location Sharing: Are More Privacy Options Really Better? In *CHI* (2013), 2667–2676.

17. Knijnenburg, B. P., Willemsen, M. C., Gantner, Z., Soncu, H., and Newell, C. Explaining the user experience of recommender systems. *User Modeling and User-Adapted Interaction 22*, 4-5 (2012), 441–504.

18. Kobsa, A. Tailoring privacy to users' needs. In *UMAP* (2001), 303–313.

19. Koren, Y. Factorization meets the neighborhood: a multifaceted collaborative filtering model. In *SIGKDD* (2008), 426–434.

20. Lipford, H. R., Besmer, A., and Watson, J. Understanding privacy settings in facebook with an audience view. In *UPSEC* (2008), 2:1–2:8.

21. Page, X., Knijnenburg, B. P., and Kobsa, A. Fyi: communication style preferences underlie differences in location-sharing adoption and usage. In *UbiComp* (2013), 153–162.

22. Paterek, A. Improving regularized singular value decomposition for collaborative filtering. In *SIGKDD Cup Workshop* (2007), 39–42.

23. Patil, S., and Lai, J. Who gets to know what when: configuring privacy permissions in an awareness application. In *CHI* (2005), 101–110.

24. Ravichandran, R., Benisch, M., Kelley, P. G., and Sadeh, N. M. Capturing social networking privacy preferences. In *PETS* (2009), 1–18.

25. Sousa, L. Facebook and your privacy: Who sees the data you share on the biggest social network? *Consumer Reports magazine* (2012).

26. Strater, K., and Lipford, H. R. Strategies and struggles with privacy in an online social networking community. In *British HCI Group Annual Conference on People and Computers* (2008), 111–119.

27. Takács, G., Pilászy, I., Németh, B., and Tikk, D. Scalable collaborative filtering approaches for large recommender systems. *J. Mach. Learn. Res. 10* (2009), 623–656.

28. Thaler, R. H., and Sunstein, C. R. *Nudge: Improving decisions about health, wealth and happiness*. Penguin, Mar. 2008.

29. Toch, E., Sadeh, N. M., and Hong, J. Generating default privacy policies for online social networks. In *CHI* (2010), 4243–4248.

30. Toch et al, E. Empirical models of privacy in location sharing. In *Ubicomp* (2010), 129–138.

31. Tsai, J., Kelley, P., Cranor, L., and Sadeh, N. Location-sharing technologies: Privacy risks and controls. *ISJLP 6* (2010), 119–317.

32. Wilson, S., Cranshaw, J., Sadeh, N., Acquisti, A., Cranor, L. F., Springfield, J., Jeong, S. Y., and Balasubramanian, A. Privacy manipulation and acclimation in a location sharing application. In *ACM UbiComp* (2013), 549–558.

33. Ye, M., Shou, D., Lee, W.-C., Yin, P., and Janowicz, K. On the semantic annotation of places in location-based social networks. In *SIGKDD* (2011), 520–528.

Audio Haptic Videogaming for Developing Wayfinding Skills in Learners Who are Blind

Jaime Sánchez
Department of Computer Science and Center for Advanced Research in Education (CARE), University of Chile Santiago, Chile
jsanchez@dcc.uchile.cl

Marcia de Borba Campos
Faculty of Informatics, Pontifical Catholic University of Rio Grande do Sul
Rio Grande do Sul, Brazil
marcia.campos@pucrs.br

Matías Espinoza
Department of Computer Science and Center for Advanced Research in Education (CARE), University of Chile Santiago, Chile
maespino@dcc.uchile.cl

Lotfi B. Merabet
Dept. Ophthalmology Massachusetts Eye and Ear Infirmary, Harvard Medical School Boston, MA, USA
lotfi_merabet@meei.har vard.edu

ABSTRACT

Interactive digital technologies are currently being developed as a novel tool for education and skill development. Audiopolis is an audio and haptic based videogame designed for developing orientation and mobility (O&M) skills in people who are blind. We have evaluated the cognitive impact of videogame play on O&M skills by assessing performance on a series of behavioral tasks carried out in both indoor and outdoor virtual spaces. Our results demonstrate that the use of Audiopolis had a positive impact on the development and use of O&M skills in school-aged learners who are blind. The impact of audio and haptic information on learning is also discussed.

Author Keywords

Haptic and Audio Interfaces; Orientation; Mobility; Navigation; People Who Are Blind.

ACM Classification Keywords

H.5.m. Information interfaces and presentation (e.g., HCI): Miscellaneous.

General Terms

Human Factors; Design; Measurement.

INTRODUCTION

The demand for innovative teaching and learning approaches has called for focused scientific research in the use of spatial audio and haptic interfaces as a means to facilitate teaching and the promotion of skill development. In particular, these technological approaches have been shown to provide both useful and contextual information needed for correct navigation and independent mobility in daily school-life contexts [8, 9, 10, 19, 20, 21]. In this direction, we aimed to develop a novel approach to allow for the development of skills/senses so that people with

visual disabilities can determine their own position in the space and understand their relationship with objects that are within that space.

To orient in a certain environment and move through it efficiently and independently requires developing basic cognition, psychomotor and emotional prequisites, including perception, attention and concentration, coding, memory, and others [2, 5].

The purpose of this research was to evaluate the impact of an audio and haptic-based videogame designed to promote the development and use of orientation and mobility (O&M) skills in both indoor and outdoor spaces by learners who are blind. The study is unique in combining and integrating interfaces based on audio + haptics for developing O&M skills. There are some studies for developing O&M skills based on just audio and other few studies based on just haptics, but the novel point of our study is the large scale and complexity of the outdoor virtual environment explored. This has not been done in previous studies.

The videogame, Audiopolis [21], requires a user to explore a fictitious environment that contains places habitually navigated by learners who are blind during their school day as well as typically prohibited places that do not include key indications needed for safe navigation. We can state that the most novel aspect of Audiopolis is the combination and integration of audio and tactile information for the purposes of exploration and navigation.

Our previous studies concentrated on audio videogaming for cognition in the blind [13][19]. Basically studies on spatial audio and the development of cognitive skills in the blind such as navigation, problem solving, memory, tempo-spatial skills. Few existing games focus on audio or haptics for this purpose, almost none of them focus on audio and haptics combined and integrated.

RELATED WORK

Orientation and mobility Problems

The ability to understand the environment, to recognize the space and relationship with other objects evolves from day to day. However, to avoid risk and to move about safely, people who are blind will typically follow the perimeter of an environment rather than move through the middle of a room. While effective, this way of exploring the environment can lead users to generate inefficient solutions to their navigational challenges [7]. It is easier for them to navigate a route by following the wall, find access points more easily, and derive a route that they would not otherwise use if moving through other spaces [8]. When a user who is blind has more time to explore and dedicate time to familiarizing themselves with an environment, they can dedicate more time to capturing relevant descriptions used to identify details that would allow for a more precise level of navigation [8].

In this navigation process, some authors such as Mazzaro [12] highlight some stages to follow to facilitate O&M in people who are blind: perception, that allows the user to perceive the information from the environment from the sensory channels; analysis, concerning the organization of the perceived information according to different degrees of confidence and familiarity; selection, to determine what information is more important to meet a navigation need in a certain moment; planning, refers to an action plan for an adequate navigation and considers the previous stages; and execution, that implies executing an action plan to navigate.

It takes that some spatial concepts are constructed by the person who is blind so he can move from one point to another safely. Masi (2003) [11] highlights the concepts of body space, action space, objects space, geometric space, and abstract space. Still, according to the same author, the child who is blind has difficulties to build spatial concepts, which interferes directly in his orientation and mobility.

Based on these issues, it is essential to establish an accurate mental map of a space in order to generate efficient O&M skills, even involuntarily. It is well known that most of the information required to form such a mental representation is generally obtained through visual channels [10, 17]. In contrast, users who are blind must rely on other sensory channels such as audio and tactile information, in addition to other strategies for efficient exploration and navigation [9, 13].

Golledge (1999) [5] use the term cognitive maps to refer to the internal spatial representation of environmental information. He discusses the relationship between cognitive maps, the actual process of cognitive mapping, the internal handling of information in the form of spatial choice and decision making, and people's actions with regard to the spatial orientation through simple and complex environments.

Lahav & Mioduser [8, 9, 10] have studied the relation between the mental representations of space generated by users who are blind through the use of virtual environments with haptic interfaces as well as the transfer of such representations to the real world. To achieve this, they utilized a virtual environment similar to a real-world environment that users who are blind habitually navigate to train them to improve their real-life navigation skills. Similarly, Merabet et al. [13] have researched the construction of mental maps and the improvement of O&M skills through the training of learners using audio-based virtual environments.

Audio and Haptic-based Videogames

AudioLink [19] is an audio-based videogame that was designed and developed to investigate the use of videogames for the development of problem solving and O&M skills.

Terraformers [24] is a videogame for players with low vision that uses high contrast 3D graphics and spatialized sound. This game was developed to test the use of such tools and to replicate experiences in other areas such as virtual reality, e-commerce and distance learning.

The videogame Access Invaders allows users who are blind to play a version of the classic Space Invaders arcade game [6]. The design takes the mental model of users who are blind into account and allows them to play together with other users (users who are blind or users who are sighted) online through a graphic and audio interface. The main objective of the study was to make areas of technology that are often inaccessible to certain people (such as the people who are blind) more accessible.

The Tactile Interactive Multimedia (TIM) project [1] is an effort to develop editing software in order to create videogames for people who are blind. This software allows designers to define the interaction that the user will have with the videogame and the interfaces that will be utilized. Some aspects that the editor strengthens are the temporal elements of the sound, the association between objects, and the sense of spatiality. One of the videogames designed with TIM is X-Tunes [3]. This game allows players who are blind to compete in various tasks such as musical composition, recording, sound manipulation and creating collections of sounds. Another videogame is Tim's Journey [3], which allows users who are blind to navigate through virtual spaces defined by specific sounds, stimulating spatial representation.

Finger Dance [14] is an audio-based videogame that allows a user who is blind to develop temporal skills through sound sequences that must be synchronized with other audio beats in order to achieve the highest possible score.

Finally, Audio-based Environment Simulator (AbES) has been developed to train and improve O&M skills in learners who are blind, promoting the construction of mental maps of indoor real spaces. In this software, two modes of interaction are highlighted. Specifically, there is a mode using directed navigation through different points in the virtual environment (with the help of a facilitator), and a videogame mode that allows for self-exploration and navigation while interacting with solving activities and tasks [13].

Haptic interfaces have also been developed to contribute to the cognitive development of learners who are blind. Interfaces include virtual reality gloves, vibrating joysticks, the Phantom Omni and the Novint Falcon. Georgios and his team [4] developed an interactive virtual reality tool by integrating the Phantom Omni and CyberGrasp (virtual reality glove), allowing users who are blind to study and interact with various virtual objects specially designed for this purpose. These devices also allow for the development of cognitive abilities [23], content specific learning [18] and writing skills [16].

Devices such as the Phantom Omni and the Novint Falcon provide a high level of feedback during interactions with virtual objects. With these devices, surfaces, objects and graphics can be represented and recognized by users who are blind through the unique haptic information that is transmitted [15, 20, 21, 22, 25]. Another use of these devices is the representation of virtual spaces for training users who are blind to navigate with more autonomy [20, 21, 22]. With both the Phantom Omni and the Novint Falcon, the user receives haptic feedback from the virtual environment so as to recognize objects, walls and hallways allowing for the generation of a mental map of the space that has been navigated [9, 10, 20].

AUDIOPOLIS

The Audiopolis videogame was designed to represent in principle any urban environment for navigation by learners who are blind. This environment can be real or fictitious, being relevant that a person who is blind can experience the space to better understand it. Various elements and co-experiencing components of a city can be included in the environment such as streets, opens spaces, and buildings. In Audiopolis, a bank, museum, jewelry store, hospital, restaurant, shops, city hall, parks, plazas, library, bookstore, school, university, hotel, supermarket, houses, apartment and office buildings can all be included in the virtual environment.

The videogame is played from a first person perspective. The user can move freely throughout the environment, including forward, backward and turning left and right. The user recognizes the various surfaces through which he or she is traveling either through audio or haptic feedback, as well as the various obstacles while moving through the virtual city. Through virtual exploration, the user can familiarize them-selves with the entire map and established routes. Basically, the user had to solve problems and answer some questions.

Turn angles of 30 degrees were defined as well as a standard length of each step taken as the user moves through the environment.

The game consists of 3 different levels of difficulty: easy, medium and advanced. These different levels are determined by the level of geographic complexity of the corresponding virtual city. In order to do this, the city was divided into three sectors. Level 1 considers tasks in sector 1. Level 2 considers tasks in sectors 1 and 2. Finally, level 3 considers tasks in sectors 1, 2 and 3 (see Figure 1). Each level implies a gradual and more difficult level of spatial information, presenting streets with different addresses and having available a wider number of buildings to explore.

For each level, the map of the city expands out on four sides, leaving more free space for the player to move about. In addition, the map integrates new elements that increase the level of complexity as the user moves through the environment.

There are 3 stages within each level. In each stage, a thief steals an object and the goal of the game is to find the thief. In each stage, the player begins at the scene of the crime and must find 3 different places within the city while "chasing" the thief. The player must also solve a series of questions that are presented in order to receive the next clue and continue moving throughout the city. Once the stolen object has been found, the player passes on to the next stage.

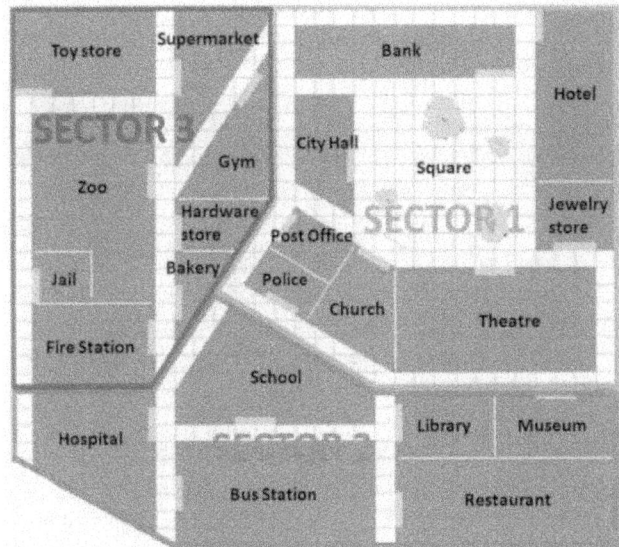

Fig. 1. Audiopolis level map.

To execute the game, a user needs a standard desktop PC or notebook running the Microsoft Windows XP operating system, the Novint Falcon haptic device, and a pair of speakers or headphones.

Interfaces

The videogame possesses 3 interface options for interaction (haptic, audio, and haptic plus audio) which operate in combination with the graphic interface. The latter graphic interface is designed for use by the facilitators that support the experiment.

Audio Interface

This interface has two main modes; environmental and instructive. The environmental component consists of a set of sounds that simulate both the indoor and outdoor environments in which the player is located. It also serves to pro-vide information that allows learners to recognize the shapes of different geometric objects. The environmental component corresponds to sound associated to a location, and its intensity depends of the position and orientation in the game. Iconic sounds and spatial localization were used. The instructive component is made up of the questions that provide clues and the instructions from the main menu, such as: "quit", "save game", etc. In addition, during the game the player can query his or her current position, or ask for the direction in which he or she is facing. All of this is answered through the audio interface.

Haptic Interface

The Novint Falcon device was used as a haptic-based force-feedback interface. With this device, we sought to simulate haptic information that could be obtained through direct touch (i.e. with the hands) and indirect touch (i.e. with a cane). The force feedback generated by the Falcon provides information regarding the physical characteristics of the place where the user is located. As the player moves about through the city (by pressing the arrow keys on the device and by dragging the cane on the floor to feel different textures that signal different paths), the user can find his or her way on a route with different levels. The player can also identify objects (e.g. a cube) by exploring their shape using the device. In this case, an object is modeled in 3D and the haptic control simulates a hand.

Haptic and Audio Interface

This interface combines the two previously mentioned sensory inputs in order to provide the user with more robust information regarding position and to provide more ample support for navigation tasks.

Graphic Interface

This interface represents a high contrast rendering of the virtual environment so that the facilitator can observe where and at what point in the game the learner who is blind is located and help the user if necessary (see Figure 2).

COGNITIVE IMPACT EVALUATION

Sample

In selecting the sample, we considered studies of Espinosa et al. (1998), who argue that the spatial knowledge of a person depends on several factors. Among these, the personal characteristics (age, cognitive development, perceptual modality used for encoding spatial information), environment characteristics (size, structure) and factors related to learning processes in relation to spatial information.

The study sample was made up of 12 learners (8 females and 4 males) between 10 and 15 years of age, with special educational needs due to visual impairment (11 learners

who are blind and 1 with low vision). All were from within the first or second cycles of General Elementary Education from the Helen Keller School and Santa Lucia Educational Center in Santiago, Chile. The sample was divided into 3 groups of 4 learners and randomized to each of the three possible interfaces of the videogame (audio group, haptic group, and haptic+audio group). These participants, because they study in the same schools, take part of the same methods to teach people who are blind to construct spatial concepts.

Figure 2. Graphic interface.

Tasks

Three training tasks and 12 cognitive tasks were established. The training tasks were designed to introduce the participants to the concepts and components used in the videogame. The training tasks were: (i) clock technique: to learn heading cues used in the videogame (see Figure 3); (ii) geometric shapes: to develop the interpretation of the shapes used during the interaction with the videogame (see Figure 4); and (iii) the elements of the videogame: to introduce the participant to the integrated use of all the elements involved in the videogame.

The cognitive tasks were focused on developing specific O&M skills based on the software interface. The cognitive tasks were: (i) Level 1: perception and dynamics; (ii) Level 1: movement, directionality and distribution; (iii) Level 1: establishment of distances; (iv) Level 2: perception and dynamics; (v) Level 2: movement, directionality and distribution; (vi) Level 2: establishment of distance; (vii) Level 3: perception and dynamics; (viii) Level 3: movement, directionality and distribution; (ix) Level 3: establishment of distances. Furthermore, the total integration of the game level was scored for (x) game 1; (xi) game 2; and (xii) game 3.

The sequential levels were a progression in complexity of the overall spatial layout of the environment. Each successive level had to be mastered before moving on to the next level. Levels 1, 2, 3 refer to game level. In each cognitive task the percentage of achievement was measured based on the total number of steps to complete a task, which resulted homogeneous all along the tasks and the different interfaces. The two interviews were conducted at the beginning of the study. In each session, the participants went through one game level, one cognitive task.

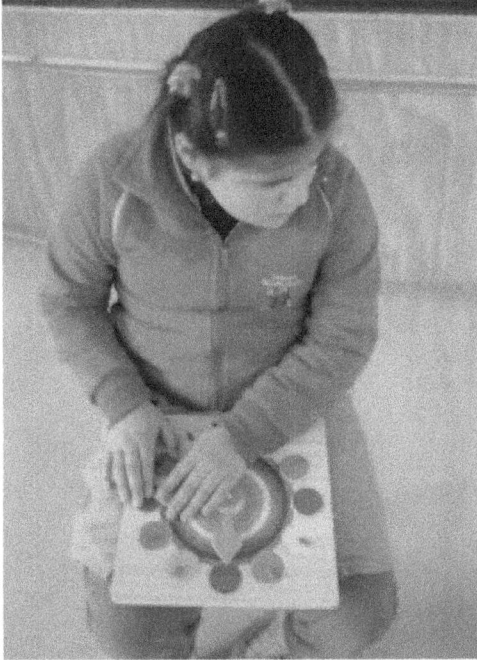

Figure 3. Training tasks: clock technique.

The objective of the cognitive tasks related to perception of the virtual space through sound, haptics, or both, depending on the interface used. Furthermore, movement, directionality and distribution were promoted through the use of turns connected to the clock system. In this way, users would learn to perceive places and how these places were in spatial relation to one another. In the case of the cognitive tasks regarding the establishment of distances, the purpose was to work on the structuring of Audiopolis and the relation between steps and distance. This means that a higher number of steps implied a longer distance between one place to another.

Instruments

The instruments of evaluation utilized for this research were created by a group of special education teachers who specialize in children who are blind and are integrated members of the research team. These instruments correspond to interviews and O&M tests.

Two interviews were carried out; one in-depth and the other structured. The in-depth interview was applied in order to analyze the O&M difficulties that the subjects faced in their daily lives. In addition, it sought to understand how they perceived the contribution of the audio and haptic-based videogame to the development of their O&M skills. This

was determined through statements that were evaluated on an appreciating numeric scale with 4 frequency categories: never, almost never, sometimes, and always. This information was also complemented by a section with open-ended questions. The objective of the structured interview was to understand the perception that the subjects have of themselves regarding their O&M skills and other variables such as their motivation and self-esteem.

The O&M test was designed to estimate the level of knowledge related to this specific area of learning. The dimensions included were: (i) Sensory development (SD) containing 35 indicators which included the sub-dimensions Audio sensory development (ASD) with 12 indicators, and Haptic sensory development (HSD) with 23 indicators, (ii) Tempo-spatial development dimension (TSD) containing 24 indicators, and (iii) O&M Techniques dimension (O&MT) containing 12 indicators, grouping together 71 indicators in total. The evaluation criteria for each indicator were: Achieved (A), In Process (IP), Not Achieved (NA), with scores of 2, 1 and 0, respectively.

Figure 4. Training tasks: geometric shapes.

Procedure

The procedure involved all of the users in the sample. In addition, two special education teachers specializing in visual impairment played the role of facilitators. These teachers aided the users and recorded their use of the instruments.

The work was carried out in 3 stages: (i) Initiation, before working with the soft-ware; (ii) Process, during the development of the activities using the computer games; (iii) Finish, at the end of the process.

In the phase prior to the use of the software, the O&M test was applied as a pre-test in order to record the subjects' initial baseline skills. Interviews were also conducted with the participants. Afterwards, the users performed the 3 training tasks related to the skills that they needed to master before using the videogame.

During the process of the intervention with the videogame, the users performed the 12 cognitive tasks during one session per task (see Figure 5). Each session involved carrying out a series of activities according to the previously described dimensions, and in accordance with the 3 levels of complexity included in the videogame.

Fig. 5. A user performing a cognitive task: playing Audiopolis.

Finally in the final stage, the O&M test was applied to the users as a post-test, in order to determine whether or not there was any change on the previously evaluated skills.

RESULTS

Interview

The interview included two sections. In the first section, 5 statements were presented related to O&M in which the participants had to respond using the frequency scale. Their answers to these statements are summarized in Table 1.

The second section included 8 open-ended questions, of which 5 were related to O&M difficulties in daily life and 3 related to the users' perception of the contribution of the videogame to their skills. In general, the users claimed experiencing difficulties in the use of cane techniques. In addition, despite knowing certain techniques, they did not always use them as a problem solving strategy. Regarding the use of their remaining senses, they preferred to use hearing as a first option in order to obtain information from their everyday surroundings. In general, to perform tasks involving independent movement through unfamiliar spaces, they required the support of third parties, which was also the case in familiar spaces when they decided to change their habitual route.

In this way, the users in the sample represented homogenous characteristics in accordance to the results of the interviews.

Training Tasks

The results obtained from the impact tests regarding the 3 training tasks (TT) are summarized in Table 2. According to these results, the participants obtained a satisfactory performance in the training tasks, attaining an average score of over 90%. In general, the positive development of the proposed activities prepared the learners for the application of the cognitive tests during the following stage, and thus

fulfilled the objective. In addition, the results of the training tasks are very similar between the different user groups, which imply that the users' initial skill level was homogenous.

Statement	Always	Someti mes	Almost Never	Never
"When I become disoriented, I generally ask for help"	5 (41.67%)	5 (41.67%)	1 (8.33%)	1 (8.33%)
"I like to explore new places"	6 (50%)	4 (33.33%)	1 (8.33%)	1 (8.33%)
"I think that it's important to use O&M techniques to move around"	9 (75%)	2 (16.67%)	0 (0%)	1 (8.33%)
"I try to protect myself if I am in a dangerous situation"	3 (25%)	7 (58.33%)	2 (16.67%)	0 (0%)
"I am attentive to the information that the environment provides me (people, fixed and moving objects)"	6 (50%)	4 (33.33%)	0 (0%)	2 (16.67%)

Table 1. Frequencies of interview responses

Cognitive Tasks

The results obtained from the impact tests through the 12 cognitive tasks (CT) are shown in Table 3.

The results show that throughout the development of the cognitive tasks, the level of achievement remained high and homogeneous, which is important when considering that the degree of complexity increased with each task.

N° Training Task	Group 1 Audio [%]	Group 2 Haptic [%]	Group 3 Audio+Haptic [%]	Average [%]
TT 1	91.67	92.19	94.27	92.71
TT 2	93.75	88.22	78.37	86.78
TT 3	90.04	89.31	86.41	88.59

Table 2. Participant performance in the 3 Training Tasks

O&M Test

For this test, the entire set of participants was analyzed according to the videogame interface group. The following dimensions and sub-dimensions of the O&M test were analyzed. Each dimension was evaluated through the sum of indicators that contained: Sensory development (SD, min-value=0, max-value =70), which included the sub-dimensions Audio sensory development (ASD, min-value=0, max-value=24) and Haptic sensory development (HSD, min-value=0, max-value=46); also the Tempo-spatial development dimension (TSD, min-value=0, max-value=48), the O&M Techniques dimension (O&MT, min-value=0, max-value=24) and the Global Indicator (min-value=0, max-value =142). The Global is the sum of SD plus TSD and O&MT. The SD dimension is the sum of ASD plus HSD.

In obtaining the results for the 12 users in the sample, a t test was performed to compare the means of the indicators obtained for the pre-test and the post-test of the entire group (see Table 4).

All of the dimensions presented increased in their post-test means com-pared to the pre-test means. However, these differences in the averages were statistically significant only in the ASD dimension (pre-test mean=21.420; post-test mean=23.250; t=-4.005; p<0.05), HSD dimension (pre-test mean=42.830; post-test mean= 44.500; t=-3.079; p<0.05), SD dimension (pre-test mean=64.250; post-test mean=67.750; t=-5.326; p<0.05), O&MT dimension (pre-test mean=16.170; post-test mean=19.080; t=-2.907; p<0.05) and the Global Indicator (pre-test mean=120.170; post-test mean=132.000; t=-4.366; p<0.05).

Complementary to this, a MANOVA test was applied to the posttest data, considering the three user groups (audio, haptics and haptic+audio) as factors. According to the MANOVA analysis, the mean vectors for the different groups did not present statistical differences between them. That is, the results for the different dimensions do not differ in function of the interface that defined the groups. It is possible that our study sample size was underpowered to detect such differences.

On this basis, we can infer that in general, the use of the videogame allowed for improving the associated cognitive

skills to the dimensions ASD, HSD, SD, O&MT and the Global Indicator. This happens in all the interfaces studied.

N° Cognitive Task	Group 1 Audio [%]	Group 2 Haptic [%]	Group 3 Audio+Haptic [%]	Average [%]
CT 1	82.91	80.54	75.83	79.76
CT 2	81.39	83.77	70.36	78.51
CT 3	83.79	78.76	77.00	79.85
CT 4	84.38	84.21	75.89	81.49
CT 5	86.97	79.88	86.51	84.46
CT 6	84.97	78.88	84.31	82.72
CT 7	87.50	79.02	80.15	82.22
CT 8	89.96	80.86	84.21	85.01
CT 9	79.92	89.86	71.00	80.26
CT 10	74.76	88.86	68.69	77.44
CT 11	86.67	82.34	72.01	80.34
CT 12	82.38	84.38	77.65	81.47

Table 3. Performance of the entire group in the 12 Cognitive Tasks

Indicator	Pre-test Mean	Post-test Mean	Diff.	t	P
ASD	21.420	23.250	1.833	-4.005	0.002
HSD	42.830	44.500	1.667	-3.079	0.010
SD	64.250	67.750	3.500	-5.326	0.001
TSD	40.080	44.000	3.917	-1.777	0.103
O&MT	16.170	19.080	2.917	-2.907	0.014
Global Indicator	120.170	132.000	11.833	-4.366	0.001

Table 4. T Test Results

DISCUSSION

As we had no true "control" group (ie. a group not playing Audiopolis), it is complex to demonstrate the beneficial effect above and beyond the training procedure. We concentrated on the pre-post assessments. Since we had a baseline of performance, our analysis is essentially a within-group comparison.

Interaction with the Audiopolis videogame led to markedly high performance levels in the users during the training tasks. This denoted a high mastering of the users concerning the concepts and components that the videogame is mainly based.

In relation to the cognitive tasks, it is important to mention that the level of complexity increases from task 1 to task 12. This is mainly due to the ramping up of the map size, producing an increase in difficulty for the activities involved in the tasks.

The virtual environment, as a simulation of a space with urban characteristics, allowed learners to work within a "safe environment". When performing the search tasks, the learners applied their prior knowledge to test and reinforce previously acquired concepts. In this way, their predisposition to learning was favored by using the videogame. The learners were observed to be highly motivated while performing the various activities.

The learners were also able to create new strategies for solving the problems regarding movement through a virtual space with Audiopolis. Such strategies included going backwards to become reoriented while on a route, circling around different objects, and guiding movements by sound or touch in order to get to know the boundaries of a space. In general, the group of learners displayed an increase in navigational skills by using the videogame, which can be observed through the speed with which they surpassed the various stages, moving through the game with increasing efficiency.

The use of different interfaces in the videogame helped to generate a positive effect on the learning of O&M skills. The statistical results regarding the difference in the means obtained between the pre-test and the post-test of the entire group resulted in an increase that was statistically significant for some dimensions. These dimensions included the Sensory Development dimension (in addition to the Audio Sensory Development and Haptic Sensory Development sub-dimensions), the O&M Techniques dimension, and the Global Indicator of O&M dimension. A second statistical analysis determined that the results did not differ by segmenting each interface group.

The level obtained in pretest indicators can be considered high, if we take into ac-count the maximum possible values. This left a small margin for improvement in posttest indicators consistent with a possible ceiling effect for performance (see Table 4).

Consequently, an increase in the sample of users employed eventually could yield would be needed to validate these findings.

CONCLUSION

The purpose of this research was satisfactorily achieved by evaluating the impact of the use of an audio and haptic-based videogame called Audiopolis on the develop-ment and use of O&M skills in both indoor and outdoor spaces. The use of Audiopolis had a positive impact on the development and use of O&M skills in school age learners

who are blind. Based on this, it can be initially inferred that the videogame's audio and/or haptic interfaces favor and aid in the development of O&M skills in learners who are blind.

The audio, haptic and combined audio-haptic stimuli aided in generating an in-creased understanding of the participants' senses. It was observed that in order to orient themselves, the users preferred the use of hearing rather than touch.

We designed Audiopolis with both, audio and haptics modes to determine the role that haptics and audio-haptics can play in developing O&M skills. The literature does not inform about robust experiences in this line of research. Haptics is relative new in the development of O&M skills. Perhaps the tactile information provided was not optimal and/or did not supplement the information that could be drawn from audio. There is still a limitation of the type haptics skills we can enhance with the devices available and usable for these end users. Future work will be directed to see what types of information are optimally provided by both audio and tactile and how they can be optimally combined.

The results with the audio interface were better perhaps due to the increased complexity involved in the use of the Novint Falcon device (audio+haptic), versus using the standard keyboard (audio interface), which probably resulted in a better outcome in audio interface.

As future work, it is proposed to increase the sample base in order to investigate potential differences between the distinct interface-groups utilized and to analyze the learning of spatial layout of unknown environments.

ACKNOWLEDGMENTS
This report was funded by the Chilean National Fund of Science and Technology, Fondecyt #1120330 and Project CIE-05 Program Center Education PBCT-Conicyt.

REFERENCES
1. Archambault, D., Olivier, D. How to make games for visually impaired children. In *Proc. ACE '05*, vol. 265. ACM, New York, NY, pp. 450-453 (2005)

2. Espinosa, M. A., Ungar, S., Ochaíta, E., Blades, M., Spencer, C. Comparing methods for introducing blind and visually impaired people to unfamiliar urban environments. Journal of Environmental Psychology, Volume 18, Issue 3, September 1998, Pages 277-287 (1998)

3. Friberg, J., Gärdenfors, D. Audio games: new perspectives on game audio. In *Proc. ACE '04*, vol. 74. ACM, New York, NY, pp. 148-154 (2004)

4. Georgios, N., Tzovaras, D., Moustakidis, S., Strintzis, M. Cybergrasp and PHANTOM integration: enhanced haptic access for visually impaired users. In *Proc. SPECOM-2004*, pp.507-513 (2004)

5. Golledge, R. G. *Wayfinding behavior: Cognitive mapping and other spatial processes*. Baltimore: Johns Hopkins University Press (1999)

6. Grammenos, D., Savidis, A., Georgalis, Y., Stephanidis, C. Access Invaders, Developing a Universally Accessible Action Game. In *Proc. ICCHP 2006*, Lecture Notes of Computer Science, LNCS 4061, pp. 388-395 (2006)

7. Kulyukin, V., Gharpure, C., Nicholson, J., Pavithran, S. RFID in robot-assisted indoor navigation for the visually impaired. In *Proc. IROS 2004*, Sendai Kyodo Printing: Sendai, Japan, pp. 1979- 1984 (2004)

8. Lahav, O., Mioduser, D. Blind Persons' Acquisition of Spatial Cognitive Mapping and Orientation Skills Supported by Virtual Environment. In *Proc. ICDVRAT 2004*, Oxford, UK, 2004, pp. 131-138 (2004)

9. Lahav, O., Mioduser, D. Haptic-feedback support for cognitive mapping of unknown spaces by people who are blind. International Journal Human-Computer Studies 66(1), pp. 23-35 (2008)

10. Lahav, O., Mioduser, D. Construction of cognitive maps of unknown spaces using a multi-sensory virtual environment for people who are blind. Computers in Human Behavior 24(3), pp. 1139-1155 (2008)

11. Masi, I. Aquisição básica para a orientação e mobilidade. In Mota, M. G. B. da. Orientação e mobilidade: conhecimentos básicos para a inclusão da pessoa com deficiência visual. Brasília: Ministério de Educação, Secretaria de Educação Especial, Brasil, (2003)

12. Mazzaro, J. Mas, afinal, o que é orientação e mobilidade?. In Mota, M. G. B. da. Orientação e mobilidade: conhecimentos básicos para a inclusão da pessoa com deficiência visual. Brasília: Ministério de Educação, Secretaria de Educação Especial, Brasil, (2003)

13. Merabet, L., Connors, E., Halko M., Sánchez, J. Teaching the Blind to Find Their Way by Playing Video Games. In PLoS ONE 7(9): e44958. Sep 2012. pp 1-6 (2012)

14. Miller, D., Parecki, A., Douglas, S. Finger dance: a sound game for blind people. In *Proc. ASSETS '07*. ACM, New York, NY, pp. 253-254 (2007)

15. Nikolakis G., Tzovaras D., Strintzis M. Object Recognition For The Blind. In *Proc. EUSIPCO2005*, Antalya, Turkey, pp. 1-4 (2005)

16. Plimmer, B., Crossan, A., Brewster, S., Blagojevic, R.: Multimodal Collaborative Handwriting Training for Visually-Impaired People. In: *Proc. CHI 2008* Proceedings Collaborative User Interfaces, April 5-10, 2008, Florence, Italy, pp. 393-402 (2008)

17. Rodrigues, C. *Um Dispositivo Háptico de Auxílio À Navegacao para Deficientes Visuais*. Trabalho de Graduacao do Centro de Informática da Universidade Federal de Pernambuco para a obtencao do grau de Bacharel em Ciência da Computacao, (2006)

18. Roth, P., Petrucci, L., Pun, T. From Dots To Shapes: an auditory haptic game platform for teaching geometry to blind pupils. In *Proc. ICCHP 2000*, Karlsruhe, pp. 603-610 (2000)

19. Sánchez, J., Elías, M. Guidelines for Designing Mobility and Orientation Software for Blind Children. In *Proc. INTERACT 2007*, Lecture Notes of Computer Science, LNCS 4662, Part I, pp. 375-388, (2007)

20. Sánchez, J., Espinoza, M. Audio haptic videogaming for navigation skills in learners who are blind. In *Proc. ASSETS '11*. ACM, New York, NY, USA, 227-228 (2011)

21. Sánchez, J., Mascaró, J. Audiopolis, navigation through a virtual city using audio and haptic interfaces for people who are blind. In *Proc. UAHCI'11*, Vol. Part II. Springer-Verlag, Berlin, Heidelberg, 362-371 (2011)

22. Sánchez, J., Tadres, A. Audio and haptic based virtual environments for orientation and mobility in people who are blind. In *Proc. ASSETS '10*. ACM, New York, NY, USA, pp. 237-238 (2010)

23. Sarmiento, L., Vargas, O. DMREI Sistema de Ayuda a Invidentes para Detectar el Color y la Posición de los Objetos Mediante Estimulación Táctil. In *Proc. VII Congreso Iberoamericano de Informática Educativa*, Monterrey, México, pp. 264-273 (2004)

24. Westin, T. Game accessibility case study: Terraformers – a real-time 3D graphic game. In *Proc. ICDVRAT 2004*, Oxford, UK, pp. 95-100 (2004)

25. Yu, W., Brewster, S. Comparing Two Haptic Interfaces for Multimodal Graph Rendering. In: *Proc. Haptics 2002*, Florida, USA, IEEE, pp. 3-9 (2002)

Triangle Charades: A Data-Collection Game for Recognizing Actions in Motion Trajectories

Melissa Roemmele
roemmele@ict.usc.edu
Inst. for Creative Technologies
University of Southern California
Los Angeles, CA USA

Haley Archer-McClellan
archermcclellanh15@mail.wlu.edu
Dept. of Computer Science
Washington and Lee University
Lexington, VA USA

Andrew S. Gordon
gordon@ict.usc.edu
Inst. for Creative Technologies
University of Southern California
Los Angeles, CA USA

ABSTRACT

Humans have a remarkable tendency to anthropomorphize moving objects, ascribing to them intentions and emotions as if they were human. Early social psychology research demonstrated that animated film clips depicting the movements of simple geometric shapes could elicit rich interpretations of intentional behavior from viewers. In attempting to model this reasoning process in software, we first address the problem of automatically recognizing humanlike actions in the trajectories of moving shapes. There are two main difficulties. First, there is no defined vocabulary of actions that are recognizable to people from motion trajectories. Second, in order for an automated system to learn actions from motion trajectories using machine-learning techniques, a vast amount of these action-trajectory pairs is needed as training data. This paper describes an approach to data collection that resolves both of these problems. In a web-based game, called Triangle Charades, players create motion trajectories for actions by animating a triangle to depict those actions. Other players view these animations and guess the action they depict. An action is considered recognizable if players can correctly guess it from animations. To move towards defining a controlled vocabulary and collecting a large dataset, we conducted a pilot study in which 87 users played Triangle Charades. Based on this data, we computed a simple metric for action recognizability. Scores on this metric formed a gradual linear pattern, suggesting there is no clear cutoff for determining if an action is recognizable from motion data. These initial results demonstrate the advantages of using a game to collect data for this action recognition task.

Author Keywords

Games and Play; Animation; Crowdsourcing

ACM Classification Keywords

H.5.m. Information interfaces and presentation (e.g., HCI): Miscellaneous.

INTRODUCTION

The human imagination generates rich meaning from simple physical observations. In 1944, Heider and Simmel [6] experimentally demonstrated this by showing people a simple animated display of triangles and a circle (Figure 1). Participants in this social psychology experiment readily described the movement of the shapes in terms of human social interaction, where the shapes were human characters with psychological states like feelings, intentions, and desires. The stories participants told about the shapes were highly similar, most commonly describing two men (the two triangles) fighting for the affection of a woman (the circle). This ability to interpret motion patterns in an anthropomorphic way has been continually revisited by social scientists in the years since Heider and Simmel's foundational study [2, 4, 5, 7].

The field of artificial intelligence is also interested in this process by which people attribute feelings, intentions, and desires to others. Here, the motive of researchers is to design software that automates this social inference task. Such software has many practical applications, such as security monitoring and expressive user interfaces. Heider and Simmel's experimental task is a representative model of what a system must do in order to automatically interpret human behavior. This task abstracts away from the full complexity of human motion, reducing it to a simple trajectory displayed by a 2-dimensional shape. This simplicity is actually an advantage for an AI system. The system does not need to process a large amount of noisy perceptual input in order to do the inference task. Rather, because motion trajectories of shapes are straightforward to represent computationally, the system can focus on solving the behavior interpretation task itself.

But even this behavior interpretation task involves a multi-layered cognitive pipeline. At some point during this pipeline, as the shapes in the animation begin to be perceived as intentional characters, people judge what the characters are doing. The characters' motion trajectories are recognized as discrete behavioral actions such as fighting, chasing, or flirting, for instance. This action recognition task is required to further infer the character's

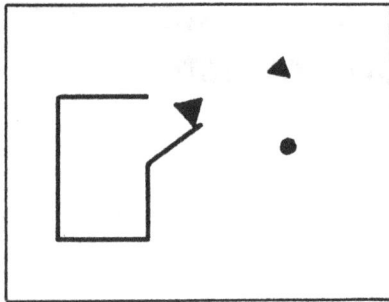

Figure 1. A frame from Heider and Simmel's film [6].

psychological states. Thus, if we want to build an AI system that does this behavior interpretation task, we first need to automatically recognize actions from motion trajectories.

There are two main challenges to performing this action recognition task. First, it is unclear exactly which human actions can be depicted with motion trajectories. No controlled vocabulary of recognizable actions currently exists, so we first need to define one. Once we have established this vocabulary, we need a large amount of motion trajectory data for each of its actions for use as training data in a supervised machine learning architecture. In this paper, we describe a game-based data-collection approach that resolves both of these problems. The game, called Triangle Charades, is a web application in which players animate shapes resembling those in Heider and Simmel's original experiment. By creating animations and evaluating other players' animations, players contribute to both of the above goals: they define which actions are recognizable from motion trajectories and they provide motion trajectory data for these actions. Using the resulting data we can then attempt to design a system that automatically perceives human actions in motion displays.

RELATED WORK

Psychologists and anthropologists have begun to more formally examine how people recognize human actions in motion trajectories, which has consequently motivated AI work on this task. There seem to be unique properties of motion displays that yield a perception of animacy, since not all displays are perceived in this way. Researchers in the visual perception community have tried to isolate the motion features that promote a human action-based interpretation [4, 5, 9, 11]. Klein et al. [7] revealed through eye-tracking methodology that animations perceived in terms of human action take longer to process than animations perceived merely as objective physical motion. This extra processing time for the animate displays may be due to people making inferences about the action the display evokes and its meaning in a social context.

Other work has focused on how, within animate displays, different motion cues yield different perceptions of action. Barrett et al. [2] collected motion trajectory data for intentional actions like fighting and playing, using a two-

person software interface similar to the one used in our game. The players were assigned agents whose movement they controlled using a mouse. They manipulated the agents' movement to perform designated actions. For instance, when the action given was "chase", one player would make their agent chase the other player's agent, while the second player made their agent evade the first player's agent. The researchers then showed the motion trajectories generated by this method to a different group of participants. They found that often participants could identify the intended action associated with the motion trajectory just by looking at the trajectory data alone. However, they were only given six possible actions to choose from (chasing, courting, following, playing, fighting, and guarding).

If humans can recognize different actions based on motion data, then possibly so can a machine equipped with that data. There has been some effort in AI on tasks related to this one. Crick and Scassellati [3] collected motion trajectory data similar to the data we collect with our game, but through a very different process. They attached sensors to individuals and objects (e.g. a ball) participating in live-action playground games, and these sensors captured participants' positions at each point in the game. From this data, they could determine the degree of attraction and repulsion between participants in the game, which in turn enabled them to identify which action was occurring at any point in the game (e.g. "player A chased player B for 10 seconds"). Further, by putting sequences of actions together, they could determine which game was being played (e.g. tag versus catch). Young et al. [13] elicited motion trajectory data from people through an animation task like ours. In this work, artists animated characters on a table-top interface using physical pucks tracked by a motion capture system. The artists had the characters perform actions that were reflective of social roles like "lover" or "bully". The motion data from these animations was used to create characters that move autonomously in styles that display their designated social role. This is highly related to our work, but we proceed in the opposite direction: whereas Young et al.'s goal was to automatically establish motion from social information, our goal is to automatically establish social information (actions) from motion.

Researchers have started creating games for artificial intelligence problems because they provide an inexpensive way to elicit a lot of data from people. Games that collect data for computational tasks have been called "games with a purpose" [12]. While people play GWAPs for entertainment, they unwittingly provide data used to automate tasks that cannot otherwise be automated. There have been GWAPs designed for perceptual and social judgment tasks similar to the one described here [1, 10]. The success of game approaches on these tasks has motivated us to apply it to the action recognition problem.

SOLUTION

Our work is unique in that we want to identify all actions that have recognizable motion trajectories. In our work, an action is represented by an English-language verb (e.g. "hop", "punch", "slide"). Most English-language verbs do not have a motion trajectory representation that people can recognize. Rather than just relying on our own intuition about which actions are recognizable, we seek to determine this empirically. We can then define a controlled vocabulary of recognizable actions.

The game we designed, Triangle Charades, is based on the classic party game Charades, in which players must convey concepts or entities using non-verbal language only. Our game utilizes the same concept, except that here players must convey actions by animating 2-D triangles on a web interface. There are two modes of play in Triangle Charades. In both modes, the interface consists of a white background, or "stage", on which solid black triangles move around, resembling the design of Heider and Simmel's classic animation. Players can create motion trajectories for actions in "authoring" mode and attempt to identify the action depicted by other players' motion trajectories in "guessing" mode. There is no requirement to play in one mode or the other, so players can simply switch modes whenever they choose.

Authoring mode

In authoring mode (Figure 2), players are presented with an action and they must create an animation depicting that action. To do this, they manipulate the movement of either one or two triangles, depending on how many characters are necessarily involved in the action. Single-character actions, such as "spin" and "tremble", only require one character to perform the action, so players are given one triangle to manipulate. In contrast, two-character actions like "hit" and "chase" describe interactions between characters where one character is performing the action and the other is receiving it. In this case, two triangles appear, and players can manipulate both in order to depict the given action. One of the triangles appears reduced in size so that players can distinguish between the "big" triangle and the "little" triangle. The player is prompted to depict a two-character action via a command that appears above the stage: "big triangle [ACTION] the little triangle". If the action is "chase", for example, the player must animate the triangles so that it appears that the big triangle chases the little triangle. The prompt for single-character actions merely shows the action that the player must depict with the triangle. The interface enables players to control the triangles' movement by simply touching them on the tablet, which establishes a dragging effect by which the triangles can be moved (translated and rotated). Since two-character actions require simultaneous animation of both triangles, a multi-touch tablet device must be used. However, a mouse-controlled device can be used to animate single-character actions. As the player drags the triangle(s), the game automatically records its successive movements to establish

an animation. Players can view this animation by selecting "playback". If a player starts animating and wishes to start over, they can select "reset" to discard their existing animation. There is a 60-second time limit for animations. If a player exceeds this time limit, their animation is automatically discarded and reset, and they receive an alert to complete the new animation within 60 seconds. When the player is satisfied with their animation for a given action, they can upload it to the game server by selecting "submit". They will then see a new action to be animated. The submitted animation will become viewable to other players in guessing mode. It is possible for authors to animate the same action more than once.

Guessing mode

In guessing mode (Figure 3), players are shown an animation authored by another player, and prompted to identify the action depicted by the animation. There is no time limit for guessing, and players can replay the animation as needed by selecting "playback". Rather than freely guessing actions for an animation, players are shown a set of six actions. From these options, the player must select which action the original author of the animation intended to depict. The other five options are randomly chosen from the set of all actions. A match between the guesser's selected action and the author's intended action is considered a correct selection. Players receive immediate feedback about whether their selection is correct. If the player is wrong, that option is removed and the player must make another selection. Players continue selecting actions until the correct one is selected. In the worst case, the only remaining action will be the correct one, which the player will have to select. As soon as the player selects the correct action, a new animation is loaded, along with a new set of options to choose from. Players are never given their own animations to guess. This process continues for as long as the player wants to keep playing in guessing mode.

Game Mechanics and UI Issues

Triangle Charades is coded in JavaScript and HTML. It is

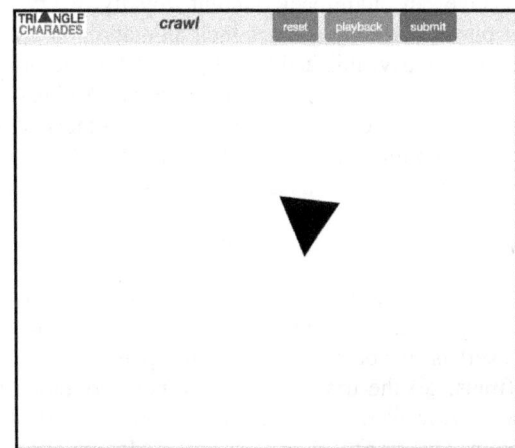

Figure 2. Triangle Charades in authoring mode. In this example, the player animates the action "crawl."

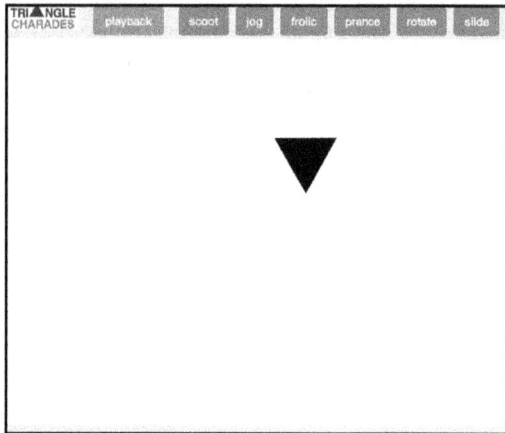

Figure 3. Triangle Charades in guessing mode. The user guesses which of six actions was intended in an animation.

accessible via the hyperlink http://charades.ict.usc.edu/. Players must log in on this page with a username and password. Accounts are required to play because Triangle Charades rewards points to players, and players' points accumulate across sessions of game play. A point scheme helps motivate players to author high-quality animations, and likewise provide careful guesses. Points rewarded in guessing mode are straightforward. If a player's first selection is correct (i.e. the one intended by the author), the guesser receives 10 points. Guessing correctly on the second, third, fourth, fifth, and final attempts yields 8, 6, 4, 2, and 0 points, respectively. Just as in live-action Charades, success in Triangle Charades requires collaboration between guessers and authors. Guessers rely on the authors to create animations whose depicted action is recognizable. Consequently, authors receive points for creating animations. Players automatically receive 10 points for every animation they author. Obviously, some actions are inherently not recognizable from animations, despite the skill of the author. However, we want to motivate players to create high-quality animations in spite of this. So, authors also receive an additional 1-point royalty every time another player correctly guesses their animation on the first attempt. Obviously, this additional reward for authoring is not immediate like the reward for guessing. Authors only see this royalty added to their score later as others players view their animation in guessing mode. To further incentivize players, we added three leaderboards to the main screen, listing players with the best acting and guessing abilities, and most overall points.

We encountered some interesting user interface design issues in programming the "dragging" behavior of the triangles. It is of course important that players be able to move (translate) the triangle from one point to another on the stage. However, it is also important to control the orientation (rotation) of the triangle. Manipulating the orientation allows players to point the triangle's "face" in different directions. This is key in expressing many of the

actions that players must author. Establishing a movement paradigm by which players can simultaneously translate and rotate the triangle is not trivial. Our solution involves computing an angle between the point at which the player "grabs" the triangle (i.e. the point where they place their finger/mouse) and the triangle's center point. As the player drags the triangle across the stage, it rotates according to this angle. The effect is that the triangle moves in a relatively intuitive way, particularly if the player grabs the triangle at one of its vertices. A problem with this approach is that if the player grabs the triangle at a point too close to its center, the angle of rotation is unpredictable, making the triangle's dragging jerky. We implemented a simple fix to this issue by making the triangle "slippery" at its center. If the player tries to grab the triangle at a point within a certain distance from the center, the triangle remains stationary until the player reaches a point outside the center. In other words, the player might start dragging from the center, but as they drag their grab point "catches" on a better control point outside the center. The effect of this is actually barely noticeable to the player but it prevents any jerkiness in the triangle's movement.

Actions

Guessing correctly in Triangle Charades can be difficult, as animations may not clearly depict their intended action. Sometimes, this is because the author did not do a good job of animating that action. However, it could be that the action is not easily depicted through triangle animation. If this is the case, the action should not be included in vocabulary of actions recognizable from motion trajectories. We define the term recognizability to mean the degree to which an action can be recognized from a motion trajectory. Triangle Charades allows us to quantitatively evaluate an action's recognizability. First, several authors animate the action. Then, those animations are presented to several players in guessing mode. In guessing mode, for each attempt, we identify how many attempts the guesser has already made, and whether or not this attempt yields the correct guess. Clearly, an action is a good depiction of an action if players typically guess that action on the first few attempts. In contrast, if it takes several attempts to identify the action represented by an animation, then the action might not be recognizable from a motion trajectory. Based on this idea, we can compute the average number of attempts it takes players to guess the action correctly from its animation. This metric represents an action's recognizability. To be clear, because recognizability is averaged over several animations, it is not subject to anomalous low-quality animations for otherwise recognizable actions.

There is another useful concept for determining membership in our action vocabulary, which we call distinguishability. Some actions have motion trajectories that are highly confusable; for instance, animations for "punch" may closely resemble animations for "hit". If an animation presented in guessing mode depicts one of these actions, users may commonly guess the other similar action, yielding an incorrect attempt. This suggests that the two similar actions should be merged in our vocabulary of actions. Distinguishability thus refers to the degree to which one action motion's trajectory is distinguishable from another action's trajectory. More formally, action X's distinguishability from action Y equals the proportion of guesses where Y is selected when X is actually the intended action. As a pairwise measure, computing distinguishability requires a lot more game data than computing recognizability, because there are only six actions to choose from for a particular guess. Each action needs several guesses before every single other action would appear in the set of options for those guesses.

Actions that are highly recognizable and highly distinguishable from all other actions should be included in a vocabulary of actions recognizable from motion trajectories. The game enables us to collect motion trajectory data for a large set of actions that potentially participate in this vocabulary. The game also enables us to filter this data: we then remove all actions/trajectories with low recognizability and low distinguishability. As mentioned above, the actions in the predefined set were all English language verbs. We knew that it was impractical to

consider all English language verbs for this set, since most such verbs are clearly not expressible in the medium of 2-D whole-body motion trajectories. To determine the best candidates for this set, we consulted a linguistic resource, Levin's [8] *English Verb Classes and Alternations*. This book is intended to be a thorough categorization of verbs according to their grammatical behavior and meaning. We examined verb classes whose semantics involve whole-body motion. An example is the "run" verb class, which includes verbs similar to "run", such as "hop", "roll", and "scramble". Verbs from the selected classes were added as potentially recognizable actions to our game. This set of potentially recognizable actions included 105 single-character actions and 89 two-character actions.

PILOT STUDY

At the time of writing, we have implemented Triangle Charades and have used it to collect an initial dataset of action and motion trajectory pairs. Upon releasing the game, we recruited 87 pilot users to play it. These users played the game in both authoring mode and guessing mode, and the set of potentially recognizable actions was limited to single-character actions only. Two-character actions are more challenging to animate than single-

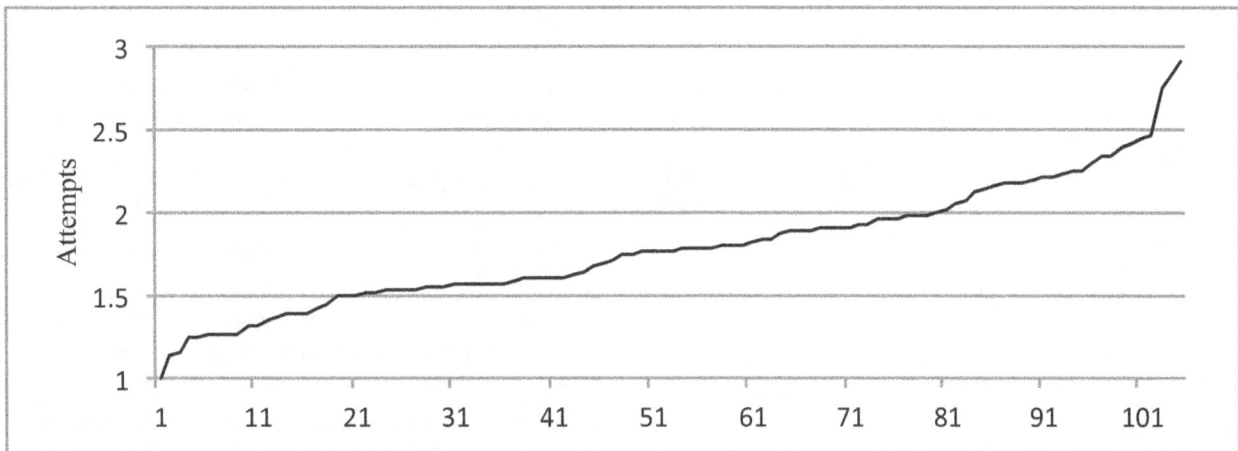

1. rotate	16. climb	31. flinch	46. hop	61. dance	76. walk	91. float
2. bolt	17. sneeze	32. meander	47. bound	62. strut	77. flap	92. traipse
3. roll	18. shake	33. bob	48. wave	63. prance	78. fly	93. trek
4. dart	19. descend	34. stroll	49. rush	64. bounce	79. scoot	94. jog
5. dash	20. zoom	35. accelerate	50. wobble	65. hurdle	80. march	95. cower
6. rise	21. swing	36. leap	51. depart	66. hurry	81. move	96. prowl
7. tremble	22. fall	37. oscillate	52. creep	67. wince	82. amble	97. promenade
8. ascend	23. limp	38. bow	53. wander	68. mosey	83. gallop	98. cringe
9. exit	24. roam	39. return	54. slither	69. hobble	84. slide	99. shuffle
10. convulse	25. vanish	40. loiter	55. frolic	70. sneak	85. hike	100. slow
11. jump	26. scramble	41. crawl	56. coast	71. scamper	86. run	101. clamber
12. wiggle	27. quake	42. scurry	57. hasten	72. trudge	87. collapse	102. swim
13. quiver	28. waddle	43. shudder	58. weave	73. stumble	88. swagger	103. skip
14. flutter	29. tiptoe	44. drift	59. recede	74. lumber	89. writhe	104. juggle
15. nod	30. turn	45. speed	60. saunter	75. glide	90. charge	105. clump

Figure 4. Recognizability scores for 105 single-character actions, represented by the mean number of attempts it takes to correctly identify that action in guessing mode. Scores are ordered lowest to highest.

character ones, because players must manipulate two different motion trajectories simultaneously. We intended to orient players to the game by asking them animate simpler actions first.

This pilot study resulted in data for 1013 authored animations and 5130 guessing attempts for animations. Based on this data, we computed the recognizability score for each action presented in the game. This data appears in Figure 4. Recognizability scores decrease by a gradual linear pattern, with no clear gap that could serve as a threshold for membership in the vocabulary of recognizable actions. This suggests that we will have to pragmatically define this threshold based on how well our machine learning paradigm can recognize actions from trajectories. The optimal threshold will maximize the number of actions in the vocabulary without compromising performance.

Distinguishability also determines vocabulary membership, by merging actions that have highly similar trajectories. However, this pilot study does not provide us with enough data to compute distinguishability scores for all actions. This is the next phase of this work, as well as collecting data for recognizable 2-character actions. Eventually, after we have determined our full vocabulary, remaining animations with low guessing performance will also be filtered from the data. This is a way of ensuring that our final dataset includes only high-quality motion trajectories.

Since actions are represented by English-language verbs, playing this game is partly dependent on English proficiency. As a tangent, we examined importance of this linguistic factor by asking 19 of the pilot users about their native language. Six of these players reported that English was not their native language. Though this is not a robust sample size, these players did seem to have more difficulty playing the game compared with native-English speakers. On average, the non-native English speakers required more guessing attempts to identify the action depicted by an animation (2.099, versus 1.733 for native speakers).

CONCLUSION
We designed a game to collect 2-D whole-body motion trajectories for human actions. This data will be used to train an AI system to automatically recognize actions from trajectories. Our pilot study shows that a game approach overcomes two existing inadequacies for this task. It provides a large set of training data, and it enables us to define a controlled vocabulary of the actions that are recognizable from motion data. For the latter, simple metrics like recognizability and distinguishability can be used to determine an action's membership in this vocabulary, though the precise membership threshold must be tuned based on system performance.

Games with a purpose are successful ways to collect data that does not require any specialized knowledge. This approach has been especially conducive to linguistic tasks, for instance. Triangle Charades benefits from this same advantage, since no special training is needed to create and interpret simple animations of triangles.

ACKNOWLEDGMENTS
This research was supported by the Office of Naval Research, grant N00014-13-1-0286.

REFERENCES
1. Ashraf, G., Why, Y. P., & Islam, M. T. (2010). Mining human shapes perception with role playing games. 3rd Annual International Conference on Computer Games, Multimedia and Allied Technology, Singapore.

2. Barrett, H., Todd, P., Miller, G., and Blythe, P. (2005) Accurate judgments of intention from motion cues alone: A cross-cultural study. Evolution and Human Behavior 26 (2005):313-331.

3. Crick, C. & Scassellati, B. (2008) Inferring Narrative and Intention from Playground Games. 7th IEEE International Conference on Development and Learning (ICDL 2008), Monterrey, California, August 2008.

4. Gao, T., McCarthy, G., and Scholl, B. (2010) The Wolfpack Effect: perception of animacy irresistibly influences interactive behavior. Psychological Science 21(12):1845-1853.

5. Gao, T., Newman, G., and Scholl, B. (2009) The psychophysics of chasing. A case study in the perception of animacy. Cognitive Psych. 59:154-179.

6. Heider, F. and Simmel, M. (1944). An experimental study of apparent behavior. American Journal of Psychology, 13, 1944.

7. Klein, A. M., Zwickel, J., Prinz, W., & Frith, U. (2009). Animated triangles: an eye tracking investigation. Quarterly journal of experimental psychology, 62(6), 1189–97.

8. Levin, B. (1993). English verb classes and alternations: A preliminary investigation. Chicago: University of Chicago Press.

9. Michotte, A. (1963) The Perception of Causality (trans. T. R. Miles & E. Miles). New York: Basic Books.

10. Pearl, L., & Steyvers, M. (2010). Identifying Emotions, Intentions, and Attitudes in Text Using a Game with a Purpose, 2010 Workshop on Computational Approaches to Analysis and Generation of Emotion in Text.

11. Tremoulet, P., and Feldman, J. (2000) Perception of animacy from the motion of a single object. Perception 29 (2000):943-951.

12. Von Ahn, L., & Dabbish, L. (2008). Designing games with a purpose. Communications of the ACM, 51(8), 57.

13. Young, J. E., Igarashi, T., & Sharlin, E. (2008). Puppet master: Designing reactive character behavior by demonstration. 2008 ACM SIGGRAPH/Eurographics Symposium on Computer Animation (pp. 183-191).

Comparison of Speech-based In-car HMI Concepts in a Driving Simulation Study

Hansjörg Hofmann, Vanessa Tobisch,
Ute Ehrlich, André Berton
Daimler AG
Ulm, Germany
hansjoerg.hofmann@daimler.com

Angela Mahr
DFKI
Saarbrücken, Germany
angela.mahr@dfki.de

ABSTRACT

This paper reports experimental results from a driving simulation study in order to compare different speech-based in-car human-machine interface concepts. The effects of the use of a command-based and a conversational in-car speech dialog system on usability and driver distraction are evaluated. Different graphical user interface concepts have been designed in order to investigate their potential supportive or distracting effects.

The results show that only few differences concerning speech dialog quality were found when comparing the speech dialog strategies. The command-based dialog was slightly better accepted than the conversational dialog, which can be attributed to the limited performance of the system's language understanding component. No differences in driver distraction were revealed. Moreover, the study revealed that speech dialog systems without graphical user interface were accepted by participants in the driving environment and that the use of a graphical user interface impaired the driving performance and increased gaze-based distraction.

In the driving scenario, the choice of speech dialog strategies does not have a strong influence on usability and no influence on driver distraction. Instead, when designing the graphical user interface of an in-car speech dialog systems, developers should consider reducing the content presented on the display device in order to reduce driver distraction.

Author Keywords

Speech dialog systems; user study; driver distraction

ACM Classification Keywords

H.5.2 Information Interfaces and Presentation (e.g. HCI): User Interfaces

INTRODUCTION

Nowaydays, people use their smartphone everywhere at anytime. In order to stay "always connected" people do not even refrain from using their smartphone's Internet functions manually while driving, which distracts and endangers the driver's

safety. According to the Governors Highway Safety Association [3] 25% of U.S. car crashes are related to drivers using their cellphones while driving. In order to increase driver safety it is essential to develop an intuitive and non-distractive in-car speech interface to the Web [14].

Before developing a new speech dialog system (SDS) in a new domain developers have to examine how users would interact with such a system. An Internet user study by Hofmann et al. [4] in which the subjects had to solve Internet tasks orally, revealed that concerning communicational (e.g. sending an Email) and transactional tasks (e.g. booking a hotel) conversational and command-based speaking styles were used with equal frequency of occurrence. Command-based utterances consist of short impersonal phrases whereas conversational utterances resemble human-human communication. Because of the equal distribution it is valuable to examine which speech dialog strategy - the command-based or the conversational - is the most suitable for these tasks. In the driving scenario the most user-friendly and the least distractive speech dialog strategy needs to be found.

First studies on the comparison of dialog strategies have been conducted by Walker et al. [16] and Devillers et al [1]. Walker et al. compared a mixed-initiative to a system-initiative dialog strategy in a voice email agent application. System-initiated dialogs are very restricted and are normally applied in command-based dialogs. Mixed-initiative dialogs allow for more flexibility and set the base for a conversational dialog. Although hypothesized by the authors the mixed-initiative strategy did not surpass the system-initiative strategy concerning the overall dialog performance. Devillers et al compare two SDS allowing the user to retrieve touristic information. One dialog strategy guides the user via system suggestions, the other does not. The evaluated dialog strategies comprise the fundamental ideas the command-based and conversational dialog strategy consist of. The authors conclude that user guidance is suitable for novices and appreciated by all kinds of users. However, both studies did not involve the use of a graphical user interface (GUI) and the speech interaction was performed as primary task. Considering the driving use case other results may be achieved.

In the TALK project, Mutschler et al.[12] compared two multimodal systems, one based on a command-based speech dialog, one based on a conversational speech dialog in a driving scenario. In the experiment, participants had to control the in-car mp3-player by speech or haptic input while driving. Each speech dialog strategy was supported by the same

GUI. The main research goal was to investigate multimodal interaction with the focuses on modality selection. Although the conversational dialog was more efficient the command-based dialog was more appreciated by the participants. According to Mutschler et al. a high error rate of the conversational strategy was the reason for the higher acceptance of the command-based dialog. There were no significant differences in the driving performance revealed when using the different SDS. However, the comparison of speech dialog strategies is only achieved on the basis of the available speech turns and is rather a side product of this experiment and therefore, the results have to be handled with care. As the speech recognizer quality has improved enormously within the last five years nowadays, the influence of the weak speech recognition performance of Mutschler et al.'s conversational dialog may be less significant. Furthermore, the use of the same GUI for different dialog strategies could have additionally influenced the result. The GUI should be adapted to the particular dialog strategy in order to benefit from the advantages of the respective strategy the most and to allow for a comparison of optimal systems.

This paper reports experimental results from a driving simulation study in order to compare different speech dialog strategies. The control of command-based and conversational SDS prototypes while driving is evaluated on usability and driver distraction. The systems allows users to perform a hotel booking by speech. Different GUIs were designed in order to support the respective dialog strategy the most and to evaluate the effect of the GUI on usability and driver distraction. Objective and subjective dialog measures are applied to assess the dialog quality and user acceptance. In order to assess driver workload, objective and subjective workload measures are applied. Additionally, visual demand is assessed by recording the participants' glances on the screen using an eye tracker. The experiments have been conducted at DFKI, Saarbrücken using the OpenDS[1] driving simulation. The research work is performed within the scope of the EU FP7 funding project GetHomeSafe[2].

The remainder of the paper is structured as follows: In Section 2, the developed SDS prototypes are briefly described. Section 3 presents the experimental setup and its results in detail. Subsequently, the results are discussed and finally, conclusions are drawn.

SDS PROTOTYPE CONCEPTS

The chosen use case for the design of the SDS concepts is booking a hotel by speech while driving since it covers many different subdialog types (parameter input, list presentation and browsing, etc.). For this purpose, the online hotel booking service HRS[3] has been used as data provider for the SDS. The systems have been developed for German users.

Each SDS prototype concept offers the same functionality: First, the user has to input his search parameter to retrieve a list of hotels. The user can browse the list and ask for detailed

information about a certain hotel. If the hotel matches his needs he is able to book the hotel. In addition, the user can change the search parameters.

In the following, the different speech dialog strategies and the corresponding GUI designs are briefly described. A detailed description of the human-machine interface (HMI) concepts can be found in [5].

Speech Dialog Strategy Design

SDS Prototypes for German language have been developed including the following SDS features: In order to speak to the system the driver has to press a Push-To-Activate (PTA) button. Furthermore, the driver is able to interrupt the system while prompting the user ("barge-in"). When designing the different dialog strategies we particularly focused our attention on the dialog initiative, the possibility to enter multiple input parameters and the acoustic feedback.

Command-based Speech Dialog Strategy

The dialog behavior of the command-based dialog strategy corresponds to the voice-control which can be found in current state-of-the-art in-car SDS. By calling explicit speech commands the speech dialog is initiated and the requested information is delivered or the demanded task is executed. There are several synonyms available for each command. By using implicit feedback in the voice prompts the driver is informed about what the system has understood. After the first command the user is guided by the system and executes the steps which are suggested and displayed by the system. The GUI supports the speech dialog by showing the "speakable" commands as widgets on the screen (see Section GUI Design). A sample dialog is illustrated in the following:

Driver:	*Book a hotel.*
System:	*Where would you like to book a hotel?*
Driver:	*In Berlin.*
System:	*When do you want to arrive in Berlin?*
Driver:	*Tomorrow.*
System:	*How long would you like to stay in Berlin?*
Driver:	*Until the day after tomorrow.*

Conversational Speech Dialog Strategy

In the conversational dialog strategy the dialog initiative switches during the speech interaction. The driver is able to speak whole sentences where multiple parameters can be set within one single utterance. Thereby, the dialog can be more natural, flexible and efficient. The driver is informed about what the system has understood by using implicit feedback. The GUI does not present the "speakable" commands on the screen. In order to indicate the possible functions icons are displayed (see Section GUI Design). A sample dialog is presented in the the following:

Driver:	*I would like to book a hotel in Berlin.*
System:	*When do you arrive in Berlin?*
Driver:	*I'll arrive tomorrow and leave the day after tomorrow.*

As illustrated in the example the driver can already indicate some input parameters when addressing the system for the first time. The system verifies which input parameters are

---

[1]http://www.opends.eu/

[2]http://www.gethomesafe-fp7.eu

[3]http://www.hrs.com

missing in order to send a hotel request. The system prompts the user and collects the missing information. Although the system asks for only one parameter, the user is able to give more or other information than requested.

GUI Design
The different GUIs have been designed in order to support the speech dialog strategies and to evaluate the effect of the GUI on usability and driver distraction. The GUI screens have been customized corresponding to the dialog strategies only as much as necessary since an objective comparison is targeted. When designing the screens we followed the international standardized AAM-Guidelines [2], which, for example, define allowed font sizes or the number of allowed widgets on a screen.

Command-based GUI Design
In the command-based dialog strategy the driver uses commands to speak to the system. In order to give the driver an idea of the "speakable" commands, the speech dialog is supported by the GUI. For that reason the currently most relevant speech commands are displayed on the screen at all times. Hence, in automotive terms the command-based speech dialog strategy is also called "speak-what-you-see" strategy.

Figure 1(a) illustrates the main screen of the hotel booking application at the beginning of the hotel booking dialog. Here, the first input parameter "destination" ("Ziel" in German) is requested by the system. Afterwards the user is guided step-by-step by the system. When the driver has given the requested information, a new widget appears on the screen and the system asks the driver for the corresponding input.

Conversational GUI Design
In the conversational dialog strategy the driver can speak freely and does not have to use certain commands. There is no need to give the driver a visual feedback of the currently "speakable" commands. For that reason, the content on the head unit screen does not have to indicate the possible options to proceed with the speech dialog. The elements of the sub-function line, which were used to indicate the available commands are replaced by symbols, which resemble the current GUI state. Figure 1(b) shows the form filling main screen at the beginning of the speech interaction where the user is already able to input several parameters at once.

Without GUI
We wanted to investigate whether it was useful or necessary to present a display at all. Therefore, we added an experimental condition with a GUI that was reduced to the minimum ("without GUI"). In this version, merely no content information is displayed on the screen. However, a visual feedback, which indicates if the user is allowed to talk is presented in the top bar of the screen (see Figure 1(c)).

EVALUATION
This Section describes briefly the experimental method followed by a detailed presentation of the results.

Method

Participants
In total, 25 German participants (mainly students) participated in the experiment. All participants possessed a valid driver's license. The participants comprised 11 male and 14 female subjects and the average age was 26.0 years (standard deviation (SD) = 6.0). 52% of the participants were driving their car at least once a week. 68% had little to no experience with speech-controlled devices.

Experimental Design
Four different HMI concept variants were evaluated in a 2x2 (speech dialog strategy: command-based vs. conversational, GUI: with vs. without) design. The Command-based and Conversational GUI were only used with the corresponding dialog strategy. The 4 HMI concepts were the following:

- Command-based speech dialog ("Comm")
  - with GUI ("CommGUI") and
  - without GUI ("CommNoGUI")
- Conversational speech dialog ("Conv")
  - with GUI ("ConvGUI") and
  - without GUI ("ConvNoGUI")

Each participant encountered all four conditions ("within-design"). For each condition, two hotel booking tasks had to be accomplished. We investigated the participants speech dialog performance and influences on driver distraction while using the SDS.

Materials
In the experiment, the speech dialog prototypes described in the preceding Section have been used. In order to explain the functionality and the control of the SDS prototypes to the user in a controlled fashion, instruction videos for each speech dialog strategy were presented. During the experiment, participants had to solve several tasks: They had to book a certain hotel according to given search parameters. The tasks were verbalized as little stories which contained the necessary parameters in a memorable manner. In total, participants had to perform 16 tasks. Eight tasks were used as sample tasks to familiarize participants with the respective speech dialog strategy after showing the instruction video. The remaining eight tasks were used for the data collection.

In the course of the experiment different questionnaires were used. In a preliminary interview demographical information (age, gender, driving experience, etc.) about the participants was collected. We applied the subjective assessment of speech-system interface usability questionnaire (SASSI) [6] (5-point Likert scale: strongly disagree: -2, .., strongly agree: 2) for subjective usability evaluation of SDS and the driving activity load index questionnaire (DALI) [13] (6-point scale: low: 0, .., high: 5) in order to evaluate the user's cognitive load. At the end of the experiment participants had to fill out a final questionnaire. This questionnaire was designed to allow for a direct comparison of the respective SDS prototypes.

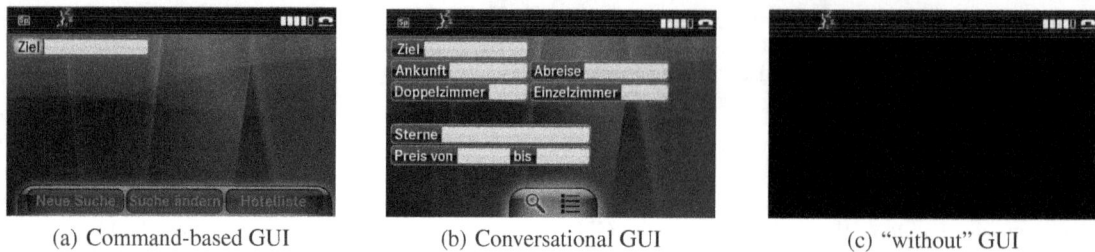

(a) Command-based GUI　　　　(b) Conversational GUI　　　　(c) "without" GUI

Figure 1. Main Screens at the Beginning of the Interaction.

Driving Simulation Setup:

The experiment was conducted in the driving simulator at DFKI's "future lab" (see Figure 2) in Saarbrücken. The participants were sitting on the driver's seat in a car which was placed in front of a canvas onto which the driving simulation was projected. The participants controlled the driving simulation by the car steering wheel and pedals. During the experiment the examiner was sitting on the passenger seat.

Figure 2. DFKI Driving Simulator Setup.

Previous driving simulation studies employ the standard Lane Change Test (LCT) by [10]. However, the LCT only includes foreseeable events and driving in the periods between events does almost not comprise any demands in terms of steering and no braking at all. This might lead to strategic task completion and to an underestimation of driver distraction. Furthermore, LCT is based on fixed tracks, which limits continuous recordings to three minutes. We employed the ConTRe (Continuous Tracking and Reaction) task as part of the OpenDS[4] driving simulation software which complements the de-facto standard LCT including higher sensitivity and a more flexible driving task without restart interruptions. The steering task for lateral control resembles a continuous follow drive which will help to receive more detailed results about effects of the two diverse dialog strategies. Furthermore, mental demand can be assessed by an additional reaction task implemented as longitudinal control. A detailed description of the ConTRe task can be found in [9]. Visual demand off the road reduces driver situation awareness [15] and negatively influences driving performance [7], as the time spent looking inside the vehicle is not spent looking at the road for

potential crash-inducing hazards. Therefore, we were interested in investigating the effects of the GUI in a speech dialog on visual distraction. In order to assess visual demand an eye tracker, which records glances on the screen, is used for gaze-based distraction evaluation. The driving performance was recorded during the baseline drives and the drives, when an SDS was used. The eye tracker data were only recorded when participants interacted with an SDS.

Procedure

In the experiment, four different conditions were evaluated. We did not randomize all four conditions, because the participants might have been confused if the speech dialog styles vary too often. Therefore, we decided to separate the experiment into two blocks. In each block, only one speech dialog variant with the two GUI variants was tested. The order of the two blocks was counterbalanced between participants to control for learning and order effects. Furthermore, the order of GUI variants within one block was balanced between participants. In each of the four conditions, the participants had to perform two tasks. The order of the hotel booking tasks was the same for all participants regardless of the system condition. When the second task was finished, participants had to fill out the SASSI and the DALI questionnaire for each condition.

The overall procedure of the experiment was as follows: at the beginning of the experiment, participants had to fill out the preliminary questionnaire. Afterwards they had the possibility to get to know the driving simulation in a test drive lasting for at least 4 minutes. After the test drive, in order to assess driver distraction without secondary task the participants completed a four minutes baseline drive and had to fill out the DALI questionnaire afterwards. Next, the participants were shown the video of their first speech dialog variant and became familiar with the SDS by performing the four explorative tasks. Subsequently, participants performed two tasks each with the first SDS variant both with and without GUI. After the first block, the second speech dialog variant was introduced by presenting its instruction video and again the explorative tasks were performed. Subsequently, participants performed tasks with the second SDS variant also with and without GUI. Finally, the participants completed a second baseline drive and filled out the final questionnaire.

Dependent Variables

Several types of data in order to evaluate the speech dialog and the driver distraction were collected. The SDS, the driving simulation software and the eye tracker produce logfiles at runtime. In the course of the experiment, the examiner was

---

[4]http://www.opends.eu/

observing the test procedure in order to take notes on hotel booking task success. Based on the collected data, the following measures were computed in order to evaluate the speech dialog and the driver distraction.

Based on the observations the task success (TS) of each speech dialog is assessed. The speech dialog logs are used to compute the Number of Turns (NoT) and the dialog duration (DD) of each dialog. In order to evaluate the system's understanding qualities, we assess the concept error rate (CER), which indicates, if the system has correctly interpreted the user's utterance. A detailed description and definition of the dialog measures can be found in [11]. A subjective usability assessment was achieved by employing the SASSI questionnaire. Based on the OpenDS logs we compute the mean lateral deviation ($MDev$) from the ideal lane and the response time upon discrete visual effects (RT). Subjective cognitive load assessment is achieved by applying the DALI questionnaire. Visual demand relates closely to driver distraction, as the time spent looking inside the vehicle is not spent looking at the road for potential crash-inducing hazards. Based on the eye tracker data the mean glance duration (MGD) and the percent dwell time (PDT) on the display is assessed. The PDT is the percentage of time that the participants spend looking at the GUI during a hotel booking task. The AAM guidelines suggest that single glance durations should generally not exceed two seconds and that the total glance duration should not exceed 20 seconds. Here, the 85th percentile of the distribution is relevant for the evaluation, which represents a common design standard in traffic engineering [2]. In order to verify if our four SDS prototypes are compliant to the AAM guidelines we additionally assess the distribution of maximum single glance durations and the distribution of total glance durations.

Overall, we expect better usability results for the conversational dialog compared with the command-based. The participants will accept the conversational dialog better than the command-based dialog because it reflects the human-human communication. Furthermore, we expect the conversational dialog to distract less than the command-based dialog as the user is able to communicate with the system as if he would talk to a human being. Thereby, users are less mentally demanded and can concentrate on the driving task. Generally, a visual feedback makes it more comfortable to interact with an SDS. Therefore, we expect the participants to accept the SDS with GUI better than without GUI. However, concerning the influence of the GUI on the driving performance, we expect the GUI to cause more driver distraction due to the glances off the road.

Results

In the following, the results concerning speech dialog quality and driver distraction are presented. Due to data loss, eight command-based dialogs and one conversational dialog could not be included in the analysis. In total, 191 dialogs (92 command-based dialogs and 99 conversational dialogs) were transcribed and analyzed. The driving data set comprised 100 drives, in which the command-based SDS was applied, 100 drives with the conversational SDS and additional 50 baseline

drives. We only recorded eye gazes, when the participants had to use an SDS prototype. Due to calibration problems, only 82 data sets when using the command-based SDS and 84 data sets when using the conversational SDS could be analyzed.

First, the most relevant results of the speech dialog evaluation are described, followed by the most relevant results of the driver distraction evaluation. The driver distraction subsection presents the results of the cognitive load and the visual demand assessment measures. Repeated measures ANOVAs have been conducted in order to compare the different conditions. In the course of a pre-test and during this experiment, we observed that a high number of understanding errors led to multiple correction dialogs. A high number of correction dialogs sometimes frustrated the users. Furthermore, we observed that participants tended to look on the screen in order to get visual help when an error occurred and when additional correction dialogs had to be performed. Therefore, concerning the two speech dialog strategies we analyzed the relationship of the CER and the NoT on other speech dialog measures and on driving distraction measures by computing Pearson product-moment correlation coefficient r_p.

Speech Dialog

In this Section, first, the results of the objective speech dialog performance measures are presented, followed by the results of the questionnaires. Afterwards, correlations between the different speech dialog measures are revealed.

Task Success:
Each of the 191 dialogs were finished with a hotel booking. If the participant booked a hotel, which did not match the task requirements the task was annotated as failed. Furthermore, if the participant input wrong parameters, which did not match the task descriptions, the task was failed, too. In total, 75% of the tasks were finished successfully. Figure 3 shows the percentage of solved tasks for both speech dialog strategies (left) and additionally split according to the two GUI conditions (right). Using the command-based SDS prototype, participants were able to solve 78% of the tasks. 71% of the tasks could be solved when using the conversational prototype. There was no significant difference revealed between the two dialog strategies. It seems that participants solved tasks more effective when a prototype with GUI than without GUI was used. However, none of the differences was found to be significant.

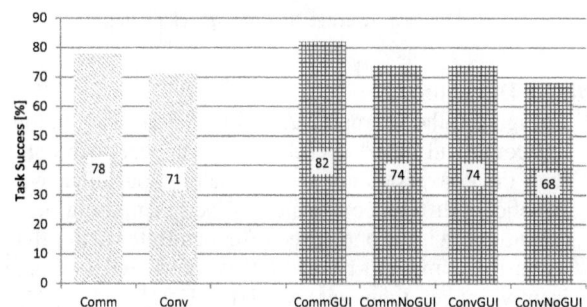

Figure 3. Overall TS rates.

Concept Error Rate:

The average CER per dialog is significantly smaller in the command-based dialogs compared to the conversational dialogs ($F(1,23) = 17.05, p < 0.001, \eta^2 = 0.43$) (see Figure 4). When comparing the GUI conditions within one speech dialog strategy, it seems that less concept errors occurred when the participants used the SDS prototypes without GUI. However, no significant differences were found.

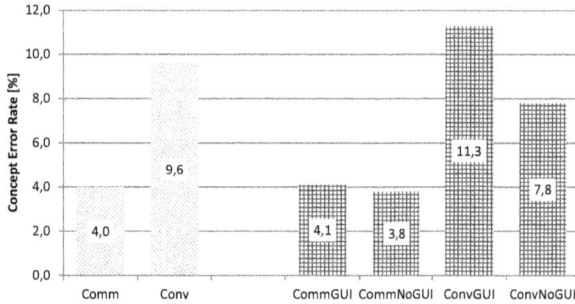

Figure 4. Average CER per speech dialog.

Number Of Turns:

Figure 5 presents the average NoT. The high number of turns is due to the list browsing the user has to perform in order to find the matching hotel. Using the conversational SDS prototype, it seems that fewer dialog turns were needed than using the command-based SDS prototype. The command-based SDS with GUI seems to need an equal number of turns as without GUI. Concerning the conversational dialog, an SDS without GUI appears to need fewer dialog turns. However, none of the differences was found to be significant.

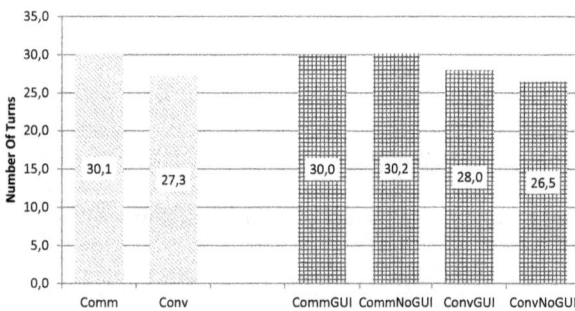

Figure 5. Average NoT per speech dialog.

Dialog Duration:

In Figure 6 the average DD is illustrated. The dialogs of the command-based speech dialogs appear to be shorter than the conversational speech dialogs, but there was no significant difference revealed. When comparing the GUI conditions within one speech dialog strategy, the dialogs using the command-based SDS without GUI took significantly longer than with GUI ($F(1,24) = 6.20, p < 0.05, \eta^2 = 0.21$). Although it seems that the dialogs of the conversational dialog without GUI take longer than with GUI, no significant differences were found.

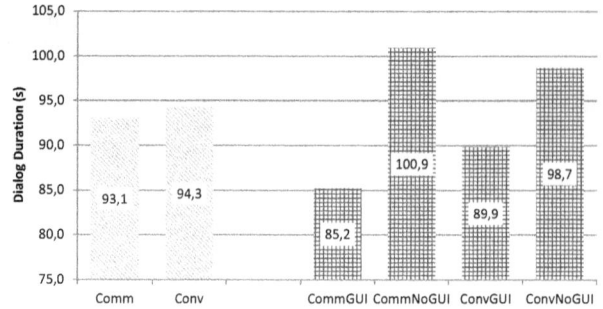

Figure 6. Average DD per speech dialog.

SASSI:

The overall result of the SASSI questionnaire is illustrated in Figure 7. All SDS achieve a positive usability assessment. The command-based dialog is significantly better accepted by the user ($F(1,23) = 10.91, p < 0.01, \eta^2 = 0.32$). It seems that the users accept the SDS supported by a GUI better than without a GUI. However, for none of the comparisons significant differences were found.

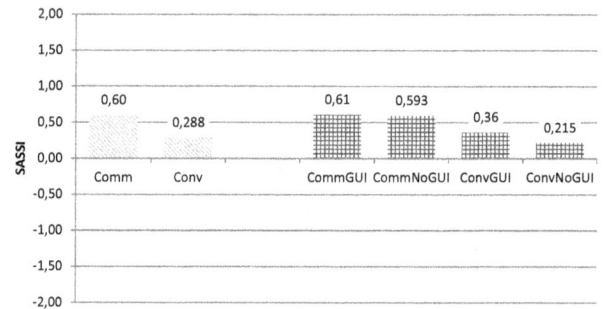

Figure 7. Overall SASSI result per speech dialog (2: strong positive user acceptance, ..., -2: strong negative user acceptance).

Correlation of Measures

As mentioned before observations during the experiment give reason to assume that the CER and the NoT might have an influence on other dialog quality measures. The CER correlates with the NoT. Concerning the command-based strategy there is a strong positive relationship ($r_p = 0.64, p < 0.001$) whereas for the conversational dialog strategy there is a moderate positive relationship ($r_p = 0.56, p < 0.01$). There is no correlation between the CER and the TS, the DD or the SASSI result. Concerning both dialog strategies there is a strong positive relationship between the NoT and the DD ("Comm": $r_p = 0.69, p < 0.001$; "Conv": $r_p = 0.78, p < 0.001$). There is a strong negative relationship between the NoT and the SASSI result of the conversational dialog ($r_p = -0.72, p < 0.001$).No other correlations between the NoT and other speech dialog measures were found.

Driver Distraction

In this Section, first the results of the cognitive load measures are presented, followed by the gaze-based distraction measures. Afterwards correlations between the CER, the NoT and the visual distraction measures are analyzed.

Mean Deviation:

Figure 8 shows the $MDev$ of the baseline drive (left), both speech dialog strategies (middle) and additionally split according to the two GUI conditions (right). The $MDev$ of the baseline drive was significantly smaller than when using any of the four SDS prototypes while driving $(F(1, 24) = 15.08, p < 0.01, \eta^2 = 0.39)$. No significant differences were found when comparing the two speech dialog strategies. The conditions without GUI achieved a significantly lower $MDev$ result than the conditions with GUI $(F(1, 23) = 43.79, p < 0.001, \eta^2 = 0.66)$.

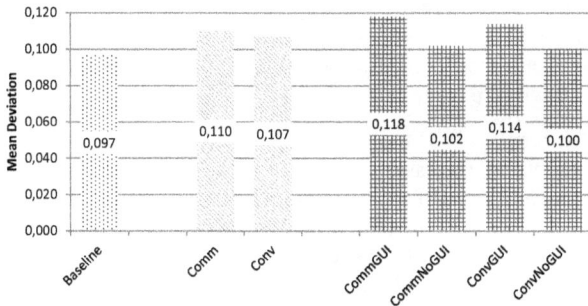

Figure 8. Average MDev per speech dialog.

Response Time:

The average RTs are illustrated in Figure 9. The RT was significantly smaller when the participants were not using any of the four SDS prototypes while driving $(F(1, 24) = 25.41, p < 0.001, \eta^2 = 0.51)$. No significant differences were found when comparing the two speech dialog strategies. The conditions without GUI achieved significantly lower RTs than the conditions with GUI $(F(1, 23) = 11.64, p < 0.01, \eta^2 = 0.34)$.

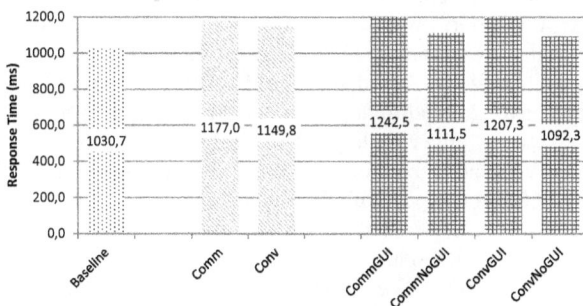

Figure 9. Average RT per speech dialog.

DALI:

Figure 10 illustrates the overall DALI result over the experiment. Driving without using any of the four SDS prototypes was perceived to be significantly less distractive $(F(1, 24) = 111.39, p < 0.001, \eta^2 = 0.82)$. All SDS are perceived as moderately distractive. As can be obtained from Figure 10 the two SDS variants and the four GUI conditions achieve similar DALI results. No significant differences were found.

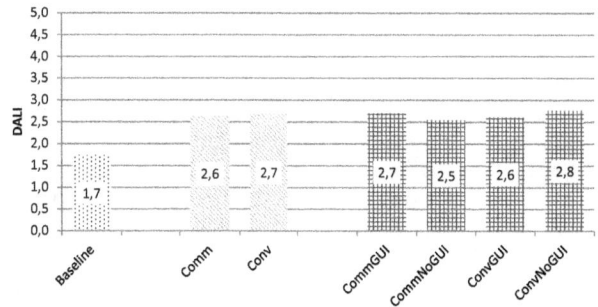

Figure 10. Overall DALI result per speech dialog (0: low cognitive load, ..., 5: high cognitive load).

Mean Glance Duration:

The MGD per speech dialog strategy and GUI condition are illustrated in Figure 11. Although it seems that the MGD is shorter when using the conversational SDS compared to the command-based SDS no significant differences were found. The glance durations were significantly shorter when there was merely no content information presented on the GUI $(F(1, 23) = 85.65, p < 0.001, \eta^2 = 0.79)$.

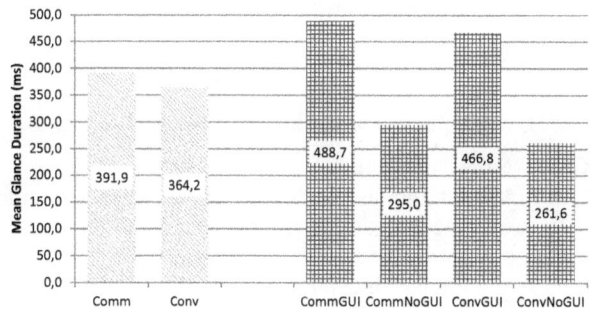

Figure 11. MGD per speech dialog.

Percent Dwell Time:

In Figure 12, the PDT is presented. No significant differences between the two speech dialog strategies were revealed. The ratio of glances on the screen was significantly higher for the SDS conditions with GUI $(F(1, 23) = 84.28, p < 0.001, \eta^2 = 0.79)$.

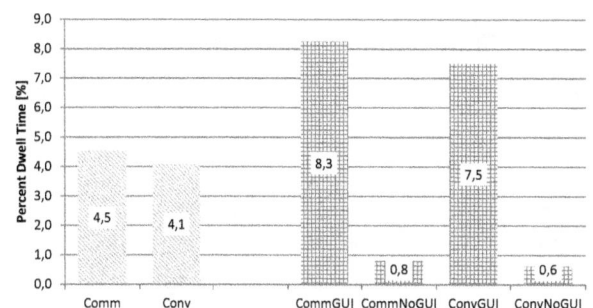

Figure 12. PDT per speech dialog.

Maximum Single Glance Duration:

Figure 13 presents the distribution of the maximum single glance durations per hotel booking task for each of the four SDS prototypes. Additionally, the 85th percentile is illustrated. In total, in the experiment only few glances exceeded the maximum glance duration of two seconds: one glance when using the command-based dialog with GUI and one glance when using the conversational dialog with GUI. As can be obtained from Figure 13, for each SDS prototype the 85th percentile of the distribution of the maximum single glance durations is below two seconds.

Maximum Glance Duration (ms)

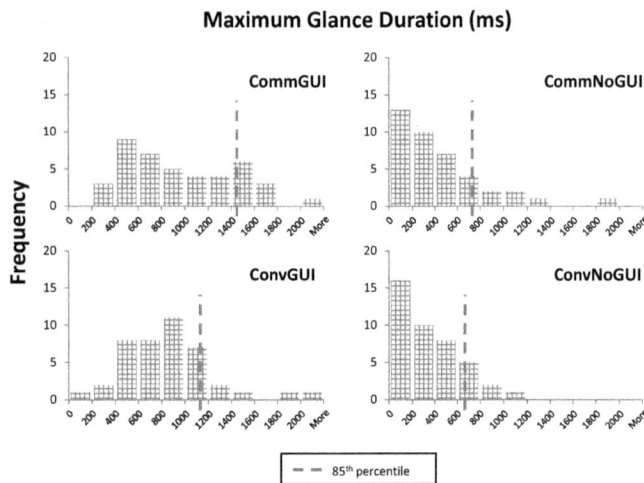

Figure 13. Distribution of maximum single glance durations.

Total Glance Duration:

In Figure 14, the distribution of the total glance durations during a hotel booking task is presented. Additionally, the 85th percentile is marked. In the course of only few hotel booking tasks the sum of participant's glances on the screen exceeded the total glance duration limit of 20 seconds: three tasks when using the command-based dialog with GUI and two tasks when using the conversational dialog with GUI. For each SDS prototype the 85th percentile of the distribution of the total glance durations is below twenty seconds.

Total Glance Duration (s)

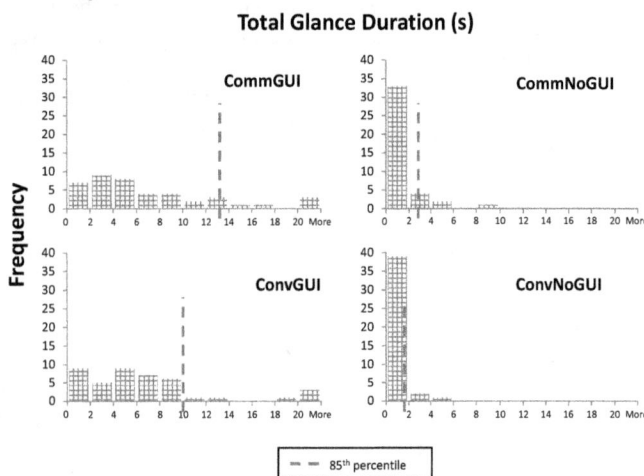

Figure 14. Distribution of total glance durations.

Correlation of Measures

The CER correlates with the MGD. Concerning the command-based strategy there is a strong positive relationship ($r_p = 0.65, p < 0.001$) whereas for the conversational dialog strategy there is a moderate positive relationship ($r_p = 0.54, p < 0.006$). There is no correlation between the CER and the PDT. The NoT moderately correlate with the MGD ("Comm": $r_p = 0.49, p < 0.01$; "Conv": $r_p = 0.50, p < 0.01$). No correlation was found between the NoT and the PDT.

DISCUSSION

In this Section the previously presented results are discussed and explained. First, the results of the speech dialog measures are discussed, followed by the discussion of the driver distraction measures.

The results show that the participants were able to successfully finish the tasks and that there were no significant differences between the different SDS and GUI concepts. The average of 75% of task success might appear to be low but is due to the fact that inputting wrong parameters or booking a wrong hotel was annotated as task fail. The flexibility and variety of conversational language poses great challenges to the speech recognition and the natural understanding module of an SDS. The understanding of conversational language is more difficult than understanding simple commands. Therefore, the CER of the conversational dialog is higher than the CER of the command-based dialog. The CER of 4.0% of the command-based dialog is an adequate result. 9.6% of CER when using the conversational dialog still leaves room for improvements. We expected a lower NoT when using the conversational dialog compared to the command-based dialog due to the multiple parameter input capabilities of the conversational dialog . However, the higher CER led to additional correction dialogs the user had to go through if an error occurred. The positive correlation between the CER and the NoT confirms this explanation. Against expectations, the command-based dialogs did not last longer than the conversational dialogs. Again, this could be due to the high CER of the conversational dialog, which led to a higher NoT, which resulted in longer dialogs. This finding is confirmed by the positive relation between the NoT and the DD. The DD of the SDS prototypes with GUI were significantly shorter than without GUI. When the SDS was supported by a GUI the users were able to gather information quicker from the screen and did not have to wait until the system delivers the content verbally. They sped up the dialog by interrupting the system's prompt. When the system was not supported by a GUI users had to let the system finish speaking because the visual source of information was not available. The command-based dialog was better accepted by the user than the conversational dialog. As observed in the experiment correction dialogs frustrated the users. Concerning the conversational dialog, the unexpectedly high NoT might have impaired the SASSI result. The strong negative correlation between the NoT and the SASSI result of the conversational dialog would confirm this hypothesis. We expected participants to accept an SDS supported by a GUI better than without a GUI. This assumption could not be confirmed. It seems that the support of an

SDS by a visual feedback does not raise the user acceptance in a driving scenario. Overall, no big differences concerning the speech dialog quality of the two speech dialog strategies were revealed. More understanding errors occurred when using the conversational dialog, which indirectly resulted in a degraded user acceptance. If the CER is reduced the conversational dialog might need fewer dialog turns and might be better accepted by the user and thereby, outperform the command-based dialog. The evaluation of the effect of the GUI on the speech dialog only revealed a difference in dialog duration. The results indicate that users seem to equally accept an SDS with GUI compared to an SDS without GUI.

The results of the objective driving performance data show that performing a secondary task by speech while driving impairs the steering performance and the RT. The use of the SDS mentally demands the user and thereby decreases the driving performance. However, previous studies show that voice interaction is still superior in terms of driving performance when compared to manual control [14]. Booking a hotel by using your smartphone manually while driving is still more dangerous than the use of an in-car SDS. Furthermore, the results of the $MDev$ and the RT did not reveal differences between the two dialog strategies although we expected the conversational dialog to distract less. The high CER of the conversational dialog might have increased the driver workload and thereby, degraded the driving performance. However, we found out that the deviation from the reference lane and the RT vary dependent on the GUI condition. If the SDS is supported by a GUI the steering performance and the reaction times are impaired. The visual feedback on the screen has a negative influence on the primary steering task performance. Furthermore, drivers cannot react on an event appearing in the driving environment if they look on the GUI screen while the stimuli happens. Thus, the RT is increased. Participants perceived the use of an SDS while driving as more distractive than only performing the primary driving task. There was no difference in subjective driver workload assessment for the two SDS variants, which matches the objective driving performance results. However, participants perceived an SDS without GUI as distractive as an SDS with GUI, which does not match the previous driving performance findings where the conditions without GUI achieve significantly better results. The absence of a visual feedback might have increased the perceived mental demand. It seems that drivers perceive interacting with an SDS, which gives only auditory feedback as mentally demanding as an SDS giving auditory and visual feedback. Concerning visual distraction, our four SDS prototypes are compliant to the rules the AAM guidelines prescribe as for each prototype the 85th percentile of the maximum single glance durations and the 85th percentile of the total glance durations are below the prescribed maximum limit. Furthermore, the analysis of the eye tracker data mirrors similar results as the objective driving performance results. Both, the MGD and the PDT did not reveal differences in the comparison of the speech dialog strategies. During the experiment we observed that people looked on the screen in order to get visual help when an error occurred. It seems that the CER has a negative influence on visual distraction. The positive correlation between the CER and the

MGD strengthens this assumption. If less understanding errors occurred, the visual demand could maybe be reduced. Especially the visual distraction results of the conversational dialog could be improved as the CER of this dialog strategy leaves more room for improvements. The use of a GUI had significant impact on visual distraction. When information is presented on the screen people tend to glance more frequently and longer at the display to get visual help. Thus, the MGD and the PDT increase. These findings are consistent with previous research [8]. Concerning the conditions without GUI one might wonder why people look on the screen although no content is displayed. As explained before, there is still a visual feedback, which indicates if the user is allowed to talk presented in the top bar of the screen. If participants were not sure if the speech dialog is still active they glanced at the screen. However, the GD and the ratio of time they look at the display is very low.

Concluding one can say that concerning speech dialog quality there are only little differences between the two speech dialog strategies. The command-based dialog was slightly better accepted than the conversational dialog. If the CER of the conversational dialog is improved this strategy might achieve better results in speech dialog performance and user acceptance. SDSs without GUI seem to be as much accepted by users as SDSs without GUI. The missing visual feedback only resulted in an increased DD as the users have to let the system finish speaking. The comparison of speech dialog strategies did not reveal differences in driver distraction measures. However, as expected, the GUI caused more driver distraction due to the glances onto the screen. Therefore, the conditions without GUI achieved better results in steering performance, reaction time and visual distraction. In the driving scenario, the choice of the speech dialog strategy for speech dialogs within one application does not have a strong influence on the driving performance. Instead, the content presentation of the GUI is important. Therefore, when designing in-car SDSs, which are supported by a GUI, developers have to consider reducing the content presented on the screen in order to reduce driver distraction.

CONCLUSIONS

This paper reports experimental results from a driving simulation study in order to compare different speech-based in-car HMI concepts. The effects of the use of a command-based and a conversational in-car speech dialog system on usability and driver distraction are evaluated. Different GUI concepts have been designed in order to investigate the effect of the GUI on the evaluation measures. The results show that only few differences concerning speech dialog quality were found when comparing the speech dialog strategies. The command-based dialog was slightly better accepted than the conversational dialog, which seems to be due to the high CER of the conversational dialog. SDSs without GUI also seem to be feasible for the driving environment and are accepted by the users. The comparison of speech dialog strategies did not reveal differences in driver distraction. However, the use of a GUI impaired the driving performance and increased gaze-based distraction.

Based on the insights a hybrid SDS concept will be designed, which employs the most feasible dialog strategy in the respective subdialog. The results of this experiment only apply for speech dialogs within one application. Further experiments on the comparison of speech dialog strategies in the driving environment for cross-application tasks are planned.

ACKNOWLEDGMENTS

The research work described in this paper is performed in the context of the project GetHomeSafe which is conducted within the scope of the Seventh Framework Program of the European Commission. We would like to thank the European Commission for funding the project GetHomeSafe.

REFERENCES

1. Devillers, L., and Bonneau-Maynard, H. Evaluation of dialog strategies for a tourist information retrieval system. In *Proc. ICSLP* (1998), 1187–1190.

2. Driver Focus-Telematics Working Group. Statement of principles, criteria and verification procedures on driver interactions with advanced in-vehicle information and communication systems. *Alliance of Automotive Manufacturers* (2002).

3. Governors Highway Safety Association. Distracted driving: What research shows and what states can do. Tech. rep., U.S. Department of Transportation, 2011.

4. Hofmann, H., Ehrlich, U., Berton, A., and Minker, W. Speech interaction with the internet - a user study. In *Proc. IE* (2012).

5. Hofmann, H., Silberstein, A., Ehrlich, U., Berton, A., and Mahr, A. Development of speech-based in-car hmi concepts for information exchange internet apps. In *Proc. IWSDS* (2012).

6. Hone, K. S., and Graham, R. Subjective assessment of speech-system interface usability. In *Proc. Eurospeech* (2001).

7. Horrey, W., Wickens, C., and Consalus, K. Modeling driver' visual attention allocation while interacting with in-vehicle technologies. *Journal of Experimental Psychology: Applied 12 2* (2006), 67–68.

8. Kun, A. L., Paek, T., Medecina, Z., Memarovic, N., and Palinko, O. Glancing at personal navigation devices can affect driving: Experimental results and design implications. In *Proc. AutoUI* (2009).

9. Mahr, A., Feld, M., Moniri, M. M., and Math, R. The ConTRe (continuous tracking and reaction) task: A flexible approach for assessing driver cognitive workload with high sensitivity. In *Adjunct Proc. AutoUI* (2012), 88–91.

10. Mattes, S. The lane-change-task as a tool for driver distraction evaluation. *Proc. IGfA* (2003), 1–30.

11. Möller, S. Parameters describing the interaction with spoken dialogue systems. ITU-T Recommendation Supplement 24 to P-Series, International Telecommunication Union, 2005. Based on ITU-T Contr. COM 12-17 (2009).

12. Mutschler, H., Steffens, F., and Korthauer, A. Final report on multimodal experiments - part 1: Evaluation of the sammie system. d6.4. talk public deliverables. Tech. rep., 2007.

13. Pauzie, A. Evaluating driver mental workload using the driving activity load index (DALI). In *Proc. European Conference on Human Centred Design for Intelligent Transport Systems* (2008), 67–77.

14. Peissner, M., Doebler, V., and Metze, F. Can voice interaction help reducing the level of distraction and prevent accidents? meta-study on driver distraction and voice interaction. Tech. rep., Fraunhofer-Institute for Industrial Engineering (IAO) and Carnegie Mellon University, 2011.

15. Rogers, M., Zhang, Y., Kaber, D., Liang, Y., and Gangakhedkar, S. The effects of visual and cognitive distraction on driver situation awareness. In *Proc. EPCE* (2011), 186–195.

16. Walker, M., Hindle, D., Fromer, J., Fabbrizio, G. D., and Mestel, C. Evaluating competing agent strategies for a voice email agent. In *Proc. Eurospeech* (1997).

Overt or Subtle? Supporting Group Conversations with Automatically Targeted Directives

Gianluca Schiavo[1&2]   Alessandro Cappelletti[1]   Eleonora Mencarini[2&3]
Oliviero Stock[1]   Massimo Zancanaro[1]

[1] FBK-irst	[2] Trento RISE	[3] University of Trento
Via Sommarive, 18	Via Sommarive, 18	Via Belenzani, 12
38123 Trento, Italy	38123 Trento, Italy	38122 Trento, Italy

{gschiavo | cappelle | mencarini | stock | zancana}@fbk.eu

ABSTRACT

In this paper, we present a system that acts as an automatic facilitator by supporting the flow of communication in a group conversation activity. The system monitors the group members' non-verbal behavior and promotes balanced participation, giving targeted directives to the participants through peripheral displays. We describe an initial study to compare two ways of influencing participants' social dynamics: overt directives, explicit recommendations of social actions displayed in the form of text; or subtle directives, where the same recommendations are provided in an implicit manner. Our study indicates that, when the participants understand how the implicit messages work, the subtle facilitation is regarded as more useful than the overt one and it is considered to more positively influence the group behavior.

Author Keywords

Conversation support; Visual Attention; Social dynamics; Implicit interaction; Persuasive Technologies.

ACM Classification Keywords

H.5.m. Information interfaces and presentation (e.g., HCI): Miscellaneous.

INTRODUCTION

Although face-to-face group discussions are very common in most workplaces as well as in informal settings, effective interaction is not always easy [7]. There has been a large amount of research into multimodal support of group conversations and many different attempts have been made to influence group activities providing real-time feedback on the group's social dynamics. We specifically aim to contribute to this research by considering a different perspective: the use of a directive approach based on subtle and minimally obtrusive directives to change the group behavior.

We use the term "directive" with reference to the illocutionary force [22] of a communicative act to have the explicit intention to induce the receiver to perform a certain action.

In this work, we present an ambient intelligence system that provides a minimal form of facilitation to foster a group of people to balance their individual participation during a face-to-face conversation. The system targets specific participants on the basis of the group behavior and gives directives to them. Specifically, we aim at providing evidence that subtle directives may be not less effective but definitely more acceptable and less obtrusive than overt directive messages.

Our approach is inspired by one of the key functions of a facilitator, namely to *"ensure that all team members contribute"* [5]. The importance of involving all the members does not always mean that all participants need to participate equally. Here, we take the simplified view of fostering equal participation for the sake of supporting group dynamics where all the points of view are equally considered. Indeed, in some contexts, such as brainstorming, the equal participations of all the members has been shown to improve the final outcome both in terms of quantity and originality of the ideas generated [17].

We adopt a "calm technology" [28] stance: designing interfaces that remain in the background providing information in a calm and unobtrusive manner. In our case we want the technology never to become prominent and to distract from the intellectual and social activity. Ultimately, we want to investigate a specific example of a persuasive technology [9] where the behavior change promoted by the technology is specifically achieved through social influence, but not through coercion, deception and with a minimal obtrusiveness.

We designed a system that monitors the behavior of the participants and assesses the level of participation of each individual. The system purposefully intervenes in the dynamics of the group by displaying the directives on personal displays embedded in a piece of furniture. The tablet devices act as peripheral displays [1] in the sense that they are not intended as the primary focus of the participants' activity, but they allow participants to be aware of information without being overburdened or distracted from their main activity.

In designing the visualizations which provide the subtle directives, we took inspiration from the information decoration approach, which aims at creating a balance between aesthetic and informational quality, and where classical aesthetical factors such as ambiguity and repetition are used to achieve interesting images that convey information in pleasant manner [8].

In a study conducted in a real-world setting, we compared the subtle directives, with and without the explanation about the information portrayed, and a control condition consisting of overt directives conveying the same communicative meaning in the form of text. The results suggest that, when the participants understand how the implicit messages work, the subtle facilitation is regarded as more useful than the overt one and it is considered to have a more substantial positive influence for changing the group behavior.

Although preliminary, these results suggest that the approach of subtle directives provided in an aesthetical and unobtrusive manner might be an effective way for persuading a group to change their behavior.

RELATED WORK

Within the domain of technology that aims at supporting group activities, many different attempts have been made to influence group conversations by providing real-time feedback on the social dynamics. Kim et al. [10] have used sociometric sensors to monitor communication patterns and other social signals during team activity, reporting a graphical representation of group dynamics to the members themselves. For example, Meeting Mediator [10] is a system that detects social interactions using sociometric badges and provides visual feedback on a mobile screen with the aim of enhancing group collaboration in tasks where balanced participation is desirable. According to the authors, cooperative behaviors can be promoted by visualizing social signals to the group members in order to increase their awareness of the communication patterns.

Situated displays and tabletops have been augmented with sensors to increase and support group activities taking place in the device proximity. For example, DiMicco et al. [6] have investigated peripheral displays that visualize the amount of participation of the member of a small group conversation. Specifically, the authors investigated the effect in group meetings of a shared display that visualizes real-time information of how much each person has spoken in relation to the others. Participation was considered in terms of vocal activity measured using close-talk microphones. This information was used to visualize each member's participation with the purpose of stimulating individual reflections on the on-going activity and harnessing social collaboration. The system was evaluated both in structured tasks (i.e. information-sharing and

decision tasks) and in real-world situations (e.g. work-meetings) showing that such technology can influence groups' behavior towards a more balanced level of participation. Specifically, the system effectively made the over-participants to decrease the amount they spoke, but the behavior of under-participants did not changed.

Other researchers have investigated the use of tabletop technologies to influence social dynamics during group conversations [26, 29, 13, 14, 4]. These interactive tables are combined with sensors for monitoring individual and group behavior, such as vocal activity, head orientation and body fidgeting. The multimodal information is used to generate unobtrusive visual feedback about the dynamics of the group conversation with the aim of supporting with various degrees of awareness, the social interactions of the users involved in the task. The visualizations include information about each individual's behavior, including quantitative measures of the physical interaction with the system [14], analysis of the vocal activity, such as the personal cumulative speaking time since the beginning of the meeting or the duration of the current turn [4], and also patterns of visual attention, such as the attention given to other participants as a listener or the attention received while speaking [26]. The visualizations are generally presented in a graphical representation displayed in real-time on the table's surface, using projected display [29, 26] or a LED board embedded on the surface [4]. The visualizations provide the participants with feedback on their performance [26, 4] or with material for supporting and sustaining the activity [29], and their applications have been explored in domains such as cultural heritage [29] and collaborative learning [12, 13].

Research in the area of smart meeting systems provides another set of examples of technologies that act to support participants in meetings by automatically analyzing the group behavior [15, 20]. For example, Pianesi et al. [18] have shown that multimodal information from meeting participants can be used to model the group dynamics and to generate post-activity summary reports that can help participants to improve their awareness on the meeting performance. Other studies have investigated how technology can facilitate turn-taking and pace of a conversation in meetings. For example, Time Aura [11] is a desktop application designed to help people to control their pace, while giving an oral presentation. Time Aura shows an overview of the presentation's structure, real-time information and suggestions about the progress of the task and feedback on speaker's performance. Different feedback modalities have been investigated in the case of Occhialini et al. [16], who presented an interactive lighting system for time management during meetings. The system was composed of halogen lights used to display a dynamic pattern on the walls, giving peripheral information to the speaker about the meeting progress. Variables of the lights, such as direction, color and intensity, were manipulated to reflect the meeting progress while blinks notified the speaker of the approaching end of the available presentation time.

Besides using graphical and explicit feedback, more subtle and indirect modalities have been investigated. Rogers et al. [21] explored the use of ambient displays to nudge behavioral change in people (i.e. whether to take the stairs or the elevator) using subtle and abstract modalities of feedback. In a further study, Balaam and colleagues [2] showed how a multi-user public display can enhance interactional synchrony by displaying peripheral subtle feedback about users' nonverbal behavior related to rapport (including simultaneous movements, posture matching, eye contact and related back channel responses). A Wizard-of-Oz study indicated that the participants showed significantly more interactional synchrony and more coordination when their nonverbal manifestations of rapport were amplified by the ambient display. According to the authors, the findings suggest that social dynamics, like rapport, can be leveraged by the technology to support group behavior, without requiring a direct and exclusive interaction with the users. Indeed, these studies showed that the effect of the technology was not always explicitly perceived by the users: the displays indirectly influenced participants' nonverbal behavior, while at the same time participants were not aware of this change.

Taken together, these studies show that dynamic feedback, presented both explicitly (e.g. through text, graphs and real-time statistics) or implicitly (e.g. using peripheral animations), can potentially foster members experience and affect group behavior.

In the present study, we present a prototype aimed at facilitating balanced conversation in groups of four people. Our system is similar to previous work in the way it adopts sensors to monitor social dynamics. The main difference is in the manner in which the system addresses the participants and influences group activity. In this regard, instead of providing real-time feedback, which requires self-reflection, we wanted to investigate a directive style of intervention: the system proactively sends messages with an illocutionary purpose to the group participants.

During the deployment of such technology, we compared two ways of influencing participants' social dynamics, namely using an overt and a more subtle style of intervention.

THE TECHNOLOGY

The system has the form factor of a small piece of furniture, such as a small table. The present prototype includes 4 Kinect cameras and 4 10-inch tablet displays which are placed in the center of the group organized in a circle (Figure 1). Each participant sits on a colored chair placed in pre-determined positions at a distance of about 1.2 m from the table. The chair's color is used to identify the different participants in the communication strategies (discussed below). The positions of the chairs were determined to make sure the perceptual capabilities of the Kinect are optimized, while allowing for a good perspective and suitable distance from the display. At present, each display is meant to be visible only to the person in front of it.

In the next two sections, we will describe in details the mechanisms for monitoring the social dynamics in the group and the visual interventions (subtle vs. overt).

Scene Analysis

The visual scene is analyzed using the 4 Kinect cameras. Each camera monitors a single participant by detecting the position of the head (as provided by a module in Microsoft Kinect API) and tracking where they are looking, using an algorithm that considers the relative positions of the other participants in the setting. Four situations are modeled: whether the person's head is directed toward the participant on the left, on the right, directly opposite, or toward no one in particular. This latter case denotes the state where the person is not looking at other participants (specifically, when the person is looking at the table). The yaw angle, used to discriminate between front and lateral orientations (left or right) and the tile angle were 35° and 5°, respectively (Figure 2). These values were based on both empirical tests and previous studies in the literature [26]. In this work, we assume that the head orientation of a person reasonably approximates the gaze and the focus of attention, as has been shown in previous studies in meeting settings with 4 people [24].

Figure 1. A group during a conversation (left) and a zoom on the prototype (right).

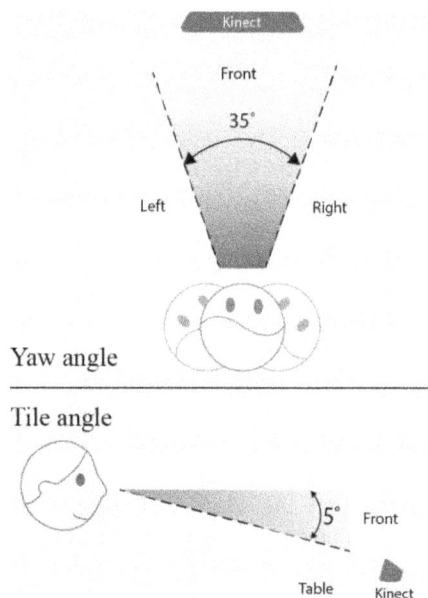

Figure 2. Diagram of the angles used to discriminate between head directions.

From the information of who is looking at whom, considered as an evidence of a participant's focus of attention, the system creates the following aggregate measures:

Visual Attraction (VAT) is defined for each participant as the relative amount of visual attention received by the other participants in a given time interval;

The *Visual Distribution Index* (VDI) in a given interval of time is defined as the degree to which each member is evenly looked at. The index is based on the minimum value of Visual Attraction in the same interval (the number 4 in the equation is given by the fact that our system at present expects exactly 4 participants)

$$VDI = \frac{min\ (VAT)}{1/4}$$

VDI values range between 1 and 0, where 1 defines a balanced attention distribution, where all participants are equally looked at, and 0 denotes an unbalanced distribution, where at least one participant is not looked at by anyone else. In the current prototype, VDI is updated every 20 seconds. VAT and VDI were then used by the system to trigger the visual intervention.

Visual intervention

As explained above, we aimed to experiment with directive interventions: that is, our system is supposed to suggest specific behaviors to the participants by delivering directive messages.

In order to compare overt, language-based, directives with subtle, aesthetically pleasant ones, we focused on a single

strategy aimed at fostering inclusion of the group members with low level of participation.

The subtle directive messages are presented by means of visualizations designed using the principle of information decoration [8]. That is, the informational content of the message is presented in a form that highlights aesthetical qualities in such a way that it can be "calmly" presented in the environment. Ambiguity and repetitions are classical means of achieving interesting representations. In our case, our messages consisted of an animation of bubbles, whose colors varied to address each different participant, while the movement of the bubbles was meant to "suggest" the performativity (in this case, directing the attention of the group toward the person who is under-participating in the conversation).

By default, the personal screen of each participant displays an animation of several bubbles of the same colors of their own chair moving toward them. This animation is not a directive per se but it represents an idle state of the system.

When the VDI drops below a minimum threshold (for the current prototype, the value has been set to 0.2, based on previous pilot studies with 4 groups), the participant with the lowest VAT in the last 20-second interval is selected as the target of the group who should be more involved in the conversation. The communicative strategy to achieve this goal is implemented as follows (Figure 3):

- The target participant sees on his/her display the bubble of his/her own color moving circularly and becoming more transparent;
- The other participants see on their displays all the bubbles changing to the color of the target chair and moving toward the target position.

As a control condition for the evaluation study, we also implemented an overt communication strategy as follow (Figure 4):

- The selected participant sees on his/her display one of the following textual messages (randomly selected to reduce repetition): "Come on! You too can contribute", "You're not participating enough! Say something!" and "What do you think about it?"
- Each other participant sees on his/her display one of the following messages (again, randomly selected to reduce repetition): "You should include everyone in the conversation!", "Maybe the person on the [red/green/yellow/purple] chair wants to say something!", "What does the person on the [red/green/yellow/purple] chair think?".

The text appeared on the screen using fading animation, remaining for 20 seconds before disappearing. The default screen for the control condition is a neutral background with no textual messages.

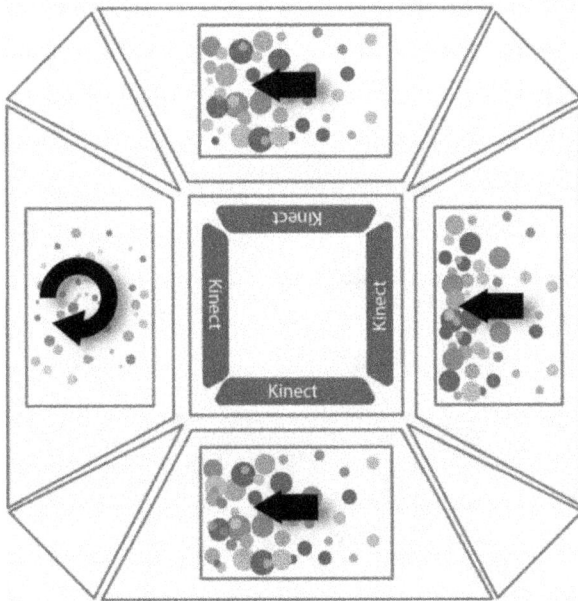

Figure 3. Visualization of the subtle strategy. The participant on the left (identified by the green color) is the current target. The arrows indicate direction of the movement.

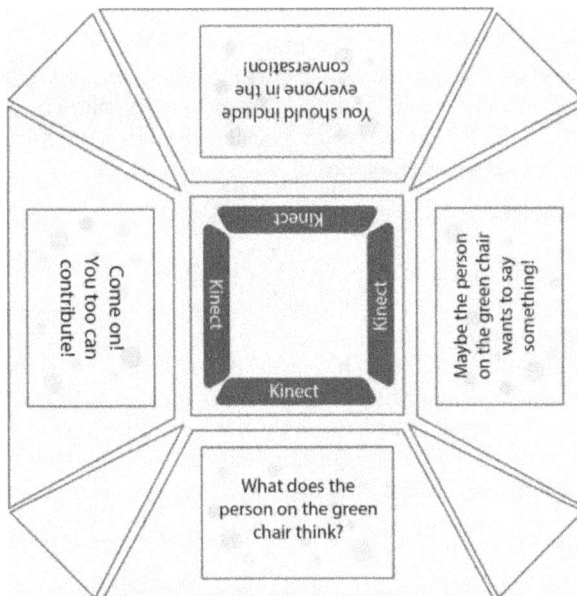

Figure 4. Visualization of the overt strategy. The participant on the left (the target) receives directive messages to participate. Other participants receive directives to include the target in the conversation.

EVALUATION STUDY

The evaluation study was organized as a quasi-experiment in the context of an ecological setting: a large science fair taking place in Trento (Italy). Visitors were invited to

participate in a brainstorming session (as a way of inducing a conversation). Groups were either formed at the moment or composed of friends. The impossibility of controlling all the variables (e.g. group composition, previous exposure to the explanation, and so on) characterizes the study as a quasi-experiment [23]. Furthermore, a *mixed methods* approach [25] has been used, in which both quantitative and qualitative data are collected.

The study used a between-subject design with 3 conditions:

- *Subtle directives with prior explanation (S_W)*. In this condition the group was informed before starting the task about the system's behavior and the information portrayed.
- *Subtle directives without any explanation (S_WO)*. The system used subtle visual directives, but the meaning was not previously explained to the group.
- *Overt directives (O)*. The system showed directives in the form of text.

Hypothesis

In comparing the subtle with the overt messages, we expect that the latter would be quite effective in changing the group dynamics and eventually lead to a more balanced participation. Thus, our first hypothesis (H1) is that the subtle condition would perform as well as the overt condition, in particular when the participants understand the meaning of the visualizations (condition S_W).

On the other hand, we expect (our second hypothesis, H2) that the subtle visualizations (conditions S_W and S_WO) would be less invasive than the overt ones (condition O). In this respect, the difference between the two subtle conditions has been introduced to evaluate the effect of an explicit understanding of the meaning of the visualization respectively on the impact of the intervention on the group dynamics and on its obtrusiveness.

Task

The system was evaluated in the context of a science fair, where brainstorming on topics related to the fair is a well-known technique for encouraging informal learning. Participants were asked to brainstorm ideas on how to improve ecological practices in daily life, such as, reducing waste and being more sustainable. Some cards with stimuli for discussion were prepared on the topic to help participants in developing their arguments. In the course of the experiment itself, only one group actually made use of them.

Procedure

At the beginning of each session, a group of participant was invited to sit and was randomly assigned to one of the three conditions. The experimenter instructed the group on the brainstorming activity and on the topic of their discussion. The participants were then asked to brainstorm for 10 minutes. All the sessions were recorded with written consent of the participants.

A short assessment session followed. First, the participants were asked to fill an individual questionnaire with 10 items that took about 5 minutes to complete (Table 1). The questions were about their experience (3 items), the disturbance of the system (2 items) and the perceived cohesiveness of the group (5-item scale adapted form the Price and Muller Work Group Cohesion Index [19]). Then, a semi-structured group interview (of around 10 minutes) was conducted to understand participants' experience with the technology. Finally participants were debriefed about the study and about all the study conditions.

Results of the study

Fifteen (15) groups, a total of 60 people (38 women and 24 men), participated in the study. Five (5) groups experienced the subtle visual intervention with prior explanation, 6 groups the subtle visual intervention without explanation and 4 groups experienced the system with the overt messages.

Assessment of the visual scene analysis

The data collected in the study was also used to assess the technical capabilities of the system in terms of monitoring functionalities. Here we report some figures about the system performance.

The Kinect cameras tracked the participants for an average of 60% (subtle condition with and without prior explanation = 57% and 58% respectively. Overt condition = 69%).

To assess the reliability of our system and head orientation tracking, three one minute meeting fragments were selected (one for each condition). For these fragments, an expert coder manually annotated head orientations for each participant using a video annotation tool. Cohen's kappa was used as a measure of reliability between automatic and manual annotations. The accuracy for classification of head direction was 68% and the resulting kappa was .67, showing good agreement.

Furthermore, in order to assess the capability of the system to correctly identify the under-participating individuals (who are the target of the of a specific type of system's interventions), two independent observers were asked to perform exactly this task by observing the videos of the conversations (excluding audio). These observers watched 20 clips (each clip was 20 seconds long) and labeled the under-participating person(s). The agreement between the observers' scores and the estimations provided by the system was good, with kappa of .65. These results show that our system provides a reasonably good estimation of the group members' participation in an ecological setting.

Distribution of Attention

According to our first hypothesis (H1), we would expect a difference in the overall balancing of the distribution of attention among conditions.

In order to measure the balancing of the group attentional behavior, we estimated the equality of the distribution of

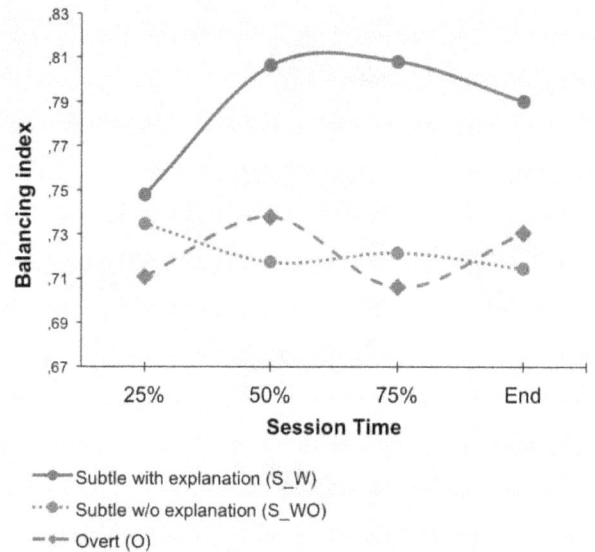

Figure 5. Average values of the Balancing index by conditions across session time.

attention at the group level by defining an index inspired by the Gini coefficient. The Gini coefficient [27] is a measure of equality that sums, over all the group members, the deviation of each member from an equal distribution, normalized by the maximum possible value of the deviation. Similar metrics inspired by the Gini coefficient have already been adopted for measuring participation equality in group conversations using speaking time [6, 12, 26] and visual attention [26].

We define the *Balancing index* as follow:

$$\text{Balancing index} = 1 - \frac{2}{3} \times \sum_i |VAT_i - 25\%|$$

The *Balancing index* represents to what extent the amount of attention received by each participant was equally distributed, considering the *Visual Attraction* (VAT) of all group participants and not only the minimum value. The index ranges between 0 (unequal distribution) and 1 (equal distribution): the more the distribution of attention deviates from an equal distribution, the lower will be the resulting value of the index.

Figure 5 shows the average distribution of the *Balancing index* across the session time. In *S_W* the index of equal attention is generally higher after the first half of the sessions (M= 0.79), while in the other conditions the index remains, relatively stable across time (subtle without explanation & overt, M= 0.72). Even though the distribution was in the expected direction, the difference was not statistically significant. These results partially support H1.

Items	Subtle with explanation S_W (N=20)	Subtle without explanation S_WO (N=24)	Overt O (N=16)	F and p values
I found the information displayed useful	2.90 (0.97)	1.17 (0.48)	2.13 (1.09)	$F_{2,57}$= 23.86 **p < .01**
I think the system had an influence on the discussion	2.90 (1.12)	1.83 (0.96)	2.50 (1.15)	$F_{2,57}$= 5.60 **p < .01**
I think the system had a negative / positive influence	3.65 (0.88)	2.88 (0.68)	3.13 (0.62)	$F_{2,57}$= 6.10 **p < .01**
I was distracted by the displays	2.20 (1.60)	2.13 (1.50)	2.31 (1.69)	$F_{2,57}$= 0.13 p > .05
I was distracted by the Kinect camera	1.60 (0.94)	1.50 (0.83)	1.69 (1.01)	$F_{2,57}$= 0.24 p > .05
Cohesion	4.08 (0.57)	4.09 (0.67)	4.07 (0.57)	$F_{2,57}$= 0.04 p > .05

Table 1. Responses (means and standard deviations) to the questions about the display on a 5-point Likert scale from 1 (*Not al all*) to 5 (*Very much*). N=60

Questionnaire results
All the groups reported high scores on the cohesion dimension (M= 4.08, SD= 0.57; the Cronbach's alpha for this scale was 0.81). Participants generally indicated that they had enough ideas on the brainstorming topic (M= 3.0, SD= 0.8) and that they were satisfied with the group work (M= 3.8, SD= 0.8). They also were not disturbed by the presence of the Kinect cameras (M= 1.58, SD= 0.91).

Regarding the perceived usefulness of the system (Table 1), an ANOVA indicates a statistically significant difference in the scores for the three conditions ($F_{2,57}$=23.86; p<.01). Post-hoc pairwise comparisons (Turkey HSD correction) showed that participants in the subtle condition with prior explanation perceived the system as more useful compared to the conditions with overt (p< .01) and subtle messages with no explanation (p< .01). This result supports H1.

In addition, participants in condition S_W (who had a prior explanation of the subtle intervention) reported that the system had stronger ($F_{2,57}$=5.60; p< .01) and more positive ($F_{2,57}$=6.1; p< .01) influence on the discussion compared to S_WO (p< .01), but no significant differences were observed compared to overt messages (p> .05). Again, this partially provides support for H1.

Participants in all conditions reported that the displays were generally slightly distracting (M= 2.20, SD= 1.11) but no significant differences across conditions were observed.

Interview results
The interviews indicate that the participants in condition S_WO noticed that the content changed over time, but they were not able to give meaning to the animation. Only one group correctly guessed that the bubble movements were related to their conversation, but they could not conceive an explanation of how the system worked.

The following excerpt from the interview illustrates this:

The system has surely some relation with our conversation, but we didn't know the meaning, so I would not say that it was useful. (from Group 5, Participant 2).

Mostly participants in this condition tended to ignore the display during the conversation. As an effect, they regarded the animation as meaningless and uninteresting; they related to it as a sort of screensaver.

In condition O, the participants clearly understood that the purpose of the system was to include everyone in the conversation. They were aware that the system showed different messages to the other participants at different times but they were not aware of what conditions led to the personalized messages. They found the messages displayed somehow distracting and intrusive, not really helpful for their activity (which is in line with the questionnaire scores). This attitude supports part of H2, as expressed in the following statement:

[The system] was useless to the communication and distracting. When I read the text I lost the thread of the conversation. (G4, P4).

In condition S_W, some participants (at least one in each group) reported that they actively used the display to monitor the conversation and to adjust their behavior accordingly. They looked at the displays purposely, monitoring the direction and the color of the bubbles to be aware of the conversation flow:

I used the system for making the conversation more balanced: I spoke more when I saw the bubbles moving in

231

circle and I tried to include the person suggested by the bubbles when they move toward someone. (G11, P3).

Yet, other participants felt uncomfortable when the system targeted them as the under-participant:

I'm a shy person. When I saw the bubbles of my color fading on the display I felt even more excluded. (G14, P4)

Most people, however, indicated that the animation adequately represented the group dynamics (e.g. targeting the person who was not really in the conversation) even though they did not constantly devote their attention to the displays. This may partially support both H1 and H2, even if it opens some issues, which will be discussed below.

DISCUSSION AND FUTURE WORK

Our research hypotheses were that (H1) the subtle directives might equally or slightly less effective than the overt ones and that would be less obtrusive (H2).

The data presented above shows some evidence, that for H1, a stronger hypothesis may hold: namely, that subtle directives may be even more effective than the overt messages provided when the participants have a prior understanding of the former's meaning. This evidence is suggested by an improvement of the Gini-like distribution of the visual attention which consistently happened in the last part of the task for the groups in the condition of subtle directives with prior explanations (yet, it is fair to note that the effect is not strong enough to be statistically significant, probably because of the small number of groups involved).

Still, the subjective measures from the questionnaires and the interviews confirmed that the explained subtle condition is perceived as more useful than the other two.

The distributions for the groups in the other two conditions do not seem to show an improvement of the balancing toward the end of the task. Indeed, the subjective measures from the questionnaires and the post-task interviews seem to indicate that this lack of improvement is for different reasons: the subtle messages (without explanation) tend to be considered meaningless and uninteresting while the language-based directives are distracting and obtrusive and not perceived as helpful for the activity.

Regarding hypothesis H2, we did not find any strong evidence from the questionnaire since all the interventions were scored as moderately distracting, but the findings from the post-task interviews support the hypothesis that the overt intervention was perceived as more distracting and not useful.

The study had some limitations: the present prototype is limited to four users and improvements in accuracy are advisable; the monitoring of the group dynamics was simple and a single communication strategy and visualization style were tested; last but not least, both the number of groups involved and the time spent in the task were relatively small. Still, the study was conducted in an ecological situation where the system was evaluated in a real-world environment.

Although still preliminary and not conclusive, our study suggests the effectiveness of subtle directives, which are non-verbal and aesthetically pleasant illocutionary acts, for changing the dynamics among a group of people.

This approach represents a different stance with respect to the extensive use of awareness feedback systems [6, 26, 4]. In our case, the system provides a directive illocutionary message that is intended to make the recipient perform a certain action. Our initial hypothesis was that a subtle directive may be not less effective than an overt directive but our results seem to exceed our hypothesis and suggest that it may work even better than the overt one when the meaning of the visualization is understood. In the study, this condition was assured by a prior explanation of the system's animation.

The idea of illocutionary force of a communicative expression is that it results from the intention of the message originator to bring about a certain state of affairs by intervening (linguistically, in the original concept) on another agent. The expression is meant to cause the receiver to perform an action. A condition is that the message originator is confident that his/her expression is recognized as a communicative message, and that the recipient has the means for understanding it (e.g. lexicon, grammar). Of course the originator may assume there can possibly be unintended ambiguity in the message (for instance the recipient may wrongly interpret the request for getting information about the time in "do you know what time is it" and answer "yes"). But the capability to correctly interpret the message by the recipient, aside from ambiguity, is assumed. At the other extreme, we have directive codes, like the illocutionary meaning of the crossroad lights which are unambiguously understood and shared.

In this work, as said, we wanted to explore subtle, minimally obtrusive influence on participants' behavior. The specific visual intervention is not the focus of attention in this paper, it is just an example of a class of modes. We noted that subtle directives might not meet the precondition of being understood as a communication mode, and, as consequence, mostly no meaning was sought for the message by the recipients. This is the reason we have introduced in the design experiment a condition where the subtle intervention was explained. This allows us to consider the case in principle, without imposing a conventional code, which tends to be very simple and without any ambiguity.

As future work, we will investigate different visualization styles to find calm, unobtrusive and aesthetically pleasant modes. We will seek among these modes those that lead to an understanding that there is a message which grant that the meaning is normally well understood, even when there is the possibility of ambiguous interpretation. We also plan to investigate the effect of different modalities for visualization: while at present we just experiment with personal display, we will also use shared or partially shared screens.

More in general, we want to pursue the study of subtle illocutionary forces. In particular, we will better explore different types of illocutionary forces in communicative strategies in order to provide a general framework for subtle intervention.

An interesting topic that emerged from the interviews is that some participants felt uncomfortable with the system because it can socially reveal their under-participation. Although this feeling is probably not only specific to directive systems (it may be applied as well to awareness systems), it might impact on acceptability of social persuasive systems in the long term. In future work, we will focus on this aspect by investigating under what condition a participant may feel uncomfortable and how we can design solutions that alleviate this aspect.

Finally yet importantly, this kind of technology might raise the issue of being manipulative by influencing participants' behavior. In our work, we are consistent with the approach discussed by Berdichevsky and Neuenschwander [3] since the intended outcome of our system is not unethical. Yet, we recognize that the method of using subtle messages may be at risk of improper use. What we aim for is an unobtrusive approach that reduces users' cognitive demand rather than an approach in which the user is not aware of being manipulated. However, it might be difficult to draw a clear line to separate the two. We believe that further investigations on the general topic of subtle illocutionary force may help in defining a general framework for better understanding this aspect.

CONCLUSION

This paper discussed a system that acts as an automatic facilitator by supporting the flow of communication in a group conversation activity. We presented a prototype that unobtrusively tracks group participation, acts in the periphery of users' attention and can targets specific group members. Previous work has mainly focused on using technology to provide feedback on the group behavior. With this study, we specifically aimed to contribute to this research area by adopting a different perspective: the use of a directive approach to change the group behavior realized through a subtle, non-distracting and aesthetically pleasant manner.

We acknowledge the limitations of this study, including the lack of variability in the type of visualizations and in the choice of different strategies. Yet, these simplifications were necessary to set up a controlled study in a real-world setting. Our main finding is that subtle directives can influence group behavior and are more positively accepted, compared to overt, language-based directives. These results

contribute to the debate on persuasive technologies and are specifically meant to lead to novel applications to support collocated groups.

ACKNOWLEDGMENTS

This work was conducted as part of the PER TE project, supported by Trento RISE. We thank Radu-Laurentiu Vieriu, Sergey Tulyakov and Nicu Sebe for helping in the design and implementation of the head tracker algorithm. We want also to thank all the participants who took part in the study.

REFERENCES

1. Bakker, S., van den Hoven, E., and Eggen, B. Acting by hand: Informing interaction design for the periphery of people's attention. *Interacting with Computers* 24, 3 (2012), 119–130.

2. Balaam, M., Fitzpatrick, G., Good, J., and Harris, E. Enhancing interactional synchrony with an ambient display. Proceedings of *CHI 2011, SIGCHI Conference on Human Factors in Computing Systems*, ACM (2011), 867–876.

3. Berdichevsky, D. and Neuenschwander, E. Toward an ethics of persuasive technology. *Communications of the ACM* 42, 5 (1999), 51–58.

4. Bergstrom, T. and Karahalios, K. Social Mirrors as Social Signals: Transforming Audio into Graphics. *IEEE Computer Graphics and Applications* 29, 5 (2009), 22–32.

5. Burns, G. The secrets of team facilitation. *Training and Development* 49 (1995), 46–52.

6. DiMicco, J.M., Hollenbach, K.J., Pandolfo, A., and Bender, W. The impact of increased awareness while face-to-face. *Human Computer Interaction* 22, 1 (2007), 47–96.

7. Doyle, M. and Straus, D. How to make meetings work. Berkley Trade (1993).

8. Eggen, B. and Mensvoort, K.V. Making Sense of What Is Going on 'Around': Designing Environmental Awareness Information Displays. In P. Markopoulos, B.D. Ruyter and W. Mackay, eds., *Awareness Systems*. Springer London, 2009, 99–124.

9. Fogg, B. J. Persuasive Technology: Using Computers to Change What We Think and Do, Morgan Kaufmann Publishers (2003).

10. Kim, T., Hinds, P., and Pentland, A. Awareness as an antidote to distance: Making distributed groups cooperative and consistent. Proceedings of *CSCW 2012, ACM conference on Computer Supported Cooperative Work*, ACM (2012), 1237–1246.

11. Mamykina, L., Mynatt, E., and Terry, M.A. Time Aura: interfaces for pacing. Proceedings of *CHI 2001, SIGCHI*

Conference on Human Factors in Computing Systems, ACM (2001), 144–151.

12. Martinez, R., Kay, J., Wallace, J.R., and Yacef, K. Modelling Symmetry of Activity as an Indicator of Collocated Group Collaboration. In J.A. Konstan, R. Conejo, J.L. Marzo and N. Oliver, eds., *User Modeling, Adaption and Personalization.* Springer Berlin Heidelberg, (2011), 207–218.

13. Martinez-Maldonado, R., Kay, J., Yacef, K., and Schwendimann, B. An Interactive Teacher's Dashboard for Monitoring Groups in a Multi-tabletop Learning Environment. In S.A. Cerri, W.J. Clancey, G. Papadourakis and K. Panourgia, eds., *Intelligent Tutoring Systems.* Springer Berlin Heidelberg, (2012), 482–492.

14. Martinez-Maldonado, R., Dimitriadis, Y., Martinez-Monés, A., Kay, J., and Yacef, K. Capturing and analyzing verbal and physical collaborative learning interactions at an enriched interactive tabletop. *International Journal of Computer-Supported Collaborative Learning* 8, 4 (2013), 455–485.

15. Nijholt, A., op den Akker, R., and Heylen, D. Meetings and meeting modeling in smart environments. *AI & Society* 20, 2 (2006), 202–220.

16. Occhialini, V., Essen, H. van, and Eggen, B. Design and Evaluation of an Ambient Display to Support Time Management during Meetings. In P. Campos, N. Graham, J. Jorge, N. Nunes, P. Palanque and M. Winckler, eds. *Human-Computer Interaction – INTERACT 2011.* Springer Berlin Heidelberg, (2011), 263–280.

17. Oxley, N.L., Dzindolet, M.T., and Paulus, P.B. The effects of facilitators on the performance of brainstorming groups. *Journal of Social Behavior & Personality* 11, 4 (1996), 633–646.

18. Pianesi, F., Zancanaro, M., Not, E., Leonardi, C., Falcon, V., and Lepri, B. Multimodal support to group dynamics. *Personal Ubiquitous Computing* 12, 3 (2008), 181–195.

19. Price, J. L., & Mueller, C. W. Handbook of organizational measurement. Pitman Publishing (1986).

20. Rienks, R., Nijholt, A., and Barthelmess, P. Pro-active meeting assistants: attention please! *AI & Society* 23, 2 (2009), 213–231.

21. Rogers, Y., Hazlewood, W.R., Marshall, P., Dalton, N., and Hertrich, S. Ambient influence: can twinkly lights lure and abstract representations trigger behavioral change? Proceedings of *Ubicomp 2010, 12th ACM international conference on Ubiquitous computing,* ACM (2010), 261–270.

22. Searle, J.R. A classification of illocutionary acts. *Language in society* 5, 1 (1976), 1–23.

23. Shadish, W., Cook, T., and Campbell, D. Experimental and Quasi-Experimental Designs for Generalized Causal Inference, Houghton-Mifflin (2002).

24. Stiefelhagen, R., Yang, J., and Waibel, A. Modeling focus of attention for meeting indexing based on multiple cues. *IEEE Transactions on Neural Networks* 13, 4 (2002), 928–938.

25. Teddlie, C.B. and Tashakkori, A. Foundations of Mixed Methods Research: Integrating Quantitative and Qualitative Approaches in the Social and Behavioral Sciences. Sage Publications, (2009).

26. Terken, J. and Sturm, J. Multimodal support for social dynamics in co-located meetings. *Personal Ubiquitous Computing* 14, 8 (2010), 703–714.

27. Weisband, S.P., Schneider, S.K., and Connolly, T. Computer-mediated communication and social information: Status salience and status differences. *Academy of Management Journal* 38, 4 (1995), 1124–1151.

28. Weiser, M. and Brown, J.S. Designing calm technology. PowerGrid Journal 1, 1 (1996), 75–85.

29. Zancanaro, M., Stock, O., Tomasini, D., and Pianesi, F. A socially aware persuasive system for supporting conversations at the museum café. Proceedings of *IUI 2011, International Conference on Intelligent User Interfaces,* ACM (2011), 395–398.

See What You Want to See: Visual User-Driven Approach for Hybrid Recommendation

Denis Parra
PUC Chile
Santiago, Chile
dparra@ing.puc.cl

Peter Brusilovsky
University of Pittsburgh
Pittsburgh, PA, USA
peterb@pitt.edu

Christoph Trattner
Know-Center
Graz, Austria
ctrattner@know-center.at

ABSTRACT

Research in recommender systems has traditionally focused on improving the predictive accuracy of recommendations by developing new algorithms or by incorporating new sources of data. However, several studies have shown that accuracy does not always correlate with a better user experience, leading to recent research that puts emphasis on *Human-Computer Interaction* in order to investigate aspects of the interface and user characteristics that influence the user experience on recommender systems. Following this new research this paper presents *SetFusion*, a visual user-controllable interface for hybrid recommender system. Our approach enables users to manually fuse and control the importance of recommender strategies and to inspect the fusion results using an interactive Venn diagram visualization. We analyze the results of two field studies in the context of a conference talk recommendation system, performed to investigate the effect of user controllability in a hybrid recommender. Behavioral analysis and subjective evaluation indicate that the proposed controllable interface had a positive effect on the user experience.

Author Keywords

Recommender systems; SetFusion; human factors; user interfaces; user studies

ACM Classification Keywords

H.5.2. Information Interfaces and Presentation (e.g. HCI): User Interfaces

INTRODUCTION

Recommender systems have emerged as an important solution to help users in finding relevant items in a large item pool [14]. These systems have been in use for over 20 years recommending items in a wide range of domains such as news, movies, music, academic articles, jobs, or social network contacts. Over the years, several principal recommendation approaches have been developed and explored. These include collaborative filtering (user-based [18] and item-based [19]),

content-based recommendation [1], as well as various hybrid-methods [5]. Nowadays, recommender systems are an essential component of many online services such as Amazon.com, Netflix, LinkedIn, Twitter, and Facebook.

Traditionally, research in this field has focused on improving the predictive accuracy of the recommendation algorithms. Recent studies have gone beyond the study of algorithms, exploring the importance of *Human-Computer Interaction* (HCI) on the user experience with recommender systems [3, 7, 10, 15, 20]. These studies have shown how visual features, enhanced interaction, and specific user characteristics affect the user engagement with the system and their decision to accept or dismiss recommendations beyond the off-line prediction accuracy paradigm. Some of the interface characteristics studied are transparency, explainability, and controllability.

In this paper we focus on one of the least explored HCI aspects of recommender systems - user controllability over the recommendation process. More specifically, we explore user controllability in the context of a hybrid recommender for conference talks. According to the experts in the area of hybrid recommenders [5], a considerable fraction of hybrid recommender systems deals with situations where the target system needs to fuse several recommendation sources to produce a single ranked list. Traditional approaches reviewed in [5] included weighted, mixed, and switching hybridization. In all these cases, the system decides how the sources should be integrated leaving the users nothing but browsing the integrated ranked list. We believe, however, that the user who understands the nature of the fused sources might be in a better position to choose the proper way to fuse them. We also believe that the final ranked list might not be the best source for the users to explore hybrid recommendation. A visual interface that offers the user a chance to control the fusion process and supports this controllability with an enhanced visualization of the fusion process might be more conductive user success and satisfaction than traditional "black box" system-driven hybridization.

To explore the value of user control and enhanced visualization in the context of hybrid recommendation we developed a novel interface that allows users to manually fuse different recommendation methods. In this paper we review the motivation behind this work, introduce our user-driven visual hybrid recommendation interface, and present the results of two studies that explored the value of this interface in the context of real research conferences.

Summarizing, the contributions of this work are: (a) presentation of a novel hybrid recommendation interface that combines Venn diagrams and sliders and allows users to fuse and inspect different recommendation methods; and (b) analysis of two field studies of the SetFusion interface in a conference talk recommendation context – a domain where user controllability has been rarely studied in the past.

BACKGROUND

This section reviews two lines of research that are related to our work: Visual Approaches for Recommendations and Recommender Systems for Research Talks or Articles.

Visual Approaches for Recommendations. We can name just a handful of interfaces that present recommended items in a visual form rather than as a traditional ranked list. Examples include SFViz [8], a sunburst visualization to allow users finding interest-based content in Last.fm, and Pharos [21] a social map visualization of latent communities. Other examples that also include a richer user interaction are PeerChooser [15], and SmallWorlds [9] which focus on representing collaborative filtering, and TasteWeights [3], an interactive visual interface for a hybrid music recommender. What differentiates SetFusion from TasteWeights [3] is the broader *depth of field* provided by the interactive Venn diagram widget, a characteristic that allows users to keep their attention on the recommended talks (the details) but also on the intersection among the recommender approaches (the high-level view) [11]. Verbert et al. [20] introduced TalkExplorer, focusing on both rich interaction and transparency of recommendation. It allowed users to explore and to find relevant conference talks by analyzing the connections of talks to different entities such as user bookmarks, recommender algorithms and user tags. A study of TalkExplorer found that the effectiveness and probability of item selection both increase when users are able to explore and interrelate multiple entities. Although TalkExplorer had good results, it had limitations: its visualization was unnecessary complex and some users had difficulty understanding the "intersections" of entities. In SetFusion, we applied a more straightforward Venn diagram rather than the *clustermaps* used in TalkExplorer to show set intersections, while adding fusing sliders to increase user control over source integration.

Recommender Systems for Research Talks or Articles. Recommending scientific and technical articles has been approached with a diverse range of methods and information sources. Basu et al. [2] used content-based (CB) filtering and collaborative filtering (CF) for recommending papers to reviewing committee members. McNee et al. [13] used the citation network to recommend citations of papers. They tested 4 CF methods (co-citation, user-item, item-item, bayesian) with two non-CF that also used articles content (graph search, google search). By performing offline evaluations and a user study, they suggested combining the algorithms or using different algorithms depending on the task: CF methods are more appropriate for recommending novel papers, while CB filtering might be more accurate when recommending familiar related work. Ekstrand et al. [6] focused on building introductory research lists by using "augmented" versions of

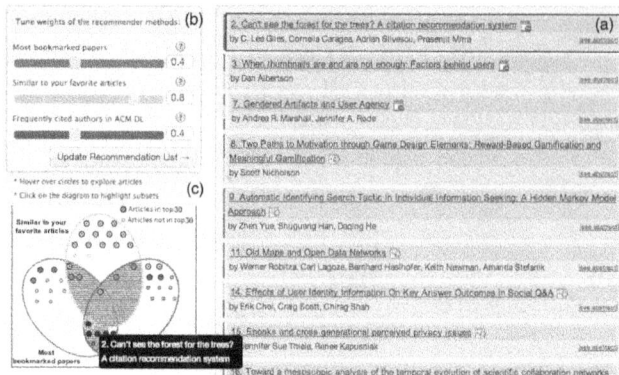

Figure 1. Screenshot of SetFusion displaying (a) a filtered list of papers recommended, (b) sliders, and (c) the Venn diagram.

CB, CF, and hybrid methods including the influence of papers within the web of citations. By conducting off-line experiments and a user study, they found that, for the task researched, CF outperformed CB and the CB-CF hybrid methods.

THE SETFUSION VISUAL RECOMMENDER

Conference Navigator

Conference Navigator 3 (*CN3*) [17] is the third version of a web system aimed at supporting conference attendees. *CN3* offers users information about talks (conference program, proceedings, paper details, most popular papers), people (list of authors, list of attendees, groups) while also collecting and representing the user's personal information (bookmarked talks, tags, connections, recommendations, and profile information). Among user-personalized features, the system offers several kinds of talk recommendations, which in the past were presented as a set of traditional ranked lists.

The Recommender Interface

CN3 leverages several sources of knowledge to generate recommendations including talk content (title and abstract), user tags, and user social connections [4]. Given their particular strengths and weaknesses, we believed that users should be aware of which sources were used to recommend a specific talk and have some level of control over the source selection in a recommender. However, the ranked lists of recommendations produced by traditional hybrid recommenders (i.e., recommender systems that fuse several sources of recommendation) do not allow the users to control and to combine them on demand. It typically does not even show which source produced which result. As mentioned above, SetFusion follows the set-based approach of TalkExplorer to visualize the sources that produced each relevant item, while using an easier-to-understand visual paradigm for set presentation – Venn diagrams. A screenshot of the SetFusion controllable recommender is presented in Figure 1. While a fused list of recommended talks is the central part of the interface (Figure 1(a)), the fusion process in SetFusion is both controllable and transparent. SetFusion allows the user to control the importance of three recommender methods by using sliders (Figure 1(b)), and provides a Venn diagram to examine and filter items recommended by one or more methods (Figure 1(c)). It also offers clear indications of the source of the recommendations in both visualization and ranked list views.

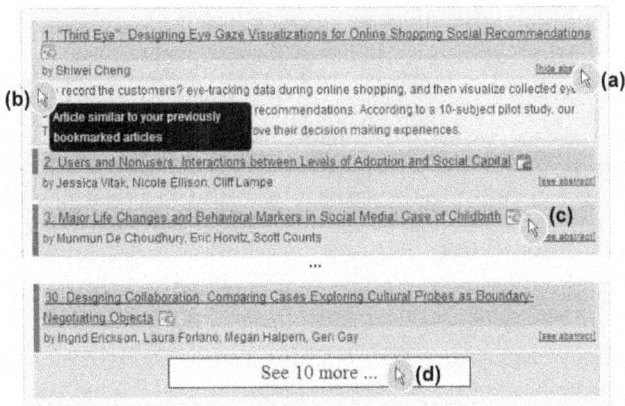

Figure 2. User interactions on the item list.

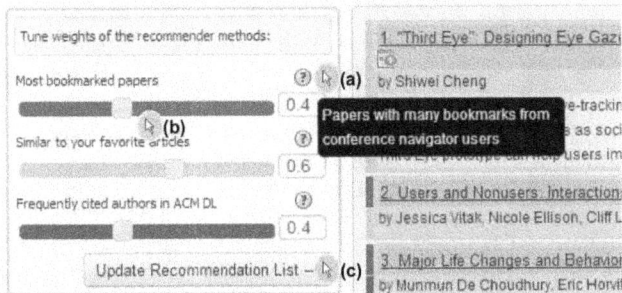

Figure 3. User interactions on the sliders widget.

SetFusion Interface Interactions

The recommender interface offered the user several interaction areas: the list or recommendations, the sliders widget and the Venn diagram:

- **List of talks recommended** (Figure 2)
  - (a) *Open and close abstract*: by clicking on the link provided by each paper title, the users could see the abstract of the article.
  - (b) *Hover over color bar*: users could hover over the color bar to obtain an explanation of the method used to recommend the paper.
  - (c) *Bookmark a paper*: at the very end of each paper's title, an icon indicates if the paper is bookmarked or not. This same icon allows the user to bookmark or remove the paper from the list of relevant items.
  - (d) *See 10 more*: By default, the system shows the top 30 recommended items. If the user wants to see more items beyond that point, she can click on the button "See 10 more".
- **Sliders widget** (Figure 3)
  - (a) *Hover over explanation icon*: this action allows the user to obtain a more detailed explanation of the method by displaying a black floating dialog.
  - (b) *Move sliders*: by moving the sliders (or typing a number in the textbox), the users change the relative importance of each method used to generate the list.
  - (c) *Update recommendation list*: after moving the sliders to adjust the importance of each method, the user must click on the button "Update Recommendation List" in order to sort the list of recommendations on the right-side panel.

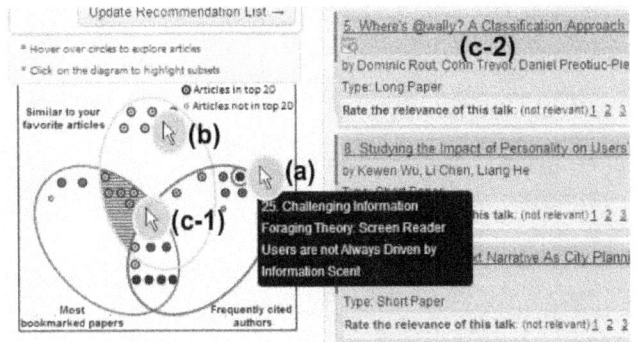

Figure 4. User interactions on the Venn diagram widget.

- **Venn diagram widget** (Figure 4)
  - (a) *Hover over the circle*: Each circle represents a talk. This action opens a small floating dialog with the title of the talk being explored.
  - (b) *Click on a circle*: with this action, the system scrolls up or down to that paper in the list on the right-side panel.
  - (c) *Clicking on a Venn diagram area (ellipse)*: When the user clicks on an area inside the Venn diagram (c-1 in Figure 4), this action allows the user to filter the list on the right panel (c-2 in Figure 4), showing only those articles that were recommended by the method or methods represented by the ellipse or intersection of ellipses. The filtering behavior differed from the preliminary study. In the prototype used at CSCW 2013, the talks selected were always visible in fixed positions in the list and the rest of talks were hidden, leaving visible empty spaces between talks. In Set-Fusion used in UMAP 2013 the list was collapsed as shown in Figure 4.

Recommendation Algorithms

Three recommendation algorithms were used to produce a fused list of talk recommendations. The methods were:

Content-based Recommendation. In this method the user profile, composed of keywords, is matched to the title and abstract of non-bookmarked talks in the conference. The user profile is represented as a vector of tokens extracted from the title and abstracts of papers that the user bookmarked from the current and previous conferences hosted in *CN3*. The user model can then be described as a vector of tokens $\vec{u} = \{w_1, w_2, ..., w_n\}$ using tf-idf weighting, and a document in the collection of conference talks is represented analogously as $\vec{d} = \{w_1, w_2, ..., w_n\}$. The recommended documents are ranked based on their similarity to the user profile. To this end, we computed the cosine-based similarity between the user profile $\vec{u}$ and each document $\vec{d}$ in the collection [12]. Apache Solr[1] was used to index the conference talks and to implement the content-based recommender. The content-filtering functions in Apache Solr receive several parameters, the following four controlled by us: (a) *min.tf*: The minimum frequency that a term must have to be considered in the user profile, (b) *min.df*: The minimum number of documents that a word must appear in the collection, (c) *min.wl*: The length

---

[1] http://lucene.apache.org/solr/

Measure	SF CSCW13	SF UMAP13
# Users exposed to recommendations	84	95
# Users who used recommender page	22	50
# Users who bookmarked	6	14
# Papers rated / avg per user	130 / 13	86 / 10.75
# Users who rated	10	8
# Users who answered survey	11	8
Average user rating	3.73	3.62
Usage at Recommender Page		
# Talks explored (user avg.)	16.84	14.9
# Talks bookmarked / user avg.	28 / 4.67	103 / 7.36
# People returning to recommender page	7 (31.8%)	14 (28%)
Average time spent in page (seconds)	261.72	353.8

Table 1. Participation and engagement metrics in the SetFusion interface of CSCW13 and UMAP13.

below which a term will not be considered as part of the user profile, (d) *max.qt*: The maximum number of terms that will be included in the user profile to match talks in the collection. Using log data from previous conferences hosted in *CN3* as ground truth, we performed 10-fold cross-validation to optimize these parameters in the UMAP 2013 study (min.tf=3, min.df=2, min.wl=4, max.qt=15).

Author-Based Popularity Recommendation. In this method, we ranked the papers considering the popularity of their authors based on the numbers of citations they had received in the ACM Digital Library. We collected a dataset from the ACM DL, and then we ranked the recommended papers following this procedure:

(a) List the papers of the conference hosted in *CN3*.
(b) Obtain the names of the authors from papers found in (a).
(c) Match the names of the authors with those in our ACM DB.
(d) For each author found in our ACM DB, obtain the number of references.
(e) Calculate the popularity of each paper found in (a) by aggregating (adding up or choosing the maximum of) the logarithm of the number of references of each of its authors.

Bookmarking Popularity. This is a non-personalized community-based recommender approach. It simply ranks papers based on their popularity in the conference community, i.e., the number of people who bookmarked the talk.

USER STUDIES

SetFusion was evaluated in the context of *CN3* talk recommendation through a sequence of two field studies. A between-subjects field study was performed during the CSCW 2013 conference. The purpose of the study was to pilot-test SetFusion in a conference context and to compare the user response to our interactive interface with a non-controllable baseline (ranked list) recommender interface. To keep a reasonable level of control, which is important for a between-subjects study, the pilot study used a rather unnatural setup stage in its recommender interface: users had to complete two steps (choosing favorite authors from previous versions of the conference and picking authors' most relevant papers) in order to see the recommendation list. Following the pilot study, we fixed some issues with the pilot SetFusion version and performed another field study of SetFusion at the UMAP 2013 conference. The availability of comparative data collected at CSCW 2013 allowed us to avoid baseline balancing and run the UMAP 2013 study in a more natural setting

(i.e., we let the users to freely interact with the interface), which was important in assessing the true impact of the visual interface. To engage users in both studies, we promoted our recommender interface by e-mail among conference attendees and also by presenting a promotion image on *CN3* home page. To measure the impact of SetFusion, we logged user activity with the systems. At the end of each conference we e-mailed all SetFusion users an invitation to answer a survey about the system.

A summary of CSCW 2013 study. Due to the lack of space, we are not able to present in detail the results of the pilot study conducted at CSCW 2013; however, these results can be found in [16]. The importance of the CSCW pilot study is that we found preliminary evidence that the controllable interface is more engaging for the conference attendees than the non-controllable one. There was also some evidence that the visual version was able to offer better ranking performance. The study logs recorded an extensive use of various SetFusion features. User questionnaires reported positive user attitudes to the SetFusion approach. Both sets of data provided good evidence that SetFusion was valuable for *CN3* users. While the remaining subsections of this paper focus on the analysis of user behavior and perception in the UMAP 2013 field study, the bottom line CSCW 2013 data are presented in all cases to compare the impact of SetFusion in a study-adjusted and natural settings.

User Participation at UMAP 2013

The analysis of user participation and engagement data shown in Table 1, in comparison with CSCW 2013 pilot study, shows a remarkable increase in most of the participation parameters following the move from less natural to more natural preference specification. While the total number of users who had a chance to notice and use the SetFusion interface was comparable (84 vs. 95), the fraction of users who used the interface more than doubled (22 vs. 50) and twice as many users made an extensive use of it by bookmarking papers (6 vs. 14). The same proportion can be observed when comparing the number of users returning to the recommender interface. In brief, we observed that the engagement impact of the visual interface is about twice as large than registered in the less natural context of the pilot CSCW study.

A comparison of user bookmarking activities also provides some evidence that the UMAP 2013 interface was highly more productive. While the number of users more than doubled, the number of bookmarks made with the visual interface increased almost 4 times. While differences between the conferences don't allow us to attribute the growth to the recommender, we could argue that in the presence of a more realistic recommender interface that properly takes into account users past bookmarked talks, the visual interface can provide better help to their users in locating relevant talks. Another interesting productivity observation is that the users were able to bookmark more talks while making fewer supportive actions such as talk ratings or talk details openings. The first kind of actions was perceived as important to improve content-based recommendation and get relevant talks closer to the top of the rating list, and the second kind was critical to choosing talks when title and authors provided insufficient relevance evidence. While increases in these parameters provide evidence of user engagement and determination to get to relevant talks, a lower yield, or ratio of bookmarked talks to the total number of supportive actions indicates that the users had to work relatively harder to end up with the same number of bookmarks (which are the true output of the process). Finally, the analysis of time spent in the system provides evidence about both engagement and productivity. While the total time spent working with the the system has further increased, along with an increase in other engagement parameters, its increase was slightly lower than the increase of the number of bookmarks (1.35 vs 1.57), i.e., the users were able to work a bit more productively spending less time per bookmark.

Action Analysis for UMAP 2013

On average, users updated the list of recommendation after manipulating the sliders 4.36 times (over 11 users), which is clearly greater than the 2.25 times average usage of the CSCW 2013 SetFusion (over 8 users). To compare the usage of specific sliders, we need to consider that the recommender methods in CSCW and UMAP were not the same. In CSCW 2013, methods A, B, and C corresponded to: (A) frequently-cited authors, (B) content-based matching, and (C) co-authors of favorite authors. On the other hand, in UMAP the mapping is: (A) talk popularity , (B) content-based matching, and (C) frequently-cited authors.

If we observe the usage distribution over sliders (*change SliderX* in Figure 5), the participants of UMAP 2013 showed a more uniform behavior, with 5.62, 6.62 and 5 changes of the sliders C (frequently-cited authors), B (content-based recommendation) and A (talk popularity), respectively. This distribution differs from CSCW 2013, where participants performed only 2.5 changes to the slider B (content-based recommender), whereas they made greater use of the sliders A (6.8 times, frequently cited authors) and C (5.5 times, articles written by co-authors).

Users increased their usage of the Venn diagram in UMAP compared with CSCW, particularly considering the *hover CircleX* actions. In UMAP, users were more likely to hover over the circles of the Venn diagram to inspect the talks recommended by a single method or by a fusion of methods. As seen in Figure 5, five areas of the Venn diagram were explored more than four times in average: A (4.75), B (7.83), C (6.9), BC (10), and ABC (5.43), compared to only two that received the same average number of user actions during the CSCW: B (6.9), and C (4.71). This behavior provides more evidence of the Venn diagram's role in identifying the papers recommended by one or more methods.

User Feedback Analysis for UMAP 2013

After UMAP 2013 had ended we e-mailed a link to the post-study survey to all *CN3* users that tried SetFusion. They rated their agreement to several statements from 1 to 5. We highlight that SetFusion users, in general, perceived that they understood why the talks were recommended (M=4.13, S.E.=0.25), that they felt in control using the sliders (M=4.25, S.E=0.4), and that they intended to recommend the system to colleagues (M=4.25, S.E.=0.33). The same survey was administered at the end of the CSCW pilot study and we found

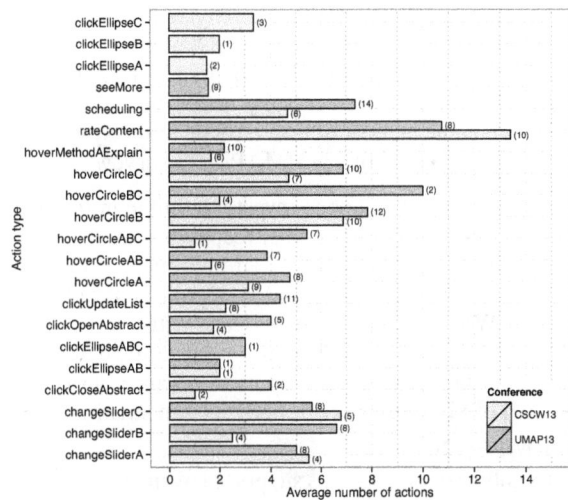

Figure 5. Average user activity and amount of people (in parenthesis) over SetFusion actions at CSCW and UMAP 2013.

two significant differences. Using t-test, we found that SetFusion users in UMAP significantly disagreed more with the statement that a talk recommender system is not necessary in *CN3* (M=1.5, S.E.=0.21) compared to CSCW users (M=2.36, S.E.=0.2), p<0.05; and they also gave a stronger indication of recommending this system to their colleagues (M=4.25, S.E.=0.33) than CSCW 2013 users (M=3.36, S.E.=0.28), p<0.05. These results might indicate that the natural setting of the UMAP study increased users' appreciation for the visual and controllable features.

DISCUSSION, CONCLUSIONS AND FUTURE WORK

This paper explores the issues of controllability and transparency in recommender system interfaces. The focus of the paper is SetFusion, a visual hybrid recommender that fuses several recommendation sources. In contrast to the traditional hybrid recommender approaches known as weighted, mixed, and switching hybridization where the recommender system decides how the sources should be integrated in the single ranked list, SetFusion uses an interactive Venn Diagram and a set of sliders to make the fusion process transparent, controllable, and explorable. To assess the value of the visual controlled hybridization, we implemented SetFusion in the context of a conference support system (*CN3*) and performed two field studies of the system at academic conferences CSCW 2013 and UMAP 2013. The CSCW study was designed to compare the impact of SetFusion with a traditional ranked list. To balance two conditions, it used a rather unnatural 2-stage preference elicitation at the start. However, it also allowed to reliably demonstrate the benefits of SetFusion over the ranked list approach [16]. UMAP study was designed as a one-condition study to assess the impact of SetFusion in natural settings. A comparison of study results provided in the paper demonstrated that SetFusion in a natural recommendation mode has an even greater impact on user motivation, performance, and attitude. First, several parameters indicated that SetFusion is more engaging to the users in its natural form – with a comparable number of users exposed to the systems, twice as many users used SetFusion, bookmarked talks with it and used it repeatedly. The users also bookmarked almost 4 times more talks and spent considerably more time with the system at average. Second, the data provided strong evidence that users worked more efficiently with SetFusion in its natural form – decreasing the ratio of support actions or total time spent to the yield of the process, i.e., number of bookmarked talks. In all, some aspects of user attitude to the system were significantly more positive in UMAP 2013 survey.

In our future work we hope to invest more time in improving SetFusion and exploring it in other recommendation contexts. In a broader scope, SetFusion is an important addition in a sequence of visual recommendation approaches explored by our team. We hope that this experience with SetFusion will allow us to distill more features that are critical for visual recommender interfaces and help us to advance our research in the area of visual user-controlled recommendation.

ACKNOWLEDGMENTS
The last author of this paper is supported by the Know-Center.

REFERENCES
1. Balabanović, M., and Shoham, Y. Fab: content-based, collaborative recommendation. *Commun. ACM 40*, 3 (Mar. 1997), 66–72.

2. Basu, C., Cohen, W. W., Hirsh, H., and Nevill-Manning, C. Technical paper recommendation: A study in combining multiple information sources. *arXiv preprint arXiv:1106.0248* (2011).

3. Bostandjiev, S., O'Donovan, J., and Höllerer, T. Tasteweights: a visual interactive hybrid recommender system. In *Proceedings of the sixth ACM conference on Recommender systems*, ACM (2012), 35–42.

4. Brusilovsky, P., Parra, D., Sahebi, S., and Wongchokprasitti, C. Collaborative information finding in smaller communities: The case of research talks. In *Collaborative Computing: Networking, Applications and Worksharing (CollaborateCom), 2010 6th International Conference on*, IEEE (2010), 1–10.

5. Burke, R. Hybrid recommender systems: Survey and experiments. *User Modeling and User-Adapted Interaction 12*, 4 (Nov. 2002), 331–370.

6. Ekstrand, M. D., Kannan, P., Stemper, J. A., Butler, J. T., Konstan, J. A., and Riedl, J. T. Automatically building research reading lists. In *Proceedings of the fourth ACM conference on Recommender systems*, ACM (2010), 159–166.

7. Faltings, B., Pu, P., Torrens, M., and Viappiani, P. Designing example-critiquing interaction. In *Proceedings of the 9th international conference on Intelligent user interfaces*, ACM (2004), 22–29.

8. Gou, L., You, F., Guo, J., Wu, L., and Zhang, X. L. Sfviz: interest-based friends exploration and recommendation in social networks. In *Proceedings of the 2011 Visual Information Communication-International Symposium*, ACM (2011), 15.

9. Gretarsson, B., O'Donovan, J., Bostandjiev, S., Hall, C., and Höllerer, T. Smallworlds: Visualizing social recommendations. In *Computer Graphics Forum*, vol. 29, Wiley Online Library (2010), 833–842.

10. Knijnenburg, B. P., Reijmer, N. J., and Willemsen, M. C. Each to his own: how different users call for different interaction methods in recommender systems. In *Proceedings of the fifth ACM conference on Recommender systems*, ACM (2011), 141–148.

11. Lurie, N. H., and Mason, C. H. Visual representation: Implications for decision making. *Journal of Marketing* (2007), 160–177.

12. Manning, C. D., Raghavan, P., and Schtze, H. *Introduction to Information Retrieval*. Cambridge University Press, New York, NY, USA, 2008.

13. McNee, S. M., Albert, I., Cosley, D., Gopalkrishnan, P., Lam, S. K., Rashid, A. M., Konstan, J. A., and Riedl, J. On the recommending of citations for research papers. In *Proceedings of the 2002 ACM conference on Computer supported cooperative work*, ACM (2002), 116–125.

14. McNee, S. M., Riedl, J., and Konstan, J. A. Being accurate is not enough: how accuracy metrics have hurt recommender systems. In *CHI '06 Extended Abstracts on Human Factors in Computing Systems*, CHI EA '06, ACM (New York, NY, USA, 2006), 1097–1101.

15. O'Donovan, J., Smyth, B., Gretarsson, B., Bostandjiev, S., and Höllerer, T. Peerchooser: visual interactive recommendation. In *Proceedings of the SIGCHI Conference on Human Factors in Computing Systems*, ACM (2008), 1085–1088.

16. Parra, D., and Brusilovsky, P. A field study of a visual controllable talk recommender. In *Proceedings of the 1st Chilean Conference on Human-Computer Interaction ChileCHI 2013* (2013).

17. Parra, D., Jeng, W., Brusilovsky, P., López, C., and Sahebi, S. Conference navigator 3: An online social conference support system. In *UMAP Workshops* (2012).

18. Resnick, P., Iacovou, N., Suchak, M., Bergstrom, P., and Riedl, J. Grouplens: an open architecture for collaborative filtering of netnews. In *Proceedings of the 1994 ACM conference on Computer supported cooperative work*, ACM (1994), 175–186.

19. Sarwar, B., Karypis, G., Konstan, J., and Riedl, J. Item-based collaborative filtering recommendation algorithms. In *Proceedings of the 10th international conference on World Wide Web*, ACM (2001), 285–295.

20. Verbert, K., Parra, D., Brusilovsky, P., and Duval, E. Visualizing recommendations to support exploration, transparency and controllability. In *Proceedings of the 2013 international conference on Intelligent user interfaces*, IUI '13, ACM (New York, NY, USA, 2013), 351–362.

21. Zhao, S., Zhou, M. X., Zhang, X., Yuan, Q., Zheng, W., and Fu, R. Who is doing what and when: Social map-based recommendation for content-centric social web sites. *ACM Transactions on Intelligent Systems and Technology (TIST) 3*, 1 (2011), 5.

Employing Linked Data and Dialogue for Modelling Cultural Awareness of a User

**Ronald Denaux[1], Vania Dimitrova[1], Lydia Lau[1], Paul Brna[1], Dhaval Thakker[1]
and Christina Steiner[2]**

[1]School of Computing, University of Leeds, United Kingdom.
[2]Knowledge Technologies Institute, Graz University of Technology, Austria.
{r.denaux, v.g.dimitrova, l.m.s.lau, d.thakker}@leeds.ac.uk, paulbrna@mac.com,
christina.steiner@tugraz.at

ABSTRACT

Intercultural competence is an essential 21st Century skill. A key issue for developers of cross-cultural training simulators is the need to provide relevant learning experience adapted to the learner's abilities. This paper presents a dialogic approach for a quick assessment of the depth of a learner's current intercultural awareness as part of the EU ImREAL project. To support the dialogue, Linked Data is seen as a rich knowledge base for a diverse range of resources on cultural aspects. This paper investigates how semantic technologies could be used to: (a) extract a pool of concrete culturally-relevant facts from DBpedia that can be linked to various cultural groups and to the learner, (b) model a learner's knowledge on a selected set of cultural themes and (c) provide a novel, adaptive and user-friendly, user modelling dialogue for cultural awareness. The usability and usefulness of the approach is evaluated by CrowdFlower and Expert Inspection.

Author Keywords

User modelling; dialogue system; linked data; cultural awareness; learning simulator.

ACM Classification Keywords

H.5 Information Interfaces and Presentation; I.2.4 Knowledge Representation Formalisms and Methods; I.3.6 Methodology and Techniques.

INTRODUCTION

Intercultural competence is an important skill in today's globalised world, and is becoming recognised as a key aspect when designing user-adaptive interactive systems and intelligent user interfaces in various domains. To adapt to cultural diversity, these systems would need to encompass robust user modelling mechanisms which should be developed and tested in representative domains. For example, the EU ImREAL project[1] which aimed to extend a learner's cultural awareness by linking to more real-life experiences.

Culture can be defined as a set of beliefs, values, behaviours and practices that characterise a given group of people [6]. The ability of being aware that there may be differences in any of these aspects and their influence by culture is important in effective interpersonal communications. According to Hofstede [4], cultural awareness is the first step towards gaining intercultural competences. It has been well-recognised that culture is a complex and ill-defined domain [1]. A way to tackle the complexity of introducing culture into intelligent interactive systems is to focus on a specific aspect, which usually aligns with the possible application.

In this line of thought, the approach presented here has selected nationality as the aspects for culture, and looks at a user's cultural awareness regarding a specific nationality (as specified by the country). This is aligned with studies in which point out that nationality and countries are reliable indicators for tackling cultural diversity [3]. Several topics attributed to national culture were identified – gestures, food, clothes as well as general knowledge about the country's socio-political system. The paper focuses on modelling a user's knowledge in these cultural topics, which we will call cultural awareness hereafter.

A key challenge in providing culture-aware adaptation is the system's ability to derive a reliable model of the user's cultural awareness. This is the well-known cold start problem. A feasible approach to tackle cold start in interactive learning systems is via probing dialogue which step by step builds up a profile of the learner.

Having a rich knowledge base is important for planning a meaningful dialogue. However, knowledge base authoring is an expensive and time consuming process. The traditional approaches develop bespoke solutions by involving relevant experts, often leading to 'knowledge

---

[1] http://www.imreal-project.eu/

bottleneck' [8]. Recent approaches begin to examine the possibility of reusing knowledge that already exists in digital forms (e.g. Linked Data) and even combining with dialogue systems [8]. New effort, such as LinkedUp, has been made to adopt this Linked Data approach for education [7]. While some have explored the cultural knowledge domain, there are no existing approaches that employ linked data for modelling user cultural awareness.

It is in this gap that the proposed approach makes its key contribution to user-adaptive learning environments, and to the general field of culture-aware intelligent adaptive systems. An ontology-based dialogue agent, Perico, probes and extracts a user's cultural awareness of selected countries by using Linked Data (in this case DBpedia) as the knowledge base. As it uses a diverse range of cultural concepts and facts, a richer user model can be generated. The paper addresses the following research question: 'How to utilise DBpedia effectively for the construction of a knowledge base that drives a dialogue agent for modelling a user's cultural awareness?'

The key aspects of the work reported here include a) the potential for the work to be utilised by many applications to derive a moderately accurate knowledge of the cultural awareness of the user; and b) the potential for the use of externally developed sources of (possibly inaccurate) knowledge about cultures rather than relying on estimates of Hofstede's five dimensions – often carried out via a lookup in a table based on the user's nationality.

OVERVIEW OF THE DIALOGUE AGENT – PERICO
Perico is a dialogue agent that interacts with the user through a chat like interface. The dialogue agent provides a set of knowledge probing and modeling dialogue plans which lead the conversation in a direction that enables (a) validation of part of the existing user model and (b)

extension of the user model. It is an implementation of a generic dialogue framework [2] that can use OWL ontologies and RDF data as its knowledge base. Figure 1 shows the main components of the Perico dialogue agent which can be grouped as follow:

- Dialogue manager (centre of Figure 1) which provides the plan and grounding of the dialogue.
- Dialogue state and knowledge base (right hand side) which keeps track of state, tasks and moves; and operates on an ontology that contains concepts about cultural variations in interpersonal communication.
- Input, output and web interface (the remaining components on the left) which handle user interfaces.

CONSTRUCT KNOWLEDGE BASE FROM DBPEDIA
Dialogue systems require access to a knowledge base for preparing dialogue and performing assessment. In our case, the knowledge base needs to contain facts about different cultures. For meaningful interaction, it needs facts about a wide variety of cultural groups. Furthermore, users of all levels should be able to understand the assertions contained in the knowledge base (even if they do not know whether the assertions are correct or not).

Intercultural Fact Extraction from DBpedia
While the literature provided key concepts based on theoretical foundations, it largely neglects the concrete cultural variations and nuances that are necessary in order to converse with a learner. For extending the core ontologies and to achieve more concrete conceptualization, we have utilized DBpedia. The extraction of intercultural facts is not straightforward, because by default DBpedia does not directly link countries with cultural aspects (e.g. Clothing, Greetings etc.). However, it provides access to the crowd-sourced categorisation of Wikipedia pages which are used to infer cultural facts.

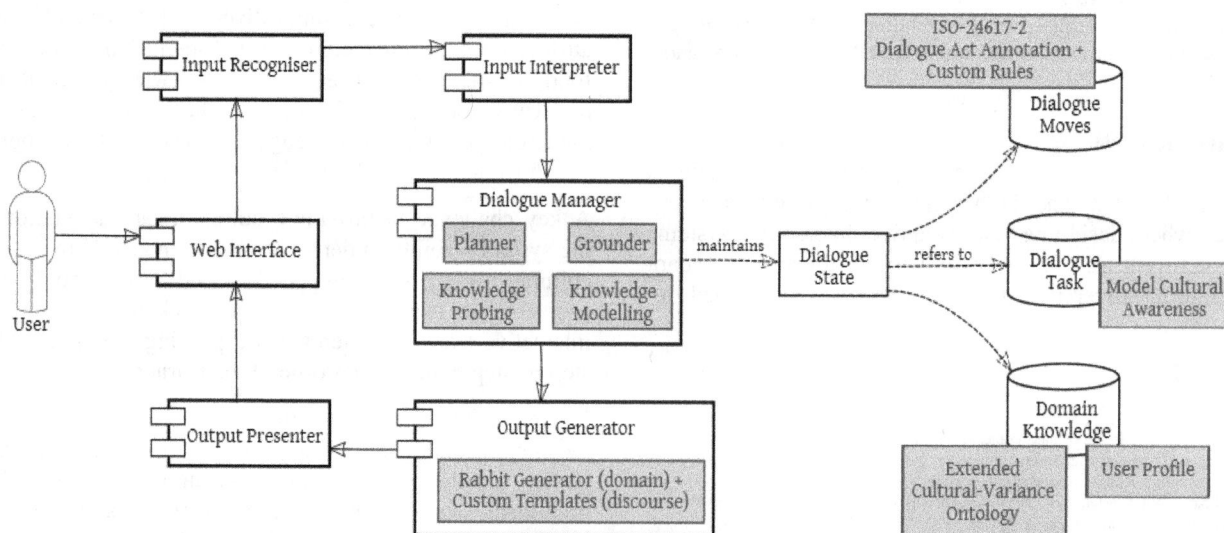

Figure 1 Component diagram for the culturally aware Perico. The main components (depicted in white) are typical of dialogue systems. Key services (shaded components) are put in place to enable the modelling of intercultural awareness.

In ImREAL, the AMOn+[2] ontology suite, developed using a theory-driven approach to conceptualize cultural variations in interpersonal communication activities [5], was used for the core vocabulary. The AMOn+ cultural variations module contains the concepts from various cultural theories and links them to Interpersonal Communication Module where appropriate. The module contains concepts such as *Cultural Norms, Stereotypes, Cultural Group* and *Behavior Primitives*.

DBpedia was used to extend the ontology with the following types of facts which have cultural variations: (a) non-verbal communication facts that relate gesture (including facial expressions and hand gestures) to a specific country, and by extension to a specific cultural group defined by nationality; (b) facts for eating norms that relate food items to countries; (c) facts for dressing norms that relate specific garments to specific countries. It was also beneficial to include other (non-cultural) facts that can be used to verify the knowledge of learners about a specific country, e.g. socio-political facts such as language and currency. Socio-political facts can easily be extracted from DBpedia since it contains a rich set of facts about countries. We used SPARQL queries to extract this knowledge[3].

In DBpedia, a page describes a topic, which may or may not be culturally relevant, and includes links to: (a) **Categories** defined for Wikipedia pages. Categories are linked to each other via sub-category relations. (b) **OWL Classes** defined in the DBpedia ontology[4] (such as Person, Organization, Music Genre, Sport, Language, Country and Currency). However DBpedia ontology does not contain culturally-relevant concepts such as *Greeting, Dressing* or *Food*. (c) **Literals** include human-readable labels and images of the topic of the page.

Extraction of DBpedia to extend the core modules is by: (a) Identifying categories that relate to concepts from the Cultural Variations module. (b) Traversing the DBpedia category network to find narrower pages with specific category and subcategories. (c) Traversing the DBpedia category network to find broader categories that are shared between the page to be extracted and a Country linked to them. (d) Inferring/adding new OWL axioms: a class assertion axiom linking the DBpedia page with an OWL class relevant to a concept from the Cultural Variations module; object property assertions linking the DBpedia page with one or more countries where this Cultural Variations concept occurs; and finally, copying relevant human-readable labels and depictions.

For example, to find concrete instantiations of the Cultural Variations module concept *Gestures*, DBpedia offers a category for Gestures[5], which has associated pages and subcategories (with their own pages). By traversing the category network, it is possible to find narrower pages like `dbpedia:Moutza`[6]. Furthermore, by searching for broader categories of `dbpedia:Moutza`, it is possible to find a category *Greek_Culture* and its super category Greece, which is connected to `dbpedia:Greece`, instance of a Country. This allows us to infer assertions that "Moutza is a `Gesture`" and that "`Moutza occursIn Greece`".

As the DBpedia category network is noisy, we apply a filter to the pages and subcategories to avoid unwanted resources. Our filter ignores resources and categories based on blacklisted parent categories or classes from the DBpedia ontology, such as OWL Classes (e.g. Person, Animal, Company) and DBpedia categories (e.g. Rooms, LivingPeople, BusinessLaw). For socio-political facts, Perico currently uses languages spoken in a country, currency, HDI (human development index) and GNI (Generalized inequality index).

Intercultural Fact Pool Generation
For a dialogue system, it is important that both types of facts, i.e. in assertive and negative forms, are available to probe a user. AMOn+ ontology suite contains assertions relating cultural aspects with specific countries (e.g. `Moutza occursIn Greece`). However, due to the Open World Assumption in OWL, it is not possible to know whether the same cultural aspects also occur in other countries (e.g. `Moutza occursIn Philippines`). In order to correctly model intercultural awareness we add extra (negation) assertions. We do this based on a list of countries that a learner may have visited to avoid generating large numbers of negation assertions. For example, if the learner has visited Greece and Germany, one of the assertions that will be generated is that "`Moutza does not occursIn Germany`". As with the facts extracted from DBpedia, it may be that links are simply missing from DBpedia or that our fact extraction algorithm failed to extract a fact. In such cases, the generated negation assertion will be incorrect.

USER EVALUATION USING CROWDFLOWER
This study examined Perico's usability. The main question addressed was: '*How do users perceive Perico's usability?*' 22 participants were recruited from CrowdFlower[7], and 4 participants recruited from the authors' institution.

The study involved: (a) *pre-study questionnaire*: for user profile information followed by an adapted version of the

---

[2]　http://imash.leeds.ac.uk/ontologies/amon/
[3]　http://dbepdia.org/sparql
[4]　http://wiki.dbpedia.org/Ontology

[5]　dbpedia.org/resource/Category:Gestures
[6]　Moutza is a traditional hand gesture of insult in Greece.
[7]　http://crowdflower.com/platform

Cultural Intelligence Scale[8] questionnaire (CQS); (b) *interaction with Perico*: for three countries; and (c) *post-study questionnaire*: repeated the adapted CQS questionnaire followed by an adapted System Usability Scale[9] (SUS) questionnaire. Participants from the authors' institution were followed-up with an interview.

Overall, the dialogue sessions covered 26 different countries in Europe, North and South America, Africa and Middle East. On average, 10 DBPedia entities were probed per dialogue session (average of 5 entities related to cultural aspects – gestures, food and clothes – and average of 5 entities related to socio-political aspects – language, currency, HDI, GNI); see Table 1.

Table 1 Distribution of DBPedia entities probed in Study 1 (total of 223 questions)

Gestures	Food	Clothes	Currency	Language	HDI	GNI
42	41	33	37	40	24	6

The participants' responses to the SUS questionnaire indicate that the participants found Perico quite usable and had no problems using it. The interviews with participants from the authors' institution resulted in following improvements: additional dialogue games to provide better feedback (e.g. indication of the correct answer and a list of countries for which the corresponding fact is correct); allow the users to indicate that the question may be confusing; more friendly tone of the dialogue; and acknowledge that content being derived from Wikipedia may not always be correct. The new version of Perico (see below) was used in the second user study, examining Perico's usefulness for user cultural awareness modelling.

EXAMPLE OF IMPROVED PERICO DIALOGUE

To illustrate the Perico components, a dialogue snippet extracted from the Expert Inspection evaluation study is presented below in which Zimbabwe was chosen by the user. Perico dialogue games are given in *italic*. The following response options were offered at every step: 'Yes', 'No', 'I don't know' or 'There's something wrong with this question'.

[Dialogue opening] In this conversation I will ask you some questions about cultural aspects related to the countries you selected. The questions are based on facts I have learned from Wikipedia.
[Episode opening] Let's first discuss Zimbabwe.
[Knowledge probing - Food] Is it true that Makdous is a typical dish in Zimbabwe?
<<*a picture with the dish*>>
User: No.

[Feedback] I agree, Wikipedia does not state this either. Makdous occurs in Jordan, Arab Federation, Mandatory Palestine and 33 other countries.

[Knowledge probing - Language] Is it true that Rama Cay Creole is spoken in Zimbabwe.?
User: I don't know

[Feedback] This is probably not true since Wikipedia does not contain this fact, maybe that's why you didn't know the answer. Rama Cay Creole is spoken in Nicaragua.
[Dialogue continues...]

[Episode closing] Your exposure to Zimbabwe is OK.

I asked you a total of 23 questions. Based on these questions, I think your overall cultural awareness is OK. Here's a breakdown of your score by topic:

Your knowledge about gestures is very good (based on 5 questions). Your knowledge about food needs improvement (based on 5 questions). Your knowledge about clothing is OK (based on 5 questions). 3 questions were on socio-political facts, your knowledge there is OK.

Your knowledge about currencies is unknown (based on 0 questions). Your knowledge about human development is very good (based on 1 question). Your knowledge about income inequality is very good (based on 1 question). Your knowledge about languages spoken in the various countries is not good (based on 1 question).

EVALUATION USING EXPERT INSPECTION

This study examined Perico's suitability for modelling user cultural awareness involving expert inspection. It addressed two questions: '*Does Perico produce an accurate user model?*' and '*What is the utility of the knowledge content for user cultural awareness modelling?*'

Two experts[10] were involved. Both had experience in user modelling and user-adaptive interactive systems and with good cultural exposure. The inspection was based on a systematically selected pool of countries based on the GLOBE model [3]. The experts conducted 10 dialogue sessions each, ensuring that one country per GLOBE cluster was selected and with varying levels of cultural knowledge in the selected countries. Possible cultural knowledge levels were: *none* (no encounter with the national culture), *low* (short visits to the country; limited contacts with people from this culture), *medium* (living in the country for a short period; sequence of regular short visits; some relationships with people from this nationality), and *high* (living in the country for a while; strong relationships with people from this nationality).

The total number of knowledge probing games in the 20 Perico dialogues was 457 (average per session = 22.85, STDV=0.6). The individual sessions were approximately twice longer than the sessions in CrowdFlower Study – this is because we changed the dialogue goals to discussing all seven DBPedia topics. Each session included one question on HDI and GNI and an average of 3 questions on language and currency and 5 questions on gestures, food and clothes.

---

[8]   http://www.linnvandyne.com/fourfac.html
[9]   http://www.measuringusability.com/sus.php

---

[10] Members of the project team who were not involved in the development of the Perico system.

User model accuracy. The experts inspected their cultural knowledge models generated by Perico at the end of the dialogue for each country (see transcript example). Four possible levels of knowledge about a topic could be return by Perico: *not-good* (the user did not answer any question correctly), *need-improvement* (less than 50% correct answers), ok (correct answers 50-70%), very good (more than 70% correct answers). Ratings for the experts to indicate accuracy level of diagnosis were: *accurate* (agree with Perico's diagnosis of their knowledge on the corresponding topic for the discussed country), *underestimated* (Perico's cultural knowledge level was lower than expected) and *overestimated* (Perico's cultural knowledge level was higher than expected).

Figure 2 gives a summary. Perico was most accurate in judging the user knowledge on food (80%) and currency (70%), followed by gestures (65%) and clothes (60%). The experts felt Perico overestimated their knowledge when correct answers could be derived from clues in the questions (see the discussion on content utility below). An error with calculation of the user model scores for language was identified – although the user answered several questions about the language, only the correct answers on normal assertions were counted – this led to the low accuracy of this topic (Perico assigned 'unknown' knowledge levels). Knowledge on human development and inequality was not properly handled by Perico (based on one question only). In several cases there were misleading values for HDI, e.g. '123 human development' or 'n/a human development' (due to noise in DBpedia), and it was unclear what was meant by 'high income inequality' and 'very high income inequality' (for a layman user).

We further examined whether the expert's familiarity with the national culture influenced their judgment of the correctness of their knowledge about that culture (see Figure 3). Experts tended to approve Perico's values on gestures, clothes and language and food when they were familiar with the country. This confirms that Perico's assessment of these topics is fairly reliable. Regarding currency, the incorrect judgment was based on having low utility content (see discussion below). Regarding HDI and GNI, the experts suggested two possible improvements – (a) instead of directly probing for a fact from DBpedia, compose a list of countries with a similar level of HDI or GNI and ask the user to compare the country against the list; and (b) combine the questions on HDI and GNI, with additional questions about the socio-political system in the country. This will require further extending the DBPdia knowledge pool.

Knowledge content utility. The quality of the resultant user model, and the overall usefulness of the approach, is dependent on the suitability of the knowledge content (i.e. the generated assertions) for assessing user's knowledge on the selected topics.

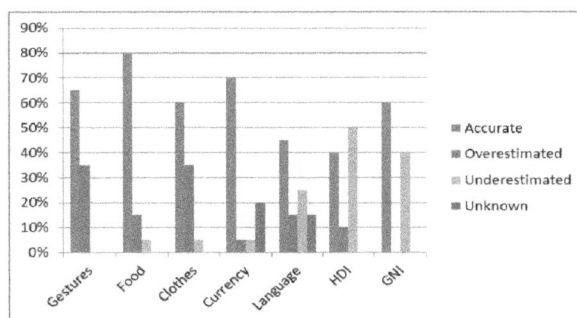

Figure 2 Summary of the experts' judgment of the accuracy of Perico's knowledge level (average values per each topic and dialogue session).

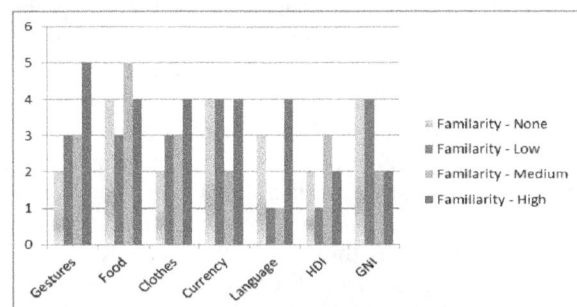

Figure 3 Frequency of cases when the experts judged that the Perico's assessment was accurate, grouped by user familiarity with the national culture.

To analyse this, the experts examined their dialogue transcripts and assigned a utility value for every knowledge probing question indicating the value of a correct answer given by the user to updating the user model. *Low utility* includes cases where the correct answer is explicitly indicated in the question (e.g. 'Is it true that Canadian Dollar is used in Canada?'). Such questions lead to inaccuracy in the user model. *Medium utility* includes cases where the correct answer can be given based on additional information in the question (e.g. the accompanying picture includes clues which help select/eliminate a country). Such questions are less cognitively demanding and in most of the cases give a good accuracy for user modelling. *High utility* questions are most valuable, as the correct answer requires good familiarity with the country culture.

The knowledge content has the highest utility for food (Figure 4). It is also suitable for gestures and clothes but leads to less cognitively demanding questions (e.g. being able to distinguish people looking as Asians or scenes which are related to Europe). While HDI and GNI were seen as usable, the limited amount of questions (only 20 per category) is insufficient to come to a conclusive answer.

The utility of currency and language questions was low – most of them superficially diagnosed a user's knowledge, as the answer could easily be guessed from the question.

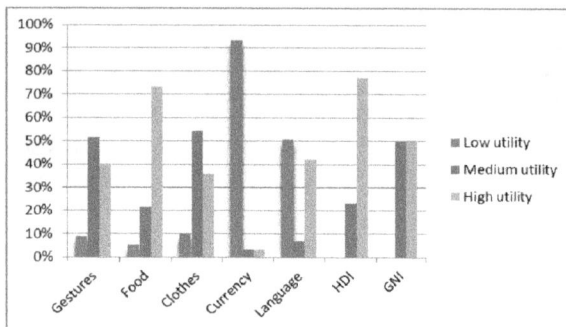

Figure 4 Knowledge content utility (% is based on the total number questions for the corresponding topic).

Further extension of Perico's knowledge probing mechanisms is needed to deal with low utility questions. The evaluation indicated some possible strategies. The first one is transforming the obviously correct statement by a syntactic transformation. For example, using currency nickname when exists in DBPedia (e.g. transforming 'Does Canada have currency Canadian dollar?' to 'Does Canada have currency loonie?') or using synonyms for entity labels. The second strategy is to go up in the ontology hierarchy (e.g. transforming 'Is Scottish Gaelic Language spoken in Scotland?' to 'Is Gaelic Language spoken in Scotland?'). For questions that are logically doubtful we need to find different solutions (e.g. 'Swedish language is spoken in Scotland' is not amenable to the three approaches described above). We can consider asking a different kind of question – such as 'Is a common kind of language shared between Sweden and Scotland?'. Similarities and dissimilarities between the ways in which countries have adopted various cultural practices can also be exploited.

CONCLUSIONS AND FUTURE WORK

The paper presents a novel approach for exploiting linked data and dialogue to deal with the cold start problem with modelling user cultural awareness. The approach is implemented in a dialogue agent Perico and has been validated in two user studies – using crowdsourcing and expert inspection. The combined findings of both studies give a strong support for the validity of the approach.

The first study indicated that layman users with various degree of cultural awareness find the system easy and intuitive to use. An in-depth expert inspection was conducted to examine the usefulness of the approach, considering the accuracy of the resultant user model and the utility of knowledge content. The inspection showed that Perico produces fairly reliable judgment of the user's knowledge of gestures, food and clothing associated with national cultures. For these topics, the extracted knowledge content had good utility (high-medium). The key challenge with modelling user's knowledge in language and currency is the low utility of generated assertions, i.e. including the country name in the question. Several strategies have been proposed for increasing the value these questions by

extending Perico's knowledge probing mechanism. There was insufficient knowledge poll for human development and inequality, requiring a further knowledge extraction from DBpedia.

Our future plans for extending Perico include looking at cross-cultural modelling taking into account other countries - not just finding out what the learner knows about a specific country but also what they know about neighbouring countries and countries that are similar/dissimilar in a number of ways (e.g. GLOBE). Eventually there is the possibility of going beyond the concept of national cultures and moving to other, perhaps more complex notions of culture. For example, seeking to understand what learners know about how minorities differentiate themselves/merge with others.

ACKNOWLEDGMENTS
The research leading to these results has received funding from the European Union Seventh Framework Programme (FP7/2007-2013) under grant agreement no ICT 257831 (ImREAL project).

REFERENCES
1. Blanchard, E.G., Mizoguchi, R., & Lajoie, S. P. Structuring the cultural domain with an upper ontology of culture. In E. Blanchard & D. Allard (eds.), *The Handbook of Research on Culturally-Aware Information Technology*. ISP (2010), 179-212.

2. Denaux, R., Dimitrova, V. & Cohn, A. G. Interacting with Ontologies and Linked Data through Controlled Natural Languages and Dialogues. In *Do-Form:Enabling Domain Experts to use Formalised Reasoning @AISB* (2013).

3. Gupta, V., Hanges, P.J., Dorfman, P. Cultural clusters: methodology and findings. In Journal of World Business, 37,2 (2002) 11-15.

4. Hofstede, G., & Hofstede, G. J. *Cultures and organizations, software of the mind, intercultural cooperation and its importance for survival* (2005).

5. Karanasios, S., Thakker, D., Lau L., Allen, D., Dimitrova, V. & Norman, A. Making Sense of Digital Traces: An Activity Theory Driven Ontological Approach. *JASIST* Sept (2013).

6. Kashima, Y. Conceptions of Culture and Person for Psychology, *J. of Cross-Cultural Psychology*. 31, 1 (2000), 14-32.

7. Keßler, C., d'Aquin, M. & Dietze, S. Linked Data for science and education. *Semantic Web* 4,1 (2013).

8. Sonntag, D. & Kiesel, M. Linked Data Integration for Semantic Dialogue and Backend Access. *AAAI Spring Symposium: Linked Data Meets Artificial Intelligence* 2010.

9. Suraweera, P., Mitrovic, A. & Martin, B. Widening the Knowledge Acquisition Bottleneck for Constraint-based Tutors. *IJAIED* 20,2 (2010), 137-173.

Who Will Retweet This? Automatically Identifying and Engaging Strangers on Twitter to Spread Information

Kyumin Lee
Department of Computer Science
Utah State University
Logan, UT 84322
kyumin.lee@usu.edu

Jalal Mahmud, Jilin Chen, Michelle Zhou, Jeffrey Nichols
IBM Research – Almaden
San Jose, CA 95120
{jumahmud, jilinc, mzhou, jwnichols}@us.ibm.com

ABSTRACT

There has been much effort on studying how social media sites, such as Twitter, help propagate information in different situations, including spreading alerts and SOS messages in an emergency. However, existing work has not addressed how to *actively* identify and engage the right strangers at the right time on social media to help effectively propagate intended information within a desired time frame. To address this problem, we have developed two models: (i) a feature-based model that leverages peoples' exhibited social behavior, including the content of their tweets and social interactions, to characterize their willingness and readiness to propagate information on Twitter via the act of retweeting; and (ii) a wait-time model based on a user's previous retweeting wait times to predict her next retweeting time when asked. Based on these two models, we build a recommender system that predicts the likelihood of a stranger to retweet information when asked, within a specific time window, and recommends the top-N qualified strangers to engage with. Our experiments, including live studies in the real world, demonstrate the effectiveness of our work.

Author Keywords

Twitter; Retweet; Social Media; Willingness; Personality.

ACM Classification Keywords

H.5.2. [Information Interfaces and Presentation]: User Interfaces.

INTRODUCTION

With the widespread use of social media sites, like Twitter and Facebook, and the ever growing number of users, there has been much effort on understanding and modeling information propagation on social media [1, 2, 6, 14, 17, 25, 27, 29, 30].

Most of the work assumes that information is propagated by a small number of influential volunteers, who possess certain qualities, such as having a large number of followers, which make them extremely effective in propagating information [28]. For example, these users can help spread emergency alerts, such as fire hazard or SOS messages like requesting blood donations, to reach more people faster.

However, prior research efforts ignore several critical factors in influencer-driven information propagation. First, influential users may be unwilling to help propagate the intended information for various reasons. For example, they may not know the truthfulness of a piece of information, and thus are unwilling to risk their reputation to spread the information. Second, an influential user may be unavailable to help propagate information when needed. For example, influential users may not be online to help propagate SOS messages when a disaster strikes.

Since everyone is potentially an influencer on social media and is capable of spreading information [2], our work aims to identify and engage the right people at the right time on social media to help propagate information when needed. We refer to these people as *information propagators*. Since not everyone on social media is willing or ready to help propagate information, our goal is to model the characteristics of information propagators based on their social media behavior. We can then use the established model to predict the likelihood of a person on social media as an information propagator. As the first step, we focus on modeling *domain-independent* traits of information propagators, specifically, their *willingness* and *readiness* to spread information.

In many situations including emergency or disastrous situations, information propagation must be done within a certain time frame to optimize its effect. To satisfy such a time constraint, we thus also develop a wait-time model based on a user's previous retweeting wait times to predict the user's next retweeting time when asked.

For the sake of concreteness, in this paper we focus on Twitter users, although our core technology can be easily applied to other social media platforms. On Twitter, the most common method for propagating information is retweeting[1], which is to repost others' tweets in your own content stream. Our work is thus reduced to the problem of finding strangers on Twitter who will retweet a message when asked.

To model one's willingness and readiness to retweet information, we first identify a rich set of features to characterize the candidate, including derived personality traits, social network information, social media activity, and previous retweeting behavior. Unlike existing work, which often uses only social network properties, our feature set includes *personality traits* that may influence one's retweeting behavior. For example, when asked by a stranger in an emergency, a person with a high level of altruism may be more responsive and willing to retweet. Similarly, a more active user who frequently posts status updates or reposts others' tweets may be more likely to retweet when asked. Our features capture a variety of characteristics that are likely to influence one's retweeting behavior.

To predict one's likelihood to retweet when asked, we train statistical models to infer the weights of each feature, which are then used to predict one's likelihood to retweet. Based on the prediction models, we also build a real-time recommender system that can rank and recommend the top-N candidates (*retweeters*) to engage with on Twitter.

To demonstrate the effectiveness of our work, we have conducted extensive experiments, including live studies in the real world. Compared to two baselines, our approach significantly improves the *retweeting rate*[2]: the ratio between the number of people who retweeted and the number of people asked. To the best of our knowledge, our work is the first to address how to *actively* identify and engage strangers on Twitter to help retweet information. As a result, our work offers three unique contributions:

- A feature-based model including one's personality traits for predicting the likelihood of a stranger on Twitter to retweet a particular message when asked.
- A wait-time model based on a person's previous retweeting wait times to estimate her next retweeting wait time when asked.
- A retweeter recommender system that uses the two models mentioned above to effectively select the right set of strangers on Twitter to engage with in real time.

RELATED WORK
Our work is most closely related to the recent efforts on actively engaging strangers on social media for accomplishing certain tasks [22, 23]. However, ours is the first on modeling and engaging strangers on social media to aid information propagation within a given time window.

Our work is also related to the effort on characterizing retweeters and their retweeting behavior [21]. However, the

existing work does not include personality features as our model does. More importantly, unlike the existing model focusing on *voluntary* retweeting behavior, ours examines a person's retweeting behavior at the request of a stranger.

There are many efforts on modeling influential behavior in social media. Such work finds influential users by their social network properties [2, 6, 14, 17, 27, 30], content of posts [1], information forwarding/propagating activity [25], and information flow [29]. In comparison, our work focuses on an individual's characteristics that influence their willingness and readiness to retweet at a stranger's request. Some of these characteristics, such as personality and readiness to retweet, have not been studied before.

As our goal is to support effective information diffusion, our work is related to efforts in this space. Bakshy et al. [3] examine the role of the social network and the effects of tie strength in information diffusion. Chaoji et al. [7] show how to maximize content propagation in one's own social network. In contrast, our approach aims at selecting a right set of *strangers* on social media to help spread information. Budak et al. [5] have studied a different type of information diffusion, which spreads messages to counter malicious influences, and hence minimize the influence of such campaigns. They proposed to identify a subset of individuals to start a counter campaign based on a set of viral diffusion features, including user virality and susceptibility, and item virality [16]. These features are complementary to the features that we use, such as personality, messaging activity, and past retweeting activity. Moreover, there is little work on automatically identifying and engaging the *right* strangers at the *right* time on social media to aid information propagation as ours does.

CREATING GROUND-TRUTH DATASETS
Since there is no publicly available ground-truth data with which we can train and build our predictive models, we collected two real-world datasets. We created a total of 17 Twitter accounts and our system automatically sent retweeting requests to 3,761 strangers on Twitter. Our first data set examines *location-based targeting*, where people who live in a particular location were asked to retweet information relevant to that location. The second examines *topic-based targeting*, where people interested in a certain topic were asked to retweet information relevant to that topic.

We hypothesize that information relevance influences a person's retweeting behavior especially at the request of a stranger. For example, people might be more likely to retweet news about public safety in an area where they live or work rather than for other locations. Similarly, a person might be more willing to retweet information on a topic in which s/he is interested.

Our dataset for location-based targeting (named *"public safety"*) and the dataset for topic-based targeting (named *"bird flu"*) are intended to examine how different types of

---

[1] We use the term "repost", "retweet" and "propagate" interchangeably

[2] We use the term "information propagation rate", "information repost rate" and "retweeting rate" interchangeably

Figure 1. An example Twitter account created for Public Safety data collection.

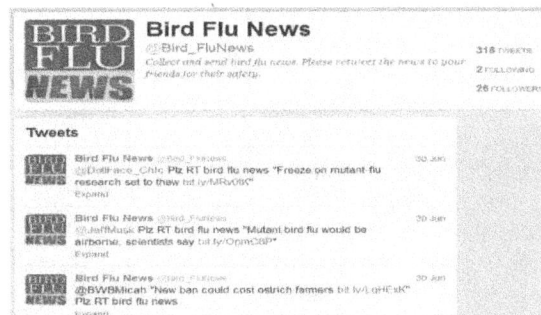

Figure 2. An example Twitter account created for Bird Flu data collection.

information (location vs. topic) may impact retweeting behavior.

Public Safety Data Collection: For location-based targeting, we chose the San Francisco bay area as the location and sent tweets about local public safety news to people whom we identified as living or staying in that area. First, we created 9 accounts on Twitter. All accounts had the same profile name, "Public Safety News" and the same description (Figure 1).

Note that we created multiple accounts to send a few messages per hour from each account in order to create a reasonable pretense of human behavior. Furthermore, previous studies have shown that if not careful, target strangers would silently flag an account as a spam to cause the suspension of the account by Twitter [22, 23]. Creating multiple accounts helped us avoid this possibility, and thus increased the number of users that we could reasonably contact per hour (each user received only one message).

Creating multiple accounts for research purposes is a commonly used methodology [18, 19]. To make these accounts appear to be genuine, all accounts followed 4~10 users and had 19 followers. We also created the following and follower accounts, and some were also followed by the original accounts. We posted 11 public safety messages using each of the 9 accounts before we contacted anyone on Twitter. We identified 34,920 bay area Twitter users using the Twitter Streaming API[3] with a geo-location filter corresponding to the bay area in June 2012. This stream retrieved only tweets that were marked as being sent within a bounding box equivalent to the bay area determined by using the Google Geocoding API[4]. We filtered out non-English tweets in this stream, and created a list of unique users whose tweets were in the stream.

Among all the identified Twitter users, we randomly selected 1,902 people. From our public safety accounts, our system automatically sent messages to those people using the Twitter API and ensured that each person received only one

message to avoid overburdening the person. Here is an example message sent:

@ SFtargetuser "A man was killed and three others were wounded in a shooting... http://bit.ly/KOl2sC" Plz RT this safety news

Each message contained the target person's screen name, the title of a news article obtained from a local news media site, a link to the article, and a phrase asking the person to retweet the message. The original link URL was shortened with the bit.ly URL shortening service to allow us to track user clicks on the link. Per our requests, 52 of the 1,902 (2.8%) people retweeted our message, which reached a total of 18,670 followers of theirs.

Bird Flu Data Collection: for topic-based targeting, we chose people who tweeted about "bird flu", a topic commonly being discussed at the time of our study. First, we created 8 accounts on Twitter (Figure 2). All accounts followed 2~5 users and had 19 followers. The following and followers accounts were created using the same method as in the public safety scenario. We then collected 13,110 people's profiles using the Twitter Search API and the queries "bird flu", "H5N1" and "avian influenza" in June 2012. We excluded non-English tweets and randomly selected 1,859 users. A message was then automatically sent to each selected person. Here is an example message sent:

@birdflutargetuser Plz RT bird flu news "Bird Flu viruses could evolve in nature http://bit.ly/MQBASY"

As in the public safety study, the news articles were obtained from the news media sites. 155 of the 1,859 users (8.4%) retweeted our messages, which reached their 184,325 followers.

For both datasets, through the Twitter API we collected publicly available information of each person whom we asked to retweet. This included their profile, people they followed, followers, up to 200 of their most recently posted messages, and whether they retweeted our message (the ground truth).

FEATURE EXTRACTION

To model a person's likelihood to retweet, we have identified six categories of features, as described below.

---

[3] http://dev.twitter.com/pages/streaming_api

[4] https://developers.google.com/maps/documentation/geocoding/

Profile Features

Profile features are extracted from a user's Twitter profile and consist of: *longevity (age) of an account, length of screen name, whether the user profile has a description, length of the description,* and *whether the user profile has a URL.* Our hypothesis behind the use of these features is that a user with a richer profile or a longer account history may be more knowledgeable in using advanced social media features, such as retweeting. Hence, when asked, they are more likely to retweet than those who have just opened an account recently or have little information in their profile.

Social Network Features

We use the following features to characterize a user's social network: *number of users following (friends), number of followers,* and the *ratio of number of friends to number of followers.* These features indicate the "socialness" of a person. Intuitively, the more social a person is (e.g., a good number of followers), the more likely the person may be willing to retweet. These features may also signal potential motivations for retweeting (e.g., an act of friendship and to gain followers) [4]. However, a person (e.g., a celebrity) with an extraordinary number of followers may be unwilling to retweet per a stranger's request.

Personality Features

Researchers have found that word usage in one's writings, such as blogs and essays, are related to one's personality [11, 13, 24]. Using the approach described in [22], we computed 103 personality features from one's tweets: 68 LIWC features (e.g., word categories such as "sadness") [24], and 5 Big5 dimensions (e.g., *agreeableness* and *conscientiousness*) with their 30 sub-dimensions [10, 32]. These features may signal potential motivations for retweeting (e.g., an act of altruism and to gain followers) [4].

Activity Features

This feature category captures people's social activities. Similar to the reasons stated earlier, our hypothesis is that the more active people are, the more likely they would retweet when asked by a stranger. Moreover, new Twitter users or those who rarely tweet may not be familiar with the retweeting feature and be less likely to reweet. To evaluate this hypothesis, we use the following features:

- *Number of status messages*
- *Number of direct mentions (e.g., @johny) per status message*
- *Number of URLs per status message*
- *Number of hashtags per status message*
- *Number of status messages per day during her entire account life (= total number of posted status messages / longevity)*
- *Number of status messages per day during last one month*
- *Number of direct mentions per day during last one month*
- *Number of URLs per day during last one month*

- *Number of hashtags per day during last one month*

These features also help us distinguish "sporadic" vs. "steady" activeness. We hypothesize that "steady" users are more dependable and are more likely to retweet when asked. For each person, we computed these features based on their 200 most recent tweets, as our experiments have shown that 200 tweets are a good representative sample for deriving one's features.

Past Retweeting Features

We capture retweeting behavior with the these features:

- *Number of retweets per status message: R/N*
- *Average number of retweets per day*
- *Fraction of retweets for which original messages are posted by strangers who are not in her social network*

Here R is the total number of retweets and N is the total number of status messages. We hypothesize that frequent retweeters are more likely to retweet in the future.

The third feature measures how often a person retweets a message originated outside of the person's social network. We hypothesize that people who have done so are more likely to retweet per a stranger's request to do so.

Readiness Features

Even if a person is willing to retweet per a request, he may not be ready to do so at the time of the request due to various reasons, such as being busy or not being connected to the Internet. Since such a context could be quite diverse, it is difficult to model one's readiness precisely. We thus use the following features to approximate readiness based on one's previous activity:

- *Tweeting Likelihood of the Day*
- *Tweeting Likelihood of the Hour*
- *Tweeting Likelihood of the Day (Entropy)*
- *Tweeting Likelihood of the Hour (Entropy)*
- *Tweeting Steadiness*
- *Tweeting Inactivity*

The first two features are computed as the ratio of the number of tweets sent by the person on a given day/hour and the total number of tweets. The third and fourth features measure entropy of tweeting likelihood of the day and the hour, respectively [26]. Below is a person's (u) entropy of tweeting likelihood of the hour $P(x_1), P(x_2), P(x_3) ... P(x_n)$:

$$Entropy(u) = -\sum_{i=1}^{n} P(x_i)\log P(x_i)$$

In the above equation, n is 24 to estimate the daily likelihood to tweet. The tweeting steadiness feature is computed as $1/\sigma$, where σ is the standard deviation of the elapsed time between consecutive tweets, computed from the most recent K tweets (where K is set to 20). The tweeting inactivity feature is the difference between the time when a retweeting request is sent and the time when user last tweeted.

PREDICTING RETWEETERS

Based on the features described above, we train a model to predict a user's likelihood to be a retweeter.

Training and Test Set. First we randomly split each dataset (public safety and bird flu) into training (containing 2/3 data) and testing sets (containing 1/3 data). The two sets were stratified, and contained the same ratio of retweeters and non-retweeters. Finally for public safety, the training set had 35 retweeters and 1,233 non-retweeters; and the test set had 17 retweeters and 617 non-retweeters. For bird flu, the training set had 103 retweeters and 1136 non-retweeters; the test data had 52 retweeters and 568 non-retweeters. For each person in the sets, we computed all the features described previously.

Predictive Models. We compared the performance of five popular models: Random Forest, Naïve Bayes, Logistic Regression, SMO (SVM), and AdaboostM1 (with random forest as the base learner). We used WEKA [15] implementation of these algorithms and trained these models to predict the probability of a person to retweet and classify a person as a retweeter or non-retweeter.

Handling Class Imbalance. Both our datasets have an imbalanced class distribution: only 52 out of 1,902 users (2.8%) in the public safety dataset and 155 out of 1,859 users (8.4%) in the bird flu dataset were retweeters. Imbalanced class distribution in a training set hinders the learning of representative sample instances, especially the minority class instances, and prevents a model from correctly predicting an instance label in a testing set. The class imbalance problem has appeared in a large number of domains, such as medical diagnosis and fraud detection. There are several approaches to the problem, including over-sampling minority class instances, under-sampling majority class instances, and adjusting the weights of instances. Currently, we used both over-sampling and weighting approaches to our class imbalance problem. For over-sampling, we used the SMOTE [8] algorithm. For weighting, we used a cost-sensitive approach of adding more weight to the minority class instances [20].

Feature Analysis. To improve the performance of our models, we analyzed the significance of our features using the training set. We computed the χ^2 value for each feature to determine its discriminative power [31], and eliminated the features that do not contribute significantly to the result. Our analyses found 21 and 46 significant features for the two data sets, respectively (Tables 1 and 2). Moreover, several feature groups have more significant power distinguishing between retweeters and non-retweeters: *activity*, *personality*, *readiness*, and *past retweeting*. Although our two datasets are quite different, we found six significant features common to both sets (bolded in Tables 1 and 2). This suggests that it is possible to build *domain-independent* models to predict retweeters. In addition, our analysis suggests that retweeters are more advanced Twitter

Feature Group	Significant Features (bolded is common to both data sets)
Profile	the longevity of the account
Social-network	|following| ratio of number of friends to number of followers
Activity	**|URLs| per day** **|direct mentions| per day** **|hashtags| per day** |status messages| |status messages| per day during entire account life |status messages| per day during last one month
Past Retweeting	**|retweets| per status message** **|retweets| per day**
Readiness	Tweeting Likelihood of the Day Tweeting Likelihood of the Day (Entropy)
Personality	7 LIWC features: **Inclusive**, Achievement, Humans, Time, Sadness, Articles, Nonfluencies 1 Facet feature: Modesty

Table 1. 21 Features Selected by χ^2 in Public Safety Dataset

Feature Group	Significant Features (bolded is common to both data sets)
Profile	the length of description has description in profile
Activity	**|URLs| per day** **|direct mentions| per day** **|hashtags| per day** |URLs| per status message |direct mentions| per status message |hashtags| per status message
Past Retweeting	**|retweets| per status message** **|retweets| per day** |URLs| per retweet message
Readiness	Tweeting Likelihood of the Hour (Entropy)
Personality	34 LIWC features: **Inclusive**, Total Pronouns, 1st Person Plural, 2nd Person, 3rd Person, Social Processes, Positive Emotions, Numbers, Other References, Occupation, Affect, School, Anxiety, Hearing, Certainty, Sensory Processes, Death, Body States, Positive Feelings, Leisure, Optimism, Negation, Physical States, Communication 8 Facet features: Liberalism, Assertiveness, Achievement Striving, Self-Discipline, Gregariousness, Cheerfulness, Activity Level, Intellect 2 Big5 features: Conscientiousness, Openness

Table 2. 46 Features Selected by χ^2 in Bird Flu Dataset

users, since they use advanced features more frequently (e.g., inclusion of URLs and hashtags in their tweets).

Incorporating Time Constraints

While our predictive models compute a person's likelihood to retweet upon request, it does not predict when that person will retweet. Some situations may require important messages to be spread quickly, such as emergency alerts and SOS messages, so we also explore how to predict when a person will act on the retweeting request. To do this, we

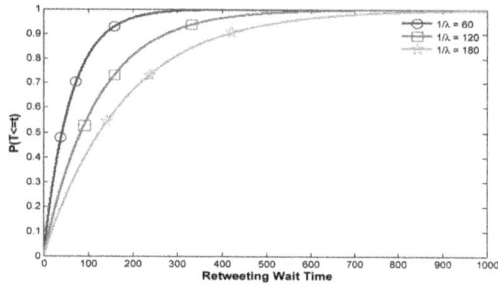

Figure 3. Three examples of the exponential distribution.

examine the person's previous temporal behavior and use this information for prediction.

In the simplest case, our model estimates the wait time for a person to respond to a retweeting request. We further assume that retweeting events follow a poisson process during which each retweeting occurs continuously and independently at a constant average rate. We thus use an exponential distribution model to estimate a user's retweeting wait time with a probability. The cumulative distribution function (CDF) of an exponential distribution is:

$$f(x; \lambda) = \begin{cases} 1 - e^{-\lambda x}, & x \geq 0, \\ 0 & , x < 0. \end{cases}$$

The distribution is on the interval from zero to infinite. We measure $\frac{1}{\lambda}$ which is the average wait time for a user based on prior retweeting wait time. For a user's specific retweeting wait time t, our model can predict the probability of the user's next retweeting $P(t)$ within that wait time. Figure 3 shows our model with three examples. The green line with stars indicates that a person's average wait time is 180 minutes based on past retweeting behavior. The retweeting probability within 200 minutes is larger than 0.6. The lower a person's average retweeting wait time t is, the higher probability of her retweeting is within time t.

In practice, given a specific time constraint t, we select a *cut-off probability* c that is then used to select people whose probability of retweeting within time t is greater than or equal to c. For example, with the cut-off probability of 0.7, our model will select only those who have at least 70% chance to retweet within the given time constraint. Incorporating the time estimation with our prediction models, we contact only people who are likely to retweet and whose cumulative probability of the retweeting wait time is greater than or equal to the *cut-off probability* c.

Incorporating Benefit and Cost

We have also explored the trade-offs between the cost of contacting a user and the benefit of a re-tweet. We assume the benefit is the number of people who are directly exposed to the message as a result of the re-tweets, which is the total number of followers of the retweeter. Using this assumption, if our system contacts N users and K retweet, the total benefit is then the sum of all followers of the K users. Assuming a unit cost per contact, the total cost is

then N. We normalize the total benefit by total cost to compute *unit-info-reach-per-person*:

$$unit\text{-}info\text{-}reach\text{-}per\text{-}person = \frac{\sum_{1}^{K} followers(i)}{N}$$

To address the case that the same person follows multiple retweeters, we count just the number of *distinct* followers for each retweeter.

REAL-TIME RETWEETER RECOMMENDATION

As mentioned earlier, our goal is to automatically identify and engage the right strangers at the right time on social media to help spread intended messages within a given time window. We thus have developed an interactive recommender system that uses our prediction model and the wait-time estimation model in *real time* to recommend the right candidates to whom retweeting requests will be sent. Figure 4 shows the interface of our system. Our system monitors the Twitter live stream and identifies a set of candidates who have posted content relevant to the topic of a retweet request (e.g., "bird flu" alerts). Such content filtering can be done by using the approaches detailed in [9]. Based on the identified candidates, our system uses the prediction model to compute the candidates' likelihood of retweeting and their probability of retweeting within the given time window t. It then recommends the top-N ranked candidates whose probability of retweeting within t is also greater than or equal to the cut-off probability c (Figure 4a). A user (e.g., an emergency worker) of our system can interactively examine and select the recommended candidates, and control the engagement process, including editing and sending the retweeting request (Figure 4b).

EXPERIMENTS

We designed and conducted an extensive set of experiments to measure the performance of various prediction models. We also compared the effectiveness of our approach with two base lines in various conditions including a live setting.

Evaluating Retweeter Prediction

To evaluate the performance of our prediction models, we used only the significant features found by our feature analysis (Tables 1-2) in our experiments.

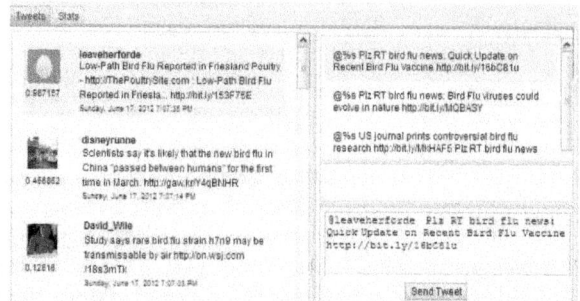

Figure 4. The interface of our retweeter recommendation system: (a) left panel: system-recommended candidates, and (b) right panel: a user can edit and compose a retweeting request.

Classifier	AUC	F1	F1 of Retweeter
Basic			
Random Forest	0.638	0.958	0
Naïve Bayes	0.619	0.939	0.172
Logistic	0.640	0.958	0
SMO	0.500	0.96	0
AdaBoostM1	0.548	0.962	0.1
SMOTE			
Random Forest	0.606	0.916	0.119
Naïve Bayes	0.637	0.923	0.132
Logistic	0.664	0.833	0.091
SMO	0.626	0.813	0.091
AdaBoostM1	0.633	0.933	0.129
Cost-Sensitive (Weighting, showing the best results in each model)			
Random Forest	**0.692**	0.954	0.125
Naïve Bayes	0.619	0.93	0.147
Logistic	0.623	0.938	0.042
SMO	0.633	0.892	0.123
AdaBoostM1	0.678	0.956	0.133

Table 3. Prediction accuracy (Public Safety).

Classifier	AUC	F1	F1 of Retweeter
Basic			
Random Forest	0.707	0.877	0.066
Naïve Bayes	0.670	0.834	0.222
Logistic	0.751	0.878	0.067
SMO	0.500	0.876	0
AdaBoostM1	0.627	0.878	0.067
SMOTE			
Random Forest	0.707	0.819	0.236
Naïve Bayes	0.679	0.724	0.231
Logistic	0.76	0.733	0.258
SMO	0.729	0.712	0.278
AdaBoostM1	0.709	0.837	0.292
Cost-Sensitive (Weighting, showing the best results in each model)			
Random Forest	**0.785**	0.815	0.296
Naïve Bayes	0.670	0.767	0.24
Logistic	0.735	0.742	0.243
SMO	0.676	0.738	0.256
AdaBoostM1	0.669	0.87	0.031

Table 4. Prediction accuracy (Bird Flu).

Accuracy Metrics. We use three metrics to assess prediction accuracy: Area under the ROC Curve (AUC), F1, and F1 of the retweeter class. We use AUC as our primary performance measure, since a higher AUC means that a model is good at correctly predicting both class instances regardless of class imbalance [12]. We report an overall F1 score as a reference measure, and F1 of the retweeter class on the performance of predicting minority class instances.

Settings. We ran all five prediction models under three settings: basic, SMOTE, and cost-sensitive.

The *basic* setting did not handle class imbalance. SMOTE was an over-sampling approach in which we over-sampled the minority class instances in the training set such that there was an equal number of majority and minority class instances. Under the *cost-sensitive* setting, we used a weighting scheme that weighted the minority class instances higher than the majority class instances. In our experiments, we tried five different weight ratios from 10:1 through 50:1 at intervals of 10. With five prediction models under three settings, we ran a total of 35 experiments: 5 in the basic setting, 5 in the SMOTE setting, and 25 using the cost-sensitive setting (5 models by 5 weight ratios).

Prediction Results. Table 3 shows the results for the public safety dataset. Overall, the cost-sensitive setting (weighting) yielded better performance than SMOTE for both AUC and F1 of the retweeter class. Both random forest and AdaBoostM1 performed particularly well under the cost-sensitive setting. We found the similar results using the bird flu dataset (Table 4). The class imbalance problem can be observed in the poor results under the basic setting. For example, SMO completely failed to predict retweeter instances (F1 of retweeter is 0). Although both SMOTE and the cost-sensitive settings outperformed the basic one, we did not observe any clear advantage of one over the other.

In summary, we have found prediction configurations that produced good results by the measures of AUC and F1. Since Random Forest in the cost-sensitive setting performed the best, we used it in the rest of our experiments.

Comparison with Two Baselines
To validate how well our prediction approach helps improve retweeting rate in practice, we compared the retweeting rates produced by our approach with those of two baselines: random people contact and popular people contact.

The *random people contact* approach randomly selects and asks a sub-set of qualified candidates on Twitter (e.g., people living in San Francisco or tweeted about bird flu) to retweet a message. This is precisely the approach that we used during our data collection to obtain the retweeting rates for both data sets. The *popular people contact* approach first sorts candidates in our test set by their follower count in the descending order. It then selects and contacts "popular" candidates whose follower count is greater than a threshold. In our experiment, we chose 100 as the threshold since a recent study reported that more than 87% of Twitter users have less than 100 followers[5]. We also considered other threshold values (e.g., 50, 500, 1000) and found that their retweeting rates were comparable.

---

[5] http://www.beevolve.com/twitter-statistics/

Approach	Retweeting Rate in Testing Set	
	Public Safety	Bird flu
Random People Contact	2.6%	8.3%
Popular People Contact	3.1%	8.5%
Our Prediction Approach	**13.3%**	**19.7%**

Table 5. Comparison of retweeting rates.

Approach	Average Retweeting Rate in Testing Set under Time Constraints	
	Public Safety	Bird flu
Random People Contact	2.2%	6.5%
Popular People Contact	2.7%	6.4%
Our Prediction Approach	13.3%	13.6%
Our Prediction Approach + Wait-Time Model	**19.3%**	**14.7%**

Table 6. Comparison of retweeting rates with time constraints.

Table 5 shows the comparison of retweeting rates produced by our approach against the two base lines. Overall, our approach produced a significantly higher retweeting rate than both baselines. Specifically, ours increases the average retweeting rate of two baselines by 375% (13.3% vs. 2.8%) in the public safety domain, and by 135% (19.7% vs. 8.4%) in the bird flu scenario.

Adding Wait Time Constraint. We also tested our wait-time model that predicts when a person would retweet after receiving a request. We compared the retweeting rate obtained using our approach with the wait-time model with that of three settings: (a) random user contact, (b) popular user contact, and (c) our approach without the use of the wait time model. In this experiment, the retweeting rate was the ratio of the people who retweeted our messages *within* the allotted time and the total number of people whom we contacted. In other words, if a person retweeted a requested message after the allotted time (e.g., 24 hours), s/he would be considered a non-retweeter as s/he did not meet the time constraint.

In our approach with the wait-time model, we set the cut-off probability at 0.7. As described previously, we first selected a subset of people who were predicted as retweeters and then eliminated those whose estimated probability to retweet within the given time window was smaller than the cut-off probability. We experimented with different time windows, such as 6, 12, 18 or 24 hours. Table 6 shows our experimental results with the averaged retweeting rates obtained for both of our data sets. Overall, our approach with the wait-time model outperformed the other three approaches in both data sets, achieving a 19.3% and 14.7% retweeting rate, respectively. Specifically, our model with wait time constraint increases the average retweeting rate of two baselines by 680% (19.3% vs. 2.45%) in the public safety domain, and by 130% (14.7% vs. 6.45%) in the bird flu scenario. This is also an improvement of 45% (19.3% vs. 13.3%) in the public safety domain and 8% (14.7% vs.

13.6%) in the bird flu domain over our own algorithm when wait time model was not used. In summary, the *combined approach* of using our prediction model and wait-time estimation further improved retweeting rates.

Effects of Benefit and Cost. As described previously, another method of evaluating the performance of our work is via a benefit-cost analysis using the notion of information reach. We compared the results obtained during data collection with the results of our best prediction results on the testing set. Table 7 shows the comparison of random user contact, popular user contact, and our approach without or with the wait-time model. The results show that our approach with/without the wait-time model achieved higher unit-info-reach per person than the two baselines. In particular, our approach with the wait-time model increased the average information reach of two baselines by 1,700% (153 vs. 8.5 = avg (6, 11)) in public safety and 54% (155 vs. 100.5 = avg (85, 116)) in bird flu case, respectively.

Live Experiments

To validate the effectiveness of our approach in a *live* setting, we used our recommender system to test our approach against the two baselines (random people contact and popular people contact). First, we randomly selected 426 candidates who had recently tweeted about "bird flu" during July 2013. We then used each approach to select 100 users among the candidates. The popular people contact and our approach selected the top 100 candidates based on their popularity (number of followers) rank and our prediction rank, respectively. If a person happened to be selected by more than one approaches, we contacted the person only once to avoid overburdening the person. Overall, we contacted a total of 232 unique people. Table 8 shows the comparison of retweeting rates for each approach. Our approach outperformed two baselines in a live setting significantly. Specifically, it increases the average retweeting rate of two baselines by more than 190% (19% vs. 6.5%). We checked the social graph of the retweeters (those who retweeted our message). They were not connected at all. Thus, our result was unlikely to be affected by their social relationship.

We also wanted to investigate the effectiveness of our approach with time constraints. Thus, we repeated the above experiment with different time windows, such as 6, 12, 18 or 24 hours. Table 9 shows the comparison of retweeting rates for each approach. Again, our approach with our wait time model outperformed all other three approaches. It in-

Approach	Unit-Info-Reach-Per-Person	
	Public Safety	Bird flu
Random People Contact	6	85
Popular People Contact	11	116
Our Prediction Approach	**106**	**135**
Our Prediction Approach + Wait-Time Model	**153**	**155**

Table 7. Comparison of information reach.

Approach	Retweeting Rate
Random People Contact	4%
Popular People Contact	9%
Our Prediction Approach	19%

Table 8. Comparison of retweeting rates in live experiment.

Approach	Average Retweeting Rate
Random People Contact	4%
Popular People Contact	8.7%
Our Prediction Approach	18%
Our Prediction Approach + Wait time model	18.5%

Table 9. Comparison of retweeting rates in live experiment (with time constraints).

creases the average retweeting rate of two baselines by more than 190% (18.5% vs. 6.35%). This is also an improvement of 3% over our own algorithm when the wait time model was not used. In summary, this result confirms that our approach consistently outperformed others in a live setting by a large margin.

DISCUSSION
Here we discuss several of observations during our investigation and the limitations of our current work.

Why People Retweet at a Stranger's Request
Although previous studies discuss various reasons why people retweet in general [4, 28], they focus on people's voluntary retweeting behavior. We were curious to find out why people retweet upon the request of a stranger. We randomly selected 50 people who retweeted per our request and asked them why they chose to retweet. 33 out of 50 replied to us. Their responses revealed several reasons why people accept our retweeting requests. One reason was the trustworthiness of the content to be spread: *"Because it contained a link to a significant report from a reputable media news source"*. Another reason is content relevance, e.g., messages about their own local area: *"Because it happened in my neighborhood"*. Interestingly, several mentioned that they retweeted because the message contained valuable information and was helpful to society: *"my followers should know this or they may think this info is valuable"*. Some of other reasons, such as to spread tweets to new audience or to entertain a specific audience, were discussed by others [4], however not mentioned in our context. In future, it would be interesting to study whether including the rationale in a retweeting request would help motivate the target strangers and affect the retweeting rate.

Retweeting with Modification
We have observed that some people retweeted our messages with modifications (e.g., adding hashtags to clarify the message or their own opinion to the original message):

#publichealth news: The Evolution of Bird Flu, and the Race to Keep Up http://nyti.ms/Qf6zsM @nytimesscience

what a shame + waste of tax $$ *"@BayPublicSafety: @esavestheworld "Hacker created fake Sierra LaMar posting http://bit.ly/Leaojo" Plz RT"*

Such behavior suggests that the target information propagators may augment/alter the original message with additional information including their personal opinions, especially if they strongly agree/disagree with the intended information. Based on this observation, it would be interesting to investigate the additional gains and risks that a potential information propagator might bring when asked to spread the message. For example, the added hashtag (#publichealth) in the re-tweet above would help propagate the message not only to the followers but also those who follow the hashtag. On the opposite, a propagator's negative opinions may affect the spread and perception of the intended message.

Generalizability
We wanted to examine how well our findings can be generalized across topics. We ran an experiment where we combined the training and test sets of public safety and bird flu. We trained prediction models on the combined training set using the significant features identified for the combined set. AUC in this experiment was 0.736, better than the original public safety result (0.692), but lower than the original bird flu result (0.785). The resulted retweeting rate was 12.5%, better than the random user contact (5.5%) and popular user contact (6%) for the combined set, but lower than the rates achieved in public safety (13.3%) and bird flu alone (19.7%). Our results suggest that it is feasible to build a domain-independent prediction model, if we have sufficient training-data from different domains. We are investigating the applicability of our models to new domains, e.g., new topics that our model is not trained on.

Optimizing Multiple Information Spreading Objectives
Currently, our work focuses on maximizing the retweeting rate in information diffusion. However, in practice, there may be multiple objectives to be satisfied, such as maximizing the expected net benefit or minimizing the reach time. We thus are investigating a model that can optimize multiple objectives at the same time. However, this is non-trivial as satisfying one objective may influence the other especially in a real world situation, where many of these objectives may be dynamically changing (e.g., the availability of retweeting candidates and the required time frame for a message to reach a certain audience).

CONCLUSIONS
In this paper, we have presented a feature-based prediction model that can automatically identify the right individuals at the right time on Twitter who are likely to help propagate messages per a stranger's request. We have also described a time estimation model that predicts the probability of a person to retweet the requested message within a given time window. Based on these two models, we build an interactive retweeter recommender system that allows a user to identify and engage strangers on Twitter who are most likely to help spread a message. To train and test our approach-

es, we collected two ground-truth datasets by *actively* engaging 3761 people on Twitter on two topics: public safety and bird flu. Through an extensive set of experiments, we found that our approaches were able to at least *double* the retweeting rates over two baselines. With our time estimation model, our approach also outperformed other approaches significantly by achieving a much higher retweeting rate within a given time window. Furthermore, our approach has achieved a higher unit-information-reach per person than the baselines. In a live setting, our approach consistently outperformed the two baselines by almost doubling their retweeting rates. Overall, our approach effectively identifies qualified candidates for retweeting a message within a given time window.

ACKNOWLEGEMENT

Research was sponsored by the U.S. Defense Advanced Research Projects Agency (DARPA) under the Social Media in Strategic Communication (SMISC) program, Agreement Number W911NF-12-C-0028. The views and conclusions contained in this document are those of the author(s) and should not be interpreted as representing the official policies, either expressed or implied, of the U.S. Defense Advanced Research Projects Agency or the U.S. Government. The U.S. Government is authorized to reproduce and distribute reprints for Government purposes notwithstanding any copyright notation hereon.

REFERENCES

1. Agarwal, N., Liu, H., Tang, L., and Yu, P. S. Identifying the influential bloggers in a community. In.*WSDM*, 2008.

2. Bakshy, E., Hofman, J. M., Mason, W. A., and Watts, D. J. Everyone's an influencer: quantifying influence on twitter, In *WSDM*, 2011.

3. Bakshy, E., Rosenn, I., Marlow, C., and Adamic, L. The role of social network in information diffusion. In *WWW*, 2012.

4. Boyd, D., Golder, S., and Lotan, G. Tweet, Tweet, Retweet: Conversational Aspects of Retweeting on Twitter. In *HICSS*, 2010.

5. Budak, C., Agrawal, D., and El Abbadi, A. Limiting the spread of misinformation in social networks. In *WWW*, 2011.

6. Cha, M., Haddadi, H., Benevenuto, F., and Gummadi, K.P. Measuring user influence in twitter: The million follower fallacy. In *ICWSM*, 2010.

7. Chaoji, V., Ranu, S., Rastogi, R., and Bhatt, R. Recommendations to boost content spread in social networks., In *WWW*, 2012.

8. Chawla, N. V., Bowyer, K. W., Hall, L. O., and Kegelmeyer, W. P. SMOTE: Synthetic Minority Over-sampling Technique. *Journal of Artificial Intelligence Research*, 16: 321-357, 2002.

9. Chen, J. Cypher, A., Drews, C. and Nichols, J. CrowdE: Filtering Tweets for Direct Customer Engagements. In *ICWSM* 2013.

10. Costa, P.T., and McCrae, R.R. Revised NEO Personality Inventory (NEO-PI-R) and NEO Five-Factor Inventory (NEO-FFI) manual. *Psychological Assessment Resources*, 1992.

11. Fast, L. A., and Funder, D. C. Personality as manifest in word use: Correlations with self-report, acquaintance report, and behavior. *Journal of Personality and Social Psychology*, Vol 94(2), 2008.

12. Fawcett, T. An introduction to ROC analysis. *Pattern Recogn. Lett.*, Vol 27(8), 2006.

13. Gill, A. J., Nowson, S., and Oberlander, J. What Are They Blogging About? Personality, Topic and Motivation in Blogs, In *ICWSM, 2009.*

14. Goyal, A., Bonchi, F., and Lakshmanan, L. V.S. Learning influence probabilities in social networks. In *WSDM*, 2010.

15. Hall, M., Frank, E., Holmes, G., Pfahringer, B., Reutemann, P., and Witten, I. The WEKA data mining software: an update. *SIGKDD Explorations Newsletter*, 11(1): 10-18, 2009.

16. Hoang, T.-A., and Lim, E.-P. Virality and Susceptibility in Information Diffiusions, In *ICWSM* 2012.

17. Huang, J., Cheng, X.-Q., Shen, H.-W, Zhou, T., and Jin, X. Exploring social influence via posterior effect of word-of-mouth recommendations. In *WSDM*, 2012.

18. Lee, K., Caverlee, J., and Webb, S. Uncovering social spammers: social honeypots + machine learning. In *SIGIR* 2010.

19. Lee, K., Eoff, B. D., and Caverlee, J. Seven Months with the Devils: A Long-Term Study of Content Polluters on Twitter. In *ICWSM*, 2011.

20. Liu, X.Y., and Zhou, Z.H. The influence of class imbalance on cost-sensitive learning: an empirical study. In *ICDM, 2006.*

21. Macskassy, S. A., and Michelson, M. Why Do People Retweet? Anti-Homophily Wins the Day!. In *ICWSM*, 2011

22. Mahmud, J., Zhou, M., Megiddo, N., Nichols, J., and Drews, C. Recommending Targeted Strangers from Whom to Solicit Information in Twitter. In *IUI*, 2013.

23. Nichols, J., and Kang, J-H. Asking Questions of Targeted Strangers on Social Networks. In *CSCW, 2012.*

24. Pennebaker, J.W., Francis, M.E., and Booth, R.J. Linguistic Inquiry and Word Count. *Erlbaum Publishers*, 2001.

25. Romero. D. M., Galuba. W., Asur. S, and Huberman, B. A. Influence and passivity in social media. In *ECML/PKDD,* 2011.

26. Shannon, C. E., A mathematical theory of communication. Bell system technical journal, Vol 27, 1948.

27. Singer, Y. How to win friends and influence people, truthfully: influence maximization mechanisms for social networks, In *WSDM*, 2012.

28. Starbird, K. and Palen, L. Pass It On?: Retweeting in Mass Emergency, In *ISCRAM*, 2010.

29. Ver Steeg, G. and Galstyan, A. Information transfer in social media. In *WWW*, 2012.

30. Weng, J. Lim. E.-P., Jiang. J, and He. Q. Twitterrank: Finding topic-sensitive influential twitterers. In *WSDM*, 2010.

31. Yang, Y., and Pedersen, O.J. A Comparative Study on Feature Selection in Text Categorization. In *ICML*, 1997.

32. Yarkoni, Tal. Personality in 100,000 words: A large-scale analysis of personality and word usage among bloggers. *Journal of Research in Personality, 2010.*

Tagging-by-Search: Automatic Image Region Labeling Using Gaze Information Obtained from Image Search

Tina Walber
Institute WeST
University of Koblenz
Germany
walber@uni-koblenz.de

Chantal Neuhaus
Institute WeST
University of Koblenz
Germany
cneuhaus@uni-koblenz.de

Ansgar Scherp
Kiel University, Germany
Leibniz Information Center for
Economics, Kiel, Germany
mail@ansgarscherp.net

ABSTRACT

Labeled image regions provide very valuable information that can be used in different settings such as image search. The manual creation of region labels is a tedious task. Fully automatic approaches lack understanding the image content sufficiently due to the huge variety of depicted objects. Our approach benefits from the expected spread of eye tracking hardware and uses gaze information obtained from users performing image search tasks to automatically label image regions. This allows to exploit the human capabilities regarding the visual perception of image content while performing daily routine tasks. In an experiment with 23 participants, we show that it is possible to assign search terms to photo regions by means of gaze analysis with an average precision of 0.56 and an average F-measure of 0.38 over 361 photos. The participants performed different search tasks while their gaze was recorded. The results of the experiment show that the gaze-based approach performs significantly better than a baseline approach based on saliency maps.

Author Keywords

Region labeling, image search, implicit user feedback, eye tracking

ACM Classification Keywords

H.5.2 User Interfaces: Input devices and strategies

INTRODUCTION

Billions of users are viewing photos on the web. Google published a number of one billion page views per day for their image search service[1]. Photo search can be performed based on simple visual similarity, e. g., on Google by the "Search by image" function. However, such low-level pixel information is often less important to the users than the content actually depicted in the image. Thus, the search is usually conducted based on techniques from text retrieval by using the photo title or the text surrounding an image, e. g., on web pages. To provide better annotations, manually added tags can be used to describe the content of an image. More detailed annotations can be conducted by tagging image regions, instead of the entire image. This information can be used for similarity search based on regions [12] or for search based on the coherence of individual image regions [15]. Additionally, a more detailed labeling can be used to display only the relevant area of a photo in the thumbnails of a search results list. Another potential use of region-based annotation data is its application as training set in object detection algorithms (e. g., [22]).

Manual labeling of image regions is a tedious task and is thus very uncommon. Automatic labeling of image regions as performed by object detection algorithms are limited to a number of trained concepts. They also need a large amount of manually created training data and they depend on the visual similarity of objects. In addition, the high computational efforts of the automatic annotation algorithms restrict their applicability.

The goal of our work is to benefit from users who are viewing photos in the results list of an image search engine to perform automatically the labeling of images at region level. It is intuitive for humans to automatically identify objects depicted in an image. Humans can easily compensate perspective distortions, occlusions, and they can also identify objects with an unusual appearance. The gaze paths of users searching for images are recorded by an eye tracking device. Subsequently, the gaze paths are analyzed and regions of the photos in the search results that caught most attention are identified. The search terms entered by the user is assigned to the most viewed image regions for describing the photo content. The gaze paths of several users are aggregated when they view the same photos with the same search term. The labeled image regions are evaluated by comparing them to ground truth regions, which are part of the experiment data sets. The recent developments of eye tracking hardware[2] supports our approach and the possibility to use eye tracking information in every-day life is expected for the next years.

Our previous research [26] showed that it is possible to annotate image regions by means of gaze information in a controlled priming experiment. In this work, we investigated the possibilities to automatically obtain labeling information

---

[1]http://www.bbc.co.uk/news/technology-10693439, (last visited Sept. 17, 2013)

[2]http://www.tobii.com/rexvip (last visited Oct. 7, 2013)

for image regions while conducting ordinary routine tasks, namely image search. We asked 23 subjects to perform 23 different search tasks with in total 361 photos from three different data sets of different origin and varying image quality. By comparing the generated region labels to ground truth data, we can show that our approach reaches a maximum average precision of $P = 0.56$ (improvement of 30 % over the best baseline result). The highest F-measure result is $P = 0.38$ (improvement of 14 % over the best baseline result). Two eye tracking approaches are used for analyzing the gaze data, one based on photo segmentation and the other one on eye tracking heat maps. Both are compared to a baseline approach which uses low-level image information to identify the most salient regions in a photo. Additionally, the results for the three photo data sets are investigated in detail.

The related work is discussed below. Subsequently, we describe the experiment design and our methods for image region labeling. The results of our experiment are presented and discussed, before we conclude the paper.

RELATED WORK

Different research has been done in the area of collecting implicit user feedback for improving retrieval quality. Joachims [10] and Jung et al. [11] used click-through data of search engine users as implicit source of information to determine the importance of search results. Other information such as how long a document was displayed were investigated, e. g., by Agichtein et al. [1]. Zhang et al. [30] identified attention times, click-through rates, and mouse movements as implicit feedback measures.

Other work, e. g., by Campbell and Flynn [4] and Viola and Jones [23], has focused on using computer vision techniques for the labeling of image regions. These works require large training data sets as well as extensive computational resources. In addition, the identification of objects is limited to the set of concepts trained on the data and to the visual similarity of the learned concepts. Humans are able to recognize objects based on — but not limited to — their visual appearance. Grabner et al. [7] constitute that objects are identified by human observers based on their function and not only on their visual appearance. This shows the limitations of object detection by visual-similarity-approaches compared to the human capabilities. A very different approach is to offer games for entertaining the users while objects are labeled. In Peekabook [24], users play together for identifying objects or parts of objects on given photos. From the collected data, words are assigned to image regions. We have presented the game EyeGrab [27], with the same goal of image region labeling, but performed in a gaze-controlled game for single users. However, these games follow an approach different from the one presented in this paper, where information is obtained from users performing the routine task of image search. No extra task has to be performed.

The use of eye tracking technology as an explicit input device was investigated in numerous studies. By gaze-control, the users explicitly control software by moving their eyes as presented, e. g., in the evaluations of gaze interaction by Sibert and Jacob [21]. Another area of usage for gaze data is

to better understand the users' behavior. For example, Chen et al. [5] analyzed gaze information to classify user behavior while performing tasks. The authors were able to identify transitions between tasks in multi-tasking situations. The research presented in this paper differs insofar as we unobtrusively observe the users' gaze paths for gaining information on the viewed objects.

Several approaches used eye tracking to obtain implicit relevance feedback in image search, e. g., [8, 14, 16]. From these works, we know that it is possible to use gaze information to detect images relevant to a given search task. Xu et al. [29] presented a recommender system based on eye tracking information for online documents, images, and videos. Buscher et al. [3] investigated the annotation of texts by means of gaze data and the usage of this information in retrieval tasks. However, their approach is limited to text documents. Putze et al. [17] combined eye tracking information with EEG data to identify events in video streams. The gaze data was used to identify the location of the perceived event (with an accuracy of 86.3 %) while EEG identified the temporal occurrence of an event. The study was performed in a controlled setting with simulated video sequences. Santella et al. [20] presented a method for semi-automatic image cropping using gaze information in combination with image segmentation. Their work showed that users preferred the gaze-based croppings over baseline croppings. Klami et al. [13] introduced an approach to identify image regions relevant in a specific task by using gaze information. Based on several gaze paths, heat maps were created, which identify regions of interest. This work revealed that these regions depended on the task, given to the subject before viewing the image. The work of Ramanathan et al. [18] aimed at localizing salient objects and actions in images by using gaze information. Image regions that were affecting the users were identified and correlated with concepts taken from a model for affection. The affective image regions were identified using segmentation and recursive clustering of the gaze fixations. The identification of image regions showing specific objects was not conducted in their analysis.

In earlier work, we investigated the potential of labeling image regions by means of gaze data [26]. The eye tracking information was collected in a controlled experiment, where the participants made decisions about the presence of a specific object on a photo. We obtained precision values of up to 65 % at pixel level for the region labeling. In this paper, we go a significant step further and investigate if it is possible to automatically obtain image region labels while asking the participants to do nothing more than performing image search tasks. To the best of our knowledge, this is the first time that the feasibility of automatic labeling of image regions by means of using eye tracking information in a real-world scenario like image search is analyzed.

EXPERIMENTAL DESIGN

We conducted an experiment to investigate the potential of photo region labeling during image search. Therefore, participants used a simulated search page for performing different search tasks.

Search task	Photos not fulfilling the task	Photos fulfilling the task
Search for a cat with black spots		
Search for a sheep with a black head		
Search for a table with a table cloth		

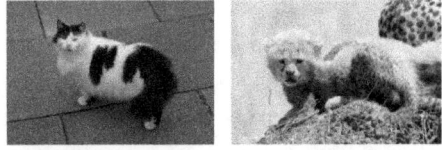

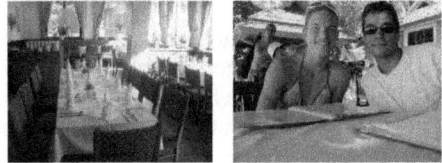

Figure 1. Sample search tasks and images not fulfilling and fulfilling the task.

Subjects

23 volunteers participated in our experiment, 11 of them were female. Their average age was 23.3 (SD: 2.09) with the youngest person being 20 and the oldest 29. Most of the participants were computer science students, but there were also students of other subjects, like mechanical engineering, biology, geology, and educational science.

Photo Sets

Photographs of natural scenes were presented to the users. These photos were taken from three data sets. All sets provided ground truth region labeling data. The VOC2012 data set [6] was made available for the Visual Object Classes Challenge. The segmentation set, which contains ground truth region labels at pixel level, contains 2913 photos and 20 classes of objects like "aeroplane", "sofa", and "dog". MSRC [28] published by Microsoft Research consists of 592 photos and 23 labeled object classes. The objects belong to simple concepts like in the VOC2012 set, e. g., "bird", "sky", and "sheep". The LabelMe [19] set with 182,657 user contributed images and 291,841 labels (download August 2010) provides images of complex indoor and outdoor scenes. The LabelMe community has manually created region labels by drawing polygons into the images and by tagging them.

The photos for the experiment data set were selected by their labels. The labels were taken from the "All time most popular tags" of the online photo sharing page Flickr[3]. Among the most frequently used tags, 23 occur in at least two of the three data sets. These labels were selected for the use in our experiment application. For each label, a random number of photos between 9 and 24 was chosen from the two resp. three data sets. 10 labels occur in all three data sets, whereas 13 labels are present in only two sets. The label-sets were composed in equal parts of the data sets.

[3]http://www.flickr.com/photos/tags/ (last visited Sept. 29, 2013)

In total, our experiment data set consists of 361 photos, with 103 photos taken from MSRC, 112 from VOC2012, and 146 from LabelMe.

Tasks

For each search set, consisting of a label and a set of photos, a search task was defined with the goal to simulate an online image search and to motivate the users to scan the image search result lists. The tasks request the participants to find an object with specific characteristics. For example for the label "bus", the search task was *"Search for a green bus"*. The tasks were created in a way that at least one photo fulfills the task. Often, even more than one photo could be selected. Also, there exist tasks where the answer depends on the subjective impression of the user. For example, a subject might chose an image showing a bird with an orange bill for the task *"Search for a bird with a red bill"*. Some more examples of search tasks can be found in Figure 1. This figure also shows examples of photos fulfilling and not fulfilling the given search task. 10 of the search tasks ask for a specific color as characteristic (e.g., *Search for a green bus*), 4 for animals with a specific coat color or pattern (e.g., *Search for a dog with black spots*), 5 tasks concentrate on other characteristics (e.g., *Search for a building with balcony*), and 4 ask for objects in specific situations (e.g., *Search for a horse with bridle*). In our analysis, we assign the named object to an image region in all photos of the search result list that were fixated, ignoring the specific characteristics. We investigate possible differences in region labeling results for photos fulfilling the search task (the photos with the *green* bus) and photos not fulfilling the task (photos depicting a bus, but not a green one).

Procedure and Experiment Application

Before starting the experiment application, the participants were introduced to the experiment tasks and the eye tracking device. A calibration of the eye tracker was performed by fixating five dots on the computer screen.

A Search task and start search   B Scrollable search results list   C Photo selection screen

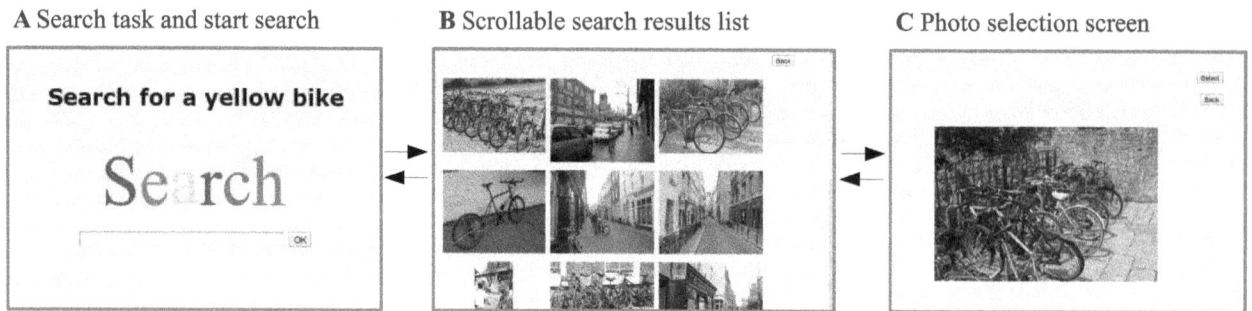

Figure 2. Cropped and scaled screen shots of the three experiment steps: A Search task and start search, B Search results, C Photo selection. The arrows show interaction options.

The experiment application was designed to resemble online image search pages. It consists of three pages. Screen shots of the application can be found in Figure 2. On the first page of the experiment application, page A in Figure 2, the search task was presented to the user. The user had to enter a search term as free text into the search input field. By pressing the OK button the simulated search was started. It was not allowed to start the search with an empty text field, but no further checks with regard to its meaning were performed on the given search query. On the second page B, the photos of the experiment data set were displayed in rows of three photos each. The photos were scaled to a maximum width and height of 450 pixels. The page was scrollable as not all photos could be shown on a static page. The user could go back to the search page by pressing the "Back" button. By clicking on the photos, page C opened. On this page, the user could select a photo by pressing the "Select" button for completing the search task. It was possible to go back to the search result page by clicking on the "Back" button.

Eye tracking data was recorded while the user performed the tasks. No time limitations were given for the 23 search tasks. The order of the tasks was randomly alternated for each participant. Also the order of the photos on the search result pages was randomized. At the end of the experiment, each user filled out a questionnaire. It comprised questions about demographic information (age, profession) and some ratings about the experiment application and tasks.

Apparatus

The experiment was performed on a 22-inch monitor. The participants' gaze paths were recorded with a Tobii X60 eye tracker at a data rate of $60\,\mathrm{Hz}$ and an accuracy of 0.5 degrees.

ANALYSIS

In this section, the two approaches for analyzing the gaze data as well as the baseline approaches, introduced in our previous work [26], are briefly presented. We extended the approach in a way that allows to assign a given search term to several image regions in one photo.

Assigning Labels to Image Regions by Gaze Analysis

We applied two gaze-based predictors for labeling image regions and one baseline predictor [26]. The two gaze-based predictors were the I Segmentation Gaze and the II Heat Map Gaze approach. By means of these approaches, we assigned

a given search term to an image region for labeling it. An overview of the calculation of both measures with one sample image is depicted in Figure 3. For all photos belonging to a search set, the input for the gaze analysis was (i) the given search term and (ii) the gaze paths of all users who fixated the photo. The I Segmentation Gaze measure additionally took (iii) (hierarchical) photo segments as input data. The photo segments for measures I Segmentation Gaze were obtained from applying the gPb-owt-ucm algorithm [2]. The different hierarchy levels describe different levels of detail and are controlled by the parameter $k = 0, 0.1 \ldots 0.7$, with $k = 0$ as highest level of detail. Please refer to the original publication by Arbeláez et al. [2] for details of the gPb-owt-ucm algorithm.

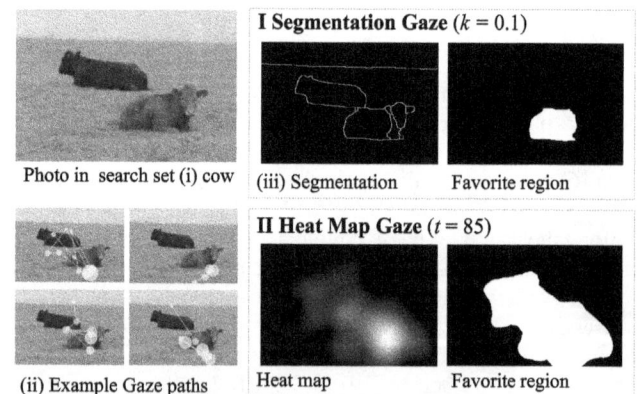

Figure 3. Gaze-based region labeling with predictors I Segmentation Gaze and II Heat Map Gaze. Input data is (i) the given search category, (ii) the users' gaze paths, and (iii) the segmented image (only for I).

The recorded gaze data was analyzed by means of so called eye tracking measures. The segment with the highest measure results was selected and the search term was assigned to it. Different eye tracking measures from literature [26, 16] could be used to perform this selection. The measure (1) fixationCount counted the number of fixations on a segment. (2) fixationDuration calculated the sum of the duration of all fixations on a segment. The measure (3) firstFixationDuration also considered the duration of a fixation, but it only took the very first fixation on a segment into account. Accordingly, (4) lastFixationDuration measured the fixation duration of the very last fixation on a segment. A visit describes the time between the first fixation on a region and the next fixation outside. (5)

visitCount counted the number of visits on a segment and (6) meanVisitDuration calculated the average duration of these visits. The segments with the highest 10 % of the measure values were selected. They were assumed to show an object or several objects described by the search query. The search term was assigned to this region. The measure results for all participants which viewed the same photos are summed up. In order to take the inaccuracies in the eye tracking data into account, we applied the region extension from previous work [26]. The region extension considers fixations in the surrounding of up to 13 pixels of a segment as belonging to the segment.

The II Heat Map Gaze approach identified intensively viewed photo regions by summing up the fixations of all gaze paths at pixel level. A value of 100 was applied to the center of each fixation. In a radius of 50 pixels, linear decreasing values were applied to the surrounding pixels. The value of all fixations were summed up for all pixels of the image for building the so-called heat map. From the created heat map, the assumed object region was calculated by applying a threshold to the data, identifying the mostly viewed pixels. The parameter t indicates the percentage of viewing intensity (e.g. $t = 10$ indicates the 10 % of all pixels with the highest values). The investigated parameters in this work were $t = 1$ and $t = 10 \ldots 100$ in steps of 10.

Baselines

We applied two baseline approaches that were compared with the gaze-based ones. The baseline approaches did not rely on eye tracking data. Furthermore, the baselines did not need training data nor a training period, just like the gaze-based approaches.

Saliency Baselines

The saliency baseline is based on the assumption that the important objects of a photo are the most salient points on an image. These points were calculated by the toolbox offered by Itti et al. [9]. The toolbox calculates salient points by means of multiscale image features. The order of the points depends on decreasing saliency values. The favorite region was selected by using the salient points and their ordering as input data. This saliency paths were interpreted as simulated gaze paths. Subsequently, the same methods as for the gaze analysis approach, described in the previous section, were used to analyze them. Thus, the investigated baseline approaches are called the III Segmentation Saliency approach and the IV Heat Map Saliency approach.

Random Baseline

Finally, for the baseline V Random, the photo was first segmented by the algorithm published by Arbeláez et al. [2]. Subsequently, one of the segments was selected randomly and the search term was assigned to this segment. This very naive baseline serves as measure for how difficult the task of selecting one favorite region was.

Calculating Precision, Recall, and F-measure

By means of ground truth data for all images and assigned labels (cf. Section Photo Sets described above), we were able to evaluate the computed object regions. For every pixel, we

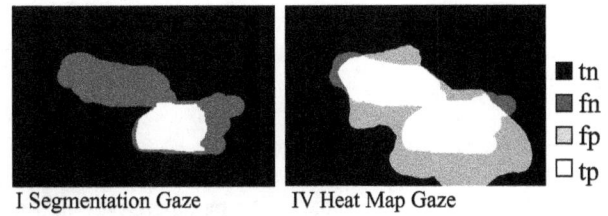

Figure 4. Comparing labeled image regions and ground truth regions at pixel level.

compared the ground truth with the labels obtained from our approaches by calculating precision, recall, and F-measure, with F-measure $= 2 \cdot \frac{precision \cdot recall}{precision + recall}$. An example photo with two object regions and their evaluation can be found in Figure 4.

RESULTS

In this section, the labeling results are presented and we compare the gaze-based methods to the saliency methods. Also the results for the three different data sets are compared. Additionally, we investigate the differences for photos fulfilling or not fulfilling the search task.

User Feedback and Behavior

The participants did not feel uncomfortable while their eye movements were recorded by the eye tracking device. Most participants gave an answer of 5 (M: 4.92, SD: 0.28) on a Likert scale from 1 ("I felt uncomfortable while my eye movements were recorded") to 5 ("I did not feel uncomfortable while my eye movements were recorded"). The users' comfort was asked in the questionnaire to check if there was a strong influence of the eye tracker recording on the participants' well-being and thus their gaze. As the users did not feel uncomfortable such an influence is not very likely.

The users did not have problems controlling the application as shown by an average answer of 1.04 (SD: 0.2) on a scale from 1 ("The application was easy to control") to 5 ("It was hard to control the application"). Also the tasks were not to difficult to perform, as the level of difficulty was in average rated with 1.33 (SD: 0.62) on a scale between 1 ("The search for images was easy") to 5 ("The search for images was difficult").

The average time the users spent on a search task was 14.6 s. The longest average search time was obtained for the search task *"Search for a road with median strip."* with 23.3 s. The shortest average time was 8.8 s for task *"Search for a chair with a red seating surface."* The searching behavior of the subjects showed that in 99.98 % of all cases the photo selection page was opened only once, namely for the final selection. Nine times subjects went from photo selection page C back to search page B before they chose an image according to the search query. With regard to the final selections, a percentage of 98.03 % correctly selected images reveals the high quality of the results.

On average, each user fixated 11.63 photos per search query. The average number of fixations over all users per photo is 2.88 (SD: 1.63). The average number of fixations on an image is highest for the search set "bottle" with 6.42 (SD: 1.91). In contrast, for the search set "car", the number of fixations on an image on average is the lowest with only 1.94 fixations (SD: 0.91).

Comparison of Eye Tracking Measures

First, the six eye tracking measures are compared for the I Segmentation Gaze predictor. As parameter for this approach, the smallest segmentation size $k = 0$ was chosen. Figure 5 depicts the detailed results. For each eye tracking measure the average precision results for each search term are depicted. The box plot diagram shows the first and third quartiles as boxes, the median is displayed inside the boxes as horizontal line, the mean as small circle, and the vertical lines show the range of all values. The measure (5) visitCount clearly performs worse than the other measures. (6) mean-VisitDuration and (3) firstFixationDuration have good mean results, but a big spread in the results over the different search terms. The measures (1) fixationCount and (2) fixationDuration perform best. As the measure (1) fixationCount has the best average result ($M = 0.48, SD = 0.13$) over all search terms compared to (2) fixationDuration ($M = 0.47, SD = 0.13$), (1) fixationCount is used in the following analysis.

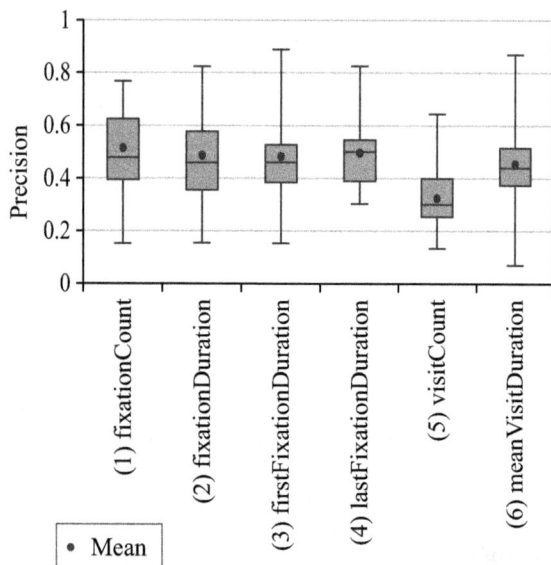

Figure 5. Precision results for I Segmentation Gaze with $k = 0$ for six different eye tracking measures.

Region Labeling Results

The results for the five region labeling approaches are compared in Figure 6. The precision and F-measure results are depicted for different parameters $k = 0 \ldots 0.7$ and $t = 1 \ldots 100$ (see Section Analysis above). Both gaze-based approaches I Segmentation Gaze and II Heat Map Gaze perform better than the baseline approaches. The saliency approach already shows better results than the random baseline. The II Heat Map Gaze approach clearly delivers the best precision and recall results over all parameters. The best F-measure was obtained for II Heat Map Gaze with 0.38 (marked as black circle in Figure 6) with $t = 90$. The overall best precision was obtained for the same measure and parameter with 0.56.

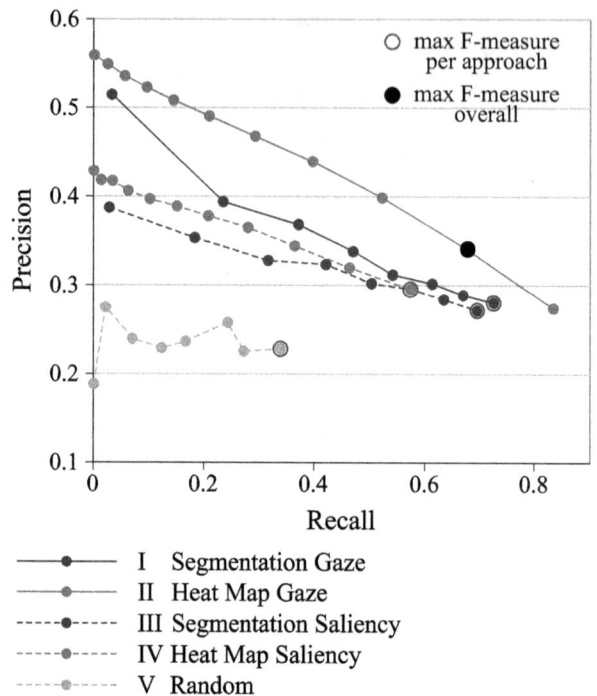

Figure 6. Precision and recall results for the two gaze-based measures I and II, the two saliency-based measures III and IV, and the V Baseline measure.

The best performing baseline approach with a F-measure result of 0.33 is IV Heat Map Saliency with $t = 100$.

A Wilcoxon signed-rank test showed a statistically significant difference with $\alpha < 0.05$ when comparing the average precision and F-measure results per search category for the best performing predictor II Heat Map Gaze with $t = 90$ and the best performing baseline predictor IV Heat Map Saliency with $t = 100$ (precision: $N = 23, Z = -3.194, p < .001$, F-measure: $N = 23, Z = -3.346, p < .001$).

Example Photos

The F-measure results for all photos are depicted in Figure 7, sorted by the F-measure values. We did not find any correlations between the number of fixations on a photo and the precision nor F-measure results. Only 9 of the 361 photos had a precision result of 0, i.e., not a single pixel of the labeled area covered a correct object.

The three photos with the best F-measure results and two photos with the lowest F-measure results are depicted in Figure 8. Besides the original photo, also the region the search tag was assigned to, as well as the ground truth regions for the given object, are depicted. Regarding the average number of fixations for the best labeling predictions one can observe that 1.47 fixations on that image were obtained by 15 subjects (the other ones did not fixate the image). In contrast, the second ranked image was fixated 9.90 times on average by 20 participants. The image placed on rank three was fixated 2.15 times by 13 subjects.

Search for a red sofa
Precision = 0.81
F-measure = 0.82

Search for a brown cow
Precision = 0.54
F-measure = 0.68

Search for a cat with black spots
Precision = 0.42
F-measure = 0.59

Search for a red sofa
Precision = 0
F-measure = 0

Search for a bottle of coke
Precision = 0.10
F-measure = 0.19

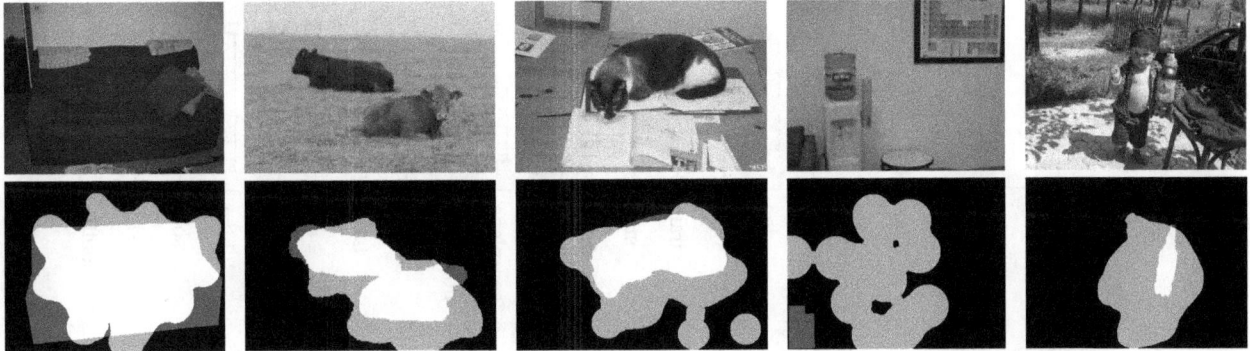

Figure 8. Example image with results for II Heat Map Gaze with $t = 90$ with evaluation of the labeled image regions.

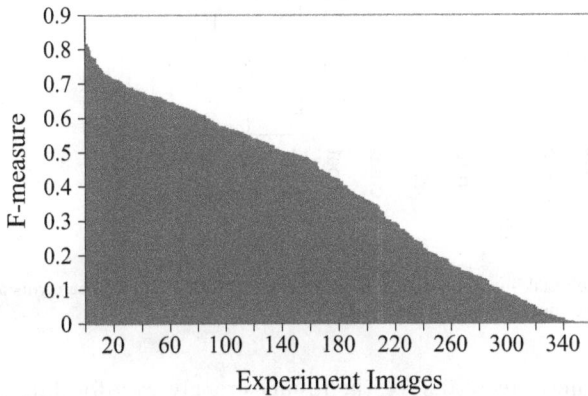

Figure 7. F-measure results for all images of the experiment data set calculated with II Heat Map Gaze with $t = 90$. The images were sorted according to their F-measure value in descending order.

Example Sets

In Figure 9, the precision and F-measure results for approach II Heat Map Gaze with $t = 90$ are split up for the different search tasks. In the diagrams, the results for all photos in each task are displayed (boxes show the area between the first and the third quartile, median as horizontal line, and the range of all photo results as vertical line). One can see that the range in the results is high. This means that the labeling results strongly depend on the given photos. The highest average precision value over all photos of one search task is obtained for "tree" with $P = 0.61$, the worst for "bottle" with $P = 0.09$. The best average F-measure value is obtained for "building" with $P = 0.63$, the worst for "sky" with $P = 0.16$.

Comparison of the Data Sets

Our experiment data was composed of photos from three different data sets, as described in Section Photo Sets. For the best performing approach II Heat Map Gaze, the best performing baseline approach IV Heat Map Saliency, and the V Random Baseline, we split up the precision and recall results for the three data sets VOC2012, MSRC, and LabelMe in Fig-

ure 10. Already the random baseline shows differences in the level of difficulty for the segmentation approach. In total, the results are much higher for the MSRC data set containing scenes of low complexity, compared to the most challenging data set LabelMe which includes images showing scenes of high complexity (i.e., many different objects). However it can be observed that the gaze-based approach improves the results for all data sets over the saliency baseline. The results of II Heat Map Gaze always lie above IV Heat Map Saliency.

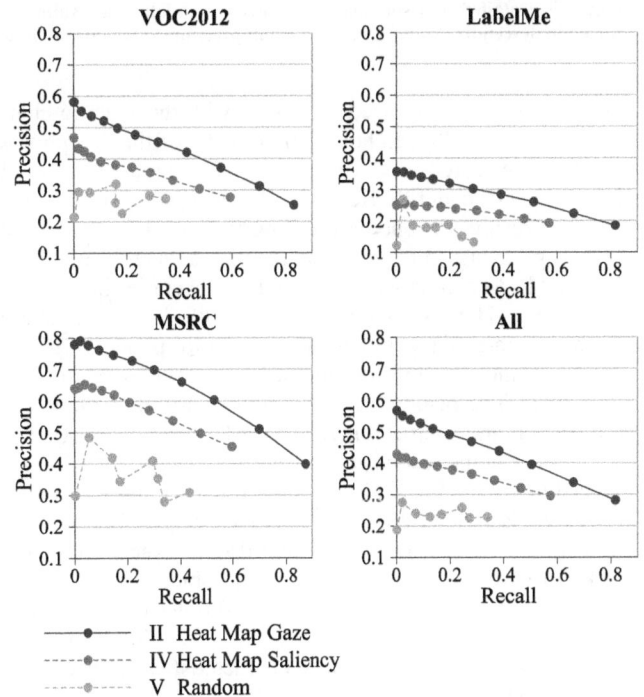

Figure 10. Compare results for the different data sets.

Comparison of True and False Images

In the experiment application, a search task was given to the participants asking for an object with specific characteristics, e.g., *"Search for a green bus"*. In the search result list, all photos depicted an object we asked for (e.g., "bus"). But

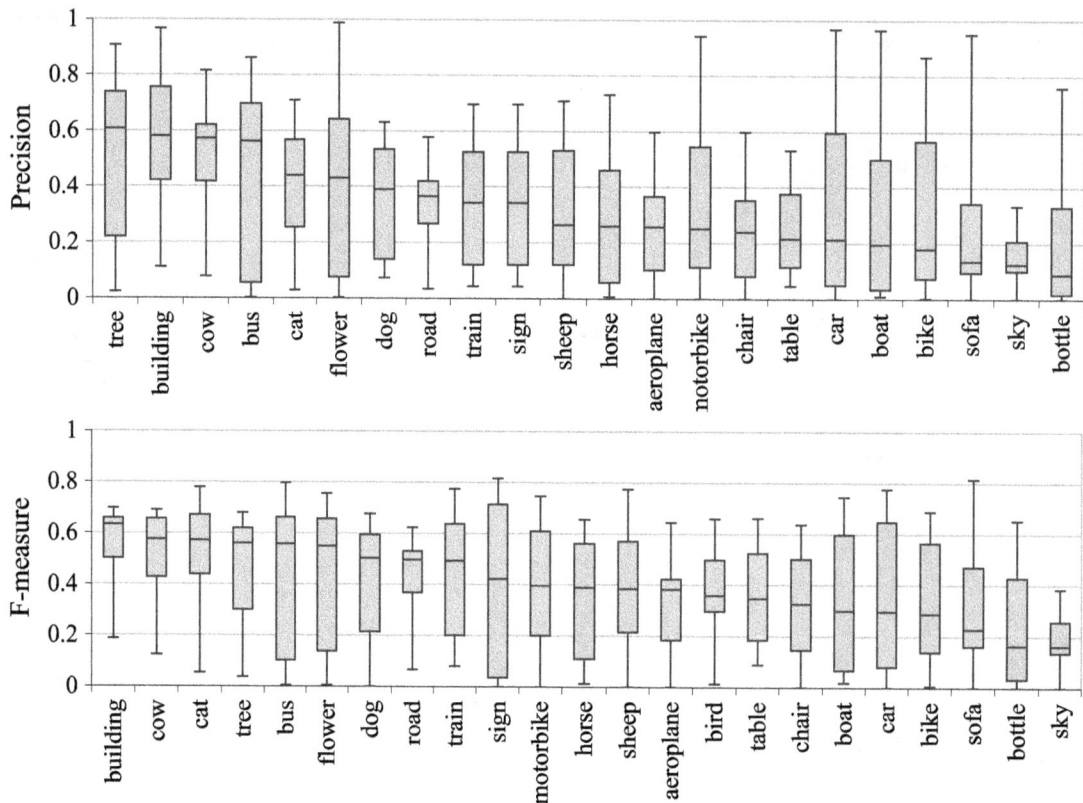

Figure 9. Detailed precision and F-measure region labeling results for each search task for approach II Heat Map Gaze with $t = 90$. The terms are sorted in descending order by their median precision value (above) and F-measure value (below), respectively.

only a few photos showed the object with the specific characteristics (e. g., "green bus") . In total, 97 of the 361 photos fulfilled the search task, 264 did not. For the approaches II Heat Map Gaze and IV Heat Map Saliency, we compared the labeling results for photos fulfilling the search task and not fulfilling the task. Precision and recall results are depicted in Figure 11. As can be seen in the figure, the curves lie close to each other. The results for the photos fulfilling the tasks are slightly higher. We compared the results for photos fulfilling the tasks and not fulfilling the tasks in a Wilcoxon signed-rank test. The results were computed using the values obtained from the approach II Heat Map Gaze with $t = 90$. The differences in the results are not significant with $\alpha < 0.05$ for precision ($N = 23, Z = -.487, p < .626$) and F-measure ($N = 23, Z = -3.346, p < .001$). This suggests that the approach also works for objects that do not exactly fulfil the task, i. e., where the photos show the object asked for but where the object does not match the additional characteristics like the color. With other words, the results imply that the labeling of objects is agnostic to characteristics of the objects the user is looking for.

DISCUSSION

Our experiment results suggest that the labeling of image regions by means of gaze data is possible. Comparing the best precision and F-measure results ($P = 0.56$, F-measure = 0.33) of this work shows slightly lower results compared to the ones obtained in previous work [26] ($P = 0.65$,

F-measure = 0.35). The results strongly vary for different search terms and photos. There are usually two reasons for difficulties in identifying objects in photos: One reason is caused by the characteristics of human visual perception. Big objects and objects that can easily be identified in the corner of ones eyes. Here, the user does not have to fixate it directly. One of the weak categories, "sky", is very likely to belong to this group of objects. Another challenge are very small objects due to inaccuracy of the eye tracking data and the segmentations of the photos. One of our previous works showed difficulties with small objects [25]. A detailed analysis of the factors influencing the results (like how many details are depicted on a photo) could be subject of a future study. More data and different photos might be needed for such a study.

We selected only "correct" photos for the search sets. Correct means that on each photo at least a correct object is depicted, even though the object does not have the specific characteristics. In a real world application, search engines reach a very high quality for simple search queries. Thus, we assume that the results may be transferred to a real search engine. However, when applying our method to real image search, this question has to be handled and wrong photos in the result set have to be considered as well.

From the two approaches for the gaze-based (I, II) and the saliency-based (III, IV) methods, the heat map approach performs better. An additional advantage of this approach is –

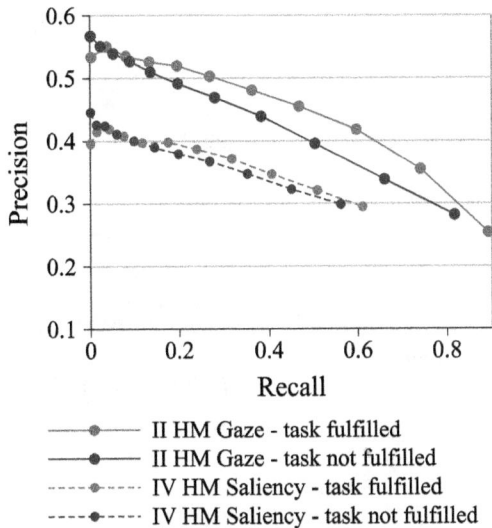

Figure 11. Precision and F-measure results for II Heat Map Gaze with $t = 90$ and IV Heat Map Saliency with $t = 100$ for photos fulfilling the search task versus not fulfilling the search task.

compared to the segmentation-based approach – that no segmentations have to be calculated. The computation of high-quality segmentations could be time-consuming. By varying the parameters of the II Heat Map Measure Gaze approach, the focus can be moved from good F-measures results (a higher parameter t which leads to bigger selected areas) to good precision values (small t values).

A further step could be the combination of I Segmentation Approach and II Heat Map Approach. For example, a segmentation inside the selected heat map areas could deliver interesting results. Until now, the II Heat Map Approach does not use any information that can be obtained from the image content.

The possibility to identify personal preferences from gaze information can also be adapted to other domains. One application could be the recommendation of products based on previous fixations on photos or objects in photos. In social media content, it could be possible to identify persons that are important to the user.

The steps forward in the development of eye tracking hardware are big and state-of-the-art open source solutions are developing rapidly. It could be an interesting next step in our work to test a low-cost device to investigate if there are differences in the accuracy and how this affects our approach.

SUMMARY

Our work shows that it is possible to assign search terms to image regions by means of gaze paths recorded by users searching for images. The usage of gaze data significantly improves the labeling results over a baseline approach using only saliency information. The method works even for photos depicting an object that was asked for, but did not fulfill the specific characteristic mentioned in the search task.

With a performance time of 14.6 s per search query, including the scanning of numerous photos, the labeling of image regions is very fast compared to the manual drawing of polygons. Also, no more effort is needed by the users than viewing search engine results. Another advantage of the suggested method is that the visual appearance of an object is not of importance and even unusual objects could be labeled as long as they are identified by the users. Also the labeling of image regions depicting more abstract concepts like "love" and "speed" could be performed by our approach.

ACKNOWLEDGMENTS
We thank all subjects for participating in our experiment. The research leading to these results has received funding from the European Community's Seventh Framework Programme (FP7/2007-2013) under grant agreement 287975.

REFERENCES

1. Agichtein, E., Brill, E., and Dumais, S. Improving web search ranking by incorporating user behavior information. In *Proceedings of the 29th annual international ACM SIGIR conference on Research and development in information retrieval*, ACM (2006), 19–26.

2. Arbeláez, P., Maire, M., Fowlkes, C., and Malik, J. Contour detection and hierarchical image segmentation. *IEEE TPAMI 33*, 5 (May 2011), 898–916.

3. Buscher, G., Dengel, A., and van Elst, L. Query expansion using gaze-based feedback on the subdocument level. In *Proceedings of the 31st annual international ACM SIGIR conference on Research and development in information retrieval*, ACM (2008), 387–394.

4. Campbell, R. J., and Flynn, P. J. A survey of free-form object representation and recognition techniques. *CVIU 81*, 2 (2001), 166–210.

5. Chen, S., Epps, J., and Chen, F. Automatic and continuous user task analysis via eye activity. In *Proceedings of the 2013 international conference on Intelligent user interfaces*, ACM (2013), 57–66.

6. Everingham, M., Van Gool, L., Williams, C. K. I., Winn, J., and Zisserman, A. The PASCAL Visual Object Classes Challenge 2012 (VOC2012) Results. http://www.pascal-network.org/challenges/VOC/voc2012/workshop/index.html.

7. Grabner, H., Gall, J., and Van Gool, L. What makes a chair a chair? In *Computer Vision and Pattern Recognition (CVPR), 2011 IEEE Conference on*, IEEE (2011), 1529–1536.

8. Hajimirza, S., and Izquierdo, E. Gaze movement inference for implicit image annotation. In *Image Analysis for Multimedia Interactive Services*, IEEE (2010).

9. Itti, L., Koch, C., and Niebur, E. A model of saliency-based visual attention for rapid scene analysis. *IEEE Transactions on Pattern Analysis and Machine Intelligence 20*, 11 (Nov 1998), 1254–1259.

10. Joachims, T., Granka, L., Pan, B., Hembrooke, H., and Gay, G. Accurately interpreting clickthrough data as implicit feedback. In *Proceedings of the 28th annual international ACM SIGIR conference on Research and development in information retrieval*, ACM (2005), 154–161.

11. Jung, S., Herlocker, J. L., and Webster, J. Click data as implicit relevance feedback in web search. *Information Processing & Management 43*, 3 (2007), 791–807.

12. Kim, D., and Yu, S. A new region filtering and region weighting approach to relevance feedback in content-based image retrieval. *Journal of Systems and Software 81*, 9 (2008), 1525–1538.

13. Klami, A. Inferring task-relevant image regions from gaze data. In *Workshop on Machine Learning for Signal Processing*, IEEE (2010).

14. Klami, A., Saunders, C., De Campos, T., and Kaski, S. Can relevance of images be inferred from eye movements? In *Multimedia information retrieval*, ACM (2008), 134–140.

15. Kompatsiaris, I., Triantafyllou, E., and Strintzis, M. A World Wide Web region-based image search engine. *Conference on Image Analysis and Processing* (2001).

16. Kozma, L., Klami, A., and Kaski, S. GaZIR: gaze-based zooming interface for image retrieval. In *Multimodal interfaces*, ACM (2009).

17. Putze, F., Hild, J., Kärgel, R., Herff, C., Redmann, A., Beyerer, J., and Schultz, T. Locating user attention using eye tracking and eeg for spatio-temporal event selection. In *Proceedings of the 2013 international conference on Intelligent user interfaces*, ACM (2013), 129–136.

18. Ramanathan, S., Katti, H., Huang, R., Chua, T.-S., and Kankanhalli, M. Automated localization of affective objects and actions in images via caption text-cum-eye gaze analysis. In *Multimedia*, ACM (New York, New York, USA, 2009).

19. Russell, B., Torralba, A., Murphy, K., and Freeman, W. Labelme: a database and web-based tool for image annotation. *International journal of computer vision 77*, 1 (2008), 157–173.

20. Santella, A., Agrawala, M., DeCarlo, D., Salesin, D., and Cohen, M. Gaze-based interaction for semi-automatic photo cropping. In *CHI*, ACM (2006), 780.

21. Sibert, L. E., and Jacob, R. J. Evaluation of eye gaze interaction. In *Proceedings of the SIGCHI conference on Human factors in computing systems*, ACM (2000), 281–288.

22. Torralba, A., Murphy, K., and Freeman, W. Sharing visual features for multiclass and multiview object detection. *Pattern Analysis and Machine Intelligence, IEEE Transactions on 29*, 5 (2007), 854–869.

23. Viola, P., and Jones, M. Rapid object detection using a boosted cascade of simple features. In *Computer Vision and Pattern Recognition, 2001. CVPR 2001. Proceedings of the 2001 IEEE Computer Society Conference on*, vol. 1, IEEE (2001), I–511.

24. Von Ahn, L., Liu, R., and Blum, M. Peekaboom: a game for locating objects in images. In *Proceedings of the SIGCHI conference on Human Factors in computing systems*, ACM (2006), 55–64.

25. Walber, T., Scherp, A., and Staab, S. Benefiting from users gaze: selection of image regions from eye tracking information for provided tags. *Multimedia Tools and Applications* (2013), 1–28.

26. Walber, T., Scherp, A., and Staab, S. Can you see it? two novel eye-tracking-based measures for assigning tags to image regions. In *Advances in Multimedia Modeling*. Springer, 2013, 36–46.

27. Walber, T., Scherp, A., and Staab, S. Exploitation of gaze data for photo region labeling in an immersive environment. In *Advances in Multimedia Modeling*. Springer, 2014.

28. Winn, J., Criminisi, A., and Minka, T. Object categorization by learned universal visual dictionary. In *Computer Vision, 2005. ICCV 2005. Tenth IEEE International Conference on*, vol. 2, IEEE (2005), 1800–1807.

29. Xu, S., Jiang, H., and Lau, F. Personalized online document, image and video recommendation via commodity eye-tracking. In *Proceedings of the 2008 ACM conference on Recommender systems*, ACM (2008), 83–90.

30. Zhang, B., Guan, Y., Sun, H., Liu, Q., and Kong, J. Survey of user behaviors as implicit feedback. In *Computer, Mechatronics, Control and Electronic Engineering (CMCE), 2010 International Conference on*, vol. 6, IEEE (2010), 345–348.

Using Eye-Tracking to Support Interaction with Layered 3D Interfaces on Stereoscopic Displays

Florian Alt[1,2], **Stefan Schneegass**[2], **Jonas Auda**[2], **Rufat Rzayev**[2], **Nora Broy**[1,2]

[1]University of Munich
Media Informatics Group
Amalienstraße 17, 80333 München
{firstname.lastname}@ifi.lmu.de

[2]University of Stuttgart
Institute for Visualization and Interactive Systems
Pfaffenwaldring 5a, 70569 Stuttgart
{firstname.lastname}@vis.uni-stuttgart.de

ABSTRACT

In this paper, we investigate the concept of gaze-based interaction with 3D user interfaces. We currently see stereo vision displays becoming ubiquitous, particularly as auto-stereoscopy enables the perception of 3D content without the use of glasses. As a result, application areas for 3D beyond entertainment in cinema or at home emerge, including work settings, mobile phones, public displays, and cars. At the same time, eye tracking is hitting the consumer market with low-cost devices. We envision eye trackers in the future to be integrated with consumer devices (laptops, mobile phones, displays), hence allowing the user's gaze to be analyzed and used as input for interactive applications. A particular challenge when applying this concept to 3D displays is that current eye trackers provide the gaze point in 2D only (x and y coordinates). In this paper, we compare the performance of two methods that use the eye's physiology for calculating the gaze point in 3D space, hence enabling gaze-based interaction with stereoscopic content. Furthermore, we provide a comparison of gaze interaction in 2D and 3D with regard to user experience and performance. Our results show that with current technology, eye tracking on stereoscopic displays is possible with similar performance as on standard 2D screens.

Author Keywords

Eye tracking; 3D; gaze interaction; stereoscopic displays

ACM Classification Keywords

H.5.2 Information Interfaces and Presentation: User Interfaces–*Input devices and strategies*

INTRODUCTION

Today, 3D technology is widely used for displays in an entertainment context, for example to play games or to watch movies in cinema or at home. At the same time, 3D is used in specialized work environments, where 3-dimensional

IUI'14, February 21–27, 2014, Haifa, Israel.
Copyright is held by the owner/author(s). Publication rights licensed to ACM.
ACM 978-1-4503-2184-6/14/02?$15.00.
http://dx.doi.org/10.1145/2557500.2557518

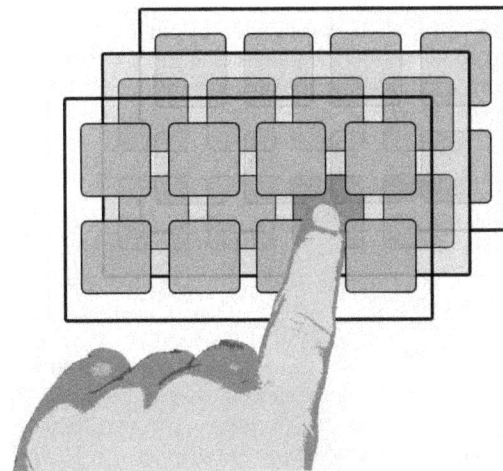

Figure 1. By using gaze to select the specific layer (gray), the user is able to interact with this layer in the same way as with 2D interfaces.

data needs to be analyzed, including CAD and medical work places. A major reason that hampers the widespread usage in other domains is the need for glasses in cases where anaglyph, polar, or shutter technology is used to create the 3D effect.

More recently, auto-stereoscopic displays entered the consumer market, making it possible to perceive content in 3D without the use of glasses. First examples, where this technology is already integrated into consumer devices include mobile phones and public displays. In such interfaces, depth can be used to highlight important information or to group information that belongs together by means of its position along the z axis. Such interfaces, that aim to enhance the users' focused attention by arranging them on distinct planes are commonly referred to as layered user interfaces [10].

At the same time, devices to track the users' gaze are becoming commercially available. Leading manufacturers recently released low-cost eye trackers, making it likely that such devices will be soon integrated with devices like laptops or displays. These devices do not only make it possible to passively monitor a user's gaze behavior but enable gaze-based interaction. For example, an interface could be adapted based on attention or users could explicitly control an application.

Using standard input devices, like touch screens, for interacting with 3D user interfaces is cumbersome due to the lack of a third (physical) dimension. Hence, we see particular potential in using gaze as an (additional) input modality. In this way, for example, a specific layer could be selected using gaze. Hence, the interaction space is reduced to the well-understood 2D space. The major challenge of this approach is to apply eye tracking to 3D, as state-of-the-art eye-trackers usually provide the gaze point in 2D space only. In this work, we compare two approaches based on the physiology of the pupil to detect the correct depth position in 3D space.

The contribution of this paper is threefold. First, we introduce the concept of interaction with layered 3D user interfaces, sketching particular application domains that could benefit from gaze as an input modality. Second, based on a study with 14 participants, we provide a comparison of two methods to calculate the gaze point in 3D space with regard to user performance. Third, we compare the user experience and performance of gaze interaction in 2D to gaze interaction in 3D.

RELATED WORK

With the advent of 3D displays, researchers started to investigate how user interfaces could benefit from this technology. Sunnari et al. investigated the user experience of 3D menus on mobile phones with auto-stereoscopic screens compared to traditional 2D displays [20]. They found that users perceived 3D menus to be more visually pleasing, entertaining, innovative, and empowering but also to be more time-consuming and difficult to control. McIntire et al. investigated human performance on stereoscopic 3D displays [17]. They found such displays to be particularly beneficial for depth-related tasks, such as judging distances or finding and identifying objects. Furthermore, stereoscopic displays improve recall of scenes and objects as well as learning of spatial relationships. On the downside, 3D visualizations were found to cause eye-strain, headache, and fatigue if not carefully applied. To avoid this, Broy et al. showed how to determine a comfort zone for layered UIs and provide insights into how to structure the displayed information in different layers in a way that increases comprehensibility [5]. Huhtala et al. showed that layering information can be used to reduce search times for information [13]. In summary, these findings show a strong benefit of 3D for accessing information if applied carefully.

Whereas 3D information is nowadays often displayed statically, researchers also looked into novel techniques to interact with the content. Direct interaction with 3D content has been investigated within the Holodesk project [12]. The Holodesk is based on a 3D projection from the top and uses depth sensors (i.e., Microsoft Kinect) to track the users' hands. Interaction with volumetric 3D displays using touch gestures has been introduced in [8]. In both cases, interaction is strongly tailored to the device. The reason is that techniques known from 2D user interfaces are in general difficult to apply to 3D. As eye trackers become commercially available, we believe that gaze as a complementary input technique could be one possible solution to this challenge. With gaze users could select a particular depth layer and then interact with it by using techniques commonly applied in 2D user interfaces.

Gaze interaction has been subject to research in several domains. Kern et al. showed how to use gaze for implicit and explicit interaction in the car [15]. Recently, eye tracking in front of public displays has received considerable attention. So far, research mainly focussed on implicitly calibrating eye trackers for passersby that approach a display [21]. Castellina et al. applied eye tracking to virtual 3D games and suggested different multimodal gaze interaction techniques. However, all those applications apply eye tracking on 2D displays only.

Research on gaze interaction with stereoscopic displays, and hence with real 3D content, is rather scarce. Prior work has looked at enabling techniques to assess gaze on stereoscopic displays. This work shows that tracking the gaze point in 3D space is in general possible by using the physiology of the eye, particularly the distance between the pupils [2, 7] and the pupil diameter [19]. Application of gaze tracking on stereoscopic displays includes the work of Ramasamy et al. who looked into how stereoscopic movies could be analyzed using gaze information [18]. Interaction using gaze for 3D displays has been explored by Ki and Kwon in [16] who control a dart game on an auto-stereoscopic display with the user's gaze.

In summary, the review of related literature shows a potential for the use of 3D technology for layered user interfaces. At the same time, eye tracking as an emerging technology is promising as a (complementary) interaction modality for such interfaces. Eye tracking in 3D has so far only been applied to a few application areas – both for analysis and interaction. Particularly for interaction, data on user performance is scarce and has as of today only been assessed qualitatively [16]. We are neither aware of any work that compared user performance and subjective perception of 2D gaze interaction to 3D gaze interaction, nor of work that compared the performance of different gaze point calculation methods. In the remainder of this paper we present our design of a prototype for gaze-based interaction on a stereoscopic display and a quantitative evaluation comparing 2D to 3D gaze interaction as well as different gaze point calculation methods.

SUPPORTING LAYERED 3D INTERFACES

Prior work has shown a combination of salient features (e.g., color and depth) to significantly decrease search times [1, 13]. A UI can hence employ depth layers to group or highlight urgent or frequently used objects. To then interact with objects on one layer we envision a multi-modal approach in which gaze is used to select a specific layer and then apply commonly used input methods (e.g., touch or keyboard and mouse) to perform actions within the selected layer (cf., Figure 1). Note, that by applying this approach, interaction is in general also possible using gaze only, e.g., by looking at an object for a certain amount of time and, thus, executing an action. In the following, we present four use cases in which our concept can be applied to ease interaction with 3D UIs.

In-car Displays

In-car interfaces have specific requirements in terms of how the user operates them [6]. While the primary goal is to keep the driver's attention on the road, the dashboard provides different types of information, necessary to operate the vehicle.

These include warnings (fuel status, doors open, handbrake not released), navigation cues, status information (temperature, time), traffic information or the currently tuned in radio station. Introducing 3D displays can decrease the cognitive load by presenting information on different layers in an easy and quick-to-perceive way. Gaze could simplify interaction through fast and intuitive interaction techniques (e.g., selection of a layer and object via gaze and execution via a button on the steering wheel).

Displays in Work Environments

Specialized work environments already employ stereoscopic displays. For example, in medical environments, 3-dimensional information in the form of layered MRT images (magnetic resonance tomography) is frequently used. During surgeries, medical staff often needs to navigate through the data but cannot do so using touch for hygienic reasons [14]. In these cases, gaze could be used to easily navigate through and access information on particular layers.

Public Displays

Popular interaction techniques for public displays include touch, gestures, and smartphones. However, many users have reservations against using touch in public due to a lack of sanitation after each user. Gestures are often cumbersome to be used for selection due to low accuracy. And smartphones are slow as they need to be taken out of the pocket and many users are not willing to install software. As a result, gaze as input modality for public displays has recently received considerable attention [21]. At the same time, the advertising industry started to deploy auto-stereoscopic displays at airports and in train stations[1]. We envision this technology to be soon deployed also for information displays, where users could access transport schedules, store directories, or city maps. Information could be presented on different layers and as displays employ sensors, users could control them via gaze.

Mobile Interfaces

Mobile devices have small displays and, thus, information placement is challenging. By integrating 3D displays the third dimension can be used to group the information on different layers (e.g., contact lists [9] on one layer and call logs on another layer). Still, small displays and touch interaction make selection cumbersome. We believe gaze to simplify interaction as it enables quick and accurate selection while at the same time allowing standard controls to be used.

APPARATUS

To enable 3D gaze interaction on stereoscopic displays and compare it to 2D, we implemented a prototype that allows gaze information to be obtained from an eye tracker, calculate the gaze position in 3D space using different methods (pupil diameter and pupil distance), and make it available to client applications. The following section introduces the architecture, describes the used gaze point calculation methods, and presents a sample application.

Architecture

Our prototype consists of an eye tracker, a gaze server that collects and processes gaze data, and a client application. The SMI RED eye tracker samples gaze data at 60Hz. An API allows the server to obtain different types of data and process it for the use in a client application. Types of data include the gaze position on the screen (x/y coordinate) for each eye, the gaze direction, and the diameter of each pupil. The communication between the components is based on UDP. The gaze server takes the gaze data, calculates additional values, such as the ocular vergence and sends them to the client. 3D client applications are created in Unity[2] using C#. The gaze point calculation is done within the client application. We use Unity 3D rays to determine the intersection of the user's gaze with an object, allowing layers or elements to be selected.

Calculating Gaze Points in 3D Space

For 2D, eye trackers calculate the x and y coordinate of the user's gaze point on the screen. In contrast, the depth (expressed as z-value) is needed to obtain a gaze point in 3D space. Different approaches have been reported to calculate this gaze point. In simple cases, where only one object is in the line of sight, an application could simply calculate the intersection of the gaze direction with the object. However, when multiple (semi-transparent) objects appear in the line of sight, more fine-grained methods are required. In this work, we implemented two such approaches.

Pupil Diameter The pupil diameter technique exploits the fact that, based on the distance of an object that is in focus, the diameter of the pupil changes, given that lighting conditions remain constant [19]. The pupil diameter ranges from 2 to 6 mm under normal photopic conditions ($> 3cd/m^2$), where the largest depth of field is obtained at 2 mm. Hence, by measuring the pupil diameter a system can calculate the depth position (or depth layer) on which the user focuses.

Pupil Distance An alternative method considers ocular vergence, that is the distance between the left and right eye pupil caused by the simultaneous inward rotation for the eyes towards each other [2, 7]. As the user focuses on an object closer to the eye, the distance decreases compared to situation where the user focuses on an object that is located further away. Prior work found this method to work best for objects near screen level [7].

The strength of the pupil diameter method is that it is applicable both to monocular as well as to binocular eye trackers, whereas the pupil distance requires a binocular device.

3D Calibration

As the cornea of each user differs, eye trackers need to be calibrated. Standard procedures depict a number of points on the screen the user needs to focus on, e.g., a regular 3x3 grid. We extend this procedure to the z-dimension by depicting calibration points also on two different depth layers. This results in 3x3x2 equally distributed calibration points. In addition we store the pupil diameter and the pupil distance for each calibration point.

---

[1]Real Eyes Website: `http://real-eyes.eu/`

[2]Unity Website: `http://unity3d.com`

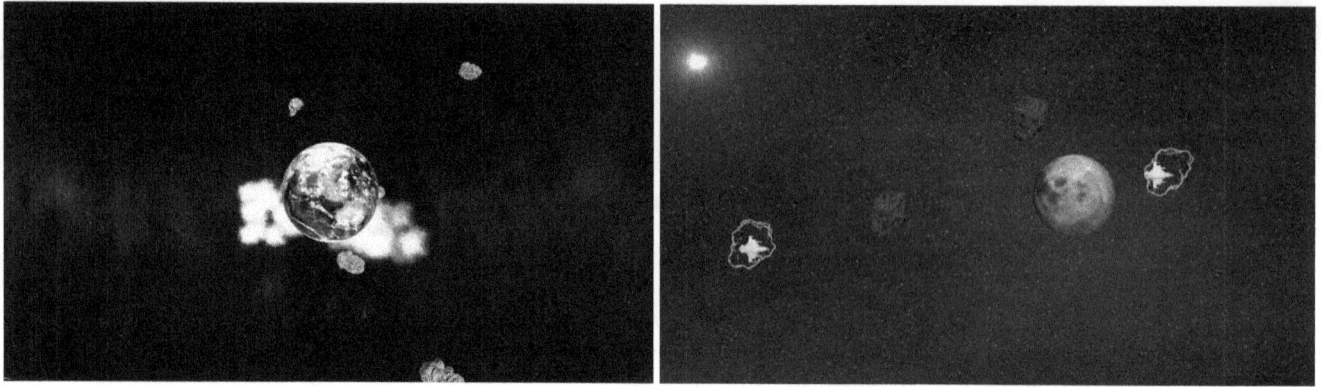

Figure 2. In the first level (left), meteoroids are flying towards earth from different angles. In the second level (right), enemy space ships are flying from left to right hiding behind meteoroids on a different depth layer.

Sample Application: Earth Defender

For our anticipated user study we implemented a simple game where users can interact with objects on different depth layers using gaze. We deliberately decided to design a playful application instead of a simple pointing task as we believe users to behave more natural when playing the game. In this way, we aim to increase the ecologic validity of our evaluation while maintaining a controlled setting.

Earth Defender is a space shooter where players need to destroy meteoroids and enemy space ships trying to attack earth. We implemented two different levels. In the first level – the *meteoroid level* – a number of meteoroids (cf. Figure 2, left) that simultaneously try to hit earth need to be destroyed via gaze (i.e., by looking at the meteoroids). The number of meteoroids, and hence the difficulty, increase throughout the levels. In the first step, only a single meteoroid approaches earth, in the second step two meteoroids, and so on. The game is over when ten meteoroids managed to hit earth. In the second level – the *enemy space ship level* – evil space ships hide behind meteoroids and need to be destroyed by the player using gaze before leaving the viewport (cf. Figure 2, right). Enemy space ships and meteoroids are placed on different depth layers. As enemy space ships hide behind meteoroids, the latter become semi-transparent so that the meteoroids and the space ship can be seen by the player. In cases where the player destroys the meteoroid instead of the hiding space ship, the space ship accelerates quickly, making it difficult to aim at it. Similar to the first level, the number of enemy space ships increases as players successfully destroy them. The game ends as ten space ships escaped the viewport.

Note that the first level can be played both in 2D and 3D, because there are no overlapping elements on the screen. Hence, we simply calculate an intersection of the user's gaze with the meteoroid to detect a hit. The second level can only be played in 3D, because elements are positioned behind each other. Either the pupil diameter method or the pupil distance method can be used to calculate the gaze point and detect a hit.

EVALUATION

The aim of our user study was twofold. First, we wanted to compare performance and user perception of gaze interaction with 2D user interfaces to interaction with 3D user inter-

faces. Second, we wanted to compare user performance for the two gaze point calculation methods for cases where elements are obscuring each other. We hence used the Earth Defender game which requires users to accurately aim at a target (the enemy space ships and the meteoroids) and to be as quick as possible. As metrics we used the number of destroyed meteoroids or space ships (i.e., the number of correctly selected targets) and the time between the target entered the scene and when it was destroyed. For the comparison between interaction in 2D and 3D, we additionally assessed usability, task load, and user experience.

Apparatus and Procedure

For the evaluation, we setup the Earth Defender game on a 55" 3D LCD TV that uses polarization glasses. The stationary SMI RED was placed in front of the user.

In the days prior to the study we recruited participants via mailing lists. As they arrived at the lab, we led them to the room where we had setup the prototype. We briefed them about the study and had them sign a consent form. After that, they filled in a demographic questionnaire on age, gender, and profession. Next, the eye-tracker was calibrated with our 3D calibration procedure. To test the calibration accuracy, nine meteoroids were shown that needed to be destroyed. If the participant was able to destroy all meteoroids, they started playing the game; else the calibration was repeated.

For the first level, participants played in 2D and 3D mode wearing the polarization glasses for both conditions. The conditions were counterbalanced, thus, half of the participants started in 2D mode before proceeding with 3D and vice versa. In each condition, participants played for 3 minutes, before filling in a questionnaire on user experience (Product Reaction Cards; PRC [4]), usability (System Usability Scale; SUS [3]) and task load (Nasa Task Load Index; NasaTLX [11]).

After that, participants proceeded with level two where they played in 3D using the pupil distance and the pupil diameter method (3 minutes each), again in counter-balanced order. We neither told participants about the two different methods nor provided technical details. After completing both conditions asked participants, which version they preferred. In addition we logged user performance in each condition.

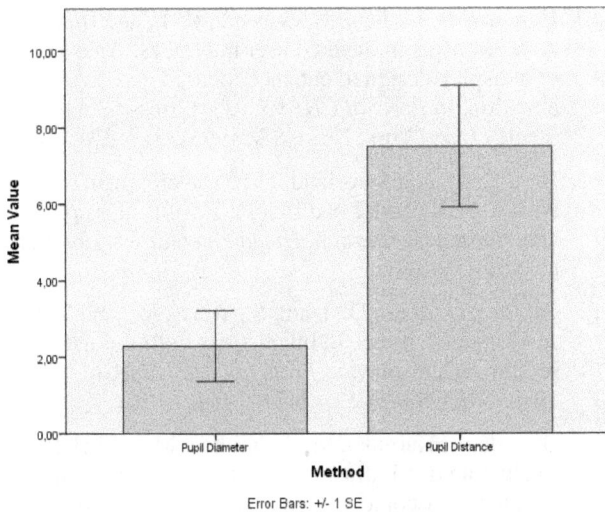

Figure 3. Comparing the number of successfully destroyed meteoroids of the pupil diameter and distance of pupils method.

Results

In total, 15 users (14 male, 1 female) aged from 22 to 28 years ($M = 24.71$, $SD = 1.73$) participated in the study. We had to exclude the data from one male participant due to tracking problems. Each participant had normal or corrected to normal eyesight and was able to perceive stereoscopic 3D.

Comparing 2D vs. 3D

In the first part of the study, we compared interaction in 2D versus 3D. Neither the results from the SUS questionnaire used to assess usability (SUS_{2D}: 74.53; SUS_{3D}: 74.33) nor from the Nasa TLX questionnaire used to assess the cognitive load on the user ($NasaTLX_{2D}$: 54.4; $NasaTLX_{3D}$: 53.3) showed any statistically significant differences. The results of the PRCs show an effect on the user experience. While the game speed was the same in both conditions, the interaction in 2D was perceived much faster compared to interaction in 3D. Furthermore, participants considered 3D interaction to be more visually pleasing and entertaining.

Finally, we compared the accuracy (number of successfully destroyed meteoroids) for all users. We found that participants performed slightly better in the 2D condition ($M = 58.57$, $SD = 17.54$) than in the 3D condition ($M = 53.79$, $SD = 14.83$). However, based on the results of a t test, statistical significance can not be reasoned, $t(13) = 1.01$, $p = .33$.

Pupil Diameter vs. Pupil Distance

When comparing the two gaze point calculation methods (cf., Figure 3), we found that participants performed better in the pupil distance condition ($M = 7.50$, $SD = 5.95$) than in the pupil diameter condition ($M = 2.29$, $SD = 3.45$). Due to a non-normal distribution of the results, we performed a non-parametric Wilcoxon tests showing statistically significant differences between the conditions, $Z = -2.138$, $p = .03$.

Looking closer at the results, the participants' accuracy increases over time using the pupil diameter method. This indicates that some kind of learning is necessary to interact with

this technique. Hence, the pupil diameter technique may be better suited for daily use, such as interaction with the mobile phone, than for interactions that happen less frequently, such as interaction with public displays. In addition, we found that the performance of the participants with the pupil distance method varies depending on the position of the space ship.

DISCUSSION

Our results suggest that in general gaze interaction in 2D is perceived equally usable and demanding as interaction in 3D. This is also backed by the fact that we did not find any significant difference in accuracy. We hence assume that tasks users currently perform in 2D could quite easily be performed also in 3D environments. Future work could look at the effects of multi-modality, for example, how performance is affected in cases where users interact with an interface based on gaze and an additional input modality. Findings from the user experience evaluation suggests that cases where task completion time is crucial could benefit from gaze-based 3D interaction as it is perceived slower by users. With regard to the gaze point calculation method, our results show that simple intersection of the gaze vector with an object works equally well in 2D and 3D. In cases of overlapping objects that require additional depth information, pupil distance outperforms the pupil diameter. Nevertheless, the accuracy when interacting using the pupil diameter method might increase in the long term, making this approach particularly suitable for cases where only monocular tracking is possible.

LIMITATIONS

We acknowledge the following limitations of our user study. First, for simplicity we only evaluated two different depth layers, leaving a thorough analysis of the impact of depth and number of layers for future work. Hence, we can not generalize our findings to an arbitrary number of layers and to cases in which objects are shown at extreme parallaxes. Nevertheless we covered a use case suitable for a multitude of applications with a limited number of depth layers at a comfortable viewing position of the user.

Second, we observed an impact of environmental influences. The pupil distance seems to be more robust to slight variances in the lightning conditions or head movement, whereas the pupil diameter seems to suffer from these changes. To obtain comparable results we ran the study under controlled lab conditions (minimal changes in position of the user and lighting). Hence, we cannot claim that the results of our evaluation generalize, for example, to outdoor settings. However, there is a strong indication, that for frequently changing environments, the pupil distance method is more robust and hence the better choice.

CONCLUSION

In this paper, we presented the first study that quantitatively compared gaze interaction with 2D interfaces and with 3D interfaces. Our findings reveal only marginal differences with regard to accuracy, usability, and mental load. With regard to user experience we observed interaction in 3D to be perceived slower, but more visually pleasing and entertaining. In addition, we compared two gaze point calculation methods to be applied in cases where multiple objects are displayed in the viewer's line of sight. We show that using the pupil distance to calculate the gaze point in 3D space is a robust method.

In this work, we decided to keep interaction simple and playful to obtain ecologically valid results. For future work, we plan to investigate more complex scenarios. For example, we are interested in how interaction on different depth layers and with a different number of objects affects performance.

ACKNOWLEDGEMENTS

The research leading to these results has received funding from the European Union Seventh Framework Programme ([FP7/2007-2013]) under grant agreement no. 600851.

REFERENCES

1. Alper, B., Höllerer, T., Kuchera-Morin, J., and Forbes, A. Stereoscopic highlighting: 2d graph visualization on stereo displays. *IEEE Trans. Vis. Comput. Graph. 17*, 12 (2011), 2325–2333.

2. Ashmore, M., Duchowski, A. T., and Shoemaker, G. Efficient eye pointing with a fisheye lens. In *Proc. of GI'05*, Canadian Human-Computer Communications Society (2005), 203–210.

3. Bangor, A., Kortum, P. T., and Miller, J. T. An Empirical Evaluation of the System Usability Scale. *International Journal on Human Computer Interaction 24*, 6 (2008), 574–594.

4. Benedek, J., and Miner, T. Measuring desirability: New methods for evaluating desirability in a usability lab setting. *Proc. of Usability Professionals Association 2003* (2002), 8–12.

5. Broy, N., Alt, F., Schneegass, S., Henze, N., and Schmidt, A. Perceiving layered information on 3d displays using binocular disparity. In *Proc. of PerDis '13*, ACM (New York, NY, USA, 2013), 61–66.

6. Broy, N., André, E., and Schmidt, A. Is stereoscopic 3d a better choice for information representation in the car? In *Proc. of AutoUI'12*, ACM (New York, NY, USA, 2012), 93–100.

7. Duchowski, A. T., Pelfrey, B., House, D. H., and Wang, R. Measuring gaze depth with an eye tracker during stereoscopic display. In *Proc. of SIGGRAPH'11*, ACM (New York, NY, USA, 2011), 15–22.

8. Grossman, T., Wigdor, D., and Balakrishnan, R. Multi-finger gestural interaction with 3d volumetric displays. In *Proc. of UIST'04*, ACM (New York, NY, USA, 2004), 61–70.

9. Häkkilä, J., Posti, M., Koskenranta, O., and Ventä-Olkkonen, L. Design and evaluation of mobile phonebook application with stereoscopic 3d user interface. In *CHI'13 Extended Abstracts on Human Factors in Computing Systems*, ACM (2013), 1389–1394.

10. Harrison, B. L., Ishii, H., Vicente, K. J., and Buxton, W. A. S. Transparent layered user interfaces: An evaluation of a display design to enhance focused and divided attention. In *Proc. of CHI'95*, ACM Press / Addison-Wesley (New York, NY, USA, 1995), 317–324.

11. Hart, S. G., and Staveland, L. E. Development of NASA-TLX (Task Load Index): Results of empirical and theoretical research. *Human mental workload 1*, 3 (1988), 139–183.

12. Hilliges, O., Kim, D., Izadi, S., Weiss, M., and Wilson, A. Holodesk: direct 3d interactions with a situated see-through display. In *Proc. of CHI'12*, ACM (New York, NY, USA, 2012), 2421–2430.

13. Huhtala, J., Karukka, M., Salmimaa, M., and Häkkilä, J. Evaluating depth illusion as method of adding emphasis in autostereoscopic mobile displays. In *Proc. of MobileHCI'11* (New York, NY, USA, 2011), 357–360.

14. Johnson, R., O'Hara, K., Sellen, A., Cousins, C., and Criminisi, A. Exploring the potential for touchless interaction in image-guided interventional radiology. In *Proc. of CHI'11*, ACM (New York, NY, USA, 2011).

15. Kern, D., Mahr, A., Castronovo, S., Schmidt, A., and Müller, C. Making use of drivers' glances onto the screen for explicit gaze-based interaction. In *Proc. of AutoUI'10*, ACM (New York, NY, USA, 2010).

16. Ki, J., and Kwon, Y.-M. 3d gaze estimation and interaction. In *3DTV Conference: The True Vision - Capture, Transmission and Display of 3D Video, 2008* (2008), 373–376.

17. McIntire, J. P., Havig, P. R., and Geiselman, E. E. What is 3d good for? a review of human performance on stereoscopic 3d displays. In *Proceedings of Head- and Helmet-Mounted Displays XVII; and Display Technologies and Applications for Defense, Security, and Avionics VI*, vol. 8383, SPIE (2012).

18. Ramasamy, C., House, D. H., Duchowski, A. T., and Daugherty, B. Using eye tracking to analyze stereoscopic filmmaking. In *Adj. Proc. of SIGGRAPH'09*, ACM (New York, NY, USA, 2009).

19. Reichelt, S., Häussler, R., Fütterer, G., and Leister, N. Depth cues in human visual perception and their realization in 3d displays. In *SPIE Defense, Security, and Sensing*, International Society for Optics and Photonics (2010), 76900B–76900B.

20. Sunnari, M., Arhippainen, L., Pakanen, M., and Hickey, S. Studying user experiences of autostereoscopic 3d menu on touch screen mobile device. In *Proc. of OzCHI'12*, ACM (New York, NY, USA, 2012).

21. Vidal, M., Bulling, A., and Gellersen, H. Pursuits: spontaneous interaction with displays based on smooth pursuit eye movement and moving targets. In *Proc. of UbiComp'13*, ACM (New York, NY, USA, 2013).

On User Behaviour Adaptation Under Interface Change

Benjamin Rosman[*]
Subramanian Ramamoorthy
M. M. Hassan Mahmud
School of Informatics
University of Edinburgh
Edinburgh, UK

Pushmeet Kohli
Machine Learning and Perception
Microsoft Research
Cambridge, UK

ABSTRACT

Different interfaces allow a user to achieve the same end goal through different action sequences, e.g., command lines vs. drop down menus. Interface efficiency can be described in terms of a cost incurred, e.g., time taken, by the user in typical tasks. Realistic users arrive at evaluations of efficiency, hence making choices about which interface to use, over time, based on trial and error experience. Their choices are also determined by prior experience, which determines how much learning time is required. These factors have substantial effect on the adoption of new interfaces. In this paper, we aim at understanding how users adapt under interface change, how much time it takes them to learn to interact optimally with an interface, and how this learning could be expedited through intermediate interfaces. We present results from a series of experiments that make four main points: (a) different interfaces for accomplishing the same task can elicit significant variability in performance, (b) switching interfaces can result in adverse sharp shifts in performance, (c) subject to some variability, there are individual thresholds on tolerance to this kind of performance degradation with an interface, causing users to potentially abandon what may be a pretty good interface, and (d) our main result – shaping user learning through the presentation of intermediate interfaces can mitigate the adverse shifts in performance while still enabling the eventual improved performance with the complex interface upon the user becoming suitably accustomed. In our experiments, human users use keyboard based interfaces to navigate a simulated ball through a maze. Our results are a first step towards interface adaptation algorithms that architect choice to accommodate personality traits of realistic users.

Author Keywords

Input and interaction technologies; usability research; usability testing and evaluation; user interface design.

---

[*]Benjamin Rosman is also affiliated with the Mobile Intelligent Autonomous Systems group at the CSIR, South Africa.

ACM Classification Keywords

H.5.m. Information Interfaces and Presentation (e.g. HCI): Miscellaneous

INTRODUCTION

Interfaces are an important component of computing applications that require interaction between man and machine, ranging from text entry based search, to configuration dialogs to emerging natural user interfaces that provide fully immersive experiences in video games, etc. In typical sequential decision making tasks, users execute sequences of atomic actions that may be configured in various ways. A set of such atomic actions defines an interface.

Given an action set/interface, and many tasks that must be performed with it, users eventually learn policies that map task specifications to sequences of actions. After significant experience, the user typically reaches a level of performance that characterises the efficiency of that interface. At this point, if a new interface were to be introduced, how should the user respond? A fully rational user might be expected to evaluate the expected efficiency of this new interface and adopt it if it could yield a better long term efficiency. In many practical settings, users seem inefficient in making this choice. A key factor here is that of learnability – evaluating the efficiency of an interface takes time, and a boundedly rational user (e.g., one with limited patience) could well arrive at a different evaluation in typical usage [13] [1]. The main aim of this paper is to study this phenomenon through empirical experiments.

The problem of devising a good alphabet of actions has been successfully addressed as one of combinatorial optimisation, e.g., in [5]. Other related work addresses design space exploration [4], determining optimal parameters within static user models [8], adaptively determining the best interface based on context variables such as mobile/desktop [6], [1] and other forms of personalization [10]. In contrast to these works that focus on estimating context from which it is clear what interface to present, our focus is on the temporal nature of the process – on how people learn to use interfaces – based on which we wish to determine how the user herself might choose an interface, which again is based on her own prior experience and private evaluation.

---

[1]See e.g., http://blogs.msdn.com/b/b8/archive/2012/05/18/creating-the-windows-8-user-experience.aspx, http://www.pcworld.com/article/2012024/the-windows-8-ui-how-do-interface-and-usability-experts-rate-all-the-changes.html, http://www.addictivetips.com/windows-tips/is-adapting-to-windows-8-and-its-metro-ui-as-hard-as-it-seems/

Our experiments are designed to test hypotheses regarding learnability of interfaces. We posit that users with limited patience and diverse prior experience will not only have different levels of initial success with different interfaces but also, given the temporal nature of their habituation [7] with interfaces and limited patience, they may incorrectly evaluate efficiency and prematurely abandon good interfaces. Finally, we hypothesize that this adoption behaviour may be improved by presenting intermediate interfaces that mitigate the initial shock and encourage learning towards the better performance level.

Our hypotheses are directly relevant to practical concerns, such as the need to minimise change aversion [12], [9], consumer choices regarding new products [11], etc. Also, we add to a literature on modelling user adaptation [14], [2], [15], [3] by empirically characterising dynamic choice behaviour.

Our Contributions

Our experiments show that users adapt to interfaces, such that their performance with a particular interface improves with time. We then show that an interface change can dramatically degrade user performance even though the new interface might be better theoretically. This performance slowly improves as the user adapts to the new interface while interacting with it repeatedly. Finally, we show that a well-designed intermediate interface can dramatically reduce the degradation in performance and can also lead to the user learning more quickly to interact with the final interface.

DOMAIN AND PROTOCOL

The aim of our experiments is twofold. Our first goal is to study how user performance and preference over interfaces varies with complexity of the interfaces. Our second goal is to test if the user's experience can be shaped to use complex but more powerful interfaces while minimising the performance hit during training by using an interface of intermediate complexity.

To that end, we implemented a system which required a user to repeatedly perform a task, using different interfaces. Each task executed by the users of our system involves navigating a ball through a simple maze of 1000×1000 pixels to a goal location in the shortest possible time, as shown in Figure 1. Obstacles block the motion of the ball, and each task ends when the goal is reached. Each user performs a number of such tasks in a set of mazes, where the mazes are standardised across users, and the time taken for each task is recorded. We used 20 such mazes, where the mazes were generated randomly initially and then fixed for all experiments.

For the above tasks, we designed three different interfaces for controlling the ball. The control scheme for the mazes is described in Table 1. The interfaces were designed to represent different tradeoffs between power and ease of use. The first interface, *I1*, is the simplest to use and the least powerful. It consists of the arrow keys, where pressing the arrow key moves the ball in the expected direction by 20 pixels. The second interface, *I2*, is in the middle in terms of power and difficulty. It requires using two counter-intuitive keys and then the arrow key to move in the expected direction by 80

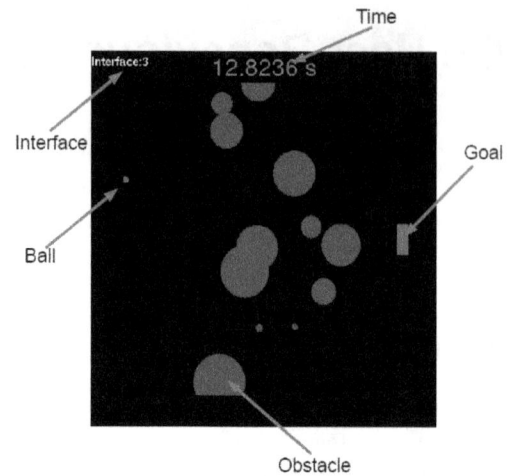

Figure 1. Depiction of the domain used in our experiments. The user navigates a ball to a goal as quickly as possible, while avoiding obstacles.

Interface 1		
Key	**Direction**	**Distance**
Left-arrow	Left	Short (20 pixels)
Right-arrow	Right	Short (20 pixels)
Up-arrow	Up	Short (20 pixels)
Down-arrow	Down	Short (20 pixels)
Interface 2		
Key	**Direction**	**Distance**
q h Left-arrow	Left	Medium (80 pixels)
w b Right-arrow	Right	Medium (80 pixels)
u g Up-arrow	Up	Medium (80 pixels)
y f Down-arrow	Down	Medium (80 pixels)
Interface 3		
Key	**Direction**	**Distance**
q h h w	Left	Long (120 pixels)
w b k f	Right	Long (120 pixels)
u g o c	Up	Long (120 pixels)
y f r e	Down	Long (120 pixels)

Table 1. The three interfaces. Interfaces 2 and 3 require sequences of key presses to execute the desired motion. Note that the first two keys for each direction match in interfaces 2 and 3.

pixels. The third interface, *I3* is the most difficult to use and also the most powerful. To move in a direction, the user needs to press four counter-intuitive keys in sequence and then her ball is moved by 120 pixels. We use the convention that if the desired motion results in hitting an obstacle, that motion is prevented.

Given the above, the effective distance moved per key press is 20, 26.67 and 30 pixels for *I1*, *I2* and *I3* respectively. Consequently, *I3* is the interface which can achieve the lowest possible times in these navigation tasks. On the other hand, this is also the interface which requires the most learning to be able to issue the commands quickly, as using this interface requires the additional cognitive load of remembering the key presses, or looking them up as needed. Alternatively, *I1* is simple and intuitive to any computer user. Finally, *I2* lies in between *I1* and *I3* in terms of simplicity and intuitiveness.

Now, our goal is to study if we can shape a user to smoothly use a powerful and complex interface, given that she is used to a simpler interface. So, we designate *I1* to be the *start interface*, *I3* to be the *target interface* and *I2* to be the *intermediate interface*. The conjectures outlined in the introduction now may be translated as follows. With practice, users will be most effective when using interface *I3*, but at the same time will initially pay a price in terms of decreased performance and increased difficulty when moving from the start interface *I1*. At the same time by using the interfaces *I1*, *I2* and *I3* in sequence, the performance loss and difficulty may be reduced. In the next section we describe experiments to test these conjectures.

EXPERIMENTS AND RESULTS

We performed five sets of experiments with a number of users. Each user was allocated to only one of the sets to ensure that the results were not corrupted by a long-term memory effect. In each experiment the user was required to use different interfaces to solve the navigation tasks according to a given schedule. The schedules are as follows:

1. **Baseline 1:** *I3* for 20 tasks, and then *I1* for 20 tasks.

2. **Baseline 2:** *I1* for 20 tasks, and then *I3* for 20 tasks.

3. **Performance Variability:** *I1* for 20 tasks, and then *I3* for 20 tasks, and again *I3* for 20 tasks.

4. **Intermediate Interface:** *I1* for 20 tasks, and then *I2* for 20 tasks, and then *I3* for 20 tasks.

5. **User Perception:** Repeat 20 times: a training task with *I1*, a training task with *I3*, and then the user's choice of *I1* or *I3* such that time taken is minimised.

We discuss each of these experiments in detail in the next four sections. Briefly, the purpose of each of these experiments is as follows. The two Baseline experiments establish the baseline user performance with the start and target interfaces when used in either order. The Performance Variability experiments establish what happens when we switch from the start to the target interface after some time and keep using it. The Intermediate Interface experiments show user performance when the intermediate interface *I2* is used to bridge the start and target interface. Finally, the User Perception experiment gives insight into which interfaces users prefer over time given prolonged experience with the interfaces. In the following, we assume the *frustration level* of a user is proportional to the time taken for a trial, and further that after some such time she would give up on an interface. We do not directly observe this in our experiments, but conjecture that it exists and state some of our conclusions based on this.

BASELINE PERFORMANCE

First we establish how using different interfaces for the same underlying action space affects performance. Here we provide a baseline performance for users with the simple interface *I1* and the powerful but complicated interface *I3*.

Eight users were tasked with 20 trials using each interface, four of which started with *I3* (Baseline 1) and the other four

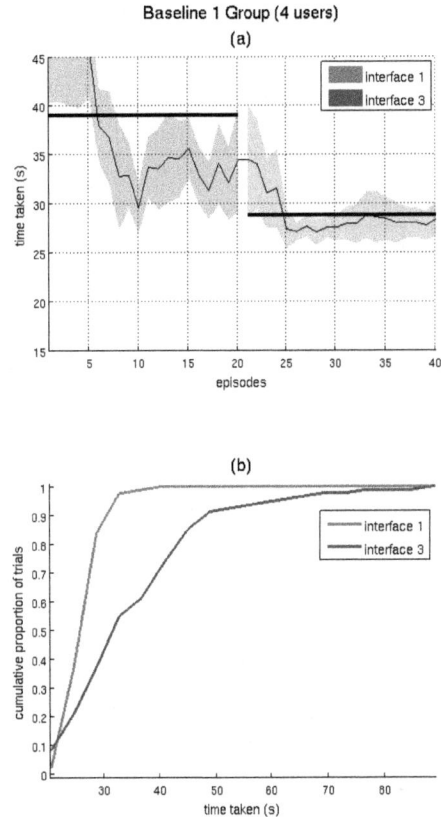

Figure 2. Results for Baseline Group 1. Figure (a) shows the averaged results when interface *I3* is used and then *I1*, for the same sequence of 20 mazes. The thin black line is the average time taken to goal in the last 5 mazes. The thick line gives the average over all the 20 mazes. This establishes the baseline for using the interfaces *I3* and *I1* in sequence. Figure (b) shows the cumulative distribution of the time taken to complete the tasks. This shows that without training *I1* is better than *I3*, because for any threshold $x > 21$s for the frustration level of the user, *I3* would breach the frustration for a greater number of tasks than *I1*.

with *I1* (Baseline 2), so as to remove any effect that the one may have on performance with the second. The results of Baseline 1 are shown in Figure 2, and Baseline 2 in Figure 3.

The results from these groups show that before the user has become familiar with the complex interface, both the mean performance and variance of *I3* are significantly higher than *I1*, although faster times are indeed possible with *I3*.

Note that there is some natural variance in the times taken for the various trials with the same interface. This is because the mazes were randomly generated, and so some were particularly easy or difficult for each interface. We did however standardise these, and each user across the entire study was presented with the same sequence of random mazes, for each interface they used.

PERFORMANCE VARIABILITY

Results in the previous section showed the performance of users in the first 20 trials. As was previously established, *I3*

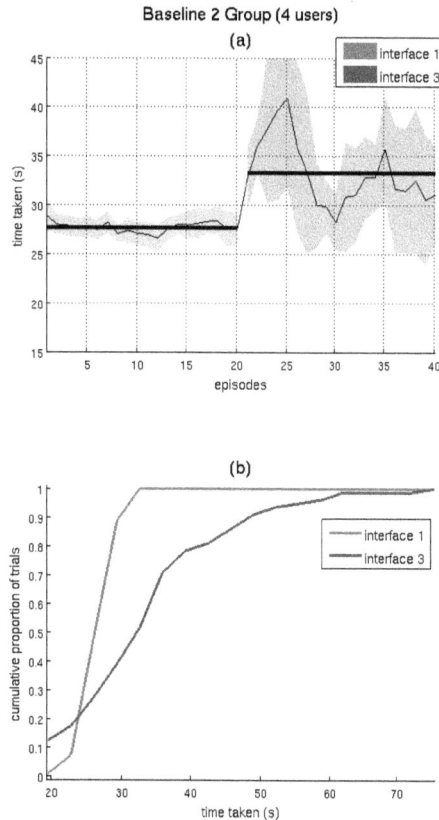

Figure 3. Results for Baseline Group 2. Figure (a) shows the averaged results when interface *I1* is used and then *I3*, for the same sequence of 20 mazes. The thin black line is the average time taken to goal in the last 5 mazes. The thick line gives the average over all the 20 mazes. This establishes the baseline for using the interfaces *I1* and *I3* in sequence. Additionally, note that the performance with *I3* is lower in this task than in Figure 2 (a). We believe that this is because the user has a chance to become familiar with the environment. On the other hand, the performance of *I1* is the same – which shows that familiarity with the domain is not especially beneficial for *I1* and so it is indeed very simple. Figure (b) shows the cumulative distribution of the time taken to complete the tasks. This shows that, again, without training *I1* is better than *I3*, because for any threshold $x > 25$s for the frustration level of the user, *I3* would breach the frustration for a greater number of tasks than *I1*.

Figure 4. Results for Performance Variability Group. In Figure (a) the thick and thin lines are the same as before. However, now each *I1* is played for the fixed 20 mazes and then *I3* for the fixed 20 mazes, twice in a row – once as a training batch, and then as the testing batch. This figure shows the effect of using *I3* for an extended period of time after using *I1*, and shows that while the user eventually learns to perform much more effectively with *I3* than with *I1*, the spike during the middle 20 mazes shows that there is a performance penalty for this. Figure (b) shows that the frustration level of the user is breached earlier for the training batch of *I3* than for the testing batch of *I3*, which ultimately outperforms *I1*.

is more difficult for the user, requiring learning of the interface. We thus provided users with a second batch of 20 trials, such that the first would constitute training with this interface. These results are shown in Figure 4.

As can be seen, after this training phase the users are able to achieve a faster mean time with *I3* than with *I1*. These is however a significant initial spike in performance times during the training phase, before the users consistently outperform their times on the simpler interface. The effect of the training is that both the mean and the variance of the trial times decrease.

INTERMEDIATE INTERFACES

As shown in the previous section, a user with a simple interface can be given a more complicated interface and ultimately achieve better performance. There is however a spike in time

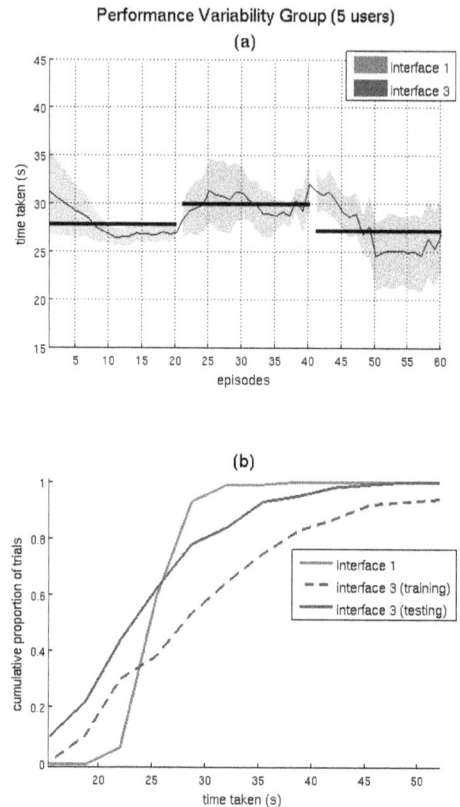

taken to complete tasks while the user adapts to the new interface. In Figure 5, we demonstrate that with the correct intermediate interface, a user can be gradually shifted to the more complicated interface, without inducing a spike in time taken.

The adoption of Interface 2 allows the user an easier transition to the full Interface 3, with only a small temporary loss in performance. Interface 2 has a slightly lower mean than Interface 1, with a minimal performance spike. Because Interfaces 2 and 3 are similar, there is also a minimal performance spike when the users make the transition to the final interface.

The key concept here is that although Interface 2 does have the ability to achieve better times than Interface 1, its strength lies mainly in bridging the cognitive divide between the simple and complicated interfaces, and that it accelerates the learning process for the user.

Intermediate Interface Group (5 users)

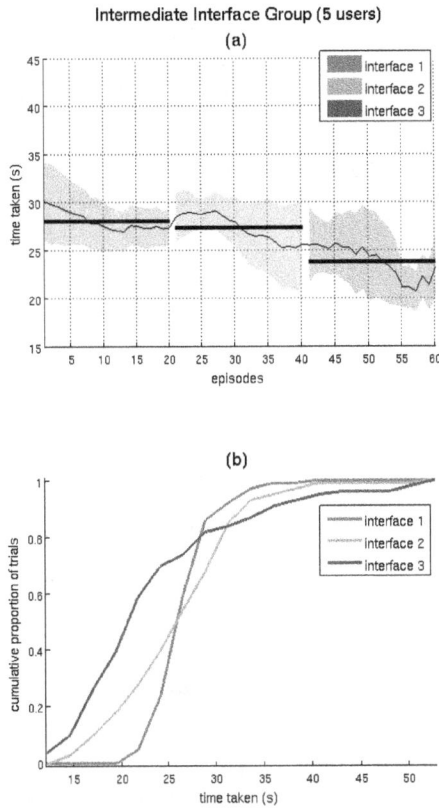

User Perception Group (13 users)

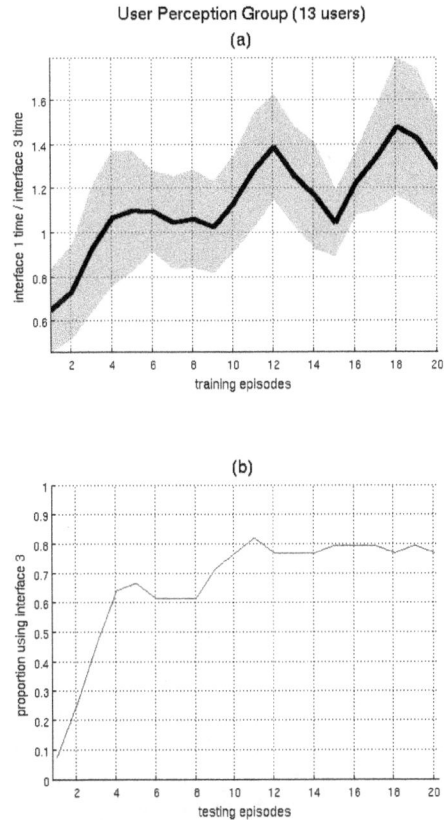

Figure 5. Results for Intermediate Interface Group. In Figure (a) the thick and thin lines are the same as before. Now the interfaces $I1$, $I2$ and $I3$ are used in sequence for 20 mazes each. $I2$ is used as a a bridge to ease transition from the simple interface $I1$ to the complex and powerful $I3$. Compared with Figure 4 (a), the user suffers a less severe performance penalty during the middle training phase, while ultimately achieving similar final performance with $I3$. Hence, using this intermediate bridge interface is highly beneficial. Figure (b) also shows a performance improvement over using $I3$ as an intermediary.

Figure 6. Results for User Perception Group. Figure (a) shows the ratio of times taken by the user during the testing episodes (recall that training and testing is interleaved, and during the training episode the user is trained with both $I1$ and $I3$, and then during testing episode, given the choice of using $I1$ or $I3$). Eventually, the user does improve with $I3$ but this only starts stabilising after episode 10. Figure (b) shows the user preference as a proportion of time they chose interface $I3$ during the testing phase. In agreement with Figure (a), this shows that within about 4 testing episodes, the proportion rises above 0.5 and then reaches the maximum 0.8 at about 10 episodes. Hence, this shows that users do eventually realise that using $I3$ is the better option, but not quickly.

USER PERCEPTION

In real applications, if a user suffers a loss in performance for more than a few episodes, the threshold being subject specific, when switching to a new and potentially better interface (as shown in Figure 4), that user is likely to abandon the new interface (or the application itself) entirely out of frustration.

We observe the effects of this in the User Perception Group. Figure 6 (a) shows the learning curve of human subjects with Interface 3 compared to Interface 1. Note that this ratio only climbs above 1.0 after 9 mazes, corresponding to the point at which users are on average more adept at Interface 3 than Interface 1, in terms of achievable times. The subsequent performance dip around episode 15 is due to mazes which were relatively more difficult for Interface 3.

Figure 6 (b) depicts the proportion of users which chose Interface 3 over Interface 1, in testing mazes. This corresponds to the percentage of users prepared to continue using the more complex interface. During the first 8 mazes, up to 40% of

users would rather use the simpler interface, which is indicative of a threshold at which they would abandon the interface. It is only after 10 episodes that about 80% of the users are satisfied with the more powerful interface.

DISCUSSION

Having presented empirical results from our experiments, we now return to our hypotheses outlined in the introduction – what implications can we draw from the data and what does it say about our conjectures?

- Experiments in Figure 4 show how the user's performance degrades when they switch from an elementary interface to a more complex interface, defined by an unfamiliar action set that must be memorised. However, we see that if they stick to this interface setting, they achieve a better performance level after the initial learning period. Although the initial performance degradation is expected from common

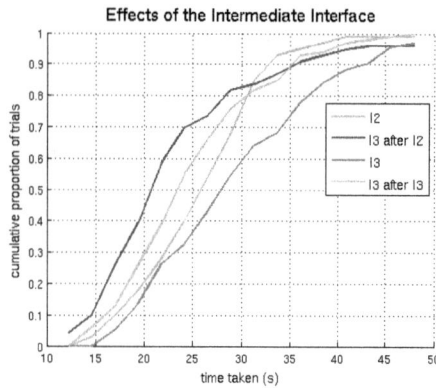

Figure 7. Comparing learning in sequences of interfaces. This figure shows how the user is more effective (more tasks solved within a specified time) in interface I3 after going through an intermediate interface, versus a control setting where they had longer experience with the same I3 interface (hence benefitted from learning), without any shaping with the intermediate interface.

sense, the fact that users may never realise the true potential of the better interface is counter to standard assumptions of expected-value based optimisation procedures that might inform interface optimisation.

- The experiments in Figure 6 show how the *perception* of the efficiency of each interface evolves over time. Although the quantitative threshold varies by user, it is clear that it takes many episodes before the user feels sufficiently comfortable with the initially unfamiliar interface to confidently choose it and realise the potential benefits. If users are impatient, in that they have a short horizon within which they need to see improved performance, they would mistakenly estimate the efficiency of the better interface and prematurely abandon it.

- Experiments in Figure 5 present a way out. If an intermediate interface were available that alleviates the initial loss in performance, the dual goals of lowering performance degradation and eventually achieving the better performance level could be achieved. This is clearly evident from the comparison in Figure 7.

CONCLUSION
The work presented in this paper represents an attempt to study temporal aspects of learning to use an interface. Many approaches to devising optimal interfaces and to adapting interfaces to context are implicitly based on a decision theoretic approach to maximising expected utility. As we show in empirical experiments, the optimal decision is made more complex by the way in which users learn and the extent to which history can play a role in their choice behaviour. This calls for a more refined user model that informs the optimisation process. Our experiments shed light on what attributes need to be captured in such a model. Moreover, we present empirical evidence to the effect that the problems raised by learning and boundedly rational user choices can be mitigated by introducing intermediate interfaces. One way in which this idea can be applied more generally is in interfaces that are continuously parametrisable, for example based on gestures

or wearable sensors. Our experiments, such as in Figures 5 and 6, are precursors to a learning algorithm that can make choices regarding sequences of interface settings in an automated fashion. Designing and implementing such algorithms is an area for future work.

ACKNOWLEDGEMENTS
The authors gratefully thank the reviewers for their insightful and constructive comments.

This work has taken place in the Robust Autonomy and Decisions group within the School of Informatics. Research of the RAD Group is supported by the European Commission (TOMSY Grant Agreement 270436, under FP7-ICT-2009.2.1 Call 6).

REFERENCES
1. Anderson, C. R., Domingos, P., and Weld, D. S. Adaptive web navigation for wireless devices. In *In Proceedings of the Seventeenth International Joint Conference on Artificial Intelligence* (2001).
2. Beaudry, A., and Pinsonneault, A. Understanding user responses to information technology: a coping model of user adaption. *MIS Quarterly 29(3)* (2005), 493–524.
3. Dessart, C.-E., Genaro Motti, V., and Vanderdonckt, J. Showing user interface adaptivity by animated transitions. In *Proceedings of the 3rd ACM SIGCHI symposium on Engineering interactive computing systems*, ACM (2011), 95–104.
4. Gajos, K. Z., Czerwinski, M., Tan, D. S., and Weld, D. S. Exploring the design space for adaptive graphical interfaces. In *Proceedings of the Working Conference on Advanced visual interfaces* (2006).
5. Gajos, K. Z., Wobbrock, J. O., and Weld, D. S. Improving the performance of motor-impaired users with automatically-generated, ability-based interfaces. In *CHI '08: Proceeding of the twenty-sixth annual SIGCHI conference on Human factors in computing systems*, ACM (New York, NY, USA, 2008), 1257–1266.
6. Hartmann, M., and Schreiber, D. Proactively adapting interfaces to individual users for mobile devices. In *Adaptive Hypermedia and Adaptive Web-Based Systems* (2008).
7. James, W. *Habit.* 1890.
8. Kohli, P., Nickisch, H., Rother, C., and Rhemann, C. User-centric learning and evaluation of interactive segmentation systems. *International Journal of Computer Vision 100(3)* (2012), 261–274.
9. Lavie, T., and Meyer, J. Benefits and costs of adaptive user interfaces. *International Journal of Human-Computer Studies 68*, 8 (2010), 508–524.
10. Mourlas, C., and Germanakos, P. *Intelligent User Interfaces: Adaptation and Personalization Systems and Technologies.* Information Science Reference, 2008.
11. Ram, S., and Sheth, J. N. Consumer resistance to innovations. *Journal of Consumer Marketing 6(2)* (1989).
12. Sedley, A., and Müller, H. Minimizing change aversion for the google drive launch. In *CHI'13 Extended Abstracts on Human Factors in Computing Systems* (2013).
13. Sinofsky, S. Creating the windows 8 user experience. http://blogs.msdn.com/b/b8/archive/2012/05/18/creating-the-windows-8-user-experience.aspx, 2012.
14. Smith, C. L., and Kantor, P. B. User adaptation: good results from poor systems. In *Proceedings of the 31st Annual International ACM SIGIR conference on Research and Development In Information Retrieval* (2008).
15. Zajonc, R. B. Attitudinal effects of mere exposure. *Journal of Personality and Social Psychology 9* (1968).

Natural Language Queries over Heterogeneous Linked Data Graphs: A Distributional-Compositional Semantics Approach

Andre Freitas
Insight Centre for Data Analytics
National University of Ireland, Galway
IDA Business Park, Lower Dangan, Galway,
Ireland
andre.freitas@deri.org

Edward Curry
Insight Centre for Data Analytics
National University of Ireland, Galway
IDA Business Park, Lower Dangan, Galway,
Ireland
ed.curry@deri.org

ABSTRACT

The demand to access large amounts of heterogeneous structured data is emerging as a trend for many users and applications. However, the effort involved in querying heterogeneous and distributed third-party databases can create major barriers for data consumers. At the core of this problem is the *semantic gap* between the way users express their information needs and the representation of the data. This work aims to provide a natural language interface and an associated semantic index to support an increased level of vocabulary independency for queries over Linked Data/Semantic Web datasets, using a *distributional-compositional semantics* approach. Distributional semantics focuses on the automatic construction of a semantic model based on the statistical distribution of co-occurring words in large-scale texts. The proposed query model targets the following features: (i) a principled semantic approximation approach with low adaptation effort (independent from manually created resources such as ontologies, thesauri or dictionaries), (ii) comprehensive semantic matching supported by the inclusion of large volumes of distributional (unstructured) commonsense knowledge into the semantic approximation process and (iii) expressive natural language queries. The approach is evaluated using natural language queries on an open domain dataset and achieved **avg. recall=0.81, mean avg. precision=0.62** and **mean reciprocal rank=0.49**.

Author Keywords

Natural Language Interface; Question Answering; Semantic Interface; Semantic Search; Distributional Semantics; Linked Data; Semantic Web; Databases

ACM Classification Keywords

H.2.5 [Heterogeneous Databases]; H.3.1 [Information Storage and Retrieval]: Content Analysis and Indexing; H.3.3 [Information Storage and Retrieval]: Information Search and Retrieval

INTRODUCTION

The demand to access large amounts of heterogeneous structured data is emerging as a trend for many users and applications on the Web [1]. Google Knowledge Graph[1] is a recent example of the benefits of enabling the use of large-scale structured data resources may bring to applications. Additionally, during the last years, Linked Data emerged as a standard for publishing structured data on the Web, playing a fundamental role in enabling the next generation of applications driven by rich Web data.

However, the effort involved in querying heterogeneous and distributed third-party Linked Data sources on the Web creates barriers for data consumers. In order to query datasets, users need to discover the datasets of interest, understand the structure and vocabularies used in these datasets, and then finally formulate the query using the syntax of a structured query language (such as SPARQL or SQL). Ideally users should be able to express their information needs without being aware of the dataset vocabulary (or 'schema'), delegating the query formulation process to a query engine.

Structured query mechanisms for datasets allow *expressive queries* at the expense of *usability*: the semantic matching process is manually done by data consumers. On the other side of the usability spectrum, information retrieval (IR) approaches allow users to search using intuitive keyword-based interfaces. In this case, the high usability comes at the expense of query expressivity and effectiveness: traditional vector space (VSM) models for IR typically do not deliver expressive and semantic queries over structured data. At the core of this *usability-expressivity trade-off* is the *semantic/vocabulary gap* between the way users express their information needs and the way structured data is represented. To address the semantic gap it is necessary to provide a semantic model which supports an effective semantic matching between users' information needs and the data representation. Additionally, from an interface perspective, natural language interfaces (NLI), i.e. query interfaces where users can express their information needs using natural language, can also support users to have more freedom and efficiency for querying large and heterogeneous data sources [7].

---

[1]http://googleblog.blogspot.ie/2012/05/introducing-knowledge-graph-things-not.html, 2012.

This paper proposes a natural language interface (NLI) approach for Linked Data targeting a greater level of *vocabulary-independency* (VoI). To cope with the semantic matching over greater levels of *lexical* and *abstraction* variations between *query* and *data*, a *distributional semantic model* is used. The *distributional semantic model* component is complemented by a *compositional semantic model* which allows the alignment of the sequence of query terms to dataset elements, respecting syntactic constraints in the queries and in the datasets. The compositional model, which is tightly coupled with the distributional model, allows the definition of expressive query capabilities required for a NLI system. The utility of the approach can be extended to any dataset which can be transformed into an *Entity-Attribute-Value* (EAV) representation abstraction.

The contributions of this paper are: (i) a NLI approach for Linked Data (LD) based on a distributional-compositional semantic model which supports greater levels of vocabulary independency, (ii) the implementation of the distributional-compositional model as a semantic inverted index, (iii) the implementation of the proposed system as a research prototype and (iv) an extensive evaluation of the proposed approach.

The Vocabulary Problem for Linked Data

The structural, categorical and lexical elements used in the representation of a proposition (triple) in a Linked Dataset depends largely on factors such as the set of usage intents for the dataset and the individual perspective of the dataset designer. Figure 1 depicts an example of the *vocabulary gap* between a user query and alternative dataset representations for triples providing answers for the query. In (a) '*United States*' composes with '*Presidents*' to form a class, while in (b) '*United States* is an instance associated with the property '*president*'. The vocabulary information related to the query term '*daughter*' is given by the property '*child*' in (a) and '*fatherOf*' in (b). The semantic gap introduced by possible conceptualizations of the reality into a database defines the *vocabulary problem for databases*.

The vocabulary problem for databases is a fundamental and practical concern for many users and information systems, as database schemas grow in size and semantic heterogeneity [7] and the time to build structured queries grows in proportion to the schema size. Addressing the vocabulary problem for databases, however, depends on the definition of a comprehensive semantic matching approach between user information needs and structured data. However, the construction of comprehensive semantic matching solutions is largely dependent on the availability of large-scale commonsense knowledge bases.

Proposed Solution

This work introduces a distributional-compositional semantic model which is used as the central element for the construction of a vocabulary-independent Natural Language Interface (NLI) for Linked Data. Figure 1 depicts the high-level workflow behind the proposed NLI approach which maps to the

outline of the paper. The first step (1) in the proposed approach is the construction of a *distributional semantic model* based on the extraction of co-occurrence patterns from large corpora, which defines a distributional semantic vector space. The distributional semantic vector space uses concept vectors to semantically represent data and queries, by mapping datasets elements and query terms to concepts in the distributional space. Once the space is built, the RDF graph data is embedded into the space (step 2), defining the $\tau - Space$, a structured distributional semantic vector space. The alignment between structured data and the distributional model allows the use of the *large-scale commonsense information* embedded in the distributional model (extracted from text) to be used in the *semantic matching/approximation* process. An introduction to distributional semantics and the construction of the $\tau - Space$ is described in section $\tau - Space$. In order to support high performance search and querying, the $\tau - Space$ is mapped into an inverted index, which is described in the section *Query Approach*.

After the data is indexed into the $\tau - Space$, it is ready to be queried. The query processing starts with the analysis of the natural language query, from which a set of *query features* and a *semi-structured query representation* is extracted (step 3). The query analysis is described in section *Query Analysis*. After the query is analyzed, a *query processing plan* is generated, which maps the set of features and the semi-structured query into a set of search, navigation and transformation *operations* (step 5) over the data graph embedded in the $\tau - Space$. These operations define the semantic matching between the query and the data, using the distributional semantic information. This corresponds to the *compositional* model associated to the distributional model. The query processing approach and the operations over the $\tau - Space$ are described in the *Query Processing* section. The approach is evaluated under a large open domain dataset in the *Evaluation* section, followed by the analysis of related work and conclusions.

DISTRIBUTIONAL SEMANTIC MODEL

Distributional Semantics

Distributional semantics is defined upon the assumption that the context surrounding a given word in a text provides important information about its meaning [5]. Distributional semantics focuses on the *automatic* construction of a semantic model based on the statistical distribution of word co-occurrence in texts, allowing the creation of an associational and quantitative model which captures the degree of semantic relatedness between words. Distributional semantic models are represented by Vector Space Models (VSMs), where the meaning of a word is represented by a weighted vector which captures the associational pattern with other words in the corpora. In this work a *distributional semantic model* is used as a core element to address the query-dataset vocabulary gap.

τ-Space

The τ-Space [3] is a *distributional structured vector space model* which allows the semantic (concept-based) indexing of labelled graphs. The distributional model under the scope of

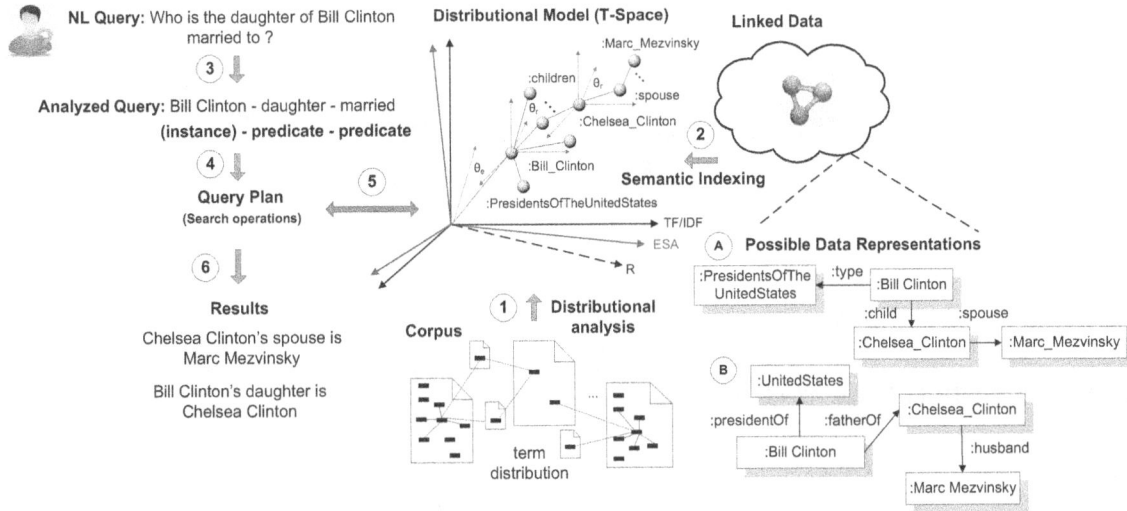

Figure 1. Example of the vocabulary gap between query and data representation.

this work is defined by the Explicit Semantic Analysis (ESA) [2] model. ESA defines a *concept coordinate basis* where the RDF(S) graph labels can be resolved into a high-dimensional concept space. Figure 1(2) depicts the $\tau - Space$ embedding an example RDF graph containing triples with instances, classes and properties. By its construction, the ESA coordinate basis can be transformed to an TF/IDF *term coordinate basis* (Figure 1) [3, 2]. Essentially, the $\tau - Space$ allows the representation of labelled graph data such as RDF with a distributional semantic grounding, using the background commonsense knowledge present in the reference corpora to support semantic search operations.

Construction

The graph data model has a signature $\Sigma = (P, E)$ formed by a pair of finite set of symbols used to represent predicates $p \in P$ and instances $e \in E$ in the graph G. It can be assumed that both elements in P and E are represented using meaningful descriptors (symbols present in the reference corpus). In this context, a predicate represent both properties (binary predicates) and classes (unary predicates). Each element in the signature Σ_G is represented as a vector in a distributional space. The semantics of G is defined by the vectors in the distributional space.

The $\tau - Space$ *coordinate system* is built from a text collection $\mathbb{C}$. The set $Term = \{k_1, \cdots, k_t\}$, of all terms available in $\mathbb{C}$ is used to define the basis $Term_{base} = \{\vec{\mathbf{k}}_1, \cdots, \vec{\mathbf{k}}_t\}$ of unit vectors that spans the *term vector space* VS^{Term}.

The set of all distributional concepts $Concept = \{c_1, \cdots, c_t\}$ are extracted from a reference corpus and each concept $c_i \in Concept$ is mapped to an identifier which represents the co-occurrence pattern in the corpus. Each identifier c_i defines a set which tracks the context where a term k_t occurred. This set is used to construct the basis $Concept_{base} = \{\vec{\mathbf{c}}_1, \cdots, \vec{\mathbf{c}}_t\}$ of vectors that spans the *distributional vector space* VS^{Dist}.

Thus, the set of contexts where a term occurs define the concept vectors associated with the term, which is a representation of its meaning based on the reference corpora. Each concept vector is weighted according to the term distribution in the corpus, allowing the concept vector space coordinate basis to be defined in terms of a term vector space coordinate basis, where each dimension maps to a word in the corpus. In order to obtain an approach that supports an approximative semantic model, the relational (labelled graph) model is linked to the distributional model, so that the distributional model could enrich and ground the semantics of the relational model.

The first step is to build the τ-*Space concept space* based on the reference corpus. The second step is to translate the elements of the signature $\Sigma = (P, E)$ of the graph G to elements VS^{Dist}. The vector representation of P, under the VS^{Dist} is defined by:

$$\vec{\mathbf{P}}_{VS^{Dist}} = \{\vec{\mathbf{p}} : \vec{\mathbf{p}} = \sum_{i=1}^{t} v_i^p \vec{\mathbf{c}}_i, \text{ for each } p \in P\} \quad (1)$$

and the vector representation of E in VS^{Term} is defined by:

$$\vec{\mathbf{E}}_{VS^{Term}} = \{\vec{\mathbf{e}} : \vec{\mathbf{e}} = \sum_{i=1}^{t} w_i^e \vec{\mathbf{k}}_i, \text{ for each } e \in E\} \quad (2)$$

where w_i^e and v_i^p are defined by a co-occurrence weighting scheme[2].

The third step refers to the translation of triple from G into the $\tau - Space$. As each predicate and instance term has a vector representation, we can define the vector representation of a triple r in the concept vector space by the following definition.

---

[2]for example, the term-frequency/inverse document frequency(TF/IDF).

Definition (Relational Vector): Let $\vec{p}$, $\vec{e_1}$ and $\vec{e_2}$ be the vector representations, respectively, of p, e_1 and e_2. A triple vector representation (denoted by $\vec{r}$) is defined by: $(\vec{p} - \vec{e_1})$ if $p(e_1)$; $(\vec{p} - \vec{e_1}, \vec{e_2} - \vec{p})$ if $p(e_1, e_2)$.

The vocabulary-independent query model uses the *distributional semantic relatedness search* as a native (and primitive) semantic approximation/equivalence operation between query terms and data elements in the $\tau - Space$. This primitive operation is coordinated with data navigation and transformation steps over the data graph, which defines the compositional model, i.e. progressively matches query structures to dataset structures.

VOCABULARY-INDEPENDENT QUERY APPROACH

Outline

To facilitate the understanding of the principles behind the query approach we start with the description of the query analysis and processing for the query example and then we follow to the description of the generalised approach.

For the example query *'Who is the daughter of Bill Clinton married to?'*, the query analysis starts with the *part-of-speech* (POS) tagging of the natural language query terms and by determining the *dependency structure* of the query. The query analysis consists in transforming the natural language query into a *partial ordered dependency structure* (PODS), a triple-like representation of the query associated with a set of *query features* (Figure 2).

With the PODS and the query features, the query processing approach starts by resolving the *core (pivot) entity* in the query (in this case *Bill Clinton*) to the corresponding database entity (*dbpedia: Bill_Clinton*) (Figure 2). The pivot determination is dependent on heuristics which take into account the query features and targets the element which is *less vague or ambiguous*, and consequently presents a higher probability of a correct matching (covered in the *Query Analysis* section).

After *Bill Clinton* is resolved, the subspace of the entity *dbpedia:Bill_Clinton* is selected, constraining the search space to elements associated with *dbpedia:Bill_Clinton*, and the next term in the PODS (*'daughter'*) is used as a query term for a distributional semantic search over the neighboring elements of *dbpedia:Bill_Clinton*. The distributional semantic search is equivalent to computing the *distributional semantic relatedness* between the query term (*'daughter'*) and all predicates associated with *dbpedia:Bill_Clinton* (*dbprop:religion*, *dbprop:child*, *dbprop:almaMater*, etc). The semantic equivalence between *'daughter'* and *dbprop:child* is determined by using the corpus-based distributional commonsense information (the words *'daughter'* and *'child'* occur in similar contexts). A *threshold* filters out unrelated relations. After the alignment between *'daughter'* and *dbprop:child* is done, the query processing *navigates to* the entity associated with the *dbprop:child* relation (*dbpedia:Chelsea_Clinton*) and the next query term (*'married'*) is taken. At this point the entity *dbpedia:Chelsea_Clinton* defines the search subspace (relations associated with *dbpedia:Chelsea_Clinton*) and the semantic search for predicates which are semantically related to *'married'* is done. The query term *'married'* is aligned

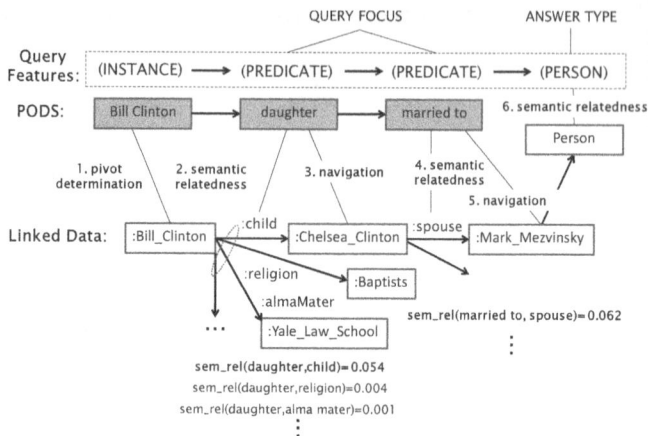

Figure 2. Query processing steps for the query example.

to *dbprop:spouse* and the answer to the query is found: the entity *dbpedia:Mark_Mezvinsky* (Figure 2).

Semantic Matching

The query processing approach has the objective of providing a mapping $m(Q, G)$ between the query terms $\langle q_0...q_n \rangle$ $\forall q_i \in Q$ and P, E elements in the graph G. This mapping is named an *interpretation* of the query Q under the graph G. In the interpretation process it is central to minimize the impact of *ambiguity*, *vagueness* and *synonymy*, which are central phenomena for the vocabulary problem for databases.

RDF(S) defines a semantic representation model which typically maps specific lexical categories to specific types of entities. Below we examine the relation between lexical categories and the representation model of RDF.

- **Instance:** Instances typically represent *named entities* such as people, places, organizations, events and are associated with proper nouns. Named entities are less bound to *vagueness* and *synonymy*. Compared to other entity types (property, relationship, class) it also presents a lower incidence of *ambiguity*. From a semantic matching perspective, instances are less bound to vocabulary variation (lower vocabulary gap) and as a consequence are more likely to match using string/term similarity approaches (under VS^{Term}).

- **Property, Class:** Represent predications, categories, relations and states. Typically map to nouns, adjectives, verbs and adverbs. Nouns, adjectives, verbs and adverbs are more bound to synonymy, vagueness, ambiguity. From a corpora perspective, predications tend to occur in a larger number of contexts. From a semantic matching perspective, properties and classes are more prone to vocabulary variation (higher vocabulary gap) and are typically dependent on more sophisticated semantic matching approaches (distributional search under VS^{Dist}).

Query Analisys

The query analysis process consists in recognizing and classifying *entities* and *operations* in the query and also in mapping the natural language query into a *PODS* (triple-like format) and into a set of *query features* (Figure 2). The query analysis operations are:

Entity detection and classification (instances, classes, complex classes): The pre-processing phase starts by determining the part-of-speech (POS) of the query terms. *POS tags pattern rules* are used to determine entity candidates' types: *instances*, *classes* and *properties*. Examples of the POS tag-based entity detection and classification mapping rules are as follows: $NNP+ \rightarrow$ Instance; $\{RB * JJ*\}$ $NN(S)* \{IN\ NNP\}* \rightarrow$ Class OR Property; $BE* VB$ $\{IN\ NN\}* \rightarrow$ Property; $\{CD+\ OR\ (NN(S*)+\ AND$ $isAfterAPropertyTerm)\} \rightarrow$ Value.

Operation detection: *POS tags* and *keyword patterns* are used in the detection of operations and associated parameters in the query. While the lexical and structural variation for dataset elements is large, the vocabulary for typical database operations can be enumerated in a knowledge base of lexical expressions of operations Op.

Triple-pattern ordering: Natural language queries are parsed using a *dependency parser*. The dependency structures are reduced to a set of *partial ordered dependency structures (PODS)* by applying two sets of operations: (i) the removal of stopwords and their associated dependencies (ii) the re-ordering of the dependencies based on the core entity position in the query (where the core entity becomes the first query term and the topological relations given by the dependencies are preserved). For the example query the PODS is *Bill Clinton - daughter - married to*. The triple-pattern processing rules are described in details in [4].

Query classification: Classifies the query according to the following *query features*: (i) *queries with instances references*, (ii) *queries with classes/complex classes references*[3], (iii) *queries with operators references*, (iv) *queries with constraint composition (property composition, conjunction & disjunction operators)*. The set of features represent database primitives in the *data representation level* (instances, properties, classes), *operational level* (e.g. aggregation, ordering) and *structural/compositional level* (conjuction, disjunction, property composition). The query features for the example query are shown in Figure 2.

Query Approach over the $\tau - Space$

Definition (Semantic Relatedness): A *semantic relatedness function* $sr : VS^{dist} \times VS^{dist} \rightarrow [0,1]$ is defined as $sr(\vec{\mathbf{p_1}}, \vec{\mathbf{p_2}}) = \cos(\theta) = \vec{\mathbf{p_1}} \cdot \vec{\mathbf{p_2}}/||\vec{\mathbf{p_1}}||\,||\vec{\mathbf{p_2}}||$. A threshold $\eta \in [0,1]$ could be used to establish the semantic relatedness between the two vectors: $sr(\vec{\mathbf{p_1}}, \vec{\mathbf{p_2}}) > \eta$. The experimental threshold η is based on the semantic differential approach for ESA proposed in Freitas et al. [6].

---

[3]complex classes are classes which contain more than two words

The *distributional semantic relatedness measure* is used to establish an approximate semantic equivalence between query-dataset elements in the context of a query matching step. The first element to be resolved in the PODS, called *the semantic pivot*, in general is a term which represents the most specific element in the query. The semantic pivot, as the more constraining element in the query, helps to reduce the search space, since just the elements in the graph associated with the pivot at a given iteration are candidates for the semantic matching. The query sequence is embedded in the vector space VS^{dist}, allowing its identification with the following sequence of vectors $< \vec{\mathbf{q'}}_0, \vec{\mathbf{q'}}_1, \cdots, \vec{\mathbf{q'}}_n >$.

Definition: Given a query q, its instances and predicates, denoted by $q_0, q_1, ..., q_n$ are ordered in a sequence $< q'_0, q'_1, \cdots, q'_n >$ using a heuristic measure of specificity $h_{specificity}$ from the most specific to the less specific, that is, $\forall i \in [0,n], h_{specificity}(q'_i) \geq h_{specificity}(q'_{i+1})$. The specificity can be computed by taking into account lexical categories (e.g. $f_{spec}(proper\_noun) > f_{spec}(noun) > f_{spec}(adjective) > f_{spec}(adverb)$) in combination with a corpus-based measure of specificity, in this case inverse document frequency (IDF) using Wikipedia as a corpus.

In the first iteration, $\vec{\mathbf{q'}}_0 \in VS^{dist}$, the vector representation of the pivot q'_0 can be resolved to a vector $\vec{\mathbf{e}}_0$. The entity e_0 defines a vector subspace which can be explored by the next query term (which spans the relations associated with the entity e_0). The second query term q'_1 can be matched with one or more predicates associated with e_0, for example p_0, considering that the *distributional semantic relatedness measure*, $sr(\vec{\mathbf{q'}}_1, \vec{\mathbf{p}}_0) \geq \eta$, where η is a semantic relatedness threshold. The entities associated with p_0 (for example e_1) are used as new semantic pivots.

At each iteration of the querying process, a set of semantic pivots are defined and are used to navigate to other points in the vector space. This navigation corresponds to the reconciliation process between the semantic intent defined by the query and the semantic intent expressed in the dataset G. The reconciliation process can be defined as the sequence of vectors $< (\vec{\mathbf{q'}}_1 - \vec{\mathbf{p}}_1), (\vec{\mathbf{q'}}_2 - \vec{\mathbf{p}}_2), \cdots, (\vec{\mathbf{q'}}_n - \vec{\mathbf{p}}_n) >$. The proposed approximate querying process can also be represented geometrically as the vectors $< (\vec{\mathbf{e}}_0 - \vec{\mathbf{p}}_0), (\vec{\mathbf{p}}_0 - \vec{\mathbf{e}}_1), ..., (\vec{\mathbf{p}}_{n-1} - \vec{\mathbf{e}}_n) >$ over the $\tau - Space$, which geometrically represents the process of finding the answer in the graph.

Query Processing

After the *Query Analysis*, the PODS and the query features are sent to the *Query Planner*, which generates the *query processing plan*. A query processing plan involves the application of a sequence $\langle op_0, ..., op_n \rangle$ of search, navigation and transformation operations over the τ-Space. The primitive operations for the *Query Planner* are:

(i) Search operations:

Consists of keyword and distributional search operations over the graph G.

- **Instance search** (VS^{Term})**:** Due to its low level of vagueness, ambiguity and synonymy and typically large number of instances, the instance search approach does not use the distributional semantic model. For a query term q^I over the term space VS^{Term}, the *ranking function* $s(\mathbf{q^I}, \mathbf{i_j})$ is given by a combination of the *dice coefficient* between the returned URI label and the query term $sim_{dice}(\mathbf{q^I}, \mathbf{i_j})$, the *node cardinality* (number of associated properties) $n(i_j)$.

- **Class search** (VS^{Dist})**:** Differently from instances, classes are more bound to synonym, vagueness and ambiguity (larger vocabulary gap), being more sensitive to vocabulary variation. The class search operation is defined by the computation of the semantic relatedness between the class candidate query term q^C and the class entities in the $\tau - Space$: $sr(\overrightarrow{\mathbf{q^C}}, \overrightarrow{\mathbf{c}})$.

- **Property search** (VS^{Dist})**:** Consists in the search operation where a set of URIs define a set of subspaces associated with instances $\mathbf{i_j}$. The property candidate query term q^P is used as an input for a distributional semantic search over the relations associated with the instance subspace. The search is defined by $sr(\overrightarrow{\mathbf{q^P}}, \overrightarrow{\mathbf{p}})$.

(ii) Graph navigation & transformation operations

- **Graph navigation:** Graph navigation elements provide the core structural compositional operations for the query processing over instances (i), properties (p), classes (c) in the graph. There are three main graph navigation elements:

  1. *Navigation (Predicate composition):* Consists in a predicate composition that defines a path query. The predicate composition is determined for a path of predicates connected through a common instance. Geometrically, the predicate composition is defined by a sequence of translations in the VS^{Dist}. This operation maps to the $(i - p_0 - v_0)(v_0 - p_1 - v_1)...(v_n - p_{n+1} - v_{n+1})$ or $(i - p_0 - v_0)(v_0 - p_1 - v_1)...(v_n - rdf : type - c)$ graph patterns, where v_i represents a variable.

  2. *Extensional class expansion (instance listing for a class):* Consists in expanding the set of instances $\mathbf{i_j}$ associated with a class $\mathbf{c}$ through the *rdf:type* predicate. This operation maps to the $(c - rdf : type - v_n)$ triple pattern, where v_n defines a set of instances associated with the class c.

  3. *Star-Shaped property composition:* Consists in the composition of triple patterns in a disjunctive $(i_0 - p_0 - v) \vee (i_1 - p_1 - v) \vee ... \vee (i_n - p_n - v)$ or conjunctive form $(i_0 - p_0 - v) \wedge (i_1 - p_1 - v) \wedge ... \wedge (i_n - p_n - v)$.

The application of the compositional constraints is done as a graph navigation over the $\tau - Space$. The query processing algorithm works as a *semantic best-effort* query system, where the algorithm tries to maximize the amount

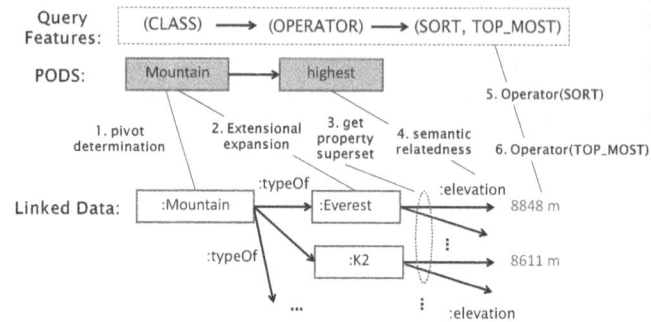

Figure 3. Execution of a query processing plan for the query '*What is the highest mountain ?*'

of semantic constraints which are matched, but eventually can return approximate or incomplete results. The search operations and the constraints application are done in a inverted index, aiming at performance and scalability. This approach can be contrasted with NLI approaches which try to satisfy all constraints in a single SPARQL query.

- **Data transformation operations:** Consists in the application of *functions* for filtering triples or mapping triples to the real domain.

  1. **Aggregation operators:** Maps a set of triples or entities from VS^{Dist} or VS^{Term} into the $\mathbb{R}$ domain, based on an enumerable set of functional operators Op (e.g. *count*, *average*, etc).

  2. **Ordering operators:** Defines a sequence for a set of triples and entities based on an ordering criteria (*ascending*, *descending*).

  3. **Conditional operators:** Filters a set of triples and entities based on a *conditional expression* (e.g. $>$, $<$, etc).

  4. **User feedback operators:** Filters a set of triples based on the user input for a set of instances, classes and properties. This operation aims at allowing users to cope with possible errors in the term and distributional search operations over the $\tau - Space$, by allowing them to select from a list matching the search criteria, a set of valid instances, classes and properties. The *user feedback dialog* define just a filtering function, where users can select from a reduced list of options (maximum 5 elements) in case there is ambiguity in the term/distributional search process.

The *query planning algorithm* (Algorithm I) orchestrates the *search & graph navigation & transformation* operations defined above.

A query plan defines multiple operations over the index. Figure 2 shows an example of a set of operations for a query with an *instance* as a pivot entity, while Figure 3 shows the execution of a query plan for a second example query ('*What is the highest mountain ?*'), which is a query with a *class* as a pivot entity.

Algorithm 1 Distributional-compositional query planning algorithm

$Q(V_Q, E_Q, Op)$: VoI query graph patterns
$G(V_G, E_G)$: Indexed LD graph
$A(V_A, E_A, P_A)$: answer graph and post-processed answer
i : set of instances URIs
c : set of classes URIs
p : related properties URIs
q : query term
$initialize(A)$
for all $q \in V_Q$ **do**
  if $(isCoreEntity(q))$ **then**
    $i \leftarrow searchInstances(q)$
    $c \leftarrow searchClasses(q)$
  end if
  if $(isAmbiguous(i, c))$ **then**
    $i, c \leftarrow disambiguatePivotEntity(i, c)$
  end if
  if $(pivotEntiyIsClass)$ **then**
    $i \leftarrow extensionalExpansion(c)$
  end if
  $p \leftarrow searchProperties(i, q)$
  if $(hasOperations(Q))$ **then**
    $p \leftarrow searchOperations(i, Op)$
  end if
  if $(isAmbiguous(p))$ **then**
    $p \leftarrow disambiguateProperty(p)$
    $triples \leftarrow selectByPivotAndProperty(i, p)$
  end if
  $i, c \leftarrow navigateTo(triples)$
  $V_A, E_A \leftarrow triples$
  $P_A \leftarrow applyOperation(triples, Op)$
end for

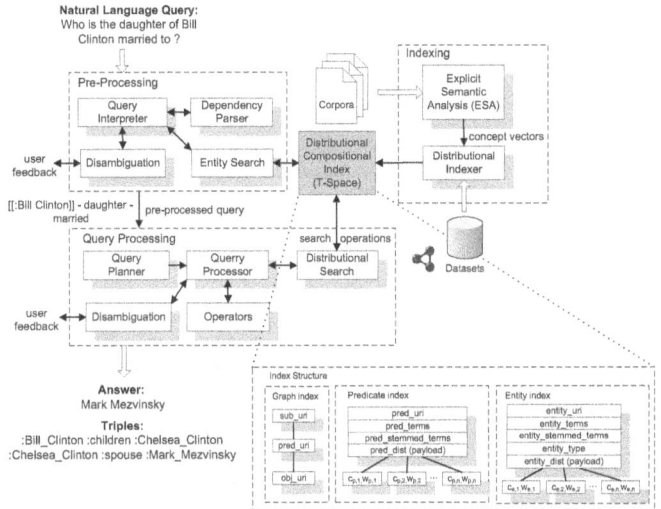

Figure 4. High-level components diagram of the vocabulary-independent query approach and distributional inverted index structure.

ARCHITECTURE

The high-level workflow and main components for the query approach are given in Figure 4. In the first phase (*query preprocessing*), the natural language query analysis process is done by the *Interpreter* component. The second phase consists in the *query processing approach* which defines a sequence of search and data transformation operations over the RDF graph embedded in the τ-Space, based on the query plan which is defined by the query features. The *Query Planner* generates the sequence of operations (the *query processing plan*) over the data graph on the semantic inverted index. The query processing plan is sent to the *Query Processor* which initialy executes the *search operations* part of the query plan over the *Distributional Search* component. The query plan also includes the application of a set of *graph navigation & transformation operations* which are implemented on the *Operators* component. The result of search operations can be disambiguated using the *Disambiguation* component for *pivot entities* and *predicates*.

Index & System Implementation

The distributional-compositional index is implemented over the *Lucene* 3.5 IR framework. The core *index* structure consists of three indexes: the *graph index* for mapping the graph topology (triples), the *entity index* (for instances and classes) and the *predicate/property index*. While *uri* stores the element URI, the field *terms/stemmed terms* covers the contents of the parsed and stemmed URIs and the *distributional concept vector* field indexes the ESA weighted concept vec-

tor. The distributional ESA concept vector is serialized as a Lucene *payload* (byte array). For elements in the entity index, only classes have a distributional field. Figure 4 depicts the distributional index structure. The index structure allows its natural parallelization: the subspaces defined by entities can serve as partition identifiers. Each entity subspace can also be partitioned and distributed given that the distributional reference corpus for each index partition is defined.

The query processing mechanism is implemented in the *Treo* NLI system following the components diagram (Figure 4). The system is implemented in Java. The *core* component contains the Lucene-based $\tau - Space$ implementation which can be used in other semantic search scenarios, while the *NLI* component contains the module for analyzing natural language queries. The *DS* component contains a distributional semantics infrastructure which implements ESA.

Figures 5 and 6 show the query interface for different query types. For the example queries we can observe the *semantic best-effort* characteristic of the approach, where other highly related elements are returned by the distributional matching. A video of a running prototype can be found online[4].

EVALUATION

The QA approach is evaluated under an open domain question answering over Linked Data scenario, using unconstrained natural language queries. The query processing approach was evaluated using the Question Answering over Linked Data 2011 test collection[5]. The dataset contains 102 natural language queries over DBpedia 3.7 and YAGO. The experiments were executed on an intel core i5 computer with 8GB of RAM. Table 1 shows the distribution of query features in the query set and the dataset statistics. In addition to the query features, the test collection was analysed in relation

---

[4] http://bit.ly/1c36LGD

[5] QALD-1, http://www.sc.cit-ec.uni-bielefeld.de/qald-1

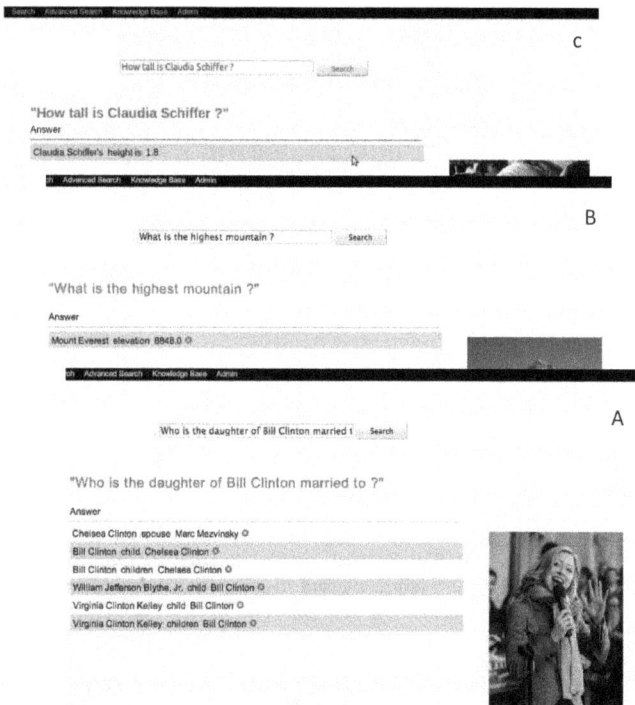

Figure 5. Screenshots of the query interface for queries returning triples.

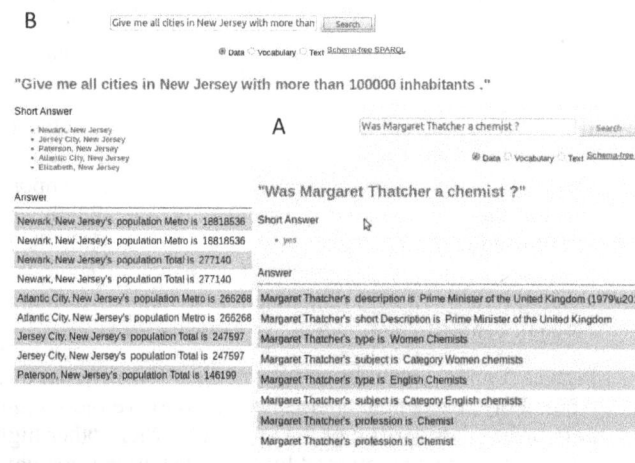

Figure 6. Screenshots of the query interface for queries returning post-processed answers.

to the presence of vocabulary gaps: 41% of the properties were aligned to different terms expressed in the queries, and only 17% of the properties had identical lexical expressions. For classes 30% had a completely different lexical expression, while 11% had an identical lexical expression. The test collection also expresses a large number of distinct query patterns. The reader is referred to [6] for the analysis of the query patterns.

The average evaluation measures are provided in the Tables 2 and 5. The first category of measurements evaluates the

[6]http://bit.ly/1c36LGD

Query Features	%
Contains instance reference	0.63
Contains class reference	0.12
Contains complex class reference	0.10
Contains operator reference	0.15
Contains constraint composition	0.84
Dataset Feature	value
# of predicates	45,767
# of classes	5,556,492
# of classes	9,434,677
dataset size	17GB

Table 1. Statistics for the test collection features.

Measure Type	Value
Mean Avg. Precision	0.62
Avg. Recall	0.81
Avg. F-Measure	0.70
Avg. MRR	0.49
% of queries answered	80%

Table 2. Relevance analysis for the QALD 2011 queries.

answer relevance using *mean avg. precision, avg. recall, mean reciprocal rank* (mrr) and the *% of answered queries* (fully and partially (recall > 0.20) answered). **80%** of the queries were answered using the distributional-compositional index. The **0.81** recall confirms the hypothesis that the distributional-compositional search provides a comprehensive semantic matching mechanism. The mean avg. precision=**0.62** and mrr=**0.49** confirms the hypothesis that the approach provides an effective approximate (semantic best-effort) NLI mechanism, also returning a limited list of unrelated results. The approach was tested under different combinations of query patterns (14 based on entity types, 57 distinct patterns based on lexical categories), showing a medium-high coverage in terms of **query expressivity**.

Table 3 shows the comparison between the distributional approach with three baseline systems. The system outperforms the existing approaches in recall and % of answered queries, showing equivalent precision to the best performing system. Analyzing the query features related to the queries with f-measure < 0.1 it is possible to observe that most of the queries which were not answered by PowerAqua have aggregations and comparisons (53% - 9 queries) and/or reference to classes (70% - 12 queries). For Freya, the same pattern could be observed: queries with aggregations and comparisons account for 50% (7 queries) of the queries with f-measure < 0.1, while queries with reference to classes account for 64% (9 queries). Comparatively, the proposed approach is able to cope with queries containing references to aggregations and comparisons and reference to classes (accounting for 40% on the queries which were not answered - 2 queries). This difference can be explained by the construction of a comprehensive query planning algorithm, which provides a mechanism to detect core query features and map them into a query execution plan (which in the context of this work, defines the compositional/interpretation model).

The second category of measurements in Table 5 evaluates individually the core search components of the approach: *instance/class(pivot) search* and *predicate search*. Queries with instances as semantic pivots have higher precision and recall

System	Avg. R	MAP	% answered queries
Treo	**0.79**	**0.63**	**79%**
PowerAqua	0.54	0.63	48%
FREyA	0.48	0.52	54%
Unger et al.	0.63	0.61	-

Table 3. Comparison with existing systems for the QALD 2011 test subset.

Measure	value
Avg. query execution time (ms)	8,530
Avg. entity search time (ms)	3,495
Avg. predicate search time (ms)	3,223
Avg. number of search operations per query	2.70
Avg. index insert time per triple (ms)	5.35
Avg. index size per triple (bytes)	250
Dataset adaptation effort (minutes)	0.00
Dataset specific semantic enrichment effort per query (secs)	0.00
Dataset specific semantic enrichment effort (minutes)	0.00

Table 4. Temporal and size measures of the distributional-compositional semantic index for the NLI approach.

compared with queries with classes pivots. The individual performance of these two components minimizes the number of *user-feedback* for disambiguation over the semantic inverted index. To support an effective user feedback dialog mechanism, the set of returned results should have high mrr and precision. From a user-interaction perspective, an average mrr higher than 0.33 (where the target result is ranked third on the list) provides a low impact disambiguation mechanism. The measured average mrr=**0.91** for *entity search* and **0.76** for *predicate search* components provide a low interaction cost disambiguation mechanism. Both entity and predicate search have a high recall value (**1.0** and **0.95** respectively). Compared with queries with instances as pivots, queries containing classes as pivots have a significantly higher number of entity disambiguation operations. The evaluation shows that the semantic matching copes with the *ability to handle lexical variation* (including non-taxonomic matchings and alignments from different POS). Most queries do not require user disambiguation. The average number of user disambiguation operations per query is **0.14** for entities and **0.05** for predicates. The system can stand on its own query processing approach, without the disambiguation functionality. Comparatively, Freya [9] has an average of 3.65 user feedback operations per query, while the proposed approach has 0.20 disambiguation operations per query.

In addition to the evaluation of the results quality, the index is evaluated in relation to its temporal performance and size (Table 4). The **8,530 ms** average query execution time supports an interactive query mechanism. This average value for the query execution time is increased by the influence of a small number of queries which have large answer sets. For queries with small answer sets, the average query execution time is less than 2,000 ms. Additionally, the approach supports a *minimum dataset adaptation effort*, neither requiring data transformations nor a dataset specific manual semantic enrichment.

RELATED WORK

PowerAqua [8] is a question answering (QA) system which uses PowerMap, a hybrid matching algorithm comprising terminology-level and structural schema matching techniques with the assistance of large scale ontological or lexical resources. In addition to the ontology structure, PowerMap uses WordNet-based similarity approaches as a semantic approximation strategy. Unger et al. [11] presents a QA approach that relies on a deep linguistic analysis which generates a SPARQL template with slots that are filled with URIs. In order to fill these slots, potential entities are identified using string similarity and natural language patterns extracted from structured data and text documents. The final result is given by a ranking of the remaining query candidates. Exploring user interaction techniques, FREyA [9] is a QA system which employs feedback and clarification dialogs to resolve ambiguities and improve the domain lexicon with the help of users. User feedback is used to enrich the semantic matching process by allowing manual query-vocabulary mappings. Yahya et al. [12] describes an approach for translating natural language questions into structured SPARQL queries. The approach uses an integer linear program to coordinate the solution of various disambiguation tasks jointly, including the segmentation of questions into phrases, the mapping of phrases to entities and the construction of SPARQL triple patterns. In the evaluation of NLI/QA systems, usually the effort involved in the adaptation, in the semantic enrichment of the dataset and the user interaction in the question-answering process is not measured, bringing additional barriers to the comparability of the approaches. Additionally, temporal performance measurements are not prioritized. This work addresses these methodological issues.

Herzig & Tran [10] propose an approach for searching heterogeneous Web datasets using a structured seed query that matches to the vocabulary of one of the datasets. They introduce the entity relevance model which is used for matching and ranking results from external datasets and for performing data integration on the fly. Novacek et al. [13] describe a distributional approach applied to Semantic Web Data targeting the description of a tensor-based model for RDF data and its evaluation on entity consolidation. Freitas et al. [3] propose an initial analysis of a distributional structured semantic space (τ-Space). The work presented in [3] had the following limitations: (i) low query expressivity - focus on IR instead of QA, (ii) lack of a more extensive evaluation, (iii) no extensive scalability/performance evaluation - lack of a robust implementation of an inverted index.

Comparatively, this work focuses on improving query expressivity while keeping query flexibility, by introducing a compositional model based on the analysis of query features. The compositional model is used to define the query planning algorithm over the distributional vector space model (which supports a flexible semantic matching mechanism). A comparative analysis with existing QA systems over Linked Data shows the improvement of query expressivity reflected by the introduction of the compositional model. Another relevant characteristic of the approach (compared to existing approaches) is the fact that it addresses each of the structural

Type	Measure	all queries	w/ in-stances	w/ classes	w/ complex classes	w/ opera-tions	w/ const. comp.
Query Processing	Mean Avg. Precision	**0.62**	0.65	0.77	0.46	0.88	0.63
	Avg. Recall	**0.81**	0.93	0.76	0.67	1.00	0.87
	MRR	**0.49**	0.59	0.44	0.19	0.92	0.56
	% of queries answered	**0.80**	0.94	0.80	1.00	0.75	0.82
	% of queries fully answered	**0.62**	0.81	0.40	0.30	0.75	0.70
	% of queries partially answered	**0.21**	0.13	0.40	0.70	0.00	0.12
Entity Search	Avg. Entity Precision	0.47	0.49	0.56	0.27	0.36	0.49
	Avg. Entity Recall	1.00	1.00	1.00	1.00	1.00	1.00
	Entity MRR	0.91	0.96	0.73	0.82	1.00	0.90
	% of entity queries fully answered	0.88	1.00	1.00	1.00	0.75	0.88
	Avg. # of entity disamb. operations per query	0.14	0.06	0.40	0.30	0.25	0.12
Predicate Search	Avg. Predicate Precision	0.45	0.36	0.18	0.52	0.43	0.42
	Avg. Predicate Recall	0.95	0.98	0.67	1.00	1.00	0.95
	Predicate MRR	0.76	0.81	0.30	0.40	0.71	0.83
	% of predicate queries fully answered	0.65	0.90	0.60	0.00	0.75	0.74
	Avg. # of predicate disamb. operations per query	0.05	0.06	0.20	0.00	0.25	0.05

Table 5. Evaluation of the query processing mechanism results using natural language queries. Measures are collected for the full query mechanism and its core subcomponents: entity search and predicate search. The measures are categorized according to the query features.

query constraints at a time (instead of generating a single SPARQL query), supporting a semantic approximation process. Compared with FREyA, the proposed approach relies 10x less on user feedback, and it can be used without user feedback. The construction of a semantic inverted index supports an interactive query execution time. The use of a distributional semantic model supports a low maintenance semantic matching mechanism, which can be automatically built from corpora, with higher vocabulary coverage. The independency of manually created linguistic resources or rich ontologies brings the potential for higher transportability across other languages or domains.

CONCLUSIONS & FUTURE WORK

This paper proposes and evaluates the suitability of the $\tau - Space$ distributional-compositional model applied to the construction of a question answering system for Linked Data. The contributions of this work are: (i) the definition of a NLI approach for Linked Data based on a distributional-compositional VSM, focusing on an additional level of vocabulary independency, (ii) the formulation and implementation of the distributional-compositional model as a semantic inverted index, and (iii) an extensive evaluation of the proposed index and query processing mechanism. The proposed approach was evaluated using the QALD 2011 dataset over DBpedia achieving an **avg. recall= 0.81, mean avg. precision=0.62** and **mrr=0.49**, outperforming existing systems in recall and query coverage. The final distributional-compositional semantic model is defined by a set of operations over a vector space model which preserves the dataset structure at the same time that supports semantically approximate queries. Future work will concentrate on the investigation of the approach under domain specific scenarios and on the verification of the impact of the use of distributional models with more constraining context windows.

Acknowledgments.

This work has been funded by Science Foundation Ireland under Grant No. SFI/08/CE/I1380 (Lion-2).

REFERENCES

1. Heath, T. and Bizer, C. Linked Data: Evolving the Web into a Global Data Space (1st edition). Synthesis Lectures on the Semantic Web, (2011), 1-136.

2. Gabrilovich, E. and Markovitch, S. Computing semantic relatedness using Wikipedia-based explicit semantic analysis, in *Proc. Intl. Joint Conf. On Artificial Intelligence*, (2007), pp. 1606-1611.

3. Freitas, A., Curry, E., Oliveira, J. G., O'Riain, S. A Distributional Structured Semantic Space for Querying RDF Graph Data. *Intl. Journal of Semantic Computing (IJSC)*, (2012), vol. 5, no. 4, pp. 433-462.

4. Freitas, A., Oliveira, J.G., O'Riain, S., Curry, E. and Pereira da Silva, J.C. Querying Linked Data using Semantic Relatedness: A Vocabulary Independent Approach, in *Proc. of the 16th Intl. Conf. on Applications of Natural Language to Information Systems*, NLDB, (2011), vol. 6716, pp. 40-51.

5. Turney, P. D. and Pantel, P. From Frequency to Meaning: Vector Space Models of Semantics, *Journal of Artificial Intelligence Research*, (2010), vol. 37, pp. 141-188.

6. Freitas, A., Curry, E. and O'Riain, S. A Distributional Approach for Terminological Semantic Search on the Linked Data Web, in *Proc. of the 27th ACM Symposium On Applied Computing (SAC)*, (2012).

7. Freitas, A., Curry, E., Oliveira, J. G. and O'Riain, S. Querying Heterogeneous Datasets on the Linked Data Web: Challenges, Approaches and Trends. *IEEE Internet Computing, Special Issue on Internet-Scale Data*, (2012).

8. Lopez, V., Motta, E., Uren, V. PowerAqua: Fishing the Semantic Web. The Semantic Web: Research and Applications, Lecture Notes in Computer Science (2006), vol. 4011, pp. 393-410.

9. Damljanovic, D., Agatonovic, M. and Cunningham, H. FREyA: An Interactive Way of Querying Linked Data Using Natural Language, in *Proc. 1st Workshop on Question Answering over Linked Data*,(ESWC), (2011).

10. Herzig, D. M. and Tran, T. Heterogeneous Web Data Search Using Relevance-based On The Fly Data Integration, in *Proc. of 21st Intl. World Wide Web Conference* (WWW), (2012).

11. Unger, C., Bühmann, L., Lehmann, J., Ngonga Ngomo, A.-C., Gerber, D. and Cimiano, P. Template-based Question Answering over RDF Data, in *Proc. of 21st Int. World Wide Web Conference*, (2012), pp. 639-648.

12. Yahya, M., Berberich, K., Elbassuoni, S., Ramanath, M., Tresp, V. and Weikum, G. Natural Language Questions for the Web of Data, EMNLP, (2012), pp. 379-390.

13. Novacek, V. Handschuh, S. and Decker, S. Getting the Meaning Right: A Complementary Distributional Layer for the Web Semantics, in *Proc. of the Intl. Semantic Web Conference*, (2011), pp. 504-519.

MILA–S: Generation of Agent-Based Simulations from Conceptual Models of Complex Systems

David A. Joyner
Design & Intelligence Laboratory
School of Interactive Computing
Georgia Institute of Technology
85 5th Street NW
Atlanta, GA 30308
david.joyner@gatech.edu

Ashok K. Goel
Design & Intelligence Laboratory
School of Interactive Computing
Georgia Institute of Technology
85 5th Street NW
Atlanta, GA 30308
goel@cc.gatech.edu

Nicolas M. Papin
Design & Intelligence Laboratory
School of Interactive Computing
Georgia Institute of Technology
85 5th Street NW
Atlanta, GA 30308
npapin3@gatech.edu

ABSTRACT

Scientists use both conceptual models and executable simulations to help them make sense of the world. Models and simulations each have unique affordances and limitations, and it is useful to leverage their affordances to mitigate their respective limitations. One way to do this is by generating the simulations based on the conceptual models, preserving the capacity for rapid revision and knowledge sharing allowed by the conceptual models while extending them to provide the repeated testing and feedback of the simulations. In this paper, we present an interactive system called MILA–S for generating agent-based simulations from conceptual models of ecological systems. Designed with STEM education in mind, this user-centered interface design allows the user to construct a Component-Mechanism-Phenomenon conceptual model of a complex system, and then compile the conceptual model into an executable NetLogo simulation. In this paper, we present the results of a pilot study with this interface with about 50 middle school students in the context of learning about ecosystems.

Author Keywords

STEM education; K6-12 education; complex systems; ecological systems; conceptual models; agent-based simulations; scientific inquiry.

ACM Classification Keywords

1.2.m **[Artificial Intelligence]**: *Miscellaneous*. K.3.1 **[Computer Uses in Education]**: *Computer-assisted instruction*. J.3 **[Life and Medical Science]**: *Biology and genetics*. I.6 **[Simulation and Modeling]**: *Miscellaneous*.

General Terms

Design; Human Factors; Experimentation.

INTRODUCTION

In the course of scientific inquiry, scientists use multiple approaches to specify, share, test, and critique their ideas [9]. Two of the most important approaches scientists use are the construction of conceptual models and the execution of simulations of the system of interest. Conceptual models are abstract, declarative representations of the components, relations, and processes of the system [1, 2, 8, 9, 16]. A conceptual model specifies a scientist's current understanding of a system, allowing externalization, sharing, and critiquing of that understanding; further, it facilitates the use of the model to guide further investigation. Most theories of scientific modeling operationalize the process in terms of multiple phases, including model construction, model usage, model evaluation, and model revision[1, 2, 5, 9, 13].

Simulations can take several forms, including mental, physical, mathematical, and computational [1, 3, 6, 9, 16]. Like models, they specify scientists' current understanding of the natural system. Simulations, however, are executable with specific values for the system's input variables to determine how the values of the system's output variables may evolve over time. If the simulation behaves differently than the actual system under the same parameters, the scientist may modify the simulation to account for the discrepancy. In this way, the process of simulation construction, use, evaluation and revision is parallel to the process of conceptual modeling outlined above. Indeed, many theorists see conceptual models and simulations simply as two different kinds of models [9, 19].

Conceptual models and simulations each have unique affordances and limitations [1, 3, 6, 9]. Conceptual models lend themselves to rapid construction, evaluation, and revision because of their abstract, declarative, often qualitative, nature. However, conceptual models are limited in their precision, detail, and rigor. Executable simulations tend to be more precise, detailed, and rigorous. However, simulations are not typically as suited to rapid construction, use, and revision as conceptual models. Thus, it is useful to leverage the affordances of conceptual models and simulations to mitigate their respective limitations. One way to do this is by generating the simulations based on the conceptual models, preserving the capacity for rapid revision and knowledge sharing allowed by the conceptual models while extending them to provide the repeated testing and feedback of the simulations. In order to facilitate the use of simulations in the modeling process, it is necessary to devise a technique by which the simulations can respond directly to changes in the conceptual models. Our goal in this paper is to report on an interactive technology that can translate users' conceptual models into computational simulations.

In this paper, we focus on ecological systems as the systems of interest, causal models that provide causal explanations for a phenomenon as the conceptual models, agent-based computational simulations as the executable simulations, and STEM students as the users. Ecological systems are comprised of many individual agents, and the observable phenomena typically are the outcomes of localized interactions among the agents. Thus, agent-based simulations tend to be well-suited for simulating ecological systems [18]. Causal models of ecological systems often emphasize a top-down approach to analyzing a system, starting with a phenomenon to be explained, and developing increasingly refined explanations of the phenomenon in terms of mechanisms and components. Vattam, Goel & Rugaber describe a method for integrating Structure-Behavior-Function causal models [4] and agent-based simulations of ecological systems in the context of an interactive learning environment called ACT for supporting middle school science [14, 15]. Their method used the notion of "behavior patterns:" first the user-generated causal model was classified into a pattern of behavior in ecological systems, and then the pattern was translated into the agent-based simulation; the interactive tool had prior knowledge of how to map behavior patterns into input variables for the simulations. In practice, that method was quite complicated and was not much used in actual middle school classrooms.

In this paper, we describe an interactive technology called MILA–S for integrating causal models and agent-based simulations of ecological systems. 'MILA' stands for Modeling & Inquiry Learning Application; the '–S' is an additional simulation layer built on top of MILA. In this paper, we present the design of this system and the process by which MILA–S converts a conceptual model into an agent-based simulation. We also present preliminary results from a pilot study with MILA–S in middle school science classrooms in near Atlanta, USA, and its use by about 50 students for modeling a local aquatic ecosystem.

DESIGN OF THE INTERACTIVE TECHNOLOGY

MILA–S has three main components. (1) A modeling tool for constructing a causal model for explaining an observed phenomenon in an ecological system. (2) An off-the-shelf tool called NetLogo [17, 18] for constructing agent-based simulations of ecological systems. (3) A translational bridge between the causal model and the simulation, whereby MILA–S automatically generates an agent-based simulation based on the contents of the user specified causal model.

Causal Models

MILA–S uses Component-Mechanism-Phenomenon (or CMP) causal models that are variants of Structure-Behavior-Function models used in ACT. Components in CMP modeling can be either biotic (that is, living, such as plants, fish, or bacteria) or abiotic (that is, non-living, such as chemicals, dead matter, or sunlight). Each component has a set of variables associated with it, four for biotic components and one for abiotic components. Biotic components are defined by their population quantity, lifespan, energy level, and likelihood to breed; abiotic components are defined only by their quantity. Figure 1 illustrates a causal model constructed by a team of 7th grade life science students early in their interaction with MILA–S. In this model, there are three components: Sunlight, Oxygen, and "Fishies". The Sunlight and Oxygen are abiotic components, and they have only Amount as a variable that is designated on the node for the component. "Fishies" is a biotic component, and thus has Population, Age, Birth Rate, and Energy as variables; Population is designated on the "Fishies" node itself, while the notations for the other three variables extend downward from the main node.

CMP modeling draws causal relations between the variables associated with the different components. For example, the presence of a chemical like ammonia in the ecosystem that is poisonous to fish may decrease the

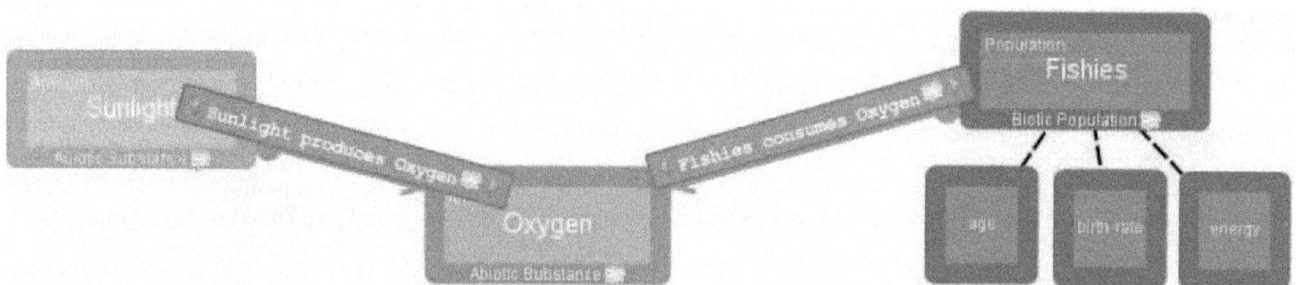

Figure 1: A causal model constructed by a team of 7th grade students using MILA–S.

lifespan of the fish, or it may directly decrease the population of the fish (additional information on the difference between the two is provided later in this paper). MILA–S provides the user with a set of prototypes that describe causal relationships among system variables. The choice among the available prototypes is determined by the variables on either end of the relation and the type or direction of the relation. For example, a relation from the Population of a biotic component to the Amount of an abiotic component, such as that from Fish Population to Oxygen Amount, may be 'consumes', 'produces', or 'becomes upon death,' etc. Similarly, a relation from an abiotic Amount to a biotic Population may be 'destroys' or 'feeds'. Similar relationship prototypes are available for links between two biotic and two abiotic components. In the model shown in Figure 1, the prototypes chosen are 'consumes' for the relationship between Fish and Oxygen, and 'produces' for the relationship between Sunlight and Oxygen. The direction of the arrow between the variables of two components indicates the direction of causal influence. For example, the arrow from Fish to Oxygen in Figure 1 indicates that the Population of Fish influences the Amount of Oxygen.

A Mechanism in CMP modeling is a causal chain of component variables connected by causal relations. For example, Figure 1 illustrates a mechanism hypothesized by a team of students according to which the Amount of Sunlight (an abiotic component) influences the Amount of Oxygen (another abiotic component) and the Population of Fish (a biotic component) also influences the Amount of Oxygen. A Phenomenon in CMP is an observation about the system of interest. For example, the phenomenon for the mechanism illustrated in Figure 1 is a change in the

Amount of Oxygen in an aquatic ecosystem. A user starts the process of CMP causal modeling using MILA–S with the goal of constructing a causal explanation of a given phenomenon. She then specifies a mechanism as the explanation for the phenomenon, incrementally composing the mechanism from the components of the system, their variables, and the relations between the variables. As Figure 1 illustrates, a CMP model in MILA–S is an external visual representation with textual annotations.

Agent-Based Simulations

MILA–S generates simulations using the popular NetLogo agent-based simulation platform [18]. NetLogo is well suited for simulating ecosystems because it models all behaviors of the ecosystem in terms of interaction among locally interacting agents in the system. Here we briefly summarize the NetLogo simulation platform and refer the reader to Wilensky & Resnick [17, 18] for details.

NetLogo can model both biotic and abiotic components. Biotic agents are organisms in an ecosystem that have intentional behaviors, such as eating, reproducing, and dying. Abiotic components have no intentionality and instead move around inside the simulation waiting for a biotic agent operate on them. Figure 2 illustrates the NetLogo simulation generated from the model illustrated in Figure 1. Note that all three components of the causal model are represented in the simulation: the Fish are in red, Sunlight hits the water at the brown dots, and the Oxygen produced by that interaction appears as blue dots.

Each biotic agent in a simulation has a set of methods or functions that describe its behaviors under different circumstances. Each agent also has variables or properties that can change as a result of these methods; in this

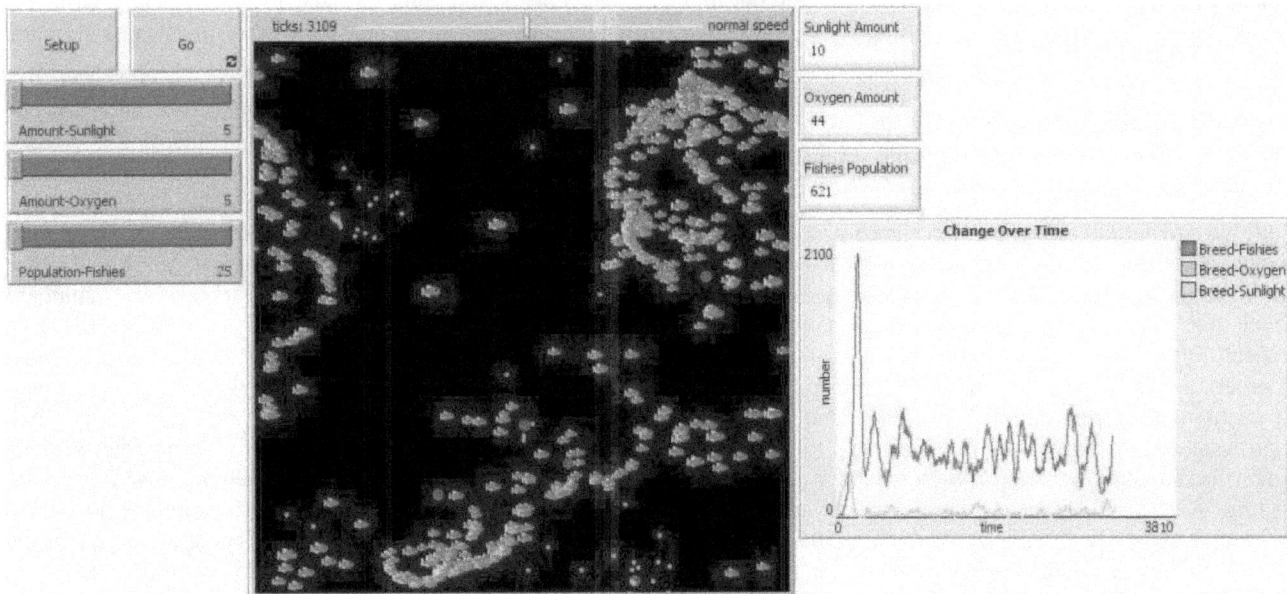

Figure 2: The simulation intelligently generated by MILA-S from the model in Figure 1.

example, an individual fish's energy level may rise when it executes its 'eat' method and fall when it executes its 'move' method. A biotic agent may also have methods dictating when it dies or when it reproduces; for example, the fish may have a method that dictates they die when their energy level drops below a certain threshold, and that they reproduce when their age and energy level are both above certain thresholds.

Each agent in a NetLogo simulation also has a special 'run' method that dictates the agent's behavior at every time step of the simulation. Every time the simulation clock ticks, the agent executes this method to determine its next behavior. Running the simulation amounts to executing this 'run' method for every agent present in the simulation. The engine iterates through every agent providing it with an opportunity to act. Upon completing the time step, the simulation advances to the next step, giving every agent the opportunity to act again. This proceeds until the user stops the simulation or the simulation reaches some built-in end condition, such as all agents dying.

As Figure 2 illustrates, NetLogo depicts the agents in a window showing their actions and behaviors. Also as Figure 2 illustrates, NetLogo provides graphs and counters for illustrating the temporal evolution of various variables of the simulation. Before running a simulation, the user sets the simulation's start condition. The input variables are set through the sliders and toggles on the left side of the simulation window illustrated in Figure 2. The user then clicks the Setup button to apply those changes to a new simulation. The user next clicks the Go button to start the time steps of the simulation.

Model-to–Simulation Bridge

As we mentioned in the introduction, one of the benefits of simulations in scientific inquiry is that they allow the user to test the predictions of their models. If a user finds that the model does not match observations of the real world, she may revise the model to more closely approximate the real world. However, this process operates most effectively when the cost of executing and revising simulations is not very high.

NetLogo simulations are typically designed with the its own dedicated programming language, which allows for enormous flexibility, However, this flexibility of designing simulations makes rapid evaluation and revision of models difficult. First, it requires at least a rudimentary background in programming. Secondly, even if the simulation designer is relatively experienced in NetLogo, it can still take significant time to make non-trivial changes to the way in which the simulation operates: these changes can involve writing all-new methods, creating new variables, or defining new agents. Clearly, it would be useful if the cost of generating NetLogo simulations could be controlled.

MILA–S provides one technique for controlling the cost of generating NetLogo simulations: it automatically generates

the simulations from the user's casual model. Note also that the generation of the CMP causal model illustrated in Figure 1 does not require any knowledge of programming. Instead, MILA–S provides a visual syntax for CMP modeling.

Managing Initial Settings

All NetLogo simulations, both those generated automatically in MILA–S and those written manually, have certain boilerplate settings and elements that must be taken care of initially. MILA–S starts the simulation generation process by generating these boilerplate settings. This includes the majority of the visible elements of the NetLogo simulation illustrated in Figure 2. The Setup and Go buttons are initialized and added to the canvas, the main simulation visualization area is created and sized in the center, and the graph area on the right is created the contain the ongoing developments on the different graphed variables. These different elements are later filled in with specific content from for simulation that is being generated; the Go button, for example, is linked to the time step functions for each agent in the simulation, the visualization is provided the locations of the different agents, and the variables to be tallied are added to the graph at the right.

Managing Agents

After initializing the boilerplate for the simulation, the simulation generation engine moves on to first gathering together the various components that are present in the model and writing the necessary methods to instantiate them as agents in the simulation. First, the generation engine compiles a list of all the different components present in the simulation, both biotic and abiotic. This also involves checking for components duplicated across multiple nodes. Then, the engine iterates over all present components and calls on each to automatically write the code necessary to define themselves as agents into the simulation file.

A noteworthy element of the automatic generation of code for agents in the NetLogo simulation is that in many ways, generating the code itself is agent-based. Within the causal model that users construct, the components themselves have certain variables in their class structures. As Figure 3 illustrates, some of these parameters are toggleable: the user can toggle whether or not certain variables are monitored by a counter on the right, graphed by a line in the chart, or controlled by a slider on the left. Other controls presented here manipulate the visualization of the specific component or the range of potential values for user input when executing the simulations. In addition to the settings presented here, there are certain predefined features within each component as well, such as the variables associated with biotic or abiotic components. These are arguably the most important among these settings as proper values for the initial state of the simulation play a significant role in determining the usefulness of the outcome. Each individual component in the model holds these parameters internally. When the generation engine is ready to write the code for these components, it calls these components one by one, passing them the file to which to write the simulation, and each one writes the code necessary to define itself as an agent. In this way, one can visualize this process as the agents writing their own code for the simulation!

When creating these agents, the generation engine applies certain assumptions to the structures and behaviors of these agents. These assumptions pertain to behaviors and other requirements that typically must be manually coded into the agents in NetLogo simulations. Thus, a major part of the work performed by the generation engine is in intelligently determining what can be assumed about these agents. While the user has control over the initial values of all of the variables present in the simulation, the assumptions herein presuppose initial conditions that would be plausible in an actual ecological system.

Abiotic agents come with a relatively simple set of assumptions. As passive, non-volitional agents, the movement of abiotic agents is assumed to be random. Upon creation, each abiotic agent is given a direction, and this direction changes pseudo-randomly throughout the duration of the agent's presence in the simulation. Abiotic agents do not reproduce to create new instances of themselves, and they do not disappear from the simulation unless removed by the activity of some agent. Abiotic agents can produce

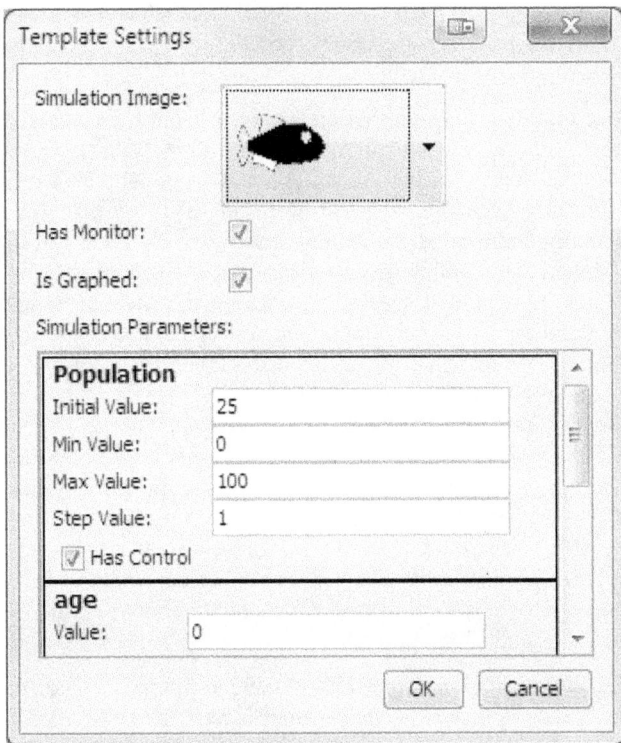

Figure 3: In this box, users annotate their model components and relationships with information for the simulation.

other biotic or abiotic agents as dictated by the model, but they do not have any automatic behaviors toward self-replication or destruction.

Biotic agents, on the other hand, come with more assumptions. First, MILA–S's simulation generation engine assumes that biotic agents have two inherent behaviors of life: reproducing and dying. All biotic agents are assumed to have a reproduction process. The user can modify the variables associated with this process, specifically the odds of reproducing (reducing it to 0 if no reproduction is desired), but the initial assumption is that any living agent in the simulation must be able to reproduce. Second, the generation engine assumes that all biotic agents have conditions under which they die. Initially, this is assumed to be a certain age threshold after which the likelihood of death increases as the agent's age increases. Agents can also die from lack of energy (the effect of a lack of food, oxygen, or carbon dioxide), although this only takes place in the presence of an external energy source, which is optional.

Managing Interactions Among Agents

With the simulation boilerplate and agent definitions in place, MILA–S' simulation generation engine proceeds to the most complex part of the simulation process: generating the interactions between agents in the simulation. Like the code for the individual agents, the code for interactions is similarly contained within the components. As we described earlier, each connection between two nodes in the CMP causal model has an origin and a destination; the component associated with the origin contains a reference to the connection itself. After iterating over all the components and writing them as agents in the simulation, the engine reiterates over all the components. In this new iteration, the generation engine iterates over all the connections of each component and writes them as interactions in the simulation. The simulation agent for each component in the causal model is called to write its interactions into the simulation code.

First, the engine defines the conditions under which the interaction will occur based on the interaction's prototype For example, a 'consumption' prototype occurs whenever a biotic agent intersects with the abiotic component it consumes while its energy level is below a certain threshold. Similarly, a 'production' prototype occurs at a regular rate as defined within the connection's properties screen (similar to that shown in Figure 3). A 'becomes upon death' prototype occurs whenever an agent's 'death' method is invoked. Thus, the engine determines when each specific interaction is triggered.

Second, the engine calls on the agents to define the actual bodies of their interactions. Each interaction prototype has an abstract definition; this abstract definition contains slots for the variables and operands of the specific components on which the interaction operates. In writing their relationships, the agents input their specific variables into the appropriate slots in the interaction prototype, then output the completed interaction definition into the simulation code itself. Then, for each such interaction definition, the agent writes the additional code necessary to realize the full spectrum of the interaction. For example, in the case of the 'consumes' interaction, the agent being consumed must call its 'death' method (if biotic) upon consumption. In this way, while the interaction is initiated by the component on the origin side of the connection, the component on the destination side must also behave in certain ways to realize the interaction in the simulation.

Like the definitions of the agents in the simulation, MILA–S's simulation generation engine also makes certain assumptions about the interactions among the agents. The most significant assumption it makes is that any time an agent is defined as consuming another agent, it is assumed that this consumption is necessary to the agent's survival. For example, the model in Figure 1 shows that fish consume oxygen. Based solely on this relationship, the simulation generation engine infers that fish rely on oxygen to survive. Oxygen, then, is connected in the simulation to the fish's energy level. This energy level decreases automatically over time and the fish relies on oxygen to replenish it. If, however, the biotic agent does not have a consumption relationship with anything else in the model, the engine infers that the agent does not rely on any external consumption to survive, and as a result the biotic agent does not die from a drop in energy.

Several similar assumptions are made based on the different types of relationships present in the models. The simulation generation engine similarly infers that if a biotic agent consumes multiple other components, the agent requires all of them to survive. When a biotic agent consumes another agent, it is inferred that that consumption provides energy to the biotic agent, and that the consumed agent ought to be removed from the simulation. When an abiotic agent, such as ammonia, is said to destroy the population of a biotic agent, such as a fish, it is inferred that contact with that agent kills the biotic agent immediately; if, on the other hand, the ammonia is drawn as destroying the energy of the fish, then contact with ammonia lowers the fish's energy level, potentially eventually leading to death. All of these assumptions and inferences are principles or relationships that would typically have to be coded into the simulation manually, and broadly represent much of the work and overhead required in such a process. By intelligently extrapolating from the model necessary details like these, MILA–S helps make it significantly easier to use and modify NetLogo simulations and thus enables the rapid construction and revision of CMP causal models.

Managing Visualization & Interactions
After creating all the agents and interactions present in the simulation, MILA–S's simulation generation engine iterates over the agents in the simulation and their interactions, and

creates the visualizations and controls necessary to observe and modify the parameters of the visualization at runtime. For each component variable that is designated to have a control (as shown in Figure 3), a slider is added on the left. Each variable that is monitored is given a monitor on the right and a line on the graph. Finally, the individual agents are added to the visualization for appropriate tracking and movement. After this, the simulation is ready to be run by the user whenever the user wants.

TESTING & ANALYSIS
MILA–S was pilot tested with about 50 7th grade life science students in a middle school in the near Atlanta, USA. The pilot study of MILA–S took place after more rigorous testing of other pieces of the MILA learning environment. In the larger experiment, about 250 students spent two weeks using MILA without the simulation generation component. During this time, they investigated the sudden death of thousands of fish in a lake in downtown Atlanta. Students were asked to use MILA to investigate this system and explain what had caused so many fish to suddenly die with no external signs of disease or trauma. For these two weeks, students posed multiple hypotheses, consulted several sources, participated in laboratory procedures regarding acidity and chemical contamination, and researched similar events in other ecological systems. During this time, students also used three static NetLogo simulations. These three simulations were not generated based on students' causal models, but rather were written by domain experts prior to the use of the system. Specifically, these simulations covered fish breeding behaviors, algae behaviors in different seasons, and the interaction between fish, algae, oxygen, and carbon dioxide.

The middle school teachers teaching the unit then selected about 50 students for the pilot study with MILA–S. These students were asked to construct a causal model that, when simulated, would give the same results as those that were actually observed in the Atlanta lake in which thousands of fish had died. In this way, students began engagement with MILA–S with two weeks of experience with conceptual modeling in MILA, manipulating NetLogo simulations, and the ecosystem which they aimed to explain. For this pilot experiment, the students worked in small teams of two to three. While students were only given 50 minutes to use MILA–S during this study, their prior experience with the learning environment and content knowledge led to quick engagement with the assignment, and all teams were able to construct and simulate non-trivial models by the end of the session. In fact, most teams were able to engage in at least one cycle of model construction, simulation use, model revision, and simulation reuse.

During interaction with MILA–S, screenshots were taken of students' workspaces, microphones were used to record students' conversations, and researchers watched in person for student behaviors. This data, along with the final projects that students constructed, log data from the software on the construction process, and feedback from students entered into the software's notepad, was used to conduct the following analysis.

Testing Analysis
The goal of this pilot study was to evaluate the usability and usefulness of MILA–S. Thus, evaluation and analysis has taken a qualitative design-based research approach, aimed at discerning the natural behaviors in which students engage while using MILA–S as well as the challenges or opportunities for future development of the process. Thus, analysis attempts to answer three questions: (1) How did students interact with MILA–S; (2) What difficulties did they encounter with MILA–S; and (3) What opportunities are there for future development of MILA–S?

Student Behavior
Students were given relatively limited advanced instruction on the process of model construction and simulation. As referenced previously, the goal provided to students was to create a simulation (by first creating a causal model) that led to the same results as the actual phenomenon. Students were told that 'same results' can mean two things: at a basic level, it means that all the fish in the simulation die as they did in the lake; at an advanced level, it means that all the fish die *and* other observed phenomena, such as the rising level of carbon dioxide, the falling level of oxygen, and the rising population of algae, also occur, with minimal coincidence of absent phenomena, such as a sudden change in weather patterns.

Given only this guidance, the majority of student teams engaged in a (surprisingly) sophisticated process of modeling and simulation. Teams began by modeling simple relationships they already believed to be true from their previous research on the system in the earlier unit; a few teams started by opening their previous projects as well to keep available for consultation and information. All teams generated their first simulation early in the engagement; no teams attempted to model the entire system accurately before attempting to run a simulation.

The projects of one particular team are used earlier in this paper in Figure 1 and Figure 2 to illustrate the workings of MILA–S. Figure 1 shows the initial model that this team constructed before every running a simulation; Figure 2 shows the first simulation this team ran after constructing that initial model. This team then ran their simulation a few more times to discern repeated patterns; they observed specifically that fish populations rise and fall with the rise and fall of oxygen concentration, and that oxygen concentrations fall and rise with the rise and fall of fish populations, creating a feedback cycle. However, they also observed that this cycle never caused the fish to die out altogether, as happened in the lake. They speculated that this relationship alone could never cause the fish to die off altogether because the oxygen would always rebound when the fish population dropped. They also noted that their simulation did not capture other substances believed to be significant, especially algae and carbon dioxide. Equipped with this feedback, they set about revising their model.

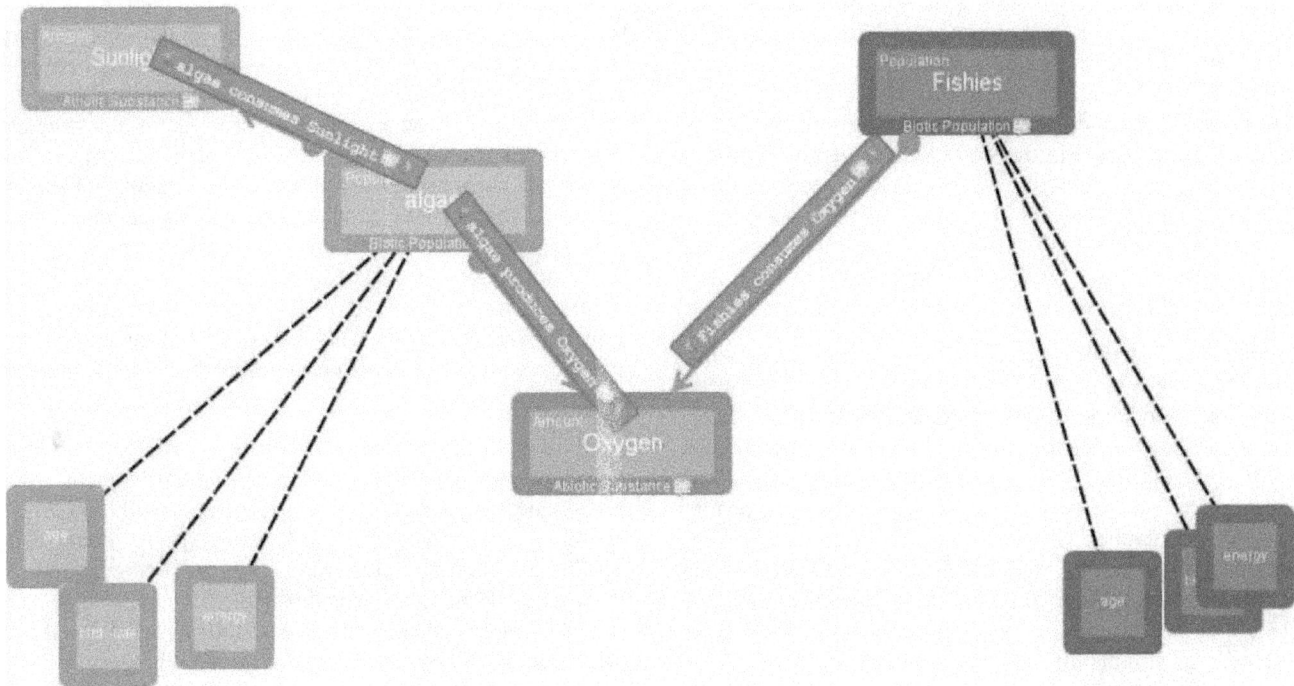

Figure 4: The revision of the model shown in Figure 1 constructed by the group after receiving feedback from the simulation shown in Figure 2.

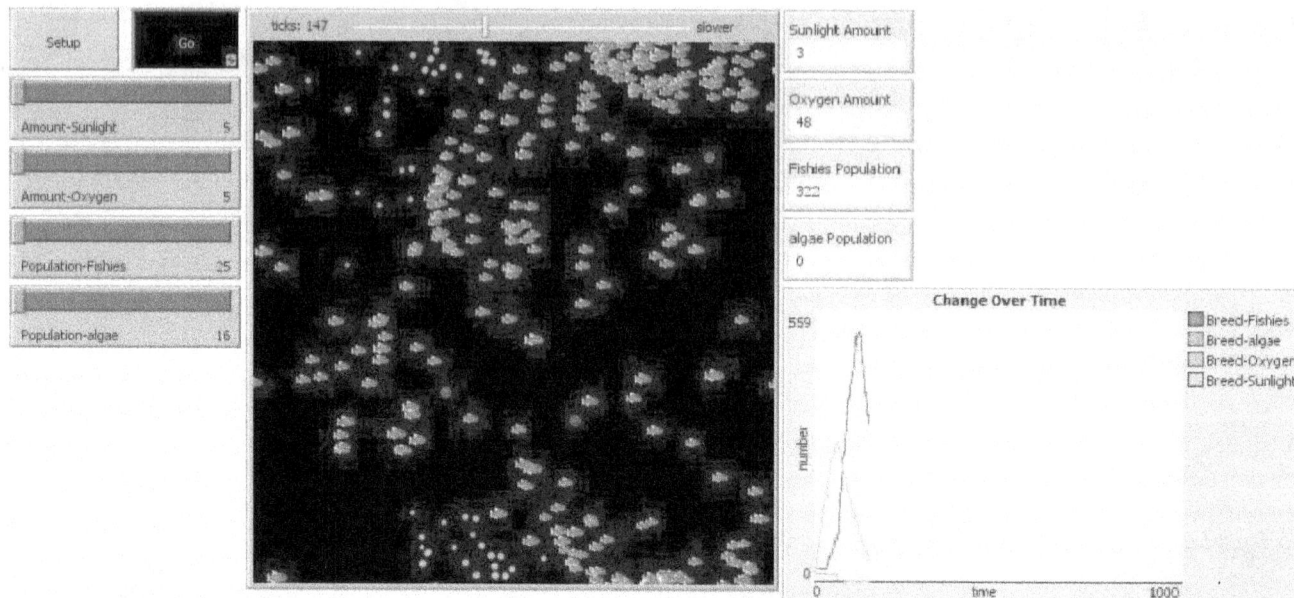

Figure 5: The simulation generated from the model shown in Figure 4.

The initial revision of the team's model is shown in Figure 4. Based on their observations, students revised their description of the way in which oxygen is generated in the system: instead of viewing it simply as being created by sunlight, they included the biotic component algae as the consumer of sunlight and producer of oxygen. Because algae is a biotic component, the simulation generated from this model inferred certain biological principles about algae, most notably that in the presence of excess sunlight, it would grow in population. Subsequently, in the presence of excess oxygen, fish, too, would grow in population given the absence of an additional limiting energy source (such as food). Then, as noted in the simulation shown in Figure 5, the spike in fish population causes the oxygen concentration to drop. Algae, serving as the intermediary in generating oxygen, does not create oxygen fast enough to prevent the fish population from crashing to extinction. The screenshot provided in Figure 5 depicts the start of this crash.

Throughout this process, students demonstrated a mature understanding and execution of the feedback cycle between conceptual modeling and simulation. Students naturally, with no specific guidance in this direction from teachers or researchers (except what was provided during the initial study preceding this study), began using observed results from the simulations to inform their continued construction of their models. In this way, students demonstrated the four cycles of model construction suggested by the literature [13]: they constructed a model initially, used the model through the simulation, evaluated the model through the results of the simulation, and revised the model for another iteration of the cycle. The process seen in this team was seen in the majority of teams as well based on preliminary

analysis of model construction logs and screenshots of interaction behaviors.

Broader Trends

To better understand the process of model construction across the various student teams, a case study analysis was conducted on the course of model construction and revision. Three significant trends were observed. First, for a majority of teams, the initial phase of model construction consisted primarily of testing out the connections between conceptual model and simulations than explicitly trying to accurately model the system. Multiple teams constructed models and made changes early on not necessarily in an attempt to more accurately describe the system, but rather to understand the way in which certain connections in the models would manifest in the simulations. For most (but not all) teams, this process preceded actual attempts to accurately model the system, and many teams completely started over once they had attained a decent working knowledge of the connection between the models and the simulations.

A second trend marked a qualitative difference in the modeling process present in the earlier engagement with MILA and that present during engagement with MILA–S. Models constructed previously in MILA could be considered "retrospective" in that they attempted to specifically capture a particular series of events that had actually transpired in the lake. Models constructed in MILA–S, on the other hand, were largely "prospective" in that they aimed to provide not only an account of what had actually happened, but also an account of what would have happened under different conditions. Although a subtle

296

difference, this shift represented a significant fundamental change in the exercise's purpose, from modeling a series of events to modeling a collection of relationships.

Finally, a third trend reflected the unique way in which conceptual models and simulations, when used together, allow students to execute the documented process of model construction [1, 5]. The literature largely breaks the process into phases of model construction, use, evaluation, and revision. Examining students' model construction activities under this framework, students can be seen using the conceptual models and generated simulations as two versions of the same underlying model. Model construction is performed in the conceptual model, while model use and evaluation are conducted using the generated NetLogo simulation. Students use these simulations to see what their model predicts would have happened under the circumstances observed in the system, then evaluate how well those predictions match the actual observations. Based on this evaluation, students then revise the original model to more accurately capture the system and repeat the cycle.

Challenges
The trajectory of model construction, use, evaluation, and revision shown in Figure 1, Figure 2, Figure 4, and Figure 5 demonstrates only approximately half of this team's interaction. Similarly, many other teams reached this stage with plenty of time to continue forward. However, a challenge arose in nearly all teams at approximately this point. MILA–S provided an effective framework at simulating the interactions between a small number of components and their variables; however, the systems that students were examining involved several more components than these, along with multiple relationships between their variables. Upon reaching a level of complexity slightly above what is shown in Figure 4, the NetLogo simulations generated by MILA–S stopped providing meaningful feedback to students. The number of agents would explode based on the multiple consumption and production relationships at play, slowing the simulation down and rendering the visualization elements indistinguishable. Repeated runs of the same simulation with the same initial parameters generated wildly varied responses as the number of agents and methods exacerbated the influence of random chance on the simulation's outcomes. These challenges are documented in similar attempts to create bridges between conceptual models and formal simulations [10, 11].

It is still likely that with the proper parameters and relationships, MILA–S could still have generated usable simulations that gave meaningful feedback; the challenge that arose is that most executions of the simulations gave limited or no feedback as to the changes that needed to be made to more closely replicate the real phenomenon. Too much noise existed in these simulations to continue to facilitate the evaluation and revision process. Future work in this direction, then, needs to improve the intelligent

generation of simulations based on these conceptual models. Additional reasoning can be used to scope and limit the simulation space to remove the majority of this noise and emphasize the useful patterns. Specifically, this additional intelligence can emphasize a natural notion of carrying capacity to prevent the populations in the simulations from exploding. It can also generate more abstract and scalable relationships in the simulation by moving away from a one-to-one matching between conceptual relationships and simulation methods.

Opportunities
In addition to these positive takeaways, this work also presents two key opportunities for future development. First, the during model construction, use, evaluation, and revision process is similar to other processes encountered in other disciplines. Computer programming, for example, involves constructing, executing, observing, and revising a program. Similarly, industrial design uses a prototyping approach in which the designer constructs a prototype, tests it with users, evaluates their results, and revises it accordingly. Thus, there is a significant opportunity to use this approach to teaching scientific inquiry to teach about underlying general design process. Indeed, in a sister project, we have developed an interactive development environment for designing game-playing agents based on the same process of rapid modeling, simulation, evaluation, and revision [12].

Secondly, the opportunity presented by bridging the gap between conceptual models and simulations is not restricted solely to science education; it is an opportunity for real-world scientific pursuits as well. This curriculum was sculpted to teach this process precisely because it is so authentically analogous to scientific research [7], and the need for a bridge between conceptual models and computational simulations exists in the real domain as well. By enhancing this framework with added flexibility to define new interaction prototypes, an ontology of a broader assortment of variables, and a more intelligently restricted simulation space, MILA–S and similar tools can provide valuable information for real research in various domains.

CONCLUSIONS
This paper has presented the design of an interactive system called MILA–S for generating agent-based simulations from conceptual models of ecological systems. MILA–S not only enables construction of causal models of components and mechanisms in an ecosystem, but it also takes as input the causal model and autonomously generates an agent-based simulation that shows the temporal evolution of the system according to the causal model. The user needs to simply use a visual syntax for generating causal models and the interactive tool automatically generates the corresponding simulation. Further, because the simulation directly corresponds to the causal model, the

results of the simulation directly evaluate the model and point to the revisions needed in the model.

Preliminary results from a pilot study in middle school science indicate that MILA–S is both useful and usable as an interactive learning environment. MILA–S was usable in that the students in our study had little difficulty in using the interactive tool for model construction, use in simulation, evaluation of the simulation results in comparison to the real world, and revising the model accordingly. Further, MILA–S was useful in that the above process of modeling led the students to significantly better causal models. On one hand, this integration of conceptual modeling and executable simulations brings authentic scientific practice to middle school classrooms. On the other, this intelligent generation of agent-based simulations from causal models can inform the construction of similar systems for use in real scientific practice.

ACKNOWLEDGMENTS

We are grateful to Vickie Bates and Lara Catall, the teachers in this study, as well as to Kristina Strickland, Angela Gula, and Connie McCrary for the support provided. We also thank our colleagues at the Design & Intelligence Laboratory for many discussions about this work, especially Rochelle Lobo, David Majerich, Spencer Rugaber, and Swaroop Vattam.

REFERENCES

1. Clement, J. (2008). *Creative Model Construction in Scientists and Students: The Role of Imagery, Analogy, and Mental Simulation*. Dordrecht: Springer.

2. Darden, L. (1998). Anomaly-driven theory redesign: computational philosophy of science experiments. In T. W. Bynum, & J. Moor (Eds.), *The digital phoenix: how computers are changing philosophy*, (pp. 62–78). Oxford: Blackwell.

3. de Jong, T., & van Joolingen, W. R. (1998). Scientific discovery learning with computer simulations of conceptual domains. *Review of Educational Research, 68*(2), 179-201.

4. Goel, A., Rugaber, S., & Vattam, S. (2009). Structure, Behavior & Function of Complex Systems: The SBF Modeling Language. *AI for Engineering Design, Analysis and Manufacturing,* 23: 23-35.

5. Halloun, I. (2007). Mediated Modeling in Science Education. *Science & Education, 16*(7), 653-697.

6. Jackson, S., Krajcik, J., & Soloway, E. (2000) Model-It: A Design Retrospective. In M. Jacobson & R. Kozma (editors), *Innovations in Science and Mathematics Education: Advanced Designs for Technologies of Learning* (pp. 77-115). Lawrence Erlbaum.

7. Joyner, D., Majerich, D., & Goel, A. (2013). Facilitating authentic reasoning about complex systems in middle

school science education. In *Proc. 11th Annual Conference on Systems Engineering Research, Procedia Computer Science 16:* 1043-1052. Elsevier.

8. Machamer, P., Darden, L., Craver, C. (2000) Thinking about Mechanisms. *Philosophy of Science, 67*(1): 1-25.

9. Nersessian, N. (2008). *Creating Scientific Concepts.* Cambridge, MA: MIT Press.

10. Norling, E. (2007). Contrasting a system dynamics model and an agent-based model of food web evolution. In *Procs. Multi-Agent-Based Simulation VII,* LNAI 4442: 57-68, Springer.

11. Parunak, H., Savit, R., & Riolo, R. (1998). Agent-based modeling vs. equation-based modeling: A case study and users' guide. In *Procs. Multi-Agent Systems and Agent-Based Simulation*, LNAI 1534: 10-25, Springer..

12. Rugaber, S., Goel, A., & Martie, L. (2013) GAIA: A CAD Environment for Model-Based Adaptation of Game-Playing Software Agents. In *Procedia Computer Science 16:*29-38.

13. Schwarz, C., Reiser, B., Davis, E., Kenyon, L., Achér, A., Fortus, D., Shwartz, Y., Hug, B., & Krajcik, J. (2009). Developing a learning progression for scientific modeling: Making scientific modeling accessible and meaningful for learners. *Journal of Research in Science Teaching, 46*(6), 632-654.

14. Vattam, S. S., Goel, A. K., & Rugaber, S. (2011). Behavior Patterns: Bridging Conceptual Models and Agent-Based Simulations in Interactive Learning Environments. In *Proc. 11th IEEE International Conference on Advanced Learning Technologies (ICALT-2011), July 2011.* 139-141. IEEE.

15. Vattam, S., Goel, A., Rugaber, S., Hmelo–Silver, C., Jordan, R., Gray, S, & Sinha, S. (2011) Understanding Complex Natural Systems by Articulating Structure-Behavior-Function Models. *Journal of Educational Technology & Society,* 14(1): 66-81.

16. White, B, & Frederiksen, J. (1990) Causal Model Progressions as a Foundation of Intelligence Learning Environments. *Artificial Intelligence*, 42(1): 99-157.

17. Wilensky, U., & Reisman, K. (2006). Thinking Like a Wolf, a Sheep, or a Firefly: Learning Biology Through Constructing and Testing Computational Theories-An Embodied Modeling Approach. *Cognition and Instruction*, 24(2), 171-209.

18. Wilensky, U., & Resnick, M. (1999). Thinking in levels: A dynamic systems approach to making sense of the world. *Journal of Science Education and Technology*, 8, 3-19.

19. Winsberg, E. (2001). Simulations, models, and theories: Complex physical systems and their representations. *Philosophy of Science*, S442–S454.

Adaptive Click-and-Cross: Adapting to Both Abilities and Task Improves Performance of Users With Impaired Dexterity

Louis Li
Harvard SEAS
33 Oxford St., Cambridge, MA, USA
louis@seas.harvard.edu

Krzysztof Z. Gajos
Harvard SEAS
33 Oxford St., Cambridge, MA, USA
kgajos@eecs.harvard.edu

ABSTRACT

Computer users with impaired dexterity often have difficulty accessing small, densely packed user interface elements. Past research in software-based solutions has mainly employed two approaches: modifying the interface and modifying the interaction with the cursor. Each approach, however, has limitations. Modifying the user interface by enlarging interactive elements makes access efficient for simple interfaces but increases the cost of navigation for complex ones by displacing items to screens that require tabs or scrolling to reach. Modifying the interaction with the cursor makes access possible to unmodified interfaces but may perform poorly on densely packed targets or require the user to perform multiple steps. We developed a new approach that combines the strengths of the existing approaches while minimizing their shortcomings, introducing only minimal distortion to the original interface while making access to frequently used parts of the user interface efficient and access to all other parts possible. We instantiated this concept as Adaptive Click-and-Cross, a novel interaction technique. Our user study demonstrates that, for sufficiently complex interfaces, Adaptive Click-and-Cross slightly improves the performance of users with impaired dexterity compared to only modifying the interface or only modifying the cursor.

Keywords: Accessibility; area cursors; adaptive user interface

ACM Classification Keywords

H.5.m. Information Interfaces and Presentation (e.g. HCI): Miscellaneous

INTRODUCTION

Computer users with impaired dexterity often have difficulty with mainstream user interfaces, especially when these user interfaces contain small, densely-packed interactive elements.

In the past few decades, a variety of software-based techniques have emerged to assist such users. These approaches fall broadly into two categories: those that modify the user interface itself (e.g., ability-based user interfaces generated with SUPPLE [8]) and those that modify the user's interaction with the mouse pointer (e.g., area cursor [15], bubble cursor [11], enhanced area cursors such as Click-and-Cross [3]).

Approaches that modify the interaction in order to adapt the user's abilities to the existing user interface make access possible without requiring substantial modifications to existing interfaces. However, these techniques may lack generality (e.g., area cursors and the bubble cursor enhance interaction only when clickable elements are sparsely laid out), or they may reduce the efficiency of the interaction (e.g., the Click-and-Cross technique from Findlater et al. [3] replaces a single click with two operations: a click in the vicinity of the desired target followed by a crossing action to make a specific selection, Figure 1a).

In contrast, approaches that adapt the user interface to the user's abilities by modifying the user interface enable efficient access to each item, optimizing the interaction to each user's strengths [8, 21]. However, adapting user interfaces to the abilities of users with impaired dexterity involves an important trade off: such adaptations typically involve making clickable elements larger at the cost of increased navigational complexity. This requires more scrolling and tab switching when navigating between user interface elements. Existing approaches often enlarge all clickable elements — even those that users rarely access — because not enlarging them might render them inaccessible. The increased navigational complexity from such a broad approach is a source of inefficiency.

We set out to combine the strengths of the two approaches: making access possible and efficient while minimizing modifications of the original design. To do this, we build on a third adaptive approach: user interfaces that adapt themselves to the user's *task* (e.g., [2, 6, 9, 18]). Such interfaces have been demonstrated to improve users' performance by leveraging predictive models for each user's actions to ease access to the features that the user is most likely to access next (e.g., by copying them to a more easily accessible location, by making them larger or more visually salient).

Building on these three ideas of adaptation, we have developed Adaptive Click-and-Cross. As illustrated in Figure 1, with Adaptive Click-and-Cross, user interface elements that are predicted to be most frequently accessed by the user are enlarged and can be accessed efficiently with a single click (adapting the interface to the user, adapting the interface to the task). The remaining elements are left unmodified and can be accessed through the Click-and-Cross technique: the user can click anywhere in the vicinity of the desired target and subsequently refine the selection with a crossing interaction (adapting the user's abilities to the interface). This approach achieves three things: it enables *efficient* access to frequently accessed user interface elements, makes access to all other

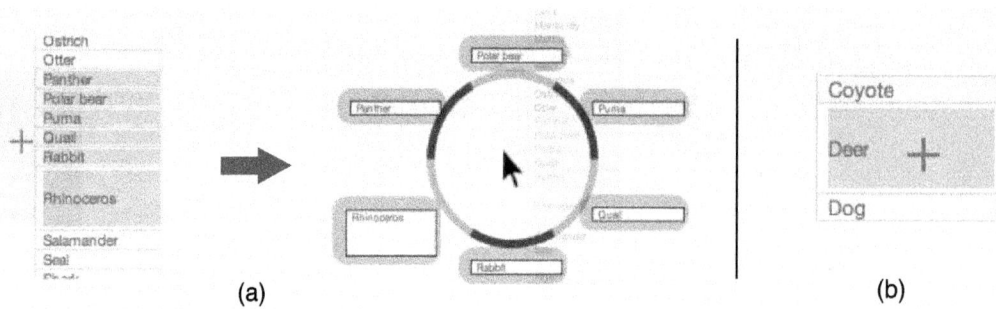

Figure 1: Adaptive Click-and-Cross. **(a)** When users click near or directly on small targets, Click-and-Cross is triggered: a circular overlay of the nearby targets appears. Users can then cross through the corresponding arc to select the item. **(b)** Users can directly click on a large target to select it.

elements *possible*, and minimizes the distortion of modifying the user interface.

The results of our study with 12 participants of impaired dexterity demonstrate that for a complex user interface (where enlarging all interface elements substantially increases the cost of navigation), Adaptive Click-and-Cross results in significantly shorter task completion times compared to either adapting the interface by enlarging all elements or Click-and-Cross alone. We observed no significant differences in error rates or subjective preference across the three techniques. However, participants subjectively perceived the interface with all elements enlarged as more efficient than either Click-and-Cross or Adaptive Click-and-Cross.

RELATED WORK

Many existing software solutions improve accessibility by modifying users' methods of interaction. Such solutions may adapt the behavior of a pointing cursor to the user (e.g., Steady Clicks [19], Angle Mouse [22]), or they may introduce entirely new interaction techniques (e.g., area cursor [15], bubble cursor [11], enhanced area cursors [3]).

Approaches that directly modify the user interface have also been investigated. These approaches advocate adapting the user interface to users' needs (e.g., EyeDraw [13] and Voice-Draw [12]). Although creating accessible designs that are well suited to a particular set of abilities can be time consuming, previous work has begun to demonstrate how such modifications could be automated [8].

However, for complex user interfaces, adapting the user interface to the abilities of users with impaired dexterity requires either reducing the available functionality to fit all elements on the screen [13, 12] or increasing navigational complexity by requiring more scrolling, switching between tab panes, etc. [8]. Recent work has examined the efficacy of on-demand expansion of targets (i.e., dynamically expanding the target after the user begins to move the cursor in its direction) [14]. This approach prevents targets from being enlarged unnecessarily, minimizing the potential increase in navigational complexity from enlarging targets. While the experimental results show that the approach improves performance, its effectiveness is likely to diminish in densely packed user interfaces.

Adaptive Click-and-Cross aims to minimize the costs of modifying the user interface by leveraging past results showing that most users only access a small subset of the available

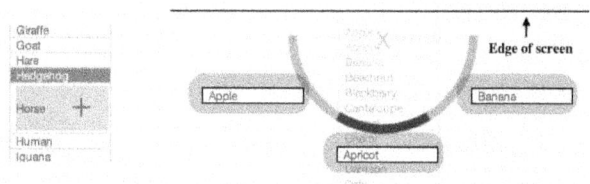

Figure 2: **(a)** In Adaptive Click-and-Cross, when target is bordered by an enlarged item, the target has a decreased amount of space for activating Click-and-Cross. **(b)** Near the edge of the screen, the Click-and-Cross cursor only displays a subset of the circle.

functionality, though each user accesses a *different* subset [10, 17]. This finding has been used to design user interfaces that enable efficient access to a subset of items that are predicted to be of most use to the user. For example, in split interfaces [5, 6, 18], the elements predicted to be most useful are duplicated to a convenient location to support more immediate access. In contrast, morphing menus [1, 20], which have been tested with able-bodied users, do not duplicate elements but instead enlarge predicted items to enable efficient access.

ADAPTIVE CLICK-AND-CROSS

The original Click-and-Cross technique [3] is illustrated in Figure 1a: when the user clicks near or directly on a user interface element, a circular overlay is displayed with several (up to six in our implementation) of the closest interface elements laid out along the circumference. Moving the mouse such that it crosses the circumference triggers a "click" on the corresponding element. If the first click was made by mistake, performing another click inside the circle cancels the interaction.

In Adaptive Click-and-Cross, a small number of the user interface elements — those predicted to be of immediate use to the user — are enlarged to enable efficient access with a direct click (Figure 1b). For the remaining elements, which may be too small for a user to access reliably, Adaptive Click-and-Cross employs the Click-and-Cross technique.

The appearance of the cursor changes depending on the position of the pointer (Figure 1). By default, the cursor is an *area cursor [15]:* a translucent, gray rectangle with a crosshair in the center. When placed directly over an enlarged item, the gray rectangle disappears, but the underlying item is highlighted in gray. When the cursor is not over an enlarged element, the cursor will resize in order to surround those targets that are projected to appear if Click-and-Cross is acti-

No.	Method	Age	Device	Gender	Condition
1	Remote	59	Mouse	M	Essential tremor
2	Remote	23	Touchpad	M	C-6 quadraplegic
3	Remote	49	Mouse	F	Spinal stenosis, ruptured cervical disks
4	Remote	62	Mouse	F	Multiple sclerosis
5	Remote	38	Mouse	F	Ankylosing spondylitis, fibromyalgia
6	Remote	42	Mouse	F	Duchene muscular dystrophy
7	Remote	65	Trackball	M	Spinal cord injury
8	Remote	38	Mouse	M	Spinal cord injury
9	Remote	43	Headmouse	M	Cerebral palsy
10	Remote	19	Mouse	F	Familiar essential tremor, Parkinson's
11	In-person	49	Trackball	F	Multiple sclerosis
12	In-person	59	Trackball	M	Multiple sclerosis

Table 1: Our participants.

vated. For useful visual feedback, these targets will also be highlighted in gray. Upon activation of the Click-and-Cross cursor, the gray rectangle disappears, revealing a traditional point cursor for making the crossing selection.

In situations where only a part of the circle can be rendered on the screen, such as when the initial click occurs near the edge of the screen (Figure 2b), the area cursor is appropriately resized to provide accurate visual feedback as to which items can be accessed.

When activated, the Click-and-Cross cursor also includes enlarged items in the overlay, meaning that enlarged items can be acquired either through Click-and-Cross or direct clicks.

EXPERIMENT

Participants. Twelve people (six male, aged 19–65) with dexterity impairments participated in the study. Table 1 provides additional details about each participant.

Two people participated in person and 10 remotely. Recent work has provided compelling evidence showing that performance evaluations of user interfaces can be performed reliably with remote participants [16], provided that a few basic safeguards (such as testing for instruction comprehension, selecting appropriate outlier removal criteria) are maintained. We have built on those insights to ensure reliability of the results collected from our remote participants.

Apparatus. The experiment was implemented as a web site written in HTML, CSS, and JavaScript. Remote participants completed the study using their own computers and devices. To ensure consistency between participants, remote participants were asked to reset the zoom levels on their browsers and make their browser windows as large as possible, and the visible portion of the scrolling menu interface (i.e., the number of items displayed at a given scroll position) was held constant at 475 pixels. A summary of the input devices used by the participants can be found in Table 1.

Tasks. Building on prior empirical research on adaptive user interfaces [1, 4, 5, 20], we chose menu selection as our experimental task. This task naturally supports manipulation of navigational complexity (i.e., by changing what fraction of the menu is visible in the application window, we could control how much scrolling was required on average to reach a menu item [5]).

We tested four designs in the study. Abbreviations for each design are used throughout the paper.

1. *Enlarged* (ENLG): traditional cursor pointing with all menu items enlarged (80×40 pixels);

2. *Click-and-Cross* (CNC): the Click-and-Cross cursor, menu items are the default size (80×10 pixels);

3. *Adaptive Click-and-Cross* (ACNC): a menu where some items are large and can be acquired directly through normal clicking, and some items are the default size and can be acquired using Click-and-Cross;

4. *Baseline* (BASE): traditional mouse pointing, menu items are the default size.

The order of the conditions was counterbalanced using a partial Latin square design. The tasks in each condition were isomorphic, but each condition used a different vocabulary (i.e., fruits, vegetables, animals, colors) and differed in the order of the sets of trials within each condition. In each design, the menu interface consisted of 60 items.

The targets that participants had to acquire during the experiment were distributed uniformly throughout the menu. In CNC and BASE conditions (where all items were the default size), this resulted in approximately 60% of the trials with targets on the first screen — those targets could be acquired without scrolling. In the ENLG condition, where all menu items were enlarged, fewer items were visible on the screen at once: in only 20% of the trials the desired targets could be reached without scrolling. In the ACNC condition, where only a small fraction of the items were enlarged while the rest were the default size, in 50% of the trials the desired targets could be accessed without scrolling.

In the ACNC condition, we simulated a system with a 70% accuracy in predicting what menu items the user would use. Similarly to others [2, 5, 6, 7], we did so by designing the experimental task such that 70% of the items that the participants were asked to select in that condition were enlarged, while the remaining 30% were not. This is a popular experimental paradigm that allows adaptive user interfaces to be evaluated under reasonable assumptions about accuracy of the predictive algorithm that might be used.

Procedure. Each participant first filled out a demographic survey containing questions about his or her computer usage and motor and/or visual impairments. Participants then proceeded to the main part of the experiment. For each participant, there were 4 conditions × 5 blocks × 10 trials = 200 trials. At the beginning of each condition, each participant was presented with an instructional video describing the cursor behavior or the condition. The first block of each condition was a practice block, allowing the participant to become accustomed to the design. Performance on the practice blocks was not included in the analysis. Thus, the analysis for each participant were performed using 4 conditions × 4 blocks × 10 trials = 160 trials. At the end of each condition, participants rated the condition on a 7-point Likert scale on how easy, tiring, or efficient they found the particular design to be. At the end of the study, each participant ranked the conditions in order of overall preference and perceived efficiency. The study took 40 to 80 minutes depending on individual abilities.

Design and Analysis. We used a within-subjects factorial design for our analysis with Design {ENLG, CNC, ACNC} as the main factor.

We did not necessarily expect to see benefits of any of the adaptations compared to the non-adaptive baseline: the results of a prior evaluation of CNC [3] suggest that the technique provides substantial performance benefits for very small targets (8 pixels or smaller) or for participants with severely impaired dexterity. In our experiment, we used larger targets (80×10 pixels) to ensure that minor visual impairments, which are common among elderly participants, would not preclude participation in our study. Additionally, most of our participants had moderate rather than severe dexterity impairments. For these reasons, we excluded the non-adaptive baseline from our analysis, but we do include those results for completeness.

The main measures in this experiment were *target acquisition time*, computed over error-free trials, and *error rate*, computed as the fraction of the trials that contained at least one error. Subjective measures for each condition also included *perceived efficiency*, *perceived fatigue*, *perceived ease of use*, *efficiency ranking*, and *overall preference ranking*.

The following (within-subjects) factors were also included in some of the follow-up analyses:

- On First Screen {Yes, No}: We recorded whether an item was *on the first screen* — the initial part of the menu presented to the participant — meaning that the participant did not have to scroll to acquire the target.

- On Edge {Yes, No}: For CNC and ACNC, we recorded whether an item was *on the edge* of the visible part of the application window at the time of acquisition. Because only part of the circular overlay is shown when there is not enough space for the circle, this could potentially impact acquisition time (Figure 2b).

- Bordered by Enlarged Item {Yes, No}: For ACNC specifically, we recorded whether the target item was *bordered by an enlarged item*. Because enlarged items could immediately be acquired by the user through a normal click, small items bordering an enlarged item had less space in which the area cursor could be triggered (Figure 2a).

In total, data were collected for 1440 acquisition trials. Trials with acquisition times outside of two interquartile ranges from the median were discarded as outliers ($42/1440 = 2.9\%$ of the trials). To account for the wide range of individual abilities, the outlier removal procedure was performed separately for each participant. This median-based approach was selected over the standard approach of discarding trials outside of ± 2 standard deviations, as it is more robust for remote experiments, where extreme outliers may heavily impact the mean and standard deviation [16]. After discarding outliers, timing data were log-transformed to account for the skewed distribution found in such data.

Analysis of acquisition time was performed using repeated measures analysis of variance. We used binomial logistic regression to examine the effect of condition on error rate, because a binary measure was used to capture whether an error occurred in each trial. The subjective results were analyzed using non-parametric Friedman tests. The findings for subjective data that were statistically significant were followed up with pairwise Wilcoxon tests with Bonferroni correction.

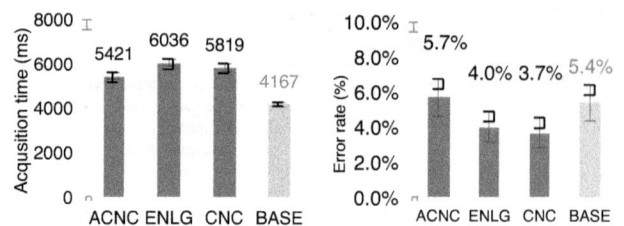

Figure 3: Mean acquisition times and error rates for each condition. Error bars represent ± 1 standard error of the mean (SEM). Baseline is included for completeness but was not included in the analysis (see Design and Analysis for further discussion)

For the analyses specific to the effect of *On Edge* and *Bordered by Enlarged Item* on performance with CNC and ACNC, paired t-tests were used. Trials with errors were included in those analyses. Because these analyses were designed to investigate whether the activation of a partial circle (On Edge) or the reduced space for activation (Bordered By Enlarged Item) affected acquisition time, we focused on the scenarios where the user was likely to make an error, either from failing to include a target near the edge or attempting to activate CNC but instead clicking an enlarged item.

RESULTS

As discussed in *Design and Analysis*, we include the baseline results for completeness but perform our analyses on the three adaptive designs: ENLG, CNC, ACNC.

Preliminaries. We first conducted an analysis to test for the presence of any prominent learning effects. We used Condition and Block Number as factors and acquisition time as the dependent variable. We observed no significant effect of block on acquisition time ($F_{3,9} = 1.322, p = 0.327$). There was also no significant interaction between condition and block number ($F_{6,6} = 0.164, p = 0.978$). These results indicate that, on average, participants' performance did not vary systematically from block to block after they had completed the practice trial for each condition. Thus, all blocks were used in the subsequent analyses.

Overall acquisition times. We observed a significant main effect of Design on acquisition time ($F_{2,10} = 1.15, p < 0.05$). ACNC had the lowest average acquisition time of the three adaptive designs: 5.4 s for ACNC, 5.8 s for CNC, and 6.0 s for ENLG. These results are illustrated in Figure 3.

There was a significant interaction effect between Design and On First Screen ($F_{2,21} = 0.67, p < 0.005$). ENLG was the slowest overall, but for trials where targets were on the first screen and required no scrolling to acquire, ENLG was the fastest with an average acquisition time of 2.6 s. ACNC (3.8 s) was still faster than CNC (4.6 s). In contrast, when users had to scroll in order to reach the target item, ACNC and ENLG had comparable acquisition times (6.6 s v 6.7 s). CNC was again slower than the other two designs (7.0 s). These results are illustrated in Figure 4.

This supports the notion that, given large menu items that require no navigation to acquire, very large menu items are easy for users with dexterity impairments to acquire. However, despite the large speed advantage of ENLG when items are on the first screen, this advantage is offset in the overall acquisition times by the increased scrolling required in ENLG.

Errors. As illustrated in Figure 3, participants were slightly more likely to make an error with ACNC than with the other conditions, but the difference was not significant ($\chi^2(2) = 2.43, p = 0.30$).

Subjective Results. After each condition, participants rated the design they interacted with on a 7-point Likert scale for how easy, efficient, or physically tiring they felt the condition to be. There was no significant effect of condition on any of these perceived traits, though the perception of efficiency was marginally significant (easy: $\chi^2_{(2,n=12)} = 3.74, p = 0.15$, efficient: $\chi^2_{(2,n=12)} = 5.87, p = 0.053$, tiring:$\chi^2_{(2,n=12)} = 2.72, p = 0.26$) with participants perceiving the ENLG condition as being more efficient than the other two.

At the end of the study, participants ranked the designs in order of overall preference and perceived efficiency. There was a significant main effect of condition on subjective efficiency rankings ($\chi^2_{(2,N=12)} = 8.17, p < 0.05$). Pairwise comparisons showed that participants perceived ENLG to be more efficient than either CNC or ACNC, but there was no significant difference in efficiency rankings between CNC and ACNC. There was no significant effect of condition on the overall preference rankings ($\chi^2_{(2,N=12)} = 4.67, p = 0.097$).

The perceived efficiency of ENLG agreed with many of the comments from participants, who cited the enlarged elements in both ACNC and ENLG as favorable. One participant stated, "I liked the combined method the most, but with the large boxes ... I found the larger boxes easier to focus on and scroll over." Regarding the ENLG design, one participant said, "[The] target was larger, but [...] lots and lots of scrolling [was] needed."

Additional Analyses

We performed two additional analyses to investigate how design choices specific to CNC and ACNC impacted participants' performance.

Performance for targets located near the edge of the screen. In both CNC and ACNC, if a user clicks on a user interface element located at the edge of the screen, only a fraction of the circular overlay can be shown on the screen (Figure 2b). We conducted an additional analysis over trials from the CNC and ACNC condition with On Edge as the within subjects factor. In ACNC condition, only those trials where the CNC technique was used to acquire the target were included in this analysis. Because we expected both CNC and ACNC to be affected in the same way by targets on the edge of the screen, these trials were analyzed together.

We observed a marginally significant main effect of On Edge on acquisition time ($t_{23} = 1.58, p = 0.06$) in the CNC and ACNC conditions. Acquisition times for items near the edge were slightly shorter (6.4 s vs 5.8 s) (Figure 5).

Performance for targets that are bordered by enlarged items. In ACNC, some small menu items were bordered by enlarged items. These items had a decreased amount of space in which the CNC cursor could be activated (Figure 2a).

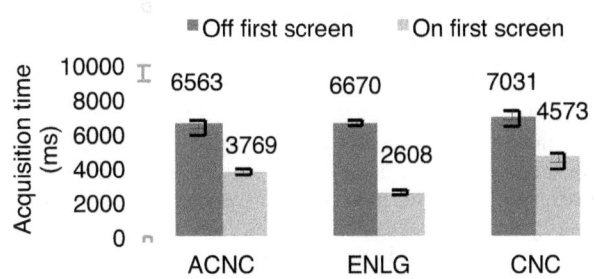

Figure 4: Mean acquisition times for each condition, grouped by whether or not the item was on the first screen presented to the user. Error bars represent ±1 SEM.

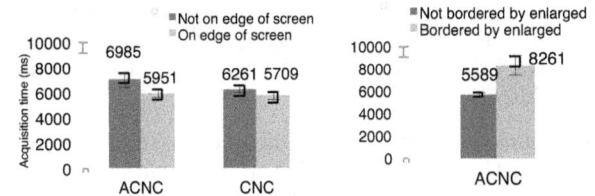

Figure 5: Mean acquisition times for ACNC and CNC, grouped by whether the target was (left) near the edge of the screen at the time of acquisition (for trials where the CNC technique was triggered) (right) bordered by an enlarged item. Error bars represent ±1 SEM.

We observed a significant main effect of whether an item was bordered by an enlarged item on acquisition time ($t_{11} = 6.33, p < 0.0001$). In examining trials where the target item was small (i.e., not predicted to be useful) but bordered by an enlarged target on either the top or bottom, acquisition times were substantially longer than for targets that were bordered only by regularly sized neighbors (8.3 s vs 5.6 s) (Figure 5).

DISCUSSION

This study explored one point in the design space of interaction techniques that combine multiple adaptations: our Adaptive Click-and-Cross technique, which combines adaptation to user's motor abilities with adaptation to a user's task, was designed to explore this concept in the context of improving the performance of users with dexterity impairments.

In our study, Adaptive Click-and-Cross was shown to result in significantly faster performance than either Enlarged or Click-and-Cross. There were no significant differences in accuracy across the three conditions. There were also no significant differences in subjective preferences across the three designs, though participants perceived the Enlarged design to be subjectively more efficient than either Adaptive Click-and-Cross or Click-and-Cross. However, participants' comments during interviews indicated that they were aware of the trade-off of enlarging all interactive elements: they commented on the ease of clicking on enlarged targets, but they also noted the increased effort required to scroll to the desired target.

Our study also allowed us to explore several practical considerations relevant to any real deployments of either Click-and-Cross or Adaptive Click-and-Cross. First, we investigated the performance of Click-and-Cross and Adaptive Click-and-Cross when used to access items near the edge of the window, where there is not enough space to display the full overlay for the subsequent crossing interaction. Our results show that performance on such targets is actually marginally faster than for targets placed in the middle of the screen where the entire circular overlay can be displayed.

Second, for Adaptive Click-and-Cross, our results show that acquisition time was negatively affected for non-enlarged targets that were bordered by an enlarged item. Because the enlarged item can be acquired through a direct click, the presence of the enlarged item reduces the available space for activating the Click-and-Cross interaction to acquire the neighboring non-enlarged item. This suggests a second design consideration for Adaptive Click-and-Cross: enlarging a larger number of items both increases the amount of scrolling required to navigate the interface *and* makes some of the non-enlarged items harder to access than they would have been with the Click-and-Cross technique alone. An important implication of this is that two enlarged items should be carefully placed such that there is enough space to acquire the non-enlarged items in between.

One limitation of our study was that most of the participants we recruited had only moderate levels of impairment. For that reason, we were not able to demonstrate the benefit of Adaptive Click-and-Cross over non-adaptive interfaces. However, we were able to meaningfully demonstrate that Adaptive Click-and-Cross improves participants' performance in comparison to two existing approaches: adapting the size of elements to users' motor abilities and Click-and-Cross, both of which had been previously shown to benefit users with severely impaired dexterity [3, 8].

While this study evaluated a single technique, Adaptive Click-and-Cross, varying further parameters can provide insight into the factors that affect such techniques, such as the choice of enhanced area cursor, different target sizes, predictive accuracy, and the severity of user impairments.

CONCLUSION

This work was spurred in part by the observation that the word "adaptive" is used to describe a multitude of different approaches in the context of interactive systems. We hypothesized that these approaches can be synergistically combined, and we explored this synergy through Adaptive Click-and-Cross, an interaction technique designed to improve the performance of users with severe dexterity impairments. Adaptive Click-and-Cross relies on knowledge of a user's task to combine two adaptive approaches: adapting frequently used interface elements to a user's motor abilities while using an adaptive accessibility technique (Click-and-Cross) to enable access to those elements that are unlikely to be used.

Our results demonstrate that Adaptive Click-and-Cross slightly improved efficiency without sacrificing accuracy compared to two previously studied adaptive approaches: enlarging all user interface elements, and Click-and-Cross. Our work explored one point in a large design space, but the results suggest that hybrid adaptive approaches are a promising area of inquiry.

Acknowledgements. We thank our anonymous participants, both those that participated remotely and those from The Boston Home. We thank Don Fredette from The Boston Home for his assistance in making this study possible. We also thank Katharina Reinecke, Pao Siangliulue, Steve Komarov and Ken Arnold for their feedback. This work was supported in part by an Alfred B. Sloan Research Fellowship and by the Mind, Brain and Behavior Faculty Award.

REFERENCES

1. Cockburn, A., Gutwin, C., and Greenberg, S. A predictive model of menu performance. In *Proc. CHI '07*, ACM (New York, NY, USA, 2007), 627–636.

2. Findlater, L., and Gajos, K. Z. Design space and evaluation challenges of adaptive graphical user interfaces. *AI Magazine 30*, 4 (2009), 68–73.

3. Findlater, L., Jansen, A., Shinohara, K., Dixon, M., Kamb, P., Rakita, J., and Wobbrock, J. O. Enhanced area cursors: reducing fine pointing demands for people with motor impairments. In *Proc. UIST '10*, ACM (New York, NY, USA, 2010), 153–162.

4. Findlater, L., and McGrenere, J. A comparison of static, adaptive, and adaptable menus. In *Proc. CHI '04* (2004), 89–96.

5. Findlater, L., and McGrenere, J. Impact of screen size on performance, awareness, and user satisfaction with adaptive graphical user interfaces. In *Proc. CHI '08*, ACM (New York, NY, USA, 2008), 1247–1256.

6. Gajos, K. Z., Czerwinski, M., Tan, D. S., and Weld, D. S. Exploring the design space for adaptive graphical user interfaces. In *Proc. AVI '06*, ACM Press (New York, NY, USA, 2006), 201–208.

7. Gajos, K. Z., Everitt, K., Tan, D. S., Czerwinski, M., and Weld, D. S. Predictability and accuracy in adaptive user interfaces. In *Proc. CHI '08*, ACM (2008), 1271–1274.

8. Gajos, K. Z., Weld, D. S., and Wobbrock, J. O. Automatically generating personalized user interfaces with Supple. *Artificial Intelligence 174* (2010), 910–950.

9. Greenberg, S., and Witten, I. Adaptive personalized interfaces: A question of viability. *Behaviour & Information Technology 4*, 1 (1985), 31–45.

10. Greenberg, S., and Witten, I. H. Supporting command reuse: mechanisms for reuse. *Intl journal of man-machine studies 39*, 3 (Sept. 1993), 391–425.

11. Grossman, T., and Balakrishnan, R. The bubble cursor: enhancing target acquisition by dynamic resizing of the cursor's activation area. In *Proc. CHI '05*, ACM (New York, NY, USA, 2005), 281–290.

12. Harada, S., Wobbrock, J. O., and Landay, J. A. Voicedraw: A voice-driven hands-free drawing application. In *Proc. ASSETS'07*, ACM Press (2007).

13. Hornof, A. J., and Cavender, A. Eyedraw: enabling children with severe motor impairments to draw with their eyes. In *Proc. CHI '05*, ACM Press (New York, NY, USA, 2005), 161–170.

14. Hwang, F., Hollinworth, N., and Williams, N. Effects of target expansion on selection performance in older computer users. *ACM Transactions on Accessible Computing (TACCESS) 5*, 1 (2013), 1.

15. Kabbash, P., and Buxton, W. A. The "prince" technique: Fitts' law and selection using area cursors. In *Proc. CHI '95*, ACM (1995), 273–279.

16. Komarov, S., Reinecke, K., and Gajos, K. Z. Crowdsourcing performance evaluations of user interfaces. In *Proc. CHI '13*, ACM (New York, NY, USA, 2013), 207–216.

17. Lafreniere, B., Bunt, A., Whissell, J. S., Clarke, C. L. A., and Terry, M. Characterizing large-scale use of a direct manipulation application in the wild. In *Proc. GI '10*, Canadian Information Processing Society (2010), 11–18.

18. Sears, A., and Shneiderman, B. Split menus: effectively using selection frequency to organize menus. *ACM Trans. Comput.-Hum. Interact. 1*, 1 (1994), 27–51.

19. Trewin, S., Keates, S., and Moffatt, K. Developing steady clicks:: a method of cursor assistance for people with motor impairments. In *Proc. ASSETS '06*, ACM (2006), 26–33.

20. Tsandilas, T., and Schraefel. An empirical assessment of adaptation techniques. In *Proc. CHI '05*, ACM Press (New York, NY, USA, 2005), 2009–2012.

21. Wobbrock, J., Kane, S., Gajos, K., Harada, S., and Froehlich, J. Ability-Based Design: Concept, Principles and Examples. *ACM Transactions on Accessible Computing (TACCESS) 3*, 3 (Apr. 2011).

22. Wobbrock, J. O., Fogarty, J., Liu, S.-Y. S., Kimuro, S., and Harada, S. The angle mouse: target-agnostic dynamic gain adjustment based on angular deviation. In *Proc. CHI '09*, ACM (New York, NY, USA, 2009), 1401–1410.

Towards a User Experience Design Framework for Adaptive Spoken Dialogue in Automotive Contexts

Pontus Wärnestål
Department of Information Science,
Computer and Electrical Engineering
Halmstad University
Box 823, SE-301 18 Halmstad, Sweden
pontus.warnestal@hh.se

Fredrik Kronlid
Talkamatic AB
Första Långgatan 18
SE-413 28 Göteborg, Sweden
fredrik@talkamatic.se

ABSTRACT

We present an initial set of design principles for designing efficient, effective, coherent, and desirable adaptive spoken interaction for traffic information and navigation. The principles are based on a qualitative analysis of driver interactions with an adaptive speech prototype along with driver interviews. The derived set of principles range from high-level fundamental design values, conceptual and behavioral principles, to low-level interface-level principles that can guide the design of adaptive spoken dialogue interaction in the car from a user experience perspective.

Author Keywords

Adaptive interfaces; interaction design; user experience; spoken interaction; natural language interaction; automotive; navigation; traffic information.

ACM Classification Keywords

H.1.2 [Models and principles]: User/Machine Systems – Human factors.

H.5.m. [Information interfaces and presentation]: Miscellaneous.

INTRODUCTION

The car has become a professional – as well as personal – space with experience-oriented attributes that must be carefully designed. Still, the primary task of a car driver – to safely operate a vehicle on the road – is a challenging task, considering the increase in traffic and driving speeds, as well as the increasing demand for the driver's attention due to the increasing complexity additional technology brought into the driving environment (e.g. texting, looking up addresses, or taking calls) [1]. This requires the driver to execute several tasks in parallel to driving, with potentially negative effects on safety [2, 3]. According to Neale et al.

[4], non-primary task distraction is the largest cause of driver inattention.

Due to the distinct differences of the driving context compared to more traditional interactive platforms (such as desktop environments), methods, tools, and design principles need to be specifically tailored to meet the challenges posed [5]. In order to design for driver safety as well as desirable user experience, researchers from both academia and industry have started exploring alternative interaction paradigms in the realm of natural user interfaces. *Spoken interaction* has been proposed as a promising candidate for safe, pleasant, and engaging driver-car interaction [6, 7]. However, contemporary speech solutions in the automotive use context are often riddled with rigid, hierarchical structures, and still suffer from usability problems and low user experience [3, 8]. To address this, *adaptive* speech systems have been proposed in the automotive design space [8]. However, the properties of adaptive interfaces also make them prone to usability problems [9-11], which can have severe effects on the system's overall success [12, 13]. Within the broad field of general user-adaptive interaction, certain initiatives towards design methodology (e.g. user-adaptive recommender systems) have been taken [14], but there is currently a lack of user experience design principles for adaptive spoken dialogue interaction in the automotive use context. This paper addresses this by proposing an initial set of empirically derived design principles that can be used as a starting point for a user experience design framework for adaptive spoken dialogue interaction in the automotive design space.

RELATED RESEARCH

This section gives a brief overview of related work within the fields of adaptive systems, natural language dialogue interaction, and user experience (UX) design perspectives, which form the interdisciplinary scene for the study reported on in this paper.

Adaptive Systems

The goal of adaptive systems is to adapt interaction and interface to a specific user based on her knowledge, skills, goals, and preferences. Adaptive systems can employ any or all of the following explicit models: user, context, and task models. The promise of adaptive systems is to provide the right information, in the right form, at the right time in relation to the user's current state. For the purpose of this work, we build on the identified usability challenges posed by Jameson [11] and incorporate the following issues in our research method:

- Diminished predictability and comprehensibility
- Diminished controllability
- Obtrusiveness
- Infringement of privacy
- Diminished breadth of experience

Designing Spoken Dialogue Interaction

Speech has been proposed as "the ideal interaction modality" for humans; on the grounds that it is considered natural, flexible, and that most humans do not need to be trained to use it [15, 16]. Even though significant progress has been achieved in speech technology, today's speech and dialogue systems do not accommodate such "natural" language conversation. The experience of natural and intuitive interaction is rather a case of design, and the interaction needs to be shaped accordingly, utilizing the pros and cons of human-computer dialogue, which is significantly different from naturally occurring human-human dialogue [17]. The notion of "natural" language and human-like speech interaction with machines has received criticism (e.g. [18]), and the systems adhering to the latter category are with very few exceptions limited to research systems and prototypes. This also means that some of the knowledge gaps regarding the user experience of such systems in specific contexts need to be addressed without having to wait for the often technology-driven development of such systems.

When it comes to design principles for spoken dialogue interaction in general, there are several initiatives, most of them based on Gricean [19] maxims for conversation, e.g. [20, 21]. Through the increasing user exposure to (mobile) spoken systems, such as Apple's Siri and Google Glass, speech solutions have become more ubiquitous. Thus, "speech" cannot be viewed as an isolated interaction modality limited to singular (research) systems. Spoken interaction has to be designed as part of a complex and authentic use-context, where the complete experience surrounding the interaction is taken into consideration.

User Experience Perspectives and Design Principles

A successful design perspective in the driving context needs to operate on both safety and user experience levels. Norman [9] suggests organizing user experience attributes according to the following levels of cognitive processing:

- **Visceral**: the most immediate level where sensory aspects of an artifact causes us to rapidly categorize it in terms of "good", "safe", "bad", "dangerous", etc.
- **Behavioral**: the functional level, where most traditional usability and interaction design efforts operate, since it constitutes the majority of human interaction with tools and artifacts.

- **Reflective**: the least immediate level, where long-term use forms a memory-based relationship with the artifact. This level allows us to integrate our (memories of) experiences into a broader perspective that associate designed artifacts with a higher level of meaning than mere functionality.

This experience-oriented model implies that designing for visceral, behavioral, and reflective levels, based on an understanding of the users' goals at all three levels, a coherent and meaningful relationship between the user and the artifact can be achieved.

For general interaction in automotive contexts, design principles exist in the form of international ANSI standards, as well as recommendations regarding text size and placement of displays [22]. However, these standards mainly address traditional interactions using buttons, knobs, and other manual interaction techniques. From a safety perspective, the aims to (a) reduce interaction time, and (b) employ interaction modalities that free eyes and hands are thus two promising design approaches. Speech has been one suggestion to address this in the automotive context [6].

The critical issue is to design the interaction in such a way that users understand the system's limitations and capabilities, and that it provides a coherent, understandable, enjoyable, and safe user experience. To this end, designers can greatly benefit from *frameworks of design principles*. A design principle framework operates on various levels, ranging from general design values to behavioral principles and interface-level interaction patterns [23] and is an important tool for human-centered design. However, UX-oriented principles that can fuel the *design* of user experience of adaptive spoken interaction in the automotive context are yet to be described in a coherent framework.

We view a "design principle" as a guideline for achieving useful and desirable interactions with systems and services, as well as ethical and human-centered design practice. In the automotive domain, this includes a prominent safety perspective on driver interfaces.

PROTOTYPING SPOKEN DIALOGUE IN THE CAR

In order to investigate experiential qualities and usability issues we devised the following method: A prototyping solution was designed as a Wizard-of-Oz (WOZ) test [24-26], which allows for simulating complex dialogue and system behavior, and generates data on the interaction between a partially implemented system and its users. By scripting the dialogue behavior in an interaction protocol and have a human "Wizard" execute the protocol unbeknownst to the user, a flexible test environment can rapidly be created. As shown in Figure 1, the setup uses a state-of-the art text-to-speech (TTS) service that runs on a (hidden) 3G mobile device hooked up to the car's loudspeakers. The TTS used a female American English voice. With the device running an open Skype connection to the Wizard's computer, text transmitted via the Skype chat is instantly read to the driver by the TTS service.

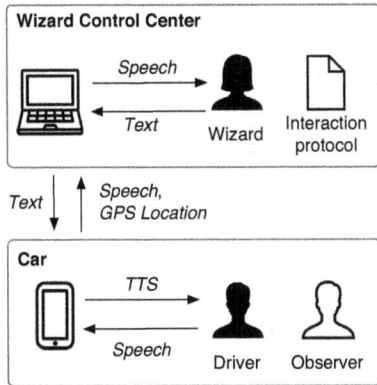

Figure 1. Wizard-of-Oz test setup.

In turn, the Wizard can hear the driver's utterances directly via the Skype call. By using the mobile device's GPS capabilities and an app that tracks the device, the Wizard can monitor the car's location in order to time responses depending on location. The driver's experience is therefore that she is interacting with a service that is part of the car's native infotainment system. The Wizard follows an interaction protocol that consists of a set of pre-canned responses based on scenarios, as well as some basic greeting and error messages. The Wizard also has the possibility to edit the messages in the chat text field directly if necessary. All interaction is logged for later analysis.

Participants
In order to get qualitative, experience-oriented input data regarding the interaction with the prototype, seven participants were recruited (see Table 1) for a driving session and post-session interview. The participants were from different age groups and gender, and were required to drive regularly (at least three times per week).

Procedure
Each participant was invited to an individual session to a parking lot where the experiment car was parked. Upon arrival they were introduced to the observer, who also gained their informed consent. The participant was briefed on the procedure, introduced to the prototype, and was given an opportunity to try a few dialogue turns of spoken interaction with the system in order to briefly familiarize with the system. Scenario 1 was introduced, and the participant's task was given: to get current traffic information about the road to his/her new workplace, and to try to find a suitable stop for coffee on the way there. The respondent was then invited to enter the car in the driver's seat, while the observer entered the passenger seat. According to the instructions, the participant started driving down the designated driveway and interacted with the system.

Upon completion of the first scenario, the participant was told to pull over and was debriefed with a short interview. The interview was semi-structured with a set of short questions concerning their initial experience with the system interaction. While the observer debriefed the respondent, the Wizard adjusted the prototype parameters and interaction protocol based on the dialogue in the first scenario to mock-up the user-adaptation that would take place in scenario 2.

Respondent	Age, Gender	Occupation
R1	22, f	Student
R2	25, m	Student
R3	38, m	Designer
R4	49, m	Sales Mgr
R5	34, f	Production Mgr
R6	27, f	Programmer
R7	32, m	Teacher

Table 1. Participant details.

After the debrief, scenario 2 was introduced, where the participant was asked to role-play that she had used the system for a period of three weeks, driving to her new workplace every weekday and regularly stopping for coffee at her favorite coffee shop (the one selected in the first driving session). The participant then "drove to work" along the test track, trying to get traffic information. This time the Wizard adapted the interaction to the learned driving behavior and suggested the stop at the coffee shop, as well as proactively reporting on traffic conditions. This scenario also included an opportunity for the Wizard to initiate a dialogue based on location. By monitoring the location of the car, the Wizard initiated suggestions on an alternative coffee shop when the car reached a specific location on the map (see S4, Figure 2). After the participant "arrived at work" s/he was debriefed with an interview regarding his/her experience with the adapted interaction.

The third and final scenario consisted of breaking a learned driving pattern. The participant was now briefed that an additional three weeks had gone by, and that she had recently started to go exercising at a health club on her way to work. Her tasks now were to drive to the gym instead of the coffee shop, and then head to her work place. The Wizard followed the learned protocol used in scenario 2, and then tried to adapt as the user corrected the assumptions.

After arriving and parking the car "at work", a slightly longer interview was held with the participant regarding her overall experience with the three scenarios. Finally, the participant was informed about the WOZ technique, and that the interaction had been mediated by a human being. The entire procedure lasted about 60 minutes (app. 40 min interview time, 15 min interaction time split on three scenarios, and 5 min introduction and briefing) for each participant.

Interviews

The post-scenario interviews conducted were semi-structured and designed to get the participants to discuss user experience qualities (encompassing visceral, behavioral, and reflective levels of experience) [9], perceived usefulness and understanding of the interaction with the prototype, as well as probe for potential usability issues derived from adaptive interface research [11]. Table 2 shows examples of interview guide themes that were discussed during the post-session interviews, and their connection to user experience and usability categories.

Category	Sample Question Themes
Predictability	*Expectations on user input effect on system output; Extent of understanding of what was being understood and modeled by the system.*
Controllability	*Extent and quality of system's understanding of user's goals and tasks. Is all desired information present?*
Obtrusiveness	*Reflections on system initiative, and its conclusions about user's tasks and goals.*
Privacy	*Extent of what the system "knows" about the user, and the effects on the interaction.*
Breadth of experience	*Reflections on narrowing in on goals "too fast", based on incomplete knowledge about the user.*
Visceral experience	*Immediate reactions to voice quality, emotional response to the services being offered by the system, etc.*
Behavioral experience	*Perceived usefulness, effectiveness, and efficiency of the services being offered by the system.*
Reflective experience	*What kind of person would like/dislike this kind of system? Is this a system you would talk about to your friends and colleagues?*

Table 2. Interview guide user experience and usability question themes.

RESULTS

Twentyone dialogues were collected (three sessions for each of the seven respondents). Scenario 1 dialogues had a mean of 16 turns. Scenario 2 had a mean of 10 turns, while scenario 3 had a mean of 12 turns. The seven post-session interviews spanned from 28 minutes (R5) to 52 minutes (R3).

All participants found the system easy to use, and easy to understand. Obtrusiveness, and behavioral experience were in general the favorite topics during the interviews. Voice quality and the system's character (see Posture, below) were also frequently discussed. Breadth of experience and reflective experience were hard to reason about due to the

time-constraints and lack of comparison with a non-adaptive system.

Figure 2 shows a dialogue excerpt from scenario 2, performed by respondent 3 (R3).

```
S1:Good morning. There is traffic congestion
   on your regular way to work. I suggest
   Interstate 6 instead. What route would you
   like to take today?

D1:Interstate 6 is fine.

S2:Ok. Do you want to stop at Starbucks,
   like you did last Tuesday morning?

D2:Yes

S3:Ok. Going south on Interstate 6 to work,
   via Starbucks on Main Street.

   [After arriving at an intersection about halfway to work]

S4:I noticed that there's just 10 minutes
   until you need to be at work. Do you want
   to go to your regular coffeeshop
   Starbucks, or would you like to go to
   George's Coffee instead? It is the closest
   to work.

D3:Ok, let's try George's Coffee.

S5:Re-routing to George's Coffee before
   going to work.
```

Figure 2. Dialogue excerpt from scenario 2 (R3). S = System, D = Driver.

The rate of wizard mishearings (i.e. what would be considered speech recognition errors in a real system) was less than 5%. This is unrealistic for a dialogue system even for this limited domain, but in order to test the experiential qualities of a high-level intelligent user interface, simulating such errors could take away focus from the user experiences we want to study in this work.

ANALYSIS: AN EMERGENT DESIGN FRAMEWORK

Three researchers qualitatively assessed the driver interview transcripts by iteratively grouping the responses into affinities. Since responses were grounded in the interview guide, affinities represented five themes related to user experience [9], as well as previously identified adaptive system usability risks [11]. The emerging themes, and resulting ten design principles are presented in this section.

Purposeful and Pragmatic Design

It is clear from the interviews that the respondents consider the driving task (i.e. getting from point A to B) to sometimes start long before getting in front of the wheel. For example, traffic congestion and weather reports affect what time the respondents choose to leave the home or workplace. This information should be available before entering the car. In addition, some of them will already be primed to have conversations with other voice-systems such as Apple's Siri. Respondents also mentioned that certain actions related to driving from point A to B could also include actions after parking the car, such as checking in at the destination venue on social media platforms.

Principle 1: Model driver-related tasks in three phases: pre-, during, and post-driving, and have the system assist the user in all three phases.

Elegance

Elegant design includes how well functional and brand attributes are expressed, or how the simplest viable solution can be realized. For the purpose of spoken interaction, the sophistication of voice quality is an important aspect. Several respondents expressed that the high quality of the female text-to-speech voice made them trust the system. It also raised the expectations of the system's capabilities. This phenomenon of anthropomorphism is well documented [27] and comes as no surprise.

Principle 2: Use sophisticated voice quality to inspire trust.

Principle 3: Match system functionality with voice quality and sophistication, and do not raise the user expectations of the system's capabilities.

By slipping in evidence of the adaptation process in order to provide context to a recommendation, the system maintains a considerate, human-like quality as S2 in Figure 2. R1 reflected: "It helps me understand why she recommended Starbucks, she noticed I usually go there."

Principle 4. Provide rich information, and motivate suggestions short and succinctly.

Levels of Expertise

Accommodation for various levels of expertise is where adaptive systems have the potential to excel by tailoring responses to suit the user's expertise. Despite the short interaction time, two respondents (R2 and R3) started using shortcuts in the dialogue:

```
S: Good morning. There is traffic congestion
   on your regular way to work. I suggest
   Interstate 6 instead. What route would you
   like to take today?

D: The usual way, and stop for coffee at
   Starbucks.
```

Principle 5: Allow the user to shortcut the dialogue protocol, by allowing several pieces of information be inputted in one go.

Posture

Posture refers to the way the system presents itself to the user [23] (e.g. to be neutral and professional, or upbeat and helpful, alert, or even flamboyant and bold). For a coherent experience, voice quality needs to match the system's posture. In our case, we used a sophisticated female voice, coupled with a competent and professional dialogue behavior. It is important to realize that traffic information and navigation in the driving context is a secondary and transient interaction. Therefore, minimalist, short, and correct interaction is desirable. R1 expressed it as: "I really need the system to be correct. Since I know she only gives

me what she thinks that I want, it's very important that she's exactly right. Otherwise I feel like I might miss information". R6 echoed this, and also added: "I don't want to have to think too much. The less she says, the better. Still, I really like talking to her!"

We designed the system to take a "bold" stance when it comes to initiative, as is illustrated by S4 in Figure 2.

R3 comments: "It felt like she really predicted my situation and had figured out where I work, and that arriving on time is important to me. Frankly it's a little scary...but awesome!"

By using the construction "your regular coffee shop" instead of just naming the location the system unobtrusively communicates the adaptive functionality.

Principle 6: Ask for forgiveness, not permission. Make suggestions, and allow for correction.

Principle 7: Use information-rich and effective language in order to reduce interaction time.

Principle 8: Organize and name functions and domain items according to user mental models.

Harmonious Interactions

Following users' mental models, and avoiding unnecessary reporting are two ways to achieve a harmonious interaction flow. Clearly communicating the inner workings of the system is also a way to cater for a well-understood interaction flow. A specific problem for adaptive systems lies in the difficulty to provide this kind of transparency of the system's functionality compared to a non-adaptive system. For this domain, the observers noted that the drivers responded quickly and effortlessly when the system gave options instead of asking open questions. Respondents reacted positively to be given choices, as long as the choices were limited to two or three options. R3 said: "She seems to have done a lot of work for me already by narrowing down a lot of choices to only two or three, which is ideal when you're focused on driving".

Principle 9: Enable users to direct, don't force them to discuss, i.e. provide a relevant but small set of choices; don't ask open questions.

R7 mentioned that it was "great" that the system did not state obvious things, and did not "confirm every little detail like most speech systems do".

Principle 10: Avoid unnecessary reporting, and don't report normalcy.

CONCLUDING DISCUSSION

We have described an emerging design principle framework based on WOZ-prototyping and user interviews from an experiential perspective on adaptive natural language interaction in the automotive context. The principles range from high-level design values to low-level interface principles and provide guidance for user experience design of adaptive spoken dialogue systems in the context of getting adapted traffic information and performing navigation.

The WOZ method allowed us to script advanced interactions that test the upper-bound limits of adaptive functionality in this domain. The downside of the WOZ approach coupled with the role-playing aspect of the scenarios is the question of validity. The design principles posed herein should therefore be verified in a longitudinal manner with a fully developed system. This study engaged seven respondents, and is limited to adapting the dialogue for traffic information and navigation tasks. This initial set of design principles must therefore be extended to cover more tasks, and take input from more respondents. The rapid prototyping WOZ-based test bed described can be used to efficiently collect such data on user experience qualities and usability issues for spoken adaptive interaction in the car. For industry researchers, the principles can be used to guide the human-centered development of systems and services that need to connect to e.g. brand values and strategic customer experiences. For academic researchers focusing on adaptive algorithms, the framework provides a foundation for designing coherent experiences for prototypes and experiments. For researchers focusing on design aspects, the design principles presented herein could serve as a knowledge gap-spotting device, and inspire to relevant research questions.

ACKNOWLEDGMENTS

This work was carried out within the FFI project "Safe Speech by Knowledge" (2012-00941), funded by VINNOVA, Volvo Car Corporation and Talkamatic.

REFERENCES

1. Pettitt, M., G. Burnett, and A. Stevens, *Defining driver distraction.* Defining Driver Distraction, 2005. **1**(1): p. 1-12.
2. Burnett, G., *Designing and Evaluating In-Car User-Interfaces*, in *Human Computer Interaction: Concepts, Methodologies, Tools, and Applications.* 2009, IGI Global. p. 532-551.
3. Dagmar, K. and S. Albrecht, *Design space for driver-based automotive user interfaces*, in *Proceedings of the 1st International Conference on Automotive User Interfaces and Interactive Vehicular Applications.* 2009, ACM: Essen, Germany.
4. Neale, V.L., et al., *The 100 car naturalistic driving study, Phase I-experimental design.* 2002.
5. Albrecht, S., et al., *Automotive user interfaces: human computer interaction in the car*, in *CHI '10 Extended Abstracts on Human Factors in Computing Systems.* 2010, ACM: Atlanta, Georgia, USA.
6. Nass, C.I. and S. Brave, *Wired for speech: How voice activates and advances the human-computer relationship.* 2005: MIT press Cambridge.
7. Peissner, M., V. Doebler, and F. Metze, *Can voice interaction help reducing the level of distraction and prevent accidents?* 2011.
8. Lavie, T. and J. Meyer, *Benefits and costs of adaptive user interfaces.* International Journal of Human-Computer Studies, 2010. **68**(8): p. 508-524.
9. Norman, D.A., *Emotional design: Why we love (or hate) everyday things.* 2007: Basic books.
10. Höök, K., *Steps to take before intelligent user interfaces become real.* Interacting with computers, 2000. **12**(4): p. 409-426.
11. Jameson, A., *Adaptive interfaces and agents.* Human-Computer Interaction: Design Issues, Solutions, and Applications, 2009. **105**.
12. McNee, S.M., J. Riedl, and J.A. Konstan. *Being accurate is not enough: how accuracy metrics have hurt recommender systems.* in *CHI'06 extended abstracts on Human factors in computing systems.* 2006. ACM.
13. Knijnenburg, B.P., et al., *Explaining the user experience of recommender systems.* User Modeling and User-Adapted Interaction, 2012. **22**(4-5): p. 441-504.
14. McNee, S.M., J. Riedl, and J.A. Konstan. *Making recommendations better: an analytic model for human-recommender interaction.* in *CHI'06 extended abstracts on Human factors in computing systems.* 2006. ACM.
15. Stefanie, T., et al., *Towards efficient human machine speech communication: The speech graffiti project.* ACM Trans. Speech Lang. Process., 2005. **2**(1): p. 2.
16. McTear, M.F., *Spoken dialogue technology: enabling the conversational user interface.* ACM Computing Surveys (CSUR), 2002. **34**(1): p. 90-169.
17. Jönsson, A., *A model for habitable and efficient dialogue management for natural language interaction.* Natural Language Engineering, 1997. **3**(2): p. 103-122.
18. Shneiderman, B., *The limits of speech recognition.* Communications of the ACM, 2000. **43**(9): p. 63-65.
19. Grice, H.P., *Logic and conversation.* 1975, 1975: p. 41-58.
20. Larsson, S., L. Santamarta, and A. Jönsson, *Using the process of distilling dialogues to understand dialogue systems*, in *6th International Conference on Spoken Language Processing ICSLP-2000.* 2000: Beijing, China.
21. Bernsen, N.O., H. Dybkjaer, and L. Dybkjaer. *Principles for the design of cooperative spoken human-machine dialogue.* in *Spoken Language, 1996. ICSLP 96. Proceedings., Fourth International Conference on.* 1996. IEEE.
22. Stevens, A., et al., *Design guidelines for safety of in-vehicle information systems.* 2002: TRL Limited.
23. Cooper, A., R. Reimann, and D. Cronin, *About face 3: the essentials of interaction design.* 2012: John Wiley & Sons.
24. Rieser, V. and O. Lemon, *Developing Dialogue Managers from Limited Amounts of Data*, in *Data-Driven Methods for Adaptive Spoken Dialogue Systems.* 2012, Springer. p. 5-17.
25. Webb, N., et al. *Wizard of Oz Experiments for a companion dialogue system: eliciting companionable conversation.* in *Lrec.* 2010.
26. Dahlbäck, N., A. Jönsson, and L. Ahrenberg, *Wizard of Oz studies—why and how.* Knowledge-based systems, 1993. **6**(4): p. 258-266.
27. Reeves, B. and C. Nass, *How people treat computers, television, and new media like real people and places.* 1996: Cambridge University Press.

A Practical Framework for Constructing Structured Drawings

Salman Cheema[1], Sarah Buchanan[1], Sumit Gulwani[2], Joseph J. LaViola Jr.[1]
[1]University of Central Florida, Orlando, FL , [2]Microsoft Research, Redmond, WA
[1]{salmanc,sarahb,jjl}@cs.ucf.edu, [2]sumitg@microsoft.com

ABSTRACT

We describe a novel theoretical framework for modeling structured drawings which contain one or more patterns of repetition in their constituent elements. We then present PatternSketch, a sketch-based drawing tool built using our framework to allow quick construction of structured drawings. PatternSketch can recognize and beautify drawings containing line segments, polylines, arcs, and circles. Users can employ a series of gestures to identify repetitive elements and create new elements based on automatically inferred patterns. PatternSketch leverages the programming-by-example (PBE) paradigm, enabling it to infer non-trivial patterns from a few examples. We show that PatternSketch, with its sketch-based user interface and a unique pattern inference algorithm, enables efficient and natural construction of structured drawings.

Author Keywords

Sketch-based Interfaces, Programming by Example, Pattern Inference, Structured Drawing

ACM Classification Keywords

H.5.2. User Interfaces: Interaction Styles

General Terms

Algorithms, Human Factors

INTRODUCTION

Images and drawings containing structured repetition are common in real-life (e.g., brick patterns, tiling patterns, and architectural drawings). We define 'Structured Drawings' as drawings that can be drawn using a CAD tool: either requiring a user to write a script using CAD APIs or perform repetitive Copy-Paste operations with some underlying mathematical logic. Figure 1 shows examples of structured drawings. Making structured drawings is hard and time consuming without software support. Although no software tools exist solely for constructing structured drawings, some commercial applications such as Microsoft PowerPoint, Ink Scape,

IUI'14, February 24–27, 2014, Haifa, Israel.
Copyright © 2014 ACM 978-1-4503-2184-6/14/02...$15.00.
http://dx.doi.org/10.1145/2557500.2557522

(a) Cog   (b) Railroad Tracks

Figure 1: Examples of structured drawings (Source: Google Images)

Adobe Illustrator and AutoDesk Inventor can be adapted for this purpose. These tools let users specify rudimentary patterns via a WIMP interface but rely mostly on variations of Copy-Paste (translation and scaling) to replicate repetitive elements.

In this paper, we describe a novel framework for modeling structure and repetition in drawings. Our framework uses a small set of abstract constructions, while giving an application developer the freedom to support different types of drawing elements and interaction methods. We leverage ideas from the domain of programming by example (PBE) [5, 9, 17] and set-theoretic constructions to create a novel algorithm that can infer patterns from a few examples highlighted by the user, and use them to complete structured drawings. We also describe PatternSketch, a sketch-based drawing tool built using our framework, that can recognize and beautify hand-drawn sketches, which users can manipulate with a series of gestures to identify and extend repetitive elements.

RELATED WORK

Programming by example (PBE) [5, 9, 17] is a popular paradigm for automating end-user programming tasks and has been used in a wide variety of domains including text-editing programs [16], spreadsheet data manipulation [10] and algebra problem generation [19]. We leverage ideas from PBE to construct a framework for modeling structured drawings, where the user provides a few examples of repetitive drawing elements, and our tool predicts the next elements in the sequence. The key technical contributions include a novel framework for representing sequences of drawing elements as well as a synthesis algorithm that infers example elements in the intended sequence from a collection of selected objects using a majority voting scheme.

We have chosen a sketch-based interface for PatternSketch so that it mimics the natural input method of pen and paper. Early work in sketch recognition focused on incorporating gesture recognition with direct manipulation [15] and on user guided recognition and beautification [2, 13]. Paulson et al. [18] have developed techniques for recognition and beautification of low-level sketch primitives. Interactive beautification [11, 22] and guided beautification [7, 8] of hand-drawn sketches have been explored in different application settings. More recently, beautification of sketched drawings involving line segments and circles by using inferred geometric constraints has been examined by [4]. PatternSketch employs a small set of drawing elements (line segments, polylines, arcs, and circles), in order to minimize interface confusion and to lower the likelihood of recognition errors. We adapted our recognition and beautification techniques from QuickDraw [4] and extended them to incorporate polylines and arcs. QuickDraw [4] was chosen as the beautification engine because it incorporates a rich set of constraints to ensure robustness.

Sketch-based interfaces have also been applied to several modeling tasks such as 3D Modeling [3, 12, 21], 3D curve sketching [1] and for animation tools for novice users [6]. Recently, Kazi et al. [14] have developed Vignette that utilizes texture synthesis and preserves individual style during sketching to generate artistic sketches. Vignette and PatternSketch both require users to specify initial examples and guide the predicted drawing but both tools differ in important ways. In Vignette, users generate texture patterns from a few examples, repeating this process a number of times for each drawing. This behavior can be modeled using our proposed framework (with its abstract representation of drawing elements and patterns) but is not entirely supported by our current prototype (PatternSketch), which instead focuses on ensuring precision. Comparing the two is difficult as both tools can probably demonstrate superior performance in different contexts, depending on whether an artistic look or precision is required. PatternSketch does not preserve individual style but uses constraint-based beautification and pattern generation to ensure precision in generated drawings.

THEORETICAL FRAMEWORK

Structured drawings contain one or more repetitive patterns in their constituent elements. Some patterns are simple and can be abstracted as linear Copy-Paste (i.e., a single element replicated many times by applying a translation and/or scaling). More often, repetition lies beyond the capability of linear Copy-Paste. Figure 1b shows a picture of railroad tracks where the planks on the inside of the rail tracks form a pattern incorporating both translation and scaling. However, the translation relating the copied planks is not constant. Additionally, an alignment operation is necessary to ensure that new planks always maintain the geometric relationship with the track lines. Figure 1b also demonstrates that repetition may not always occur in a straight line, thus requiring either clever inference or user intervention. Linear Copy-Paste can only extend patterns in a single direction.

We consider repetition as a generative operation starting from an initial sequence of drawing elements sketched by a user. From a theoretical perspective, the choice of how to define the generative operation is inconsequential and we leave this choice open to application developers. It can either be defined explicitly by the user or it may be inferred from a sufficient number of examples by using programming-by-example techniques. Additionally, the operation encodes information about how new elements are to be aligned with respect to existing elements. It can also be manipulated by a user to create new elements in one or more directions. We now define a few key ideas related to structured drawings:

Drawing Element (e) is a basic component of a sketched drawing. Examples are points, line segments, circles and composite shapes.

Collection ($\overline{E}$) is a set of drawing elements. A single drawing may contain zero or more collections.

Filter An operation used to select a subset of a collection's elements in a particular order.

Pattern (ϕ) is a spatial relationship inherent in an ordered sequence of drawing elements. A pattern is a generative operation that can extend the sequence by creating new drawing elements. The relationship can either be inferred from the entire initial sequence, a filtered subset, or can be explicitly defined by the user.

Frame of Reference A geometrical construct that serves as a frame of reference for a pattern within a structured drawing. It can potentially be used to denote boundaries within which a pattern can be extended. Additionally, new drawing elements generated by a pattern may have to be aligned or positioned relative to the frame of reference.

Copy-Paste (ϕ_{copy}) A special generative operation that creates a copy of a selected drawing element at a specified location. Any required alignment must be performed manually by the user.

These abstract entities enable us to model complicated structured drawings. From our perspective, the choice of which drawing elements and patterns to support, as well as interaction metaphors for creating collections, performing filtering, and extending patterns are implementation details that can vary from system to system, depending on context. Our framework permits the use of any type of drawing element. Potentially, even collections of elements can act as building blocks in a larger pattern. Similarly, we place no restrictions on interaction metaphors for creating collections, performing filtering, inferring/defining, or extending patterns. User interaction may be enabled via WIMP interfaces, sketch-based interaction, 3D gestures or even voice input. The notion of a frame-of-reference is also abstract. It can either be a drawing element or a path drawn by a user or even some virtual geometrical construct. Our framework also supports Copy-Paste functionality in its traditional form. The notion of collections that combine a sequence of drawing elements with a generative operation is very powerful and affords users the freedom to extend the pattern as they see fit or till some condition is met. Collections combined into hierarchical relationships can be used to create chains of generative patterns which can enable interesting effects.

PATTERNSKETCH: AN OVERVIEW

PatternSketch can recognize and beautify sketched drawings containing line segments, polylines, arcs and circles. A series of gestures can be used to interact with the drawing. The 'Lasso' gesture is used to group drawing elements into a collection. It can also be used to select existing collections. Once a collection is selected, the user can filter it by selecting a subset of its elements and assigning them an explicit ordering. For inferring patterns, users can either have the system consider the filtered collection or all possible ordered subsets. Once a pattern is inferred, the 'Drag' gesture can be used to generate new drawing elements.

Recognition and Beautification

Recognition is triggered by hitting the 'Recognize' button, after which the sketched drawing is parsed into its component elements (line segments, polylines, arcs, and circles). We use the IStraw [20] cusp finding algorithm to enumerate cusps in each ink stroke within the sketch, followed by a series of heuristics to classify each ink stroke as either a line segment, a circle, an arc, or a polyline. Our recognition heuristics and beautification system are based on ideas presented in [4], but have been extended to include polylines and arcs.

Constraints used for Beautification	
Applicable To	Constraint
Line Segments	Vertical line segment
	Horizontal line segment
	Parallel line segments
	Perpendicular line segments
	Touching line segments
	Line segments with same length
Circles	Circles with same radius
	Concentric circles
	Circles touching at their circumference
	Circle passing through the center of another circle
PolyLines	Similar structure (interior angles)
	Regular convex polygon
	Polygon
Circles, Line Segments & PolyLines	Line segment tangent to circle
	Line segment passing through center of circle
	Line segment touching circumference with an endpoint
	Line segment touching circle center with an endpoint
	PolyLine point touching a line segment
	PolyLine point touching a circle

Table 1: List of constraints that are inferred for beautifying drawings

After a drawing is recognized, our beautification subsystem infers geometric constraints between its recognized elements, which are used to beautify the drawing. In comparison to [4], we utilize a smaller set of constraints relating line segments and circles and have incorporated new constraints relating polylines with line segments and circles (See Table 1). After beautification, ink strokes are replaced by beautified drawing elements on the screen. For details of the beautification algorithm, please refer to [4].

Collections

Users can enable a special mode called 'Lasso' via the system menu. In 'Lasso' mode, a user can create a collection, select a element/collection, do Copy-Paste, or filter a subsequence from a collection for pattern inference. The user initially draws an ink stroke that encloses one or more drawing elements. If the encircled elements are part of an existing collection, the collection is selected. If selected elements belong to different collections, a new collection is created. Newly created collections are automatically selected (Selected collections are displayed with a colored bounding box). If a single element is lassoed, it is considered only for Copy-Paste. After selection, the user can either trigger pattern inference via the 'Infer' button on the menu or use the 'Tap' gesture to paste the selection at a new location. New elements created by Copy-Paste can be manually aligned by selecting 'Edit' mode via the menu and manipulating the element. PatternSketch allows the construction of the following collections of drawing elements:

Collection of Line Segments Homogeneous collection containing only line segments

Collection of Circles Homogeneous collection containing only circles

Collection of Polylines Homogeneous collection containing only polylines

Super Collection A collection containing other collections

Mixed Collection A collection containing several different types of drawing elements

With a selected collection, users can draw a line from the boundary of one element to the boundary of another element within the collection to assign an explicit ordering to the two elements thus creating a sequence within a collection. Sequences of drawing elements thus created can be extended by drawing another line from one of the elements within the sequence to another element outside the sequence but within the same collection. User defined orderings are rendered as dotted arrows. In this manner, PatternSketch merges the two steps (selection and ordering) of the filter operation into a single step which is intuitive and makes it easy for the user to indicate the intended ordering of elements within a collection.

Pattern Inference

Pattern inference is triggered by hitting the 'Infer' button from the menu. If the selected collection is filtered, the inference system tries to infer a pattern from the filtered elements. For an unfiltered collection, our inference system considers all possible ordered subsets of its elements. Within each subset, our inference algorithm considers ordered pairs (forming an input-output example) of drawing elements in isolation and uses a simple voting mechanism to determine the dominant pattern (See Algorithm 1).

We define the fundamental unit of each pattern as a 'PointSet' (ζ), which is a sequence of points that encodes one of the following relationships:

PointSet on Circle (ζ_C) Sequence of points along a circle's circumference separated by a constant non-zero arc length.

PointSet on Line Segment (ζ_L) Sequence of points along a line segment separated by a constant non-zero translation.

PointSet on Polyline (ζ_P) Sequence of points along a polyline separated by a constant non-zero distance.

PointSets form the basis for the following high-level patterns in PatternSketch:

1. Concentric Circles: A sequence of circles with a constant difference in radii whose centers are the same point.
2. Moving Lines: A sequence of line segments whose respective endpoints either form a PointSet or are the same point.
3. Moving Polylines: A sequence of polylines whose respective endpoints either form a PointSet or are the same point.
4. Moving Circles: A sequence of circles whose centers form a PointSet.
5. Moving Collections: A sequence of composite drawing elements or collections whose centroids form a PointSet.

PointSets are extremely useful because they capture low-level relationships between drawing elements and also encapsulate a frame of reference, as described in our theoretical framework. They enables us to model patterns as sets of low-level geometric transformations that are easy to visualize and can have one or more frames of reference.

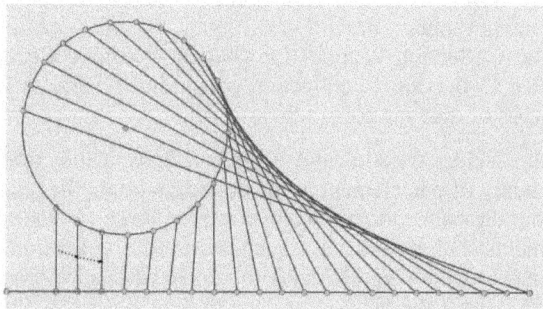

Figure 2: Example of a pattern of line segments that has two different frames of reference encoded by two different PointSets.

With patterns that leverage PointSets, we can enable powerful construction mechanisms. Figure 2 depicts a collection of line segments whose endpoints form PointSets along two different surfaces with different increments. As each of these PointSets encodes the relevant surface as a frame of reference, alignment is an implicit part of the repetition. It is also possible to use the frame of reference itself as a way to replicate a given pattern. For example, a collection of circles that form a pattern along the circumference of a larger circle can be selected for replication via the system menu. By selecting a target circle or even a collection of circles, the entire pattern can be duplicated onto the target. This is a non-trivial context-sensitive replication operation whose rules are encoded in our patterns and PointSets, enabling a very modular and powerful architecture.

Algorithm 1 gives the outline of our inference algorithm, which looks at each ordered pair (an input-output example pair) of elements and tries to determine the geometric relationship between them. The $InferRelationShip$ procedure

Algorithm 1 Algorithm to infer a pattern from an unordered set of drawing elements

```
1: function INFER(E̅)          ▷ E̅ are ordered drawing elements
2:     Φ := ∅                  ▷ Φ is the list of inferred patterns
3:     for i = 1 → ‖E̅‖ do
4:         for j = 1 → ‖E̅‖ do
5:             φ_i ← InferRelationShip(e_i, e_j)    ▷ i ≠ j
6:             if Φ Contains φ_i then
7:                 Get φ_k from Φ       ▷ φ_k is similar to φ_i
8:                 φ_k ← Merge(φ_k, φ_i)
9:                 Score(φ_k) += 1
10:            else
11:                Score(φ_i) = 1
12:                Φ ← Φ ∪ φ_i
13:            end if
14:        end for
15:    end for
16:    Select φ_best ∈ Φ with highest score
17:    return φ_best
18: end function
```

looks at the ordered pair (e_i, e_j), and determines if they constitute an example for one of the five patterns supported by the system. This is tested by applying the following rules:

- If e_i and e_j are circles and have the same center, they are considered an example of 'Concentric Circles'.
- If e_i and e_j are circles and their centers lie on the same line segment, polyline or circle, they are considered an example of 'Moving Circles'.
- if e_i and e_j are line segments, they are considered an example of 'Moving Lines', if two PointSets (ζ_C, ζ_L, or ζ_P) can be formulated involving both endpoints of both segments.
- if e_i and e_j are polylines, they are considered an example of 'Moving Polylines', if two PointSets (ζ_C, ζ_L, or ζ_P) can be formulated involving the first and last points of both polylines.
- if e_i and e_j are collections, they are considered an example of 'Moving Collections', if we can formulate a PointSet (ζ_L only with a virtual line as frame of reference) involving the centroids of both collections.

If the newly inferred pattern ϕ_i is similar to an existing pattern ϕ_k, then the score of ϕ_k is incremented and ϕ_i is merged with ϕ_k along with its example (e_i, e_j). If ϕ_i is not similar to any existing pattern, it is added to the set of possible patterns Φ with a score of one. Determining if two example pairs are part of the same pattern is difficult because users may not draw the elements with perfect spacing. Hence we introduce a similarity metric to infer patterns from noisy user input. We leverage PointSets and their unifying structure for this purpose. A pattern (ϕ_i) in our system contains one or more PointSets ($\zeta_1(\phi_i)\ldots\zeta_n(\phi_i)$) and a list of numeric values $\delta(\phi_i)$ (to denote pattern-specific information such as scaling coefficients, rotation values, alignment hints, etc). Each PointSet $\zeta_1(\phi_i)$ also has a list of interesting numerical values such as distances, arc length, vector offset, etc. Consequently, each pattern in our system can be represented as an

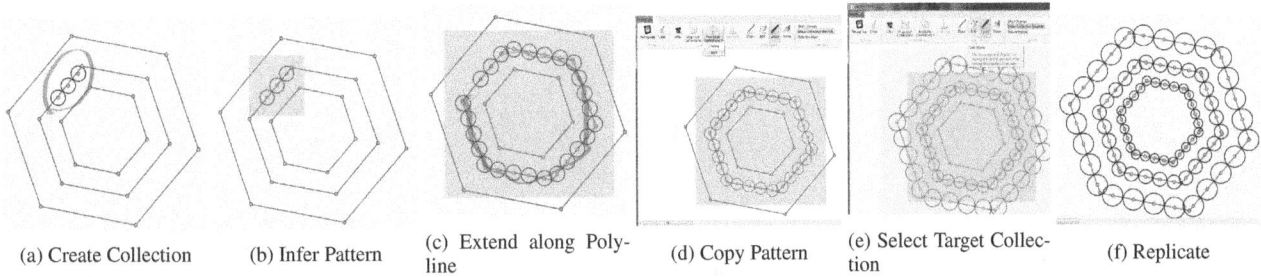

(a) Create Collection   (b) Infer Pattern   (c) Extend along Poly-line   (d) Copy Pattern   (e) Select Target Collection   (f) Replicate

Figure 3: Example scenario showing how mathematical art can be created using PatternSketch. The user draws three hexagons and creates a collection of circles on the surface of one of them. The 'Lasso' and 'Drag' gestures are used to extend the circles along the entire hexagon. Afterwards, the user can quickly replicate this pattern onto the other hexagons.

n-dimensional numeric vector:

$$\langle \phi_i \rangle = [\zeta_1(\phi_i) \ldots \zeta_n(\phi_i), \delta(\phi_i)]$$

Testing similarity among patterns simply constitutes comparing their vector representations using context-specific threshold values:

$$\text{Similarity}(\phi_1, \phi_2) = \langle \phi_1 \rangle - \langle \phi_2 \rangle \leq \varepsilon(\phi_1, \phi_2)$$

Where $\varepsilon(\phi_1, \phi_2)$ is a function to determine context-specific threshold values for comparing ϕ_1 and ϕ_2. Context-specific information can include things like touch constraints, distance thresholds, etc. Once all ordered pairs have been examined, the highest ranked pattern ϕ_{best} is picked as the most-likely candidate. It should be noted that, ideally, with programming-by-example, three examples are needed to determine if a set of drawing elements forms a pattern. As our system only considers pairs of elements in isolation, it can yield false positives, e.g., if two interesting points in a selection lie on a drawing element, they will always be considered a PointSet (ζ_C, ζ_L or ζ_P). Such erroneous cases are mitigated automatically because our algorithm picks the highest voted pattern. Erroneous PointSets will get few votes and be automatically suppressed. Also, as our algorithm only considers pairs of points, it will never consider a set of points in unison, rendering it unable to infer movement along a virtual circle. The workaround for this is to draw the virtual circle initially and erase it after creating the pattern. Virtual lines are deducible because each equidistant set of points on a virtual line will contribute higher votes to the same translation offset, making it a candidate for highest ranked pattern ϕ_{best}.

After a candidate pattern ϕ_{best} is chosen, the system first uses it to align the initial sequence. This involves aligning the elements with respect to the inferred frame(s) of reference. After alignment, our system uses the inferred pattern ϕ_{best} to predict the next element in the sequence and renders it on the screen with a dotted blue line. The 'Drag' gesture can then be used to extend the pattern. The user can drag the stylus to intersect the predicted item, causing the system to add it to the currently selected collection and predict a new item. This lets a user extend a collection as needed. Figure 3 shows a scenario where a sequence of circles is being extended along the edge of a polyline by continually dragging the stylus across the predicted elements.

Interactive Editing

Our beautification engine can make mistakes due to incorrectly inferred constraints, which can be corrected by entering 'Edit' mode, and manipulating the positions/sizes of beautified elements. For a circle, moving its center changes its position and moving its circumference changes its radius. For a line segment, moving the segment itself changes its position while moving either endpoint changes its length. For polylines, users can change the positions of its points by moving them as needed. Moving the boundary of a polyline moves the entire polyline to a new position. For severe beautification errors, the user can erase and redraw part or all of the drawing. We support the 'Scribble-Erase' gesture for erasing elements from the drawing. We also provide an intelligent 'Erase' mode which lets users delete parts of drawing elements. In intelligent 'Erase' mode, a user draws a region and any portions of recognized line segments falling within the region are clipped. PatternSketch also provides a method to break all groupings of drawing elements within a sketch by hitting the 'Ungroup Collections' button from the menu.

DISCUSSION AND CONCLUSION

Figure 4 shows a variety of structured drawings constructed with PatternSketch. Our framework provides a general way to describe structured drawings with a small set of abstract entities yet it leaves several important questions unanswered from an application developer's perspective. These questions include:

- What set of drawing elements should be supported?
- What types of patterns to support?
- What is a good method to instantiate supported drawing elements?
- What interaction metaphors are suitable for creating collections and filtering them?
- What is a good interaction metaphor for describing repetitive patterns explicitly?
- What algorithms may be used to infer patterns automatically?
- How can a user be empowered to extend and manipulate patterns?

We have addressed these practical questions with our prototype system, PatternSketch. It should be noted that PatternSketch is the first step toward the realization of our theoretical

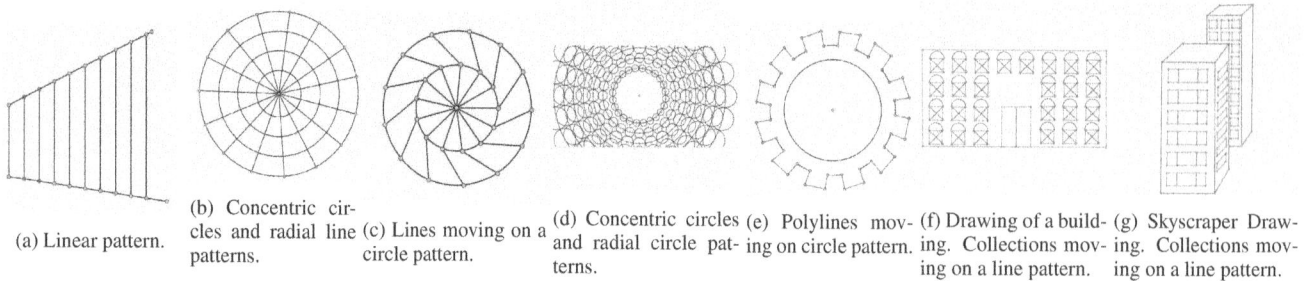

(a) Linear pattern.   (b) Concentric circles and radial line patterns.   (c) Lines moving on a circle pattern.   (d) Concentric circles and radial circle patterns.   (e) Polylines moving on circle pattern.   (f) Drawing of a building. Collections moving on a line pattern.   (g) Skyscraper Drawing. Collections moving on a line pattern.

Figure 4: Examples of drawings created using PatternSketch

framework and does not use the framework to its full potential. Our prototype system highlights the expressive power of our framework for modeling structured drawings. However, design trade-offs such as the use of sketch-based interaction can introduce errors in input (due to recognition and beautification), which can degrade drawing performance by requiring editing and redrawing. These errors can also cause problems with our pattern inference algorithm. Additionally, our choice of supporting a small set of drawing elements limits our system's capability to support all possible structured drawings that can be modeled using our framework.

PatternSketch uses a sketch-based interaction method to enable users to draw drawing elements in a natural manner. It supports four different types of drawing elements, and also enables composite elements by using collections. For creating and selecting collections, users can use the 'Lasso' gesture and can draw lines between drawing elements to perform filtering. PatternSketch supports five different types of patterns to cater to supported drawing elements. The patterns are built using the notion of PointSets that describe each pattern as a collection of low-level geometric transformations and implicitly encapsulate the notion of frame(s) of reference. We also provide the details of a novel inference algorithm that leverages concepts from the programming-by-example paradigm and exploits geometric constraints with a simple voting mechanism to identify dominant patterns. Our inference algorithm can work with both filtered and unfiltered collections.

ACKNOWLEDGEMENTS

This work is supported in part by NSF CAREER award IIS-0845921 and NSF awards IIS-0856045 and CCF-1012056.

REFERENCES

1. Bae, S.-H., Balakrishnan, R., and Singh, K. Everybodylovessketch: 3d sketching for a broader audience. In *Proceedings of the 22nd annual ACM symposium on User interface software and technology*, ACM (2009), 59–68.

2. Baudel, T. A mark-based interaction paradigm for free-hand drawing. In *Proceedings of the 7th annual ACM symposium on User interface software and technology*, ACM (1994), 185–192.

3. Bernhardt, A., Pihuit, A., Cani, M.-P., and Barthe, L. Matisse: Painting 2d regions for modeling free-form shapes. In *SBIM '08* (2008), 57–64.

4. Cheema, S., Gulwani, S., and LaViola, J. Quickdraw: improving drawing experience for geometric diagrams. In *CHI '12* (2012), 1037–1046.

5. Cypher, A., Ed. *Watch What I Do – Programming by Demonstration*. MIT Press, 1993.

6. Davis, R. C., Colwell, B., and Landay, J. A. K-sketch: a 'kinetic' sketch pad for novice animators. In *CHI '08* (2008), 413–422.

7. Fernquist, J., Grossman, T., and Fitzmaurice, G. Sketch-sketch revolution: an engaging tutorial system for guided sketching and application learning. In *Proceedings of the 24th annual ACM symposium on User interface software and technology*, ACM (2011), 373–382.

8. Fung, R., Lank, E., Terry, M., and Latulipe, C. Kinematic templates: end-user tools for content-relative cursor manipulations. In *Proceedings of the 21st annual ACM symposium on User interface software and technology*, ACM (2008), 47–56.

9. Gulwani, S. Synthesis from examples: Interaction models and algorithms. In *14th International Symposium on Symbolic and Numeric Algorithms for Scientific Computing* (2012). Invited talk paper.

10. Gulwani, S., Harris, W. R., and Singh, R. Spreadsheet data manipulation using examples. *Commun. ACM 55*, 8 (2012), 97–105.

11. Igarashi, T., Matsuoka, S., Kawachiya, S., and Tanaka, H. Interactive beautification: a technique for rapid geometric design. In *UIST '97* (1997), 105–114.

12. Igarashi, T., Matsuoka, S., and Tanaka, H. Teddy: a sketching interface for 3d freeform design. In *SIGGRAPH '99* (1999), 409–416.

13. Julia, L., and Faure, C. Pattern recognition and beautification for a pen based interface. In *Document Analysis and Recognition, 1995., Proceedings of the Third International Conference on*, vol. 1, IEEE (1995), 58–63.

14. Kazi, R. H., Igarashi, T., Zhao, S., and Davis, R. Vignette: interactive texture design and manipulation with freeform gestures for pen-and-ink illustration. In *CHI '12* (2012), 1727–1736.

15. Kurtenbach, G., and Buxton, W. Issues in combining marking and direct manipulation techniques. In *Proceedings of the 4th annual ACM symposium on User interface software and technology*, ACM (1991), 137–144.

16. Lau, T. A., Domingos, P., and Weld, D. S. Version space algebra and its application to programming by demonstration. In *Machine Learning (ICML)* (2000), 527–534.

17. Lieberman, H. *Your Wish Is My Command: Programming by Example*. Morgan Kaufmann, 2001.

18. Paulson, B., and Hammond, T. Paleosketch: accurate primitive sketch recognition and beautification. In *IUI '08* (2008), 1–10.

19. Singh, R., Gulwani, S., and Rajamani, S. Automatically generating algebra problems. In *AAAI* (2012).

20. Xiong, Y., and LaViola Jr., J. J. Technical section: A shortstraw-based algorithm for corner finding in sketch-based interfaces. *Comput. Graph. 34* (October 2010), 513–527.

21. Yang, C., Sharon, D., and van de Panne, M. Sketch-based modeling of parameterized objects. In *SIGGRAPH 2005* (2005).

22. Zeleznik, R. C., Bragdon, A., Liu, C.-C., and Forsberg, A. Lineogrammer: creating diagrams by drawing. In *UIST '08* (2008), 161–170.

Minimizing User Effort in Transforming Data by Example∗

Bo Wu
Computer Science Department
University of Southern
California
4676 Admiralty Way
Marina del Rey,CA
bowu@isi.edu

Pedro Szekely
Information Sciences Institute
University of Southern
California
4676 Admiralty Way
Marina del Rey, CA
pszekely@isi.edu

Craig A. Knoblock
Information Sciences Institute
University of Southern
California
4676 Admiralty Way
Marina del Rey, CA
knoblock@isi.edu

Table 1: Text Format Transformation Scenario

Raw Data	Target Data
Lois Anderson	Anderson, Lois
knud Merrild	Merrild, knud
robert boardman howard	howard, robert boardman
...	...
William J. Forsyth	Forsyth, William J.
John G. Dunn	Dunn, John G.

ABSTRACT

Programming by example enables users to transform data formats without coding. To be practical, the method must synthesize the correct transformation with minimal user input. We present a method that minimizes user effort by color-coding the transformation result and recommending specific records where the user should provide examples. Simulation results and a user study show that our method significantly reduces user effort and increases the success rate for synthesizing correct transformation programs by example.

Author Keywords

Data Transformation, Programming by Example, Recommendation

ACM Classification Keywords

H.5.m. Information Interfaces and Presentation: User Interfaces

INTRODUCTION

Many mashup applications rely on data from multiple sources. Unfortunately, using data from multiple sources often requires format transformation, which is highly task dependent. It often requires the user to specify the transformation, which is typically done by writing scripts [4] or demonstrating a sequence of edit operations [5] [6]. In order to ease the burden of specifying the transformations, Gulwani [3] developed a programming by example approach.

Programming by example approach asks a user to provide examples to synthesize the transformation program instead of having her write a program directly. In Table 1, a user wants to change the name format. To do this, a user only needs to provide an example for a record showing the target value. For instance, she would provide "Anderson, Lois" for the first record. Once she provides that example, the approach automatically generates the transformation program that is consistent with the examples. It then applies this program to the rest of the data and transforms those records automatically. The user then examines the results. If any record is transformed incorrectly, she enters the target value for that record. This process goes through multiple rounds until all the results are correct. During the process, she actively takes part in these activities:

1. Examining the results
2. Deciding which example to provide

All these activities repeat for several rounds until the user stops. Since a dataset can easily have thousands of records, the activities listed above can be very labor intensive and error prone. We identify several challenges as follows.

Firstly, the user needs to find incorrectly transformed results from possibly thousands of records. These records can either cause the transformation program to exit abnormally or simply have incorrect results. The user must identify these records so that the synthesizing approach can refine the program to handle the unseen cases correctly.

Secondly, the user cannot easily tell which record to label. Using different records as examples provides different amounts of information for the program to learn. Using the most informative record reduces the total number of examples that the user needs to provide.

Thirdly, the user does not know whether the synthesized transformation is as she expected. As the user generally does

∗This research was supported in part by the Intelligence Advanced Research Projects Activity (IARPA) via Air Force Research Laboratory (AFRL) contract number FA8650-10-C-7058. The U.S. Government is authorized to reproduce and distribute reprints for Governmental purposes notwithstanding any copyright annotation thereon. The views and conclusions contained herein are those of the authors and should not be interpreted as necessarily representing the official policies or endorsements, either expressed or implied, of IARPA, AFRL, or the U.S. Government.

not want to read the synthesized program, the system does not typically show it. She usually has no idea of what transformations are synthesized and applied.

In order to address the challenges above, we developed an approach to recommend records for the user and visualize the transformation to facilitate the decision-making on which example she should provide. By recommending records and color-coding the transformations, our system can reduce user effort in making decisions on which record to provide as an example and make the user aware of incorrectly transformed results. This approach to recommending records and visualizing the transformations provides the following contributions:

1. Reduces the number of iterations
2. Reduces the effort in examining the results
3. Increases the success rate

SYNTHESIZING TRANSFORMATION PROGRAMS
Gulwani [3] developed a programming by example approach that defines a string transformation language. This language supports a restricted, but expressive form of regular expressions, which includes conditionals and loops. The approach synthesizes transformation programs from this language using examples. The transformation program is a concatenation of several segments. Each segment consists of a start and an end position expression.

As shown in Figure 1, the program consists of four segments: last name, comma, blank space and first name segment. A segment can either be a constant string like the comma segment or describe how to extract the corresponding parts from the raw data. The second type of segment has two position expressions: start and end position expressions. The positions can be specified using (1) an absolute position, or (2) restricted regular expressions that identify the context of the given position, which can be represented as (leftcxt, rightcxt, occ). "leftcxt" describes the left context of the position, "rightcxt" describes the right context and"occ" is the occurrence of the position. For example, the start position of "Lois" can be specified as (START, UWRD, 1) or an absolute position 0. Here, "START" represents the beginning of the raw value. "END" is for the end of the raw value. "UWRD" represents an uppercase letter. "LWRD" means a continuing sequence of lower letters. The "BNK" means a blank space. Therefore, (START,UWRD, 1) means the first occurrence of a position, which is at the beginning of the raw data and has a uppercase token at its right.

In order to generate such transformation programs, Gulwani's approach first tokenizes the original value and target value of an example into two token sequences. He then groups the target token sequence into different segments. The approach then determines different ways to generate these segments from the original token sequence. As shown in Figure 1, "Anderson, Lois" is divided into multiple segments. The segments shown in the brackets are "Anderson", ",", " ", and "Lois". These segments are then concatenated in order to make up the transformation program.

If there are multiple examples, the approach uses an efficient algorithm to construct a version space for each example and

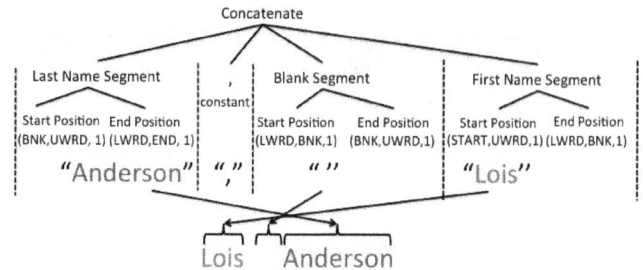

Figure 1: Transformation Program for Generating Target Values from Raw Values

to merge them into a version space consistent with the maximum number of examples. However, if the examples cannot be covered by a single version space, the algorithm partitions the examples and generates a version space for each partition individually. A conditional expression can be learned to distinguish multiple different version spaces. This approach also supports loop expressions by detecting whether continuous segments of one program can be merged.

APPROACH OVERVIEW
Our approach builds upon Gulwani's approach [3] to recommend incorrectly transformed records using active learning. Our system first recommend the most informative record from the records that cause transformation program to exit with error. When all the records are successfully transformed, it will then recommend the most questionable record that may have incorrect results.

The screenshot of our user interface in Figure 2 has the following areas. (1) "Examples You Entered" shows all previous examples. (2) "Recommended for Examining" shows our recommended record. (3) "All Records" shows all the records in a multi-page table. On the left are raw data and on the right are transformed values.

The user first checks whether the recommended record is correct. If it is not, she can provide the target value for this entry to teach the system to learn this new variation. If the result is already correct, she can then check the transformed values in the "All Records" area to identify any incorrect result. As she might type an incorrect example by accident, she can easily find all the previous examples and cancel the one with an error.

We can see that all the original values and transformed values are color coded, which shows the correspondence between substrings in the transformed values and substrings in the original values. This color-coding can help the user understand what transformation is currently applied to the data and also makes it easier to identify incorrect results by displaying irregular color patterns.

RECOMMENDING INFORMATIVE RECORDS
Certain records can cause the transformation program to exit abnormally. For example in Figure 2, the user entered "Anderson, Lois" as the target value for "Lois Anderson". The synthesized program exits with an error on both record A and B. (Our system keeps the values the same as the raw values

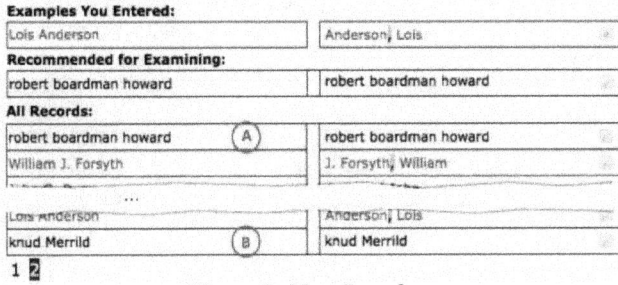

Figure 2: User Interface

Table 2: Fail or Success for Each position Expression

Record	LStart	LEnd	BStart	BEnd	FStart	FEnd
A	0	1	1	0	0	1
B	1	1	1	1	0	1

and will not color-code these records.) Choosing the informative record to provide an example can minimize the number of examples to synthesize the correct program.

Our approach recommends such informative records for the user. As we mentioned before, the transformation program consists of a number of position expressions, which specify how to locate the start or end position of a segment. Any position expression that fails to locate any position on a record will cause the transformation program to fail in that record. By tracking the interpretation results of each individual position expression, we can get the number of failed position expressions for each record and then identify the record with the largest number of failed position expressions.

Table 2 shows the interpreted results for each position expression on two records. L represents last name, B represents blank and F represents first name. "LStart" means the start position expression for last name. According to Table 2, record A fails on both the last name and first name start position expression, while the record B fails on the first name start position. As seen from Figure 1, the last name start position expression is (BNK, UWRD, 1) and the first name start position is (START, UWRD). Both expressions require the right context to be an upper case token. However, record B has a lower case first name, while both the first name and last name in record A are lower case token. Therefore, if we provide an example for record A, we can teach the transformation program that both first name and last name can be lower case words.

Our program may contain conditional expression and loop expression. For conditional expression, our approach evaluates the condition of the record and chooses the correct program for the record. We then calculate the score as described before. For loop expression, the loop will break if any mismatch happens. Therefore, we actually use the number of mismatches in the last iteration to calculate the score for the record.

To identify the most informative record, we count the number of failed position expressions for each record and recommend the one with the largest number of failed position expressions.

RECOMMENDING QUESTIONABLE RECORDS

Records can have incorrect results, which requires the user to examine the results more carefully to detect the error. For example, in Figure 3 the synthesized program generates results for all records. However, after scrutinizing the data, we can see the results for record C and record D are still incorrect. The end position expression of the first or middle name is (LWRD,BNK,-1) after entering two examples as shown in Figure 3. The expression aims to find a location, whose left is a lower case token and right is a blank. "-1" means the first occurrence when searching backwards. As record C and D use "." as the left context for the end position, which doesn't match the condition, the expression cannot match at the correct position. Instead, it keeps scanning backwards until it reaches the end of the first word. Although the result satisfies the position expression, it is incorrect.

To capture these incorrect results, we found the transformation can also be evaluated based on the content before and after the transformation. From Figure 3, we can see that the examples keep all the content in the raw value. However, for record C and D, the middle names do not get copied to the transformed value. We can compare other records against the examples. Thus, the record that is the most different from the examples is most likely to be incorrect. We recommend this record as questionable record for the user to examine.

We represent the transformation using a set of features. There are two types of features:

Transformation features: These features aim to capture the content changed after applying the transformation program. We use these features to represent the transformation.

1. Token count difference: this type of features calculates the difference between the token counts before and after the transformation. Taking "." as an example, it appears once in record C before transformation and appears 0 times after. Thus, the feature value for "." count difference is 1 for record C. We track the count difference for a set of tokens such as all the punctuation, numbers and tokens appearing in at least 10% records. Each token in this set will be a feature in the final feature vector.

2. Reorder: this type of feature calculates the inversion number of the target string. We assign each token in the result a number o_i, which is its order in the original token sequence. We then compute the inversion number using $count(\{(o_i, o_j) \mid i < j \, and \, o_i > o_j\})$.

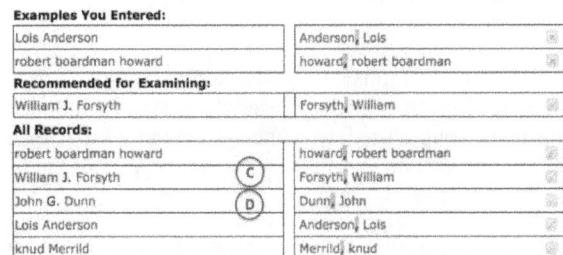

Figure 3: Transformed Results are Incorrect

Result format features: these features aim to capture the format of transformed result. Using these features, we can identify the records that have different formats from examples. We use the counts of various tokens in the result for these features. Each token count corresponds to one result format feature. The tokens used in this type of feature are the same as the tokens used in token count difference features.

Given the feature set, we follow these steps to detect the questionable record:

1. Convert all pairs of raw and transformed values into feature vectors V_i using the features defined above. Convert all examples into features vectors E_i in the same way.
2. Obtain the mean vector $\bar{E}$ of the m examples by $\bar{E} = \frac{\sum_i^m E_i}{m}$
3. Calculate the Euclidean distance of each record V_i with the mean vector $\bar{E}$ of examples and identify the questionable record V^* by $\|V^* - \bar{E}\| = max_{V_i}\{\|V_i - \bar{E}\|\}$

After identifying the questionable record, we will recommend it for the user to examine. As our program can contain conditional expressions, our approach will partition the records based on the conditions. We then identify the candidate questionable record for each partition and recommend the record with maximal distance to its partition's mean vector.

EVALUATION

In this section, we present the results of two experiments. One is a real user study and the other is a simulated evaluation. [1]

User Study

To test whether our approach reduces user effort and increases the likelihood that a user can correctly transforms a real dataset, we conducted a comparative user study between the system with and without extensions in real world transformation scenarios. The system without extensions hid the suggested records and color coding from users.

Dataset

The data came from 5 museums with thousands of records of artworks and artists represented in different formats. The goal was to extract the common properties across the 5 museums and convert them into the same format.

We identified 41 scenarios and grouped them based on the 8 common properties. We then randomly chose 1 from each group and used these 8 scenarios for the user study. We kept a maximum of 500 records and the average number of records was 300. We give the first several examples for each scenario to demonstrate the transformations in Table 3.

Participants and Method

We recruited 10 graduate students and randomly divided them into 2 equal groups. Group 1 used the system without extensions and Group 2 used the same system but with extensions. We first trained participants using a simple scenario and then asked them to work on the 8 scenarios by orally describing

[1] Data is available at www.isi.edu/integration/data/IUI2014. The code is available as the data transformation tool of Karma(http://www.isi.edu/integration/karma/).

Table 4: User Study Results

Scen	Without Extensions (group 1)		With Extensions (group 2)	
	Avg time (sec.)	Success rate	Avg time (sec.)	Success rate
s1	30	1.0	35	1.0
s2	119	0.6	41	1.0
s3	110	0.6	40	1.0
s4	unsolved	0.0	unsolved	0.0
s5	201	0.2	95	1.0
s6	unsolved	0.0	142	1.0
s7	unsolved	0.0	unsolved	0.0
s8	191	0.4	95	1.0
All	130.2	0.35	74.6	0.75

the task. We asked Group 2 participants to use the recommendation if it were applicable. If the user could not finish the scenario in 5 minutes, that scenario is regarded as a failure.

Results

We used the following metrics to measure how each group performed on each scenario.

1. Average Time: the average time in seconds used by the users who transformed all the records in the scenario correctly.
2. Success Rate: the ratio of the users in the group that transformed all the records in the scenario correctly.

According to Table 4, both systems failed on s4 and s7, where the success rate was 0 and average time was "unsolved" as no user transformed the two scenarios correctly. We can see that group 2 used less time and achieved a higher rate on all the other scenarios except s1. Users saved 55 seconds on average of all successfully transformed scenarios and increased their success rate for 0.4 on average across all scenarios.

The time saving shown in the user study was largely because the user in group 2 did not need to examine all records to identify the ones with bad results. The more examples a scenario required, the more rounds it took the user to examine the results. Taking scenario 1 as example, because the user only needed to provide one example to derive the correct program and both groups examined the results before submitting, the group 1 users did not spend more time examining the results. The two groups had very close average times as seen in Table 4. On the other hand, for the rest of scenarios (s2, s3, s5 and s8), an average of 8.2 examples were required for group 1 users to correctly synthesize the program, while the users in group 2 only used an average of 6.5. The users in group 2 not only spent less time examining the results in each round, but also used fewer rounds. Therefore, these scenarios showed significant time savings.

The user study also showed the group 2 users achieved higher success rate. For group 1 users, many reported it was very exhausting to examine hundreds of records. They generally needed to provide 8.2 examples to synthesize the correct program. Even after providing a new example, they still needed to recheck all the records as previously correctly transformed records may have become incorrect this time. Many users simply did not check whether all the results are correct. They

Table 3: Scenarios used in the user study

Scenario	Orignal Value	Target Value
s1:extract the artist birth date	1860-1945	1860
	1870-1955	1870
s2:extract the artist death date	active c. 1859 - 1910	1910
	born 1936	none
s3:extract the first degree of the art work dimension	15 3/8 in.	15 3/8
	20 x 24 1/4 in.	20
s4: extract the width of the artwork dimension	W: 26 in, H: 36 in.	26
	H: 28 in, W: 50 in	50
	H: 5 1/2 in, W: 8 1/2 in	8 1/2
s5: extract the third degree of the artwork dimension	11.5 in WIDE x 1.5 in DEEP(29.21 cm WIDE x 3.81 cm DEEP)	1.5
	24 in HIGH(60.96 cm HIGH)	none
s6: extract the content in the parenthesizes	Despair	none
	Untitled (Grindelia)	Grindelia
	California Landscape ((Hills around Sonoma))	Hills around Sonoma
s7: extract the date that the artwork was made	California,1970	1970
	Los Angeles, Calif.,July 7, 1970	July 7, 1970
	Los Angeles, Calif., Los Angeles, Calif.,	none
s8: change the format to put surname at the end	Wyeth, Andrew Newell	Andrew Newell Wyeth
	C. C. Bohm	C. C. Bohm

randomly chose several pages and browsed the results. They submitted the results when they found all the records in those pages were correct. However, they missed records with bad results in the pages that they did not check.

The reason that both groups failed on s4 and s7 is because the two scenarios were beyond the ability of Gulwani's approach. For s4, the approach cannot learn the end position expression for extracting the number after width. The right context for the end position is " in.", while the number after the "H" also has same context. The left context for the end position cannot be learned either. The first row's left context is ("W" ":" BNK NUM). The third row's left context is ("W" ":" NUM BNK NUM "/" NUM). After generalization over these two contexts, we get (NUM), which also has a false match position in the second row. As both the left and right context of the end position expression cannot locate the correct position, a transformation program cannot be learned in this case. For scenario 7, we want to extract the date or the year from the string. The start position is indiscernible here. The target substring may appear after the third comma, second comma or first comma. The substring itself may also start with a word or a digit too. As s4 and s7 are beyond the synthesizing programs capability, both our system and the baseline system cannot derive a correct program.

Finally, the system with recommendations succeeded in all the scenarios that can be solved by using more than one example with significantly less time and higher success rate compared to the system without recommendation.

Simulation Experiment

Our simulation tests whether our approach uses fewer examples and examines fewer records to transform all the records correctly, when compared to three other simulated record selection strategies.

Dataset

The dataset consists of 20 scenarios that we collected from Google user forum and the 6 solvable scenarios from the museum dataset. We went through all the posts from July 2012 to July 2013 and randomly collected 20 scenarios. As some

posts may not post the data directly, we created the data based on the description in the post. The number of records for each scenario is 75.

Method

We designed three alternative record examining strategies to approximate user record examining behaviors and compare them with our recommendation-based strategy. Each strategy examines the results in the order described below till it identifies a record with an incorrect result.

1. Longest record: examine the record with the longest result first.
2. Shortest record: examine the record with the shortest result first.
3. Top down: examine the record from top down order.

Results

In this experiment, we measured the average number of examples and examined records on 2 datasets (Tables 5).

The "Example" shows the average number of examples for each strategy to solve each dataset. The percentage in the parenthesizes shows the percentage of examples that can be saved by using recommendation. The "Record" shows the average number of examined records. The percentage in the parenthesizes presents the percentage of examined records that can be saved by using recommendation. On average, our strategy needed 3 examples and examined 3 records on forum dataset; it needed 6.5 examples and examined 17 records on museum dataset. Our recommendation cannot alway identify the incorrect result. We noticed that for our strategy examined more records than the number of examples in scenario 6 of museum dataset. Our strategy used the first row as the first examples. The synthesized program transformed all the records to "none". Our approach cannot recommend the right record then, as our system did not know the transformation was to extract the content within parenthesizes before getting such examples.

In Tables 5, by using recommendation, the system used fewer examples and examined a lower percentage of records than

Table 5: Comparing Recommendation with Other Strategies

Datasets		Longest	Shortest	Top_Down	Recmd
Forum	Example	4.1 (26%)	4.3 (30%)	4.2 (29%)	3
	Record	48 (94%)	21 (86%)	18 (83%)	3
Museum	Example	8.3 (21%)	8.8 (26%)	9.2 (29%)	6.5
	Record	186 (91%)	162 (90%)	154 (89%)	17

the three alternative strategies. One tail t test suggested the improvements were statistically significant ($p < 0.05$).

RELATED WORK

In this section, we review the most related data transformation systems and active learning approaches. OpenRefine [4] and Potter's wheel [8] allow the user to specify edit operations. OpenRefine [4] is a tool for cleaning messy data. Its language supports regular expression style of string transformation and data layout transformation. Potter's Wheel [8] defines a set of transformation operations and let users gradually build transformations by adding or undoing transformations in an interactive GUI. Many PBD [2] approaches can learn edit operations by asking the user to demonstrate the operations. Lau's system [6] and Data Wrangler [5] learn from the user's edit operations. Lau [6] described a system that can learn from a user's edit operations and generate a sequence of text editing programs using the version space algebra. Data Wrangler [5] is an interactive tool for creating data transformation. It uses the transformation operations defined in Potter's wheel [8]. Besides supporting string level transformation, it also supports data layout transformation including column split, column merge, fold and unfold. Our approach is different from these two types of systems as it only requires users to enter the target data.

Gulwani [3] developed an approach to synthesis a program through input and output string pairs. Gulwani mentioned that his approach can highlight the entry, which has two or more alternative transformed results. This method needs to generate multiple programs and evaluate these programs on all the records, which requires more processing time. Our approach improves Gulwani's work by providing recommendation. To generate the recommendation, we only need one program and its results on the records. Topes [9] let the user specify the data pattern or learn the pattern from examples. Programmers can implement transformation functions between patterns to perform data transformation across different formats.

CueFlik [1] shows users an overview of the learned concept. Users can examine this overview to provide new examples. This overview is essentially a high level abstraction of the instances in the image feature space. Our approach recommends records from two spaces: program space and text feature space. LAPIS [7] highlight the texts that have potentially incorrect matches. Their approach identifies the matches that are different from the majority of matches. Besides helping the user identify problematic inputs, our approach also identifies the most informative record. Wolfman [10] extends Lau's [6] work by reducing the user effort using a mix initiative approach combining several interaction modes. Our work is inspired by his work of shifting the user's attention to

a particular example. His approach suggests those examples that can reduce the ambiguity of the version space. However, our approach focus on acquiring the unseen examples. As our program can be a disjunct of multiple transformations, the new example does not necessarily reduce the ambiguity of version space.

CONCLUSION AND FUTURE WORK

This paper presents a general data transformation tool aiming to minimize user effort in synthesizing transformation programs by example. This tool recommends records to help the user avoid examining a large quantity of transformed results. In our simulated experiment and user study, the experimental results show the tool saves user time, reduces number of examples and increases success rates significantly.

We identified one interesting problem for the future work. When the users were working on the two unsolvable cases, they complained that adding new examples may correct some incorrect result but also make some previous correct results incorrect. It was very frustrating for the users. They did not know whether they were making progress in transforming the dataset toward the target format in general. However, the system can show the status of the current results so that the user can quit when most of the records are transformed into a good shape. It may be easier for user to process these semi-finished data than handle the raw data directly.

REFERENCES

1. Amershi, S., Fogarty, J., Kapoor, A., and Tan, D. Overview based example selection in end user interactive concept learning. In *UIST* (2009), 247–256.

2. Cypher, A., Halbert, D. C., Kurlander, D., Lieberman, H., Maulsby, D., Myers, B. A., and Turransky, A., Eds. *Watch what I do: programming by demonstration.* MIT Press, 1993.

3. Gulwani, S. Automating string processing in spreadsheets using input-output examples. In *POPL* (2011), 317–330.

4. Huynh, D. F., and Stefano, M. *OpenRefine* http://openrefine.org.

5. Kandel, S., Paepcke, A., Hellerstein, J., and Heer, J. Wrangler: interactive visual specification of data transformation scripts. In *CHI* (2011), 3363–3372.

6. Lau, T., Wolfman, S. A., Domingos, P., and Weld, D. S. Programming by demonstration using version space algebra. *Mach. Learn.* (2003), 111–156.

7. Miller, R. C., and Myers, B. A. Outlier finding: Focusing user attention on possible errors. In *UIST* (2001), 81–90.

8. Raman, V., and Hellerstein, J. M. Potter's wheel: An interactive data cleaning system. In *VLDB* (2001).

9. Scaffidi, C., Myers, B., and Shaw, M. Topes: Reusable abstractions for validating data. In *ICSE* (2008), 1–10.

10. Wolfman, S. A., Lau, T. A., Domingos, P., and Weld, D. S. Mixed initiative interfaces for learning tasks: Smartedit talks back. In *IUI* (2001), 167–174.

Exploring Head Tracked Head Mounted Displays for First Person Robot Teleoperation

Corey Pittman
University of Central Florida
Orlando, FL 32816 USA
cpittman@knights.ucf.edu

Joseph J. LaViola Jr.
University of Central Florida
Orlando, FL 32816 USA
jjl@eecs.ucf.edu

ABSTRACT

We explore the capabilities of head tracking combined with head mounted displays (HMD) as an input modality for robot navigation. We use a Parrot AR Drone to test five techniques which include metaphors for plane-like banking control, car-like turning control and virtual reality-inspired translation and rotation schemes which we compare with a more traditional game controller interface. We conducted a user study to observe the effectiveness of each of the interfaces we developed in navigating through a number of archways in an indoor course. We examine a number of qualitative and quantitative metrics to determine performance and preference among each metaphor. Our results show an appreciation for head rotation based controls over other head gesture techniques, with the classic controller being preferred overall. We discuss possible shortcomings with head tracked HMDs as a primary input method as well as propose improved metaphors that alleviate some of these drawbacks.

Author Keywords

3D Interaction; User Studies; Robots

ACM Classification Keywords

H.5.m. Information Interfaces and Presentation (e.g. HCI): Miscellaneous

General Terms

Design, Experimentation

INTRODUCTION

As the cost of Virtual Reality technologies fall, new applications for these once unaffordable technologies are being found in a number of diverse areas of study. One such area is Human Robot Interaction. Manipulating robots using gestural inputs has been an oft studied area [3][4][10] in recent years, with interactivity and naturalness being among the observed benefits of this modality. A mode of control that has not been thoroughly explored as a primary input method for teleoperation is head tracking. Head tracked HMDs have often been used in virtual environments to increase a user's

sense of immersion and proprioception [3]. Using head tracking in addition to a head mounted display (HMD) as a means to improve a user's experience in virtual environments has been detailed in prior work, with evaluations of different settings to determine the effects of different HMD configurations being among the more recent work in the area [7][11].

One area that has not seen a significant amount of work with head tracking and head mounted displays is robot teleoperation. In this paper, we focus on direct teleoperation of a robot using egocentric head movements. The robot selected as the test robot for this study was a low cost quadrotor, as it is well represented in entertainment as a toy and possesses similarities to military unmanned aerial vehicles (UAV) in potential applications. Using commonly observed vehicles and VR control techniques as inspiration, we developed five head tracking based metaphors for flying the UAV using simply an HMD with head tracking and compared against a game controller. We designed and conducted a user study that asked users to complete a navigation task by flying around a hexagonal course. We then analyzed the qualitative and quantitative results of the study.

RELATED WORK

Pfeil et al. [10] have previously developed full body gesture interfaces for controlling an AR Drone using a depth camera and joint information. Multiple metaphors for controlling a UAV were proposed, and a number of interfaces were compared in a formal user study. One significant problem with the system as described was the user's view of the drone, which was from a third person perspective. Our system addresses this problem by placing users in the first person, making our controls more meaningful to users given the difference in relative viewpoints.

Higuchi et al. [4] have developed a head tracking solution for the teleoperation of a Parrot AR Drone using synchronized optical trackers attached to the head and drone chassis called Flying Head. Users wore a head mounted display which featured a view from the front mounted camera of the drone, giving the user a first person view of the world through the drone's eyes. One of the techniques we implemented was based on this work with some modifications. However, we do not use any visual sensors thereby avoiding potential occlusion problems. The authors also did not conduct a systematic study comparing their approach with a traditional joystick interface.

Koeda et al. [6] tested the benefit of providing a user with a first person view from a teleoperated small helicopter. Their system placed an omni-directional camera on the helicopter so that the user can turn his head while wearing an HMD and see as if looking around from within the helicopter. They did not utilize head tracking for any sort of teleoperation controls instead opting for an RC controller.

The Robonaut, a humanoid designed for use in space, was designed with a teleoperation technique for control of the entire robot, including the head with two degrees of freedom [1]. Users wore an HMD with head tracking and were able to send commands to the Robonaut by rotating head yaw and pitch. This control scheme is comparatively simple, as it only tracks two axes of rotation of the head, while our techniques makes use of three axes of head rotation and three translation axes. Other work has explored using head mounted displays for controlling robots, such as [8][9].

INTERACTION TECHNIQUES

We developed five gestural navigation techniques, with one of them being inspired by prior work [4]. All techniques were created under the assumption that the user is standing. For all techniques that use head gestures, additional controls for takeoff, landing, and resetting the drone were placed on a Nintendo Wiimote to give a supervisor control of the drone in case of emergencies.

Head Translation

This technique was inspired by commonly used techniques for navigating a virtual environment by moving the upper body in the desired direction of motion [2]. In our context, this means that by taking a step forwards and shifting the head over that foot, the head will translate from its original position and the UAV will then move forwards. This can be done in all four cardinal directions, meaning the user needs only to shift one foot in a direction and then shift their weight over that foot to translate the UAV in that direction relative to its current heading. Once the user returns their foot and head to their original position, the UAV will cease moving and return to its resting position. The user can also move in the ordinal directions to cause the UAV to move along a combination of two cardinal directions. To turn the UAV, the user can turn their head to the left or right and the drone will turn until the user returns to looking forwards relative to their initial orientation. The user can stand on their toes to increase the elevation of the UAV and squat down slightly to decrease the elevation of the UAV.

Head Rotation

This technique was inspired by observing people playing video games in a casual environment. Occasionally when people play first person perspective video games, they tilt or turn their head slightly while playing in an attempt to will their avatar to move more than what the constraints of the game controls will allow [12]. To control the drone using these movements, we made use of the rotational axes of the head. If the user tilts his head forwards, the UAV will move forwards; tilts his head backward then the UAV will move back; and tilts his head to the left or right to cause the UAV to strafe in the corresponding the direction. The user can also turn his head to cause the drone to turn in the corresponding

direction. In order to move the drone up or down, the user stands on their toes or squats down slightly.

Modified Flying Head

Higuchi et al. designed an interaction technique based on a visual tracking system that allowed for a UAV to synchronize its movements with a user's movements [4]. A major shortcoming with this method of interaction is that the size of the user's control area would have to match the UAV's environment. A number of methods were proposed to alleviate this shortcoming. We made use of the turning technique proposed in their work, which uses direct manipulation of the UAV's heading based on the heading of the user, allowing them to turn 360 degrees within their control space. To cause the drone to turn, the user rotates his entire body the same amount that they would like the drone to rotate, which will rotate to match the movements of the user. This is the largest difference between this technique and the previous two described techniques. To move the drone forwards, the user needed to step forwards along the direction their head was facing. This remains true regardless of how turned the user is from their initial heading: shifting the head forwards will always move the drone forwards. The user can also shift their head in the other three major directions to translate the drone in other directions. To control elevation, the user can stand on their toes or squat down.

Flying Car and Plane

One initial assumption that was made when designing these techniques was that when a user is standing in a neutral position, the UAV should not be moving and therefore require the user to make a pronounced movement to trigger any sort of change in its behavior. In some cases, this could be considered a hindrance, including the control of vehicles that spend a majority of their time in motion, such as a car. Therefore we designed the Flying Car metaphor based around the idea that when sitting in a car that is engaged in a forward gear, it will move forwards slowly using the motion generated by its idling engine. When the user is standing idly, the UAV will move forwards at a slow pace. If the user shifts back, it is synonymous with applying the brakes in a car, therefore causing the UAV to come to a stop. If the user shifts forwards or presses the accelerator, the drone will accelerate at full speed. To turn the car, the user simply looks to the left or right with their head. The user may also look up to move the drone upward or look down to move the drone downwards—this being similar to theoretical controls for a flying car from popular entertainment media. Because a car cannot strafe, there is no ability to strafe in this control scheme. The Plane technique is similar to flying car except that instead of turning the head to control the drone's rotation, the user must tilt their head.

Wiimote

A classic control scheme was implemented as a baseline for comparison with our head tracking interfaces. Pfeil et al. showed that gestural interfaces were preferred to the packaged smartphone application for the AR Drone with regards to naturalness, fun, and overall preference [10]. For that reason we developed our own simple control configuration using a Nintendo Wiimote. The D-pad was mapped to drone translations within the horizontal axis, elevation was mapped to the A and B buttons, and turning the drone was mapped to the 1 and 2 buttons. The other three commonly used controls (takeoff, land, and reset/emergency) were mapped to the remaining buttons on the controller. Figure 1 shows these settings mapped to a controller.

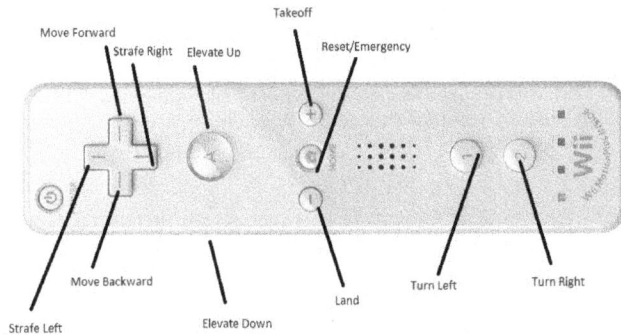

Figure 1. Control configuration for Wiimote interface.

USER STUDY

We designed a user study around a simple navigation task for a robot in a physical environment. Our goal was to analyze the performance and ergonomics of our developed interaction techniques compared to a traditional interface.

Subjects

Eighteen students (16 male, 2 female) from the University of Central Florida were recruited to participate in the study. Ages ranged from 18 to 38 with a median age of 22. Of all participants, 16 had experience with remote controlled vehicles, five had worn a head mounted display prior to participating in the study, and five had experience with position tracking devices. Two of the eighteen students were graduate students.

Devices and Apparatus

We used an Oculus Rift, a low cost HMD with a stereoscopic display and a resolution of 1280 by 800. We used a Polhemus PATRIOT tracker to track the users head movements. The sensor was placed on the upper headband of the Oculus Rift and the source was placed at a position over the user's head to minimize electromagnetic interference from the electronics within the HMD. A Nintendo Wiimote was used for all non-gesture commands, in addition to being used as the basis for the control interaction technique for the study. The UAV we used to test our metaphors was the Parrot AR Drone 2.0. The AR Drone possesses two on board cameras: one forward facing and one downwards facing. The raw front camera feed from the UAV was displayed in the HMD with no additional modification or overlay. The system was set up on a laptop running Ubuntu 12.04 LTS, 4 GB of RAM, a 2.53 GHz Intel Core i5 processor, and an NVIDIA GeForce 310m graphics card.

Environment Layout

The study took place in a 10m by 10m open area with six archways of varying heights arranged in a regular hexagon

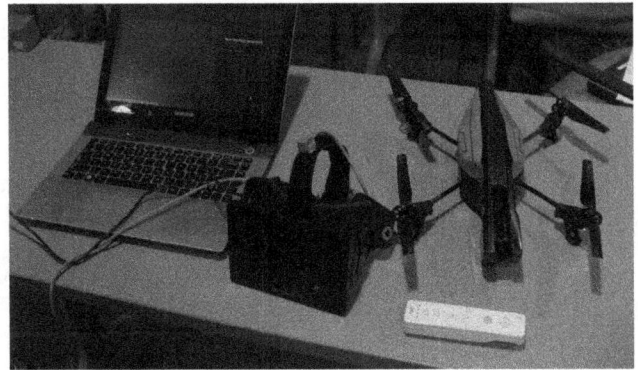

Figure 2. The devices used for our system. From left to right: Laptop, Oculus Rift with Polhemus PATRIOT sensor attached, Parrot AR Drone 2.0, Nintendo Wiimote.

with a 3 meter gap between each arch. The archways were 1.2 meters wide and between 1.5 meters and 2 meters in height. These arches were arranged in alternating height along the hexagon. The size of these arches was determined in a pilot study in which circular hoops of various heights were placed in a similar environment. It was determined that a larger rectangular shape was more fitting for a flying navigation task. The participant stood 3 meters away from the course in the same room. The tracking system, HMD, and laptop were all set up in this designated area, allowing the participant to move around a designated area to give commands to the drone unimpeded. The participant's space was approximately 1.5 meters by 1.5 meters, giving ample space to freely execute head gestures without impedance. Though they could hear the drone in the environment, participants were asked to look away from the course and towards the control setup at all times. The starting position of the drone was in an adjacent corner to the participant's position, approximately 6 meters away. A diagram illustrating this layout can be seen in Figure 3.

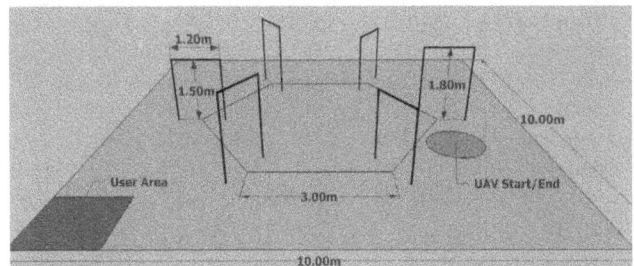

Figure 3. A diagram of the study environment layout.

Experimental Procedure

We used a six-way within-subjects comparison where the independent variable was the interface being used to complete the course. The dependent variables were the completion time of the navigation task and responses to a post-questionnaire that rated a users agreement to nine statements on a seven point Likert scale for each of the six interfaces. These statements are listed in Table 1. A Simulator Sickness Questionnaire (SSQ) [5] was also completed after each run to check for any sort of nausea caused by the use of a head mounted display. The six interfaces tested were Head Translation, Head Rotation, Modified Flying Head, Flying Car, Plane, and Wiimote. The interface order was assigned using replicated Latin Squares.

Participants were given a practice run at the course to become familiar with the nuances of the current control scheme. Once the participant declared that they felt confident in their abilities to complete the course for time, the drone was placed back at the initial point of the course. This typically occurred after one run, though there were examples of participants needing upwards of three practice runs to feel comfortable enough with the controls to be willing to attempt a timed run. With the drone at the starting point of the course, the proctor of the study used the Wiimote to give the takeoff command to the drone. Once the drone was in the air, the participant was informed that time would start on their mark. Participants were allowed to make heading adjustments to the drone prior to the start of a run to correct for any unintended movement or drift that occurred on takeoff.

Once the participant gave the command to move the drone forwards, the proctor began timing the run. The participant was asked to move the drone through the six arches in counter clockwise order. If at any time the participant passed by an arch without flying through it, they were asked to continue on to the next arch and proceed through an additional arch after passing through what would have been the sixth arch. If the participant crashed the drone mid-run, there was no time penalty: the timer was stopped and the drone was returned to a point on the optimal flight path. Timing was continued once the participant began moving the drone forwards again. No penalty was given to participants who touched the arches while passing through them without crashing. Time was stopped once the entire drone passed through the final arch. A human was placed at the position of the last arch to ensure that an accurate time was recorded. Participants were given a break after each run to fill out a questionnaire.

When the Wiimote control interface was used to complete a run, the participant did not wear the HMD. They instead were asked to sit in front of a monitor with the controller in their hands. This was done to ensure that the interface we were comparing to most accurately represented a standard interface, which typically allow participants to freely look at the controller in their hands to confirm the button configuration.

ANALYSIS OF DATA

Quantitative Metrics

Figure 4 shows the mean completion time of the course for each technique. Using a 6-way repeated measures ANOVA analysis, we tested for significant differences in the mean completion times between each of the six interaction techniques. We found that there was significance ($F_{5,13} = 5.885, p < 0.05$), and therefore went on to compare the Wiimote control technique to each of the head gesture based techniques. The Wiimote was found to be significantly faster around the course than each of the gesture based techniques based on a paired samples t-test of the mean completion times with $\alpha = 0.05$.

Between Runs Survey Questions
The interface to fly the Drone was comfortable to use.
The interface to fly the Drone did not confuse me.
I liked this interface for flying the Drone.
The interface to fly the drone felt natural to me.
It was fun to use this interface to control the drone.
I did not feel frustrated using the interface.
I did not feel discomfort or pain while using this interface.
It was easy to use this interface.
The Drone always flew in a predictable way.

Table 1. Survey questions asked after each run of the study. The questions used a 7-point Likert scale, with one being strongly disagree and seven being strongly agree.

To determine if there was any significant difference among the remaining techniques, we then ran a paired samples t-test with each of the remaining pairings. We found that there was significant difference between Plane and Flying Head ($t_{17} = 2.858, p < 0.05$), Plane and Head Translation ($t_{17} = 2.353, p < 0.05$), Head Rotation and Head Translation ($t_{17} = 2.617, p < 0.05$), and Head Rotation and Flying Head ($t_{17} = -2.457, p < 0.05$). This implies that though they were not nearly as fast as the Wiimote, Head Rotation and Plane were both better than Flying Head and Head Translation.

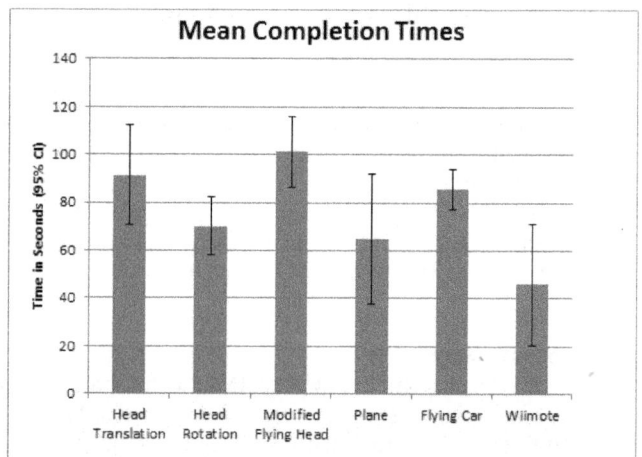

Figure 4. Mean completion time for each technique. There are three tiers of performance displayed here with Wiimote being significantly faster than all others, and Head Rotation/Plane being faster than the remaing three.

Qualitative Metrics

To determine if there was any significant difference between median results on our qualitative ranking metrics, we used a non-parametric Friedman test. If it was determined that there was significant differences, we then employed Wilcoxon's signed rank test to look at significant differences between the Wiimote technique and the head tracking based techniques. We found that the Wiimote was rated highest along a number of different measures.

Wiimote was significantly more predictable, easy to use, and comfortable than every other interface. These findings match up with the completion time results, as navigation tasks will typically be best completed with an interface that is accurate and familiar. Participants had a clear preference for the strain-free button presses of the controller overhead movements. Wiimote was significantly less frustrating, less confusing, more fun, and more likable than Modified Flying Head and Plane, based on analysis of the medians of ranking. One possible explanation for this is the large number of users who have previously used a remote control vehicle. All eighteen of the users also own at least one game system, so there is familiarity with similar controls to the one that was given to them in this experiment.

In order to determine a ranking of preference among participants, we used a Chi-Squared test to determine which techniques were liked more than expected. The Wiimote is ranked as the most likable interface of the six used in the study ($\chi^2_{5,17} = 21.333, p < 0.05$). The most liked of the remaining techniques is shown to be the Head Rotation interface ($\chi^2_{5,17} = 12.667, p < 0.05$). Head Translation and Modified Flying Head were the least liked interfaces.

Analysis of the SSQ scores shows significant difference among the six interfaces. The Wiimote was determined to have lower total SSQ scores than Head Rotation ($t_{17} = -2.250, p < 0.05$), Plane ($t_{17} = -3.296, p < 0.05$), and Flying Car ($t_{17} = -2.148, p < 0.05$). There is significantly less sickness in the Wiimote technique than three of the head-tracked HMD interfaces, most likely because participants are not wearing an HMD when using it. Only five of the participants reported experiencing any amount of sickness that achieved a total SSQ score greater than 25 with any of the techniques. Eye strain scores were more prominent than any other measure, most likely due to the low resolution of the HMD and the motion blur from the camera feed. Another interesting pattern is that anytime a user had to wear the HMD for long periods of time to complete a run, their SSQ scores were notably higher. We base this observation solely on the completion time of the run, though participants typically wore the HMD for longer than the reported numbers when factoring in practice time.

A number of comments about the interfaces were recorded by participants between runs and after the study. Four of the 18 participants explicitly mentioned enjoying the natural feeling of the head tracked interfaces. Two each mentioned that they found the head gestures a fun and intuitive method of controlling a robot. Three participants mentioned that the drone felt like an extension of their body, verifying that they indeed felt immersed while wearing the HMD. There were two participants who explicitly mentioned that Head Rotation is most likely the most interesting of the interfaces, while simultaneously requiring the least energy to use.

Seven participants reported a lack of sensitivity or precision when using the head gestures. One explanation for this could be incorrect calibration, as participants tended to calibrate their head turning thresholds at an exaggerated position even after being informed that all thresholds should be comfortable and easily met using ordinary head movements. Only two of the participants reported having problems with the HMD being blurry in written form, though more than two mentioned

it while running the studies. Multiple participants mentioned drifting, difficulty returning to their original position while wearing the HMD, while using the Head Translation and Flying Head techniques. These problems stem from the use of an HMD, which completely occludes the users immediate surroundings, thereby preventing them from returning to their original position based on environmental references.

DISCUSSION

Two interaction techniques (Flying Car, Plane) were based on metaphors that could not be meaningfully used in a large number of interaction contexts, as they assume that the robot will be moving forwards and therefore they are most suited for controlling robots designed around their namesakes: cars and planes. Our study did show some shortcomings when comparing these interfaces, particularly the lack of precision that participants mentioned. Our concerns about the size of the arches users were expected to navigate through with a limited field of view were confirmed to be true even with the larger archways. A larger FOV would have helped users to perform the task, as users often felt that they were smaller than the onboard camera which did not give a proper sense of the scale of the robot. These findings were expected, as prior studies have found that a larger field of view assists users in a number of different tasks [3] [11]. The other problem users had with the HMD was low resolution. Users stated that they had trouble discerning distant objects from their surroundings. When using the Wiimote, users did not experience any loss of visual information. This could have contributed to the users' preferences.

A few problems were caused by the AR Drone itself. Because we relied solely on the onboard magnetometer for heading information, interfaces that relied on it occasionally stuttered or wobbled anytime there was loss of information. The only time this occurred was when Flying Head was the interface being tested. There were oscillations in the sensor information, which caused a side to side vibration in the UAV as it turned while using Flying Head. Both of these contributed to the general disfavor of the Flying Head interface. The UAV also tended to drift to one side when given a forwards command with too small of a magnitude, which particularly affected Plane and Flying Car, as they were the only two techniques that primarily employed slower speeds.

We believed that Head Translation and Flying Head would be easy to use because stepping in a direction seemed to be a simple command for people to give. People easily drifted away from their starting position when they were unable to see their surroundings and then lose their original heading, therefore causing their controls to be less responsive. There was some praise for the one-to-one turning controls of the Flying Head technique, but combined with the recentering problem, the controls became inaccurate or unresponsive quickly. The large movements required to trigger a command also caused problems for users who wanted to give rapid commands to the UAV. A possible solution to these problems would be to combine the turning of these two techniques, allowing for direct control for fine adjustments of heading and a point at which the drone will begin turning continuously until the user returns to a point below a threshold head yaw value.

Participants found Head Rotation to be a fun and responsive technique. A couple of participants found this interface to be more nausea inducing than other techniques, though not enough to negatively impact performance. This technique was originally designed to be used while sitting, and a number of users commented that it would have been easier to use while sitting. This mapping would be easiest to adapt to a number of different robot configurations and, if used from a sitting position and combined with a higher resolution HMD, could be used for extended periods of time

Both Flying Car and Plane received middling preference due to quirks in their design. Users felt that the lack of strafing and moving backwards was restricting and made it difficult to move the UAV in certain situations, such as when the user was stuck on an arch or wall. That Plane recorded such low completion times can be attributed to the automatic forwards movements of the interface. Users spent less time aiming for the arch and more time adjusting on the fly when they did not have to give a separate command to move forwards. This promoted a more reckless approach to the course that was also seen with Flying Car. Although these techniques would not be viable for many other interfaces, it is clear that when applicable, it is worth determining what sort of effect having automatic forwards movement would have on a user's experience.

Generally, our results lead us to believe that so long as the mapping is contextually sound, head tracking is worthy of exploring when attempting to teleoperate a flying robot. Though some findings of our study are limited to UAVs, we can infer that others will equally benefit other types of robots. The key design requirements for such an interface would be to limit the magnitude of the movements of the head to preserve user comfort. Ensuring that there is a logical correspondence between head movements and robot movements allows for a natural connection between the user and the teleoperated robot. This can be literal as in the direct axial mapping of Head Rotation or symbolic as in the Flying Car and Plane interfaces.

In the future, we aim to explore how to improve our head tracking techniques by improving their precision and adding stereoscopic view of the environment. We would also like to look at the possible design implications of adding an additional sensor to the user's torso. We also plan on making use of the Head Rotation technique to control the head of a humanoid robot along with a system for tracking the skeleton to allow for direct teleoperation of the humanoid in a human-robot team.

CONCLUSION

We developed head tracking based interaction techniques using a Polhemus Patriot 6DOF tracker attached to an Oculus Rift HMD to control an AR Drone 2.0. Following a user study designed to evaluate the performance of the technique based on a number of quantitative and qualitative metrics, we found that users felt that a traditional game controller interface was

superior to our head tracking interfaces. Users consistently selected the Wiimote along almost all measures. However, users did find that Head Rotation was the most likeable of the non-traditional interfaces, although it did not perform as well as the Wiimote based on completion time and preferences. We can say that Head Rotation is a viable interface for controlling a quadrotor when users stay within the bounds of calibration. From this, we infer that Head Rotation is a possible alternative control scheme for a number of robot configurations, due to the many parallels that could be drawn between head rotations and movements of the robot platform.

ACKNOWLEDGEMENTS
This work is supported in part by NSF CAREER award IIS-0845921 and NSF awards IIS-0856045 and CCF-1012056.

REFERENCES
1. Bluethmann, W., Ambrose, R., Diftler, M., Askew, S., Huber, E., Goza, M., Rehnmark, F., Lovchik, C., and Magruder, D. Robonaut: A robot designed to work with humans in space. *Autonomous Robots 14*, 2-3 (2003), 179–197.

2. Bowman, D. A., Kruijff, E., LaViola Jr, J. J., and Poupyrev, I. *3D user interfaces: theory and practice.* Addison-Wesley, 2004.

3. de Vries, S. C., and Padmos, P. Steering a simulated unmanned aerial vehicle using a head-slaved camera and hmd. In *AeroSense'97*, International Society for Optics and Photonics (1997), 24–33.

4. Higuchi, K., and Rekimoto, J. Flying head: a head motion synchronization mechanism for unmanned aerial vehicle control. In *CHI '13 Extended Abstracts on Human Factors in Computing Systems*, CHI EA '13, ACM (New York, NY, USA, 2013), 2029–2038.

5. Kennedy, R. S., Lane, N. E., Berbaum, K. S., and Lilienthal, M. G. Simulator sickness questionnaire: An enhanced method for quantifying simulator sickness. *The international journal of aviation psychology 3*, 3 (1993), 203–220.

6. Koeda, M., Matsumoto, Y., and Ogasawara, T. Development of an immersive teleoperating system for unmanned helicopter. In *Robot and Human Interactive Communication, 2002. Proceedings. 11th IEEE International Workshop on*, IEEE (2002), 47–52.

7. Lee, S., and Kim, G. J. Effects of haptic feedback, stereoscopy, and image resolution on performance and presence in remote navigation. *International Journal of Human-Computer Studies 66*, 10 (2008), 701–717.

8. Martins, H., and Ventura, R. Immersive 3-d teleoperation of a search and rescue robot using a head-mounted display. In *Emerging Technologies & Factory Automation, 2009. ETFA 2009. IEEE Conference on*, IEEE (2009), 1–8.

9. Mollet, N., and Chellali, R. Virtual and augmented reality with head-tracking for efficient teleoperation of groups of robots. In *Cyberworlds, 2008 International Conference on*, IEEE (2008), 102–108.

10. Pfeil, K., Koh, S. L., and LaViola, J. Exploring 3d gesture metaphors for interaction with unmanned aerial vehicles. In *Proceedings of the 2013 international conference on Intelligent user interfaces*, IUI '13, ACM (New York, NY, USA, 2013), 257–266.

11. Ragan, E., Kopper, R., Schuchardt, P., and Bowman, D. Studying the effects of stereo, head tracking, and field of regard on a small-scale spatial judgment task.

12. Wang, S., Xiong, X., Xu, Y., Wang, C., Zhang, W., Dai, X., and Zhang, D. Face-tracking as an augmented input in video games: enhancing presence, role-playing and control. In *Proceedings of the SIGCHI conference on Human Factors in computing systems*, ACM (2006), 1097–1106.

A Mixed Reality Head-Mounted Text Translation System Using Eye Gaze Input

Takumi Toyama, Daniel Sonntag,
Andreas Dengel
German Research Center for AI (DFKI)
Trippstadter Str. 122, 67663 Kaiserslautern,
Germany
firstname.lastname@dfki.de

Takahiro Matsuda, Masakazu Iwamura,
Koichi Kise
Osaka Prefecture University
1-1 Gakuen-cho, 599-8531Osaka, Japan
{masa,kise}@cs.osakafu-u.ac.jp,
matsuda@m.cs.osakafu-u.ac.jp

ABSTRACT

Efficient text recognition has recently been a challenge for augmented reality systems. In this paper, we propose a system with the ability to provide translations to the user in real-time. We use eye gaze for more intuitive and efficient input for ubiquitous text reading and translation in head mounted displays (HMDs). The eyes can be used to indicate regions of interest in text documents and activate optical-character-recognition (OCR) and translation functions. Visual feedback and navigation help in the interaction process, and text snippets with translations from Japanese to English text snippets, are presented in a see-through HMD. We focus on travelers who go to Japan and need to read signs and propose two different gaze gestures for activating the OCR text reading and translation function. We evaluate which type of gesture suits our OCR scenario best. We also show that our gaze-based OCR method on the extracted gaze regions provide faster access times to information than traditional OCR approaches. Other benefits include that visual feedback of the extracted text region can be given in real-time, the Japanese to English translation can be presented in real-time, and the augmentation of the synchronized and calibrated HMD in this mixed reality application are presented at exact locations in the augmented user view to allow for dynamic text translation management in head-up display systems.

Author Keywords

Augmented Reality and Projection; Ubiquitous Computing; Smart Environments; Visualization; Mobile and embedded devices

ACM Classification Keywords

H.5.2 Information Interfaces and Presentation: Input devices and strategies

INTRODUCTION

Optical Character Recognition (OCR) available today provides us with a great deal of opportunities to access digital

resources by simply taking a picture of textual objects existing in the real world. For example, people nowadays can use the cameras integrated in their phones to translate texts written in a foreign language when they travel. However, the existing applications of these systems often require the user to click the shutter of the camera or to indicate the region of the objective texts by hand in order to obtain a preferable output. This paper presents an approach to use the persons eyes for more intuitive and efficient input for an OCR application. The user can use his/her eyes to indicate where the region of interest is and to activate the recognition. Visual feedback is presented in a see-through head-mounted display (HMD), not only for the provision of the recognition result but also for a navigation of the interaction process. The experiment results and the user study show the benefits of the proposed approach.

A profound growth of computer vision (CV) technologies observed today can change our everyday life drastically. People nowadays can access to a vast amount of information resources on the Internet, by simply taking a picture of texts in the environment. A number of applications, such as Google Goggles[1], make use of OCR technology in order to supply the user with digital information of textual objects in an Augmented Reality (AR) manner. It is true that the fusion of CV and AR has a great potential for enhancing people's everyday life.

OCR has an important role to play when it comes to automatic ubiquitous text translation services. But translations as a result of the OCR reading and translation process should only be provided upon the users request. We motivate the use of eye gaze instead of pressing a button or clicking a shutter to implement a direct manipulation intelligent user interface for the purpose of displaying text translations in a HMD. The important side effect is that the translations in the synchronized and calibrated HMD are presented at precise locations in the augmented user view. In OCR applications, we always have to inform the system about the interested text regions, mainly by cropping the text region manually. As an intelligent user interface, computers should understand eye gaze information in this context, and anticipate when the user wants translation help and provide it instantly where it is needed, as an augmentation in a HMD at a precise location relative to the real document. In this paper, we propose such a gaze based interactive OCR system, which extends the work in [5], by com-

---

[1]http://www.google.com/mobile/goggles/

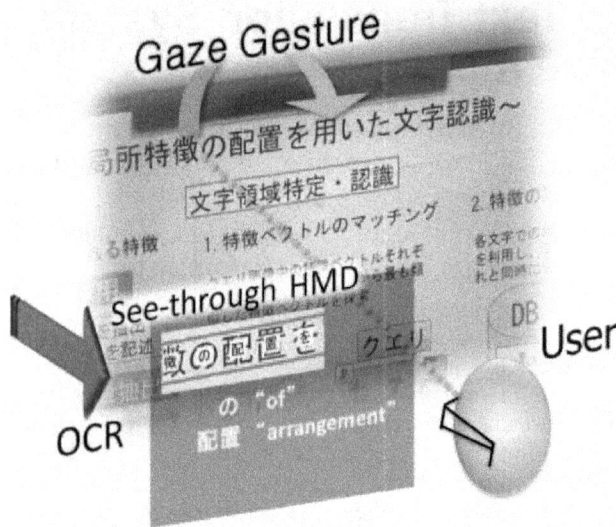

Figure 1. Proposed mixed reality translation application system. English translations of Japanese texts snippets the user is looking at in the real scene are presented in a see-through HMD.

bining the wearable eye tracking system with an AR system. The mixed reality translation application, which would be incomplete without both its real and virtual text components in Japanese and English, respectively, is shown in figure 1. We focus on a product for travelers who go to Japan or a foreign company and need to read signs and posters. One of the drawbacks of gaze interaction with a real scene environment is that the user cannot know instantly whether the computer correctly understands his input without any feedback. In our solution presented in this paper, the OCR reading feedback is presented as a red box superimposed on the source text of the real world, together with the translation result at the exact position (figure 1, grey box).

The paper is structured as follows: first, we presents related work; second, we present the technical approach of the translation system: the gaze gestures for a text in a real scene is discussed and gaze guided OCR techniques are presented. Then, the translation function and the visual feedback on the see-through HMD is presented. Third, we describe the experimental setup and the evaluation of the feasibility of the proposed approach and provide a conclusion. We focus on three contributions, the two methods for selecting/interacting with text in the ORC scenario, the design of the related translation capability, and an evaluation to test the selection methods, followed by a discussion whether these translation capabilities are useful.

BACKGROUND AND RELATED WORK

It is quite natural for humans to read a text with uniform eye movements, which means that we can leverage this phenomenon to create new input methods using OCR systems and head-mounted activation triggers, where the intelligence mainly rests in the head-mounted user interface.

By using human gaze as input, we can design an intuitive interface which uses eye gaze gestures as indicators of the text region of interest, which the user wants the system to recognize (trigger OCR) and translate in real-time. Research such as the idea presented in [10] suggests that eye gaze analysis would benefit text oriented interaction systems.

Additionally, there is another advantage of using gaze in this OCR context: current character recognition methods (even detection method) are still computationally costly, especially when they are applied to high resolution images. Since our method utilises gaze input, we can quickly obtain the region of interest and reduce the computational cost of OCR (see evaluation).

Additionally, it is essential to present information to the user in a fashion that allows clear viewing of the text without obstructing the main reading task. Research on text management systems such as the one recently developed in [7] clearly show the importance of managing information in the users field of view in an unobtrusive, yet viewable manner. We consequently follow in these footsteps in order to improve a users ability to read and translate on the fly without affecting the reading experience.

Eye tracking technology has been used in intelligent user interfaces (IUIs) more and more frequently in recent years. For example, the task of communicating with the user based on eye-gaze patterns [9] introduced an interesting idea: the possibility to sense users' interest based on eye-gaze patterns and manage computer information output accordingly. Following up on this essential observation, we bring eye gaze patterns into the context of translation help in mixed reality settings. Also motivated by previous findings showing the relevance of eye-gaze in multimodal conversational interfaces [8], we extended the passive eye gaze input idea to active eye gaze user input in the mixed reality realm.

Some previous works have contributed to the combination of an eye tracking device with a see-through HMD. A see-through HMD has better compatibility with an eye tracker, since a see-through HMD does not obstruct the user's view and affixing the HMD to the tracker can reduce or eliminate calibration errors. The user can then focus on an object in a real scene through the display. In [12], an augmented reality system for knowledge-intensive location-based expert work is presented. The multi-modal interaction system combines multiple on-body input and output devices (a speech-based dialogue system, a head-mounted augmented reality display, and a head-mounted eye- tracker) in a similar way, but focusses on speech recognition instead of eye gaze while reading to trigger a context-related function and its interpretation.

More recently, several studies and works have shown the benefits of utilizing human (eye) gaze in several HCI contexts, e.g., [6], [5], and [13] focus on the interaction using the objects in the real world and suggest many possibilities of gaze based interaction in a real world scenario. In [5], eye gaze is used to find relevant text passages in a scene and support a subsequent OCR process accordingly. Bringing this technology together to form a combined real-time translation-based interaction system is the unique contribution of the work presented here.

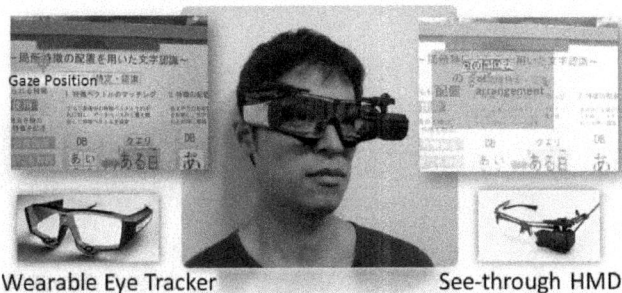

Figure 2. Technical HCI setup. The HMD screen size is limited and does not cover the whole user view (grey region).

Our attention recognition system (active gaze-based user input to trigger the translation function) is based on an eye control system such as [1]. If somebody's eyes are moving from left to right (or vice versa) and if the movement is repeated several times, the user is considered to be reading text. Using this methodology we provide two novel methods for interacting with text, and evaluate their potential for use with HMD systems.

TECHNICAL APPROACH

Figure 2 shows the technical HCI setup. We combine two different devices (head-mounted eye tracker and HMD) by mounting the HMD frame on the top of the wearable eye tracker frame; the HMD should be placed in front of the user's dominant eye which provides a more accurate eye gaze focus. The two scene images shown in figure 2 (left and right, the user is reading a poster) are captured by the scene camera of the eye tracker, which is integrated in the center of the eye tracker frame, and the eye tracker software computes the gaze position in the captured scene image (left). The see-through HMD translation output is show on the right hand side. We use SMIs Eye Tracking Glasses (ETG)[2] and Brothers Airscouter[3] in this work. However, the proposed approach is not limited to this hardware setting; it can be applied to any calibrated other eye tracking and HMD device combination. The resolution of the scene camera is 1280×960 and the gaze accuracy we can obtain via our calibration method is $0.5°$.

The usage procedure is as follows: in a first step to use the eye tracker, the user has to calibrate the system. The eye tracking calibration is done by looking at one reference point in the scene and by clicking a mouse on the reference point in the scene camera image (which is displayed in a computer screen editor that must be used before the real-time usage, similar to the method explained in [12]). After the calibration, the eye tracking server streams scene images with the exact gaze position. Our text-based gaze gesture recognition module receives them and processes the data accordingly, as explained next.

Text-based Gaze Gesture Recognition

By integrating eye gaze gesture recognition (as an extension to [2]), the system can detect the user's intention in a specific context. A typical smartphone-based AR application

[2]http://www.eyetracking-glasses.com
[3]http://www.brother.co.uk/g3.cfm/s_page/888150

such as Wikitude SDK applications, www.wikitude.com/, presents additional location and orientation-specific information whenever the AR objects (for a travel guide for example) are in focus.

In our wearable computing HMD / eye-tracker scenario, we try to provide related the information of a more narrowed interaction context.

An intelligent head-mounted interface should filter out the irrelevant information and provides the information only when it is needed and about what is needed in the context of the text reading and translation scenario. Eye gaze input is a useful input method in such a scenario. On the other hand, using eye gaze input also contains an inherent problem, as known as *Midas touch problem* [3], when using it as a direct substitute for the mouse. It it not desirable for each eye move during normal visual perception to initiate a computer command.

Because of this, we employ a more complex eye gaze gesture recognition system, which recognizes rather complex gaze movement patterns, and we propose two new domain-specific eye gaze gestures for the text reading scenario in order to tackle these problems. First, eye gaze patterns observed during text reading are quite symptomatic compared to other gaze activities. Thus, we can utilize these representative and discriminatory gaze patterns as gestures for controlling the translation system and triggering the OCR system. Second, OCR on a high resolution image is still computationally costly. When we apply the OCR recognition (in combination with the text window detection) to the entire images obtained from the scene camera, it cannot be processed in real-time. By focusing on a particular region in a scene, we can reduce the computational cost required in the recognition process. Gaze gestures can easily indicate where text exists in the scene, because a gaze path can draw lines onto the text regions. Third, without a proper gaze gesture implementation, no text window detection and text snippet -based translation are possible in this head-mounted input context.

We propose two gaze gestures for an OCR text reading and translation scenario and investigate which type of gesture suits our OCR scenario best. Essentially, the first looks at the beginning and the end of the text line alternately and repeatedly (*gaze repetitive leap*), and the other is to move gaze from the beginning to the end gradually (*gaze scan*). These two types of gaze gestures can be divided into two groups based on the deliberateness and the complexity of the gesture. The gaze scan gesture is less complex and can occur less deliberately, whereas gaze repetitive leap is more complex and hardly occurs without intention. It can be that the less complex the gesture is, the more false recognitions (false positives) occur. However, if the gesture is too complex, it is also quite demanding for the user. Thus, we need to explore and evaluate the trade-off of the deliberateness and the complexity of the text-based gaze gesture.

The recognition algorithm of each gaze gesture is as follows: *Gaze Repetitive Leap (GRL)*: If a fixation that lasts one second is detected, it activates the recognition process and set the fixation as the start point. If the next detected fixation is right

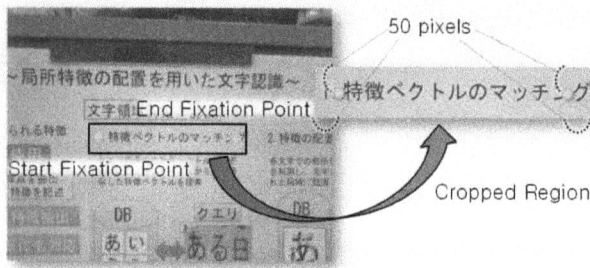

Figure 3. Text snippet extraction for translation guided by gaze gesture.

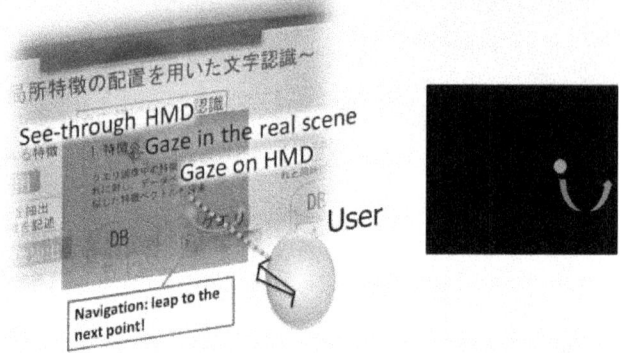

Figure 4. The interaction navigation is presented near the gaze position. In this example, GRL navigation is shown in the HMD.

from the start fixation within $\pm 30°$, it is set as the end point fixation. If the third fixation is within d pixels from the start point, it continues the recognition; otherwise the recognition process is discarded. If the following fixations are within d from either the end point or the start point (switches alternately) and n of such fixations are detected in total, the gesture is recognized. (By changing n in the GRL gesture, we can increase the complexity of the gesture. If n is small, the gesture can also occur less deliberately.)

Gaze Scan (GS): If a fixation that lasts one second is detected, it activates the recognition process and set the fixation as the start point. If the next detected fixation is right from the start fixation within $\pm 30°$, it continues the recognition; otherwise the recognition process is discarded. If such a fixation (within $\pm 30°$ to the right) is detected continuously more than three times, it is recognized as a gesture. The end point is determined when the fixation point swerved from $\pm 30°$.

Gaze Guided OCR

When the end of the gesture is recognized, the system extracts the text region indicated by the start fixation point and the end fixation point as shown in figure 3. Scene image tracking of the used KLT tracker [11] is running as a background process. It tracks reference points in scenes and computes the relative distances between the scene image frames. While tracking the image, we can estimate the position of the start point even at a later frame[4].

The cropping rectangle area is determined by a heuristic as follows: Left: 50 pixels left from the start point, Top: 50 pixels above from the higher point of either of the start point or the end point, Right: 50 pixels right from the end point, and Bottom: 50 pixels under from the lower point of either of the start point or the end point. The cropped text image is sent to the character recognition module.

Visual Feedback in HMD Screen

Once the start of the gaze gesture is recognized, a navigation image is presented in the HMD screen (figure 4). In this way, the user can ensure that the start of the gesture command is correctly recognized by the system. When the end of the gesture is recognized, the OCR module is triggered and returns

the result of the text recognition of the given textual image (this step may include more complex natural language preprocessing steps).

The resulting selected text snippet, which also includes the cropped image, is visualized in the HMD screen (figure 1), so that the user can check if the correct region-of-interest is recognized; the visual feedback is given instantly as augmented reality (AR) boxes (figure 1, red, green and blue boxes). If no Japanese (Kanji) character is recognized in the given region, no boxes are presented in AR.

Hence, false gesture recognition is rejected based on the character recognition result (if gaze gesture is recognized mistakenly (false positive), and no text is read, it will be classified as gaze detection error (false positive).

By taking the relative position of the HMD in a scene image in the system into account, we can present the navigation near the gaze position as shown in figure 4. Dynamitic text management and intuitive positioning of the augmented translations in the users field of view to migrate user-centric text content is important because if the visualization is far from the user's focus, it cannot be perceived easily; and therefore, the see-through feature of the HMD plays an important role in this system. Another consideration is the position of the translated text throughout a users mobile environment ([7]).

EMBEDDED TRANSLATION SERVICE

Our Japanese-English translation system provides the user with a translated Japanese text snippet as a direct translation from the Japanese text snippet indicated by the eye gaze gesture figure 1).

For the test system presented in this paper, we implemented our own translation function. First, we built a Japanese-English dictionary using 10000 Japanese characters (Kanji)[5]. We selected 10000 common Japanese words from a common Japanese dictionary service and translated them into English using the Microsoft Bing Translator API[6]. The simple translation process, see *Translation Module* in the architecture

---

[4]To obtain the entire image from the beginning, one sometimes has to apply mosaicing; however, it is not integrated in this work because we focus on rather short texts and they can be captured by one image frame.

[5]Actually, it contains Kanji, Katakana, and Hiragana Japanese characters mixtures. For the sake of simplicity, we say Kanji.
[6]http://www.bing.com/translator

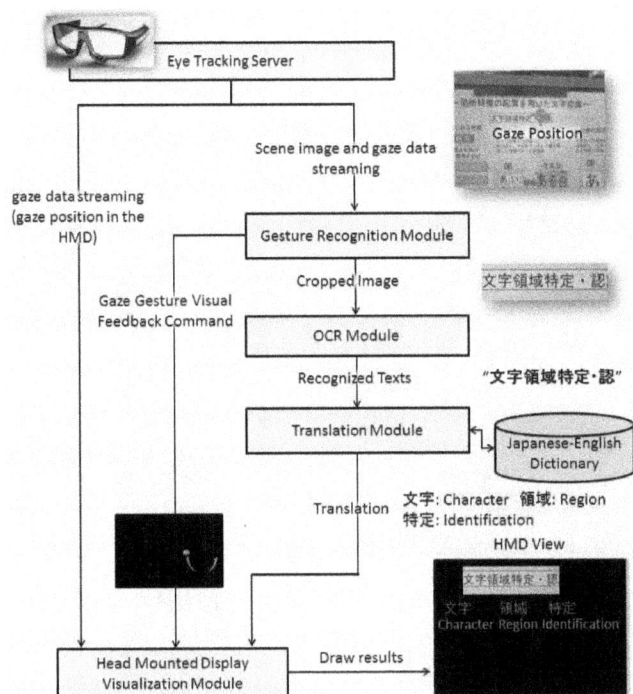

Figure 5. Architeture of embedded translation service

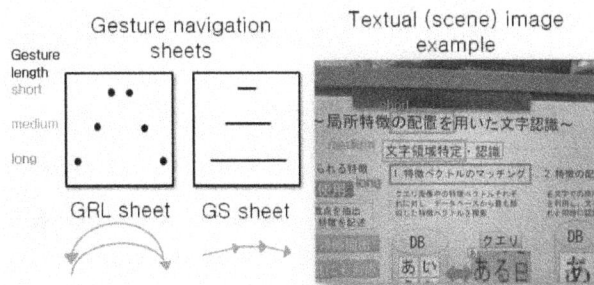

Figure 6. Gesture navigation sheets (left) and an example of actual scene image (right). The scene image contains a complex background.

Table 1. Gesture recognition accuracy.

length	GRL gaze gesture		GS gaze gesture	
	sheet	scene image	sheet	scene image
short	80%	83%	67%	77%
medium	60%	60%	80%	80%
long	60%	33%	87%	83%

in figure 5, works as follows: 1) The recognized OCR text is preprocessed by a very shallow text processing pipeline for Japanese tokenization. In the evaluation, we used the OCR method presented in [4]. This method is specialized to Japanese characters; 2) The individual Kanji tokens (possibly compounds) are matched against an approximate Kanji index that uses a Levenshtein distance metric; 3) The token-by-token translation of the nearest Kanji compounds in the dictionary according to the distance metric are presented; and 4) If the Levenshtein distance exceeds a threshold, no translation is returned (we assume a bad OCR result). It is to be noted that complex linguistic-based translation pipelines (e.g., [14]) can easily be integrated into the architecture. We relied on a fast on-board solution for the translation integration test. There are also several online translation services available, but they are dependent on the speed of the wireless network and are blackbox processes. Their utility evaluation is beyond the reach of evaluating the real-time feature of the mixed reality head-mounted text translation system using eye gaze input.

EVALUATION

We provide an initial evaluation of the proposed gesture recognition approach; we sought to determine whether the two proposed eye gestures are adequate for triggering the eye gaze based translation function while reading the text.

Gesture Recognition

To test this, a user evaluation under realistic circumstances has been conducted including the following steps: First, we tested the gesture recognition without using any textual real-world image or document in order to evaluate the acceptability of the proposed gestures for the users, i.e., how well peo-

ple can perform those gestures and how much the system can recognize them in general. The experiment included 10 participants, ranging from age 22 to 56, with an approximately even number of males and females. The participants were asked to perform the the two gestures in order to trigger the translation function. Two types of gesture navigation sheets (as shown in figure 6) were presented to the user and we asked them to perform each gesture (GRL and GS) on each sheet. In addition to the gesture type, three types of gesture length are prepared here (short, medium and long), to compare the recognition performance of each gesture with a different length. The overall result of each gesture is shown in table 1. For *GRL*, n was set to 4 and d was set to 50. In general, the results show that the longer the gesture length is, the less accurate the *GRL* gesture becomes; contrariwise, the longer the GS gesture is, the more accurate the recognition is. We hypothesize that this is because the user cannot find the end point easily when the distance of two reference points becomes greater; contrariwise, using the *GS gesture* it is easier to track a path (line) by eye gaze when it is longer.

In a second evaluation step, we tested the recognition on a textual (scene) image example of proper Japanese text of different lengths. An example image that we used is shown in figure 6 (right), and the result is also shown in table 1. Here, we asked the users to perform the gesture on proper text of length: short, medium, or long. Compared to the non-textual image, it can be said that it becomes even harder to find the end point with proper texts. The *GS* gesture slightly gets better with texts. Some users mentioned that to move eyes along a text line is easier than to move it along a normal straight line. Since these experiments were conducted without a training phase (for the users to try and learn these gestures over time), it would be interesting to see how the performance to use those two proposed gestures improves over time. Though some users had difficulties because they had to concentrate more than usual and felt stressed, these gestures were rather easy and intuitive to perform for the majority of users. We might switch the gesture depending on the length of text, since *GRL* suits short text length, while *GS* suits long text length. Furthermore, the visual feedback could reasonably navigate the user for the correct gesture throughout the experiment. Many users failed the gesture without the visual feedback in the HMD. This result shows the benefit of a see-through AR screen for visual feedback in the proposed system though the experiment we conducted is only adequate to show the basic effectiveness of our algorithm.

Gaze Guided OCR Time Performances

Similar to this image, most of the texts were cropped correctly if the gestures were correctly recognized. Some users had difficulties in gazing on a particular point if there is no characteristic point (reference point), which is sometimes the case when we focus on texts in a real scene. In a third part of the evaluation, we compared the processing time required for the OCR of an entire video image vs. the cropped video. The entire video image required $4.77sec$ on average, the cropped image OCR required only $0.19sec$ on average. This result shows that we can effectively reduce the computational cost by using the gaze gesture guided image cropping to present a translation result in real-time.

CONCLUSION

We proposed a mixed reality system with the ability to provide translations to the user in real-time. The eyes can be used to indicate regions of interest in text documents and activate optical-character-recognition (OCR) text recognition and translation functions. For this purpose, we proposed and evaluated two gaze-based image region selection and OCR activation functions. The experimental results showed the feasibility of the gaze gesture recognition and the utility of gaze gesture as an automatic indicator of the text region of interest. Image cropping guided by gaze also reduced the computational cost of the OCR in order to perform the whole triggering-OCR-translation processing workflow in real-time. Future work includes further user studies for a comprehensive evaluation of the approach in combination with other dynamic text management capabilities of see-through wearable display systems. The system can also be adapted for professional translators or learners of a foreign language, potentially for full translation of documents for the general public. Additionally, visitors in foreign countries can use the method to translate signs that may provide essential safety or navigation information. Lastly, industry workers will gain the ability to read warning labels or instructions on products which may not be translated to into their native language.

Acknowledgements
This research has been supported by the ERmed project, see http://www.dfki.de/RadSpeech/ERmed.

REFERENCES

1. J. M. Henderson. Human gaze control during real-world scene perception. *Trends in Cognitive Sciences*, 7(11):498–504, 2003.

2. M. Hopmann, P. Salamin, N. Chauvin, F. Vexo, and D. Thalmann. Natural activation for gesture recognition systems. In *CHI '11 Extended Abstracts on Human Factors in Computing Systems*, CHI EA '11, pages 173–183, New York, NY, USA, 2011. ACM.

3. R. J. K. Jacob. Eye movement-based human-computer interaction techniques: Toward non-command interfaces. In *Advances in Human-Computer Interaction*, volume 4, pages 151–190. Ablex Publishing Co, 1993.

4. T. Kobayahsi, M. Iwamura, and K. Kise. An anytime algorithm for faster camera-based character recognition. In *Proceedings of the 12th International Conference on Document Analysis and Recognition (ICDAR)*, 2013.

5. T. Kobayashi, T. Toyamaya, F. Shafait, M. Iwamura, K. Kise, and A. Dengel. Recognizing words in scenes with a head-mounted eye-tracker. *IAPR International Workshop on Document Analysis Systems*, pages 333–338, 2012.

6. M. Kumar, A. Paepcke, and T. Winograd. Eyepoint: Practical pointing and selection using gaze and keyboard. In *Proceedings of the SIGCHI Conference on Human Factors in Computing Systems*, CHI '07, pages 421–430, New York, NY, USA, 2007. ACM.

7. J. Orlosky, K. Kiyokawa, and H. Takemura. Dynamic text management for see-through wearable and heads-up display systems. In *Proceedings of the International Conference on Intelligent user interfaces*, IUI '13, pages 363–370, New York, NY, USA, 2013. ACM.

8. Z. Prasov and J. Y. Chai. What's in a gaze?: the role of eye-gaze in reference resolution in multimodal conversational interfaces. In *Proceedings of the 13th international conference on Intelligent user interfaces*, IUI '08, pages 20–29, New York, NY, USA, 2008. ACM.

9. P. Qvarfordt and S. Zhai. Conversing with the user based on eye-gaze patterns. In *Proceedings of the SIGCHI Conference on Human Factors in Computing Systems*, CHI '05, pages 221–230, New York, NY, USA, 2005. ACM.

10. K. Rayner. Eye movements in reading and information processing: 20 years of research. *Psychological Bulletin*, pages 372–422, 1998.

11. J. Shi and C. Tomasi. Good features to track. In *Computer Vision and Pattern Recognition, 1994. Proceedings CVPR '94., 1994 IEEE Computer Society Conference on*, pages 593–600, 1994.

12. D. Sonntag and T. Toyama. On-Body IE: A Head-Mounted Multimodal Augmented Reality System for Learning and Recalling Faces. In *9th International Conference on Intelligent Environments (IE)*, pages 151–156, 2013.

13. T. Toyama, T. Kieninger, F. Shafait, and A. Dengel. Gaze guided object recognition using a head-mounted eye tracker. In *Proc. of the Symposium on Eye Tracking Research and Applications*, pages 91–98, 2012.

14. W. Wahlster, editor. *VERBMOBIL: Foundations of Speech-to-Speech Translation*. Springer, 2000.

AllAboard: Visual Exploration of Cellphone Mobility Data to Optimise Public Transport

Giusy Di Lorenzo, Marco Luca Sbodio, Francesco Calabrese,
Michele Berlingerio, Rahul Nair, Fabio Pinelli
IBM Research
IBM Technology Campus, Damastown Industrial Estate, Dublin, Ireland
{giusydil, marco.sbodio, fcalabre, mberling, rahul.nair, fabiopin } [at] ie [dot] ibm [dot] com

ABSTRACT

The deep penetration of mobile phones offers cities the ability to opportunistically monitor citizens' mobility and use data-driven insights to better plan and manage services. In this context, transit operators can leverage pervasive mobile sensing to better match observed demand for travel with their service offerings. In this paper we present AllAboard, an intelligent tool that analyses cellphone data to helps city authorities in exploring urban mobility and optimizing public transport. An interactive user interface allows transit operators to explore the travel demand in both space and time, evaluate the quality of service that a transit network provides to the citizens, and test scenarios for transit network improvements. The system has been tested using real telecommunication data for the city of Abidjan, Ivory Coast, and evaluated from a data mining, optimisation and user prospective.

Author Keywords

spatio-temporal mining; cellphone data; visual exploration; urban data; mobility

ACM Classification Keywords

H.5.2 [Information Interfaces and Presentation]: User Interfaces; H.5.8 [Database Management]: Database applications - Data Mining.

INTRODUCTION

Transportation planning and management is often a top priority for many cities around the world. Increased urbanisation, as well as traffic congestion and associated pollution push several cities to invest in building new public transport networks, or extending their existing ones. Usually, transit authorities involved in planning tasks have to rely on several semi-automatic steps. One challenge is provided by the poor availability of data to be used to create travel demand models.

If transit agencies could have an effective tool to quantify the travel demand and recommendations on how to better design and optimize the transit network to accommodate it, cities would be able to better support the mobility demand through an efficient, and more sustainable public transport system.

In recent years, the deep penetration of mobile phones is offering cities the ability to opportunistically monitor citizens' mobility and use data-driven insights to better plan and manage transportation services. Accurately assessing travel demand through mobile phones offers key benefits and a true alternative to classical survey-based approaches. The high level of penetration of mobile phones provides samples that are several order of magnitudes larger that manual surveys. It could potentially be less biased by survey sampling limitations, embracing a wider classes of users that are represented proportionally with their own statistical significance. It is faster than surveys, as mobile phone data can be gathered instantaneously. It allows for dynamic assessment of the travel demand, as the data follows a streaming paradigm, with the potential to make urban services more responsive.

We propose AllAboard[1], a system which puts together, in a novel way, the following:

- A mobility mining module, that extracts mobility demand and shared route patterns from coarse-grain and un-evenly sampled location data (opportunistically collected from cellphones);

- An optimization module that recommends extensions to the city's transit network, to improve travelers experience.

- An interactive tool to allow transit operators to explore the travel demand, and test different scenarios for transit optimisation.

AllAboard is designed to provide the above features all together, thus making the final user (a city or transport authority) independent from other external tools for analysis, reporting, optimization, and planning.

The system is presented by means of a case study conducted on a large scale telecommunication dataset for the city of Abidjan, in Ivory Coast, and on the SOTRA transportation

---

[1] http://www.youtube.com/watch?v=9givVEcxnEE shows a video of the AllAboard system

network running the city's bus service. To the best of our knowledge, this is the first time that such an interactive tool has been developed, and tested with real large scale data.

RELATED WORK

Several tools have been proposed to support transit authorities in analysing individual mobility data, and to extract knowledge from them. Most of them use visual analytics, or Data Mining, to measure, extract patterns, and gain insights on mobility data. We present here some examples of such systems. In [10], a tool to explore urban mobility dynamics by visualising individual and aggregated activity and trajectories extracted from cell phones traces is proposed. Key features of this system include combining aggregated mobility patterns and individual traces in real time, visualizing massive dynamic datasets in both spatial and temporal scale, and automatic detection of homophily between mobility patterns of people's traces. In [3], a tool to extract traffic related information from social media and linked data, and semantically describe them is presented. To this end, static data from event providers, planned road works together with dynamically emerging events such as a traffic accidents, localized weather conditions or unplanned obstructions are captured through social media to provide users real-time feedback to highlight the causes of traffic congestion. In [5], the authors present a system to explore spatio-temporal urban data visually. They present the system on a case study on real taxi data. The use interface allows to visually query the data, by means of selectors for time, space, and features to analyze. Besides standard analytics queries, the system supports origin-destination queries that enable the study of mobility across the city. The query is then translated into a DB query, and the results are then filtered and mapped for visualization.

The main differences provided by AllAboard with respect to all the above works are: i) we work on both mobility and transport data; ii) our final users are mainly city and transport authorities and iii) our tool does not only provide mining and insights from data, but also solves the transport optimization problem.

THE DATA

Cell phone data

The D4D Orange challenge[2] made available data collected in the Ivory Coast over a five month period, from December 2011 to April 2012. The original dataset contains 2.5 billion records, calls and text messages exchanged between 5 million users. The data released in the challenge contains samples from this original data and contains four separate datasets, each with information on different aspects and at different spatio-temporal resolutions. To safeguard personal privacy, individual phone numbers were anonymized by the operator before leaving storage facilities. Our system specifically uses a mobility dataset extracted from the Call Detail Records, that describes call activity of a randomly chosen sample of 50,000 users every two weeks, for a total period of 20 weeks. Specifically, the data contains the cell phone tower and a timestamp at which a user (identified by an anonymized id) sent

or received a text message (SMS) or a call. The dataset consists of tuples in the form <UserID, Day, Time, Antenna>. An auxillary dataset that describes the spatial location (latitude and longitude) of antennas was used to map each tuple spatially. Since this work presents a specific case study on the city of Abidjan (largest city in Ivory Coast, with 4.5 million inhabitants) a spatial bounding box defined by $(5.2089, -4.2557)$ and $(5.4937, -3.7389)$ was considered. The number of users over the five month period shows a minimum in March (columns 6 and 7), but it is consistently around 18,000 distinct users. The dataset contained some antennas with obfuscated codes which were omitted from the analysis. Additionally, in some occasions multiple antenna identifiers were used to reference the same location (antennas attached to the same cell tower, most likely covering distinct sectors). As we had no data to distinguish between them, these antennas were combined and treated as one. As a result, 407 distinct antennas were selected within the bounding box for Abidjan. To evaluate the quality of the dataset, the cumulative distribution of interleaving time between two calls and the cumulative distribution of the number of distinct visited towers were studied. We saw that 50% of time there is less than ten minutes between two consecutive calls of the same user, highlighting that users are frequently tracked. Moreover, 50% of the users do not visit more than 6 cell towers on a period of 14 days. This demonstrates that while users are recorded often, their spatial movement is relatively limited, as already shown in [7].

Public transport data

To model the existing public transportation network, information from SOTRA, the local public transport agency, was gathered from its website[3]. The website provided bus route information in the form of bus line, and street names for each bus stop. Since the route information was not geo-referenced, Open Street Maps (OSM)[4] and other geo-localization toolkits were employed to locate bus stops across Abidjan. From a set of 301 distinct bus stops, 203 were able to be located in this manner. These bus stops represent 17 express bus routes, 67 regular bus routes (called the *monbus*), and 1 special route meant for trader with heavy goods (called *marche bus*). This represents our baseline transit network.

Road network

To model travel time for vehicles, and walking time, we used Open Street Maps to extract the road network of the city.

THE ALLABOARD PLATFORM

The system is composed of:
- a mobility mining component in charge of manipulating the data, and extract travel demand models and candidate routes
- a transit assignment component in charge of evaluating ridership and other KPIs for a given transit network and a given demand model
- an optimisation component in charge of recommending new routes, given a transit network, a demand model, a set of candidate routes, and budget constraints

[2]http://www.d4d.orange.com/

[3]http://sotra.ci

[4]http://www.openstreetmap.org

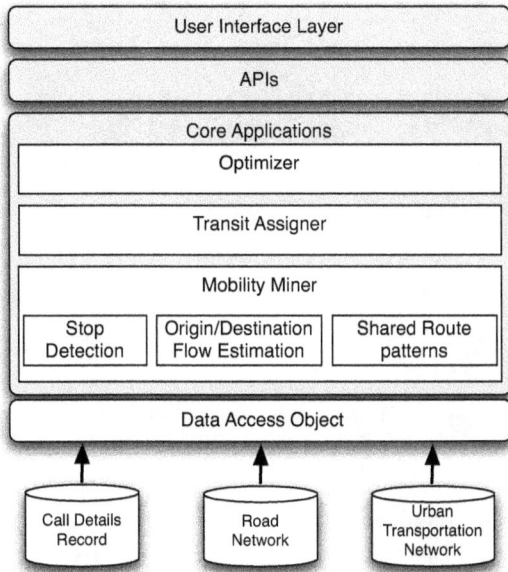

Figure 1. Architecture of the AllAboard platform

- a user interface component that allows operators (our end users) to interrogate the underlying components to perform the visual explorations.

Architectural Design Choices

We privileged modularity in the architecture of our system (see Figure 1). We decided to implement the Mobility Miner, the Transit Assigner and the Optimizer components as separate back-end modules exposing their functionalities as REST services. The entire front-end and visualization capabilities of our application are based on asynchronous calls to these REST services. This approach allows us to improve or change the algorithms of our components without affecting the application front-end. We developed a lighteweight data abstraction layer, which shields our core components from the details of how raw data (maily CDRs - Call Detail Records) are stored on disks. We also observe that our current application is not processing CDRs in real-time, and therefore we did not optimize the data storage and retrieval part (for which several dedicated solutions exist). We decided to have a Web based front-end, as opposed to a custom rendering application. We mainly use (i) CSS and SVG rendering capabilities of modern Web browser to build graphs, (ii) OpenLayers[5] for map rendering, and (iii) Javascript for client-side data processing, UI interactivity, and asynchronous REST services invocation. The major rationale behind these design choices was to have a technology stack relying as much as possible on consolidated standards to simplify future possible integration with existing and emerging products for monitoring, managing, simulating and improving urban environments.

Mobility Miner

---
[5]`http://openlayers.org/`

The Mobility Miner component processes mobile phone location data, and extracts information on users' stops, origin/destination flows, and shared route patterns. The methodology consists of the following steps: i) we extract the location of the stops performed by each user; ii) we estimate the aggregated Origin/Destination (O/D) flows between those stops; iii) we extract shared route patterns from the sequences of stops visited by each user, that we use as candidate new routes for public transport optimisation. The last two datasets are then fed to the optimization component. We now present each step in more details.

Stop detection and Origin/Destination flows estimation

A first insight into the mobility within a city can be captured by extracting users' stops and origin/destination (O/D) flows, as they can be used to model the mobility demand. In several works, such as [6] and [2], the authors proposed methodologies to estimate the O/D flows using GPS data as well as mobile phone data. We apply a similar methodology in order to estimate the stops and the flows between each pair of origin and destination antennas within a certain temporal interval. In particular, all the antennas are considered as either origin or destination, and the time is divided into hourly intervals. In order to define the flow between the antenna O and the antenna D, we first introduce the concept of trip. A trip $trip(u, O, D, t)$ is the path between two consecutive stops O and D where $O \neq D$. A trip is characterized by the user u, the stop O as starting point of the trip, the stop D as destination of the trip, and the time t corresponding to the last time associated to O. Therefore, the estimated flow between a pair of antennas O and D, in a time interval h, is defined as the count of all user trips $trip(u, O, D, t), t \in h$.

Shared route patterns

Together with a model of travel demand, the optimization component also requires a set of candidate routes on which the optimizer can evaluate which best combination of new routes will provide the greatest improvement of the performance indications, while respecting the constraints on budget (e.g. number of new buses) and feasibility (e.g. end-to-end travel time). Thus, an adequate choice of candidate routes is fundamental to provide the best optimization results. In current practice, candidate routes are usually chosen by subject matter experts, mainly as shortest paths connecting different parts of the city [4]. Our proposal is to use the patterns extracted from the mobile phone data to come up with candidate routes. Given the quality of the mobile phone data, for which we are not able to extract actual trajectories but only sequences of visited places, we decided to adopt a traditional sequential pattern mining algorithm [11]. We first defined the daily activity sequence of a user as the concatenation of the different trips performed by a user in a single day. We take into account only sequences with at least 3 different locations (as sequences of two locations are already modeled in the O/D flows). As we are interested in producing potential new routes for public transport, we constrain sequences not to involve the same location more than once, discarding loops. This builds the set of transactions used as input for the sequential pattern mining algorithm. Moreover, we need to input a threshold of minimum support min_{sup} in order to extract all the sequences with a frequency higher than min_{sup}.

Transit Assigner

This module is in charge of evaluating, given a transit network and a model of travel demand, the traveller behaviours in terms of route chooses. This allows extracting transit KPIs, such as ridership for each bus link (connecting two consecutive bus stops), wait time for each bus stop, and overall travel time for each O/D pair. Modeling user behavior in transit systems involves added complexity of waiting processes and the frequency of routes. Further, users are likely to dynamically change travel paths, depending on which service arrives at a particular bus stop. Instead of shortest path, users are therefore assumed to follow *optimal strategies* [12]. The process of assigning users to paths along a network, termed transit assignment in the transportation literature, therefore reflects user behavior and allocates flows based on frequency. Readers are referred to reviews on transit network design [4, 8] that show the prior work, which is omitted for brevity. Our proposed model builds on the *optimal strategies* work by [12], that models how transit users are likely to board services.

Optimizer

The objective of the optimizer is to minimize system wide journey times for users, which includes travel and waiting time. More specifically, given (a) an existing transit network, (b) O/D flows derived from mobile data representing travel demand, (c) a set of candidate new routes, (d) travel time estimates across the network, and (d) a resource budget, in terms of fleet size, we seek to determine an optimal set of new routes and their associated service frequencies, such that passenger journey times city-wide are minimized. A new route is defined by a sequence of bus stops and has an associated frequency during peak periods. The optimization process takes into account several contraints, including (i) flow conservation, (ii) allocation of flows on existing services based on frequency of service, (iii) relating flows for new services and their respective frequencies, (iv)fleet size, and (v) upper bounds on frequency. Some of these constraints are non-linear (for example allocation of flows on existing services based on frequency of service). For the AllAboard system, a heuristic procedure is developed that first picks a set of routes from major origin-destination flows by using the separable programming approximation. Then, the optimal strategies flows for all OD pairs are determined using the new set of routes. The model is executed using IBM ILOG CPLEX v12.4.

User Interface

As the system is intended to be used by transit operators, who may not have a background in computer science, the tool should be expressive enough to support: visual spatio-temporal exploration at different scale of mobility data; the selection of different mobility data parameters; visual exploration of the public transport network; visual exploration of different public transport KPIs; and capability to redefine, validate and compare different optimisation strategies. We have designed and implemented a user interface to allow an

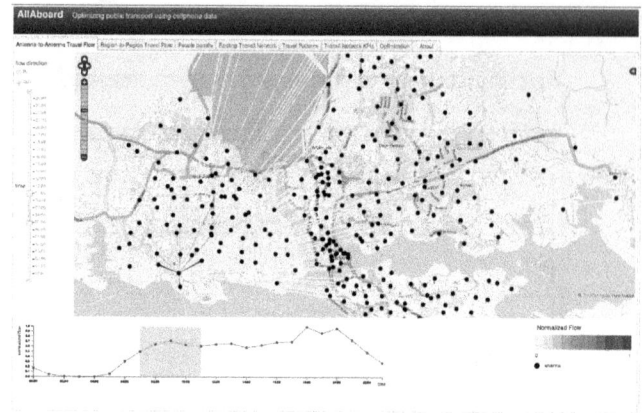

Figure 2. Origin/Destination Panel

operator to explore mobility data, validate them and evaluate different optimisation strategy by interacting with maps, density heat maps and other visual representations. The following subsections describe in details the different components.

O/D flows exploration

This visualisation allows the operator to explore the travel demand model that our tool is able to compute. The model is in the form of time-varying O/D flows, and different spatio-temporal visualisations are provided. From the spatial prospective, the data can be visualised at the level of aggregation of the cellphone antenna. Due to the large scale of the data, the operator can select the time interval for which he/she wants to evaluate the origin-destination flow (simply by selecting the time interval using the time bar (see Figure 2), where the minimum time interval is one hour), then use the radio bottom to select incoming or outgoing flow from an antenna. The flow for a selected antenna can be visualised by clicking on an antenna represented with a black dot on the map. The flow is pictured with arrows (darker ones indicate higher amount of trips between two antennas). Such visualisation can help answering questions like "where do people go from a given location?".

Regarding the temporal perspective, a temporal data summary of origin/destination flows from/to a selected antenna is presented through the line-chart (see Figure 2) where the x-axis represents time and the y-axis the total number of trips. The temporal interval is also highlighted with a grey box.

Optimization

The operator can run different optimisation scenarios expressed in terms of budget (number of buses to be added) to improve the public transport system. To do so, the operator can specify the number of buses to add, upper bound services frequencies and a measure of ticket cost per kilometer[6] by using the text boxes *Number of buses to add*, *Upper bound on bus frequencies*, and *Ticked cost* respectively on the left side of the optimisation panel and click on the *optimize* bottom (see Figure 3).

---

[6]While more complex ticket cost options are usually applied in cities, this measure was validated in our user study to be significant for comparing different scenarios.

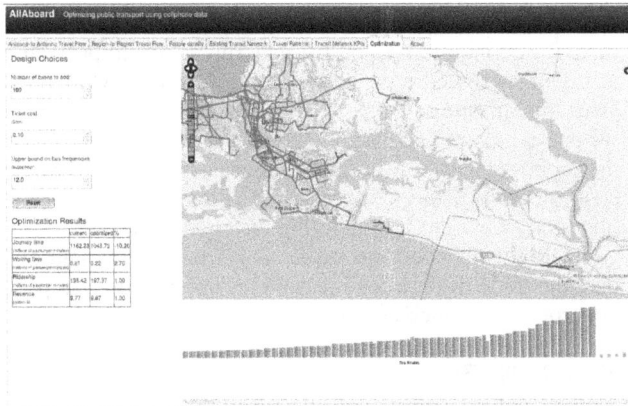

Figure 3. Optimization Panel

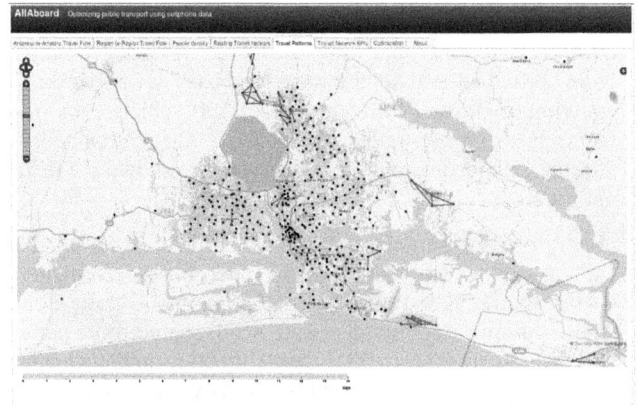

Figure 4. Extracted shared route patterns. Colours range from blue (low) to red (high) as function of the frequency.

As output, the Optimizer will provide network-wide KPIs for the current and optimised network, including Total Journey time, Total Waiting time, Ridership (all expressed in passenger-minutes) and Revenue (in $) that transportation authorities could get by actuating the optimisation strategy. Percentage increases are also displayed. Moreover, the map will display the current public transport network in magenta and the new routes provided by the Optimizer in blue. This will help the operator to quickly figure out where the adjustments have been recommended.

A visual summary of the impact of the optimisation strategy on the current public transit network is provided through the bar chart on the bottom of the Optimization panel, where the brown bars represent the ridership of the current routes instead the orange ones the ridership of the optimised ones. The bars are sorted by increasing value of the ridership for the current network. New routes are shown on the extreme right of the chart. The operator can then quickly figure out which routes are positively impacted by the extended network, and which others see a decrease in ridership. Moreover, by moving the mouse on a bar, the operator can get more details on the ridership, and the selected route is also highlighted on the map. In this way an operator could select routes which see an increase or decrease of ridership, and, looking at the map, see how close that route is to the proposed new ones.

EXPERIMENTAL EVALUATION

Origin-Destination Data Evaluation
We validate the process of estimation of O/D flows through a comparison with the gravity model (the basic model used in transportation [9]) that we define as

$$G(O,D) = \frac{O_{out} * D_{in}}{distance(O,D)^2}$$

where O_{out} represents the sum of all the flows going out from the node O and D_{in} indicates the sum of all the flows ending in D. We report a R^2 (coefficient of determination) between the flows detected by our method and the gravity model of 0.59, indicating that the mobility flows in Abidjan follow a similar behaviour as already seen in other cities [2].

Shared route patterns Evaluation

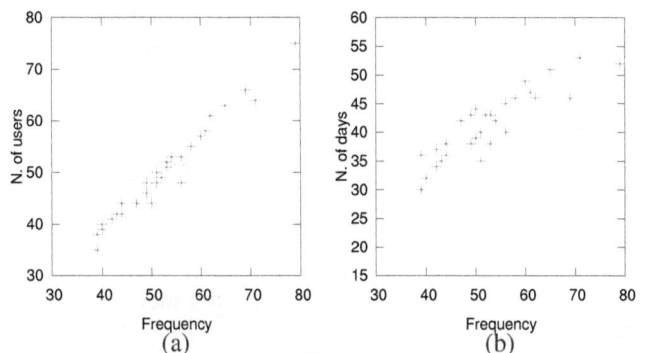

Figure 5. Relationship between the frequency of a sequence and the user traveling along that sequence (left) and the frequency with the number of days when the sequence was performed.

Starting from 199,767 sequences longer than 2 stops (whose maximum length was 12), the algorithm has been executed on with min_{sup} equal to 0.2%, thus obtaining 30 sequences of length 3 (i.e., there were no frequent sequences longer than 3 stops), see Figure 4.

We tuned the min_{sup} parameter to a low value (0.2%) due to the fact that the presence of a given user id is not guaranteed across different periods, thus every user has virtually only 14 days to support a given sequence. In other terms, there are only 14 days of mobility data for every single user, and the frequency threshold must be kept low, if we consider that the entire period covers 5 months. However, these sequences present interesting properties as shown in Figure 5. On the left, we report on the x-axis the frequency of the sequences and on the y-axis the number of users performing those sequences. As we can easily see, the sequences are performed by several distinct users, and so are not an artefact of a particular user's mobility. The sequences are also performed on distinct days, as reported in 5(b), showing that they are not specific of a few peculiar days of the year. For these reasons, we consider this set of sequences, which we call shared route patterns, interesting and usable from the optimization module since they are able to describe mobility patterns shared by different users and conducted on several days.

Optimization Evaluation

We evaluated the optimisation module on the recommendations provided to extend the existing SOTRA network, for a maximum allowed fleet increase of 100 vehicles, and maximum bus frequency of 12 buses/hour. The aggregated KPIs for the existing and optimised network are shown in the Table in Figure 3.

For the optimisation scenario, the tool used as candidate new routes a combination of 35 randomly selected shortest paths among already used bus stops (as it's usually done in these optimization models), and the 30 shared route patterns. Please note that these routes are connecting antenna locations instead of existing bus stops (since they are based on users' trajectories with antenna location resolution). The current implementation uses map-matching techniques to associate antenna locations to the road network, and a shortest path between stop locations to create route shapes. However, such a mapping might not be optimal. Thus, a post optimization phase would be required, where the operator could manually adjust the shape of the route and the location of the stops, also to take into account other criteria including the width of the streets, locations of shops, etc. This is currently not implemented in the tool, and will be part of future work.

The optimal assignment of new routes and their associated frequencies are determined using the optimization model presented above. The model recommends four additional routes, shown in Figure 3, with service headways of 12 minutes. Interestingly, the new routes (in blue) represent Feeder services that allow improving the overall ridership. Indeed, in the optimized network, system-wide travel times were found to reduce by 10.2%, while waiting time systemwide increased by 2%, on account of new bus stops that were introduced. While there was no change in bus route schedules in areas not impacted by the new services, they did have an impact on passenger flows on 22 existing routes. The ridership difference between existing and optimized services is shown in bottom of Figure 3. Interestingly, all four new selected routes belong to the shared route patterns.

End-User-based Evaluation

We showed the tool at the European congress on Intelligent Transportation Systems[7], where the main attendees are cities, transport authorities, and technology companies. Attendees were invited at our lab, where they were presented this and other demonstrators. We summarize here several questions that were asked during the demonstration of the tool.

One transit agency asked: "I know that my transit network was designed several years ago, and so might not be fully optimal with respect to the current travel demand. Can I use this tool to find gaps in my current transit network, i.e. areas of the city which are not currently well served?" To answer this question, we showed the panel in Figure 3, highlighting the location of the 4 new routes our system was able to suggest. There routes are indeed representing areas of the city where current public transport was not well developed.

Another transit agency asked: "Can I use this tool to estimate the economic impact that new routes would provide, in terms of increased revenue for the transit agency?" To answer this question, we showed the panel in Figure 3, where we can evaluate, line by line, the ridership of the current and the proposed new network. Once given a nominal $/km ticket cost, this information is turned into revenue estimate for the operator. We were told that this information would be very valuable for transport operators, as it would help them evaluate the tradeoff between investments in new buses/stops for new routes, and increased incomes from fares.

FUTURE WORK

The presented system allows to assess how a current transit system supports urban mobility demand, extracted by means of mobile phone location data. It further determines gaps in the current transit network, and recommends adjustments to it (e.g. in terms of new routes) with the goal to improve travellers' satisfaction both in terms of travel and wait time. In the future, the system could be extended to support decisions on different transport aspects, including better fares, dynamic road or congestion pricing, multi-modal data collection, and user incentives to encourage behavioral switch.

REFERENCES

1. Borndörfer, R., Grötschel, M., and Pfetsch, M. E. A column-generation approach to line planning in public transport. *Transportation Science 41*, 1 (2007), 123–132.

2. Calabrese, F., Di Lorenzo, G., Liu, L., and Ratti, C. Estimating origin-destination flows using mobile phone location data. *Pervasive Computing, IEEE 10*, 4 (april 2011), 36 –44.

3. Daly, E. M., Lécué, F., and Bicer, V. Westland row why so slow?: fusing social media and linked data sources for understanding real-time traffic conditions. In *IUI* (2013).

4. Desaulniers, G., and Hickman, M. Public transit. *Handbooks in operations research and management science 14* (2007), 69–128.

5. Ferreira, N., Poco, J., Vo, H. T., Freire, J., and Silva, C. T. Visual exploration of big spatio-temporal urban data: a study of new york city taxi trips. *IEEE Trans Vis Comput Graph 19*, 12 (2013), 2149–58.

6. Giannotti, F., Nanni, M., Pedreschi, D., Pinelli, F., Renso, C., Rinzivillo, S., and Trasarti, R. Unveiling the complexity of human mobility by querying and mining massive trajectory data. *The VLDB Journal 20*, 5 (Oct. 2011), 695–719.

7. Gonzalez, M., Hidalgo, C., and Barabasi, A.-L. Understanding individual human mobility patterns. *Nature 453*, 7196 (2008), 779–782.

8. Guihaire, V., and Hao, J. Transit network design and scheduling: A global review. *Transportation Research Part A: Policy and Practice 42*, 10 (2008), 1251–1273.

9. Levinson, D. M., and Kumar, A. Multimodal trip distribution: Structure and application. transportation research record 1446. transportation research board. In *Transportation Research Record 1466, 124* (1995), 131.

10. Martino, M., Calabrese, F., Di Lorenzo, G., Andris, C., Liang, L., and Ratti, C. Ocean of information: fusing aggregate and individual dynamics for metropolitan analysis. In *IUI* (2010).

11. Pei, J., Han, J., Mortazavi-asl, B., Pinto, H., Chen, Q., Dayal, U., and chun Hsu, M. Prefixspan: Mining sequential patterns efficiently by prefix-projected pattern growth. In *ICDE* (2001), 215–224.

12. Spiess, H., and Florian, M. Optimal strategies: A new assignment model for transit networks. *Transportation Research Part B: Methodological 23*, 2 (1989), 83–102.

---

[7]http://www.itsineurope.com/its9/

Exploring Customer Specific KPI Selection Strategies for an Adaptive Time Critical User Interface

Ingo R. Keck
Applied Intelligence Research Centre
Dublin Institute of Technology
ingo.keck@dit.ie

Robert J. Ross
School of Computing
Dublin Institute of Technology
robert.ross@dit.ie

ABSTRACT

Rapid growth in the number of measures available to describe customer-organization relationships is presenting a serious challenge for Business Intelligence (BI) interface developers as they attempt to provide business users with key customer information without requiring users to painstakingly sift through many interface windows and layers. In this paper we introduce a prototype Intelligent User Interface that we have deployed to partially address this issue. The interface builds on machine learning techniques to construct a ranking model of Key Performance Indicators (KPIs) that are used to select and present the most important customer metrics that can be made available to business users in time critical environments. We provide an overview of the prototype application, the underlying models used for KPI selection, and a comparative evaluation of machine learning and closed form solutions to the ranking and selection problems. Results show that the machine learning based method outperformed the closed form solution with a 66.5% accuracy rate on multi-label attribution in comparison to 54.1% for the closed form solution.

Author Keywords

Data Analytics; Information Filtering; Machine Learning

ACM Classification Keywords

H.5.2. User Interfaces: User-Centered Design

General Terms

Human Factors; Design

INTRODUCTION

Key Performance Indicators (KPIs) are numeric or categorical measures which are used to describe the operating performance of an organization or individual [11]. In the area of Customer Relationship Management (CRM) (see for example [5] for an introduction) KPIs are frequently used to characterize the relationship between a client and an organization. KPI measures in the CRM domain range from long term properties such as the total net sales made to a customer, to short term measures such as the length of time that a customer has been left on hold waiting to speak with a company representative.

KPIs are used by organizations to both assess the organization's performance and to tune services and products for clients. Within an organization's Customer Call Centers for example, appropriate KPI information can facilitate a call center agent to: (a) provide tailored service to customers; (b) to inform the customer of relevant special offers; and (c) to provide quick and efficient support. The importance of common KPI metrics in the CRM domain has been recognized by the developers of CRM and contact center software who have where possible integrated KPI measures into their software platforms.

As the area of Data Analytics and Information Sciences has expanded over the past ten years, the range and quantity of KPIs available to describe the relationship between customer and organization has expanded enormously (see for example [2]). This expansion in the number of useful KPIs presents a challenge to Contact Center Agents and to the developers of Contact Center Software alike. Namely, while it is possible to collect and provide 100s of KPIs to an agent via a conventionally designed CRM interface, a typical Call Center Agent is required to meet stringent throughput-based service level goals, and hence does not have the time available to review a large number of KPI metrics in the first seconds of answering a telephone call or chat based customer inquiry.

In our work we have been investigating solutions to the above class of problem through the use of machine learning techniques and other data analytics techniques. In this paper we introduce a specific solution that we have developed to identify the most important KPIs that should be provided to a call center agent at the initial stage of a customer inquiry. This is a description of work in progress and as such we limit our discussion to a short technical overview of this solution and an initial evaluative comparison of a machine learning based selection strategy against a closed form analytic solution. We proceed by first providing a brief overview of the state of the art in intelligent user interfaces for Business Intelligence systems. We then present an overview of our proposed solution before introducing a publicly available synthesized data set that we have developed for this study. Following this we provide details on the developed KPI selection strategies, as well as a comparative evaluation of those strategies on the synthesized data set. A brief discussion is also provided before we conclude and outline potential future work.

RELATED WORK

The aggregation and presentation of Key Performance Indicators within call center systems or other customer relationship management applications broadly falls into the class of Business Intelligence (BI) [3] software. User Interfaces design for BI software has historically been less than intelligent but has in recent years slowly embraced intelligent features in order to improve usability for less technical users. This work has been industry and development led rather than research led, and initially focused on the embedding of context-sensitive information displays alongside traditional business process interfaces. The presentation of alerts based on business measures moving beyond some acceptable bounds is for a example a simple but important aspect of *intelligence* in BI software; however in such cases these alerts are limited in scope and are typically hard coded event triggers [8]. More recently, active development in Business Intelligence interfaces has began to move towards the incorporation of more intelligent techniques such as the incorporation of improved visualization methods, speech based communication, and multi-touch and multi-modal interfaces[1]. While these developments represent progress, BI interfaces generally remain bloated and often require a user to navigate through many pages of content to find important information.

Adaptive Graphical User Interfaces (see for example [6] for an overview) self-modify to provide users with the most appropriate interface for their needs, and are thus of particular relevance to us. There are a number of different types of adaptations possible. These include: (a) device adaptation where an application adapts and conforms to the parameters of the display; (b) presentation adaptation where visual settings are for example automatically modified to accommodate users with eyesight limitations; to (c) content adaptation wherein displayed options available to a user vary based on a model of the user's previous interactions with the system. The dynamically selected collection of programme menu options available in Windows XP through Windows 7 is a classic example of such content based selection. Within the broad CRM and BI domain, Singh recently examined the role of the adaptive user interface in Enterprise Resource Planning systems [14]. While Singh's analysis was comprehensive, it did however stay focused on issues far removed from our question of information selection for adaptive prompting, and focused instead on issues such as the partial activation of menus based on usage context.

Underlying technologies in the recommender domain (see e.g., [13]) such as collaborative filtering provide a useful foundation for information filtering and provision to business users in the BI software domain. For example, personalization and adaptation have been used extensively in CRM applications for the identification of customized services or products that can be offered to the customer [5]. Indeed one of the great applications of data science in the business domain has been the targeting of products and special offers to specific customers. For our purposes however, the output of recommender systems in the classical sense is inappropriate for KPI selection. In our case the selection of appropriate output is linked to the intrinsic properties of current data rather than the specific preferences of an individual customer or service agent. The selection of appropriate KPIs for display is therefore closer from a modeling perspective to the content selection process as used in the natural language or text generation communities [12], i.e., our task is to select the most salient of items to present to the user.

SOLUTION ARCHITECTURE

In order to investigate alternative strategies for the selection of key information to be provided to service agents, we have developed a prototype KPI recommendation application. Intended to run alongside a traditional CRM solution, the prototype application provides company agents with the most appropriate information generated at run-time and customized to each specific customer and case.

An essential part of the design of the system is that for a given company or even division, the recommendation strategies can be tailored for the given environment. While we provide specific details on the selection strategies later in the paper, it is worth noting at this point that we have adopted a *Managed Selection Strategy*. By this we mean that strategies are not learned based on feedback from individual Contact Center Agents or indeed customers. Instead we have adopted a semi-automatic learning system that can be used by IT personnel and Contact Center management to bootstrap and supervise the assistance provided. Our primary reason for doing so was due to feedback from industry partners who indicated that gathering accurate feedback from Contact Center Agents is rarely feasible in a high throughput environment.

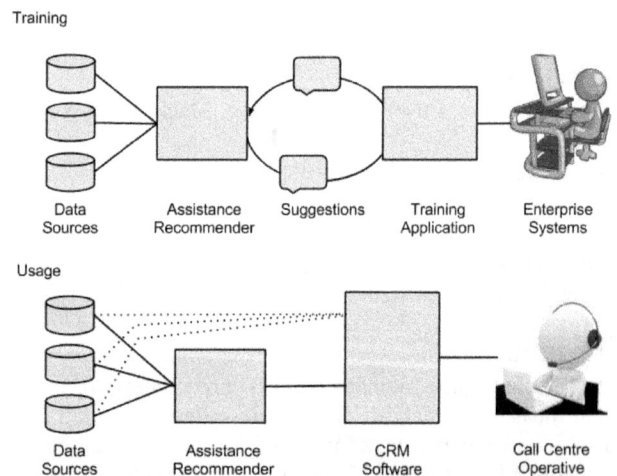

Figure 1. The high-level architecture of the proposed system.

Figure 1 outlines the training and usage models for the enterprise assistance system. During training the assistance recommender is customized by Enterprise Systems or IT personnel through the use of a training application which augments the models used in the assistance system. An Active Learning based approach to training has been adopted in the prototype system to take best advantage of occasional designer involvement in the modeling process. Once trained, or partially trained, the assistance recommender can then be integrated alongside CRM software to provide key insights from individual customer histories to call center agents at the beginning of a user interaction.

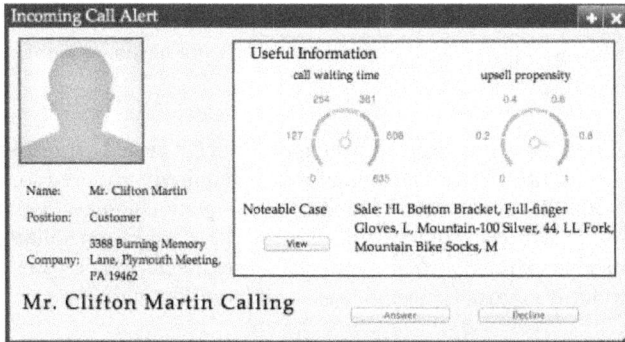

Figure 2. End User Interface to the Selector.

Selected summary items are provided in 'screen pop' style information bursts alongside traditional summary information. This information is made available briefly to the sales or service agent on the initiation of a call or chat based interaction by a customer. Figure 2 shows this interface as implemented for the prototype solution. Call center agents can accept the incoming call or chat, reject it, or accept it while clicking through the provided summary items to more comprehensive CRM information screens. While the use of 'screen pop' type interfaces are already in use in existing applications to provide end users with a static selection of information items, our work has concerned the extension of this idea to dynamic content selection and the development of optimal selection strategies.

As indicated earlier, the selection of relevant metrics and customer history is based on training by IT users or customer service managers. For our prototype design we have implemented an explicit labeling interface which can be used by non-technical users to select the most important items to display to a sales or service agent for a given customer. Specifically this interface displays for a given customer at a given point in time: (a) their key contact and role information; (b) context information such as whether the customer is making a sales or service call; and (c) a selection of metrics that are available to describe the customer-organization relationship at that particular point in time. Designated system developers or managers can then select the most relevant information items for each of a number of training cases.

DATA CREATION & LABELING

While this project has been developed in part with collaborations with industry partners who have a significant interest in the CRM and call center domains, legal and moral restrictions due to Data Governance and Data Protection legislation mean that it is not always feasible to integrate directly with deployed CRM applications. Moreover, in deploying any solution it is wherever possible useful to evaluate systems and algorithms on publicly available data. In light of these two issues, for this work we have synthesized a comprehensive CRM data set that is indicative of the data used in industry. The complete data set is openly available online along side detailed documentation regarding its synthesis and structure

[1]. In the following we provide a very brief overview of the synthesized data, but interested readers are encouraged to review the data and documentation provided elsewhere.

As indicated earlier the data model itself is typical of many common CRM systems, and has in fact been designed with a view to easy compatibility with existing systems. With respect to the parametrization or population of the model, the most important issue to consider here relates to the interactive and behavioral aspects of user actions that are captured by the data set. Here the simulated data is based on 5 commonly quoted customer classes (*innovators, early adopters, early majority, late majority and laggards*) with corresponding characteristics. Customers can buy products and services, ask for information and for quotes. Sold products can fail and thus generate customer requests for service or new sales (based on the characteristics of the customer). These constitute contexts for customer call and chat sessions.

For test purposes we simulated a data set of roughly 104.000 interactions, 10.000 customers, 20 agents and 590 products, covering a time span of 2 years. Each customer has 9 KPIs as inherent values (*churn probability, profit generated, upsell propensity, social influence, service load, service contract, sale probability, profit per order and number of sales*), while one KPI value (*call waiting time*) is interaction specific. The distribution type of each KPI varies greatly: Univariate, gaussian, exponential and multimodal distributions are generated in the simulation by the combination of the distinct customer segment characteristics.

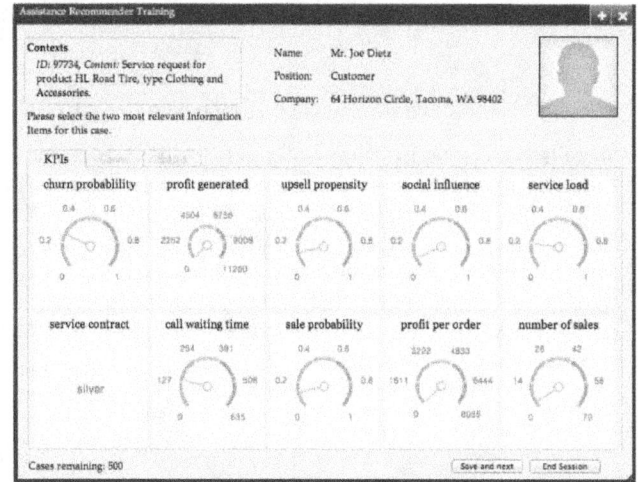

Figure 3. The labeling interface.

The raw dataset thus defines a customer's state in terms of a number of KPI types. For any such point the KPI recommendation system should select the most appropriate KPIs. For model generation and evaluation it is necessary to label a subset of the dataset such that the most important KPIs are highlighted. For this purpose a custom front-end has been implemented to aid with the direct labeling of cases from the data set (see Figure 3). Each KPI is presented either in form of a gauge or as text in case of the KPI *service contract*. A

---

[1]http://www.comp.dit.ie/aigroup/?page_id=729

Measure	Annotator Weights	Nelder-Mead-A	Nelder-Mead-B
All Labels	**54.2**	51.9	54.1
Both Labels	**21.6**	19.6	**21.6**
Either Label	**86.6**	84.2	**86.6**

Measure	SVM
All Labels	66.5
Both Labels	39.1
Either Label	93.4

Table 1. Accuracy for Closed Form Solution results (left) and Multi-Label Classification using SVM (right). Values in bold give the highest within closed form solution.

human expert can then select up to two KPIs to label as the most important KPIs in the given context of the simulated customer call.

SELECTION STRATEGIES

From the perspective of intelligent user interfaces the primary technical problem to be addressed is the selection of KPI measures for presentation to the call center agents at the start of every call[2]. For this work we have implemented and evaluated two types of selection strategy for this purpose, i.e., a closed form solution and a classifier based ranking solution.

Closed Form Solution

By assuming that KPI measures obey a normal distribution or other well defined distribution we can characterize the problem of most relevant measure selection as a problem of identifying those KPI measures which have the greatest deviation from the location parameter (mean in the case of normal distributions). Namely for a given KPI, x, we can measure the deviation of the ith instance of that parameter from the mean for that parameter $\bar{x}$ as:

$$\delta(x_i) = \frac{x_i - \bar{x}}{\sigma_x} \qquad (1)$$

where σ_x is the standard deviation for the parameter x.

Since the deviation measure δ accounts for the relative deviation of a parameter from the mean, we can use δ to provide relative prominence values for each KPI. Scoring each KPI measure and ranking the values for δ for the given instance we gain a very simple method for estimating the relative deviation of KPI from its expected value. Generalizing over each KPI $x \in X$ the most prominent KPI is simply that which maximizes the δ function, i.e.,

$$\arg \max_{x} \delta(x_i) = \frac{x_i - \bar{x}}{\sigma_x} \qquad (2)$$

Within a given organization all KPIs will not be equally relevant. Moreover, within a given context difference KPIs will have greater or lesser importance in different contexts. For example, within a sales context an *upsell* propensity is more important than *call waiting time*. We therefore assign individual weights w_x for each KPI, x as follows:

$$\arg \max_{x} \delta(x_i) = w_x \frac{x_i - \bar{x}}{\sigma_x} \qquad (3)$$

There are a number of advantages to such a closed form solution. Primarily no labeling of data is required for closed form solutions, thus allowing rapid implementation and evaluation of closed form solutions. Moreover, the closed form solution is also extremely transparent and allows business users to explicitly control the weights assigned to different KPIs.

Classifier Based Ranking Solution

In addition to the closed form solution just outlined, we also implemented a supervised learning based solution to the KPI selection problem. Specifically we can treat KPI selection as a multi-label classification problem [16] where the most relevant n KPIs for a given instance are labels. This multi-label classification treatment is necessary since it is generally appropriate to display more than one KPI instance for every given incoming call. In the current case we selected n=2 and subsequently both labeled each instance with the two most applicable labels, and implemented the selection strategy to select the two most appropriate labels. While this constraint is necessary for evaluation purposes, it is generally not necessary to constraint the number of labeled KPIs and selected KPIs in this way. However, recent research in Psychology [4] showed that the human working memory is limited to 3–5 independent items depending on personal capabilities. Given that the call center agent must at least handle the customer's name and the context of the case, this already sums up to at least 2 items. Therefor no more than 3 additional information items should be presented to a user.

We first labeled 500 instances from our synthesized data set using the labeling interface introduced earlier. For each of the 500 cases the annotator selected the two most important KPIs based on a specific business rational. This business rational, outlined in the annotation instructions, explained that the priority of the business was to maximize profits while maintaining brand quality perception in customers. Within a real deployment we would expect a more prescriptive and company specific description of objectives to be made available to an annotator in line with business requirements.

The features used for training in the unsupervised learning case were the KPI values themselves and a context feature which defines the business context in which the call was made. Following a standard multi-label classification approach, one binary classifier was then trained per target KPI label. For classification we used Support Vector Machine instances with a sigmoid kernel function [7][3]. As well as a binary classification decision for the given target KPI, each SVM also provides a class probability based on distance to

---

[2]From this point we are generalizing the use of the term call to telephone based or chat based conversations.

[3]Our choice of the Support Vector Machine as the baseline classifier was due to its well established accuracy, but other robust high-performance classifiers such as Random Forests [15] would also be applicable.

the class boundary. Comparing class probabilities across SVMs, we may then select the n most probable KPIs for a given instance.

RESULTS

The closed form solution described earlier requires relative weights to be assigned to each KPI. We approached the assignment of weights in three ways. In the first approach annotator provided post-hoc estimates were assigned to each KPI weight. In the second approach the weights were instead learned directly from the annotated data using a global Nelder-Mead search [10] starting from 0.5 for all KPI weights (Nelder-Mead-A). As a third method we also applied the Nelder-Mead optimization method but with the annotator provided post-hoc weights as starting point (Nelder-Mead-B). In the latter two cases, 10-fold cross validation was applied in the training and testing process.

For this multi-label classification problem we apply three distinct measures of accuracy in assessing the performance of the KPI selection process:

- **All Label Accuracy -** A count of the total number of correctly attributed labels divided by the total number of attributed labels in the sample.

- **Both Label Accuracy -** A count of the number of cases in which both labels were correctly attributed divided by the total number of cases.

- **Either Label Accuracy -** A count of the number of cases in which either one or both labels were correctly attributed divided by the total number of cases.

Table 1 (left) summarizes the results of the closed form solution application for the three weight assignment methods. We can see from the table that the annotator provided weights alone provided the overall best accuracy, with Nelder-Mead-B or the optimization algorithm with annotator provided weights as starting point coming in second. Referring to the individual measures, both methods performed well on either label accuracy with 86.6% of cases having at least one correctly attributed label. Results for the correct attribution of both labels for a given case are however considerably worse, with only 21.6% of cases having both labels correctly attributed.

For the machine learning based approach we similarly applied 10-fold cross validation for training and testing. Table 1 (right) summarizes accuracy results for the multi-label classification problem. In this 2 label identification problem, 66.5% of labels were identified correctly. In other words, in the case of 50 test cases and hence 100 labels to be identified, on average 66.5 of these 100 labels were correctly attributed. In the case of successfully identifying both labels for a given sample, the raw accuracy rate drops to 39.1% . While this is a poor result if the overall problem is viewed as a single class classification problem, it is less problematic in the multi-label context. This is evidenced when we instead consider the number of cases in which at least one label was identified successfully. For the current data set either of the attributed labels were correct in 93.4% of cases. This means

that in the vast majority of cases at least one of the KPIs presented to a call center agent would have been selected by the expert.

While our main consideration is the multi-label results, it is worth also considering results on a class by class basis. Figure 4 presents the F-score (F1) for each individual SVM based classifier. From the results we see that many of the classifiers performed moderately well with F-score values greater than 0.6 in 7 cases. Individual classification for 3 KPIs were however poor. Further investigation shows that this poor performance is most likely due to unbalanced target labels with certain KPIs under represented in the data set. For example KPI-10 accounted for less than 5% of all labels in the current data set.

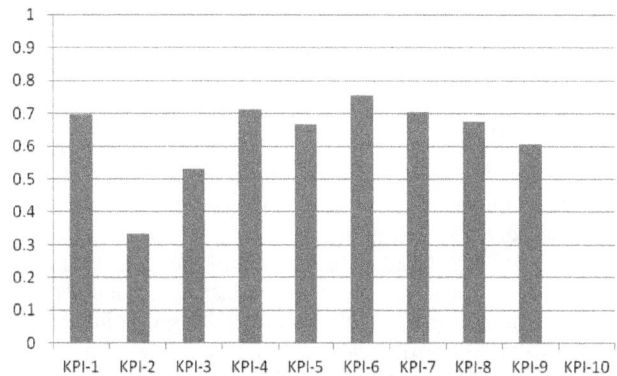

Figure 4. F1 Scores for individual classifiers

DISCUSSION

The automated provision of business metrics and customer case summary information is far from novel in either a research or industrial setting (consider for example the use of 'screen pops' in *Salesforce.com*'s CRM solution[4] for details.).. Thus, the question we are investigating in our work is not whether information should be intelligently provided to users through the user interface, but rather what are the best methods which can be used in selecting and summarizing that information for users in time critical environments. The selection of KPIs as outlined here is a starting point in this work.

Considering first the results for the classifier based approach, we see these as a good starting point in terms of KPI recommendation scores. We recognize however that under represented target labels in the training and test data are a problem for the method. With a larger labeled data set and appropriate sampling, we do however expect to lessen this problem. Related to this issue we also recognize the limitation of depending on synthesized data. While we expect real data to be naturally more noisy and necessarily different in nature to the data we have synthesized and worked with, we see the synthesized data as being a necessary and useful first test bed in developing the methods presented here.

The SVM-based supervised learning method considerably outperformed the closed form solution based method in this

[4]See http://www.salesforce.com

study. While poor performance in closed form results will be due in part to deficiencies in optimization, it is far more likely that the poor performance is due chiefly to the inaccuracy of annotator based weightings and the invalid nature of the assumptions being made with respect to the data set. Essentially the closed form solution assumes that KPIs are well defined by a normal distribution and that notable values are directly proportional to deviation from a well defined mean. In practice such assumptions do not hold in many cases. Multi-modal data, uniformly distributed data, or data that fits other well defined distributions such as logarithmic distributions will each violate the assumptions made by the basic closed solution model. However we are hopeful that unsupervised learning methods such as those used in novelty detection can provide a more robust framework on which to base an improved closed form solution [9].

CONCLUSIONS & FUTURE WORK

The model and results presented in this paper are contributed as work in progress rather than a presentation of completed or finalized work. Nevertheless we believe that the work presented constitutes a useful starting point in our analysis in the development and improvement of intelligent interfaces for call center agents and other workers dealing with large volumes of structured data in a time-critical environment. Perhaps unsurprisingly the machine learning based selection strategy outperformed the closed form based solution. Despite this we do see the closed form based approach as being worthy of further development. We note in particular that the closed form solution presented made a number of assumptions about the statistical assumptions of a given KPI. By broadening the nature of the closed form method to automatically select appropriate measures for a given distribution, we expect a considerable improvement in performance.

With respect to the machine learning based selection methods we believe that type of labeling required does not place a great burden on organizations. That said, the policy of pre-labeling a large data set is only a starting point for our deployment method. We are currently developing an active learning based solution which allows training to be performed on a periodic basis, and also provide a more robust framework which can account for potential drift in KPI measures over time.

ACKNOWLEDGMENTS
We would like to thank Enterprise Ireland and IDA Ireland for funding this research under their Technology Centres programme (TC 2013 0013).

REFERENCES
1. Alotaibi, M., and Rigas, D. Fostering the user interface acceptance in customer relationship management: A multimedia-aided approach. In *Information Technology: New Generations (ITNG), 2012 Ninth International Conference on* (2012), 796–801.

2. Baroudi, R. *KPI Mega Library: 17,000 Key Performance Indicators*. CreateSpace, 2010.

3. Chaudhuri, S., Dayal, U., and Narasayya, V. An overview of business intelligence technology. *Communications of the ACM 54*, 8 (2011), 88–98.

4. Cowan, N. The magical mystery four: How is working memory capacity limited, and why? *Current Directions in Psychological Science 19*, 1 (2010), 51–57.

5. Dyche, J. *The CRM Handbook: A Business Guide to Customer Relationship Management*. Addison Wesley, 2001.

6. Findlater, L., and Gajos, K. Z. Deisgn space and evaluation challenges of adaptive graphical user interfaces. *AI Magazine 30 (4)* (2009), 68–73.

7. Hearst, M. A., Dumais, S., Osman, E., Platt, J., and Scholkopf, B. Support vector machines. *Intelligent Systems and their Applications, IEEE 13*, 4 (1998), 18–28.

8. Kang, J. G., and Han, K. H. A business activity monitoring system supporting real-time business performance management. In *Third International Conference on Convergence and Hybrid Information Technology* (2008).

9. Markou, M., and Singh, S. Novelty detection: a review – part 1: statistical approaches. *Signal processing 83*, 12 (2003), 2481–2497.

10. Olsson, D. M., and Nelson, L. S. The nelder-mead simplex procedure for function minimization. *Technometrics 17*, 1 (1975), 45–51.

11. Parmenter, D. *Key Performance Indicators: Developing, Implementing, and Using Winning KPIs*. John Wiley & Sons, Inc., 2010.

12. Reiter, E., and Dale, R. *Building Natural Language Generation Systems*. Cambridge University Press, Cambridge, U.K., 2000.

13. Ricci, F., Rokach, L., Shapira, B., and Kantor, P. B., Eds. *Recommender Systems Handbook*. Springer, 2011.

14. Singh, A. *Designing Adaptive User Interfaces for Enterprise Resource Planning Systems for Small Enterprises*. PhD thesis, Nelson Mandela Metropolitan University, 2013.

15. Svetnik, V., Liaw, A., Tong, C., Culberson, J. C., Sheridan, R. P., and Feuston, B. P. Random forest: a classification and regression tool for compound classification and qsar modeling. *Journal of chemical information and computer sciences 43*, 6 (2003), 1947–1958.

16. Tsoumakas, G., and Katakis, I. Multi-label classification: An overview. *International Journal of Data Warehousing and Mining (IJDWM) 3*, 3 (2007), 1–13.

Improving Cross-domain Information Sharing for Care Coordination using Semantic Web Technologies

Spyros Kotoulas
spyros.kotoulas@ie.ibm.com

Vanessa Lopez
vanlopez@ie.ibm.com

Marco Luca Sbodio
marco.sbodio@ie.ibm.com

Pierpaolo Tommasi
ptommasi@ie.ibm.com

Martin Stephenson
martin_stephenson@ie.ibm.com

Pol Mac Aonghusa
aonghusa@ie.ibm.com

Smarter Cities Technology Centre
IBM Research Ireland

ABSTRACT

We present an approach to access and consolidate complex information spanning multiple specialist domains and make it available to non-experts. We are using a combination of business rules and contextual exploration to reduce interface complexity and improve consumability. We present a use case and a prototype on top of a real-world enterprise solution for coordinating Social care and Health care. We evaluate our system through a user study. Our results indicate that our approach reduces the time required to obtain business results compared to a baseline graph exploration approach.

INTRODUCTION

Healthcare and Social Care are unique domains in terms of economic magnitude and complexity. In economic terms, for 2009, total expenditure on healthcare in the United States was 2.6 trillion USD or 17.4% of the GDP[1]. Total expenditure on social care was 2.98 trillion USD or 19.90% of the GDP[2]. In terms of complexity, organizations that are involved in providing social and health care are numerous and span a very wide domain (ranging from public safety to income support). For example, AHIP, the trade association of health insurers numbers some 1300 members[3]; the number of hospitals registered with the American Hospital Association is 5724[4] and the number of homeless shelters surpasses 4000[5]. In addition, medical information is vastly complex: Nuance reports that LinkBase®[6] contains more than 1 million concepts.

Coordinating Social Care and Health Care has been identified both as a major pain point and a significant opportunity

[1]http://dx.doi.org/10.1787/888932523215

[2]http://www.oecd.org/els/social/expenditure

[3]http://www.ahip.org

[4]http://www.aha.org/research/rc/stat-studies/fast-facts.shtml, retrieved 19/04/2013

[5]http://www.shelterlistings.org/

[6]http://www.nuance.com/for-healthcare/resources/clinical-language-understanding/ontology/index.htm

in modern health and social systems [12]. Several studies have shown that costs can be contained and outcomes improved with a more holistic approach to care [10]. As a simple motivating example, consider an individual quartered in inappropriate housing while suffering from a relatively minor health issue, aggravated by the housing condition. As a result, the given individual frequently resorts to visiting emergency rooms, resulting in significant cost to the healthcare system and a less effective treatment. By itself, the housing situation does not warrant state intervention. Nevertheless, resolving it would dramatically improve the health situation, resulting in a better quality-of-life for the individual and lower costs for the health system.

In this paper, we investigate the challenges presented in Care Coordination as a characteristic complex, multi-domain information access problem space. We propose a novel technical solution to augment applications with cross-domain context, based on an intelligent semantics-based user interface. Although we focus on the specific use-case, the approach presented in this paper is applicable to any domain with similar characteristics (e.g. public safety).

The main contribution of this paper lies in an abstract, standards-compliant and transferable definition of hybrid business rules and context-driven data exploration. Our approach marries the usability of business rules with the flexibility, ability to represent abstract information and interoperability of Semantic technologies.

We present a proof of concept on top of an enterprise solution for care management, IBM Cúram. For privacy reasons, all personal information shown in this paper is fictional, although it has been retrieved from internal system deployments. This paper is an extension to the demo in [8], showing a user evaluation and a more extensive description of the Vulnerability Indicators.

BACKGROUND

In this Section, we are giving an overview of the main characteristics, pain points, research efforts and technologies for the domains targeted in this paper.

Healthcare is a very complex domain where numerous organizations are involved during the care providing process: medical research institutes, hospitals, clinics, pharmaceutical companies, nursing facilities, medical equipment manufactures etc. With the wide adoption of information technology solutions, medical records are scattered among different archives both within and across institutions, often based on proprietary formats. Even within the same hospital, patient records may be stored in different systems such as Electronic Health Records (EHRs) or Hospital Information Systems (HIS) or Laboratory Information Systems (LIS).

Semantic Web-related technologies have gained popularity because they facilitate integration of heterogeneous data using rich explicit semantics and the ability to infer additional information [2]. In [5, 9], information is standardized using ontologies. In [4], they surveyed the feasibility and state of the art for using semantic technology to represent, integrate and analyze knowledge in a range of biomedical networks. Recognizing that a single ontology for healthcare is not an achievable goal, [11] investigates alignment techniques to better support data integration at a large scale. The closest system to our approach is InfoSleuth [3], which provides semantic integration across an open set of sources in the healthcare domain. Unlike InfoSleuth, our approach focuses on making information spanning multiple domains accessible to non-experts.

Social Care is usually organized and managed separately from healthcare, and through different legal entities. While healthcare records are deep but narrow, with a wealth of technical and biomedical details, social care records capture a very broad spectrum of information [7], ranging from family relations, vulnerability, social programs and received benefits to accommodation descriptions. The citizen engagement process in social care starts by identifying needs and strengths, assessing risk and priority through evidence-based models and ends with outcome evaluation and monitoring. This process involves disparate types of organizations such as social service administration, educational institutions, homeless shelters and public safety authorities. As a result, the Social care domain is highly fragmented and standardisation efforts sparse (with the notable exception of the UK Social care online taxonomy[7]).

Care Coordination generally refers to combining social care and healthcare to improve outcomes and lower costs. Although it is one of the major cornerstones of health reform, it lacks a common definition and is recognized as a modern-day Tower of Babel [7]. For instance, in Camden, New Jersey, 1% of patients account for a third of the city's medical costs [6]. According to Gawande [6], the routinely higher cost and lower quality of care for high cost/high need people are due to lack of integrated health and social services. Taking high-cost situations into coordinated care requires considering multiple sources, from different domains. There are two recent examples implementing a patient centric view of care coordination for special high-need patient populations: the *patient-centered Medical Home* in NY [1] - a primary care model to contain healthcare costs by promoting patient-centered care-, and the *Common Ground organization*, focused on homelessness, veterans' affairs, mental illness, and health care. Common Ground launched a campaign[8] to place

chronically homeless people into permanent housing, using vulnerability indexes to prioritize care for the homeless population that faced the greatest risk of dying on the streets.

SCENARIO

In this Section, we present a motivational use-case that sets the ground for further discussion regarding contextual access to healthcare and social information. It captures a situation where a social worker wants an overview and exploration capability of the situation of an individual across several dimensions, so as to get insight on their needs and potential vulnerabilities.

As an illustrative example, a patient named Bob visits a physician and is diagnosed with pre-CHF (Congestive Heart Failure) condition and obesity. He has an unhealthy diet and sedentary life style. The physician can access the different medical information from various systems to obtain a complete clinical view. The physician can see vitals (e.g., weight, pressure), symptoms (such as cough, wheezing and shortness of bread), medications, allergies, lab tests, care plans, and family history of CHF as well as analytics results (risk stratification). His care plan requires implementing lifestyle changes, such as healthy heart diet and exercise.

Bob's clinical issues are complicated with social issues - unemployment - and signs of depression. Thus, Bob is referred to *integrated care* by the physician to help him achieve necessary lifestyle changes and receive proper counseling and services (e.g., social benefits or referral to a nutritional programme). Bob has been registered on the system and he has given his consent to accept services through the health home[9].

The assigned care manager can review Bobs medical, social and behavioral situation, across both health and social care systems. Individual risks variables that influence care include: social needs (e.g., does the person own a house, are they homeless?), personal details (age, gender, ethnicity), health history, entire family situation and even places or communities where she belongs (deprivation and morbidity indexes). Based on the information above, the care manager can make informed decisions concerning treatments plans, involving additional services (e.g. social service, income support) or including family members.

Challenges

This use-case brings forth a set of challenges. Although we are investigating these challenges in the context of the health care and social care domains, we believe that they are pervasive in several complex domains.

- **Models are complex and span multiple domains.** Creating a model for a single addressed domain is a very challenging task (take HL7, for example). A model encapsulating all relevant domains would be very difficult to develop and very difficult to use.

- **Data consumability is challenging.** Traditional UI techniques do not cope well with schema heterogeneity, while

---

[7]http://www.scie-socialcareonline.org.uk
[8]http://100khomes.org/

[9]A health home is an organization to coordinate care

if:	an individual has been homeless in the last 6 months
and one of:	more than three hospitalizations or emergency room visits in a year
	more than three emergency room visits in the previous three months
	aged 60 or older
	cirrhosis of the liver, end-stage renal disease
	history of frostbite, immersion foot, or hypothermia
	HIV+/AIDS
	tri-morbidity: co-occurring psychiatric, substance abuse, and chronic medical condition
then:	they have a 40% chance of dying prematurely

Table 1. Example factors that put individuals at high morbidity risk.

generic semantic browsing does not cope well with accessibility to non-expert users. In addition, users with various roles require information at a different granularity: while a medical professional needs exact information about a disease, a social worker only needs to know about complicating environmental of psychological factors.

- **Context and semantics go beyond space, time, identity and datatypes.** Aggregating or abstracting from information at the level presented in the use-cases requires machine understanding of the exact relationships between records or entities.

OUR APPROACH

We describe an approach addressing the challenges presented in the previous section, consisting of the following main elements: (a) To abstract from the complexity of each source, and to allow incremental integration, we use a set of *reference ontologies* to partially map our data against. (b) To *facilitate navigation* across very complex cross-domain information, we use a set of expert-defined business rules. These business rules are defined in terms of the reference ontologies and are reusable across deployments (and possibly systems). (c) To enable users to access information *not* captured by the business rules, we are using a *graph exploration approach.* (d) To abstract from the infrastructure of each source, and to allow enforcement of policies defined by each organization, we use a *semantic data management* layer. The semantic data management layer allows accessing information from distributed sources as RDF. Data resides in the source systems, is integrated on demand and is queried through a federation mechanism. Further detail is out of scope for this paper.

Navigating needs and vulnerabilities

Care workers need to be able to assess the needs and vulnerabilities of individuals. The related information is: (a) *broad*, coming from different domains (e.g. healthcare, social care, public safety, citizen records), (b) *voluminous*, comprising many factors in the life on the individual and (c) *complex*, often expressed in specialist terms (e.g. medical conditions).

Vulnerability Indexes have been used to model potential risks of individuals. For example, Table 1 shows some factors that contribute to the risk that a given homeless individual is at

highly increased morbidity risk (taken from [1]). In general, vulnerability indexes may rely on information from multiple domains. For example, consider the factors contributing to *food insecurity*: low income, family size, physical or behavioral health problems, in particular, obesity, disabilities or chronic diseases that affect diet (e.g., diabetes and CHF); substance abuse, which can affect eating habits and money available for food; poor housing, which affects access/preparation/storage of food; lower levels of education; social services received, in particular food stamps or school lunches; safety issues, such as domestic violence or youth in foster care; or other barriers related to the population, such as single parent households and access to food in impoverished urban and rural areas.

We augment the concept of Vulnerability Indexes into what we call Decomposable Vulnerability Indicators (DVIs). DVIs have a *formal representation*, drawn from concepts in an ontology, allowing transferability across systems (e.g. the unemployment can be grounded at a specific term in an OWL ontology). In addition, they are *decomposable* into contributing factors, represented as an acyclic graph the nodes of which represent contributing factors to a vulnerability (e.g. vulnerability regarding health can be influenced by substance abuse, allergies, known medical problems etc). Finally, DVIs are *computable* on the basis of their formal semantics, their acyclic graph structure and weights on the edges of the graph.

Figure 1 (A) shows the DVI for Bob on the left. At a glance, the care manager can see that Bob is facing problems in multiple dimensions, with Health and Food being the most important ones, indicated by the size and colour of the circles. Clicking on a node (circle) expands it, revealing the contributing factors and their relative importance.

Contextual access and exploration

DVIs can help users abstract from the volume and domain heterogeneity of information. Nevertheless, in some scenarios, they need to retrieve relevant *facts* that are difficult to capture in a business rule. For example, a social worker is looking at the family situation of an individual. They see that the individual suffers from mobility problems and has early symptoms of Alzheimer. Their family members do not live in the vicinity, so as to provide assistance, while they need to visit a hospital on a weekly basis for some treatments. In addition, their closest family member suffers from serious social deprivation issues, so they are less likely to help. Although none of the problems listed above is life-threatening by itself, their combination is. A social worker will need to *explore relevant information*, identify the problem, based on their domain experience, and take appropriate measures.

Additional semi-structured sources can be used to uncover connections between factors and records. For example, for all factors that are also described as entities in DBpedia, we have added links (owl:sameAs) to the corresponding DBpedia term. In turn, for each topic linked to a DBpedia term, we extract the social care topics that are also mentioned in the descriptions of the corresponding Wikipedia page, so as to add links to commonly co-related factors. These correlations,

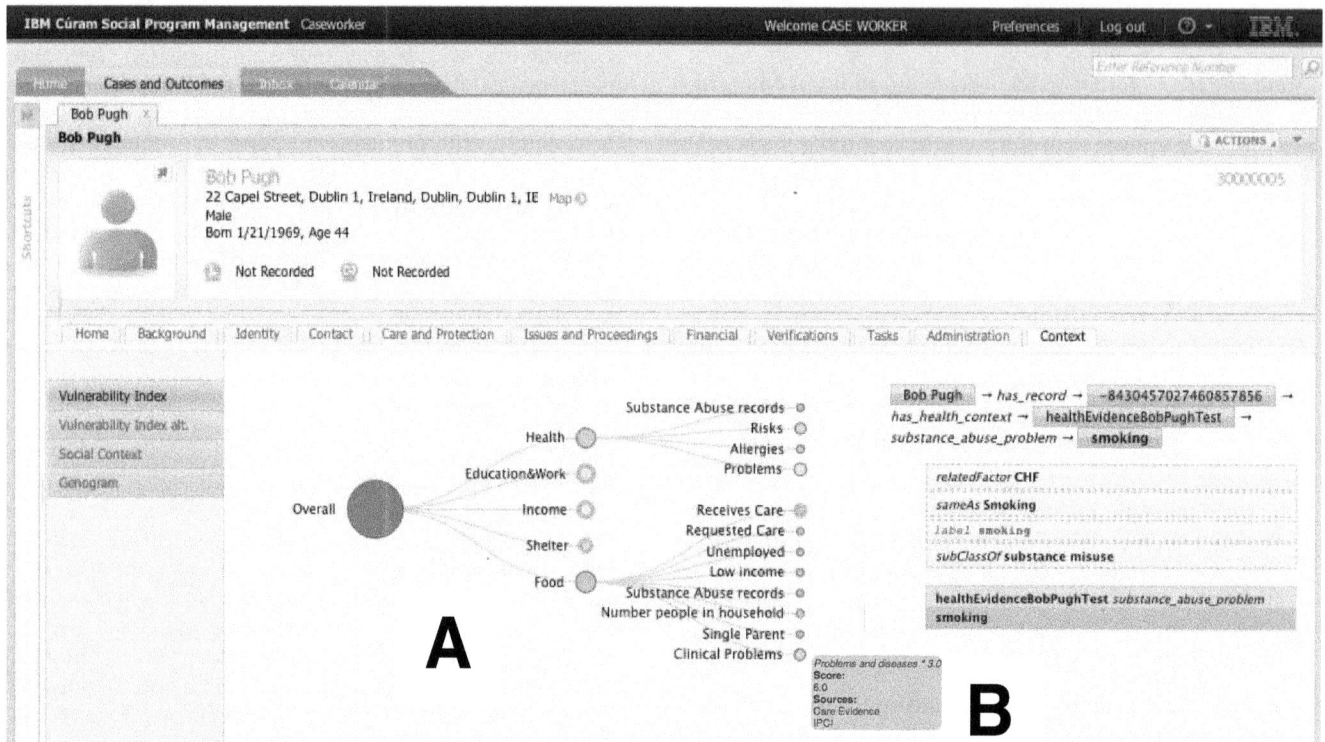

Figure 1. DVI and contextual exploration view

although do not necessarily imply causality, can be used to uncover and present relevant content for the user to explore.

Figure 1 (B) shows the exploration pane on the right. The care manager can drill into the specific vulnerabilities of Bob. Hovering over a node provides a description of the node and provenance information while clicking on a node updates the navigation pane on the right. For example, the care manager can see that Bob smokes, and that smoking is a type of substance abuse. More importantly, the care manager can see that smoking is correlated to CHF (which is abstracted into the understandable term Heart Disease), so it is particularly important to try to convince Bob to implement a lifestyle change (i.e. quit smoking).

Furthermore, contextual exploration surfaces facts related to the DVIs but not necessarily covered by them. Drilling down on income, the social worker can see that Bob is receiving income support. Clicking further, the fact that he is receiving child benefit weekly and that he is unemployed for the past 6 months is surfaced.

Application

In this section, we are providing technical detail regarding the approach described in the previous section. DVIs are used to calculate and present vulnerability scores relative to the level of functioning and risk across the six core needs of an individual, as well as to understand the dependencies across them. The six needs that influence care are: Health (e.g. known diseases, mental health problems, prescriptions, substance abuse, etc.), Education and Work, Shelter, Safety and Food.

While business rules are grounded to the data in different systems to create multi-dimensional views of the citizen and family, interactive contextual access gets all the relevant information for an entity when the structure is not known - i.e., not modeled though business rules. Due to the lack of standards in the social care domain and the complexity of it, we use a flexible architecture based on extensible models and interlinked schemas to represent relevant data, following the Linked Data principles and without the requirement to come up with a common shared model(s) to suit all parties involved. Potentially useful data sources are published by populating and extending the existent schemas, and by reusing reference ontologies/vocabularies that act as common anchors connecting topics and datatypes (no silos). In this set up, dynamic contextual access allows exploring all the known information for an entity in a given context (e.g., context around mental health issues for a given patient), by following the relationships across the data sources, collecting the triples in the vicinity of the search node or between nodes. Table 2 shows the ontologies we have used in our deployment. We have aimed for maximizing re-use. Nevertheless, given that some domains have not been traditionally addressed in Semantic Web deployments, we have had to develop some ontologies or adapt existing taxonomies. Although, on a more general view, aligning these ontologies might be necessary, in this paper, since the ontologies cover different domains, we only had to do limited linking between concepts in the ontologies.

DVIs are calculated using a graph of SPARQL templates and a set of aggregation functions for each node, together with a text explanation of each node. For each node in the DVI, we (optionally) associate a SPARQL SELECT query to calculate scores (e.g. a query to count the number of diseases a person is suffering from) and a SPARQL CONSTRUCT query to retrieve related information. The SELECT queries operate either on properties of concepts, using either existential quantifiers or values (e.g. is a person unemployed? what was their income during the past year?), using operators such as BOUND, SUM, COUNT etc. Their results are aggregated using arbitrary functions (e.g. logical AND, sum, average). The CONSTRUCT queries capture information in the vicinity of some given concepts as well as justification for the values captured by the SELECT queries. In addition, for both cases, provenance information is displayed.

Prototype

We have implemented a prototype of the approach described in this paper on top of a set of enterprise systems.

The IBM Cúram Social Program Management Platform is a business and technology solution that delivers prebuilt social program components, business processes, toolsets and interfaces on top of a dynamically configurable architecture. With connection to this paper, the information of interest mainly regards social relationships, known problems concerning employment, substance abuse, participation in social assistance programs and information concerning housing, education and safety.

IBM software Patient Care and Insights provides data driven population analysis and multi-party collaboration to support patient-centered care processes. With connection to this paper, we are mainly interested in clinical summaries and analytics results (for example, a person having a high risk of developing some medical condition).

Information from these two systems, as well as data from an example source with information from a homeless shelter is accessed using a Linked Data infrastructure.

EVALUATION

We have compared the DVI-based user interface to a generic graph exploration approach based on a set of timed tasks. Users were called to gain insight on a variety of subjects concerning two test persons, one of them being highly vulnerable and the other being homeless.

We have simulated an intake scenario, where a social worker is called to gather information about various aspects of somebody's life. Currently, this is done manually, by means of an interview[10]. Considering that the related information already exists in *some* system, we have asked users to retrieve it. We have used a subset of the actual intake questions to test the ability of our system to retrieve this information.

We have asked 10 users to retrieve the answers to the questions in Table 3, using our user-interface and a generic RDF exploration user interface[11]. We note that we have not tuned

---

[10]Questionnaires for self-sufficiency assessment in order to identify barriers preventing a household from self-sufficiency. The results feed into a process to create an outcome plan.

[11]http://wifo5-03.informatik.uni-mannheim.de/pubby/

our approach to correspond to the input questions. For each question, we started a timer once the user was given the question and stopped the timer when the user would give up or report the answer, essentially measuring the time the user needs to get some business insight, Time to Insight (TTI). Each user used both systems but the order was randomized (i.e. each system was used first in 50% of the cases).

The results are reported in Figure 2, as a box plot showing the minimum, 25th percentile, median, 75th percentile and maximum. The results for one-way ANOVA ($F(1,104)=8.366, p=0.005$) indicate that the TTI difference for the two systems is statistically significant. We observe that our approach required significantly less time to acquire the required information, although, for both systems, there is significant variance. On average, using the baseline system took 54.1% more time than our system. In addition, for Pubby, there were 3 cases where users gave up, not being able to find the answer and 3 more cases where the users reported a result that was wrong. In contrast, for our system, users always succeeded in finding the correct answer. Path lengths were comparable between the two systems. User comments included: (a) The baseline Pubby UI was often confusing, since it was displaying too much information. (b) The presence of multiple records in the baseline and the exploration interface was difficult to navigate. (c) There was sometimes confusion regarding property values and descriptions of properties.

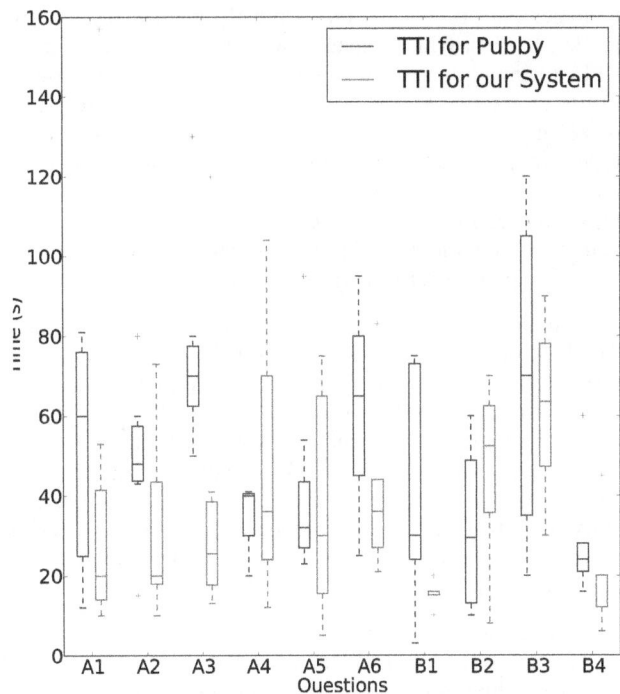

Figure 2. Time to insight.

DISCUSSION AND CONCLUSIONS

We have showcased an approach in which, Health Care and Social Care data coming from several heterogeneous and large systems can been accessed and queried in an seamlessly

Ontology	Description
Clinical	Captures clinical summaries, medical data analytics and care plans
Social Care Reference taxonomy and vocabulary	Partially extracted from the taxonomy of topics in the social care online taxonomy to annotate datatypes and values in all 6 different dimensions for evidences or needs. These values are also manually linked to DBpedia.
Family Ontology	We have extended the family relationships ontology described in [13].
FOAF, VCARD	Personal details and addresses.
Common Ground	Used to model health questionnaires from the 100khomes campaign [1]
WSG84, Time	Representation of geospatial and temporal features.
Social care evidence ontology	Created to model the relevant contextual data stored in social care systems.
Human Disease Ontology	Used to ground and simplify information pertaining to diseases.

Table 2. Set of ontologies used in our use-case

ID	Domain	Question
A1	Employment	When did you last work? (never/in the last x months / over x years)
A2	Education	What is the highest grade of education that you have completed? (primary/ secondary/ ..)
A3	Income	What type of services is your family receiving?
A4	Housing	What is your current housing situation (homeless/ eviction / poor housing / temporary shelter / home ownership / (non)-subsidized rental / ..
A5	Substance abuse	Do you or have you ever had a problem with alcohol or drugs? (yes / no)
A6	Physical health	Do you have any health or medical conditions? (no / yes - list diseases)
B1	Housing	What is your primary reason for homelessness? (eviction / poor housing / domestic violence / release from jail/ natural disaster/ ..)
B2	Housing	How long have you been living on the street (x months/ years)
B3	Child Welfare	Do you currently have children in foster care ?
B4	Mental health	Do you have any emotional issues, personal problems or strees? (no / yes - list)?

Table 3. Intake questions for user study. A1 to A6 refer to the vulnerable individual, B1 to B4 refer to the homeless individual.

integrated way, using a set of reference ontologies and business rules. We have applied this approach to the presentation and exploration of vulnerabilities for individuals.

Unlike traditional ETL, data warehousing and master data management approaches that typically fit data on a global model, RDF provides a natural way to implement an extensible information space within the enterprise, while allowing re-use of assets from the Web. Such assets include reference ontologies and vocabularies to standardize datatypes, define types , ranges etc. In some cases, these ontologies and vocabularies facilitate querying and allow displaying information in a more consumable way, even when lacking pre-defined and common structures, through common or related (linked) values - e.g., broader or narrower topics.

Nevertheless, a semantic approach also bears significant cost. The lack of a global model raises challenges with regard to user interfaces, since the application can not longer assume a given structure for query results. In our work, we have tried a middle ground between an easy-to-use user interface based on business rules and a powerful exploration interface that can access the entire information space. Our evaluation results show that our approach indeed allows users to get the required insight from the data in less time, while maintaining generality, at least within the given domain.

For the future, we are planning to apply the approach presented in this paper in similar complex domains. Urban planning and public safety are of particular interest. Both domains present similar challenges regarding information sources and domain complexity, but pose additional requirements concerning managing geospatial information.

REFERENCES

1. 100000 Homes Campaign. Vulnerability index, prioritizing the street homeless population by mortality risk. http://www.naph.org/Main-Menu-Category/Our-Work/Quality-Overview/ 100000-Homes-Campaign/Vulnerbility-Index.aspx. Accessed: 2013-05-01.

2. Baker, C. J., and Cheung, K.-H. *Semantic web: Revolutionizing knowledge discovery in the life sciences*. Springer, 2007.

3. Bayardo Jr, R. J., Bohrer, W., Brice, R., Cichocki, A., Fowler, J., Helal, A., Kashyap, V., Ksiezyk, T., Martin, G., Nodine, M., et al. Infosleuth: agent-based semantic integration of information in open and dynamic environments. In *ACM SIGMOD Record*, vol. 26, ACM (1997), 195–206.

4. Chen, H., Ding, L., Wu, Z., Yu, T., Dhanapalan, L., and Chen, J. Y. Semantic web for integrated network analysis in biomedicine. *Briefings in bioinformatics 10*, 2 (2009), 177–192.

5. Cheung, K.-H., Prudhommeaux, E., Wang, Y., and Stephens, S. Semantic web for health care and life sciences: a review of the state of the art. *Briefings in bioinformatics 10*, 2 (2009), 111–113.

6. Gawande, A. The hot spotters. *New Yorker 86* (2011), 41.

7. Kodner, D. L., and Spreeuwenberg, C. Integrated care: meaning, logic, applications, and implications–a discussion paper. *International journal of integrated care 2* (2002).

8. Kotoulas, S., Lopez, V., Stephenson, M., Tommasi, P., Shen, W., Hu, G., Sbodio, M. L., Bicer, V., Kementsietsidis, A., Rafique, M. M., Ellis, J. B., Erickson, T., Srinivas, K., McAuliffe, K., Xie, G. T., and Aonghusa, P. M. Coordinating social care and healthcare using semantic web technologies. In *ISWC* (2013), 169–172.

9. Manning, M., Aggarwal, A., Gao, K., and Tucker-Kellogg, G. Scaling the walls of discovery: using semantic metadata for integrative problem solving. *Briefings in bioinformatics 10*, 2 (2009), 164–176.

10. Peikes, D., Chen, A., Schore, J., and Brown, R. Effects of care coordination on hospitalization, quality of care, and health care expenditures among medicare beneficiaries. *JAMA: the journal of the American Medical Association 301*, 6 (2009), 603–618.

11. Puri, C., Gomadam, K., Jain, P., Yeh, P. Z., and Verma, K. Multiple ontologies in healthcare information technology: Motivations and recommendation for ontology mapping and alignment. In *Proceedings of the Workshop on Working with Multiple Biomedical Ontologies (at ICBO)*, vol. 26 (2011).

12. Rigby, M., Hill, P., Koch, S., and Keeling, D. Social care informatics as an essential part of holistic health care: A call for action. *I. J. Medical Informatics 80*, 8 (2011), 544–554.

13. Stevens, R., and Stevens, M. A family history knowledge base using owl 2. In *OWLED* (2008).

AR Lamp: Interactions on Projection-based Augmented Reality for Interactive Learning

Jeongyun Kim
Media System Lab.
Yonsei University, 50
Yonsei-ro, Seodaemun-gu,
Seoul, Republic of Korea
jeongyunkim@gmail.com

Jonghoon Seo
Media System Lab.
Yonsei University, 50
Yonsei-ro, Seodaemun-gu,
Seoul, Republic of Korea
jonghoon.seo@msl.yonsei.ac.kr

Tack-Don Han
Media System Lab.
Yonsei University, 50
Yonsei-ro, Seodaemun-gu,
Seoul, Republic of Korea
hantack@msl.yonsei.ac.kr

ABSTRACT

Today, people use a computer almost everywhere. At the same time, they still do their work in the old-fashioned way, such as using a pen and paper. A pen is often used in many fields because it is easy to use and familiar. On the other hand, however, it is a quite inconvenient because the information printed on paper is static. If digital features are added to this paper environment, the users can do their work more easily and efficiently.

AR (augmented reality) Lamp is a stand-type projector and camera embedded system with the form factor of a desk lamp. Its users can modify the virtually augmented content on top of the paper with seamlessly combined virtual and physical worlds. AR is quite appealing, but it is difficult to popularize due to the lack of interaction.

In this paper, the interaction methods that people can use easily and intuitively are focused on. A high-fidelity prototype of the system is presented, and a set of novel interactions is demonstrated. A pilot evaluation of the system is also reported to explore its usage possibility.

Author Keywords

Pen computing; bimanual interaction; projection-based augmented reality; finger gesture;

ACM Classification Keywords

H.5.2. [User Interfaces]: Input devices and strategies, interaction styles

INTRODUCTION

There are many fields that still use physical tools more than computers. Education is one of them. More people studying with paper-books are seen than people studying with e-books. Especially, when studying, many people prefer using paper documents because they feel more comfortable writing something on paper rather than on an electronic panel. At the same time, however, more people use a

computer rather than a paper-book to look for additional information, and people understand some concepts more easily and quickly by watching a video or an animation than by just reading a paper-book.

The current augmented reality (AR), such as MagicBook [1], provides dynamic contents to static paper, but it is difficult for the users to give an input and to obtain feedback according to their input. Although there have been many researches about AR, less research works have been conducted on AR interaction techniques.

This paper focuses on the need for interactions especially in a learning environment. A system (Figure 1) that meets the following requirements was developed:

- it provides a way of creating informal animations;
- the users can manipulate the static information written on paper; and
- the users can obtain multimodal feedback according to their input.

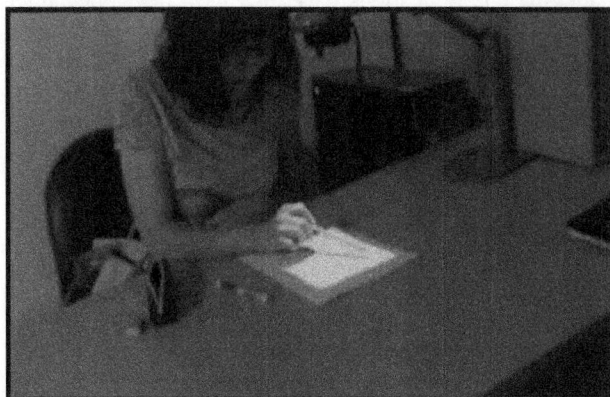

Figure 1. Studying with the developed system.

The developed system is called *AR Lamp*. In this system, the virtual contents are projected on paper by the pico-projector, and the camera recognizes the physical objects on paper through computer vision techniques. Paper and pen are used in the system as interface tools. As they have been used for a long time, they are familiar to all people.

RELATED WORKS

Paper-based Interface and Digital Pen

The digital pen was originally designed to digitize the users' handwritings on physical paper. But it can be used in other way such as a means to combine the virtual and physical worlds. For example, PapierCraft [2] and PaperPoint [3] use the anoto digital pen to directly interact with physical paper. Using the digital pen, the users can query relevant functions using a separate display. AR Lamp differs from them in that the query results are projected on the paper. Therefore, the users do not need to move their eyes to a different display.

Spatial Augmented Reality

Spatial AR promises the integration of digital information in the real world through projection. Shader Lamps [4] projects color or texture to the physical model, which has the proper structure or shape. iLamps [5] indicates the electronic-data items that have been attached to the environment.

The type of feedback provided by the commercialized digital pen is mainly audio feedback, and even if there is visual feedback, it uses the separate display nearby, like the laptop screen. By adapting spatial AR, the two different elements can be more seamlessly combined, together with proper visual feedback, which will stick in the real world.

Sketch-based Interfaces

Understanding free-form sketches is a difficult problem because of the variation in the users' handwriting. Sezgin et al. [6] explains the conversion of the original digitized pen strokes in a sketch into the intended geometric objects. Sketch-based applications have also been developed for a variety of contexts. K-Sketch [7] allows novice users to create a wide range of animations quickly. SKETCH [8] bridges the gap between hand sketches and computer-based modeling programs.

AR Lamp recognizes simple geometric objects like ovals, circles, rectangles, and squares from the pen strokes. If the physical writing is converted to digital data, it can be used in many meaningful ways.

Finger Gestures

This paper explores the interaction possibilities when users use their non-dominant hand while studying with a pen. Not only the pen but also the non-dominant hand can be a good interface medium in the developed system.

Multi-finger gestures have become popular since the smartphone became widely used. For example, if a user spreads out his thumb and index finger, it can be appreciated as a zoom-out.

DESIGN CHARACTERISTICS

Bimanual Interaction

The non-dominant hand is free while the other hand grabs a pen. Some interfaces that can be done using the non-dominant hand and a pen simultaneously are defined herein.

Figure 2 shows three examples. First, two different objects can be moved at the same time using a pen for one object and a finger for the other (Figure 2(a)). Second, the wheel can be rotated by moving it to a specific direction. A pen can express the trace of the wheel, and a finger can indicate the wheel's rotation (Figure 2(b)). Third, if you want to describe the movement of a character from far to near, the character should be getting bigger while coming closer. The route of a character can be expressed as the trace of a pen tip, and the size of a character can be tuned by spreading out the fingers (Figure 2(c)).

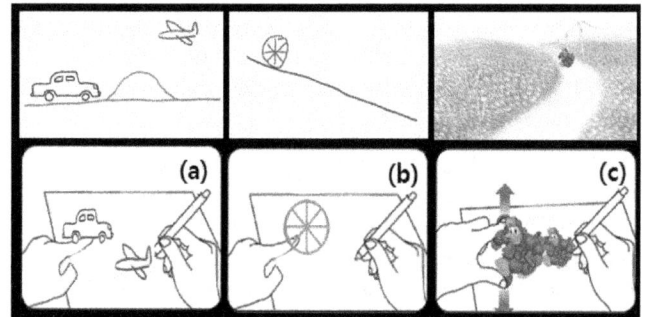

Figure 2. Example of bimanual interaction.

Capturing an Object's Attributes and the User's Actions

Capturing a physical object's attributes or the user's actions as digital data will be very beneficial. The developed system can easily pick up color from the physical object through the camera. Figure 3 explains how the developed system captures the physical color. The proposed system can also capture other virtual attributes such as texture.

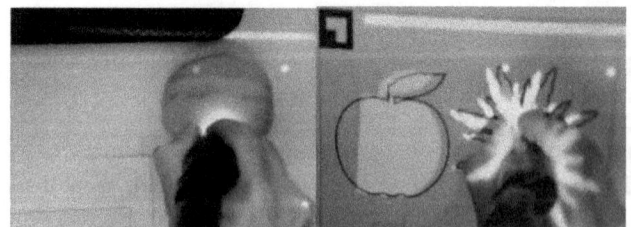

Figure 3. Example of picking up physical color.

The developed system can also capture figure gestures done by the non-dominant hand. One example is that the object can be resized by "pinching it close" to make it smaller or by "pinching it open" to make it larger.

SCENARIOS FOR INTERACTIVE LEARNING

The following are the scenarios that were introduced into the developed system. Here, some interfaces for an interactive book are introduced. The following figures were all captured from the embedded camera to AR Lamp. The full scenarios can be checked in the video prototype.

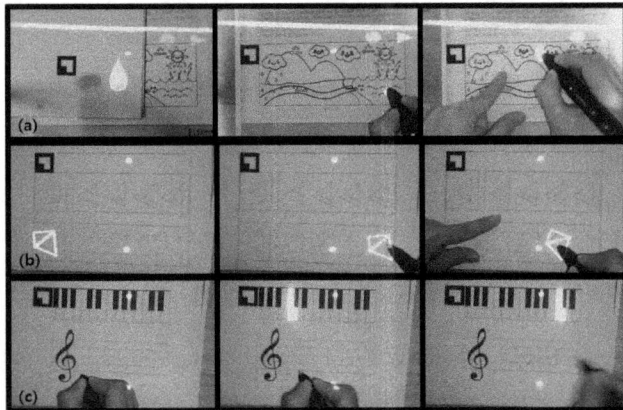

Figure 4. Scenarios for interactive learning. Animation-based explanation (a); procedure-centric problem-solving (b); and inference relationship between different notions (c).

Animation-based Explanation

Animation is effective for conveying concepts of change. For example, weather patterns, circuit diagrams, and circulatory systems can be explained more efficiently when expressed with animation. A paper-book, however, can contain only static pictures and text. Even though an AR book shows animated contents, it cannot create such contents by itself.

AR Lamp provides the user with a way of creating informal animation. In the following scenario, animated content explaining the flow of water is created (Figure 4(a)). It is assumed that the teacher or friend, or whoever will explain the content, will create an animated explanation in an intuitive way using a pen and paper. Then a student follows that up and understands the content much more easily.

Capturing the Physical Image

An analogue image can be transformed into a digital captured image using computer vision technology. Figure 5 shows the process of capturing the image (left) and of projecting it on paper (right). In this scenario, the water image is grabbed from the physical cartoon and is used in the animated content.

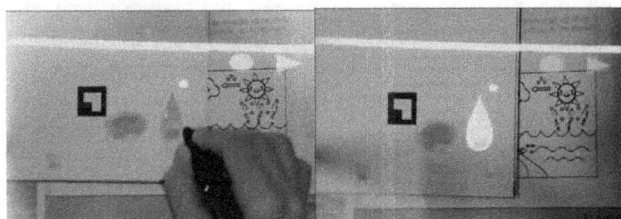

Figure 5. Capturing the image.

Recording and Playing the Movement of the Object

Once the physical image is captured, it can be moved to the other position by moving a pen. The trace of a pen can be recorded by calculating the changes in the relative position to the marker on the paper (left part of Figure 6). It is saved as a video clip in the system. Therefore, it can be played in a different book (right part of Figure 6).

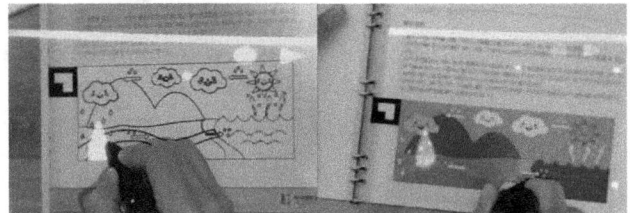

Figure 6. Recording and playing the video clip.

The way of creating animations was adapted from sketch-based interfaces. One of the difficulties of creating an animation is expressing more than one action at the same time. This issue was addressed by suggesting "bimanual interaction," which was explained in the previous section with some examples.

Procedure-centric Problem-Solving

AR Lamp enables its users to solve problems, and then animates the procedure to show that the solution is correct. Not only the final answer but also the procedure until finding the answer is important, but there is no way of recording such procedure. In the developed system, as with the creation of an animation, it can be recorded simply and can be checked later by a tutor.

In this scenario, the educational content for enhancing spatial skills is introduced (Figure 4(b)). Children who see this kind of problem for the first time may find it difficult to directly come up with the answer to it, but if the user can manipulate the figure tangibly, it can be solved more easily. Additionally it can be proven that the user solved the problem in the right way.

Recognizing Geometric Objects

AR Lamp recognizes the geometric objects sketched by the users. If a computer knows what the object is, it will be helpful in solving many other problems. For example, it can give an instruction to calculate the area or volume of the figure based on the recognized geometric objects.

Figure 7. Recognizing geometric objects.

Manipulating the Object
If one hand grabs a pen, the non-dominant hand can be used for other functionalities. Figure 8 shows an example of this. After selecting or drawing a figure, the figure is turned by rotating the non-dominant fingers. If the user twists his thumb and index finger clockwise or counterclockwise, the selected figure is rotated.

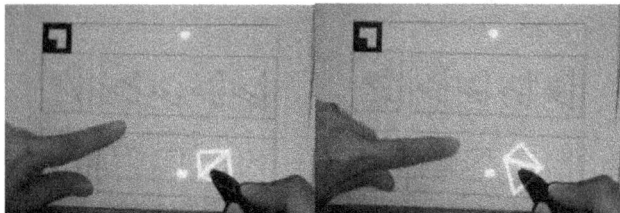

Figure 8. Manipulating the object.

It is believed that if students can manipulate static contents in their own way, it will attract their attention more and will make them understand the content more easily. Designing interfaces such as pinching gestures for resizing, twisting fingers for rotation, and pen strokes are all familiar and intuitive.

Inference Relationship between Different Notions
It is difficult to explain the relationship between different notions. One example of this is the relationship between a musical scale and a piano keyboard.

One of the weak points of static paper is visual feedback. Visual effect is very important and effective in conveying knowledge. Projection-based AR was adapted because it can provide immersive visual effects.

In this scenario, there is not only visual feedback from the projector but also sound feedback from the speaker. The pico-projector, which was installed in the developed system, has a speaker. Thus, the matched sound can be played. In the developed system, diverse inputs and feedback can be made.

Calculating the Position of the User Sketch
In this scenario, if a user writes music on manuscript paper, the position of the piano keyboard is highlighted by the projector. At the same time, the matched tone is played through the speaker. To do this, the exact position of the user's sketch on paper should be known right away. The anoto technology was used for this purpose [9]. We've used the commercialized anoto pen [10]. A piece of paper with an anoto pattern is printed, and if the anoto digital pen points somewhere on the paper, it gives its exact position to the computer.

PROTOTYPE

Hardware Configuration
Diverse types of projection-based AR have proposed different hardware configurations. DigitalDesk [11] suspends a projector from the ceiling. PenLight [12]

explains new interfaces by simulating the projector-mounted pen. In practice, however, it uses a projector hung from the ceiling. MouseLight [13] introduces a movable projector. The users move a mouse-type projector that is separated from a pen.

Pico-projector has already become small enough to be embedded in the mobile phone and as such, a small component similar in size to the smartphone can already be easily made. Moreover, this small component can be installed in a desk lamp. Figure 9 is a conceptual sketch explaining the hardware set-up of the developed system. The pico-projector was used for displaying the digital contents. The camera is for capturing and recognizing physical pictures and non-dominant finger gestures.

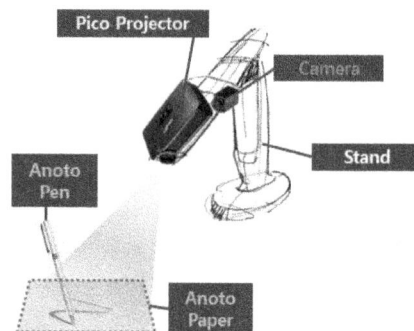

Figure 9. Sketch of the hardware configuration.

Calculation of the Projected Area
While some of previous systems support navigation of virtual contents by a fixed viewing window, AR Lamp's viewing dynamically changes relative to the position of the paper and the location of the pen.

For the developed system, two different calibrations are needed. One is between the camera and the projector. The relative position between the camera and projector is fixed. Therefore, there is no need to consider the calibration between them while running the system. At first, however, it was done with four dots projected from the projector. Their positions were predefined under the projector coordinate. Their positions under the camera coordinate can be calculated by detecting the projected four dots through the camera.

The other calibration is between the camera and the physical world. Physical world here refers to the paper position under the developed system. Stabilization of the projected image is required because the paper is movable. Presenting spatial information can only make sense if information is presented at a specific position. The developed system projects an image in a constant position. In other words, the image drawing position is updated based on the fluctuation of the paper's position. To do this, a physical marker printed on paper is used. The camera can easily detect the marker and update the projected image accordingly in real time.

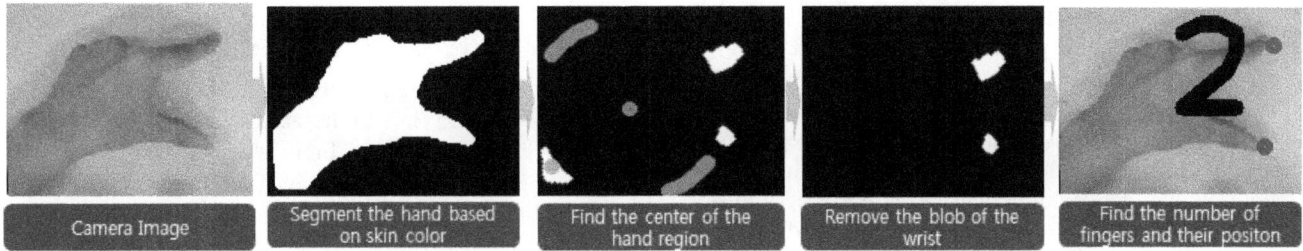

Figure 10. Workflow of finger gesture recognition

Recognition of Finger Gestures

To recognize the finger gestures, a simple algorithm based on computer vision was adapted [14]. Actually there is another way of implementing finger gestures. For example, SixthSense [15] requires the users to wear colored markers at the tips of their fingers. If a user wears something on his fingers or hands, it becomes much easier to recognize the finger gestures. But we do not want to make a user wear anything on his fingers, because it is inconvenient. It is quiet complicated if you want to recognize diverse types of finger gestures for general usages. But if you set up some constraints, you can implement it easily even if you are not wearing anything on your fingers. We have limited the types of finger gestures based on our designed scenarios and assumed they are being used by a right-handed user only.

EVALUATION

What was focused on in the developed system was designing new interfaces that were believed to be useful in the learning environment. Therefore, there was a need to obtain the end users' opinions to ascertain the usefulness and practicality of the related ideas. To do this, a prototype of the developed system was created quickly using an easy-to-implement technique, e.g., using a physical marker.

Diverse users were asked to obtain many different opinions. First, expert interviews were done. As the suggested scenarios focused on the education domain, the opinions of education experts were obtained. Second, young students were asked to fill out a special questionnaire. Finally, usability evaluation was investigated with graduate students who knew AR well.

Tutor Interview

A teacher, an academy lecturer, and a parent with a young child were interviewed to assess the usefulness and applicability of each introduced interaction to their respective practices. The developed system was demonstrated to provide the participants with an overall understanding of the system and of its functionality.

In general, the feedback from the interviewees validated the fact that the design choices would apply well to learning environment. They agreed that the use of animation-based explanation is an effective way of teaching, and the teacher said that it is important for young students to actually manipulate elements. Therefore, the concepts that were shown with a "matching polygon" and a "piano and musical scale" were appealing.

Students' Feedback

To get opinions of children with AR Lamp, 20 students aged 10-12 were asked to participated in the present study. In the first couple of minutes, an introduction of how to use a pen and how to interact with the system was given. Then a researcher asked some questions that had been extracted from the ARCS model [16]. ARCS is short for Attention, Relevance, Confidence, and Satisfaction. It is used for measuring and studying the effect of a newly introduced teaching method. One of the questions was if the developed system captured the participant's attention.

The overall results were good. Especially, the younger students were more interested in the developed system and were more satisfied with it. It is believed, however, that more time is needed to obtain objective results. This will be considered in the future research work.

AR Experts' Opinions

Interviews were conducted with people who knew the AR concepts well. It was found from such interviews that the AR experts felt that this tool would be useful and easy to use. One of the interviewees suggested that an additional sensor be installed.

All the implemented interactions happened on a two-dimensional paper surface, but if a new sensor like leap motion [17] is supplemented, the movement of the Z-axis can be measured. This is being considered for the next step.

CONCLUSION AND FUTURE WORK

A new system combining the physical and digital world was explored in this study. The developed system has the power to recognize physical objects and to display digital contents. It is believed that these features will be helpful in coming up with augmented-reality (AR) books. It is difficult to create contents for AR books, and there are few ways of interacting with them. We believe that our system can help find a solution to this kind of issues.

It is believed that AR Lamp will have several interesting usage scenarios for paper-based interaction, but its implementation was focused on a single application domain, allowing the development of a working application supporting specific tasks. Many of the core concepts can be easily generalized to other domains. For example, paper is often used in architectural designs because it is easy to read and is portable, but it is quite inconvenient to modify.

The design is updated several times while having a meeting, but the attendees of the meeting use the early version of the blueprint. It is quite bothersome if this is done with a paper blueprint. With the use of similar finger gestures and forms of pen usages, we believe our system can provide clues for the resolution of this issue.

For the evaluation of the developed system, there is a plan to measure the system performance, such as the finger-tracking, in the next evaluation, after improving the system. Specifically, some tasks will be designed to compare the system with existing tools, such as a tablet PC or a blackboard.

ACKNOWLEDGEMENT

This work was supported by the National Research Foundation of Korea(NRF) grant funded by the Korea government(MEST) (No. 2012R1A2A2A01014499).

REFERENCES

1. Billinghurst, M., H. Kato, and I. Poupyrev. "The MagicBook - Moving Seamlessly Between Reality and Virtuality." *IEEE Computer Graphics and Applications* 21, no. 3 (2001): 6–8.

2. Liao, C., Guimbreti`ere, F., and Hinckley, K. Papiercraft: a command system for interactive paper. In *Proceedings of the 18th annual ACM symposium on User interface software and technology,* ACM (2005), 241–244.

3. Signer, Beat, and Moira C. Norrie. "PaperPoint: a Paper-based Presentation and Interactive Paper Prototyping Tool." In *Proceedings of the 1st International Conference on Tangible and Embedded Interaction*, 57–64. TEI '07. New York, NY, USA: ACM, 2007.

4. Raskar, Ramesh, Greg Welch, Kok-Lim Low, and Deepak Bandyopadhyay. "Shader Lamps: Animating Real Objects With Image-Based Illumination." In *Rendering Techniques 2001*, edited by Prof Dr Steven J. Gortler and Professor Dr Karol Myszkowski, 89–102.

5. Raskar, Ramesh, Jeroen van Baar, Paul Beardsley, Thomas Willwacher, Srinivas Rao, and Clifton Forlines. "iLamps: Geometrically Aware and Self-configuring Projectors." In *ACM SIGGRAPH 2006 Courses*. SIGGRAPH '06. New York, NY, USA: ACM, 2006.

6. Sezgin, Tevfik Metin, Thomas Stahovich, and Randall Davis. "Sketch Based Interfaces: Early Processing for Sketch Understanding." In *ACM SIGGRAPH 2006 Courses*. SIGGRAPH '06. New York, NY, USA: ACM, 2006.

7. Davis, Richard C., Brien Colwell, and James A. Landay. "K-Sketch: A 'Kinetic' Sketch Pad for Novice Animators." In Proceedings of the SIGCHI Conference on Human Factors in Computing Systems, 413–422. CHI '08. New York, NY, USA: ACM, 2008.

8. Zeleznik, Robert C., Kenneth P. Herndon, and John F. Hughes. "SKETCH: An Interface for Sketching 3D Scenes." In *ACM SIGGRAPH 2007 Courses*. SIGGRAPH '07. New York, NY, USA: ACM, 2007.

9. Anoto, Development Guide for Service Enabled by Anoto Functionality. 2002, Anoto.

10. http://www.pengenerations.com

11. Wellner, Pierre. "Interacting with Paper on the DigitalDesk." *Commun. ACM* 36, no. 7 (July 1993): 87–96.

12. Song, Hyunyoung, Tovi Grossman, George Fitzmaurice, Fran\ccois Guimbretiere, Azam Khan, Ramtin Attar, and Gordon Kurtenbach. "PenLight: Combining a Mobile Projector and a Digital Pen for Dynamic Visual Overlay." In *Proceedings of the SIGCHI Conference on Human Factors in Computing Systems*, 143–152. CHI '09. New York, NY, USA: ACM, 2009.

13. Song, Hyunyoung, Francois Guimbretiere, Tovi Grossman, and George Fitzmaurice. "MouseLight: Bimanual Interactions on Digital Paper Using a Pen and a Spatially-aware Mobile Projector." In *Proceedings of the SIGCHI Conference on Human Factors in Computing Systems*, 2451–2460. CHI '10. New York, NY, USA: ACM, 2010.

14. Malima, A., E. Ozgur, and M. Cetin. "A Fast Algorithm for Vision-Based Hand Gesture Recognition for Robot Control." In *Signal Processing and Communications Applications, 2006 IEEE 14th*, 1 –4, 2006.

15. Mistry, Pranav, and Pattie Maes. "SixthSense: a Wearable Gestural Interface." In *ACM SIGGRAPH ASIA 2009 Sketches*, 11:1–11:1. SIGGRAPH ASIA '09. New York, NY, USA: ACM, 2009.

16. Keller, John M. "Development and Use of the ARCS Model of Instructional Design." *Journal of Instructional Development* 10, no. 3 (September 1, 1987): 2–10.

17. https://www.leapmotion.com/

Steptorials:
Mixed-Initiative Learning
of High-Functionality Applications

Henry Lieberman
MIT Media Lab
Cambridge, MA, USA
lieber@media.mit.edu

Elizabeth Rosenzweig
Bentley University
Waltham, MA, USA
erosenzweig@bentley.edu

Christopher Fry
MIT Media Lab
Cambridge, MA, USA
cfry@media.mit.edu

ABSTRACT

How can a new user learn an unfamiliar application, especially if it is a *high-functionality (hi-fun)* application, like Photoshop, Excel, or programming language IDE? Many applications provide introductory videos, illustrative examples, and documentation on individual operations. Tests show, however, that novice users are likely to ignore the provided help, and try to learn by exploring the application first. In a hi-fun application, though, the user may lack understanding of the basic concepts of an application's operation, even though they were likely explained in the (ignored) documentation.

This paper introduces *steptorials* ("stepper tutorials"), a new interaction strategy for learning hi-fun applications. A steptorial aims to teach the user how to work through a simple, but nontrivial, example of using the application. Steptorials are unique because they allow varying the autonomy of the user at every step.

A steptorial has a control structure of a reversible programming language stepper. The user may choose, at any time, to be shown how to do a step, be guided through it, use the application interface without constraint, or to return to a previous step. It reduces the risk in either trying new operations yourself, or conversely, the risk of ceding control to the computer. It introduces a new paradigm of mixed-initiative learning of application interfaces.

Author Keywords

Steptorials; tutorials; help; documentation; program stepper

ACM Classification Keywords

H.5.m. Information interfaces and presentation (e.g., HCI): Miscellaneous.

HI-FUN VS. LO-FUN APPLICATIONS

As the range of tasks that people want to do with computers expands, and the capability of software grows, we are faced with the development of *hi-fun* interfaces. We are not going to give a precise definition of hi-functionality interfaces here. Roughly, we mean those that provide large command sets, long menus, large or numerous icon bars, many data types, and complex patterns of use. *Low-functionality (lo-fun)* interfaces are much simpler, acting on just a few kinds of data, and providing reasonably small command sets, where the name and effect of each command are expected to be immediately apparent to the user. Apple's *Preview* is an example of a relatively lo-fun application for images; it can, for example, print, crop, and rotate images, but it has relatively few operations (about 9 top-level operations, 7 menus of 5-15 items, few subsidiary dialogs). Adobe's *Photoshop* is a hi-fun image application (25 top level operations (+ modifier keys on many), 4 palettes of 2-3 tabs each, 8 menus of 10 to >25 items, many subsidiary dialogs). It has many different image types, and the total number of operations reaches into the thousands. It has a number of abstract concepts that it is necessary to learn, such as layers. It is user customizable, can record and play macros, has numerous plug-ins, etc.

The paper proceeds with a discussion of the problem of learning hi-fun interfaces, with identification of the ability to dynamically vary the autonomy of the user as a key. We then present *steptorials*, a new interaction strategy that allows this variation, and show steptorials implemented in the decision-support system Justify. We then report usability testing.

THE CHALLENGE OF LEARNING HI-FUN APPLICATIONS

Applications that become popular tend to grow into hi-fun interfaces over time as users desire more features and companies continually try to improve their products.

The most successful, like Photoshop or Microsoft Excel, become languages and programming environments in their own right. They become as powerful (and as difficult to learn for new users) as interactive development environments for programming languages.

The UI for hi-fun applications is typically designed for the expert, habitual user. It aims to make all the operations that the expert user would want to use easily accessible. But then the new user doesn't know where to start. And users who try to learn an interface by sequential exploration get confused because they are tempted to try many things for which they won't have use until much later, if at all.

THE PARADOX OF HELP

Developers of hi-fun interfaces are well aware that novice users may have trouble learning them. So they provide help, in a variety of forms. Applications may be introduced to new users with an introductory video, which shows an example of a typical use of the application. Tutorials may be presented, which guide the users step-by-step. The tutorials may take the form of a set of screenshots, with explanations of each one, or, more recently, various kinds of interactive tutorials may allow the user a more participatory role. Within the application itself, help may be provided with a help menu with index and search on particular topics. You may be able to point to a particular interface element and receive so-called "tooltips" by hovering the pointing device at that location. There are a wide variety of ways of offering help, and some complex applications essentially offer them all.

So why do users still have trouble? We know that people learn in both top-down and bottom-up ways [12] and for that reason some users may need to learn by exploring. User studies [9] reinforce this concept, but surprisingly, show that the majority of users are persistent in trying to use an application without first seeking help. This is especially true for novice users, and for complex applications, precisely the situation in which help would provide the most benefit. So what's wrong, and what do we do about it?

AUTONOMY, CONTEXT, RISK, AND STYLE IN LEARNING INTERFACES

We would like to focus on four major issues that affect whether users will be able to make effective use of help: *autonomy*, *context*, *risk,* and *cognitive style*.

Different forms of help provide different levels of *autonomy* to the user. At one extreme, watching a video affords the user no autonomy at all-they can only sit there, eat popcorn, and watch. If they get tired or bored, they can stop the video but that's all. Similarly, reading a manual is also passive. The reluctance to give up control is a principal reason why users are reluctant to view prepared material before attempting to use an interface.

At the other extreme, forms of help that are embedded in the application's interface provide the most autonomy. The user is free to use any part of the application they wish, and call up the help at any time and place they want. This is fine if the subject of the help is localized to a particular interface element, but is often unhelpful when the user has to consider patterns of use that might stretch across several operations or several interface elements. Between these extremes, interactive tutorials provide an intermediate level of autonomy, and are often preferable for that reason.

But it is hard to choose an appropriate level of autonomy that is right for all situations. Most people learn best by doing, that is, when they have a maximal level of autonomy. But novice users may get lost if left on their own, and it may be necessary to cede some autonomy to a more knowledgeable teacher for effective learning. Users may be more or less expert, or more or less confident in various aspects of an interface. The problem with traditional forms of help is that you have to choose a fixed level of autonomy at the start.

The second problem is *context*. Watching a video, reading a manual, or looking at help that appears in pop-up windows, all take you out of the context of using the actual application. In-place help, such as tool tips, and some forms of interactive tutorials, such as stencils [5], are much better at preserving relevant contexts of use. However, providing in-place help might be constrained by screen real estate or the disadvantage of obscuring portions of the interface.

The third problem is *risk*. When users cede autonomy to the computer, they take the risk that it will not be rewarded. The video may go too fast to get an effective understanding or too slow, boring the user. When the user launches a tutorial, they are often not sure how much time they are committing. The well has been poisoned by marketing-hype videos, or poorly written documentation, making users reluctant to turn to documentation for help. Much documentation and help is written in technical jargon.

The last problem we would like to consider is that of *cognitive style*. Users vary enormously in their preferred style of learning. Some people are top-down learners. They like to understand things conceptually before embarking on practical procedures. Others are bottom-up learners. They need to start exploring and doing first. Conventional help doesn't provide enough flexibility for learners of different cognitive styles.

VARIABLE AUTONOMY IN USER HELP

The solution we propose in this paper is to allow the user to *vary the autonomy level at every step in the interaction*. At every step of the way, users can choose whether they would like to sit back and have the computer present something automatically, whether they would like to do it themselves, or whether they choose some point in between, leading to a mixed-initiative interaction.

Not having to choose a fixed level of autonomy in advance means that interactions can be tailored to the level of expertise of the individual user for that particular part of the application, supporting different *cognitive styles*. Depending on the situation at the moment, the user can choose help either in or out of *context*.

Finally, having a variable level of autonomy reduces the *risk*, since the user can always go back and choose a different level of autonomy without any penalty.

LEARNING GOALS

The goal for introducing a hi-fun application should be to get a new user "up to speed" in the time they would plausibly allocate for a session with a new program; say 20 minutes to an hour at most. They should be able to gain the skills to complete a simple example that seems realistic to them. To motivate them to continue learning, they need to experience the "magic" of having the system be able to do something for them that they would have found difficult or impossible to do by paper-and-pencil, or other manual means.

After successful completion of the introductory example, they should also be able to understand what the paths are to learn more about the interface. It's usually not possible for them to learn any significant portion of an entire hi-fun interface in an introductory session, but they should get a sense that there is a world of functionality at their fingertips just waiting to be discovered.

INTRODUCING STEPTORIALS

This paper introduces the idea of a *steptorial* ("stepper tutorial"). A steptorial is a kind of interactive tutorial based on the control structure of a reversible programming language stepper.

The idea is that the interface steps necessary to complete the introductory example are like a "program" (described by English sentences and/or interaction with the application rather than programming language code). The steptorial allows the user to step through the example, as a programmer steps through code. The steptorial is completely reversible, inspired by the control structure of the program stepper ZStep [6]. In extending the stepper metaphor beyond its origins in program debugging, we are enabling learning by *end-user debugging* [7] of application use-cases.

THE CONTROL STRUCTURE OF A STEPTORIAL

The control structure of a steptorial follows the control structure of a program stepper. Steppers traditionally display the code for a program, with a program counter indicating the expression that is just about to be executed.

The user has the choice of *Stepping Over* the current expression, which executes it, returns the result, and moves the program counter forward to point to the next expression. The user also has the choice of *Stepping Into* the current expression, which dives down into the details of evaluating the expression, which, recursively, are stepped. The *Step Over/Step Into* choice represents a mechanism for control over the level of detail. In debugging, this prevents the programmer from getting drowned in detail while preserving the ability to see any particular detail if the need arises.

The fully reversible ZStep debugger [6] introduced the insight that it's often hard to make the choice about whether or not you want to see detail of an expression until *after* you see its result. If you choose not to see detail, and it turns out an error did in fact occur in execution, you can back up the stepper, and only then go through the detail of what may have caused it. Though there have been several reversible stepper implementations, none of today's most popular programming language IDEs come with a reversible stepper as standard equipment.

We aim to bring the same kind of flexibility to choices about how much autonomy and risk the user wants to take while following an introductory tutorial. The steps of a steptorial are represented in English sentences rather than the program code found in a stepper. Both represent, in some sense "instructions".

At each step of the tutorial, the user is given choices that vary in autonomy, from "have the computer do it" to "let me do it myself". Since the steptorial is reversible, the user can always back up and make a different decision. A good learning strategy for top-down learners is often to passively watch a step at first, then increase autonomy by trying it themselves. For bottom-up learners, they might want to try a step first, then retreat to more guided modes if they run into problems.

AUTHORING STEPTORIALS

At the moment, steptorials are hand-authored for each example. Each example is described as a set of steps, each roughly representing a user interaction which satisfies a single goal. The step is represented to the user by an English sentence describing the goal. Each step describes the interface operations necessary to accomplish it. Steps may have substeps, each of which corresponds to a subgoal. Justify has an interpreter for running a steptorial from the list-based representation that contains the steptorial description as above.

Future work will consider the possibility of generating steptorials automatically or semi-automatically from program demonstrations or from user-supplied examples.

STEPTORIALS IN JUSTIFY

The remainder of this paper will present a steptorial for the decision-support application *Justify* [4]. Justify is a hi-fun application that helps manage structured online discussions about important issues. Justify has a total of 4808 interface operations, making it comparable to Photoshop (whose documentation index contains 4032 entries, almost all of which describe a particular tool or interaction).

Justify is organized around threaded discussions composed of *points* (like *posts* in an online forum). Each point represents a single idea, fact, or opinion. Points have a rich ontology of types, which represent the role of that point in the argument, such as *pro* or *con*. Each point also has an *assessment*, the result of applying a rule (based on the type of point) that is intended to compute a summary or possible decision for that point, taking into account the points below it.

Like a spreadsheet, creating, deleting, or changing points propagates changes automatically to other points that depend on it. Justify is actually a *language* for representing arguments, and the interface is really an interactive development environment (IDE) for that language [4], which is what makes it hi-fun.

CHOICES IN THE JUSTIFY STEPTORIAL

The Justify steptorial window (Figure 1) provides, as we mentioned earlier, the standard stepper controls: Forward and back one step or to the beginning or end (arrows along left side), and the *"Dive In"* icon, which steps *into* the current step, revealing its details. For each step, we provide three choices (along bottom): *Show Me How to Do It*, *Guide Me Through It*, and *Let Me Do It Myself*. The purple right-pointing arrow is the "program counter" indicating the current step.

If the user chooses *Show Me How to Do It*, it runs a predefined video that corresponds to the current step. If the user does *Step Over* (down arrow) on that step, it runs the entire step to completion. If the step happens to have substeps, videos for *all* of the substeps are concatenated and run continuously.

If the user instead chooses *Dive In* for that step, the substeps for that step are opened up, and the first substep is indicated. In this way, the user may choose any of the three presentation options for each substep independently. When all the substeps for the main step are finished, control returns up to the previous level, following the control structure of a standard stepper.

Future versions of the steptorial will replace the video segments with execution of the procedure in the actual application itself (in its own window and affecting its own internal data structures). This requires the application to be externally scriptable. Reversing the stepper will fully restore application state.

Guide Me Through It launches a *stencil* based interactive tour [5]. Stencils "gray out" all interface elements except the one with which the user is expected to interact at that particular step. Stencils permit interaction in the proper application context, and direct the user's attention to avoid distraction. Again, the level of detail seen is determined by the *Step Over/Step Into* distinction. If we step into a substep, we play only that part of the stencil tour that is relevant to that substep.

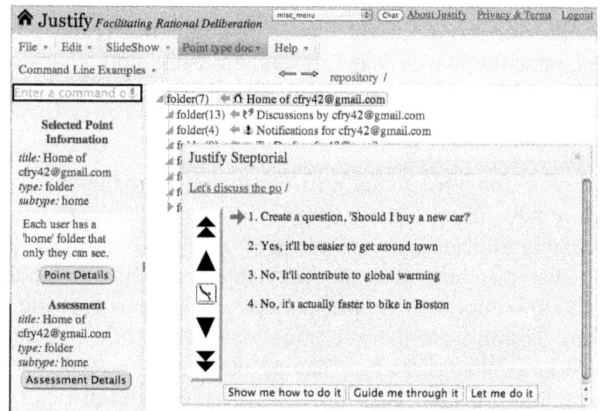

Figure 1. A *steptorial* (lower right pane) in the decision support system Justify.

Stencil tours can vary in the level of interaction they permit the user. Allowing the user more autonomy in operating the interface means that the application has to check to make sure the user isn't getting "off track".

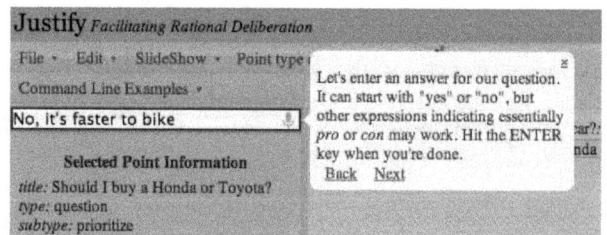

Figure 2. A *stencil* guided tour. Most of the interface is "grayed out", except for the particular element that the tour wants the user to interact with at that step.

Finally, there's *Let Me Do It Myself*. This allows the user pretty much unconstrained use of the application, with the understanding that they will try to accomplish the goal represented by that particular step themselves. The stepper controls are replaced by two options: *I Did It*, and *Oops!*, indicating, respectively, the user declaring success or failure of the goal.

If the application is scriptable and recordable, it may be able to determine for itself whether the user accomplished the goal, rather than wait for the user to click *I Did It*. This may obviate the need for the user to explicitly mark the end of the interaction.

Oops! simply returns to the previous application state, so there's little risk for the user in at least attempting to perform the task themselves. There's also potential, as in Intelligent Tutoring Systems, for an intelligent program to try to diagnose what may have gone wrong with the user's attempt, and try to provide more targeted help.

EVALUATION

First, we ran a usability test on the Justify system itself. This study had 6 participants, over an hour each, and focused on the introductory experience. Justify provided help in a variety of conventional forms: video, side-panel help, and tool tip help on interface elements. Though this study is not the subject of this paper, we uncovered problems typical of introducing hi-fun interfaces to new users: disorientation, distraction, and unwillingness to consult the provided help. This motivated the introduction of steptorials.

We then ran two kinds of formative evaluation on Justify steptorials. The first was a Heuristic Review [8] performed by two experienced User Experience (UX) professionals. We also performed a walkthrough with a single novice user, experienced with Microsoft Office and other complex applications, but not a programmer. We were most interested in the question of whether a steptorial would support the preferred learning style of the user, regardless of whether it was top-down or bottom-up.

Heuristic review

The two UX reviewers represented two contrasting learning styles: one preferred a learning style that starts with exploration; the other preferred to read or view explanatory material before exploration. Both found that the Steptorial interaction allowed them to learn about the interface using their preferred style. Each felt that they were more "engaged" with the interface than with conventional help systems, and that the interface provided more "motivation for pushing through complexities in the interface".

User walkthrough

The novice user walkthrough, (and user testing of new help paradigms in general) provides some interesting challenges. Most users' experience with conventional help is so discouraging, that if we merely offer a steptorial as an alternative to traditional forms of documentation, we run the risk that they will ignore steptorials in the same way they've been shown to decline other forms of help.

This test was *not* designed to see if users could pick up the concept of a steptorial from scratch and spontaneously choose it over conventional help. Therefore, the session started out with an introduction to the steptorial methodology, and we verified that the participant understood the operation of the steptorial window. We were interested to see whether the participant could achieve a better understanding of Justify than was possible with conventional help methods.

Participant A. was able to learn the steptorial methodology easily after the initial presentation. She then embarked on learning Justify. The task was to encode a simple argument, with one yes-or-no question, one reason in favor, one reason opposed, and a reply to refute one of the first two reasons presented.

There were some problems with orientation and context. A. had some trouble distinguishing real-world or problem-focused concepts from interface concepts. For example, a *question* refers both to a (real-world) topic the user wishes to discuss using Justify, and a technical concept in the Justify interface that the steptorial is trying to teach you how to create. A. sometimes got confused about what constituted a "step". After introducing the question, the intent of the steptorial was to make three sequential entries, each professing an opinion for or against the question. But A. at first interpreted them as three different options from which she should select just one. Writing steptorials is an art, just like writing other kinds of documentation, and care is needed to keep terminology straight.

Because of the "low-fidelity" of the prototype (all modes were not fully implemented), A. sometimes got out of sync between the various modes. Running a video looks almost identical to actions in the interface, but when you return to the interface, the effects of the actions aren't there! Similarly, we were unable in the current implementation to keep the stencil guided tour in perfect sync with the stepper navigation. We hope to correct that in future when we are able to fully script the application.

Before the test, we had asked participant A. about how she normally approached learning new applications. She said that she preferred to "dive right in" rather than preparing by reading manuals or watching videos. However, we observed that during the test, whenever she was presented with a choice between watching the video, guided tour, and unconstrained application use, she chose to watch the video first. But it also shows that, even though a user might have a preferred overall strategy, they may choose in the moment to adopt a different strategy for a specific situation. This confirms our hypothesis that it is valuable to offer varying autonomy alternatives at every step.

At the end, A. demonstrated that she was able to operate the interface to enter her own example with little or no help, analogous to the example she was shown. We take this as a positive result, especially as the previous tests had shown that users who did not follow tutorials had trouble with similar problems.

RELATED WORK

The most closely related work is Chi et. al's MixT, [2] which provided the user a choice between static (screenshot+text) tutorials and video tutorials. In both cases, the tutorials were presented linearly, rather than with the structure of the task hierarchy, as here, and there is no reversibility.

We employ Kelleher and Pausch's stencil [5] technique as an intermediary between fully scripted and fully flexible options for the user. Selker's Coach [10] system pioneered the use of user-generated examples and mixed-initiative tutorials in teaching rather than predefined tutorial material. We see opportunity in incorporating more user-generated examples and input into steptorials.

Carroll and Rosson [1] and Fischer [3] have long advocated for users taking an active role in learning interfaces. We have been inspired by their user-centered design principles, relevance to user goals over techno-centrism, and advocacy of learning by doing.

We see this work in the tradition of Intelligent Tutoring Systems [11] and many opportunities arise for trying to better understand user behavior and provide personalized help. VanLehn [13] surveys contemporary ITS'es and compares with human instruction. Wiedenbeck and Zila [14] systematically tested guided vs. exploratory approaches.

CONCLUSION

Hi-functionality applications are here to stay. If we're going to enable new users to be productive quickly, we need better ways of introducing users to them. They need to be able to quickly succeed at small, but nontrivial and relevant examples that best show off the use of the application, to motivate them to continue learning and using it. But we can't teach them everything at once.

This paper introduced the *steptorial*, a new paradigm for mixed-initiative learning of complex applications. It allows users to choose at any moment, between passively watching a demonstration of that step, trying it themselves without help, or via one or more mixed-initiative learning modes. Whether you prefer a top-down learning style, or a bottom-up learning style, we'll get you on the road to success.

ACKNOWLEDGMENTS

We would like to acknowledge Dani Nordin and Heather Wright Karlson for their help with the usability evaluation.

REFERENCES

1. Carroll, J., Rosson, M. B., The Paradox of the Active User, in *Intefacing Thought: Cognitive Aspects of Human-Computer Interaction*, MIT Press, 1987.

2. Chi, P., Ahn, S., Ren, A., Dontcheva, M., Li, W., Hartmann, B., MixT: Automatic Generation of Step-by-Step Mixed Media Tutorials, ACM User Interface Software Technology (UIST), 2012.

3. Fischer, G., Lemke, A. C., & Schwab, T. (1985) Knowledge-Based Help Systems in L. Borman, & B. Curtis (Eds.), CHI 1985, pp. 161-167.

4. Fry, C., Lieberman, H., Decision-Making Should Be More Like Programming, Int'l Symposium on End-User Development, Copenhagen, June 2013.

5. Kelleher, C. and Pausch, R., Stencil Based Tutorials: Design and Evaluation, CHI 2005,pp 541-550

6. Lieberman, H. and Fry, C., ZStep 95: A Reversible, Animated, Source Code Stepper, in *Software Visualization*, John Stasko, John Domingue, Marc Brown, and Blaine Price, eds., MIT Press, 1997.

7. Lieberman, H., and Wagner, E., End-User Debugging for Electronic Commerce, Int'l Conference on Intelligent User Interfaces, 2003.

8. Nielson, J, Technology Transfer of Heuristic Evaluation and Usability Inspection, IFIP INTERACT'95 International Conference on Human-Computer Interaction, Lillehammer, Norway, 1995.

9. Pashler, H, McDaniel, M, Rohrer, D, Bjork, R., Learning styles: Concepts and Evidence, Psychological Science in the Public Interest, 9, pp 105-119, 2008.

10. Selker, T., Coach: A Teaching Agent that Learns, Communications of the ACM, July 1999, Vol.37 No.7, pp. 92-99.

11. Sleeman, D. and Brown, J.S., *Intelligent Tutoring Systems*, Academic Press, 1982.

12. Sun, R., Zhang, Xi, Top-down versus bottom-up learning in cognitive skill acquisition, *Cognitive Systems Research* Vol. 5, pp. 63-89, 2004.

13. Van Lehn, K., The Relative Effectiveness of Human Tutoring, Intelligent Tutoring Systems, and Other Tutoring Systems, Educational Psychologist 46(4), 197-221.

14. Wiedenbeck, S. & Zila, P. L. Hands-on practice in learning to use software: a comparison of exercise, exploration, and combined formats, ACM Transactions on Computer-Human Interaction, Vol. 4., No. 2, pp. 169-196, 1997.

MIXPLORATION: Rethinking the Audio Mixer Interface

Mark Cartwright
Northwestern University
mcartwright@u.northwestern.edu

Bryan Pardo
Northwestern University
pardo@northwestern.edu

Joshua D. Reiss
Queen Mary University of
London
josh.reiss@eecs.qmul.ac.uk

ABSTRACT

A typical audio mixer interface consists of faders and knobs that control the amplitude level as well as processing (e.g. equalization, compression and reverberation) parameters of individual tracks. This interface, while widely used and effective for optimizing a mix, may not be the best interface to facilitate exploration of different mixing options. In this work, we rethink the mixer interface, describing an alternative interface for exploring the space of possible mixes of four audio tracks. In a user study with 24 participants, we compared the effectiveness of this interface to the traditional paradigm for exploring alternative mixes. In the study, users responded that the proposed alternative interface facilitated exploration and that they considered the process of rating mixes to be beneficial.

Author Keywords

Audio; music; mixing; exploratory interfaces

ACM Classification Keywords

H.5.2. User Interfaces: Interaction styles; H.5.5. Sound and Music Computing: Systems

INTRODUCTION

Mixing refers to processing and combining multiple audio recordings (tracks) together into a single recording (the mix). Mixing is an integral part of how modern video and music production is done, where it is common to combine dozens of tracks into a single final mix.

In its most basic form, mixing consists of applying gain (a change in volume) to each track and summing all tracks together into the mix. Existing mixing interfaces in widespread use all start from the same underlying paradigm: the interface should provide one controller (fader) per track and this should control the gain applied to that track. Figure 1 shows an example of a typical mixing interface, whose design emulates existing hardware mixing boards.

If we think of each track as an independent dimension, and the gain of each track as the relevant feature, a mix of N tracks with a static gain for each track can be described as a point in

Figure 1. The fader view of a mix in ProTools, a typical mixing interface.

an N-dimensional vector space. Similarly, a mix with varying gain on one or more tracks traces a path through a vector space. For simplicity we will assume static-gain mixes, where we are setting the rough volume levels for a set of N tracks.

Given this paradigm, we can now consider how one explores this N-dimensional space using the conventional N-fader approach. Typically, the user will set the faders to an initial position of roughly equal gain and then move one fader at a time to improve the mix. This is a form of N-dimensional hill-climbing where only a single dimension is varied at any one time. This is illustrated in Figure 2. Note that grouping tracks to be controlled by a single fader just changes this walk to allow diagonal travel at a fixed angle.

One common issue with hill-climbing approaches to optimizing a set of parameters is getting stuck in a local maximum which is not the global maximum. In search algorithms, this problem is typically ameliorated through multiple random restarts. Since mixing takes significant time, people do not take this approach. Instead, they either trust to luck or to the experience of a good mixing engineer (if they can afford one and the project allows for this) to ensure that they mix to at least a local optimum. This approach may miss artistically satisfying alternatives, since they may lie outside the space falling within the local maximum's basin of attraction or the mixing engineers prior experience.

In this work we rethink the interaction paradigm for mixing to facilitate the discovery of diverse, high-quality rough mixes. We define a "high-quality rough mix" as one whose gain and equalization parameters are set approximately correctly to achieve a pleasing sound, though there might still be some fine-tuning to do. Therefore, we seek an interface that facilitates high-level exploration of the mixing space (see Figure 2) so the user can quickly and easily reach places in the

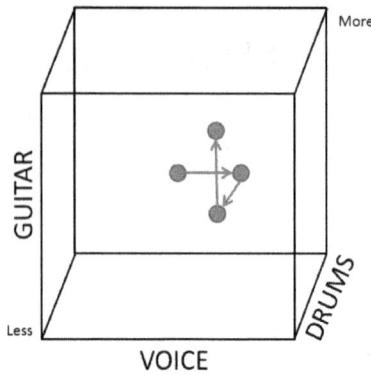

Figure 2. The 3-dimensional space representation of a three-track mixing session using faders. First, gain on the voice is raised, then drum gain is decreased, then guitar gain is raised.

mixing space they would be unlikely to reach with the conventional interface.

In addition to *facilitating broad exploration*, we designed our interface with two other goals in mind. We wanted users to *trust their ears* by listening to the whole mix, rather than trusting their eyes by focusing on individual parameter settings reported by a level meter or knob. We also wanted to make *explicit evaluation of alternatives* an integral and easy part of the process. We argue that an interface that supports exploration, evaluation and trusting one's ears will enhance and support the creativity of artists involved in mixing.

RELATED WORK

In the current digital audio workstation marketplace, products like Apples GarageBand may simplify the user interface, but the essential mixing paradigm is the same "hill-climbing" procedure as described earlier. One approach to simplify the mixing problem is to fully automate the mixing process [13, 14, 15, 20, 9, 2]. This however takes the user completely out of the loop, removing any creative input by the user, and assumes there is one ideal mix rather than multiple solutions to the problem. However, [7] shows that there may be multiple preferred mixes for a given piece.

Researchers in recent years have attempted to eliminate slider/knob-based interfaces for music and audio production by using machine learning and optimization to map gestures [3], examples [4, 11, 5, 6, 22], and language [16, 17] to control spaces. While these interfaces potentially allow users to explore parameter spaces without the distraction of a slider/knob-based interface, it is not clear that these interfaces would translate well to the mixing task.

Interfaces such as the Tenori-On [12] and TC-11 [19] provided inspiration for the two-dimensional interface in this work, but these interfaces are typically used for sequencing and synthesis rather than mixing, and there is no inherent tie-in to evaluation of what is being produced. There have been previous interfaces for controlling equalizers (a component of mixing) with a 2D space [18, 10]. Both of these interfaces mapped a high dimensional space down to a two-dimensional, square interface, but both of these interfaces were concerned with only the equalization of a single audio

object, not mixing multiple objects. Further, their focus was on mapping descriptive terms (e.g. a "warm" sound) onto equalization, not facilitating exploration of mixing options.

A NEW MIXING INTERFACE

Our interface is illustrated in Figure 3. To *facilitate broad exploration*, we eliminated the one-dimensional sliders/knobs that one finds in a traditional interface. Instead the user changes the mix by moving a ball around a two-dimensional map, which changes multiple parameters at once. Each point in the map represents some setting of the gain and equalization parameters of all the audio tracks. This map is a two-dimensional reduction of the high-dimensional level and equalization parameter space. The map broadly covers the space of possible mixes, letting the user quickly move to very different points in the mixing space using a single control.

At any point in the map, the user hears the resulting audio, without seeing the individual parameter settings. This is done to encourage the user to *trust their ears* and listen to the whole mix, rather than trusting their eyes and focusing on individual parameter settings.

To encourage *explicit evaluation of alternatives*, the interface incorporates evaluation of mixes directly into the interface by encouraging users to rate each point on the map using a 9-level scale from *dislike* to *like*. The users rate mixes using their keyboard while navigating the map using their mouse. The instructions encourage the user to re-rate mixes as their preferences become more defined. The rating process may help the user to remember preferred mixes, and concretize their preferences. We believe it may also aid the user in transitioning from divergent thinking (exploring the diversity of mixes in the two-dimensional map) to convergent thinking (concretizing a specific mix idea).

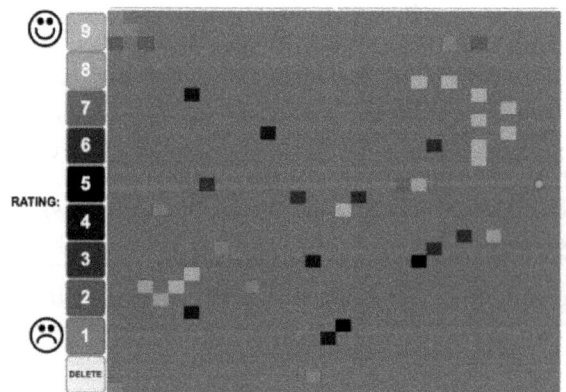

Figure 3. The proposed mixing interface.

The 2-dimensional map

When creating a 2-dimensional map, we wanted the topology of our 2-dimensional space to be similar to the topology of the original parameter space, i.e. the relative distance between points is similar in both spaces. We did not want the parameter values to jump dramatically and seem random. Instead we wanted the user to feel as if they were in control of their navigation through the space.

For the experiment in this paper, the interface controlled the equalization and gain parameters of 4 audio tracks. We reduced the dimensionality of the equalization parameters down to one parameter, the weighting coefficient for the first principal component of a 40 band graphic equalizer learned from data collected by Cartwright and Pardo [1]. This curve essentially represents a spectral tilt with a pivot point around 630 Hz. It is similar to the first dimension of the equalizer presented in [18]. Therefore, in total there were 8 mix parameters (one gain parameter and one EQ parameter per track).

We then used a self-organizing map (SOM a.k.a Kohonen map) [8] to map these 8 dimensions down to 2 dimensions (a 30x30 grid). The inputs to the SOM were 10,000 8-dimensional vectors sampled randomly from a 6-level quantized space. We used an initial neighborhood of 7 and allowed 400 iterations. Since our training examples were sampled from a uniform distribution, the goal of the SOM was not to learn a manifold as is typical with an SOM but rather to create a coarsely sampled but smooth map. While this map only contains 900 points from a much larger space, we think that such a broad, coarse sampling encourages the user to explore a wide variety of mixes before becoming focused on fine tuning one potential mix.

Refining the mix

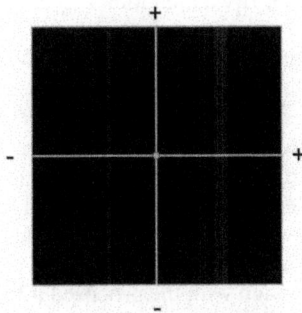

Figure 4. The refinement controller. The x and y axes respectively map to gain and equalization.

Having such a coarse map of the space encourages high-level exploration, but it does not allow for fine-tuning of the mix. Therefore, once a user rates several mixes and picks one *favorite mix*, the machine uses the ratings the user provided, along with their corresponding mix parameters (i.e. the 8-dimensional vector) to learn a weighting function of what the user finds important. This approach is similar to the equalization learning approach taken in [17]. For each individual control parameter, we perform a separate least-squares linear regression between the mix parameter values and the user's ratings of the mixes (i.e. find the least squares fit of α_i and β_i to the model $\mathbf{y} = \alpha_i + \beta_i \mathbf{x_i}$ where $\mathbf{y}$ is the vector of mix ratings and $\mathbf{x_i}$ is the vector of the ith mix parameter's values (e.g. the gain parameters for track 1)). The slope of the resulting line, β_i, is used as the weighting coefficient for the ith mix parameter.

We group the learned coefficients of the gain and equalization parameters into their respective weight vectors, β_{gain} and β_{EQ}. We then provide the user with a 2-dimensional

mix refinement controller (see Figure 4), where the x and y axes respectively control ω_{gain} and ω_{EQ} in the following equation:

$$\mathbf{z} = \left[\begin{array}{c} \mathbf{z_{gain}} \\ \mathbf{z_{EQ}} \end{array} \right] = \left[\begin{array}{c} \mathbf{x_{gain}} \\ \mathbf{x_{EQ}} \end{array} \right] + \left[\begin{array}{c} \omega_{\mathbf{gain}}\beta_{\mathbf{gain}} \\ \omega_{\mathbf{EQ}}\beta_{\mathbf{EQ}} \end{array} \right] \quad (1)$$

where $\mathbf{x} = \left[\begin{array}{c} \mathbf{x_{gain}} \\ \mathbf{x_{EQ}} \end{array} \right]$ is the mix parameter vector of the user's chosen *favorite mix*, z is the mix parameter vector of the refined mix. Therefore, when the controller is set in the middle ($\omega_{gain} = \omega_{EQ} = 0$), the refiner has no effect, and the the *favorite mix* is left untouched. At other settings, this controller allows the user to refine their favorite mix by increasing/decreasing the gains and EQs the machine believes to be important (depending on the sign of ω_{gain} and ω_{EQ}).

Similar to how navigation through the coarse map could be considered a coarse tuning of the mix, this refinement stage could be considered a medium precision tuning of this mix since it changes multiple parameters at once. True fine-tuning of the mix is not the goal of this interface.

EXPERIMENT

To validate our proposed interface, we compared it against the traditional mixing interface, with a focus on answering the following questions:

1. Which interface facilitates creating more satisfying mixes?

2. Which interface better facilitates exploration of alternative mixes?

The Mixing Interfaces

To evaluate whether the explicit rating of mixes or the refinement controller added value, we evaluated two variants of the *proposed* interface: 1) the complete proposed interfaces with ratings and refinement (*2D rater*) and 2) just the exploratory 2-dimensional map portion of the proposed interface (*2D map*), with no explicit rating of mixes and no refinement controller. We compared them to a traditional mixer interface (*traditional*), similar to that in Figure 1. The *traditional* interface had three controls for each audio track: an overall gain slider, a low frequency gain knob, and a high frequency gain knob.

Audio Sources

We used one musical excerpt from each of three different genres for the mixing source material: one pop (electro-pop), one rock (shoe-gaze), and one electronic (techno) excerpt. All excerpts were between 17 and 32s long musical sections obtained from [21]. Each excerpt consisted of 4 temporally aligned, stereo "stems" (i.e. subgroup recordings).

We chose these genres to support a variety of mixing styles. Genres like jazz or classical were not included since the engineer may likely strive for a realistic-sounding mix, recreating how it would be heard in a live setting. We instead chose genres which we believe can support a variety of artistic mixes without the constraint of "realism" as an aesthetic .

Participant Pool

Since we seek a fair test for the new interface, we chose not to focus on professional mixing engineers, who would be experts in using the standard paradigm. Instead, we recruited critical listeners without significant mixing experience. We defined critical listeners as either experienced musicians, audio researchers, or music enthusiasts who passed our critical listening pre-test, in which they had to identify small differences in mixes. We believe this population is capable of judging the quality of mixes but does not have years of experience to bias their judgment of interfaces. Participants were recruited through personal contacts.

Mixing Procedure

Each participant took part in one session that lasted about an hour. Sessions were conducted in a quiet room using a laptop computer and high-quality headphones. Each session consisted of two trials: one trial with the *traditional* interface and one trial with one of the proposed interfaces. Half the participants were assigned the *2D rater* interface and half of the participants were assigned the *2D map* interface. The order of presentation of interfaces was random, with half of participants using a proposed interface first and half using the traditional interface first.

Prior to each trial, participants were given a minimum of one minute (no maximum) of training on the interface used in the trial. As there were three musical excerpts and only two trials per participant, each trial used a unique excerpt and the training was conducted on the third excerpt. This prevented learning the details of a musical excerpt on one interface affecting the results for the next interface. Combinations of musical excerpt and interface were balanced across participants so that all excerpt/interface pairs were equally represented.

In a single trial, the participant was presented with one of the three song excerpts (e.g. the "pop" excerpt) and asked to create three diverse, but "good," mixes with the given interface (e.g. three distinct "pop" mixes with the *2D rater*). Participants were given 10 minutes to create each mix.

After each mix, participants completed a survey regarding the diversity, satisfaction, and objectives of their mix. At the end of the entire session, participants were asked additional questions regarding their preferences and experiences working with the interfaces.

For the *traditional* interface, prior to the start of each mix, the settings of the sliders and knobs were all randomized. Similarly, the mapping function for the proposed interfaces was randomly chosen from a set of 24, prior to each mix. The map was randomized to prevent associating particular map locations with particular sounds because we want the users to mix with their ears not their eyes. Controllers on the *traditional* interface were randomized to make things fair.

RESULTS

24 participants performed the experiment. There were two trials per participant and each trial had three mixes. Therefore each participant created 6 mixes. Ideally this would yield 24 mixes for each excerpt/*traditional* pair and 12 mixes for each excerpt/*proposed* pair, for a total of 144 mixes. However, two participants did not finish their mixes in time, reducing the total number of mixes to 142. The participants reported having an average of 169 (SD=148, median=204) months of experience playing music, 23 months (SD=37, median=3) mixing audio, and 56 (SD=63, median=24) months using audio recording equipment. Three participants reported significantly more experience mixing than the others, causing a large difference between median mixing experience (3 months) and mean mixing experience(23 months). However, these participants did not skew the data and therefore were not removed/replaced.

Participant Feedback

To answer our first question ("Which interface facilitates creating more satisfying mixes?"), each participant was asked "How satisfied are you with the quality of this mix?" after completing each mix. Responses were chosen from a seven-level scale: *completely satisfied, mostly satisfied, somewhat satisfied, neither satisfied nor dissatisfied, somewhat dissatisfied, mostly dissatisfied, completely dissatisfied*. The median value for all of the three tested interfaces was the same: *somewhat satisfied*. However, if we perform a Kruskal-Wallis sum-rank test on the group of distributions, we reject the null hypothesis that the location parameters of the distributions are equal ($p=0.0017$). If we then look at the two distributions we are most concerned with, mix satisfaction of *traditional* and the *2D rater*, and perform a one-sided Wilcoxon sum-rank test, we find that the distribution of *traditional*'s mix satisfaction is greater than that of the *2D rater* mix satisfaction ($p=0.0357$). However, while this difference is statistically significant, with the medians the same, it is not discouraging. Recall that the goal of the proposed interface was not to make an interface that supports fine-tuning of mixes, but rather one that facilitates broad exploration of the mixing space. If a user can get close enough with the proposed interface, they can always use the traditional mixer after the *2D rater* in order to fine-tune a novel mix.

At the end of the experiment participants were also asked to complete a survey in which they were asked a number of questions regarding their interface preferences, the physical/mental demands of the interface, etc. The results of these questions are shown in Figure 5. In this survey we directly asked them our second question ("Which interface better facilitates exploration of alternative mixes?"). As shown in the plot, it seems clear that participants think that the proposed interfaces facilitate exploration and that the traditional interface facilitates precise mixing. The results on which interface is less distracting are not clear, but there does seem to be some agreement that the proposed interface is more mentally demanding. The participants were only a bit more inclined to think that the traditional interface is more physical demanding and the proposed interface. Unfortunately, the majority of participants preferred working with the traditional mixer over the proposed mixers, but they gave plenty of feedback as to why, which will help in a future iteration.

From the participants' feedback, it seems that many users found the proposed interfaces great for "exploring possibil-

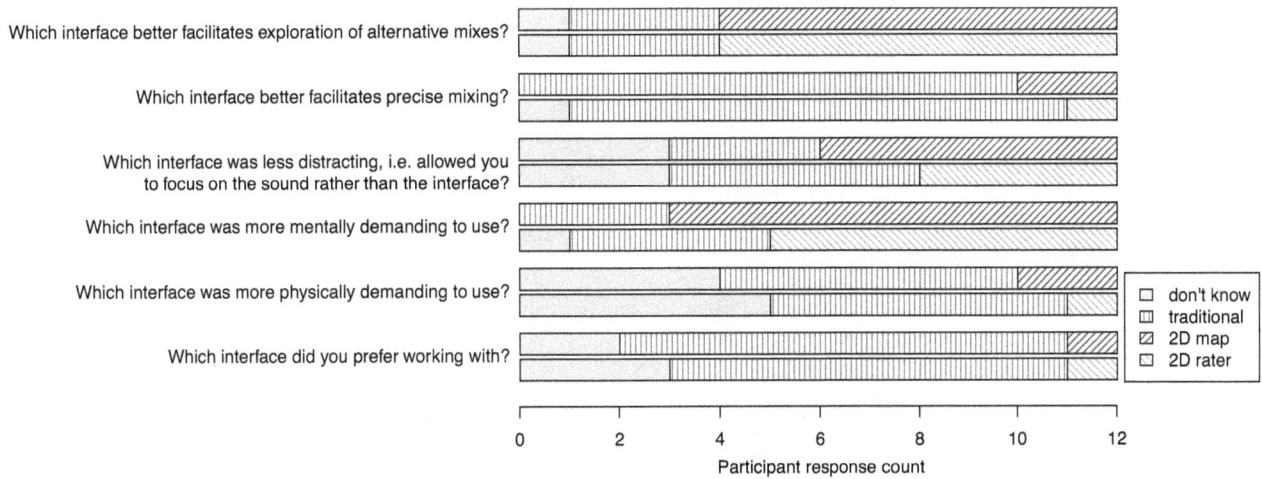

Figure 5. Interface survey response data. The first stacked bar for each question is the response data from participants given *2D map*, and the second is from those given *2D rater*.

ities quickly", "finding ideas I hadn't anticipated", and ideas that they "would not necessarily think of" themselves. However, once they did have an idea in mind, they preferred the traditional interface because they could express their idea in "terms of balance and EQ" and "easily isolate the sounds" to play with. The proposed interface's strength for exploration was its weakness for precision. As one participant put it, "Whenever I found something I liked I, but wanted to tweak one thing, I couldn't find that one tweak." Or as another participant reported, "While at first interface B was really cool in the way that I just wiggle my finger around and get different mixes without actually mixing, I felt frustrated when trying to achieve something specific." This seems to be because many users found the lack of labeled axes on the proposed interface frustrating and caused the mixes to seem random. From this feedback it seems that a combination of the two interfaces may be a good approach for a future iteration. In fact, participants reported this preference as well: "I'd use B (*the 2D rater*) followed by A (*the traditional mixer*) in an ideal mixing situation" reported one participant. The *2D map* and *2D rater* responses were similar, with only a couple of more participants listing *2D map* as more mentally demanding, but less distracting.

Figure 6 shows the results of questions specific to the *2D rater* variant of the proposed interface. It seems that there is little agreement on whether rating mixes helps user concretize their ideas. For instance, one participant reported that "it helped most when my objectives were quite vague to begin with." Whereas other participants reported that their "mixing objectives were not influenced by the ratings" and that "actually rating mixes makes your mixing objectives less clear". There also seemed to be little consensus on how burdensome the rating process was. Some found rating mixes very easy and others didn't. One participant reported, "Rating a mix is difficult when you have no criteria of how to quantify it. It's a difficult task to say I like this, or I don't like this." However, participants did generally agree that rating mixes was useful, especially for the purpose of providing visual feedback in order to remember where and what preferred mixes were. This

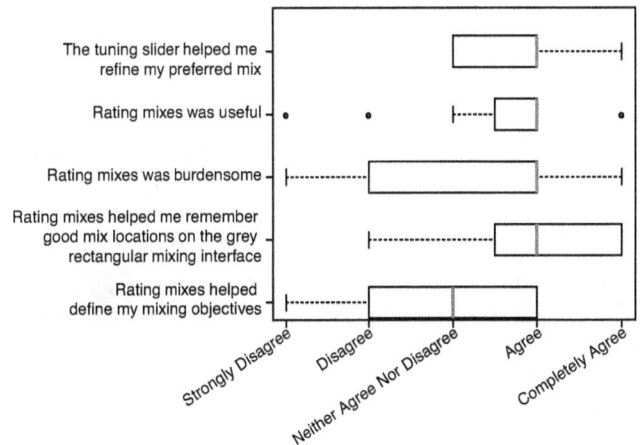

Figure 6. *2D rater*-specific survey response data.

benefit could also be why participants reported the *2D rater* as mentally demanding less often than the *2D map*. Lastly, participants found the refinement controller helpful. One participant reported that it "definitely helped me get closer to something I was happier with." However, participants also reported that they "would have liked more control over separate tracks." In general, the perceived benefit of rating mixes seems to be very participant dependent. Some people finding it useful, others not. This implies that making both the rating stage and the learned refinement stage optional would be a good approach, especially in a hybrid traditional/2D map interface.

DATASET

The mixing data from the study is available for download at http://music.eecs.northwestern.edu/data/mixploration/.

This dataset includes:

1. source audio files

2. mixing parameters of final mixes

369

3. survey response data of the final mixes

4. time series of mixing parameters during the mixing process

CONCLUSION

This paper presented a new mixing interface that facilitates broad exploration of the mixing space. From the survey response data, it seems that most participants were able to explore the mixing space more easily with the proposed interface than a traditional mixer. Participants found rating mixes to be useful for both remembering good mixes and creating the refinement controller. This let them to get closer to their preferred mix. While the refinement controller helped, participants generally preferred the traditional interface, especially for precision mixing due to its clearly defined dimensions. Participant feedback indicates that in a future iteration we should combine the two interfaces and provide more guidance and feedback when navigating the 2-dimensional map.

This work was supported by National Science Foundation Grant Nos. IIS-1116384 and DGE-0824162 and EPSRC grant EP/K007491/1, "Multisource audio-visual production from user-generated content."

REFERENCES

1. Cartwright, M., and Pardo, B. Social-eq: Crowdsourcing an equalizaiton descriptor map. In *Proc. of International Society for Music Information Retrieval* (Curitiba, Brazil, 2013).

2. De Man, B., and Reiss, J. D. A knowledge-engineered autonomous mixing system. In *Audio Engineering Society Convention 135*, Audio Engineering Society (Year).

3. Fiebrink, R. A. *Real-time human interaction with supervised learning algorithms for music composition and performance*. PhD thesis, Princeton Univ., 2011.

4. Garcia, R. Growing sound synthesizers using evolutionary methods. In *Proc. of ALMMA 2002 Workshop on Artificial Life Models for Musical Applications* (Cosenza, Italy, 2001).

5. Heise, S., Hlatky, M., and Loviscach, J. Automatic adjustment of off-the-shelf reverberation effects. In *Proc. of Audio Engineering Socienty Convention 126* (2009).

6. Heise, S., Hlatky, M., and Loviscach, J. Automatic cloning of recorded sounds by software synthesizers. In *Proc. of Audio Engineering Society Convention 127* (2009).

7. King, R., Leonard, B., and Sikora, G. Consistency of balance preferences in three musical genres. In *Proc. of Audio Engineering Society Convention 133* (2012).

8. Kohonen, T. The self-organizing map. *Proceedings of the IEEE 78*, 9 (1990), 1464–1480.

9. Mansbridge, S., Finn, S., and Reiss, J. D. Implementation and evaluation of autonomous multi-track fader control. In *Proc. of Audio Engineering Society Convention 132*, Audio Engineering Society (2012).

10. Mecklenburg, S., and Loviscach, J. subjeqt: controlling an equalizer through subjective terms. In *Proc. of CHI '06 Extended Abstracts on Human Factors in Computing Systems* (Montreal, Canada, 2006).

11. Mintz, D. Toward timbral synthesis: a new method for synthesizing sound based on timbre description schemes. Master's thesis, University of California, 2007.

12. Nishibori, Y., and Iwai, T. Tenori-on. In *Proc. of New Interfaces for Musical Expression*, IRCAM (Paris, France, 2006), 172–175.

13. Perez-Gonzalez, E., and Reiss, J. Automatic equalization of multichannel audio using cross-adaptive methods. In *Proc. of Audio Engineering Society Convention 127*, Audio Engineering Society (2009).

14. Perez-Gonzalez, E., and Reiss, J. Automatic gain and fader control for live mixing. In *Proc. of Applications of Signal Processing to Audio and Acoustics, 2009. WASPAA'09. IEEE Workshop on*, IEEE (2009), 1–4.

15. Perez-Gonzalez, E., and Reiss, J. Automatic mixing. In *DAFX : digital audio effects*, U. Zlzer, Ed., 2nd ed. Wiley, Chichester, U.K., 2011.

16. Reed, D. A perceptual assistant to do sound equalization. In *Proc. of the 5th international conference on Intelligent user interfaces*, ACM (2000), 212–218.

17. Sabin, A., Rafii, Z., and Pardo, B. Weighting-function-based rapid mapping of descriptors to audio processing parameters. *Journal of the Audio Engineering Society 59*, 6 (2011), 419–430.

18. Sabin, A. T., and Pardo, B. 2deq: an intuitive audio equalizer. In *Proc. of ACM Creativity and Cognition*, ACM (Berkeley, USA, 2009).

19. Schlei, K. Tc-11: A programmable multi-touch synthesizer for the ipad. In *Proc. of New Interfaces for Musical Expression* (Ann Arbor, USA, 2012).

20. Scott, J., Prockup, M., Schmidt, E., and Kim, Y. Automatic multi-track mixing using linear dynamical systems. In *Proc. of Sound and Music Computing* (Padova, Italy, 2011).

21. Senior, M. The 'mixing secrets' free multitrack download library.
`http://www.cambridge-mt.com/ms-mtk.htm`.

22. Yee-King, M. J. *Automatic sound synthesizer programming: techniques and applications*. PhD thesis, Univ. of Sussex, 2011.

Author Index

www.ingramcontent.com/pod-product-compliance
Lightning Source LLC
Chambersburg PA
CBHW080708220326
41598CB00033B/5347